CURRENT LAW STATUTES ANNOTATED
1987

VOLUME THREE

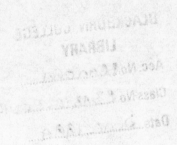

AUSTRALIA AND NEW ZEALAND
The Law Book Company Ltd.
Sydney : Melbourne : Perth

CANADA AND U.S.A.
The Carswell Company Ltd.
Agincourt, Ontario

INDIA
N. M. Tripathi Private Ltd.
Bombay
and
Eastern Law House Private Ltd.
Calcutta and Delhi

M.P.P. House
Bangalore

ISRAEL
Steimatzky's Agency Ltd.
Jerusalem : Tel Aviv : Haifa

CURRENT LAW

STATUTES

ANNOTATED

1987

VOLUME THREE

EDITOR IN CHIEF

PETER ALLSOP, C.B.E., M.A.

Barrister

GENERAL EDITOR

KEVAN NORRIS, LL.B.

Solicitor

ASSISTANT GENERAL EDITORS

GILLIAN BRONZE, LL.B.

SUSAN SHUAIB, B.A.

LONDON

SWEET & MAXWELL   STEVENS & SONS

EDINBURGH

W. GREEN & SON

1988

Published by
SWEET & MAXWELL LIMITED
and **STEVENS & SONS LIMITED**
of 11 New Fetter Lane, London,
and **W. GREEN & SON LIMITED**
of St. Giles Street, Edinburgh,
and Printed in Great Britain
by The Eastern Press Ltd.,
London and Reading

ISBN This Volume only : 0 421 39670 9
As a set : 0 421 39680 6

©
Sweet & Maxwell Limited
1988

CONTENTS

Chronological Table . . . . *page* v
Index of Short Titles vii
Statute Citator . . . . (1)
Index . . . . [1]

CHRONOLOGICAL TABLE

STATUTES 1987

VOLUME ONE

c. 1. Teachers' Pay and Conditions Act 1987
  2. Licensing (Restaurant Meals) Act 1987
  3. Coal Industry Act 1987
  4. Ministry of Defence Police Act 1987
  5. Rate Support Grants Act 1987
  6. Local Government Finance Act 1987
  7. Social Fund (Maternity and Funeral Expenses) Act 1987
  8. Consolidated Fund Act 1987
  9. Animals (Scotland) Act 1987
  10. Broadcasting Act 1987
  11. Gaming (Amendment) Act 1987
  12. Petroleum Act 1987
  13. Minors' Contracts Act 1987
  14. Recognition of Trusts Act 1987
  15. Reverter of Sites Act 1987
  16. Finance Act 1987
  17. Appropriation Act 1987
  18. Debtors (Scotland) Act 1987
  19. Billiards (Abolition of Restrictions) Act 1987
  20. Chevening Estate Act 1987
  21. Pilotage Act 1987
  22. Banking Act 1987
  23. Register of Sasines (Scotland) Act 1987
  24. Immigration (Carriers' Liability) Act 1987
  25. Crown Proceedings (Armed Forces) Act 1987

VOLUME TWO

26. Housing (Scotland) Act 1987
27. Fire Safety and Safety of Places of Sport Act 1987
28. Deer Act 1987
29. Agricultural Training Board Act 1987
30. Northern Ireland (Emergency Provisions) Act 1987
31. Landlord and Tenant Act 1987
32. Crossbows Act 1987
33. AIDS Control Act 1987
34. Motor Cycle Noise Act 1987
35. Protection of Animals (Penalties) Act 1987
36. Prescription (Scotland) Act 1987
37. Access to Personal Files Act 1987
38. Criminal Justice Act 1987
39. Parliamentary and Health Service Commissioners Act 1987
40. Registered Establishments (Scotland) Act 1987
41. Criminal Justice (Scotland) Act 1987

VOLUME THREE

42. Family Law Reform Act 1987
43. Consumer Protection Act 1987
44. Local Government Act 1987
45. Parliamentary and other Pensions Act 1987
46. Diplomatic and Consular Premises Act 1987
47. Abolition of Domestic Rates Etc. (Scotland) Act 1987
48. Irish Sailors and Soldiers Land Trust Act 1987
49. Territorial Sea Act 1987
50. Appropriation (No. 2) Act 1987
51. Finance (No. 2) Act 1987
52. British Shipbuilders (Borrowing Powers) Act 1987
53. Channel Tunnel Act 1987
54. Consolidated Fund (No. 2) Act 1987
55. Consolidated Fund (No. 3) Act 1987
56. Scottish Development Agency Act 1987
57. Urban Development Corporations (Financial Limits) Act 1987

INDEX OF SHORT TITLES

STATUTES 1987
References are to chapter numbers of 1987

Abolition of Domestic Rates Etc. (Scotland) Act 1987 47
Access to Personal Files Act 1987 37
Agricultural Training Board Act 1987 29
AIDS Control Act 1987 33
Animals (Scotland) Act 1987 9
Appropriation Act 1987 17
Appropriation (No. 2) Act 1987 50
Banking Act 1987 22
Billiards (Abolition of Restrictions) Act 1987 19
British Shipbuilders (Borrowing Powers) Act 1987 52
Broadcasting Act 1987 10
Channel Tunnel Act 1987 53
Chevening Estate Act 1987 20
Coal Industry Act 1987 3
Consolidated Fund Act 1987 8
Consolidated Fund (No. 2) Act 1987 54
Consolidated Fund (No. 3) Act 1987 55
Consumer Protection Act 1987 43
Criminal Justice Act 1987 38
Criminal Justice (Scotland) Act 1987 41
Crossbows Act 1987 32
Crown Proceedings (Armed Forces) Act 1987 25
Debtors (Scotland) Act 1987 18
Deer Act 1987 28
Diplomatic and Consular Premises Act 1987 46
Family Law Reform Act 1987 42
Finance Act 1987 16
Finance (No. 2) Act 1987 51
Fire Safety and Safety of Places of Sport Act 1987 27
Gaming (Amendment) Act 1987 11
Housing (Scotland) Act 1987 26
Immigration (Carriers' Liability) Act 1987 24
Irish Sailors and Soldiers Land Trust Act 1987 48
Landlord and Tenant Act 1987 31
Licensing (Restaurant Meals) Act 1987 2
Local Government Act 1987 44
Local Government Finance Act 1987 6
Ministry of Defence Police Act 1987 4
Minors' Contracts Act 1987 13
Motor Cycle Noise Act 1987 34

Index of Short Titles

Northern Ireland (Emergency Provisions) Act 1987 30
Parliamentary and Health Service Commissioners Act 1987 39
Parliamentary and other Pensions Act 1987 45
Petroleum Act 1987 12
Pilotage Act 1987 21
Prescription (Scotland) Act 1987 36
Protection of Animals (Penalties) Act 1987 35
Rate Support Grants Act 1987 5
Recognition of Trusts Act 1987 14
Register of Sasines (Scotland) Act 1987 23
Registered Establishments (Scotland) Act 1987 40
Reverter of Sites Act 1987 15
Scottish Development Agency Act 1987 56
Social Fund (Maternity and Funeral Expenses) Act 1987 7
Teachers' Pay and Conditions Act 1987 1
Territorial Sea Act 1987 49
Urban Development Corporations (Financial Limits) Act 1987 57

FAMILY LAW REFORM ACT 1987*

(1987 c. 42)

Arrangement of Sections

Part I

General Principle

SECT.
1. General principle.

Part II

Rights and Duties of Parents etc.

Parental rights and duties: general

2. Construction of enactments relating to parental rights and duties.
3. Agreements as to exercise of parental rights and duties.

Parental rights and duties where parents not married

4. Parental rights and duties of father.
5. Exercise of parental rights and duties.
6. Appointment of guardians.
7. Rights with respect to adoption.
8. Rights where child in care etc.
9. Consents to marriages.

Orders for custody

10. Orders for custody on application of either parent.
11. Orders for custody in guardianship cases.

Orders for financial relief

12. Orders for financial relief on application of either parent.
13. Orders for financial relief in guardianship cases.
14. Orders for financial relief for persons over eighteen.

Alteration of maintenance agreements

15. Alteration during lives of parties.
16. Alteration after death of one party.

Supplemental

17. Abolition of affiliation proceedings.

Part III

Property Rights

18. Succession on intestacy.
19. Dispositions of property.
20. No special protection for trustees and personal representatives.
21. Entitlement to grant of probate etc.

---

* Annotations by M. D. A. Freeman, Professor of English Law at University College London: of Gray's Inn, Barrister.

Part IV

Determination of Relationships

SECT.
22. Declarations of parentage.
23. Provisions as to scientific tests.

Part V

Registration of Births

24. Registration of father where parents not married.
25. Re-registration where parents not married.
26. Re-registration after declaration of parentage.

Part VI

Miscellaneous and Supplemental

Miscellaneous

27. Artificial insemination.
28. Children of void marriages.
29. Evidence of paternity in civil proceedings.

Supplemental

30. Orders applying section 1 to other enactments.
31. Interpretation.
32. Text of 1971 Act as amended.
33. Amendments, transitional provisions, savings and repeals.
34. Short title, commencement and extent.

Schedules:
Schedule 1—Text of 1971 Act as amended.
Schedule 2—Minor and consequential amendments.
Schedule 3—Transitional provisions and savings.
Schedule 4—Repeals.

An Act to reform the law relating to the consequences of birth outside marriage; to make further provision with respect to the rights and duties of parents and the determination of parentage; and for connected purposes. [15th May 1987]

Parliamentary Debates
Hansard, H.L. Vol. 482, cols. 23, 647, 1251; Vol. 483, col. 635; Vol. 484, col. 515; Vol. 487, col. 783; H.C. Vol. 114, col. 254; Vol. 116, col. 215.
The Bill was considered in Standing Committee F from April 30 to May 5, 1987.

General Note
Background and Sources
The subject of this Act is illegitimacy. The policy underlying it is that 'to the greatest extent possible the legal position of a child born to unmarried parents should be the same as that of one born to married parents' (*per* Lord Chancellor, *Hansard*, H.L. Vol. 482, col. 647). The Act is a product of two Law Commission Reports (Nos. 118 and 157), published respectively in 1982 and 1986. The recommendations of the first report were the object of considerable criticism, not least from women's rights organisations. The recommendations of the second report take account of these criticisms and of the Scottish approach to the problem, embodied in the Scottish Law Commission report on Illegitimacy (Scot. Law Com. No. 82) and now in the Law Reform (Parent and Child) (Scotland) Act 1986. The English Law Commission's second report is influenced by the Scottish report: it saw 'significant advantages' in the Scottish approach and also believed that, in so far as was possible, there

should be 'consistency' between the two legal systems on 'such an important subject' (Law Com. No. 157, para. 1.1).

The Act does not abolish the status of illegitimacy. Its aim is to remove "so far as possible . . . any avoidable discrimination against, or stigma attaching to, children born outside wedlock" (*per* Lord Chancellor, *Hansard*, H.L. Vol. 482, col. 647). Some discrimination remains, as will be shown. Perhaps, more importantly, it should be stressed that the real discrimination suffered by children in one-parent families is poverty and its multi-faceted correlates. The Act is, of course, tangential to these problems which remain and, indeed, are exacerbated by other policies of the government which passed this Act. (See, to like effect, M. Drummond, "The Reality of Being Illegitimate", *Sunday Times*, January 28, 1987, and *per* Mr. N. Brown M.P., *Hansard*, H.C. Vol. 114, cols. 261–2).

Nevertheless, the Act follows the world trend towards the elimination of discrimination against those born out of wedlock. There has been reform in New Zealand (Status of Children Act 1969, s.3(1) declaring that "for all the purposes of the law of New Zealand the relationship between every person and his father and mother shall be determined irrespective of whether the father and mother are or have been married to each other, and all other relationships shall be determined accordingly"), Australia, Switzerland, Netherlands, West Germany, France. In addition, the European Court of Human Rights has held that laws discriminating against those born outside marriage are, unless justifiable on some special ground, inconsistent with the guarantees provided by the Convention (Art. 8) (see *Marckx* v. *Belgium* (1979–80) 2 E.H.H.R. 330, on which see S. Maidment (1979) 9 Fam. Law 228 and see also Law Com. No. 118, para. 4.11). Further, in the U.S.A., there have been many decisions striking down legislation which treats illegitimate children differently from others as inconsistent with the constitutional guarantee of equal protection (*e.g. Levy* v. *Louisiana*, 391 U.S. 68 (1968); *Trimble* v. *Gordon*, 430 U.S. 762 (1977) and see Perry (1979) 79 Col.L.R. 1023).

The Act is not the first to tackle discrimination against the illegitimate. The Family Law Reform Act 1969 undertook a number of major reforms in the area of succession in particular. But even in this area important distinctions remained (see E. C. Ryder (1971) C.L.P. 157). The Second Reading debate in the House of Commons on that Bill remains an important source of concern for the plight of the illegitimate (see, in particular, *Hansard*, H.C. Vol. 778, cols. 46, 58–62, 70, 74, 97, 99). Reference should also be made to the Children Bill 1979, introduced by Mr. James White M.P., which sought unsuccessfully, to eliminate legal discrimination against illegitimate children (*Hansard*, H.C. Vol. 963, cols. 807–845).

Summary of the Act's Provisions

S.1 lays down the general principle that, in the absence of a contrary intention, a relationship between two persons is to be construed without regard to whether either of them, or any person through whom the relationship is deduced, is or is not legitimate. This principle is applied to the provisions of the Act and is to apply to all future enactments and instruments.

Pt. II of the Act is concerned with the *rights and duties of parents*. The principle established by s.1 is to govern a number of specific enactments which relate to the allocation of parental rights and duties (see s.2).

Perhaps the most important consequence of this is that the principle (in s.1 of the Guardianship of Minors Act 1971 (GMA 1971)) that, in custody and related proceedings, the child's welfare is the first and paramount consideration is now to apply to proceedings affecting illegitimate as well as legitimate children (see s.2(1)(c)). There is extended to all parents, irrespective of whether they are married or not, and whether divorced or not, the right to make agreements about the exercise of parental rights while the parents are separated (see s.3). In many ways the key provision in the Act is contained in s.4. This empowers the father of an illegitimate child to apply to share with the child's mother all the parental rights and duties which, short of an order being made, she has, as is the case at the present time (see s.85(7) of the Children Act 1975) alone. S.4 provides that the court may order that the father shall have all the parental rights and duties with respect to the child. The court's direction may be sought in relation to an illegitimate child where the parents disagree on a question affecting its welfare, provided the father has all the rights (as a result of a s.4 order) or a right to custody or legal or actual custody as a result of an order made under any other Act (for example, the GMA 1971, ss.9 and 14) (see s.5). Similarly, where there has been a s.4 order or the father has a right to custody, etc., as a result of an order made under another Act, the father may become a guardian on the death of the mother, may appoint a testamentary guardian and may object to a testamentary guardian appointed by the mother (s.6). In addition, where a s.4 order is in existence or the father has a right to custody, etc., by virtue of an order made otherwise than under this Act, the father's agreement to the child's adoption or to the freeing of the child for adoption is required (s.7). S.8 provides that the father of an illegitimate child who has the right to actual custody of him shall be treated as a "parent" for the purposes of the Children and Young Persons Act 1969 and for certain purposes of the Child Care Act 1980. The right of the father to give consent to the marriage of his illegitimate child under 18 is also extended (see s.9). The right of the father of an illegitimate child to apply to the court for legal custody or access to his child is also strengthened (see s.10). This section also *removes* the existing provision (in s.9 of the GMA 1971) which directs the court to have regard specifically to the conduct and wishes of the parents. Provision is made by s.11 for a child's legal custody and access where the court makes an order that a testamentary guardian be a guardian to the exclusion of the surviving parent, or where there is a disagreement between joint guardians one of whom is a parent.

The remainder of Pt. II is concerned with matters relating to *financial provision*. Affiliation proceedings are abolished by s.17. In their place is substituted a new code dealing with financial relief for children, whether or not legitimate. Thus, courts are allowed (under s.12) to make a variety of orders for financial provision, on the application of either parent of a child and under s.13 there is similar provision in cases where there is a guardian to the exclusion of the surviving parent, or where there is a disagreement between joint guardians one of whom is a parent. In addition, there is provision for children over 18, irrespective of their legitimacy, whose parents are not living together, to apply (in certain circumstances) for financial relief from their parents (s.14). S.15 makes provision for the alteration of maintenance agreements made in respect of illegitimate children during the lives of either of the parties to such agreements; s.16 makes similar provision for the situation after the death of one party to such an agreement.

Pt. III of the Act deals with rights of succession to property on intestacy. Illegitimacy is not to be taken into consideration in determining:

 (i)   the rights of succession of an illegitimate person;
 (ii) rights of succession to the estate of an illegitimate person; and
 (iii) rights of succession traced through an illegitimate relationship.

Rights under the intestacy of a person dying before the implementation of s.18 are not affected (see s.18(4)).

S.19 effects certain reforms which are intended to benefit illegitimate persons in relation to succession under wills and other dispositions including entailed interests. S.17 of the Family Law Reform Act 1969, which enable trustees and personal representatives to distribute property without having ascertained that no person whose parents were not married to each other at the time of his birth, or who claims through such a person, is or may be entitled to an interest in the property, is repealed: thus the special protection formerly enjoyed by such persons is removed (see s.20). A new presumption is created by s.21: for the purposes of obtaining a grant of probate or administration there is now to be a rebuttable presumption that the deceased left no surviving illegitimate relatives, or relatives whose relationship is traced throught an illegitimate person.

Pt. IV of the Act deals with the *determination of relationships*. S.22 provides for the making of declarations of parentage. As with the Family Law Act 1986, s.56 (which is not yet in force), the court is to have jurisdiction to entertain an application if, and only if, the applicant is either domiciled or habitually resident for the preceding year in England and Wales. Four declarations may be made: (i) that a person named is or was his parent; (ii) that he is the legitimate child of his parents; (iii) that he has become a legitimated person; (iv) that he has not become legitimated person. Scientific developments, particularly the new DNA tests, are taken account of in s.23. This confers on the court the power in any civil proceedings in which questions of parentage fall to be determined to require the use of scientific tests on bodily fluids or bodily tissue.

Pt. V of the Act is concerned with the *registration of births*. Their object is to facilitate the recording of paternity on the birth certificate of an illegitimate child. The sections deal with the first registration of an illegitimate child, the re-registration of the birth of such a child, and the re-registration of birth after a declaration of parentage.

Pt. VI of the Act, entitled "Miscellaneous and Supplemental", contains a number of significant changes in the law. S.27 provides that a child born to a married woman as a result of A.I.D. is to be treated in law as the child of his mother and her husband, and as a child of their marriage. This is only to apply where the mother's husband has consented to the insemination. The provision has implications for surrogacy arrangements: a future "Baby Cotton" (see *Re C.* [1985] F.L.R. 846) would now be legitimate, but a child produced for a surrogacy arrangement by means of natural intercourse would be illegitimate. S.28 creates a new presumption that in void marriages at least one of the parties believed the marriage to be valid. This will have the effect that any child of such a marriage will be legitimate. The section also provides that a mistake of law as to the validity of the marriage does not prevent such a belief from being reasonable so as to make the child legitimate.

S.12 of the Civil Evidence Act 1968 is amended (by s.29) so that an adjudication of paternity made in the course of all proceedings brought under the Guardianship of Minors Act 1971 (and in the course of all proceedings brought by public bodies) is to constitute prima facie evidence of paternity.

The Significance of the Act

There are a large number of illegitimate births. In 1985 126,000 children were born illegitimate (19 per cent. of births and twice the rate of a decade earlier). It must not be assumed that the majority of these births occur in one-parent families. In 1979 the Law Commission assumed (W.P. No. 74, para. 1.4) that as many as half of the illegitimate children then born were the offspring of stable cohabitations outside marriage. In 1985 65 per cent. of all illegitimate births were registered jointly by both parents. Furthermore, as Poulter indicates (*English Law and Ethnic Minority Customs*, 1986 para. 4–05), it may also be the case that birth outside marriage is more readily accepted as a social and cultural norm amongst some of the immigrant communities in this country, particularly those of Afro-Caribbean origin, than has been the case traditionally in this country. All this suggests that *real* discrimination may not be as great as potentially the law has allowed hitherto. Nevertheless, the *symbolic* importance of the 1987 Act cannot be underestimated.

The Act does not, however, abolish the status of illegitimacy. Rather, it adopts the general principle that the question whether a person's mother and father have been married to each other is legally irrelevant. But, although the Act applies this principle to any future legislation, it only affects existing legislation in so far as it expressly so provides. Accordingly, there remain a number of areas where the old concept of legitimacy is still relevant to a child's rights (in particular, citizenship: see below). Secondly (and this is more significant), the father of a child born outside marriage does not automatically have parental authority over the child. He can acquire this by application to the court (see s.4), but not otherwise. Furthermore, there is no presumption of parentage where parents are unmarried. There is a presumption that a child born in wedlock to a married woman is the child of her husband. Developments in blood-testing and the new genetic finger-printing should make it relatively easy to establish paternity in most cases, but where it is contested, proof of parentage will remain a pre-requisite to any further action taken by the "father".

The most important of existing laws which discriminate between legitimate and illegitimate children and which remain after the passing of the 1987 Act is the law on *citizenship*. Under the British Nationality Act 1981, the relationship of parent and child exists only between a man and his legitimate child (British Nationality Act 1981, s.50(9)(*b*)). An illegitimate child cannot, therefore, acquire British citizenship through his father. So, a child born outside marriage in the U.K. to a British father and a foreign mother is not entitled to British citizenship. Nor is a child born overseas to a British father and a foreign mother (or to a mother who is British by descent only). The Law Commission (Law Com. No. 118, para. 11.20) thought that "as a matter of policy" a child born outside marriage should be entitled to British citizenship on the "same terms" as a marital child. The Act does not embody this policy.

Hereditary peerages are also unaffected by the 1987 Act. They have been limited (there is no reason why any future ones should) to heirs "lawfully begotten" (see further Law Com. No. 118, para. 8.26). Succession to the throne is also unaffected by the Act. This is governed by the Act of Settlement 1701, which restricts the right of succession to the legitimate. The new Act does not alter this.

Marital status thus remains relevant and the status of illegitimacy has *not* been abolished. The Scottish Law Commission observed (Scot. Law Com. No. 82, para. 9.3) that "it would be a matter for argument whether it was any longer justifiable to refer to a legal status of illegitimacy . . . whether minor differences in the rules applying to different classes of persons justify the ascription of a distinct status is a matter for commentators rather than legislators". But differences do remain. Although the Act discriminates between *fathers* rather than children, the terminology "legitimate" and "illegitimate" has not been extirpated. The original Law Commission proposal (see Law Com. No. 118, para. 4.51) would have done this by distinguishing the "marital" and "non-marital" child. The value of this would have been to do away with the word "illegitimate" with the connotation that this has of illegality and unlawfulness. But "a rose by any other name . . .". Marital status is not irrelevant: nor is legitimacy (a fact recognised by the Act itself in s.22, which provides for applications to the Court for a declaration that a person is the "legitimate" child of his parents).

EXTENT

This Act, with minor exceptions, extends to England and Wales only (see s.34(5)).

S.33(1) and paras. 12, 13 and 74 of Schedule 2; s.33(2) and para. 7 of Sched. 3 (so far as relating to the question of the Maintenance Orders Act 1950); s.33(4) and Sched. 4 (so far as relating to that Act and the Interpretation Act 1978) extend to Scotland and Northern Ireland (see s.34(4)).

The relevant Scottish legislation is the Law Reform (Parent and Child) (Scotland) Act 1986, on the principles embodied in which this Act is largely modelled.

COMMENCEMENT

This Act is not yet in force. It will come into force on such a day or days as the Lord Chancellor may by order made by Statutory Instrument appoint (see s.34(2)).

SOURCES

The essential preliminary material relating to this Act are two Law Commission reports (Nos. 118 and 157) and the Scottish Law Commission report (No. 82). On the extent to which these may be consulted for the purpose of interpreting this Act see the House of Lords' decisions in *Black-Clawson* v. *Papierwerke Waldhof-Aschaffenberg* [1975] A.C. 591 and *Davis* v. *Johnson* [1979] A.C. 264. An attempt by Lord Simon of Glaisdale to move an amendment that would have permitted reference to the Law Commission reports (see *Hansard*, H.L. Vol. 482, col. 1297–1300) failed (as ever).

ABBREVIATION

GMA 1971: Guardianship of Minors Act 1971.

PART I

GENERAL PRINCIPLE

General principle

1.—(1) In this Act and enactments passed and instruments made after the coming into force of this section, references (however expressed) to any relationship between two persons shall, unless the contrary intention appears, be construed without regard to whether or not the father and mother of either of them, or the father and mother of any person through whom the relationship is deduced, have or had been married to each other at any time.

(2) In this Act and enactments passed after the coming into force of this section, unless the contrary intention appears—

    (a) references to a person whose father and mother were married to each other at the time of his birth include; and

    (b) references to a person whose father and mother were not married to each other at the time of his birth do not include,

references to any person to whom subsection (3) below applies, and cognate references shall be construed accordingly.

(3) This subsection applies to any person who—

    (a) is treated as legitimate by virtue of section 1 of the Legitimacy Act 1976;

    (b) is a legitimated person within the meaning of section 10 of that Act;

    (c) is an adopted child within the meaning of Part IV of the Adoption Act 1976; or

    (d) is otherwise treated in law as legitimate.

(4) For the purpose of construing references falling within subsection (2) above, the time of a person's birth shall be taken to include any time during the period beginning with—

    (a) the insemination resulting in his birth; or

    (b) where there was no such insemination, his conception,

and (in either case) ending with his birth.

GENERAL NOTE

This lays down "a new rule of construction" (see Law Com. No. 157, para. 2.4). It is that references to relationships, for example between parent and child or brother and sister, are to be construed, unless a contrary intention appears, without regard to whether or not any person's mother and father were married to each other at any particular time. This rule is to apply to all future enactments and instruments. As the Law Commission indicates (*idem*): "this approach enables [the Act] to achieve the legislative changes needed to implement the basic policy without using adjectives which describe the child".

The section establishes an important point of principle for the future. Henceforth "it will be unnecessary to use . . . adjectives [legitimate and illegitimate] in order to encompass the children of unmarried parents or those claiming through them" since they will be covered unless a contrary intention is shown.

It must be noted that the new rule of construction does not apply to existing legislation except where it is expressly so provided. It is expressly so provided in s.2 (relating to parental rights and duties), s.18 (succession on intestacy) and s.19 (dispositions of property). It should also be noted that it is not a consequence of the new rule of construction that all fathers are treated alike: only the fathers of children born in lawful wedlock automatically have parental authority over their children. Others may apply for this as a result of s.4 of this Act. Further, it will still be necessary to establish parentage; in the case of parents married to each other this is presumed, but not where they are not.

Subs. (1)

Enactments . . . instruments made after. But not before save as expressly so provided by this Act (see ss.2, 18, 19).

Coming into force of this section. On a date to be appointed (see s.34(2)).

Whether or not. "Or not" is strictly otiose. See, for agreement, *Hansard*, H.L. Vol. 482, col. 1251–1252.

The father. It will be necessary to establish *who* this is, when a relationship which has come into being outside marriage is in question.

Any person through whom the relationship is deduced. There may be great difficulties in providing that someone several generations previously was the father.

Subs. (2)

At the time of his birth. In construing this see s.1(4).

Subs. (3)

Treated as legitimate. Under s.1(1) of the Legitimacy Act 1976 the child of a void marriage is treated as the legitimate child of his parents if at least one of his parents reasonably believed that the marriage was valid (the doctrine of the putative marriage). For amendments to s.1 of the 1976 Act see s.28 and commentary thereon.

Legitimate person . . . section 10. That is a person legitimated or recognised as legitimated under s.2 or s.3 of the 1976 Act or under s.1 or s.8 of the Legitimacy Act 1926 or by a legitimation recognised by the law of England and Wales and effected under the law of any other country.

Adopted child. See s.39 of the Adoption Act 1976.

Subs. (4)

Insemination. Either by natural intercourse or artificially.

Where there was no such insemination. This provides for situations of *in vitro* fertilisation. See in general the debate at Report stage in the Lords (*Hansard*, H.L. Vol. 483, cols. 637–644). The period of time between *in vitro* fertilisation and birth may, with the development of freezing techniques, be lengthy. Indeed, in such a case, if it were allowed to proceed, a child might be born years after conception and, indeed, long after the father's death (and even, presumably, after the mother's re-marriage and the birth of other children later conceived.

PART II

RIGHTS AND DUTIES OF PARENTS ETC.

Parental rights and duties: general

Construction of enactments relating to parental rights and duties

2.—(1) In the following enactments, namely—
    (a) section 42(1) of the National Assistance Act 1948;

    (b) section 6 of the Family Law Reform Act 1969;
    (c) the Guardianship of Minors Act 1971 (in this Act referred to as "the 1971 Act");
    (d) Part I of the Guardianship Act 1973 (in this Act referred to as "the 1973 Act");
    (e) Part II of the Children Act 1975;
    (f) the Child Care Act 1980 except Part I and sections 13, 24, 64 and 65;
    (g) section 26(3) of the Social Security Act 1986,
references (however expressed) to any relationship between two persons shall be construed in accordance with section 1 above.

(2) In subsection (7) of section 1 of the 1973 Act (equality of parental rights) for the words from "or be taken" to the end there shall be substituted the words "and nothing in subsection (1) above shall be taken as applying in relation to a child whose father and mother were not married to each other at the time of his birth".

GENERAL NOTE

    This section applies to the general principle enunciated in s.1 to a list of specific existing enactments relating to the allocation of parental rights and duties. Excluded from the list is any reference to the British Nationality Act 1981. For criticism of this omission see Lord Silkin at *Hansard*, H.L. Vol. 482, cols. 1262–1264. The Lord Chancellor's response is that this Act is not "about nationality: it is now about the position of children born out of wedlock" (*idem*, col. 1266).

Subs. (1)

    Section 42(1). This states (*inter alia*) that a man is liable to maintain his children (see s.42(1)(a)). The reference to children is said to include "a reference to children of whom he has been adjudged to be the putative father" (s.42(2)). There will still need to be proof of paternity.

    Section 6. This states (*inter alia*) that the court may make an order requiring "either parent" of a ward of court to pay the "other parent" or requiring "either parent or both parents" of a ward to pay to any other person having care and control of the ward weekly or other periodical sums towards the maintenance etc., of the ward (see s.6(2)).

    The Guardianship of Minors Act 1971. As amended by s.32 of this Act and Sched. 1. The importance of listing the 1971 Act is that in all disputes about custody the child's welfare will now be first and paramount, irrespective of the status of his parents. The previous wording of s.9 of the 1971 Act empowered the court to make such orders regarding custody and access as the court thought fit "having regard to the welfare of the minor and to the conduct and wishes of the mother and father". In practice courts applied the paramountcy principle (as enunciated in *J.* v. *C.* [1970] A.C. 668) to applications concerning illegitimate children, and the wording of s.9 was not thought to erode this principle. Nevertheless, the Law Commisison thought (see Law Com. No. 118, paras. 7.22–7.23) there was "some advantage in making it clear by means of a suitable declaratory provision" that the welfare principle applies to children born out of wedlock. Commentators, it noted, had noted a tendency to attach excessive weight to the legal relationship between the parents in disputes where the child was illegitimate.

    This provision, *inter alia*, puts the matter beyond doubt.

    Part 1 of the Guardianship Act 1973. This confers equality of parental rights (s.1(1)), deals with agreements thereto (s.1(2)), provides for courts to be seised of disagreements between parents (s.1(3)). There are also provisions relating to orders on applications under the GMA 1971, on supervision orders, on committing the care of a minor to the local authority, etc.

    Part II of the Children Act 1975. This deals with custodianship. On this see M. D. A. Freeman, *Law and Practice of Custodianship*, 1986.

    Child Care Act 1980. Pt. I deals with the powers and duties of local authorities in relation to the welfare and care of children, s.13 with penalties for assisting a child in care under s.2 (reception) to run away, etc., s.24 with the power of local authorities to arrange emigration, and ss.64 and 65 with voluntary organisations and parental rights and duties (resolution and transfer).

    Social Security Act 1986. S.26(3) states (*inter alia*) that "a man shall be liable to maintain his children". "Children" includes those of whom he has been adjudged to be the father" (s.26(4)).

Agreements as to exercise of parental rights and duties

3. For subsection (2) of section 1 of the 1973 Act (agreements between parents to give up parental rights) there shall be substituted the following subsection—

"(2) Notwithstanding anything in section 85(2) of the Children Act 1975, an agreement may be made between the father and mother of a child as to the exercise by either of them, during any period when they are not living with each other in the same household, of any of the parental rights and duties with respect to the child; but no such agreement shall be enforced by any court if the court is of opinion that it will not be for the benefit of the child to give effect to it."

GENERAL NOTE

This section substitutes a new s.1(2) of the Guardianship Act 1973. Under the previous law the right of a parent to make an enforceable agreement relating to his or her parental rights is restricted by s.1(2) of the 1973 Act and s.85(2) of the Children Act 1975. S.1(2) provides that a parent cannot enforce any agreement to give up parental rights made between himself and the other parent unless the agreement is in contemplation of their separation while married. In this *exceptional* case only, the agreement is enforceable, but the court can refuse to enforce the agreement if it is not for the benefit of the child to do so. S.85(2) of the 1975 Act provides that "subject to s.1(2) of the 1973 Act . . . a person cannot surrender or transfer to another any parental right or duty he has as respects a child". The result was that, while a husband and wife might make an enforceable separation agreement, including provisions about their parental rights (subject to the court's power in the interest of the child not to enforce it), unmarried parents and divorced parents could make such an agreement.

This section extends to *all* parents, whether married or not, and whether divorced or not, the right to make agreements about the exercise of parental rights while the parents are separated. Such agreements remain subject to the power of the court, in the interest of the child, to refuse to enforce them. The value of this provision is that it provides a framework for out-of-court discussion and negotiation on such matters as access arrangements.

Note the section applies to legitimate as well as to illegitimate children.

Notwithstanding . . . section 85(2). S.85(2) states that a person cannot surrender or transfer to another any parental right or duty he has as respects a child. This prohibition remains: the section in the 1987 Act deals merely with the *exercise* of parental rights.

The father and mother. Note: (i) the agreement may be made only *between* father and mother and not between one of them and anybody else with parental rights or some of them (*e.g.* a custodian); (ii) all fathers and mothers are included, irrespective of marital status (they may be unmarried or divorced).

Exercise. But not surrender or transfer.

By either of them. But not by anyone else.

Not living with each other in the same household. They may, nevertheless, be living in the same house, in which case the question is: are they living separate lives, living in two "households", rather than one (see *Hopes* v. *Hopes* [1949] P. 227, *Mouncer* v. *Mouncer* [1972] 1 All E.R. 289). A couple living in chronic discord may well be living together and thus not within this provision (though it seems unlikely that they would be able to formulate an agreement). If parents are living together, and wish to regulate rights and duties, they should use s.1(3) of the Guardianship Act 1973 (and see s.5 of this Act).

Parental rights and duties. There is, of course, no statutory definition of these (save the unhelpful attempt in s.85 of the Children Act 1975). A recent attempt to list them is M.D.A. Freeman, *Law and Practice of Custodianship* (1986), pp. 42–50. The importance of parental rights is waning, in particular after the House of Lords' decision in *Gillick* v. *West Norfolk Area Health Authority* [1985] 3 All E.R. 402. It is now said (by Lord Fraser at p.410) that they "do not exist for the benefit of the parent. They exist for the benefit of the child and they are justified only in so far as they enable the parent to perform his duties toward the child, and towards other children in the family" (see also Lord Scarman's speech at pp. 420–422). But, nevertheless, they "clearly do exist, and they do not wholly disappear until the age of majority" (*per* Lord Scarman at p.420). However, the "parental right yields to the child's right to make his own decisions when he reaches a sufficient understanding and intelligence to be capable of making up his own mind on the matter requiring decision (*per* Lord Scarman at p.422). It has also been said (by Lord Templeman in *Gillick* at p.435) that "parental rights cannot be insisted on by a parent who is not responsible for the custody and upbringing of an infant or where the parent has abandoned or abused parental rights". Access is clearly a parental right (see Children Act 1975, s.85(1): "shall include a right of access"). Given the difficulty of enforcing court orders on access, a problem which continues to exercise the minds of the courts, agreement on access may be particularly desirable.

Benefit of the child. It is not clear what test regarding "benefit" is to be applied by the court. It is suggested that the paramountcy principle in s.1 of the GMA 1971, as interpreted by Lord MacDermott in *J.* v. *C.* [1970] A.C. 668, should govern. The court should not enforce an agreement unless its terms are motivated by a desire to promote the best interests of the child. But how many such agreements will be so motivated? It is also important to bear in mind that if the court refuses to enforce an agreement, it may lead to greater disagreements between parents, out of which no "benefit" to the child is likely to emerge.

Parental rights and duties where parents not married

Parental rights and duties of father

4.—(1) Where the father and mother of a child were not married to each other at the time of his birth, the court may, on the application of the father, order that he shall have all the parental rights and duties with respect to the child.

(2) Where the father of a child is given all the parental rights and duties by an order under this section, he shall, subject to any order made by the court otherwise than under this section, have those rights and duties jointly with the mother of the child or, if the mother is dead, jointly with any guardian of the child appointed under the 1971 Act.

(3) An order under this section may be discharged by a subsequent order made on the application of the father or mother of the child or, if the mother is dead, any guardian of the child appointed under the 1971 Act.

(4) This section and the 1971 Act shall be construed as if this section were contained in that Act.

GENERAL NOTE

This section is central to the whole Act. The Law Commission considered (and rejected) the suggestion that the unmarried father should be placed in the same position as his married counterpart. Its concern (and in particular that of feminist organisations) was that the "unmeritorious father" would exercise parental rights contrary to the child's interest (let alone those of the mother) (Law Com. No. 118, paras. 4.24–4.51). The Act accordingly stops short of conferring upon the unmarried father the same status as the married father enjoys (see, further, Law Com. 157, paras. 3.1–3.3).

This section permits the court to order that the father shall have all parental authority, sharing it with the mother. The Law Commission believes successful applications will be rare (Law Com. No. 118, para. 7.27). Under the previous law, an unmarried father could be granted "legal custody", but could not share it with the mother (Guardianship of Minors Act 1971 ss.9(i) and 11A11). The position of the unmarried father will still differ from that of a married father in one respect: the court will have the power to revoke the order under s.4(3). The value of this power is that it may encourage courts to make orders in the first place, knowing that if they turn out unsuccessfully they can be discharged subsequently.

Subs. (1)

Father. He will first have to establish that he is the father.

The Court. See GMA 1971, s.15 (in Sched. 1 of this Act).

May. The court has a discretion. It may be assumed that it will only exercise this in favour of a deserving father, that is one who is contributing (and not just financially) to the care and upbringing of the child. It is expected that the majority of applicants will be living in stable unions with the mother and child. The existence of a discretion is important: there is no reason why an order should be made save where it will be of positive value to the "family" as such.

All the parental rights and duties. Note it is "all or nothing". The Court cannot confer on the father any one or more of parental rights and duties (*cf.* the wording of s.8(4) of the Domestic Proceedings and Magistrates' Courts Act 1978). It either confers upon him parental rights and duties or it does not. The "split order" is thus frowned upon (and see also *Dipper* v. *Dipper* [1981] Fam. 31, 45 *per* Ormrod L.J. and *Caffell* v. *Caffell* [1984] F.L.R. 169, 171 *per* Ormrod L.J.)

It should be emphasised that where a father is granted all parental rights and duties he *shares* them with the mother (see s.4(2)) or in certain circumstances with the guardian. Disputes between the parents can be dealt with by orders under the Guardianship Act 1973, s.1(3) (where they relate to specific issues) or by custody and access orders under the GMA 1971.

Subs. (2)

Otherwise than under this section. So, on an application by a father under s.4, the court cannot remove the mother's parental authority.

Jointly with the mother. But rights are exercisable by either without the other. Either of two persons jointly entitled to a parental right may exercise it if the other has not signified disapproval" (Children Act 1975, s.85(3)).

Guardian . . . 1971 Act. Appointed by the mother (or the father if he first gets a s.4 order) under s.4 of the GMA 1971 or by the court, where a child has no parent, guardian of the person or any other person having parental rights with respect to him, under s.5 of the GMA 1971.

Subs. (3)

Applications for discharge may be made by the father, mother, testamentary guardian or court-appointed guardian. Applications for discharge may well be made by a parent on the break-up of a cohabitation. The courts lack powers equivalent to those they possess on divorce to protect children (for example, the power to commit the child to the care of a local authority or to make a supervision order—see s.43 and 44 of the Matrimonial Causes Act 1973).

Application. Most applications are likely to be made by the mother when the relationship with the father comes to an end. The subsection offers the court no assistance as to how to deal with an application.

Any guardian. I.e. a testamentary guardian (s.4 of the GMA 1971) or a court-appointed guardian (s.5 of the GMA 1971).

Exercise of parental rights and duties

5. At the beginning of subsection (3) of section 1 of the 1973 Act (which enables application to be made for the direction of the court where parents disagree on a question affecting the child's welfare) there shall be inserted the words "Subject to subsection (3A) below" and after that subsection there shall be inserted the following subsection—

"(3A) Where a child's father and mother were not married to each other at the time of his birth, subsection (3) above does not apply unless—

(a) an order is in force under section 4 of the Family Law Reform Act 1987 giving the father all the parental rights and duties with respect to the child; or

(b) the father has a right to custody, legal or actual custody or care and control of the child by virtue of an order made under any other enactment."

GENERAL NOTE

Under s.1(3) of the Guardianship Act 1973 an application can be made for the court to make a decision where the parents disagree on a question affecting a legitimate child's welfare. This section allows such applications to be made in relation to illegitimate children if the father has parental rights and duties under s.4 of this Act or a right to custody, legal or actual custody or care and control of the child by virtue of other enactments.

Right to custody . . . . But not where he has a right to access only.

Under any other enactment. I.e. Guardianship of Minors Act 1971, Matrimonial Causes Act 1973 or Domestic Proceedings and Magistrates' Courts Act 1978.

Legal custody. See s.86 of Children Act 1975.

Actual custody. See s.87 of Children Act 1975.

Appointment of guardians

6.—(1) At the end of section 3 of the 1971 Act (rights of surviving parent as to guardianship) there shall be added the following subsections—

"(3) Where the father and mother of a child were not married to each other at the time of his birth, this section does not apply unless the father satisfies the requirements of subsection (4) of this section.

(4) The father of a child satisfies the requirements of this subsection if—

(a) an order is in force under section 4 of the Family Law Reform Act 1987 giving him all the parental rights and duties with respect to the child; or

(b) he has a right to custody, legal or actual custody or care and control of the child by virtue of an order made under any other enactment."

(2) At the end of section 4 of that Act (power of father and mother to appoint testamentary guardians) there shall be added the following subsection—

"(7) Where the father and mother of a child were not married to each other at the time of his birth—

(a) subsection (1) of this section does not apply, and subsection (3) of this section does not apply in relation to a guardian appointed by the mother, unless the father satisfies the requirements of section 3(4) of this Act; and

(b) any appointment under subsection (1) of this section shall be of no effect unless the father satisfies those requirements immediately before his death."

(3) At the end of section 5 of that Act (power of court to appoint guardian for child having no parent etc.) there shall be added the following subsection—

"(3) Where the father and mother of a child were not married to each other at the time of his birth, subsection (1) of this section shall have effect as if for the words 'no parent' there were substituted the words 'no mother, no father satisfying the requirements of section 3(4) of this Act'."

GENERAL NOTE

This section deals with the appointment of guardians for illegitimate children under respectively ss.3 and 4 of the GMA 1971. S.3 of the GMA 1971 provides that on the death of a parent, the surviving parent is the child's guardian either alone or jointly with any guardian appointed by the deceased parent, and that where no guardian has been appointed or in the event of death or refusal to act, the court may appoint a guardian to act jointly with the surviving parent. This is extended by this section to illegitimate children where there is a s.4 order or where the father has a right to custody, legal or actual custody or care and control of a child by virtue of other legislation.

S.4 of the GMA 1971 confers a power on parents to appoint testamentary guardians. This section extends this power to the father of an illegitimate child, where there is a s.4 order or where the father has a right to custody, legal or actual custody or care and control of a child by virtue of other legislation and this condition is satisfied immediately before the father's death.

Subs. (1)

Right to custody. . . . But not where he has a right to access only.

Legal custody. Defined in s.86 of the Children Act 1975.

Actual custody. Defined in s.87 of the Children Act 1975.

Under any other enactment. I.e. under the Guardianship of Minors Act 1971, Matrimonial Causes Act 1973 or Domestic Proceedings and Magistrates' Courts Act 1978.

Subs. (2)

Subsection (1) . . . does not apply. Subs. (1) states that the father may appoint a testamentary guardian.

Subsection (3) . . . mother. Subs. (3) states: "Any guardian so appointed shall act jointly with the mother or father, as the case may be, of the child so long as the mother or father remains alive unless the mother or father object to his so acting".

Unless the father satisfies . . . I.e. a s.4 order is in force or he has a right of custody, legal or actual custody or care and control of the child by virtue of an order made under any other enactment.

Requirements immediately before his death. Thus indicating a link between the father and child, though it by no means follows for there will be situations where a s.4 order, though not revoked, is a dead letter.

Subs. (3)

"No parent". An unmarried father without a s.4 order or a right to custody, legal or actual custody or care and control is *not* a parent for the purposes of s.5 of the GMA 1971, which confers upon the court a power to appoint a guardian where the child has no parent or guardian and no other person with parental rights (it is irrelevant for these purposes that a local authority or voluntary organisation has parental rights under a resolution passed under the Child Care Act 1980, ss.3 or 64).

Rights with respect to adoption

7.—(1) In section 18 of the Adoption Act 1976 (which relates to orders declaring a child free for adoption), for subsection (7) there shall be substituted the following subsection—

"(7) Before making an order under this section in the case of a child whose father and mother were not married to each other at the time of his birth and whose father is not his guardian, the court shall satisfy itself in relation to any person claiming to be the father that either—

(a) he has no intention of making—

(i) an application under section 4 of the Family Law Reform Act 1987 for an order giving him all the parental rights and duties with respect to the child; or

(ii) an application under any other enactment for an order giving him a right to custody, legal or actual custody or care and control of the child; or

(b) if he did make such an application, the application would be likely to be refused."

(2) In section 72(1) of that Act (interpretation), in the definition of "guardian" for paragraph (b) there shall be substituted the following paragraph—

"(b) in the case of a child whose father and mother were not married to each other at the time of his birth, includes the father where—

(i) an order is in force under section 4 of the Family Law Reform Act 1987 giving him all the parental rights and duties with respect to the child; or

(ii) he has a right to custody, legal or actual custody or care and control of the child by virtue of an order made under any enactment."

GENERAL NOTE

This section makes changes in the legal position of the father of an illegitimate child as regards the making of an adoption order in respect of that child and as regards the making of an order freeing the child for adoption. It provides that before a freeing order is made in relation to an illegitimate child, where the father is not the guardian, the court is to satisfy itself in relation to any person claiming to be the father that he has no intention of applying for a s.4 order or applying for custody, etc., under any other enactment, or if he did apply, the application would be likely to be refused. The section also provides a new definition of "guardian" in s.72(1) of the Adoption Act 1976; as regards an illegitimate child "guardian" is now to include the father where there is a s.4 order in force or where he has a right to custody, legal or actual custody or care and control by virtue of an order made under any enactment. Where he is a "guardian" his agreement, or the dispensing thereof, becomes a pre-requisite to the making of an adoption order.

Subs. (1)

Not his guardian. See s.72(1) of the Adoption Act 1976 and subs. (2) below.

Satisfy. On balance of probabilities.

Any person to be the father. He will need to establish his paternity first.

All parental rights. Which include the right to consent to a freeing order (and agree to the making of an adoption order.)

Application . . . custody . . . child. It is not relevant that he has the right to access or intends to apply for one. However, a father with access can be heard on the merits of the adoption order anyway (see Adoption Rules 1984, rr.4(2), 9, 10, 15(2), 21 and 23; and Magistrates' Courts (Adoption) Rules 1984, rr.4(2), 9, 10, 15(2), 21 and 23; see also Law Com. No. 157, para. 3.4 for an explanation of why the Act does not extend to fathers who only have access rights).

Likely to be refused. Experience suggests that applications for custody are likely to be refused (one notorious reported example of success is *Re C. (M. A.)* [1966] 1 All E.R. 838). It is difficult to predict whether applications for s.4 orders are likely to succeed. The Law Commission expects only rare applications but I suspect they will be more common than this pessimistic prognosis would suggest. Of course, if courts do not think they are likely to succeed, they will not succeed!

Subs. (2)

Guardian. The agreement of the guardian is a pre-requisite to the making of an adoption order. It may be dispensed with on statutory grounds.

Rights where child in care etc.

8.—(1) In section 70 of the Children and Young Persons Act 1969 (interpretation), after subsection (1) there shall be inserted the following subsection—

> "(1A) Where, in the case of a child whose father and mother were not married to each other at the time of his birth, an order of any court is in force giving the right to the actual custody of the child to the father, any reference in this Act to the parent of the child includes, unless the contrary intention appears, a reference to the father.
>
> In this subsection 'actual custody', in relation to a child, means actual possession of his person."

(2) In section 8 of the Child Care Act 1980 (application of Part I to children subject to orders of court), for subsection (2) there shall be substituted the following subsections—

> "(2) Subject to subsection (3) below, where an order of any court is in force giving the right to the actual custody of a child to any person, the provisions of this Part of this Act shall have effect in relation to the child as if for references to the parents or guardians of the child or to a parent or guardian of his there were substituted references to that person.
>
> (3) Where, in the case of a child whose father and mother were not married to each other at the time of his birth, an order is in force under section 4 of the Family Law Reform Act 1987 by virtue of which actual custody is shared between the mother and the father, both the mother and the father shall be treated as parents of the child for the purposes of the provisions of this Part.
>
> (4) In this section 'actual custody', in relation to a child, means actual possession of his person."

(3) In section 13 of that Act (penalty for assisting children in care to run away etc.), for subsection (4) there shall be substituted the following subsection—

"(4) Subsections (2) and (3) of section 8 of this Act shall apply for
the purposes of this section as they apply for the purposes of the
provisions of Part I of this Act."

(4) In section 24 of that Act (emigration of children), after subsection
(4) there shall be inserted the following subsection—

"(4A) Subsections (2) and (3) of section 8 of this Act shall apply
for the purposes of subsection (2) above as they apply for the purposes
of the provisions of Part I of this Act."

(5) At the end of section 64 of that Act (transfer of parental rights and
duties to voluntary organisations) there shall be added the following
subsection—

"(8) Subsections (2) and (3) of section 8 of this Act shall apply for the
purposes of this section and section 65 of this Act as they apply for
the purposes of the provisions of Part I of this Act."

GENERAL NOTE

This section amends provisions in care legislation so as to strengthen the legal position of
the unmarried father in relation to the child in care.

Subs. (1)

This subsection lays down that the father of an illegitimate child is to be treated as a
"parent" for the purpose of the Children and Young Persons Act 1969 if he has an order
giving him the right to actual custody of the child. The significance of this is that he must
then receive notice of care proceedings (Magistrates' Courts (Children and Young Persons)
Rules 1970, as amended, s.14(1), (2), (3)), and can make various applications on behalf of
the child (under Children and Young Persons Act 1969, ss.2(12), 15(1), 16(8), 21(2) and (4),
22(4) and 28(5)). There are a number of other provisions in the 1969 Act where being a
"parent" is relevant:

(i)	s.1(2)(*d*)	:	care order where beyond parental control;
(ii)	s.1(3)(*a*)	:	requirement to enter into recognisance on infant's behalf;
(iii)	s.2(9)	:	notice of proceedings where infant is under five;
(iv)	s.3(6)(*b*)	:	payment of compensation on infant's behalf;
(v)	s.7(7)(*c*)	:	recognisances in cases where criminal offence proved;
(vi)	s.18(3)	:	service of supervision order;
(vii)	s.24(8)	:	duty to keep local authority informed as to address;
(viii)	s.25(1) and (2)	:	transfer to or from Northern Ireland dependent on party's residence;
(ix)	s.28(3) and (4)	:	right to be informed of child's detention or arrest;
(x)	s.29(2)	:	entry into recognisances;
(xi)	s.32A	:	conflict of interest between parent and child.

Actual custody: the definition of this as actual possession is in accordance with s.87 of the
Children Act 1975.

Subs. (2)

Under the Child Care Act 1980 "parent" in relation to an illegitimate child has been
defined to mean mother to the exclusion of father (see s.87(1)). Only if the father had
obtained a "custody" order (see s.8(2)) or if he had been appointed "guardian" by deed or
will or by court order (see s.87(1)) was he treated as a parent for the purposes of the Act.
He is, however, included in the definition of "relative". As a consequence of these provisions
a father has had to have had a "custody" order or to be a "guardian" in order to request the
return of a child received into "voluntary" care (s.2(1)) or to contest the assumption of
parental rights by the local authority under s.3 (though his "rights" could not be assumed
because he didn't have any; see *R.* v. *Oxford Justices, ex p. H.* [1974] 2 All E.R. 356).

This subsection makes a number of changes to the 1980 Act. It re-enacts s.8(2) of the
1980 Act with the following changes. The concept of "custody" is replaced by the concept
of the "right to actual custody". This brings the provision into line with other legislation. It
covers "custody" orders made by divorce courts which deal with the right to actual custody
by making orders for "custody" or "care and control". Secondly, it provides that where a s.4
order is in force, by virtue of which actual custody is shared between the mother and the
father, both of them are to be treated as parents for the purposes of the provisions of the
1980 Act.

Subs. (3)

This subsection applies s.8(2) of the 1980 Act (as amended by s.8(2) of *this* Act) to s.13 of the 1980 Act. Under s.13, it is a criminal offence to assist a child in care to run away, to remove him without lawful authority or to harbour him. Under s.13(2), the ambit of the offence is extended to children in "voluntary care": a parent does not have "lawful authority" to remove a child who has been in care for the preceding six months though a parent may give 28 days' written notice of his intention to remove the child. The new s.13(4) (which is substituted by *this* subsection) provides that any person, including the father of an illegitimate child who has the right to actual custody under a court order or who has obtained a s.4 order under this Act, qualifies as a "parent" for this purpose, as under s.8(2).

Subs. (4)

This subsection applies s.8(2) of the 1980 Act, as substituted by s.8(2) of *this* Act, to the power of a local authority to arrange for the emigration of children in care. It provides that anyone who is a parent within the meaning of the substituted s.8(2), that is any person with a right to actual custody or in possession of a s.4 order, has a right to be consulted as to the question of the child's emigration.

Subs. (5)

This subsection applies s.8(2) of the 1980 Act, as substituted by s.8(2) of *this* Act, to cases of transfer of parental rights and duties to voluntary organisations (s.64) and from voluntary organisations to the local authority (s.65). It provides that anyone who is a parent within the meaning of s.8(2), that is any person with a right to actual custody or the recipient of a s.4 order, is a parent for the purposes of ss.64 and 65 of the Child Care Act 1980.

Consents to marriages

9. In Schedule 2 to the Marriage Act 1949 (consents required to marriages of persons under eighteen), for Part II there shall be substituted the following provisions—

"II. WHERE THE PARENTS OF THE CHILD WERE NOT MARRIED TO EACH OTHER AT THE TIME OF HIS BIRTH

Circumstances	*Person or persons whose consent is required*
1. Where both parents are alive:	
(a) if the father has been given by an order of any court the right to the actual custody of the child or the right to consent to the marriage of the child, or both those rights;	The mother and the father.
(b) if the father has not been given either of those rights.	The mother.
2. Where the mother is dead:	
(a) if the father is a guardian under the Guardianship of Minors Act 1971 and there is no other guardian;	The father.
(b) if the father is a guardian as mentioned in paragraph (a) above and another guardian has been appointed by the mother or by the court under the Guardianship of Minors Act 1971;	The father and the guardian if acting jointly, or the father or the guardian if the father or guardian is the sole guardian of the child.

Circumstances	*Person or persons whose consent is required*
(c) if the father is not a guardian and a guardian has been appointed by the mother or by the court under the Guardianship of Minors Act 1971.	The guardian.
3. Where the father is dead:	
(a) if there is no other guardian;	The mother.
(b) if a guardian has been appointed by the father or by the court under the Guardianship of Minors Act 1971.	The mother and the guardian if acting jointly, or the mother or the guardian if the mother or guardian is the sole guardian of the child.
4. Where both parents are dead.	The guardian or guardians appointed by the mother or father or by the court under the Guardianship of Minors Act 1971.

In this Part of this Schedule 'actual custody', in relation to a child, means actual possession of his person.''

GENERAL NOTE

This section deals with consents to marriage of illegitimate children under s.18. It substitutes a new Pt. II of Sched. 2 to the Marriage Act 1949 to deal with parental consent to the marriage of the illegitimate child. It should be read together with Sched. 2, paras. 9–11 which effects certain minor and consequential amendments.

The section deals with *four* cases:

    (i)   Where both parents are alive;
    (ii) Where the mother is dead;
    (iii) Where the father is dead;
    (iv) Where both parents are dead.

(i) Where both parents are alive, the consent of the mother alone is required *unless* the father has been given by court order the right to actual custody or the right to consent to the marriage of the child (or both those rights). If he has, the consent function is vested in both parents.

(ii) Where the mother is dead, the power to consent if vested in the guardian or guardians, whether the surviving father (if a guardian) or a non-parent guardian. If the father had parental rights under a court order before the mother's death, he will normally become a guardian.

(iii) Where the father is dead, the power to consent is vested in the surviving mother and in the non-parent guardian, if there is one.

(iv) Where both parents are dead, the power to consent to marry is vested in the child's guardian or guardians.

Orders for custody

Orders for custody on application of either parent

10. For section 9 of the 1971 Act and the heading preceding that section there shall be substituted the following heading and section—

"*Orders for custody and financial relief*

Orders for custody on application of either parent

    9.—(1) The court may, on the application of either parent of a child, make such order regarding—

    (a) the legal custody of the child; and
    (b) access to the child by either parent,

as the court thinks fit; and an order under this section may be varied or discharged by a subsequent order made on the application of either parent or, after the death of either parent, on the application of any guardian appointed under this Act.

(2) An order under this section—

(a) shall not give legal custody to a person other than a parent of the child; and

(b) shall not be made at any time when the child is free for adoption by virtue of an order made under section 18 of the Adoption Act 1976 or section 18 of the Adoption (Scotland) Act 1978."

GENERAL NOTE

This section re-enacts with amendments s.9 of the GMA 1971 to deal with orders for legal custody and access on the application of a parent. The court cannot give legal custody to a non-parent, though such a person (if qualified) may apply for a custodianship order, which vests legal custody in the successful applicant. Further, on a parent's application, the court may treat the application as if there were one for a custodianship order and give legal custody to a person other than a parent (see Children Act 1975 s.37(3)).

Subs. (1)

This subsection re-enacts s.9(1) of the GMA 1971 subject to two changes. First, it applies to all children, whether legitimate or illegitimate. Secondly, the reference to the "conduct and wishes of the mother and father" is removed, so that the welfare paramountcy test is affirmed.

The Court. See s.15 of the GMA 1971.

Either parent. Irrespective of whether they are married to each other or not.

Legal custody. As defined in s.86 of the Children Act 1975.

Access. On the importance of the child's welfare in relation to access, see Wrangham J. in *M.* v. *M.* [1973] 2 All E.R. 81, 85. It is wrong to suspend access until the court welfare officer considered it was appropriate it should take place. Courts must take access decisions (*Orford* v. *Orford* [1979] 1 F.L.R. 260). The normal order is "reasonable access" but it may be defined. It may also be supervised (if so, it should be by a person who is mutually agreeable to the parties—*Practice Direction* [1980] 1 W.L.R. 334). The court may deny access, where it is in the interests of the child so to do. It may also limit the right to re-apply for access, though for how long it is not clear (see *Re N.* [1983] 4 F.L.R. 150 and *Re C.* [1985] F.L.R. 1114).

As court thinks fit. Although this gives the court *carte blanche*, in practice they apply the paramountcy principle. The clearest statement of this is by Lord MacDermott in *J.* v. *C.* [1970] A.C. 668, 710–11: The words [first and paramount] "can note a process whereby, when all the relevant facts, relationships, claims and wishes of parents, risks, choices and other circumstances are taken into account and weighed, the course to be followed will be that which is most in the interests of the child's welfare as that term is now understood That is the first consideration because it is of first importance and the paramount consideration because it rules upon or determines the course to be followed".

Guardian appointed. See ss.3, 4, 5.

Subs. (2)

There are two limitations on the court. First, only a parent may be granted legal custody. Secondly, an order cannot be made at any time when the child is free for adoption.

A person other than the parent. This was possible under the GMA 1971 and remained possible until the custodianship provisions of the 1975 Children Act became operative in December 1985. Thus, in one case, custody (as it then was) was awarded to a great-aunt (see *Re R.* [1974] 1 All E.R. 1033). Now, on the application of a parent for legal custody under this section, the court may treat the application as if it were an application for custodianship (see Children Act 1975, s.37(3) and grant legal custody to a person other than a parent of the child. Where a direction is given in this way, the applicant is to be treated, if not anyway the case, *as if* he were qualified to apply for a custodianship order (s.37(4)). The conditions set out in s.33 therefore need not be satisfied. See, further, on custodianship, M. D. A. Freeman, *Law and Practice of Custodianship,* 1986.

Free for adoption. A child is free for adoption if he is the subject of an order under s.14 of the Children Act 1975 (or s.18 of the Adoption Act 1976, when it comes to operation) and the order has not been revoked under s.16 of the 1975 Act (s.20 of the 1976 Act) (see s.12(6) of the 1975 Act).

Orders for custody in guardianship cases

11. For sections 10 and 11 of the 1971 Act there shall be substituted the following section—

"Orders for custody in guardianship cases

10.—(1) Where the court makes an order under section 4(4) of this Act that a person shall be sole guardian of a child to the exclusion of a parent, the court may make such order regarding—
  (a) the legal custody of the child; and
  (b) access to the child by the parent,
as the court thinks fit; and the powers conferred by this subsection may be exercised at any time and include power to vary or discharge any order previously made.

(2) The powers of the court under section 7 of this Act to make orders regarding matters in difference between joint guardians shall include, where a parent of the child is one of the joint guardians—
  (a) power to make such order regarding—
    (i) the legal custody of the child; and
    (ii) access to the child by the parent,
    as the court thinks fit; and
  (b) power to vary or discharge any order previously made by virtue of this subsection.

(3) An order shall not be made under or by virtue of this section at any time when the child is free for adoption by virtue of an order made under section 18 of the Adoption Act 1976 or section 18 of the Adoption (Scotland) Act 1978."

GENERAL NOTE

This section gives the court power to make orders regarding legal custody and access when it makes an order that a person shall be sole guardian to the exclusion of a parent. It also gives courts the power, in resolving differences between joint guardians (where a parent is one of those guardians) to make orders relating to legal custody and access.

An order under section 4(4). I.e. an order that a testamentary guardian be a guardian to the exclusion of the surviving parent. Such orders are made but rarely.

Legal custody. See s.86 of the Children Act 1975.

Where a parent . . . is one of the joint guardians. But only where this is so.

Free for adoption. See s.12(6) of the Children Act 1975 and note on s.10 above.

Orders for financial relief

Orders for financial relief on application of either parent

12. After section 11A of the 1971 Act there shall be inserted the following section—

"Orders for financial relief on application of either parent

11B.—(1) The court may, on the application of either parent of a child, make—
  (a) in the case of proceedings in the High Court or a county court, one or more of the orders mentioned in subsection (2) of this section;
  (b) in the case of proceedings in a magistrates' court, one or both of the orders mentioned in paragraphs (a) and (c) of that subsection;
and an order mentioned in paragraph (a) or (b) of that subsection may be varied or discharged on the application of either parent or, after the death of either parent, on the application of any guardian appointed under this Act.

(2) The orders referred to in subsection (1) of this section are—

   (a) an order requiring one parent to make to the other parent for the benefit of the child, or to the child, such periodical payments, and for such term, as may be specified in the order;

   (b) an order requiring one parent to secure to the other parent for the benefit of the child, or to secure to the child, such periodical payments, and for such term, as may be so specified;

   (c) an order requiring one parent to pay to the other parent for the benefit of the child, or to the child, such lump sum as may be so specified;

   (d) an order requiring either parent to transfer to the other parent for the benefit of the child, or to the child, such property as may be so specified, being property to which the first-mentioned parent is entitled, either in possession or reversion;

   (e) an order requiring that a settlement of such property as may be so specified, being property to which either parent is so entitled, be made to the satisfaction of the court for the benefit of the child."

GENERAL NOTE

This section provides powers for the court to make orders for financial relief on the application of either parent. The orders it can make depend on the court hearing the application, the powers of the High Court and County Court being more extensive than those vested in Magistrates' Courts. The significance of the provision is that courts will have the power to make financial orders whether or not any other order is sought or made. It will thus not be necessary to put custody in issue on an application for financial provision.

Either parent. Whether or not the child is legitimate.

Any guardian appointed under the Act. I.e. under ss.3, 4 or 5.

Order requiring one parent. A parent may seek an order against him- (or her-) self. See *Simister* v. *Simister* [1987] 1 All E.R. 233. On the tax advantages of this see *Sherdley* v. *Sherdley* [1987] 2 All E.R. 54.

To the child. This has tax advantages.

Orders for financial relief in guardianship cases

13. After section 11B of the 1971 Act there shall be inserted the following section—

"Orders for financial relief in guardianship cases

11C.—(1) Where the court makes an order under section 4(4) of this Act that a person shall be sole guardian of a child to the exclusion of a parent, the court may make—

   (a) in the case of proceedings in the High Court or a county court, one or more of the orders mentioned in subsection (3) of this section;

   (b) in the case of proceedings in a magistrates' court, one or both of the orders mentioned in paragraphs (a) and (c) of that subsection;

and the powers conferred by this subsection may be exercised at any time and include power to vary or discharge any order mentioned in paragraph (a) or (b) of that subsection previously made.

(2) The powers of the court under section 7 of this Act to make orders regarding matters in difference between joint guardians shall include, where a parent of the child is one of the joint guardians—

   (a) power to make—

      (i) in the case of proceedings in the High Court or a county court, one or more of the orders mentioned in subsection (3) of this section;

      (ii) in the case of proceedings in a magistrates' court, one or both of the orders mentioned in paragraphs (a) and (c) of that subsection; and

(b) power to vary or discharge any order mentioned in paragraph (a) or (b) of that subsection previously made.

(3) The orders referred to in subsections (1) and (2) of this section are—

(a) an order requiring the parent to make to the guardian or other guardian for the benefit of the child, or to the child, such periodical payments, and for such term, as may be specified in the order;

(b) an order requiring the parent to secure to the guardian or other guardian for the benefit of the child, or to secure to the child, such periodical payments, and for such term, as may be so specified;

(c) an order requiring the parent to pay to the guardian or other guardian for the benefit of the child, or to the child, such lump sum as may be so specified;

(d) an order requiring the parent to transfer to the guardian or other guardian for the benefit of the child, or to the child, such property as may be so specified, being property to which the parent is entitled, either in possession or reversion;

(e) an order requiring that a settlement of such property as may be so specified, being property to which the parent is so entitled, be made to the satisfaction of the court for the benefit of the child."

GENERAL NOTE

This section makes similar provision (to s.12) in cases where there is a guardian to the exclusion of the surviving parent or where there is a disagreement between joint guardians one of whom is a parent.

An order under s.4(4). I.e. an order that a testamentary guardian be a guardian to the exclusion of the surviving parent.

The powers of the Court under s.7. I.e. to make orders regarding differences between joint guardians.

Where the parent . . . one of the joint guardians. But not otherwise.

Order requiring one parent. See note on s.12.

Orders for financial relief for persons over eighteen

14. After section 11C of the 1971 Act there shall be inserted the following section—

"Orders for financial relief for persons over eighteen

11D.—(1) If, on an application by a person who has attained the age of eighteen and whose parents are not living with each other in the same household, it appears to the High Court or a county court—

(a) that the applicant is, will be or (if an order were made under this section) would be receiving instruction at an educational establishment or undergoing training for a trade, profession or vocation, whether or not he also is, will be or would be in gainful employment; or

(b) that there are special circumstances which justify the making of an order under this section,

the court may make one or both of the orders mentioned in subsection (2) of this section.

(2) The orders referred to in subsection (1) of this section are—

(a) an order requiring either or both of the applicant's parents to pay to the applicant such periodical payments, and for such term, as may be specified in the order; and

(b) an order requiring either or both of the applicant's parents to pay to the applicant such lump sum as may be so specified.

(3) An application may not be made under this section by any person if, immediately before he attained the age of sixteen, a periodical payments order was in force with respect to him.

(4) No order shall be made under this section at a time when the parents of the applicant are living with each other in the same household.

(5) Any order made under this section requiring the making of periodical payments shall, notwithstanding anything in the order, cease to have effect on the death of the person liable to make payments under the order.

(6) An order under this section requiring the making of periodical payments may be varied or discharged by a subsequent order made on the application of any person by or to whom payments were required to be made under the previous order.

(7) In subsection (3) of this section 'periodical payments order' means an order made under—

(a) this Act,
(b) section 6(3) of the Family Law Reform Act 1969,
(c) section 23 or 27 of the Matrimonial Causes Act 1973,
(d) section 34 of the Children Act 1975, or
(e) Part I of the Domestic Proceedings and Magistrates' Courts Act 1978,

for the making or securing of periodical payments."

GENERAL NOTE

This section provides that children over 18, whether or not legitimate, whose parents are not living together, may in certain circumstances, have the right to apply for financial relief from their parents.

It was possible under the law for maintenance orders made in matrimonial (see Matrimonial Causes Act 1973, s.29(3) and Domestic Proceedings and Magistrates Courts Act 1978, s.5(3), guardianship (see GMA 1971, s.12) and affiliation proceedings (see Affiliation Proceedings Act 1957, s.6) to continue beyond the compulsory school leaving age and after 18 if the child was undergoing further education or training, or if there were special circumstances, such as disability. But, whether a child can be the beneficiary of a financial provision order when he is already *over 18* on application depended upon the legislation under which the application was made. It could be made in divorce proceedings (see Matrimonial Causes Act 1973, s.29(3) and *Downing* v. *Downing* [1976] Fam. 288) or in matrimonial proceedings in the magistrates' court (Domestic Proceedings and Magistrates Courts Act 1978, s.5(3)). But it couldn't be made under the guardianship legislation or the affiliation legislation. This section, which extends previously existing powers to guardianship legislation, is necessary to eliminate differences between legitimate and illegitimate children.

Because this is a "far-reaching step" (Law Com. No. 118, para. 6.32), jurisdiction has been confined to the High Court and County Court (*cf.* ss.12, 13 where magistrates' courts have jurisdiction) and powers limited to the making of periodical payment and lump sum orders. Powers to make property adjustment orders are not conferred on the courts under this provision. Further, the powers under this section may only be activated when the parents are living apart (s.11D(4)), and an application may not be made if, immediately before the applicant attained the age of 16, a periodical payments order was in force with respect to him (s.11D(3)).

Application by a person. This section deals only with applications at their own instance by adult children.

Attained the age of eighteen. Attained at the commencement of the eighteenth anniversary of birth (see Family Law Reform Act 1969, s.9).

Whose parents are not living with each other . . . same household. The test, where they are living under the same roof, is: are they living as two households or one? There is a difference between chronic discord or neglect and separate lives (see *Hopes* v. *Hopes* [1949] P. 227 and *Mouncer* v. *Mouncer* [1972] 1 All E.R. 289). Parents will not be living with each other if they are living with someone else (see *Fuller (orse Penfold)* v. *Fuller* [1973] 2 All E.R. 650).

Is . . . will be . . . would be. Note the section provides for the situation where the applicant requires financial provision *in order to* continue education or training.

Trade. This "has the technical meaning of buying or selling" (*per* Willes J. in *Harris* v. *Amery*, L.R. 1 C.P. 148. It has been said that even an illegal business may be a "trade" (*Southern* v. *A.B.* [1944] 1 K.B. 713).

Profession. It is "impossible to lay down any strict legal definition of what is a profession" (*per* Scrutton L.J. in *Currie* v. *I.R.C.* [1921] 2 K.B. 332). According to du Parcq L.J. in *Carr* v. *I.R.C.* [1944] 2 All E.R. 163 it is "the intention of the legislature, when it refers to a profession, to indicate what the ordinary intelligent subject . . . will think that 'profession' means"! He did not think the lawyer could help him very much (see pp.166–167).

Special circumstances. Most obviously that he is handicapped.

The court may make. "The court, on examining the merits of the case, may not think it appropriate to make an order." See *Downing* v. *Downing* [1976] Fam. 288, 293. The Law Commission thinks the discretion needs to be "sparingly exercised" (Law Com. No. 118, para. 6.32).

The orders. These are the only orders. Property adjustment orders may not be made.

Immediately before . . . 16. The order will have lapsed at that date or at some time thereafter. A child over 18 may apply to revive an earlier order, even if his parents are living together (see s.12(C)(5) of the GMA 1971).

Attained the age of 16. At the commencement of the sixteenth anniversary of his birth (Family Law Reform Act 1969, s.9).

Periodical payments order. See s.11D(7).

No order . . . parents . . . living with each other. S.11B(1) above provides that an *application* cannot be made by a person over 18 if his parents are living together. This provision provides that an *order* cannot be made at a time when the parents are living together, so that it covers the case where cohabitation is resumed between the application and the order. If parents cohabit *after* the making of the order, this will not affect the order.

Cease on death. Orders are thus personal and expire on the payer's death. This is in line with s.12(3) of the GMA 1971.

Periodical payments order. This supplements s.11B(3) and defines "periodical payments order" by reference to the proceedings in which a particular payments order may have been made.

Alteration of maintenance agreements

Alteration during lives of parties

15.—(1) In this section and section 16 below "maintenance agreement" means any agreement in writing made in respect of a child, whether before or after the commencement of this section, being an agreement which—

(a) is or was made between the father and mother of the child; and

(b) contains provision in respect of the making or securing of payments, or the disposition or use of any property, for the maintenance or education of the child;

and any such provisions are in this section and that section referred to as "financial arrangements".

(2) Where a maintenance agreement is for the time being subsisting and each of the parties to the agreement is for the time being either domiciled or resident in England and Wales, then, subject to subsection (4) below, either party may apply to the High Court, a county court or a magistrates' court for an order under this section.

(3) If the court to which the application is made is satisfied either—

(a) that, by reason of a change in the circumstances in the light of which any financial arrangements contained in the agreement were made (including a change foreseen by the parties when making the agreement), the agreement should be altered so as to make different financial arrangements; or

(b) that the agreement does not contain proper financial arrangements with respect to the child,

then, subject to subsections (4) and (5) below, that court may by order make such alterations in the agreement by varying or revoking any financial arrangements contained in it as may appear to that court to be just having regard to all the circumstances; and the agreement shall have effect thereafter as if any alteration made by the order had been made by agreement between the parties and for valuable consideration.

(4) A magistrates' court shall not entertain an application under subsection (2) above unless both the parties to the agreement are resident in England and Wales and at least one of the parties is resident in the commission area (within the meaning of the Justices of the Peace Act 1979) for which the court is appointed, and shall not have power to make any order on such an application except—

  (a) in a case where the agreement contains no provision for periodical payments by either of the parties, an order inserting provision for the making by one of the parties of periodical payments for the maintenance of the child;

  (b) in a case where the agreement includes provision for the making by one of the parties of periodical payments, an order increasing or reducing the rate of, or terminating, any of those payments.

(5) Where a court decides to alter an agreement, by an order under this section—

  (a) by inserting provision for the making or securing by one of the parties to the agreement of periodical payments for the maintenance of the child, or

  (b) by increasing the rate of periodical payments required to be made or secured by one of the parties for the maintenance of the child,

then, in deciding the term for which under the agreement as altered by the order the payments or, as the case may be, the additional payments attributable to the increase are to be made or secured for the benefit of the child, the court shall apply the provisions of subsections (1) and (2) of section 12 of the 1971 Act as if the order were an order under section 11B(2)(a) or (b) of that Act.

(6) For the avoidance of doubt it is hereby declared that nothing in this section affects any power of a court before which any proceedings between the parties to a maintenance agreement are brought under any other enactment to make an order containing financial arrangements or any right of either party to apply for such an order in such proceedings.

GENERAL NOTE

    This section (and the next) make provision for the alteration of maintenance agreements made in respect of illegitimate children during the lives of the parties to such agreements (s.15), and after the death of one of the parties to such an agreement (s.16).

    The section essentially reproduces the law contained in ss.35 and 36 of the Matrimonial Causes Act 1973 relating to the alteration of written maintenance agreements, which only applied to parties to a marriage (see s.34(2) of the 1973 Act) and thus placed agreements relating to the maintenance of a child of unmarried parents outside its scope.

    This extension should facilitate and encourage out of court agreements. The consideration for the father's promise to pay sums towards the child's maintenance has been said to be the mother's agreement not to institute affiliation proceedings. Denning L.J. in *Ward* v. *Byham* [1956] 1 W.L.R. 496 said (at p.498) that the mother's promise to perform her existing legal obligations towards the child provided sufficient consideration, but that view is thought to be too wide. Affiliation proceedings were abolished by this Act (s.17). Consideration will now be found in the mother's agreement not to bring proceedings for financial provision.

Subs. (1)

    This subsection defines maintenance agreement for the purpose of this section and s.16. It must:

    (i) be in writing;

    (ii) be between father and mother of the child;

    (iii) contain provision in respect of the making or securing of payments or the disposition or use of any property for the maintenance or education of the child.

It is not necessary (*cf.* Law Com. No. 118, para. 6.43) that the agreement contains an acknowledgment of paternity by the father.

Subs. (2)

This subsection, which provides for application to the High Court, a county court or a magistrates' court to vary a maintenance agreement, corresponds to s.35(1) of the Matrimonial Causes Act 1973.

Subs. (3)

This subsection reproduces the effect of s.35(2) of the Matrimonial Causes Act 1973. There are two differences. First, some modifications are made to reflect the fact that the powers are only exercisable in relation to children. Secondly, it is necessary that some financial arrangements were originally made in the agreement the terms of which it is desired to alter.

Subs. (4)

This subsection (corresponding to s.35(3) of the Matrimonial Causes Act 1973) provides that magistrates' courts may only exercise jurisdiction where the parties are resident in England and Wales and one is resident in the relevant commission area. An order cannot be made unless the agreement concerns unsecured periodical payments.

Subs. (5)

The purpose of this subsection is to ensure the same rules apply to the duration of maintenance agreements for illegitimate children as for legitimate ones, when the agreements are altered by an order under this section.

Subs. (6)

This subsection reproduces with necessary modifications the effect of s.35(6) of the Matrimonial Causes Act 1973. It ensures that any other financial proceedings between parties to a maintenance agreement should not be prejudiced by the powers conferred in this section.

Alteration after death of one party

16.—(1) Where a maintenance agreement provides for the continuation, after the death of one of the parties, of payments for the maintenance of the child and that party dies domiciled in England and Wales, the surviving party or the personal representatives of the deceased party may, subject to subsections (2) and (3) below, apply to the High Court or a county court for an order under section 15 above.

(2) An application under this section shall not, except with the permission of the High Court or a county court, be made after the end of a period of six months from the date on which representation in regard to the estate of the deceased is first taken out.

(3) A county court shall not entertain an application under this section, or an application for permission to make an application under this section, unless it would have jurisdiction to hear and determine proceedings for an order under section 2 of the Inheritance (Provision for Family and Dependants) Act 1975 in relation to the deceased's estate by virtue of section 25 of the County Courts Act 1984 (jurisdiction under the said Act of 1975).

(4) If a maintenance agreement is altered by a court on an application under this section the like consequences shall ensue as if the alteration had been made, immediately before the death, by agreement between the parties and for valuable consideration.

(5) The provisions of this section shall not render the personal representatives of the deceased liable for having distributed any part of the estate of the deceased after the expiration of the period of six months referred to in subsection (2) above on the ground that they ought to have taken into account the possibility that a court might permit an application by virtue of this section to be made by the surviving party after that period;

but this subsection shall not prejudice any power to recover any part of the estate so distributed arising by virtue of the making of an order in pursuance of this section.

(6) In considering for the purposes of subsection (2) above the question when representation was first taken out, a grant limited to settled land or to trust property shall be left out of account and a grant limited to real estate or to personal estate shall be left out of account unless a grant limited to the remainder of the estate has previously been made or is made at the same time.

GENERAL NOTE
This section is supplementary to s.15. It provides for the case where it is desired to alter a maintenance agreement after one of the parties to the agreement has died.

It corresponds to s.36 of the Matrimonial Causes Act 1973 and extends to illegitimate children the powers already available under the 1973 Act in respect of legitimate children.

Subs. (1)
This subsection allows the surviving party or a personal representative of the deceased party to apply to the court for an order varying a maintenance agreement, where the agreement provides for the continuation after death of payments.

This corresponds to s.31 of the 1973, with necessary modifications.

Apply. See s.16(2).

Subs. (2)
This subsection is identical to s.36(2) of the Matrimonial Causes Act 1973.

Permission. The onus lies on the applicant and an extension of time should be sought promptly. It has been said (in relation to the Inheritance (Provision for Family and Dependants) Act 1975) that solicitors acting for an applicant may be liable in negligence if an application is not made in time (*Re Salmon* [1981] Ch. 167).

Subs. (3)
This subsection limits the jurisdiction of the county court in line with that court's powers to deal with applications for reasonable financial provision out of the deceased's estate under the Inheritance (Provision for Family and Dependants) Act 1975.

Subs. (4)
This section is identical to s.36(4) of the Matrimonial Causes Act 1973.

Subs. (5)
This subsection gives personal representatives the same immunity from liability, and the applicants a similar right to recover property, as in relation to variation of secured periodical payments. It is in identical terms to s.36(5) of the Matrimonial Causes Act 1973.

Subs. (6)
This subsection reproduces, with necessary modifications, the effect of s.36(6) of the Matrimonial Causes Act 1973. It also corresponds to s.12D(4) of the GMA 1971.

Supplemental

Abolition of affiliation proceedings

17. The Affiliation Proceedings Act 1957 (the provisions of which are superseded by this Part) shall cease to have effect.

GENERAL NOTE
This section abolishes affiliation proceedings. The demise of affiliation (formerly bastardy) proceedings, rooted in the Poor Law and tainted with criminality, is unlikely to be mourned by anyone. It was in the area of maintenance that the illegitimate child encountered the most serious discrimination. Maintenance could only be obtained by the child's mother (or, since December 1985 his custodian), only in the magistrates' court, and only if certain requirements were satisfied (*e.g.* the mother had to be a "single woman", proceedings had to be brought within three years of the child's birth and the mother's evidence had to be

corroborated). The orders that could be made were limited. In fact few applications were made.

The distinctive procedure for the maintenance of illegitimate children is thus abolished. Henceforth, orders for financial provision of a child are obtainable, whatever the marital status of the parents, under the GMA 1971. So far as the law is concerned, all children, whether legitimate or illegitimate, will have equal rights to financial provision from both their parents. The only difference (and it is a major one) is that it will still be necessary to prove that the "father" is the father. There will continue to be denials, and thus trials, of paternity: in practice this happens comparatively rarely where the parents are married to each other.

Cease to have effect. For transitional provisions and savings see Sched. 3, paras. 6 and 7. One of the consequences of abolishing affiliation proceedings is that certain orders will no longer be enforceable as "affiliation orders". The abolition of affiliation proceedings means that the expression will no longer apply and such orders will henceforth be enforceable as "magistrates' courts maintenance orders" (see para. 88 of Sched. 2).

Other provisions which will cease to have effect are:
—s.44 of the National Assistance Act 1948 (para. 7 of Sched. 2);
—s.45 of the Children Act 1975 (para. 66 of Sched. 2);
—ss.49 and 50 of the Child Care Act 1980 (para. 76 of Sched. 2);
—s.25 of the Social Security Act 1986 (para. 92 of Sched. 2);

and (presumably) s.19 of the Supplementary Benefits Act 1976 (but by oversight *semble* this is left intact).

Part III

Property Rights

Succession on intestacy

18.—(1) In Part IV of the Administration of Estates Act 1925 (which deals with the distribution of the estate of an intestate), references (however expressed) to any relationship between two persons shall be construed in accordance with section 1 above.

(2) For the purposes of subsection (1) above and that Part of that Act, a person whose father and mother were not married to each other at the time of his birth shall be presumed not to have been survived by his father, or by any person related to him only through his father, unless the contrary is shown.

(3) In section 50(1) of that Act (which relates to the construction of documents), the reference to Part IV of that Act, or to the foregoing provisions of that Part, shall in relation to an instrument inter vivos made, or a will or codicil coming into operation, after the coming into force of this section (but in relation to instruments inter vivos made or wills or codicils coming into operation earlier) be construed as including references to this section.

(4) This section does not affect any rights under the intestacy of a person dying before the coming into force of this section.

GENERAL NOTE

This section deals with the rights of succession to property on intestacy. It embodies the principle that illegitimacy is not to be taken into consideration in determining: (i) the rights of succession of an illegitimate person; (ii) the rights of succession to the estate of an illegitimate person; and (iii) the rights of succession traced through an illegitimate relationship.

Subs. (1)

Shall be construed. And without reference to whether or not the father and mother of the relevant person were married to each other or not. In effect illegitimacy becomes irrelevant for the purpose of entitlement on intestacy, whether *by* an illegitimate person or *to* his estate.

Subs. (2)

The Family Law Reform Act 1969, s.14(4) created, for the purposes of intestate succession, a rebuttable presumption that the father of an illegitimate intestate had not survived his child. It followed a recommendation of the Russell committee (Cmnd. 3051, 1966). In effect, the presumption places the burden of proof upon the man claiming to be entitled to succeed as the intestate's father. The Law Commission (Law Com. No. 118, paras. 8, 32–8, 33) recommended that the presumption be retained and extended to all relatives of an illegitimate deceased on the paternal side. This is enacted by this subsection. The justification for so extending this rule of convenience is that rights of intestate succession have been extended by the Act to such relatives.

Subs. (3)

S.50(1) of the Administration of Estates Act 1925 deals with the construction of documents. It states, *inter alia*, that "references . . . to statutory next of kin shall be construed . . . as referring to the person who would take beneficially on an intestacy . . ."

Subs. (4)

This states that this section has prospective force only and only applies to those who die intestate after this section comes into operation.

Dispositions of property

19.—(1) In the following dispositions, namely—
  (a) dispositions inter vivos made on or after the date on which this section comes into force; and
  (b) dispositions by will or codicil where the will or codicil is made on or after that date,
references (whether express or implied) to any relationship between two persons shall be construed in accordance with section 1 above.

(2) It is hereby declared that the use, without more, of the word "heir" or "heirs" or any expression which is used to create an entailed interest in real or personal property does not show a contrary intention for the purposes of section 1 as applied by subsection (1) above.

(3) In relation to the dispositions mentioned in subsection (1) above, section 33 of the Trustee Act 1925 (which specifies the trust implied by a direction that income is to be held on protective trusts for the benefit of any person) shall have effect as if any reference (however expressed) to any relationship between two persons were construed in accordance with section 1 above.

(4) Where under any disposition of real or personal property, any interest in such property is limited (whether subject to any preceding limitation or charge or not) in such a way that it would, apart from this section, devolve (as nearly as the law permits) along with a dignity or title of honour, then—
  (a) whether or not the disposition contains an express reference to the dignity or title of honour; and
  (b) whether or not the property or some interest in the property may in some event become severed from it,
nothing in this section shall operate to sever the property or any interest in it from the dignity or title, but the property or interest shall devolve in all respects as if this section had not been enacted.

(5) This section is without prejudice to section 42 of the Adoption Act 1976 (construction of dispositions in cases of adoption).

(6) In this section "disposition" means a disposition, including an oral disposition, of real or personal property whether inter vivos or by will or codicil.

(7) Notwithstanding any rule of law, a disposition made by will or codicil executed before the date on which this section comes into force shall not be treated for the purposes of this section as made on or after

that date by reason only that the will or codicil is confirmed by a codicil executed on or after that date.

GENERAL NOTE

This section effects reforms for benefiting illegitimate persons in relation to succession under wills and other dispositions. It continues the moves begun by the Family Law Reform Act 1969.

Subs. (1)

This lays down that in construing wills and codicils and dispositions *inter vivos* no account is to be taken of whether the relationship between two persons is established through or outside marriage. Thus, the rule in s.15(2) of the Family Law Reform Act 1969 that words of relationship were only to be construed presumptively to include an illegitimate person where that person was a potential beneficiary or where the beneficiary's relationship to the deceased depended on an intermediate illegitimate link. Thus, the appointment of "my eldest surviving son" as an executor was governed by the law as it stood pre-1969, with the result that the eldest surviving *legitimate* son alone qualified as executor. Similarly, if property was settled on A for life, with remainder to A's estate if he dies leaving any child surviving him, followed by a gift over to X, the gift over to X took effect if A left illegitimate, but not legitimate, issue (and see *Re Paine* [1940] Ch. 46). This discrimination against those born outside marriage is removed by this subsection.
    Dispositions. See s.19(6).
    Disposition by will or codicil . . . on or after that date. See s.19(7).

Subs. (2)

This subsection makes it clear that the reforms effected by this section extend to entailed interests. See, further, Law Com. No. 157, para. 3.7.

Subs. (3)

Where income is held in protective trusts, and the interest fails or determines during the trust period, the income is to be applied at the trustees' discretion for the maintenance and support, or otherwise for the benefit of the principal beneficiary and his or her wife or husband, if any, and his or her children or remote issue, etc. In determining "children" and "issue", no account must now be taken of legitimacy. Trustees have absolute discretion (see *Re Powles* [1954] 1 W.L.R. 336).

Subs. (4)

Titles of honour are unaffected by this legislation. See further Law Com. No. 118, para. 8.26.

Subs. (5)

A useful discussion of s.42 of the Adoption Act 1976 is Cretney, 126 New L.J. 7.

Subs. (7)

This makes it clear that where a will is made before the implementation of this section, the fact that a codicil confirming the will may be made *after* the section is implemented will not prevent the will from being treated as having been made *before* implementation of the section. Without this provision, it is possible that dispositions in the will might be governed by the law in force at the date of the later codicil (*cf. Re Rayner* [1903] 1 Ch. 685).

No special protection for trustees and personal representatives

20. Section 17 of the Family Law Reform Act 1969 (which enables trustees and personal representatives to distribute property without having ascertained that no person whose parents were not married to each other at the time of his birth, or who claims through such a person, is or may be entitled to an interest in the property) shall cease to have effect.

GENERAL NOTE

This section *removes* the special protection, formerly found in s.17 of the Family Law Reform Act 1969, for trustees and personal representatives to distribute property without inquiring whether any illegitimate relationship existed which might affect the distribution. The Law Commission changed its mind on this in the period between its first and second reports (see respectively Law Com. No. 118, paras. 8.29–8.33 and Law Com. No. 157, paras. 3.8–3.13).

Protection for trustees and personal representatives is still found in s.27 of the Trustee Act 1925. He may advertise for claims and is then exempt from liability to all claimants except those of whom he has notice (including constructive notice; *Re Land Credit Company of Ireland* (1872) 21 W.R. 135). Advertisement should be prompt: it was judicially regarded as "late" where there was a delay of five months after the death (*Re Kay* [1897] 2 Ch. 518, 523). The advertisement should ask for "any person interested" (see *Re Aldhous* [1955] 2 All E.R. 80). Note also the court has power to relieve a personal representative of liability where he has "acted honestly and reasonably, and ought fairly to be excused. . ." (Trustee Act 1925, s.61).

It should be stressed also that the beneficiary's right to claim against the recipients of the property remains.

Entitlement to grant of probate etc.

21.—(1) For the purpose of determining the person or persons who would in accordance with probate rules be entitled to a grant of probate or administration in respect of the estate of a deceased person, the deceased shall be presumed, unless the contrary is shown, not to have been survived—

(a) by any person related to him whose father and mother were not married to each other at the time of his birth; or

(b) by any person whose relationship with him is deduced through such a person as is mentioned in paragraph (a) above.

(2) In this section "probate rules" means rules of court made under section 127 of the Supreme Court Act 1981.

(3) This section does not apply in relation to the estate of a person dying before the coming into force of this section.

GENERAL NOTE

This section lays down that, for the purposes of obtaining a grant of probate or administration, there should be a rebuttable presumption that the deceased left no surviving relatives who are illegitimate or whose relationship is traced through illegitimacy. The section is not retrospective. See, further, Law Com. No. 118, paras. 8.40–8.42.

PART IV

DETERMINATION OF RELATIONSHIPS

Declarations of parentage

22. For section 56 of the Family Law Act 1986 (declarations of legitimacy or legitimation) there shall be substituted the following section—

"Declarations of parentage, legitimacy or legitimation

56.—(1) Any person may apply to the court for a declaration—

(a) that a person named in the application is or was his parent; or

(b) that he is the legitimate child of his parents.

(2) Any person may apply to the court for one (or for one or, in the alternative, the other) of the following declarations, that is to say—

(a) a declaration that he has become a legitimated person;

(b) a declaration that he has not become a legitimated person.

(3) A court shall have jurisdiction to entertain an application under this section if, and only if, the applicant—

(a) is domiciled in England and Wales on the date of the application; or

(b) has been habitually resident in England and Wales throughout the period of one year ending with that date.

(4) Where a declaration is made on an application under subsection (1) above, the prescribed officer of the court shall notify the Registrar General, in such a manner and within such period as may be prescribed, of the making of that declaration.

(5) In this section 'legitimated person' means a person legitimated or recognised as legitimated—

(a) under section 2 or 3 of the Legitimacy Act 1976;
(b) under section 1 or 8 of the Legitimacy Act 1926; or
(c) by a legitimation (whether or not by virtue of the subsequent marriage of his parents) recognised by the law of England and Wales and effected under the law of another country."

GENERAL NOTE

This section provides for the making of declarations of parentage. The jurisdictional basis is the same as that for declarations of legitimacy or legitimation in s.56 of the Family Law Act 1986 (which is not yet in force).

Subs. (1) of the new s.56

This subsection gives the court power to grant a declaration that the applicant is legitimate or that a person named in the application is or was his parent.

The Court. I.e. the High Court or a county court (see s.63 of the 1986 Act).

Parent. Whether that person was married to other parent or not.

He is. The court does not have the power to make a declaration as to the legitimacy of any other person than the applicant.

Legitimate child. But not to make a declaration that the applicant, is or was, illegitimate (see s.58(5)(b) of the Family Law Act 1986). Included within legitimacy is the concept of the putative marriage rendered legitimate by s.1 of the Legitimacy Act 1976 (see *F. and F.* v. *Att.-Gen.* [1980] 10 Fam. Law 60).

Subs. (2) of new s.56

This subsection gives the court power to grant a declaraton that the applicant has, or has not, become a legitimated person, as the case may be. For jurisdiction see the new subsection (3).

The court. I.e. the High Court or a county court (see s.63 of the 1986 Act).

He has. Only the person whose legitimation is in issue may apply.

Legitimated person. As to which see the new subsection (5).

Not become a legitimated person. The Law Commission (Law Com. No. 132, p.18 No. 124) believes: "there may well be cases in which such a declaration could serve a useful purpose, particularly where the alleged legitimation has occurred as a result of formal acknowledgement, or governmental act, in a foreign country".

Subs. (3) of new s.56

Domiciled. The domicile of origin of a legitimate child is that of his father (*Udny* v. *Udny* [1869] L.R. 1 Sc. and Div. 441). Until the child attains the age of 16 (or marries under that age), his domicile will follow that of his mother, as it will where the parents are separated and the child has his home with his mother and has no home with his father (Domicile and Matrimonial Proceedings Act 1973, s.4). A circular argument will, accordingly, develop when considering whether the court has jurisdiction where the applicant for a declaration of legitimacy is an unmarried child under 16. His domicile depends on whether he is legitimate. Jurisdiction to entertain the application depends on his domicile. The Law Commission (Law Com. No. 132, p.33, n.224) envisages that courts will resolve this problem by not declaring jurisdiction until it has been ascertained whether or not the alleged fact upon which the jurisdiction is found is true. It notes (*idem*): "In practice this will mean that jurisdiction will depend on the domicile of the child's mother or father, as the case may be". See also for an analogy the case. of *Garthwaite* v. *Garthwaite* [1964] P. 356. It should, perhaps, be pointed out that the law of domicile is unaffected by the reforms in the 1987 Act. See, further, Law Com. No. 118, paras. 13.1–13.3, where it is pointed out that to reform the law would affect more legitimate that illegitimate children and would have implications for the law of taxation.

Habitually resident. There is no authoritative definition of this. The word "habitual" indicates a quality of residence, rather than a period of residence (see *Cruse* v. *Chittum* [1974] 2 All E.R. 940, 942–943). It was defined as regular physical presence enduring for some time. In more recent cases (*R.* v. *London Borough of Barnet, ex p. Shah* [1983] 2 A.C. 309, at p.340 and 342 and *Kapur* v. *Kapur* [1984] F.L.R. 920) it has been suggested that there is no substantial difference between ordinary residence and habitual residence. But it has been said that one can be ordinarily resident in more than one country at the same time (see *Inland Revenue Commission* v. *Lysaght* [1928] A.C. 234). It surely cannot be right that one can be habitually resident in more than one country at the same time.

Throughout the period. This does not mean that the applicant must have lived in England and Wales throughout the whole of the one year period preceding the application. An applicant could be "habitually resident" in England and Wales for the preceding year without living in England and Wales for any of that period. What is in question are "durable ties" (Law Com. No. 48, para. 42) and not actual residence.

Subs. (4) of new s.56
As may be prescribed. This has not yet been done.

Subs. (5) of new s.56
This section defines "legitimated person" for the purposes of this section. The definition corresponds to that in s.10(1) of the Legitimacy Act 1976. The effect of paras. (a) and (b) is that a declaration of legitimacy may be granted in respect of a legitimation by virtue of the Legitimacy Act 1976, or recognised under either that Act or the Legitimacy Act 1926. Para. (c) makes it clear that a declaration may also be granted that the applicant is recognised as legitimated at common law.

Not by virtue of the subsequent marriage. For example by recognition (see *Re Luck's Settlement* [1940] Ch. 864).

Recognised by the law of England . . . effected under the law of any country. Note where the legitimation is by an act other than marrige, the Legitimacy Act has no application. It will be recognised only if the common law rules are satisfied, *i.e.* the father must be domiciled in a country, the law of which accepts the validity of the legitimation, both at the time of the child's birth and at the time of the act effecting the legitimation (see *Re Luck's Settlement* [1940] Ch. 864).

Provisions as to scientific tests

23.—(1) For subsections (1) and (2) of section 20 of the Family Law Reform Act 1969 (power of court to require use of blood tests) there shall be substituted the following subsections—

    "(1) In any civil proceedings in which the parentage of any person falls to be determined, the court may, either of its own motion or on an application by any party to the proceedings, give a direction—

      (a) for the use of scientific tests to ascertain whether such tests show that a party to the proceedings is or is not the father or mother of that person; and

      (b) for the taking, within a period specified in the direction, of bodily samples from all or any of the following, namely, that person, any party who is alleged to be the father or mother of that person and any other party to the proceedings;

and the court may at any time revoke or vary a direction previously given by it under this subsection.

    (2) The person responsible for carrying out scientific tests in pursuance of a direction under subsection (1) above shall make to the court a report in which he shall state—

      (a) the results of the tests;

      (b) whether any party to whom the report relates is or is not excluded by the results from being the father or mother of the person whose parentage is to be determined; and

      (c) in relation to any party who is not so excluded, the value, if any, of the results in determining whether that party is the father or mother of that person;

and the report shall be received by the court as evidence in the proceedings of the matters stated in it.

(2A) Where the proceedings in which the parentage of any person falls to be determined are proceedings on an application under section 56 of the Family Law Act 1986, any reference in subsection (1) or (2) of this section to any party to the proceedings shall include a reference to any person named in the application."

(2) In section 25 of that Act (interpretation of Part III)—

    (a) for the definitions of "blood samples" and "blood tests" there shall be substituted the following definition—

        "'bodily sample' means a sample of bodily fluid or bodily tissue taken for the purpose of scientific tests;"; and

    (b) after the definition of "excluded" there shall be inserted the following definition—

        "'scientific tests' means scientific tests carried out under this Part of this Act and made with the object of ascertaining the inheritable characteristics of bodily fluids or bodily tissue."

GENERAL NOTE

This section confers on the court the power in any civil proceedings in which questions of parentage fall to be determined to require the use of scientific tests on bodily fluids or bodily tissues. It also provides for the person responsible for carrying out the scientific tests to report to the court.

The new power replaces that in s.20 of the Family Law Reform Act 1969 and makes the following changes:

    (i) the court may give a direction for the use of scientific tests of its own motion;

    (ii) the court may direct that a bodily sample be taken from any party to the proceedings;

    (iii) tests may be used to determine parentage, including maternity, and are not, as under the previous law, limited to paternity.

Note also the purpose of a scientific test direction is expressed to be to determine whether or not a person *is* a parent, and not merely whether a person is excluded from being a parent.

These changes reflect scientific developments, in particular the new DNA testing procedure, which has been readily available since June 1987.

Subs. (1) of new s.20

This corresponds in part to s.20(1) of the Family Law Reform Act 1969. It provides for the court hearing any civil proceedings in which parentage falls to be determined (ranging from an application for a declaration to a matter of succession) to give a direction for the use of scientific tests and for the taking of bodily samples from the person whose parentage falls to be decided, any person alleged to be his parent and any such party to the proceedings. Directions may be revoked or varied.

Civil proceedings. But not criminal proceedings.

Parentage. Not just paternity. Maternity is rarely in doubt, but where it is, it comes within the provision.

Court may. It has a discretion. The Act does not specify how this discretion should be exercised. As to how discretion should be exercised in relation to a child see *S.* v. *S.* [1972] A.C. 24 (court should allow a blood test of a child unless satisfied that such a course would be against the interests of the child).

Own motion. See Law Com. No. 118, para. 10.29, where the risk of collusive claims being presented is referred to. The Law Commission believes the court would be "influenced by the views of the Attorney-General".

Scientific tests. Including the new DNA test. See s.23(2)(b).

Whether such tests show. On a balance of probabilities. See *Blyth* v. *Blyth* [1966] A.C. 643; *Bastable* v. *Bastable* [1968] 1 W.L.R. 1684. Nevertheless, however it is conveyed, the court should not draw conclusions without clear and convincing evidence. On the relevance of tests generally see Law Com. No. 118, paras. 5.2–5.7 and B. Dodd, "When Blood is Their Argument" (1980) 20 Med.Sci. and Law 231. Good examples of the usefulness of blood testing are *R.* v. *R.* [1968] P. 414 and *Dixon* v. *Dixon* [1982] 4 F.L.R. 99.

For the taking. No test may be carried out on a person aged 16 or over without his consent (and arguably in certain circumstances after *Gillick* on a person under 16). A direction is not compulsory but a refusal to comply will entitle the court to draw such inferences as the circumstances may properly warrant (see s.23 of the Family Law Reform Act 1969).

Any other party in the proceedings. E.g. mother's husband. And see s.23(2A) in relation to s.22.

Subs. (2) of s.25 of the 1969 Act

This lays down new definitions for the purpose of Pt. III of the Family Law Reform Act 1969. These new definitions are made necessary by the new bio-technological developments, in particular by the new technique of blood finger-printing (the so-called DNA tests).

PART V

REGISTRATION OF BIRTHS

Registration of father where parents not married

24. For section 10 of the Births and Deaths Registration Act 1953 (in this Act referred to as "the 1953 Act") there shall be substituted the following section—

> **"Registration of father where parents not married**
>
> 10.—(1) Notwithstanding anything in the foregoing provisions of this Act, in the case of a child whose father and mother were not married to each other at the time of his birth, no person shall as father of the child be required to give information concerning the birth of the child, and the registrar shall not enter in the register the name of any person as father of the child except—
>
> (a) at the joint request of the mother and the person stating himself to be the father of the child (in which case that person shall sign the register together with the mother); or
>
> (b) at the request of the mother on production of—
>> (i) a declaration in the prescribed form made by the mother stating that that person is the father of the child; and
>> (ii) a statutory declaration made by that person stating himself to be the father of the child; or
>
> (c) at the request of that person on production of—
>> (i) a declaration in the prescribed form by that person stating himself to be the father of the child; and
>> (ii) a statutory declaration made by the mother stating that that person is the father of the child; or
>
> (d) at the request of the mother or that person (which shall in either case be made in writing) on production of—
>> (i) a certified copy of a relevant order; and
>> (ii) if the child has attained the age of sixteen, the written consent of the child to the registration of that person as his father.
>
> (2) Where, in the case of a child whose father and mother were not married to each other at the time of his birth, a person stating himself to be the father of the child makes a request to the registrar in accordance with paragraph (c) or (d) of subsection (1) of this section—
>
> (a) he shall be treated as a qualified informant concerning the birth of the child for the purposes of this Act; and
>
> (b) the giving of information concerning the birth of the child by that person and the signing of the register by him in the presence of the registrar shall act as a discharge of any duty of any other qualified informant under section 2 of this Act.
>
> (3) In this section and section 10A of this Act references to a child whose father and mother were not married to each other at the time

of his birth shall be construed in accordance with section 1 of the Family Law Reform Act 1987 and 'relevant order', in relation to a request under subsection (1)(d) that the name of any person be entered in the register as father of a child, means any of the following orders, namely—

(a) an order under section 4 of the said Act of 1987 which gives that person all the parental rights and duties with respect to the child;

(b) an order under section 9 of the Guardianship of Minors Act 1971 which gives that person any parental right with respect to the child; and

(c) an order under section 11B of that Act which requires that person to make any financial provision for the child."

GENERAL NOTE

This section (and the next two) are designed to facilitate the recording of paternity on the birth certificate of an illegitimate child. They deal respectively with the first registration of an illegitimate child (s.24), the re-registration of the birth of such a child (s.25) and the re-registration of birth after a declaration of parentage (s.26).

This section substitutes a new s.10 for the Births and Deaths Registration Act 1953, which deals with the circumstances in which paternity may be recorded on first registration in the case of an illegitimate child. There are two changes of significance: (i) a person acknowledging himself to be the father of an illegitimate child may be registered as the child's father if he has a court order under which he has parental rights and duties (a s.4 order), an order under the GMA 1971, s.9, giving him any parental right or an order under s.11B of that Act requiring him to make financial provision for the child, and (ii) he may be so registered if he has a statutory declaration as to his paternity made by the mother.

Subs. (1) of new s.10

This re-states the principle that the father of an illegitimate child is not to be required to give information concerning the birth of the child. Other parents are so required (1953 Act, ss.2 and 36). Only in the circumstances set out will the person claiming to be the father be *entitled* to register the child's birth: there is no general right (or duty) to register. This subsection sets out in paras. (a) to (d) the circumstances in which the name of the father of an illegitimate child may be registered on first registration.

Paras. (a) and (b) re-enact existing paras. (a) and (b) in s.10(1) of the 1953 Act (as substituted by s.27(1) of the Family Law Reform Act 1969).

Para. (c) provides that, just as the mother of an illegitimate child can register the child's birth on the strength of declarations made by herself and by the man acknowledging himself to be the father, so the acknowledging father can register the birth with such declarations. It assists the situation where the mother cannot or does not wish to attend the register office to register the birth, but the father can do so. (See Law Com. No. 118, para. 10.74.)

Para. (d) replaces para. (c) of s.10 of the 1953 Act (as substituted by s.93(1) of the Children Act 1975) which provides for registration of a child's birth upon production of an affiliation order. It is now provided that either the mother or the person acknowledging himself to be the father may on written request have the child's birth registered, so as to show that person's name as father, on production of an order giving him parental rights (s.4 of this Act) or any parental right (see s.9 of the GMA 1971) or an order requiring him to make any financial provision for the child. The written consent of a child over 16 is required (as it was in s.93(1) of the Children Act 1975, but this is extended to cases where there is a s.4 order or an order under s.9 of the 1971 Act).

Subs. (2) of new s.10

This subsection is necessary because the father of an illegitimate child is not, as such, a "qualified informant" concerning the birth of the child. This subsection makes him a "qualified informant" where he makes a request under para. (c) or (d) of subs. (1). Registration at the instance of the father of an illegitimate child in this way discharges the duty of any other qualified informant.

Subs. (3) of new s.10

This subsection incorporates s.1 of the 1987 Act into the 1953 Act and defines "relevant order" (see the new s.10(1)(d)) as one of these orders: (i) a s.4 order, (ii) an order under s.9 of the GMA 1971 giving "any parental right", (iii) an order under s.11B of the 1971 Act requiring the person to make any financial provision for the child.

Re-registration where parents not married

25. For section 10A of the 1953 Act there shall be substituted the following section—

"Re-registration where parents not married

10A.—(1) Where there has been registered under this Act the birth of a child whose father and mother were not married to each other at the time of the birth, but no person has been registered as the father of the child, the registrar shall re-register the birth so as to show a person as the father—

(a) at the joint request of the mother and that person; or

(b) at the request of the mother on production of—
    (i) a declaration in the prescribed form made by the mother stating that that person is the father of the child; and
    (ii) a statutory declaration made by that person stating himself to be the father of the child; or

(c) at the request of that person on production of—
    (i) a declaration in the prescribed form by that person stating himself to be the father of the child; and
    (ii) a statutory declaration made by the mother stating that that person is the father of the child; or

(d) at the request of the mother or that person (which shall in either case be made in writing) on production of—
    (i) a certified copy of a relevant order; and
    (ii) if the child has attained the age of sixteen, the written consent of the child to the registration of that person as his father;

but no birth shall be re-registered under this section except in the prescribed manner and with the authority of the Registrar General.

(2) On the re-registration of a birth under this section—

(a) the registrar shall sign the register;

(b) in the case of a request under paragraph (a) or (b) of subsection (1) of this section, or a request under paragraph (d) of that subsection made by the mother of the child, the mother shall also sign the register;

(c) in the case of a request under paragraph (a) or (c) of that subsection, or a request made under paragraph (d) of that subsection by the person requesting to be registered as the father of the child, that person shall also sign the register; and

(d) if the re-registration takes place more than three months after the birth, the superintendent registrar shall also sign the register."

GENERAL NOTE

This section substitutes a new section for s.10A of the Births and Deaths Registration Act 1953, which provides for the re-registration of the birth of an illegitimate child where no person has previously been registered as the child's father.

Subs. (1) of the new s.10A

This subsection sets out the cases where the father's name may be shown in the births register on re-registration. Paras. (a) to (d) correspond to paras. (a) to (d) of s.10(1) of the 1953 Act, as re-enacted in s.24 above, with modifications necessary because for re-registration there is no requirement that there be a "qualified informant". Re-registration requires the authority of the Registrar General.

Paras. (a) and (b) re-enact paras. (a) and (b) of s.10A(1) of the 1953 Act (as substituted by Children Act 1975, s.93(2)).

Paras. (c) to (d) correspond to para. (c) and (d) of s.10(1) of the 1953 Act (see commentary on s.24 above).

Subs. (2) of new s.10A
This subsection re-enacts with modifications the existing subsection which deals with the signing of the births register on re-registration. The signing of the register (whether by mother, person acknowledging himself to be father or both) takes place where there has been a request that the birth be re-registered. The requirement (in para. (d)) that the superintendent registrar sign the register, if the re-registration takes place more than three months after the birth, reproduces the existing law (s.10A(2)(c)).

Re-registration after declaration of parentage

26. After section 14 of the 1953 Act there shall be inserted the following section—

"Re-registration after declaration of parentage

14A.—(1) Where, in the case of a person whose birth has been registered in England and Wales—
(a) the Registrar General receives, by virtue of section 56(4) of the Family Law Act 1986, a notification of the making of a declaration of parentage in respect of that person; and
(b) it appears to him that the birth of that person should be re-registered,
he shall authorise the re-registration of that person's birth, and the re-registration shall be effected in such manner and at such place as may be prescribed.
(2) This section shall apply with the prescribed modifications in relation to births at sea of which a return is sent to the Registrar General."

GENERAL NOTE
This section provides for the re-registration of a person's birth following a declaration of parentage. Re-registration of the birth under the new s.14A of the Births and Deaths Registration Act 1953 will be effected by the authority of the Registrar General and will follow the receipt by him of a notification from the Court of a declaration of parentage.
The place and manner of such re-registration is to be prescribed by rules.

PART VI

MISCELLANEOUS AND SUPPLEMENTAL

Miscellaneous

Artificial insemination

27.—(1) Where after the coming into force of this section a child is born in England and Wales as the result of the artificial insemination of a woman who—
(a) was at the time of the insemination a party to a marriage (being a marriage which had not at that time been dissolved or annulled); and
(b) was artificially inseminated with the semen of some person other than the other party to that marriage,
then, unless it is proved to the satisfaction of any court by which the matter has to be determined that the other party to that marriage did not consent to the insemination, the child shall be treated in law as the child of the parties to that marriage and shall not be treated as the child of any person other than the parties to that marriage.

(2) Any reference in this section to a marriage includes a reference to a void marriage if at the time of the insemination resulting in the birth of the child both or either of the parties reasonably believed that the marriage was valid; and for the purposes of this section it shall be presumed, unless the contrary is shown, that one of the parties so believed at that time that the marriage was valid.

(3) Nothing in this section shall affect the succession to any dignity or title of honour or render any person capable of succeeding to or transmitting a right to succeed to any such dignity or title.

GENERAL NOTE

This section provides that a child born to a married woman after A.I.D. with the consent of her husband is to be treated in law as the child of his mother and her husband and as a child of their marriage.

The section follows recommendations of the Law Commission (Law Com. No. 118, paras. 12.1–12.27) and, more tentatively, in the later report (Law Com. No. 157, para. 3.20). In between the two reports the Warnock Committee of Enquiry into Human Fertilization and Embryology ((1984) Cmnd. 9314) endorsed the Law Commission's earlier proposals in principle and recommended that a similar approach be adopted in relation to ovum donation and embryo transfer (see paras. 4.17, 4.22, 4.24, 4.25 and 6.8).

S.27 was the most debated clause in the Bill, and the most controversial. It is inconsistent with the rest of the Act, which is informed by a desire to recognise the true father as the lawful father of a child. By contrast, what this section does is recognise someone who is not the true father as the child's father. It should be stressed also that the section only applies to married couples: a child produced by A.I.D. to a cohabiting couple is illegitimate (see also Law Com. No. 118, para. 12.10). So is a child produced by natural intercourse (in effect by adultery) where this is done with the husband's consent to create a family where the husband is infertile. Thus, a child produced as a result of a surrogacy arrangement will be legitimate if A.I.D. is used, but illegitimate if natural intercourse is used. It should be stressed also that, with no comparable provision in the equivalent Scottish legislation, a child born in Gretna Green as a result of A.I.D. will be illegitimate and one born a couple of miles south will be legitimate (it is irrelevant where the insemination took place). Women living in Scotland, about to give birth to A.I.D. babies, must be advised to book into Carlisle maternity hospital if they want their children to be legitimate! The statute is clear that the status of legitimacy (in the case of A.I.D. births) depends on place of birth, and not, for example, on personal law (*e.g.* the domicile of the father or husband). It will thus be advantageous to a child's status to give birth to him in England and Wales. Whether this will lead to women abroad seeking entry merely to confer legitimate status on an A.I.D. child can only remain in the realm of speculation. It should be added that, with our immigration laws, they are hardly likely to be greeted sympathetically.

The main criticism of the provision, voiced in both Houses, is to the effect that it legitimates a form of perjury. As Lord Denning put it (*Hansard*, H.L. Vol. 482, col. 1282): "Is it right to tell a lie on the birth certificate? Is it fair for the child itself to be told and to be led to believe that the husband is the father when in truth some other man is the father?" Lord Denning asked how it squared with the Warnock Committee recommendation (para. 4.21) that "on reaching the age of 18 the child should have access to the basic information about the donor's ethnic origin and genetic health".

Subs. (1)

A child is born in England and Wales. The place of the child's birth is critical, not his personal law or that of his parents or the mother's husband.

As a result of . . . artificial insemination. If the woman does not refrain from sexual intercourse with the husband at the relevant time, it will not be known whether the child was produced by A.I.D. or intercourse. This has been relied on in the past to support the registering of the husband of the mother as the father of the child.

Marriage. See also s.27(2).

Dissolved or annulled. It is not clear whether this refers only to dissolved or annulled in England and Wales or also under the English rules of private international law.

Proved to the satisfaction of any Court. Though the standard must be the civil test, it seems (given what turns on it) that the evidence of consent will have to be very clear.

Shall be treated in law. Note the section does *not* state that the child is the child of the husband. But see s.1(3)(d).

Subs. (2)

This subsection makes it clear that marriage (for these purposes) includes putative marriage (see Legitimacy Act 1976, s.1). The subsection also incorporates the presumption (now also found in s.28(4)) that for the purposes of this section, it is to be presumed, unless the contrary is shown, that one of the parties did believe at the time that the marriage was valid.

Subs. (3)

This subsection purports to exclude children produced by A.I.D. from succeeding to dignities or titles of honour. Whether it is capable of doing so is, to say the least, highly dubious, since it is unlikely that investigations can or will take place to determine how a particular person came into the world.

Children of void marriages

28.—(1) In subsection (1) of section 1 of the Legitimacy Act 1976 (legitimacy of children of certain void marriages), for the words "the act of intercourse resulting in the birth" there shall be substituted the words "the insemination resulting in the birth or, where there was no such insemination, the child's conception".

(2) At the end of that section there shall be added the following subsections—

"(3) It is hereby declared for the avoidance of doubt that subsection (1) above applies notwithstanding that the belief that the marriage was valid was due to a mistake as to law.

(4) In relation to a child born after the coming into force of section 28 of the Family Law Reform Act 1987, it shall be presumed for the purposes of subsection (1) above, unless the contrary is shown, that one of the parties to the void marriage reasonably believed at the time of the insemination resulting in the birth or, where there was no such insemination, the child's conception (or at the time of the celebration of the marriage if later) that the marriage was valid."

GENERAL NOTE

This section makes *three* amendments to the law relating to the putative marriage, contained in s.1 of the Legitimacy Act 1976. First, the language of s.1 is altered to take account of the new biology. Secondly, it makes it clear that a mistake of law as to the validity of a marriage does not prevent a belief that the marriage is valid from being reasonable so as to make the child legitimate. Thirdly, proof of legitimacy is facilitated by the creation of a new presumption that at the material time one of the parties did reasonably believe in the validity of the marriage.

Subs. (1)

Insemination. Either by natural intercourse or by means of *in vitro* fertilisation.

Subs. (3)

Mistake of Law. It has been suggested that a mistake of law (*e.g.* as to the prohibited degrees of marriage or the validity of a divorce) cannot found a reasonable belief (see, *e.g.* Bromley, *Family Law* (6th ed.), 1981, p.267). This subsection now puts the matter beyond doubt.

Subs. (4)

It shall be presumed. This is to overcome the problem that the question of a child's legitimacy may only arise years after the marriage ceremony and it might by then have become difficult to establish the existence of a reasonable belief.

Reasonably believed. Reasonable belief is to be judged objectively. See *Hawkins* v. *Att.-Gen.* [1966] 1 W.L.R. 978.

Evidence of paternity in civil proceedings

29.—(1) Section 12 of the Civil Evidence Act 1968 (which relates to the admissibility in evidence in civil proceedings of the fact that a person has been adjudged to be the father of a child in affiliation proceedings) shall be amended as follows.

(2) For paragraph (b) of subsection (1) there shall be substituted the following paragraph—

"(b) the fact that a person has been found to be the father of a child in relevant proceedings before any court in England and Wales or has been adjudged to be the father of a child in affiliation proceedings before any court in the United Kingdom;".

(3) In subsection (2) for the words "to have been adjudged" there shall be substituted the words "to have been found or adjudged" and for the words "matrimonial or affiliation proceedings" there shall be substituted the words "other proceedings".

(4) In subsection (5) after the definition of "matrimonial proceedings" there shall be inserted the following definition—

"'relevant proceedings' means—

(a) proceedings on a complaint under section 42 of the National Assistance Act 1948 or section 26 of the Social Security Act 1986;

(b) proceedings on an application for an order under any of the following, namely—

    (i) section 6 of the Family Law Reform Act 1969;
    (ii) the Guardianship of Minors Act 1971;
    (iii) section 34(1)(a), (b) or (c) of the Children Act 1975;
    (iv) section 47 of the Child Care Act 1980; and
    (v) section 4 of the Family Law Reform Act 1987;

(c) proceedings on an application under section 35 of the said Act of 1975 for the revocation of a custodianship order;".

GENERAL NOTE

This section amends s.12 of the Civil Evidence Act 1968, so that an adjudication of paternity made in the course of all proceedings brought by public bodies should constitute prima facie evidence of paternity.

Subs. (1)

Section 12. A finding of paternity constitutes prima facie evidence of paternity, so that the burden will lie in future proceedings on any party seeking to disprove it. The standard of proof is on the balance of probabilities (see *Sutton* v. *Sutton* [1969] 3 All E.R. 1348).

Subs. (2)

Found. As opposed to an express finding of fact, such as when a man was "adjudged" to be the father in affiliation proceedings.

Relevant proceedings. For the meaning of this see s.29(4).

Adjudged . . . in affiliation proceedings. This preserves the existing rule.

Subs. (3)

For the words. This provision is consequential and reflects the fact that a finding of paternity made be made in an extended range of proceedings, as set out in s.29(4).

Supplemental

Orders applying section 1 to other enactments

30.—(1) The Lord Chancellor may by order make provision for the construction in accordance with section 1 above of such enactments passed before the coming into force of that section as may be specified in the order.

(2) An order under this section shall so amend the enactments to which it relates as to secure that (so far as practicable) they continue to have the same effect notwithstanding the making of the order.

(3) An order under this section shall be made by statutory instrument which shall be subject to annulment in pursuance of a resolution of either House of Parliament.

GENERAL NOTE
This section gives the Lord Chancellor the power (by statutory instrument) to apply the principle in s.1 to past enactments. In doing so, no change may be made to the substance of the law.

Interpretation

31. In this Act—
  "the 1953 Act" means the Births and Deaths Registration Act 1953;
  "the 1971 Act" means the Guardianship of Minors Act 1971;
  "the 1973 Act" means the Guardianship Act 1973.

GENERAL NOTE
This is the interpretation section.

Text of 1971 Act as amended

32. The 1971 Act (excluding consequential amendments of other enactments and savings) is set out in Schedule 1 to this Act as it will have effect, subject to sections 33(2) and 34(3) below, when all the amendments and repeals made in it by this Act come into force.

GENERAL NOTE
This section makes provision for a "Keeling" Schedule. This (Sched. 1) contains the Guardianship of Minors Act 1971, as amended by all subsequent legislation including this Act.

Amendments, transitional provisions, savings and repeals

33.—(1) The enactments mentioned in Schedule 2 to this Act shall have effect subject to the amendments there specified, being minor amendments and amendments consequential on the provisions of this Act.
  (2) The transitional provisions and savings in Schedule 3 to this Act shall have effect.
  (3) The inclusion in this Act of any express saving or amendment shall not be taken as prejudicing the operation of sections 16 and 17 of the Interpretation Act 1978 (which relate to the effect of repeals).
  (4) The enactments mentioned in Schedule 4 to this Act are hereby repealed to the extent specified in the third column of that Schedule.

GENERAL NOTE
This section, together with the Schedules to which it refers, makes minor and consequential amendments to other legislation, provides for savings and repeals and sets out transitional provisions.

Subs. (2)
Transitional provisions. See Sched. 3, particularly para. 1 which states that this Act (including its repeals and amendments) is not to have effect in relation to applications made under enactments repealed or amended by this Act if the application is *pending* when the particular provision in question comes into force. In particular it should be noted that *existing* affiliation orders are not affected (para. 6), but where there is an application for an order under s.11B of the GMA 1971 the court may direct that the affiliation order shall cease to have effect (para. 7). Also of importance is para. 8 which states that already accrued rights arising under the intestacy of a person dying before the coming into force of the repeal of s.14 of the Family Law Reform Act 1969 are not affected. There are similar provisions preserving the operation of s.15 of that Act (dealing with dispositions *inter vivos* and by will or codicil (para. 9) and protecting trustees and personal representatives in

respect of any conveyance or distribution made before the coming into force of the repeal of s.17 of the Family Law Reform Act 1969 (para. 10)).

Short title, commencement and extent

34.—(1) This Act may be cited as the Family Law Reform Act 1987.

(2) This Act shall come into force on such day as the Lord Chancellor may by order made by statutory instrument appoint; and different days may be so appointed for different provisions or different purposes.

(3) Without prejudice to the transitional provisions contained in Schedule 3 to this Act, an order under subsection (2) above may make such further transitional provisions as appear to the Lord Chancellor to be necessary or expedient in connection with the provisions brought into force by the order, including—

(a) such adaptations of the provisions so brought into force; and

(b) such adaptations of any provisions of this Act then in force,

as appear to him necessary or expedient in consequence of the partial operation of this Act.

(4) The following provisions of this Act extend to Scotland and Northern Ireland, namely—

(a) section 33(1) and paragraphs 12, 13 and 74 of Schedule 2;

(b) section 33(2) and paragraph 7 of Schedule 3 so far as relating to the operation of the Maintenance Orders Act 1950;

(c) section 33(4) and Schedule 4 so far as relating to that Act and the Interpretation Act 1978; and

(d) this section.

(5) Subject to subsection (4) above, this Act extends to England and Wales only.

SCHEDULES

Section 32

SCHEDULE 1

TEXT OF 1971 ACT AS AMENDED

ARRANGEMENT OF SECTIONS

General principles

1. Principle on which questions relating to custody, upbringing etc. of children are to be decided.

Appointment, removal and powers of guardians

3. Rights of surviving parent as to guardianship.
4. Power of father and mother to appoint testamentary guardians.
5. Power of court to appoint guardian for child having no parent etc.
6. Power of High Court to remove or replace guardian.
7. Disputes between joint guardians.

Orders for custody and financial relief

9. Orders for custody on application of either parent.
10. Orders for custody in guardianship cases.
11A. Further provisions relating to orders for custody.
11B. Orders for financial relief on application of either parent.
11C. Orders for financial relief in guardianship cases.
11D. Orders for financial relief for persons over eighteen.
12. Duration of orders for periodical payments.
12A. Matters to which court is to have regard in making order for financial relief.
12B. Provisions relating to lump sums.
12C. Variation etc. of orders for periodical payments.

12D. Variation of orders for secured periodical payments after death of parent.
13. Enforcement of orders for custody and maintenance.
13A. Restriction on removal of child from England and Wales.
13B. Direction for settlement of instrument by conveyancing counsel.

Access to children by grandparents

14A. Access to children by grandparents.

Jurisdiction and procedure

15. Courts having jurisdiction under this Act.
15A. Financial provision for child resident in country outside England and Wales.
16. Appeals and procedure.
17. Saving for powers of High Court and other courts.

Supplementary

20. Short title, interpretation, extent and commencement.

An Act to consolidate certain enactments relating to the guardianship and custody of minors.

(Formal enacting words)

General principles

Principle on which questions relating to custody, upbringing etc. of children are to be decided
1.—(1) Where in any proceedings before any court (whether or not a court as defined in section 15 of this Act)—
(a) the legal custody or upbringing of a child; or
(b) the administration of any property belonging to or held on trust for a child, or the application of the income thereof,
is in question, the court, in deciding that question, shall regard the welfare of the child as the first and paramount consideration, and shall not take into consideration whether from any other point of view the claim of the father in respect of such legal custody, upbringing, administration or application is superior to that of the mother, or the claim of the mother is superior to that of the father.

Appointment, removal and powers of guardians

Rights of surviving parent as to guardianship
3.—(1) On the death of the father of a child, the mother, if surviving, shall, subject to the provisions of this Act, be guardian of the child either alone or jointly with any guardian appointed by the father; and—
(a) where no guardian has been appointed by the father; or
(b) in the event of the death or refusal to act of the guardian or guardians appointed by the father,
the court may, if it thinks fit, appoint a guardian to act jointly with the mother.
(2) On the death of the mother of a child, the father, if surviving, shall, subject to the provisions of this Act, be guardian of the child either alone or jointly with any guardian appointed by the mother; and—
(a) where no guardian has been appointed by the mother; or
(b) in the event of the death or refusal to act of the guardian or guardians appointed by the mother,
the court may, if it thinks fit, appoint a guardian to act jointly with the father.
(3) Where the father and mother of a child were not married to each other at the time of his birth, this section does not apply unless the father satisfies the requirements of subsection (4) of this section.
(4) The father of a child satisfies the requirements of this subsection if—
(a) an order is in force under section 4 of the Family Law Reform Act 1987 giving him all the parental rights and duties with respect to the child; or
(b) he has a right to custody, legal or actual custody or care and control of the child by virtue of an order made under any other enactment.

Power of father and mother to appoint testamentary guardians

4.—(1) The father of a child may by deed or will appoint any person to be guardian of the child after his death.

(2) The mother of a child may by deed or will appoint any person to be guardian of the child after her death.

(3) Any guardian so appointed shall act jointly with the mother or father, as the case may be, of the child so long as the mother or father remains alive unless the mother or father objects to his so acting.

(4) If the mother or father so objects, or if the guardian so appointed considers that the mother or father is unfit to have the custody of the child, the guardian may apply to the court, and the court may either—

(a) refuse to make any order (in which case the mother or father shall remain sole guardian); or

(b) make an order that the guardian so appointed—

(i) shall act jointly with the mother or father; or

(ii) shall be the sole guardian of the child.

(5) Where guardians are appointed by both parents, the guardians so appointed shall, after the death of the surviving parent, act jointly.

(6) If under section 3 of this Act a guardian has been appointed by the court to act jointly with a surviving parent, he shall continue to act as guardian after the death of the surviving parent; but, if the surviving parent has appointed a guardian, the guardian appointed by the court shall act jointly with the guardian appointed by the surviving parent.

(7) Where the father and mother of a child were not married to each other at the time of his birth—

(a) subsection (1) of this section does not apply, and subsection (3) of this section does not apply in relation to a guardian appointed by the mother, unless the father satisfies the requirements of section 3(4) of this Act; and

(b) any appointment under subsection (1) of this section shall be of no effect unless the father satisfies those requirements immediately before his death.

Power of court to appoint guardian for child having no parent etc.

5.—(1) Where a child has no parent, no guardian of the person, and no other person having parental rights with respect to him, the court, on the application of any person, may, if it thinks fit, appoint the applicant to be the guardian of the child.

(2) A court may entertain an application under this section to appoint a guardian of a child notwithstanding that parental rights and duties with respect to the child are vested in a local authority or a voluntary organisation by virtue of a resolution under section 3 or 64 of the Child Care Act 1980.

(3) Where the father and mother of a child were not married to each other at the time of his birth, subsection (1) of this section shall have effect as if for the words "no parent" there were substituted the words "no mother, no father satisfying the requirements of section 3(4) of this Act".

Power of High Court to remove or replace guardian

6. The High Court may in its discretion on being satisfied that it is for the welfare of the child remove from his office any testamentary guardian or any guardian appointed or acting by virtue of this Act, and may also, if it deems it to be for the welfare of the child, appoint another guardian in place of the guardian so removed.

Disputes between joint guardians

7. Where two or more persons act as joint guardians of a child and they are unable to agree on any question affecting the welfare of the child, any of them may apply to the court for its direction and the court may make such order regarding the matters in difference that it may think proper.

Orders for custody and financial relief

Orders for custody on application of either parent

9.—(1) The court may, on the application of either parent of a child, make such order regarding—

(a) the legal custody of the child; and

(b) access to the child by either parent,

as the court thinks fit; and an order under this section may be varied or discharged by a subsequent order made on the application of either parent or, after the death of either parent, on the application of any guardian appointed under this Act.

(2) An order under this section—
   (a) shall not give legal custody to a person other than a parent of the child; and
   (b) shall not be made at any time when the child is free for adoption by virtue of an order made under section 18 of the Adoption Act 1976 or section 18 of the Adoption (Scotland) Act 1978.

Orders for custody in guardianship cases

10.—(1) Where the court makes an order under section 4(4) of this Act that a person shall be sole guardian of a child to the exclusion of a parent, the court may make such order regarding—
   (a) the legal custody of the child; and
   (b) access to the child by the parent,
as the court thinks fit; and the powers conferred by this subsection may be exercised at any time and include power to vary or discharge any order previously made.

(2) The powers of the court under section 7 of this Act to make orders regarding matters in difference between joint guardians shall include, where a parent of the child is one of the joint guardians—
   (a) power to make such order regarding—
      (i) the legal custody of the child; and
      (ii) access to the child by the parent,
      as the court thinks fit; and
   (b) power to vary or discharge any order previously made by virtue of this subsection.

(3) An order shall not be made under or by virtue of this section at any time when the child is free for adoption by virtue of an order made under section 18 of the Adoption Act 1976 or section 18 of the Adoption (Scotland) Act 1978.

Further provisions relating to orders for custody

11A.—(1) An order shall not be made under section 9 or 10 of this Act giving the legal custody of a child to more than one person; but where the court makes an order under one of those sections giving the legal custody of a child to any person it may order that a parent of the child who is not given the legal custody of the child shall retain all or such as the court may specify of the parental rights and duties comprised in legal custody (other than the right to the actual custody of the child) and shall have those rights and duties jointly with the person who is given the legal custody of the child.

(2) Where the court makes an order under section 9 or 10 of this Act the court may direct that the order, or such provision thereof as the court may specify, shall not have effect until the occurrence of an event specified by the court or the expiration of a period so specified; and where the court has directed that the order or any provision thereof shall not have effect until the expiration of a specified period, the court may, at any time before the expiration of that period, direct that the order, or that provision thereof, shall not have effect until the expiration of such further period as the court may specify.

(3) Any order made in respect of a child under section 9 or 10 of this Act shall cease to have effect when the child attains the age of eighteen.

Orders for financial relief on application of either parent

11B.—(1) The court may, on the application of either parent of a child, make—
   (a) in the case of proceedings in the High Court or a county court, one or more of the orders mentioned in subsection (2) of this section;
   (b) in the case of proceedings in a magistrates' court, one or both of the orders mentioned in paragraphs (a) and (c) of that subsection;
and an order mentioned in paragraph (a) or (b) of that subsection may be varied or discharged on the application of either parent or, after the death of either parent, on the application of any guardian appointed under this Act.

(2) The orders referred to in subsection (1) of this section are—
   (a) an order requiring one parent to make to the other parent for the benefit of the child, or to the child, such periodical payments, and for such terms, as may be specified in the order;
   (b) an order requiring one parent to secure to the other parent for the benefit of the child, or to secure to the child, such periodical payments, and for such term, as may be so specified;

    (c) an order requiring one parent to pay to the other parent for the benefit of the child, or to the child, such lump sum as may be so specified;

    (d) an order requiring either parent to transfer to the other parent for the benefit of the child, or to the child, such property as may be so specified, being property to which the first-mentioned parent is entitled, either in possession or reversion;

    (e) an order requiring that a settlement of such property as may be so specified, being property to which either parent is so entitled, be made to the satisfaction of the court for the benefit of the child.

Orders for financial relief in guardianship cases

11C.—(1) Where the court makes an order under section 4(4) of this Act that a person shall be sole guardian of a child to the exclusion of a parent, the court may make—

    (a) in the case of proceedings in the High Court or a county court, one or more of the orders mentioned in subsection (3) of this section;

    (b) in the case of proceedings in a magistrates' court, one or both of the orders mentioned in paragraphs (a) and (c) of that subsection;

and the powers conferred by this subsection may be exercised at any time and include power to vary or discharge any order mentioned in paragraph (a) or (b) of that subsection previously made.

(2) The powers of the court under section 7 of this Act to make orders regarding matters in difference between joint guardians shall include, where a parent of the child is one of the joint guardians—

    (a) power to make—

        (i) in the case of proceedings in the High Court or a county court, one or more of the orders mentioned in subsection (3) of this section;

        (ii) in the case of proceedings in a magistrates' court, one or both of the orders mentioned in paragraphs (a) and (c) of that subsection; and

    (b) power to vary or discharge any order mentioned in paragraph (a) or (b) of that subsection previously made.

(3) The orders referred to in subsections (1) and (2) of this section are—

    (a) an order requiring the parent to make to the guardian or other guardian for the benefit of the child, or to the child, such periodical payments, and for such term, as may be specified in the order;

    (b) an order requiring the parent to secure to the guardian or other guardian for the benefit of the child, or to secure to the child, such periodical payments, and for such term, as may be so specified;

    (c) an order requiring the parent to pay to the guardian or other guardian for the benefit of the child, or to the child, such lump sum as may be so specified;

    (d) an order requiring the parent to transfer to the guardian or other guardian for the benefit of the child, or to the child, such property as may be so specified, being property to which the parent is entitled, either in possession or reversion;

    (e) an order requiring that a settlement of such property as may be so specified, being property to which the parent is so entitled, be made to the satisfaction of the court for the benefit of the child.

Orders for financial relief for persons over eighteen

11D.—(1) If, on an application by a person who has attained the age of eighteen and whose parents are not living with each other in the same household, it appears to the High Court or a county court—

    (a) that the applicant is, will be or (if an order were made under this section) would be receiving instruction at an educational establishment or undergoing training for a trade, profession or vocation, whether or not he also is, will be or would be in gainful employment; or

    (b) that there are special circumstances which justify the making of an order under this section,

the court may make one or both of the orders mentioned in subsection (2) of this section.

(2) The orders referred to in subsection (1) of this section are—

    (a) an order requiring either or both of the applicant's parents to pay to the applicant such periodical payments, and for such term, as may be specified in the order; and

    (b) an order requiring either or both of the applicant's parents to pay to the applicant such lump sum as may be so specified.

(3) An application may not be made under this section by any person if, immediately before he attained the age of sixteen, a periodical payments order was in force with respect to him.

(4) No order shall be made under this section at a time when the parents of the applicant are living with each other in the same household.

(5) Any order made under this section requiring the making of periodical payments shall, notwithstanding anything in the order, cease to have effect on the death of the person liable to make payments under the order.

(6) An order under this section requiring the making of periodical payments may be varied or discharged by a subsequent order made on the application of any person by or to whom payments were required to be made under the previous order.

(7) In subsection (3) of this section "periodical payments order" means an order made under—

    (a) this Act,

    (b) section 6(3) of the Family Law Reform Act 1969,

    (c) section 23 or 27 of the Matrimonial Causes Act 1973,

    (d) section 34 of the Children Act 1975, or

    (e) Part I of the Domestic Proceedings and Magistrates' Courts Act 1978,

for the making or securing of periodical payments.

Duration of orders for periodical payments

12.—(1) The term to be specified in an order for periodical payments made by virtue of section 11B(2)(a) or (b) or 11C(3)(a) or (b) of this Act in favour of a child may begin with the date of the making of an application for the order in question or any later date; but—

    (a) shall not in the first instance extend beyond the date of the birthday of the child next following his attaining the upper limit of the compulsory school age (that is to say, the age that is for the time being that limit by virtue of section 35 of the Education Act 1944 together with any Order in Council made under that section) unless the court thinks it right in the circumstances in the case to specify a later date: and

    (b) shall not in any event, subject to subsection (2) below, extend beyond the date of the child's eighteenth birthday.

(2) Paragraph (b) of subsection (1) above shall not apply in the case of a child if it appears to the court that—

    (a) the child is, will be or (if an order were made without complying with that paragraph) would be receiving instruction at an educational establishment or undergoing training for a trade, profession or vocation, whether or not he also is, will be or would be in gainful employment; or

    (b) there are special circumstances which justify the making of an order without complying with that paragraph.

(3) An order for periodical payments made by virtue of section 11B(2)(a) or 11C(3)(a) of this Act shall, notwithstanding anything in the order, cease to have effect on the death of the person liable to make payments under the order.

Matters to which court is to have regard in making orders for financial relief

12A. In deciding whether to exercise its powers under section 11B, 11C or 11D of this Act and, if so, in what manner, the court shall have regard to all the circumstances of the case including the following matters, that is to say—

    (a) the income, earning capacity, property and other financial resources which the mother or father of the child has or is likely to have in the foreseeable future;

    (b) the financial needs, obligations and responsibilities which the mother or father of the child has or is likely to have in the foreseeable future;

    (c) the financial needs of the child;

    (d) the income, earning capacity (if any), property and other financial resources of the child;

    (e) any physical or mental disability of the child.

Provisions relating to lump sums

12B.—(1) Without prejudice to the generality of section 11B and 11C of this Act, an order under any of those provisions for the payment of a lump sum may be made for the purpose of enabling any liabilities or expenses reasonably incurred before the making of the order to be met, being liabilities or expenses incurred in connection with the birth of the child or in maintaining the child.

(2) The amount of any lump sum required to be paid by an order made by the magistrates' court under section 11B, 11C or 11D of this Act shall not exceed £500 or such larger amount

as the Secretary of State may from time to time by order fix for the purposes of this subsection.

Any order made by the Secretary of State under this subsection shall be made by statutory instrument and shall be subject to annulment in pursuance of a resolution of either House of Parliament.

(3) The power of the court under section 11B, 11C or 11D of this Act to vary or discharge an order for the making or securing of periodical payments by a parent shall include power to make an order under the said section 11B, 11C or 11D, as the case may be, for the payment of a lump sum by that parent.

(4) The amount of any lump sum which a parent may be required to pay by virtue of subsection (3) above shall not, in the case of an order made by a magistrates' court, exceed the maximum amount that may at the time of the making of the order be required to be paid under subsection (2) above, but a magistrates' court may make an order for the payment of a lump sum not exceeding that amount notwithstanding that the parent was required to pay a lump sum by a previous order under this Act.

(5) An order made under section 11B, 11C or 11D of this Act for the payment of a lump sum may provide for the payment of that sum by instalments and where the court provides for the payment of a lump sum by instalments the court, on an application made either by the person liable to pay or the person entitled to receive that sum, shall have power to vary that order by varying the number of instalments payable, the amount of any instalment payable and the date on which any instalment becomes payable.

Variation etc. of orders for periodical payments

12C.—(1) In exercising its powers under section 11B, 11C or 11D of this Act to vary or discharge an order for the making or securing of periodical payments the court shall have regard to all the circumstances of the case, including any change in any of the matters to which the court was required to have regard when making the order.

(2) The power of the court under section 11B, 11C or 11D of this Act to vary an order for the making or securing of periodical payments shall include power to suspend any provision thereof temporarily and to revive any provision so suspended.

(3) Where on an application under section 11B, 11C or 11D of this Act for the variation or discharge of an order for the making or securing of periodical payments the court varies the payment required to be made under that order, the court may provide that the payments as so varied shall be made from such date as the court may specify, not being earlier than the date of the making of the application.

(4) An application for the variation of an order made under section 11B or 11C of this Act for the making or securing of periodical payments to or for the benefit of a child may, if the child has attained the age of sixteen, be made by the child himself.

(5) Where an order for the making of periodical payments made under section 11B or 11C of this Act ceases to have effect on the date on which the child attains the age of sixteen or at any time after that date but before or on the date on which he attains the age of eighteen, the child may apply—

(a) in the case of an order made by the High Court or a county court, to the court which made the order, or

(b) in the case of an order made by a magistrates' court, to the High Court or a county court,

for an order for the revival of the first mentioned order.

(6) If on such an application it appears to the High Court or county court that—

(a) the child is, will be or (if an order were made under this subsection) would be receiving instruction at an educational establishment or undergoing training for a trade, profession or vocation, whether or not he also is, will be or would be in gainful employment; or

(b) there are special circumstances which justify the making of an order under this subsection,

the court shall have power by order to revive the first mentioned order from such date as the court may specify, not being earlier than the date of the making of the application.

(7) Any order made under section 11B or 11C of this Act by the High Court or a county court which is revived by an order under subsection (5) above may be varied or discharged under section 11B or 11C of this Act, as the case may be, on the application of any person by whom or to whom payments are required to be made under the order.

(8) Any order made under section 11B or 11C of this Act by a magistrates' court which is revived by an order of the High Court or a county court under subsection (5) above—

(a) for the purposes of the variation and discharge of the order, shall be treated as an order of the court by which it was revived and may be varied or discharged by that court on the application of any person by whom or to whom payments are required to be made under the order; and

(b) for the purposes of the enforcement of the order, shall be treated as an order of the magistrates' court by which the order was originally made.

Variation of order for secured periodical payments after death of parent

12D.—(1) Where the parent liable to make payments under a secured periodical payments order has died, the persons who may apply for the variation or discharge of the order shall include the personal representatives of the deceased parent, and no application for the variation of the order shall, except with the permission of the court, be made after the end of the period of six months from the date on which representation in regard to the estate of that parent is first taken out.

(2) The personal representatives of a deceased person against whom a secured periodical payments order was made shall not be liable for having distributed any part of the estate of the deceased after the expiration of the period of six months referred to in subsection (1) of this section on the ground that they ought to have taken into account the possibility that the court might permit an application for variation to be made after that period by the person entitled to payments under the order; but this subsection shall not prejudice any power to recover any part of the estate so distributed arising by virtue of the variation of an order in accordance with this section.

(3) Where an application to vary a secured periodical payments order is made after the death of the parent liable to make payments under the order, the circumstances to which the court is required to have regard under section 12C(1) of this Act shall include the changed circumstances resulting from the death of that parent.

(4) In considering for the purposes of subsection (1) of this section the question when representation was first taken out, a grant limited to settled land or to trust property shall be left out of account and a grant limited to real estate or to personal estate shall be left out of account unless a grant limited to the remainder of the estate has previously been made or is made at the same time.

(5) In this section "secured periodical payments order" means an order for secured periodical payments made by virtue of section 11B(2)(b) or 11C(3)(b) of this Act.

Enforcement of orders for custody and maintenance

13.—(1) Where an order made by a magistrates' court under this Act contains a provision committing to any person the actual custody of any child, a copy of the order may be served on any person in whose actual custody the child may for the time being be, and thereupon the provision may, without prejudice to any other remedy open to the person given the custody, be enforced under section 63(3) of the Magistrates' Courts Act 1980 as if it were an order of the court requiring the person so served to give up the child to the person given the custody.

(2) Any person for the time being under an obligation to make payments in pursuance of any order for the payment of money made by a magistrates' court under this Act shall give notice of any change of address to such person (if any) as may be specified in the order, and any person failing without reasonable excuse to give such a notice shall be liable on summary conviction to a fine not exceeding level 2 on the standard scale.

(3) Any order for the payment of money made by a magistrates' court under this Act shall be enforceable as a magistrates' court maintenance order within the meaning of section 150(1) of the Magistrates' Courts Act 1980.

Restriction on removal of child from England and Wales

13A.—(1) Where the court makes

(a) an order under section 9 or 10 of this Act regarding the legal custody of a child, or

(b) an interim order under section 2(4) of the Guardianship Act 1973 containing provision regarding the legal custody of a child,

the court, on making the order or at any time while the order is in force, may, if an application is made under this section, by order direct that no person shall take the child out of England and Wales while the order under this section is in force, except with the leave of the court.

(2) An order made under subsection (1) above may be varied or discharged by a subsequent order.

(3) An application for an order under subsection (1) above, or for the variation or discharge of such an order, may be made by any party to the proceedings in which the order mentioned in paragraph (a) or (b) of that subsection was made.

Direction for settlement of instrument by conveyancing counsel

13B. Where the High Court or a county court decides to make an order under this Act for the securing of periodical payments or for the transfer or settlement of property, it may direct that the matter be referred to one of the conveyancing counsel of the court for him to settle a proper instrument to be executed by all necessary parties.

Access to children by grandparents

Access to children by grandparents

14A.—(1) The court, on making an order under section 9 of this Act, or at any time while such an order is in force, may on the application of a grandparent of the child make such order requiring access to the child to be given to the grandparents as the court thinks fit.

(2) Where one parent of a child is dead, or both parents are dead, the court may, on an application made by a parent of a deceased parent of the child, make such order requiring access to the child to be given to the applicant as the court thinks fit.

(3) Section 11A(2) of this Act shall apply in relation to an order made under this section as it applies in relation to an order under section 9 or 10 of this Act.

(4) The court shall not make an order under this section with respect to a child who is for the purposes of Part III of the Child Care Act 1980 in the care of a local authority.

(5) Where the court has made an order under subsection (1) above requiring access to a child to be given to a grandparent, the court may vary or discharge that order on an application made—

    (a) by that grandparent, or

    (b) by either parent of the child, or

    (c) if before 1st December 1985 the court has made an order under section 9 of this Act giving the legal custody of the child to a person other than one of the parents, by that person.

(6) Where the court has made an order under subsection (2) above requiring access to a child to be given to a grandparent, the court may vary or discharge that order on an application made—

    (a) by that grandparent, or

    (b) by any surviving parent of the child, or

    (c) by any guardian of the child.

(7) Section 6 of the Guardianship Act 1973 shall apply in relation to an application under this section as it applies in relation to an application under section 5 or 9 of this Act, and any reference to a party to the proceedings in subsection (2) or (3) of the said section 6 shall include—

    (a) in the case of an application under subsection (1) or (2) above, a reference to the grandparent who has made an application under either of those subsections.

    (b) in the case of an application under subsection (5) or (6) above, a reference to the grandparent who has access to the child under the order for the variation or discharge of which the application is made.

(8) Where, at any time after an order with respect to a child has been made under subsection (1) above, no order is in force under section 9 of this Act with respect to that child, the order made under subsection (1) above shall cease to have effect.

Jurisdiction and Procedure

Courts having jurisdiction under this Act

15.—(1) Subject to the provisions of this section "the court" for the purposes of this Act means the High Court, any county court or any magistrates' court, except that provision may be made by rules of court that in the case of such applications to a county court, or such applications to a magistrates' court, as are prescribed, only such county courts, or as the case may be such magistrates' courts, as are prescribed shall be authorised to hear those applications.

(2) A magistrates' court shall not be competent to entertain—

    (b) any application involving the administration or application of any property belonging to or held in trust for a child or the income thereof.

(2A) It is hereby declared that any power conferred on a magistrates' court under this Act is exercisable notwithstanding that any party to the proceedings is residing outside England and Wales.

(2B) Where any party to the proceedings on an application to a magistrates' court under this Act resides outside the United Kingdom and does not appear at the time and place appointed for the hearing of the application, the court shall not hear the application unless it is proved to the satisfaction of the court, in such manner as is prescribed, that such steps as are prescribed have been taken to give to that party notice of the application and of the time and place appointed for the hearing of it.

(2C) In this section "prescribed" means prescribed by rules of court.

Financial provision for child resident in country outside England and Wales

15A.—(1) Where one parent of a child resides in England or Wales and the other parent and the child reside outside England and Wales, the court shall have power, on an application made by that other parent, to make one or both of the orders mentioned in section 11B(2)(a) and (b) of this Act against the parent resident in England and Wales; and in relation to such an application section 11B(2)(a) and (b) shall have effect as if for any reference to the parent excluded from actual custody there were substituted a reference to the parent resident in England and Wales.

(2) Any reference in this Act to the powers of the court under section 11B(2) of this Act or to an order made under the said section 11B(2) shall include a reference to the powers which the court has by virtue of subsection (1) above or, as the case may be, to an order made by virtue of subsection (1) above.

Appeals and procedure

16.

(3) Subject to subsection (4) of this section, where on an application to a magistrates' court under this Act the court makes or refuses to make an order, an appeal shall lie to the High Court.

(4) Where an application is made to a magistrates' court under this Act, and the court considers that the matter is one which would more conveniently be dealt with by the High Court, the magistrates' court shall refuse to make an order, and in that case no appeal shall lie to the High Court.

(5) In relation to applications made to a magistrates' court under section 14A of this Act regarding access to a child by a grandparent or under section 3(3) or 4(3A) of the Guardianship Act 1973 for the discharge or variation of a supervision order or, as the case may be, an order giving the care of a child to a local authority or an order requiring payments to be made to an authority to whom care of a child is so given, rules made under section 144 of the Magistrates' Courts Act 1980 may make provision as to the persons who are to be made defendants on the application; and if on any such application there are two or more defendants, the power of the court under section 64(1) of the Magistrates' Courts Act 1980 shall be deemed to include power, whatever adjudication the court makes on the complaint, to order any of the parties to pay the whole part of the costs of all or any of the other parties.

(6) On an appeal under subsection (3) of this section the High Court shall have power to make such orders as may be necessary to give effect to its determination of the appeal including such incidental or consequential orders as appear to the court to be just, and, in the case of an appeal from a decision of a magistrates' court made on an application for or in respect of an order for the making of periodical payments, the High Court shall have power to order that its determination of the appeal shall have effect from such date as the court thinks fit, not being earlier than the date of the making of the application to the magistrates' court.

(7) Without prejudice to the generality of subsection (6) above, where, on an appeal under subsection (3) of this section in respect of an order of a magistrates' court requiring a parent of a child to make periodical payments, the High Court reduces the amount of those payments or discharges the order, the High Court shall have power to order the person entitled to payments under the order of the magistrates' court to pay to that parent such sum in respect of payments already made by the parent in compliance with the order as the High Court thinks fit and if any arrears are due under the order of the magistrates' court, the High Court shall have power to remit the payment of those arrears or any part thereof.

(8) Any order of the High Court made on an appeal under subsection (3) of this section (other than an order directing that an application shall be re-heard by a magistrates' court) shall for the purposes of the enforcement of the order and for the purposes of any power to vary, revive or discharge orders conferred by section 9(1), 10(1) or (2)(b), 11B(1), 11C(1) or (2)(b), 11D(6), 12B(5) or 12 C(2) of this Act or section 3(3) or 4(3A) of the Guardianship Act 1973 be treated as if it were an order of the magistrates' court from which the appeal was brought and not of the High Court.

Saving for powers of High Court and other courts

17.—(1) Nothing in this Act shall restrict or affect the jurisdiction of the High Court to appoint or remove guardians or otherwise in respect of children.

Supplementary

Short title, interpretation and extent

20.—(1) This Act may be cited as the Guardianship of Minors Act 1971.

(2) In this Act, unless the context otherwise requires—

"actual custody", as respects a child, means the actual possession of the person of the child;

"child" except where used to express a relationship, means a person who has not attained the age of eighteen;

"legal custody" shall be construed in accordance with Part IV of the Children Act 1975;

"maintenance" includes education.

(2A) In this Act—

(a) references (however expressed) to any relationship between two persons; and

(b) references to the father and mother of a child not being married to each other at the time of his birth,

shall be construed in accordance with section 1 of the Family Law Reform Act 1987.

(3) References in this Act to any enactment are references thereto as amended, and include references thereto as applied, by any other enactment.

(4) This Act—

(a) so far as it amends the Maintenance Orders Act 1950 extends to Scotland and Northern Ireland,

but, save as aforesaid, extends to England and Wales only.

Section 33(1)   SCHEDULE 2

Minor and Consequential Amendments

The Maintenance Orders (Facilities for Enforcement) Act 1920 (c.33)

1. In section 6(2) of the Maintenance Orders (Facilities for Enforcement) Act 1920—

(a) for the words "in like manner as an order of affiliation" there shall be substituted the words "as a magistrates' court maintenance order";

(b) at the end of that subsection there shall be inserted the words—

"In this subsection 'magistrates' court maintenance order' has the same meaning as in section 150(1) of the Magistrates' Courts Act 1980."

The Trustee Act 1925 (c.19)

2. At the end of section 33 of the Trustee Act 1925 there shall be added the following subsection—

"(4) In relation to the dispositions mentioned in section 19(1) of the Family Law Reform Act 1987, this section shall have effect as if any reference (however expressed) to any relationship between two persons were construed in accordance with section 1 of that Act."

The Administration of Estates Act 1925 (c.23)

3. At the end of section 50 of the Administration of Estates Act 1925 there shall be added the following subsection—

"(3) In subsection (1) of this section the reference to this Part of this Act, or the foregoing provisions of this Part of this Act, shall in relation to an instrument inter vivos made, or a will or codicil coming into operation, after the coming into force of section 18 of the Family Law Reform Act 1987 (but not in relation to instruments inter vivos made or wills or codicils coming into operation earlier) be construed as including references to that section."

4. At the end of section 52 of that Act there shall be added the words "and references (however expressed) to any relationship between two persons shall be construed in accordance with section 1 of the Family Law Reform Act 1987".

The National Assistance Act 1948 (c.29)

5. In section 42 of the National Assistance Act 1948 (liability to maintain spouse and children), for subsection (2) there shall be substituted the following subsection—
"(2) Any reference in subsection (1) of this section to a person's children shall be construed in accordance with section 1 of the Family Law Reform Act 1987."

6. In section 43 of that Act (recovery of cost of assistance from persons liable for maintenance), for subsection (6) there shall be substituted the following subsection—
"(6) An order under this section shall be enforceable as a magistrates' court maintenance order within the meaning of section 150(1) of the Magistrates' Courts Act 1980."

7. Section 44 of that Act (affiliation orders) shall cease to have effect.

8. In section 56(1) of that Act (legal proceedings), after the words "any sum due under this Act to a local authority" there shall be inserted the words "(other than a sum due under an order made under section 43 of this Act)".

The Marriage Act 1949 (c.76)

9. In the Marriage Act 1949 for the words "an infant", wherever they occur in section 3, 16 or 28 or in Schedule 2, there shall be substituted the words "a child" and for the words "the infant", wherever they occur in section 3 or in Schedule 2, there shall be substituted the words "the child".

10. In section 78 of that Act—
    (a) in subsection (1) for the definition of "infant" there shall be substituted the following definition—
    "'child' means a person under the age of eighteen;";

    (b) after that subsection there shall be inserted the following subsection—
    "(1A) References in this Act to the parents of a child being or not being married to each other at the time of his birth shall be construed in accordance with section 1 of the Family Law Reform Act 1987."

11. In Schedule 2 to that Act for the heading to Part I there shall be substituted the following heading—

"I. WHERE THE PARENTS OF THE CHILD WERE MARRIED TO EACH OTHER AT THE TIME OF HIS BIRTH."

The Maintenance Orders Act 1950 (c.37)

12. In section 16(2)(a) of the Maintenance Orders Act 1950—
    (a) for sub-paragraph (iii) there shall be substituted the following sub-paragraph—
    "(iii) section 11B, 11C(1) or 11D of the Guardianship of Minors Act 1971 or section 2(3) or 2(4A) of the Guardianship Act 1973;";
    (b) sub-paragraph (iv) shall cease to have effect;
    (c) the sub-paragraph (vi) inserted by the Children Act 1975 shall cease to have effect;
    (d) in the sub-paragraph (vi) inserted by the Supplementary Benefits Act 1976 the words from "or section 4 of the Affiliation Proceedings Act 1957" to the end shall cease to have effect;
    (e) in sub-paragraph (viii) the words from "or section 4 of the Affiliation Proceedings Act 1957" to the end shall cease to have effect.

13. In section 18 of that Act for subsection (2) there shall be substituted the following subsection—
"(2) Every maintenance order registered under this Part of this Act in a magistrates' court in England and Wales shall be enforceable as a magistrates' court maintenance order within the meaning of section 150(1) of the Magistrates' Courts Act 1980."

The Reserve and Auxiliary Forces (Protection of Civil Interests) Act 1951 (c.65)

14. In section 2(1) of the Reserve and Auxiliary Forces (Protection of Civil Interests) Act 1951, for paragraph (d) of the proviso there shall be substituted the following paragraph—
    "(d) an order for alimony, maintenance or other payments which has been made under sections 21 to 33 of the Matrimonial Causes Act 1973 or under section 11B, 11C(1) or 11D of the Guardianship of Minors Act 1971 or section 2(4A) of the Guardianship Act 1973;".

The Births and Deaths Registration Act 1953 (c.20)

15. In section 9(4) of the 1953 Act for "(b) or (c)" there shall be substituted "(b), (c) or (d)".

16. In the proviso to section 14(1) of that Act—
   (a) in paragraph (a) for the word "acknowledging" there shall be substituted the word "stating";
   (b) in paragraph (b) the words "by an affiliation order or otherwise" shall cease to have effect;
   (c) at the end of paragraph (c) there shall be added the words "or section 56 of the Family Law Reform Act 1987".

17. In section 34(2) of that Act for the words "required by law" there shall be substituted the words "required or permitted by law".

The Maintenance Orders Act 1958 (c.39)

18. In section 3 of the Maintenance Orders Act 1958 for subsection (2) there shall be substituted the following subsection—
   "(2) Subject to the provisions of the next following subsection, an order registered in a magistrates' court shall be enforceable as a magistrates' court maintenance order within the meaning of section 150(1) of the Magistrates' Courts Act 1980."

The Domestic and Appellate Proceedings (Restriction of Publicity) Act 1968 (c.63)

19. In section 2 of the Domestic and Appellate Proceedings (Restriction of Publicity) Act 1968 (restriction of publicity for certain proceedings)—
   (a) in subsection (1) the word "and" following paragraph (b) shall cease to have effect and there shall be inserted at the end the following paragraph—
   "(e) proceedings under section 56(1) of the Family Law Act 1986 (declarations of parentage);";
   (b) in subsection (3) for the words "subsection (1)(d)" there shall be substituted the words "subsection (1)(d) or (e)".

The Family Law Reform Act 1969 (c.46)

20.—(1) Section 6 of the Family Law Reform Act 1969 (maintenance for wards of court) shall be amended as follows.

(2) At the end of subsection (1) there shall be added the words "and references (however expressed) to any relationship between two persons shall be construed in accordance with section 1 of the Family Law Reform Act 1987".

(3) For subsection (3) there shall be substituted the following subsection—
   "(3) Section 12 of the Guardianship of Minors Act 1971 (duration of orders for maintenance) and subsections (4), (5) and (6) of section 12C of that Act (variation and revival of orders for periodical payments) shall apply in relation to an order made under subsection (2) of this section as they apply in relation to an order made by the High Court under section 11B of that Act."

(4) In subsection (5) (which provides that an order under that section shall cease to have effect if the parents of the ward reside together for a period of three months after the making of the order) for the words "three months" there shall be substituted the words "six months".

(5) Subsection (6) (which provides that no order shall be made under that section requiring any person to make any payment towards the maintenance or education of an illegitimate child) shall cease to have effect.

21. In section 20(6) of that Act, for the words "blood samples" there shall be substituted the words "bodily samples".

22. In section 21 of that Act, for the words "blood sample", in each place where they occur, there shall be substituted the words "bodily sample" and for the words "blood tests" there shall be substituted the words "scientific tests".

23.—(1) Section 22(1) of that Act shall be amended as follows.

(2) For the words "blood sample", "blood samples" and "blood tests", in each place where they occur, there shall be respectively substituted the words "bodily sample", "bodily samples" and "scientific tests".

(3) After paragraph (a) there shall be inserted the following paragraph—
   "(aa) prescribe the bodily samples to be taken;".

(4) In paragraph (d) after the words "any such illness" there shall be inserted the words "or condition or undergone any such treatment".

(5) After paragraph (i) there shall be inserted the following paragraph—

"(j) make different provision for different cases or for different descriptions of case."

24. In section 23 of that Act—

(a) in subsection (2), for the word "paternity" there shall be substituted the word "parentage"; and

(b) in subsection (3), for the words "blood sample" there shall be substituted the words "bodily sample".

25. In section 24 of that Act, for the words "blood sample" there shall be substituted the words "bodily sample".

The Children and Young Persons Act 1969 (c.54)

26. In section 70 of the Children and Young Persons Act 1969, after subsection (1A) there shall be inserted the following subsection—

"(1B) In subsection (1A) of this section the reference to a child whose father and mother were not married to each other at the time of his birth shall be construed in accordance with section 1 of the Family Law Reform Act 1987 and 'actual custody', in relation to a child, means actual possession of his person."

The Administration of Justice Act 1970 (c.31)

27. In Schedule 8 to the Administration of Justice Act 1970—

(a) for paragraph 4(a) there shall be substituted—

"(a) section 11B, 11C or 11D of the Guardianship of Minors Act 1971 or section 2(3) or 2(4A) of the Guardianship Act 1973 (payments for maintenance of persons who are or have been in guardianship);";

(b) paragraph 5 shall cease to have effect.

The Guardianship of Minors Act 1971 (c.3)

28. Without prejudice to any other amendment of the 1971 Act made by this Act, for the words "minor", "minor's" and "minors", wherever occurring in that Act otherwise than in the expression "the Guardianship of Minors Act 1971", there shall be substituted the words "child", "child's" and "children" respectively.

29. In section 5(2) of that Act for the words from "notwithstanding" to the end there shall be substituted the words "notwithstanding that parental rights and duties with respect to the child are vested in a local authority or a voluntary organisation by virtue of a resolution under section 3 or 64 of the Child Care Act 1980".

30. In section 11A of that Act for the words "section 9(1), 10(1)(a) or 11(a)", wherever they occur, there shall be substituted the words "section 9 or 10".

31.—(1) Section 12 of that Act shall be amended as follows.

(2) In subsection (1) for the words "an order made under section 9, 10 or 11 of this Act for the making of periodical payments" there shall be substituted the words "an order for periodical payments made by virtue of section 11B(2)(a) or (b) or 11C(3)(a) or (b) of this Act".

(3) In subsection (2) for paragraph (a) there shall be substituted the following paragraph—

"(a) the child is, will be or (if an order were made without complying with that paragraph) would be receiving instruction at an educational establishment or undergoing training for a trade, profession or vocation, whether or not he also is, will be or would be in gainful employment; or".

(4) In subsection (3) for the words "Any order made under section 9, 10 or 11 of this Act requiring the making of periodical payments" there shall be substituted the words "An order for periodical payments made by virtue of section 11B(2)(a) or 11C(3) of this Act".

32. In section 12A of that Act for the words "section 9(2), 10(1)(b) or 11(b)" there shall be substituted the words "section 11B, 11C or 11D".

33.—(1) Section 12B of that Act shall be amended as follows.

(2) In subsection (1) for the words "section 9(2), 10(1)(b) and 11(b)" there shall be substituted the words "sections 11B and 11C", the words "in maintaining the minor" shall cease to have effect and there shall be added at the end the words "being liabilities or expenses incurred in connection with the birth of the child or in maintaining the child".

(3) In subsection (2) for the words "section 9(2), 10(1)(b) or 11(b)" there shall be substituted the words "section 11B, 11C or 11D".

(4) In subsections (3) and (5) for the words "section 9, 10 or 11", in each place where they occur, there shall be substituted the words "section 11B, 11C or 11D".

(5) In subsection (3) after the words "for the making" there shall be inserted the words "or securing" and the words "of a minor" shall cease to have effect.

34.—(1) Section 12C of that Act shall be amended as follows.

(2) In subsections (1) to (3) for the words "section 9, 10 or 11" there shall be substituted the words "section 11B, 11C or 11D" and after the words "for the making" there shall be inserted the words "or securing".

(3) In subsection (4) for the words "section 9, 10 or 11" there shall be substituted the words "section 11B or 11C" and after the words "for the making" there shall be inserted the words "or securing".

(4) For subsection (5) there shall be substituted the following subsections—

"(5) Where an order for the making of periodical payments made under section 11B or 11C of this Act ceases to have effect on the date on which the child attains the age of sixteen or at any time after that date but before or on the date on which he attains the age of eighteen, the child may apply—

(a) in the case of an order made by the High Court or a county court, to the court which made the order, or

(b) in the case of an order made by a magistrates' court, to the High Court or a county court,

for an order for the revival of the first mentioned order.

(6) If on such an application it appears to the High Court or county court that—

(a) the child is, will be or (if an order were made under this subsection) would be receiving instruction at an educational establishment or undergoing training for a trade, profession or vocation, whether or not he also is, will be or would be in gainful employment; or

(b) there are special circumstances which justify the making of an order under this subsection,

the court shall have power by order to revive the first mentioned order from such date as the court may specify, not being earlier than the date of the making of the application.

(7) Any order made under section 11B or 11C of this Act by the High Court or a county court which is revived by an order under subsection (5) above may be varied or discharged under section 11B or 11C of this Act, as the case may be, on the application of any person by whom or to whom payments are required to be made under the order.

(8) Any order made under section 11B or 11C of this Act by a magistrates' court which is revived by an order of the High Court or a county court under subsection (5) above—

(a) for the purposes of the variation and discharge of the order, shall be treated as an order of the court by which it was revived and may be varied or discharged by that court on the application of any person by whom or to whom payments are required to be made under the order; and

(b) for the purposes of the enforcement of the order, shall be treated as an order of the magistrates' court by which the order was originally made."

35. After that section there shall be inserted the following section—

"Variation of orders for secured periodical payments after death of parent

12D.—(1) Where the parent liable to make payments under a secured periodical payments order has died, the persons who may apply for the variation or discharge of the order shall include the personal representatives of the deceased parent, and no application for the variation of the order shall, except with the permission of the court, be made after the end of the period of six months from the date on which representation in regard to the estate of that parent is first taken out.

(2) The personal representatives of a deceased person against whom a secured periodical payments order was made shall not be liable for having distributed any part of the estate of the deceased after the expiration of the period of six months referred to in subsection (1) of this section on the ground that they ought to have taken into account the possibility that the court might permit an application for variation to be made after that period by the person entitled to payments under the order; but this subsection shall not prejudice any power to recover any part of the estate so distributed arising by virtue of the variation of an order in accordance with this section.

(3) Where an application to vary a secured periodical payments order is made after the death of the parent liable to make payments under the order, the circumstances to which the court is required to have regard under section 12C(1) of this Act shall include the changed circumstances resulting from the death of that parent.

(4) In considering for the purposes of subsection (1) of this section the question when representation was first taken out, a grant limited to settled land or to trust property shall be left out of account and a grant limited to real estate or to personal

estate shall be left out of account unless a grant limited to the remainder of the estate has previously been made or is made at the same time.

(5) In this section 'secured periodical payments order' means an order for secured periodical payments made by virtue of section 11B(2)(b) or 11C(3)(b) of this Act."

36. In section 13 of that Act for subsection (3) there shall be substituted the following subsection—

"(3) Any order for the payment of money made by a magistrates' court under this Act shall be enforceable as a magistrates' court maintenance order within the meaning of section 150(1) of the Magistrates' Courts Act 1980".

37. In section 13A(1) of that Act, for the words "section 9(1), 10(1)(a) or 11(a)" there shall be substituted the words "section 9 or 10".

38. After that section there shall be inserted the following section—

"Direction for settlement of instrument by conveyancing counsel

13B. Where the High Court or a county court decides to make an order under this Act for the securing of periodical payments or for the transfer or settlement of property, it may direct that the matter be referred to one of the conveyancing counsel of the court for him to settle a proper instrument to be executed by all necessary parties."

39. Section 14 of that Act and the heading preceding that section shall cease to have effect.

40.—(1) Section 14A of that Act shall be amended as follows.

(2) In subsection (1) for the words "section 9(1)" there shall be substituted the words "section 9".

(3) In subsection (3) for the words "section 9(1), 10(1)(a) or 11(a)" there shall be substituted the words "section 9 or 10".

(4) In subsection (5) for the words "the court has made an order under section 9(1)(a)" there shall be substituted the words "before 1st December 1985 the court has made an order under section 9".

41.—(1) Section 15A of that Act shall be amended as follows.

(2) In subsection (1)—

(a) for the words "section 9(2)(a) and (b)", in both places where they occur, there shall be substituted the words "section 11B(2)(a) and (b)"; and

(b) the words from "notwithstanding" to "custody of the child" shall cease to have effect.

(3) In subsection (2) for the words "section 9(2)", in both places where they occur, there shall be substituted the words "section 11B(2)".

42. In section 16(8) of that Act for the words "section 9(4), 10(2), 11(c), 12B(5) or 12C(5) of this Act or section 3(3) or 4(3A) or (3D)" there shall be substituted the words "section 9(1), 10(1) or 11B(1), 11C(1) or (2)(b), 11D(6), 12B(5) or 12C(2) of this Act or section 3(3) or 4(3A)".

43. In section 20 of that Act for subsection (2) there shall be substituted the following subsections—

"(2) In this Act, unless the context otherwise requires—

'actual custody', as respects a child, means the actual possession of the person of the child;

'child', except where used to express a relationship, means a person who has not attained the age of eighteen;

'legal custody' shall be construed in accordance with Part IV of the Children Act 1975;

'maintenance' includes education.

(2A) In this Act—

(a) references (however expressed) to any relationship between two persons; and

(b) references to the father and mother of a child not being married to each other at the time of his birth,

shall be construed in accordance with section 1 of the Family Law Reform Act 1987."

The Attachment of Earnings Act 1971 (c.32)

44. In Schedule 1 to the Attachment of Earnings Act 1971—

(a) for paragraph 5(a) there shall be substituted the following paragraph—

"(a) section 11B, 11C or 11D of the Guardianship of Minors Act 1971 or section 2(3) or 2(4A) of the Guardianship Act 1973 (payments for maintenance of persons who are or have been in guardianship);";

(b) paragraph 6 shall cease to have effect.

The Maintenance Orders (Reciprocal Enforcement) Act 1972 (c.18)

45. In section 8 of the Maintenance Orders (Reciprocal Enforcement) Act 1972, for subsection (4) there shall be substituted the following subsection—

"(4) An order which by virtue of this section is enforceable by a magistrates' court shall be enforceable as if it were a magistrates' court maintenance order made by that court.

In this subsection 'magistrates' court maintenance order' has the same meaning as in section 150(1) of the Magistrates' Courts Act 1980."

46. In section 27 of that Act—

(a) in subsection (2) for the words from "appointed for the commission area" to the words "as the case may be" there shall be substituted the words "acting for the petty session district";

(b) in subsection (9) the words "section 5(5) of the Affiliation Proceedings Act 1957" shall cease to have effect.

47. In section 28 of that Act after "19(1)(ii)" there shall be inserted "20A".

48. In section 28A(3) of that Act, in paragraph (e) after "19(1)(ii)" there shall be inserted "20A".

49.—(1) Section 30 of that Act shall be amended as follows.

(2) For subsection (1) there shall be substituted the following subsection—

"(1) Section 12C(5) of the Guardianship of Minors Act 1971 (revival by High Court or county court of orders for periodical payments) shall not apply in relation to an order made on a complaint for an order under section 11B of that Act."

(3) In subsection (2) for the words "to which subsection (1) above applies" there shall be substituted the words "for an order under section 11B of that Act".

(4) In subsection (3) the words "the Affiliation Proceedings Act 1957 or", the words "paragraph (b) of section 2(1) of the said Act of 1957 (time for making complaint) or", the words "(provision to the like effect) as the case may be", the words "three years or" and the words "in the case of a complaint under the said Act of 1924" shall cease to have effect.

(5) In subsection (5) the words "the said Act of 1957 or" and the words "as the case may be" shall cease to have effect.

(6) In subsection (6) the words "or an affiliation order under the said Act of 1957" shall cease to have effect.

50. In section 33 of that Act, for subsection (3) there shall be substituted the following subsection—

"(3) An order which by virtue of subsection (1) above is enforceable by a magistrates' court shall be enforceable as if it were a magistrates' court maintenance order made by that court.

In this subsection 'magistrates' court maintenance order' has the same meaning as in section 150(1) of the Magistrates' Courts Act 1980."

51.—(1) Section 41 of that Act shall be amended as follows.

(2) Subsection (1) shall cease to have effect.

(3) In subsection (2) for the words "section 9, 10 or 11" there shall be substituted the words "section 11B or 11C".

(4) In subsection (2A), paragraph (a) shall cease to have effect and for paragraph (b) there shall be substituted the following paragraph—

"(b) an application made under section 11B or 11C of the Guardianship of Minors Act 1971 for the revocation or variation of an order for the periodical payment of money made under the said section 11B or 11C.".

(5) In subsection (2B), paragraph (a) shall cease to have effect and in paragraph (b) for the words "section 9, 10 or 11" there shall be substituted the words "section 11B or 11C".

The Matrimonial Causes Act 1973 (c.18)

52. In section 27 of the Matrimonial Causes Act 1973 for subsection (6B) there shall be substituted the following subsection—

"(6B) Where a periodical payments order made in favour of a child under this section ceases to have effect on the date on which the child attains the age of sixteen or at any time after that date but before or on the date on which he attains the age of eighteen, then if, on an application made to the court for an order under this subsection, it appears to the court that—

(a) the child is, will be or (if an order were made under this subsection) would be receiving instruction at an educational establishment or undergoing training for a trade, profession or vocation, whether or not he also is, will be or would be in gainful employment; or

(b) there are special circumstances which justify the making of an order under this subsection,

the court shall have power by order to revive the first mentioned order from such date as the court may specify, not being earlier than the date of the making of the application, and to exercise its power under section 31 of this Act in relation to any order so revived."

The Guardianship Act 1973 (c.29)

53. Without prejudice to any other amendment of Part I of the 1973 Act made by this Act, for the words "minor" and "minors", wherever occurring in that Part otherwise than in the expression "the Guardianship of Minors Act 1971", there shall be substituted the words "child" and "children" respectively.

54.—(1) Section 2 of that Act shall be amended as follows.

(2) For subsection (2) there shall be substituted the following subsection—

"(2) Where an application is made under section 9 of the Guardianship of Minors Act 1971 for the legal custody of a child, then subject to sections 3 and 4 below—

(a) if by virtue of the making of, or refusal to make, an order on that application the actual custody of the child is given to, or retained by, a parent of the child, but it appears to the court that there are exceptional circumstances making it desirable that the child should be under the supervision of an independent person, the court may make an order that the child shall be under the supervision of a specified local authority or under the supervision of a probation officer;

(b) if it appears to the court that there are exceptional circumstances making it impracticable or undesirable for the child to be entrusted to either of the parents, the court may commit the care of the child to a specified local authority."

(3) In subsection (3B) for the words "section 9(2)" there shall be substituted the words "section 11B".

(4) For subsections (4) and (5) there shall be substituted the following subsections—

"(4) Subject to the provisions of this section, where an application is made under section 9 of the Guardianship of Minors Act 1971 the court, at any time before it makes a final order or dismisses the application, may, if by reason of special circumstances the court thinks it proper, make an interim order containing any such provision regarding the legal custody of and right of access to the child as the court has power to make under that section.

(4A) Subject to the provisions of this section, where an application is made under section 11B of the Guardianship of Minors Act 1971, the court, at any time before it makes a final order or dismisses the application, may make an interim order requiring either parent to make to the other or to the child such periodical payments towards the maintenance of the child as the court thinks fit.

(5) Where under section 16(4) of the Guardianship of Minors Act 1971 the court refuses to make an order on an application under section 9 or 11B of that Act on the ground that the matter is one that would more conveniently be dealt with by the High Court, the court shall have power—

(a) in the case of an application under section 9 of that Act, to make an order under subsection (4) above,

(b) in the case of an application under section 11B of that Act, to make an order under subsection (4A) above".

(5) In subsection (5B) for the words "section 9" there shall be substituted the words "section 11B".

(6) For subsection (5E) there shall be substituted the following subsection—

"(5E) On an application under section 9 or 11B of the Guardianship of Minors Act 1971 the court shall not have power to make more than one interim order under this section with respect to that application, but without prejudice to the powers of the court under this section on any further such application."

(7) Subsection (6) shall cease to have effect.

55. In section 4 of that Act—

(a) in subsection (3) after the words "section 9" there shall be inserted the words "of 11B"; and

(b) subsection (3D) shall cease to have effect.

56.—(1) Section 5 of that Act shall be amended as follows.

(2) For subsections (1) and (2) there shall be substituted the following subsections—

"(1) There shall be no appeal under section 16 of the Guardianship of Minors Act 1971 from an interim order under subsection (4A) of section 2 above.

(2) Section 9 of the Guardianship of Minors Act 1971 shall apply in relation to an interim order made under this Act on an application under that section as if the interim order had been made under that section.

(2A) Section 13 of the Guardianship of Minors Act 1971 shall apply in relation to an interim order made under this Act as if the interim order had been made under that Act."

57. In section 5A of that Act for subsections (1) and (2) there shall be substituted the following subsections—

"(1) Where any of the following orders is made, that is to say—

(a) an order under section 9 of the Guardianship of Minors Act 1971 which gives the right to the actual custody of a child to one of the parents of the child,

(b) an order under section 11B of that Act which requires periodical payments to be made or secured to a parent of the child,

(c) an interim order under section 2(4) above which gives the right to the actual custody of a child to a parent of the child,

(d) an interim order under section 2(4A) above which requires periodical payments to be made to a parent of the child,

that order shall be enforceable notwithstanding that the parents of the child are living with each other at the date of the making of the order or that, although they are not living with each other at that date, they subsequently live with each other; but that order shall cease to have effect if after that date the parents of the child marry each other or live with each other for a period exceeding six months.

(2) Where any of the following orders is made, that is to say—

(a) an order under section 11B of the Guardianship of Minors Act 1971 which requires periodical payments to be made or secured to a child,

(b) an order under section 2(2) or (3) above,

(c) an interim order under section 2(4A) requiring periodical payments to be made to a child,

then, unless the court otherwise directs, that order shall be enforceable notwithstanding that the parents of the child are living with each other at the date of the making of the order or that, although they are not living with each other at that date, they subsequently live with each other.

(2A) Where an order is made under section 11D of the Guardianship of Minors Act 1971 requiring periodical payments to be made to a person who has attained the age of eighteen, then unless the court otherwise directs, that order shall be enforceable notwithstanding that the parents of that person, although they are not living with each other at the date of the order, subsequently live with each other."

58. Before section 9 of that Act there shall be inserted the following section—

"Interpretation of Part I

8A.—(1) In this Part of this Act 'child', except where used to express a relationship, means a person who has not attained the age of eighteen.

(2) In this Part of this Act—

(a) references (however expressed) to any relationship between two persons; and

(b) references to the father and mother of a child not being married to each other at the time of his birth,

shall be construed in accordance with section 1 of the Family Law Reform Act 1987."

The Social Security Act 1975 (c.14)

59. At the end of section 25(1) of the Social Security Act 1975 there shall be added the words "or

(c) if the woman and her late husband were residing together immediately before the time of his death, the woman is pregnant as the result of being artificially inseminated before that time with the semen of some person other than her husband."

The Children Act 1975 (c.72)

60. In section 33 of the Children Act 1975, after subsection (9) there shall be inserted the following subsection—

"(9A) In this Part of this Act references (however expressed) to any relationship between two persons shall be construed in accordance with section 1 of the Family Law Reform Act 1987."

61.—(1) Section 34 of that Act shall be amended as follows.

(2) Subsections (3) and (4) shall cease to have effect.

(3) In subsection (5) for the words "(5A), (5B), (5C), (5D), (5E) and (6)" there shall be substituted the words "(4A), (5A), (5B), (5C), (5D) and (5E)" and for the words "section 2(2)(b) and (4)(a)" there shall be substituted the words "section 2(2)(b) and (4A)".

62. In section 35 of that Act, for subsection (10) there shall be substituted the following subsections—

"(10) Where an order under section 34(1)(b) ceases to have effect on the date on which the child attains the age of 16 or at any time after that date but before or on the date on which he attains the age of 18, the child may apply to an authorised court, other than a magistrates' court, for an order for the revival of that order, and if, on such an application, it appears to the court that—

(a) the child is, will be or (if an order were made under this subsection) would be receiving instruction at an educational establishment or undergoing training for a trade, profession or vocation, whether or not he also is, will be or would be in gainful employment; or

(b) there are special circumstances which justify the making of an order under this subsection,

the court shall have power by order to revive the order made under section 34(1)(b) from such date as the court may specify, not being earlier than the date of the making of the application and to vary or revoke under this section any order so revived.

(10A) Any order made by a magistrates' court under section 34(1)(b) which is revived by an order under subsection (10) shall for the purposes of the enforcement of the order be treated as an order made by the magistrates' court by which the order was originally made."

63. In section 36 of that Act, subsection (5A) shall cease to have effect.

64. In section 37(3) of that Act, for the words "section 9 (orders for custody and maintenance)" there shall be substituted the words "section 9 (orders for custody)".

65. In section 43 of that Act, for subsection (3) there shall be substituted the following subsection—

"(3) An order for the payment of money made by a magistrates' court under section 34 shall be enforceable as a magistrates' court maintenance order within the meaning of section 150(1) of the Magistrates' Courts Act 1980."

66. Section 45 of that Act (affiliation order on application of custodian) shall cease to have effect.

The Adoption Act 1976 (c.36)

67. At the end of section 18 of the Adoption Act 1976 there shall be added the following subsection—

"(8) In subsection (7) the reference to a child whose father and mother were not married to each other at the time of his birth shall be construed in accordance with section 1 of the Family Law Reform Act 1987."

68. In section 72 of that Act, after subsection (1) there shall be inserted the following subsection—

"(1A) In the definition of 'guardian' in subsection (1) the reference to a child whose father and mother were not married to each other at the time of his birth shall be construed in accordance with section 1 of the Family Law Reform Act 1987."

The Domestic Proceedings and Magistrates' Courts Act 1978 (c.22)

69. After section 20 of the Domestic Proceedings and Magistrates' Courts Act 1978 there shall be inserted the following section—

"Revival of orders for periodical payments

20A.—(1) Where an order made by a magistrates' court under this Part of this Act for the making of periodical payments to or in respect of a child (other than an interim maintenance order) ceases to have effect on the date on which the child attains the age of 16 or at any time after that date but before or on the date on which he attains the age of 18, the child may apply to the High Court or a county court for an order for the revival of the order of the magistrates' court, and if, on such an application, it appears to the High Court or county court that—

(a) the child is, will be or (if an order were made under this subsection) would be receiving instruction at an educational establishment or undergoing training for a trade, profession or vocation, whether or not he also is, will be or would be in gainful employment; or

    (b) there are special circumstances which justify the making of an order under this subsection,

the court shall have power by order to revive the first mentioned order from such date as the court may specify, not being earlier than the date of the making of the application.

    (2) Where an order made by a magistrates' court is revived by an order of the High Court or a county court under subsection (1) above, then—

    (a) for the purposes of the variation and discharge of the revived order, that order shall be treated as an order of the court by which it was revived and may be varied or discharged by that court on the application of any person by whom or to whom payments are required to be made under the order, and

    (b) for the purposes of the enforcement of the revived order, that order shall be treated as an order of the magistrates' court by which the order was originally made."

70. In section 32 of that Act, for subsection (1) there shall be substituted the following subsection—

    "(1) An order for the payment of money made by a magistrates' court under this Part of this Act shall be enforceable as a magistrates' court maintenance order."

71. In section 88(1) of that Act, after the definition of "local authority" there shall be inserted the following definition—

    " 'magistrates' court maintenance order' has the same meaning as in section 150(1) of the Magistrates' Courts Act 1980,".

72. In Schedule 1 to that Act—

    (a) after paragraph 3 there shall be inserted the following paragraph—

        "3A. Any order for the payment of money in force under the Matrimonial Proceedings (Magistrates' Courts) Act 1960 (including any such order made under that Act by virtue of paragraph 1 above) shall be enforceable as a magistrates' court maintenance order."

    (b) in paragraph 4 for the words "paragraph 2 or 3" there shall be substituted the words "paragraph 2, 3 or 3A".

The Interpretation Act 1978 (c.30)

73. At the end of Schedule 1 to the Interpretation Act 1978, there shall be added the following heading and entry—

"Construction of certain references to relationships

In relation to England and Wales—

    (a) references (however expressed) to any relationship between two persons;

    (b) references to a person whose father and mother were or were not married to each other at the time of his birth; and

    (c) references cognate with references falling within paragraph (b) above,

shall be construed in accordance with section 1 of the Family Law Reform Act 1987. [The date of the coming into force of that section]".

74. In paragraph 4 of Schedule 2 to that Act, the words "earlier than the commencement of this Act" shall cease to have effect and after the word "specified", wherever it occurs, there shall be inserted the words "or described".

The Child Care Act 1980 (c.5)

75. In section 47 of that Act, for subsection (4) there shall be substituted the following subsections—

    "(4) A contribution order shall be enforceable as a magistrates' court maintenance order within the meaning of section 150(1) of the Magistrates' Courts Act 1980, except that any powers conferred on a magistrates' court by that Act shall as respects a contribution order be exercisable, and exercisable only, by a magistrates' court appointed for the commission area where the contributor is for the time being residing.

    (5) Where a contribution order is made requiring the father of a child whose parents were not married to each other at the time of his birth to make contributions in respect of the child, the father shall keep the local authority to whom the contributions are required to be made informed of his address; and if he fails to do so, he shall be guilty of an offence and liable on summary conviction to a fine not exceeding level 1 on the standard scale."

76. Sections 49 and 50 of that Act (affiliation orders) shall cease to have effect.

77. In section 55 of that Act—
    (a) subsection (3) shall cease to have effect;
    (b) in subsection (5) the words from "and any jurisdiction conferred by this section in affiliation proceedings" to the end shall cease to have effect.

78. In section 86 of that Act for paragraphs (a) and (b) there shall be substituted the words "of an order made by a court under section 47 or 48 of this Act".

79.—(1) Section 87 of that Act shall be amended as follows.

(2) In subsection (1), in the definition of "relative" the words from "and includes" to the end shall cease to have effect.

(3) After subsection (1) there shall be inserted the following subsection—
"(1A) In this Act—
    (a) references to a child whose father and mother were not married to each other at the time of his birth; and
    (b) except in Part I and sections 13, 24, 64 and 65, references (however expressed) to any relationship between two persons,
shall be construed in accordance with section 1 of the Family Law Reform Act 1987."

The Magistrates' Courts Act 1980 (c.43)

80. In section 58(2)(a) of the Magistrates' Courts Act 1980, for the words "an affiliation order or order enforceable as an affiliation order" there shall be substituted the words "a magistrates' court maintenance order".

81. In section 64 of that Act, for subsection (4) there shall be substituted the following subsection—
"(4) Any costs awarded on a complaint for a maintenance order, or for the enforcement, variation, revocation, discharge or revival of such an order, against the person liable to make payments under the order shall be enforceable as a sum ordered to be paid by a magistrates' court maintenance order."

82. In section 65(1) of that Act, after paragraph (1) there shall be inserted the following paragraph—
"(m) section 4 or 15 of the Family Law Reform Act 1987;".

83. In section 80(1) of that Act, for the words "an affiliation order or an order enforceable as an affiliation order" there shall be substituted the words "a magistrates' court maintenance order".

84. In section 93(1) of that Act, for the words "an affiliation order or order enforceable as an affiliation order" there shall be substituted the words "a magistrates' court maintenance order".

85. In section 94 of that Act, for the words "an affiliation order or order enforceable as an affiliation order" there shall be substituted the words "a magistrates' court maintenance order".

86. In section 95 of that Act, for the words "an affiliation order or an order enforceable as an affiliation order" there shall be substituted the words "a magistrates' court maintenance order".

87. In section 100 of that Act, for paragraph (b) there shall be substituted the following paragraph—
"(b) on any application made by or against that person for the making of a magistrates' court maintenance order, or for the variation, revocation, discharge or revival of such an order".

88. In section 150(1) of that Act—
    (a) the definition of "affiliation order" shall cease to have effect;
    (b) after the definition of "London Commission area" there shall be inserted the following definitions—
        "'magistrates' court maintenance order' means a maintenance order enforceable by a magistrates' court;
        'maintenance order' means any order specified in Schedule 8 to the Administration of Justice Act 1970 and includes such an order which has been discharged, if any arrears are recoverable thereunder;".

The Civil Jurisdiction and Judgments Act 1982 (c.27)

89.—(1) Section 5 of the Civil Jurisdiction and Judgments Act 1982 shall be amended as follows.

(2) After subsection (5) there shall be inserted the following subsection—
"(5A) A maintenance order which by virtue of this section is enforceable by a magistrates' court in England and Wales shall be enforceable in the same manner as a magistrates' court maintenance order made by that court.

In this subsection 'magistrates' court maintenance order' has the same meaning as in section 150(1) of the Magistrates' Courts Act 1980."

(3) In subsection (6) the words "England and Wales or" shall cease to have effect.

The Child Abduction and Custody Act 1985 (c.60)

90. In Schedule 3 to the Child Abduction and Custody Act 1985—
    (a) in paragraph 1(1)(d) for the words "section 9(1), 10(1)(a) or 11(a)" there shall be substituted the words "section 9 or 10";
    (b) in paragraph 1(1)(f) for the words "(4)(b) or (5)" there shall be substituted the words "(4) or (5)(b)".

The Social Security Act 1986 (c.50)

91. In section 24 of the Social Security Act 1986 (recovery of expenditure on supplementary benefits from persons liable for maintenance), subsections (2) and (3) shall cease to have effect and for subsection (7) there shall be substituted the following subsection—
    "(7) An order under this section shall be enforceable as a magistrates' court maintenance order within the meaning of section 150(1) of the Magistrates' Courts Act 1980."

92. Section 25 of that Act (affiliation orders) shall cease to have effect.

93. In section 26 of that Act, for subsection (4) there shall be substituted the following subsection—
    "(4) Any reference in subsection (3) above to a person's children shall be construed in accordance with section 1 of the Family Law Reform Act 1987."

The Family Law Act 1986 (c.55)

94. In section 1 of the Family Law Act 1986—
    (a) in subsection (1)(a)(i) for the words "section 9(1), 10(1)(a), 11(a)" there shall be substituted the words "section 9, 10" and for the words "section 2(4)(b) or 2(5)" there shall be substituted the words "section 2(4) or (5)(a)";
    (b) in subsection (1)(a)(iv) for the words "section 2(4)(b)" there shall be substituted the words "section 2(4)";
    (c) in subsection (4)(a) for the words "sections 9(1)" there shall be substituted the words "sections 9".

95. In section 3(5) of that Act for the words "section 9(1)" there shall be substituted the words "section 9".

96. At the end of section 60(2)(c) of that Act (supplementary provisions as to declarations) there shall be added the words "and on persons who may be affected by any declaration applied for".

Section 33(2)   SCHEDULE 3

TRANSITIONAL PROVISIONS AND SAVINGS

Applications pending under amended or repealed enactments

1. This Act (including the repeals and amendments made by it) shall not have effect in relation to any application made under any enactment repealed or amended by this Act if that application is pending at the time when the provision of this Act which repeals or amends that enactment comes into force.

References to provisions of Adoption Act 1976

2. In relation to any time before the coming into force of section 38 of the Adoption Act 1976, the reference in section 1(2) of this Act to Part IV of that Act shall be construed as a reference to Schedule 1 to the Children Act 1975.

3. In relation to any time before the coming into force of section 18 of the Adoption Act 1976, any reference—
    (a) in section 7(1) of or paragraph 67 of Schedule 2 to this Act; or
    (b) in section 9(2) or 10(3) of the 1971 Act as substituted by this Act,
to or to subsection (7) of the said section 18 shall be construed as a reference to or to subsection (8) of section 14 of the Children Act 1975.

4. In relation to any time before the coming into force of section 72(1) of the Adoption Act 1976, any reference in section 7(2) of or paragraph 67 of Schedule 2 to this Act to the said section 72(1) shall be construed as a reference to section 107(1) of the Children Act 1975.

5. In relation to any time before the coming into force of section 42 of the Adoption Act 1976, the reference in section 19 of this Act to the said section 42 shall be construed as a reference to paragraph 6 of Schedule 1 to the Children Act 1975.

Affiliation orders

6.—(1) Neither section 17 of this Act nor any associated amendment or repeal shall affect, or affect the operation of any enactment in relation to—

(a) any affiliation order made under the Affiliation Proceedings Act 1957 which is in force immediately before the coming into force of that section; or

(b) any affiliation order made under that Act by virtue of paragraph 1 above.

(2) Any reference in this paragraph or paragraph 7 below to an affiliation order made under the Affiliation Proceedings Act 1957 includes a reference to—

(a) an affiliation order made, by virtue of section 44 of the National Assistance Act 1948, section 19 of the Supplementary Benefits Act 1976, section 49 or 50 of the Child Care Act 1980 or section 25 of the Social Security Act 1986; and

(b) any order made in relation to such an order.

7. Where—

(a) an application is made to the High Court or a county court for an order under section 11B of the 1971 Act in respect of a child whose parents were not married to each other at the time of his birth, and

(b) an affiliation order made under the Affiliation Proceedings Act 1957 and providing for periodical payments is in force in respect of the child by virtue of this Schedule,

the court may, if it thinks fit, direct that the affiliation order shall cease to have effect on such date as may be specified in the direction.

Property rights

8. The repeal by this Act of section 14 of the Family Law Reform Act 1969 shall not affect any rights arising under the intestacy of a person dying before the coming into force of the repeal.

9. The repeal by this Act of section 15 of the Family Law Reform Act 1969 shall not affect, or affect the operation of section 33 of the Trustee Act 1925 in relation to—

(a) any disposition inter vivos made before the date on which the repeal comes into force; or

(b) any disposition by will or codicil executed before that date.

10. The repeal by this Act of section 17 of the Family Law Reform Act 1969 shall not affect the liability of trustees or personal representatives in respect of any conveyance or distribution made before the coming into force of the repeal.

Registration of births

11. Where—

(a) a child whose parents were not married to each other at the time of his birth has been born in England and Wales before the date on which section 24 of this Act comes into force;

(b) the birth has not been registered under the 1953 Act before that date; and

(c) an order has been made under section 4 of the Affiliation Proceedings Act 1957 naming any person as the putative father of the child,

the mother of the child, on production of a certified copy of the order, may request the registrar to enter the name of that person as the father of the child under section 10 of the 1953 Act as if the order made under the said section 4 were an order under section 11B of the 1971 Act.

12. Where—

(a) the birth of a child whose parents were not married to each other at the time of his birth has been registered under the 1953 Act before the date on which section 25 of this Act comes into force;

(b) no person has been registered as the father of the child; and

(c) an order has been made under section 4 of the Affiliation Proceedings Act 1957 naming any person as the father of the child, the mother of the child, on production of a certified copy of the order, may request the registrar to re-register the birth so as to show as the father of the child the person named in the order.

Section 33(4)   SCHEDULE 4

REPEALS

Chapter	Short title	Extent of repeal
11 & 12 Geo. 6 c.29	The National Assistance Act 1948.	Section 42(2). Section 44.
14 Geo. 6 c.37.	The Maintenance Orders Act 1950.	Section 3. In section 16(2)(*a*)— (*a*) sub-paragraph (iv); (*b*) the sub-paragraph (vi) inserted by the Children Act 1975; (*c*) in the sub-paragraph (vi) inserted by the Supplementary Benefits Act 1976, the words from "or section 4 of the Affiliation Proceedings Act 1957" to the end; (*d*) in sub-paragraph (viii), the words from "or section 4 of the Affiliation Proceedings Act 1957" to the end.
3 & 4 Eliz. 2 c.18.	The Army Act 1955.	In section 150(5), the words from "references to a sum ordered to be paid" to the end.
3 & 4 Eliz 2 c.19.	The Air Force Act 1955.	In section 150(5), the words from "references to a sum ordered to be paid" to the end.
5 & 6 Eliz. 2 c.53.	The Naval Discipline Act 1957.	In section 101(5), the words "and includes an affiliation order within the meaning of the Affiliation Orders Act 1914".
5 & 6 Eliz. 2 c.55.	The Affiliation Proceedings Act 1957.	The whole Act.
6 & 7 Eliz. 2 c.39.	The Maintenance Orders Act 1958.	In section 21(1), the words "affiliation order".
7 & 8 Eliz. 2 c.73.	The Legitimacy Act 1959.	The whole Act.
1968 c.63.	The Domestic and Appellate Proceedings (Restriction of Publicity) Act 1968.	In section 2(1), the word "and" following paragraph (*c*).
1969 c.46.	The Family Law Reform Act 1969.	Sections 14 and 15. Section 17. Section 27.
1970 c.31.	The Administration of Justice Act 1970.	In Schedule 8, paragraph 5.
1971 c.3.	The Guardianship of Minors Act 1971.	In section 12B, in subsection (1), the words "in maintaining the minor" and, in subsection (3), the words "of a minor". Section 14 and the heading preceding that section.
1971 c.32.	The Attachment of Earnings Act 1971.	In Schedule 1, paragraph 6.
1972 c.18.	The Maintenance Orders (Reciprocal Enforcement) Act 1972.	Section 3(3). In section 27(9), the words "section 5(5) of the Affiliation Proceedings Act 1957".

Chapter	Short title	Extent of repeal
1972 c.18— *cont.*	The Maintenance Orders (Reciprocal Enforcement) Act 1972—*cont.*	In section 30— (*a*) in subsection (3), the words "the Affiliation Proceedings Act 1957 or", the words "paragraph (*b*) of section 2(1) of the said Act of 1957 (time for making complaint) or", the words "(provision to the like effect), as the case may be", the words "three years (or" and the words "in the case of a complaint under the said Act of 1924)"; (*b*) in subsection (5), the words "the said Act of 1957" and the words "as the case may be"; (*c*) in subsection (6), the words "or an affiliation order under the said Act of 1957". In section 41— (*a*) subsection (1); (*b*) in subsection (2A), paragraph (*a*); (*c*) in subsection (2B), paragraph (*a*).
1972 c.49.	The Affiliation Proceedings (Amendment) Act 1972.	The whole Act.
1973 c.29.	The Guardianship Act 1973.	Section 2(6). Section 4(3D).
1974 c.4.	The Legal Aid Act 1974.	In Schedule 1, in Part I, paragraph 2.
1975 c.72.	The Children Act 1975.	In section 34, subsections (3) and (4). Section 36(5A). Section 45. In section 85(2), the words "(which relate to separation agreements between husband and wife)". In section 93, subsections (1) and (2). In Schedule 3, paragraphs 14 and 75(1).
1976 c.36.	The Adoption Act 1976.	In Schedule 3, paragraph 16.
1978 c.22.	The Domestic Proceedings and Magistrates' Courts Act 1978.	In section 20, subsections (10) and (13). In section 36(1), paragraph (*c*). Section 38(2). Section 41. In section 45, subsections (2) and (3). In Schedule 2, paragraphs 30 and 44.
1978 c.30.	The Interpretation Act 1978.	In Schedule 2, in paragraph 4, the words "earlier than the commencement of this Act".
1980 c.5.	The Child Care Act 1980.	Sections 49 and 50. In section 52(1), paragraph (*b*). In section 54, in subsections (1) and (2), the words "49, 50". In section 55, subsection (3) and, in subsection (5), the words from "and any jurisdiction conferred by this section in affiliation proceedings" to the end. In section 87(1), in the definition of "relative", the words from "and includes" to the end. In Schedule 2, paragraphs 4 and 5 and, in paragraph 7, the words "49, 50". In Schedule 5, paragraphs 6 to 8.

Chapter	Short title	Extent of repeal
1980 c.43.	The Magistrates' Courts Act 1980.	In section 59(2), the words "an affiliation order". In section 65(1)— (*a*) in paragraph (*b*), the words "or section 44"; (*b*) paragraph (*d*); (*c*) in paragraph (*i*), the words "or section 19"; (*d*) in paragraph (*k*), the words 49 or 50". Section 92(3). In section 150(1), the definition of "affiliation order".
1981 c.54	The Supreme Court Act 1981.	In Schedule 1, in paragraph 3(*b*)(iii), the words "affiliation or".
1982 c.24.	The Social Security and Housing Benefits Act 1982.	In Schedule 4, paragraph 1.
1986 c.50.	The Social Security Act 1986.	In section 24, subsections (2) and (3). Section 25.

CONSUMER PROTECTION ACT 1987*

(1987 c. 43)

ARRANGEMENT OF SECTIONS

PART I

PRODUCT LIABILITY

SECT.
 1. Purpose and construction of Part I.
 2. Liability for defective products.
 3. Meaning of "defect".
 4. Defences.
 5. Damage giving rise to liability.
 6. Application of certain enactments etc.
 7. Prohibition on exclusions from liability.
 8. Power to modify Part I.
 9. Application of Part I to Crown.

PART II

CONSUMER SAFETY

10. The general safety requirement.
11. Safety regulations.
12. Offences against the safety regulations.
13. Prohibition notices and notices to warn.
14. Suspension notices.
15. Appeals against suspension notices.
16. Forfeiture: England and Wales and Northern Ireland.
17. Forfeiture: Scotland.
18. Power to obtain information.
19. Interpretation of Part II.

PART III

MISLEADING PRICE INDICATIONS

20. Offence of giving misleading indication.
21. Meaning of "misleading".
22. Application to provision of services and facilities.
23. Application to provision of accommodation etc.
24. Defences.
25. Code of practice.
26. Power to make regulations.

PART IV

ENFORCEMENT OF PARTS II AND III

27. Enforcement.
28. Test purchases.
29. Powers of search etc.
30. Provisions supplemental to s.29.
31. Power of customs officer to detain goods.
32. Obstruction of authorised officer.
33. Appeals against detention of goods.
34. Compensation for seizure and detention.
35. Recovery of expenses of enforcement.

* Annotations by Paul Dobson, Principal lecturer, Polytechnic of North London.

PART V

MISCELLANEOUS AND SUPPLEMENTAL

SECT.
36. Amendments of Part I of the Health and Safety at Work etc. Act 1974.
37. Power of Commissioners of Customs and Excise to disclose information.
38. Restrictions on disclosure of information.
39. Defence of due diligence.
40. Liability of persons other than principal offender.
41. Civil proceedings.
42. Reports etc.
43. Financial provisions.
44. Service of documents etc.
45. Interpretation.
46. Meaning of "supply".
47. Savings for certain privileges.
48. Minor and consequential amendments and repeals.
49. Northern Ireland.
50. Short title, commencement and transitional provision.

Schedule 1—Limitation of actions under Part I.
    Part   I—England and Wales.
    Part II—Scotland.
Schedule 2—Prohibition notices and notices to warn.
    Part   I—Prohibition notices.
    Part II—Notices to warn.
    Part III—General.
Schedule 3—Amendments of Part I of the Health and Safety at Work etc. Act
    1974.
Schedule 4—Minor and consequential amendments.
Schedule 5—Repeals.

An Act to make provision with respect to the liability of persons for
damage caused by defective products; to consolidate with amendments
the Consumer Safety Act 1978 and the Consumer Safety (Amendment)
Act 1986; to make provision with respect to the giving of price
indications; to amend Part I of the Health and Safety at Work etc. Act
1974 and sections 31 and 80 of the Explosives Act 1875; to repeal the
Trade Descriptions Act 1972 and the Fabrics (Misdescription) Act
1913; and for connected purposes.

[15th May 1987]

PARLIAMENTARY DEBATES
Hansard, H.L. Vol. 482, cols. 233, 1003; Vol. 483, cols. 715, 781, 818, 865, 1463; Vol. 485,
cols. 824, 840, 886, 1140, 1519; Vol. 487, col. 784; H.C. Vol. 115, col. 51; Vol. 116, col.
345.
The Bill was considered by Standing Committee D from May 25 to 12, 1987.

GENERAL NOTE
The Act changes the Law in three main respects. Pt. 1, headed Product Liability, deals
with damage caused by defective products. It imposes strict liability upon producers, own-
branders and those who imported the products into the EEC. Pt. 2, headed Consumer
Safety, consolidates some earlier legislation and also creates a new criminal offence of
supplying consumer goods which are not reasonably safe. Pt. 3, headed Misleading Price
Indications, replaces earlier legislation by making it a criminal offence for a trader to give
a consumer a misleading price indication as to goods, services, accommodation or facilities.
A fuller note is given at the beginning of each of these Parts of the Act.

COMMENCEMENT
The Act received the Royal Assent on May 15, 1987. It will come into force on days to
be appointed (s.50(2)).

Part I

Product Liability

GENERAL NOTE

This Part implements the Product Liability Directive (85/374/EEC). These provisions and the Directive which they implement are the culmination of commissions, reports and debates, the stimulus for which was the Thalidomide tragedy in the late 1960's and early 1970's. That tragedy left hundreds of newly born children limbless as a result of their mothers having been given the Thalidomide drug during pregnancy. The Royal Commission on Civil Liability and Compensation for Personal Injury (the Pearson Committee) produced its report in 1976 (Cmnd. 7054). The Law Commissions produced their report "Liability For Defective Products" in 1977 (Cmnd. 6831). Also in 1977 the Council of Europe's "Strasbourg Convention on Products Liability in Regard to Personal Injury and Death" was opened for signature. This convention was produced as Appendix A to the above mentioned report of the Law Commissions. All of these various bodies recommended that manufacturers' liability for injury caused by defective products should be strict liability; liability should not depend upon proof of any fault or negligence; importers and own branders should be under a similar liability. This also was the position taken in the Directive. This Part of the Act makes it law.

Three matters proved particularly controversial during discussions before the Directive was finally adopted. First was the development risks defence, sometimes referred to as the "state of the art" defence. The compromise reached was that the Directive allows each member state to decide for itself whether to incorporate this defence into its law. The British government opted for the defence which is, accordingly, stated in s.4(1)(e). Second was the issue of whether the liability should extend to primary agricultural products. In the result the Directive excluded primary agricultural products but nevertheless left member states free, if they wished, to extend liability to include them. The British government opted for the exclusion, which, accordingly, appears in s.2(4). Third was the issue of whether there should be an overall financial limit on a producer's liability for damage caused by identical items each with the same defect. The Directive allowed member states the option to include such a limit. The British government opted against any such limit and none appears in the Act.

A further matter of debate was the question of whether the strict liability should extend to property damage as well as to death and personal injuries caused by the defective product. The Directive came down on the side of extending the strict liability to property damage provided that the property damaged was of a type ordinarily intended (and mainly used) for private use, occupation or consumption and provided the damage was worth at least a certain minimum figure. This is enacted in s.5 where the minimum figure is £275. The reason for this threshold is to exclude trivial claims for property damage.

COMMENCEMENT

It is not expected that Pt. 1 will be brought into force (by order under s.50(2)) before, at the earliest, November 15, 1987. It will not apply to damage suffered after it has come into force where that damage was caused by a defect in a product which was supplied by its producer before Pt. 1 came into force (s.50(7)).

Purpose and construction of Part I

1.—(1) This Part shall have effect for the purpose of making such provision as is necessary in order to comply with the product liability Directive and shall be construed accordingly.

(2) In this Part, except in so far as the context otherwise requires—

"agricultural produce" means any produce of the soil, of stock-farming or of fisheries;

"dependant" and "relative" have the same meaning as they have in, respectively, the Fatal Accidents Act 1976 and the Damages (Scotland) Act 1976;

"producer", in relation to a product, means—

(a) the person who manufactured it;

(b) in the case of a substance which has not been manufactured but has been won or abstracted, the person who won or abstracted it;

(c) in the case of a product which has not been manufactured, won or abstracted but essential characteristics of which are attributable to an industrial or other process having been carried out (for example, in relation to agricultural produce), the person who carried out that process;

"product" means any goods or electricity and (subject to subsection (3) below) includes a product which is comprised in another product, whether by virtue of being a component part or raw material or otherwise; and

"the product liability Directive" means the Directive of the Council of the European Communities, dated 25th July 1985, (No. 85/374/EEC) on the approximation of the laws, regulations and administrative provisions of the member States concerning liability for defective products.

(3) For the purposes of this Part a person who supplies any product in which products are comprised, whether by virtue of being component parts or raw materials or otherwise, shall not be treated by reason only of his supply of that product as supplying any of the products so comprised.

DEFINITIONS
"goods": s.45(1).
"product": subs. (2).
"supplies", "supply": s.45(1) and s.46.
"the product liability Directive": subs. (2).

GENERAL NOTE
It is thought that this is the first time that primary legislation has been used in Britain to implement a Directive. Implementation is normally done by order under the European Communities Act 1972.

Subs. (1)
Suppose an English court were faced with a provision in Pt. 1 of the Act which was unambiguous and plainly inconsistent with a requirement of the Directive. In that case the English court would have a choice. On the one hand it could decide that the provision, being inconsistent with the Directive, was thus inconsistent also with s.1(1); it could resolve that inconsistency in favour of s.1(1) which is drafted in mandatory terms and could thus attribute an effect to the provision in question contrary to its plain and unambiguous meaning. On the other hand it could decide that the provision in question, being plain and unambiguous, gave rise to no problem of *construction*. Hence it could give effect to the provision despite its inconsistency with the Directive. In the event of such an unfortunate result, a plaintiff might find himself unable to succeed under the Act when, if the Act had been consistent with the Directive, he would have been successful. Could such a plaintiff maintain an action based, not on the Act, but on the Directive? Certainly not in respect of damage occurring before July 25, 1988, (the date by which the Directive has to be implemented in the member states), see *Ratti* Case 148/78, [1979] E.C.R. 1629, [1980] 1 C.M.L.R. 96. Even in respect of damages occurring after that date an action probably could not be based solely on the Directive. Whereas a Directive can have direct effect upon a *government* of a member state (see *Van Duyn* v. *Home Office (No. 2),* Case 41/74, [1974] E.C.R. 1337, [1975] 1 C.M.L.R. 1, [1975] 3 All E.R. 190), it seems unlikely that the European Court would hold that a Directive could have direct effect in the sense that it could impose obligations on a private individual.

Subs. (2)
Agricultural produce. Under s.2(4) no liability under Pt. 1 of the Act will attach to someone who supplies agricultural produce which has not undergone an industrial process. See also "producer" below.
Producer. Unless the product has been either imported into the EEC or else "own-branded," the producer is the person primarily liable under s.2 for damage caused by a defective product. Subs. (2)(b) catches a person who mines or quarries the product. Sea salt would probably be another example of a substance "abstracted", the person who abstracts the salt from the water being the "producer." Could game (*e.g.* wild rabbits and ducks) be an example of a product "won," the person who shoots or ensnares it being the winner, *i.e.* producer? Or is "winning" confined to winning substances like coal or oil or sea salt? If the

latter is the case, it is difficult to see much distinction between something being "won" and something being "abstracted." But see comment below on Subs. (2)(c).

Subs. (2)(c) makes it clear that someone who puts agricultural produce through an industrial process will be regarded as a producer, provided the process gives the product essential characteristics. Despite the use of the plural, presumably it will be sufficient that the process gives the product just one essential characteristic. Someone canning peas would be a "producer" of the peas. S.2(4) will not prevent him from being liable if the peas are defective. That, apparently, is so, even if the defect is not attributable to the processing and even if the peas had the defect before coming into his possession. The same would be true of someone who freezes peas. To be canned or frozen is, it is suggested, to have an essential characteristic. Presumably mere wrapping does not add an essential characteristic. What then of "cooked" beetroot, "dried" onions and "washed" carrots?

Does subs. (2)(c) apply to game which has been processed, *e.g.* ready cooked pheasant or ready jugged hare? The answer depends upon whether the game has been "manufactured, won or abstracted." If it has (*i.e.* because it has been "won"), then subs. (2)(c) does not apply; it seems clear that it has not been manufactured or abstracted. As already observed, if it has been "won," the person who "won" it will be the person who ensnared or shot it. That person will not be a "producer" within any of the paragraphs of s.1(2)—not para. (a) because he did not "manufacture" the game, not para. (b) because, in shooting or ensnaring the game, he did not win a "substance", not para. (c) because that paragraph applies only to products which have not been manufactured, won or abstracted. This would have the effect of excluding all liability, under this Part of the Act, in respect of game, *i.e.* because there would be no "producer" to be held liable. It would exclude that liability even on the part of someone carrying out industrial processing, *e.g.* cooking the pheasant or jugging the hare. That would mean that the Act distinguished between game and agricultural produce, making the industrial processor of only the latter liable. It is reasonably clear from the preamble to the Directive (though not from the text) that the Directive intended that liability be imposed upon the processor of game (as well as the processor of agricultural produce). It is therefore suggested that the better view is that game is not "won" by being shot, ensnared, etc., and that therefore someone who subsequently processes the game thereby giving it some essential characteristic, will be a producer within subs. 2(c)).

Product. The definition of "product" is wider than that of the definition of "goods" in the Sale of Goods Act 1979, s.61(1). The definition includes not only electricity but also gas, since "product" includes "goods" and "goods" are further defined in s.45(1) to include "substances" and "substance" is defined in s.45(1) to mean any substance "whether in solid, liquid or gaseous form or in the form of a vapour". Also "goods" are defined in s.45(1) to include "growing crops and things comprised in land by virtue of being attached to it and any ship, aircraft or vehicle". Whereas the Sale of Goods Act 1979 applies to things attached to the land only if they are agreed to be severed from it, there is no such qualification to liability for defective products under Pt. 1 of the Consumer Protection Act 1987. Such liability can, it seems, arise in relation to a fixture (*e.g.* a fence) supplied with land, though the liability will attach to the producer (*i.e.* the manufacturer) of the fence. Although the Act applies to "things attached to the land," it does not apply to the land itself. There can be no liability under this Part of the Act where the defect is merely in the land and not in the things attached to it. Is a house "land" or is it a "thing attached to land"? The Directive states that a producer shall be liable for damage caused by a defect in his product and, in Art. 2, provides "For the purposes of this Directive 'product' means all moveables with the exception of primary agricultural products and game, even though incorporated into another movable or an immovable." It would seem that the bricks, cement, tiles, etc., used in a house are all products. They are incorporated in an immovable, the house. The house, being an immovable, is not itself a "product." It follows that if the house falls upon someone because it is badly built, the builder is not liable under the Act as the producer of a defective *product*. He may, of course, be liable under the common law of contract or tort. If, on the other hand, a tile, because it was defective, fell upon someone's head, the manufacturer of the tile *could* be liable as the producer of the defective *product*, the tile. For whether the builder would then be a "supplier", see note to s.2(3) below.

Subs. (3)

Suppose a car dealer has sold and supplied to a customer a new car with a defective tyre. The manufacturer of the car had not manufactured the tyre himself but had bought it from a tyre manufacturer. Suppose also, as is likely, that the tyre, being defective, thereby renders the car defective. In this situation the car dealer is a "supplier" of a defective car but is not a "supplier" of the defective tyre. Thus if he receives a request under s.2(3), he can escape liability under this Part by identifying the person who supplied him with the *car*.

Liability for defective products

2.—(1) Subject to the following provisions of this Part, where any damage is caused wholly or partly by a defect in a product, every person to whom subsection (2) below applies shall be liable for the damage.

(2) This subsection applies to—

    (a) the producer of the product;

    (b) any person who, by putting his name on the product or using a trade mark or other distinguishing mark in relation to the product, has held himself out to be the producer of the product;

    (c) any person who has imported the product into a member State from a place outside the member States in order, in the course of any business of his, to supply it to another.

(3) Subject as aforesaid, where any damage is caused wholly or partly by a defect in a product, any person who supplied the product (whether to the person who suffered the damage, to the producer of any product in which the product in question is comprised or to any other person) shall be liable for the damage if—

    (a) the person who suffered the damage requests the supplier to identify one or more of the persons (whether still in existence or not) to whom subsection (2) above applies in relation to the product;

    (b) that request is made within a reasonable period after the damage occurs and at a time when it is not reasonably practicable for the person making the request to identify all those persons; and

    (c) the supplier fails, within a reasonable period after receiving the request, either to comply with the request or to identify the person who supplied the product to him.

(4) Neither subsection (2) nor subsection (3) above shall apply to a person in respect of any defect in any game or agricultural produce if the only supply of the game or produce by that person to another was at a time when it had not undergone an industrial process.

(5) Where two or more persons are liable by virtue of this Part for the same damage, their liability shall be joint and several.

(6) This section shall be without prejudice to any liability arising otherwise than by virtue of this Part.

Definitions
    "agricultural produce": s.1(2).
    "business": s.45(1).
    "damage": s.5.
    "defect": s.3.
    "mark": s.45(1), s.45(4).
    "producer": s.1(2).
    "product": s.1(2).
    "supplied", "supplier", "supply": s.45(1), s.46.
    "trade mark": s.45(1).

General Note
Subs. (1)

This is the central provision of this Part. It imposes a strict liability. The plaintiff does not have to prove any negligence or fault. The plaintiff must prove (on a balance of probabilities):

    (a) that a "product" contained a "defect."

    (b) that the plaintiff suffered "damage."

    (c) that the "damage" was caused by the "defect."

    (d) that the defendant was either "producer" of the "product" or someone else falling within subs. (2).

The requirement that the plaintiff has to prove that the damage was *caused* by the defect brings in the legal principles of causation which have been worked out mainly in negligence cases. These principles would include those relating to a possible *novus actus interveniens*.

Thus an intelligent person of sound mind and full age who recognises a product to be defective, fully appreciates the danger it poses and who nevertheless unreasonably goes on to use the product, could be held to have committed a *novus actus interveniens* and to have been the sole cause of his own damage, *McKew* v. *Holland & Hannen & Cubitts* [1969] 3 All E.R. 1621. The principles in *McGhee* v. *National Coal Board* [1973] 1 W.L.R. 1 would also apply. So, if, for example, a defect in a product materially increased the risk that the plaintiff would suffer dermatitis and the plaintiff did indeed suffer dermatitis, the plaintiff would not, in the absence of available scientific evidence, have to establish that it was more probable than not that the dermatitis was caused by the defect. The *McGhee* principle has been extended by the Court of Appeal in *Wilsher* v. *Essex Area Health Authority* [1987] 2 W.L.R. 425 and *Fitzgerald* v. *Lane* [1987] 2 All E.R. 455 and has been distinguished by the House of Lords in *Kay* v. *Ayrshire and Arran Health Board* [1987] 2 All E.R. 417 and in *Hotson* v. *East Berkshire Health Authority* [1987] 3 W.L.R. 232.

In a situation where a plaintiff suffered damage and then suffered a subsequent futher injury, it would again seem likely that court would adopt the same aproach as in negligence cases (*McKew* v. *Holland & Hannen & Cubitts, supra; Wieland* v. *Cyril Lord Carpets* [1969] 3 All E.R. 1006; *Baker* v. *Willoughby* [1970] A.C. 467). Yet another matter, sometimes closely related to the latter, is the risk that the defendant would, or might, have suffered accidentally the very same damage even if it had not been caused by the defect. Clearly deductions for such contingencies and eventualities should be made in just the same way as in other actions for damages in tort, *Jobling* v. *Associated Dairies* [1982] A.C. 794; *Hotson* v. *East Berkshire Health Authority* [1987] 3 W.L.R. 232.

More problematical is the question whether the same rules on *remoteness* of damage apply to this new strict statutory liability as apply to actions in negligence. To put it another way, do the *Wagon Mound* [1961] A.C. 388 and all its works apply? Put it in at least two further ways: (i) is the recoverable damage limited to damage which is of a generally foreseeable kind occurring in a generally (though not necessarily precisely) foreseeable sort of way?; and (ii) is the recoverable damage limited to damage which was within the *foreseeable* risk created by the defect? Against such a suggestion it may be said that this Part incorporates no such restriction on the defendant's liability and that according to the words of subs. (1) the defendant is liable for damage *caused* by the defect, *i.e.* irrespective of whether the damage was foreseeable. Nevertheless when courts have had to decide whether X *caused* Y, they had tended to answer the question by asking whether Y was a *foreseeable* consequence of X. For example in *Australian Coastal Shipping* v. *Green* [1977] 1 All E.R. 353 at 358 Lord Denning, M.R. said "If the master when he does a 'general average act' ought reasonably to have foreseen that a subsequent accident of the kind might occur—or even that there was a distinct possibility of it—then the subsequent accident does not break the chain of causation. The loss or damage is the direct consequence of the original general average act". Cases such as this, however, are not a complete answer because they tend to be dealing with *subsequent* losses and injuries or whether there has been a break in the chain of causation. They do not deal with the situation where, say, a product is defective because it presents a given risk but a totally different item of damage occurs which would not, and could not, have been foreseen even if the defect had been known to the defendant. Suppose mineral water is defective in that it contains an alien substance which means that, if drunk, the mineral water will effectively burn up part of the victim's inside. Suppose, however, that the plaintiff chooses to use the mineral water to wash the leaves of his rare prize plants and that the alien substance kills the plants by depriving them of essential rays of the sun. Clearly, given the strict nature of the liability, even if a test of reasonable foresight is correct, the matter can not be as simple as "Could the defendant have foreseen this loss?" for the presence of the alien substance in the mineral water may in the circumstances have been something he could not have known about. If a test of reasonable foresight is appropriate, it would have to be something like "Could a defendant who was aware of the presence of the defect have reasonably foreseen damage occurring in this kind of way?". It is submitted that a test of reasonable foresight is, in fact, not appropriate other than to decide whether there has been a break in the chain of causation in the sense of whether there has been a *novus actus interveniens*. Thus one *does* ask whether it was reasonably foreseeable that mineral water would be used to wash plant leaves. If such use was reasonably foreseeable, then the defect (the alien substance) has caused the loss of the plants even if it would not have been foreseeable that the alien substance could damage plants—either in the way it did or in any other way. In other words, the decision in *Doughty* v. *Turner Manufacturing* [1964] 1 All E.R. 98 does not apply. In *Millard* v. *Serck Tubes* [1969] 1 W.L.R. 1, the Court of Appeal held, in relation to the strict duty (under the Factories Act) to fence dangerous machinery, that provided the machinery is dangerous (*i.e.* may foreseeably cause injury if unfenced), it is irrelevant that the plaintiff's injury occurs in an unforeseeable way; it is sufficient that the injury would not have occurred if the machinery had been fenced.

Subs. (2)

Neither subs. (2)(a) (unlike subs. (2)(c)), nor the definitions in s.1(2) of "producer" and "product" contain any reference to a product having to be produced *in the course of a business*. Therefore at first sight it might seem that someone, *e.g.* a d-i-y person or someone with a hobby (but not a business) of sculpting, could be liable under s.2. He would, in fact, have a defence under s.4(1)(c), unless he produced the goods for profit.

Subs. (2)(b) is intended to catch the person who is termed in the trade an "own-brander," *i.e.* an organisation, such as a supermarket chain, which does not manufacture a product but who buys it and has it "got up" in his own name and, maybe, with his own logo on it. However, the own-brander will fall within subs. (2)(b) only if by thus labelling the product he has "held himself out to be the producer". If the goods carrying the name and logo of Eatmore Supermarkets also bore the statement "Manufactured for Eatmore Supermarkets", this would surely displace any suggestion that Eatmore Supermarkets had held itself out as producer. In that case Eatmore Supermarkets, assuming that they had not imported the goods into the EEC, would not be within subs. (2) and could not be liable under this Part other than as supplier under s.2(3).

Subs. (2)(c) does not catch someone who imports the product from one member state of the EEC to another. For cases on "in the course of any business" see the notes to s.4(1)(c).

Subs. (3)

This is intended to make the supplier liable if the producer (or own-brander or importer into the EEC) can not be identified. There may be cases where the supplier is simply unable to satisfy the conditions in subs. (3) necessary to escape liability. This could, for example, occur where he has himself bought similar or identical goods from different sources. The policy of the subsection is to make the supplier liable in those circumstances irrespective of whether it is his fault that he cannot identify the source of the particular item in question. This is not however, a vicarious liability. If, for example, the supplier has bought direct from the manufacturer and identifies that manufacturer within a reasonable time of the request, the supplier will escape liability. That is still so even if the manufacturer is now bankrupt, dead or untraceable.

In the note to s.1 above the example was discussed of a defective tile which, having been used by a builder on the roof of the house, later, because the tile was defective, fell upon the head of someone. Is the builder a "supplier"? He will not be a "supplier" if he built the house on his, the builder's, land and then conveyed the land (and house) to the house buyer, see s.46(3) and (4).

For whether a finance company can be liable as "supplier," see s.46(2).

Subs. (4)

The Directive excluded game and primary agricultural produce from its ambit but nevertheless allowed member states to include such products when legislating to implement the Directive. The British government chose not to adopt the latter option. The preamble to the Directive says "it is appropriate to exclude liability for agricultural products and game, except where they have undergone processing of an industrial nature which could cause a defect in those products." Nevertheless the text of the Directive and also the drafting of subs. (4) would seem to have the result that the "producer" (*i.e.* industrial processor, s.1(2)) of agricultural produce will be liable for damage caused by any defect in them even if the defect was not attributable to the industrial processing and even though it had been present in the goods before the industrial processor acquired the products.

Whereas the Directive refers to "initial" processing, the Act refers to someone carrying out an "industrial" process. It gives no guidance upon what amounts to an industrial process. It is thought that the spraying of crops before they are ready for harvest would not come within that expression because the expression does not cover a process unless it be a process undergone by "produce" and, arguably, until the crop is ready for harvest it is still in nature's production process and is not yet "produce." In any case, the person carrying out an industrial process upon agricultural produce or game will not be a "producer" (and therefore will not be liable as such) unless the industrial process has imparted some essential characteristic to the product, s.1(2)(c). See further the notes to the latter subsection.

Subs. (6)

The most obvious other causes of action are negligence and breach of contract, a good example of the latter being liability for breach of the implied terms (in sale of goods, hire-purchase, hire and analogous contracts) as to the merchantable quality and fitness for purpose of goods supplied. Another possible cause of action is a claim for breach of duty imposed by the Health and Safety at Work etc. Act 1974 (which is amended by s.36 and Sched. 3 of this Act).

Meaning of "defect"

3.—(1) Subject to the following provisions of this section, there is a defect in a product for the purposes of this Part if the safety of the product is not such as persons generally are entitled to expect; and for those purposes "safety", in relation to a product, shall include safety with respect to products comprised in that product and safety in the context of risks of damage to property, as well as in the context of risks of death or personal injury.

(2) In determining for the purposes of subsection (1) above what persons generally are entitled to expect in relation to a product all the circumstances shall be taken into account, including—

(a) the manner in which, and purposes for which, the product has been marketed, its get-up, the use of any mark in relation to the product and any instructions for, or warnings with respect to, doing or refraining from doing anything with or in relation to the product;

(b) what might reasonably be expected to be done with or in relation to the product; and

(c) the time when the product was supplied by its producer to another; and nothing in this section shall require a defect to be inferred from the fact alone that the safety of a product which is supplied after that time is greater than the safety of the product in question.

DEFINITIONS
"damage": s.5.
"mark": s.45(1), s.45(4).
"personal injury": s.45(1).
"producer": s.1(2).
"product": s.1(2).
"supplied", "supply": s.45(1), s.46.

GENERAL NOTE
There can be said to be three different types of defect: design defects; manufacturing or processing defects; the presence of an inherent risk without a warning being given. They are all treated the same way. Any alleged defect is subject to the same test. Products are not "defective" simply because they wear out quickly or do not function properly. Defectiveness is measured in terms of safety, *i.e.* of the risks of damage to persons or property. Whatever the alleged defect, the test is "Was the safety of the product such as persons generally were entitled to expect?". There is no limit to the circumstances which a court may take into account in deciding this question. Subs. (2) merely articulates some of them.

It may be that manufacturing defects will be the easiest to establish because there will often be yardsticks of comparison. When with mass produced items one or some of them are flawed these may clearly be seen as defective since they deviate from the norm of the rest of the production. With mass produced, as with non-mass produced, items there will often be a design specification; an item which is less safe because it has not been produced in accordance with that specification will surely not be as safe as one is entitled to expect.

Turning to design defects, a consideration of whether a characteristic of design is a "defect" may well have the court taking into account factors (including a "social utility" factor) similar to some that are considered in cases of negligence. A product may, for example, have a characteristic that creates a risk of injury. Relevant questions might be the following: (1) If the risk was not known at the time of production, how many more months or years of research would it have taken to discover it? (2) How many more months or years of development would have been needed to eliminate the risk? (3) Would it have cost so much to eliminate the risk that any profit in marketing the product would also have been eliminated? (4) Would the cost have been prohibitively expensive from the consumer's point of view? (5) Was the product urgently needed? (6) Was the product produced to meet an emergency? (7) What was the general utility of the product? Suppose that to control the disease, Aids, there were developed and marketed a drug which subsequently was discovered to have had a serious unfortunate side effect upon some individuals causing them some injury. A court might well hold, having considered factors such as those just listed, that persons generally were not entitled to expect the drug to be any safer than in fact it was. Thus the producer might not even have to rely upon the development risks defence in s.4(1)(e).

One might ask "Are persons generally entitled to expect the product to be any safer than reasonable care and skill can make it?" If the answer is no, then this new provision will, in relation to design defects, hardly have made any change in the law at all! Maybe the answer to the question is yes, since the preamble to the Directive states "liability without fault on the part of the producer is the sole means of adequately solving the problem, peculiar to our age of increasing technicality, of a fair apportionment of the risks inherent in modern technological production."

Turning to inherent risks, some are clearly unavoidable and require no warnings. A knife is not defective simply because it is dangerous. No doubt other products which are inherently dangerous, *e.g.* inflammable glue or paint, would not be as safe as one is entitled to expect if they were supplied without a warning of the inherent danger.

Hindsight—When the Product must be Defective
Subs. (2)(c) also is redolent of the established judicial approach in negligence cases. In *Roe* v. *Minister of Health* [1954] 2 Q.B. 66 at 86, Denning L.J., said "Nowadays it would be negligence not to realise the danger, but it was not then". One does not assess whether a defendant's actions were negligent with the benefit of knowledge which he could not reasonably have been expected to have. It seems that a similar approach is to be taken in deciding whether a product is defective.

However, the plaintiff does not have to prove that the product was defective when it left the producer. Rather the plaintiff needs to prove that a feature of the product caused the damage complained of and that that feature amounted to a "defect." The qualification provided by subs. (2)(c) is that in determining whether the feature amounted to a defect, one asks what persons generally were entitled to expect of a product produced when the defendant produced (or rather, supplied) it. If the defendant wishes to escape liability it is for *him* to prove that the defect did not exist when he, the defendant, supplied the product (s.4(1)(d) and s.4(2)).

Unreasonable usage
It seems possible that subs. (2)(b) was intended to exclude unreasonable uses of the product when assessing its safety or defectiveness. There is an argument, however, that it has not entirely done so. The word "reasonably" qualifies the expression "what might be expected", not the expression "to be done." It is submitted that a manufacturer of glue these days might reasonably *expect* that people, including youngsters, will sniff his product, even though sniffing it is clearly an unreasonable thing to do. To qualify as a factor under subs. (2)(b), it is the expectation that has to be reasonable, not the sniffing. It may be that the product will be defective if no warning is printed on it or if it could just as easily and cheaply have been made without toxic fumes. An unreasonable use which was also unforeseeable might well, however, break the chain of causation (see notes to s.2(1) above) or at least allow the partial defence of contributory negligence (see s.6(4) and notes thereto).

Defences

4.—(1) In any civil proceedings by virtue of this Part against any person ("the person proceeded against") in respect of a defect in a product it shall be a defence for him to show—

    (a) that the defect is attributable to compliance with any requirement imposed by or under any enactment or with any Community obligation; or

    (b) that the person proceeded against did not at any time supply the product to another; or

    (c) that the following conditions are satisfied, that is to say—

        (i) that the only supply of the product to another by the person proceeded against was otherwise than in the course of a business of that person's; and

        (ii) that section 2(2) above does not apply to that person or applies to him by virtue only of things done otherwise than with a view to profit; or

(d) that the defect did not exist in the product at the relevant time; or

(e) that the state of scientific and technical knowledge at the relevant time was not such that a producer of products of the same description as the product in question might be expected to have discovered the defect if it had existed in his products while they were under his control; or

(f) that the defect—

   (i) constituted a defect in a product ("the subsequent product") in which the product in question had been comprised; and

   (ii) was wholly attributable to the design of the subsequent product or to compliance by the producer of the product in question with instructions given by the producer of the subsequent product.

(2) In this section "the relevant time", in relation to electricity, means the time at which it was generated, being a time before it was transmitted or distributed, and in relation to any other product, means—

(a) if the person proceeded against is a person to whom subsection (2) of section 2 above applies in relation to the product, the time when he supplied the product to another;

(b) if that subsection does not apply to that person in relation to the product, the time when the product was last supplied by a person to whom that subsection does apply in relation to the product.

DEFINITIONS
  "business": s.45(1).
  "defect": s.3.
  "person proceeded against": subs. (1).
  "producer": s.1(2).
  "product": s.1(2).
  "relevant time": subs. (2).
  "supplied", "supply": s.45(1), s.46.

GENERAL NOTE
Burden of proof
  The introductory words of subs. (1) make it clear that the burden of proof in relation to the defences rests upon the defendant.

Subs. (1)(a)
  Typical requirements with which producers will have to comply will be those in Safety Regulations made under Pt. 2 of this Act, as well as those made under the Consumer Protection Acts 1961 and 1971 and the Consumer Safety Act 1978. To establish the defence, it will not be sufficient for the defendant to show that the producer complied with the requirements of the Regulations. He will have to show that the defect was attributable to that compliance. If it had been possible to comply with the Regulations without leaving the product with the defect in question, this defence could not be established.

Subs. (1)(b)
  An airline buys and uses in its fleet an aircraft which it has bought in the U.S.A. The aircraft, in landing at Heathrow, crashes because it is defective and injures passengers. The airline is not a producer, *i.e.* is not an importer into the EEC within s.2(2)(c)—see s.46(9). Even if it were a producer, it would have a defence under s.4(1)(b). Anyone who makes for his own use an article which is defective will qualify for this defence if during that use the defect causes damage to someone else.

Subs. (1)(c)
  A granddad who makes a toy and gives it to his grandson for Christmas would clearly have this defence. Sometimes products disposed of as gifts are nevertheless supplied in the course of a business, *e.g.* promotional gifts. In those circumstances the defence would not be available.

The expression "in the course of a business," or a similar expression, has appeared in a number of statutes providing for consumer protection. The case law relating to it has arisen mainly under statutes imposing criminal liability. *John* v. *Matthews* [1970] 2 Q.B. 443, *Havering London Borough* v. *Stevenson* [1970] 3 All E.R. 609, *Blackmore* v. *Bellamy* [1983] R.T.R. 303 and *Corfield* v. *Sevenways Garage* [1985] R.T.R 109 all arose under the Trade Descriptions Act 1968 as did the House of Lords decision in *Davies* v. *Sumner* [1984] 1 W.L.R. 1301. See also *Southwark London Borough* v. *Charlesworth* (1983) 2 Tr.L. 95, a case under the Consumer Protection Act 1961. Consumer protection measures dealing with civil liability and also containing the expression "in the course of a business" include the Unfair Contract Terms Act 1977 (notably ss.1 and 12) and the Sale of Goods Act 1979, s.14. In the latter section the expression "in the course of a business" dates only from the Supply of Goods (Implied Terms) Act 1973 when the expression replaced more convoluted and restricted wording (in s.14 of the Sale of Goods Act 1893). Since that amendment in 1973 there appears to have been no case law upon the expression in the Sale of Goods Act. The Unfair Contract Terms Act has thrown up one decision of tangental significance, *Rasbora* v. *J.C.L. Marine* [1977] 1 Lloyd's Rep. 645.

Subs. (1)(d)

If there is a dispute as to *when* an alleged defect became present in the product, the plaintiff does not have to prove any more than that the defect was present when it caused his damage. The defendant can escape liability if *he* proves that the defect was not present when *he* supplied the product. That is the position where the defendant is someone within s.2(2), *i.e* producer, own-brander or importer into the EEC. The rule is slightly different where the defendant is being sued under s.2(3), *i.e.* as a supplier who has both failed to identify the person who supplied the product to him and also failed to comply with a request to identify the producer, own-brander or importer into the EEC. Such a defendant has the defence if he shows that the defect was not present when the goods were last supplied by the producer, own-brander or importer into the EEC. That is the effect of subss. (1)(d) and (2) combined. In short—and if the goods were not own-branded or imported into the EEC—it is a defence for any defendant to show that the defect was not present in the product when it left the producer.

Subs. (1)(e)

This defence is sometimes known as the "state of the art" defence or "development risks" defence. The relationship between this defence and the basis of liability is a curious one. The basis of liability is that the product is defective, *i.e.* its safety is not such as persons generally are entitled to expect. Are persons generally entitled to expect that a product will be free of a defect (risk) which, in the state of scientific and technical knowledge at the time, was not discoverable when the product was put into circulation? Logically the answer must be yes, since otherwise the defence is otiose. A drug manufacturer may say "When I supplied the drug, the state of scientific and technical knowledge was such that I could not have been expected to have discovered that this drug had this particular side effect which it has since been shown to have and which has caused the injury complained of." He will, however, have to show not merely that this side effect of the drug was not at the time known to science but also that he could not have been expected to discover it, *e.g.* by further research, before putting the drug on the market.

The drafting of this defence is not more favourable to the defendant than the corresponding wording of the Directive. On the wording of subs. (1)(e), it will not be enough for the defendant to prove that the defect was one which a producer of products of that description might not have discovered. To establish the defence the defendant must prove a negative, namely that the defect was *not* one which such a producer might have been expected to discover. The only practicable way of proving this is to establish that the defect was, at the time, undiscoverable. If it was discoverable, then surely a producer of such a product might have been expected to discover it.

Subs. (1)(f)

A product may include component products. A component product may be defective and thereby render defective the product in which it is a component. For example an electrical switch may be defective in that it can spark off a fire. That switch might subsequently be used as a component in a new car. Then we will have two dangerous, "defective," products, a switch and a car. The car is defective because it includes the switch. Suppose the switch catches fire, which fire not only damages the car but also seriously burns a passenger. If the car manufacturer (*i.e.* producer) is proceeded against by the passenger, it seems he will have no defence although he may have a claim for indemnity (*e.g.* under the Sale of Goods Act

1979, s.14) against the switch manufacturer or whoever else the car manufacturer bought the switch from.

The passenger could alternatively proceed against the switch manufacturer, *i.e.* the producer of the switch, a defective product (see definition of "product" in s.1(2)). In that case the switch manufacturer would be entitled to the defence in subs. 1(f) if he were to show either that the defect was due to the design of the *car* or that the defect in the switch was due to his having complied with instructions given him by the car manufacturer. (For liability for the damage done to the car, see note to s.5(2) below.)

The same principles as apply to components, also apply to any other product, *e.g.* a raw material, which is comprised in another product—see "product" in s.1(2).

Subs. (2)

The relevant time. This is the relevant time not only for the purposes of the defence in s.4(1)(d) but also for the purposes of s.11A(3) of the Limitation Act 1980 (as inserted by Sched. 1 of this Act). The effect of s.11A(3) is that any right of action for damages under this Part is absolutely extinguished after the expiry of ten years from "the relevant time". That is so, even if otherwise the limitation period would not have run out. For a fuller note on the limitation period, see the note to s.6 below.

Damage giving rise to liability

5.—(1) Subject to the following provisions of this section, in this Part "damage" means death or personal injury or any loss of or damage to any property (including land).

(2) A person shall not be liable under section 2 above in respect of any defect in a product for the loss of or any damage to the product itself or for the loss of or any damage to the whole or any part of any product which has been supplied with the product in question comprised in it.

(3) A person shall not be liable under section 2 above for any loss of or damage to any property which, at the time it is lost or damaged, is not—

(a) of a description of property ordinarily intended for private use, occupation or consumption; and

(b) intended by the person suffering the loss or damage mainly for his own private use, occupation or consumption.

(4) No damages shall be awarded to any person by virtue of this Part in respect of any loss of or damage to any property if the amount which would fall to be so awarded to that person, apart from this subsection and any liability for interest, does not exceed £275.

(5) In determining for the purposes of this Part who has suffered any loss of or damage to property and when any such loss or damage occurred, the loss or damage shall be regarded as having occurred at the earliest time at which a person with an interest in the property had knowledge of the material facts about the loss or damage.

(6) For the purposes of subsection (5) above the material facts about any loss of or damage to any property are such facts about the loss or damage as would lead a reasonable person with an interest in the property to consider the loss or damage sufficiently serious to justify his instituting proceedings for damages against a defendant who did not dispute liability and was able to satisfy a judgment.

(7) For the purposes of subsection (5) above a person's knowledge includes knowledge which he might reasonably have been expected to acquire—

(a) from facts observable or ascertainable by him; or

(b) from facts ascertainable by him with the help of appropriate expert advice which it is reasonable for him to seek;

but a person shall not be taken by virtue of this subsection to have knowledge of a fact ascertainable by him only with the help of expert advice unless he has failed to take all reasonable steps to obtain (and, where appropriate, to act on) that advice.

(8) Subsections (5) to (7) above shall not extend to Scotland.

DEFINITIONS
"damage": subs. (1).
"defect": s.3.
"personal injury": s.45(1).
"product": s.1(2).
"supplied", "supply": s.45(1), s.46.

GENERAL NOTE
Subs. (1)

Presumably purely financial loss is not recoverable even if that loss was consequential upon physical damage to property. So, if because of a defect in it, a toaster catches fire and the fire badly damages the plaintiff's house, the plaintiff will be entitled to claim the cost of repairing the house and replacing the burnt contents but will not be able to claim the cost of alternative accommodation rendered necessary because the house was uninhabitable until repaired. This is because the damages recoverable are limited to "damage to property" and, apparently, do not include financial loss flowing from that damage (though such consequential financial loss would be recoverable in negligence, *Spartan and Steel Alloys* v. *Martin* [1973] 1 Q.B. 27). If that is right, then the same rule would, at first sight, seem to apply to loss of earnings, since they are not personal injuries but would merely be consequential upon personal injuries. The court could, however, overcome this drafting defect by construing personal injuries (despite its definition in s.45(1)) to include such consequences of those injuries as are normally compensatable in the law of tort. Such a construction is seemingly required by s.1 since, in the Directive, Art. 9 defines "damage" as "(a) damage caused by death or by personal injuries; (b) damage to, or destruction of, any item of property . . .". This wording of the Directive seems not to require the same approach to the consequences of damage to property.

Subs. (2)

The example given in the General Note to s.4(1)(f), of a defective switch which is incorporated by a car manufacturer in a car, is useful here. Both the switch and the car are defective products because the switch is liable to ignite a fire. Both the switch manufacturer and the car manufacturer are producers and can be liable under this Part. That liability does not, however, include liability for any damage sustained by the switch or the car.

The result might, of course, be different in another cause of action. The owner of the car might well have a claim for such damage, against the dealer from whom he bought the car, under s.4 of the Sale of Goods Act 1979. It is unlikely that in a negligence action he could recover for such damage from the car manufacturer (even if negligence by the car manufacturer could be established). However, the damage to the car might well be recoverable in a successful negligence action against the *switch* manufacturer, see *per* Lloyd L.J., in *Aswan Engineering Co.* v. *Lupdine* [1987] 1 W.L.R. 1 at 21. If the defective switch had not been incorporated by the car manufacturer but had, say, been bought by the car owner as a spare part from a spare parts dealer, then the same problem would not arise. In that case subs. (2) would not prevent the switch manufacturer being liable under this Part of the Act for damage to the car.

Subs. (3)

For damage to any given piece of property to be compensatable under this Part, that property must fall within both (a) and (b) of this subsection. Imagine a man who buys a house for himself and his wife and two children to live in. Suppose it is damaged by a defective product. Can it be said (assuming the house is entirely his) that the house was intended by him "*mainly* for his own private use, occupation or consumption" when he is only one out of four occupants? It is to be hoped that the court would hold that private occupation by himself includes private occupation also by his family. What, however, is the position if he buys another house, this one being for his elderly parents to live in, and if it is this second house which is damaged by a defective product? It could hardly be said here that it was intended for the man's own private occupation when he is himself not going to occupy it at all. Could it be said that it was intended "mainly for his own use", his use of it being his having his parents live there?

Subs. (4)

This is intended to cut out trivial claims for property damage. If the amount of damage done to property of the plaintiff is worth £275 or more, then the whole amount is recoverable including the first £275.

Subss. (5), (6), (7)

These subsections (taken with s.6(6) and the relevant parts of Sched. 1) mirror provisions in s.14A of the Limitation Act 1980 (as inserted in that Act by the Latent Damage Act 1986). For the background to them, see the notes to the Latent Damage Act 1986 in Current Law Statutes Annotated. Briefly and broadly, the effect of these provisions, in relation to damage to property, is to prevent time from starting to run (*i.e.* for limitation purposes) until the damage is such that the plaintiff realised, or ought reasonably to have realised, that the damage had occurred and was serious enough to justify proceedings. There is, however, an important qualification to that in the case of proceedings under this Part. It is that there is an absolute bar to the commencement of proceedings after *10* years from when the producer (own-brander or importer into the EEC) supplied the defective product—see s.11A(3) of the Limitation Act 1980 (as inserted by s.6 and Sched. 1 of this Act). See further the note following s.6 below, on limitation.

Application of certain enactments etc.

6.—(1) Any damage for which a person is liable under section 2 above shall be deemed to have been caused—

(a) for the purposes of the Fatal Accidents Act 1976, by that person's wrongful act, neglect or default;

(b) for the purposes of section 3 of the Law Reform (Miscellaneous Provisions) (Scotland) Act 1940 (contribution among joint wrong-doers), by that person's wrongful act or negligent act or omission;

(c) for the purposes of section 1 of the Damages (Scotland) Act 1976 (rights of relatives of a deceased), by that person's act or omission; and

(d) for the purposes of Part II of the Administration of Justice Act 1982 (damages for personal injuries, etc.—Scotland), by an act or omission giving rise to liability in that person to pay damages.

(2) Where—

(a) a person's death is caused wholly or partly by a defect in a product, or a person dies after suffering damage which has been so caused;

(b) a request such as mentioned in paragraph (a) of subsection (3) of section 2 above is made to a supplier of the product by that person's personal representatives or, in the case of a person whose death is caused wholly or partly by the defect, by any dependant or relative of that person; and

(c) the conditions specified in paragraphs (b) and (c) of that subsection are satisfied in relation to that request,

this Part shall have effect for the purposes of the Law Reform (Miscellaneous Provisions) Act 1934, the Fatal Accidents Act 1976 and the Damages (Scotland) Act 1976 as if liability of the supplier to that person under that subsection did not depend on that person having requested the supplier to identify certain persons or on the said conditions having been satisfied in relation to a request made by that person.

(3) Section 1 of the Congenital Disabilities (Civil Liability) Act 1976 shall have effect for the purposes of this Part as if—

(a) a person were answerable to a child in respect of an occurrence caused wholly or partly by a defect in a product if he is or has been liable under section 2 above in respect of any effect of the occurrence on a parent of the child, or would be so liable if the occurrence caused a parent of the child to suffer damage;

(b) the provisions of this Part relating to liability under section 2 above applied in relation to liability by virtue of paragraph (a) above under the said section 1; and

(c) subsection (6) of the said section 1 (exclusion of liability) were omitted.

(4) Where any damage is caused partly by a defect in a product and partly by the fault of the person suffering the damage, the Law Reform

(Contributory Negligence) Act 1945 and section 5 of the Fatal Accidents Act 1976 (contributory negligence) shall have effect as if the defect were the fault of every person liable by virtue of this Part for the damage caused by the defect.

(5) In subsection (4) above "fault" has the same meaning as in the said Act of 1945.

(6) Schedule 1 to this Act shall have effect for the purpose of amending the Limitation Act 1980 and the Prescription and Limitation (Scotland) Act 1973 in their application in relation to the bringing of actions by virtue of this Part.

(7) It is hereby declared that liability by virtue of this Part is to be treated as liability in tort for the purposes of any enactment conferring jurisdiction on any court with respect to any matter.

(8) Nothing in this Part shall prejudice the operation of section 12 of the Nuclear Installations Act 1965 (rights to compensation for certain breaches of duties confined to rights under that Act).

DEFINITIONS
"damage": s.5.
"defect": s.3.
"dependant": s.1(2).
"fault": subs. (5).
"product": s.1(2).
"relative": s.1(2).
"supplier", "supply": s.45(1), s.46.

GENERAL NOTE
Subss. (1) to (5) apply the statutes mentioned in them to an action under Pt. 1. S.2 makes the liability of a "supplier" dependent upon the supplier's failure to respond (or respond appropriately) to a request to identify the producer, own-brander or importer into the EEC. Where the victim of the defect has died without having made such a request, s.6(2) preserves for the victim's personal representatives (or relatives and dependants) the opportunity to make the request and, if the appropriate response is not forthcoming, to maintain an action against the supplier.

Contributory negligence
Subs. (4) applies the Law Reform (Contributory Negligence) Act 1945. Contributory negligence is, put simply, such a failure by the plaintiff to take reasonable care as to have rendered the damage in respect of which he is suing a foreseeable risk. If the court holds that there is contributory negligence, it is saying that the damage was caused not merely by the defendants' tort but also by the plaintiff's failure to take reasonable care. The court must then make an apportionment between the plaintiff and the defendant. In doing this, it must have in mind two things: (i) the relative causative potency of the two causes; and (ii) the relative blameworthiness of each (*Davies* v. *Swan Motor Co.* [1949] 2 K.B. 291, 326 and *Stapley* v. *Gypsum Mines* [1953] A.C. 633, 682). This is regularly done by courts in negligence cases. Then, however, the court is comparing two *negligent* causes. Under Pt. 1 of this Act, on the other hand, the plaintiff does not have to prove that the defendant was negligent (see the note to s.3 above). How is the court to measure the relative *blameworthiness* of a defendant who is made liable irrespective of negligence and plaintiff who is contributorily *negligent*? The answer is that the plaintiff's contributory negligence is not to be judged as harshly as it would be in an action in negligence. This should, in turn, have one of two effects; either his actions will not be found to be contributorily negligent at all (*i.e.* when in a negligence action they would be) or, more likely, the reduction in the award of damages will not be as great as it would be in a negligence action—see *Mullard* v. *Ben Line Steamers* [1970] 1 W.L.R. 1414, C.A., an action for breach of statutory duty under the Shipping and Ship-Repairing Regulations 1960.

Limitation
With two exceptions, the limitation rules for claims under this Part are the same as they now are in other tort claims (*i.e.* under the Limitation Act 1980 as amended by the Latent Damage Act 1986). The first exception is that the limitation period for a claim under this Part for damage to property is the same as that for personal injuries (namely three years).

The other exception is that there is an absolute and overriding rule that no claim can be brought more than 10 years after the defective product in question was supplied by the producer (or, if later, by the own-brander or importer into the EEC)—see Sched. 1 and, therein s.11A(3). No extension of the limitation period for disability, no later discovery of previously latent damage, no fraud, concealment or mistake, no exercise of discretion, can allow proceedings to be commenced after the expiry of that 10 year period. The 10 year period expires 10 years after the producer supplied the particular defective product in question, *i.e.* even though the producer may have gone on producing similar or identical products for many years afterwards.

Prohibition on exclusions from liability

7. The liability of a person by virtue of this Part to a person who has suffered damage caused wholly or partly by a defect in a product, or to a dependant or relative of such a person, shall not be limited or excluded by any contract term, by any notice or by any other provision.

DEFINITIONS
   "damage": s.5.
   "defect": s.3.
   "dependant": s.1(2).
   "product": s.1(2).
   "relative": s.1(2).

GENERAL NOTE
   Under s.2 the persons who can be liable to the plaintiff under this Part are the producer, the own-brander, the importer into the EEC and, in certain circumstance, the supplier. By s.2(5) their liability is joint and several. Thus the plaintiff is entitled to recover fully against any one of them, leaving them to sort out, and enforce, between themselves any right to indemnity or contribution. This section prevents any of them excluding or limiting his liability "to a person who has suffered damage caused wholly or partly by a defect in a product." It does not prevent them, as between two or more of themselves, altering by contract their respective rights to indemnity and/or contribution. This is clear from the wording of s.7. See also *Thompson* v. *Lohan (T.) (Plant Hire)* [1987] 1 W.L.R. 694, distinguishing *Phillips Products* v. *Hyland* [1987] 1 W.L.R. 659, both cases on the Unfair Contract Terms Act 1977.

Power to modify Part I

8.—(1) Her Majesty may by Order in Council make such modifications of this Part and of any other enactment (including an enactment contained in the following Parts of this Act, or in an Act passed after this Act) as appear to Her Majesty in Council to be necessary or expedient in consequence of any modification of the product liability Directive which is made at any time after the passing of this Act.
   (2) An Order in Council under subsection (1) above shall not be submitted to Her Majesty in Council unless a draft of the Order has been laid before, and approved by a resolution of, each House of Parliament.

DEFINITIONS
   "the product liability Directive": s.1(2).

GENERAL NOTE
   After 10 years' operation the Directive, including in particular the development risk defence, is to be reviewed. This section will enable any resulting amendments to the Directive to be implemented by way of amendment to the Act by Order in Council.

Application of Part I to Crown

9.—(1) Subject to subsection (2) below, this Part shall bind the Crown.
   (2) The Crown shall not, as regards the Crown's liability by virtue of this Part, be bound by this Part further than the Crown is made liable in

tort or in reparation under the Crown Proceedings Act 1947, as that Act has effect from time to time.

GENERAL NOTE

This section means that medicines provided under the National Health Service will be subject to this Part in just the same way as any other product.

PART II

CONSUMER SAFETY

GENERAL NOTE

Prior to the White Paper "The Safety of Goods" published in July 1984 (Cmnd. 9302), the safety of goods was covered by the provisions of the Consumer Safety Act 1978 (itself replacing the earlier Consumer Protection Acts 1961 and 1971). The 1978 Act contained (as had the earlier Acts) powers enabling the Secretary of State to make Safety Regulations relating to the types of goods specified in the Regulations. A trader supplying goods in breach of Safety Regulations would expose himself to the risk of a criminal prosecution and also to the risk of a civil suit for breach of statutory duty by anyone suffering in consequence of the breach. The 1978 Act also conferred new powers upon the Secretary of State, namely to issue the following three sorts of order and notice: (i) a "prohibition order", to prevent any trader from supplying specified types of goods considered unsafe by the Secretary of State; (ii) a "prohibition notice", similar to a prohibition order but applying only to the trader upon whom it is served; (iii) a "notice to warn", requiring the trader upon whom it is served to take specified action to warn customers about unsafe goods already supplied by the trader.

Against this background the White Paper made two main sets of recommendations, one designed to improve enforcement arrangements and the other, more radical, to make it a criminal offence for a trader to supply unsafe consumer goods. The first of these two main sets of recommendations was implemented by the Consumer Safety (Amendment) Act 1986. This Part consolidates the provisions previously in the 1978 and 1986 Acts and also implements the remaining recommendations in the White Paper including, principally, the introduction of a new offence of supplying consumer goods which do not comply with a general safety requirement.

The general safety requirement

10.—(1) A person shall be guilty of an offence if he—

(a) supplies any consumer goods which fail to comply with the general safety requirement;

(b) offers or agrees to supply any such goods; or

(c) exposes or possesses any such goods for supply.

(2) For the purposes of this section consumer goods fail to comply with the general safety requirement if they are not reasonably safe having regard to all the circumstances, including—

(a) the manner in which, and purposes for which, the goods are being or would be marketed, the get-up of the goods, the use of any mark in relation to the goods and any instructions or warnings which are given or would be given with respect to the keeping, use or consumption of the goods;

(b) any standards of safety published by any person either for goods of a description which applies to the goods in question or for matters relating to goods of that description; and

(c) the existence of any means by which it would have been reasonable (taking into account the cost, likelihood and extent of any improvement) for the goods to have been made safer.

(3) For the purposes of this section consumer goods shall not be regarded as failing to comply with the general safety requirement in respect of—

(a) anything which is shown to be attributable to compliance with any requirement imposed by or under any enactment or with any Community obligation;

(b) any failure to do more in relation to any matter than is required by—

　(i) any safety regulations imposing requirements with respect to that matter;

　(ii) any standards of safety approved for the purposes of this subsection by or under any such regulations and imposing requirements with respect to that matter;

　(iii) any provision of any enactment or subordinate legislation imposing such requirements with respect to that matter as are designated for the purposes of this subsection by any such regulations.

(4) In any proceedings against any person for an offence under this section in respect of any goods it shall be a defence for that person to show—

(a) that he reasonably believed that the goods would not be used or consumed in the United Kingdom; or

(b) that the following conditions are satisfied, that is to say—

　(i) that he supplied the goods, offered or agreed to supply them or, as the case may be, exposed or possessed them for supply in the course of carrying on a retail business; and

　(ii) that, at the time he supplied the goods or offered or agreed to supply them or exposed or possessed them for supply, he neither knew nor had reasonable grounds for believing that the goods failed to comply with the general safety requirement; or

(c) that the terms on which he supplied the goods or agreed or offered to supply them or, in the case of goods which he exposed or possessed for supply, the terms on which he intended to supply them—

　(i) indicated that the goods were not supplied or to be supplied as new goods; and

　(ii) provided for, or contemplated, the acquisition of an interest in the goods by the persons supplied or to be supplied.

(5) For the purposes of subsection (4)(b) above goods are supplied in the course of carrying on a retail business if—

(a) whether or not they are themselves acquired for a person's private use or consumption, they are supplied in the course of carrying on a business of making a supply of consumer goods available to persons who generally acquire them for private use or consumption; and

(b) the descriptions of goods the supply of which is made available in the course of that business do not, to a significant extent, include manufactured or imported goods which have not previously been supplied in the United Kingdom.

(6) A person guilty of an offence under this section shall be liable on summary conviction to imprisonment for a term not exceeding six months or to a fine not exceeding level 5 on the standard scale or to both.

(7) In this section "consumer goods" means any goods which are ordinarily intended for private use or consumption, not being—

(a) growing crops or things comprised in land by virtue of being attached to it;

(b) water, food, feeding stuff or fertiliser;

(c) gas which is, is to be or has been supplied by a person authorised to supply it by or under section 6, 7 or 8 of the Gas Act 1986 (authorisation of supply of gas through pipes);

(d) aircraft (other than hang-gliders) or motor vehicles;

   (e) controlled drugs or licensed medicinal products;
   (f) tobacco.

DEFINITIONS
   "aircraft": s.45(1).
   "business": s.45(1).
   "consumer goods": subs. (7).
   "controlled drugs": s.19(1).
   "feeding stuff": s.19(1).
   "fertiliser": s.19(1).
   "food": s.19(1) and (2).
   "gas": s.45(1).
   "goods": s.45(1) and (3).
   "in the course of carrying on a retail business": subs. (5).
   "licensed medicinal product": s.19(1).
   "mark": s.45(1), (4).
   "motor vehicle": s.45(1).
   "safe": s.19(1).
   "safety regulations": s.45(1).
   "supplies", "supply": s.45(1), s.46.
   "the general safety requirement": subss. (2) and (3).
   "tobacco": s.19(1).

GENERAL NOTE

Subs. (1)

Unlike liability under Pt. 1, this section applies to anyone who supplies goods, provided the goods are supplied in the course of a business (s.46(4)) and unless they are supplied as not being new (s.10(4)(c)). There are one or two other exceptions in s.46. Thus a finance company, which supplies goods only in the sense that it supplies them on hire-purchase (or credit sale, conditional sale or hire) terms as a means of financing the customer's acquisition of those goods from a dealer, is not caught; instead the dealer is treated as the person who "supplies" the goods to the customer (s.46(2)). The dealer might, like any other retail supplier, be able to rely upon the defence in s.10(4)(b). Anyone charged under this section may seek to rely upon the defence of due diligence in s.39.

The word "offers" will be interpreted in the contract law sense, *Fisher* v. *Bell* [1967] 1 Q.B. 394. For a discussion of "exposes or possesses . . . for supply" see the commentary to *Haringey London Borough* v. *Piro Shoes* at [1976] Crim.L.R. 462.

Subs. (2)

Safety is defined (see s.19(1)) in terms of risks of death or personal injury. Therefore supplying new furniture which has woodworm would not be caught as the only threat it would pose would be to other property. Also the goods will not be rendered unsafe merely because it would be dangerous to put them to a use which could not reasonably be expected, s.19(2).

Subs. (2) means that in deciding whether the goods complied with the general safety requirement the court can have regard to standards such as those published by the British Standards Institute and can do so irrespective of whether those standards have been incorporated in Safety Regulations or approved for the purpose of s.10(3).

Subs. (3)

Under subs. (3)(a) the burden of proof appears clearly to be cast upon the defendant (*cf.* "shown"). Under subs. (3)(a) it will not be sufficient to show that the goods complied with the requirement or enactment in question; the defendant will have to show that the risk of death or personal injury relied upon by the prosecution was attributable to that compliance, *i.e.* was a consequence of, or was inherent in, compliance.

Under subs. (3)(b), on the other hand, there is no need for the risk to have been attributable to the compliance. It will be a defence that the goods complied with the Safety Regulations, *approved* standards of safety or *designated* requirements of legislation. Any such approval or designation will be in Safety Regulations made under s.11(1) below.

Subs. (4)

The burden of proof is clearly cast upon the defendant. Subs. (4)(a) lets off the supplier of goods intended for export. Subs. 4(b) is a defence which recognises that a retailer may be unable to know or discover that the goods he supplies are unsafe. There is no equivalent defence for traders further back up the line of distribution, *e.g.* wholesalers or distributors. Even a retailer will not qualify for this defence if his business consists, to a significant extent, of supplying goods which he has himself manufactured or which he has acquired direct from a source outside the U.K., s.10(5). Curiously, it seems that a retailer, who in his business both supplies consumer goods of his own manufacture and also supplies consumer goods of other U.K. manufacture, can not rely on the defence in subs. (4)(b) even in relation to goods in the latter category. At least, that is so, if the supply of his own manufactured goods is of a "significant extent."

Subs. (7)

It is thought that the safety of most of the products listed here is adequately covered by other statutes. Tobacco is excluded, presumably, because it is, arguably, unsafe by definition and, if it were not excluded, would be effectively banned.

Safety regulations

11.—(1) The Secretary of State may by regulations under this section ("safety regulations") make such provision as he considers appropriate for the purposes of section 10(3) above and for the purpose of securing—
  (a) that goods to which this section applies are safe;
  (b) that goods to which this section applies which are unsafe, or would be unsafe in the hands of persons of a particular description, are not made available to persons generally or, as the case may be, to persons of that description; and
  (c) that appropriate information is, and inappropriate information is not, provided in relation to goods to which this section applies.
  (2) Without prejudice to the generality of subsection (1) above, safety regulations may contain provision—
  (a) with respect to the composition or contents, design, construction, finish or packing of goods to which this section applies, with respect to standards for such goods and with respect to other matters relating to such goods;
  (b) with respect to the giving, refusal, alteration or cancellation of approvals of such goods, of descriptions of such goods or of standards for such goods;
  (c) with respect to the conditions that may be attached to any approval given under the regulations;
  (d) for requiring such fees as may be determined by or under the regulations to be paid on the giving or alteration of any approval under the regulations and on the making of an application for such an approval or alteration;
  (e) with respect to appeals against refusals, alterations and cancellations of approvals given under the regulations and against the conditions contained in such approvals;
  (f) for requiring goods to which this section applies to be approved under the regulations or to conform to the requirements of the regulations or to descriptions or standards specified in or approved by or under the regulations;
  (g) with respect to the testing or inspection of goods to which this section applies (including provision for determining the standards to be applied in carrying out any test or inspection);
  (h) with respect to the ways of dealing with goods of which some or all do not satisfy a test required by or under the regulations or a standard connected with a procedure so required;
  (i) for requiring a mark, warning or instruction or any other information relating to goods to be put on or to accompany the goods or to be used or provided in some other manner in relation to the goods, and for securing that inappropriate information is not given

in relation to goods either by means of misleading marks or otherwise;

(j) for prohibiting persons from supplying, or from offering to supply, agreeing to supply, exposing for supply or possessing for supply, goods to which this section applies and component parts and raw materials for such goods;

(k) for requiring information to be given to any such person as may be determined by or under the regulations for the purpose of enabling that person to exercise any function conferred on him by the regulations.

(3) Without prejudice as aforesaid, safety regulations may contain provision—

(a) for requiring persons on whom functions are conferred by or under section 27 below to have regard, in exercising their functions so far as relating to any provision of safety regulations, to matters specified in a direction issued by the Secretary of State with respect to that provision;

(b) for securing that a person shall not be guilty of an offence under section 12 below unless it is shown that the goods in question do not conform to a particular standard;

(c) for securing that proceedings for such an offence are not brought in England and Wales except by or with the consent of the Secretary of State or the Director of Public Prosecutions;

(d) for securing that proceedings for such an offence are not brought in Northern Ireland except by or with the consent of the Secretary of State or the Director of Public Prosecutions for Northern Ireland;

(e) for enabling a magistrates' court in England and Wales or Northern Ireland to try an information or, in Northern Ireland, a complaint in respect of such an offence if the information was laid or the complaint made within twelve months from the time when the offence was committed;

(f) for enabling summary proceedings for such an offence to be brought in Scotland at any time within twelve months from the time when the offence was committed; and

(g) for determining the persons by whom, and the manner in which, anything required to be done by or under the regulations is to be done.

(4) Safety regulations shall not provide for any contravention of the regulations to be an offence.

(5) Where the Secretary of State proposes to make safety regulations it shall be his duty before he makes them—

(a) to consult such organisations as appear to him to be representative of interests substantially affected by the proposal;

(b) to consult such other persons as he considers appropriate; and

(c) in the case of proposed regulations relating to goods suitable for use at work, to consult the Health and Safety Commission in relation to the application of the proposed regulations to Great Britain;

but the preceding provisions of this subsection shall not apply in the case of regulations which provide for the regulations to cease to have effect at the end of a period of not more than twelve months beginning with the day on which they come into force and which contain a statement that it appears to the Secretary of State that the need to protect the public requires that the regulations should be made without delay.

(6) The power to make safety regulations shall be exercisable by statutory instrument subject to annulment in pursuance of a resolution of either House of Parliament and shall include power—

(a) to make different provision for different cases; and

(b) to make such supplemental, consequential and transitional provision as the Secretary of State considers appropriate.

(7) This section applies to any goods other than—

(a) growing crops and things comprised in land by virtue of being attached to it;

(b) water, food, feeding stuff and fertiliser;

(c) gas which is, is to be or has been supplied by a person authorised to supply it by or under section 6, 7 or 8 of the Gas Act 1986 (authorisation of supply of gas through pipes);

(d) controlled drugs and licensed medicinal products.

DEFINITIONS

"contravention": s.45(1).
"controlled drug": s.19(1).
"feeding stuff": s.19(1).
"fertiliser": s.19(1).
"food": s.19(1), (2).
"gas": s.45(1).
"goods": s.45(1).
"information": s.45(1).
"licensed medicinal products": s.19(1).
"magistrates' courts": s.45(1).
"mark": s.45(1), (4).
"safe": s.19(1).
"supplied", "supply", "supplying": s.45(1), s.46.
"unsafe": see "safe" in s.19(1).

Offences against the safety regulations

12.—(1) Where safety regulations prohibit a person from supplying or offering or agreeing to supply any goods or from exposing or possessing any goods for supply, that person shall be guilty of an offence if he contravenes the prohibition.

(2) Where safety regulations require a person who makes or processes any goods in the course of carrying on a business—

(a) to carry out a particular test or use a particular procedure in connection with the making or processing of the goods with a view to ascertaining whether the goods satisfy any requirements of such regulations; or

(b) to deal or not to deal in a particular way with a quantity of the goods of which the whole or part does not satisfy such a test or does not satisfy standards connected with such a procedure,

that person shall be guilty of an offence if he does not comply with the requirement.

(3) If a person contravenes a provision of safety regulations which prohibits or requires the provision, by means of a mark or otherwise, of information of a particular kind in relation to goods, he shall be guilty of an offence.

(4) Where safety regulations require any person to give information to another for the purpose of enabling that other to exercise any function, that person shall be guilty of an offence if—

(a) he fails without reasonable cause to comply with the requirement; or

(b) in giving the information which is required of him—

(i) he makes any statement which he knows is false in a material particular; or

(ii) he recklessly makes any statement which is false in a material particular.

(5) A person guilty of an offence under this section shall be liable on summary conviction to imprisonment for a term not exceeding six months or to a fine not exceeding level 5 on the standard scale or to both.

DEFINITIONS
"business": s.45(1).
"contravenes", "contravention": s.45(1).
"goods": s.45(1), (3).
"information": s.45(1).
"mark": s.45(1), (4).
"safety regulations": s.11, s.45(1).
"supply", "supplying": s.45(1), s.46.

GENERAL NOTE
Note the defence of due diligence in s.39.

Subs. (1)
For comment on "offering" and "exposing or possessing . . . for supply" see the note to s.10 above.

Subs. (2)
For comment on "in the course of carrying on a business" and similar phrases see the note to s.4(1)(c) above.

Subs. (4)
The formulation of the offence is very similar to that in s.14 of the Trade Descriptions Act 1968. It would seem that, where a corporate body (*e.g.* a public or private company) is charged, the knowledge or recklessness required must be that of the corporate body *i.e.* of one of its directors or, perhaps other superior officer of the company (*Wings* v. *Ellis* [1984] 1 W.L.R. 731, D.C.; *Tesco Supermarkets* v. *Nattrass* [1972] A.C. 153). That knowledge or recklessness must have been present when the statement was made. However, it seems that a statement once put out (*e.g.* on a brochure or leaflet or on goods) is "made" every time the brochure or leaflet, etc., is read. Put another way, the statement once made is a continuing one and continues to be made to anyone who later reads it. So, if the defendant did not have the necessary knowledge (or recklessness) when he first published the statement but acquired the knowledge later, he might still commit the offence if after he had acquired that knowledge, the statement was read by someone (*Wings* v. *Ellis* [1985] A.C. 272, H.L.). Recklessness does not necessarily involve dishonesty. The duty not to be reckless casts upon the defendant the positive obligation to have regard to whether the statements in the information are true or false, *M.F.I. Warehouses* v. *Nattrass* [1973] 1 All E.R. 162; *Cowburn* v. *Focus Television Rentals* [1983] Crim.L.R. 563. It is not thought that that proposition is undermined by anything in the leading case of *R.* v. *Caldwell* [1982] A.C. 341, where the House of Lords considered the meaning of the word "recklessly" in a modern statute.

Prohibition notices and notices to warn

13.—(1) The Secretary of State may—
    (a) serve on any person a notice ("a prohibition notice") prohibiting that person, except with the consent of the Secretary of State, from supplying, or from offering to supply, agreeing to supply, exposing for supply or possessing for supply, any relevant goods which the Secretary of State considers are unsafe and which are described in the notice;
    (b) serve on any person a notice ("a notice to warn") requiring that person at his own expense to publish, in a form and manner and on occasions specified in the notice, a warning about any relevant goods which the Secretary of State considers are unsafe, which that person supplies or has supplied and which are described in the notice.

(2) Schedule 2 to this Act shall have effect with respect to prohibition notices and notices to warn; and the Secretary of State may by regulations

make provision specifying the manner in which information is to be given to any person under that Schedule.

(3) A consent given by the Secretary of State for the purposes of a prohibition notice may impose such conditions on the doing of anything for which the consent is required as the Secretary of State considers appropriate.

(4) A person who contravenes a prohibition notice or a notice to warn shall be guilty of an offence and liable on summary conviction to imprisonment for a term not exceeding six months or to a fine not exceeding level 5 on the standard scale or to both.

(5) The power to make regulations under subsection (2) above shall be exercisable by statutory instrument subject to annulment in pursuance of a resolution of either House of Parliament and shall include power—

(a) to make different provision for different cases; and

(b) to make such supplemental, consequential and transitional provision as the Secretary of State considers appropriate.

(6) In this section "relevant goods" means—

(a) in relation to a prohibition notice, any goods to which section 11 above applies; and

(b) in relation to a notice to warn, any goods to which that section applies or any growing crops or things comprised in land by virtue of being attached to it.

DEFINITIONS

"contravenes": s.45(1).

"goods": s.45(1).

"information": s.45(1).

"relevant goods": subs. (6).

"supplied", "supplies", "supply", "supplying": s.45(1), s.46.

"unsafe": see "safe" in s.19(1), (2).

GENERAL NOTE

The provision enabling the Secretary of State to issue prohibition *orders*, previously contained in the Consumer Safety Act 1978, has now gone. It is rendered unnecessary by the new offence created by s.10 above.

Subs. (1)

For comment on "offering" and "exposing" or "possessing" for supply, see the note to s.10 above.

Subs. (4)

Note the defence of due diligence in s.39.

Suspension notices

14.—(1) Where an enforcement authority has reasonable grounds for suspecting that any safety provision has been contravened in relation to any goods, the authority may serve a notice ("a suspension notice") prohibiting the person on whom it is served, for such period ending not more than six months after the date of the notice as is specified therein, from doing any of the following things without the consent of the authority, that is to say, supplying the goods, offering to supply them, agreeing to supply them or exposing them for supply.

(2) A suspension notice served by an enforcement authority in respect of any goods shall—

(a) describe the goods in a manner sufficient to identify them;

(b) set out the grounds on which the authority suspects that a safety provision has been contravened in relation to the goods; and

(c) state that, and the manner in which, the person on whom the notice is served may appeal against the notice under section 15 below.

(3) A suspension notice served by an enforcement authority for the purpose of prohibiting a person for any period from doing the things mentioned in subsection (1) above in relation to any goods may also require that person to keep the authority informed of the whereabouts throughout that period of any of those goods in which he has an interest.

(4) Where a suspension notice has been served on any person in respect of any goods, no further such notice shall be served on that person in respect of the same goods unless—

    (a) proceedings against that person for an offence in respect of a contravention in relation to the goods of a safety provision (not being an offence under this section); or

    (b) proceedings for the forfeiture of the goods under section 16 or 17 below,

are pending at the end of the period specified in the first-mentioned notice.

(5) A consent given by an enforcement authority for the purposes of subsection (1) above may impose such conditions on the doing of anything for which the consent is required as the authority considers appropriate.

(6) Any person who contravenes a suspension notice shall be guilty of an offence and liable on summary conviction to imprisonment for a term not exceeding six months or to a fine not exceeding level 5 on the standard scale or to both.

(7) Where an enforcement authority serves a suspension notice in respect of any goods, the authority shall be liable to pay compensation to any person having an interest in the goods in respect of any loss or damage caused by reason of the service of the notice if—

    (a) there has been no contravention in relation to the goods of any safety provision; and

    (b) the exercise of the power is not attributable to any neglect or default by that person.

(8) Any disputed question as to the right to or the amount of any compensation payable under this section shall be determined by arbitration or, in Scotland, by a single arbiter appointed, failing agreement between the parties, by the sheriff.

DEFINITIONS
"contravened", "contravention": s.45(1).
"enforcement authority": s.45(1).
"goods": s.45(1), (3).
"safety provision": s.45(1).
"supply", "supplying": s.45(1), s.46.
"suspension notice": subs. (1).

GENERAL NOTE

Subs. (1)
For comment on "offering" and "exposing" see note to s.10 above.

Appeals against suspension notices

15.—(1) Any person having an interest in any goods in respect of which a suspension notice is for the time being in force may apply for an order setting aside the notice.

(2) An application under this section may be made—

    (a) to any magistrates' court in which proceedings have been brought in England and Wales or Northern Ireland—

        (i) for an offence in respect of a contravention in relation to the goods of any safety provision; or

      (ii) for the forfeiture of the goods under section 16 below;
   (b) where no such proceedings have been so brought, by way of complaint to a magistrates' court; or
   (c) in Scotland, by summary application to the sheriff.

(3) On an application under this section to a magistrates' court in England and Wales or Northern Ireland the court shall make an order setting aside the suspension notice only if the court is satisfied that there has been no contravention in relation to the goods of any safety provision.

(4) On an application under this section to the sheriff he shall make an order setting aside the suspension notice only if he is satisfied that at the date of making the order—
   (a) proceedings for an offence in respect of a contravention in relation to the goods of any safety provision; or
   (b) proceedings for the forfeiture of the goods under section 17 below, have not been brought or, having been brought, have been concluded.

(5) Any person aggrieved by an order made under this section by a magistrates' court in England and Wales or Northern Ireland, or by a decision of such a court not to make such an order, may appeal against that order or decision—
   (a) in England and Wales, to the Crown Court;
   (b) in Northern Ireland, to the county court;
and an order so made may contain such provision as appears to the court to be appropriate for delaying the coming into force of the order pending the making and determination of any appeal (including any application under section 111 of the Magistrates' Courts Act 1980 or Article 146 of the Magistrates' Courts (Northern Ireland) Order 1981 (statement of case)).

DEFINITIONS
  "contravention": s.45(1).
  "goods": s.45(1), (3).
  "magistrates' court": s.45(1).
  "safety provision": s.45(1).
  "suspension notice": s.14(1), s.45(1).

Forfeiture: England and Wales and Northern Ireland

16.—(1) An enforcement authority in England and Wales or Northern Ireland may apply under this section for an order for the forfeiture of any goods on the grounds that there has been a contravention in relation to the goods of a safety provision.

(2) An application under this section may be made—
   (a) where proceedings have been brought in a magistrates' court for an offence in respect of a contravention in relation to some or all of the goods of any safety provision, to that court;
   (b) where an application with respect to some or all of the goods has been made to a magistrates' court under section 15 above or section 33 below, to that court; and
   (c) where no application for the forfeiture of the goods has been made under paragraph (a) or (b) above, by way of complaint to a magistrates' court.

(3) On an application under this section the court shall make an order for the forfeiture of any goods only if it is satisfied that there has been a contravention in relation to the goods of a safety provision.

(4) For the avoidance of doubt it is declared that a court may infer for the purposes of this section that there has been a contravention in relation to any goods of a safety provision if it is satisfied that any such provision has been contravened in relation to goods which are representative of

those goods (whether by reason of being of the same design or part of the same consignment or batch or otherwise).

(5) Any person aggrieved by an order made under this section by a magistrates' court, or by a decision of such a court not to make such an order, may appeal against that order or decision—

    (a) in England and Wales, to the Crown Court;

    (b) in Northern Ireland, to the county court;

and an order so made may contain such provision as appears to the court to be appropriate for delaying the coming into force of the order pending the making and determination of any appeal (including any application under section 111 of the Magistrates' Courts Act 1980 or Article 146 of the Magistrates' Courts (Northern Ireland) Order 1981 (statement of case)).

(6) Subject to subsection (7) below, where any goods are forfeited under this section they shall be destroyed in accordance with such directions as the court may give.

(7) On making an order under this section a magistrates' court may, if it considers it appropriate to do so, direct that the goods to which the order relates shall (instead of being destroyed) be released, to such person as the court may specify, on condition that that person—

    (a) does not supply those goods to any person otherwise than as mentioned in section 46(7)(a) or (b) below; and

    (b) complies with any order to pay costs or expenses (including any order under section 35 below) which has been made against that person in the proceedings for the order for forfeiture.

DEFINITIONS
"contravened", "contravention": s.45(1).
"enforcement authority": s.45(1).
"goods": s.45(1), (3).
"magistrates' court": s.45(1).
"safety provision": s.45(1).
"supply": s.45(1), s.46.

Forfeiture: Scotland

17.—(1) In Scotland a sheriff may make an order for forfeiture of any goods in relation to which there has been a contravention of a safety provision—

    (a) on an application by the procurator-fiscal made in the manner specified in section 310 of the Criminal Procedure (Scotland) Act 1975; or

    (b) where a person is convicted of any offence in respect of any such contravention, in addition to any other penalty which the sheriff may impose.

(2) The procurator-fiscal making an application under subsection (1)(a) above shall serve on any person appearing to him to be the owner of, or otherwise to have an interest in, the goods to which the application relates a copy of the application, together with a notice giving him the opportunity to appear at the hearing of the application to show cause why the goods should not be forfeited.

(3) Service under subsection (2) above shall be carried out, and such service may be proved, in the manner specified for citation of an accused in summary proceedings under the Criminal Procedure (Scotland) Act 1975.

(4) Any person upon whom notice is served under subsection (2) above and any other person claiming to be the owner of, or otherwise to have an interest in, goods to which an application under this section relates

shall be entitled to appear at the hearing of the application to show cause why the goods should not be forfeited.

(5) The sheriff shall not make an order following an application under subsection (1)(a) above—

(a) if any person on whom notice is served under subsection (2) above does not appear, unless service of the notice on that person is proved; or

(b) if no notice under subsection (2) above has been served, unless the court is satisfied that in the circumstances it was reasonable not to serve notice on any person.

(6) The sheriff shall make an order under this section only if he is satisfied that there has been a contravention in relation to those goods of a safety provision.

(7) For the avoidance of doubt it is declared that the sheriff may infer for the purposes of this section that there has been a contravention in relation to any goods of a safety provision if he is satisfied that any such provision has been contravened in relation to any goods which are representative of those goods (whether by reason of being of the same design or part of the same consignment or batch or otherwise).

(8) Where an order for the forfeiture of any goods is made following an application by the procurator-fiscal under subsection (1)(a) above, any person who appeared, or was entitled to appear, to show cause why goods should not be forfeited may, within twenty-one days of the making of the order, appeal to the High Court by Bill of Suspension on the ground of an alleged miscarriage of justice; and section 452(4)(a) to (e) of the Criminal Procedure (Scotland) Act 1975 shall apply to an appeal under this subsection as it applies to a stated case under Part II of that Act.

(9) An order following an application under subsection (1)(a) above shall not take effect—

(a) until the end of the period of twenty-one days beginning with the day after the day on which the order is made; or

(b) if an appeal is made under subsection (8) above within that period, until the appeal is determined or abandoned.

(10) An order under subsection (1)(b) above shall not take effect—

(a) until the end of the period within which an appeal against the order could be brought under the Criminal Procedure (Scotland) Act 1975; or

(b) if an appeal is made within that period, until the appeal is determined or abandoned.

(11) Subject to subsection (12) below, goods forfeited under this section shall be destroyed in accordance with such directions as the sheriff may give.

(12) If he thinks fit, the sheriff may direct that the goods be released, to such person as he may specify, on condition that that person does not supply those goods to any other person otherwise than as mentioned in section 46(7)(a) or (b) below.

DEFINITIONS
"contravened", "contravention": s.45(1).
"goods": s.45(1), (3).
"notice": s.45(1).
"safety provision": s.45(1).
"supply": s.45(1), s.46.

Power to obtain information

18.—(1) If the Secretary of State considers that, for the purpose of deciding whether—

(a) to make, vary or revoke any safety regulations; or

    (b) to serve, vary or revoke a prohibition notice; or

    (c) to serve or revoke a notice to warn,

he requires information which another person is likely to be able to furnish, the Secretary of State may serve on the other person a notice under this section.

(2) A notice served on any person under this section may require that person—

    (a) to furnish to the Secretary of State, within a period specified in the notice, such information as is so specified;

    (b) to produce such records as are specified in the notice at a time and place so specified and to permit a person appointed by the Secretary of State for the purpose to take copies of the records at that time and place.

(3) A person shall be guilty of an offence if he—

    (a) fails, without reasonable cause, to comply with a notice served on him under this section; or

    (b) in purporting to comply with a requirement which by virtue of paragraph (a) of subsection (2) above is contained in such a notice—

       (i) furnishes information which he knows is false in a material particular; or

      (ii) recklessly furnishes information which is false in a material particular.

(4) A person guilty of an offence under subsection (3) above shall—

    (a) in the case of an offence under paragraph (a) of that subsection be liable on summary conviction to a fine not exceeding level 5 on the standard scale; and

    (b) in the case of an offence under paragraph (b) of that subsection be liable—

       (i) on conviction on indictment, to a fine;

      (ii) on summary conviction, to a fine not exceeding the statutory maximum.

DEFINITIONS
  "information": s.45(1).
  "notice": s.45(1).
  "notice to warn": s.13(1)(b), s.45(1).
  "prohibition notice": s.13(1)(a), s.45(1).
  "safety regulations": s.11, s.45(1).

GENERAL NOTE

Subs. (3)

  Note that the defence of due diligence in s.39 is not available (s.39(5)). For comment on the need for knowledge or recklessness, see the note to s.12 above.

Interpretation of Part II

19.—(1) In this Part—

    "controlled drug" means a controlled drug within the meaning of the Misuse of Drugs Act 1971;

    "feeding stuff" and "fertiliser" have the same meanings as in Part IV of the Agriculture Act 1970;

    "food" does not include anything containing tobacco but, subject to that, has the same meaning as in the Food Act 1984 or, in relation to Northern Ireland, the same meaning as in the Food and Drugs Act (Northern Ireland) 1958;

    "licensed medicinal product" means—

       (a) any medicinal product within the meaning of the Medicines Act 1968 in respect of which a product licence within the meaning of that Act is for the time being in force; or

(b) any other article or substance in respect of which any such licence is for the time being in force in pursuance of an order under section 104 or 105 of that Act (application of Act to other articles and substances);

"safe", in relation to any goods, means such that there is no risk, or no risk apart from one reduced to a minimum, that any of the following will (whether immediately or after a definite or indefinite period) cause the death of, or any personal injury to, any person whatsoever, that is to say—

(a) the goods;
(b) the keeping, use or consumption of the goods;
(c) the assembly of any of the goods which are, or are to be, supplied unassembled;
(d) any emission or leakage from the goods or, as a result of the keeping, use or consumption of the goods, from anything else; or
(e) reliance on the accuracy of any measurement, calculation or other reading made by or by means of the goods,

and "safer" and "unsafe" shall be construed accordingly;

"tobacco" includes any tobacco product within the meaning of the Tobacco Products Duty Act 1979 and any article or substance containing tobacco and intended for oral or nasal use.

(2) In the definition of "safe" in subsection (1) above, references to the keeping, use or consumption of any goods are references to—

(a) the keeping, use or consumption of the goods by the persons by whom, and in all or any of the ways or circumstances in which, they might reasonably be expected to be kept, used or consumed; and

(b) the keeping, use or consumption of the goods either alone or in conjunction with other goods in conjunction with which they might reasonably be expected to be kept, used or consumed.

DEFINITIONS
"goods": s.45(1), (3).
"personal injury": s.45(1).
"substance": s.45(1).
"supplied": s.45(1), s.46.
"tobacco": subs. (1).

PART III

MISLEADING PRICE INDICATIONS

GENERAL NOTE

This Part when brought into force will replace provisions in s.11 of the Trade Descriptions Act 1968 and the Price Marking (Bargain Offers) Order 1979. Those provisions had been found unsatisfactory: they contained loopholes which enabled some traders to publish misleading statements without falling foul of the law; the Price Marking (Bargain Offers) Order was obscure, giving rise to difficulties of interpretation and enforcement; s.11 of the Trade Descriptions Act did not apply to services or accommodation and the 1979 Order did not apply to accommodation. This Part applies to misleading price indications relating to "goods, services, accommodation or facilities" and it adopts a new approach to the problem of defining the mischief which it seeks to stamp out, *i.e.* the giving out of *misleading* price information. Thus it contains a definition (in s.21) in general (though not brief) terms of "misleading" and also provides for an approved code (or codes) of practice, non-compliance or compliance with which can be relied upon at any trial as tending to show that a particular price indication was or was not misleading. In addition there is, in s.26, a regulation-making power whereby specific practices can be banned and the giving of specific information can be made mandatory.

Offence of giving misleading indication

20.—(1) Subject to the following provisions of this Part, a person shall be guilty of an offence if, in the course of any business of his, he gives (by any means whatever) to any consumers an indication which is misleading as to the price at which any goods, services, accommodation or facilities are available (whether generally or from particular persons).

(2) Subject as aforesaid, a person shall be guilty of an offence if—

  (a) in the course of any business of his, he has given an indication to any consumers which, after it was given, has become misleading as mentioned in subsection (1) above; and

  (b) some or all of those consumers might reasonably be expected to rely on the indication at a time after it has become misleading; and

  (c) he fails to take all such steps as are reasonable to prevent those consumers from relying on the indication.

(3) For the purposes of this section it shall be immaterial—

  (a) whether the person who gives or gave the indication is or was acting on his own behalf or on behalf of another;

  (b) whether or not that person is the person, or included among the persons, from whom the goods, services, accommodation or facilities are available; and

  (c) whether the indication is or has become misleading in relation to all the consumers to whom it is or was given or only in relation to some of them.

(4) A person guilty of an offence under subsection (1) or (2) above shall be liable—

  (a) on conviction on indictment, to a fine;

  (b) on summary conviction, to a fine not exceeding the statutory maximum.

(5) No prosecution for an offence under subsection (1) or (2) above shall be brought after whichever is the earlier of the following, that is to say—

  (a) the end of the period of three years beginning with the day on which the offence was committed; and

  (b) the end of the period of one year beginning with the day on which the person bringing the prosecution discovered that the offence had been committed.

(6) In this Part—

"consumer"—

    (a) in relation to any goods, means any person who might wish to be supplied with the goods for his own private use or consumption;

    (b) in relation to any services or facilities, means any person who might wish to be provided with the services or facilities otherwise than for the purposes of any business of his; and

    (c) in relation to any accommodation, means any person who might wish to occupy the accommodation otherwise than for the purposes of any business of his;

"price", in relation to any goods, services, accommodation or facilities, means—

    (a) the aggregate of the sums required to be paid by a consumer for or otherwise in respect of the supply of the goods or the provision of the services, accommodation or facilities; or

(b) except in section 21 below, any method which will be or has been applied for the purpose of determining that aggregate.

DEFINITIONS
"accommodation": s.22.
"business": s.45(1).
"consumer": subs. (6).
"facilities": s.22, s.23.
"goods": s.45(1).
"misleading": s.21.
"price": subs. (6).
"services": s.22.
"supplied", "supply": s.45(1), s.46.

GENERAL NOTE
Someone charged under subs. (1), but not someone charged under subs. (2), may rely on the defence of due diligence in s.39. There are a few other limited defences. in s.24. For cases on "in the course of any business of his" and similar expressions, see note to s.4(1)(c) above.

Suppose a trader has put out an advertisement or brochure giving price information which was accurate when the advertisement or brochure was first published but which has become misleading whilst the advertisement or brochure is still current. Suppose that after the information has become misleading a consumer reads the advertisement or brochure. The appropriate charge in such a case is under subs. (1) and not subs. (2). This is because a brochure or other publication does not involve just a single, "once-off" giving of an indication of the information in it but a continuous giving of such an indication or, alternatively, a repeated giving of an indication to each person who reads it (see *Wings* v. *Ellis* [1985] A.C. 272). Thus the consumer is given an indication (which is by then misleading) when he *reads* the brochure or advertisement. Subs. (2) will be the appropriate charge in circumstances where the advertisement or brochure is still absolutely accurate when the customer reads it but becomes inaccurate (and "misleading") before the customer enters a transaction in reliance on its accuracy. In that situation, the trader could be liable under subs. (2) if that reliance by the customer might reasonably be expected and the trader has not taken all reasonable steps to prevent the customer relying on the misleading indication. It is important that the charge be laid under the correct subsection because, *inter alia*, the defences in s.39 and s.20(4) are not available to someone charged under s.20(2).

Meaning of "misleading"

21.—(1) For the purposes of section 20 above an indication given to any consumers is misleading as to a price if what is conveyed by the indication, or what those consumers might reasonably be expected to infer from the indication or any omission from it, includes any of the following, that is to say—

(a) that the price is less than in fact it is;

(b) that the applicability of the price does not depend on facts or circumstances on which its applicability does in fact depend;

(c) that the price covers matters in respect of which an additional charge is in fact made;

(d) that a person who in fact has no such expectation—
  (i) expects the price to be increased or reduced (whether or not at a particular time or by a particular amount); or
  (ii) expects the price, or the price as increased or reduced, to be maintained (whether or not for a particular period); or

(e) that the facts or circumstances by reference to which the consumers might reasonably be expected to judge the validity of any relevant comparison made or implied by the indication are not what in fact they are.

(2) For the purposes of section 20 above, an indication given to any consumers is misleading as to a method of determining a price if what is

conveyed by the indication, or what those consumers might reasonably be expected to infer from the indication or any omission from it, includes any of the following, that is to say—

(a) that the method is not what in fact it is;

(b) that the applicability of the method does not depend on facts or circumstances on which its applicability does in fact depend;

(c) that the method takes into account matters in respect of which an additional charge will in fact be made;

(d) that a person who in fact has no such expectation—

(i) expects the method to be altered (whether or not at a particular time or in a particular respect); or

(ii) expects the method, or that method as altered, to remain unaltered (whether or not for a particular period); or

(e) that the facts or circumstances by reference to which the consumers might reasonably be expected to judge the validity of any relevant comparison made or implied by the indication are not what in fact they are.

(3) For the purposes of subsections (1)(e) and (2)(e) above a comparison is a relevant comparison in relation to a price or method of determining a price if it is made between that price or that method, or any price which has been or may be determined by that method, and—

(a) any price or value which is stated or implied to be, to have been or to be likely to be attributed or attributable to the goods, services, accommodation or facilities in question or to any other goods, services, accommodation or facilities; or

(b) any method, or other method, which is stated or implied to be, to have been or to be likely to be applied or applicable for the determination of the price or value of the goods, services, accommodation or facilities in question or of the price or value of any other goods, services, accommodation or facilites.

DEFINITIONS

"accommodation": s.22.

"consumer": s.20(6).

"facilities": s.22, s.23.

"goods": s.45(1).

"services": s.22.

"price": s.20(6).

GENERAL NOTE

As under the old s.11 of the Trade Descriptions Act, the price indication is to be looked at through the eyes of a consumer. The question is not "What did the trader intend to convey?" but "How might a consumer reasonably understand what he reads or is told?" It is up to the trader to resolve ambiguities in the price information he gives. The section catches, *inter alia*: (a) an understatement of the price; (b) the stating of a price without making it clear that, if that is the case, it applies only to cash customers or without making it clear that, if that is the case, it does not apply on part-exchange deals; (c) stating a price without making it clear that service is charged extra; (d) falsely saying that the price is expected to go up; (e) comparing the price of a car with that of another model without stating that the price given for the other model has since been reduced. Paras. (d) and (e) of subs. (1) are worded in very general language and it is in relation to them in particular that reference to an approved code of practice is likely to be most helpful.

Application to provision of services and facilities

22.—(1) Subject to the following provisions of this section, references in this Part to services or facilities are references to any services or facilities whatever including, in particular—

(a) the provision of credit or of banking or insurance services and the provision of facilities incidental to the provision of such services;

(b) the purchase or sale of foreign currency;

(c) the supply of electricity;

(d) the provision of a place, other than on a highway, for the parking of a motor vehicle;

(e) the making of arrangements for a person to put or keep a caravan on any land other than arrangements by virtue of which that person may occupy the caravan as his only or main residence.

(2) References in this Part to services shall not include references to services provided to an employer under a contract of employment.

(3) References in this Part to services or facilities shall not include references to services or facilities which are provided by an authorised person or appointed representative in the course of the carrying on of an investment business.

(4) In relation to a service consisting in the purchase or sale of foreign currency, references in this Part to the method by which the price of the service is determined shall include references to the rate of exchange.

(5) In this section—

"appointed representative", "authorised person" and "investment business" have the same meanings as in the Financial Services Act 1986;

"caravan" has the same meaning as in the Caravan Sites and Control of Development Act 1960;

"contract of employment" and "employer" have the same meanings as in the Employment Protection (Consolidation) Act 1978;

"credit" has the same meaning as in the Consumer Credit Act 1974.

DEFINITIONS

"appointed representative": subs. (5).

"authorised person": subs. (5).

"caravan": subs. (5).

"contract of employment": subs. (5).

"credit": subs. (5).

"employer": subs. (5).

"investment business": subs. (5).

"motor vehicle": s.45(1).

Application to provision of accommodation etc.

23.—(1) Subject to subsection (2) below, references in this Part to accommodation or facilities being available shall not include references to accommodation or facilities being available to be provided by means of the creation or disposal of an interest in land except where—

(a) the person who is to create or dispose of the interest will do so in the course of any business of his; and

(b) the interest to be created or disposed of is a relevant interest in a new dwelling and is to be created or disposed of for the purpose of enabling that dwelling to be occupied as a residence, or one of the residences, of the person acquiring the interest.

(2) Subsection (1) above shall not prevent the application of any provision of this Part in relation to—

(a) the supply of any goods as part of the same transaction as any creation or disposal of an interest in land; or

(b) the provision of any services or facilities for the purposes of, or in connection with, any transaction for the creation or disposal of such an interest.

(3) In this section—

"new dwelling" means any building or part of a building in Great Britain which—

(a) has been constructed or adapted to be occupied as a residence; and

     (b) has not previously been so occupied or has been so occupied only with other premises or as more than one residence,

and includes any yard, garden, out-houses or appurtenances which belong to that building or part or are to be enjoyed with it;

"relevant interest"—

     (a) in relation to a new dwelling in England and Wales, means the freehold estate in the dwelling or a leasehold interest in the dwelling for a term of years absolute of more than twenty-one years, not being a term of which twenty-one years or less remains unexpired;

     (b) in relation to a new dwelling in Scotland, means the *dominium utile* of the land comprising the dwelling, or a leasehold interest in the dwelling where twenty-one years or more remains unexpired.

DEFINITIONS
"business": s.45(1).
"facilities": s.22.
"goods": s.45(1).
"new dwelling": subs. (3).
"relevant interest": subs. (3).
"supply": s.45(1), s.46.

Defences

24.—(1) In any proceedings against a person for an offence under subsection (1) or (2) of section 20 above in respect of any indication it shall be a defence for that person to show that his acts or omissions were authorised for the purposes of this subsection by regulations made under section 26 below.

(2) In proceedings against a person for an offence under subsection (1) or (2) of section 20 above in respect of an indication published in a book, newspaper, magazine, film or radio or television broadcast or in a programme included in a cable programme service, it shall be a defence for that person to show that the indication was not contained in an advertisement.

(3) In proceedings against a person for an offence under subsection (1) or (2) of section 20 above in respect of an indication published in an advertisement it shall be a defence for that person to show that—

     (a) he is a person who carries on a business of publishing or arranging for the publication of advertisements;

     (b) he received the advertisement for publication in the ordinary course of that business; and

     (c) at the time of publication he did not know and had no grounds for suspecting that the publication would involve the commission of the offence.

(4) In any proceedings against a person for an offence under subsection (1) of section 20 above in respect of any indication, it shall be a defence for that person to show that—

     (a) the indication did not relate to the availability from him of any goods, services, accommodation or facilities;

     (b) a price had been recommended to every person from whom the goods, services, accommodation or facilities were indicated as being available;

     (c) the indication related to that price and was misleading as to that price only by reason of a failure by any person to follow the recommendation; and

(d) it was reasonable for the person who gave the indication to assume that the recommendation was for the most part being followed.

(5) The provisions of this section are without prejudice to the provisions of section 39 below.

(6) In this section—

"advertisement" includes a catalogue, a circular and a price list;

"cable programme service" has the same meaning as in the Cable and Broadcasting Act 1984.

DEFINITIONS

"accommodation": s.23.
"advertisement": subs. (6).
"business": s.45(1).
"cable programme service": subs. (6).
"facilities": s.22, s.23.
"goods": s.45(1).
"misleading": s.21.
"price": s.20(6).
"services": s.22.

GENERAL NOTE

The defences in this section are additional to the defence of due diligence in s.39. In each of them the burden of proof is clearly cast on the defendant (*cf.* the word "show").

Subs. (1)

This does not make it a defence simply that the defendant complied with regulations. The compliance must consist of acts or omissions "authorised for the purposes of this subsection" by regulations. This, in other words, allows the Secretary of State to spell out certain things which if the trader does them will provide him with a defence. Such regulations will mean that where they apply, the trader will be given certainty and will be able to ensure that he does not fall foul of s.20.

Subs. (2)

This should ensure that, for example, an author who is interviewed on the radio about his new book will have a defence if during the interview he should misstate the price of the book.

Subs. (3)

This is a defence of innocent publication available for newspapers, radio, television and others who publish advertisements and available also for advertising agencies who do not themselves create the advertisement.

Subs. (4)

This provides a limited defence for someone, say a manufacturer, who recommends a retail price for his product and publishes that price to the public. The defence is limited because it does not apply if it was not reasonable for the manufacturer to assume that the recommendation was for the most part being followed. What then is the position of the car manufacturer who advertises the price of his model? Presumably if he knows that there is a discount war going on among retailers, he cannot rely on this defence.

Code of practice

25.—(1) The Secretary of State may, after consulting the Director General of Fair Trading and such other persons as the Secretary of State considers it appropriate to consult, by order approve any code of practice issued (whether by the Secretary of State or another person) for the purpose of—

(a) giving practical guidance with respect to any of the requirements of section 20 above; and

(b) promoting what appear to the Secretary of State to be desirable practices as to the circumstances and manner in which any person gives an indication as to the price at which any goods, services, accommodation or facilities are available or indicates any other matter in respect of which any such indication may be misleading.

(2) A contravention of a code of practice approved under this section shall not of itself give rise to any criminal or civil liability, but in any proceedings against any person for an offence under section 20(1) or (2) above—

(a) any contravention by that person of such a code may be relied on in relation to any matter for the purpose of establishing that that person committed the offence or of negativing any defence; and

(b) compliance by that person with such a code may be relied on in relation to any matter for the purpose of showing that the commission of the offence by that person has not been established or that that person has a defence.

(3) Where the Secretary of State approves a code of practice under this section he may, after such consultation as is mentioned in subsection (1) above, at any time by order—

(a) approve any modification of the code; or

(b) withdraw his approval;

and references in subsection (2) above to a code of practice approved under this section shall be construed accordingly.

(4) The power to make an order under this section shall be exercisable by statutory instrument subject to annulment in pursuance of a resolution of either House of Parliament.

DEFINITIONS
"accommodation": s.22.
"contravention": s.45(1).
"facilities": s.22, s.23.
"goods": s.45(1).
"misleading": s.21.
"price": s.20(6).
"services": s.22.

GENERAL NOTE
It is expected that before this Part is brought into force, a code of practice drawn up by the Director General of Fair Trading will be approved under this section. During the passage of the Bill through Parliament the role for such a code of practice became a controversial issue and the government was forced to withdraw its proposal that compliance with the code of practice should be a complete defence. The effect of subs. (2) is that compliance or non-compliance with the code will simply be something to be taken into account by the court in determining whether an offence contrary to s.20 has been committed. It will therefore be possible, in theory at least, for a court to find that a trader has complied with the code but that such compliance nevertheless involved making a misleading indication. In such a case, no doubt, compliance would be a strong factor in mitigation of sentence.

Power to make regulations

26.—(1) The Secretary of State may, after consulting the Director General of Fair Trading and such other persons as the Secretary of State considers it appropriate to consult, by regulations make provision—

(a) for the purpose of regulating the circumstances and manner in which any person—

(i) gives any indication as to the price at which any goods, services, accommodation or facilities will be or are available or have been supplied or provided; or

(ii) indicates any other matter in respect of which any such indication may be misleading;

(b) for the purpose of facilitating the enforcement of the provisions of section 20 above or of any regulations made under this section.

(2) The Secretary of State shall not make regulations by virtue of subsection (1)(a) above except in relation to—

(a) indications given by persons in the course of business; and

(b) such indications given otherwise than in the course of business as—

   (i) are given by or on behalf of persons by whom accommodation is provided to others by means of leases or licences; and

   (ii) relate to goods, services or facilities supplied or provided to those others in connection with the provision of the accommodation.

(3) Without prejudice to the generality of subsection (1) above, regulations under this section may—

(a) prohibit an indication as to a price from referring to such matters as may be prescribed by the regulations;

(b) require an indication as to a price or other matter to be accompanied or supplemented by such explanation or such additional information as may be prescribed by the regulations;

(c) require information or explanations with respect to a price or other matter to be given to an officer of an enforcement authority and to authorise such an officer to require such information or explanations to be given;

(d) require any information or explanation provided for the purposes of any regulations made by virtue of paragraph (b) or (c) above to be accurate;

(e) prohibit the inclusion in indications as to a price or other matter of statements that the indications are not to be relied upon;

(f) provide that expressions used in any indication as to a price or other matter shall be construed in a particular way for the purposes of this Part;

(g) provide that a contravention of any provision of the regulations shall constitute a criminal offence punishable—

   (i) on conviction on indictment, by a fine;

   (ii) on summary conviction, by a fine not exceeding the statutory maximum;

(h) apply any provision of this Act which relates to a criminal offence to an offence created by virtue of paragraph (g) above.

(4) The power to make regulations under this section shall be exercisable by statutory instrument subject to annulment in pursuance of a resolution of either House of Parliament and shall include power—

(a) to make different provision for different cases; and

(b) to make such supplemental, consequential and transitional provision as the Secretary of State considers appropriate.

(5) In this section "lease" includes a sub-lease and an agreement for a lease and a statutory tenancy (within the meaning of the Landlord and Tenant Act 1985 or the Rent (Scotland) Act 1984).

DEFINITIONS

"accommodation": s.23.
"business": s.45(1).
"contravention": s.45(1).
"enforcement authority": s.45(1).
"facilities": s.22, s.23.
"goods": s.45(1).
"information": s.45(1).
"lease": subs. (5).
"misleading": s.21.
"officer": s.45(1).
"price": s.20(6).
"services": s.22.
"supplied": s.45(1), s.46.

PART IV

ENFORCEMENT OF PARTS II AND III

Enforcement

27.—(1) Subject to the following provisions of this section—
  (a) it shall be the duty of every weights and measures authority in Great Britain to enforce within their area the safety provisions and the provisions made by or under Part III of this Act; and
  (b) it shall be the duty of every district council in Northern Ireland to enforce within their area the safety provisions.

(2) The Secretary of State may by regulations—
  (a) wholly or partly transfer any duty imposed by subsection (1) above on a weights and measures authority or a district council in Northern Ireland to such other person who has agreed to the transfer as is specified in the regulations;
  (b) relieve such an authority or council of any such duty so far as it is exercisable in relation to such goods as may be described in the regulations.

(3) The power to make regulations under subsection (2) above shall be exercisable by statutory instrument subject to annulment in pursuance of a resolution of either House of Parliament and shall include power—
  (a) to make different provision for different cases; and
  (b) to make such supplemental, consequential and transitional provision as the Secretary of State considers appropriate.

(4) Nothing in this section shall authorise any weights and measures authority, or any person on whom functions are conferred by regulations under subsection (2) above, to bring proceedings in Scotland for an offence.

DEFINITIONS
  "goods": s.45(1).
  "safety provision": s.45(1).

Test purchases

28.—(1) An enforcement authority shall have power, for the purpose of ascertaining whether any safety provision or any provision made by or under Part III of this Act has been contravened in relation to any goods, services, accommodation or facilities—
  (a) to make, or to authorise an officer of the authority to make, any purchase of any goods; or
  (b) to secure, or to authorise an officer of the authority to secure, the provision of any services, accommodation or facilities.

(2) Where—
  (a) any goods purchased under this section by or on behalf of an enforcement authority are submitted to a test; and
  (b) the test leads to—
      (i) the bringing of proceedings for an offence in respect of a contravention in relation to the goods of any safety provision or of any provision made by or under Part III of this Act or for the forfeiture of the goods under section 16 or 17 above; or
      (ii) the serving of a suspension notice in respect of any goods; and
  (c) the authority is requested to do so and it is practicable for the authority to comply with the request,

the authority shall allow the person from whom the goods were purchased or any person who is a party to the proceedings or has an interest in any goods to which the notice relates to have the goods tested.

(3) The Secretary of State may by regulations provide that any test of goods purchased under this section by or on behalf of an enforcement authority shall—

(a) be carried out at the expense of the authority in a manner and by a person prescribed by or determined under the regulations; or

(b) be carried out either as mentioned in paragraph (a) above or by the authority in a manner prescribed by the regulations.

(4) The power to make regulations under subsection (3) above shall be exercisable by statutory instrument subject to annulment in pursuance of a resolution of either House of Parliament and shall include power—

(a) to make different provision for different cases; and

(b) to make such supplemental, consequential and transitional provision as the Secretary of State considers appropriate.

(5) Nothing in this section shall authorise the acquisition by or on behalf of an enforcement authority of any interest in land.

DEFINITIONS
   "accommodation": s.23.
   "contravened", "contravention": s.45(1).
   "enforcement authority": s.45(1).
   "facilities": s.22, s.23.
   "goods": s.45(1).
   "officer": s.45(1).
   "safety provision": s.45(1).
   "services": s.22.
   "suspension notice": s.14, s.45(1).

Powers of search etc.

29.—(1) Subject to the following provisions of this Part, a duly authorised officer of an enforcement authority may at any reasonable hour and on production, if required, of his credentials exercise any of the powers conferred by the following provisions of this section.

(2) The officer may, for the purpose of ascertaining whether there has been any contravention of any safety provision or of any provision made by or under Part III of this Act, inspect any goods and enter any premises other than premises occupied only as a person's residence.

(3) The officer may, for the purpose of ascertaining whether there has been any contravention of any safety provision, examine any procedure (including any arrangements for carrying out a test) connected with the production of any goods.

(4) If the officer has reasonable grounds for suspecting that any goods are manufactured or imported goods which have not been supplied in the United Kingdom since they were manufactured or imported he may—

(a) for the purpose of ascertaining whether there has been any contravention of any safety provision in relation to the goods, require any person carrying on a business, or employed in connection with a business, to produce any records relating to the business;

(b) for the purpose of ascertaining (by testing or otherwise) whether there has been any such contravention, seize and detain the goods;

(c) take copies of, or of any entry in, any records produced by virtue of paragraph (a) above.

(5) If the officer has reasonable grounds for suspecting that there has been a contravention in relation to any goods of any safety provision or of any provision made by or under Part III of this Act, he may—

(a) for the purpose of ascertaining whether there has been any such contravention, require any person carrying on a business, or employed in connection with a business, to produce any records relating to the business;

(b) for the purpose of ascertaining (by testing or otherwise) whether there has been any such contravention, seize and detain the goods;

(c) take copies of, or of any entry in, any records produced by virtue of paragraph (a) above.

(6) The officer may seize and detain—

(a) any goods or records which he has reasonable grounds for believing may be required as evidence in proceedings for an offence in respect of a contravention of any safety provision or of any provision made by or under Part III of this Act;

(b) any goods which he has reasonable grounds for suspecting may be liable to be forfeited under section 16 or 17 above.

(7) If and to the extent that it is reasonably necessary to do so to prevent a contravention of any safety provision or of any provision made by or under Part III of this Act, the officer may, for the purpose of exercising his power under subsection (4), (5) or (6) above to seize any goods or records—

(a) require any person having authority to do so to open any container or to open any vending machine; and

(b) himself open or break open any such container or machine where a requirement made under paragraph (a) above in relation to the container or machine has not been complied with.

DEFINITIONS
  "business": s.45(1).
  "contravention": s.45(1).
  "enforcement authority": s.45(1).
  "goods": s.45(1).
  "officer": s.45(1).
  "premises": s.45(1).
  "records": s.45(1).
  "safety provision": s.45(1).
  "supplied", "supply": s.45(1), s.46.

Provisions supplemental to s.29

30.—(1) An officer seizing any goods or records under section 29 above shall inform the following persons that the goods or records have been so seized, that is to say—

(a) the person from whom they are seized; and

(b) in the case of imported goods seized on any premises under the control of the Commissioners of Customs and Excise, the importer of those goods (within the meaning of the Customs and Excise Management Act 1979).

(2) If a justice of the peace—

(a) is satisfied by any written information on oath that there are reasonable grounds for believing either—

    (i) that any goods or records which any officer has power to inspect under section 29 above are on any premises and that their inspection is likely to disclose evidence that there has been a contravention of any safety provision or of any provision made by or under Part III of this Act; or

    (ii) that such a contravention has taken place, is taking place or is about to take place on any premises; and

(b) is also satisfied by any such information either

    (i) that admission to the premises has been or is likely to be refused and that notice of intention to apply for a warrant under this subsection has been given to the occupier; or

(ii) that an application for admission, or the giving of such a notice, would defeat the object of the entry or that the premises are unoccupied or that the occupier is temporarily absent and it might defeat the object of the entry to await his return,

the justice may by warrant under his hand, which shall continue in force for a period of one month, authorise any officer of an enforcement authority to enter the premises, if need be by force.

(3) An officer entering any premises by virtue of section 29 above or a warrant under subsection (2) above may take with him such other persons and such equipment as may appear to him necessary.

(4) On leaving any premises which a person is authorised to enter by a warrant under subsection (2) above, that person shall, if the premises are unoccupied or the occupier is temporarily absent, leave the premises as effectively secured against trespassers as he found them.

(5) If any person who is not an officer of an enforcement authority purports to act as such under section 29 above or this section he shall be guilty of an offence and liable on summary conviction to a fine not exceeding level 5 on the standard scale.

(6) Where any goods seized by an officer under section 29 above are submitted to a test, the officer shall inform the persons mentioned in subsection (1) above of the result of the test and, if—

(a) proceedings are brought for an offence in respect of a contravention in relation to the goods of any safety provision or of any provision made by or under Part III of this Act or for the forfeiture of the goods under section 16 or 17 above, or a suspension notice is served in respect of any goods; and

(b) the officer is requested to do so and it is practicable to comply with the request,

the officer shall allow any person who is a party to the proceedings or, as the case may be, has an interest in the goods to which the notice relates to have the goods tested.

(7) The Secretary of State may by regulations provide that any test of goods seized under section 29 above by an officer of an enforcement authority shall—

(a) be carried out at the expense of the authority in a manner and by a person prescribed by or determined under the regulations; or

(b) be carried out either as mentioned in paragraph (a) above or by the authority in a manner prescribed by the regulations.

(8) The power to make regulations under subsection (7) above shall be exercisable by statutory instrument subject to annulment in pursuance of a resolution of either House of Parliament and shall include power—

(a) to make different provision for different cases; and

(b) to make such supplemental, consequential and transitional provision as the Secretary of State considers appropriate.

(9) In the application of this section to Scotland, the reference in subsection (2) above to a justice of the peace shall include a reference to a sheriff and the references to written information on oath shall be construed as references to evidence on oath.

(10) In the application of this section to Northern Ireland, the references in subsection (2) above to any information on oath shall be construed as references to any complaint on oath.

DEFINITIONS
"contravention": s.45(1).
"enforcement authority": s.45(1).

"goods": s.45(1).
"information": s.45(1).
"notice": s.45(1).
"officer": s.45(1).
"premises": s.45(1).
"records": s.45(1).
"safety provision": s.45(1).
"suspension notice": s.14, s.45(1).

Power of customs officer to detain goods

31.—(1) A customs officer may, for the purpose of facilitating the exercise by an enforcement authority or officer of such an authority of any functions conferred on the authority or officer by or under Part II of this Act, or by or under this Part in its application for the purposes of the safety provisions, seize any imported goods and detain them for not more than two working days.

(2) Anything seized and detained under this section shall be dealt with during the period of its detention in such manner as the Commissioners of Customs and Excise may direct.

(3) In subsection (1) above the reference to two working days is a reference to a period of forty-eight hours calculated from the time when the goods in question are seized but disregarding so much of any period as falls on a Saturday or Sunday or on Christmas Day, Good Friday or a day which is a bank holiday under the Banking and Financial Dealings Act 1971 in the part of the United Kingdom where the goods are seized.

(4) In this section and section 32 below "customs officer" means any officer within the meaning of the Customs and Excise Management Act 1979.

DEFINITIONS
"customs officer": subs. (4).
"enforcement authority": s.45(1).
"goods": s.45(1).
"officer": s.45(1).
"safety provision": s.45(1).

Obstruction of authorised officer

32.—(1) Any person who—
   (a) intentionally obstructs any officer of an enforcement authority who is acting in pursuance of any provision of this Part or any customs officer who is so acting; or
   (b) intentionally fails to comply with any requirement made of him by any officer of an enforcement authority under any provision of this Part; or
   (c) without reasonable cause fails to give any officer of an enforcement authority who is so acting any other assistance or information which the officer may reasonably require of him for the purposes of the exercise of the officer's functions under any provision of this Part,
shall be guilty of an offence and liable on summary conviction to a fine not exceeding level 5 on the standard scale.

(2) A person shall be guilty of an offence if, in giving any information which is required of him by virtue of subsection (1)(c) above—
   (a) he makes any statement which he knows is false in a material particular; or
   (b) he recklessly makes a statement which is false in a material particular.

(3) A person guilty of an offence under subsection (2) above shall be liable—

(a) on conviction on indictment, to a fine;

(b) on summary conviction, to a fine not exceeding the statutory maximum.

DEFINITIONS
"customs officer": s.31(4).
"enforcement authority": s.45(1).
"information": s.45(1).
"officer": s.45(1).

Appeals against detention of goods

33.—(1) Any person having an interest in any goods which are for the time being detained under any provision of this Part by an enforcement authority or by an officer of such an authority may apply for an order requiring the goods to be released to him or to another person.

(2) An application under this section may be made—

(a) to any magistrates' court in which proceedings have been brought in England and Wales or Northern Ireland—

(i) for an offence in respect of a contravention in relation to the goods of any safety provision or of any provision made by or under Part III of this Act; or

(ii) for the forfeiture of the goods under section 16 above;

(b) where no such proceedings have been so brought, by way of complaint to a magistrates' court; or

(c) in Scotland, by summary application to the sheriff.

(3) On an application under this section to a magistrates' court or to the sheriff, an order requiring goods to be released shall be made only if the court or sheriff is satisfied—

(a) that proceedings—

(i) for an offence in respect of a contravention in relation to the goods of any safety provision or of any provision made by or under Part III of this Act; or

(ii) for the forfeiture of the goods under section 16 or 17 above, have not been brought or, having been brought, have been concluded without the goods being forfeited; and

(b) where no such proceedings have been brought, that more than six months have elapsed since the goods were seized.

(4) Any person aggrieved by an order made under this section by a magistrates' court in England and Wales or Northern Ireland, or by a decision of such a court not to make such an order, may appeal against that order or decision—

(a) in England and Wales, to the Crown Court;

(b) in Northern Ireland, to the county court;

and an order so made may contain such provision as appears to the court to be appropriate for delaying the coming into force of the order pending the making and determination of any appeal (including any application under section 111 of the Magistrates' Courts Act 1980 or Article 146 of the Magistrates' Courts (Northern Ireland) Order 1981 (statement of case)).

DEFINITIONS
"contravention": s.45(1).
"enforcement authority": s.45(1).
"goods": s.45(1).
"magistrates' court": s.45(1).
"officer": s.45(1).
"safety provision": s.45(1).

Compensation for seizure and detention

34.—(1) Where an officer of an enforcement authority exercises any power under section 29 above to seize and detain goods, the enforcement authority shall be liable to pay compensation to any person having an interest in the goods in respect of any loss or damage caused by reason of the exercise of the power if—

 (a) there has been no contravention in relation to the goods of any safety provision or of any provision made by or under Part III of this Act; and

 (b) the exercise of the power is not attributable to any neglect or default by that person.

(2) Any disputed question as to the right to or the amount of any compensation payable under this section shall be determined by arbitration or, in Scotland, by a single arbiter appointed, failing agreement between the parties, by the sheriff.

DEFINITIONS
 "contravention": s.45(1).
 "enforcement authority": s.45(1).
 "goods": s.45(1).
 "officer": s.45(1).
 "safety provision": s.45(1).

Recovery of expenses of enforcement

35.—(1) This section shall apply where a court—

 (a) convicts a person of an offence in respect of a contravention in relation to any goods of any safety provision or of any provision made by or under Part III of this Act; or

 (b) makes an order under section 16 or 17 above for the forfeiture of any goods.

(2) The court may (in addition to any other order it may make as to costs or expenses) order the person convicted or, as the case may be, any person having an interest in the goods to reimburse an enforcement authority for any expenditure which has been or may be incurred by that authority—

 (a) in connection with any seizure or detention of the goods by or on behalf of the authority; or

 (b) in connection with any compliance by the authority with directions given by the court for the purposes of any order for the forfeiture of the goods.

DEFINITIONS
 "contravention": s.45(1).
 "enforcement authority": s.45(1).
 "goods": s.45(1).
 "safety provision": s.45(1).

PART V

MISCELLANEOUS AND SUPPLEMENTAL

Amendments of Part I of the Health and Safety at Work etc. Act 1974

36. Part I of the Health and Safety at Work etc. Act 1974 (which includes provision with respect to the safety of certain articles and substances) shall have effect with the amendments specified in Schedule

3 to this Act; and, accordingly, the general purposes of that Part of that Act shall include the purpose of protecting persons from the risks protection from which would not be afforded by virtue of that Part but for those amendments.

<small>DEFINITIONS</small>
  "enforcement authority": s.45(1).
  "goods": s.45(1).
  "information": s.45(1).
  "officer": s.45(1).
  "safety provisions": s.45(1).

Power of Commissioners of Customs and Excise to disclose information

37.—(1) If they think it appropriate to do so for the purpose of facilitating the exercise by any person to whom subsection (2) below applies of any functions conferred on that person by or under Part II of this Act, or by or under Part IV of this Act in its application for the purposes of the safety provisions, the Commissioners of Customs and Excise may authorise the disclosure to that person of any information obtained for the purposes of the exercise by the Commissioners of their functions in relation to imported goods.

(2) This subsection applies to an enforcement authority and to any officer of an enforcement authority.

(3) A disclosure of information made to any person under subsection (1) above shall be made in such manner as may be directed by the Commissioners of Customs and Excise and may be made through such persons acting on behalf of that person as may be so directed.

(4) Information may be disclosed to a person under subsection (1) above whether or not the disclosure of the information has been requested by or on behalf of that person.

Restrictions on disclosure of information

38.—(1) Subject to the following provisions of this section, a person shall be guilty of an offence if he discloses any information—
  (a) which was obtained by him in consequence of its being given to any person in compliance with any requirement imposed by safety regulations or regulations under section 26 above;
  (b) which consists in a secret manufacturing process or a trade secret and was obtained by him in consequence of the inclusion of the information—
    (i) in written or oral representations made for the purposes of Part I or II of Schedule 2 to this Act; or
    (ii) in a statement of a witness in connection with any such oral representations;
  (c) which was obtained by him in consequence of the exercise by the Secretary of State of the power conferred by section 18 above;
  (d) which was obtained by him in consequence of the exercise by any person of any power conferred by Part IV of this Act; or
  (e) which was disclosed to or through him under section 37 above.

(2) Subsection (1) above shall not apply to a disclosure of information if the information is publicised information or the disclosure is made—
  (a) for the purpose of facilitating the exercise of a relevant person's functions under this Act or any enactment or subordinate legislation mentioned in subsection (3) below;
  (b) for the purposes of compliance with a Community obligation; or
  (c) in connection with the investigation of any criminal offence or for the purposes of any civil or criminal proceedings.

(3) The enactments and subordinate legislation referred to in subsection (2)(a) above are—

  (a) the Trade Descriptions Act 1968;
  (b) Parts II and III and section 125 of the Fair Trading Act 1973;
  (c) the relevant statutory provisions within the meaning of Part I of the Health and Safety at Work etc. Act 1974 or within the meaning of the Health and Safety at Work (Northern Ireland) Order 1978;
  (d) the Consumer Credit Act 1974;
  (e) the Restrictive Trade Practices Act 1976;
  (f) the Resale Prices Act 1976;
  (g) the Estate Agents Act 1979;
  (h) the Competition Act 1980;
  (i) the Telecommunications Act 1984;
  (j) the Airports Act 1986;
  (k) the Gas Act 1986;
  (l) any subordinate legislation made (whether before or after the passing of this Act) for the purpose of securing compliance with the Directive of the Council of the European Communities, dated 10th September 1984 (No. 84/450/EEC) on the approximation of the laws, regulations and administrative provisions of the member States concerning misleading advertising.

(4) In subsection (2)(a) above the reference to a person's functions shall include a reference to any function of making, amending or revoking any regulations or order.

(5) A person guilty of an offence under this section shall be liable—

  (a) on summary conviction, to a fine not exceeding the statutory maximum;
  (b) on conviction on indictment, to imprisonment for a term not exceeding two years or to a fine or to both.

(6) In this section—

"publicised information" means any information which has been disclosed in any civil or criminal proceedings or is or has been required to be contained in a warning published in pursuance of a notice to warn; and

"relevant person" means any of the following, that is to say—

  (a) a Minister of the Crown, Government department or Northern Ireland department;
  (b) the Monopolies and Mergers Commission, the Director General of Fair Trading, the Director General of Telecommunications or the Director General of Gas Supply;
  (c) the Civil Aviation Authority;
  (d) any weights and measures authority, any district council in Northern Ireland or any person on whom functions are conferred by regulations under section 27(2) above;
  (e) any person who is an enforcing authority for the purposes of Part I of the Health and Safety at Work etc. Act 1974 or for the purposes of Part II of the Health and Safety at Work (Northern Ireland) Order 1978.

DEFINITIONS
"information": s.45(1).
"notice to warn": s.13(1)(b), s.45(1).
"publicised information": subs. (6).
"relevant person": subs. (6).
"safety regulations": s.11, s.45(1).

Defence of due diligence

39.—(1) Subject to the following provisions of this section, in proceedings against any person for an offence to which this section applies it shall be a defence for that person to show that he took all reasonable steps and exercised all due diligence to avoid committing the offence.

(2) Where in any proceedings against any person for such an offence the defence provided by subsection (1) above involves an allegation that the commission of the offence was due—

(a) to the act or default of another; or

(b) to reliance on information given by another,

that person shall not, without the leave of the court, be entitled to rely on the defence unless, not less than seven clear days before the hearing of the proceedings, he has served a notice under subsection (3) below on the person bringing the proceedings.

(3) A notice under this subsection shall give such information identifying or assisting in the identification of the person who committed the act or default or gave the information as is in the possession of the person serving the notice at the time he serves it.

(4) It is hereby declared that a person shall not be entitled to rely on the defence provided by subsection (1) above by reason of his reliance on information supplied by another, unless he shows that it was reasonable in all the circumstances for him to have relied on the information, having regard in particular—

(a) to the steps which he took, and those which might reasonably have been taken, for the purpose of verifying the information; and

(b) to whether he had any reason to disbelieve the information.

(5) This section shall apply to an offence under section 10, 12(1), (2) or (3), 13(4), 14(6) or 20(1) above.

DEFINITIONS
"information": s.45(1).
"notice": s.45(1).

GENERAL NOTE
This defence is a refinement of the defence in s.24 of the Trade Descriptions Act 1968.

Liability of persons other than principal offender

40.—(1) Where the commission by any person of an offence to which section 39 above applies is due to an act or default committed by some other person in the course of any business of his, the other person shall be guilty of the offence and may be proceeded against and punished by virtue of this subsection whether or not proceedings are taken against the first-mentioned person.

(2) Where a body corporate is guilty of an offence under this Act (including where it is so guilty by virtue of subsection (1) above) in respect of any act or default which is shown to have been committed with the consent or connivance of, or to be attributable to any neglect on the part of, any director, manager, secretary or other similar officer of the body corporate or any person who was purporting to act in any such capacity he, as well as the body corporate, shall be guilty of that offence and shall be liable to be proceeded against and punished accordingly.

(3) Where the affairs of a body corporate are managed by its members, subsection (2) above shall apply in relation to the acts and defaults of a member in connection with his functions of management as if he were a director of the body corporate.

DEFINITION
"business": s.45(1).

GENERAL NOTE
This section is the equivalent in this Act of s.23 of the Trade Descriptions Act 1968. Clearly it is intended to catch the real culprit where the person who at first sight appears to have committed an offence has a good defence under s.39, namely that he took all reasonable steps and exercised all due diligence but it was someone else's fault. This section, in saying "Where the commission by any person of an offence to which section 39 applies. . . ." means "Where the commission by any person of one of the offences listed in section 39(5), or what would have been such an offence but for the defence in section 39. . . ." (see *Coupe* v. *Guyett* [1973] 1 W.L.R. 669).

The inclusion of the phrase "in the course of any business of his" means that the person referred to above as the real culprit can not be caught unless he was acting in the course of a business. This is different from the position under s.23 of the Trade Descriptions Act 1968, where no similar phrase appears with the result that non-traders can get caught, as occurred in *Olgeirsson* v. *Kitching* [1986] 1 W.L.R. 304. For cases on "in the course of any business" and similar expressions, see the note to s.4(1)(c) above.

Civil proceedings

41.—(1) An obligation imposed by safety regulations shall be a duty owed to any person who may be affected by a contravention of the obligation and, subject to any provision to the contrary in the regulations and to the defences and other incidents applying to actions for breach of statutory duty, a contravention of any such obligation shall be actionable accordingly.

(2) This Act shall not be construed as conferring any other right of action in civil proceedings, apart from the right conferred by virtue of Part I of this Act, in respect of any loss or damage suffered in consequence of a contravention of a safety provision or of a provision made by or under Part III of this Act.

(3) Subject to any provision to the contrary in the agreement itself, an agreement shall not be void or unenforceable by reason only of a contravention of a safety provision or of a provision made by or under Part III of this Act.

(4) Liability by virtue of subsection (1) above shall not be limited or excluded by any contract term, by any notice or (subject to the power contained in subsection (1) above to limit or exclude it in safety regulations) by any other provision.

(5) Nothing in subsection (1) above shall prejudice the operation of section 12 of the Nuclear Installations Act 1965 (rights to compensation for certain breaches of duties confined to rights under that Act).

(6) In this section "damage" includes personal injury and death.

DEFINITIONS
   "contravention": s.45(1).
   "damage": subs. (6).
   "personal injury": s.45(1).
   "safety provision": s.45(1).
   "safety regulations": s.45(1).

GENERAL NOTE
The possibility of an action for statutory duty exists where there is a contravention of safety regulations, but not, apparently, where there is a contravention of, or failure to comply with, a suspension notice, prohibition notice or a notice to warn.

Reports etc.

42.—(1) It shall be the duty of the Secretary of State at least once in every five years to lay before each House of Parliament a report on the exercise during the period to which the report relates of the functions which under Part II of this Act, or under Part IV of this Act in its application for the purposes of the safety provisions, are exercisable by the Secretary of State, weights and measures authorities, district councils in Northern Ireland and persons on whom functions are conferred by regulations made under section 27(2) above.

(2) The Secretary of State may from time to time prepare and lay before each House of Parliament such other reports on the exercise of those functions as he considers appropriate.

(3) Every weights and measures authority, every district council in Northern Ireland and every person on whom functions are conferred by regulations under subsection (2) of section 27 above shall, whenever the Secretary of State so directs, make a report to the Secretary of State on the exercise of the functions exercisable by that authority or council under that section or by that person by virtue of any such regulations.

(4) A report under subsection (3) above shall be in such form and shall contain such particulars as are specified in the direction of the Secretary of State.

(5) The first report under subsection (1) above shall be laid before each House of Parliament not more than five years after the laying of the last report under section 8(2) of the Consumer Safety Act 1978.

DEFINITIONS
"safety provision": s.45(1).

Financial provisions

43.—(1) There shall be paid out of money provided by Parliament—
    (a) any expenses incurred or compensation payable by a Minister of the Crown or Government department in consequence of any provision of this Act; and
    (b) any increase attributable to this Act in the sums payable out of money so provided under any other Act.

(2) Any sums received by a Minister of the Crown or Government department by virtue of this Act shall be paid into the Consolidated Fund.

Service of documents etc.

44.—(1) Any document required or authorised by virtue of this Act to be served on a person may be so served—
    (a) by delivering it to him or by leaving it at his proper address or by sending it by post to him at that address; or
    (b) if the person is a body corporate, by serving it in accordance with paragraph (a) above on the secretary or clerk of that body; or
    (c) if the person is a partnership, by serving it in accordance with that paragraph on a partner or on a person having control or management of the partnership business.

(2) For the purposes of subsection (1) above, and for the purposes of section 7 of the Interpretation Act 1978 (which relates to the service of documents by post) in its application to that subsection, the proper address of any person on whom a document is to be served by virtue of this Act shall be his last known address except that—
    (a) in the case of service on a body corporate or its secretary or clerk, it shall be the address of the registered or principal office of the body corporate;
    (b) in the case of service on a partnership or a partner or a person having the control or management of a partnership business, it shall be the principal office of the partnership;
and for the purposes of this subsection the principal office of a company registered outside the United Kingdom or of a partnership carrying on

C.L. STATS.—3 B.V.S.—5

business outside the United Kingdom is its principal office within the United Kingdom.

(3) The Secretary of State may by regulations make provision for the manner in which any information is to be given to any person under any provision of Part IV of this Act.

(4) Without prejudice to the generality of subsection (3) above regulations made by the Secretary of State may prescribe the person, or manner of determining the person, who is to be treated for the purposes of section 28(2) or 30 above as the person from whom any goods were purchased or seized where the goods were purchased or seized from a vending machine.

(5) The power to make regulations under subsection (3) or (4) above shall be exercisable by statutory instrument subject to annulment in pursuance of a resolution of either House of Parliament and shall include power—

(a) to make different provision for different cases; and

(b) to make such supplemental, consequential and transitional provision as the Secretary of State considers appropriate.

DEFINITIONS
  "information": s.45(1).

Interpretation

45.—(1) In this Act, except in so far as the context otherwise requires—

"aircraft" includes gliders, balloons and hovercraft;

"business" includes a trade or profession and the activities of a professional or trade association or of a local authority or other public authority;

"conditional sale agreement", "credit—sale agreement" and "hire-purchase agreement" have the same meanings as in the Consumer Credit Act 1974 but as if in the definitions in that Act "goods" had the same meaning as in this Act;

"contravention" includes a failure to comply and cognate expressions shall be construed accordingly;

"enforcement authority" means the Secretary of State, any other Minister of the Crown in charge of a Government department, any such department and any authority, council or other person on whom functions under this Act are conferred by or under section 27 above;

"gas" has the same meaning as in Part I of the Gas Act 1986;

"goods" includes substances, growing crops and things comprised in land by virtue of being attached to it and any ship, aircraft or vehicle;

"information" includes accounts, estimates and returns;

"magistrates' court", in relation to Northern Ireland, means a court of summary jurisdiction;

"mark" and "trade mark" have the same meanings as in the Trade Marks Act 1938;

"modifications" includes additions, alterations and omissions and cognate expressions shall be construed accordingly;

"motor vehicle" has the same meaning as in the Road Traffic Act 1972;

"notice" means a notice in writing;

"notice to warn" means a notice under section 13(1)(b) above;

"officer", in relation to an enforcement authority, means a person authorised in writing to assist the authority in carrying out its functions under or for the purposes of the enforcement of any of the safety provisions or of any of the provisions made by or under Part III of this Act;

"personal injury" includes any disease and any other impairment of a person's physical or mental condition;

"premises" includes any place and any ship, aircraft or vehicle;

"prohibition notice" means a notice under section 13(1)(a) above;

"records" includes any books or documents and any records in non-documentary form;

"safety provision" means the general safety requirement in section 10 above or any provision of safety regulations, a prohibition notice or a suspension notice;

"safety regulations" means regulations under section 11 above;

"ship" includes any boat and any other description of vessel used in navigation;

"subordinate legislation" has the same meaning as in the Interpretation Act 1978;

"substance" means any natural or artificial substance, whether in solid, liquid or gaseous form or in the form of a vapour, and includes substances that are comprised in or mixed with other goods;

"supply" and cognate expressions shall be construed in accordance with section 46 below;

"suspension notice" means a notice under section 14 above.

(2) Except in so far as the context otherwise requires, references in this Act to a contravention of a safety provision shall, in relation to any goods, include references to anything which would constitute such a contravention if the goods were supplied to any person.

(3) References in this Act to any goods in relation to which any safety provision has been or may have been contravened shall include references to any goods which it is not reasonably practicable to separate from any such goods.

(4) Section 68(2) of the Trade Marks Act 1938 (construction of references to use of a mark) shall apply for the purposes of this Act as it applies for the purposes of that Act.

(5) In Scotland, any reference in this Act to things comprised in land by virtue of being attached to it is a reference to moveables which have become heritable by accession to heritable property.

DEFINITIONS

"aircraft": subs. (1).
"contravention": subs. (1).
"enforcement authority": subs. (1).
"goods": subs. (1).
"prohibition notice": subs. (1).
"safety provision": subs. (1).
"safety regulations": subs. (1).
"ship": this section, subs. (1).
"substances": subs. (1).
"supplied", "supply": subs. (1), s.46.
"suspension notice": subs. (1).

Meaning of "supply"

46.—(1) Subject to the following provisions of this section, references in this Act to supplying goods shall be construed as references to doing any of the following, whether as principal or agent, that is to say—

(a) selling, hiring out or lending the goods;

(b) entering into a hire-purchase agreement to furnish the goods;

(c) the performance of any contract for work and materials to furnish the goods;

(d) providing the goods in exchange for any consideration (including trading stamps) other than money;

(e) providing the goods in or in connection with the performance of any statutory function; or

(f) giving the goods as a prize or otherwise making a gift of the goods;

and, in relation to gas or water, those references shall be construed as including references to providing the service by which the gas or water is made available for use.

(2) For the purposes of any reference in this Act to supplying goods, where a person ("the ostensible supplier") supplies goods to another person ("the customer") under a hire-purchase agreement, conditional sale agreement or credit-sale agreement or under an agreement for the hiring of goods (other than a hire-purchase agreement) and the ostensible supplier—

(a) carries on the business of financing the provision of goods for others by means of such agreements; and

(b) in the course of that business acquired his interest in the goods supplied to the customer as a means of financing the provision of them for the customer by a further person ("the effective supplier"),

the effective supplier and not the ostensible supplier shall be treated as supplying the goods to the customer.

(3) Subject to subsection (4) below, the performance of any contract by the erection of any building or structure on any land or by the carrying out of any other building works shall be treated for the purposes of this Act as a supply of goods in so far as, but only in so far as, it involves the provision of any goods to any person by means of their incorporation into the building, structure or works.

(4) Except for the purposes of, and in relation to, notices to warn or any provision made by or under Part III of this Act, references in this Act to supplying goods shall not include references to supplying goods comprised in land where the supply is effected by the creation or disposal of an interest in the land.

(5) Except in Part I of this Act references in this Act to a person's supplying goods shall be confined to references to that person's supplying goods in the course of a business of his, but for the purposes of this subsection it shall be immaterial whether the business is a business of dealing in the goods.

(6) For the purposes of subsection (5) above goods shall not be treated as supplied in the course of a business if they are supplied, in pursuance of an obligation arising under or in connection with the insurance of the goods, to the person with whom they were insured.

(7) Except for the purposes of, and in relation to, prohibition notices or suspension notices, references in Parts II to IV of this Act to supplying goods shall not include—

(a) references to supplying goods where the person supplied carries on a business of buying goods of the same description as those goods and repairing or reconditioning them;

(b) references to supplying goods by a sale of articles as scrap (that is to say, for the value of materials included in the articles rather than for the value of the articles themselves).

(8) Where any goods have at any time been supplied by being hired out or lent to any person, neither a continuation or renewal of the hire or loan (whether on the same or different terms) nor any transaction for the transfer after that time of any interest in the goods to the person to whom they were hired or lent shall be treated for the purposes of this Act as a further supply of the goods to that person.

(9) A ship, aircraft or motor vehicle shall not be treated for the purposes of this Act as supplied to any person by reason only that services consisting in the carriage of goods or passengers in that ship, aircraft or vehicle, or in its use for any other purpose, are provided to that person in pursuance of an agreement relating to the use of the ship, aircraft or vehicle for a particular period or for particular voyages, flights or journeys.

DEFINITIONS
  "aircraft": s.45(1).
  "business": s.45(1).
  "conditional sale agreement": s.45(1).
  "credit sale agreement": s.45(1).
  "gas": s.45(1).
  "goods": s.45(1).
  "hire-purchase agreement": s.45(1).
  "notice to warn": s.13(1)(b), s.45(1).
  "prohibition notice": s.13(1)(a), s.45(1).
  "suspension notice": s.14, s.45(1).
  "vehicle": s.45(1).

GENERAL NOTE

Subs. (1)
  Subs. (1) sets out what amounts to "supplying" and the later subsections are exceptions or qualifications to that general provision. Subs. (1) makes clear, *inter alia*, that British Gas are "suppliers" of gas and the water boards, *e.g.* Thames Water, are "suppliers" of water.

Subs. (2)
  This deals with the commonplace triangular transaction where a finance company or leasing company buys goods from a dealer in order to supply them to a customer on hire, hire-purchase, conditional sale or credit sale terms. Such a finance or leasing company is, in this subsection, referred to as the "ostensible supplier." The effect of the subsection is that the finance or leasing company is not for the purposes of this Act regarded as a supplier. At least, that is the case where the reason that the finance or leasing company acquired the goods was so that it could thereby finance the acquisition of the goods by the customer from the dealer. Thus the finance company can not be liable as supplier under Pts. 1 or 2 of this Act. The dealer is instead regarded as the "supplier" who supplies the goods to the customer.

Subss. (3) and (4)
  The effect of these two subsections seems to be to make an important distinction between a builder who carries out work on a customer's land and a builder who carries out work on his own land and then conveys the land (together with the work already carried out in it) to a customer. The former will be a "supplier" of the bricks, tiles and cement, etc., used in the building work. The latter apparently will not, except in relation to certain matters in Pt. 2 of the Act.

Subs. (5)
  For cases on "in the course of a business" and similar expressions, see the note to s.4(1)(c).

Subs. (7)
  A repairer could be a "supplier". When he returns goods which had been left with him for repair he would not be a supplier of those goods because that would not fall within the governing subsection (subs. (1)). He would, however, be a supplier of any goods, *e.g.* replacement parts, which had been incorporated by him in the repair. Subs. (7)(a) merely refers to the repairer who *buys* goods and then reconditions or repairs them; if such a repairer re-sells the goods he is a "supplier". The person who sold them *to* the repairer will not be.

Subs. (9)
  If British Airways fly a passenger in one of their planes, they do not thereby become a "supplier" of the plane. They will therefore not be liable under Pt. 1 as supplier of a

defective plane (if it is defective). Nor will they be liable as "importer" unless they had (a) imported it from outside the EEC, and (b) done so in order to "supply", *e.g.* lease or sell, it (see s.2(2)(c) and the note to s.4(1)(b)).

Savings for certain privileges

47.—(1) Nothing in this Act shall be taken as requiring any person to produce any records if he would be entitled to refuse to produce those records in any proceedings in any court on the grounds that they are the subject of legal professional privilege or, in Scotland, that they contain a confidential communication made by or to an advocate or solicitor in that capacity, or as authorising any person to take possession of any records which are in the possession of a person who would be so entitled.

(2) Nothing in this Act shall be construed as requiring a person to answer any question or give any information if to do so would incriminate that person or that person's spouse.

Definitions
  "information": s.45(1).
  "records": s.45(1).

Minor and consequential amendments and repeals

48.—(1) The enactments mentioned in Schedule 4 to this Act shall have effect subject to the amendments specified in that Schedule (being minor amendments and amendments consequential on the provisions of this Act).

(2) The following Acts shall cease to have effect, that is to say—
    (a) the Trade Descriptions Act 1972; and
    (b) the Fabrics (Misdescription) Act 1913.

(3) The enactments mentioned in Schedule 5 to this Act are hereby repealed to the extent specified in the third column of that Schedule.

Northern Ireland

49.—(1) This Act shall extend to Northern Ireland with the exception of—
    (a) the provisions of Parts I and III;
    (b) any provision amending or repealing an enactment which does not so extend; and
    (c) any other provision so far as it has effect for the purposes of, or in relation to, a provision falling within paragraph (a) or (b) above.

(2) Subject to any Order in Council made by virtue of subsection (1)(a) of section 3 of the Northern Ireland Constitution Act 1973, consumer safety shall not be a transferred matter for the purposes of that Act but shall for the purposes of subsection (2) of that section be treated as specified in Schedule 3 to that Act.

(3) An Order in Council under paragraph 1(1)(b) of Schedule 1 to the Northern Ireland Act 1974 (exercise of legislative functions for Northern Ireland) which states that it is made only for purposes corresponding to any of the provisions of this Act mentioned in subsection (1)(a) to (c) above—
    (a) shall not be subject to paragraph 1(4) and (5) of that Schedule (affirmative resolution procedure and procedure in cases of urgency); but
    (b) shall be subject to annulment in pursuance of a resolution of either House of Parliament.

Short title, commencement and transitional provision

50.—(1) This Act may be cited as the Consumer Protection Act 1987.

(2) This Act shall come into force on such day as the Secretary of State may by order made by statutory instrument appoint, and different days may be so appointed for different provisions or for different purposes.

(3) The Secretary of State shall not make an order under subsection (2) above bringing into force the repeal of the Trade Descriptions Act 1972, a repeal of any provision of that Act or a repeal of that Act or of any provision of it for any purposes, unless a draft of the order has been laid before, and approved by a resolution of, each House of Parliament.

(4) An order under subsection (2) above bringing a provision into force may contain such transitional provision in connection with the coming into force of that provision as the Secretary of State considers appropriate.

(5) Without prejudice to the generality of the power conferred by subsection (4) above, the Secretary of State may by order provide for any regulations made under the Consumer Protection Act 1961 or the Consumer Protection Act (Northern Ireland) 1965 to have effect as if made under section 11 above and for any such regulations to have effect with such modifications as he considers appropriate for that purpose.

(6) The power of the Secretary of State by order to make such provision as is mentioned in subsection (5) above, shall, in so far as it is not exercised by an order under subsection (2) above, be exercisable by statutory instrument subject to annulment in pursuance of a resolution of either House of Parliament.

(7) Nothing in this Act or in any order under subsection (2) above shall make any person liable by virtue of Part I of this Act for any damage caused wholly or partly by a defect in a product which was supplied to any person by its producer before the coming into force of Part I of this Act.

(8) Expressions used in subsection (7) above and in Part I of this Act have the same meanings in that subsection as in that Part.

DEFINITIONS
  "damage": s.5.
  "defect": s.3.
  "producer": s.1(2).
  "product": s.1(2).
  "supplied", "supply": s.45(1), s.46.

SCHEDULES

Section 6   SCHEDULE 1

LIMITATION OF ACTIONS UNDER PART I

PART I

ENGLAND AND WALES

1. After section 11 of the Limitation Act 1980 (actions in respect of personal injuries) there shall be inserted the following section—

"**Actions in respect of defective products**
    11A.—(1) This section shall apply to an action for damages by virtue of any provision of Part I of the Consumer Protection Act 1987.

    (2) None of the time limits given in the preceding provisions of this Act shall apply to an action to which this section applies.

    (3) An action to which this section applies shall not be brought after the expiration of the period of ten years from the relevant time, within the meaning of section 4 of the said Act of 1987; and this subsection shall operate to extinguish a right of action

and shall do so whether or not that right of action had accrued, or time under the following provisions of this Act had begun to run, at the end of the said period of ten years.

(4) Subject to subsection (5) below, an action to which this section applies in which the damages claimed by the plaintiff consist of or include damages in respect of personal injuries to the plaintiff or any other person or loss of or damage to any property, shall not be brought after the expiration of the period of three years from whichever is the later of—

(a) the date on which the cause of action accrued; and

(b) the date of knowledge of the injured person or, in the case of loss of or damage to property, the date of knowledge of the plaintiff or (if earlier) of any person in whom his cause of action was previously vested.

(5) If in a case where the damages claimed by the plaintiff consist of or include damages in respect of personal injuries to the plaintiff or any other person the injured person died before the expiration of the period mentioned in subsection (4) above, that subsection shall have effect as respects the cause of action surviving for the benefit of his estate by virtue of section 1 of the Law Reform (Miscellaneous Provisions) Act 1934 as if for the reference to that period there were substituted a reference to the period of three years from whichever is the later of—

(a) the date of death; and

(b) the date of the personal representative's knowledge.

(6) For the purposes of this section 'personal representative' includes any person who is or has been a personal representative of the deceased, including an executor who has not proved the will (whether or not he has renounced probate) but not anyone appointed only as a special personal representative in relation to settled land; and regard shall be had to any knowledge acquired by any such person while a personal representative or previously.

(7) If there is more than one personal representative and their dates of knowledge are different, subsection (5)(b) above shall be read as referring to the earliest of those dates.

(8) Expressions used in this section or section 14 of this Act and in Part I of the Consumer Protection Act 1987 have the same meanings in this section or that section as in that Part; and section 1(1) of that Act (Part I to be construed as enacted for the purpose of complying with the product liability Directive) shall apply for the purpose of construing this section and the following provisions of this Act so far as they relate to an action by virtue of any provision of that Part as it applies for the purpose of construing that Part."

2. In section 12(1) of the said Act of 1980 (actions under the Fatal Accidents Act 1976), after the words "section 11" there shall be inserted the words "or 11A".

3. In section 14 of the said Act of 1980 (definition of date of knowledge), in subsection (1), at the beginning there shall be inserted the words "Subject to subsection (1A) below," and after that subsection there shall be inserted the following subsection—

"(1A) In section 11A of this Act and in section 12 of this Act so far as that section applies to an action by virtue of section 6(1)(a) of the Consumer Protection Act 1987 (death caused by defective product) references to a person's date of knowledge are references to the date on which he first had knowledge of the following facts—

(a) such facts about the damage caused by the defect as would lead a reasonable person who had suffered such damage to consider it sufficiently serious to justify his instituting proceedings for damages against a defendant who did not dispute liability and was able to satisfy a judgment; and

(b) that the damage was wholly or partly attributable to the facts and circumstances alleged to constitute the defect; and

(c) the identity of the defendant;

but, in determining the date on which a person first had such knowledge there shall be disregarded both the extent (if any) of that person's knowledge on any date of whether particular facts or circumstances would or would not, as a matter of law, constitute a defect and, in a case relating to loss of or damage to property, any knowledge which that person had on a date on which he had no right of action by virtue of Part I of that Act in respect of the loss or damage."

4. In section 28 of the said Act of 1980 (extension of limitation period in case of disability), after subsection (6) there shall be inserted the following subsection—

"(7) If the action is one to which section 11A of this Act applies or one by virtue of section 6(1)(a) of the Consumer Protection Act 1987 (death caused by defective product), subsection (1) above—

(a) shall not apply to the time limit prescribed by subsection (3) of the said section 11A or to that time limit as applied by virtue of section 12(1) of this Act; and

(b) in relation to any other time limit prescribed by this Act shall have effect as if for the words 'six years' there were substituted the words 'three years'."

5. In section 32 of the said Act of 1980 (postponement of limitation period in case of fraud, concealment or mistake)—

(a) in subsection (1), for the words "subsection (3)" there shall be substituted the words "subsections (3) and (4A)"; and

(b) after subsection (4) there shall be inserted the following subsection—

"(4A) Subsection (1) above shall not apply in relation to the time limit prescribed by section 11A(3) of this Act or in relation to that time limit as applied by virtue of section 12(1) of this Act."

6. In section 33 of the said Act of 1980 (discretionary exclusion of time limit)—

(a) in subsection (1), after the words "section 11" there shall be inserted the words "or 11A";

(b) after the said subsection (1) there shall be inserted the following subsection—

"(1A) The court shall not under this section disapply—

(a) subsection (3) of section 11A; or

(b) where the damages claimed by the plaintiff are confined to damages for loss of or damage to any property, any other provision in its application to an action by virtue of Part I of the Consumer Protection Act 1987.";

(c) in subsections (2) and (4), after the words "section 11" there shall be inserted the words "or subsection (4) of section 11A";

(d) in subsection (3)(b), after the words "section 11" there shall be inserted the words ", by section 11A"; and

(e) in subsection (8), after the words "section 11" there shall be inserted the words "or 11A".

Part II

Scotland

7. The Prescription and Limitation (Scotland) Act 1973 shall be amended as follows.

8. In section 7(2), after the words "not being an obligation" there shall be inserted the words "to which section 22A of this Act applies or an obligation".

9. In Part II, before section 17, there shall be inserted the following section—

"Part II not to extend to product liability

16A.—This Part of this Act does not apply to any action to which section 22B or 22C of this Act applies."

10. After section 22, there shall be inserted the following new Part—

"Part IIA

Prescription of Obligations and Limitation of Actions under Part I of the Consumer Protection Act 1987

Prescription of Obligations

Ten years' prescription of obligations

22A.—(1) An obligation arising from liability under section 2 of the 1987 Act (to make reparation for damage caused wholly or partly by a defect in a product) shall be extinguished if a period of 10 years has expired from the relevant time, unless a relevant claim was made within that period and has not been finally disposed of, and no such obligation shall come into existence after the expiration of the said period.

(2) If, at the expiration of the period of 10 years mentioned in subsection (1) above, a relevant claim has been made but has not been finally disposed of, the obligation to which the claim relates shall be extinguished when the claim is finally disposed of.

(3) In this section a claim is finally disposed of when—

(a) a decision disposing of the claim has been made against which no appeal is competent;

(b) an appeal against such a decision is competent with leave, and the time limit for leave has expired and no application has been made or leave has been refused;

(c) leave to appeal against such a decision is granted or is not required, and no appeal is made within the time limit for appeal; or

(d) the claim is abandoned;

'relevant claim' in relation to an obligation means a claim made by or on behalf of the creditor for implement or part implement of the obligation, being a claim made—

(a) in appropriate proceedings within the meaning of section 4(2) of this Act; or

(b) by the presentation of, or the concurring in, a petition for sequestration or by the submission of a claim under section 22 or 48 of the Bankruptcy (Scotland) Act 1985; or

(c) by the presentation of, or the concurring in, a petition for the winding up of a company or by the submission of a claim in a liquidation in accordance with the rules made under section 411 of the Insolvency Act 1986;

'relevant time' has the meaning given in section 4(2) of the 1987 Act.

(4) Where a relevant claim is made in an arbitration, and the nature of the claim has been stated in a preliminary notice (within the meaning of section 4(4) of this Act) relating to that arbitration, the date when the notice is served shall be taken for those purposes to be the date of the making of the claim.

Limitation of actions

3 year limitation of actions

22B.—(1) This section shall apply to an action to enforce an obligation arising from liability under section 2 of the 1987 Act (to make reparation for damage caused wholly or partly by a defect in a product), except where section 22C of this Act applies.

(2) Subject to subsection (4) below, an action to which this section applies shall not be competent unless it is commenced within the period of 3 years after the earliest date on which the person seeking to bring (or a person who could at an earlier date have brought) the action was aware, or on which, in the opinion of the court, it was reasonably practicable for him in all the circumstances to become aware, of all the facts mentioned in subsection (3) below.

(3) The facts referred to in subsection (2) above are—

(a) that there was a defect in a product;

(b) that the damage was caused or partly caused by the defect;

(c) that the damage was sufficiently serious to justify the pursuer (or other person referred to in subsection (2) above) in bringing an action to which this section applies on the assumption that the defender did not dispute liability and was able to satisfy a decree;

(d) that the defender was a person liable for the damage under the said section 2.

(4) In the computation of the period of 3 years mentioned in subsection (2) above, there shall be disregarded any period during which the person seeking to bring the action was under legal disability by reason of nonage or unsoundness of mind.

(5) The facts mentioned in subsection (3) above do not include knowledge of whether particular facts and circumstances would or would not, as a matter of law, result in liability for damage under the said section 2.

(6) Where a person would be entitled, but for this section, to bring an action for reparation other than one in which the damages claimed are confined to damages for loss of or damage to property, the court may, if it seems to it equitable to do so, allow him to bring the action notwithstanding this section.

Actions under the 1987 Act where death has resulted from personal injuries

22C.—(1) This section shall apply to an action to enforce an obligation arising from liability under section 2 of the 1987 Act (to make reparation for damage caused wholly or partly by a defect in a product) where a person has died from personal injuries and the damages claimed include damages for those personal injuries or that death.

(2) Subject to subsection (4) below, an action to which this section applies shall not be competent unless it is commenced within the period of 3 years after the later of—

(a) the date of death of the injured person;

(b) the earliest date on which the person seeking to make (or a person who could at an earlier date have made) the claim was aware, or on which, in the opinion of the court, it was reasonably practicable for him in all the circumstances to become aware—

(i) that there was a defect in the product;

(ii) that the injuries of the deceased were caused (or partly caused) by the defect; and

(iii) that the defender was a person liable for the damage under the said section 2.

(3) Where the person seeking to make the claim is a relative of the deceased, there shall be disregarded in the computation of the period mentioned in subsection (2) above any period during which that relative was under legal disability by reason of nonage or unsoundness of mind.

(4) Where an action to which section 22B of this Act applies has not been brought within the period mentioned in subsection (2) of that section and the person subsequently dies in consequence of his injuries, an action to which this section applies shall not be competent in respect of those injuries or that death.

(5) Where a person would be entitled, but for this section, to bring an action for reparation other than one in which the damages claimed are confined to damages for loss of or damage to property, the court may, if it seems to it equitable to do so, allow him to bring the action notwithstanding this section.

(6) In this section 'relative' has the same meaning as in the Damages (Scotland) Act 1976.

(7) For the purposes of subsection (2)(b) above there shall be disregarded knowledge of whether particular facts and circumstances would or would not, as a matter of law, result in liability for damage under the said section 2.

Supplementary

Interpretation of this Part

22D.—(1) Expressions used in this Part and in Part I of the 1987 Act shall have the same meanings in this Part as in the said Part I.

(2) For the purposes of section 1(1) of the 1987 Act, this Part shall have effect and be construed as if it were contained in Part I of that Act.

(3) In this Part, 'the 1987 Act' means the Consumer Protection Act 1987."

11. Section 23 shall cease to have effect, but for the avoidance of doubt it is declared that the amendments in Part II of Schedule 4 shall continue to have effect.

12. In paragraph 2 of Schedule 1, after sub-paragraph (gg) there shall be inserted the following sub-paragraph—

"(ggg) to any obligation arising from liability under section 2 of the Consumer Protection Act 1987 (to make reparation for damage caused wholly or partly by a defect in a product);".

Section 13   SCHEDULE 2

PROHIBITION NOTICES AND NOTICES TO WARN

PART I

PROHIBITION NOTICES

1. A prohibition notice in respect of any goods shall—

(a) state that the Secretary of State considers that the goods are unsafe;

(b) set out the reasons why the Secretary of State considers that the goods are unsafe;

(c) specify the day on which the notice is to come into force; and

(d) state that the trader may at any time make representations in writing to the Secretary of State for the purpose of establishing that the goods are safe.

2.—(1) If representations in writing about a prohibition notice are made by the trader to the Secretary of State, it shall be the duty of the Secretary of State to consider whether to revoke the notice and—

(a) if he decides to revoke it, to do so;

(b) in any other case, to appoint a person to consider those representations, any further representations made (whether in writing or orally) by the trader about the notice and the statements of any witnesses examined under this Part of this Schedule.

(2) Where the Secretary of State has appointed a person to consider representations about a prohibition notice, he shall serve a notification on the trader which—

(a) states that the trader may make oral representations to the appointed person for the purpose of establishing that the goods to which the notice relates are safe; and

(b) specifies the place and time at which the oral representations may be made.

(3) The time specified in a notification served under sub-paragraph (2) above shall not be before the end of the period of twenty-one days beginning with the day on which the notification is served, unless the trader otherwise agrees.

(4) A person on whom a notification has been served under sub-paragraph (2) above or his representative may, at the place and time specified in the notification—

(a) make oral representations to the appointed person for the purpose of establishing that the goods in question are safe; and

(b) call and examine witnesses in connection with the representations.

3.—(1) Where representations in writing about a prohibition notice are made by the trader to the Secretary of State at any time after a person has been appointed to consider representations about that notice, then, whether or not the appointed person has made a report to the Secretary of State, the following provisions of this paragraph shall apply instead of paragraph 2 above.

(2) The Secretary of State shall, before the end of the period of one month beginning with the day on which he receives the representations, serve a notification on the trader which states—

(a) that the Secretary of State has decided to revoke the notice, has decided to vary it or, as the case may be, has decided neither to revoke nor to vary it; or

(b) that, a person having been appointed to consider representations about the notice, the trader may, at a place and time specified in the notification, make oral representations to the appointed person for the purpose of establishing that the goods to which the notice relates are safe.

(3) The time specified in a notification served for the purposes of sub-paragraph (2)(b) above shall not be before the end of the period of twenty-one days beginning with the day on which the notification is served, unless the trader otherwise agrees or the time is the time already specified for the purposes of paragraph 2(2)(b) above.

(4) A person on whom a notification has been served for the purposes of sub-paragraph (2)(b) above or his representative may, at the place and time specified in the notification—

(a) make oral representations to the appointed person for the purpose of establishing that the goods in question are safe; and

(b) call and examine witnesses in connection with the representations.

4.—(1) Where a person is appointed to consider representations about a prohibition notice, it shall be his duty to consider—

(a) any written representations made by the trader about the notice, other than those in respect of which a notification is served under paragraph 3(2)(a) above;

(b) any oral representations made under paragraph 2(4) or 3(4) above; and

(c) any statements made by witnesses in connection with the oral representations,

and, after considering any matters under this paragraph, to make a report (including recommendations) to the Secretary of State about the matters considered by him and the notice.

(2) It shall be the duty of the Secretary of State to consider any report made to him under sub-paragraph (1) above and, after considering the report, to inform the trader of his decision with respect to the prohibition notice to which the report relates.

5.—(1) The Secretary of State may revoke or vary a prohibition notice by serving on the trader a notification stating that the notice is revoked or, as the case may be, is varied as specified in the notification.

(2) The Secretary of State shall not vary a prohibition notice so as to make the effect of the notice more restrictive for the trader.

(3) Without prejudice to the power conferred by section 13(2) of this Act, the service of a notification under sub-paragraph (1) above shall be sufficient to satisfy the requirement of paragraph 4(2) above that the trader shall be informed of the Secretary of State's decision.

Part II

Notices to Warn

6.—(1) If the Secretary of State proposes to serve a notice to warn on any person in respect of any goods, the Secretary of State, before he serves the notice, shall serve on that person a notification which—

(a) contains a draft of the proposed notice;

(b) states that the Secretary of State proposes to serve a notice in the form of the draft on that person;

(c) states that the Secretary of State considers that the goods described in the draft are unsafe;

(d) sets out the reasons why the Secretary of State considers that those goods are unsafe; and

(e) states that that person may make representations to the Secretary of State for the purpose of establishing that the goods are safe if, before the end of the period of fourteen days beginning with the day on which the notification is served, he informs the Secretary of State—

    (i) of his intention to make representations; and

    (ii) whether the representations will be made only in writing or both in writing and orally.

(2) Where the Secretary of State has served a notification containing a draft of a proposed notice to warn on any person, he shall not serve a notice to warn on that person in respect of the goods to which the proposed notice relates unless—

(a) the period of fourteen days beginning with the day on which the notification was served expires without the Secretary of State being informed as mentioned in sub-paragraph (1)(e) above;

(b) the period of twenty-eight days beginning with that day expires without any written representations being made by that person to the Secretary of State about the proposed notice; or

(c) the Secretary of State has considered a report about the proposed notice by a person appointed under paragraph 7(1) below.

7.—(1) Where a person on whom a notification containing a draft of a proposed notice to warn has been served—

(a) informs the Secretary of State as mentioned in paragraph 6(1)(e) above before the end of the period of fourteen days beginning with the day on which the notification was served; and

(b) makes written representations to the Secretary of State about the proposed notice before the end of the period of twenty-eight days beginning with that day,

the Secretary of State shall appoint a person to consider those representations, any further representations made by that person about the draft notice and the statements of any witnesses examined under this Part of this Schedule.

(2) Where—

(a) the Secretary of State has appointed a person to consider representations about a proposed notice to warn; and

(b) the person whose representations are to be considered has informed the Secretary of State for the purposes of paragraph 6(1)(e) above that the representations he intends to make will include oral representations,

the Secretary of State shall inform the person intending to make the representations of the place and time at which oral representations may be made to the appointed person.

(3) Where a person on whom a notification containing a draft of a proposed notice to warn has been served is informed of a time for the purposes of sub-paragraph (2) above, that time shall not be—

(a) before the end of the period of twenty-eight days beginning with the day on which the notification was served; or

(b) before the end of the period of seven days beginning with the day on which that person is informed of the time.

(4) A person who has been informed of a place and time for the purposes of sub-paragraph (2) above or his representative may, at that place and time—

(a) make oral representations to the appointed person for the purpose of establishing that the goods to which the proposed notice relates are safe; and

(b) call and examine witnesses in connection with the representations.

8.—(1) Where a person is appointed to consider representations about a proposed notice to warn, it shall be his duty to consider—

(a) any written representations made by the person on whom it is proposed to serve the notice; and

(b) in a case where a place and time has been appointed under paragraph 7(2) above for oral representations to be made by that person or his representative, any representations so made and any statements made by witnesses in connection with those representations,

and, after considering those matters, to make a report (including recommendations) to the Secretary of State about the matters considered by him and the proposal to serve the notice.

(2) It shall be the duty of the Secretary of State to consider any report made to him under sub-paragraph (1) above and, after considering the report, to inform the person on whom it was proposed that a notice to warn should be served of his decision with respect to the proposal.

(3) If at any time after serving a notification on a person under paragraph 6 above the Secretary of State decides not to serve on that person either the proposed notice to warn or that notice with modifications, the Secretary of State shall inform that person of the decision; and nothing done for the purposes of any of the preceding provisions of this Part of this Schedule before that person was so informed shall—

(a) entitle the Secretary of State subsequently to serve the proposed notice or that notice with modifications; or

(b) require the Secretary of State, or any person appointed to consider representations about the proposed notice, subsequently to do anything in respect of, or in consequence of, any such representations.

(4) Where a notification containing a draft of a proposed notice to warn is served on a person in respect of any goods, a notice to warn served on him in consequence of a decision made under sub-paragraph (2) above shall either be in the form of the draft or shall be less onerous than the draft.

9. The Secretary of State may revoke a notice to warn by serving on the person on whom the notice was served a notification stating that the notice is revoked.

PART III

GENERAL

10.—(1) Where in a notification served on any person under this Schedule the Secretary of State has appointed a time for the making of oral representations or the examination of witnesses, he may, by giving that person such notification as the Secretary of State considers appropriate, change that time to a later time or appoint further times at which further representations may be made or the examination of witnesses may be continued; and paragraphs 2(4), 3(4) and 7(4) above shall have effect accordingly.

(2) For the purposes of this Schedule the Secretary of State may appoint a person (instead of the appointed person) to consider any representations or statement, if the person originally appointed, or last appointed under this sub-paragraph, to consider those representations or statements has died or appears to the Secretary of State to be otherwise unable to act.

11. In this Schedule—

"the appointed person" in relation to a prohibition notice or a proposal to serve a notice to warn, means the person for the time being appointed under this Schedule to consider representations about the notice or, as the case may be, about the proposed notice;

"notification" means a notification in writing;

"trader", in relation to a prohibition notice, means the person on whom the notice is or was served.

Section 36   SCHEDULE 3

AMENDMENTS OF PART I OF THE HEALTH AND SAFETY AT WORK ETC. ACT 1974

1.—(1) Section 6 (general duties of manufacturers etc. as regard articles and substances for use at work) shall be amended as follows.

(2) For subsection (1) (general duties of designers, manufacturers, importers and suppliers of articles for use at work) there shall be substituted the following subsections—

"(1) It shall be the duty of any person who designs, manufactures, imports or supplies any article for use at work or any article of fairground equipment—

(a) to ensure, so far as is reasonably practicable, that the article is so designed and constructed that it will be safe and without risks to health at all times when it is being set, used, cleaned or maintained by a person at work;

(b) to carry out or arrange for the carrying out of such testing and examination as may be necessary for the performance of the duty imposed on him by the preceding paragraph;

(c) to take such steps as are necessary to secure that persons supplied by that person with the article are provided with adequate information about the use for which the article is designed or has been tested and about any conditions necessary to ensure that it will be safe and without risks to health at all such times as are mentioned in paragraph (a) above and when it is being dismantled or disposed of; and

(d) to take such steps as are necessary to secure, so far as is reasonably practicable, that persons so supplied are provided with all such revisions of information provided to them by virtue of the preceding paragraph as are necessary by reason of its becoming known that anything gives rise to a serious risk to health or safety.

(1A) It shall be the duty of any person who designs, manufactures, imports or supplies any article of fairground equipment—

(a) to ensure, so far as is reasonably practicable, that the article is so designed and constructed that it will be safe and without risks to health at all times when it is being used for or in connection with the entertainment of members of the public;

(b) to carry out or arrange for the carrying out of such testing and examination as may be necessary for the performance of the duty imposed on him by the preceding paragraph;

(c) to take such steps as are necessary to secure that persons supplied by that person with the article are provided with adequate information about the use for which the article is designed or has been tested and about any conditions necessary to ensure that it will be safe and without risks to health at all times when it is being used for or in connection with the entertainment of members of the public; and

(d) to take such steps as are necessary to secure, so far as is reasonably practicable, that persons so supplied are provided with all such revisions of information provided to them by virtue of the preceding paragraph as are necessary by reason of its becoming known that anything gives rise to a serious risk to health or safety."

(3) In subsection (2) (duty of person who undertakes the design or manufacture of an article for use at work to carry out research), after the word "work" there shall be inserted the words "or of any article of fairground equipment".

(4) In subsection (3) (duty of persons who erect or install articles for use at work)—

(a) after the words "persons at work" there shall be inserted the words "or who erects or installs any article of fairground equipment"; and

(b) for the words from "it is" onwards there shall be substituted the words "the article is erected or installed makes it unsafe or a risk to health at any such time as is mentioned in paragraph (a) of subsection (1) or, as the case may be, in paragraph (a) of subsection (1) or (1A) above."

(5) For subsection (4) (general duties of manufacturers, importers and suppliers of substances for use at work) there shall be substituted the following subsection—

"(4) It shall be the duty of any person who manufactures, imports or supplies any substance—

(a) to ensure, so far as is reasonably practicable, that the substance will be safe and without risks to health at all times when it is being used, handled, processed, stored or transported by a person at work or in premises to which section 4 above applies;

(b) to carry out or arrange for the carrying out of such testing and examination as may be necessary for the performance of the duty imposed on him by the preceding paragraph;

(c) to take such steps as are necessary to secure that persons supplied by that person with the substance are provided with adequate information about any risks to health or safety to which the inherent properties of the substance may give rise, about the results of any relevant tests which have been carried out on or in connection with the substance and about any conditions necessary to ensure that the substance will be safe and without risks to health at all such times as are mentioned in paragraph (a) above and when the substance is being disposed of; and

(d) to take such steps as are necessary to secure, so far as is reasonably practicable, that persons so supplied are provided with all such revisions of information provided to them by virtue of the preceding paragraph as are necessary by reason of its becoming known that anything gives rise to a serious risk to health or safety."

(6) In subsection (5) (duty of person who undertakes the manufacture of a substance for use at work to carry out research)—

    (a) for the words "substance for use at work" there shall be substituted the word "substance"; and

    (b) at the end there shall be inserted the words "at all such times as are mentioned in paragraph (a) of subsection (4) above".

(7) In subsection (8) (relief from duties for persons relying on undertakings by others)—

    (a) for the words "for or to another" there shall be substituted the words "for use at work or an article of fairground equipment and does so for or to another";

    (b) for the words "when properly used" there shall be substituted the words "at all such times as are mentioned in paragraph (a) of subsection (1) or, as the case may be, in paragraph (a) of subsection (1) or (1A) above"; and

    (c) for the words "by subsection (1)(a) above" there shall be substituted the words "by virtue of that paragraph".

(8) After the said subsection (8) there shall be inserted the following subsection—

"(8A) Nothing in subsection (7) or (8) above shall relieve any person who imports any article or substance from any duty in respect of anything which—

    (a) in the case of an article designed outside the United Kingdom, was done by and in the course of any trade, profession or other undertaking carried on by, or was within the control of, the person who designed the article; or

    (b) in the case of an article or substance manufactured outside the United Kingdom, was done by and in the course of any trade, profession or other undertaking carried on by, or was within the control of, the person who manufactured the article or substance".

(9) In subsection (9) (definition of supplier in certain cases of supply under a hire-purchase agreement), for the words "article for use at work or substance for use at work" there shall be substituted the words "article or substance".

(10) For subsection (10) (meaning of "properly used") there shall be substituted the following subsection—

"(10) For the purposes of this section an absence of safety or a risk to health shall be disregarded in so far as the case in or in relation to which it would arise is shown to be one the occurrence of which could not reasonably be foreseen; and in determining whether any duty imposed by virtue of paragraph (a) of subsection (1), (1A) or (4) above has been performed regard shall be had to any relevant information or advice which has been provided to any person by the person by whom the article has been designed, manufactured, imported or supplied or, as the case may be, by the person by whom the substance has been manufactured, imported or supplied."

2. In section 22 (prohibition notices)—

    (a) in subsections (1) and (2) (notices in respect of activities which are or are about to be carried on and involve a risk of serious personal injury), for the word "about", in each place where it occurs, there shall be substituted the word "likely";

    (b) for subsection (4) (notice to have immediate effect only if the risk is imminent) there shall be substituted the following subsection—

"(4) A direction contained in a prohibition notice in pursuance of subsection (3)(d) above shall take effect—

    (a) at the end of the period specified in the notice; or

    (b) if the notice so declares, immediately."

3. After section 25 there shall be inserted the following section—

"Power of customs officer to detain articles and substances

25A.—(1) A customs officer may, for the purpose of facilitating the exercise or performance by any enforcing authority or inspector of any of the powers or duties of the authority or inspector under any of the relevant statutory provisions, seize any imported article or imported substance and detain it for not more than two working days.

(2) Anything seized and detained under this section shall be dealt with during the period of its detention in such manner as the Commissioners of Customs and Excise may direct.

(3) In subsection (1) above the reference to two working days is a reference to a period of forty-eight hours calculated from the time when the goods in question are seized but disregarding so much of any period as falls on a Saturday or Sunday or on Christmas Day, Good Friday or a day which is a bank holiday under the Banking and Financial Dealings Act 1971 in the part of Great Britain where the goods are seized."

4. After section 27 (power to obtain information) there shall be inserted the following section—

"**Information communicated by the Commissioners of Customs and Excise**

27A.—(1) If they think it appropriate to do so for the purpose of facilitating the exercise or performance by any person to whom subsection (2) below applies of any of that person's powers or duties under any of the relevant statutory provisions, the Commissioners of Customs and Excise may authorise the disclosure to that person of any information obtained for the purposes of the exercise by the Commissioners of their functions in relation to imports.

(2) This subsection applies to an enforcing authority and to an inspector.

(3) A disclosure of information made to any person under subsection (1) above shall be made in such manner as may be directed by the Commissioners of Customs and Excise and may be made through such persons acting on behalf of that person as may be so directed.

(4) Information may be disclosed to a person under subsection (1) above whether or not the disclosure of the information has been requested by or on behalf of that person."

5. In section 28 (restrictions on disclosure of information) in subsection (1)(a), after the words "furnished to any person" there shall be inserted the words "under section 27A above or".

6. In section 33(1)(h) (offence of obstructing an inspector), after the word "duties" there shall be inserted the words "or to obstruct a customs officer in the exercise of his powers under section 25A".

7. In section 53(1) (general interpretation of Part I)—

(a) after the definition of "article for use at work" there shall be inserted the following definition—

"'article of fairground equipment' means any fairground equipment or any article designed for use as a component in any such equipment;"

(b) after the definition of "credit-sale agreement" there shall be inserted the following definition—

"'customs officer' means an officer within the meaning of the Customs and Excise Management Act 1979;"

(c) before the definition of "the general purposes of this Part" there shall be inserted the following definition—

"'fairground equipment' means any fairground ride, any similar plant which is designed to be in motion for entertainment purposes with members of the public on or inside it or any plant which is designed to be used by members of the public for entertainment purposes either as a slide or for bouncing upon, and in this definition the reference to plant which is designed to be in motion with members of the public on or inside it includes a reference to swings, dodgems and other plant which is designed to be in motion wholly or partly under the control of, or to be put in motion by, a member of the public;"

(d) after the definition of "local authority" there shall be inserted the following definition—

"'micro-organism' includes any microscopic biological entity which is capable of replication;"

(e) in the definition of "substance", after the words "natural or artificial substance" there shall be inserted the words "(including micro-organisms)".

Section 48   SCHEDULE 4

MINOR AND CONSEQUENTIAL AMENDMENTS

The Explosives Act 1875

1. In sections 31 and 80 of the Explosives Act 1875 (prohibitions on selling gunpowder to children and on use of fireworks in public places), for the words from "shall be liable" onwards there shall be substituted the words "shall be guilty of an offence and liable on summary conviction to a fine not exceeding level 5 on the standard scale".

The Trade Descriptions Act 1968

2.—(1) In section 2 of the Trade Descriptions Act 1968 (meaning of trade description)—

(a) for paragraph (g) of subsection (4) (marks and descriptions applied in pursuance of the Consumer Safety Act 1978) there shall be substituted the following paragraph—

"(g) the Consumer Protection Act 1987;" and

(b) in subsection (5)(a) (descriptions prohibited under certain enactments), for the words "or the Consumer Safety Act 1978" there shall be substituted the words "or the Consumer Protection Act 1987".

(2) In section 28(5A) of the said Act of 1968 (disclosure of information authorised for purpose specified in section 174(3) of the Consumer Credit Act 1974), for the words from "section 174(3)" onwards there shall be substituted the words "section 38(2)(a), (b) or (c) of the Consumer Protection Act 1987."

The Fair Trading Act 1973

3. In section 130(1) of the Fair Trading Act 1973 (notice of intended prosecution by weights and measures authority to Director General of Fair Trading), after the words "that Act," there shall be inserted the words "or for an offence under any provision made by or under Part III of the Consumer Protection Act 1987,".

The Consumer Credit Act 1974

4. In section 174(3)(a) of the Consumer Credit Act 1974 (exceptions to general restrictions on disclosure of information), after the words "or the Airports Act 1986" there shall be inserted the words "or the Consumer Protection Act 1987".

The Torts (Interference with Goods) Act 1977

5. In section 1 of the Torts (Interference with Goods) Act 1977 (meaning of "wrongful interference"), after paragraph (d) there shall be inserted the following words—

"and references in this Act (however worded) to proceedings for wrongful interference or to a claim or right to claim for wrongful interference shall include references to proceedings by virtue of Part I of the Consumer Protection Act 1987 (product liability) in respect of any damage to goods or to an interest in goods or, as the case may be, to a claim or right to claim by virtue of that Part in respect of any such damage."

The Estate Agents Act 1979

6. In section 10(3)(a) of the Estate Agents Act 1979 (exceptions to general restrictions on disclosure of information), after the words "or the Airports Act 1986" there shall be inserted the words "or the Consumer Protection Act 1987."

The Competition Act 1980

7. In section 19(3) of the Competition Act 1980 (enactments specified in exceptions to general restrictions on disclosure of information), after paragraph (i) there shall be inserted the following paragraph—

"(j)　the Consumer Protection Act 1987."

The Employment Act 1982

8. In section 16(2) of the Employment Act 1982 (proceedings against trade unions in relation to which the appropriate limit does not apply), after paragraph (b) there shall be inserted the following words—

"or to any proceedings by virtue of Part I of the Consumer Protection Act 1987 (product liability)."

The Telecommunications Act 1984

9.—(1) In sections 28(6) and 85(5)(b) of the Telecommunications Act 1984 (meaning of "supply"), for the words "be construed in accordance with section 9 of the Consumer Safety Act 1978" there shall be substituted the words "have the same meaning as it has in Part II of the Consumer Protection Act 1987".

(2) In section 101(3) of the said Act of 1984 (enactments specified in exceptions to general restrictions on disclosure of information), after paragraph (g) there shall be inserted the following paragraph—

"(h)　the Consumer Protection Act 1987."

The Airports Act 1986

10. In section 74(3) of the Airports Act 1986 (enactments specified in exceptions to general restrictions on disclosure of information), after paragraph (h) there shall be inserted the following paragraph—
"(i) the Consumer Protection Act 1987."

The Gas Act 1986

11. In section 42 of the Gas Act 1986—
    (a) in subsection (3) (restrictions on disclosure of information except for the purposes of certain enactments), at the end there shall be inserted the following paragraph—
        "(j) the Consumer Protection Act 1987.";
    (b) after subsection (5) there shall be inserted the following subsection—
        "(6) In relation to the Consumer Protection Act 1987 the reference in subsection (2)(b) above to a weights and measures authority shall include a reference to any person on whom functions under that Act are conferred by regulations under section 27(2) of that Act."

The Insolvency Act 1986

12. In section 281(5)(a) of the Insolvency Act 1986 (discharge from bankruptcy not to release bankrupt from liability in respect of personal injuries), for the word "being" there shall be substituted the words "or to pay damages by virtue of Part I of the Consumer Protection Act 1987, being in either case".

The Motor Cycle Noise Act 1987

13. For paragraphs 3 to 5 of the Schedule to the Motor Cycle Noise Act 1987 (enforcement) there shall be substituted the following paragraph—
"3. Part IV of the Consumer Protection Act 1987 (enforcement), except section 31 (power of customs officers to detain goods), shall have effect as if the provisions of this Act were safety provisions within the meaning of that Act; and in Part V of that Act (miscellaneous and supplemental), except in section 49 (Northern Ireland), references to provisions of the said Part IV shall include references to those provisions as applied by this paragraph."

SCHEDULE 5

Repeals

Chapter	Short title	Extent of repeal
3 & 4 Geo. 5. c. 17.	The Fabrics (Misdescription) Act 1913.	The whole Act.
1967 c. 80.	The Criminal Justice Act 1967.	In Part I of Schedule 3, the entry relating to the Fabrics (Misdescription) Act 1913.
1967 c. 29. (N.I.).	The Fines Act (Northern Ireland) 1967.	In Part I of the Schedule, the entry relating to the Fabrics (Misdescription) Act 1913.
1968 c. 29.	The Trade Descriptions Act 1968.	Section 11.
1972 c. 34.	The Trade Descriptions Act 1972.	The whole Act.
1972 c. 70.	The Local Government Act 1972.	In Part II of Schedule 29, paragraph 18(1).
1973 c. 52.	The Prescription and Limitation (Scotland) Act 1973.	Section 23.
1973 c. 65.	The Local Government (Scotland) Act 1973.	In Part II of Schedule 27, paragraph 50.
1974 c. 37.	The Health and Safety at Work etc. Act 1974.	In section 53(1), the definition of "substance for use at work".
1976 c. 26.	The Explosives (Age of Purchase etc.) Act 1976.	In section 1, in subsection (1), the words from "and for the word" onwards and subsection (2).
1978 c. 38.	The Consumer Safety Act 1978.	The whole Act.
1980 c. 43.	The Magistrates' Courts Act 1980.	In Schedule 7, paragraphs 172 and 173.
1984 c. 12.	The Telecommunications Act 1984.	In section 101(3)(f), the word "and".
1984 c. 30.	The Food Act 1984.	In Schedule 10, paragraph 32.
1986 c. 29.	The Consumer Safety (Amendment) Act 1986.	The whole Act.
1986 c. 31.	The Airports Act 1986.	In section 74(3)(g), the word "and".
1986 c. 44.	The Gas Act 1986.	In section 42(3), paragraphs (a) and (g) and, in paragraph (h), the word "and".

LOCAL GOVERNMENT ACT 1987*

(1987 c. 44)

ARRANGEMENT OF SECTIONS

Capital expenditure

SECT.
1. Payments in respect of capital expenditure.

Block grant: education

2. Adjustments between England and Wales.
3. Adjustments for advanced further education.

General

4. Citation and extent.

SCHEDULE:
   Amendments of Part VIII of the Local Government, Planning and Land Act 1980.

An Act to amend Part VIII of the Local Government, Planning and Land Act 1980; to make further provision about the adjustment of block grant in connection with education; and for connected purposes.

[15th May 1987]

PARLIAMENTARY DEBATES
   Hansard: H.C. Vol. 110, col. 924; Vol. 111, col. 760; Vol. 116, col. 223; H.L. Vol. 487, cols. 636, 798.
   The Bill was considered in Standing Committee B from March 12 to April 2, 1987.

GENERAL NOTE
   The Local Government Bill which was ultimately enacted as this Act was originally a somewhat larger measure, containing provisions relating to financial assistance for privately let housing accommodation and to land held by public bodies. By the time the Bill reached Report Stage in the House of Commons the dissolution of Parliament was imminent and those provisions, which were the subject of contention between the parties, were dropped. The opposition parties accepted the remaining provisions, relating to capital expenditure and block grant, and the Bill as now enacted passed through its remaining stages in the House of Commons on May 12, 1987, and through all its stages in the House of Lords on May 13–14, 1987.

Capital expenditure

Payments in respect of capital expenditure

   1. Part VIII of the Local Government, Planning and Land Act 1980 (capital expenditure of local authorities etc.) shall have effect in relation to the year beginning with 1st April 1987 and subsequent years, and shall be deemed to have had effect in relation to the year beginning with 1st April 1986—
   (a) with the insertion after section 80 of the sections set out in Part I of the Schedule to this Act; and
   (b) with the further amendments set out in Part II of that Schedule (being amendments consequential on the insertion of those sections).

* Annotations by Reginald Jones, Barrister, former Inspector of Audit, District Audit Service.

The Secretary of State for the Environment announced in Parliament on July 22, 1986, that he proposed to take action to prevent local authorities from circumventing the local authority capital expenditure control system (contained in Pt. VIII of the Local Government, Planning and Land Act 1980) by using devices such as advance and deferred purchase agreements to incur prescribed expenditure in earlier or later years than would ordinarily be the case. Local authorities were so informed in a Department of the Environment Circular of the same date.

S.1 and the Schedule effect this intention by the insertion of new ss.80A and 80B in the 1980 Act, together with consequential amendments. These sections provide, broadly, that in respect of contracts and other arrangements entered into after July 22, 1986 (the date of the original announcement) payment for works shall be deemed for the purpose of Pt. VIII of the 1980 Act to have been made in the year in which the works are carried out, or, in certain circumstances, in the year immediately following. For more detailed notes on the new sections, see the General Notes to Pt. I of the Schedule, below.

Block grant: education

Adjustments between England and Wales

2.—(1) Schedule 10 to the 1980 Act (block grant adjustment for education) shall be amended as follows—

(a) in paragraphs 1(2), (3)(a) and (b) and (4) for "education expenditure" there shall be substituted "qualifying education expenditure",

(b) in paragraph 1(3)(a) and (b) the words "(after taking account of recoupment)" shall be omitted, and

(c) paragraph 3(4) shall be omitted.

(2) In that Schedule the following shall be substituted for paragraph 3(3)—

"(3) References to the qualifying education expenditure for a year are to the aggregate of the following amounts of expenditure in connection with further education of an advanced character, including the training of teachers, namely—

(a) such amount of expenditure to which paragraph 5 below applies as the Secretary of State estimates has been or will be incurred for the year by all local authorities in England and Wales, and

(b) such amounts of expenditure to which paragraph 6 below applies as are, or he estimates will be, specified for the year by or under regulations made under paragraph 6(1)(a) and (b) below.

(3A) References to the qualifying education expenditure for a year of local authorities in England or Wales (as the case may be) are to such of the qualifying education expenditure for the year as the Secretary of State estimates has been or will be incurred for the year by all local authorities in England or Wales (as the case may be)."

(3) Subsections (1) and (2) above shall have effect in relation to the year beginning in 1988 and subsequent years.

(4) In relation to the year beginning in 1986 and to that beginning in 1987—

(a) after the passing of this Act Part I of Schedule 10 to the 1980 Act shall have effect with the amendments mentioned in subsections (1) and (2) above, and

(b) anything done (including an adjustment made) after the passing of this Act under that Part shall be done by reference to that Part with those amendments.

(5) In this section "the 1980 Act" means the Local Government, Planning and Land Act 1980 and "year" has the same meaning as in Part VI of that Act.

DEFINITIONS
"the 1980 Act": subs. (5).
"year": subs. (5); Local Government, Planning and Land Act, s.68(1).

GENERAL NOTE
This section makes new provision for the adjustments to block grant which arise out of expenditure by local education authorities and are required by s.63 of, and Sched. 10 to, the Local Government, Planning and Land Act 1980. It deals with the adjustments required to avoid an uneven burden falling on local education authorities in England and those in Wales; the section confines the adjustments to those which relate to expenditure on advanced further education, and authorises adjustments to be made on this basis for years beginning on and after April 1, 1986.

Adjustments for advanced further education

3.—(1) When the Secretary of State pays 1987 block grant to an English local education authority he may make an adjustment designed to conclude the course of action adopted by him before the passing of this Act as regards 1981 block grant in purported compliance with paragraph 6 of Schedule 10 to the 1980 Act and regulations under that paragraph.

(2) Any adjustment under subsection (1) above shall be made by a method determined by the Secretary of State.

(3) Any method determined under subsection (2) above shall be determined in accordance with principles to be applied to all English local education authorities.

(4) Before he determines any method under subsection (2) above the Secretary of State shall consult such associations of local authorities as appear to him to be concerned and any local education authority with whom consultation appears to him to be desirable.

(5) References in this section to 1981 block grant and 1987 block grant are respectively to block grant for the year beginning in 1981 and block grant for the year beginning in 1987.

(6) In this section "the 1980 Act" means the Local Government, Planning and Land Act 1980, "local authority" means any body which is a local authority for the purposes of Part VI of that Act, and "year" has the same meaning as in that Part.

(7) This section shall come into force at the end of the period of two months beginning with the day on which this Act is passed.

DEFINITIONS
"local authority": subs. (6); Local Government, Planning and Land Act 1980, s.53(5).
"the 1980 Act": subs. (6).
"year": subs. (6); Local Government, Planning and Land Act 1980, s.68(1).

GENERAL NOTE
This section makes further provision in respect of the education adjustments to block grant referred to in the note to s.2. It deals with the adjustments relating to expenditure on advanced further education incurred in the year 1981–82; the section authorises the making, in the year 1987–88, of final adjustments, which are needed in relation to that expenditure, by methods to be determined by the Secretary of State after consultation with those concerned.

General

Citation and extent

4.—(1) This Act may be cited as the Local Government Act 1987.

(2) This Act extends to England and Wales only.

SCHEDULE

AMENDMENTS OF PART VIII OF THE LOCAL GOVERNMENT, PLANNING AND LAND ACT 1980

PART I

SECTIONS INSERTED AFTER SECTION 80

Payment for works

80A.—(1) Subject to the following provisions of this section, where any works are or are to be carried out for any authority or, by virtue of subsection (9) below, are to be treated as if they were or were to be so carried out, the authority in question—

(a) shall be taken for the purposes of this Part of this Act to make payments in respect of expenditure on the works at the times and of the amounts determined in accordance with subsection (3) or, as the case may be, subsection (4) below; but

(b) shall not be taken for those purposes to pay or to have paid any other amount in respect of expenditure on those works, either at those times or at any other times.

(2) An amount which is taken in pursuance of this section to have been paid at any time by an authority shall accordingly be treated as an item of account within the meaning of section 19 of the Local Government Finance Act 1982 (declaration that item of account is unlawful).

(3) Where any works are carried out in the course of a single year ("the relevant year"), the payments that the authority shall be taken to make in respect of expenditure on the works are—

(a) a payment in the relevant year of an amount equal to the aggregate of—

(i) the amount (if any) which was actually paid in the relevant year by the authority in respect of expenditure on the works; and

(ii) the amount (if any) which was actually paid before the beginning of the relevant year by the authority in respect of expenditure on the works; and

(b) a payment in the year following the relevant year of an amount equal to the amount (if any) by which the value of the works exceeds the aggregate amount which is taken by virtue of paragraph (a) above to have been paid in the relevant year by the authority in respect of expenditure on the works.

(4) Where any works are carried out in the course of two or more years ("the relevant years"), the payments that the authority shall be taken to make in respect of expenditure on the works are—

(a) a payment in the first of the relevant years of an amount equal to the aggregate of—

(i) the amount (if any) which was actually paid in the first of the relevant years by the authority in respect of expenditure on the works; and

(ii) the amount (if any) which was actually paid before the beginning of the first of the relevant years by the authority in respect of expenditure on the works;

(b) a payment in each of the relevant years after the first of an amount equal to the aggregate of—

(i) the amount (if any) which was actually paid in the year in question by the authority in respect of expenditure on such of the works as were carried out in the year in question; and

(ii) the amount (if any) by which the value of such of the works as were carried out before the beginning of the year in question exceeds the aggregate of the amounts which are taken by virtue of this subsection to have been paid before the year in question by the authority in respect of expenditure on any of the works; and

(c) a payment in the year following the last of the relevant years of an amount equal to the amount (if any) by which the value of all the works exceeds the aggregate amount taken by virtue of this subsection to have been paid in the relevant years by the authority in respect of expenditure on those works.

(5) For the purposes of subsections (3) and (4) above the value at any time of any works shall be taken to be equal to the aggregate of—

(a) the amounts which have actually been paid by the authority in question in respect of expenditure on the works; and

(b) the amounts which have not been so paid but are determined by that authority to have fallen due for actual payment by the authority in respect of expenditure on the works or to be likely to fall due for such payment;

and, if the Secretary of State has given to any authority, to authorities of any description or to authorities generally any directions as to the manner of making determinations for the purposes of paragraph (b) above, the authority or authorities to whom the directions have been given shall make their determinations for those purposes in accordance with those directions.

(6) Subsection (1) above shall not apply in relation to any works in so far as they consist in an acquisition for the purposes of section 80 above of an interest in or right over property or in works the value of which is treated as paid at a particular time in accordance with subsection (6) of that section.

(7) Subsection (1) above shall not apply in relation to such cases, to such works or to such authorities as may be specified in or determined under regulations; and regulations under this subsection may contain provision which—

(a) for the purposes of this Part of this Act treats amounts determined under the regulations as paid, at the times so determined, in respect of expenditure on any works in relation to which subsection (1) above does not apply by virtue of this subsection; and

(b) requires payments actually made in respect of expenditure on any such works to be disregarded for those purposes.

(8) Subsection (1) above shall not apply in relation to any works in so far as they consist in works in respect of expenditure on which the authority in question makes actual payment by virtue of an obligation arising under arrangements entered into on or before 22nd July 1986, unless the obligation arises as the result of the exercise after that date of any option conferred by the arrangements.

(9) Without prejudice to section 82 below, works shall be treated for the purposes of subsection (1) above as carried out for an authority in such cases as may be specified in or determined under regulations.

DEFINITION

"year": Local Government, Planning and Land Act 1980, s.85(2).

GENERAL NOTE

For the background to the enactment of this section, see General Note to s.1 of this Act, above.

The detailed provisions as to the year in which payments for works are deemed to be made are contained in subss. (3) to (5) of this section. Any payments made in a year before that in which works are commenced are deemed to be made in the year in which the works are commenced (subss. (3)(a)(ii), (4)(a)(ii)). Payments made in a year in respect of works carried out in that year are treated, without adjustment, as made in that year (subss. 3)(a)(i), (4)(a)(i), (4)(b)(i)). Payments made in the year in which work commenced, in respect of works carried out in subsequent years, are treated as paid in the first year (subs. 4)(a)(i)). Finally, the authority, at the end of each year in which works are carried out but have not yet been treated as paid for, must estimate the value of works completed at that date. To the extent that the estimate exceeds the amounts already treated as paid it is to be treated as paid in the following year (subss. (3)(b), (4)(b)(ii), (4)(c)). The method of valuation of works is set out in subs. (5); the Secretary of State may issue directions in this respect (after consultation, see Sched., Pt. II, para. 6, below).

The foregoing provisions do not apply to obligations arising from arrangements made before July 22, 1986, except for subsequent exercise of options (subs. (8)); nor do they apply to building works on leasehold land, covered by s.80(6) of the 1980 Act (subs. (6)—but see Sched., Pt. II, para. 3(3), below).

Subss. (7) and (9) provide for regulations in supplementation. The Government have announced that regulations will be made enabling authorities to use deferred purchase schemes to finance one project each, up to £3 million in cost, beginning in any one period of five consecutive years; there will also be exemptions for schemes under which builders build or improve houses under licence on local authority land (*Hansard,* Standing Committee 3, March 17, 1987, cols. 46–47).

Payments of grants and advances

80B. Provision may be made by regulations which, in relation to such cases, to such grants or advances or to such authorities as may be specified in or determined under the regulations—

(a) for the purposes of this Part of this Act treats amounts determined under the regulations as paid, at the times so determined, in respect of expenditure on the making of grants or advances; and

(b) requires payments actually made in respect of any such expenditure to be disregarded for those purposes.

GENERAL NOTE

This section enables regulations to be made making similar provisions in respect of grants and advances to those of section 80A in respect of works.

PART II

FURTHER AMENDMENTS OF PART VIII

1.—(1) In subsection (1)(a) of section 78 of the Local Government, Planning and Land Act 1980 (directions prohibiting the making of payments), for the words from "make" to "aggregate" there shall be substituted the words "do anything the effect of which is that the aggregate of the payments made in any year by the authority in respect of prescribed expenditure exceeds the aggregate of".

(2) Subsection (2) of that section (power to vary or revoke directions) shall be omitted.

2.—(1) In subsection (1) of section 79 of that Act (contravention of Part VIII not in itself beyond the powers of an authority), for the words from "make" to "exceeding" there shall be substituted the words "do anything on the ground only that to do that thing would have the effect that the aggregate of the payments made in any year by the authority in respect of prescribed expenditure exceeds".

(2) In subsection (2) of that section (contravention of direction is beyond powers of authority), for the words from "make" to "contract" there shall be substituted the words "do anything".

3.—(1) In subsection (1) of section 80 of that Act (payments in respect of acquisition of property), for the words from "shall be taken" onwards there shall be substituted the words—

"(a) shall be taken to pay an amount calculated in accordance with subsections (3) and (4) and (8) to (13) below at the time of, and in respect of expenditure on, the acquisition but

(b) shall not be taken to pay or to have paid any other amount in respect of expenditure on the acquisition at that or any other time."

(2) In subsection (2) of that section (deemed payments treated as items of account), for the words "A payment of an amount so calculated" there shall be substituted the words "An amount which is taken in pursuance of this section to have been paid at any time by an authority".

(3) After subsection (6) of that section (work on land in which a leasehold interest is acquired), there shall be inserted the following subsection—

"(6A) For the purposes of subsection (6) above the value at any time of any work carried out in respect of a building to be erected on land in which an authority has acquired a leasehold interest shall be taken to be equal to the aggregate of—

(a) the amounts which have actually been paid by the authority in respect of expenditure on the work; and

(b) the amounts which have not been so paid but are determined by the authority to have fallen due for actual payment by the authority in respect of expenditure on the work or to be likely to fall due for such payment;

and if the Secretary of State has given to any authority, to authorities of any description or to authorities generally any directions as to the manner of making determinations for the purposes of paragraph (b) above, the authority or authorities to whom the directions have been given shall make their determinations for those purposes in accordance with those directions."

4.—(1) After paragraph (a) of subsection (1) of section 82 of that Act (application of Part VIII to Passenger Transport Executives) there shall be inserted the following paragraph—

"(aa) any works which are or are to be carried out for an Executive or, by virtue of subsection (1A) below, are to be treated as if they were or were to be so carried out shall be treated as if they were or were to be carried out for that authority;".

(2) After that subsection there shall be inserted the following subsection—

"(1A) Works shall be treated for the purposes of subsection (1)(aa) above as carried out for an Executive in such cases as may be specified in or determined under regulations."

5. In section 84 of that Act (regulations under Part VIII), after subsection (5) there shall be inserted the following subsection—

"(5A) Regulations made by virtue of section 80A, 80B or 82(1A) above may be made so as to have effect in relation to times before the regulations were made, including times before the Local Government Act 1987 (by virtue of which those provisions have effect) was passed."

6. In section 85 of that Act (supplementary provisions for Part VIII), after subsection (1) there shall be inserted the following subsections—

"(1A) Before giving any direction under section 80(6A) or 80A(5) above the Secretary of State shall consult such associations of authorities as appear to him to be concerned and any authority with whom consultation appears to him to be desirable.

(1B) Any power of the Secretary of State to give directions under this Part of this Act shall include power to vary or revoke a direction given in exercise of that power."

GENERAL NOTE

Pt. II of the Schedule makes sundry amendments to Pt. VIII of the Local Government, Planning and Land Act 1980, for the most part in necessary adaptations consequent on the provisions of the new sections inserted by Pt. I.

Para. 3(3) inserts a new subs. (6A) in s.80 of the 1980 Act, making similar provision to that of the new s.80A in respect of building works on leasehold land covered by s.80(6).

Para. 6 requires the Secretary of State to consult as appropriate before issuing directions as to methods of valuation of works under the new s.80A(5) or 80(6A).

PARLIAMENTARY AND OTHER PENSIONS ACT 1987

(1987 c. 45)

ARRANGEMENT OF SECTIONS
SECT.
1. Continuance of Fund.
2. Power to provide for pensions.
3. Exchequer contributions to Fund.
4. Amendment of Mr Speaker King's Retirement Act 1971.
5. Interpretation.
6. Minor and consequential modifications, savings and repeals.
7. Short title, commencement and extent.

  SCHEDULES:
    Schedule 1—Provisions that may be included in regulations.
    Schedule 2—Existing enactments etc. continued in force.
    Schedule 3—Consequential modifications and savings.
    Schedule 4—Repeals.

An Act to provide for the continuance in existence of the Parliamentary Contributory Pension Fund; to confer power on the Leader of the House of Commons to make regulations with respect to that Fund and with respect to the application of the assets of that Fund in or towards the provision of pensions; to amend Mr Speaker King's Retirement Act 1971; and for connected purposes.   [15th May 1987]

PARLIAMENTARY DEBATES
  Hansard: H.C. Vol. 111, col. 432; Vol. 115, col. 94; Vol. 116, col. 242; H.L. Vol. 487, col. 801.

Continuance of Fund

1.—(1) Subject to the following provisions of this Act, the Parliamentary Contributory Pension Fund (in this Act referred to as "the Fund") shall continue to exist on and after the day on which this section comes into force with the same trustees as it had immediately before that day.

(2) The House of Commons shall have power by Order of the House to remove a trustee of the Fund and, subject to any provision made under section 2 below as to the qualification or number of trustees, to fill any vacancy in the trustees and to appoint additional trustees.

(3) The trustees of the Fund may invest the assets of the Fund, whether at the time in a state of investment or not, in any investment whatever and may also from time to time vary any such investments.

Power to provide for pensions

2.—(1) The Leader of the House of Commons may, with the consent of the Treasury, by regulations make provision with respect to the Fund and with respect to the application of the assets of the Fund in or towards the provision of pensions for or in respect of persons with service to which this section applies.

(2) Subject to subsection (3) below, the service to which this section applies is service as any of the following, that is to say—

  (a) a Member of the House of Commons;
  (b) the holder of any of the offices specified in Parts I to IV of Schedule 1 to the Ministerial and other Salaries Act 1975 (ministerial offices);

(c) the holder of any office specified in Part I of Schedule 2 to that Act (Opposition leaders and whips); or

(d) the holder of the office of Chairman of Ways and Means, Deputy Chairman of Ways and Means, Chairman of Committees of the House of Lords or Deputy Chairman of Committees of the House of Lords.

(3) Regulations under this section shall not provide for the application of any of the assets of the Fund in or towards the provision of pensions for or in respect of persons with service as Lord Chancellor, Prime Minister and First Lord of the Treasury or Speaker of the House of Commons.

(4) Without prejudice to the generality of subsection (1) above, regulations under this section may—

(a) include all or any of the provisions specified in Schedule 1 to this Act;

(b) subject to subsection (5) below, make provision which has effect—

(i) from a date earlier than the date of the making of the regulations containing the provision; or

(ii) in relation to service before the passing of this Act (including, in the case of service falling within subsection (2)(b) or (c) above, service before the passing of the Ministerial and other Salaries Act 1975);

(c) make different provision in relation to different cases, circumstances or persons; and

(d) make such incidental, consequential and transitional provision as the Leader of the House of Commons considers appropriate.

(5) No regulation made under this section shall be construed as restricting the powers of the trustees of the Fund under section 1(3) above.

(6) The Leader of the House of Commons shall not under this section make any regulations in relation to an accrued right which put any person in a worse position than he would have been in apart from the regulations unless the Leader of the House of Commons is satisfied—

(a) that the person in respect of whose service the right has accrued or, as the case may be, will have accrued by the time when the regulations come into force is, at the time of the making of the regulations, in service to which this section applies; or

(b) that an opportunity is given under the regulations for that person or (where that person has died) for the persons who are or may become entitled by virtue of that right to or to the benefit of any pension, or for a person acting on behalf of that person or those persons, to opt for the accrued right to remain unaffected by the regulations.

(7) The power to make regulations under this section shall be exercisable by statutory instrument subject to annulment in pursuance of a resolution of either House of Parliament; but no such regulations shall be made unless the trustees of the Fund and persons appearing to the Leader of the House of Commons to represent persons likely to be affected by the regulations have first been consulted about them.

(8) Where the Leader of the House of Commons has made any proposals for the making of regulations under this section, a copy of any representations made to him by the trustees of the Fund about the proposals shall be laid before the House of Commons.

(9) Schedule 2 to this Act shall have effect for the purpose of treating the enactments and subordinate legislation which relate to the Fund and the payment of pensions out of the Fund and which are in force immediately before the coming into force of this section as if they were contained in regulations made under this section.

(10) In this section "accrued right", in relation to any regulations made under this section, means so much of any right or entitlement to or in respect of a pension payable out of the Fund (including any future or contingent right or entitlement) as—

(a) has accrued under the Parliamentary pension scheme in respect of so much of any person's service as was before the making of the regulations; or

(b) by the time when the regulations come into force, will have accrued under that scheme in respect of any service of a person whose service to which this section applies includes a period of service before the making of the regulations.

Exchequer contributions to Fund

3.—(1) In respect of each financial year an Exchequer contribution shall be paid out of money provided by Parliament into the Fund.

(2) Subject to subsection (6) below, the amount of the contribution to be paid under subsection (1) above in respect of any financial year shall be calculated in accordance with the recommendations for that year contained in a report made under this section by the Government Actuary.

(3) As soon as practicable after the beginning of the period of three years beginning with the relevant date and of each succeeding period of three years, the Government Actuary shall make a report to the trustees of the Fund and to the Treasury on the general financial position of the Fund as at the commencement of the period of three years in which the report is made.

(4) Each report under this section shall contain a recommendation of the Government Actuary as to the rate at which Exchequer contributions should (subject to any subsequent report under this section) be paid into the Fund under this section in respect of any financial year beginning after the report is made; and that rate shall be expressed by reference to such matters as the Government Actuary considers appropriate.

(5) A copy of every report made by the Government Actuary under this section shall be laid before the House of Commons.

(6) Notwithstanding the repeals made by this Act, section 5 of the Parliamentary and other Pensions Act 1972 shall continue to have effect after the coming into force of this section for the purpose—

(a) of requiring a report to be made by the Government Actuary in accordance with that section in respect of any three year period which is current for the purposes of that section when this section comes into force and in respect of which no report has already been made;

(b) of requiring any report so made to be laid before the House of Commons; and

(c) of determining the amount of the Exchequer contribution to be paid into the Fund in respect of any financial year beginning before the making of the first report to be made under this section;

and for the purposes of this subsection any recommendation contained in a report made under that section in respect of the three year period mentioned in paragraph (a) above shall, so far as it relates to the last year of that period (and except in so far as the Government Actuary otherwise recommends in the report), be treated as the recommendation to be taken into account under that section in relation to any financial year beginning after the end of the said last year and before the making of the said first report.

(7) In this section "the relevant date" means the date immediately following the end of the three year period which is current for the purposes of the said section 5 when this section comes into force.

Amendment of Mr Speaker King's Retirement Act 1971

4.—(1) Subsection (2) of section 1 of Mr Speaker King's Retirement Act 1971 shall have effect as from the coming into force of this subsection as if the annuity which would have been payable to Una, the late Lady Maybray-King, if she had survived the late Lord Maybray-King were required to be paid, during her life, to Sheila, Lady Maybray-King, his widow.

(2) In the proviso to the said subsection (2) (application of terms and conditions applying under Part I of the Parliamentary and other Pensions Act 1972), for the words from "Part I" onwards there shall be substituted the words "the Parliamentary pension scheme (within the meaning of the Parliamentary and other Pensions Act 1987)".

(3) There shall be charged on and paid out of the Consolidated Fund any increase attributable to this section in the sums so charged and paid under the said Act of 1971.

Interpretation

5.—(1) In this Act, except in so far as the context otherwise requires—

"the Fund" means the Parliamentary Contributory Pension Fund;

"the Leader of the House of Commons" means the Minister of the Crown who is for the time being designated as Leader of the House of Commons by the Prime Minister and First Lord of the Treasury;

"modifications" includes additions, alterations and omissions, and cognate expressions shall be construed accordingly;

"the Parliamentary pension scheme" means the provisions of any regulations made under section 2 above or of any enactment or subordinate legislation which by virtue of this Act has effect as if it were contained in regulations so made;

"pension" includes gratuity;

"subordinate legislation" has the same meaning as in the Interpretation Act 1978.

(2) For the purposes of this Act a person shall be treated as a Member of the House of Commons at any time if, at that time, a salary is or was payable to him under such resolutions of the House of Commons relating to the remuneration of Members as are or were for the time being in force.

Minor and consequential modifications, savings and repeals

6.—(1) Schedule 3 to this Act, which in connection with the provisions of this Act makes certain modifications and savings, shall have effect.

(2) Subject to section 3(6) above and Schedules 2 and 3 to this Act, the enactments mentioned in Schedule 4 to this Act are hereby repealed to the extent specified in the third column of that Schedule.

Short title, commencement and extent

7.—(1) This Act may be cited as the Parliamentary and other Pensions Act 1987.

(2) This Act shall come into force on such day as the Leader of the House of Commons may by order made by statutory instrument appoint, and different days may be so appointed for different provisions or for different purposes.

(3) This Act extends to Northern Ireland.

SCHEDULES

SCHEDULE 1

Provisions that may be Included in Regulations

1. Provision as to the administration of the Fund, as to the management and application of the assets of the Fund as to the number, qualification and proceedings of the trustees of the Fund.

2. Provision authorising or requiring contributions and other sums to be paid into the Fund by or on behalf of persons in service to which section 2 of this Act applies, including provision for those contributions and sums to be paid by means of deductions from salary and, in the case of a person who does not draw a salary, provision for them to be paid out of money provided by Parliament.

3. Provision as to the circumstances in which there is to be entitlement to a pension payable out of the Fund, as to the conditions of any such entitlement, as to the persons to or for the benefit of whom such a pension is to be payable, as to the calculation of the amount of any such pension and as to the payment or commutation of any such pension.

4. Provision for the application of assets of the Fund in or towards the provision of pensions to be paid otherwise than out of the Fund and, in connection with any such provision, provision for the payment into the Fund out of money provided by Parliament of sums in addition to those paid into the Fund under section 3 of this Act.

5. Provision for the payment and receipt of transfer values by the trustees of the Fund (including provision for the payment of such values into the Consolidated Fund), and provision for the transfer and receipt by those trustees, in lieu of transfer values, of funds or policies of insurance.

6. Provision authorising service other than service to which section 2 of this Act applies to be taken into account, in addition to service to which that section does apply, for the purposes of any of the regulations.

7. Provision as to the circumstances and manner—

   (a) in which amounts equal to some or all of the contributions and other sums paid by or on behalf of a person into the Fund may be repaid or paid to him; and

   (b) in which any such amounts are to be paid out of the Consolidated Fund in respect of any transfer values paid into that Fund,

and provision as to whether any repayment or payment made out of either Fund is to be made with or without interest.

8. Provision which, in relation to such cases, circumstances or persons as may be specified in or determined under the regulations, authorises any sum due to be paid out of the Fund in respect of a person who has died to be paid without probate or other proof of title.

9. Provision rendering void any assignment (or, in Scotland, assignation) of or charge on, or any agreement to assign or charge, any pension which is or may become payable out of the Fund; and, without prejudice to paragraph 13 below, provision modifying the effect in relation to any such pension of so much of any enactment or subordinate legislation (whether passed or made before or after the passing of this Act) as relates to bankruptcy or, in Scotland, to the sequestration of a debtor's estate.

10. Provision conferring functions under the regulations on such persons as may be specified in or determined under the regulations.

11. Provision making the approval, satisfaction or opinion of persons on whom functions are conferred by or under the regulations material for the purposes of any provision of the regulations.

12. Provision which, with or without modifications, applies in relation to a pension payable out of the Fund so much of any enactment or subordinate legislation (whether passed or made before or after the passing of this Act) as relates to any other pension, being a pension payable out of money provided by Parliament.

13. Provision making such modifications of any enactment or subordinate legislation (whether passed or made before or after the passing of this Act) as the Leader of the House of Commons considers appropriate in consequence of any provision of the regulations.

SCHEDULE 2

Enactments

1.—(1) Notwithstanding the repeals made by this Act, on and after the appointed day the
existing enactments shall have effect, subject to the following provisions of this Schedule, as
if they were contained in regulations made under and in accordance with section 2 of this
Act and could be modified accordingly.

(2) In any enactment contained in Part I of the Parliamentary and other Pensions Act
1972, as that enactment has effect under sub-paragraph (1) above, any reference to section
31 of that Act shall have effect as a reference to the provisions, as from time to time
modified by virtue of paragraph 3 of Schedule 3 to this Act, of the Pensions (Increase) Act
1971 and sections 59 and 59A of the Social Security Pensions Act 1975.

(3) In subsection (1) of section 24 of the said Act of 1972 (payments due to deceased
persons), as it has effect under sub-paragraph (1) above, the reference to the amount
payments in excess of which cannot (except in so far as they are due by way of interest) be
made under that subsection shall have effect as a reference to the amount of the limit for the
time being specified by virtue of orders made from time to time under section 6 of the
Administration of Estates (Small Payments) Act 1965 in the enactments listed in Part I of
Schedule 1 to the said Act of 1965.

Subordinate legislation

2. Where any of the existing enactments contains any power to make subordinate
legislation, that power shall cease to have effect on the appointed day, but on and after that
day any subordinate legislation which was made under that power and is in force immediately
before that day shall have effect, with the necessary modifications, as if it were contained in
regulations made under and in accordance with section 2 of this Act and could be modified
accordingly.

Commencement and transitional provisions

3.—(1) Where for the purpose of determining the enactments and subordinate legislation
which have effect under paragraphs 1 and 2 above it is necessary to take account of any
modifications or successive modifications of any enactment or subordinate legislation as
originally enacted or made—
   (a) neither paragraph 1 nor paragraph 2 above shall apply in relation to any commence-
       ment or transitional provision or saving made in connection with any such modifica-
       tions; but
   (b) notwithstanding the repeals made by this Act, on and after the appointed day any
       such provision or saving (whether contained in, or in subordinate legislation made
       under, any existing enactment or not) shall continue to have effect, in so far as it
       relates to any enactment or subordinate legislation which has effect under paragraph
       1 or 2 above, for the purpose of determining the cases, circumstances or persons in
       relation to which that enactment or subordinate legislation so has effect.

(2) On and after the appointed day so much of any enactment or subordinate legislation
as, notwithstanding its modification by any other enactment or subordinate legislation, is
continuing immediately before that day to have effect, in relation to particular cases,
circumstances or persons—
   (a) by virtue of any commencement or transitional provision or saving made in connection
       with any such modifications as are mentioned in sub-paragraph (1) above; or
   (b) by virtue of section 36(2) of the Parliamentary and other Pensions Act 1972
       (transitional provisions),
shall continue to have effect in accordance with the provision or saving, or with the said
section 36(2), as if it too were contained in regulations made under and in accordance with
section 2 of this Act and could be modified accordingly.

(3) Sub-paragraph (2) above shall apply to the provisions of section 8 of the Parliamentary
Pensions Act 1978 (as they have effect by virtue of sections 3(1) and 5(7) of the Parliamentary
Pensions etc. Act 1984) as it applies to the other enactments repealed by virtue of the said
section 3(1).

(4) In subsection (2) of section 14 of the Ministerial Salaries and Members Pensions Act
1965 (payments due to deceased persons), as it has effect under sub-paragraph (2) above,
the reference to the amount payments in excess of which cannot (except in so far as they are

due by way of interest) be made under that subsection shall have effect as a reference to the amount of the limit for the time being specified by virtue of orders made from time to time under section 6 of the Administration of Estates (Small Payments) Act 1965 in the enactments listed in Part I of Schedule 1 to the last-mentioned Act of 1965.

Supplemental

4.—(1) Anything done before the appointed day under or for the purposes of any provision which by virtue of this Schedule has effect as if it were contained in regulations made under section 2 of this Act shall have effect on and after that day as if it had been done under or for the purposes of that provision as so contained.

(2) Subject to any regulations made under section 2 of this Act, any reference in any enactment or subordinate legislation, or in any deed or other instrument or document, to any provision which by virtue of this Schedule has effect as if it were contained in regulations so made shall have effect, so far as necessary for the purposes of or in connection with the provisions of this Schedule, as a reference to the corresponding provision having effect as if so contained.

(3) Where any period of time specified in any enactment or subordinate legislation having effect under this Schedule as if it were contained in regulations made under section 2 of this Act is current on the appointed day, this Schedule shall have effect in relation to that period as if the appointed day had been before the period began to run.

Interpretation

5. In this Schedule—

"the appointed day" means the day on which section 2 of this Act comes into force;

"commencement or transitional provision" includes so much of any provision as provides for, or is to be construed as providing for, any enactment or subordinate legislation to come into force only with effect from a particular time or only in relation to particular cases, circumstances or persons; and

"the existing enactments" means the following enactments as they have effect immediately before the appointed day, namely—

(a) the enactments contained in Part I of the Parliamentary and other Pensions Act 1972 (including Schedules 1 and 2), other than sections 1(1) to (4) and (7), 5, 23 and 24(4);

(b) sections 30, 33 and 35 of the said Act of 1972; and

(c) without prejudice to section 20(2) of the Interpretation Act 1978 (references to enactments) in its application in relation to paragraphs (a) and (b) above, sections 2 to 5, 6(2), 7, 11, 12(8) and 18(2) and (3) of the Parliamentary Pensions Act 1978 and sections 3(4) to (6), 4(3) to (6), 5(1) and (2) and 6 of the Parliamentary Pensions etc. Act 1984.

Section 6   SCHEDULE 3

CONSEQUENTIAL MODIFICATIONS AND SAVINGS

The Superannuation (Miscellaneous Provisions) Act 1948

1.—(1) For the purposes of section 2 of the Superannuation (Miscellaneous Provisions) Act 1948 (pensions of persons transferring to different employment) a person's service—

(a) as a Member of the House of Commons of the United Kingdom during any period in respect of which he is a participant in relation to his membership of that House in arrangements contained in the Parliamentary pension scheme; or

(b) as the holder of an office mentioned in subsection (2)(b), (c) or (d) of section 2 of this Act during any period in respect of which he is a participant in relation to that office in any such arrangements; or

(c) as a Member of the House of Commons of the United Kingdom or the holder of an office so mentioned during any period in respect of which his service was treated as employment by virtue of section 23 of the Parliamentary and other Pensions Act 1972; or

(d) as a Member of the House of Commons of Northern Ireland,

shall be treated as employment within the meaning of the said Act of 1948, whether or not it would be so treated apart from this paragraph.

(2) Without prejudice to the power conferred by virtue of paragraph 13 of Schedule 1 to this Act, regulations under section 2 of this Act may make provision specifying the circumstances in which any person is to be regarded for the purposes of this paragraph as being a participant in relation to his membership of the House of Commons of the United Kingdom, or in relation to any office, in arrangements contained in the Parliamentary pension scheme.

(3) In relation to any time before the coming into force of the first regulations to be made containing any such provision as is mentioned in sub-paragraph (2) above a person shall be treated as a participant in arrangements contained in the Parliamentary pension scheme—

   (a) in relation to his Membership of the House of Commons, if he is a Member of that House;

   (b) in relation to any office, if he is a participant under section 2 of the Parliamentary and other Pensions Act 1972, as that section has effect by virtue of Schedule 2 to this Act.

(4) Nothing in this Act shall affect the validity of any rules which are in force at the coming into force of this paragraph under section 2 of the said Act of 1948 or which have effect under section 36(4) of the Parliamentary and other Pensions Act 1972 as if they were so in force.

The Income and Corporation Taxes Act 1970

2.—(1) In section 211(2) of the Income and Corporation Taxes Act 1970 (exemption from income tax of Parliamentary pension funds), for paragraph (b) there shall be substituted the following paragraph—

   "(b) the Parliamentary Contributory Pension Fund;".

(2) Subsection (1) of section 229 of the said Act of 1970 (annuity premiums of Ministers and other officers) shall have effect with the following amendments, that is to say—

   (a) in paragraph (b), for the words "elects not to be a participant under section 2 of the Parliamentary and other Pensions Act 1972" there shall be substituted the words "is not a participant in relation to that office in arrangements contained in the Parliamentary pension scheme but is a participant in relation to his membership of the House of Commons in any such arrangements"; and

   (b) for the words from "(in accordance with any" to "that resolution)" there shall be substituted the words "and the salary which (in accordance with any such resolution as is mentioned in subsection (1B)(a) below)";

   (c) for the words from "In this subsection" onwards there shall be substituted the following subsections—

   "(1A) In this section—

      'Member's pensionable salary' means a Member's ordinary salary under any resolution of the House of Commons which, being framed otherwise than as an expression of opinion, is for the time being in force relating to the remuneration of Members or, if the resolution provides for a Member's ordinary salary thereunder to be treated for pension purposes as being at a higher rate, a notional yearly salary at that higher rate;

      'qualifying office' means an office mentioned in paragraph (b), (c) or (d) of subsection (2) of section 2 of the Parliamentary and other Pensions Act 1987;

      'the Parliamentary pension scheme' has the same meaning as in that Act;

     and, without prejudice to the power conferred by virtue of paragraph 13 of Schedule 1 to that Act, regulations under section 2 of that Act may make provision specifying the circumstances in which a person is to be regarded for the purposes of this section as being or not being a participant in relation to his Membership of the House of Commons, or in relation to any office, in arrangements contained in the Parliamentary pension scheme.

   (1B) In subsection (1A) above 'a Member's ordinary salary', in relation to any resolution of the House of Commons, means—

      (a) if the resolution provides for salary to be paid to Members at different rates according to whether or not they are holders of particular offices, or are in receipt of salaries or pensions as the holders or former holders of particular offices, a Member's yearly salary at the higher or highest rate; and

      (b) in any other case, a Member's yearly salary at the rate specified in or determined under the resolution."

The Pensions (Increase) Act 1971

3.—(1) In section 5(3) of the Pensions (Increase) Act 1971 (power to modify Act in relation to certain official pensions), the reference to the provisions of that Act and of sections 59 and 59A of the Social Security Pensions Act 1975 shall include a reference to those provisions as they have effect in consequence of the following provisions of this paragraph.

(2) Notwithstanding the repeal by this Act of Part I and section 34(1) of the Parliamentary and other Pensions Act 1972, section 19(2)(a) of the said Act of 1971 shall continue to have effect, after the coming into force of the repeal, with the amendment made by the said section 34(1).

(3) In Schedule 2 to the said Act of 1971, for paragraph 3A there shall be substituted the following paragraph—

"3A. A pension which under the Parliamentary pension scheme (within the meaning of the Parliamentary and other Pensions Act 1987) is payable out of the Parliamentary Contributory Pension Fund."

(4) Without prejudice to paragraph 4 of Schedule 2 to this Act—

(a) any regulations made under section 5(3) of the said Act of 1971 which immediately before the day on which this paragraph comes into force have effect in relation to pensions payable under any enactment the effect of which is continued under Schedule 2 to this Act shall have effect on and after that day, with the necessary modifications, as if they had effect in relation to pensions payable under the corresponding provision of the Parliamentary pension scheme; and

(b) any increases made before that day under the said Act of 1971 and sections 59 and 59A of the Social Security Pensions Act 1975 shall be taken into account in determining the amount of any pension which was being paid before that day and continues to be paid on and after that day under that scheme.

(5) Subject to any regulations made under section 2 of this Act, the provisions of the said Act of 1971 and of the said sections 59 and 59A shall not be taken into account in calculating any amount—

(a) in accordance with subsection (1) of section 8 of the Parliamentary and other Pensions Act 1972 (alternative calculation of pension by reference to the 1965 Act), as that subsection has effect by virtue of Schedule 2 to this Act; or

(b) for the purposes of subsection (2) of section 25 of the said Act of 1972 (meaning of "basic or prospective pension or pensions"), as that subsection so has effect.

Parliamentary and other Pensions Act 1972

4.—(1) In section 27 of the Parliamentary and other Pensions Act 1972 (pensions for dependants of Prime Minister or Speaker) for the words from "the provisions of sections 13 to 15" in subsection (1) to the end of subsection (2) there shall be substituted the words "the designated provisions shall have effect as if—

(a) at the time of his death that person had been entitled in respect of service as a Member of the House of Commons to receive a pension payable under the provisions of the Parliamentary pension scheme out of the Parliamentary Contributory Pension Fund;

(b) the annual amount of that pension had been an amount equal to the annual amount of such pension calculated in accordance with subsection (3) or (in the case of a person who held office as Speaker) subsection (4) of section 26 of this Act as would have been payable to him at the time of his death if he had ceased to hold office immediately before his death and subsection (2) of that section and section 31 of this Act were disregarded; and

(c) references in the designated provisions to the trustees of the Fund were references to the Treasury.

(2) For the purposes of subsection (1) above the designated provisions are such of the provisions contained in the Parliamentary pension scheme as—

(a) have effect for the purposes of, or in connection with, the payment out of the Parliamentary Contributory Pension Fund of a pension in respect of service as a Member of the House of Commons—

(i) to the widow or widower of a person with such service; or

(ii) for the benefit of any children of any person;

and

(b) are designated for the purposes of this section by regulations made by the Leader of the House of Commons.

(2A) The power to make regulations designating any provisions for the purposes of this section shall be exercisable by statutory instrument subject to annulment in pursuance of a resolution of either House of Parliament."

(2) After subsection (4) of the said section 27 there shall be inserted the following subsection—

"(5) In this section—

'children' includes adopted children, stepchildren and illegitimate children; and

'the Leader of the House of Commons' and 'the Parliamentary pension scheme' have the same meanings as in the Parliamentary and other Pensions Act 1987."

(3) This paragraph shall not apply in relation to a person who, having held office as Prime Minister and First Lord of the Treasury or Speaker of the House of Commons, died before the coming into force of this paragraph; and in relation to such a person section 27 of the said Act of 1972, and the provisions applied by that section, shall have effect as if this Act had not been passed.

(4) There shall be charged on and paid out of the Consolidated Fund any increase attributable to this paragraph in the sums so charged and paid under section 27 of the said Act of 1972.

The European Parliament (Pay and Pensions) Act 1979

5. In section 8(1) of the European Parliament (Pay and Pensions) Act 1979 (interpretation), for the words "section 3(6) of the Parliamentary and other Pensions Act 1972" there shall be substituted the words "subsections (1A) and (1B) of section 229 of the Income and Corporation Taxes Act 1970".

The House of Commons Members' Fund and Parliamentary Pensions Act 1981

6. In section 1(5)(b) of the House of Commons Members' Fund and Parliamentary Pensions Act 1981 (disqualification from benefit of certain office holders and persons receiving pensions), for the words from "a qualifying office" to "that Act" there shall be substituted the words "an office mentioned in paragraph (b), (c) or (d) of section 2(2) of the Parliamentary and other Pensions Act 1987 or is in receipt of a pension under the Parliamentary and other Pensions Act 1972."

Section 6   SCHEDULE 4

REPEALS

Chapter	Short title	Extent of repeal
1965 c.32.	The Administration of Estates (Small Payments) Act 1965.	In section 6(1)(b), the words from "section 14(2)" to "1972".
1972 c.48.	The Parliamentary and other Pensions Act 1972.	Part I. Section 30. In section 31, subsection (1), in subsection (4) the words "and by section 22(3) of the Act of 1978" and subsection (5). Sections 33 and 34. In section 35(1), the definitions of "the Act of 1978", "contribution", "effective resolution" and "interest". Section 36(1), (2) and (4). Schedules 1 to 4.
1975 c.72.	The Children Act 1975.	In Schedule 3, paragraph 77.
1976 c.48.	The Parliamentary and other Pensions Act 1976.	Sections 1 to 4.
1978 c.56.	The Parliamentary Pensions Act 1978.	The whole Act.
1981 c.7.	The House of Commons Members' Fund and Parliamentary Pensions Act 1981.	Section 4. Section 5(2).
1983 c.20.	The Mental Health Act 1983.	In Schedule 4, paragraph 31.
1984 c.52.	The Parliamentary Pensions etc. Act 1984.	Sections 1 to 11. Section 15(2)(a). Section 16. The Schedule.
1986 c.50.	The Social Security Act 1986.	In section 17(3), paragraph (f).

DIPLOMATIC AND CONSULAR PREMISES ACT 1987

(1987 c. 46)

ARRANGEMENT OF SECTIONS

PART I

DIPLOMATIC AND CONSULAR PREMISES

ECT.
1. Acquisition and loss by land of diplomatic or consular status.
2. Vesting of former diplomatic or consular premises.
3. Duty of sale.
4. Provisions supplementary to sections 2 and 3.
5. Interpretation of Part I.

PART II

AMENDMENTS OF DIPLOMATIC PRIVILEGES ACT 1964, CONSULAR RELATIONS ACT 1968, AND CRIMINAL LAW ACT 1977

6. Amendments of 1964 and 1968 Acts.
7. Amendments of 1977 Act.

PART III

SUPPLEMENTARY

8. Financial provision.
9. Short title, commencement and extent.

SCHEDULES:
   Schedule 1—Provisions supplementary to sections 2 and 3
      Part I—England and Wales
      Part II—Scotland
      Part III—Northern Ireland
   Schedule 2—Amendments of 1964 and 1968 Acts

An Act to make provision as to what land is diplomatic or consular premises; to give the Secretary of State power to vest certain land in himself; to impose on him a duty to sell land vested in him in the exercise of that power; to give certain provisions of the Vienna Convention on Diplomatic Relations and the Vienna Convention on Consular Relations the force of law in the United Kingdom by amending Schedule 1 to the Diplomatic Privileges Act 1964 and Schedule 1 to the Consular Relations Act 1968; to amend section 9(2) of the Criminal Law Act 1977; and for connected purposes.

[15th May 1987]

PARLIAMENTARY DEBATES
   Hansard: H.C. Vol. 115, col. 483; Vol. 116, col. 237; H.L. Vol. 487, cols. 618, 804.

PART I

DIPLOMATIC AND CONSULAR PREMISES

Acquisition and loss by land of diplomatic or consular status

1.—(1) Subject to subsection (2) below, where a State desires that land shall be diplomatic or consular premises, it shall apply to the Secretary of State for his consent to the land being such premises.

(2) A State need not make such an application in relation to land if the Secretary of State accepted it as diplomatic or consular premises immediately before the coming into force of this section.

(3) In no case is land to be regarded as a State's diplomatic or consular premises for the purposes of any enactment or rule of law unless it has been so accepted or the Secretary of State has given that State consent under this section in relation to it; and if—

(a) a State ceases to use land for the purposes of its mission or exclusively for the purposes of a consular post; or

(b) the Secretary of State withdraws his acceptance or consent in relation to land,

it thereupon ceases to be diplomatic or consular premises for the purposes of all enactments and rules of law.

(4) The Secretary of State shall only give or withdraw consent or withdraw acceptance if he is satisfied that to do so is permissible under international law.

(5) In determining whether to do so he shall have regard to all material considerations, and in particular, but without prejudice to the generality of this subsection—

(a) to the safety of the public;

(b) to national security; and

(c) to town and country planning.

(6) If a State intends to cease using land as premises of its mission or as consular premises, it shall give the Secretary of State notice of that intention, specifying the date on which it intends to cease so using them

(7) In any proceedings a certificate issued by or under the authority of the Secretary of State stating any fact relevant to the question whether or not land was at any time diplomatic or consular premises shall be conclusive of that fact.

Vesting of former diplomatic or consular premises

2.—(1) Where—

(a) the Secretary of State formerly accepted land as diplomatic or consular premises but did not accept it as such premises immediately before the coming into force of this section; or

(b) land has ceased to be diplomatic or consular premises after the coming into force of this section but not less than 12 months before the exercise of the power conferred on the Secretary of State by this subsection,

the Secretary of State may by order provide that this section shall apply to that land.

(2) The Secretary of State shall only exercise the power conferred by subsection (1) above if he is satisfied that to do so is permissible under international law.

(3) In determining whether to exercise it he shall have regard to all material considerations, and in particular, but without prejudice to the generality of this subsection, to any of the considerations mentioned in section 1(5) above that appears to him to be relevant.

(4) An order under subsection (1) above shall be made by statutory instrument, and a statutory instrument containing any such order shall be

subject to annulment in pursuance of a resolution of either House of Parliament.

(5) The Secretary of State may by deed poll vest in himself such estate or interest in land to which this section applies as appears to him to be appropriate.

(6) A deed poll under this section may also comprise any portion of a building in which the former diplomatic or consular premises are situated.

(7) In relation to land in Scotland this section shall have effect with the substitution of references to an order for references to a deed poll, and such an order shall take effect immediately it is made.

(8) Subject to subsection (9) below, in a case falling within paragraph (a) of subsection (1) above the Secretary of State may only exercise the power conferred by that subsection before the end of the period of two months beginning with the date on which this section comes into force.

(9) In such a case the power continues to be exercisable after the end of that period if the Secretary of State within that period—

  (a) certifies that he reserves the right to exercise it; and

  (b) unless he considers it inappropriate or impracticable to do so, serves a copy of the certificate on the owner of any estate or interest in the land.

(10) Where—

  (a) circumstances have arisen in consequence of which the power conferred by subsection (1) above is exercisable; but

  (b) the Secretary of State serves on the owner of the land in relation to which it has become exercisable notice that he does not intend to exercise the power in relation to that land,

it shall cease to be exercisable in relation to it in consequence of those circumstances.

(11) If—

  (a) the Secretary of State has exercised the power conferred by subsection (1) above in relation to land; but

  (b) serves on the owner notice that he does not intend to execute a deed poll under this section, or if the land is in Scotland to make an order under it, relating to the land,

the power to vest conferred by this section shall cease to be exercisable.

Duty of sale

3.—(1) Where an estate or interest in land has vested in the Secretary of State under section 2 above, it shall be his duty to sell it as soon as it is reasonably practicable to do so, taking all reasonable steps to ensure that the price is the best that can reasonably be obtained.

(2) The Secretary of State shall apply the purchase money—

  (a) firstly in payment of expenses properly incurred by him as incidental to the sale or any attempted sale;

  (b) secondly in discharge of prior incumbrances to which the sale is not made subject or in the making of any payments to mortgagees required by Schedule 1 to this Act;

  (c) thirdly in payment of expenses relating to the land reasonably incurred by him on repairs or security;

  (d) fourthly in discharge of such liabilities to pay rates or sums in lieu of rates on the land or on any other land as the Secretary of State thinks fit;

  (e) fifthly in discharge of such judgment debts arising out of matters relating to the land or to any other land as he thinks fit,

and, subject to subsection (3) below, shall pay any residue to the person divested of the estate or interest.

(3) Where a State was divested but there is no person with whom Her Majesty's Government of the United Kingdom has dealings as the Government of that State, the Secretary of State shall hold the residue until there is such a person and then pay it.

(4) A sum held by the Secretary of State under subsection (3) above shall be placed in a bank account bearing interest at such rate as the Treasury may approve.

Provisions supplementary to sections 2 and 3

4. Part I of Schedule 1 to this Act shall have effect to supplement sections 2 and 3 above in England and Wales, Part II shall have effect to supplement them in Scotland and Part III shall have effect to supplement them in Northern Ireland.

Interpretation of Part I

5. In this Part of this Act—
"consular post" and "consular premises" have the meanings given by the definitions in paragraph 1(a) and (j) of Article 1 of the 1963 Convention as that Article has effect in the United Kingdom by virtue of section 1 of and Schedule 1 to the Consular Relations Act 1968;
"diplomatic premises" means premises of the mission of a State;
"mortgage" includes a charge or lien for securing money or money's worth, and references to mortgagees shall be construed accordingly;
"premises of the mission" has the meaning given by the definition in Article 1(i) of the 1961 Convention as that Article has effect in the United Kingdom by virtue of section 2 of and Schedule 1 to the Diplomatic Privileges Act 1964;
"the 1961 Convention" means the Vienna Convention on Diplomatic Relations signed in 1961; and
"the 1963 Convention" means the Vienna Convention on Consular Relations signed in 1963.

Part II

Amendments of Diplomatic Privileges Act 1964, Consular Relations Act 1968, and Criminal Law Act 1977

Amendments of 1964 and 1968 Acts

6. Schedule 2 to this Act shall have effect for the purpose of making amendments in Schedule 1 to the Diplomatic Privileges Act 1964 and Schedule 1 to the Consular Relations Act 1968 (provisions of 1961 and 1963 Conventions having force of law in the United Kingdom).

Amendments of 1977 Act

7.—(1) In section 9(2) of the Criminal Law Act 1977—
(a) the following paragraph shall be inserted after paragraph (a)—
"(aa) the premises of a closed diplomatic mission;" and
(b) the following paragraph shall be inserted after paragraph (b)—
"(bb) the premises of a closed consular post;".

(2) The following subsection shall be inserted after that subsection—

"(2A) In subsection (2) above—

"the premises of a closed diplomatic mission" means premises which fall within Article 45 of the Convention mentioned in subsection (2)(a) above (as that Article has effect in the United Kingdom by virtue of the section and Schedule mentioned in that paragraph); and

"the premises of a closed consular post" means premises which fall within Article 27 of the Convention mentioned in subsection (2)(b) above (as that Article has effect in the United Kingdom by virtue of the section and Schedule mentioned in that paragraph);".

PART III

SUPPLEMENTARY

Financial provision

8. There shall be paid out of money provided by Parliament any expenses of the Secretary of State under this Act.

Short title, commencement and extent

9.—(1) This Act may be cited as the Diplomatic and Consular Premises Act 1987.

(2) This Act shall come into force on such day as the Secretary of State may by order made by statutory instrument appoint and different days may be appointed in pursuance of this section for different provisions or different purposes of the same provision.

(3) This Act extends to Northern Ireland.

SCHEDULES

Section 4   SCHEDULE 1

PROVISIONS SUPPLEMENTARY TO SECTIONS 2 AND 3

PART I

ENGLAND AND WALES

Interpretation

1. In this Part of this Schedule—

"the registrar" means the Chief Land Registrar;

"the registry" means Her Majesty's Land Registry;

"the searches rules" means the Land Registration (Official Searches) Rules 1986 and any rules amending or replacing them;

and expressions defined in section 3 of the Land Registration Act 1925 have the meanings assigned to them by that section.

General

2.—(1) If the Secretary of State gives notice to the registrar that he has reason to believe that any register or document in the custody of the registrar may contain information relating to any person or property specified in the notice which would be of assistance to him in connection with the exercise of the power conferred on him by section 2 above, the registrar shall permit him to inspect and make copies of and extracts from any such register or document so far as it relates to any such person or property.

(2) The following paragraph shall be inserted after subsection (1)(a) of section 112 of the Land Registration Act 1925 (inspection of register and other documents at Land Registry)—

"(aa) to paragraph 2(1) of Schedule 1 to the Diplomatic and Consular Premises Act 1987 (power of Secretary of State to inspect register in connection with exercise of power to vest in himself former diplomatic or consular premises);".

3. A deed poll under section 2 above shall have effect to vest in the Secretary of State the benefit of any covenant touching and concerning the land to which the deed relates but not annexed to it if, immediately before the vesting of the estate to which the deed relates, the covenant was enforceable by the person divested of that estate.

4. Where—

(a) a term of years has vested in the Secretary of State under section 2 above; and

(b) assignment of the term is absolutely prohibited,

the prohibition shall be treated, in relation to an assignment on sale under section 3 above as if it were a provision to the effect that the term may not be assigned without the consent of the landlord and that such consent shall not be unreasonably withheld.

Registered land

5.—(1) If an estate which the Secretary of State proposes to vest in himself is registered land—

(a) he shall be treated for the purposes of the searches rules as a purchaser within the meaning of those rules; and

(b) the deed vesting the registered land in him shall be treated for the purposes of those rules as the instrument effecting the purchase.

(2) If after vesting registered land in himself the Secretary of State lodges the vesting deed at the registry the registrar shall register him as the proprietor of the land.

Unregistered land

6. A conveyance by the Secretary of State under this Act shall have effect if the estate conveyed is not registered land—

(a) to vest the estate conveyed in the purchaser free from any mortgage to which the sale is not made subject; and

(b) to extinguish any other person's title to the estate conveyed.

7.—(1) Where by virtue of paragraph 6 above land is discharged from a mortgage, the mortgagee shall be entitled, subject to the following provisions of this paragraph and to the claims of any prior mortgagee, to have the proceeds of sale applied in payment of the sums secured by the mortgage.

(2) The Secretary of State may by publishing such notice or notices as he thinks appropriate require any person who claims to be entitled to a payment under sub-paragraph (1) above to send particulars of his claim to the Secretary of State within the time, not being less than two months, fixed in the notice or, where more than one is published, in the last of them.

(3) At the end of the time fixed by the notice or, where more than one is published, the last of them, the Secretary of State shall not be liable to any person of whose claim he has not then received particulars.

8. Where, after land has become vested in the Secretary of State under section 2 above, a person retains possession of any document relating to the title to the land, he shall be deemed to have given the Secretary of State an acknowledgment in writing of the Secretary of State's right to production of that document and to delivery of copies thereof and (except where he retains possession of the document as mortgagee or trustee or otherwise in a fiduciary capacity) an undertaking for safe custody thereof; and section 64 of the Law of Property Act 1925 shall have effect accordingly, and on the basis that the acknowledgment and undertaking did not contain any such expression of contrary intention as is mentioned in that section.

PART II

SCOTLAND

9. In this Part of this Schedule "order" means an order under section 2(5) above.

10. An order shall contain a particular description of the lands affected or a description

by reference of those lands in the manner provided by section 61 of the Conveyancing (Scotland) Act 1874.

11. On the date on which an order is made, the land specified in the order, together with the right to enter upon and take possession of it, shall vest in the Secretary of State.

12.—(1) Where the Secretary of State has effected a sale of the premises or any part thereof and grants to the purchaser or his nominee a disposition of the subjects sold, which bears to be in implement of the sale and which does not bear to be subject to a prior security, then, on that disposition being duly recorded or (as the case may be) registered, those subjects shall be disburdened of any heritable security or diligence affecting the subjects.

(2) Where on a sale as aforesaid the premises remain subject to a prior security, the recording of a disposition under sub-paragraph (1) above shall not affect the rights of the creditor in that security, but the Secretary of State shall have the like right as the debtor to redeem the security.

13. Where a lease has vested in the Secretary of State by virtue of an order and that lease prohibits assignation absolutely, that prohibition shall be treated as if it were a prohibition to the extent only that the lease shall not be assigned without the consent of the landlord, such consent not to be unreasonably nor unfairly withheld nor delayed.

14. Where, after land has become vested in the Secretary of State under section 2 above, a person retains possession of any document relating to the title to the land, he shall be deemed to have given to the Secretary of State an acknowledgment in writing of the right of the Secretary of State to production of that document and to delivery of copies thereof and (except where he retains possession of the document as heritable creditor or as trustee or otherwise in a fiduciary capacity) an undertaking for safe custody thereof.

15. After an order has been made it may be recorded in the General Register of Sasines or (as the case may be) in the Land Register of Scotland.

Part III

Northern Ireland

Interpretation

16. In this Part of this Schedule—
"estate" includes interest;
"registered land" means land the title to which is registered under the Land
Registration Act (Northern Ireland) 1970;
"unregistered land" means land the title to which is not registered under the Land
Registration Act (Northern Ireland) 1970.

General

17.—(1) Where—
(a) a tenancy has vested in the Secretary of State under section 2 above; and
(b) assignment of the tenancy is absolutely prohibited,
the prohibition shall be treated, in relation to an assignment on sale under section 3 above, as if it were a provision to the effect that the tenancy may not be assigned without the consent of the landlord and that such consent shall not be unreasonably withheld.

(2) In this paragraph "tenancy" includes a fee farm grant.

18. A deed poll under section 2 above shall have effect to vest in the Secretary of State the benefit of any covenant touching and concerning the land to which the deed relates but not annexed to it if, immediately before the vesting of the estate to which the deed relates, the covenant was enforceable by the person divested of that estate.

Registered land

19.—(1) If an estate which the Secretary of State proposes to vest in himself under section 2 above is registered land—
(a) he shall have a right, in accordance with the prescribed procedure, to inspect and make copies of the whole or any part of any register or document in the custody of the registrar relating to that estate; and
(b) he shall be treated for the purposes of the priority search provisions as if he were a person who has entered into a contract to purchase that estate, and any reference in those provisions to purchase shall be construed accordingly.

(2) If after vesting registered land in himself the Secretary of State lodges the vesting deed at the registry, the registrar—

(a) shall register him as the owner of the estate specified in the deed poll; and

(b) shall issue him a certificate showing the title to the estate.

(3) The registrar may, if he thinks fit, register the title of the Secretary of State to an estate under sub-paragraph (2) above notwithstanding that the Secretary of State has not produced to him the land certificate relating to the land in which the estate subsists and, where the registrar does so, he shall enter a note to that effect in the register.

(4) In this paragraph—

"the priority search provisions" means section 81(3) and (4) of the Land Registration Act (Northern Ireland) 1970 and the provisions of the Land Registration (Northern Ireland) Rules 1977 relating to priority searches and any rules amending or replacing those provisions;

"the registrar" means the Registrar of Titles in Northern Ireland;

"the registry" means the Land Registry in Northern Ireland;

and expressions defined in section 94 of the Land Registration Act (Northern Ireland) 1970 have the meanings assigned to them by that section.

Unregistered land

20. A conveyance by the Secretary of State under this Act of unregistered land shall have effect—

(a) to vest the estate conveyed in the purchaser free from any mortgage to which the sale is not made subject; and

(b) to extinguish any other person's title to the estate conveyed.

21. Where, after land has become vested in the Secretary of State under section 2 above, a person retains possession of any document relating to the title of the land, he shall be deemed to have given the Secretary of State an acknowledgment in writing of the Secretary of State's right to production of that document and to delivery of copies thereof and (except where he retains possession of the document as mortgagee or trustee or otherwise in a fiduciary capacity) an undertaking for safe custody thereof; and section 19 of the Conveyancing Act 1881 shall have effect accordingly, and on the basis that the acknowledgment and undertaking did not contain any such expression of contrary intention as is mentioned in that section.

22.—(1) Where by virtue of paragraph 20 above land is discharged from a mortgage, the mortgagee shall be entitled, subject to the following provisions of this paragraph and to the claims of any prior mortgagee, to have the proceeds of sale applied in payment of the sums secured by the mortgage.

(2) The Secretary of State may, by publishing such notice or notices as he thinks appropriate, require any person who claims to be entitled to a payment under sub-paragraph (1) above to send particulars of his claim to the Secretary of State within the time, not being less than two months, fixed in the notice or, where more than one notice is published, in the last of them.

(3) At the end of the time fixed by the notice or, where more than one is published, the last of them, the Secretary of State shall not be liable to any person of whose claim he has not then received particulars.

(4) If after executing a deed poll under section 2 above with respect to unregistered land, the Secretary of State lodges it at the registry of deeds, the registrar shall register it.

Section 6   SCHEDULE 2

Amendments of 1964 and 1968 Acts

1. The following shall be inserted at the end of Schedule 1 to the 1964 Act—

"ARTICLE 45

If diplomatic relations are broken off between two States, or if a mission is permanently or temporarily recalled:

(a) the receiving State must, even in case of armed conflict, respect and protect the premises of the mission, together with its property and archives;

(b) the sending State may entrust the custody of the premises of the mission, together with its property and archives, to a third State acceptable to the receiving State;

(c) the sending State may entrust the protection of its interests and those of its nationals to a third State acceptable to the receiving State.".

2. Schedule 1 to the 1968 Act shall have effect subject to the following amendments.

3. The following shall be inserted after the heading "CHAPTER 1.—CONSULAR RELATIONS IN GENERAL"—
"SECTION I.—ESTABLISHMENT AND CONDUCT OF CONSULAR RELATIONS".

4. The following shall be inserted after Article 17—
"SECTION II.—END OF CONSULAR FUNCTIONS

ARTICLE 27

Protection of consular premises and archives and of the interests of the sending State in exceptional circumstances

1. In the event of the severance of consular relations between two States:
   (a) the receiving State shall, even in case of armed conflict, respect and protect the consular premises, together with the property of the consular post and the consular archives;
   (b) the sending State may entrust the custody of the consular premises, together with the property contained therein and the consular archives, to a third State acceptable to the receiving State;
   (c) the sending State may entrust the protection of its interests and those of its nationals to a third State acceptable to the receiving State.

2. In the event of the temporary or permanent closure of a consular post, the provisions of sub-paragraph (a) of paragraph 1 of this Article shall apply. In addition,
   (a) if the sending State, although not represented in the receiving State by a diplomatic mission, has another consular post in the territory of that State, that consular post may be entrusted with the custody of the premises of the consular post which has been closed, together with the property contained therein and the consular archives, and, with the consent of the receiving State, with the exercise of consular functions in the district of that consular post; or
   (b) if the sending State has no diplomatic mission and no other consular post in the receiving State, the provisions of sub-paragraphs (b) and (c) of paragraph 1 of this Article shall apply.".

5. The following paragraph shall be inserted after paragraph 2 of Article 31—
"3. Subject to the provisions of paragraph 2 of this Article, the receiving State is under a special duty to take all appropriate steps to protect the consular premises against any intrusion or damage and to prevent any disturbance of the peace of the consular post or impairment of its dignity.".

6. The following shall be inserted after Article 58—

"ARTICLE 59

Protection of the consular premises

The receiving State shall take such steps as may be necessary to protect the consular premises of a consular post headed by an honorary consular officer against any intrusion or damage and to prevent any disturbance of the peace of the consular post or impairment of its dignity.".

ABOLITION OF DOMESTIC RATES ETC. (SCOTLAND) ACT 1987*

(1987 c. 47)

Arrangement of Sections

Part I

Abolition of Domestic Rates: Rating and Valuation

SECT.
1. Abolition of domestic rates.
2. Valuation roll not to include domestic subjects.
3. Non-domestic rates.
4. Valuation of premises part of which occupied as dwelling house.
5. Statutory and other references to rateable values etc.
6. Minor and consequential amendments.

Part II

Community Charges

General

7. Creation and purpose of community charges.

Personal Community Charge

8. Liability for personal community charge.
9. Determination of amount of personal community charge.

Standard Community Charge

10. Liability for and calculation of standard community charge.

Collective Community Charge

11. Liability for and calculation of collective community charge.

Community Charges Registration Officer

12. Community Charges Registration Officer.

Community Charges Register

13. Community Charges Register.
14. Setting up of register.
15. Amendment of register.
16. Registration appeals.

Duties in relation to registration

17. Duties in relation to registration.
18. Obtaining of information from individual residents.
19. Effect of register.
20. Inspection of register.

Levy, collection, payment and recovery of community charges

21. Levy, collection, payment and recovery of community charges.

Reduction of community charges
22. Reduction of community charges.

---

* Annotations by Christopher Himsworth and Neil Walker, University of Edinburgh.

PART III

REVENUE SUPPORT GRANTS

SECT.
23. Replacement of rate support grants by revenue support grants.

PART IV

REBATES

24. Rebates from community charges.

PART V

WATER AND SEWERAGE CHARGES

25. Water and sewerage charges.

PART VI

MISCELLANEOUS AND GENERAL

26. Interpretation.
27. Grant for rate relief given to certain recreational clubs.
28. Prohibition on arrangements for making of certain determinations under this Act.
29. Appeals.
30. Crown application.
31. Additional powers exercisable by, and procedure for, regulations.
32. Finance.
33. Amendments to Debtors (Scotland) Act 1987.
34. Repeals.
35. Citation, commencement and extent.

SCHEDULES
    Schedule 1 Valuation and rating.
        Part I Part residential subjects.
       Part II General.
      Part III Amendment of enactments.
    Schedule 2 Levy, collection, payment and recovery of community charges.
    Schedule 3 Reduction of community charges.
    Schedule 4 Revenue support grants.
    Schedule 5 Water and sewerage charges.
        Part I Charges for water services.
       Part II Charges for sewerage services.
      Part III Miscellaneous provisions.
      Part IV Amendments to the Water (Scotland) Act 1980 (c.45).
    Schedule 6 Repeals.

An Act to abolish domestic rates in Scotland; to provide as to the finance of local government in Scotland; and for connected purposes.

[15th May 1987]

PARLIAMENTARY DEBATES
   Hansard, H.C. Vol. 106, col. 464; Vol. 107, col. 200; Vol. 110, col. 320; Vol. 111, cols. 875, 1051; Vol. 116, col. 292; H.L. Vol. 485, cols. 822, 1319; Vol. 486, cols. 361, 461, 706, 903, 984, 1118, 1364, 1434, 1610, 1683; Vol. 487, cols. 13, 423.
   The Bill was considered in the First Scottish Standing Committee from December 16, 1986, to February 19, 1987.

GENERAL NOTE
   This Act implements in relation to Scotland the Government's proposals for the restructuring of local taxation forecast in their Green Paper *Paying for Local Government* published in January 1986 (Cmnd. 9714 (1986)). Chapter 8 of the Green Paper contained proposals which were specific to Scotland but, for the most part, these were in line with the general proposals for Great Britain as a whole.

The Green Paper, mocked by Lord Ross of Marnock as the "talk of the Gorbals", was not a document based on substantial research or analysis. Compared with such massive investigations into the problems of local taxation as the Royal Commission reports of 1901 (Cd. 638 for England and Wales) and 1902 (Cd. 1067 for Scotland) or, in our own time, the report of the Layfield Committee of Enquiry into Local Government Finance (Cmnd. 6543 (1976)), the Green Paper was a relative lightweight. It was, for instance, a document which managed to encapsulate a "historical perspective" on local government finance in just under a page. On the other hand, it must have contributed some of the most colourful pie charts to the official literature of local finance (Lord Ross called it a "glossy magazine") and it was, above all, a document which knew where it was going and went there in a direct, no-nonsense manner.

Non-domestic rates needed a new stability and uniformity of application. Their level should be nationally determined, and the income pooled and redistributed on the basis of the needs of local authorities. Local domestic taxes had to be assessed in terms of three principal criteria: technical adequacy, fairness, and the encouragement of local democratic accountability. Domestic rates passed the tests of technical adequacy (more fully elaborated in the 1981 Green Paper on *Alternatives to Domestic Rates* (Cmnd. 8449 (1981)) but were fair only to the extent that "as a broad generalisation" people in valuable houses could more easily afford to pay local taxes. On accountability, the 1986 Green Paper came to a different conclusion from that reached in 1981. Rates were highly perceptible to ratepayers but much less so to those not directly liable to pay them. The burden of rates fell on too few shoulders. They also failed "the test of giving clear signals to those who pay". Slippage in the process of valuation (much more true of England and Wales than Scotland) and unevenness in the spread of rateable value per head produced a lack of directness in the chain of accountability. As alternatives, a local sales tax and local income tax were quickly reviewed but abandoned. The "way forward" was the community charge. No tax could reconcile the conflicting demands of the "redistributive principle" of fairness and the "beneficial principle" but a flat-rate charge for local services payable by all the adult residents of a local authority satisfied, it was argued, most of the important criteria of a local tax. The charge would be perceptible. It would be locally determined. All adult residents would pay. Accountability would be achieved through clear and comprehensible price signals to all local taxpayers. The community charge was to be introduced. Domestic rates were to be abolished.

Ss.7 and 1 of this Act are designed to achieve those purposes for Scotland with effect from April 1, 1989. In the Bill as originally introduced there was to have been a transitional period between 1989 and 1992 during which the two taxes would have coexisted but this was dropped at the Commons Report Stage.

Starting with s.7, Pt. II of the Act makes provision, subject to regulations yet to be made, for liability to the three forms of community charge—personal, standard and collective (ss.7–11). It provides for the Community Charges Registration Officer, and the Register itself (ss.12–20). Incorporating Sched. 2, it provides for the levy, collection, payment and recovery of community charges (s.21). It also contains provision for the reduction of an authority's community charges by the Secretary of State (s.22 and Sched. 3).

Meanwhile Pt. I of the Act and Sched. 1 make the changes in valuation law to accommodate the abolition of domestic rates and to construct the dividing line which, from April 1, 1989, will distinguish those premises (domestic subjects) whose occupants will pay community charges from those which will remain in rating.

Pt. III (*i.e.* s.23) of the Act and Sched. 4 introduce a new system of revenue support grants and Pt. IV (s.24) makes skeleton provision for a system of rebates. Pt. V (s.25) and Sched. 5 put water and sewerage charges in Scotland on to an entirely new basis and Pt. VI contains a number of miscellaneous but important provisions.

The notes on each section discuss the provisions in detail, drawing, where appropriate, upon parliamentary debates. There is some attempt to provide the material upon which could be based a preliminary assessment of the extent to which the new arrangements for local taxation in Scotland will satisfy the Green Paper's criteria of technical adequacy, fairness and accountability.

COMMENCEMENT

The Act is brought into force (S.I. 1987 No. 1489) in stages on September 14, 1987; October 1, 1988; April 1, 1989 and April 1, 1994. Unless otherwise stated in the note to a particular section, the commencement date is September 14, 1987. For details see notes on s.35.

EXTENT

The Act extends to Scotland only.

PART I

ABOLITION OF DOMESTIC RATES: RATING AND VALUATION

Abolition of domestic rates

1. With effect from 1st April 1989 domestic rates shall be abolished.

DEFINITION
   "domestic rates": see s.26(1) and, for "domestic subjects", s.2(3).

GENERAL NOTE
   Although this section has a simplicity enjoyed by no other section, it is the symbolic flagship of the whole Act. It declares the greatest single change brought about by the Act and from which the later provisions flow.
   But it is a curious sort of change which first creates "domestic rates" and then, in the same line, abolishes them. "Domestic rates", a term which figures only in this section, the long and short titles, and the interpretation section, is not one recognised in the rating law of Scotland hitherto. "Domestic rates" will be paid only between September 14, 1987 (the date of commencement of this section) and March 31, 1989. They are created only to be abolished with effect from April 1, 1989.
   There is a sense, of course, in which this is a highly artificial argument. Common sense tells us that "domestic rates" or something very like them have been paid since rates were first introduced and can meaningfully be abolished—whether or not "domestic rates" and the "domestic subjects" on which they are levied are newly created by ss.1, 2 and 26 of this Act.
   On the other hand, the argument is not wholly artificial. It is for the very reason that "domestic subjects", "domestic rates" and "domestic ratepayers" are not precise terms of art in the existing law (a "domestic subject" is not necessarily one presently valued as a dwelling house) that so much attention has to be given (especially in s.2 and the regulations which will be made under it) to drawing the distinction between "domestic subjects" and "domestic rates" on the one hand and, on the other hand, all other subjects on the valuation roll (the term "non-domestic subjects" is not used in Act) and the "non-domestic rates" which are to continue to be levied on them.
   In its original version, cl. 1 of the Bill provided for the abolition of domestic rates with effect from April 1, 1992. The original cl. 3 (later deleted) however, went on to make elaborate provision for the gradual reduction in the levels of domestic rates to be determined by local authorities during the financial years 1989–90, 1990–91 and 1991–92. During those transitional years domestic rates were to be fixed at 60 per cent., 40 per cent. and 20 per cent. respectively of the "base rate" which was to be the rate (less, where appropriate, the reduction due to the domestic element in the rate support grant) fixed by an authority for the year 1988–89, unless the Secretary of State prescribed a different "base rate". During the same transitional period the authority was also to draw upon community charges levied under later provisions of the Act.
   Those transitional arrangements were dropped from the Bill by means of a series of amendments introduced at the House of Commons Report stage. The Government had apparently been impressed by arguments from local authority financial officers that the years in which the two systems ran in parallel would be administratively very complicated.
   In the House of Lords, Lord Glenarthur explained, for the Government, that the three advantages of a "clean break" were that it was simpler for individual taxpayers, simpler to administer and that it would enable local authorities to plan more effectively (*Hansard*, H.L. Vol. 486, col. 370). The Government was, unsurprisingly, not inclined to accept the other amendments that would have delayed abolition until after consideration by the First Scottish Select Committee (col. 114); or until 1991 or 1992 (*e.g. Hansard*, H.L. Vol. 486, col. 361); or until a date to be appointed by the Secretary of State (*Hansard*, H.L. Vol. 486, col. 1386; Vol. 487, col. 424); or until all necessary regulations had been drafted (*Hansard*, H.L. Vol. 486, col. 1398); or until a scheme of local income tax had been established (*Hansard*, H.L. Vol. 486, col. 382); or until also implemented in England and Wales (*Hansard*, H.L. Vol. 486, col. 398); or until approved by a referendum (*Hansard*, H.L. Vol. 486, col. 1391); or until a Scottish Assembly was established (*Hansard*, H.L. Vol. 486, col. 398). The Government also refused to allow a pilot scheme of abolition of domestic rates to proceed in the area of one authority alone (*Hansard*, H.C. Vol. 111, col. 877).

ADDENDUM

In addition to providing for the abolition of domestic rates, s.1 is an abrupt introduction to the complex legal regime of valuation and rating. A full account of valuation and rating law cannot be provided in these notes (for that see Armour, *Valuation for Rating* (edited by Clyde and Hope, 5th ed., 1985)) but, because the concepts and terminology of valuation constantly recur in the Act and notes, a very brief resume is presented:

1. Rating as a form of local property tax is one in which each local authority calculates the amount of income from rates necessary to fund its expenditure in a financial year taking account of other sources of income (especially central government grants) which are available. Currently that calculation is made in terms of s.108 of the Local Government (Scotland) Act 1973 (to be repealed by Sched. 6 to this Act and to be replaced, in effect, by ss.3(1) and 9).

2. The rate is levied (by islands councils, and also by regional councils on behalf of themselves and districts in their areas) by reference to (and expressed as an amount in the pound of) the rateable value of all "lands and heritages" on the valuation roll for the area (see especially s.7 of the Local Government (Scotland) Act 1975).

3. This, in turn, requires the creation of that valuation roll which is the task of the assessor, an officer of the islands or regional council but acting under independently conferred statutory powers. For the roll and assessor see the Local Government (Scotland) Act 1975, s.1, and the Local Government (Scotland) Act 1975, s.116(2).

4. Decisions on which "lands and heritages" go onto the roll and at what value are for the assessor in the light of the Valuation Acts (see s.26(1)) subject to appeal to valuation appeal committees and, from them, to the Lands Valuation Appeal Court. For more on appeals see the notes on s.2(6).

5. "Lands and heritages" appear on the roll as commercial subjects, industrial subjects (separately identified because they attract reduced values on the roll through "derating"), dwelling houses and others. Some subjects, principally agricultural lands and heritages, do not go on the roll at all and are, therefore, exempt from rates.

6. The "rateable value" for most subjects on the roll is identical to the "net annual value" placed on them by the assessor (see especially s.6 of the Valuation and Rating (Scotland) Act 1956). As explained, however, in the notes on s.2, dwelling houses are initially valued to a "gross annual value" which is subsequently converted to a net value.

Valuation roll not to include domestic subjects

2.—(1) Domestic subjects shall not be entered in the valuation roll in respect of the financial year 1989–90 or any subsequent financial year.

(2) Domestic subjects in respect of which there is an entry in the valuation roll immediately before 1st April 1989 shall be deleted from the roll with effect from that date.

(3) Subject to subsection (4) below, for the purposes of the Valuation Acts "domestic subjects" means—

    (a) any lands and heritages consisting of one or more dwelling houses with any garden, yard, garage, outhouse or pertinent belonging to and occupied along with such dwelling house or dwelling houses; and

    (b) such class or classes, or such parts of any class or classes, of other lands and heritages as may be prescribed.

(4) There shall be excepted from paragraph (a) of subsection (3) above such class or classes, or such parts of any class or classes, of lands and heritages as may be prescribed.

(5) Where a part of any lands and heritages falls within a class or part of a class prescribed under subsection (3)(b) or (4) above—

    (a) the part so affected and the remainder shall be treated for the purposes of the Valuation Acts as separate lands and heritages, and

    (b) the part of those lands and heritages which does not constitute domestic subjects shall be entered in the valuation roll accordingly.

(6) Any proprietor, tenant or occupier of any lands and heritages may appeal to the valuation appeal committee for the area in which the lands and heritages are situated against any decision of the assessor—

    (a) to alter the valuation roll with effect from 1st April 1989 by deleting those lands and heritages on the ground that they constitute domestic subjects; or

(b) not so to alter the roll.

(7) Parts I and II of Schedule 1 to this Act have effect in relation to the provisions of this Part of this Act.

DEFINITIONS

"assessor": see Local Government (Scotland) Act 1973, s.116(2).

"financial year": see s.26(1) and s.96(5) of the Local Government (Scotland) Act 1973 as amended; *i.e.* the year from April 1.

"lands and heritages": see Lands Valuation (Scotland) Act 1854, s.42.

"prescribed": see ss.26(1) and 31(3).

"the Valuation Acts": see s.26(1).

"valuation appeal committee": see Local Government (Scotland) Act 1975, s.4.

"valuation roll": see Local Government (Scotland) Act 1975, s.1.

GENERAL NOTE

The purpose of this section together with the provisions in Pts. I and II of Sched. 1 (see separate notes on that Schedule) is to ensure that, in order to achieve the abolition of domestic rates under s.1, "domestic subjects" (a new term in Scottish rating law) are deleted from the valuation roll and that no new "domestic subjects" are entered. "Domestic subjects" join agricultural lands and heritages and certain other subjects (see Valuation and Rating (Scotland) Act 1956, ss.7–8AA) in being excluded from the roll. This leaves, in principle, those subjects not defined as "domestic" and which (principally in terms of s.3 of the Act) continue to be liable to non-domestic rates.

The technique adopted for achieving this, and other consequential purposes, is, on its face, fairly straightforward. Subss. (1) and (2) are designed to get domestic subjects off the valuation roll. Subs. (3) starts the process of defining "domestic subjects" and the core definition is supplied by subs. (3)(a)—"lands and heritages consisting of one or more dwelling houses etc." By means of regulations under subs. (3)(b) and subs. (4), however, certain types of "lands and heritage" may be added to or subtracted from the core in subs. (3)(a). Subs. (3)(b) allows the Secretary of State to designate premises as "domestic" and the Government have indicated that this power will be used for two main purposes (see, *e.g.*, Lord Glenarthur at *Hansard*, H.L. Vol. 486, col. 1449). One is to take in private lock-up garages which are detached from any dwelling house and, therefore, not necessarily included within subs. (3)(a). The Government believe that it would be anomalous to leave some private garages in the non-domestic category and liable to rates whilst others would be "domestic subjects".

The other purpose is to add to the core category of "domestic subjects" premises for institutional living such as student halls of residence and nurses' homes. Such premises, therefore, go off the valuation roll from 1989. Thus no rates will be leviable but, jumping ahead to Pt. II of the Act and the rules on liability to the personal community charge, the same prescription of student residences and nurses' homes will ensure that their occupants (who are solely or mainly resident there) are liable to pay community charges. Taking the premises out of rating ensures that their occupants (who are in other respects liable) will pay the community charge.

The same principle applies in reverse in relation to subs. (4) which authorises the Secretary of State to prescribe categories of "land and heritage" which will *not* be "domestic subjects" with the necessary consequence that they *will* remain on the valuation roll; they will be rated and their occupants *will not* pay community charges. Once again, precise categories will be known only when regulations are published but the Government have indicated that the power will be used to keep holiday caravans and small holiday huts within rating (see *Hansard*, H.L. Vol. 486, col. 423).

Thus we have in subss. (3) and (4) the elements of the scheme of classification between "domestic" and other premises. The section goes on to make two further forms of provision. The first (in subs. (5)) is to enable any lands designated as "domestic" subjects under subs. (3)(b), or alternatively excepted from being "domestic subjects" under subs. (4) to be sub-divided if necessary. Thus, in an example provided by Lord Glenarthur in the House of Lords Committee (*Hansard*, H.L. Vol. 486, col. 424), there may be, within the site of a student residence, some retail or other commercial premises. These should not come off the valuation roll and will continue to attract non-domestic rates. Subs. (5) operates as an instruction to assessors to treat such "parts" of lands and heritages separately and to place them on the roll. (But for continuing uncertainties about what sorts of division of "domestic subjects" will be possible see below and the note on subs. (5)).

One result of the new definition of subjects as "domestic" or not, whether by s.2 itself or by regulations made under it, is that new categories of aggrieved person will emerge and, by subs. (6), they are given a right of appeal to valuation appeal committees.

S.2 does not, as is evident from the notes above, operate in isolation from the rest of the Act. In particular, ss.8, 10 and 11 which define liability to the personal, standard and collective community charge respectively should be referred to. All contain definitions which refer, in part, to the question of whether the relevant residence or other premises are subject to non-domestic rating. The dichotomy between liability to non-domestic rates and to a community charge has to be maintained at both points in the Act. One problem in the observance of that dichotomy is that of the premises which appear to straddle the two categories. This arises, for instance, in the case of premises which, on the one hand, are defined, under one or other limb of s.2, as being not "domestic subjects" and are, therefore, liable to non-domestic rates but which are, on the other hand, used in part for residential purposes in a way which cannot be handled by the separation of "lands and heritages" under subs. (5). The "domestic" cannot be hived off physically from the "non-domestic". One example is that of the hotel which contains a flat used by the manager as his home. This was cited by Lord Glenarthur in debate (*Hansard,* H.L. Vol. 486, col. 463) as a typical example of the hybrid category created by the Act—the "part residential subject".

Part-residential subjects are defined in s.26(1) and then treated substantively in Pt. I of Schedule 1 to which effect is given by s.2(6). The core definition of part residential subjects is premises (lands and heritages) which are not domestic subjects but "which are used partly as the sole or main residence of any person". This requires them to remain subject to non-domestic rating but with their value abated by the extent of their residential use. The process of apportionment is treated in Sched. 1. Such an apportionment also creates a liability in those who are resident to the personal or collective community charge (ss.8, 11). However, another of the Secretary of State's powers of prescription is found in the definition of the part residential subject enabling him to exclude categories of premises which might otherwise be included. Thus, it has been indicated (*Hansard,* H.L.Vol. 486, cols. 1654 and 1665) that, when residential care homes and nursing homes are retained by exemption under subs. (3)(b) subjects, as "non-domestic" they will also be prescribed as *not* part residential subjects. Their rateable value will *not* be apportioned. Their residents will *not* be liable to pay any community charge. Just as the power to prescribe their residences and homes as "domestic" under subs. (3)(b) ensures that students and nurses will, by the operation of s.8, pay the personal community charge, the exclusion of their homes by prescription under s.3(b) and their prescription as not part residential under s.26(1) ensures that long-stay residents in nursing homes will not pay a community charge. (The prescription of prisoners and long stay patients in N.H.S. hospitals under s.30(2) will ensure a parallel exemption for them).

Whatever their merits in policy terms (*i.e.* in terms of the allocation of liability to local taxation by rates or community charge), the pragmatic route to these designations under the Act or regulations is not without its difficulties. The difficulties arise from the uneasy co-existence of one tax based on property and another based on individual liability—but with that liability closely linked with the use or occupation of property.

Subs. (1)

The structure of the present system of valuation and rating has already been sketched out in the General Note on s.1. The changes effected by this and subsequent sections leave intact the essentials of that structure. However, in terms of this subsection, "domestic subjects" (to be defined below) are to join agricultural subjects in not being entered in the valuation roll.

This was regarded by the Government as essential to the abolition of liability to rates on such subjects although there were attempts (see *Hansard,* H.L. Vol. 486, cols. 411, 1419) to keep *all* properties on the valuation roll but with zero values entered against domestic subjects. There was a feeling that, whatever happened to domestic rates, a fully comprehensive property roll was useful for other purposes—perhaps including implementation of the community charge. That argument was rejected—although it should be noted that there is a statutory obligation on assessors to preserve and keep open for inspection the complete roll as it stands immediately prior to April 1, 1989 (see s.5(8)). The roll, still containing domestic subjects at that point, will be frozen and kept available for the purposes of s.5. Notice that s.5 does, in some circumstances, also require the updating of information in the roll.

It will become apparent in the notes on the following subsections that the definition of what are, and are not, domestic subjects is not precise and some entries (or decisions against an entry) are bound to be contested. Appeals are dealt with in subs. (6) below.

Subs. (2)

Just as subs. (1) is designed to prevent new entries of domestic subjects, this subsection instructs the deletion of those already in the roll immediately prior to April 1, 1989. See also the requirement to remove parts of lands and heritages under subs. (5) and also under s.4 of the Act.

Subs. (3)

This subsection serves two purposes. Para. (a) provides what has been referred to as the core definition of domestic subjects. Para. (b) gives the Secretary of State the power to add further classes or parts of classes to that core.

Para. (a)

As explained in the notes on s.1, the concept of domestic subjects has to be created before domestic rates can be abolished. The concept is new to the Valuation Acts but the concept of the "lands and heritages consisting of one or more dwelling houses . . ." is wholly familiar. The term "lands and heritages" is defined in s.42 of the Lands Valuation (Scotland) Act 1854 and is the generic term for the entity recognised by the Valuation Acts for the purposes of making up the roll. "Lands and heritages" extend to and include, *inter alia,* lands and houses; shootings; fishings; woods; ferries; piers; harbours and "all buildings and pertinents thereof, and all machinery fixed or attached to any lands or heritages."

Unless they are statutorily exempted all such lands and heritages must, in terms of s.1 of the Local Government (Scotland) Act 1975, be entered in the valuation roll by the assessor.

"Lands and heritages consisting of one or more dwelling houses" are separately identified already. This is partly because they, uniquely since changes under s.3 of the Local Government (Miscellaneous Provisions) (Scotland) Act 1981 are differently valued. In terms of s.6 of the Valuation and Rating (Scotland) Act 1956, they are first given a gross annual value (*i.e.* a valuation derived from the rent at which the premises might reasonably be let upon the assumption that the *landlord* undertook to bear the cost of repairs, insurance and other expenses). From this gross annual value is derived a net annual value by making a prescribed percentage reduction. The net annual value is then treated as the rateable value of the premises. Other "lands and heritages" are given a net annual value direct. Dwelling houses also attract domestic rates relief (s.7 of the Local Government (Scotland) Act 1966) and a domestic water rate levied on their full net annual value (see also s.4 and Sched. 5).

Thus the existing concept of the dwelling house is the natural starting point for the definition of domestic subjects. It is not only already available but it is clearly a very close approximation to the ideal target of the Government's abolition plans. Whatever other marginal categories have to be included or excluded, it must above all, be those who pay rates on dwelling houses who are intended to benefit from the abolition of domestic rates—and also made subject to the poll tax. In these notes, the definition in para. (a) need not be exhaustively examined. Some aspects of it have, however, attracted the attention of the courts and relevant decisions are fully treated in the principal authoritative work— Armour, *Valuation for Rating* (edited by Clyde and Hope, 5th ed., 1985) especially Pt. IV. Despite the longstanding use of the term "dwelling-house", its precise meaning remains a matter of considerable uncertainty in the existing law. It has not been made the subject of further statutory definition as it has, for England and Wales, in the General Rate Act 1967, s.115(1) and Sched. 13.

There a dwelling-house is immediately defined as a hereditament "used wholly for the purposes of a private dwelling or private dwellings" and in Sched. 13 guidance is provided on the question of whether premises are so used. One consideration is the extent to which a building is made up of rooms let out singly. If it is wholly or substantially let on this basis then it will not normally be a dwelling house. On the other hand, the inclusion within the hereditament of other land or buildings not used for the purposes of a private dwelling does not prevent the hereditament as a whole being so regarded.

These rules in the General Rate Act 1967 are not part of the law of Scotland. This means, *inter alia*, that there is no explicit indication that, for lands and heritages to be a dwelling house, they have to be occupied and used for the purposes of "dwelling". There is no indication of whether, if there has to be such occupation, it has to be "private". There is no guidance on whether or not multiple lets of single rooms preclude a building from being a "dwelling house".

Rather the courts in Scotland have been forced to proceed on a piece-meal basis in the wake of decisions by assessors and have had to grasp at precedents from other areas of the law including, interestingly in the context of the new poll tax, the Representation of the People (Scotland) Act 1868 which conferred the franchise on the occupiers of a "separate dwelling". Despite attempts at greater precision, the editors of Armour are compelled to conclude (at para. 17–07): "From what has been said it follows that for a subject to qualify as a dwelling-house it must be suitable for human habitation. But it is more difficult to say what further conditions, if any, must be satisfied for it to come within the meaning of 'dwelling-house' in the 1956 Act. For example, should hotels and other establishments of that kind, boarding houses or hostels, be included . . .?".

After discussion of *Assessor for Dundee* v. *Sisters of St. Vincent de Paul* [1968] R.A. 515 (question raised but not decided whether institutional accommodation for nuns was a dwelling house) and *Assessor for Lothian Region* v. *Viewpoint Housing Association*, 1983 S.L.T. 479 (separate bed-sitters with bathrooms but shared kitchenettes and shared amenity rooms held to be separate dwelling houses) they conclude further (para. 17–08): "For the present the question whether the word 'dwelling-house' as used in section 6(2) of the 1956 Act is wide enough to include not only ordinary private dwelling-houses but also residences of an institutional character remains an open one. On balance however it is thought that s.6(4) provides a sufficient indication that only ordinary private dwelling-houses are to be taken to be included, and that subjects which are properly described as a hotel, hostel or institution should now be valued directly to net annual value under section 6(8)."

As Armour points out (paras. 17–09 to 17–10) the position has been further complicated in relation to certain communal accommodation not used for profit-making purposes which (under s.4 of the Local Government (Scotland) Act 1962 and S.I. 1983 No. 534) may be valued *as if* they were dwelling houses.

Of greater general importance is Armour's observation (in para. 17–07) that the significance of whether or not premises constitute a dwelling house has varied over time. Thus, the reason why the term has remained so vaguely understood is that it has only rarely been necessary (*i.e.* in anyone's interest) to press for a firmer definition. One consequence of the 1987 Act will be to give an immediate and compelling significance to the distinction between those lands and heritages which are a dwelling house and those which are not.

On the extent to which caravans are dwelling houses, see the notes on subs. (4) below.

As to the words in para. (a) other than "dwelling house", two strands of earlier authority may be referred to. One, which is very thin, may be used to assist in the interpretation of the "garden, yard, garage, outhouse, or pertinent" referred to. Under s.6(11) of the 1956 Act the term " 'pertinent' in relation to a dwelling-house or to a school, college or other educational establishment shall be taken to include all land occupied therewith and used for the purposes thereof". This is not a very helpful addition to the original definition of a dwelling-house (although, by Sched. 1, para. 18 of this Act, retained for the purposes of s.7 of the 1956 Act). It is clear (Armour, para. 10–17) that, in addition to the items specified, things such as adjoining stables and (heritable) greenhouses will be treated as a part of the relevant lands and heritages.

The definition of "pertinent" above, as well as the phrase "belonging to and occupied along with" are both useful in alerting us to the second, and much more problematic, line of authority on the unit of valuation and the *unum quid* (see Armour, chapter 10). It is by means of the concept of the "unit of valuation" that the law distinguishes one set of lands and heritages from another and gives them separate entries on the roll or, alternatively, insists that they are, as a *unum quid*, not distinguishable and that they should be entered together as a single entry. A mixture of relevant factors—geographical identification on the ground; jointness or separateness of ownership, occupation or use; capacity for separate letting; intentions of the ratepayer—have all been, to a greater or lesser degree acknowledged. Many will have little to do in practice with the identification of "domestic subjects" under the 1987 Act but there are bound to be problems. Because they will be regarded as part of the *unum quid* most garages and the like which adjoin dwelling houses will be swept off the valuation roll. For those which are not, special provision will be made under subs. (3)(b) below. Potentially much more difficult will be divisions within premises used for residential purposes (only parts of which may be judged under this section to be "domestic subjects") and then between residential (and probably "domestic") premises and commercial premises. These points are pursued a little further below.

As mentioned above, it is the sudden new significance to be given to these matters which will open or reopen questions which have remained dormant. It will be extremely interesting to see how the rather shaky ideas of the pre-1987 *unum quid* survive under the new regime. It has, in the past been urged (see Armour, para. 10–01 citing *Bank of Scotland* v. *Assessor for Edinburgh* (1890) 17 R. 839) that "the possible consequences to value are not a relevant consideration in deciding whether to enter subjects separately or together". We shall see.

At the very least, some aspects of the core definition of "dwelling houses" need the benefit of further refinement. To some extent, this is statutorily acknowledged and some matters are resolved in the Act itself and in the regulations to be made under it. Others will be left to be resolved in practice by assessors and, on appeal from assessors, by valuation appeal committees, the Lands Tribunal for Scotland and the Lands Valuation Appeal Court. See note on subs. (6). Some are questions about (a) what more precisely, will be the limits of a "dwelling-house" once identified. Others are about (b) what can reasonably be identified as a "dwelling-house" and what should be deliberately added to or subtracted from it to constitute the whole class of domestic subjects.

As to (a) these will be matters for resolution by assessors at the point of making decisions under subss. (1) and (2). In the vast majority of cases there will doubtless be no dispute. In others, however, where significant questions of value will depend on the limits of the subjects in question, disputes are bound to arise and especially as to what constitutes the appropriate unit of valuation and, on the other hand, what part of existing subjects might be hived off as domestic subjects.

As to (b) some answers will be provided by regulations under subss. (3)(b) and (4) and are considered below. Others will not be and there was much parliamentary debate about the desirability or otherwise of leaving so much in the lap of either the Secretary of State or of the assessors and the appeal system (see, *e.g.*, *Hansard,* H.L. Vol. 486, col. 1449).

It was argued that a much fuller list of domestic subjects should be set out in the Act itself. Apart from subjects likely to be prescribed (in one direction or the other), mobile homes and residential caravans will probably be viewed as domestic subjects but attempts (on behalf of the caravan site owners) to remove from the roll the whole of the sites on which such mobile homes and caravans are parked were resisted (see, *e.g.*, *Hansard,* H.L. Vol. 111, col. 943; H.L. Vol. 486, col. 1438). On the other hand holiday caravans are likely to remain in rating (see subs. (4) below). Other parliamentary concerns ranged from National Trust for Scotland properties—they may be designated domestic subjects or not by assessors according to their character (see *Hansard,* H.L. Vol. 486, cols. 428, 1444)—to womens' aid refuges (see below). Another category debated was houses owned by the churches (see *Hansard,* H.L. Vol. 485, cols. 1335, 1394). The question was whether the equivalent of rating relief on such properties could be maintained by retaining them in rating and protecting their occupants from community charges. The Government, however, saw no justification for such a direct carry-over of relief for individuals benefiting from existing rules.

Perhaps the type of property which became the most controversially doubtful "domestic subjects" in Parliament was the "second home" or "holiday home" or "holiday cottage". Most such properties might, at first blush, appear to fit fairly happily within the definition of the "dwelling house" in para. (a)—a definition which on its face, demands no particular degree or type of use as a house or home. Indeed, it is plain that the Government's own logic acknowledges that there are "dwelling houses" not used as a sole or main residence, the archetypal "second homes", and this led them to insist on the need for the standard community charge (see s.10). Although the standard community charge is to be, in effect, a property tax but at a flat rate, it is essential to the rates *versus* community charge dichotomy that the standard charge be payable only on properties taken out of rating. This is automatically achieved for "second homes" if they are accepted as "domestic subjects" and, in its original version, the Bill defined a property subject to the standard charge simply as, firstly, one within the definition in para. (a) and not excluded by prescription under subs. (4) and, secondly, not the sole or main residence of any person. This definition was subsequently changed at House of Commons Committee stage (1st Scot. S.C., cols. 685–686). Although it was described as a "tightening up of the drafting approach", the change does seem to acknowledge that some "second homes" may (with the consent of ratepayer and assessor) remain on the roll. The rate bill may be less than two personal charges. (see. s.10).

At all events, what that change of definition accommodates is the possibility, indeed probability, that many subjects which look very much like "dwelling houses" will nevertheless be entered on the valuation roll! Some commercially-let holiday cottages are, under the existing law, entered as commercial subjects rather than dwelling-houses. They are, despite their structural resemblance to dwelling-houses, not viewed as such. The same approach is adopted towards premises run as small (or, for that matter, large) boarding houses rather than as dwelling houses.

Under this Act, where "domestic subjects" must come right off the valuation roll, the disadvantages of a definition aimed primarily at structure and only secondarily at use ("dwelling"), in a way which fails to distinguish properties adequately in what is a very grey area, become apparent. Who can say with confidence whether a cottage in Argyll owned by a person normally resident in Edinburgh, occupied by her for two weeks in the summer, and let out, through an agency, to holiday-makers for the rest of the year should be, as a matter of law, on the valuation roll or not?

Experience will tell. Perhaps some further guidance will yet come in the form of prescription by the Secretary of State. If not, there may be a long round of appeals to valuation appeal committees against assessors' decisions—but only where the taxpayer sees an advantage in dislodging an assessor's decision to enter subjects on the roll or not. Such appeals and their outcomes at the level of the Lands Valuation Appeal Court if necessary may be paralleled by appeals to the sheriff (and thence to the Court of Session) against liability to community charge and perhaps even by applications (from interested ratepayers or community chargees) for judicial review of assessors' decisions?

Para. (b)

It is under this power of prescription that the Secretary of State will probably extend the scope of "domestic subjects" in two respects (see, *e.g.*, *Hansard*, H.L. Vol. 486, col. 1449). One is to take in the private lock-up garage. This is to try to avoid the anomaly of taking a garage as a "domestic subject" out of rating simply because it adjoins a dwelling house but leaving others in. How precisely the premises will be defined is not yet known but, however it is done, there will almost certainly be a need for careful inspection of the use of a garage before the assessor is persuaded to take it off the roll.

The other broad use of the power of prescription which has been indicated will be to take into the category of "domestic subjects" many types of communal living accommodation. As indicated above, such accommodation has normally been commercially rated in the past and, unless prescribed, would be expected to remain on the roll and rated. The disadvantage of this would be that the residents in such accommodation would not be liable to pay a community charge even though they were solely or mainly resident—unless (rather inappropriately in these circumstances) they become liable as residents in part residential subjects (see below and Sched. 1).

Such accommodation will, therefore, be prescribed as "domestic subjects" under para. (b). The exact scope of the prescription has not been defined but the two prime examples given in debate were nurses' homes and student residences. Logically it would seem that a class of subjects containing nurses' homes would carry with it other accommodation owned by employers for occupation by their employees. All such accommodation would come off the valuation roll.

Students' residences may be more troublesome because of the alternative commercial uses to which many are put during university and college vacations. Once the residences are prescribed as domestic subjects, their student occupants will, as intended, become liable to pay community charges. It seems unlikely that, when residences are then let out to conferences and holiday makers, there will be any way of returning them to rating at that stage. Presumably the instruction to assessors to identify "parts" of lands and heritages under subs. (5) cannot include the possibility of putting subjects on the roll for a "part" of that year?

Another complication concerning the prescriptions under para. (b), which was anticipated in debate, is that of accommodation for those people whom the Government wished to see exempted from community charges and thus resident in subjects defined as "non-domestic". The people involved here are the residents of nursing homes and of residential care homes. Because such homes are commercially rated and "non-domestic" subjects to start with, they cannot be simply confirmed in that status by prescription under s.2(4) which can be directed only at dwelling houses.

Thus, the accommodation will instead have to be specifically excepted from whatever classes of accommodation are prescribed under para. (b). Most types of long-stay accommodation will doubtless join nurses' homes and student residences as "domestic subjects". Nursing homes and residential care homes will not. Additionally these homes will have to be prescribed (under s.26(1)) as *not* part residential to complete the immunity of their residents from community charges.

Although the precise categories of nursing homes and others have yet to be prescribed, an indication was given in Parliament (Lord Glenarthur, *Hansard*, H.L. Vol. 486, col. 1665) that they were likely to be "first, nursing homes registered under the Nursing Homes Registration (Scotland) Act 1938; secondly, staffed houses provided by a local authority under section 59 of the Social Work (Scotland) Act 1968 or section 27 of the National Health Service (Scotland) Act 1947 and staffed houses provided by the private or voluntary sector and registered under section 61 of the Social Work (Scotland) Act 1968".

Another category might presumably be private hospitals registered under s.12 of the Mental Health (Scotland) Act 1984.

It may be difficult for the Government to draw up the final list of categories of accommodation to be kept in rating by means of this prescription and this could be particularly troublesome in that the main target is not, of course, the accommodation but the residents. This is part of the package of measures to ensure exemption from community charges of people temporarily or permanently removed from the democratic process. Communal living is not synonymous with the need for care nor with the inability to exercise a political choice and the question may arise as to why those who are in a nursing home are exempt from a community charge and those who are nursed by son or daughter at home will not be.

The remaining loose end in that process which has been foreseen is that the *staff* accommodation in these specially exempted homes will have to be further extracted from the homes themselves since there is no reason why the staff housed there should not join nurses and the rest of the population in paying community charges. The "notes on clauses" accompanying the Bill indicated that one use to be made of the power to prescribe a "part" of a class would be to identify specific types of accommodation such as "staff accommodation in private hospitals". They would be separately prescribed as "domestic subjects" while the accommodation for patients is left on the roll. (In passing, it may be noted that this represents an unusual use of the concept of a "part" of a class, *i.e.* as part of the lands and heritages which constitute the class as a whole).

One category of residential accommodation which will not, it seems, be the subject of prescription under either subss. (3)(b) or (4) is premises used as a women's aid refuge. There was, however, some debate in Parliament (see especially *Hansard*, H.L. Vol. 486, cols. 439, 1451) about what the status of such accommodation and its residents should be. In the end, the Government resisted an attempt to make all refuges definitely rateable (normally securing exemption for residents from community charges) on two grounds. In the first place it would be wrong for those residents who are using a refuge as their sole or main residence to avoid altogether any liability to a community charge—whereas women using the refuge briefly, whilst solely or mainly resident elsewhere, would be liable to a charge through that other address. It was also argued that keeping refuges in rating would mean that in many cases they would be the only ordinary dwelling houses which remained on the valuation roll—with adverse consequences for confidentiality.

Instead the Government have said that "the most equitable treatment of women's refuges would be that they should be subject to liability for the collective community charge". (*Hansard*, H.L. Vol. 486, col. 1452). This, they say, should ensure consistency of treatment for all refuges and that women paying collective community charges contributions would be paying at the same rate as women registered for the personal charge at their home address. Thus women's aid refuges will be prescribed under s.11(2). It has also been indicated that they would be prescribed under s.20(2)(iii) to ensure that their multiplier does not appear on the register (*Hansard*, H.L. Vol. 486, col. 1453).

Although this approach is designed to achieve some consistency of treatment, it seems possible that there may yet be further difficulties in its application. In particular, the Government's policy cannot rule out the possibility that, in the absence of prescription under para. (b), a refuge might be treated by an assessor like many boarding houses and be put or kept on the roll as commercial subjects. This would not prevent its also being subject to the collective community charge—as part residential subjects—but would raise again the issue of confidentiality of the address.

For the additional opportunity to separate "lands and heritages" under subs. (5), see below.

Subs. (4)

This subsection is almost the mirror image of subs. (3)(b) in that it permits the restriction rather than the extension of "domestic subjects" required not to be entered on the valuation roll. It is not, however, precisely to the opposite effect. Under subs. (3)(b), the Secretary of State may prescribe classes (or parts of classes) as "domestic subjects" either if they are plainly not, in themselves, "dwelling houses" or if they would arguably be regarded as such but, perhaps to achieve a uniform response from assessors, the Secretary of State prescribes a class for that purpose. He will, of course, be as much concerned about the liability of occupants to community charges as about the rating of the premises.

Subs. (4) operates more narrowly. It enables the Secretary of State to except only classes (or parts of classes) of "lands and heritages" within subs. (3)(a), *i.e.* those which, the prescription apart, are in law dwelling houses.

In Parliament, it was stated on behalf of the Government that the power would primarily be used to ensure that holiday caravans and small holiday huts would remain on the valuation roll and be rated (see 1st Scot. S.C., col. 322).

The general position of caravans in the light of s.2 is not easy but an indication of the Government's overall view was given. In the first place, there are residential caravans licensed for year-round occupation. These are valued as dwelling houses at present and the

Government's expectation and wish is that these should, therefore, be treated as domestic subjects simply through the operation of subs. (3)(a) and taken off the valuation roll. Their occupants would become liable to the personal or standard community charge as the case may be. (For unsuccessful attempts to get any site infrastructure and related facilities taken off the roll as well, see *Hansard,* H.L. Vol. 486, col. 1438.)

Otherwise, the general intention of the Government is that caravans and their sites should remain on the valuation roll. They would be rated and, unless a caravan was actually occupied as a sole or main residence in which case the site would be regarded as "part residential subjects" and its value apportioned, there would be no liability to a community charge. Such liability would, in the Government's view be normally unfair. Caravans should not routinely become liable to the standard community charge like "second homes".

However, achieving this position is complicated by the fact that, at present, some of the caravans involved are separately valued as dwelling houses and some are not. Those that are valued as dwelling houses have to be prescribed under subs. (4) and, therefore, kept on the roll.

The sites of the remainder would simply continue on the roll. The ones in this category are mobile caravans and also static leisure caravans on sites of not less than 400 square metres overall which are not licensed for occupation throughout the year.

The caravans presently separately valued and treated as dwelling houses are either (a) those static leisure caravans which are on the same (fairly) large sites of over 400 square metres but *whose owners have opted* for separate valuation under s.3(8A) of the Rating (Caravan Sites) Act 1976; or (b) those caravans on small sites (less than 400 square metres) not licensed for all-year occupation but which have, in some cases, been separately valued.

The prescription under subs. (4) will keep these caravans on the roll and liable to non-domestic rates. It has been pointed out that the caravan site operators (of sites of over 400 square metres valued as a whole under the 1976 Act) will continue to have the advantage of the 40 per cent. reduction of rate prescribed (S.I. 1984 No. 1881) under section 3A of that Act (added by s.15 of the Rating and Valuation (Amendment) (Scotland) Act 1984 in response to the relatively high valuation of sites confirmed in *Bourne Leisure (Seton Sands)* v. *Assessor for Lothian Region,* 1983 S.L.T. 298) (see *Hansard,* H.L. Vol. 486, col. 436). Notice the amendment to the 1976 Act in Sched. 1, para. 37 and repeals in Sched. 6.

Even though the subs. (4) prescription will ensure that most of the caravan sites (and also holiday huts) referred to in the regulations will remain on the roll and rated (in some cases with benefit of the 40 per cent. reduction) there will, as mentioned, be the possibility that, because some caravans and huts are occupied as sole or main residences, they will have to be treated as part residential subjects (see Sched. 1). In the case of individual caravans, they will presumably be "wholly part residential"? Equally, prescription under subs. (4) might lead to the need for the further separation of lands and heritages under subs. (5).

Subs. (5)

It will already have been noticed that both subs. (3)(b) and (4) enable the Secretary of State to prescribe "*parts* of any class or classes" of lands and heritages. Presumably this is to avoid any doubt about his power to be selective in the categories he chooses and to ease their designation. Thus, if a "residence" is a class of "lands and heritages", students' residences and nurses' residences or homes are two parts of the class.

The power in those cases to prescribe a "part" is by reference to a "part" of a "class". However, what is envisaged in subs. (5) is that a part of particular lands and heritages falling within the prescribed class (or part of class) does not truly belong within it and should be differently treated as separate lands and heritages.

The example given in debate was that of the commercial outlets on the site of a student residence (see *Hansard,* H.L. Vol. 486, col. 424). Although the residence may, as a whole be prescribed as "domestic" subjects, the commercial element should, as non-domestic subjects, be put on the valuation roll (subs. (5)(b)).

Such a result is no doubt logical within the context of the overall scheme of the Act and it may be fairly easily achieved in most cases. A difficulty which may arise in some cases will presumably be, however, that of satisfactorily dividing the two (or more) parts to produce "separate lands and heritages" (see note on subs. (3)(a)).

Other problems may arise in the process of discerning what precisely has been prescribed as "domestic" under subs. (3)(b) or as "excepted from paragraph (a)" under subs. (4). These cannot be fully addressed until the regulations to be interpreted are promulgated but it may, for instance, be by no means obvious which, if indeed any, "parts" of the site of a student residence should be retained on the valuation roll. Since *any* type of subjects could validly be prescribed—a shop *could* be prescribed as "domestic"—there will be no absolutely clear interpretative guidelines for construing the regulations.

A division of another kind is made by means of the concept of "part residential subjects" (see Sched. 1). It is possible that, rather than undertake the difficulties of prescription under subs. (3)(b) and the difficulties of further separating the premises under subs. (5), "part residential subjects" might have provided an easier solution to the problem of (*e.g.*) student residences.

Subs. (6)

It is plain that the application of the rules in earlier subsections will not be a totally smooth process. It is inevitable that there will be disputes about the division between domestic subjects and others, whether lands and heritages should or should not go on the valuation roll.

Many of these disputes will arise in the form of a challenge to the decision of an assessor and this subsection confirms that such challenge will be by way of appeal to the valuation appeal committee. These committees are established under s.4 of the Local Government (Scotland) Act 1975 and S.I. 1975 No. 1220. It will be noticed that the relevant "proprietor, tenant or occupier" may appeal against either a decision to delete lands and heritages from the valuation roll or not to delete them. This reflects the general position under the Act that an individual's exact circumstances will determine his potential liability to community charges or rates and thus his reasons for opting for one rather than the other.

The designation "proprietor, tenant, or occupier" is wholly familiar in valuation law. It is proprietors, tenants and occupiers whose names are required to be entered by the assessor in the valuation roll (Local Government (Scotland) Act 1975, s.1 and S.I. 1984 No. 1505, Art. 3) and who are given the right of appeal to the valuation appeal committee (1975 Act s.3(2), (2A), (2B)). The terms have been the subject of further statutory (see especially on "proprietors" the Lands Valuation (Scotland) Act 1854, s.42) and judicial interpretation (see generally Armour, chapters 12 and 13). They may not be expected to cause any difficulty as deployed in this subsection, save that they may be difficult to interpret after April 1, 1989, in the case of subjects (and relevant names) deleted from the roll. It is not made clear when appeals are to be lodged.

Other related questions concerning appeals may arise. Subs. (6) refers only to appeals against decisions to *delete* or not to *delete* with effect from April 1, 1989. Presumably, if premises are entered in the roll after that date, an appeal under s.3 of the 1975 Act will be competent if a proprietor wishes to claim that they are domestic subjects. If premises are *not* entered at some point after April 1, 1989, and the "proprietor" wishes to object, his remedy would presumably be to complain as a "person interested" under s.22 of the Local Government (Scotland) Act 1966 that "particular lands and heritages are not included in the valuation roll for that area and that they ought to be included".

This, in turn, raises the general question of the scope for a "complaint", as opposed to an appeal in relation to the issues potentially in dispute under s.2. Under s.13 of the Lands Valuation (Scotland) Act 1854, it is possible for complaints to be made to the valuation appeal committee on the grounds (normally) that a valuation entered in the roll is fixed too low. Such a complaint can be made by any party having an interest (for examples, see Armour, para. 5–12) and has usually been a ratepayer. Presumably a community chargee will also become someone with a sufficient interest to make a complaint under the 1854 Act or, as above, under the 1966 Act? Complaints are also competently made by any person interested under s.6 of the Valuation of Lands (Scotland) Amendment Act 1879 that particulars other than the valuation itself are wrongly stated in the valuation roll.

Complaints of all these varieties are handled by the valuation appeal committees in the same way as appeals. Under s.1 of the Lands Tribunal Act 1949 (as amended by the Rating and Valuation (Amendment) (Scotland) Act 1984) appeals and complaints may be referred by a valuation appeal committee to the Lands Tribunal for Scotland for determination (see also S.I. 1984 No. 1506). A further appeal, whether direct from a valuation committee, or from the Lands Tribunal, may be taken to the Lands Valuation Appeal Court consisting of three (or sometimes only one since the Rating and Valuation (Amendment) (Scotland) Act 1984) Court of Session judges. Normally only questions of value (or questions necessary to be decided in order to establish value) can be taken at the Lands Valuation Appeal Court (for the procedure, see Valuation Appeal Rules, S.I. 1952 No. 1906 as amended). Such questions can include whether subjects should be entered as a *unum quid* where that affects their valuation (see *Rootes Motors (Scotland)* v. *Assessor for Renfrewshire*, 1971 S.L.T. 67 and generally at Armour, para. 5–42).

Two other forms of challenge should be borne in mind. In the first place, it should be noted that, at some points, the rules on liability to rates and those on liability to community charges overlap and yet they are handled within different decision-making and appellate systems. Questions of valuation are, as described, matters for the assessor and then, on appeal, for the valuation appeal committee and beyond. Questions of liability to the community charge are for the community charge registration officer and, thereafter, for the sheriff and ultimately, on a point of law, the Court of Session and House of Lords (see s.29). It is not, therefore, impossible that questions of whether two adjoining (and apparently similar) houses are "dwelling houses" could be answered differently if one is taken on appeal (under s.2) from the assessor and the other on appeal in relation to a standard charge (under sections 10 and 16) from the community charges registration officer.

The other important form of challenge potentially available to someone aggrieved by a decision of the assessor (or indeed the community charges registration officer) is that of an application for judicial review in the Court of Session. Since April 30, 1985, this has been a procedure governed by Rule 260B which was designed to make judicial review quicker and more efficient. Recourse to judicial review is not, however, a new thing in valuation practice (see Armour, paras. 5–6) and, in circumstances where an individual has no obvious access to the statutory forms of appeal or complaint but does have the title and interest to apply for judicial review on the grounds of, *e.g.*, the *ultra vires* act of an assessor or registration officer, the procedure may yet acquire a new significance. For a full discussion of the grounds for judicial review, the questions of title and interest, the procedure and the remedies available, see A. W. Bradley "Administrative Law" in the *Stair Encyclopaedia of the Laws of Scotland*, Vol. 1, 1987.

Subs. (7)

Pts. I and II of Sched. 1 are concerned with part residential subjects. See the notes on those Parts below.

Non-domestic rates

3.—(1) Subject to the provisions of this section, each local authority shall, in respect of the financial year 1989–90 and each subsequent financial year, determine, before such rate as may be prescribed in relation to each of those years, a non-domestic rate, which shall be levied, in respect of lands and heritages—

(a) which are subjects (other than part residential subjects) in respect of which there is an entry in the valuation roll, according to their rateable value; or

(b) which are part residential subjects, according to that part of their rateable value which is shown in the apportionment note as relating to the non residential use of those subjects,

and for the purposes of this subsection "rateable value" shall be construed in accordance with the provisions of section 7(1) of the 1975 Act (which relates to the levying of rates).

(2) The Secretary of State shall with the consent of the Treasury prescribe, in relation to each local authority, the maximum non-domestic rate which may be determined by that authority in respect of each financial year.

(3) The maximum prescribed under subsection (2) above in relation to each local authority in respect of the financial year 1989–90 shall be calculated in accordance with the formula—

$$(B-S) \times I$$

where—

(a) B is the base rate;

(b) S is, in the case of

(i) a regional or islands council, the Secretary of State's estimate of the amount of the rate determined by that council in respect of the financial year 1988–89 which is attributable to the provision, by that council in that year, of the sewerage services mentioned in section 1(1) of the 1968 Act (which requires local authorities to provide such services), and

(ii) a district council, zero; and

(c) I is the ratio of the retail prices index for September 1988 to the retail prices index for September 1987.

(4) The maximum prescribed under subsection (2) above in relation to each local authority in respect of the financial year 1990–91 and each subsequent financial year shall be calculated in accordance with the formula—

$$M \times I \times R$$

where—

(a) M is the maximum prescribed under subsection (2) above in respect of the immediately preceding financial year;

(b) I is the ratio to the retail prices index for September of the immediately preceding year to the retail prices index for September 12 months earlier; and

(c) R is, where the financial year in respect of which the maximum non-domestic rate is being prescribed is—

(i) a year of revaluation, the Secretary of State's estimate of the proportion which the aggregate rateable value of lands and heritages in Scotland in respect of which the non-domestic rate is leviable on the last day of the financial year immediately preceding that year will be of the aggregate rateable value of those lands and heritages on the first day of the year of revaluation; and

(ii) a year other than a year of revaluation, 1.

(5) For the purposes of this section—

(a) "the base rate" means—

(i) the rate determined by that local authority in respect of the financial year 1988–89 less, in the case of a regional or islands council, such portion of that rate as they have determined to be their public water rate for that year under section 39 of the 1980 Act (which relates to the levying of rates in respect of expenditure on water supply); or

(ii) where, before 1st April 1989, the Secretary of State prescribes a base rate in respect of that authority for the purposes of this section, the amount so prescribed;

(b) "retail prices index" has the meaning assigned to it in section 24(8) of the Finance Act 1980 (which relates to the indexation of income tax thresholds and allowances); and

(c) "year of revaluation" has the meaning assigned to it by section 37(1) of the 1975 Act (which defines terms used in that Act).

(6) Where the calculation required by subsection (3) or (4) above produces a sum which includes a fraction of a tenth of a penny, the Secretary of State shall increase or, as the case may be, reduce the sum to the nearest tenth of a penny.

(7) Before determining a non-domestic rate under this section, a local authority shall, in accordance with such procedure as the Secretary of State may direct—

(a) make available to the persons mentioned in subsection (8) below such information as he may direct; and

(b) consult those persons on that information and on the rate which the local authority propose to determine.

(8) The persons referred to in subsection (7) above are—

(a) persons liable to pay the non-domestic rate; and

(b) bodies appearing to the local authority to be representative of persons so liable.

(9) A direction made under subsection (7) above may be revoked or amended by a further direction so made.

(10) The rates determined by local authorities under subsection (1) above shall be known in the case of—

(a) a regional council, as the non-domestic regional rate;

(b) a district council, as the non-domestic district rate; and

(c) an islands council, as the non-domestic islands rate.

Definitions
    "apportionment note": see Sched. 1, para. 2.
    "financial year": see s.26(1) and Local Government (Scotland) Act 1973, s.96(5) (as amended), *i.e.* the year from April 1.
    "local authority": see s.26(1).
    "part residential subjects": see s.26(1).
    "prescribe", "prescribed": see ss.26(1), 31(3).
    "rate", "non-domestic rate": see s.26(2).
    "rateable value": see s.3(1) and s.7(1) of the Local Government (Scotland) Act 1975.
    "retail prices index": see s.3(5)(b).
    "valuation roll": see Local Government (Scotland) Act 1975, s.1.
    "year of revaluation": see s.3(5)(c).

General Note
    The abolition of domestic rates and their replacement by community charges is a process which leaves in place rates levied on non-domestic property as the second principal source of locally derived revenue available to local authorities. (For the separate provision to be made for water and sewerage charges, see s.25 and Sched. 5.)
    The Green Paper (Cmnd. 9714 (1986)) described the proposals it contained on the future of the non-domestic rate as central to the Government's proposals for the reform of local government finance as a whole (para. 2.45). It showed local government income in Scotland coming from domestic rates (13 per cent.) and non-domestic rates (28 per cent.) (with 59 per cent. from central grants (para. 8.13)). It looked forward to a situation which the Government would itself set a non-domestic rate poundage common to all areas. This would avoid, they said, wide variations and fluctuations within and between different areas—a feature which they believed to have had an adverse effect upon the business community. Once collected, the nationally prescribed rate income would be redistributed to local authorities as a standard level of grant.
    Although the government claimed this centrally directed scheme of non-domestic rating to be their long term aim, they accepted that, because of variations in valuation procedures and practice between Scotland and England and Wales, the full implementation of their plans would have to wait until after revaluations proposed for both jurisdictions in 1990 and any necessary statutory adjustments to valuation rules made to achieve their harmonisation.
    Thus the scheme to come into effect in 1989 is one which requires all local authorities to continue to levy a rate, the non-domestic rate, on all those "lands and heritages" which remain in the valuation roll (including "part-residential subjects" to the extent of their value which is non-residential). The level at which the non-domestic rate is to be levied is not in all respects prescribed in the Act. There is no minimum level of non-domestic rate. There is no duty to relate the level of non-domestic rate to a level of "total estimated expenses" (*cf.* the duty in relation to the community charge in s.9(2)) nor to the amount of the community charge for the year in question. What *is* fixed—by the Secretary of State in accordance with s.3(2)–(6)—is the *maximum* non-domestic rate. A permanent "rate-cap" is imposed.
    The machinery for doing this is, first, to enable the Secretary of State to prescribe a maximum rate for each authority in 1989–90 which will normally be the rate for 1988–89 (reduced, for regional and islands councils by certain amounts attributable to water and sewerage services) *increased* by the increase in the level of retail prices between September 1987 and September 1988 (subs. (3)). Thereafter, the maximum permitted increase is calculated again by reference to increases in retail prices from year to year but with special account taken of years of revaluation—in which values may be expected to rise but (to achieve the same revenue) rates poundages to fall (subs. (4)).
    Provision is also made in this section for local authorities to supply information to and to consult with those people liable to pay non-domestic rates and their representatives (subss. (7)–(9)).
    More detailed notes on each subsection follow but it is important, if the effects of s.3 are to be fully understood, to take account of some other provisions in the Act. As part of a pattern of central control over local expenditure, the section should be seen alongside the powers available to the Secretary of State under Sched. 3 to take selective action against local authorities by ordering a reduction in the level of their community charges. Provisions of even greater importance are contained in Sched. 4 which concerns the Secretary of State's revenue support grants to local authorities. There is no doubt that the powers of the Secretary of State in that Schedule to determine both aggregate levels of grant and the rules for its distribution will continue to be the most significant regulators of the financial fortunes of the Scottish authorities. One particularly interesting feature (discussed in the notes on the

Schedule) is that, in a much revised form of "needs" assessment of authorities, their income from non-domestic rates is apparently to be incorporated as a significant variable. To have a relatively low non-domestic rate income (presumably, in most cases, assumed to be the maximum permissible under s.3) will result, if relative expenditure "needs" are constant, in a higher revenue support grant entitlement than that of an authority with a high rate income. Thus, although in form there is no national rate poundage or national pool of rate income for redistribution, the Secretary of State is, in practice, preparing to achieve virtually the same result from 1989. Instead of gathering in income centrally for redistribution, rate income is left with the levying authorities and topped up with differing amounts of grant. There is no explicit requirement of a uniform rate poundage but the prescription of maximum levels under s.3 is a strong substitute.

Subs. (1)

Ss.1 and 2 provided for the abolition of domestic rates and for the exclusion of domestic subjects from the roll. Pt. II of the Act provides for the substituted system of community charges. As a result of those changes, the principal rating provisions in the Local Government (Scotland) Act 1973 (ss.107–108C) are repealed by Sched. 6 and, in their place from 1989–90, is put the new duty in this subsection to levy a rate. For the full names of these non-domestic rates by reference to the tier of local government, see subs. (10).

Although "non-domestic subjects" are occasionally referred to in these notes, that is not a term of art in the Act itself. Non-domestic rates are levied on all those subject remaining on the roll (*i.e.* after the removal of domestic subjects) and having a rateable value. For most such subjects, that is (in terms of subs. (1)(a)) the "rateable value" shown in the roll. For those part-residential subjects whose value has been apportioned in accordance with Sched. 1 (in order to remove from rating those parts of premises used by a person as a sole or main residence) it is, of course, only those non-residential parts of the rateable value shown in the apportionment note upon which rates are levied. For the consequent adjustment of the definition of "rateable value" in the Local Government (Scotland) Act 1975 by the addition of a new s.7(1A), see Sched. 1, para. 32.

It will be noted that the final three lines of the subsection instruct that it is in accordance with s.7(1) of the 1975 Act that the term "rateable value" for the purposes of this subsection alone must be construed. In other provisions in the Act, s.26(1) ensures that the term will be construed in accordance with s.6 of the Valuation and Rating (Scotland) Act 1956. What s.7(1) of the 1975 Act contributes is that (subject to a proviso in relation to new entries and entries altered during the year) for the purposes of levying a rate the "rateable value" of lands and heritages is that "appearing in the valuation roll in force at the beginning of the year in respect of which the rate is levied".

The date by which the non-domestic rate is to be determined is to be prescribed. It will be before the level of revenue support grant is fixed which will, in turn, be before the date on which the authority determines its community charge (see *Hansard,* H.C. Vol. 111, col. 1093 *et seq.*).

For the level at which the rate is to be fixed, see succeeding subsections. Notice that, in terms of s.56(6) of the Local Government (Scotland) Act 1973 (as amended by s.28 of this Act), it continues to be the full council (rather than, *e.g.,* a committee) which must determine the rate under this subsection.

Subs. (2)

As mentioned in the General Note, this section gives no general guidance to an authority on the level of rate which it should determine. There is no statutory minimum. There is no obligation to relate the level of rate to the total estimated expenses of the authority (*cf.* s.9 and the community charge). There is no obligation to maintain any sort of balance between the amount to be derived from the non-domestic rate and the community charge (*cf.* the obligation not to show undue preference or to discriminate in relation to water and sewerage charges—see Sched. 5 paras. 4 and 17).

Each year, however, the Secretary of State will prescribe the *maximum* non-domestic rate for each authority. For the relationship between this maximum rate and the level of revenue support grant, see the General Note and Sched. 4.

Prescription is by regulations subject only to negative resolution procedure (s.31(3)). It is perhaps a curiosity that a financial order of this sort could be annulled by the House of Lords (*cf.* rate-capping under the Local Government (Scotland) Act 1973, s.108B which requires an affirmative resolution in the Commons). There were amendments proposed to make the regulations subject to the affirmative procedure but the Government's response was that all the terms of the regulations would be dictated by the statutory formula (*Hansard,* H.L. Vol. 486, col. 510)—except the "base rate" in the first year.

For the effect of this rate-capping by the Government upon the obligation of authorities to consult with ratepayers, see subss. (7)–(9).

Subs. (3)
This subsection and subs. (4) are the most crucial in the section. They define the maximum rates to be prescribed for 1989–90 and for subsequent years respectively.

For 1989–90, the maximum non-domestic rate is, subject to certain qualifications, the rate determined for 1988–89 plus an inflation supplement expressed in the formula as the ratio of the R.P.I. in September 1988 to that in September 1987.

The 1988–89 rate is subject to adjustment. Firstly, there is a need, in the case of regional and islands councils, to deduct the portion of the rate determined to be their public water rate. This is because, in terms of Sched. 5, water charges are to be put on entirely separate footing from 1989–90 and the "base-rate" (see subs. (5)(a)) is adjusted accordingly.

Staying with the "base-rate", that is capable of being wholly prescribed by the Secretary of State (subs. (5)(a)(ii)). This power is crucial to the whole rate-capping exercise because, after 1989–90, the Secretary of State lacks any power to intervene directly in the calculation of the permissible increase. By using this power to prescribe a (lower) base rate before April 1, 1989, he can impose an initial control which will affect all future years. In Parliament it was stated that a base rate would be prescribed "in circumstances where the 1988–89 figure is distorted—for example, through the abnormal use of balances" (*Hansard,* H.L. Vol. 485, cols. 1321–1322). However, the uses to which the power may be put are not restricted by subs. (5) and there can be little doubt that it could be widely used to restrain local authority income from non-domestic rates. Until 1988–89, the powers will be available under s.5 of the Local Government (Scotland) Act 1966 to take selective action against authorities (Lord Glenarthur mentioned these—*Hansard,* H.L. Vol. 486, col. 485—as a measure of protection to non-domestic ratepayers before 1989) and even those under s.108B of the Local Government (Scotland) Act 1973 to impose a general rate cap.

Once the base rate is fixed, by whichever route in subs. (5), it is subject to a further deduction ("S") in the case of regional and islands councils. Sewerage charges (like water charges) go on to a separate basis from 1989–90 (Sched. 5) and an amount equivalent to the cost of sewerage services in 1988–89 has to be deducted. Since, unlike the public water rate, that amount does not have to be separately fixed, the Secretary of State is empowered to make his own estimate of the amount (subs. (3)(b)). In Parliament it was said that the estimate would be derived from figures published in the *Rating Review* (*Hansard,* H.L. Vol. 486, col. 510). This is not an amount separately prescribed but is incorporated in the prescription under subs. (2). For district councils there is no deduction for water or sewerage costs as these services are not a part of their responsibilities.

The final element in the formula—"I", representing inflation—was the most controversial in Parliament. The central objection was that the "retail prices index" (see subs. (5)(b)) was irrelevant as a measure of the increase of local authority costs. The principal measures suggested in substitution were links to an index of average earnings or to an index of local authority costs (see, *e.g., Hansard,* H.L. Vol. 486, col. 513). These, it was argued, would be a better indication of the actual additional needs of local authorities from year to year. This, however, was also the main reason why the Government preferred a general index such as the R.P.I.—"that it would break the link between rates and local authority spending so that non-domestic ratepayers would then be able to rely on local authority rates moving in line with the costs generally" (*Hansard,* H.L. Vol. 486, cols. 1467–1468)—but not necessarily in line with local authority costs. Furthermore, the other proposed index (a local authority cost index which is drawn up by the Scottish Office in consultation with the Convention of Scottish Local Authorities—C.O.S.L.A.) would be "entirely informal with the result that it does not have the same status the R.P.I. which is subject to external monitoring and scrutiny through the Retail Price Index Advisory Committee" (*Hansard,* H.L. Vol. 486, col. 1468).

In addition to attempts to dislodge the R.P.I. as the statutory measure, it was argued that there should be a method built into the formula by which *some* further increase in the non-domestic rate could be secured in respect of A.S.P. (for Additional Service or Special Provision rather than A.S.S. for Additional Special Services!) (see Lord Ross, *Hansard,* H.L. Vol. 486, cols. 1469–1470). The intention here was to allow for the possibility that an authority might be making available an additional service of greater benefit to non-domestic ratepayers than the community chargees—*e.g.* a conference or exhibition centre. This was rejected (*Hansard,* H.L. Vol. 486, col. 1470) largely on the basis that attempts to apportion benefits between different categories of taxpayer would be a novelty and one which would be impossible to operate. It may, however, be observed that, at a lesser level, this sort of balancing exercise is expected in relation to water and sewerage services. More importantly, the totally rigid capping of non-domestic rates does imply that any new service provision or any increase in the cost of an old service will escape the shoulders of non-domestic ratepayers entirely. Any such burden (including, presumably, the additional financial burden of the community charge system itself) will be borne by community charges and central grants.

Subs. (4)

This subsection ensures that the maximum prescribed non-domestic rate will rise in the years from 1990–91 onwards in accordance with exactly the same formula as for 1989–90 (*i.e.* by the amount of increase in the R.P.I.) but with the maximum prescribed rate for the previous year substituted for the original "base rate".

The only obvious complication which arises is the one addressed in subs. (4)(c) which relates to the years of revaluation. In those years, there has to be inserted into the formula an element ("R") which will lower the maximum prescribed rate precisely in proportion to the amount by which the overall increase in property revaluations would have otherwise increased the rate product had the formula been left unadjusted in those years. In terms of subs. (5)(c), the definition of "year of revaluation" the year in respect of which under s.1 of the Local Government (Scotland) Act 1975 the assessor must make up a new valuation roll, is incorporated from section 37(1) of that Act, *i.e.* "the year 1985–1986 and each fifth year thereafter". Under s.37(3), the Secretary of State may, by order, substitute a different financial year.

It should be noted that subs. (4)(c)(i) makes the necessary adjustment by reference to estimated national rather than local figures for the amount of increase in rateable values. Severe local fluctuations at the point of revaluations could, therefore, result in an authority's maximum rate yield rising or falling against the national average. It should, however, be recalled that, if non-domestic rate income is to be taken into account in the revenue support grant process under Sched. 4, a fluctuation of this sort may be accommodated at that stage (see General Note above and the notes on Sched. 4).

In debate, it was stated that the Secretary of State's estimate under subs. (4)(c)(i) would be based on returns submitted by assessors under s.7(4) of the Local Government (Financial Provisions) (Scotland) Act 1963 (see *Hansard,* H.L. Vol. 486, col. 510).

Subs. (5)

The significance of all the terms defined in this subsection has already been discussed.

Subs. (6)

Since the calculations are multiplications perhaps the "sums" should be "products"?

Subs. (7)

In an earlier phase of the attempts of the Government to achieve what they viewed as the greater financial accountability of local authorities to their ratepayers, they introduced a new duty to be imposed upon all local authorities to consult with "non-domestic ratepayers" before the determination of the rate. Non-domestic ratepayers were seen as disenfranchised and yet vulnerable to rate increases. S.4 of the Rating and Valuation (Amendment) (Scotland) Act 1984 inserted new subss. (3)–(6) in s.108 of the Local Government (Scotland) Act 1973. Now ss.107 to 108C of the 1973 Act are to be repealed by Sched. 6 to this Act but the effect of those subsections is retained by subss. (7)–(9) of this section.

The questions raised in debate on the new subsections focussed on the continuing relevance of the consultation process under the new rules in earlier subsections. It was argued that, since local authorities would have very little room for manoeuvre in the fixing of the level of their non-domestic rate, there would be very little on which to consult. Indeed it was suggested that, because of the dominant role of the Secretary of State, he should be made a party to the consultation process. These arguments were, unsurprisingly, rejected by the Government who instead maintained that, because authorities could if they wished fix a rate below the maximum (but see subs. (2) above), the process of consultation remained important. (See 1st Scot. S.C. col. 402).

Subss. (8) and (9)

See note on subs. (7).

Subs. (10)

This gives names to the rates to be determined under subs. (1). For related definitions, see s.26(2).

Under s.108(1) of the Local Government (Scotland) Act 1973 (repealed by Sched. 6) the name of the rate determined by an islands council was the "general rate". It has now been redubbed the "islands rate".

Valuation of premises part of which occupied as dwelling house

4.—(1) Where, by virtue of section 45 of the 1980 Act (which makes provision as to the apportionment of the net annual value of premises occupied partly as a dwelling house) or of section 7(3) of the 1966 Act (which relates to the reduction of rates on premises occupied partly as a dwelling house by reference to the domestic element)—

(a) the net annual value of any premises has been apportioned as between the part occupied as a dwelling house and the remainder; and

(b) the net annual value of each of the parts is shown separately on the valuation roll prior to 1st April 1989,

then, with effect from that date, the part occupied as a dwelling house and the remainder shall each be treated for the purposes of the Valuation Acts as separate lands and heritages.

(2) Where premises are required by subsection (1) above to be treated as separate lands and heritages, the assessor shall, with effect from 1st April 1989, enter in the valuation roll only the part not occupied as a dwelling house, at the value resulting from the apportionment mentioned in that subsection.

DEFINITIONS
"assessor": see Local Government (Scotland) Act 1973, s.16(2).
"domestic element": see Local Government (Scotland) Act 1966, s.2(4).
"net annual value": see s.26(1) and the Valuation and Rating (Scotland) Act 1956, s.6.
"the 1980 Act": see s.26(1).
"the 1966 Act": see s.26(1).
"the Valuation Acts": see s.26(1).
"valuation roll": see Local Government (Scotland) Act 1975, s.1.

GENERAL NOTE
For some purposes, it is already necessary, under the law in force until April 1, 1989, to distinguish premises occupied as a dwelling house from those which are not. On the one hand, premises valued as dwelling houses suffer the levy of a domestic water rate under s.40 of the Water (Scotland) Act 1980 according to their full net annual value whereas commercial premises are (normally) charged on half of their net annual value. On the other hand, dwelling houses attract the domestic rate relief under s.7 of the Local Government (Scotland) Act 1966 consequent upon the payment to authorities of the domestic element of the rate support grant.

Dwelling houses are, normally, shown on the valuation roll separately from other premises. In some cases, however, premises *occupied partly as a dwelling house* are shown on the roll as a single subject having a single net annual value. To achieve the purposes of s.41(3) of the 1980 Act (read with s.45 of that Act) and s.7 of the 1966 Act, the assessor is obliged (under para. 3(g) of the Valuation Roll and Valuation Notice (Scotland) Order 1984 S.I. 1984 No. 1505) to show apportioned net annual values under the two Acts. It is upon the basis of those that the domestic water rate and the domestic rate relief can be calculated.

The typical illustrative example is that of the shop with flat above but other mixtures of commercial and residential subject may be involved. Depending largely upon the practice of the local assessor, such a shop and flat may appear as either completely separate entries on the register or else as a single subject but (as explained above) with an indication of the apportioned values.

What this section now requires is that, where a *single* such subject appears on the roll, the two parts of the premises must be treated with effect from April 1, 1989, not merely as subject to an apportionment of value but as separate lands and heritages. Only that part not occupied as a dwelling house should be entered in the roll after April 1, 1989.

S.4 is, thus, a piece of statutory tidying up which supplements the more radical measures taken in s.2, the regulations to be made under that section and Sched. 1 (especially Pt. I on part residential subjects) to divide existing premises on the valuation roll into domestic and

non-domestic subjects. The section takes advantage of pre-existing criteria for apportionin
value to achieve the same purpose.

A possible draw-back may be, however, that those pre-existing criteria are not precisel
those which determine, under s.2, that subjects are domestic or non-domestic. "Occupied a
a dwelling house" is not coterminous with "domestic subject". Thus the simple instructio
to the assessor to "enter in the valuation roll only the part not occupied as a dwelling-house"
could conceivably amount to an instruction to enter a subject defined under s.2 as (wholl
or, more probably, in part) "domestic".

If, for instance, the premises in question were not a dwelling house plus shop but a
dwelling house plus rooms let to boarders (perhaps students) it might be at least arguabl
that those rooms could be viewed as domestic subjects (especially if so prescribed in the cas
of students) and thus not appropriately entered on the roll under subs. (2)? Presumably th
practical answer is that there will be scope for appeal to the valuation appeal committe
under s.2(6) in any such cases?

Subs. (1)

As explained in outline above, s.40 of the Water (Scotland) Act 1980 provides for liability
for domestic water rate on dwelling houses based on their net annual value. S.41 provide
for similar liability (but based normally on half of net annual value) for commercial premises
S.41(3) as supplemented by s.45 provides for how premises containing a mixture of dwelling
house and commercial premises should appear on the roll with its net annual value
apportioned in order that the calculation can be made. A similar arrangement is made to
produce an apportioned value on which the domestic rate relief under the 1966 Act can be
made.

With effect from April 1, 1989, the two "parts" of the premises must be treated as separate
lands and heritages. In many cases this has, in practice, already occurred in typical house
and shop combinations—avoiding the need for apportionment of a single value and, thus,
also avoiding the application of this section.

In some other cases where the separation is ordered under this section, it may not always
produce "parts" which would in the past have been viewed as capable of being separate
units of valuation. (See notes on s.2 and especially s.2(4)).

For arrangements after April 1, 1989, see Sched. 5. In the substituted s.40 of the 1980
Act, a non-domestic water rate replaces the present domestic water rate and, normally, is
payable on all those premises remaining on the roll. The community water charge is payable
by those who pay the community charge. The need for apportionment disappears and
ss.41(3) and 45 are repealed by Sched. 6.

With the abolition of domestic rates, domestic rating relief also disappears from April 1,
1989, and s.7 of the 1966 Act is repealed.

Subs. (2)

This subsection completes the process by ensuring that the assessor, with effect from April
1, 1989, enters only the "part not occupied as a dwelling house" on the roll—subject to the
possibility of appeal mentioned in the general note.

Notice also that the commercial part goes on to the roll "at the value resulting from the
apportionment". This makes for simplicity. Whether such a separate unit *should* necessarily
be given the same value it enjoyed as a part of a larger unit is another question. Perhaps the
normal opportunities for the assessor, on his own motion or following appeal or complaint,
to alter the valuation will be available. These may, however, not be competent to displace
the original mode of valuation.

Statutory and other references to rateable values etc.

5.—(1) Where—

(a) in any deed relating to heritable property executed before 1st April
1989 there is any provision which apportions any liability according
to the assessed rental or, as the case may be, the gross annual, net
annual or rateable value of any properties; and

(b) all the properties involved in the apportionment appear in the
valuation roll in force immediately before 1st April 1989; and

(c) one or more of the properties constitute domestic subjects,

then, with effect from 1st April 1989, any reference to the assessed rental
or, as the case may be, to any of those values in any such deed shall,
unless the context otherwise requires, be construed as a reference to the

net annual value or, as the case may be, to the gross annual, net annual or rateable value which appears in relation to any of those properties in the valuation roll in force immediately before that date.

(2) Where in any document executed before 1st April 1989 there is a reference to the assessed rental or, as the case may be, to the gross annual, net annual or rateable value of any property which—

(a) constitutes domestic subjects; and

(b) appears in the valuation roll in force immediately before 1st April 1989,

then, with effect from that date that reference shall, unless the context otherwise requires, be construed as a reference to the net annual value or, as the case may be, to the gross annual, net annual or rateable value which appears in relation to that property in the valuation roll in force immediately before that date.

(3) Where in any enactment there is a reference to the gross annual value, net annual value or rateable value of any property which constitutes domestic subjects, then, with effect from 1st April 1989, that reference shall, unless the context otherwise requires, be construed as a reference to the gross annual value, net annual value or rateable value—

(a) subject to subsection (4) below, which appears in relation to that property in the valuation roll in force immediately before that date; or

(b) subject to subsection (5) below, in the case of such property which does not come into existence or occupancy as domestic subjects until after that date, which would have appeared in the roll in respect of it had it been in existence or occupancy as such immediately before that date.

(4) Where, before or after 1st April 1989, there is a material change of circumstances, within the meaning of section 37(1) of the 1975 Act—

(a) in relation to any such property as is mentioned in subsection (3)(a) above; and

(b) in respect of which no alteration has been made to the valuation roll in force immediately before that date,

references in that subsection to the gross annual, net annual or rateable value of that property which appears in the roll in force immediately before that date shall be construed as references to the gross annual, net annual or rateable value which would have so appeared had that roll been altered to take account of that material change of circumstances.

(5) Where there is a material change of circumstances, within the meaning of section 37(1) of the 1975 Act, in relation to any such property as is mentioned in subsection (3)(b) above, references in that subsection to the gross annual, net annual or rateable value of that property which would have appeared in respect of it in the roll in force immediately before 1st April 1989 shall be construed as references to the gross annual, net annual or rateable value which would have so appeared had that material change of circumstances been taken into account.

(6) The assessor shall, at the request of any person and on payment of such fee as may be prescribed, certify—

(a) what would have appeared in the valuation roll in force immediately before 1st April 1989 as the gross annual value, net annual value or rateable value of any such property as is mentioned in subsection (3)(b) above; or

(b) what would have appeared in that roll as the gross annual value, net annual value or rateable value of any such property as is mentioned in subsection (3) above had that roll been altered to take account of any material change of circumstances, within the meaning of section 37(1) of the 1975 Act, occurring before or after that date.

(7) An appeal shall lie—

(a) against any certificate issued by the assessor under subsection (6) above; or

(b) against any refusal by the assessor to issue a certificate under tha subsection,

and the provisions of the Valuation Acts in regard to appeals and complaints shall apply, subject to such modifications and adaptations as may be prescribed, for the purposes of this subsection.

(8) Without prejudice to section 35 of the Lands Valuation (Scotland) Act 1854 (which relates to the preservation of valuation rolls by the Keeper of the Records of Scotland), the assessor for each valuation area shall retain a copy of the valuation roll in force immediately before 1st April 1989 for the purposes of this Act; and the copy so retained shall be made available for public inspection at the assessor's offices during ordinary business hours.

(9) Where the net annual value of any property does not appear, or would not have appeared, in the valuation roll in force immediately before 1st April 1989, references in this section to the appearance in that roll of the net annual value of that property shall be taken as references to the appearance of its rateable value.

(10) For the purposes of this section "gross annual value", "net annual value" and "rateable value" shall continue to be construed in accordance with the provisions of section 6 of the 1956 Act as those provisions have effect immediately before 1st April 1989.

DEFINITIONS

"assessor": see Local Government (Scotland) Act 1973 s.116(2).
"domestic subjects": see ss.26(1) and 2(3).
"gross annual value": see Valuation and Rating (Scotland) Act 1956, s.6.
"net annual value": see s.26(1).
"the 1956 Act": see s.26(1).
"the 1975 Act": see s.26(1).
"prescribed": see ss.26(1) and 31.
"rateable value": see s.26(1).
"valuation roll": see Local Government (Scotland) Act 1975, s.1.

GENERAL NOTE

The process of abolishing domestic rates, replacing them with community charges and restructuring non-domestic rates is one which requires the enactment of much new law and the amendment and repeal of old law. This is the primary purpose of this Act and the regulations made under it—including, if it is used, the power under s.31(1) to make provisions "necessary or expedient for the purposes of rendering this Act of full effect".

For the most part, the specific amendments and repeals in the Act are directed towards those provisions in existing law which may be said to concern the primary purpose of the valuation and rating of properties—to provide a source of locally-derived, property-based tax income for local authorities. However, the very existence of the valuation system, rateable and other values on properties and the ratepayers which the valuation system identifies has generated a number of dependant or secondary purposes for them. On the one hand, Parliament has taken advantage of the existence of ratepayers and property valuations to enable it to achieve other purposes. Historically, the right to vote was attached to the payment of rates. Ratepayers (or prescribed numbers of them) were given rights to appeal against certain types of local authority action (see, *e.g.*, Public Health (Scotland) Act 1897 s.146). They were given rights of access, not then available to other members of the public, to local authority accounts and to make objections to them (see, *e.g.*, Local Government (Scotland) Act 1929, Sched. 3). Valuations for rating have been, and still are, used in statutory schemes for, *e.g.*, the payment of compensation on compulsory purchase (Housing (Scotland) Act 1987, s.306) and eligibility for house improvement grants (Housing (Scotland) Act 1987, s.240).

In addition, valuations for rating have been extensively used for defining the legal relations between private individuals. There are, therefore, countless contracts and dispositions (especially those affecting tenement properties) which define and apportion liability for such things as repairs to roofs and stairs in terms of the value placed upon the different properties.

In so far as these documents (statutory or private) make reference to the value of subjects or which there will continue to be an entry in the valuation roll (*i.e.* non-domestic subjects) to problem need arise. As far as "domestic subjects" are concerned, however, they will ease by virtue of s.2(1), to be on the roll from April 1, 1989, and they will cease to be alued. The term "gross annual value", which now has relevance only in relation to the aluation of dwelling houses, ceases to have meaning after April 1, 1989, when it is deleted om the Valuation and Rating (Scotland) Act 1956 (see Sched. 6). Nor will dwelling houses continue to have either a net annual value or rateable value.

Plainly something has to be done both to restrict the use of these terms of valuation in ture and to ensure that, when they survive either in statute or private documents after pril 1, 1989, some meaning is attributed to them. So far as statutes are concerned, a start made in this Act to amend the law to reduce dependance upon rateable values—see hed. 2, para. 39 (Civic Government (Scotland) Act 1982, s.90(9)). Another example is the ecific amendment made by Sched. 1, para. 27 to freeze local authority powers to incur xpenditure under s.83 of the Local Government (Scotland) Act 1973 at 1988–89 levels and o doubt other adjustments will be made, perhaps before 1989. In the meantime, however, 5(3)–(7) provides rules for the construction of references to valuations after April 1, 1989. is, in principle, the equivalent value of the domestic subjects concerned immediately prior April 1, 1989, but with supplementary provisions to deal, *inter alia*, with "material change f circumstances" thereafter. Similar provision is made by subss. (1)–(2) in relation to ocuments (subs. (2)) and to deeds which apportion liability (subs. (1)).

Subs. (8) ensures that valuation rolls in force immediately prior to April 1, 1989, survive nd can be inspected for the purposes of the section.

ubs. (1)

This deals with the questions raised by deeds which relate to heritable property and which pportion liability (*e.g.* for the maintenance of roof or stairs) by reference to gross annual alue, net annual value or rateable value. It is concerned only (subject to one qualification elow) with the problems of interpretation to which this Act may give rise.

Thus it is concerned only with deeds in which at least one of the properties constitutes omestic subjects—otherwise all would remain on the roll producing no difficulty.

The properties must all be on the roll immediately prior to April 1, 1989—the changes rought about by the Act come into effect only on that date.

It is also concerned only with deeds executed prior to April 1, 1989. The subsection makes o attempt to solve the problem of a deed executed after April 1, 1989, which misguidedly efers to non-existent values.

It then translates, for purposes *after* April 1, 1989, the terms mentioned into the equivalent alues they had on that date. The apportionment is frozen. There is no machinery under this ubsection for alterations or deemed alterations in the values to take account of subsequent material changes of circumstances" (*cf.* subss. (4)–(7) below in relation to statutory eferences).

See subs. (8) for the obligation on assessors to maintain in existence copies of the roll in orce immediately prior to April 1, 1989.

The references to "assessed rental" in this subsection and in subs. (2) were added in the Iouse of Lords (see *Hansard,* H.L. Vol. 486, cols. 521–522) and are a little anomalous. The dditions were said to be made on the suggestion of the Property Owners and Factors ssociation and the Law Society of Scotland. These bodies had "pointed out that this term ssessed rental' is found in deeds and conditions of tenement properties in the West of cotland where responsibility for bearing the costs of common repairs is frequently allocated ccording to the assessed rental of the properties in the tenement". Although it was accepted aat it was sensible to clear up doubts about the use of the term, those doubts appear to ave nothing to do with the changes operative from April 1, 1989.

ubs. (2)

This subsection makes equivalent provision to that in subsection (1) in relation to any ocument executed prior to April 1, 1989, in which there is a reference to the value of remises which are to become domestic subjects on that date.

See also subs. (8) for the preservation of the roll.

ubs. (3)

This subsection addresses the same problem but, this time, in relation to enactments"—a term not defined in this Act (nor in the Interpretation Act 1978) but one early capable of embracing any Act of Parliament. It has been held that the question of hether "enactment" includes delegated legislation depends on the context—see *Rathbone*

v. *Bundock* [1962] 2 All E.R. 257 at 259. It is submitted that, as used here, the term shou
include delegated legislation.

The section contains, in para. (a), substantially the same provision as for documents
subs. (2) save that the enactment need not have been passed prior to April 1, 1989. A
enactment is included—thus enabling a meaning to be given to references to valuations f
domestic subjects in an Act passed *after* April 1, 1989, by which time domestic subjects w
not be on the roll.

There are two other associated extensions. In the first place para. (a) is made subject
subs. (4) which, with subss. (6) and (7), allows the value attached by subs. (3)(a) to
varied in the light of a "material change of circumstances" whether before April 1, 198
(provided this has not already given rise to an alteration of the valuation in the roll) or aft
April 1, 1989.

The "material change of circumstances" is a term incorporated from s.37 (interpretatio
of the Local Government (Scotland) Act 1975. In that Act the concept is importa
principally because it is on the basis of such a material change of circumstances that t
assessor is authorised (under s.2(1)(d)) to alter the roll while it is in force and the ratepay
(under s.3(4)) is permitted to appeal against an entry in the roll.

The actual definition of the term in the 1975 Act (as significantly amended by s.20 of t
Rating and Valuation (Amendment) (Scotland) Act 1984) is as follows:—

"Material change of circumstances" means in relation to any lands and heritages a chan
of circumstances affecting their value and, without prejudice to the foregoing generalit
includes any alteration in such lands and heritages, any relevant decision of the Lan
Valuation Appeal Court or a valuation appeal committee for the valuation area in which t
lands and heritages are situated or the Lands Tribunal for Scotland under s.1(3A) of t
Lands Tribunal Act 1949, and any decision of that Court, committee or Tribunal whi
alters the gross or net annual value or rateable value of any comparable lands and heritage

Most aspects of this definition have been subjected to extensive judicial interpretation ar
this cannot be examined here. See Armour, *Valuation for Rating*, edited by Clyde and Ho
(5th ed., 1985) paras. 3–12 to 3–31. That jurisprudence has to be regarded as incorporate
by reference, into the construction of this section.

Thus, picking up the earlier argument, subs. (4) enables the valuation immediately pri
to April 1, 1989, to be treated as if altered to take account of a "material change" whic
had the property remained on the roll, would have given rise to an alteration by the assess
or, on appeal, by a valuation appeal committee. For the equivalent procedure under th
Act to secure such an alteration, see subss. (6)(b) and (7).

The second extension introduced in relation to enactments but not documents is express
in subs. (3)(b). This accommodates within the general rule, property (being, of cours
domestic subjects) which comes into existence (or occupation as domestic subjects) on
after April 1, 1989—if it would have been on the roll had it then existed or been so occupie

In respect of this class, too, "material changes" have to be taken into account—this tin
in terms of subs. (5) and, procedurally, subss. (6)(b) and (7). What is also available for th
class of properties is the procedure (under subss. (6)(a) and (7)) under which the assess
may certify what the relevant valuation *would have been* immediately before April 1, 198

See subs. (8) for the rule requiring preservation of the roll.

Subs. (4)

See the note on subs. (3) above. For the assessor's power to certify the effect of
"material change of circumstances", see subs. (6)(b) and, for appeals, subs. (7).

Subs. (5)

This provides the same rule in relation to those "yet to be created" properties in sub
(3)(b) as that set out for the others in subs. (4).

Subs. (6)

In the preceding subsections are anticipated these duties of the assessor to issue th
necessary certificates. In response to "any person" but on payment of whatever fee
prescribed, the assessor must (under (a)) certify a hypothetical value at April 1, 1989, fo
the properties coming into existence (or occupation) after that date. Para. (b) provides fo
the power to certify, as appropriate, the altered value resulting from a "material change
circumstances".

Appeals against certificates and refusals to certify lie under subs. (7).

ubs. (7)

For the circumstances out of which the appeals referred to arise, see subss. (3)–(7).

The system into which these appeals feed has been described in relation to s.2(6). The initial appeal is to the valuation appeal committee with the possibility of reference to the ands Tribunal for Scotland and with a further right of appeal to the Lands Valuation ppeal Court on a valuation matter. (See s.3 of the Local Government (Scotland) Act 1975 id S.I. 1984 No. 1506; s.7 of the Valuation of Lands (Scotland) Amendment Act 1879 and .I. 1982 No. 1506).

ubs. (8)

S.35 of the Lands Valuation (Scotland) Act 1854, as substituted by the Local Government cotland) Act 1975, Sched. 6, Pt. II, para. 4, requires that the "assessor for each valuation ea shall as soon as is reasonably practicable after a valuation roll has ceased to be in force ansmit that roll to the Keeper of the Records of Scotland for preservation by him".

This subsection is stated to be without prejudice to that obligation of the assessor but he , in addition, required to retain a copy—for how long is not stated—at his own office and ade available for public inspection during ordinary business hours. This will be in addition the assessor's obligation to deliver copies of the current valuation roll to the rating uthority which is obliged to keep copies of that roll for inspection at its offices during the urrency of the roll.

The need for the new duty to keep a copy of the last valuation roll with all domestic abjects still recorded is evident from its importance to preceding subsections.

ubs. (9)

This subsection was added at Committee stage in the Lords (*Hansard,* H.L. Vol. 486, col. 37). It was explained that it is intended to deal with the situation in which no entry for a et annual value (necessary to implement preceding subsections) actually appears in the oll. This can arise where the assessor is permitted to enter only a rateable value when it is lentical to the net annual value. The subsection permits that rateable value to be used for ae purposes of the section.

ubs. (10)

With the repeal by Sched. 6 of those parts of s.6 of the Valuation and Rating (Scotland) ct 1956 which deal with the valuation of dwelling houses (including all references to "gross nnual value") it is necessary to preserve the effect of the terms used in s.6 of that Act to nable the provisions of this section to be applied.

Iinor and consequential amendments

6. The enactments specified in Part III of Schedule 1 to this Act shall ave effect subject to the amendments specified in that Part, being minor mendments and amendments consequential upon the provisions of this art of this Act.

OMMENCEMENT

This section came into force on September 14, 1987, but only for the purpose of bringing ato force the paragraphs of Sched. 1 to the Act which were themselves prescribed as coming ato force on that date and subject to any restriction of purpose indicated in relation to aem. The section is brought wholly into force on April 1, 1989.

ENERAL NOTE

S.2(7) gives effect to Pts. I and II of Sched. 1. Those deal with part residential subjects id were brought into force on September 14, 1987.

Pt. III of the Schedule contains amendments which are consequential upon the earlier rovisions in Pt. I of the Act. For brief notes on the amendments, see the Schedule itself. he note on each paragraph indicates its date of commencement.

PART II

COMMUNITY CHARGES

General

Creation and purpose of community charges

7.—(1) Each local authority shall impose, in accordance with this Part of this Act, three community charges, to be known respectively as the personal community charge, the standard community charge and the collective community charge.

(2) The expenses of a local authority in discharging functions under any public general Act, so far as not met otherwise or so far as not otherwise provided for in any such Act, shall be met out of the community charge due to the local authority under this Act.

DEFINITIONS
"community charge": see s.26(1).
"local authority": see s.26(1).

COMMENCEMENT
September 14, 1987, but only for the purposes of, and in relation to, the community charges (and community water charges) in respect of 1989–90 and subsequent financial years.

GENERAL NOTE
This section provides the mainspring for Pt. II of the Act. It provides for the introduction and imposition of community charges, the form of poll tax first mooted in the Green Paper *Paying for Local Government* (Cmnd. 9714, 1986, Paras. 3.33–3.38). Community charges are intended to replace domestic rates which are to be abolished by s.1 of this Act.

Subs. (1)
This specifies the three types of community charge which are to be imposed, the personal community charge, the standard community charge and the collective community charge. The nature, scope and amount of these three charges are dealt with in ss.8 and 9, 10, and 11 respectively.
Notice that Sched. 5, para. 6, creates the three parallel community water charges and that, by virtue of para. 11 of that Schedule, this and other sections in Pt. II of the Act are to be applied, with modifications, to those charges.

Subs. (2)
This subsection explicitly confirms the fiscal significance of the three new community charges. It stipulates that the expenses of a local authority, in carrying out its functions under any public general Act, shall be met out of the new community charges in so far as they are not otherwise met.
In this respect, the subsection replaces s.107 of the Local Government (Scotland) Act 1973 (repealed by Sched. 6 to this Act), which required a local authority's expenses (unless met from another source) to be met out of rates.
Non-domestic rates will continue to be levied (s.3) and, with the revenue support grant from central government (Sched. 4), will be the principal other sources of local authority income. As explained, however, in the notes to s.9 below, the new community charges will become the "balancing element in a local authority's budgeting".

Personal Community Charge

Liability for personal community charge

8.—(1) Subject to the following provisions of this section, any person aged 18 or over who is solely or mainly resident in the area of a local authority in any financial year shall be liable to pay the personal community charge determined by that authority in respect of that year.

(2) A person who—

(a) becomes solely or mainly resident in the area of a local authority; or

(b) attains the age of 18,

during the course of a financial year shall be liable, as from the date on which he becomes so resident or (as the case may be) attains the age of 18, to pay the personal community charge for the remainder of that year.

(3) A person who ceases to be solely or mainly resident in the area of a local authority shall remain liable to pay the personal community charge determined by that authority in respect of any financial year until the date on which the removal of his name from the register takes effect.

(4) For the purposes of this section, a person undertaking a full-time course of education shall be regarded as being solely or mainly resident in the area of the local authority in which he is resident during term time for the purpose of undertaking the course, until he ceases to undertake the course.

(5) A person undertaking a full-time course of education shall, in respect of the period beginning when he undertakes the course and ending when he ceases to do so, be liable for only such percentage as may be prescribed of the amount of the personal community charge for which he would otherwise be liable.

(6) The—

(a) meanings of "full-time course of education", "person undertaking a full-time course of education", "term time" and "ceases to undertake the course"; and

(b) manner in which the registration officer shall determine when a person ceases to undertake such a full-time course of education,

shall be such as may be prescribed.

(7) Persons who—

(a) are married to each other and live together; or

(b) being a man and a woman, live together as if they were husband and wife,

shall be jointly and severally liable for the personal community charges, relating to the period during which they live together, for which each of them is liable.

(8) The following are exempt from liability to pay the personal community charge—

(a) persons aged 18 in respect of whom child benefit is payable under the Child Benefit Act 1975;

(b) persons who are severely mentally handicapped within the meaning of subsection (9) below;

(c) persons other than those mentioned in subsection (4) above who are solely or mainly resident in premises in respect of which a collective community charge is payable;

(d) persons whose sole or main residence is subject to non-domestic rates other than persons who are solely or mainly resident in part residential subjects.

(9) In subsection (8)(b) above, "persons who are severely mentally handicapped" has the following meaning, that is to say, persons suffering from a state of arrested or incomplete development of mind which includes severe impairment of intelligence and social functioning, or such other meaning as may, in substitution, be prescribed.

DEFINITIONS

"community charge": ss.26(1) and 7.

"financial year": s.26(1) and s.96(5) of the Local Government (Scotland) Act 1973 as amended, *i.e.* the year from April 1.

"local authority": s.26(1).

"part residential subjects": s.26(1).
"prescribed": ss.26(1) and 31.

COMMENCEMENT

The section came into force in September 14, 1987, but only for the purposes of and in relation to the community charges (and as applied by para. 11 of Sched. 5 to the Act, the community water charges) in respect of the financial year 1989–90 and each subsequent financial year. The section as a whole will come into force on April 1, 1989.

GENERAL NOTE

The central proposal of the Green Paper, "Paying for Local Government" (Cmnd. 9714 (1986)) was that all adult residents in a local authority area should be liable to pay the personal community charge. This section defines the general nature of this charge, introduces a number of modifications thereto, and specifies a number of criteria which qualify or exempt a person from liability.

Subs. (2) provides that the personal community charge shall be a charge on individuals, and that it should be payable on a "rolling basis", *i.e.* liability as a matter of fact should faithfully reflect liability in theory on an ongoing, day-to-day basis, rather than representing a fixed term (*e.g.* annual) liability reflective of a person's tax status on a specific date. Subs. (3) consolidates the idea of a rolling liability. It provides that liability within the area of a local authority during a financial year may be terminated, but only on the removal of the relevant person's name from the register, so introducing the concept of the "rolling register" as the administrative complement of the idea of "rolling" liability (see also s.19 below).

Modifications to these two definitive characteristics of the new tax—individual liability and rolling liability—are introduced in subss. (7) and (4) respectively. Subs. (7) modifies the doctrine of individual accountability and liability by providing that both married couples who live together and unmarried couples who co-habit in a heterosexual relationship are to be jointly and severally liable for the personal community charges of each other. Subs. (4) modifies the principle of "rolling" liability by providing that full-time students will, for the duration of their course, be deemed to be resident in the area of the local authority in which they are resident during term time for the purposes of undertaking the course, irrespective of whether they are actually resident in that area throughout the entire period in question.

The remainder of the section is concerned with the criteria of liability for the personal community charge. In order to understand fully the implications of these criteria it is necessary to examine the overall scheme provided by the Act to determine people's liability. This scheme is not exclusively contained within the present section, and, therefore, for the sake of completeness, the following discussion will contain references to rules and conditions provided for, or partly provided for, in other sections.

For analytical purposes, the various factors bearing upon the question of liability to pay the personal community charge may be divided into three different categories. In the first place, there is a set of generic qualifying attributes, of personal factors which provide universally necessary but insufficient conditions of liability. The second and third categories both deal with different types of exemptions from payment of the charge. The second category refers to class-based disqualifying attributes, again focussing on personal factors, but in this context, those of a disqualifying rather than a qualifying kind, and applying to selected groups of persons rather than across the board. Thirdly, and finally, there is a category of property-related disqualifying factors. As the description suggests, these factors refer to features of heritable property rather than the attributes of persons, but, as will be demonstrated, the distinction is somewhat muddied in practice as the purpose of focussing on the characteristics of property is often to gain an indirect purchase on additional personal factors deemed to be consequential in relation to the question of liability.

The class of generic qualifying attributes is reducible to a mere two characteristics. First, that the person is an adult, aged 18 or over, and, secondly, that he is solely or mainly resident in the area of a local authority in Scotland (s.8(1)).

The class-based disqualifying attributes are three in number. Eighteen-year-olds in respect of whom child benefit is payable (subs. (8)(a)) together with persons classified as severely mentally handicapped (subss. (8)(b) and (9)) are totally exempt. On the other hand, students undertaking full-time courses of education are partially exempt (subs. (5)).

Finally, the property related disqualifying factors are rather more complex and take us at points outwith the remit of the present section.

First, these are persons other than students who are solely or mainly resident in premises in respect of which a collective community charge is payable (subs. (8)(c)). Significantly, by virtue of s.11(11)(c), a condition of such persons being liable to pay a collective community charge contribution, is that, but for their residence in premises which attract the collective charge, they would be liable to pay the personal community charge. As such, the qualifying conditions of personal community charge liability presently under discussion, are equally relevant to the question of liability for the collective community charge contribution.

The next category of persons exempt under this heading, consists of those persons whose sole or main residence is subject to non-domestic rates other than persons who are solely or mainly resident in part residential subjects (subs. (8)(d)). On account of ss.2(1) and 3(1), the only persons under this heading who are exempt are those who are resident in non-domestic subjects, and then only if they are also resident in subjects which are not part residential subjects. By means of the use of the powers of prescription to define domestic subjects (s.2(3)(b)) and, also, in relation to the definition of part residential subjects under s.26(1), it is envisaged that, *inter alia*, residents of residential care homes and nursing homes will meet the two criteria necessary to permit them exemption under subs. (8)(d). (See s.2(3)(b) above and subs. (8)(d) below). The final category of persons exempt on account of the premises in which they live are those who are solely or mainly resident in Crown land such as prisons or National Health Service hospitals, by virtue of s.30(2).

Even if the situation of a person meets all of the above qualifying criteria, his liability may be reduced by the operation of the rebate system under s.24. That section, together with the regulations to be made thereunder, also contributes to the overall structure through which liability to pay the personal charge is determined and measured and so is also worthy of consideration in order to place the set of conditions of liability contained in this section in their proper legislative context.

Subs. (1)

This subsection states the fundamental principle underpinning the new tax system, that of a generalised liability to pay throughout the adult population. Specifically, it states that any person aged 18 or over who is solely or mainly resident in an area of a local authority, or local authorities, in any financial year shall be liable for the personal community charge determined by the authorities for that year. However, the tax though generally based, is not universal, as its application is subject to and qualified by subss. (2)–(8) below, and to the various additional qualifying criteria which are not articulated in these subsections but which are referred to.

Solely or mainly resident. It was suggested at the Second Reading in the Commons by Mr. Malcolm Rifkind, M.P., Secretary of State for Scotland, that with reference to the definition of this phrase, "a body of case law will be allowed to build up, just as has happened for electoral registration and mortgage tax relief", (*Hansard*, H.C. Vol. 107, col. 205) in order to resolve hard cases. It was made clear by the Government both in the course of this debate, and at various other points in the gestation of the Bill, (see Green Paper Annex G8, also 1st Scot.S.C., cols. 648–649, *per* Michael Ancram M.P.) that no great problems were envisaged in the application of the test. However, in so far as it is experience of the use of this concept in other contexts which sustains this argument, then it may be contested on the grounds that the analogy is inappropriate. This may be so for two reasons.

First, there is the practical matter of the extent of use. In the other legal contexts in which this or a similar term is utilised, which include, apart from examples cited by Mr. Rifkind, the Leasehold Reform Act 1967 in relation to the securing of the freehold or an extended lease of a leasehold property under English law, the Capital Gains Tax Act 1979 in relation to the scope of application of that tax, and the Mobile Homes Act 1983 in relation to security of tenure in mobile homes, (see further E. M. Scobbie, "The residence test and the personal community charge", SCOLAG (1987) pp. 125–126) the test is applicable to much more limited categories of persons than in the present case. Accordingly, the number of hard cases and active disputes will be correspondingly higher in this new context of use.

Secondly, there is the question of the appropriateness of the precise test as developed in other situations to the present context. The determination of a sole or main residence of a person has traditionally been treated as a matter of fact, dependent upon the particular circumstances of the case and irreducible to any categorical formula. However, in so far as guidelines have been laid down, it has been made clear that it is not just the objective question of residence which is salient, but also subjective factors. For instance, in *Frost* v. *Feltham* (1981 S.T.C. 115) it was stipulated that the key question:

"... is not whether it was his only or main residence during that period, but whether it was used as such ... If someone lives in two houses, the question which does he use as the principal or more important one cannot be determined solely by reference to the way in which he divides his time between the two".

The use of this "mixed" model, would appear to be a sensible approach. Merely to make an objective judgment based upon quantitative criteria would be to ignore the views of the owner or occupier, and thus would eliminate an integral element in the definition of "home", with its affective connotations. Equally, however, since there must be some factual core to the beliefs and attitudes in question, and in particular, since, both in the traditional context of use and in this new context, the person in question may have an interest in maintaining that his sole or main residence is this place rather than that place, there are dangers in relying entirely upon the stated opinion of the party in question. For example, under the new Act each local authority may determine and impose its own level of personal community charge (s.9(1)), and by inference, its own level of collective community charge contribution (s.11(11)) and so whether or not he is solely or mainly resident in local authority area A or local authority B will be a question whose answer may often be financially significant to a person. As the level of the standard community charge payable on "second homes" (s.11) may also vary between local authorities and, furthermore, may be set at a higher point than the personal community charge, then, as liability to pay this charge is dependent upon the premises in question not being the sole or main residence of any person (s.10(2)(c)), the determination of this latter question may be of significance in this context too.

However, although in order to remain within the range of the ordinary meaning denoted by the term in question, the test as applied in the present context must remain a balance between subjective and objective factors, there are sound reasons for suggesting that the balance should be struck at a point in the continuum closer to the pole represented by objective factors than is the case in respect of the other legislative contexts. Since the policy of the new Act, on the grounds of fairness and accountability, is to forge on intimate connection between the liability of the individual tax payer and the expenditure of a relevant local authority then it would be possibly inappropriate to hold someone liable to pay the community charge to a local authority from whose services he derived little benefit.

As such, it may be the subject of much uncertainty and debate as to how faithfully the development of the text in the present context should mirror its development in other contexts and this together with the sheer scope of the new legislation, may entail that the question of the meaning of this legal concept will attract more controversy than it has in the past, and that many of the cases of appeal against registration under s.17 will turn upon this very point. (On whether this issue may constitute a question of law which may be appealed to the Court of Session, see s.29 below).

Subs. (2)

This subsection deals with the position of a person who comes to fulfil the age criterion or the residential criterion at a point during the financial year, and stipulates that such a person will become liable for the charge due in respect of that area as of that date. As such, it introduces the idea of "rolling" liability, which is reflected at the administrative level by the introduction of a "rolling register". (See s.15 below). Liability is not to be reassessed annually or for a set period of any duration, but it is instead intended to reflect immediately and faithfully all changes in the circumstances or characteristics of a person which are relevant for the purposes of determining liability. To this end, the register which documents liability must be similarly sensitive to relevant changes, and cannot simply be renewable on an annual basis as is the case with the electoral register.

The concept of "rolling" liability is not specifically extended to the situation where the liability of a person is affected one way or the other on account of a salient change of circumstance in relation to any of the four exemptions specified in subs. (8) below. However, it would be anomalous if the rolling system were not to incorporate all possible sources of changes in liability including these in subs. (8). Read together, s.13 which is intended to include in the register all considerations relevant to liability (see especially s.13(1)(f) below), s.15 which permits amendments to be made to the register at any time and with immediate or retrospective effect, and s.19 which provides that the register for the time being is to be conclusive as to the fact and date of liability, function so as to allow the tax to be operated and administered in such a way as assumes the endemic application of the rolling principle. Accordingly, even though it is not provided for in the present section, the intention of the statute read as a whole is to extend the rolling principle to instances of liability which are terminated or initiated in accordance with the operation of the exemptions under subs. (8) below or otherwise.

Subs. (3)

This subsection deals with the position of a person leaving the area of a local authority in the course of the financial year. In such a case, liability for the personal community charge of a person who ceases to be solely or mainly resident in the area of the authority is to continue until the date at which he ceases to be registered as so liable.

Read in isolation, this subsection would seem to suggest that registration is a test of liability, and the former is co-extensive with the latter. However, it is clear from subss. (1)

and (2) above, that registration is not a relevant consideration within the test of liability. The (significance of the) date of cessation of registration under this subsection, is merely a message to the registration officer, and ultimately to the levying authority (see s.21 and Sched. 2 below), that they are no longer entitled to treat the said party as liable. As such, it merely underscores the effect of s.19, by permitting the register to be used as a trigger for liability for administrative purposes, and so ensuring that any dispute about liability will not lead to interruption in the payment of the charge. Once a person's liability in respect of any particular period has been ultimately determined, there is no provision in the Act by virtue of s.15(1) and s.16(4) to permit the register to be amended retrospectively. As such, while this provision ensures that liability remains linked to registration, and will continue pending the removal of a person's name from the register irrespective of where that person is solely or mainly resident, if the name of a person is removed tardily, then he need not be subject to dual liability in two separate areas. Such a possibility would be incompatible with the basic purpose of the section, which is to ensure that every liable person can only be liable for the personal charge in respect of one locality at any one time.

Removal . . . from the register. The register is defined by s.26(1) as the community charges register, as established under s.13 of the Act. S.13 stipulates that there shall be a community charges register for each registration area, which in turn is defined in s.26 as meaning that of a "regional or islands council". A local authority, on the other hand, is defined by s.26(1) as a regional, islands, or district council.

This raises interesting questions concerning the nature of the liability of a person whose sole or main residence changes from one local authority to another but who remains within a particular registration area, *i.e.* where he moves from one district to another within the same region. In such a case, the community charges register applicable in the new district is the same as that applicable in the old, yet the level of community charge liability of a person may change on account of the capacity of district councils to determine their own levels of community charge by virtue of s.9. Obviously, the appropriate way of intimating such a change on the face of the register is by altering rather than removing the entry of the person in the same register. However, under this subsection the only competent way of terminating liability within any particular area is by removal of one's name from the register. Unless "removal" is interpreted to mean, "removal from that part of the register referring to premises within the area of a particular district council", as well as actual removal from the register, then a liable person will never be able to adjust his liability within a financial year to reflect a change of residence between districts within the area of a single regional authority. This is obviously anathema to the idea of a system of "rolling" liability sensitive to local conditions, and it is submitted that the wider interpretation of "register" will have to be endorsed in order to ensure that the intentions of the Act are promoted.

Subs. (4)

This subsection deals with the position of full time students. It provides that a person undertaking a full time course of education is to be deemed to be solely or mainly resident at his term time address for the duration of the course.

This provides the only circumstance under the Act in which residence for the purposes of assessing liability will be automatically deemed to be within a particular area, rather than subject to discovery by assessment and evaluation of the particular circumstances of the case (see subs. (2) above). The rationale for making the exception and laying down a fixed place of residence in the case of students is the particularly and predictably high degree of mobility on their part during any financial year, between the area of the parental home or other non study-related accommodation, and the area in which they reside for the purposes of study, which need not necessarily be the area within which the place of study is actually situated. It might be argued, nevertheless, that the inclusion of the deeming provision is of negligible significance or is even unnecessary, since the general test of sole or main residence is impervious to temporary changes in address and that its application would, therefore, in any case, result in students being treated as resident at their term time addresses throughout the financial year. However, this could not be guaranteed in every case, given the sheer variety of living arrangements by students on the one hand, and the uncertainty surrounding the application and interpretation of the sole or main residence test on the other (see subs. (2) above).

In general terms, the deeming provision in this subsection dovetails with a number of other provisions under the Act which ensure or which may be acted upon to ensure that the atypicality of the situation of many students for residential purposes, does not prevent the provisions and purposes of this Act being applied to them in a coherent, methodical and uniform manner. Thus, the combined effect of subs. (8)(c) below and s.11(11)(c) is to ensure that where they are resident in premises attracting the collective charge, students will not be liable to pay the collective charge contribution, but instead, will remain liable to pay the personal charge. As explained below (subs. (8)(c)) this prevents students, in some circumstances, from avoiding liability to pay any part of a community charge for part of the year. While subs. (8) insulates the student from the sphere of the collective charge, the effect of the use of prescriptive powers under s.2(3)(b) will be to insulate them from the sphere of rating. It is intended that students' residences shall fall within that sub-category of the category of communal accommodation which might otherwise not be classed as domestic subjects under s.2(3)(a), and so will specifically be prescribed to be domestic subjects under s.2(3)(b). This will ensure that their residents will not be exempt from the personal community charge under s.8(8)(d) (see, *e.g.*, *Hansard*, H.L. Vol. 486, col. 1449). How widely the category of the students residences will be defined, by virtue of these powers of prescription, remains to be seen.

Overall, then, it is plain that the policy of the Government is to ensure that this subsection, together with subs. (5) below, shall constitute a universal method of treating students under the Act, irrespective of the details of their personal circumstances.

Although this subsection ensures that a student cannot be liable to pay a number of personal community charges in respect of different addresses simultaneously, he may, like anyone else, still be liable to pay the personal community charge and a standard community charge, or a number of standard community charges, concurrently. This legitimate form of dual liability would be incurred if he is the owner or tenant of a property or properties in addition to the study related property on which his residential qualification is based, provided the additional property is neither subject to non-domestic rates nor is the sole or main residence of any other person or persons, such as his parents (see s.10(1) and (2) below).

Subs. (5)

This subsection provides that a full time student, for the duration of his course, shall be liable for only such percentage as may be prescribed by the Secretary of State of the personal community charge determined in respect of that area.

This provision was not inserted until Report Stage in the House of Lords (*Hansard*, H.L. Vol. 486, cols. 1633–1650, *per* Lord Glenarthur). It was always intended that students be partially exempt from the personal community charge, but it was planned initially that this should be achieved by purely administrative and fiscal means, by providing for a compensatory increase in grant from the Scottish Education Department or other local education authorities in the U.K., in order to offset partially the cost of the new charge. Ultimately, however, the idea of a directly applied partial exemption prevailed as it was seen to have a number of advantages over a grant supplement system. First, it involves no extra administrative burden for the relevant education authorities. Secondly, it permits a simplification of the budgeting practices of students in relation to the payment of the charge, therefore, reducing the number of potential defaulters. Thirdly, being presented as a percentage reduction rather than a standard rate discount, it is sensitive to local differences in the amount of community charge payable, and so retains the direct link significant for the purposes of the accountability thesis (see Green Paper) between the expenses incurred by a local authority in providing a particular level of service, and the cost borne by the individual tax payer. Fourthly, it extends the principle of equality of treatment to overseas students, for whom reimbursement through a domestic students grant scheme would have been particularly difficult given that the relative funding body in their case would normally be of non-U.K. origin.

The disadvantages of the partial exemption scheme lies in its exclusion of other possible avenues of financial aid to students. It is intended by the government that the system set in place should be supplemented neither by the topping-up of educational grants, nor by access to payment of social security and to rebates (*Hansard*, H.L. Vol. 486, cols. 1634 and 1645). Therefore, the possibility of a student being fully compensated for any liability to pay the community charge—a principle which is extended to all other groups in the community through the intended operation of the social security system and the rebates system under s.24 below—is categorically ruled out. The inflexibility of this system will inevitably militate against students who are most disadvantaged in economic terms.

Subs. (6)

This subsection makes provision for the Secretary of State to prescribe in regulations the meanings of certain key phrases mentioned in subss. (4) and (5). These prescriptions are necessary to give effect to the provisions as to the place of registration of students in subs. (4), and as to their degree of liability in subs. (5). Apart from providing for the interpretation of these key terms, this subsection also provides that the Secretary of State shall prescribe the manner in which the registration officer is to determine when a person ceases to undertake a full time course of education.

Subs. (7)

This subsection provides that married persons living together and couples living together as if they were man and wife are to be jointly and severally liable for each other's personal community charges.

The extension of this provision at Report Stage in the Commons (*Hansard*, H.C. Vol. III, cols. 982–939) to include, not only married persons living together, but also other cohabiting couples in a heterosexual relationship, prevents the anomaly whereby cohabitees who choose not to marry avoid the mutual financial responsibility assumed by those who are married, and so gain what might be perceived as an unfair advantage. The inclusion of unmarried couples also ensures that the rules concerning liability for community charge will dovetail with those concerning payment of housing benefit, including rebates of community charges in that under the housing benefits system unmarried couples who occupy a dwelling together are already assessed as a single unit for the purposes of the specification of needs allowance and weekly income, and the subsequent computation of the appropriate rebate or allowance. (See Social Security and Housing Benefits Act 1982; Housing Benefit Regulations 1982 (S.I. 1982 No. 1124, regs. 11–14) (Repealed and replaced by Sched. 11 and ss. 28–31 respectively of the Social Security Act 1986)).

The definitions of a married couple and of an unmarried couple for the purposes of this section are very similar to those contained in social security legislation (Supplementary Benefits Act 1976, s.34(1)). In both cases it is the factual relationship rather than the legal relationship which is of significance. Presumably, the considerations deemed relevant in ascertaining whether a couple are a single unit in the case law and administrative practice deriving from the area of social security law, will also be relevant to the present case. Accordingly, the most salient considerations will include actual membership of the same household, the existence of children and of a sexual relationship, the degree of stability and of financial inter-dependence within the relationship and public acknowledgement of the nature of the relationship (Supplementary Benefits Handbook, 1984 ed.).

In general terms, the principle of joint and several liability as applied to this or any other field of social interaction (note that the principle of joint and several liability in the landlord/tenant relationship for purposes of the payment of both the standard community charge and the collective community charge was discarded during the passage of the Bill; see ss.10(4) and 11(5) below) may be seen to be at odds with one of the three criteria stipulated in the Green Paper as indicative of the value of any new system of local taxation, namely that of maximum local democratic accountability (Green Paper, paras. 3.11–3.12). This is so because it effectively excepts from the category of persons with a direct financial interest in the decisions of the local authority those persons within a cohabiting relationship who are economically dependant. However, it may well be that this is more an indictment of the attempt to give substance to the democratic principle through the notion of a fiscal relationship, than it is of this specific provision, in that the initial assumption of a universal ability to forge such a financial relationship may be argued to be economically naïve. From such a perspective, introduction of a principle of joint and several liability might be seen to be necessary to patch over the threadbare premises of this argument by providing a means of avoiding widespread default of payment. Of course, the practical consequence of this pragmatic solution to the problem of giving substance to the democratic principle, will not merely be to erode such a principle, but also to place a disproportionate financial burden on the economically dominant partner in relationships in which only one party has a significant independent source of income, so also breaching the fairness principle, which is one of the other standards invoked by the Government for judging the new scheme (see Green Paper paras. 3.11–3.12).

Subs. (8)

This subsection provides for a number of exemptions from liability to pay the personal community charge. Specifically, it introduces four classes of exempt persons: persons aged 18 for whom child benefit is still payable; severely mentally handicapped persons; persons other than full time students who are solely or mainly resident in premises in respect of which a collective community charge is payable; persons who live in premises which are subject to non-domestic rates unless such premises are also part residential subjects.

Even by the standards of what was a controversial section, this subsection excited particularly heated and extensive debate. Being concerned with exemption from liability for a personal community charge, it provided a focal point for both parliamentary and extra parliamentary special pleading. Among those groups whom it was mooted should be entirely exempt from the new tax were persons in the receipt of income support or state pensions, persons employed on government youth training schemes or on M.S.C. schemes and persons falling under various categories of physical disability, mental handicap, or mental illness. In the final analysis, although some members of such groups will receive relief through the operation of the rebate system (s.24), only the four categories specified above were prescribed as exempt categories under this subsection, and only two of these are directly related to personal characteristics.

Para. (a)

This category consists of persons aged 18 in respect of whom child benefit is payable under the Child Benefit Act 1975. By virtue of ss.2 and 24, of that Act and of reg. 2 of the Child Benefit (General) Amendment Regulations 1983, this is defined to include young persons of 18 who are in receipt of full time non-advanced education. Most persons falling withing this category will still be at school, but it will also cover other persons attending other educational institutions and pursuing such non-advanced qualifications as Higher Grade certificates of Education, Scottish Certificates of 6th Year Studies, Ordinary National Diplomas, Scottish Vocational Educational Council Diplomas, etc. Persons pursuing degree courses, teaching qualifications, diplomas of higher education, and other advanced diplomas, will not be covered.

Para. (b)

This exempt category consists of persons who are severely mentally handicapped as defined in subs. (9) below.

Para. (c)

This exemption refers to persons, other than students undertaking full time courses of education as specified in subs. (4), who are solely or mainly resident in premises in respect of which the collective community charge is payable.

The rationale for the general principle in this subsection is straightforward and uncontroversial: that the categories of persons liable to pay the personal community charge and collective community charge contributions as should be distinct, and no-one should suffer from double liability. The rationale for the proviso, or the exemption from the exemption, which was only introduced at Committee Stage in the Lords (*Hansard*, H.L. Vol. 486, cols, 910–913) is somewhat more complex. Basically, the aim of the proviso is to ensure that a consequence of the general provision against double prejudice is not to provide double indemnity for one specific group, namely students.

In the original Bill, the position of students resident in premises attracting collective charge was not distinguished from that of any other such resident, and accordingly, such students would be liable to pay the collective charge contribution in the normal way. The Bill therefore contemplated the construction of two classes of students for the purposes of community charge liability, on the one hand, those who resided in accommodation which did not attract collective community charge and who would therefore be treated in a manner specifically provided under subs. (4) and so would be liable for the personal community charge at their term time addresses, and on the other, those who did stay in accommodation attracting the collective charge and would therefore be liable to pay a collective charge contribution under s.11(11). This construction of a second and residual class of students raised the possibility of a partial and unintended exemption from community charge liability on the part of members thereof. This would happen if and when, probably during the vacation, a student left the premises in respect of which he paid a collective community charge contribution. If a student was deemed in these circumstances to have ceased to be solely or mainly resident in such accommodation, which matter would have to be decided on the facts of the case, and if he moved back to the parental home or to any other place outwith the area of his term time address, then the deeming provision in subs. (4) would entail that he could not be held liable for the personal community charge during such periods on account of his lack of a residential qualification.

Accordingly, the proviso in question was inserted in order to remove this possibility of partial exemption by ensuring that all students are to be treated in uniform manner, as prescribed under subs. (4), and that there shall be no residual class of students liable to pay the collective charge contribution.

All that is achieved by the proviso in this section, analysed in its own terms, is to ensure that students are not to be treated as exempted from the personal community charge merely by dint of residence in premises attracting the collective charge. However, merely to be excepted from a category which is exempt from paying the personal charge, does not in itself entail that one is exempted from paying a collective community charge contribution.

However, as was postulated by the Government (*Hansard*, H.L. Vol. 486, cols. 910–913), this further effect will be achieved by the operation of s.11(11) in the light of this newly amended subsection. S.11(11)(a) lays down the basic rule that only persons solely or mainly resident in premises in respect of which the collective community charge is payable shall pay a collective community charge contribution. S.11(11)(c) further qualifies the category of persons liable to pay a collective charge contribution, by restricting it to those persons who would be liable to pay a personal community charge under the Act but for the operation of the present subsection, as now amended. Therefore, the major effect of that subsection is to restrict the class of persons liable to pay a collective charge contribution to those persons who have all other qualifying attributes of persons liable to pay the personal charge, apart from the fact of their residence in premises attracting the collective charge.

However, as the precise import of the words "but for section 8(8)(c)" is to designate as liable to pay the collective charge contribution only those persons who are not, in fact, liable to pay the personal charge on account of their residence in premises attracting the collective charge, then an additional and subsidiary effect of s.11(11)(c) will be to exclude students who, on account of the proviso to s.8(8)(c) remain liable to pay the personal charge *irrespective* of their residence in premises attracting the collective charge.

Para. (d)

This subsection refers to persons whose sole or main residence is subject to non-domestic rates other than persons who are solely or mainly resident in part residential subjects.

The immediate purpose of this provision is to maintain the dichotomy between liability to pay non-domestic rates and liability to pay the community charge. This is an underlying theme of the Act, and reflects the policy aim that the community charge should function as a replacement for, rather than an addition to, rates in its appropriate sphere of operation, namely (that which might be tentatively described as) the domestic sector. This task is begun in ss.1, 2 and 3 which respectively abolish domestic rates, distinguish between domestic and non-domestic subjects, and provide that the latter, in that only they shall stay on the valuation roll, shall remain within rating. The present subsection, together with ss.10(2)(b) and 11(2) ensure that each of the three types of community charge will not be payable by persons on account of their having the type of connection with premises which, by virtue of ss.8, 10 and 11 respectively, would normally result in their having to pay the personal, standard or collective charge, provided such premises are subject to non-domestic rates in terms of s.3. (In the case of the personal charge and the collective charge contribution, this exemption will not apply if the premises resided in are part residential subjects.)

What are the substantive implications of this exemption? In order to answer this question, reference must be made to the key provisions in Pt. I of the Act, and in particular, to s.2(3) and (4) which provides the test as to whether lands and heritages are "domestic subjects" which, as said, is axiomatic in determining liability to rates.

The definition of domestic subjects is treated in great detail under s.2(3) and 2(4) above. Briefly, however, the technique for differentiating between domestic and non-domestic subjects is as follows: a core definition of "domestic subjects" is provided by subs. (3)(a) and refers to "lands and heritages consisting of one or more dwelling houses etc.". Thereafter by means of regulations under subs. (3)(b) and subs. (4), certain types of "lands and heritages" may be added to or subtracted from that core.

As such, for the purposes of this subsection, the basic message to be drawn is that if a person is solely or mainly resident in premises which cannot be described as a dwelling-house, then, unless such premises are part residential subjects, (to be dealt with below) he will not be liable to pay a personal community charge. However, by the operation of s.2(4) which provides that certain dwelling houses will not be treated as domestic subjects, the exemption in the present subsection may be extended in certain respects, while by the operation of s.2(3)(b) which provides that certain premises other than dwelling houses will be treated as domestic subjects, the scope of the present subsection is in other respects contracted, and also more precisely delineated. As both of these effects are to be achieved through the use of prescriptive powers, it is difficult to specify their precise implications. However, certain undertakings were made by the Government in the course of debate as to the matters it is intended to deal with by prescription, and in the light thereof, the implications of ss.2(3)(b) and 2(4) for present purposes may be specified in rather more detail.

It was stated by the Government that the power of prescription in s.2(4) would primarily be used to ensure that holiday caravans and small holiday huts remain on the valuation roll and be rated, (1st Scot.S.C., col. 322). The net effect of this undertaking on the scope of the present subsection is nil. This is so as it is highly unlikely that such caravans or holiday huts would be the sole or main residence of any person in any case, and even if they are, as it has not been intimated that such lands and heritages will be exempted by the power of prescription contained therein, from the definition of part residential subjects in s.26(1), then anyone who is solely or mainly resident will by virtue of the proviso to the present subsection, remain liable to pay the personal charge (see further below). As is intended, s.2(4) is much more consequential when read together with the equivalent exemption to that contained in the present subsection which is prescribed in relation to the standard charge by virtue of s.10(2)(b), its effect in that context being to exempt the owners of most caravans or holiday huts from payment of the standard charge, so distinguishing them from owners of "second homes".

S.2(3)(b), on the other hand, does have implications for the extent of the exemption under the present subsection. It is the intention of the Government to ensure that lock-up garages, and, more importantly here, certain types of communal living accommodation will be treated as domestic subjects (see, *e.g. Hansard*, H.L. Vol. 486, col. 1449). For present purposes this entails that the exemption from personal community charge under the present subsection will not extend to residents of those types of communal living accommodation to be prescribed including residents of nurses' homes and students' residences.

This does not exhaust the possible implications of s.2(3)(b) for the scope of the present subsection, as it is the intention of the Government to use their prescriptive powers under the subsection to define categories of domestic subjects *exclusively* as well as *inclusively*. As such, it is intended that certain types of nursing homes and residential care homes, although forms of communal accommodation, will be specifically excluded from the category of domestic subjects. As it is further intended that powers will be used under subs. 26(1) to ensure that such premises are not treated as part residential subjects, then their residents, in so far as they are not solely or mainly resident elsewhere (by definition, extremely unlikely) will be exempt from the personal community charge (*Hansard*, H.L. Vol. 486, col. 1655, *per* Lord Glenarthur).

In turn, in order to complete the chain of reasoning employed by the Government, this use of s.2(3)(b) for *exclusionary* purposes requires an additional use of the said powers for *inclusionary* purposes. The aim here is to ensure that residential staff of these types of communal accommodation which are specifically exempted from the status of domestic subjects will themselves, unlike the long-stay residents, not be exempt from the personal charge. In order to achieve this, it was indicated in the "notes on clauses" accompanying the Bill, that use would be made of the power to prescribe a "part of a class" under s.2(3)(b) in order to include staff accommodation in such homes within the category of domestic subjects, so ensuring that the residents of such accommodation would not fall within the terms of the exemption contained in this provision.

Other than persons who are solely or mainly resident in part residential subjects. "Part residential subjects" represent a hybrid category under the Act, in that, in terms of the type of liability to which they give rise, they straddle the distinction between non-domestic rates and the community charge. By virtue of s.26(1) they are defined as being lands and heritages, which, although they are used partly as the sole or main residence of any person, are neither domestic subjects nor such other class or classes of lands and heritages as may be prescribed. If such a category of premises had not been constructed under the Act, and the sole or main residents thereof had not been excepted from the exemption under the present subsection, then those persons who happened to live in premises which could not be physically distinguished and hived off from the non-domestic, would have been immune from payment of the personal community charge. The classic example of the type of case which is captured by this conceptual innovation is that of the hotel which contains a flat used by the manager as his home. (*Hansard*, H.L. Vol. 486, col. 463, *per* Lord Glenarthur). The effect of the application of this new category of lands and heritages to this type of case would be that the manager in question would be liable to pay the personal community charge in the normal way.

To move away from mainstream examples, two special types of lands and heritages should be mentioned, to which the concept of part residential subjects is relevant in a rather more unusual way, in both cases having implications for liability under the present provision.

First, there are those lands and heritages which although prima facie domestic subjects, have been exempted from this category under s.2(4). In the absence of the use of prescriptive powers to bring about a parallel exemption from the category of part residential subjects, it is possible, given the affinity between the core definition of domestic subjects in s.2(3)(a) and the notion of sole or main residence, that such lands and heritages might paradoxically be described as wholly residential part residential subjects if they are, in fact, occupied as the sole or main residence of a person. Types of premises to which this paradoxical description might apply include caravans and holiday huts which are solely or mainly occupied by one or more persons, which persons would, of course, be liable to pay the personal community charge.

Secondly, there are those lands and heritages which, although being the sole or main residence of a person or persons, and not being domestic subjects, are to be specifically prescribed as not being part residential subjects. As stipulated above, within this category will fall those parts of residential homes and nursing homes which are used as long-stay accommodation by residents, and in respect of whom it is Government policy to exempt from payment of the personal community charge. For the procedure for the apportionment of value of part residential subjects, see Sched. 1.

Subs. (9)

This subsection attempts to define the category of severely mentally handicapped persons exempted from liability to pay the personal community charge under subs. (8). Exemption was only extended to this category of persons at Report Stage in the Lords, after much pressure had been exerted at earlier points during the parliamentary proceedings (*Hansard*, H.L. Vol. 486, cols. 1653–1668, *per* Lord Glenarthur). The inclusion of this category graphically illustrates the tensions and inconsistencies between the criteria for liability to pay a form of local taxation set out in the Green Paper. Given their inability to understand the concept and mechanics of accountability, severely mentally handicapped persons are justifiably exempted in accordance with the criterion of local democratic accountability, but given also their undoubted status as beneficiaries of local services, it is difficult to equate this with the operation of the fairness principle.

The definition is an abbreviated form of that which applies under s.1(2) of the Mental Health (Scotland) Act 1984 as descriptive of a state of severe mental impairment. The element of the earlier definition which has been omitted in the present context is that which stipulates the association of the condition of severe mental impairment with "abnormally aggressive or seriously irresponsible conduct on the part of the person concerned". This aspect of the definition has been criticised as erroneously conflating the categories of persons suffering from mental impairment and psychopathic disorder. As such, its omission is to be welcomed. However, the new definition itself is not immune from criticism in terms both of its internal consistency and of the extent of its application.

To explain: the use of the phrase "arrested or incomplete development of mind" implies the existence of a congenital mental handicap, while the phrase "severe impairment" implies loss or abnormal development of psychological or physiological structure or function. Thus, one part of the definition appears to denote a subcategory of persons suffering from congenital disorders, while another appears to denote a subcategory of persons suffering from non-congenital disorders. If the principle of like treatment of like cases is to be upheld on the grounds of the consistent application of the argument as to the absence of a relationship of democratic accountability, then subcategories within *both* congenital and non-congenital types of mental disorder require to be exempted. Some of the difficulties in this respect were conceded by the Government who indicated that the power to prescribe an alternative definition, which is also contained within the subsection, might be of use in resolving certain of these problems. However, the ambitions of the Government in this respect would appear to be fairly restricted. In their view, while it may be conceivable that the definition might extend, or might by prescription be extended, to cover cases of severe mental impairment on account of a physical or chemical accident, it is not intended that it should cover categories of persons who are otherwise mentally ill. Some members of such categories would, instead, be exempt on account of their residence in hospitals, nursing homes or residential care homes (see s.30 below for hospitals, and s.2(3)(b) and subs. (8)(d) above for nursing homes and residential care homes) (*Hansard*, H.L. Vol. 486, cols. 439–440, *per* Lord Glenarthur).

Determination of amount of personal community charge

9.—(1) Every local authority shall, in respect of the financial year 1989–90 and of each subsequent financial year, determine, before such date as may be prescribed in relation to each of those years, the amount of the personal community charge to be imposed by them in respect of that year.

(2) The amount determined under subsection (1) above shall be such as will provide (account having been taken of the moneys to be produced by the standard and collective community charges) sufficient moneys to meet such part of the total estimated expenses to be incurred by the local

authority during the financial year in respect of which the personal community charge is to be levied as falls to be met out of their community charges, together with such additional sum as is, in their opinion, required—

(i) to cover expenses previously incurred;

(ii) to meet contingencies;

(iii) to meet any expenses which may fall to be met before the moneys to be received in respect of their community charges for the next following financial year will become available.

(3) In calculating, for the purposes of subsection (2) above, such part of the total estimated expenses to be incurred by a local authority as falls to be met out of community charges, account shall be taken of any means by which those expenses may otherwise be met or provided for.

DEFINITIONS

"community charge": see ss.26(1) and 7.

"financial year": see ss.26(1) and 96(5) of the Local Government (Scotland) Act 1973 as amended, *i.e.* the year from April 1.

"local authority": see s.26(1).

"prescribed": see ss.26(1) and 31.

GENERAL NOTE

This section may be seen as the successor to s.108 of the Local Government (Scotland) Act 1973 which is repealed by Sched. 6. It contains, in subs. (1), the instruction to all local authorities to determine the amount of their community charge (in the 1973 Act is was their rate) and in subss. (2) and (3) directions as to the level of charge to be chosen.

The date by which the amount of the personal community charge has to be determined each year will be prescribed but it has been made clear that it will follow (a) the determination by the authority of its non-domestic rate under s.3(1) and (b) the making of the revenue support grant order by the Secretary of State under Sched. 4 (see *e.g. Hansard*, H.C. Vol. 111, col. 1093 *et seq.*)

It is the Government's stated intention (on which, see also the notes on s.3 and Sched. 4) that, by the time each authority comes to determine its community charge, it will do so from a financial position which is the same as other authorities of its type (see also the Green Paper paras. 4.38–4.39)—that is to say that initial differences between authorities will have been ironed out by the revenue support grant. The grant is supposed to take account both of differences of "need" in the provision of services (through the application of the "client group" calculation of relative needs) and differences in non-domestic rateable resources (through the device of "netting-off" the non-domestic rate product prior to the fixing of individual grants). Thus, at the point of determining their community charges, authorities of the same type are supposed to be able to impose the same level of charge to achieve the same level of service provision. On this basis, authorities will need to impose a high charge if their "total estimated expenses" are high—and will be accountable to their tax payers for doing so. Conversely, the lower the "total estimated expenses", the lower the charge. As the Earl of Dundee, for the Government, pointed out, "under the new system the community charges will become the balancing element in a local authority's budgeting, rather than rates" (*Hansard*, H.L. Vol. 486, col. 935).

Three final general observations. In the first place, it should be remembered that the general intention of the Government is that community charges should be a substitute for domestic rates in providing only about 13 per cent. of the average annual income of local authorities (see Cmnd. 9714, (1986) para. 8.13). Thus, for most authorities, a fairly marginal percentage increase or decrease in "total estimated expenses" will produce a much larger percentage increase or decrease in the level of community charge.

Secondly, the powers of the Secretary of State under Sched. 3 should be borne in mind. If he believes an authority's total estimated expenses to be "excessive and unreasonable" he may order a reduction in the level of community charge. This power is discussed in detail in the notes on that Schedule. Its existence is not without consequences for the operation of local democratic financial accountability.

Thirdly, to fix the level of personal community charge is not to determine completely the liability of every taxpayer. The system of rebates under s.24 will reduce the liability of some. An element in authorities' total expenses will be that part of the rebates made which is not refunded by the Secretary of State by subsidy under s.24(b).

Subs. (1)

As a result of the amendment made to s.56(6) of the Local Government (Scotland) Act 1973 by s.28 of this Act, the determination by an authority of the amount of its personal community charge (and also the standard community charge multiplier under s.10(6)–(7)) is a decision for the full council. It cannot be made on behalf of the council by a committee.

There is no explicit means of enforcing the duty of the authority to determining the charge by the prescribed date but a failure to do so might attract the use by the Secretary of State of default powers under s.211 of the Local Government (Scotland) Act 1973, an application for judicial review in the Court of Session under Rule 260B, or action by the Controller of Audit under s.102 of the 1973 Act.

Once the amount of charge is determined, the process of levying and collection under Sched. 2 is set in motion—starting, in the case of district councils, with intimation to the regional council as levying authority of the amount of the charge.

There is no general power to amend or remake the determination of an amount of community charge. An authority cannot, for instance, make a supplementary determination during the year. The only exceptions to this general position arise in the circumstances created in Sched. 3, *i.e.* either after the Secretary of State has taken action under para. 3 or in anticipation of such action under para. 5. Paras. 4(2) and 5(3) provide that references to the determination of community charges include references to amended determinations made under those paragraphs.

Subss. (2), (3)

As indicated in the general note, these subsections relate the amount of charge to the level of expenses.

As to expenditure, the subsection makes the starting point the level of total estimated expenses of the authority and the part of those expenses to be met from community charges. The total level is a matter (subject to Sched. 3) for the authority and will reflect levels of service provision and political priorities.

Paras. (i)–(iii) in subs. (2) explicitly empower the authority to add to their total estimated expenses the provision for contingencies, etc., referred to (N.B. the similar formula adopted in Sched. 5, paras. 3 and 15 in relation to water and sewerage charges).

Subs. (3) then requires authorities to take account of other available means for the meeting of the total expenses. Plainly this includes grants from central government (whether in revenue support grant or specific grants), the income from the authority's own non-domestic rate under s.3 and income from charges for services. It will also include balances brought forward from the previous year (something formerly made explicit in s.108 of the 1973 Act) (see 1st Scot.S.C., col. 679).

The deductions of income from other sources from the total estimated expenses leaves the amount to be raised in community charges. Fixing the actual figure for the individual personal charge will not, however, be a simple matter of dividing that amount by the number of adults on the register. In the first place, as subs. (2) makes clear, the calculation must take account of the standard and collective charges. The amount which will be derived from standard charges will depend upon the number of relevant premises in the area of the authority and the multiplier to be determined by the authority under s.10(7). The amount from collective charges will also depend on the number of premises and their multipliers determined by the registration officer under s.11(9).

Secondly, authorities will have to allow for the partial exemptions from the charge for students under s.8(5).

Thirdly, there will have to be allowance for movement on and off the register during the year and for slippage in the levying and collection of the charges. The Green Paper admitted that "there would inevitably be less than 100 per cent. compliance with the community charge, as with all taxes" (para. 3.44). Some have suggested that authorities will not succeed in gathering more than 80 per cent. of the national total of charges imposed and will have to adjust the initial amount of the personal charge accordingly.

An important factor in this process of determining the correct level of charge will be access to the register. Under s.20(2)(b), a local authority is "entitled to inspect such part of the register as relates to premises within their area for the purpose of determining, levying or collecting any community charge". (But see the note on that subsection.)

Standard Community Charge

Liability for and calculation of standard community charge

10.—(1) The standard community charge shall be payable in respect of premises to which this section applies.

(2) This section applies to premises which—

(a) are a dwelling house with any garden, yard, garage, outhouse or pertinent belonging to and occupied along with such dwelling house;

(b) are not subject to non-domestic rates; and

(c) are not the sole or main residence of any person,

but not to such class or classes of those premises as may be prescribed.

(3) The prescribing of a class or classes of premises under subsection (2) above may be by reference to such factors as may be prescribed.

(4) The person liable to pay the standard community charge in respect of any premises shall be—

(a) subject to paragraphs (b) and (c) below, the owner of the premises

(b) subject to paragraph (c) below, if the premises are let for a period of 12 months or more, the tenant; or

(c) if the premises are sub-let for such a period, the sub-tenant,

and that liability shall, in the case of a tenant or sub-tenant, be in respect of the period of his tenancy or, as the case may be, sub-tenancy.

(5) The standard community charge shall be due to—

(a) each local authority; or

(b) (in the case of an islands council) the local authority

in the area of which the premises in respect of which it is payable are situated.

(6) The standard community charge due to a local authority in respect of any premises in respect of any financial year shall be the product of—

(a) the personal community charge; and

(b) the standard community charge multiplier,

determined in respect of that year by the local authority.

(7) In subsection (6) above, "the standard community charge multiplier" means such number, being neither smaller than 1 nor greater than 2, as the local authority which determines the personal community charge to which the multiplier is applied shall, before such date in each year as may be prescribed, determine.

(8) Where—

(a) premises to which this section applies are unoccupied and unfurnished; and

(b) a person liable to pay the standard community charge in respect of the premises notifies the levying authority that they are unoccupied and unfurnished,

then, subject to subsection (9) below, the standard community charge shall not be payable in respect of the premises in respect of whichever is the shorter of the following—

(i) the period for which the premises are unoccupied and unfurnished

(ii) a period of 3 months or such longer period as the local authority to which it is due may determine.

(9) Any period for which the standard community charge is, under subsection (8) above, not payable shall not begin earlier than one month before the receipt of notification under paragraph (b) of that subsection.

(10) The person liable to pay the standard community charge in respect of any premises in respect of a financial year shall be entitled to recover from any person to whom he lets or sub-lets the premises or whom he permits to occupy them an amount equal to the product of—

(a) the number of days in that year for which the premises are let or sub-let to or, as the case may be, permitted to be occupied by that other person (excluding any which fall within a period in respect of which the standard community charge is, under subsections (8) and (9) above, not payable); and

(b) the amount of the standard community charge payable in respect of the premises in respect of that year divided by the number of days in that year

and such an amount is referred to in this section as a "standard community charge contribution").

(11) A standard community charge contribution recovered from a person—

(a) shall be in addition to any obligation of his to make other payments (whether by way of rent or otherwise) in respect of the premises in respect of which that contribution is made;

(b) is not affected by any enactment relating to the control or restriction of any such other payment, and shall not, for the purposes of any such enactment, be regarded as such a payment or part thereof.

DEFINITIONS

"community charge": s.26.

"financial year": s.26. See ss.26(1) and 96(5) of the Local Government (Scotland) Act 1973 as amended; *i.e.* the year from April 1.

"levying authority": s.26.

"local authority": s.26.

"prescribed": s.26.

COMMENCEMENT

This section came into force in September 14, 1987, but only for the purposes of and in relation to the community charges (and, as applied by para. 11 of Sched. 5 to the Act, the community water charges) in respect of the financial year 1989–90, and each subsequent financial year. The section is brought wholly into force on April 1, 1989.

GENERAL NOTE

The purpose of this section is to specify in detail the nature of and the conditions of liability of the standard community charge, which was introduced by virtue of s.7(1).

This section provides that either the owner or the tenant, depending on the circumstances of the case, of domestic premises which are neither the sole or main residence of any person nor subject to non-domestic rates is to be liable to pay a standard community charge of between one and two units of the personal community charge. The standard charge is due to the local authorities in whose area the premises are situated.

In general terms, the introduction of this charge honours a commitment made by the Government in the *Green Paper* (Annex G) that the owners of second homes should make financial contribution to the provision of local authority services, the benefits of which they enjoy in the environment of these second homes. This would be a charge additional to any personal community charge which such persons would be liable to pay in the local authority area in which their sole or main residence was situated. At the Committee stage in the Commons, (*Hansard*, 1st Scot.S.C., cols. 689–696) a debate developed over whether the term 'property tax' was a more appropriate appellation for the new standard charge. The standard charge is something of a hybrid. It is a property tax in the sense that a necessary condition of liability on the part of a person is his or her ownership or use of heritable property over and above that consisting of his or her main home. However, being a flat-rate charge, it lacks one of the characteristics normally associated with a property tax and in particular with the rating system which it is intended to replace, namely, variability with the value of the property. Furthermore, it may be plausibly argued that, especially since most of the services provided by the modern local authority such as education, recreation and road maintenance are in the nature of personal benefits rather than relating directly to any property controlled by the beneficiary, the standard charge merely extends the implementation of the property independent accountability and beneficial principles articulated in the Green Paper and primarily instanced in the personal community charge.

Paradoxically, however, the same factors, which allow the Government to claim a degree of success as regards the internal consistency of their approach and in respect of the above semantic debate, may also provide the basis for the most incisive critique of the new system. A flat-rate charge is entirely insensitive to differences, however great, between the values of different properties. Accordingly, in so far as such differences in value are indicative of ability to pay, a tried and tested method of measuring the latter has been discounted. It is conceivable that the operation of the rebates system under s.24 may provide an alternative means of achieving the same end. In the absence, however, of the explicit extension of

rebates to the standard charge (as opposed to standard charge contributions) this seem
most unlikely. As such, the fear remains that the new charge may have harsh consequence:
for those owners or users of second homes of a more modest nature in areas whose loca
authorities nevertheless demand a high yield from local taxation. The widespread nature o
the disquiet occasioned by the anticipation of such anomalies is indicated by the fact tha
amendments were unsuccessfully moved by the Government's own supporters in botl
Houses aimed at modifying the inequitable effect of this section (1st Scot.S.C., cols. 702–705
see also subs. (2)(b) and (7) below).

In all cases where liability to pay the standard community charge is established, there wil
also arise a liability to pay standard community water charge, provided that the water is no
wholly supplied to the premises in question by meter. (Sched. 5, para. 8.)

Subs. (1)

This subsection provides for a standard community charge to be payable in respect of th
premises specified in subs. (2). The use of the term "premises" in this section, and also i
s.11, is at odds with the terminology adopted in Pt. I of the Act to denote heritable property

In Pt. I, heritable property is described instead as "lands and heritages" or, wher
appropriate, "domestic subjects", the relationship of which concepts to one another i
stipulated (see s.2(3)). However, at no point in the Act is the relationship between either o
these concepts and the term "premises" directly specified.

In an indirect and rather untidy way, however, a degree of terminological continuity i:
retained in that "premises" are described in subs. (2)(a) below as including the singular forn
of that which is definitive of "domestic subjects" in s.2(3)(a), except that the term "land:
and heritages" is not included at the beginning of the description contained in the presen
section.

Whether or not there exists a continuity in the usage of terms becomes consequential i
subs. (2)(b) below, and also in s.11(3), where status originally defined with reference t(
concepts used in Pt. I (*i.e.* being subject to non-domestic rates, and also in s.11(2), bein,
part residential subjects) are instead defined with reference to the concept "premises". Fo
the purposes of construing these provisions, "premises" may be taken as the functiona
equivalent of the relevant Pt. I concepts, although such an interpretation would hav(
emerged more clearly if the relationship of the various concepts to one another had beer
defined on the face of the Act in a more explicit and precise manner.

Subs. (2)

This subsection specifies the premises in respect of which the standard community charg(
shall be payable in accordance with subs. (1).

Para. (a)

The definition provided is identical to the description of "domestic subjects" in s.2(3)(a
except that it specifically refers only to a single dwelling house. This identification of th
independent dwelling unit rather than the lands and heritages as a whole as significant fo
taxing purposes is consistent with the general intention of the section to link liability to th
derivation of benefit from services the supply of which is consequent upon the use o
property, rather than to the bare fact of ownership of property.

Under the Valuation Acts, from which the definition contained in s.2(3)(a) is derived, an(
from which, in turn, the definition in the present subsection is distinguished, it is permissibl(
for a single entry in the valuation roll to consist of more than one dwelling house. As such
that there exists only a single entry in the valuation roll will not constitute evidence for th(
purposes of this paragraph of the fact that such an entry refers to only one dwelling house
and a person running a number of dwelling houses other than his sole or main residence wil
be liable to pay the standard charge in respect of each one of them whether or not they ar(
entered separately in the valuation roll (prior to April 1, 1989).

Para. (b)

The aim of this subsection is to distinguish "second homes", which may be let out fo
longer or shorter periods during periods of absence of the owner, from properties which ar(
let out on a commercial basis as holiday homes. Only the former type will attract th(
standard charge, the latter remaining within the non-domestic rating sector and being subjec
to rates by virtue of s.3 above. It may be a moot point, and one of considerable financia
significance for the owner of the relevant property, whether a particular letting is a
sufficiently viable commercial proposition to attract non-domestic rates. Any such decisio
will fall within the discretion of the local assessor subject to s.2(3)(a), and ss.2(3)(b) an(
2(4) which respectively provide a core definition of "domestic subjects" and variou:

prescriptive powers which may vary this core definition (which "domestic subjects", by virtue of ss.2(1) and 3(1), cannot be subject to rates). In this context, it is worthy of note that the Government has intimated that most caravans and holiday huts will be prescribed under s.2(4) as not being "domestic subjects". (*Hansard*, H.L. Vol. 487, col. 322). As such, they represent types of property which although ostensibly similar to "second homes" will not, unlike them, attract the standard charge but will instead continue to attract rates. The potential attractions of such a state of affairs for owners of caravans and holiday huts are discussed under s.2(4) above.

Para. (c)

This paragraph provides that no standard charge shall be payable in respect of premises which are the sole or main residence of any person. This provision is central to the policy aim of identifying and taxing second homes, and ensures that where one or more personal community charges are payable in respect of premises, there can be no additional liability for the standard charge in respect thereof. As is commented upon above (see s.8(1)), the definition of "sole or main residence" may prove problematical under the Act, the precise mix of subjective and objective factors which will be required to constitute the above status being difficult to anticipate, particularly in the light of the specific concern of the Act to link liability to the objective fact of use of local services. One fertile area for dispute under the present paragraph concerns those cases where members of the one family own more than one home, but where there is variety amongst family members as to the pattern of occupation as between the various residences. In such cases, it may be in the interests of some or all members of the family, for each of the family homes to be deemed to be the sole or main residence of at least one family member, in which case, even if such a home is used as a second home by other family members, it will not attract a standard charge.

The "sole or main residence" proviso also entails that if a person lets out his main residence as a holiday home for a limited period of the year, no tax of any type will be due specifically on account of its use as a holiday home unless the assessor decides that the premises do not comprise of "domestic subjects" by virtue of s.2(3)(a) and (4) in which case they will fall within the definition of part residential subjects contained in s.26(1), and will accordingly attract both personal community charge and an element of non-domestic rates calculated to that part of the net annual value of the premises attributable to its non-domestic use (see Sched. 1).

But not to such class or classes of those premises as may be prescribed. It is envisaged that the power of prescription will be used to exempt uninhabitable property from the scope of the clause and thus from standard community charge liability. (*Hansard*, H.L. Vol. 486, col. 943, *per* Lord Glenarthur.)

Subs. (3)

This is a rather curious adjunct to subs. (2). The Secretary of State's power to prescribe a class or classes of premises as exempt from the standard charge (intended to be used to exempt premises on the grounds that they are uninhabitable) *may* be exercised by reference to such factors as *may* be prescribed by him. Presumably the two "may"s are permissive and, therefore, there is the possibility that no such factors will ever be prescribed and, even if they are, their status will be unclear. Certainly the subsection appears neither effectively to circumscribe the power under subs. (2) nor to augment or clarify it. Under that subsection, if it stood alone, the Secretary of State would be able to prescribe a class by reference to any, legally relevant, factors if he wished to do so. The addition of subs. (3) does not even appear to add further protection from judicial review, should the exercise of the power under subs. (2) be challenged.

Lord Morton of Shuna described the subsection as making "the muddle even more muddled; it is an Alice-in-Wonderland or Alice-through-the Looking Glass type of Bill. It is quite difficult to work out what is happening. What is supposed to be meant?" (*Hansard*, H.L. Vol. 486, col. 941). Lord Ross (at col. 947) said that "This has got to the point of utter nonsense. We do not understand the clause at all".

This type of two-tier prescription (*i.e.* prescription by the Secretary of State governing the exercise of another prescriptive power by himself) is not wholly unfamiliar. A rather similar device occurs, for instance, in ss.2(5) and 3(2) of the Rates Act 1984.

Subs. (4)

This subsection further develops the idea that liability should be related to use rather than the bare fact of ownership. It provides that liability for the standard charge should fall on the owner of the premises, the tenant, or the sub-tenant, depending on the circumstances of the case. Where a sub-tenant has a lease for a continuous period of 12 months or more, he is to be liable; where a tenant has such a lease, and he has no sub-tenant with a lease of such duration, he is to be liable; and in any other case, the owner is to be liable.

In the original Bill, it was stipulated that in the case of longer leases, the owner and the tenant should be jointly and severally liable. However, it was felt that such provision might lead to the adoption of different and inconsistent procedures within and between local authorities and attendant confusion and uncertainty. It was also anticipated that this measure might subject the landlord to an unacceptable level of risk in cases of default by the tenant, on account of the fact that the tenant might often be difficult to trace since the property under consideration, by definition, would not be his sole or main residence. Therefore, an amendment introducing the principle of separate liability according to circumstances was introduced by the Government at Report Stage in the House of Commons. (*Hansard*. H.C. Vol. 111, cols. 990–991, *per* Ian Lang M.P.).

Subs. (5)
This subsection provides that the standard charge is due to each local authority in whose area are situated the premises for which liability for the standard charge arises.

Each local authority. This phrase makes it clear that elements of the standard community charge shall be due to both the district council and the regional council within those areas, which include the whole of Scotland (except those parts covered by the three islands councils), where two separate tiers of local government exist and operate concurrently. The wider implications of this will be considered under subs. (7).

Subs. (6)
This subsection stipulates the means of calculation of the standard community charge in any financial year. This will be the product of the personal community charge determined by the authority for the year, and the standard community charge multiplier determined in respect of that year by the local authority.

Standard community charge multiplier. This is defined in subs. (7) below.

Subs. (7)
The original intention of the Government as stated in the Green Paper (Annex G) was that the multiplier should be universally set at 2. This was intended as a rough method of avoiding the revenue shortfall which would otherwise occur if a local authority attempted to reduce the base of the personal community charge in comparison to the average rates bill in recognition of and in compensation for its much broader base of application—all adult persons rather than all ratepayers—yet was compelled also to use this as a standard for taxing this additional residential source, which, of course, reverts to the more restricted property base as opposed to the individual as a basic unit of taxation. However, it was recognised that such a stipulation would introduce an unnecessary element of rigidity into the system, and so the subsection acknowledges this by permitting an element of local authority discretion, though still circumscribed by the need to exact a yield from the second home sector which is proportionately at least equivalent to if not greater than that exacted from sole or main residences.

This subsection also became the focus for those concerns articulated in the general note on the section as to the inability of a flat-rate charge to reflect capacity to pay. Both amendments tabled by supporters of the Government seeking to reduce the flat rate and amendments tabled by the Opposition aimed at introducing a differential rate akin to that applicable within the rating system were resisted during the passage of the Bill. (*Hansard*, H.C. Vol. 111, cols. 991–993, H.L. Vol. 487, cols. 443–446.)

Such number . . . as the local authority which determines the personal community charge to which the multiplier is applied shall . . . determine. Just as it is the function of every local authority to determine the personal community charge applicable within its area (s.9), it is provided herein that it is also and equally the function of the local authority to determine the standard community charge multiplier applicable within its area. Taken together with subs. (5) this means that, in most cases, the standard community charge applicable in respect of property in any financial year will be the sum of two separate calculations made by the district authority and the regional authority respectively, which calculations will involve both different base figures (equivalent to the different personal community charges set by the two tiers) and different multipliers. It is possible that, in practice, it will be agreed that a single multiplier should operate throughout a region, (both between all the district authorities within the region and between these district authorities and the regional authority). However, he likelihood of this is diminished by the fact that such an agreement will compromise the ability of each local authority to determine independently the particular balance of its local tax burden which is to be distributed between the personal sector and the second property sector. However, if such an agreement is not forthcoming, it will be difficult to reconcile the complex calculations which will be required in assessing the tax burden of certain individuals with the claim made in the Green Paper under the criterion of local democratic accountability that, from the perspective of the tax payer, the link between changes in local expenditure and changes in one's personal local tax burden should be direct and clear. (See also s.9 above, and, expecially, s.28 below which prohibits a local authority from making arrangements for any other body, including one of its own committees or another local authority, to discharge its functions of determining the personal community charge and the standard community charge multiplier.)

Subs. (8)

This subsection provides that the standard charge should not be payable for a period, not necessarily continuous, of up to three months in any one financial year in respect of property which is unoccupied and unfurnished and where the levying authority has been notified of the fact by the person liable to pay the charge.

As Sched. 2, para. 1 defines the "levying authority" for the purposes of collection of the regional and district community charges as the regional authority, this subsection might involve the regional authority in determining questions which affect the level of community charges income received by the district council. Any appeal in relation to this provision, would presumably have to be against the decision of the levying authority as reflected in the contents of the demand notice by virtue of Sched. 2, para. 3(b).

Subs. (9)

This subsection provides that any period of exemption under subs. (8) above, shall not commence more than one month prior to the receipt of notification by the levying authority of the relevant information from the person liable to pay the charge. Together with subs. (8), subs. (9) further develops the link between liability and the use of services and in so doing provides a variation of a similar exemption which was previously available under the rating system (Local Government (Scotland) Act 1947, s.243).

Subs. (10)

This subsection extends the logic of subs. (4) by specifying that, in cases of leases or other more informal occupancy arrangements of less than 12 months, the person directly liable to pay the standard community charge may recover contributions towards that liability from such short term tenants or occupiers. Apportionment is on a daily basis, with the proviso that if the person directly liable has claimed exemption under subss. (8) and (9) above, he is unable to claim contributions for periods covered by the exemption from any short-term tenant or occupier.

The rationale underpinning this subsection, which was not introduced until Report Stage in the Commons (*Hansard*, H.C. Vol. 111, cols. 993–996), is unclear. On the one hand, it may be argued to be necessary in order to regulate the payment of a rebate to persons contributing to the payment of a standard community charge, as is specifically provided for under s.24. However, given that the premises in respect of which a person is liable to pay a standard community charge contribution, by definition, cannot be his sole or main residence (subs. (2)(c)), the eligibility of such a person for housing benefit would surely be in respect of the premises that did constitute his sole or main residence, and would be unlikely to extend to any other property. In the absence of detailed regulations under s.24 this cannot be confirmed, but it seems probable that the reference to the standard community charge contribution in s.24 will, in practice, prove to be redundant, and, accordingly, the present subsection will be incapable of justification as being necessary to regulate the application thereof.

Another possible justification for the present subsection, and the one specifically invoked by the Government (*Hansard*, Vol. 111, col. 994, *per* Ian Lang, M.P.) is to ensure that the payment of a standard community charge contribution will not be affected by any restriction on other payments made in respect of the property, such as payments of fair rents made under Pt. V of the Rent (Scotland) Act 1984. Indeed, this explanation of the present subsection is implicit in the section itself, as subs. (11) explicitly provides that the payment of contributions will not be affected in the manner specified. However, it is difficult to envisage circumstances where the Rent Acts would be applicable where the tenant is liable to pay a standard charge contribution. S.2(1)(d) of the 1984 Act specifically exempts from the class of protected tenancies, to which, *inter alia*, the fair rent provisions apply, a tenancy whose purpose is to confer on the tenant the right to occupy the dwelling-house for a holiday. It is at least arguable that any accommodation in respect of which one is liable to pay a standard charge contribution must be holiday accommodation, as the degree of permanence implied by residence in accommodation which could not be appropriately so described would appear to be such as to entail that it be regarded as the sole or main residence of the person concerned, so excluding the accommodation from the class of premises in respect of which the standard charge is payable. Accordingly, as the Rent Acts would not appear to be applicable in this context, it would appear that this subsection does not permit the person liable to pay the standard charge to do anything which he would not be able to do by contractual means in any event. Therefore, a final set of possible justifications for this subsection relate to the regulation of matters which the liable person could have regulated, but did not regulate by contractual means, or to the regulation of matters between the liable person and a third party arising out of the relationship between the liable person and the person making the standard charge contribution. On the first count, liability for the standard charge contribution on the part of the short-term tenant will be treated as an implied contractual term between the two parties, and so will give rise to an obligation to pay on the part of the short-term tenant even if not specifically agreed between them. In the second place, the explicit stipulation that a standard community charge contribution is recoverable may usefully regulate the position of the liable person for income tax purposes. On account of his direct liability for the standard charge, if the standard charge contributions were commuted into rent then it would constitute an allowable expense deductible from gross rent for tax purposes in any case. Accordingly, this same result is achieved more efficiently and straightforwardly by providing that the payment of the standard charge contribution shall be considered separately from the payment of rent in the first instance.

Subs. (11)

This subsection provides that a contribution payable under subs. (10) shall be in addition to any other payment, such as rent, which a tenant or occupier is liable to make in respect of the premises. In particular, as it is a separate charge, any such payment of "a standard community charge contribution" will not be affected by any statutory provisions, such as those contained in the Rent (Scotland) Act 1984, which control or restrict such other payments (see further s.11(12) below). (The question whether such considerations are at all applicable to the payment of the standard charge contribution is discussed in subs. (10) above.)

Presumably the payment of "a standard community charge contribution" will include a proportionate contribution to the standard community water charge as determined by Sched. 5, Part I, paras. 9–11, (and the payment of this contribution will likewise not be affected by any statutory provisions which control or restrict payments).

Collective Community Charge

Liability for and calculation of collective community charge

11.—(1) The collective community charge shall be payable in respect of premises to which this section applies.

(2) This section applies to—

> (a) premises which are not subject to non-domestic rates and either are designated by the registration officer under subsection (3) below or fall within such class or classes or premises as may be prescribed;

> (b) premises which are part residential subjects and either are so designated or fall within such class or classes of premises as may be prescribed.

(3) Premises may be designated under this subsection if, in the opinion of the registration officer—

> (a) in the case of premises not subject to non-domestic rates, they are used, or

> (b) in the case of part residential subjects, the residential use made of them is,

wholly or mainly as the sole or main residence of persons most or all of whom reside there only for short periods.

(4) In determining whether to designate any premises under subsection (3) above, the registration officer shall have regard to such factors as may be prescribed.

(5) The person liable to pay the collective community charge in respect of any premises shall be—

    (a) subject to paragraphs (b) and (c) below, the owner of the premises;

    (b) subject to paragraph (c) below, if the premises are let for a period of 12 months or more, the tenant; or

    (c) if the premises are sub-let for such a period, the sub-tenant,

and that liability shall, in the case of a tenant or sub-tenant, be in respect of the period of his tenancy or, as the case may be, sub-tenancy.

(6) The collective community charge shall be due to—

    (a) each local authority; or

    (b) (in the case of an islands council) the local authority

in the area of which the premises in respect of which it is payable are situated.

(7) Subject to subsection (8) below, the collective community charge due to a local authority in respect of any premises in respect of any financial year shall be the product of—

    (a) the personal community charge determined by them in respect of that year; and

    (b) the collective community charge multiplier specified in the register as having effect in relation to the premises.

(8) If, in the course of a financial year, the collective community charge multiplier specified in the register as having effect in relation to any premises is changed, it shall be assumed, for the purposes of subsection (7) above, that the new multiplier shall remain in effect in relation to those premises from the date when it takes effect until the end of that year.

(9) In this Act, "the collective community charge multiplier" means, in respect of any premises, such number as the registration officer for the registration area in which the premises are situated determines in respect of the premises.

(10) In determining the collective community charge multiplier in respect of any premises, the registration officer shall have regard to—

    (a) the number of persons who are solely or mainly resident in the premises and would, but for section 8(8)(c) of this Act, be liable to pay a personal community charge; and

    (b) such other factors as may be prescribed.

(11) A person—

    (a) who is, at any time in a financial year, solely or mainly resident in premises in respect of which the collective community charge is payable; and

    (b) who is not liable to pay it; and

    (c) who would, but for section 8(8)(c) of this Act, be liable under this Act to pay a personal community charge

shall, for each day of his residence in the premises, pay to the person liable under this section for that collective community charge an amount equal to the amount mentioned in paragraph (i) below divided by the number in paragraph (ii) below—

    (i) the amount in this paragraph is—

        (A) the sum of the personal community charges determined in respect of that year by each local authority; or

        (B) (in the case of an islands council) the amount of the personal community charge determined in respect of that year by the local authority

    in the area of which the premises are situated;

    (ii) the number of days in that year,

(and such a payment is referred to in this section as a "collective community charge contribution").

(12) A collective community charge contribution made by a person—

    (a) shall be in addition to any obligation of his to make other payments (whether by way of rent or otherwise) in respect of his residence in the premises in respect of which that contribution is made;

    (b) is not affected by any enactment relating to the control or restriction of any such other payment, and shall not, for the purposes of any such enactment, be regarded as such a payment or part thereof.

(13) The person to whom a collective community charge contribution is made shall issue a receipt therefor showing the amount paid and the day or days to which the contribution relates.

(14) The person liable under this section to pay a collective community charge in respect of any premises shall keep, or cause to be kept, a record of all persons who are or have been solely or mainly resident there showing the periods for which they were so resident and the amounts paid to him by them by way of collective community charge contributions.

(15) A person who, but for this subsection, would be liable under this section to pay a collective community charge contribution to another in respect of any premises—

    (a) shall not be so liable until; and

    (b) shall have no such liability in respect of any days before,

that other person has given him notification of the amount he is liable to pay by way of such contribution for each day of his residence in the premises.

(16) Without prejudice to any rule of law, where a person—

    (a) in respect of his residence in any premises, pays, by way of collective community charge contribution, any sum which (for whatever reason) is not due; and

    (b) within 3 months of that payment, claims reimbursement of the sum from the person who, at the time of the payment, was liable to pay the collective community charge in respect of the premises,

the person so liable shall reimburse the other in that sum.

DEFINITIONS

    "community charge": s.26.

    "financial year": See s.26(1) and Local Government (Scotland) Act 1973 s.96(5) *i.e.* the year from April 1.

    "local authority": s.26.

    "part residential subjects": s.26.

    "prescribed": s.26.

    "register": s.26.

    "registration area": s.26.

    "registration officer": ss.12 and 26.

COMMENCEMENT

    This section came into force on September 14, 1987, but only for the purposes of and in relation to the community charges (and as applied by para. 11 of Sched. 5 to the Act, the community water charges) in respect of the financial year 1989–90 and each subsequent financial year. The section as a whole will come into force on April 1, 1989.

GENERAL NOTE

    This section was described by John Home Robertson M.P. in Committee as "the Heineken Clause" (1st Scot.S.C., col. 734)—intended to refresh the parts that other clauses cannot reach! In certain respects this is a very apt label as there is an unmistakably residual quality attached to this provision. Basically, it derives from a commitment made by the Government in the Green Paper (Annex G, paras. 32–36) to bring within the ambit of the new tax that part of the population to whom it would be extremely difficult to apply the personal community charge, with its emphasis on individual local registration, on account of their extreme mobility. This is to be done by making the relevant classes of people subject to an appropriate fraction of the personal community charge in the local authority area(s) in which are located the premises in which they reside from time to time, which amounts are to be paid collectively to those responsible for the management of the appropriate premises who, in turn, will be liable to the local authority for the payment of the aggregate sum.

In the course of the enactment of the present measure, the original commitment was refined and modified in two minor respects, both of which serve to enforce the residual quality. In the first place, it was made clear by ministers on a number of occasions in the course of debate (*e.g.* 1st Scot.S.C., col. 721 *per* Michael Ancram M.P.) that, in response to comments received after the publication of the Green Paper, there would in all cases be a strong presumption in favour of the application of the personal community charge and, therefore, against the application of the collective charge. As such, what was always intended to be a very limited class of persons to which this tax would be applicable—a notional figure of 3 per cent. of the population was mooted in the Green Paper—is intended to be restricted still further. Secondly, powers were assumed under subs. (2)(b) to permit the extension of the collective charge to other groups, and it was suggested that the purpose of this was to bring at least some members of the class of very dependent persons living in institutions within the scope of this tax (although subsequent amendments to other parts of the Bill seem to have restricted its potential scope, see s.11(2) below). In the light of this, it would seem that the true criterion for invoking the collective charge is not the mobility of the taxpayer, but the degree of practical difficulty involved in holding him/her personally liable, a condition with potentially a significantly broader range of application and of which mobility is merely an example. It is also a condition which is defined in negative terms—the absence of qualities attributable to the individual and her or his lifestyle which would make normal taxing mechanisms appropriate—and this further underlines the intent of its authors to identify and isolate the exceptional and residual case to whom the main principles and thrust of the legislation would be inappropriate.

The reason why the residual tone of this provision has been emphasised is that it would appear to be the source of most reservations which might be expressed about it. Insofar as such an idea has connotations which trivialise both the size and significance of the relevant client group and the nature of what is being done to its members, the notion of treating separately and differently merely for administrative purposes and as a practical expedient a small percentage of the population contains dangers. The client group may be small in percentage terms but is not insignificant. However, its overall minority status and its inability as a group with a membership of the type described to raise an effective political voice on most occasions, entails that any Government may act in a manner potentially at odds with its interests with relative impunity. And if one turns to the substance of what is attempted in the section, it may be concluded that that which may be passed off under the rubric of administrative efficiency and technical reform may have profound consequences in individual and general terms.

To begin with, we may refer to the concept of technical adequacy, including within it the notion of practical efficacy, which was one of the criteria established by the Government itself in the Green Paper (paras. 3.6–3.7) to judge the adequacy of any new local tax, and so cannot be lightly discounted. In terms of this criterion, the provision would appear to suffer from a number of drawbacks, precipitating certain inefficiencies and operational difficulties to be described below. Furthermore, the inadequacy of the administrative and technical assumptions underpinning the provision would appear to have implications for its adequacy in relation to the other two evaluative criteria set out in the Green Paper. To make particular individuals, namely those who run institutions of a type referred to in the present section, responsible for the community charge liability of the occupants of these institutions, in circumstances where the appropriate payments by the latter to the former cannot be guaranteed, would appear to place an unfairly onerous burden on the former group. (See note on subs. (10) below.)

From the perspective of the collective community charge contributor also, technical inadequacies and anomalies would appear to cast doubts on the fairness of the system. His marginal status extends to the Community Charges Register (s.13), within which he is unrecognised, so depriving him of certain consequential rights of appeal (s.16) and inspection of the register (s.20) which may make his position more vulnerable (see, *e.g.*, note on s.11(11) below).

Still with reference to the collective charge contributor, the section would appear to be at odds with the aspirations underlying the principle of accountability, in that by introducing an intermediary it involves an attenuation of the link between the payer and the ultimate source and recipient of the tax, and thus a blurring of that perception on the part of the taxpayer of the direct relationship between the spending activities of local government and his personal tax burden, a perception which, it is claimed, adds to the keenness with which the taxpayer scrutinises the merits of the relevant local administration and to the care with which and the base of knowledge from which he exercises his democratic judgment. (Green Paper, paras. 3.11–3.12 and Annex G, para. 16.)

Liability for the collective community charge gives rise to certain other and consequential rights and liabilities. Community charge rebates will be available by virtue of s.24 to reduce the amounts of collective charge contributions. Also, liability for the collective community charge triggers an additional liability for the collective community water charge (see note on subs. (11) below).

Subs. (1)

This subsection provides that the collective community charge is to be paid in respect of premises to which the section applies. As such, as with the standard charge, the criterion for differentiating between liability under this head and liability for the personal community charge relates to certain characteristics of the premises in question and the typical mode of occupation thereof.

The use of the term "premises" is again indicative of a degree of terminological discontinuity between Pts. I and II of the Act. In Pt. I, the key term used to describe heritable subjects is "lands and heritages" (s.2(3)(a)). However, as suggested above, despite the lack of conceptual rigour, this need not lead to ambiguity or unintended consequences in the interpretation of "premises" in the context of this Part of the Act (see note on s.10(2) above).

Subs. (2)

This subsection defines the categories of premises to which the collective charge will be applied. There is both a negative and positive element to this definition. As to the negative element, it is provided that those premises which are subject to non-domestic rates are not premises in respect of which the collective charge is payable unless they are part residential subjects, *i.e.* lands and heritages which are used partly as the sole or main residence of any person, other than domestic subjects or such other class or classes of lands and heritages as may be prescribed (s.26(1)). Accordingly, premises which remain subject to non-domestic rates on account of their not being "domestic subjects" within the meaning of s.2(3)–(4) will not be subject to the collective charge, unless they are part residential subjects. Thus, premises which are not dwelling houses such as hotels, guest houses, construction camps provided by an employer for workers deployed in a particular location on a short term basis, (1st Scot.S.C., cols. 781–782, *per* Michael Ancram M.P.) and other accommodation of a temporary nature run on commercial grounds which might otherwise fall within the ambit of the collective charge, will not be liable to the collective charge, unless they are part residential subjects. This will probably occur infrequently in the case of the examples mentioned. If such premises are judged to be part residential, this is likely to be because some of the residents in *e.g.* a guest house are long-term guests. This degree of permanence, however, is likely to prevent the premises from being made subject to the collective charge. The residents will instead be liable to the personal charge.

In order to find an example of premises which do not constitute a dwelling house, but which, nevertheless, might constitute part residential subjects in respect of which the collective charge would be payable, we must look to examples outwith the sector which provides exclusively residential services. Thus, for example, "part residential subjects might be designated as suitable for the collective community charge . . . in cases where premises housed both a hostel and an associated day centre providing a service for people other than its residents" (*Hansard*, H.L. Vol. 486, col. 1699, *per* The Earl of Dundee).

Other premises which, unless part residential subjects, would not attract the collective charge on account of their not being "domestic subjects" include those premises which are to be specifically excluded from those classes of premises which are not dwelling houses but which are, nevertheless, to be prescribed as domestic subjects by virtue of s.2(3)(b), together with those classes of premises which are dwelling houses but which are, nevertheless, to be prescribed as not being domestic subjects under s.2(4). Within the former category are certain types of communal accommodation such as nursing homes and residential care homes, in relation to which premises prescriptive powers will also be used under s.26(1) to stipulate that they are not treated as part residential subjects (*Hansard,* H.L. Vol. 486, col. 1665) (see above, notes on ss.2(3)(b) and 8(8)(d) above). Within the latter category are to be included holiday caravans and small holiday huts (1st Scot.S.C., col. 332) (see also, notes on ss.2(4) and 8(8)(d) above).

If we turn to the positive element in the definition, the categories of premises to which the collective charge is applicable are firstly, those which are to be designated by the registration officer under subs. (3) below, and secondly, those which fall within such other class or classes of premises yet to be prescribed. As indicated, it was originally intended that the power of prescription would be used to bring within the ambit of the section those residents of institutions for whom it would be impracticable to have individual registration for the community charge, on account of their being very dependent. At Committee stage in the House of Commons, it was suggested by the Under Secretary of State for Scotland, Mr. Ian Lang, that the mentally handicapped might provide one group which would be classified as dependent under the said powers of prescription (1st Scot.S.C., col. 752). However, this observation, and indeed, the original rationale for introducing the powers of prescription in this context seem to have been somewhat overtaken by events, in particular, the undertaking referred to above, to exempt certain vulnerable groups from all forms of the community charge by ensuring that the premises in which they reside remain or become subject to non-domestic rates, and the extension of the categories of persons exempt from payment of personal community charge or a collective charge contribution to include persons who are severely mentally handicapped (s.8(8)(b) above). Neither the undertaking nor the amendment was made until Report Stage in the Lords (*Hansard*, H.L. Vol 486, cols. 1653 and 1665, *per* Lord Glenarthur).

Nevertheless it would be wrong to suggest on such tentative grounds that this or any other particular power of prescription is redundant. Indeed, at the Lords Report Stage, while certain options for use of these prescriptive powers were being foreclosed, others were being opened up. In response to a debate as to the appropriate status of women's aid hostels under the new Act which had gained momentum within and outwith Parliament during the passage of the Bill, the Government made an undertaking that such premises would be prescribed as being subject to the collective charge by virtue of this subsection (*Hansard*, Vol. 486, cols. 1452–1453, *per* Lord Glenarthur) (for a full discussion of the scope of this undertaking, its legal implications, and its appropriateness as a response to the concerns expressed on behalf of residents of these hostels, see note on subs. (3) below). Overall, then, when considering the precise scope of this section, one is confronted with a provisional and flexible structure, where a number of categories of persons may or may not be exempt under a variety of potentially overlapping provisions, the definitive package stipulating the proper relationship and the lines of demarcation between each having yet to be settled.

Subs. (3)

This subsection defines and describes the main category of premises, the residents of which will be subject to the collective charge, namely those premises which in the opinion of the registration officer are used wholly or mainly as the sole or main residence of persons most or all of whom reside there only for short periods.

The Government resisted attempts at various points during the passage of the Bill to specify the particular types of premises which would fall within this definition. It was argued that under the criterion set out, some, but not all instances of premises falling within the categories of common boarding houses, half-way houses, homeless persons units, house in multiple occupancy, etc., would attract a collective charge, and, therefore, to stipulate that all premises within any of these particular categories should be treated in the uniform manner would lead to unnecessary rigidity and to results at odds with the objectives of the section (1st Scot.S.C., cols. 728–731, *per* Michael Ancram M.P.).

Particular concern was voiced over the position of womens' refuges, and over the possibility that they might attract the collective charge, on account of two special considerations which relate to such premises (see, *e.g.*, 1st Scot.S.C., cols. 713–727). In the first place, whereas in the other examples cited above, one is dealing with classes of persons with characteristically itinerant life-styles, and who, therefore, are unlikely to be registered anywhere for the personal community charge in the same financial year as they are liable to pay a collective charge contribution, the same is not true of typical residents of womens' refuges. For the most part, the locus of the violent or otherwise turbulent domestic situation from which they seek to escape will be premises which previously provided their permanent residence, and in many of these cases they will subsequently return to these same premises. Accordingly, it will often be difficult to decide in advance, or even retrospectively, whether a particular resident of a refuge is liable to pay a collective charge contribution. Therefore, the application of the section to refuges will both create administrative difficulties for those involved in management of such refuges and, in the case of the residents themselves, may involve them in making payments of collective charge in circumstances where they are not liable and thereafter having to make use of the procedure provided under subs. (16) to obtain repayment, a rather cumbersome and precarious protection against double indemnity.

(Problems in this respect might be exacerbated by the anomalous position of the collective charge contributor in respect of the availability of appeals mechanisms under the Act. See the note on subs. (11) below.)

In the second place, concern was expressed about the ease with which potentially hostile spouses or ex-cohabitees could trace the whereabouts of women who enter refuges, if those refuges were to be entered onto the community charges register as being subject to the collective charge.

Scottish Women's Aid believed that the best way to counter these problems and dangers would be to provide that residents of premises used as refuges should be made exempt from any form of the community charge in respect of these premises (by means of prescribing under s.2(4) that such premises should remain in rating, and under s.26(1), that they should be treated as part residential subjects thus bringing their residents within the ambit of the exemption provided in s.8(8)(d)). Such provision would avoid administration complexities and avert the danger of double liability. It would also prevent the leakage of information so as to threaten the safety of a woman.

After some deliberation (see, *e.g., Hansard*, Vol. 486, col. 957–958, *per* Earl of Dundee), the Government decided against this particular remedy, and instead, opted in favour of refuges being prescribed (under subs. (2) above) as subject to the collective charge (*Hansard*, Vol. 486, cols. 1452–1453, *per* Lord Glenarthur). It was argued that this would make for administrative simplicity, in that it would avoid any distinction in liability between those who are solely or mainly resident in a refuge and those who are not. Furthermore, as it was simultaneously undertaken that women's refuges would be prescribed as a class of premises whose multiplier would not appear on the public part of the register under s.20(2)(a)(iii), the fact that residents of such premises were not to be excluded from liability to pay the charge would not entail any consequent danger of publication of their whereabouts to their detriment. Despite these advances, the Government's preferred solution does not address the problem of double liability.

Sole or main residence of persons most or all of whom reside there only for short periods. Given the meaning normally attributed in law to the words "sole or main residence" (see above, s.8(1)) which is based upon the idea of the contemplation of permanent residence, the use of this term to describe the nature of the tenure of property in situations where it is explicitly stated is for a short period only, would appear to be something of a contradiction in terms. Presumably, this will be resolved in practice by the registration officer also assuming that where a person does not appear to have any home of a permanent nature, then the location at which he happens to reside presently will be deemed to be his sole and main residence, providing that it consists of premises which can reasonably be described as providing accommodation. Accordingly, only the genuine itinerant, the person who "lives under a railway arch" (1st Scot.S.C., col. 725, *per* Michael Ancram M.P.) or somewhere equally uncongenial, would be exempt.

One further effect of this provision is to provide that it is the typical pattern of the occupation of premises rather than the particular pattern of occupation of any individual which is significant for the purposes of determining the appropriate type of liability. Accordingly, it will follow that some people whose residence at a particular address is as longstanding and permanent in intent as a person liable to pay the personal charge, will, nevertheless, be liable to pay a collective charge contribution. This will be so, for example, in the case of a long-term resident of a hostel which is otherwise used as the sole or main residence of persons most or all of whom reside there only for short periods.

Subs. (4)

This subsection provides the registration officer with some guidance in arriving at his decisions under subs. (3) by stipulating that in so doing he shall have regard to such factors to be prescribed in regulations. It is envisaged that the factors to be prescribed will develop the criterion of practical expediency as the appropriate yardstick for these purposes, referring to the extent to which residents are transient and to the difficulty, or potential difficulty, of achieving individual registration for the personal community charge in such cases (*Hansard*, H.L. Vol. 486, cols. 1701–1702).

Subs. (5)

This subsection sets out who is liable for payment for a collective charge, and is identical in form and similar in intent to that which is provided in relation to the standard charge under s.10(4) above. It provides that liability for payment of a collective community charge is to fall on the owner of the premises in respect of which the collective charge is payable, the tenant, or sub-tenant, depending on the circumstances of the lease. Where a sub-tenant

ias a lease for a continuous period of 12 months or more, he is to be liable; when there is
io sub-tenant with such a lease, but there is a tenant who has one, he is liable; and in any
other case, the owner is liable.

Despite the similarity with s.10(4), the present measure has more of an anti-avoidance
flavour to it, since the collection and processing of the collective community charge due in
respect of particular premises may involve the liable person in dealing with sizeable sums of
money. As such, the stipulation that, under appropriate circumstances, a tenant or sub-
tenant may be liable and is, therefore, the person to whom collective community charge
contributions are to be paid under subs. (11) below, by linking responsibility for the tax with
a *de facto* responsibility for the premises, will help to prevent abuses. An owner resident
abroad could not be relied on to collect the contributions from residents, and thereafter to
remit them to the local authority, to whom they are ultimately due under subs. (6) below
without acting through an intermediary.

The basic idea of holding responsible, for a residential tax, the person who may be
deemed to be in charge of the premises rather than their transient occupier(s) is not entirely
innovative, in that this subsection in particular and the section in general may be construed
to be roughly analogous in intent to s.240 of the Local Government (Scotland) Act 1947
which provides that in cases of lets of a year or less the owner rather than the occupier of
the premises may be held liable for the rates by the relevant local authority.

Subs. (6)

This provides that, as in the case of the standard charge under s.10(5) above, the collective
community charge is due to each local authority (regional and district council, or islands
council) in whose area the premises are situated.

Subs. (7)

This subsection provides that it is the personal community charge which is to constitute
the base figure from which is to be determined the collective community charge for the
financial year in question. Specifically, it provides that the collective community charge for
the year shall be the product of the personal community charge and the collective community
charge multiplier, the latter figure to be determined in accordance with subs. (9).

Subs. (8)

This subsection provides that where, in the course of a financial year the collective
community charge multiplier for any premises is changed, it is to be assumed for the
purposes of calculating the collective charge, that the new multiplier specified will not be
further altered for the remainder of that year.

By virtue of Sched. 2, para. 4(1), any community charge will, subject only to the
exceptional circumstances specified in Sched. 2, paras. 3, 8, 9 and 10, be payable by twelve
equal monthly instalments to the levying authority. However, in the case of the collective
charge, the basis of liability in respect of particular premises may change during the course
of the financial year by means of alteration of the collective community charge multiplier,
principally in accordance with the criteria set out in subs. (10) below. In general, alterations
may be made with retrospective, immediate or prospective effect by the registration officer
at any time to correct a clerical or typographical error (s.15(2)) or to give effect to the
decisions of a sheriff or higher judge on a registration appeal (s.16(4)–(5)), or at intervals
of not less than three months or such other period as may be prescribed for any other reason
(s.15(1)(b)). Accordingly, in the case of such an alteration, a device is required to re-
establish the terms of periodical liability, and so avoid a breakdown in the system of levy of
charge. Such a device is provided under this subsection, since the assumption that the
collective charge will remain stable for the remainder of the financial year permits the
recalculation of the total amount due and the set monthly yield for that period.

Subs. (9)

This subsection provides that the collective community charge multiplier in respect of any
premises is to be such a figure as the registration officer for the registration officer for the
registration area in which the premises are situated determines.

Taken with subs. (7), the effect of this provision is that the overall collective community
charge payable in respect of premises is to be a figure calculated by reference to the
discretionary judgment of the registration officer, albeit circumscribed by factors to be
specified in subs. (10), rather than reflecting the precise sum actually received by the person
responsible for the collective charge, as was the method envisaged by Opposition amendments in both Houses. (1st Scot.S.C., cols. 789–802; *Hansard*, H.L. Vol. 486, cols. 984–999).

The advantage of the latter approach would have been that the possibility of a mis-matc
between the amount of collective community charge legally due and the actual amount pai
in respect of premises would have been eliminated, the person in charge of those premise
bearing no responsibility and suffering no financial penalty in the case of default on the pai
of any residents liable to pay a contribution or of any other eventuality which would caus
a projection of collective charge to be inaccurate. The disadvantage of such an approach i
that it provides no incentive on the part of the person responsible to administer and collec
the tax efficiently and effectively, so exacerbating the danger of a shortfall in the actua
amount of tax paid, whether as a result of neglectful inefficiency by the liable person or c
an altruistic desire on his part to ease the tax burden of already impoverished groups c
persons. Whether on balance the merits of the system in place outweigh its demerits
depends upon whether one believes it is legitimate to treat the owner or manager of premise
within this section as a tax collecting agent or whether one believes that this imposes a
unfair administrative burden on such persons and places them in an invidious position i
respect of the development of what are often already precarious personal relationships wit
the occupiers of such premises. What does *not* appear to be a consideration relative to th
above debate, despite the protestations of both pro-Bill and anti-Bill lobbyists in Parliament
is the issue of the potential for financial exploitation on the part of the person in charge c
the premises. The introduction of this theme in the arguments of the protagonists of bot
positions would seem to be something of a red herring. This is so, because, all else bein
equal, the same potential for abuse exists under both systems: While not supposed to be
record of the actual amount of contributions paid, the calculation of the collective charg
payable under the method chosen is still firmly based on, and derived from the sum of th
liabilities of persons who are actually solely or mainly resident in premises attracting th
collective charge at any time (subs. 10)). Therefore, in both cases, financial exploitatio
depends upon the falsification of the records which a liable person is required to keep unde
subs. (14) of contributors and the amounts of their contributions, so as to convey a
impression that less contributions were paid than actually was the case, or less probably, b
overcharging contributors. Accordingly, the prevention of abuse does not depend upon th
method of calculating the collective charge but upon the vigilance of the registration officer
and the enthusiasm and diligence with which is enforced the duty upon the liable person t
keep comprehensive records of the persons who have occupied relevant premises and of th
collective community charge contributions which they have made, and possibly also upo
the knowledge of contributors of the proper level of their liability and their willingness t
complain if they are being overcharged.

Subs. (10)

This subsection provides that when the registration officer determines the collectiv
community charge multiplier in respect of any premises he is to have regard to the numbe
of persons who are solely or mainly resident in the premises and who would be liable to pa
the personal community charge but for the fact that the premises in which they reside attrac
a collective charge (see s.8(8)(c), and such other factors as the Secretary of State may hav
prescribed.

Para. (a)

This makes it clear that an important criterion for determining the multiplier is to be th
actual number of persons solely or mainly resident in the premises at any time, and s
dovetails with subs. (11) below which provides the basis of the liability of such persons t
make a collective community charge contribution to the person responsible for the premise
and *directly* liable to pay the tax. The proviso that persons living in the premises should b
otherwise liable to pay the personal charge or may be of significance in the deliberations o
registration officers on occasions; for example, in relation to womens' refuges, given that th
women who seek accommodation in such places are often accompanied by members of thei
family under the age of 18; or in relation to hostels, homeless persons unit, or stop-ove
units, given that, on account of the limited nature of the duties of local authorities to suc
persons under Pt. II of the Housing (Scotland) Act 1987, a significant portion of the resident
of such places fall within the category of the young, single homeless, many of whom ma
also be under the age of 18.

Two other points should be noted which may be pertinent to the deliberations of th
registration officer under this paragraph. First, the form of words used does not discriminat
between persons who are solely or mainly resident for short periods, and those who are s
on a more permanent basis. All should be taken into account, and this is in keeping wit
subs. (3) which suggests that it is the typical mode of residence within the premises rathe
than the mode of residence of the particular individual which is significant in determinin

ether all residents should be liable to pay collective charge contributions. Secondly, any
idents residing in the premises should not be included in the calculation, since, by virtue
s.8(8)(c) they are excepted from the category of persons exempted from the personal
arge on account of being resident in premises attracting the collective charge, and so, are
t persons who "would, but for section 8(8)(c) of this Act, be liable to pay a personal
mmunity charge" (see note on s.8(8)(c) above). Instead, these students will be liable to
y the personal community charge, provided that the premises are in the area of the local
thority in which they are resident during term-time for the purpose of undertaking their
urse (s.8(4)). If the premises fall outwith such an area, they will not be liable to pay any
rm of the community charge in respect of their residence there.

Notice that the formula used in this paragraph does not exclude from the calculation the
rson liable to pay the collective community charge itself. He is not, however, liable to pay
mself a contribution (see subs. 11(b) below).

ara. (b)

This provides that other factors to be prescribed by the Secretary of State may be taken
to account in determining the multiplier. It is envisaged that such factors will include
ictuations in the number of persons solely or mainly resident in premises and other costs
an administrative nature.

Obviously, the obligation to take into account seasonal fluctuations will inform any
ljustments made by the registration officer in the collective community charge multiplier
der s.15(1)(b) which permits him to make such adjustments at intervals of not less than
ree months, and may even give him cause to exercise his power under s.15(1) to make
ich adjustments retrospectively.

As to matters of and administrative nature, what are mainly referred to here are the
iancial implications of the difficulties involved in collecting the collective charge. These
fficulties may give rise to two distinct sets of costs, both of which, it may be inferred from
e tenor of the Government's comments during the passage of the Bill, may be identified
 factors to be taken into account in calculating the net charge, (see, *e.g.*, 1st Scot.S.C.,
ols. 797–798). In the first place, incidents of default of payment of contributions will cause
 element of shortfall which may only be avoided by undue administrative effort or by the
loption of unreasonable conditions of admission to and the continued occupation of
remises attracting the collective charge. In the second place, the processes of tax determi-
ation and collection and the effort to minimise loss under the above heading will inevitably
use management costs to be incurred, and these ought to be set against the estimation of
oss receipts for the purposes of calculating the appropriate multiplier.

ubs. (11)

This subsection provides for the payment by persons who occupy premises subject to the
llective community charge and who would be liable to pay personal community charge but
r that fact, of an amount of money described as a collective community charge contribution
 the person directly liable for the collective community charge payable in respect of these
remises. The amount of this contribution is to be arrived at by apportioning, on a daily
asis, the personal community charge(s) of the local authority or authorities in whose area
ie premises are situated and by multiplying the daily figure by the number of days that the
erson is solely and mainly resident in the premises. The amount of the collective community
iarge contribution then arrived at, may be reduced by the amount of any rebate of
ommunity charge payable by virtue of s.24.

Liability to pay a collective community charge contribution may trigger an additional
ability to pay a contribution to the collective community water charge. By virtue of s.25
id Sched. 5, paras. 7–8, such a charge is payable provided that the water for domestic
irposes is not supplied to the premises wholly by meter. Although the person liable in the
rst instance to pay the collective community water charge is the person directly liable to
ay the collective community charge (Sched. 5, para. 8(a)(ii)), the collective charge
ontributor may, by use of prescriptive powers under para. 11 of Sched. 5, be held directly
ible to make a contribution thereto.

There exists no mechanism under the Act for persons liable to pay a collective charge
ontribution to appeal against the designation of premises as attracting the collective charge.
his is in contrast to the position of the person directly liable to pay the collective charge,
ho may appeal against such a designation under the registration appeals provisions in s.16.
s such, any person who feels that his interests as a payer of community charge might be
etter served if he were liable to pay a personal charge rather than a collective contribution
ould presumably have to raise an action of judicial review against the decision of the
egistration officer in order to have the matter judicially determined.

Para. (a)

This ensures that any person who is not otherwise exempt from payment of a contributi
to the collective charge on account of the grounds set out in (b) and (c) below, is not lial
to make such a contribution solely on account of being resident in the premises subject
charge. For liability to arise, it must be his/her sole or main residence. Accordingly if,
example, a person leaves a permanent address to take up an occupation which involves h
in staying at various working men's hostels (all of which happen to attract the collecti
charge) around Scotland, and never returns to his previous address, then he cannot be he
liable to pay a collective charge contribution in respect of any such premises until such tir
as he is no longer mainly resident at his previous address—which may be a difficult matr
to decide.

Particular difficulties may arise in the case where someone is seeking temporary accon
modation while still retaining his/her sole or main residence elsewhere, as with wom
seeking accommodation in a refuge on account of temporary relationship breakdown or w
young persons seeking accommodation in a hostel of some description having temporar
vacated the family home. They will not be liable to pay a collective community char
contribution during the time of the temporary residence. Unfortunately, however, in ma
cases the determination of the degree of permanency and legal status of the accommodati
may depend upon subsequent developments in the relevant relationships and living patter
of the person concerned and the light that this sheds upon his or her attitude to t
accommodation in question at the beginning of the period of residence, and may therefo
only be satisfactorily determined retrospectively. This complexity makes for an element
intrinsic uncertainty as to the appropriate form of charge that a person is liable to pay at
particular time, and indeed, given that in most such cases the person in question will ha
been registered to pay the personal community charge on the basis of the previously stab
accommodation which they have left, raises the spectre of double jeopardy. In such
event, subs. (13)–(16) below provide, respectively, for evidential safeguards (subs. (13) ar
(14)), for notification of liability (subs. 15)), and a mechanism for claiming reimburseme
(subs. 16)), all of which devices combine to provide a package of safeguards agair
permanent loss. However, such measures do not alleviate the temporary hardship ar
inconvenience which may be caused, and, indeed, in terms of subs. (16), depend upon tl
initiative of the aggrieved person within a strict time limit of three months within which ar
undue sum of money may be recovered.

The absence of rights of appeal under the Act against liability for a collective char,
contribution (see the note on s.16(1) below) may also affect the position of the person at tl
interface between liability for the personal charge and liability for a collective communi
charge contribution and threatened by double jeopardy. If a woman, having left her ma
residence for a short period and then returned, and who in the interim has paid bo
personal charge in respect of her permanent address and a collective charge contribution
respect of a refuge accommodation, wishes to challenge her liability for the collective char,
contribution retrospectively, the only action open to her will be an ordinary action f
payment in the Sheriff Court. If the action is unsuccessful on the grounds that she is held
have been resident in the collective charge premises for the relevant period and so is not dr
any repayment, there exists no mechanism, such as that which is available to the sheri
under s.16(5) in the case of a registration appeal (over which of two competing liabilities fr
personal charge shall subsist), for the court to ensure that the register entry in respect of h
personal community charge liability is altered so that she is relieved of liability for tl
personal charge for such period as she has been required to pay the collective char,
contribution. It cannot be guaranteed that the registration officer for the area in respect
which she pays the personal charge will adjust the register accordingly in any case; nor th
her appeal against a refusal so to do under s.16(2) will be successful, so triggering a directic
from the sheriff that the relevant register entry be altered under s.16(4).

Because all relevant and interconnected questions of liability cannot be determine
together in the one forum, the possibility exists of mutually inconsistent decisions which mi
lead to double prejudice. Of course, it would be highly unlikely that one sheriff would con
to a decision which, by suggesting that a person's sole or main residence was in a differe,
area than had been determined by another sheriff, effectively contradicted that earlir
decision. However, the absence of an integrated appellate system to deal with this type
situation, might prove very inconvenient for a person affected and make it very difficult fr
her to vindicate her rights.

Para. (b)

This exception creates an element of uncertainty as to the personal liability of a persc
who is directly liable for the collection and payment of the collective community charge

ation to premises, and who is solely or mainly resident in these premises, as in the case
a resident warden of a hostel. Such a person cannot be held liable to pay the personal
mmunity charge on account of the operation of s.8(8)(c). Yet s.11(1)(b) makes it clear
t there exists no mechanism for him to pay a collective community contribution to
self. As such, a persuasive interpretation might support the view that under certain
:umstances a resident manager of premises in respect of which the collective community
arge is payable is not liable to any form of community charge.
There exist two possible alternative ways of avoiding this conclusion. First, subs. (11) may
read as being purely of an administrative nature concerned mainly to provide the
chanism whereby certain persons liable to pay a collective charge contribution actually
ke such payment, rather than to provide a legal foundation for such an obligation. If this
re the case, the exclusion of the person in charge of the premises would be explicable in
ninistrative terms. Given that he occupies the role of intermediate tax collecting agent,
night appear redundant to suggest that he be obliged to go through a separate process of
ying his contribution to himself prior to the payment of the overall amount due to is local
hority. This interpretation is reinforced by the fact that subs. (10)(a) requires that *all*
se resident (*i.e.* presumably including a resident warden) are included in the calculation
ding to the determination of the multiplier for the premises—which creates a notional
rtfall between total collective charge and the total contributions. Thus the person liable
the charge itself, whilst not formally required to make a contribution, may be deemed
make one at the point that he pays the charge itself. This seems clumsy and, in denying
warden the opportunity to pay a contribution, he may be deprived of the right to a
ate under s.24. Perhaps a "deemed contribution" might have been the answer?
A second and perhaps more plausible way of avoiding the conclusion that a resident
nager is exempt, is to surmise that the part of the relevant premises in which he resides
l be treated as separate premises and, as he will not therefore be deemed to be resident
premises in respect of which the collective charge is payable, he will not fall within the
mpt category in s.8(8)(c) and so will be liable to the personal charge in the normal way.
thin rating and valuation law, an authoritative line of judicial reasoning suggests that the
um quid, that is, the separate subjects for the purposes of entry onto the valuation roll,
y be constituted by the unit of occupation regardless of whether this is only one section
the physical structure of the building occupied, as is often the case in multiple occupancy
angements. (See for example *Wright* v. *Assessor for Glasgow,* 1936, S.C. 344.)
Of course, these matters have traditionally fallen within the jurisdiction of the assessor,
d on appeal, the valuation appeal committee. (See note to s.2(6) above.) Under the
esent Act, the question of liability for the personal charge is one for the registration
icer to determine, and on appeal, the sheriff (see s.16 below). However, despite the
ferent personnel, or in the case of the assessor, at least different roles involved (s.12(2)),
would appear that the issue of the definition of the *unum quid* for rating purposes is
sonably analogous to the question of separate premises for the purpose of ascertaining
mmunity charge liability, and that the registration officer, while not obliged to follow the
soning applicable in the former area of law, ought to be informed and influenced thereby.
cordingly, it would appear that one legally persuasive avenue for the registration officer
follow in the case of the resident manager of premises in respect of which the collective
mmunity charge is payable, would be to hold him liable for the personal charge. The
nager or warden would not then slip through the conceptual net erected by the Act, the
ction of which is to provide universal liability for the new tax with the exception only of
cifically exempted categories.

a. (c)
This provides that, apart from meeting the criteria specified in paras. (a)–(b) above, in
der to be liable to pay a collective community charge contribution, a person must be
neone who would have been liable to pay the personal community charge but for the fact
his residence in premises attracting the collective charge. Thus, all the categories of
emption from the personal charge specified in the General Note to s.8 above, apply
ually to the case of the collective charge contributor. Also, as, by virtue of s.8(8)(c), they
not persons who would be liable for the personal charge but for their residence in
mises attracting the collective charge, but are instead persons whose liability for the
rsonal charge subsists regardless of their residence in such premises. Students are exempt
m the collective community charge contribution under this provision. (See ss.8(8)(c) and
(10)(a) above.)

Subs. (12)

This provision is identical in form and intent to that provided under s.10(11) in relation to the standard charge. It provides that the collective community charge contribution which a person makes is additional to any other payments for which he is liable, such as rent. also provides that the contribution is not affected by any statutory control (for example, relation to regulated tenancies under Pts. 4 and 5 of the Rent (Scotland) Act 1984) upon such payments and that it is not to be considered as comprising or forming part of those other payments.

Subs. (13)

This subsection requires the person liable to pay the collective community charge and whom collective community charge contributions are to be made, to issue a receipt anyone making such a contribution showing the amount paid and the day or days to which the contribution relates. Together with subss. (15) and (16), and to a lesser extent sub (14), the subsection contributes to a package of measures designed to safeguard the interest of persons liable to make collective community charge contributions.

Subs. (14)

This subsection provides that the person liable to pay the collective community charge respect of any premises shall maintain a record of all persons who are or have been sole or mainly resident therein (*i.e.* deemed by him to be so resident?), and of the periods their residence and of the amounts of the collective charge contributions which they paid him. As well as providing evidence, additional to the receipt provided for under subs. (1. above, of payment by the person liable of the relevant amount of collective community charge contribution, this record will provide an important source of evidence and informatio for the registration officer for the purposes of determining the collective community charg multiplier under subs. (10) above, in negotiation of the periodic alterations permitted unde s.(15)(1)(b) below. Furthermore, if a person feels aggrieved at the result of any such period redetermination and adjustment, then he may appeal to the registration officer and then the sheriff under s.16, and the record will obviously be an important source of evidence any such proceedings.

Subs. (15)

This subsection provides that a person shall not be liable to make a collective communit charge contribution unless and until, and with any attempt to impose a retrospective liabili excluded, he has been given notification of the daily amount he will be liable to pay by th person directly liable for the collective charge.

The provision purports to safeguard the resident of premises from any form of retrospectiv liability, or from any form of indeterminate liability unaccompanied by advance notificatio of the amount due. Unfortunately, the practical consequence of this provision may be th the person directly liable to pay the collective charge, in order to safeguard himself, w automatically charge every resident of the premises who may *appear to* fall within th category of persons liable to make the contribution from the date of commencement of the residence. This may cause (at least) temporary financial loss and administrative inconvenienc to persons such as battered women seeking refuge who may validly claim to maintain the main residence elsewhere, or hostel residents under the age of 18, who may truthfully clai to be under that age but whose case may raise sufficient doubts to encourage the perso directly liable for the community charge to charge them pending resolution thereof, in th knowledge that any revenue lost through delay in making such a decision may not be claime back retrospectively.

Subs. (16)

This subsection requires a person to whom has been paid a collective community charg contribution to repay it, if it should not have been paid, provided that the claim f reimbursement by the relevant person is made within three months of the payment question. The introduction of a three month time bar is an attempt to balance fairness to th person wrongly charged against fairness to the hard pressed administrator of the collectiv charge within the premises who may wish to limit the contingency fund to be put aside f the repayment of undue charge to a level consistent with maintenance of an accountir system which permits reasonably accurate projections of future outlays and of the resourc available to meet them.

For comments on the limitations of this right to recover, see notes on subs. (11)(a).

Community Charges Registration Officer

Community Charges Registration Officer

12.—(1) There shall be a Community Charges Registration Officer (to be known as such but, in this Act, referred to as "the registration officer") or every region and islands area.

(2) The assessor appointed for each region or islands area under section 116(2) or (5) of the Local Government (Scotland) Act 1973 shall be the registration officer for that area and any depute assessor appointed under he said section 116(2) or (5) shall be a depute registration officer and hall have all the functions of a registration officer.

(3) A regional or islands council may appoint such additional number of depute registration officers as they consider necessary to enable the registration officer to perform his functions under this Act, and any depute registration officer so appointed shall have all the functions of a registration officer.

(4) The registration officer shall prepare, maintain and keep up-to-date he register for his registration area.

(5) A regional or islands council shall secure the provision of sufficient staff, accommodation and other resources to enable the registration officer o perform his functions under this Act.

DEFINITIONS
"register": ss.13 and 26.
"registration area": s.26.
"registration officer": ss.12 and 26.

GENERAL NOTE
This section provides for the creation of the key office required in order for the new charges to be rendered operable. Specifically, it provides for the creation of a community charges registration officer for every region and islands area, and stipulates that the assessor or the region or islands area should hold that office. Depute registration officers are also provided for, and these are to be the depute assessor(s) for the area together with such additional officers as may be appointed by the regional or islands council to which the new office relates for the purpose of enabling the functions of the new office to be carried out. In general terms, the functions of the new office consist of the preparation and maintenance of the community charges register for the area, which is created by s.13 below. The duties of the registration officer and the characteristics of the register are described in more detail in ss.14 to 20 below. Finally, this section provides that the regional or islands council in question shall secure the provision of the infrastructure of administrative resources and services required for the registration officer to perform his functions. It does not, however, create the council as registration authority (*cf.* 1973 Act s.116(1)).

Subs. (1)
This subsection provides that there shall be a community charges registration officer for all the nine mainland and three islands areas, who is referred to at all other places within the Act as "the registration officer".

Subs. (2)
This subsection provides that the assessor for each region or islands area, appointed under s.116(2) or (5) of the Local Government (Scotland) Act 1973, shall be the registration officer for that area. (Under s.116(5) and S.I. 1974 No. 1565 the Highland Region is combined with he Western Isles, and Orkney and Shetland Islands areas are combined.) It also provides that any depute assessor appointed under the same section of the 1973 Act, is to be a depute registration officer, with all the functions of the registration officer. The justification for combining the offices of assessor and registration officer in the one role appears to rest on arguments based upon autonomy and expertise.
As regards the issue of autonomy, it was a constant theme of the Government throughout he parliamentary debates that matters relating to the calculation of the tax base, including questions concerning the liability of individuals, should be kept apart from matters relating o the setting of the tax rate and the collection of the tax. In particular, officers of the body,

which has a financial interest in the extent of the tax return, namely the local authority, while they should obviously be involved in matters falling within the latter set of functions, should be debarred from involvement in the former function on account of the fact that calculation of the tax base involves questions of fairness and equity to the individual tax payer, and an officer concerned to maximise the return to local authority might encounter difficulties in looking at such matters objectively. As such, one could look to the example of the assessor, who although appointed by a local authority carries out independent functions in relation to issues of valuation, as a model of autonomy. A sure way to incorporate the beneficial aspects of this model would be directly to endow this already existing official with the functions of the registration officer.

The office of assessor would also be a convenient locus for the new set of responsibilities on account of the degree of relevant knowledge and the number of related existing practices attached to the former role. Issues which have traditionally fallen within the remit of the assessor and which continued to do so under this Act (see especially s.2 above) concerning the identification of domestic and non-domestic subjects, together with issues arising out of his new functions relating to the identification and apportionment of part residential subjects (see Sched. 1 below) are directly relevant to questions as to whether and in what manner particular persons should be registered in the new community charges register and as to their consequent liability for any of the new taxes.

In particular, the registration officer's duty to maintain an updated record of liability in the register under subs. (4) below requires him to decide the following questions which are also pertinent to the office of assessor: whether premises are domestic subjects and, therefore, not subject to non-domestic rates in relation to the tests of both personal community charge liability and standard community charge liability by virtue of ss.8(8)(d) and 10(2)(b) respectively; whether premises are part residential subjects in relation to the test of personal community charge liability, again by virtue of s.8(8)(d); and whether premises constitute a dwelling house in relation to standard community charge liability by virtue of s.10(2)(a). Apart from this direct functional inter-dependence, it should also be noted that, as a matter of administrative fact though not of legal necessity (Representation of the People Act 1983 s.8(3)), the roles of assessor and electoral registration officers are already combined in Scotland. Thus, according to the then Under Secretary of State, Mr. Michael Ancram M.P., "the expertise in registration procedures associated with those functions will be useful in setting up and maintaining an accurate community charges register", (1st Scot.S.C., col. 823).

The merits of the autonomy argument are undeniable, although certain qualifications may be made. First, given that in aggregate terms the capacity of the assessor and registration officer to affect the tax yield of the local authority under the new system is limited, the dangers of role conflict, in the absence of an element of independence from the local authority, should not be over-played. Secondly, the use of the existing office of the assessor is not the only means whereby the Government could have achieved its aim in this respect, and indeed, given that the assessor is technically an appointee of the local authority albeit independent in his professional function, it is perhaps not the ideal model on which to draw.

The expertise argument is much more contentious. Functional interdependence is not necessarily a good argument in favour of the collapsing of differences between, and the fusion of, roles. The roles of assessor and community charge registration officer may overlap but are not identical, and particularly as the statutorily required rating revaluation in 1990 will coincide with the early stages of implementation of the community charge and maintenance of the new community charges register, a not inconsiderable burden will be placed on the incumbent of both roles immediately on assumption of the dual responsibility. Also, even within the area of overlap, the combination of roles may promote conflict rather than harmony and economy of effort. Appeals from the assessor are to local valuation appeal committees, and from these by reference to the Lands Tribunal for Scotland and, ultimately, the Lands Valuation Appeal Court (see s.2(6) above), while appeals from the registration officer concerning questions relating to the validity of register entries and consequent liability to pay the new charge are to the sheriff court and from there to the Court of Session and, ultimately, to the House of Lords (see ss.16 and 19 below). The existence of these disparate avenues of appeal may mean that the authoritative directives being relayed to the two officers are at variance with one another, so placing their sole incumbent in an invidious position. Furthermore, as regards the functions of the assessor in relation to electoral registration, it might be argued that the heavy reliance upon the electoral register as a data base for the community charges register as is contemplated by this conjunction of roles and as is directly encouraged under s.17(2), may tempt some potential voters to refrain from having their names placed on the electoral register in order to attempt to avoid payment of the new tax. Under such circumstances, the label "poll-tax" would become an accurate reflection of the administrative reality if not the formal legal status of the new measure.

For each region or islands area. This entails that, in all areas other than those covered by the islands councils, the task of registration shall be performed at a regional level. As such, it is part of a wider policy pursued under the Act to provide that where there are within one geographical area two local authorities—regional and district—the administration of the tax is to be in large part the responsibility of the regional authority. This extends beyond matters of registration to those of levy, collection, payment and recovery under s.21 and Sched. 2 below. In the context of financial restrictions upon local government, this may, in the light of the technical inadequacies and administrative complexities of the new measure, prove to be a particularly heavy onus, and may cause a degree of friction between the two levels of local government. (See further, s.21 and Sched. 2 below.)

Subs. (3)

This subsection allows the regional or islands council to appoint as many depute registration officers as it considers necessary, in addition to the depute assessors who are automatically deemed to be depute registration officers by virtue of subs. (2) above, to enable the registration officer to perform his functions under the Act. It also provides that depute registration officers appointed by virtue of the subsection shall have all the functions of the registration officer.

Subs. (4)

This subsection requires the registration officer to prepare, maintain and keep up-dated the community charges register for his registration area. This is the foundation of the functional independence of the registration officer. The local authority cannot compel or prevent performance of these functions. Accordingly, any legal action to ensure compliance with his responsibilities, including an action of judicial review, would be against the officer directly.

Subs. (5)

This subsection requires the regional or islands council to ensure that the registration officer has sufficient staff, accommodation and other resources to perform his registration functions. It does not, however, create them registration authorities (see above).

Given the high degree of opposition to the new measure within Scottish local authorities, as articulated by the Convention of Scottish Local Authorities, (see for example, 'Paying for Local Government: the Convention's responses', C.O.S.L.A. 1986), this is one of the critical provisions within the Act which, by imposing significant financial and administrative obligations on the local authorities, appears to institutionalise a degree of conflict within the system which is required to operate the new measure. Partly this is a question of principle, in that it is possible that opposition to the philosophy underpinning the Act may be translated into practice by omitting to carry out, or to carry out sufficiently diligently or enthusiastically, these actions which are required of local authorities in order to make the Act viable. Partly, and relatedly, it is a question of fiscal pressure, in that one element in the critique of the new Act is that in technical and administrative terms it is not cost effective. To require the very agencies who are the authors of such a critique to bear the financial burden of administrative inefficiency, may compound the error in their eyes, and may risk providing a significant tactical and ideological platform for those within such local authorities who contemplate resisting the implementation of the Act. In anticipation of some of these objections and dangers, the Government did stipulate that the cost of registration is to be treated as relevant expenditure for the purposes of the new revenue support grant to be introduced under s.23 of, and Sched. 4 to this Act, and that, as such, the above administrative costs would ultimately be met centrally. (1st Scot.S.C., col. 825, *per* Michael Ancram, M.P.) However, as the debates on the Bill amply illustrate, the element of genuine uncertainty as to the administrative and financial implications of registration together with the opposing perspectives and interests of the proponents and opponents of the measure in relation to the question of the cost and feasibility of the new administrative infrastructure, including the register, entail that this area of dispute will not easily be resolved. As such, with regard to the question of the overall fate and legitimacy of the new measure, much could yet turn on the attitudes and strategy of local authorities in relation to the fulfilment of their obligations under this subsection.

Secure the provision of. This allows the regional or islands authority either to provide the relevant staff, accommodation and other items required from its own resources, or to agree with another body that they should make such provision on its behalf. This leaves the way open for collaboration between regional and district authorities as regards the administration of the new register and indeed between the regional authority and any agency outwith local government. In the latter case at least, any such arrangement would presumably be on a commercial basis.

Community Charges Register

Community Charges Register

13.—(1) There shall be a Community Charges Register (to be known as such but, in this Act, referred to as "the register") for each registration area which shall specify—

(a) in relation to the personal community charge—
  (i) the name of every person liable to pay the personal community charge in the registration area; and
  (ii) the address of his sole or main residence;

(b) in relation to the standard community charge—
  (i) the name and address of every person liable to pay the standard community charge in the registration area;
  (ii) the address of the premises in the registration area in respect of which the standard community charge for which he is liable is payable;

(c) in relation to the collective community charge—
  (i) the name and address of every person liable to pay the collective community charge in the registration area;
  (ii) the address of the premises in the registration area in respect of which the collective community charge for which he is liable is payable;
  (iii) the collective community charge multiplier determined in respect of those premises for the time being by the registration officer under section 11(9) of this Act;

(d) in relation to each natural person registered in the register, his date of birth;

(e) in relation to each person registered, the date (which may be before, on, or after the date on which the entry is made) from which he is liable to pay any of these community charges; and

(f) such other matters as may be prescribed.

(2) There shall not be specified in the register any information relating to a person's liability, by virtue only of section 8(7) of this Act, for a personal community charge.

(3) The register shall be kept in such form (which need not be documentary form) as may be prescribed.

DEFINITIONS
"collective community charge multiplier": s.11(9), (10).
"community charge": ss.7 and 26.
"community charges register": ss.13 and 26.
"prescribed": ss.26 and 31.
"registration area": s.26.

GENERAL NOTE
This section provides for the creation of a single community charges register for each registration area and specifies that it is to contain the names and addresses of the persons liable to pay any of the community charges, the dates from which such liability commences, and in the case of natural persons, their dates of birth. In the case of the standard and the collective community charges, the address of the premises in respect of which the charge is to be payable is also to be entered, while in the case of the collective community charge, the register will record the multiplier for the time being applicable. The register will also contain such additional information as may be prescribed, with the exception of information relating to joint and several liability under s.8(7) and will be kept in a form which is again subject to prescription at a future date.

By specifying the data to be contained in the register, this section begins to elaborate upon the nature of the information base required for the administration of the new charge. As such, it introduces us to a tension endemic in the Act between the difficulties of obtaining sufficient information for the effective and comprehensive application of the new tax and the need to ensure the relevance, accuracy, and confidentiality of such personal information as is held concerning individuals. Accordingly, for a full understanding of these issues and of how they may be resolved in terms of the legislative scheme adopted, this section should be read together with other sections relevant to this set of questions, ss.14, 17, 18, 19 and 20, and in particular with ss.17 and 20 which deal respectively with matters relating to the nature and limits of the access of the registration officer to information from public and private sources for the purposes of compiling the register and carrying out his duties, and with matters relating to the powers of inspection of the register enjoyed by various persons.

Subs. (1)
This provides that there is to be one community charges register for each registration area, and specifies the entries which are to be made in the register in respect of the three community charges. It was contended by the Government that the creation of a single register was preferable to the creation of a number of registers—one for each type of community charge—on a number of grounds.

First, a change in the use of premises might require a corresponding alteration in the type of community charge which they attract, and the documentation of such a change is achieved much more easily and conveniently within one register than between several. Secondly, the creation of several registers would expedite the identification of properties such as refuges and second homes by persons who might thereby be in a position to harm the interests of the occupants or owners of such premises. (1st Scot.S.C., cols. 840–841). In theory, the mere existence of a single register does not shield the identity of such properties, but the restrictions on public access contained in s.20 (see especially s.20(2)(a)(iii)) together with the difficulty involved in gleaning information from a larger internally undifferentiated register would suggest that in practice the process of identification will be decidedly more difficult under the system as constituted.

Para. (a)
This specifies that entries relating to the personal community charge are to comprise the name of every person liable to pay it and the address of his sole or main residence (see s.8 above).

Para. (b)
This specifies that entries relating to the standard community charge are to comprise the name and address of every person liable to pay it together with the address of the premises in the registration area in respect of which he is liable to pay the standard community charge. The fact that, in so far as the address of the person liable to pay the standard charge is interpreted as being his sole or main residence or otherwise differentiated from the address of the residence for which the standard charge is payable, two addresses will be placed against his entry and will thereby distinguish it from a personal community charge or collective community charge entry, is not inconsistent with the intention of avoiding a "burglar's charter" by preventing the general disclosure as to whether a particular residence is being used as a second home. This is so because the effect of s.20(2)(a)(ii) will be to ensure that such information will only be specified in that part of the register, the contents of which are not generally available.

Para. (c)
This paragraph specifies that entries relating to the collective community charge are to comprise the name and address of every person liable to pay it, the address of the premises in respect of which a charge is payable, and the collective community charge multiplier which the registration officer has determined in relation to these premises in terms of s.11(9) and (10). The rationale for making available the information as to the multiplier, to a larger or smaller audience depending upon circumstances yet to be prescribed (see s.20(2)(a)(iii)), is that it will provide a safeguard additional to those already provided in s.11(13)–(16) against exploitation of the system of administration and payment of the collective charge by those directly liable to pay it, to the detriment either of local authorities to whom the collective charge is due under s.11(6) or those individuals liable to make a collective community charge contribution under s.11(11). It is envisaged that by checking the figure of the multiplier as specified in the register against his own first hand knowledge of the number of persons normally resident within the premises in question, the person liable to make a

contribution, or for that matter, any other informed observer, will be in a position to discern abuses of the system (1st Scot.S.C., col. 870). However, in the absence of the use of prescriptive powers under s.20(3) to make details of the multiplier available for inspection on the premises in question, it is doubtful whether the assumptions concerning the vigilance of those making collective community charge contributions on which the justification of the provision depends will be borne out in practice.

Para. (d)

This provision, which was introduced as a Government amendment at Report Stage in the Commons, provides that the register should show the date of birth of each individual registered. Its purpose is to provide for those involved in the administration of the tax, an additional aid to the identification of liable persons in circumstances of potential confusion, such as where a number of members of a family and household are known by the one name, or where a liable person enters his name on the register claiming to have recently moved from another registration area and the registration officer wishes to confirm the veracity of his claim by inspecting the records from the other area as he will be entitled to do under s.17(3).

The term "natural person" is used in recognition of the fact that while it is possible that bodies having artificial personality such as companies may be liable to pay the standard or the collective charges and so may be named under subs. (1)(b)–(c) above, this category must be specifically exempted from this requirement as it is obviously inapplicable to their situation.

Para. (e)

This provides that the entry for each person should specify the date from which his liability to pay any of the community charges shall run. This date may be the same as the date on which the entry was made or it may be before or after it. This is one of a package of flexible measures which is required on account of the operation of s.19, which provides that, subject only to the provisions for appeal contained in s.16 and 29, the register will be treated as conclusive on matters relating to the identity of the person liable for any of the taxes and the date from which they are to be treated as so liable. The attribution of such a status to the register is important both for the purposes of predictability in the administration of the tax, and also in order that the register can be treated as a reliable guide to the overall picture of tax payment within the area by those persons legitimately interested therein and within the limits and safeguards provided by the restrictions on powers of inspection under s.20. However, the danger exists that such certainty is purchased only at the expense of a certain rigidity and of occasional anomalies and injustices to individuals. Accordingly, the aim of this measure is to help to prevent these costs from accruing. It does so by admitting of the possibility that the point of commencement of liability of an individual will not and cannot always be simultaneous with the point of entry of his name onto the register, largely because of the impossibility of maintaining an up to date record of all information bearing upon questions of liability which is entered in the register, and so provides for this distinction to be recognised. This introduces an element of flexibility in respect of decisions to be made as regards entries within and the uses of the register. The attempt within this provision to combine flexibility with uncertainty in an appropriate mix, is complemented by the operation of s.15 which deals with amendments to the register.

Para. (f)

This allows for the register to include such other matters as the Secretary of State may prescribe. It is envisaged that matters to be prescribed may include information as to whether or not the person on the register is a student or whether child benefit is paid under the Child Benefit Act 1975. (*Hansard*, H.C. Vol. III, col. 1000, *per* Ian Lang M.P.). As may be inferred from these two examples, and as is evident from the comments of ministers, (see also, 1st Scot.S.C., cols. 851–853, *per* Michael Ancram M.P.), the rationale underpinning the assumption of powers of prescription in this context is the desire to include in the register information directly relevant to and necessary for the resolution of questions of whether a particular person is or is not liable to pay any charge, and if so, which type or types of charge are due and in what form they are payable. (For example, information on which answers to questions as to the applicability of the conditions specified in s.8(4) and s.8(8) depend.) This type of information relating to matters which are directly constitutive of liability and indicative of its form may be contrasted with information whose possession by the registration officer would merely be administratively convenient, such as whether a person is to be treated as a responsible person (s.17(5)), or the national insurance number of the person (possibly relevant as an additional aid to identification of the person and, in particular, in relation to the recovery of community charge debt). In the course of the debate cited above, this latter category of information and items which fall within it were explicitly rejected by the Government as matters requiring to be entered onto the face of the register.

In the light of the above considerations, it is unclear why the aims of this subsection could not have been satisfied by means of the stipulation of an exhaustive list or, at least, bearing in mind that the categories of persons exempt from the charge may effectively be varied by the use of prescriptive powers (for example those in s.2(3)(b) and 2(4) bearing upon the distinction between domestic and non-domestic subjects), by means of a principle relating the contents of the register directly to such modifications. Such an approach would have obviated the need for the inclusion of open ended prescriptive powers in a sensitive area such as this, concerned as it is with the gathering and the retention by a public agency of private information. Ss. 17 and 20 afford some protection against the abuse of this facility: furthermore, the laws of confidentiality, and of defamation and negligence, together with certain of the provisions in the Data Protection Act 1984 provide some safeguards in situations where private information is unlawfully disseminated or used for purposes other than originally intended. Nevertheless, the identification of unlawful and negligent acts and/or breaches of confidence is notoriously problematic in the domain of public agencies. This is so because the unlawful passing or improper use of information often involves agencies which have a degree of functional interdependence and each of whom has an independent capacity to access a vast amount of information relating to members of the public which may be potentially useful to its fellow agencies. Accordingly, it may be perceived to be in both or all of their interests either to endorse or at least not explicitly to frustrate or oppose such an action either on the basis of a sense of perceived common interest or of a calculation of future mutual benefit. Accordingly, any measure which extends the obligation of or increases the capacity of any public agency to collect private information may be seen to heighten the possibility of the development of relationships where such abuses may be contemplated, and so should be carefully scrutinised in order to determine its necessity in principle and its proper scope of application. These themes are further developed in ss.14, 17, and 20 below.

Subs. (2)

This subsection provides that no information concerning joint and several liability, which arises in respect of the personal community charge in the case of married or co-habiting couples under s.8(7) of this Act, is to be shown on the register. This is the only type of information which is specifically prohibited from inclusion on the register.

Subs. (3)

This subsection provides that the Secretary of State may prescribe the form in which a register is to be kept, and that it need not be documentary in nature. Accordingly, it is envisaged that the style and layout of the register shall be uniform across all registration areas.

Which need not be documentary form. This qualification is in recognition of the fact that, increasingly, it will become expedient for registration officers to hold the register and information contained therein on a computerised file or files. Such a development, however, may also precipitate certain problems relating to issues of confidentiality on the one hand, and of accessibility of information to data subjects on the other.

The general problem of confidentiality in this context has already been touched upon under s.13(1)(f) above. Such is the nature of computer technology, that its use for the purposes of maintaining the register may facilitate unauthorised access to data by third parties, with or without the consent of the data holder. By the same token, the transcription of the register into computerised form will render it subject to the provisions of the Data Protection Act 1984. Basically, the aim of that Act is to provide against the illegitimate use and unlawful disclosure of information held on computer, by means of the elaboration of a number of data protection principles (Data Protection Act 1984, Sched. 1, Pt. I). These principles provide a regulatory code which applies to all registered data users (ss.1 and 4), which category effectively includes all persons or bodies holding data for the purposes of automatic processing, including the registration officer under this Act, since under s.5 of the 1984 Act it is a criminal offence to hold data in the relevant form yet remain unregistered. The principles in question provide, *inter alia*, that personal data should be held only for one or more specified lawful purposes (Sched. 1, Pt. I, para. 1), that it shall not be used or disclosed in any manner incompatible with that purpose or those purposes (Sched. 1, Pt. I, para. 3) that it shall be adequate, relevant and not excessive in relation to that purpose or those purposes (Sched. 1, Pt. I, para. 4), that it shall be accurate, and where necessary, kept up to date (Sched. 1, Pt. I, para. 5), that it shall not be kept for any longer than is necessary for the said purpose or purposes (Sched. 1, Pt. I, para. 6), that an individual shall be entitled at reasonable intervals and without undue delay or expense to be informed by any data user whether any information at which he is the subject is held, and to access such data and, where appropriate, have it corrected or erased (Sched. 1, Pt. I, para. 6), and that appropriate security measures shall be taken against unauthorised access to, or alteration, disclosure or destruction of, personal data and against its accidental loss or destruction (Sched. 1, Pt. I, para. 8). The main responsibility for enforcing the above principles lies with the Data Protection Registrar (s.3), who may issue enforcement notices (s.10). Breach of the principles may also constitute a criminal offence to be prosecuted by the Procurator Fiscal (s.19). Finally, unauthorised disclosure may give rise to a civil claim for compensation (s.23). As such, on account of the information being held in computerised form, there exists a more specific package of statutory rules and sanctions dovetailing with the common law protections contained in the laws of confidence, defamation, and negligence. The statutory scheme described above is in its early stages of implementation and, thus, its effectiveness for the purposes of the present Act cannot as yet be predicted. However, its impact is bound to be somewhat diluted—by virtue of the operation of s.28 of the D.P.A. which, *inter alia*, exempts personal data from the subject-access (s.28(1)) and non-disclosure (s.28(3)) provisions where the data are held for the purpose of the assessment or collection of any tax or duty and subject-access or disclosure would be likely to be prejudicial thereto, which exemptions might presumably embrace certain forms of information storage and passage relating to the various community charges. In particular, the effect of this proviso may be to undermine two safeguards against abuse of privacy which would otherwise exist in respect of the community charges.

First, there is the question of the "second life . . . behind the register" (N.C.C.L.: "The Privacy Implications of the Poll Tax", October 1987) which might be required to supplement the official register in order to assist the registration officer in the performance of his functions. If such a "file behind the file" is compiled, then, even if it is stored in computerised form, it might be argued that the information contained therein should not be made accessible to the subject for the reasons outlined above, thus reducing the value of the right granted to the registered person under s.20(1) of the present Act to inspect the whole of his entry. In short, he may only be entitled to examine the tip of the information iceberg. Secondly, the exemption in question may prejudice the position of the individual in relation to whom information is held in a computerised form by one of the persons or bodies specified under s.17(2)–(4) as being obliged to supply the registration officer with information required by him to discharge his functions under the Act. Under the terms of s.28(3) of the D.P.A., such persons and bodies (*i.e.* the local assessor and electoral registration officer; the regional or islands council, any district council, or any housing body in the registration area of the community charges registration officer; or the registration officer of any other registration area) will not be in breach of the non-disclosure provisions in the event of divulging information concerning a subject to the registration officer, even without prior intimation of such a purpose to the subject in question, provided that they can justify such disclosure on the basis of the need to avoid prejudicing the assessment or collection of the community charges. However, in the circumstances described, it may be that the individual may be afforded some protection under the common law of confidence. (See also notes on ss.17(3) and 20(1) below.)

As suggested, the facility to maintain the register in computerised form raises issues of accessibility of the information to data subjects themselves. S.20(1), (3), (6) and (7) make it clear that a data subject has power to inspect the whole of each entry in the register relating to him and, upon payment of a fee, to request a copy. However, fears have been expressed that such information will not be capable of easy recovery and assimilation by some persons unless it is available in documentary form, and that this is not guaranteed by s.20, subs. (7) of which provides that a "copy (need only be) in a form in which it is legible and can be taken away". This condition could be met by the provision of a "tablet of stone . . . or [a] microfiche" (1st Scot.S.C., col. 889, *per* John Home Robertson M.P.) just as adequately by the provision of a document. Similarly, s.21 of the Data Protection Act 1984, merely empowers the data subject to require a copy of information constituting personal data referring to him, but does not specify the form in which such a copy is to be provided. Nevertheless, the Under Secretary of State, Mr. Ian Lang, M.P., did undertake that the copy of personal information to be available to be taken away under s.20 would be in documentary form, "almost certainly in the form of a computer print-out". (1st Scot.S.C., col. 889.)

Setting up of register

14.—(1) The registration officer shall, as from such date as may be prescribed, undertake such inquiries as he considers necessary to enable him to determine—

(a) the names and addresses of persons who will be liable to pay any of the community charges on 1st April 1989;

(b) the premises in respect of which the standard community charge and the collective community charge will be payable on 1st April 1989,

and thereafter shall prepare the register by such date as may be prescribed as the date of coming into force of the register.

(2) After the date of coming into force of the register the registration officer shall, within such period and in such manner as may be prescribed, send to each person whose name is entered in the register a copy of each entry relating to that person together with a notice in such form as may be prescribed informing him of—

(a) the effect of the entry in the register;

(b) the rights of appeal under section 16 of this Act; and

(c) the requirement imposed by section 18(2) of this Act to notify the registration officer of any changes to be made to the entry.

DEFINITIONS

"community charge": s.26.
"prescribed": s.26.
"register": s.26.
"registration officer": s.26.

GENERAL NOTE

This is the crucial paving section of the Act, in that it makes provision for the initial establishment of the register which is the key document for the purposes of determining liability in relation to all of the new charges (see s.19 below). It provides that the registration officer is to make inquiries in order to determine to his satisfaction both the names and addresses of all persons who will be subject to any of the three new charges as of April 1, 1989, being the date when the new system of taxation comes into operation (see s.9 above), and the identity of those premises in respect of which the standard and collective charges will become payable on that date. It further provides that the registration officer has a duty thereafter to notify persons who have been entered on the register of the fact and contents of such an entry and of its implications for the incurrence of liability to pay a charge, the acquisition of rights of appeal, and the assumption of an obligation to inform the registration officer of future changes in circumstances relevant to one's entry.

In general terms, this section is relevant to an understanding of the substantive means to be employed by the registration officer in administering the Act, the nature of certain procedural checks which are to be introduced in respect of such methods, and the timetabling of the initial stages of the operation. However, none of these matters is fully resolved or provided for within the four corners of this section as presently constituted, but, as shall be demonstrated below, requires in order to be fully understood, elaboration by reference to delegated powers or to the operation of other sections of the Act.

Subs. (1)

This provides that, from such date as the Secretary of State may prescribe, the registration officer will make the inquiries he considers necessary to allow him to determine the names and addresses of persons who will be liable to pay a community charge as of April 1, 1989, and the premises which will be subject to either the collective or the standard charge as of the same date. It also provides for the preparation of the register to be completed by a date to be prescribed by the Secretary of State, which will be the date that the register comes into force. During the passage of the Bill, it was estimated that the prescribed date for the commencement of inquiries would be May or June 1988, and that for the register coming into force would be around October 1988 (presumably now confirmed as October 1, 1988, by the commencement of ss.18–20 on that date). The idea of providing a timetable of universal application was defended on the grounds that it would prevent the confusions and resulting omissions and inaccuracies which would otherwise arise under a scheme which permitted the exercise of local discretion, in those cases where the sole or main residence of a person liable to pay charge changed at a point during the gestation period of the register after initial inquiries had been carried out by the registration officer in the area of one's previous residence but before inquiries had been initiated by that officer in the area of one's new residence (1st Scot.S.C., col. 894, *per* Michael Ancram, M.P.).

The registration officer shall . . . undertake such inquiries as he considers necessary. The nature and extent of the powers conferred by this provision should be construed in the light of s.17. It is envisaged that the initial thrust of the inquiries of the registration officer will take the form of a mass canvass of "responsible persons" under s.17(6) of the Act. Any subsequent inquiries required to complete the preparation of the initial register, and indeed to maintain and update the register thereafter, may involve the requesting of information from various persons or bodies under duties imposed and powers conferred by s.17(1)–(3) of the Act. However, the exercise of such powers *vis-à-vis* any local authority within his area or any department or area of functional responsibility within such a local authority, any local housing body, or the registration officer of any other area, will be subject to the power of the Secretary of State to prescribe that certain classes of information will not be supplied by such persons or bodies, (see s.17(4) below). Furthermore, the data protection principles enumerated under Sched. 1, Pt. I of the Data Protection Act 1984 will function so as to complement these restrictions by placing limits and conditions upon the storage of information by the registration officer and the passage of information to him by the relevant persons and bodies, subject to the operation of s.28 of that Act which provides exemption from the subject-access and non-disclosure provisions where these would be likely to prejudice the assessment or collection of the charge (see s.13(3) above).

The practicability of the set of methods for the pursuit of inquiries envisaged above very much depends upon the efficiency of the canvass. Comparisons with other widely based canvasses such as those undertaken in relation to the electoral register and the census are not necessarily helpful as in those cases there will be an incentive or at least no disincentive to provide accurate and comprehensive information, something which cannot be guaranteed when the consequence of such full and frank disclosure is the imposition of tax liability on a person or persons. As such, the value to be attributed to the canvass as a tool for gathering information is very much a matter of speculation at present. Given that the effectiveness of the back-up methods is an equally unknown quantity in the absence of any experience of their operation or, indeed, of specification of their legitimate scope under s.17(4), and that what will constitute a satisfactory level of accuracy and comprehensiveness of coverage as regards the initial coverage from the point of view of the Government remains similarly unspecified, it is very difficult to know what to make of the claim by the Government that they envisage that the extra cost incurred in setting up the register in 1988–89 will be "about £6 million" (1st Scot.S.C., col. 911, *per* Michael Ancram, M.P.). In any attempt to evaluate the exercise of setting up the register, it has to be recognised that the efficacy of canvassing techniques, the scope of investigative powers, the amount of financial resources deployed, and the accuracy and the comprehensiveness of the final record are all interrelated variables. Accordingly, values relating to financial efficiency in public administration, the protection of private information, and the creation of an information base of a quality to ensure optimal achievement of the ends of fairness and accountability specified as among the main criteria against which the success of the Act should be measured, cannot be simultaneously maximised, and choices will have to be made in practice as to which are to be accorded the greatest priority.

Subs. (2)

This subsection provides that, after the register comes into force, the registration officer is to send to every person whose name is entered on the register a copy of each entry relating to him together with notification of three other items of information relating to the incurrence of obligations and the acquisition of rights attendant upon registration: first, the effect of the entry, namely that he will be liable to pay a charge from the date specified on the register, and in the case of the collective charge, at the rate specified by the multiplier in terms of s.19: secondly, his rights of appeal against the entry to the registration officer and, thereafter, to the sheriff, in terms of s.16 of the Act: thirdly, the requirement placed upon him by s.18(2) of the Act to notify the registration officer of any changes to be made to any entry relating to him within one month of the event which has given rise to the change.

The notification is to be carried out within such period and in such manner as the Secretary of State may prescribe. It is envisaged that a period of some four to six weeks after the register has come into force will be prescribed for notification. Amendments were moved by the Opposition in Committee Stage in the Commons in the attempt both to have specified in advance a date before which notification would have to take place and to ensure that such notification would require the person in question to be "informed personally" of the relevant information (1st Scot.S.C., cols. 896–908). The justification for the first of these mooted alterations was that unless such a discipline was introduced there was a danger that the period of negotiation of the accuracy of the initial register would overlap with the period from which liability would commence, so inevitably leading to a higher incidence of wrongful payment and non-payment of tax in the earlier stages than would otherwise occur. The justification for the second, which would appear to involve the assumption of an additional onerous administrative responsibility by the registration officer, was that if notification by post were deemed to be adequate then it might result in a situation in which the very persons who were most likely to have legitimate grounds to appeal against the initial register would be least likely to be able to do so. Persons erroneously registered at a particular address might not be in a position to receive a communication posted to that address intended to inform them of that fact and so would be unable to correct the original mistake. In resisting these amendments and insisting that these matters would be dealt with by regulation, the Government did not provide any guarantees that these or similar safeguards would be enshrined in such regulations. Indeed, it may well be that given the enormity of the task involved in setting up the initial register, any such guarantees would not be proof against the dangers contemplated by the Opposition unless a longer period of preparation than has been countenanced under the Act were allowed prior to the charges coming into effect.

The Secretary of State may also prescribe the form in which the notification of the information specified in this subsection is to be given.

It should be noted that this subsection is intended only to refer to persons who are entered in the register at the point at which it initially comes into force. Individual residents who become liable at a later date, together with those who are liable at the point when the register comes into force but whose liability is not recorded at that time, possess no rights under the Act to be notified by the registration officer of any matter relating to any entry in respect of them in the register until such time as that entry is amended (see s.15(5) below). As is specified under s.18 below, individual residents have an active rather than a passive role in relation to the provision of registration information (s.18(1) and (2)), and this is underlined by the absence of any obligation towards them under this subsection.

Amendment of register

15.—(1) As from the date of coming into force of the register, it may be amended by the registration officer at any time and amendments may be made with retrospective, immediate or prospective effect, except that—

(a) the maximum period for which an amendment can be made with retrospective effect is two years; and

(b) no amendment of the collective community charge multiplier in respect of any premises shall be made or take effect until three months, or such other period as may be prescribed, after the date when the current entry is made or takes effect, whichever is later.

(2) The registration officer may at any time alter the register to correct any clerical or typographical error in any entry and subsection (1)(b) above and subsections (3) and (5) below shall not apply to any such alteration.

(3) The registration officer shall before amending an entry in the register ensure that a record (which need not be in documentary form) is made of the entry and shall retain this record for two years from the date on which it was made.

(4) The record made under subsection (3) above may be inspected in like manner as the register may be inspected under section 20 of this Act.

(5) The registration officer shall not be obliged to consult the person registered or to be registered before making any amendment to the register which might affect that person, but he shall, within such period and in such manner as may be prescribed, send to the person who is or was registered—

(a) a copy of the amendment; or

(b) where the amendment is a deletion or substitution of the whole or

      part of an existing entry, a notification of the deletion or substitution,
together with a notice in such form as may be prescribed informing him of—

(i) the effect of the amendment in the register;
(ii) the rights of appeal under section 16 of this Act;
(iii) the requirement imposed by section 18(2) of this Act to notify the registration officer of any changes to be made to the entry.

DEFINITIONS
"collective community charge multiplier": s.11(9) and (10).
"prescribed": ss.29 and 31.
"register": ss.13 and 26.
"registration officer": ss.12 and 26.

GENERAL NOTE
This section provides for the register to be substantively amended at any time by the registration officer with retrospective, immediate or prospective effect, subject to limited restrictions as to the frequency of certain types of amendments and the extent of back-dating of corrections permitted (subs. (1)). Pursuant upon this power of amendment, the registration officer also acquires a number of duties under this section. He is required to preserve records of entries for two years after the amendment thereof (subs. (3)), which historical records will be made available for inspection under the same conditions as those applicable to the current register as specified in s.20(4). He is also required to notify the person, whose entry has been amended, of the amendment, the effect thereof, his rights of appeal and his duty under s.18(2) to report the need for any further changes in the amended register. He need not, however, consult the person in question before making any amendment to the register which might affect him (subs. (5)). Finally, in the case of non-substantive amendment—those of a clerical or a typographical nature—the registration officer may make alterations without any frequency bar, and without any requirement to maintain a record or inform the person affected by the change in the manner required in the case of substantive amendments (subs. (2)).
In the Green Paper, there was expressed a preference for the concept of a "rolling register" recording changes in the liability to pay the community charge in respect of the tests laid down in ss.8, 10 and 11, as they occur. This concept is given legislative expression through the provision of the facilities necessary to introduce a system of continuous amendment in the present section, and through s.19, the effect of which is to provide that the "rolling" record of liability at any point in time is conclusive of the actual detailed pattern of liability at that time.

Subs. (1)
This subsection provides the registration officer with the power to amend the register at any time after it comes into force, with retrospective, immediate, or prospective effect. The retrospective application of amendments is limited to a period of two years. In the particular case of the collective charge multiplier, with the exception of clerical and typographical errors under subs. (2), it is further stipulated that no amendments are to be made or take effect until three months, or such other period as may be prescribed by the Secretary of State, after the later of the dates on which any existing entry was made or took effect.
This subsection provides the statutory fulcrum for the rolling register. Opinion both within and outwith Parliament remained divided during the period of the passage of the Bill as to the relative merits of rolling and fixed annual registers (see also, s.8 above). Indisputably, with its greater degree of responsiveness to change, the rolling register meets the criteria of fairness and accountability much more effectively than the fixed register. In the case of the electoral register—an example of a fixed register—the degree of inaccuracy at the point immediately prior to the annual readjustment may be as much as 15 to 20 per cent. Even allowing that a significant proportion of such inaccuracies would relate to changes of residence within the boundaries of particular district or islands authorities and thus would be irrelevant to the question of liability for the community charge, the fixed register would still result in a substantial number of persons who, for the part of the financial year after which they moved house and area, would be paying tax to a local authority from whose services they did not benefit and would be receiving services from a local authority to whose budget they did not contribute. However, these considerations must be balanced against considerations of technical adequacy which may tip the scales in the other direction. The

maintenance of an ongoing record may impose an unacceptable administrative and financial burden upon the registration officer and the regional and islands councils who are required to support him under s.12(5). Furthermore, the device of the canvass which it is intended to employ in the construction of the register (see ss.14 above and 17 below), is more suited to the fixed register. Logistical problems inherent in the mass canvass may be highlighted and may prove particularly problematic if the aim is to produce a rolling register. Such logistical problems, arising from the timescale involved in carrying out such a canvass, exist equally in the case of a fixed register, but the inaccuracies that they produce do not offend against the principle of fixed liability, which acknowledges an in-built margin of error in any case).

Para. (a)

While the general principle of retrospective alteration must be conceded in order to provide an administrative remedy both for persons who have been erroneously held liable to pay charge at an earlier point and for registration officers who have failed to establish the liablity of a person until after its commencement, the more detailed question of the maximum period within which such a retrospective amendment should be competent is more difficult to resolve. By a process of negotiation based upon rather obscure reasoning, the Government were prevailed upon, first, to jettison the idea of placing no restriction upon the back-dating period in favour of a definite three-year maximum, and then to reduce the three-year threshold to one of two years (*Hansard*, H.L. Vol. 486, cols. 1709–1710). In so far as any rationale emerged, the final choice of two years appears to have been made on the basis that it minimises the possibility both of successful avoidance techniques and of imposing an undue financial burden upon persons who have inadvertently escaped liability in the past. A period of more than two years was seen as exposing to the risk of considerable financial penalty persons whose liability had not been recognised due to administrative error at a much earlier date. Conversely, a period of less than two years was seen as providing an incentive for persons to contemplate techniques of tax evasion with a reasonable chance of success: equally, it could be argued that such a threshold unreasonably restricts the time limit within which a person erroneously held liable to pay tax at an earlier date might challenge the original decision of the registration officer. Of course, a person who has a legitimate grievance concerning the decision of a registration officer may appeal under s.16 to the sheriff, whose power to require the registration officer to amend the register retrospectively is unrestricted (s.16(4)). However, it would be absurd if the person had to undergo court proceedings in a case where there might conceivably be no longer any matter in dispute between the appellant and the registration officer, merely in order to trigger the amendment of the register. Such a possibility is still conceivable under the legislation as it stands in cases where errors are not detected until two years have passed, but it is much less likely to be realised in practice than it would have been if a period of, say, one year had been stipulated as a maximum within which a purely administrative correction was competent.

Para. (b)

The justification for imposing this special restriction in the case of the collective community charge multiplier derives from the method of calculation of the multiplier and the practical context in which it operates. The multiplier is an artifice, calculated with reference to factors to be prescribed under s.11(10), and is not intended to be a direct reflection of the actual number of persons within premises who are liable to pay collective community charge contributions at a particular time. The excessive buoyancy of the base of calculation which would otherwise be permitted and the need to place limits on the administrative burden to be imposed upon those liable to pay the collective community charge are the factors which support the use of such a device. As such, as it is the one example of a condition relevant to a test of liability of any of the charges which does not have an immediate and transparent empirical reference, and as there are sound administrative reasons why this should be the case, then to provide a power to amend the multiplier without any restriction upon frequency of use would be both to provide a capacity inappropriate to the tool being used—in that there is no direct requirement to respond to events as they happen—and also to reintroduce the administrative problems which the construction of the artifice was designed to eradicate. The three-month period is also provided for reasons of administrative convenience in relation to the alteration of apportionment notes in respect of part residential subjects under Sched. 1, para. 9).

Subs. (2)

This subsection enables the registration officer to correct clerical or typographical errors in any entry in the register. The two-year time bar upon the retrospective effect of amendment applies to these amendments just as it applies to those of a substantive nature but the requirement in the latter case that changes to the collective community charg multiplier should not be made at intervals more frequent than three months, does not apply Moreover, the requirements to preserve a record under subs. (3) and to notify the perso to whom the entry relates of any amendment made under subs. (5), do not apply. In th original Bill, "arithmetical errors" also fell within the ambit of the subsection. However, a amendment was successfully moved by John Maxton at Committee stage (1st Scot. S.C cols. 936–937) to delete this reference. It would appear that one of the intentions behind th amendment was to ensure that the figure of the collective community charge multiplier coul not be altered without the safeguards of recording and notification, since, unlike th amendments competent under the heads of clerical and typographical errors, an amendmen of this figure could be significant in terms of the liability of a person for community charge Ironically, however, the reasons given for accepting this amendment were other than thos initially advanced in favour of its inclusion; they were based on the assertion that nothin which would appear on the register, including the multiplier, could be properly described a "arithmetical" and, therefore, the term was redundant in this context. If the terms of thi argument are correct then the purpose of the Opposition in moving the amendment wil manifestly not have been achieved, as many errors in recording the collective communit charge multiplier will be subsumed under one of the other two categories of cosmetic errors An inaccuracy deriving from a more fundamental error in the calculation of liability will not however, be open to correction in this way.

Subs. (3)

This subsection requires the registration officer to preserve a record of any entry as it wa before amendment for a period of two years from the date that the entry was made. Just a with the "live" register itself, this record need not be in documentary form (see s.13(3)).

As is obvious from the history of its parliamentary development, which mirrors exactl that of subs. (1)(a), the provision of a two-year limit in this subsection is intended to dove tail precisely with the two-year limit in respect of retrospective amendments. There is a obvious rationale underpinning this process of matching, namely, that the information o the basis of which an administrative amendment may be advocated must be available for th entire period with reference to which the power of administrative amendment may b competently exercised, otherwise the evidential basis upon which certain changes, althoug theoretically possible, may be argued for may already have been erased. However, strictl speaking, this line of reasoning only sustains the thesis that the period of retention of th records should be at least as long as the period for which amendments are competent. I does not support the more specific thesis that the two periods should be identical. Thi logical jump between premise and conclusion may be significant, because there would appea to be grounds, independent of these considerations, for arguing that the period of retentio of the records should in fact be longer than two years.

First, there is a disalignment between administrative powers of amendment and judicia powers of amendment, which has already been noted under s.15(1), as a potential source c anomalies. Under s.16(4), the registration officer is obliged to amend the register in lin with the decision of a sheriff in determination of an appeal, without any restriction of tim whether it be retrospective or prospective (given the possibility of appeal to the Court o Session from the sheriff court on a point of law under s.29, presumably the registratio officer will be similarly required to give effect to the decision of that Court irrespective o the extent of retrospective or prospective application, although this is not specificall provided for. It is also presumably the case that, in the interim, he would still be require to give effect to the sheriff's decision). As such, on account of the two-year limit it is no inconceivable that the appeal process could be frustrated because of the absence of proof o the earlier entry unless the precaution had been taken at an earlier date to retain the cop of an initial entry under s.14(2) or of an amendment under s.15(5).

Secondly, there is the question of the utility of the register as a historical archive, as modern doomsday book of use to later scholars. Strict adherence to a two-year time limi would erase this unique source of information.

In response to both these arguments several points may be made. First, it might b pointed out that there is nothing in the section which *requires* the registration officer t dispose of the record after two years, he is simply permitted to do so, and it may well b that the record of the register will be available for the above purposes. If this response i met with the riposte that the caprice of the local registration officer is not a sound basis o which to provide for policy objectives, then considerations of relevance to the protection o private information may be invoked. Using a utilitarian calculus, the advantages to be gaine through the retention of records for the above purposes may be outweighed by the danger

d disadvantages involved in widening the scope for breaches of confidence. More
ecifically, one of the data protection principles enshrined in the Data Protection Act 1984
ates that "personal data held for any purpose or purposes shall not be held for longer than
is necessary for that purpose, or those purposes" (Sched. 1, Part I, para. 6) and this would
pear to place a legal limit, albeit not of determinate duration, upon the permissible length
retention of the relevant record, if it is to be held in computerised form. This restriction
ould not apply to those parts of the register which are publicly available for inspection at
point when they constitute the current record under s.20(2) since s.34(1) of the Data
otection Act exempts from the operative provisions of that Act," information which a
rson is required by or under any enactment to make available to the public." As such, a
mprehensive historical record of the names and addresses of persons within the register
ould not be prohibited by the terms of the Data Protection Act, and so for the purposes
archival research, if a historical record was retained to an extent permitted by statute, this
ould appear to strike a useful balance between the needs and interests of the researcher
d the desire to minimise disclosure of confidential information.

Additional safeguards, relating not to time limits within which records may be kept but to
e power of access to them during a period that they must be kept are spelled out in subs.
) below.

Finally, there is available under the Act another mechanism for preserving the record for
e purposes of appeals and archival research while respecting the confidentiality of private
formation. Under s.20(10), as inserted at Committee stage in the Lords (*Hansard*, H.L.
ol. 486, cols. 1148–1149), it is provided that the registration officer shall as soon as is
asonably practicable send a copy of the whole register as in force on April 1, each year to
e Keeper of the Records of Scotland for preservation by him. By virtue of s.20(11) it is
en provided that the keeper shall not make the register available for inspection nor issue
y extracts or certified copies except as may be prescribed.

This provision will not necessarily resolve all the problems mentioned above. In the first
ace, for a potential appellant, the record as at some point in time other than April 1 might
 important. Secondly, it was undertaken by the Government that the powers of prescription
 make the register publicly available would be used to provide that a period of 30 years
ould be required to elapse before publication of any particular record (*Hansard*, H.L. Vol.
6, col. 1149, *per* the Earl of Dundee). If honoured, this undertaking would seem to
ustrate both the person making a late appeal and the historian of the recent past.

Accordingly, although the provision under s.20(10)–(11) may open another avenue for
solving some of the problems and dilemmas considered above, it provides by no means a
ll answer, and so the possibilities and limitations of the present subsection remain relevant.

bs. (4)
This subsection specifies that any record made under subs. (3) may be inspected in terms
 s.20 below, in the same way as the register itself. Accordingly, as with the register itself,
ree different status generating three different levels of inspection rights will be created. At
e highest level, persons who appear on the register will have the right to inspect the whole
 each entry relating to them. Then there is a level of rights of access which are qualified
 considerations of functional necessity; a representative of the local authority, assessor, or
ectoral registration officer will be entitled to inspect the register to an extent necessary for
e exercise of his official functions. Finally, at the lowest level, members of the public will
ve access to the names and addresses of those persons who appear on the register and in
me cases, to the size of the collective community charge multiplier in respect of premises
hich attract the collective charge.

As such, this subsection extends the system of safeguards against breach of confidences
ntained in the register to the historical record of the register. In so far as such a system
 safeguards is effective, since it functions to restrict access to rather than to destroy the
cord, it provides a useful device which permits the preservation of the record for the
rposes of achieving the two functions specified in our discussion of subs. (3) above, *i.e.* of
rmitting change to any other decision on liability and of preserving useful historical data,
ithout generating corresponding problems and dangers of breaches of confidentiality on a
sproportionate scale.

bs. (5)
This subsection imposes one set of obligations on the registration officer, and specifically
empts him from another. The exemption is in respect of any requirement of consultation,
e registration officer not being obliged to consult in advance the person who will be
fected by any amendment of the register. The set of obligations imposed relates to various
atters of which the registration officer must notify, and materials which he must send to

the person affected by the amendment within a period to be prescribed of the making of th
amendment, and in a manner to be prescribed. The materials to be sent are a copy of th
amendment, or where the amendment takes the form of a deletion or substitution of all o
part of the entry, a notification of the deletion or substitution. The matters of which notic
is to be provided at the same time are the effects of the amendment in the register, th
rights of appeal provided under s.16, and the duty of a person under s.18(2) of this Act t
notify the registration officer of any further changes to be made in the register.

The registration officer shall not be obliged to consult. The Government resisted amend
ments moved by the opposition in both Houses which were aimed at removing this exemptio
and imposing a specific obligation to consult (*Hansard*, H.L. Vol. 486, cols. 945–948 an
1014–1015). It might reasonably be argued that an amendment which may significantly alte
the tax burden of someone and, moreover, may do so retrospectively up to a limit of tw
years, is of sufficient moment to warrant the prior consultation of that person. The argumen
of Lord Glenarthur that such a provision would be unnecessary in that most amendmen
would be triggered by persons whose entry was subject to amendment themselves notifyin
the registration officer of the need for such amendment under s.18(2), appears disingenuou
in that it relies upon rather tentative and disputable assumptions as the source of th
majority of amendments to the register, and in that it is unable to explain and justify th
failure to consult in that class of cases, however small, in which the affected person does nc
have prior knowledge (*Hansard*, H.L. Vol. 486, cols. 1014–1015). A much more persuasiv
justification for not imposing a duty of prior consultation, albeit not one drawn upon durin
the parliamentary debate, relates to the practical difficulties involved in fulfilling such a
obligation, and highlights one of the problems inherent in the system of regulation an
enforcement of a tax which is neither property dependent like rates, nor income dependen
like income tax. In the most general of terms, the absence of a source other than th
personhood of the relevant subject, which source would provide both a means of tracin
that person and an indication of his ability to pay, provides preconditions for default on
wider scale than would otherwise be the case. One way of countering this is to provide
framework of rules of liability which, while it does not provide any means of overcomin
such practical difficulties, does not provide any concessions in the face of them, and s
ensures that the tax payer is responsible for, or at least the cost of, any technical inadequac
of the system by which he has been adversely affected. The omission of a duty to consult i
an example of the strategy not to specify duties of notification on the part of the registratio
officer or under s.14 in relation to initial registration (whether in this present subsection i
relation to amendments) in too onerous a manner—as is also the absence of any exemptio
from the community surcharge provisions in s.18(3) in respect of someone unable to fulfi
his obligation under s.18(1) because unaware of his liability. To provide otherwise in any c
these cases, and in particular, in the present case, to impose a duty to consult and thus t
make contact in advance, would reveal the logistical difficulties involved in keeping track c
the vast majority of the adult population on a register the character of which does not revea
any obvious method of monitoring their whereabouts. Indeed, the whole thrust of Part II c
the Act is to ensure that liability in practice will follow from liability in theory (see especially
ss.14, 15, 18 and 19) and that, in the case of error, the onus lies upon the taxpayer to obtai
redress retrospectively (s.16). Perhaps the provision of a comprehensive appeals system i
the only way to combine efficiency with requirements of individual justice in the case of th
administration of a tax fraught with such practical difficulties, but perhaps also it might b
argued that the degree of temporary hardship which such a system countenances, i
unreasonable, in which case a compromise situation would have to be rejected as inadequat
and the general principle underlying such a system of liability would have to be called int
question.

Within such period and in such manner as may be prescribed. It is envisaged that th
prescribed period within which notification under the subsection must take place will be on
of "weeks rather than months" (1st Scot.S.C., col. 955). As regards the power to prescrib
the manner in which the notice is to be sent, in response to an amendment tabled by th
Opposition, Michael Ancram M.P. suggested that a "requirement to notify by recorde
delivery could be very onerous" (1st Scot.S.C., col. 948), so implying that ordinary posta
delivery would be sufficient and that there would be no obligation to ensure that the perso
to whom notice is sent actually receives that notice. This reluctance to enshrine administrativ
"best practice" in the legislation or even in the regulations is a further example of th
minimalist attitude of the Government towards the technical complexities and inadequacie
of the new Act commented upon above, and in particular, their desire to ensure that th
costs of any inefficiencies of the new system will be borne by the tax payer rather than b
the parties who collect the tax or to whom the tax is due.

Paras. (a) and (b)

In broad conceptual terms, an amendment of any piece of text may take one of three forms: addition, deletion, or substitution. Para. (b) deals with deletions and substitutions, and so by implication, since its function is to deal with that residual category of amendments which are neither deletions nor subsections, para. (a) deals with additions. Now, the reason for differentiating between the forms in which amendments are to be notified under paras. (a) and (b) relates to certain intrinsic characteristics of the amendments in question. Para. (b) refers to types of amendments, namely deletions and substitutions, which it is logically impossible fully to describe without reference to the words of the text as it was prior to amendment, whereas (a) refers to types of amendment, established by deductive reasoning to be additions, which can be formally described without any reference to text prior to amendment except that which is necessary to identify points at which the insertion begins and ends.

In neither case is there an obligation to present a full text of the entry either prior to or after amendment, still less in both forms. However, the degree of decontextualisation permitted and curtailment of understanding countenanced is exacerbated in the case of amendments in the form of additions under para. (a), as in these cases, even the relevant part of the text prior to amendment will not necessarily be made available to illuminate the sense and purpose of the amendment. Such matters may be of little moment while the register remains a minimal record of liability (although this does not necessarily guarantee against misunderstanding but merely makes it less likely by making it easier for people to maintain an accurate mental image of the register) but if the powers of prescription under s.13(1)(f) are used generously, then instances of confusion or incomplete understanding may proliferate. Of course, persons will be able to acquire full knowledge of the record before and after amendment by utilising the combination of powers to inspect and to require copies of current and past entries under s.20 and s.15(4) or, where appropriate, by retaining the copy of the original entry received by virtue of s.14(2). However, it is at least arguable that where the amendment of a register entry may substantially affect the financial liability of a person and may trigger rights of appeal, and moreover, the commencement of a limited period within which such an appeal may be made (see s.16(1) below), then the registration officer has an obligation to inform the affected person fully and unambiguously of the nature and overall effect of the amendment, a right which is probably not guaranteed by this section. If such were the case, then the registered person would be in a position to draw his own conclusions as to the import of the amendment in the register, rather than having to rely upon the interpretation and judgment of its effect made by the registration officer, which he is obliged to relay to the registered person under subs. (5)(i).

Registration appeals

16.—(1) A person who is registered in the register as being liable to pay any of the community charges may appeal—

    (a) against any entry or amendment of an entry in the register in respect of his liability to pay any of the community charges, in such manner and within such period as may be prescribed, to the registration officer, who shall determine that appeal in such manner and within such period as may be prescribed; and

    (b) against such a determination by the registration officer of an appeal by that person, to any sheriff of any sheriffdom which wholly or partly falls within the registration area.

(2) Where a person requests the registration officer to make or to amend an entry in the register relating to him and—

    (a) the registration officer refuses to do so, the person may appeal to the sheriff against that refusal; or

    (b) the registration officer fails to notify the person of the determination of the request within such period as may be prescribed, he shall be deemed to have refused the request and the person may appeal to the sheriff against the deemed refusal.

(3) In any case where a question arises as to which one of two or more registers for different registration areas a person is or should be registered in as being liable to pay the personal community charge the person may appeal to the sheriff of any sheriffdom which wholly or partly falls within any of the registration areas.

(4) If the sheriff upholds an appeal under subsection (1) or (2) above, the registration officer shall amend the register to give effect to the decision with effect from such date (which may be retrospective, immediate or prospective) as the sheriff may determine.

(5) In an appeal to which subsection (3) above applies, the registration officer of any registration area to which the appeal relates shall be given the opportunity to become a party to the appeal, and all the entries in the registers in which the person is entered as being liable to pay the personal community charge shall be made subject to the appeal proceedings.

(6) Subject to subsection (7) below, where an entry in the register shows that a person is liable to pay any of the community charges, that person shall pay the community charge notwithstanding that he has appealed against the entry, pending the determination of the appeal.

(7) Where a person is registered as being liable to pay the personal community charge in two or more registers and he has appealed against one or more registration, he shall be required to pay only the personal community charge relating to the first registration made, pending the determination of the appeal.

(8) In Schedule 8 of the Civil Jurisdiction and Judgments Act 1982 (rules as to jurisdiction in Scotland) in paragraph 4(1)(c) after the word "proceedings" there shall be inserted the words "(other than proceedings under section 16 of the Abolition of Domestic Rates Etc. (Scotland) Act 1987)".

Definitions
   "community charge": ss.7 and 26.
   "prescribed": ss.26 and 31.
   "register": ss.13 and 26.
   "registration area": s.26.
   "registration officer": ss.12 and 26.

GENERAL NOTE
   The aim of this section is to specify the procedural arrangements for appeals to the registration officer, or, as the case may be, to the sheriff, on matters relating to registration. The initial right of appeal of a person who is dissatisfied with anything specified in an entry or amendment to an entry in the register is to the registration officer, and if still dissatisfied, from him to the sheriff (subss. (1) and (2)). If the issue in question relates to a person's liability as between two different registration areas then he may appeal to the sheriff in either area (subs. (3)) and all the entries in the registers in which the person is entered in respect of his liability to pay the personal charge will be made subject to the appeal proceedings. In either case, the registration officer may become a party to the appeal (subs. (5)). In the case of all appeals, any registration officer will amend the register for his registration area as required in accordance with the determination of the sheriff (subss. (4) and (5)). Any liability to pay a charge which is established by the register will continue pending the resolution of an appeal (subs.(6)) except that where a person is registered as being liable to pay the community charge in two or more registers and he has made an appeal against one or more of these registrations, he will be required to pay only the personal community charge relating to the earlier registration until such time as the appeal is decided (subs. (7)). Finally, in recognition of the fact that, in determining liability as between different registration areas located in different sheriffdoms, the sheriff will be required to assess the validity of entries in public registers for areas outside the sheriffdom of the court or courts over which he presides, the provisions of this Act require to be excepted from earlier legislation conferring exclusive jurisdiction upon the local sheriff courts in such matters (subs. (8)).
   The choice of the sheriff court as the major forum within which registration appeals are to be determined has been justified on a number of grounds relating to appropriateness and economy. It was argued that since the majority of cases going to appeal would be concerned with matters of fact concerning, for example, sole or main residence (ss.8(1) and 10(2)(c) or the size of the collective community charge multiplier (s.11(10)), no technical expertise, such as that possessed by local valuation committees, would be required in resolving such appeals. The sheriff court, with its tradition of deciding matters of fact in a wide variety of

civil and criminal cases, and with its more specific experience of deciding similar questions in the case of electoral registration law under the Representation of the People Act 1983, would thus be the body most suited technically to deciding such matters (1st Scot.S.C., cols. 980 and 984–985, *per* Ian Lang, M.P.). It was estimated in the explanatory and financial memorandum to the Bill that up to forty additional staff would be required in the sheriff courts in order to handle appeals under this section (and under ss.17 and 18 in relation to the imposition of civil penalties) and that those extra staffing requirements would generate a cost of £1 million in a full year. Unquantified additional costs on legal advice and assistance were also contemplated as a consequence of using the sheriff court as the appropriate forum, although it was predicted by Michael Ancram, M.P. that this would merely amount to "an initial surge of expenditure which would begin to drop off as the system became known and the register began to settle down" (1st Scot.S.C., col. 1004), on the assumption that registration officers would be able to deal with hard cases more consistently, predictably and uncontroversially once a body of relevant case law had been built up. In overall terms, it was argued, if an entirely new tribunal was set up to deal with these matters, the administrative and financial implications would be even greater (1st Scot.S.C., cols. 979–980 *per* Ian Lang, M.P.).

Are there any countervailing arguments which would support the establishment of a new tribunal for registration appeals, or even the hiving off of the relevant caseload to an existing forum other than the sheriff court? First, it might be argued, as indeed it was by the Law Society of Scotland in its Memorandum of Observations on the Abolition of Domestic Rates Etc. (Scotland) Bill as prepared by its Working Party on Rating Reform, that to leave open-textured questions of interpretation to the mercy of the 90 permanent sheriffs and the 50 temporary sheriffs operating in the 49 sheriff court districts in Scotland would be to provide a recipe for acute local variations and inconsistencies which would require the expense and inconvenience of frequent resort to the Court of Session under s.29 of this Act in order to be resolved. To avoid this, direct appeal to one centralised decision-making forum should be provided, either by establishing a new tribunal or by extending the jurisdiction of an already centralised body such as the Electoral Registration Court. Secondly, it might be argued that the neat division between technical questions of rating and valuation law and broader questions of fact upon which the force of the argument for utilising a forum of more general competence such as the sheriff court depends, cannot in practice be sustained. As was indicated in the comment on s.11(11)(b), lines of reasoning and conceptual distinctions relevant to rating and valuation law may be pertinent to the determination of questions of registration, although this overlap is unlikely to apply very frequently.

As such, on the basis of the criteria stipulated by the Government, the answer to the question of whether the sheriff court is the appropriate forum for resolving registration disputes is one of fine judgment, and is at least partially dependent upon the validity and strength of certain hypothesis which can only be tested in practice.

Subs. (1)

This subsection provides that any person, who is registered as being liable to pay any of the community charges, may appeal against that registration. In relation to a new entry in the register or an amendment to an existing entry, the initial appeal is to the registration officer. The appeal is to be made in such manner and within such period as the Secretary of State prescribes, and the manner in which and period within which the registration officer must determine the appeal is also to be decided by prescription. As regards the timetabling arrangements, it is intended that the lengths of the periods to be prescribed will take account of and endeavour to balance, the need to allow reasonable time to make an appeal and for their consideration and disposal on the one hand, and on the other, the need to ensure that disputes are resolved as expeditiously as possible. It was suggested by the then Under Secretary of State, Michael Ancram, M.P., that the period within which an appeal must be lodged "could be 28 days" from the point of notification of the original entry under s.14(2)(c) or of the amendment of the register under s.15(5)(iii), and "that a period of six weeks will be appropriate" as a limit within which the appeal must be thereafter determined (1st Scot.S.C., col. 969). As regards the manner in which the appellant is required to pursue his case and the registration officer is required to respond, it is intended that the former party must state his grounds of appeal and that the latter party must give reasons for his decision.

If a person is dissatisfied with the initial determination of his appeal by the registration officer, then he may appeal to the sheriff of any sheriffdom which wholly or partly falls within the relevant registration area. By virtue of s.29, such an appeal must be lodged with the sheriff clerk within 28 days of the determination or such longer period as the sheriff may permit.

For an individual to be permitted to appeal, he must be "registered in the register as being liable to pay" a community charge, and the entry must be "in respect of his liability to pay" a charge. Accordingly, it is intended that the effect of this subsection, together with subss. (2) and (3) below, will be to ensure that all questions of personal registration which affect the liability of that person to pay any of the charges may competently be dealt with on appeal by either the registration officer or the sheriff. On the other hand, questions relating to the registration of another person which affect the liability of a person to pay any of the charges may not be dealt with under this provision. This limitation would appear to affect two classes of person.

First, there is the category of persons liable to pay collective community charge contributions under s.11(11) to the person directly liable to pay the collective community charge. The Government resisted amendments moved at Committee stage in the Commons (1st Scot.S.C., cols. 894 and 869–870, *per* Michael Ancram, M.P.) which would have required their names to be entered in the register, and accordingly, they have no rights of appeal under this section. This does not necessarily mean, however, that such persons will be unable to vindicate their rights under the Act in the courts. For example, if someone believes that he is entitled to be repaid collective charge contributions which he contends not to have been due, then he may do so through an ordinary action for payment in the sheriff court. However, as was noted in the comment on s.11(11), the absence of an integrated appeal system specifically provided under the Act may conceivably make more vulnerable the position of certain categories of persons—including battered women and young single homeless people—positioned at the interface between liability to pay the personal community charge and liability to pay the collective community charge contribution, and may also weaken the position of a contributor wishing to challenge the designation of the premises in which he resides as attracting the collective community charge.

The second category of persons unable to challenge a register entry which affects their liability on account of the fact that the register entry does not personally relate to them, consists of those persons who may be held liable for the personal community charge of their spouses or co-habitees by virtue of the provisions relating to joint and several liability under s.8(7). This is so because s.13 prohibits the specification of any information relating to liability under s.8(7). This omission is unlikely to cause prejudice to members of the relevant category, since they may challenge any decision on the question of joint and several liability at the point of payment of the charge. Indeed, by specifically disallowing the use of summary warrant procedure in relation to debts arising out of joint and several liability (Sched. 2, para. 7(4)), the Act guarantees that a person held liable in such circumstances by the levying authority will have the opportunity to contest this liability in the courts.

Accordingly, although a degree of prejudice of the position of the collective community charge contributor may be envisaged on account of the absence of rights of appeal under this section, this is not true in the case of a person held jointly and severally liable for the community charge debt of another.

Subs. (2)

This subsection provides that any person who has asked the registration officer to make or amend a register entry relating to him, may, if the request is refused, appeal against this refusal to the sheriff. Quite apart from the situation of actual refusal, it also provides for the situation of constructive refusal—that is, where a person has asked the registration officer to make or amend a register entry relating to him, and the registration officer fails to notify his determination of such a request within a period to be prescribed by the Secretary of State, he will be deemed to have refused the request and the person concerned may appeal against the deemed refusal to the sheriff. It is envisaged that, in order to ensure consistency between the various timetables, the period to be prescribed in this subsection after which the assumption of refusal is triggered is to be the same as that which is to be prescribed under subs. (1) as the period within which the registration officer must determine an appeal.

The general purpose of this subsection is to provide for the appeal process to operate in those situations where the person liable to pay the community charge rather than the registration officer takes the initiative and wishes to have what he believes to be a pertinent change in circumstances reflected in the entry relating to him. If this facility were not provided, then a person who felt aggrieved would only be able to challenge what he believed to be errors of commission on the part of the registration officer but not errors of omission.

However, while errors of commission and errors of omission can be empirically distinguished, it may be submitted that, in the context of the register, all errors of commission have the potential *to become* errors of omission, and that this change may be precipitated by the potential appellant, so permitting him to use the procedure under subs. (2) in relation to a dispute, the initial catalyst for which was an entry or amendment to the register by the registration officer, even although it is intended that subs. (1) should provide the appropriate method of proceeding in such cases. This is so because the addition or amendment specified in subs. (2) can only be an addition or amendment of a record containing the original entry with or without amendments made by the registration officer; as there is no proviso in subs. (2) that the point of dispute dealt with by the proposed addition or amendment shall not be the same point as was dealt with by the previous entry or amendment by the registration officer, and accordingly, the suggested change need not be with reference to a *novus actus* which has intervened since the relevant register entry was last changed, then the appeal under subs. (2) may concern precisely the same point as would have been capable of being appealed under subs. (1).

The significance of this overlapping of appeal structures is that it may provide a means to circumvent the time limit for the lodging of appeals under subs. (1). If a person wishes at a later date to challenge the action of a registration officer in relation to an entry in the register affecting him, having failed to appeal timeously against such an entry or change under subs. (1) procedure at the time of the entry or change, then he need only frame an amendment which if accepted would have the same effect upon his entry as would a successful initial appeal under subs. (1), in order to be able to take advantage of the subs. (2) procedure and effectively defeat the procedural time bar.

The need to resort to this alternative procedure might arise on account of indolence or misunderstanding at the earlier point, or because the implications of the alterations appear more detrimental to his interests now than they did initially; for example, as in the case of a person, who having originally paid a personal charge in registration area A and a standard charge in registration area B, finds that decisions made by the relevant registration officers have resulted in this pattern of liability being reversed, and at a later date feels that it is in his interests to challenge this reversal because the policies of the relevant local authorities in relation to the setting of their personal charges (s.9(1)) and standard community charge multipliers (s.10(6)) have altered in such a way that his overall community charge bill is now more onerous than it would have been under the previous determination of his status, even though when the charge was first made the tax consequences favoured him.

Para. (b)

In the course of the parliamentary debates the Opposition tabled and the Government resisted a number of amendments designed to strengthen the rights of the aggrieved person in circumstances of constructive refusal by providing that in the case of failure to respond by the registration officer to a requirement to alter the register he would be deemed to have allowed the request (*Hansard*, H.L. Vol. 486, cols. 1118–1122, *Hansard*, H.L. Vol. 487, cols. 13–15). Although the practice actually adopted under this subsection is not an unusual way of responding to this type of situation within appeals systems, one telling point in favour of inverting the presumption in the manner proposed by the Opposition, is that without such an inversion the procedurally incorrect registration officer is made less vulnerable to legitimate challenge than the procedurally correct registration officer. Failure to notify also entails failure to give reasons and failure to notify rights of appeal, both of which omissions will reduce the likelihood of an adequate appeal actually being made. Although the alternative may be rather drastic, any system which rewards procedural incorrectness and encourages rule cynicism on the part of the body on whom the greatest burden rests to render the main tax structure operational is obviously flawed.

Subs. (3)

This subsection provides that, where the question at issue is which one of two or more registers a person should be registered in as being liable to pay the personal community charge, then he may appeal to the sheriff of any sheriffdom which overlaps with any of the registration areas. The subsection recognises that many of the disputes which cannot be resolved without recourse to the sheriff court will involve dual registration since, in such cases, any single registration officer does not have the capacity to deal with the problem personally whether administratively or on formal appeal under subs. (1). Accordingly, it attempts to expedite the resolution of what will be a large group of cases, by providing that it may be any sheriff of any of the sheriffdoms which falls wholly or partly within any of the registration areas whose register is affected by the dispute who hears the appeal. The provision of an element of choice as to the appeal forum is not unusual in circumstances such as this, and applies in a similar fashion, for example, in electoral registration appeals under the Representation of the People Act 1983.

Subs. (4)

This subsection provides that where the sheriff upholds an appeal under subss. (1) or (2), the registration officer is obliged to amend the register in accordance with the sheriff's decision. The amendment is to take effect from such date as the sheriff determines, and may be retrospective, immediate or prospective. The purpose of this provision derives from the recognition of the status of the register under s.19 as conclusive on questions of liability, and the consequent need to ensure that the determinations of the sheriff are given effect in the register. Under s.15(1) a necessary element of flexibility is built in to the amendment process, permitting the registration officer himself to amend the register with retrospective, immediate or prospective effect, subject to a two-year limit in the case of retrospective amendments and to a stipulation that alterations should not be effected at intervals of less than three months in the case of the collective community charge multiplier. The power of the sheriff under the present subsection to order such alterations as "he may determine" is not made subject to s.15(1), and therefore he is not bound by these restrictions. As commented upon under s.15(1), this assymetry of power may be of consequence at least as regards the period of retrospective amendment: on the one hand, it would appear to provide a remedy where there would otherwise be none for a person who wishes to challenge the accuracy of the record from a date a considerable time beforehand, a challenge whose success or failure could be of considerable significance to that person in financial terms; on the other hand, by stipulating that this remedy be uniquely available through the judicial process, it would appear to require an otherwise time-barred person to pursue the process of appeal in order to remedy longstanding errors in the register even when there is no substantive point of dispute and no justifiable issue between him and the registration officer who maintains the register in question. The means required would accordingly appear to be inappropriate to and entirely disproportionate to the end sought.

Although it is not expressly provided for, presumably on a further appeal on a point of law to the Court of Session from the sheriff court under s.29 further amendments of the register beyond the scope of the present subsection will be permitted. Indeed, this would appear to be implicit in s.19 which provides for the conclusiveness of the register "subject to the provisions of ss.16 and 29 of this Act." This additional liability to amend the register is necessary in order to ensure that a remedy granted in the Court of Session is effective. Furthermore, it would not appear to be vulnerable to the criticisms of disproportionality which apply to the powers of amendment explicitly provided for under the present subsection, in that any amendment would be bound to flow from the resolution of a substantive justifiable issue, as any merely procedural error would have been corrected after the initial case heard before the lower court, and in any case, it would not be competent to the Court of Session to hear an appeal which did not concern a point of law.

Subs. (5)

This subsection allows the registration officer for any of the registration areas to which an appeal under subs. (3) relates, to be a party to the appeal, and provides that all entries in respect of the personal liability of a person shall be made subject to the appeal proceedings.

Accordingly, the subsection anticipates the situation where an appeal is made against only one registration officer, even though the question of liability at issue is also relevant to entries in registers held by registration officers in other registration areas. It is recognised that both they and the court may have an interest in making available their relevant submissions and relevant documentary evidence in the records that they hold, in order to aid the determination of the dispute. It is also recognised that, given that under s.8(1) liability for the personal community charge can only exist in respect of the area where a person is "solely or mainly resident", and so may exist only in respect of one registration area at any one time, in order to maintain the principle of exclusive liability adjustment of an entry in respect of one register may require consequential adjustments in respect of others.

The integrative potential of this subsection is, however, limited. Although it allows all matters relating to the personal liability of a person to be resolved in the one forum, it does not, for example, prevent the person's spouse or cohabitee pursuing a completely separate appeal, even although in many such cases identical considerations will require to be taken into account in resolving the appeal.

Subs. (6)

This subsection provides that a register entry which demonstrates the liability of a person to pay the community charge shall remain effective in establishing liability to pay any community charge even if the entry is the subject of an appeal, until such time as the appeal is determined, subject only to subs. (7) below. Again, this provision underlines the primacy to be accorded to the register as the test of liability. It ensures that no-one may exploit the appeals procedure as a mechanism to delay payment of the charge, but, equally, it means that a person with legitimate grounds for contesting his liability must continue to meet the liability triggered by the disputed entry unless and until the entry is demonstrated to be erroneous. Only then will he receive any repayment due as determined by reference to any amendment to the register ordered by the sheriff under subs. (4) above and in accordance with the duty of the levying authority to repay any sum not due under para. 9 of Sched. 2.

Subs. (7)

This subsection, which was introduced at Report Stage in the House of Commons, introduces an exception to the provision in subs. (6) in the case where a person is registered as being liable to pay the community charge in two or more registers and the appeal is against one or more of these registrations. In that case he is to be required to pay only the personal community charge relating to the first registration made.

In so far as it purports to provide a clear prescription against dual liability, this subsection is unsatisfactory in a number of respects. First, the meaning of the phrase "first registration" would appear to be ambiguous. It may refer to the entry which was made at the earliest date; or, given that, by virtue of s.13(1)(e), an entry may stipulate a date other than the date of entry at which liability is to commence, it may refer to the entry which stipulates the earliest effective date of liability; or given the powers of the registration officer under s.15(1) to amend the register the retrospective, immediate or prospective effect, it may refer to the entry which, in amended form, is with reference to the earliest date.

Secondly, the wording of the subsection assumes that multiple registration, and therefore multiple liability, may only result from a person's name being entered in more than one register. The possiblity of muliple entries within the one register is not provided for, even although the possibility of administrative error entails that such an eventuality cannot be ruled out.

Thirdly, the use of the term "registration" is inconsistent with the nomenclature used elsewhere in Pt. II and, indeed, even in s.16 (*i.e.* subs. (1), (2) and (6)), where the term "entry" is employed to describe the set of references to a particular individual within a register. Although insignificant in itself, this linguistic sloppiness would appear to be symptomatic of the degree of carelessness with which the task of framing this amendment was approached, which may in turn explain the more significant inadequacies discussed above.

Subs. (8)

This subsection is consequential upon other provisions in the section, and attempts to ensure that their effect is not prejudiced by other legislation. Para. 4(1)(c) of Sched. 8 to the Civil Jurisdiction and Judgments Act 1982 confers exclusive jurisdiction "in proceedings which have as their object the validity of entries on public registers, [upon] the courts of the place where the register is kept". Since, in determining appeals under the section, the sheriff's jurisdiction may extend to entries in registers for areas outwith the sheriffdom, it is necessary to exclude such proceedings from the general rule.

Duties in relation to registration

Duties in relation to registration

17.—(1) The general duty of the registration officer under section 12(4) of this Act shall include the duty to take all reasonable steps to obtain such information as is reasonably required by him.

(2) The registration officer shall for the purpose of discharging his functions under this Act have access to and the use of any information which the assessor or electoral registration officer for the area which comprises or includes the registration area of the registration officer may have acquired in connection with any of his functions.

(3) Subject to subsection (4) below, the registration officer may require—

(a) the registration officer of any other registration area;

(b) the regional or islands council, any district council, or any housing body in his registration area,

to supply him with such information as he may reasonably require in connection with his functions, being information which the other registration officer has in connection with his functions or, as the case may be, the local authority or housing body have in connection with any of their functions; and the registration officer, regional, islands or district council or housing body shall comply with such a requirement.

(4) A local authority, housing body, or other registration officer shall not be required under subsection (3) above to supply to the registration officer such information as may be prescribed, and such prescription may be by reference to classes of functions of a local authority or housing body or to classes of information.

(5) The registration officer shall, at such times and in such manner as may be prescribed, require any responsible person to give him such information in respect of any premises in his registration area in such form and within such period as may be prescribed.

(6) For the purposes of this section, "responsible person" means, subject to subsections (7) to (9) below—

  (a) where the premises are occupied by the owner or by a tenant, the occupier of the premises;

  (b) where the premises are not occupied by the owner or by a tenant, the owner or, if there is a tenant whose lease is for a period of 12 months or more, the tenant;

  (c) in any case, such other person as the registration officer considers it appropriate to designate from time to time as the responsible person.

(7) Where, in the case of premises occupied by the owner or by a tenant as referred to in subsection (6)(a) above, there is more than one occupying owner or tenant, both or, as the case may be, all of them shall be responsible persons.

(8) Where there is more than one responsible person and both or, as the case may be, all of them agree with the registration officer that one of them is to be the responsible person, then that one alone shall be the responsible person.

(9) Where, under subsection (6) above, the registration officer designates a person to be the responsible person in relation to any premises, he shall notify that person that he has been so designated and the person so designated may appeal—

  (a) against his designation, in such manner and within such period as may be prescribed, to the registration officer who shall determine that appeal in such manner and within such period as may be prescribed; and

  (b) against such a determination by the registration officer of an appeal by that person, to the sheriff of any sheriffdom which wholly or partly falls within the registration area.

(10) Where the registration officer is satisfied that a responsible person—

  (a) has failed to comply with the duty to provide the information required within the prescribed period; or

  (b) has given false information,

he shall, unless satisfied that the responsible person has a reasonable excuse, impose upon the responsible person a civil penalty of £50 or such other sum as may, in substitution, be prescribed, which shall be a debt due to the regional or islands council, recoverable by them as such as if it were arrears of community charges.

(11) Where—

  (a) a civil penalty has been imposed upon a responsible person under subsection (10) above; and

  (b) the registration officer has repeated his requirement under subsection (5) above; but

  (c) the registration officer is satisfied that the responsible person

has failed to comply with the duty to provide the information
required within the prescribed period or has given false
information,
the registration officer shall, unless satisfied that the responsible person
has a reasonable excuse, impose upon him a civil penalty of £200 or such
other sum as may, in substitution, be prescribed, which shall be a debt
due to the regional or islands council, recoverable by them as such as if
it were arrears of community charges; and the provisions of this subsection
shall apply to any subsequent failures to provide information within the
prescribed period or to any subsequent provision of false information.

(12) The responsible person may appeal to the sheriff against the
imposition of a civil penalty under this section.

DEFINITIONS

"community charge": ss.7 and 26.
"housing body": s.26.
"local authority": s.26.
"registration area": s.26.
"registration officer": ss.12 and 26.
"responsible person": s.17(6).

GENERAL NOTE

This section develops the framework laid down in ss.13–15 as to the nature, construction
and regulation of the database from which the register is derived by setting out in some
detail the duties and powers of the registration officer in relation to the process of
registration. His primary duty is to take all reasonable steps to obtain such information as
is required by him in order to carry out his functions of preparing and maintaining the
register (subs. (1)).

The powers accorded to him may be divided into two basic categories, namely those
which allow him to require information from certain public bodies and those which allow
him to require information from private individuals, conditional in both cases on such
information being necessary in order for him to perform his functions.

The provision of information under the first category falls under subss. (2)–(4). These
provide that the registration officer is to have access to relevant information held by the
local assessor and electoral registration officer, by the registration officer of any other
registration area, and by local authorities and housing bodies within his registration area
(subss. (2) and (3)). In relation to information held by other registration officers and to local
authorities and housing bodies within the registration area, certain exemptions may be
prescribed (subs. (4)). The parliamentary stages of the Bill witnessed a number of heated
debates on the general justification and proper extent of the power to require information
from public bodies. This debate again illustrates the tension referred to in the general note
to s.13 between the difficulties of ensuring sufficient information for the adequate application
of the new tax and the need to minimise the possibility of the illegitimate retention and/or
use of information concerning individuals by public bodies. In the present context, however,
the debate is enriched by a further complexity, in that a third set of variables become
relevant. The question of the appropriate level of access to information held by other public
agencies has implications not only for the degree of effectiveness with which the tax is
administered, but also for the weight which will have to be attached to the other method of
developing an adequate database, namely the attribution of responsibility to individual
citizens for the provision of relevant information, which is the technique with which the
second part of this section is concerned. If, for the sake of argument, the need to ensure
that the tax be administered in a consistent, comprehensive and efficient manner is conceded,
then it has to be acknowledged that any critique of the public sphere as a source of
information implies the need for greater reliance on the private sphere as a source and
vice-versa. Any stance which is critical of the use of both sources must be cognisant of this
inverse relationship, and so must seek to strike the right balance.

As suggested, the second category of powers of the registration officer introduced by this
section consists of those which enable him to require individuals to provide information
relevant to the registration process. Indeed, within this category may be included not only
the powers conferred by subss. (5)–(12) but also those powers to require individual residents
to provide information under s.18. However, it is only with those stipulated in subss.
(5)–(12) that we are presently concerned.

Subss. (5) and (6) introduce the concepts of the "responsible person", defined as the owner, occupier or long-term tenant of premises, or such other person as the registration officer may consider it appropriate to designate. It is the function of the responsible person to provide such information as is required by the registration officer relating to all persons residing at the premises. Provision is made for the possibility of a number of responsible persons for the same premises (subs. (7)), and, in such cases, for such persons to decide among themselves whether anyone wishes to assume sole responsibility (subs. (8)). Subss. (10) and (11) allow for a sanction to be invoked against a responsible person by the registration officer if he fails in his responsibilities, namely a civil penalty. Subs. (9) and (12) provide for appeals against designation as a responsible person and the imposition of the civil penalty respectively.

The introduction of the concept of a responsible person and of the idea of a civil penalty represent alterations of the Government's original intentions in the Green Paper. They replace the concept of "head of household" and a criminal sanctions respectively. Both of these were dropped at least partly for symbolic reasons, the former because it was perceived to be anachronistic and the latter because it was perceived to lead to stigmatisation. Whether their replacement have preferable connotations and otherwise represent improvements on the ideas contained in the Green Paper, are questions which will be explored in the detailed comments on the subsections.

Subs. (1)

This subsection provides that the general duty imposed upon the registration officer to prepare, maintain and keep up-to-date the register for his registration area under s.12(4) shall include the specific duty to take all reasonable steps to obtain information reasonably required.

The terms "reasonable" and "reasonably" introduce the qualifications to the duty specified under the subsection, in turn placing similar qualifications on the types of powers required to perform the duty adequately. The term "reasonable" qualifies the measures which the registration officer is required to adopt in pursuit of his duty, and its insertion was a result of an amendment successfully moved by the Opposition in Committee Stage in the House of Lords (*Hansard*, H.L. Vol. 486, col. 112). The term "reasonably" qualifies his judgment of what the general duty demands by way of obtaining information, and will presumably restrict the scope of the duty to provide information. Both qualifications may place some check on the over-zealous registration officer, although the constraint may be more effectively performed directly through the provisions restricting the scope of information-gathering powers and providing for appeal against their use.

Subs. (2)

This subsection provides that the registration officer, in order to facilitate the discharge of his functions under the Act, is to have access to and the use of any information collected by the assessor or electoral registration officer for the area which comprises or includes his registration area in the pursuit of their functions.

This provision is the only one in the Act (other than s.20(2)(c)) to ensure that the relationship between the two officers and registers, for the purpose of passage of information, is a reciprocal one. Thus it acknowledges the connection, however tenuous, between the community charge register and the electoral register and, therefore, between the administration of the new tax and the right to vote. In debate, it fuelled suggestions that the "poll tax" might indeed become a tax on voting! For the Government, it was contended that information held by the assessor and electoral registration officer would be of limited value. In the former case, the valuation roll contained limited information of relevance and, in the latter case, as a fixed register, the electoral register was too inaccurate.

Nevertheless, it was argued, within these limits they would still constitute a significant source and, in any case, as regards the occupation of the roles of assessor, electoral registration officer and community charge registration officer, "they will be the same person so there is a certain logic in saying that the information which is available to that person when he has one hat on should be equally available when wearing his registration officer's hat" (1st Scot.S.C., col. 103, *per* Michael Ancram, M.P.). That the availability of the electoral register as a source of information will encourage some people to keep their names off that register because they perceive it to be, in effect, a tax on the right to vote, is not a hypothesis which can be entirely discounted. Much will depend upon whether the claim of the Government that the public registers will only be of secondary significance—to be consulted in order to supplement the information from the canvass as the primary means of constructing and maintaining the database of the register—is borne out in practice. It is not, of course, strange that, in a scheme which quite explicitly links liability to be taxed to the power of electors as taxpayers to hold councils accountable for their actions, the connection between the two processes is made at this point. Any critique levelled at the use of the electoral register as a source of information should not be as to its use in principle but rather its inadequacy in practice and, in particular, the danger of affording people the opportunity to disenfranchise themselves for gain. To say this is not, however, to concede that there is "a certain logic" in allowing the incumbent of a number of roles to use the information acquired in the pursuit of one role for the purposes of another. The logic in question is circular and, therefore, spurious, since it is the present Act itself which specifies by virtue of s.12(2) that the incumbents of the offices of community charge registration officer and assessor (and thus, also, in practice, electoral registration officer) should be one and the same person. Accordingly, by permitting a flow of information between officers, the Government is not simply responding to a given state of affairs, but rather, is acting pursuant to a state of affairs which has itself enacted.

Indeed, not only might it be argued that the conjunction of roles does not provide any separate justification for the use of information held by the assessor or electoral registration officer, but that it tempers the force of such justification as does exist. The aim of both subss. (2) and (3) is to impose two types of check upon the abuse of information on the part of the registration officer. One check is largely a matter of self-discipline, that he should request and make use of only such information as he requires for the purpose of discharging his functions. The other check is provided by the donor of the information, in that he need allow access only to information which he may have acquired in connection with any of his functions and which he believes the registration officer may reasonably require in the exercise of his functions. Where the distinction between donor and recipient collapses, as under subs. (2), only self-discipline remains, and, accordingly, the technique of autolimitation will be required to bear a much more onerous load. A system of checks and balances which allocates different responsibilities to different individuals rather than to the one individual in his various personae, unquestionably provides a more comprehensive set of safeguards against the illegitimate use of private information and demands less exacting standards of the persons involved.

Subs. (3)

This subsection empowers the registration officer to require the registration officer of any other registration area, and the local authorities and housing bodies in his area, to provide him with information he may reasonably require, in connection with his functions, from information which they have obtained in connection with their own functions. As a corollary of this power, any local authority, housing body or registration officer which, or who, is the object of such a requirement is specifically placed under a duty to comply with it. The power and duty in question are both made subject to subs. (4), which permits the Secretary of State to prescribe that certain types of information or, in the case of local authorities and housing bodies, all information deriving from certain functional units thereof, shall not be made available to the registration officer.

The registration officer of any other registration area. The rationale and justification for the inclusion of other registration officers within the class of persons and agencies who may be consulted is straightforward. In order to fulfil their duty to prepare, maintain and keep up-to-date their registers under s.12(4) registration officers will be continually required to check with one another on the registration details of persons who have moved or who claim to have moved from one area to another. However, in the absence of any express right of access to the register in another registration area, it is a moot point whether the powers under this subsection are sufficient to allow comprehensive rights of inspection (see also s.20(2)).

The regional or islands council, any district council. The inclusion of local authorities as potential sources of information is somewhat less straightforward. It is envisaged that the type of information sought would include local authority housing records concerning tenancies (presumably including records of the details of transfer requests which might provide rather fuller information, for example on the number of inhabitants of a particular let, than the bare details of the contract of let itself) and improvement and repair grant applications in the private sector. Other areas covered would include applications for bus passes, library tickets or season tickets for other local authority facilities (1st Scot.S.C., col. 1022).

Within s.17 there exist two safeguards against abuse of privacy. First in terms of the present subsection, the local authority is required to divulge only such information as is reasonably required by the registration officer in the performance of his functions. Secondly, under subs. (4), the passing of certain types of information may be absolutely proscribed by prescription. The Government has undertaken that these powers will be used to prevent the disclosure of police records and social work records under any circumstances (see generally subs. (4) below).

Other areas of law may also be relevant to the restriction of the flow of information from the local authority to the registration officer. In the extreme case, the laws of defamation and of negligence may provide an aggrieved party with a remedy where incorrect information defamatory of an individual is made available by the local authority or where it otherwise processes the personal data of an individual in a manner which is negligent and causes harm. More generally, the law of confidence may apply. This prohibits the unauthorised use of disclosure of information which is confidential in nature and which was originally provided in circumstances involving a relationship of confidentiality. The prohibition refers not only to the original party to the confidential relationship, but to any third party, such as the registration officer in the present context, to whom the information is subsequently divulged, even if the third party has acquired it without knowledge of any impropriety (*Malone* v. *Commissioner of Police (No. 2)* [1979] 2 All E.R. 620). If, however, the information in question consists only of the name and address of a person liable to the charge and such other information as is to be part of the public record of the register under s.20(2), then the law of confidence is unlikely here to be applicable, as it may be argued that the requirement that the information be inherently confidential in nature cannot be met if the information is required by statute to be made public. Finally, it is unlikely that the data protection principles set out in Sched. 1, Pt. I of the Data Protection Act may be invoked in aid here in relation either to the public or the non-public parts of the register, on account of the exception to the non-disclosure provisions in cases where disclosure is required to avoid prejudicing the collection or assessment of any duty or tax, such as the community charge (Data Protection Act 1984, s.28(3)). (See also the note on s.13(3) above).

In general, a combination of factors, including the complex overdetermination of this area by a number of discrete branches of law together with the difficulty in predicting the precise types of requests which will be made to different branches of the various local authorities for the purposes of maintaining the register, make it difficult to envisage the degree of conflict which will be engendered by this provision, and also its overall implications for standards of confidentiality of information and for the relationship of local authorities and their electors.

One interesting example, which highlights these issues was provided by Lord Carmichael of Kelvingrove at Committee Stage in the Lords (*Hansard*, H.L. Vol. 486, cols. 1129–1130). He cited the practice followed by a number of regional councils of carrying out a voluntary population survey covering matters such as the age and sex of local residents, as a management information exercise allowing the authority to engage in forward planning as to the provision of services. The request for information under the survey is typically accompanied by a written undertaking that the confidentiality of any information will be respected. As such, both the law of confidence and, in so far as such information is retained on computer, the Data Protection Act, would appear to be applicable, yet, under the operation of the present Act, the local authority would be unable to refuse access to information gleaned from the survey which was reasonably required by the registration officer, a condition which would permit him access to much of the information in question. Accordingly, unless a local authority adds an explicit proviso to any undertaking of confidentiality that such confidentiality will be subject to the powers of the registration officer to request information under s.17 of this Act, it will be placed in the invidious situation of being in breach of one or a number of legal duties whichever course it pursues. If, on the other hand, it does include such a proviso, its information base, vital to any programme of rational forward planning, could be severely undermined as people become more reluctant to volunteer information.

The dangers and dilemmas involved in this type of situation are perhaps placed in an even starker perspective if a scenario involving one of the more specific functions of a local authority is presented. If, for example, a district council housing department obtains a request for a transfer to a smaller home in a different area from a person on account of the fact that her or his spouse has been hospitalised on a long-term basis, as this could affect liability to the personal charge under s.8 on account of the exemptions contained in s.8(8)(d) and s.30, such information could presumably be reasonably requested by the registration officer as information he required in order to fulfill his functions. Again, in order to ensure that it is in breach of its duty neither to provide information to the registration officer nor to respect of the confidence of the individual, the local authority might be required to insert a rider in any communications with the individual to the effect that certain information might be vulnerable to disclosure. As such, the pervasive potential of the Act to infringe upon the relationships of candour with members of the general public upon which the efficient execution of local authority business depends is demonstrated. Of course, it may be that in time awareness of the powers of the registration officer will become widespread, and

ince, as in the above example, the exercise by the registration officer at these new powers
f access may often be of benefit to the individual and the accommodatory practices
escribed above may become commonplace or uncontroversial. Nevertheless, it might be
rgued that, at the level of general principle, the concession of the possibility that information
rimarily divulged to one public body for a specific purpose may be utilised by another body
or a secondary purpose, represents a significant erosion of an important right of privacy.

Any housing body. The extension of the principles embodied in this section to housing
odies, which under s.26 include (as well as district councils which are already covered by
his subsection) the Scottish Special Housing Association and the New Town Development
Corporations, was effected by means of a Government amendment at Committee Stage in
he Lords. It was justified on the grounds that such bodies will be able to provide similar
nformation in relation to their tenants as district councils (*Hansard*, H.L. Vol. 486, col.
132). The same dilemmas which were highlighted and reservations which were expressed
n relation to local authorities apply, albeit on a somewhat more modest scale.

Such information as he may reasonably require in connection with his functions. The
arliamentary debates on this section appeared to be predicated upon the assumption that
he capacity of the registration officer to request information was limited to information
equired in pursuit of his duty to prepare, maintain and keep up-to-date the register under
.12(4), the duty specifically referred to under s.17(1). However, the words "in connection
vith his functions" denote a wider range of activities which may relate to (*e.g.* concerning
esponsible persons under s.17(6)) which it has specifically been guaranteed will not appear
n the register (see s.13(1)(f) above). This should be borne in mind in any assessment of
ssues of confidentiality of communication between local authorities and their clients and
electors.

Subs. (4)

This subsection relieves a registration officer, local authority or housing body of the duty
o comply with requests from the registration officer under subs. (3) if the information
equested falls within a category which has been prescribed by the Secretary of State. Such
nformation may be prescribed by reference to classes of functions of the local authority or
o classes of information. It is envisaged that this power will be used to prescribe information
uch as social work or police records which contain personal data of a particularly sensitive
nature and which it is not thought appropriate to expose beyond the confines of the
department in question (1st Scot.S.C., col. 1026).

While it is apparent from the parliamentary debates that it is intended by the Government
hat prescribed information *cannot* be made available under any circumstances, the subsec-
ion in fact achieves a rather more limited objective, namely that the body or person in
question *need not* reveal information to the registration officer. Accordingly, the guarantee
of absolute prohibition rests on the assumption that the interests and standpoint of the
oublic body in question will never dictate that it should reveal, rather than retain as
confidential, information in a prescribed category. That this may be an unwarranted
assumption has already been commented upon (see s.13(1)). In particular, it should be
oorne in mind that in terms of Sched. 2, the regional council and, to a lesser extent, the
district council and other housing bodies are responsible for matters relating to the levy,
collection, payment and recovery of the community charge. Thus there may develop a
common interest in the administration of the tax. More concretely, authorities may conclude
quite legitimately that the efficiency with which they can carry out their functions depends
n part upon the accuracy of the database (*i.e.* the register) from which they operate, which
n turn depends upon the contribution made by bodies such as themselves to the development
of that database. Accordingly, the interrelationship of functional responsibilities in relation
:o the new community charge as between the registration officer and these other bodies
orovides a forceful argument for the imposition of a mandatory prohibition—rather than the
nere withdrawal of the right to request certain types of information on the part of the
registration officer.

Of course, it could be argued that the law of confidence is capable of filling the lacunae
eft by the legislation. However, the validity of such an argument is in doubt. The law of
confidence requires the demonstration of a confidential relationship and that the information
n question is of a confidential nature. In any case, even to draw upon the argument as to
alternative legal mechanisms is to indict the wording of the subsection, since its very purpose
was to render the use of such alternative measures unnecessary by providing a foolproof
orotection.

Subs. (5)

This subsection introduces us to the concept of a "responsible person", a term which i defined in subs. (6). It imposes a duty on the registration officer to require any responsibl person to provide him with information in respect of premises in his registration area. The subsection merely provides us with a bare outline of the measures which are intended to be introduced. The information which is to be required, the frequency and manner in which i is to be required and the form in which, and time within which, it is to be provided, are al matters to be prescribed. It is envisaged that these powers of prescription will be used to provide for periodic canvasses—including the initial canvass—and other *ad hoc* inquiries to be undertaken in his area by the registration officer; for requiring that names of resident and other information necessary for their registration are given to the registration officer for a uniform procedure to be undertaken in relation to canvasses; for the form and conten of inquiry forms and for the determination of the period in which, after delivery to the responsible person, the forms are to be returned completed.

As stated in the general note, the introduction of the concept of a "responsible person" represents a change in policy from the stated intention in the Green Paper, which was to focus on the "head of household" as the key figure in the registration procedure. This shift which was in response to criticisms by bodies such as the Scottish Consumer Council, was presented as being due to dissatisfaction with the archaic nature of the term "head o household" and its resistance to precise definition. Whether or not the new concep represents a more effective fulcrum for a system which attempts to place a significan administrative burden on a selected group of persons is a point which will be considere under subs. (6) below. The more general point of principle raised by this subsection i whether it is appropriate that any private citizen, however defined, should be held primaril responsible for procuring information concerning the registration details of other persons.

The argument advanced by the Government in favour of the introduction of a status such as that of the responsible person, is linked to their preference for the canvass as the main source of information from which the register would be constructed and, to a lesser extent maintained. It was argued that, for the canvass to be effective, there must be prio identification of persons likely to be able to provide the information required. Such prio identification is possible by two means. It could be by empirical inquiry, in a preliminary canvass before the main canvass, but that would be a cumbersome and costly procedure Alternatively it could be by the designation of a particular category of persons, who car thereafter be identified during the process of canvassing itself.

If this second method is followed, as the Government has advocated (1st Scot.S.C., cols 1051–1054, *per* Michael Ancram, M.P.) then the category may be defined by reference to al persons actually liable, or to a smaller group. On practical grounds, the solution adopted involves the initial identification of a smaller group, whose members have a close connectior with premises in the area and who are thereby likely to have knowledge of other resident of the premises in question, as a source of data relevant to the register.

Against those practical advantages of the use of "responsible persons" have to be weighed some other considerations—considerations as to the need to encourage the responsibility o the *individual* taxpayer (consistent with the theme of the Green Paper itself to enhance democractic accountability), as to the possible detrimental effect upon relationship betweer informants and those persons about whom they must provide information, and as to the encroachment on the privacy of individuals by other private persons. However, the logistica difficulties involved if a system such as this were not adopted, and the fact that its non adoption would necessitate greater reliance on methods of information gathering from publi bodies (which raise as many problems of confidentiality—see subss. (2)–(4) above) place a heavy onus on anyone attempting to argue against the principle of "responsible persons".

It appears that it is intended that the major function of the responsible persons will be ir relation to the initial construction of the register. For example, there is no duty on a responsible person to notify changes in the composition of the household as they occur, and thus, any role he may have in relation to the mature register will be reactive rather thar proactive (1st Scot.S.C., col. 1050, *per* Michael Ancram, M.P.). Accordingly, once the initial logistical problems have been successfully negotiated, the balance of the argumen will alter and it will become more difficult to sustain a case for the retention of the concep of the responsible person. However, questions concerning the frequency of subsequen canvasses or of *ad hoc* inquiries are matters yet to be prescribed and it is very difficult to anticipate the precise role to be occupied by the responsible person in the future.

Subs. (6)

This subsection defines the term "responsible person". The responsible person is to be the owner-occupier of the premises, or, where there is neither, the owner, or tenant having a ease for at least 12 months, or, in any case, such other person whom the registration officer considers it appropriate to designate as the responsible person. These provisions are subject o subss. (7)–(9) which regulate the legal position of persons who are jointly responsible in espect of particular premises (subss. (7) and (8)) and provide an appeals procedure for persons aggrieved by decisions of the registration officer under this subsection (subs. (9)).

The overarching idea which unites all three definitions of responsible person is that of the xistence of a close contact between the responsible person and the premises in question. It s envisaged that, in most cases, the responsible person will be within the category referred o in subs. (6)(a). The categories in subss. (6)(a) and (6)(b) are mutually exclusive. However, f there exist persons within these categories, the registration officer need not rely upon hem but may instead designate a further person whom he considers appropriate under subs. 6)(c).

It is envisaged that para. (c) will be invoked for the most part in situations where there s a responsible person, qualified only under para. (b) rather than para. (a), for the traightforward reason that such a person is less likely to have the required degree of contact with the premises and degree of knowledge of its inhabitants, to be able to provide the nformation that the registration officer requires. For example, in a case of multiple occupancy involving young persons where the identity of the tenant is unclear, or where the enant has sub-let the premises, one or more of the residents may be designated as esponsible persons (1st Scot.S.C., cols. 1051–1052, *per* Michael Ancram, M.P.). Alternaively, the responsible person designated under para. (c) may be someone who is not esident on the premises but holds a position of responsibility for the management of them and is accordingly well placed to provide the information necessary, such as the manager of a sheltered housing development or of a hostel or a lodging house (1st Scot.S.C., col. 1054, *per* Michael Ancram, M.P.).

However, para. (c) may also be invoked where there is a responsible person under para. a). This might happen, for example, where a person lives with and cares for elderly parents who might own the premises in question but neither of whom wishes to take on the burdens associated with being the responsible person (*Hansard*, H.L. Vol. 487, col. 18, *per* Lord Glenarthur). In such a case, it is not a question of one person being more knowledgeable about domestic details relevant to registration than others, but rather of a person, who is as knowledgeable as the owner-occupier or tenant-occupier about relevant details, and who is designated on grounds of convenience.

Subs. (7)

This subsection provides that where there is more than one occupying owner or tenant falling within the category specified in subs. (6)(a), all of them shall be responsible persons.

Subs. (8)

This provides that where there is more than one responsible person, all of them may agree with the registration officer that one of them alone is to be the responsible person.

Presumably this is a situation which may normally arise either by the operation of subs. (7) or in circumstances where, in addition to a responsible person by virtue of subs. (6)(a) or (b), there has been another designated under subs. (6)(c).

Once the agreement is concluded, it is only the one agreed person who is subject to the obligations imposed by subs. (5) and to the sanctions under subss. (10)–(12). The subsection does not provide for the ending of the arrangement but this would presumably occur if the identity of the responsible person under subss. (6)–(7) changed or by the termination of the agreement by any party to it. For this, there is no formal provision and it is possible that difficulties may arise.

Subs. (9)

This subsection provides that where he designates (see subs. (6)(c)) a person to be a responsible person, the registration officer is to notify that person accordingly. After notification, that person may appeal against the decision to the registration officer in a manner and within a period to be prescribed, and the latter will determine that appeal, again in a manner and within a period which is to be prescribed by the Secretary of State. Thereafter, a further appeal lies to the sheriff by means of summary application in accordance with the procedure set out in s.29 below.

In the original, provision was made for direct appeal to the sheriff. The insertion of a procedure for initial appeal to the registration officer and the consequent construction of a two-stage appeal system which mirrors the appeals structure set up in section 16, was only made by the Earl of Dundee at Report Stage in the House of Lords (*Hansard*, H.L. Vol. 487, col. 19). One perhaps unintended consequence of the amendment was the removal of the specification of the grounds of appeal to the sheriff, namely "that it is not appropriate that he should be so designated". No doubt, the "appropriateness" of the designation will nevertheless remain the principal area of dispute.

It should be noted that the appeals mechanism relates only to "designations". There is no appeal against the operation of subs. (6)(a) or (b). Presumably if a person claims not to be a responsible person under those paragraphs, his remedy must lie in the operation of subss. (10)–(12).

Subs. (10)

This subsection provides for the imposition of a civil penalty of £50 or such other sum as may be prescribed by the Secretary of State where a responsible person has either failed to comply with the duty to provide information or has provided false information. It is envisaged that the power to vary the civil penalty will be used to increase the penalty in line with inflation from time to time. The penalty imposed is to be a debt payable to the regional or islands council, recoverable by them in the same way as arrears of community charge under para. 7 of Sched. 2 to the Act.

As stated in the general note, the introduction of the civil penalty represents a change of policy from the Green Paper which had originally suggested that criminal sanctions be applied in this area (Annex G, para. 9). The rationale for the change was stated as being the desire to avoid the imposition of the stigma of a criminal record in such a sensitive area. It was emphasised by the Government that the approach to be taken is not unprecedented and is in line with the recommendations of the Keith Committee on the Reform of the Enforcement of Powers enjoyed by Revenue Departments (1983, Cmnd. 8822 and 9120) which suggested the greater use of civil rather than the criminal sanctions (see also Finance Act 1985, ss.13 and 15 in relation to civil penalties for evasion of Value Added Tax) (1st Scot.S.C., col. 1049, *per* Michael Ancram, M.P.). Against the arguments expressed by the Government must be balanced certain considerations which would suggest that criminal procedure might incorporate more safeguards than the civil penalty procedure. John Maxton, M.P. was not the only Opposition member to point out that in relation to the civil penalty provisions under this section, at the initial stage, the registration officer played "three roles—the policeman, the prosecutor and the judge" (1st Scot.S.C., col. 1041) so permitting a dense concentration of power in his hands. Although a two-tier appeals procedure is provided thereafter, it could be argued that this contrasts unfavourably with the criminal process, which would have required a trial before any penalty was imposed and where also a higher standard of proof would have been required prior to any finding which could justify such a penalty. While there may be a great deal of substance in these points, the same cannot be said of another element of the critique of the civil penalty which was voiced at various points in the debates, namely that the civil penalty procedure might ultimately attract the sanction of imprisonment in the same way as the criminal process, but without the same standard of procedural and evidential checks available in the latter. The civil penalty is to be treated as a debt, and since under s.4 of the Debtors (Scotland) Act 1880 civil imprisonment was abolished as a sanction in relation to the non-payment of all forms of debt (with the exception of a limited number of specified cases), it is not available here. The types of action which are available under this section as regards the non-payment of the civil penalty are limited to those types of recovery of debt which are available in relation to arrears of community charge under Sched. 2, para. 7. Recovery may be initiated through summary warrant procedure or through an action for payment in the sheriff court. All the usual forms of diligence are available thereafter in order to secure the payment of the debt.

Unless satisfied that the responsible person has a reasonable excuse. This represents an important qualification of the powers of a registration officer to impose a civil penalty. Presumably, to provide false information unknowingly and in good faith (or to fail to provide information because of prolonged absence from the premises and ignorance of a request for information under subs. (5)) would constitute examples of reasonable excuses. Arguments such as this would provide the nub of any issue before the sheriff in the course of any appeal by a responsible person under subs. (12) against the imposition of a civil penalty.

Subs. (11)

This provides that, where there is a repeated failure by a responsible person to perform his duty, either in the form of a failure to provide information or of the provision of false information (both of which infractions are specified in subs. (10)), then the registration officer may, following the initial imposition of a £50 civil penalty under subs. (10), impose a larger penalty of £200 or such other sum as may be prescribed. Once again, it is envisaged that the power of prescription will be used to revise the penalty in line with inflation. This further penalty is again to be treated as a debt to the regional or islands council, recoverable in the same way as the initial penalty under subs. (10) above. The defence of reasonable excuse is available in the same manner as under subs. (10) above and may be relevant to court proceedings under subs. (12). Any further infraction of the rules specified in subs. (10) will again trigger the procedures for the imposition of the enhanced penalty under this subsection. Thus, while there will be no incremental increase in the severity of the penalty beyond the figure of £200 or such other figure as may be prescribed, there will be no limit to the number of occasions on which the maximum penalty may be incurred.

Subs. (12)

This provides for an appeal to the sheriff in terms of s.29 against the imposition of a civil penalty under subs. (10) or (11) of this section.

Obtaining of information from individual residents

18.—(1) Every person who—
  (a) will be liable on 1st April 1989; or
  (b) becomes liable on or after that date,
to pay the personal or standard community charge in a registration area and who is not already entered in the register for that area as being so liable shall—
  (i) notify the registration officer of the fact that he will be so liable on 1st April 1989 or (as the case may be) that he has become so liable on or after that date, within one month of the occurrence of the fact; and
  (ii) supply the registration officer with such information as the registration officer may require for the purpose of preparing the entry in the register relating to the person within such period as may be prescribed.
(2) Every person registered as being liable to pay any of the community charges shall notify the registration officer of any change which requires to be made to any entry relating to him in the register within one month after the event which gives rise to the change.
(3) Where an entry in the register shows that a person is liable to pay any of the community charges for a period ("the backdated period") commencing on a date prior to the date on which the entry is made and no such payment has been made—
  (a) he shall pay to the levying authority the amount of any of the community charges which he is liable to pay for the backdated period, together with interest thereon at such rate or rates as may be prescribed, in respect of the period commencing one month after the date shown on the register as the date from which he is liable to pay the community charge and ending on the date on which the entry is made in the register; and
  (b) if the backdated period is three months or more the levying authority, unless the person satisfies them that he has a reasonable excuse for not having been registered, shall require the person to pay to them, in addition to the amount to be paid under paragraph (a) above, a surcharge equal to 30 per cent of the amount of the community charge which the person is liable to pay for the backdated period or, if it is greater, a surcharge of £50,
which shall be a debt due to the levying authority recoverable by them as such as if it were arrears of community charges; and where the levying authority is a regional council they shall account to the council of each district in their region for any sum paid under paragraph (a) above which relates to any of the district community charges.
(4) For the purposes of subsection (3) above—
  (a) different rates of interest may be prescribed from time to time; and

(b) for the amount of 30 per cent or £50 (or for such amount as may be substituted for them under this subsection) there may be substituted such amount as may be prescribed.

(5) A person who is required to pay any sum of money under subsection (3) above may appeal to the sheriff.

DEFINITIONS
"community charge": ss.7 and 26.
"levying authority": s.26 and Sched. 2, para. 1.
"prescribed": ss.26 and 31.
"registration": ss.13 and 26.
"registration area": s.26.
"registration officer": ss.12 and 26.

COMMENCEMENT
October 1, 1988.

GENERAL NOTE
This section requires every person who will be liable on April 1, 1989, or who becomes liable on or after that date to pay the personal or standard community charge in a registration area, and who is in any case not already registered in respect of that liability, to notify the registration officer within one month of becoming so liable and to provide the information which the registration officer requires to make an entry in the register (subs. (1)). Moreover, every person registered as being liable to pay any of the community charges, including in this case any person registered to pay the collective charge, is required to notify the registration officer of any change in circumstances which would require the register entry to be amended, again within one month of the event in question (subs. (2)). If the period between the change in circumstances and the notification thereof exceeds one month, then interest will be payable in respect of charge due for any period in excess thereof and, if the backdated period is in excess of three months, in the absence of a reasonable excuse, a surcharge will become payable over and above the interest payment (subs. (3)). Both the interest rates and the rate of and minimum amount of surcharge may be varied from time to time (subs. (4)). Backdated payments, together with any payments of interest and surcharge, will be treated as debts due to the levying authority, with the proviso that in the case of interest payments but not of payments of surcharge, the levying authority must account to the district authority for any sum which relates to the element of community charge imposed by it under s.7. Any person who is required to pay any sum of money under subs. (3) may appeal to the sheriff (subs. (5)).

As suggested in the general note to s.17 above, the duty imposed on individual residents by this section complements the duty imposed on responsible persons under s.17(5), and together these two provisions constitute the overall strategy of utilising private citizens to provide data relevant to the register. These in turn, must be looked at together with s.17(1)–(4), which deal with the utilisation of public agencies for the same purpose, in order to afford one a panoramic view of the enterprise involved in providing the documentary basis for the construction and maintenance of the register. As with the discussion of these other methods of gaining information, it must be borne in mind that a critique levelled at one branch of the strategy places greater pressure on the remaining branches, and so to avoid contradiction it has to be ensured that the consequence of such pressure is not to make these remaining elements equally or more vulnerable to the types of criticism which led to the commitment to discard or to minimise reliance upon the other methods in the first instance.

It is difficult to predict in advance just how much reliance will be placed on this section. For reasons described above (see s.17(5)) great reliance will be placed upon the responsible person at the stage of setting up the register. Thereafter, although the Government would not be drawn on this matter (*Hansard*, H.L. Vol. 486, cols. 1099–1100) the individual resident is likely to become a more significant figure. Once he is identified, his duties are of a proactive nature—he must notify the registration officer of relevant changes in his circumstances—while those of the responsible person are of a reactive nature, merely responding to the requests made by the registration officer. This proactive role is one which is underlined by ss.14(2)(c) and 15(5)(iii) which provide that after the setting up of the register and the making of any amendments to the register respectively, the registration officer will send affected persons a notice reminding them of their duty to notify him of any change to be made in the entry. As such, the legislative strategy appears to be geared towards a system where individual residents gradually become sufficiently informed of their duties as to be able to assume a greater share of the responsibility for keeping the register up-to-date.

In the light of the assumptions underpinning the legislative intent, the opinion voiced by Lord Howie of Troon that "people can decently be asked to claim a right but I am not sure that they can be decently asked to claim a liability" (*Hansard*, H.L. Vol. 487, col. 21) takes on some significance. It could be argued that any policy aimed at an incremental movement towards self-registration is a naive and indeed an irrational and unjust one, since the inevitable inefficiency of the regulatory system thereby produced will make the sanctioning of irregularly identified infractions appear arbitrary and anomalous. However, this argument in turn might be countered by the view that, for the very reason that individual residents will not assume a significant role until the register has become a relatively mature document, they will by then have had time to assimilate the new law. Accordingly, the various terms and assumptions which it introduces and embodies, such as the general attribution of greater responsibility to the individual citizen in matters of local taxation, of which the allocation of duties in relation to registration is a specific instance, will no longer appear alien but will be accepted and incorporated into his normal life practices so far as is necessary.

Subs. (1)

This subsection imposes the duty on every person in a registration area who is already liable to pay the personal or standard community charge on April 1, 1989, or who becomes liable on or after that date and who is not already entered in the register for that area as being so liable, to notify the registration officer of the fact that he will be liable on that date, or that he is to become liable on or after that date, as the case may be. Beyond the initial notification of the registration officer in the relevant circumstances, the person in question will be required to give to him, within such period as may be prescribed, whatever information he requires to make a register entry. For the sake of parity of treatment, it is envisaged that the period will be similar to the period to be prescribed under s.17(5) for the provision of information by a responsible person.

Thus, the aim of this subsection is to specify the duties of the individual person at the point of initial registration. In the majority of cases, a person who falls within the category specified in subs. (1)(a) will have been identified by the initial canvass envisaged under ss.14 and 17(5) and will already have been entered in the register, so making this provision inapplicable and, indeed, irrelevant. However, subs. (1)(a) will still be necessary to regulate the position of liable persons who have moved into an area after the register has come into force on October 1, 1988, but before April 1, 1989, or of liable persons whose names have otherwise inadvertently been omitted from the initial register.

Para. (b)

The majority of persons covered by this provision will be those who have attained the age of 18 or left school after April 1, 1989. As Lord Ross of Marnock put it in the Lords, the effect of this stipulation will be that "every person now in Scotland who becomes 18 on or after April 1, 1989, instead of receiving a birthday greetings card, has to send one!" (*Hansard*, H.L. Vol. 486, col. 1141). The humour of the above remark lies in its depiction of a situation which will strike many people as counter-intuitive. While the self-registration of persons liable prior to the date of commencement of the tax may also be difficult to guarantee, their relative youth and the decline of the level of publicity which will follow the early stages of the administration of the new charge ensure that these considerations apply *a fortiori* in the case of young persons on the point of entering the taxation system in later years. How realistic is it to expect extensive self-registration in these circumstances? What administrative supports may be required to avoid the danger of widespread default? The Government appeared sufficiently confident that these questions could be answered in a positive and constructive manner to resist on two separate occasions, amendments moved by Lord Ross which would have deleted para. (b) (*Hansard*, H.L. Vol. 486, cols. 1141–1143; Vol. 487, cols. 20–23).

Another category which will be subsumed under para. (b) consists of persons who become liable after April 1, 1989, to pay the standard community charge within a registration area. Many such persons may have their sole or main residence abroad, and, as such, a high incidence of default may be anticipated.

Within one month of the occurrence of that fact. The Government resisted an Opposition amendment moved at Committee Stage in the Commons intended to increase this period to one of three months (1st Scot.S.C., cols. 1073–1076). In arriving at a period of one month (as the margin of tolerance to be allowed), the Government was concerned to balance the need to allow some leeway prior to notification on account of the fact that the relevant person might well be in a situation where subs. (1) applied because he was in the process of moving house and area and so had many other administrative tasks to contend with, against the need to ensure that the register retained its character as a "rolling register" and did not become seriously out-of-date. As described below, the choice of one month as the pivotal period under this subsection has implications for the section as a whole.

Subs. (2)

This requires every person who is registered to notify any change which requires to be made to his entry within one month of the event which gives rise to the change. This places an active responsibility on the registered person to help keep the register up-to-date after the period of initial construction. In the light of remarks made in the general note as to the probable shift towards individual responsibility as the register matures, this provision will probably be ultimately more significant than subs. (1).

Subs. (3)

This subsection provides that where a person is registered as liable to pay a community charge from a date prior to the date when the entry is made and no such payment has been made, then he is liable to pay to the levying authority the amount of any of the community charges for the backdated period, together, in certain circumstances, with payments of interest and of surcharge. The payment of interest arises in respect of any period commencing one month after the date of liability and ending on the date of the entry. The payment of surcharge arises in respect of any period commencing three months after the date of liability. The amount of surcharge is to be 30 per cent. of the community charge payable in respect of the entire period between the date of liability and the date of entry, or £50, whichever is greater. The surcharge will not be applied if the levying authority is satisfied that the person has a reasonable excuse for not having been registered. The surcharge is to be recoverable, as if it were arrears of community charge, under para. 7 of Sched. 2 to the Act. Where the levying authority is a regional council, it is to account to each district council for any principal sum (relating to that council's charge) paid to it in respect of the backdated period together with any interest thereon—but not for any surcharge recovered.

Para. (a)

This provision was the subject of a major amendment successfully made at Committee Stage in the Lords as a result of representations made by the Scottish Rating Forum of the Rating and Valuation Association (*Hansard*, H.L. Vol. 486, cols. 1143–1144, *per* Baroness Carnegy of Lour). One major thrust of the amendment was to simplify the procedure for payment of interest, so as both to ease the administrative burden and to facilitate understanding of the system on the part of the liable person. Its other more substantive purpose was to ensure that the liability of a person to make intererst payments would not commence until the completion of a period of one month's grace in respect of notification of initial registration and changes therein, as is permitted in respect of both subss. (1) and (2). In the original Bill, interest was to have been payable in respect of the entire backdated period. The effect of this change is to ensure that, in a literal sense, the punishment fits the crime (or perhaps this should be rephrased in terms having less punitive connotations, for reasons which will become obvious in the discussion under para. (d) below).

Para. (b)

In relation to the payment of the surcharge, the defence of reasonable excuse is available. In the discussion in Committee Stage in the Commons, it was suggested that the practical impossibility of or degree of difficulty of notification might constitute a reasonable excuse under this section. Thus, for example, someone resident abroad, who purchases a second home in Scotland and thereby becomes liable to the standard charge, may not visit Scotland as his new home for some period of time thereafter, and so may not be in a position easily to notify the registration officer of his liability (1st Scot.S.C., cols. 1083–1085). Of course, it may well be that in the situation described, an alternative or additional explanation of default is ignorance of the law, which on account of the maxim *ignorantia juris haud excusat* could not excuse him from liability. As such, it is only the somewhat fortuitous combination of circumstances that would allow the person in question a defence in this particular context. However, in a variety of other cases which might be argued to be intrinsically no less deserving that the example cited above, such as that of a person moving from shared facilities in a hostel, where he would be liable to pay a collective community charge contribution, to his own rented accommodation where he should be entered on the register for the first time as liable to pay the personal community charge, the defence of reasonable excuse might not be available as ignorance of the law would be the sole reason for the failure to notify.

The reason why the doctrine in question appears so draconian in this context is because the very fact that someone is ignorant of the notification provisions may in many cases be an indictment of the system of administration and communication created by this Act to apply the new tax. Under ss.14(2)(c) and 15(5)(iii), a person will be given notice of his duty to notify any changes to be made to his entry once he has been recorded on the register, and so, as a matter of fact, unawareness of the law is unlikely to be an excuse here. However, prior to registration, there is no provision for a person to be informed of his duties, but instead it is hoped that the responsible person under s.17(5) will trigger the registration process so ensuring that the date of entry of the individual of the register will be sufficiently prompt to escape penalty under the present subsection. Thus, the only occasions on which a person may, as a matter of fact, be entirely unaware of the relevant law and be registered tardily are where the registration officer either fails to designate a responsible person timeously or ask him for registration details sufficiently frequently to allow him to intimate timeously the new liability of any resident of the premises (including situations, such as that of our tenant newly come from the hostel, where the individual resident under this section might also be the responsible person as regards his own liability) or where a responsible person, having been designated, fails in his duty to supply the registration officer with registration details of persons residing at the premises in question. Thus, under this subsection, the individual resident may be penalised either for the direct failure of the registration officer to perform his duties timeously or at sufficiently regular intervals or for the failure of the responsible person to perform his. This anomaly could have been avoided without encroaching upon the maxim of *ignorantia juris haud excusat* by focussing upon the failure of the registration officer or the responsible person, as the case may be, to perform their duties rather than upon the effect of such failures, and to provide that if either of them failed in the ways prescribed above, the individual resident would not be surcharged.

As it stands, the section constitutes another example of the trend within the legislation to attributable responsibility for any systemic shortcomings to the individual taxpayer. Nor can this be excused by suggesting that the assumption of knowledge of the law is no more or less of an artifice that it is, for example, in the case of many statutory offences under the Road Traffic Acts or Finance Acts, since in the present situation there is imposed an administrative structure which purports to provide a system capable of informing all individuals of their responsibilities under the Act, thus indicating that it is not intended to punish ignorance of the law as a matter of strict liability but rather to ensure that such a circumstance is an empirical impossibility.

Another reservation which may be expressed concerning the "reasonable excuse" provision, relates to its scope of application. It provides a defence against the payment of surcharge under para. (b), but not against the payment of interest under para. (a). This restriction was justified by the Government on the grounds that the surcharge is intended as a penalty while the payment of interest is merely an acknowledgment of compensation for the fact that a debt is overdue as in normal business practice, and has no punitive connotations (1st Scot.S.C., cols. 1080–1081, *per* Michael Ancram, M.P.). If one focuses on the nature of the charges in question, this argument appears correct, but if one focuses instead on their consequences for the debtor, both function as penalties and so the distinction appears less clear. From this latter perspective, an argument in favour of extending the "reasonable excuse" provision to para. (a) might be sustained. The relevance of this argument may be underlined by the operation of the appeals provision in respect of this section, namely subs. (5), which is discussed below.

And where the levying authority is a regional council they shall account to the council of each district in their region for any sum paid under para. (a) above which relates to any of the district community charges. In the original Bill, all payments under s.18(3) were due directly to each local authority in proportion to the amount of charge due to them. In other words, payments would be due to the district council for the district community charges and to the regional council for the regional charges. The potential for administrative complexity and confusion inherent in such an arrangement was exacerbated by the fact that different local authorities might come to different conclusions regarding the imposition of surcharge in situations where the defence of reasonable excuse was claimed.

To avoid this, a Government amendment was introduced so that a single levying authority, defined under Sched. 2, para. 1, for the purposes of levy, collection, payment and recovery of regional and district community charges, as the regional authority, would be responsible for collecting all payments of backdated charge, with interest and surcharge thereon, under this subsection (1st Scot.S.C., cols. 1086–1089, *per* Ian Lang, M.P.). Such a solution is not without its own complexities and difficulties, both in a practical sense and as regards principles of fairness in distribution.

On the first count, it has to be borne in mind that, although the regional authority may be the *de lege* levying authority, it may arrange with the district council for the latter to be the *de facto* authority for the purposes of levy, collection, payment and recovery of community charge under Sched. 2, para. 5. Thus, by virtue of that paragraph, some district council housing department tenants may, on the one hand, pay their community charge to the district council in the normal course of events, but may, on the other, be required to pay any backdated payment under this subsection directly to the regional council as levying authority. It would not be open to them also to make these backdated payments to the district council, acting for the levying authority under Sched. 2, para. 5, since the powers of delegation in that paragraph do not extend to functions not prescribed under that Schedule (Sched. 2, para. 5(1))—although such delegation is possible under s.56 of the Local Government (Scotland) Act 1973.

On the second count, while the levying authority has to account to the district council for backdated payments plus interest under para. (a), it is permitted to retain the whole of the surcharge payments under para. (b). This was justified as allowing the levying authority to meet its overheads under this subsection (*Hansard*, H.L. Vol. 486, cols. 1088–1089). It is at least arguable that, in terms of equity, this is too crude a rule of thumb to apply in the apportionment of moneys in compensation for administrative costs. If practicable, the ideal solution would be to distribute all sums received under subs. (3) on a proportionate basis, with the levying authority thereafter receiving any recompense due from the district council for administrative overheads on a "real costs" basis.

Subs. (4)

This specifies that, for the purposes of subs. (3), different rates of interest may be prescribed from time to time and that for the surcharge of 30 per cent. of arrears or £50 there may also be prescribed different amounts in substitution, which may themselves be varied from time to time. It is envisaged that these powers of prescription will be used to correct the payment of interest to reflect interest rates generally prevailing, and to update the surcharge in line with inflation.

Subs. (5)

This subsection allows a right of appeal to the sheriff to any person "who is required to pay any sum of money under subsection (3)". Such an appeal is to be by way of summary application in terms of s.29(1) of the Act.

While the issue of reasonable excuse is pertinent to any appeal against payment of surcharge within subs. (3)(b) it is difficult to glean from the face of the Act the grounds of appeal under subs. (3)(a). (Assuming there is a right of appeal at all under subs. (3)(a). Subs. (5) gives a right of appeal to a person "who is required to pay"—language used only in subs. (3)(b) and arguably applicable to the surcharge alone?) The right of appeal cannot be with reference to substantive questions concerning the accuracy of the relevant entry in the register, (which questions would have implications for payment since the register entry is conclusive of liability under s.19), as rights of appeal in respect of these substantive questions are dealt with under s.16. So it has to be concluded that either the reference to any sum of money under subs. (3) is unnecessarily wide and in so far as it refers to any sum of money other than surcharge, is redundant, or that certain potentially justiciable issues do arise in relation to the very process of payment of backdated charge and/or interest under sub. (3)(b). As they stand, the rules governing payment under this subsection are straightforward and uncontroversial. It is only if the existence of criteria by which the decision to request payment of backdated charge or interest may be challenged are implied, that one might contemplate the possibility of disputes requiring to be resolved by the sheriff. Questions relating to the payment of the principal amount of backdated charge are either substantive and so dealt with under s.16, or uncontroversial, and so do not require to be resolved in a court of law. However, in relation to interest payments, it might be argued that a defence of "reasonable excuse" should be read into this provision in the same manner as is explicitly provided for under subs. (3)(b), on account of the fact, that in line with the arguments presented under subs. (3) above, payments of interest and of surcharge are variations on the same punitive theme and so should attract the same conditions of liability and of exemption from liability. As such, by a process of analogy and implication, it is possible that questions concerning the appropriateness of the levy of payments of interest under subs. (3)(a) could be competently brought before the sheriff. (For appeals generally, see s.29. For general discussion of the range of statutory appeals to the sheriff on administrative matters; see A. W. Bradley "Administrative Law" in the *Stair Memorial Encylopaedia of the Laws of Scotland*, Vol. 1, 1987, para. 338.)

Effect of register

19. Subject to the provisions of sections 16 and 29 of this Act, the register shall for the purposes of this Act be conclusive on the following matters—
   (a) that a person registered in it as being liable to pay any community charge is so liable;
   (b) the date as from which a person so registered is so liable;
   (c) the collective community charge multiplier for the time being specified in the register as having effect in relation to any premises in respect of which the collective community charge is payable.

DEFINITIONS
   "collective community charge multiplier": ss.11(9) and 13(c)(iii).
   "community charge": ss.7 and 26(1).
   "register": ss.13 and 26(1).

COMMENCEMENT
   October 1, 1988.

GENERAL NOTE
   This section provides that, subject only to the rights of appeal under ss.16 and 29, the register is to be conclusive, as to the liabilities of persons to pay any of the community charges, as to the date from which such liabilities commence, and as to collective community charge multipliers recorded.
   Liability in principle for any of the community charges depends on the circumstances set out in ss.8, 10 and 11 above. It does not depend upon what appears on the face of the register. Therefore, the function of this provision is only to secure the evidential status of the register. As explained by Ian Lang, M.P. the stipulation as to the conclusiveness of the register for evidential purposes allows it to operate as "the trigger mechanism for the preparation and despatch of billing notices", and thus for the collection of the tax (1st Scot.S.C., col. 1105). This distinction between the contents of the register as a prima facie accurate statement of the liability of persons for the various charges and the actual pattern of liability for the charge throughout the adult population, entails that in order to ensure that the fundamental liability sections—ss.8, 10 and 11—remain sovereign, provision will be required to be made to permit both the retrospective demonstration of the erroneous nature of a register entry, and the consequent adjustment of the record to ensure that the correct liability can be acknowledged and so enforced.
   Provision is made in the Act for the achievement of these two objectives by virtue of ss.16 and 29 which provide an appeals structure and so aid the achievement of the first end, and by virtue of s.15 which allows for amendment of the register by the registration officer and so expedites the achievement of both ends in question. As suggested in the notes on previous sections (see especially ss.15 and 16 above), there is a tension endemic in the Act between the need to secure the efficient administration and enforcement of the new tax, and the need to ensure fairness and equality of treatment as between individual taxpayers. To the extent that the present provision merely acknowledges the undoubted value of the efficient administration principle, by giving to the register "the substance and standing that it needs as a mechanism for the implementation of the registration officer's powers in collecting the charges" (1st Scot.S.C., col. 1105, *per* Ian Lang, M.P.), this section is in itself uncontroversial. Significant questions as to the relative merits of this principle and that of fairness to, and equality between, individuals only arise when the section is looked at in conjunction with those sections—primarily ss.15, 16 and 29—which are concerned with the latter principle and which seek to reflect, at a practical level, the appropriate balance between the values in question.
   Subject to the provisions of ss.16 and 29 of this Act, the register shall . . . be conclusive. Ss.16 and 29 are concerned with appeals, and for the most part the manner in which they impinge upon and qualify the conclusiveness of the register is retrospective, by providing fora and mechanisms for the *post hoc* adjustment of the register and of the liabilities to which it gives rise. The one exception to this rule is to be found in s.16(7) which requires someone who is registered as being liable to pay the personal community charge in two or

more registers and who has lodged an appeal against one or more of them, only to pay the charge in respect of the earlier registration made, pending the determination of the appeal. In this one instance, the conclusiveness of the register for the purposes of triggering liability is qualified with immediate rather than retroactive effect.

Para. (a)

This paragraph provides that any person registered as being liable to pay any community charge is liable to pay the charge. In effect, this provision means that, for evidential purposes, the register is to be conclusive as to the minimum necessary conditions which require to be ascertained in order to demonstrate liability. Some of the implications of this, both positive and negative, may be gleaned from a debate conducted through Committee and Report Stages of the Lords as to whether it was necessary, in order to make this section effective for the purposes for which it was intended, to include a provision that the register was conclusive as to the address at which liability was incurred (*Hansard*, H.L. Vol. 486, cols. 1144–1145; Vol. 487, col. 26). It was argued by the Government that such an insertion is unnecessary as it is already implicit in the conclusive finding that someone is liable, say, for the personal community charge, that that person is solely or mainly resident in the registration area in question (s.8(1)), and, therefore, it was unnecessary to specify further the conclusiveness of the particular address within that registration area in respect of which liability arose. This point would be unarguable if all that was required to be verified on the face of the record in order to trigger the application of any of the three taxes was the fact of liability itself. This would indeed be the case if the levels of liability for each of the three categories were uniform throughout the registration area. However, in the case of areas which are covered by both regional and district councils this is not so, as each regional and district council determines its three community charges separately by virtue of s.7(1) so ensuring that the total amount of liability for each charge will vary across district council boundaries within the one region, which is, of course, coterminous with the registration area. Accordingly, given that the pertinent questions to be answered in order to trigger liability in any registration area for any of the three charges concern both the fact and *extent* of liability, the latter being incapable of being derived from the former, then it would appear that, strictly speaking, a separate and additional provision as to the conclusiveness of the specific address is necessary to render this section fully effective for its purposes. It may well be that, in practice, the address as specified in the register and for the purposes specified in the register will be deemed to constitute sufficient evidence of these matters in order to trigger liability. However, such assumptions could equally have been made about the evidential status of the matters which are specified in this section, in which case there would have been no need for the section at all. Logically, if it is assumed that this section, which guarantees the evidential status of the register, is necessary to secure the liability of registered persons against the possibility of contemporaneous challenge (and for the reasons set out by Ian Lang, M.P. and commented upon in the general note it would appear that such an assumption is valid) then it must be concluded that such a guarantee should extend to the address of premises in respect of which liability arises, otherwise basic questions as to the extent of liability whose resolution provides the remainder of the information necessary to identify the salient features of the basic liability in question, will remain unanswered.

In a more straightforward vein, it must also be acknowledged that this section does nothing to underpin forms of liability constituted by the Act which are not acknowledged on the face of the register. This is unimportant if the nature of the liability in question is otherwise guaranteed. This is so, for example, in the case of the liability to make a collective community charge contribution by virtue of s.11(11). The constituent features in the identification and computation of such a contribution are either guaranteed in the register entry of another person (the identification on the register of the direct liability of the person liable for the collective community charge), or are matters of public knowledge and so beyond dispute (the number of days in the year and the size of the personal community charge determined by the relevant local authorities in respect of that financial year), or are matters the very nature of which is such as to permit the person to whom payment is due to enforce payment timeously in any case by making such payment a necessary condition of a benefit to be granted to the liable person, where the conferral of such a benefit is crucial in constituting a necessary condition of liability (the question whether the premises are the sole or main residence of the person who, if they are deemed so to be, will be liable to pay a collective community contribution charge).

However, the restricted remit of this section might be significant in one particular case, where such alternative guarantees are not available and whose details cannot be recorded on the register as its documentation is absolutely prohibited by virtue of s.13(2), namely liability for the community charge of another person under the joint and several liability provisions in s.8(7) of the Act. Although, in practice, this provision is intended to be invoked only in the case of default by the main debtor and so liability will not arise contemporaneously with the constitution of liability under s.8, it might be argued that, since in practice the invocation of the principle of joint and several liability will be the only means of recovering the personal community charge from the economically dependent partner in a relationship and so will not be an infrequent occurrence, there ought still to be an administrative mechanism for ensuring liability prior to any judicial determination of liability. That there is not, particularly given the existence of a judicial safeguard against the abuse of this principle by levying authorities by virtue of Sched. 2, para. 7(4), which prevents consideration of the substantive merits of an action for recovery of debt from being circumvented by the use of summary warrant procedure (see Sched. 2, para. 7(1)(a) and (4), below) is perhaps indicative of a degree of reluctance on the part of the Government to confront the full implications of s.8(7), in light of its inconsistency with the principles underpinning the Act (see s.8(7) above).

Para. (b)

This paragraph stipulates that the register is to be conclusive as to the date from which a person so registered is liable.

Para. (c)

This paragraph stipulates that the register is to be conclusive as to the level of the collective community charge multiplier for the time being specified in the register as having effect in relation to any premises to which the charge applies.

Inspection of register

20.—(1) Subject to subsection (2) below, only the person registered in the register shall have the right to inspect the whole of each entry in the register relating to him.

(2) The following persons shall also be entitled to inspect the register to the extent specified—

(a) a member of the public shall be entitled to inspect only those parts of the register which specify—

   (i) a list of addresses in the registration area;

   (ii) the name or names of any person or persons relating to each address (but not so as to ascertain whether that person resides at that address); and

   (iii) the address of, and collective community charge multiplier for the time being determined in relation to, any premises in respect of which a collective community charge is payable (but not the collective community charge multiplier relating to premises within such class or classes as may be prescribed);

(b) a local authority shall be entitled to inspect such part of the register as relates to premises within their area for the purpose of determining, levying or collecting any community charge;

(c) the assessor or electoral registration officer shall be entitled to inspect the whole register for the registration area which comprises or forms part of their area for the purposes of exercising the functions of either of those offices.

(3) The register shall be available for inspection to the extent permitted by subsections (1) and (2) above at the office of the registration officer and at such other places as may be prescribed at all reasonable hours; and, in relation to any portion of the register kept otherwise than in documentary form the right of inspection conferred by subsections (1) and (2) above is a right to inspect the information in the register.

(4) Without prejudice to the provisions of subsection (3) above, a record of those parts of the register which a member of the public may inspect under subsection (2)(a) above shall be made by the registration officer and copies thereof made available for public inspection or, on payment of such fee as may be prescribed, for sale by the regional or islands council at such places as may be prescribed.

(5) The—

(a) date on which a record is to be made under subsection (4) above; and

(b) dates, times, places and manner in which it is to be available for inspection by the public,

shall be such as may be prescribed.

(6) A person shall be entitled to obtain a copy, or a copy certified by or on behalf of the registration officer (a "certified copy"), of any entry in the register which he is entitled by virtue of subsection (1) or (2) above to inspect, on payment of the fee.

(7) Where the register is kept otherwise than in documentary form the reference to a copy (other than a copy made available for sale under subsection (4) above) or certified copy is a reference to a copy or certified copy in a form in which it is legible and can be taken away.

(8) A copy of an entry in the register which is supplied under subsection (6) above and which purports to be a certified copy shall be deemed, unless the contrary is shown, to be so certified and shall be sufficient evidence of the matters contained in the entry.

(9) The fee payable for a copy or a certified copy shall be such as may be prescribed and different fees may be prescribed for a copy and for a certified copy and it may be prescribed that no fee shall be payable in any case or classes of case.

(10) The registration officer shall as soon as is reasonably practicable send a copy of the whole register as in force on 1st April each year to the Keeper of the Records of Scotland for preservation by him.

(11) The Keeper shall not, except as may be prescribed—

(a) make any register sent to him under subsection (10) above available for inspection; nor

(b) issue under section 9 of the Public Records (Scotland) Act 1937 extracts or certified copies of such a register.

DEFINITIONS

"collective community charge multiplier": ss.11(9) and (10).
"community charge": ss.7 and 26(1).
"local authority": s.26(1).
"prescribed": s.26(1).
"register": ss.13 and 26(1).
"registration area": s.26(1).
"registration officer": ss.12 and 26(1).

COMMENCEMENT

October 1, 1988.

GENERAL NOTE

This section specifies the circumstances and forms in which access to various types of information in the register may be provided to various parties. The Green Paper envisaged that the register would, as with the electoral register, be a public document containing no more information than was necessary to list individuals liable. The Act achieves a similar result by other means. Under s.13, the information contained in the register is to be more comprehensive in nature than originally intended, containing all matters deemed to be necessary for registration purposes. However, full details of the expanded register will not be available for public inspection. Instead, varying degrees of access are to be provided, on the basis of a "need to know" approach.

Basically the overall scope of provision of access to registration under the section may be likened to a pyramidical structure. At the base of the pyramid, the most comprehensive rights of access belong to persons in respect of entries relating to themsleves. They possess full rights of access to these particular entries (subs. (1)). The middle section of the pyramid refers to the rights of access of a number of public bodies and officials, the local authority, the assessor and the electoral registration officer. Their rights are generally less comprehensive and may vary across a wide range and may on specific occasions encroach downwards into the base or upwards towards the apex, since they are dependent entirely upon what such bodies or officials need to know in order to meet their functional responsibilities (subs. (2)(b) and (2)(c)). At the apex of the pyramid, the most restricted right of access is available to the widest audience, the general public. A member of the public is entitled to inspect the names and addresses of persons associated with all addresses in the registration area entered on the register, together with the collective community charge multiplier, if any, of those addresses, but with certain restrictions so as to ensure that in no cases may he thereby ascertain whether it is a standard community charge or a personal community charge which is payable, and, in only certain cases, may he ascertain whether a collective community charge is payable (subs. (2)(a)).

The remainder of the section deals with the various procedures through which the rights of access described above may be exercised. The register is to be made available to the extent permitted to the various categories of persons at the office of the registration officer, and at other places to be prescribed (subs. (3)). A record of the public aspect of the register is to be made, and copies thereof are to be made available with or without a fee at such places as may be prescribed (subs. (4)). The date on which the public record is to be made, and the date, times, place and manner in which it is to be available for inspection by the public are to be prescribed (subs. (3)). The right to purchase a copy extends to a copy of any information to which one is entitled to have access (subs. (6)). The copy may or may not be certified. Any copy which purports to be a certified copy shall be deemed to be so unless otherwise demonstrated (subs. (8)) and different prescribed fees may be payable for such a copy depending upon whether it is certified or not (subs. (9)). In either case, where the register, from which the copy is drawn, is kept in other than documentary form, the copy should be available in a form which is legible and can be taken away (subs. (7)). The Keeper of the Records of Scotland shall be sent a copy of the whole register on an annual basis (subs. (10)) but may not make available for inspection or issue any copies of this register except to the extent prescribed (subs. (11)).

Subs. (1)

This subsection lays the base of the pyramid (see general note). It stipulates that the person, and only the person, to whom an entry in the register relates has the right to inspect the whole of that entry. Obviously, a right of inspection is necessary in this context so that a person may understand, verify or, if appropriate, suggest modifications of or otherwise challenge the basis of his liability. It complements his rights to receive a copy of any entry relating to him in the initial register under s.14(2) and to receive a copy of any amendment to his register entry under s.15(5). However, it is arguable that, notwithstanding its appearance of comprehensiveness, this right of access to one's own personal registration information may, in practice, be less than absolute and, accordingly, that any benefits which may accrue from such a right are not fully guaranteed. This is so on account of the possibility of the compilation by the registration officer of a "file behind the file" for all or some registered individuals—a fund of background information perceived by the registration officer as necessary to permit him to perform his functions adequately. This secondary file might include information gleaned from housing waiting lists and housing benefit records, education authority records (including information on grant awards), planning and building control records, rent rolls of housing bodies, etc., all being examples of information which the registration officer could lawfully require under s.17(2) and (3). (See N.C.C.L., "The Privacy Implications of the Poll Tax", October 1987.) The registered person would have no right of access to such information under the terms of the present Act. Nor, it is submitted, would he be entitled, in many circumstances, to access by virtue of the operation of the data protection principles contained in Sched. 1, Pt. I of the Data Protection Act 1984 in the case where such background information was held in computerised form, on account of s.28(1) of the same Act which permits exemptions to the subject-access provisions where such access would be likely to prejudice the assessment or collection of any duty or tax, such as the community charge. (See also the note on s.13(3) above.)

Subject to subs. (2) below. This proviso entails that it is contemplated that certain rights of access to the register on the part of public bodies under subs. (2) below in pursuit of their functions, will be rights of access to the whole of the relevant entry or entries.

Each entry in the register relating to him. The words "relating to him" again raise the doubts and provoke the ambiguities occasioned by the use of similar phraseology in s.16 (see especially, s.16(2) above). Are the rights of comprehensive inspection confined to personal entries, or do they extend to entries in respect of which one has an indirect interest? The relevance of this question to the circumstances outlined below is probably more immediate than in respect of s.16, since as regards the appeals issue, the redress will be obtainable in the courts by other means in the relevant cases, whereas, as regards the issue of access to information, this section provides the only means of providing the type required in these circumstances.

Does a person who is jointly and severally liable for the community charge of another person have rights of access to the entire register entry of that other person? *Per conversam* the answer would appear to be no, since the original Bill made specific and separate provision for such rights of access, thus implying that subs. (1) did not extend to such cases. However, this provision was removed at Report Stage in the Commons, which deletion entails that the *per conversam* argument, while still logically sound, has no legal basis. As such, the possibility remains that despite the fact that this matter was the subject of a specific policy decision by the Government in order to lessen the likelihood of a person's being traced by their ex-partner after relationship breakdown (see also subs. (2)(a)(iii) below), the section may be construed as permitting access to the ex-partner in such situations.

What of someone who is not directly liable to pay the collective community charge and who, therefore, does not appear on the register, but who nevertheless is liable to pay a collective community charge contribution in respect of the premises in question? As was suggested in the commentary to s.13(1)(c) above, one of the rationales for the specification of the multiplier on the face of the register, is to provide a check exercisable by the residents of such a property against possible abuse of the system by a person directly liable to pay the collective charge (1st Scot.S.C., col. 1124, *per* Ian Lang, M.P.).

However, as the effect of s.20(2)(a)(iii) will be to prevent members of the public gaining access to the information as to the collective community charge multiplier in certain situations, unless the contributor can gain access to the relevant information under the present subsection, then the aim of the Government will have been frustrated in respect of these premises. Furthermore, under the power of prescription in s.13(1)(f), other information relevant to premises in respect of which the collective charge is payable may be added to the register. Again, unless means provided in the present subsection can be argued to be sufficient, there will be no mechanism for any contributor to gain access thereto. In such circumstances, if, for example, it were to be prescribed that the average number of person over a period who were resident in such premises and who were under the age of 18 were to be recorded in the register, then although such information might be useful as a further aid to the monitoring functions mentioned above, it could not be made available to the person capable of performing such a function. As such, it can be argued that there are good reasons for providing the person with a collective community charge contribution with access to the entire register entry relating to the premises in question under this subsection. However, as said, the words "relating to" will probably be taken to denote only personal entries rather than all entries in which one has a direct interest, and the additional fact that the collective charge contributor (unless also liable to pay the standard charge) is not a "person registered in the register" would appear to provide a conclusive argument against comprehensive rights of access on his part. Therefore, even if the more restrictive interpretation is avoided in the case of joint and several liability it will not be in the present case regardless of whatever persuasive practical arguments may be advanced as to why these positions ought, if anything, to be reversed.

Subs. (2)

This subsection introduces the middle section and the apex of the pyramid (see general note). It specifies the other categories of persons who will be entitled to inspect the register. First, members of the public, and, secondly, various public bodies and officials for whom access to the register is deemed necessary for the performance of their functions. The subsection also specifies the degree of access to be extended to these two groups.

In the original Bill, there was included a further power to provide access to other prescribed groups to an extent to be prescribed. However, this was removed at Report Stage in the Lords on acceptance by the Government of an Opposition amendment to that effect (*Hansard*, H.L. Vol. 487, cols. 27–28). One category of persons not specifically provided for in this subsection, and, with the removal of the open-ended power of prescription, incapable of being provided for, is that consisting of other registration officers. Under s.17(3)(a) each registration officer is under a duty to supply to other registration officers such information as they may necessarily require to perform their functions, subject to limitations specified in s.17(4). On account of the operation of this section, it would seem that, strictly speaking, this duty cannot be fulfilled, by simply permitting the other registration officer such access to the register in question as is requested and permitted, to be divulged in accordance with the qualifications contained in s.17(3) and (4). Instead, the registration officer charged with maintaining the register in question must take responsibility for extracting the relevant information and making it available to the other registration officer. The distinction between the right to inspect the register and the right of access to information contained in the register may appear to be a fine one, but it is one which may be of some consequence. It might be argued that the perhaps unintended omission of the category of other registration officers from this subsection would appear to be to provide a legal impediment against any possible development of a centralised computer list incorporating the information on all the local registers and accessible to all such officers, even if the restrictions upon access contained in s.17(3) and (4) were taken into account and provided for.

However, such a conclusion might be avoided in two ways. First, it could be argued that the right of access to information in a register is tantamount to a right to inspect the register itself, and indeed that a legitimate means of exercising the former right would be by acting in the manner sanctioned by the latter right; on such an analysis, the latter right would be parasitic upon the former right, and, therefore, its existence would be presupposed by the existence of the former right.

Secondly, even if the reasoning set out were not accepted, and it was conceded that there was no right on the part of a registration officer to inspect entries pertaining to registers in other areas, access for all registration officers to a centralised computer facility might still be possible. This would be so if the software used in this centralised facility, while containing identical information to that contained in the register, was not itself designated as the register. The register itself might exist in the form of a documentary record or another item or items of software and, although the difference would be merely a nominological one, this might be sufficient to distinguish it from copies of the register.

Para. (a)

This provision deals with the apex of the pyramid, the minimal degree of access to be extended to members of the general public. A member of the public is to be allowed to inspect only those parts of the register which show addresses in the registration area, the names of persons relating to each address, the addresses of premises in relation to which a collective community charge is payable and the collective community charge multiplier applicable to such premises. However, in the case of the list of names and addresses, a member of the public should be unable to determine therefrom whether a person lives at the address in question. Also, the right to inspect the collective community charge multiplier relating to premises will not be available in respect of classes of premises to be prescribed by the Secretary of State.

The right of the general public to have access to these minimum registration details was explained and justified by Lord Glenarthur thus: "unless a member of the public has this right, he will not be able to satisfy himself that the persons who appear to reside at an address are shown as registered in relation to it, and therefore as being liable to pay the personal community charge. It is right that a person who is paying any of the community charges should be able to satisfy himself that the charges are being fairly applied, and that those who appear to him to be liable to pay any of these charges are also shown on the register. Otherwise, there is a very grave risk that the whole system of community charge could be brought into disrepute. I do not think that this can be thought of by anybody as some sort of snooper's charter or anything like that. It is a matter of legitimate public interest" (*Hansard*, H.L. Vol. 486, col. 1146).

It is beyond argument that there is a "legitimate public interest" in ensuring that the law is applied evenly and equally over the population. Nor is the register unique as a public document providing information of this sort. A similar role is performed by the valuation roll and by the electoral register. If any criticism can be levelled at this aspect of the legislative scheme, then it cannot be with reference either to the aspiration of universal application of and conformity to the law, or to the concept of a public register containing a skeletal framework of information, treated in isolation. Rather, such ideals and provisions must be placed in context.

The community charge register, unlike the electoral register, records a liability rather than a benefit, and the community charge itself, not being limited in its range of application to persons having easily identifiable qualifying attributes, is peculiarly dependent upon information drawn from third parties for its successful application. This element of contextualisation may permit the drawing of a distinction between intrinsic quality and functional potential when evaluating the publicly available aspect of the register, and may permit the dismantling of the dichotomy set up by Lord Glenarthur. Intrinsically, the idea of a public register may be consonant with a "legitimate public interest" but given the vulnerability of the new tax to evasion and the consequent dependence on third parties for enforcement to a potentially greater extent than is the norm in our system of law enforcement, in terms of functional possibilites the notion of a "snooper's charter" may also resonate with certain well-founded fears. In light of these thoughts, it is interesting to note that types of information which are contained in the full register but to which general access is not to be permitted include the date from which the liability of a person to pay the community charge commences (s.13(1)(e)) as well as information as to which of the personal or standard community charge is payable (s.20(2)(a)(ii)), and in some cases, as to whether the collective community charge is payable (s.20(2)(a)(iii)). Surely, if the argument of the Government in favour of this provision is to be taken to its logical conclusion, in order for a person to "be able to satisfy himself that the charges are being fairly applied", he thought to have access to these types of information. That the Government did not take this final step may be evidence of the fact that it was aware that the same provisions eyed from different perspectives, could be viewed equally as the endorsement of a "legitimate public interest" and as a "snooper's charter", and, as such, a policy of moderation would enable a balance to be struck and potential dangers to be avoided. The only other item of information which it is specifically provided for to be part of the register in terms of s.13 and which is to be excluded from the public part of the register under the present subsection, is the date of birth of registered persons (s.13(1)(d)). This may be justified both on grounds of general privacy and by the desire not to aid the identification of persons—particularly old person living alone—who may be vulnerable to particular types of crimes.

Subpara. (ii)

The intention behind the proviso contained in this paragraph is similar to that underlying the omission of dates of birth, namely, the prevention of crime. The literal aim of the proviso is to ensure that one cannot glean from the public part of the register whether or no someone resides at an address to which his name relates. This can only be achieved by excluding from the publicly available aspect of the register the sole or main residence or other registered addresses of a person liable to pay the standard community charge (specified as part of the register under s.13(1)(b), for if this information were available, then two addresses would appear alongside the name of such a person, and one would be able to deduce that he was liable for a standard charge and, therefore, that he was not resident at the address within the registration area, or if more than one address within the registration area was listed, that he was not mainly resident at at least one of them. This would aid the identification of empty homes and second homes, so exposing the register to the accusation that it provided a burglar's charter, or even, to borrow from the Welsh experience, a fireraiser's charter!

Subpara. (iii)

The proviso contained in this paragraph was introduced at Committee Stage in the Lords in an amendment sponsored by Scottish Women's Aid and moved by Lord Strathclyde, and is specifically aimed at women's refuges in which battered women may live, in that "the existence of the multiplier on the public record could jeopardise the confidentiality of the addresses of such refuges and allow husbands, boyfriends or anyone else wishing to see such women to trace them to that address" (*Hansard*, H.L. Vol. 486, col. 1148). As explained above (see s.13(1)(c)) an unfortunate side effect of this could be to remove the means by which contributors to the collective community charge payable in respect of these premises might check on the accuracy of the multiplier and on the probity of the person in charge of the premises and directly liable for the charge. However, as the value of such a check and the degree of enthusiasm with which it must be practiced are in doubt, it might be thought that this sacrifice is worth making in light of the benefit to be gained.

However, the question remains, is the provision actually effective in guaranteeing that such a benefit would be gained? Apart from the obvious point that it is dependent upon future prescription rather than being inscribed in the Act, the rather clumsy drafting of subs. (2) casts a certain doubt on whether the anonymity even of these premises which are prescribed will be secured. To explain, sub-para. (iii) refers to the publication of the address and collective community charge multiplier of premises in respect of which the collective charge is payable. Read in isolation, the instruction that the address of any premises in respect of which the collective charge is payable is to be made available to the general public does not appear to imply that publication of the address should include a specification that the collective charge is payable in respect thereof. However, if sub-para. (i) of subsection (2)(a) is examined, it would appear that provision is already made for the publication of all the addresses in question, since they must be included in any comprehensive list of addresses in the registration area. As such, the reference in sub-para. (iii) to the publication of the address of premises in respect of which the collective charge is payable is either redundant or is meant to imply that something more than the bare address is to be supplied, namely, the very fact that the address is of premises in respect of which the collective charge is payable. Thus, reading the subsection as a whole, it is arguable that the material to be published under sub-para. (iii) includes the identification of the address as premises in espect of which the collective charge is payable. If this is indeed the case, then the omission of the multiplier will not disguise the nature of the premises in question and so preserve their anonymity. In fact, it will identify them as premises whose multiplier must not be revealed. This would not be merely ironic but also counterproductive, as the distinct form of the public record in respect of these premises would further ease their identification.

Para. (b)

This paragraph, together with para. (c) below, refers to the middle section of the information pyramid (see general note). It stipulates that the local authority is to be permitted to inspect that part of the register which relates to premises within its area, for the purposes of determining, levying or collecting any community charge.

Two interrelated sets of questions arise in the interpretation and evaluation of this paragraph. First, what level of access is required for the purposes specified? Secondly, to whom is such access to be granted? Which persons or bodies may represent the local authority for the purposes of these provisions?

As regards the first question, each of the functions specified is determined elsewhere in the Act. S.9(1) stipulates that it is the function of every local authority to determine the amount of the personal community charge each year, which amount also provides the basis for the collective community charge (s.11(7)). Moreover, s.10(6)(b) states that it is the function of the local authority to determine its standard community charge each year, by means of multiplying the personal community charge by the standard community charge multiplier, which latter figure is also to be determined by the local authority. In relation to the functions of levy and collection of community charges, Sched. 2, para. 1 specifies that such functions will be the duty of the levying authority, which is either the regional or islands council. However, the other type of local authority, the district council, is not necessarily thereby excluded from these spheres of responsibility as para. 5 of Sched. 2 permits the delegation of these functions by the regional council to the district council.

As it is intended that the register will contain only information which is required in order to identify liable persons and determine their liability, then for the purposes of levy and collection and, in particular, the issue of demand notices, (Sched. 2, para. 2) it would appear that the local authority as levying authority would also require virtually comprehensive access. The one exception to this would appear to be the date of birth of the registered person (s.13(1)(d)) since this is information which will require to be made available to registration officers and between registration officers for the purpose of identifying persons with the same name, but which, beyond that stage of the administrative process, and in particular, for the purposes of issuing demand notices, would appear to be irrelevant.

For the purposes of determining the community charge, the access of the local authority might arguably be unlimited. Under s.7(2) the three community charges must produce sufficient revenue to cover its statutory expenditure in so far as this is not met from other sources, and with specific reference to the personal community charge, s.9(2) states that the amount produced should be sufficient to meet total estimated expenditure for the financial year and various other outlays and potential outlays. As such, it has an interest in calculating the levels of community charge and of standard community charge multiplier required in order to yield the appropriate level of revenue. To perform such a calculation, it would require to have access to information which would demonstrate the precise nature and size "of the community charge raising base—that is, how many people were liable to pay and under what different categories" (1st Scot.S.C., col. 1116, *per* Ian Lang, M.P.). The overall number of liable persons refers to the number of persons mentioned on the register less those who may have disqualifying attributes, such as persons who are currently in prison (s.30). The categorical distinctions in question relate to the three different community charges: the local authority requires to distinguish between persons liable to pay the collective charge and the other two categories, as the income from the first will be larger than from the latter two to the extent described in the multiplier; also, it requires to distinguish between persons liable to pay the standard charge and the other two categories, as the amount of the former, and so the proportionate yield may be made larger in the former case than in the case of the latter two. All such information will be required to be gleaned from the register (see s.13 above).

Quite apart from these classes of information, for the immediate purposes of determining the community charge, other items of registered data might be necessary aids to long-term financial planning by allowing projections of variations in the "charge raising base" in the future, matters which may be deemed to be relevant to the future determination of the amount of the charges. For example, an analysis of the age composition of the charge paying population might reveal the balance between projected mortality rates and projected new registration rates. Or an analysis of trends in rates of long-term hospitalisation (s.30) or in the number of students entering the local authority area to study (s.8(4)) might permit significant projections in this context.

Although the question of provision of information for the immediate purposes of the annual determination of the charges given a settled level of expenditure, is uncontentious the question of provision for more general financial planning purposes is more dubious. In the last analysis, on account of the fact that under s.20(3)–(6) the power to make the register available for inspection and provide in the form of a copy relevant information contained therein lies with the registration officer, it is he who has the effective power to reject or accept, claims for access by local authorities.

Given the degree of access which may be available to the local authority for various purposes, who may be deemed to be representative of the local authority for those purposes? The answer to this question has a number of implications. First, for the issue of the relationships of confidentiality between the registered person, the registration officer and the local authority and, secondly, for issues concerning the relationship between the local authority and its officers and the individual councillor, in particular the appropriate balance to be struck between those same considerations of confidentiality and the right of individual councillors to be informed of such matters as are necessary for the performance of their duties as elected representatives.

Under s.2(1) of the Local Government (Scotland) Act 1973, a regional, district, or islands council, each of which is, by s.235(1) of that Act, a local authority, comprises a chairman and councillors, and the body corporate thereby created has all the functions vested in a local authority by any Act. Under s.56(1) of the same Act, the local authority as constituted can arrange for the discharge of the majority of its functions by a committee, sub-committee, officer or by any other local authority in Scotland. In principle, any committee of the local authority can arrange for the discharge of its functions by a sub-committee, and any committee or sub-committee can arrange for the discharge of their respective functions by an officer (s.56(2), as amended by Local Government and Planning (Scotland) Act 1982, s.32).

As stated by the Under Secretary of State, Ian Lang, M.P., the functions of levy and collection of the community charge would probably be delegated to the finance officer, who would, therefore, exercise the power of access under the subsection on behalf of the local authority (1st Scot.S.C., col. 1116). The function of determining the community charge cannot be discharged by any body other than the local authority itself by virtue of s.28 of this Act which achieves this effect by amending s.56(6) of the Local Government (Scotland) Act 1973. However, the aggregated data pertinent to the understanding of the nature and size of the community charge raising base and so necessary to effect a reasoned determination, would probably also be collected by local authority officers on behalf of the council itself.

However, in either case the decision as to who shall discharge its functions is, within the limits set by s.56 of the 1973 Act, that of the local authority itself. In general, it will not be for the registration officer to decide which is the appropriate functional element within the local authority to seek information under this subsection, but for the local authority itself. If, for example, a local authority decided that, in performance of its functions of determining the charge its members needed to be able to consult the register and not simply rely upon a précis of significant findings from its finance department—on the view that the council would not have a comprehensive grasp of which factors were significant in the determination or estimation of the present and projected raising base unless it had sight of the register itself—then it would seem unlikely that the registration officer could legitimately object. Nor, to take a further example, could he object if a regional authority delegated its functions of levy and collection of the community charge and the corresponding rights of access to the register to a number of district authorities within its area, as this is generally permitted under s.56(1) of the 1973 Act and is specifically provided for under Sched. 2, para. 5 of the present Act. Any concerns which he might have about possible breaches of the Data Protection Act 1984, or of the law of confidence if access was requested by the local authority or a particular body or person representative of that local authority could presumably only be dealt with at the point of entering into the confidential relationship with the private person concerned. With regard to the Data Protection Act, if the register is computerised, the registration officer will be required by s.4(3) of that Act to specify in the Data Protection Register that the data in the Community Charges Register might be used by the local authority, and by s.4(3)(b), to specify the purposes for which the latter body might use it. Under s.9 of the same Act a member of the public has a right to inspect such an entry in the Data Protection Register.

With regard to the law of confidence generally, the registration officer could protect himself by intimating at the point of receipt of information to the person to whom the nformation related the possibility of access by the local authority. In neither case do the demands of the relevant areas of law permit a direct challenge to the power of access of the ocal authority. Of course, as stated in the *Malone* case (see above) the local authority will also, as a third party, be bound by the confidential nature of the relationship in so far as it was so, and will be no more entitled to use or disclose such information unlawfully than the registration officer himself. Furthermore, in the particular case of false or defamatory nformation, any qualified privilege enjoyed by the local authority would similarly be subject to the limitation that disclosure be reasonably necessary to the performance of the functions of the local authority. Overall then, a number of mechanisms exist to protect the confidentiality of registration information pertaining to a particular person, but whether they are as effective as would be a more comprehensive safeguard at the point of access is a moot point.

As to the position of individual councillors, the local authority has no power to arrange for them to discharge its functions. However, at common law, individual members are under a duty to keep themselves informed of council business which relates to their role as elected representatives and which they are required to know, and from this duty springs a corresponding right to inspect such documents addressed to the council as are necessary to perform the member's duties (*R.* v. *Hampstead Borough Council, ex p. Woodward* (1917) 15 L.G.R. 309).

Would such a right extend to the inspection of those parts of the register of which the local authority had obtained copies under subs. (6) below in pursuit of its right under the present subsection? The answer to this question very much depends upon the attitude of the local authority. Recent case-law (see, for example, *R.* v. *Lancashire County Council Police Authority, ex p. Hook* [1980] Q.B. 603; *R.* v. *Birmingham City Counci, ex p. O.* [1983] 1 A.C. 578, H.L.) has suggested that if a local authority believes that its individual councillors require access to information then this decision cannot be challenged unless, in accordance with *Wednesbury* principles (*Associated Provincial Picture Houses* v. *Wednesbury Corporation* [1948] 1 K.B. 223), it is quite clear that no reasonable authority could have reached the conclusion which was reached. So, for example, if a local authority concluded that, as a body corporate, it could perform its function of determining the community charge on the basis of information and analysis gleaned from the register by the finance officer, but also respected the wish of an individual councillor, as a member of the local authority, to have independent access to the register in order to form his own judgments and attempt an alternative or supplementary analysis of its implications for present and future determination of the raising base, then it would appear that it could permit him access thereto. If, on the other hand, although the individual councillor believed that such disclosure was necessary, this belief was not shared by the local authority itself, then he would not appear to be in a strong position to require disclosure. Quite apart from the existence of *Wednesbury* discretion, it could be argued that as the councillor's common law right to know is linked to and circumscribed by the duties associated with his position, and as such duties are defined with reference to the functions of the local authority in general, then the local authority is the best judge of what he requires to know in pursuit of such a duty. Furthermore, in the *Hook* case it was stated that where it is doubtful whether the right of the councillor to be informed extends to a particular document, a salient consideration might be the possible ill-effects on innocent people of allowing documents to be inspected (see generally, Patrick Birkinshaw: "Freedom of Information. The Elected Member and Local Government" [1981] P.L. 545–558)).

Accordingly, questions of confidentiality are here allowed to influence the initial decision whether or not to divulge. Thus, it would appear that, as regards the confidentiality of his entry in the register, the private individual is in a much stronger position in relation to the individual councillor than in relation to the council as such. At the point where the attempt is made to gain access, the limits of the councillor's powers are within the discretion of the local authority, and even if the local authority is not unequivocally opposed to the idea of disclosure, it ought to take into account considerations of confidentiality when coming to a decision. Additionally, as in the case of the position of the individual in relation to the local authority generally, remedies under the Data Protection Act, the law of confidence, and the law of defamation (for the loss of qualified privilege where disclosure is not reasonably necessary for the performance of a councillor's duties, see *Hook* (above), at pp.624–625, *per* Waller L.J.) may be available in the case of unlawful disclosures which have already been made. However, unlike the situation of the local authority itself in relation to the registration officer, the capability here exists for the stable door to be locked before, and not merely after, the horse has bolted.

Of course, it might be argued that too intense a concern with questions of confidentiality might prejudice the legitimate interests of the councillor in informing himself of matters relevant to his duties. To permit the local authority to be the best judge of the individual councillor's need to know, it might be added, might functions less as a means of protecting the confidences of private persons than as a means of cocooning the political judgments of the majority political party within the council and insulating them against informed critical appraisal by councillors either representative of minority parties or simply loathe to toe the official line within the majority party. The facility on the part of councillors to question intelligently the basis on which the local authority seeks to determine the community charge in the present and future years is obviously in the public interest and is, arguably, as important as the need to secure the protection of confidential information, and so should be balanced carefully against it.

Para. (c)

This stipulates that the assessor or electoral registration officer is to be entitled to inspect the whole register for any registration area which comprises or forms part of his area, for the purposes of exercising his functions.

Of course, the three offices will, at any rate for the immediate future, be occupied by one and the same person. The fusion of roles in the case of the Community Charges Registration Officer and the assessor is provided for under s.12(2) of the present Act. The fusion of roles as between the assessor and the electoral registration officer, and so between the community charges registration officer and the electoral registration officer, has no longer been required in law since the passage of the Local Government (Scotland) Act 1973, but the arrangement is still retained as a matter of universal practice. In a sense, therefore, the rationale for this provision derives from an acceptance of the practical reality of the situation and a consequent desire to put the issue of the passage of information from the office of Community Charge Registration Officers to the other two offices occupied by that person on a footing which is legitimate, but only within the proper requirements of the latter two roles. If the distinction is artificial in relation to the triple role incumbent himself, it is not necessarily so in relation to the staff of his three offices, who may consist of different persons for whom the legal constraints upon access may correspond to actual constraints upon access (1st Scot.S.C., col. 1114, *per* Ian Lang, M.P.). For this to be guaranteed, what is required is a variation of the "Chinese Wall", a concept and mechanism which originated in the domain of corporate finance and which has attracted increased attention and interest in the wake of the "big bang" of October 1, 1986, at which point various rules demarcating functions relating to dealings in securities and restricting membership of the Stock Exchange were removed. One of the consequences of this was to facilitate the process of agglomeration and the construction of financial supermarkets, and to increase the possibility of persons within the one organisation simultaneously acting for clients wishing to buy and sell the same type of securities, so giving rise to possible conflict of interests. Accordingly, "Chinese Walls" refer to the administrative means whereby these different functions within the same organisation are sealed off from one another by dint of their allocation to different personnel, so that the advantages of scale remain but the disadvantages are removed, and, in the words of Lord Carmoys, the various functions are "tolerably linked, but not intolerably linked" (quoted in M. Clarke, *Regulating the City?*, 1986). In our present context, the rules under this subsection would appear to provide a supportive legal substructure for the "Chinese Wall" to be extended into the office of our triple role incumbent.

Again, while it is appropriate, given the division of roles, to regulate the passage of information in this manner, as was suggested in relation to the complementary provision under s.17(2) which permits reciprocal rights of access to information pertinent to the other two offices on the part of the Community Charges Registration Officer, the protection against abuse of a system permitting limited passage of information between offices is in principle more likely to be guaranteed where the offices are held by separate persons having separate interests and so more able and inclined to operate as meaningful checks upon the activities of one another.

The whole register for the registration area. This is a rather clumsy formulation, in that the adjective "whole" is used elsewhere in the section to refer to the entire detail of each entry. In this context it is intended instead to refer to the area covered by the register (1st Scot.S.C., col. 1113, *per* Ian Lang, M.P.). However, for the avoidance of doubt it would have been preferable if a different adjective, such as "entire", had been employed in this context, or even if the term "whole had simply been omitted. As it stands, it is unclear whether the meaning of the provision is as the Government intended.

Subs. (3)

This subsection provides that the register shall be available for inspection to the extent set out in subss. (1) and (2) at the office of the registration officer and at such other places as may be prescribed by the Secretary of State at all reasonable hours. It also specifies that the nformation contained in that part of the register which is kept in computerised rather than documentary form is also subject to those same rights of inspection. It is envisaged that the powers of prescription will be used to permit access to the register at local authority and branch offices, and possibly at other public offices such as post offices and public libraries. As such, the pattern of availability would be similar to that which already exists in the cases of the electoral register and the valuation roll. The Government declined to stipulate in advance the precise range of locations at which the register was to be made available on account of the fact that some members of classes of premises which might, in principle, be appropriate locations would be unsuitable for practical reasons, such as lack of space in small post offices (1st Scot.S.C., col. 1132, *per* Ian Lang, M.P.). Presumably, if the register is to be available in computerised form, the expense and practical difficulties involved in installing computer terminals and services at the relevant locations might also be an important consideration.

A right to inspect the information in the register. The verb and the predicate contained within this clause would appear to be couched at different levels of abstraction. Only physical objects may be inspected, and the term "information" does not refer to a physical object, but, rather, is an abstract norm referring to matter which may be contained within a physical object. As such, a semantically more appropriate formulation would either have pitched the main verb at a higher level of abstraction, as in "a right of access to the information in the register", or alternatively, would have incorporated a tangible predicate, as in "a right to inspect a record of the information in the register".

Subs. (4)

This subsection deals with those parts of the register which are to be open to the public under subs. (2)(a). Without prejudice to the rights of inspection under subs. (3), a record will be made of the public parts of the document and it must be made available for inspection and for sale by the regional or islands council, in the latter case at places and a fee to be prescribed. It is envisaged that the various powers of prescription under this subsection will be used to provide that copies should be made available for sale at certain regional and islands council offices, at a fee sufficient to cover the costs incurred by the authority in providing them. As, by virtue of s.13(3), the register need not be kept in documentary form, presumably a record thereof need not be in documentary form either. Furthermore, in accordance with subs. (7) below, a copy of the public part of the register which is to be made available for sale under this subsection need not be in documentary form either, and so may take the form of software.

The idea of making the public part of the register available for sale as well as inspection attracted some criticism in the parliamentary debates. It was argued that this encouraged the indiscriminate use of the register for commercial purposes, something which proved a source of annoyance to many people. In reply to the argument that such a facility was already available in respect of the electoral register under the Representation of the People (Scotland) Regulations 1986 (S.I. No. 1111) it was pointed out that the availability for purchase of the entire electoral register for an area served the legitimate ends of political canvassing, its use for commerical purposes merely being an incidental consequence, but that no such wider justification could be put forward in the case of the present register (*Hansard*, H.L. Vol. 487, cols. 29–31).

For public inspection or . . . for sale. Presumably "or" in this context means "and". Against this presumption it might be argued that, even though it is obviously intended in the section to provide, *inter alia*, a right of inspection of the public part of the register as well as a right to purchase a copy thereof, the right of inspection of the public record is already covered by subs. (3), and so all that subs. (4) does is to provide the registration officer with a duty to make the public record available, either for inspection or for sale by the council at the particular places to be stipulated in this subsection. However, countering this argument and in favour of the view that the options are additive rather than alternative it may be contended that subs. (5) below assumes that the facility to inspect the public record in terms of subs. (4) will be provided.

Subs. (5)

This subsection specifies that the date on which a record under subs. (4) is to be made and the dates, times, places and manner in which it is to be made available for public inspection are to be prescribed. It is envisaged that these powers will be used, *inter alia*, to prescribe that a record of what the register contains should be produced at regular intervals and that it should be made available for inspection at branch offices of the local authorities for the area, and possibly at other public offices (see also, subs. (3) above).

Subs. (6)
This subsection gives the right to obtain a copy, or a copy certified by or on behalf of the registration officer, to any person who is entitled to inspect a register entry under subss. (1) and (2), on payment of the appropriate fee as specified under subs. (9).

Subs. (7)
This subsection provides that where the register is kept in computerised rather than documentary form, a copy or certified copy made under subs. (6) refers to one which is in legible form and can be taken away. It has been confirmed by the Government that this copy will be in the form of a computer print-out (1st Scot.S.C., col. 889) (see also, s.13(3) above). This provision does not apply to a copy of the public part of the register made available for sale under subs. (4); in such a case the copy may presumably take the form of computer software.

Subs. (8)
The effect of this subsection is to create a presumption that a copy of a register entry supplied under subs. (6) which appears to be a certified copy is to be regarded as a certified copy, and is to provide sufficient evidence of the matters contained in the register, unless it is demonstrated otherwise. If this provision had not been inserted then the rationale for certification—to render a copy sufficient proof of the contents of the original and so to avoid the delay, expense and inconvenience involved in the registration officer being required to speak to the authenticity of the original would have been defeated, as the grounds of challenge would merely have shifted from the contents of the register entry to the authenticity of the certification itself, so giving rise to precisely the same types of problems as the certification process was designed to avoid.

Subs. (9)
This subsection specifies that the fee payable for a copy or a certified copy is to be prescribed, that different fees may be prescribed for an uncertified copy and a certified copy, and that it may be prescribed that no fee is to be payable in certain cases or classes of case. It is envisaged that the fees prescribed should be sufficient to cover the administrative costs incurred by the authority in providing and certifying copies, but that there should remain open the possibility of requiring authorities to provide copies free of charge in certain circumstances.

Subs. (10)
Subss. (10) and (11) were inserted at Committee Stage in the Lords in order to resolve the problem, first raised in debate on s.15 (see s.15(4) above) of securing the preservation of the record of the Community Charges Register for the purposes of historical research while ensuring that there was no breach of the principles of confidentiality generally applied under the Act (*Hansard*, H.L. Vol. 486, cols. 1148–1149). To this end, the present subsection provides that the Keeper of the Records of Scotland shall receive a copy of the entire Community Charges Register from every registration officer in Scotland as it stands on April 1, each year as soon as is reasonably practicable after that date. The Keeper of the Records shall preserve these records, just as he already preserves other records such as the valuation roll.
The form in which the record is to be kept is not specified under this subsection, nor does it provide that this may be determined by prescription. Another area of uncertainty relates to the precise meaning of the preservation of the register "as in force on April 1 each year". Does this refer to the register as actually in force on that date, or to the register formally pertaining to that date as retrospectively amended under ss.15(1) and 16(4)?
The introduction of this mechanism in order to create an important database for future research would also appear to have been a significant factor in the decision to permit the removal from the original Bill of the general power of prescription of further grounds of access and categories of persons permitted access, as one of the few articulated justifications for this open-ended power was the need to be able to cater for the needs of historians (1st Scot.S.C., col. 118, *per* Ian Lang, M.P.).

Subs. (11)
While subs. (10) provides the mechanism for preservation of the record of the register for historical purposes, this subsection deals with the conditions of access for those purposes. It provides that, except in circumstances to be prescribed by the Secretary of State, the Keeper of the Records of Scotland shall not make any register sent to him under subs. (10) above

vailable for inspection nor issue any extracts or certified copies of any such register under
.9 of the Public Records (Scotland) Act 1937.

The purpose of this subsection is to ensure that the elaborate protective structure created
inder subss. (1) and (2) to ensure that access to the register should be limited for reasons
of confidentiality should not be capable of being breached by the indirect method of
onsulting the record preserved by the Keeper of the Records of Scotland. It is envisaged
that, in accordance with the standard closure period for government records, the powers of
prescription will provide that no part of the register as sent to the Keeper should be made
ivailable for inspection or for copies to be taken before 30 years from the date of receipt of
the record have elapsed (*Hansard*, H.L. Vol. 486, col. 1149, *per* The Earl of Dundee). It is
o be hoped that successive governments do not abide by this undertaking too literally and
oo conscientiously, otherwise even the public part of the register, which may comprise the
nost interesting and useful section for historical purposes, and which, by virtue of the
Government's own criteria, raises no issues of confidentiality, will not be available. If that
s to be the fate of the Keeper's record, then an anomalous situation will arise where the
historical record of the register will be deemed to be available for inspection and indeed will
be required to be open to inspection if it is two years old or less (s.15(3) and (4)) or 30 years
old or more (present subsection), but will be entirely unaccessible during the intermediate
period of maturation!

Levy, collection, payment and recovery of community charges

Levy, collection, payment and recovery of community charges

21. Schedule 2 to this Act has effect.

GENERAL NOTE
This section gives effect to Sched. 2.

Reduction of community charges

Reduction of community charges

22. Schedule 3 to this Act has effect for the purpose of making provision
as to the reduction of community charges where the Secretary of State is
satisfied, in accordance with that Schedule, that the total estimated
expenses mentioned in section 9(2) of this Act of a local authority are
excessive and unreasonable, and for related purposes.

GENERAL NOTE
For discussion of this power of the Secretary of State to require the reduction of
community charges, see the notes on Sched. 3 where the substantive provisions appear.

In its original version, the section stated simply that "Schedule 3 to this Act has effect".
This survived until, after criticism in the Lords at Committee Stage (*Hansard*, H.L. Vol.
486, col. 1170) and Report stage (*Hansard*, H.L. Vol. 487, col. 35), the wording was
expanded into its final form at Third Reading (*Hansard*, H.L. Vol. 487, col. 455). There had
been objections to confining such an important part of the Bill to a Schedule at all, and the
Government finally conceded that it was not inappropriate to include a more informative
section in the body of the Act.

PART III

REVENUE SUPPORT GRANTS

Replacement of rate support grants by revenue support grants

23.—(1) Rate support grants shall not be payable in respect of the
financial year 1989–90 and subsequent financial years.

(2) For the financial year 1989–90 and each subsequent financial year,
the Secretary of State may make a grant (to be known as a "revenue
support grant") to each local authority.

(3) Schedule 4 to this Act has effect with respect to revenue support
grants.

A consequence of the abolition of domestic rates is a restructuring (and renaming) of the annual grants made by central government to local authorites. Since 1967–68 these grants have been made under the Local Government (Scotland) Act 1966 (as subsequently amended and, in particular, by the Local Government (Scotland) Act 1975) and have been known as rate support grants. These grants cease to be payable in respect of financial years from 1989–90 and are replaced by grants to be known as "revenue support grants". Subs. (3) gives effect to Sched. 4 which contains the detailed provisions on the grants (see the notes on the Schedule).

One small point to be noted at this stage, however, is that, whilst the formula in s.2 of the 1966 Act is that the Secretary of State "*shall*, for each year, make grants", the wording in s.23 is that he "*may* make a grant". As explained for the Government by Lord Glenarthur (*Hansard*, H.L. Vol. 487, col. 45), this is designed "to cover the remote possibility that an authority might one day have so much income from non-domestic rates and other sources that it would be fairer to give all the grant to other authorities. That position might arise from a massive industrial development in a small authority".

PART IV

REBATES

Rebates from community charges
24. The Secretary of State shall, by regulations, modify the provisions relating to housing benefit in the Social Security Act 1986 so as to provide—

(a) for the making by local authorities of rebates in respect of payments made by way of community charges (including payments of standard community charge contributions under section 10 and collective community charge contributions under section 11 of this Act) by such persons as are entitled, by or under that Act as so modified, to such rebates; and

(b) for the payment by the Secretary of State to each local authority in respect of each year of a subsidy, calculated by reference to such factors as are specified in or under that Act as so modified.

DEFINITIONS
"community charge": see s.7.
"local authority": see s.26(1).
"regulations": see s.31.

GENERAL NOTE
One of the essential elements of community charges as a form of poll tax, a tax per skull, is that they should be levied at a flat rate. Everyone liable to pay the personal community charge in the area of a particular local authority should pay the same amount and that principle can be extended with necessary modification into both the standard and collective charges.

It was, nevertheless, conceded from the start that the system would have to contain some recognition of the poverty of many potential community chargees. In the Green Paper (Cmnd. 9714, paras. 3.45–3.46) the Government said that "it would be better for there to be an explicit income support scheme operated through the social security system than to obscure the true cost of the local contribution to services by, for example, having a lower level of community charge for those with low incomes. Either approach would require a test of income. Direct income support would be the most efficient way of helping the poor without distorting the signals to the majority of taxpayers who do not require special assistance . . . The Community charge would have a different impact from domestic rates because it would reflect the size of the household. The Government would therefore have to consider how best to provide support for those on low incomes. The new housing benefit scheme set out in "Reform of Social Security" (Cmnd. 9691) provides help with domestic rates to low income householders but requires every householder to make a minimum contribution of 20 per cent. towards them. For illustrative purposes in the Green Paper it is assumed that the White Paper scheme is extended to bring in those on low incomes, non-householders as well as householders, who would be liable to the community charge. The Government will however be considering other options which are consistent with the principles in the White Paper and the objective of enhancing the accountability of local authorities to their electors".

In the result it is the incorporation of those White Paper proposals which is achieved, in skeletal fashion, by s.4 but, in two main respects, things have moved on since January 1986. In the first place, it should now be borne in mind that other dents in the "flat rate" principle have been built in to the statutory scheme for the community charge. Students, though liable to the personal charge, have their partial exemption guaranteed by s.8(5). People who are severely mentally handicapped are totally exempt under s.8(8)(b). By means of the prescriptions under s.2(3)(b), the residents of nursing homes and residential care homes will, in effect, be exempted as will prisoners and long stay patients in N.H.S. hosiptals by prescription under s.30(2).

Without suggesting that there is a total overlap between those affected by the exemptions listed and those who may benefit from rebates, the rules will be, to an extent complementary. Some of those not fully or partially exempted from the community charge will be entitled to rebates.

In the area of rebates too, things have moved on since January 1986 and, in particular, the Social Security Act 1986 implementing the proposals in Cmnd. 9691 is on the statute book.

Ss.20(1) and 28–31 of the 1986 Act provide for the making of a scheme for housing benefits and that scheme will be effective from April 1988. What s.24 of this Act does is to empower the Secretary of State (the power would be exercised by the Secretary of State for Social Services) to make regulations (by statutory instrument and subject, in terms to s.31, to only negative resolution procedure in Parliament) to modify the 1986 Act to provide for both the payment by authorities of the rebates themselves (para. (a)) and for the payment by the Secretary of State of subsidies to authorities (para. (b)).

Para. (a)

The rebates will be payable only in respect of "payments made by way of community charges" and not, for instance, community water charges under Sched. 5. This is in line with present practice (see *e.g.* the Housing Benefits Regulations 1985 (S.I. 1985 No. 677) which define "rates" on which rebates are payable as not including domestic water rates under the Water (Scotland) Act 1980, and the Social Security Act 1986, s.84(1)).

On the other hand, by virtue of an amendment made in the House of Commons (1st Scot.S.C., col. 1096) payments of standard community charge contributions and of collective community charge contributions are specifically referred to and included. This is vital in the case of collective charge contributions since it should normally be those who pay the contributions (under s.11) and not those liable to pay the collective charge itself who benefit from rebates—although it might have been even more satisfactory for the position of a person who is both resident and liable to pay the charge itself to be specifically recognised. The case for rebates of standard community charge contributions is less clear.

Beyond these general statements, it is impossible to say anything with complete certainty since everything else—the details of the rebate rules—depends upon regulations yet to be made.

Two further general comments can, however, be added. In the first place, because the rebates are to become payable by way of amendments to the scheme under the 1986 Act many aspects of which had been publicised prior to parliamentary debates on this Act, ministers were able to give a fairly full account of the principles which will apply. The 1986 Act itself categorises (s.20(1)) housing benefit as one of the three "income-related benefits" which the Act establishes—the other two being "income support" and "family credit" which are to replace supplementay benefit and family income supplement. Thus, in relation to housing benefit itself, the s.20(7) of the 1986 Act defines entitlement principally in terms of a person's liability "to make payments in respect of a dwelling in Great Britain which he occupies as his home", and that person's income. No doubt the principal amendment to be made to the 1986 Act will be in s.28 (and also s.30 in relation to subsidies) in order to substitute community charge rebates for rate rebates in a system which also provides for rent rebates and rent allowances. As Lord Glenarthur explained (*Hansard*, H.L. Vol. 485, col. 1392) "We have made it crystal clear that the rebate scheme will follow closely the reformed housing benefit scheme for rates that is to be introduced on 1st April, 1988". Going on to explain the scheme he continued (col. 1393):

"Its starting point will be a system of income thresholds which will take account of personal and family circumstances such as age, number of children and any permanent disability. These income thresholds will be closely linked to the income support levels which include personal allowances designed to give special help to vulnerable groups such as single parents and the disabled. Having established the income threshold, the operation of a rebate scheme means that someone whose income is equal to or below the threshold for his own circumstances will be entitled to the maximum rebate, and for illustrative purposes the Government have set a figure of 80 per cent. for that rebate. For those whose income exceeds the threshold for their own personal circumstances there will be a downward taper. The proposed figure in the scheme of housing benefit for rates will be 20 per cent. and that is therefore the figure we envisage including in the community charges rebate scheme".

Absolutely central to the rebate scheme (both before and after the modifications for community charges) is the idea of the 20 per cent. minimum contribution. Resisting amendments which might have permitted rebates of up to 100 per cent., Lord Glenarthur said (*Hansard*, H.L. Vol. 486, col. 1193) "This provision for a minimum contribution therefore really must be an essential part of the improvements in accountability which the new system will bring. It will indeed already have been included in principle in the rating system before the community charge is introduced, but the carry-over of the principle into the community charge arrangements will reinforce the improvements in accountability that the broadening of the tax base will bring".

The adverse consequences for individuals affected led to opposition criticism of the minimum contribution especially in the case of some groups (notably people who are severely physically disabled) who benefit at present from 100 per cent. rate rebates. The Government's response to these criticisms was to give an assurance that, whilst the idea of the minimum contribution would be retained, the fixing of the income thresholds would ensure that "vulnerable groups" would, through increased income support, be compensated for the amount of community charge payable. Thus there would be no complete exemptions (*cf.* the exemption for people who are "severely mentally handicapped" under s.8(8)(b)) but those who are physically handicapped and others will be compensated by higher income support (*Hansard*, H.L. Vol. 486, col. 1667). In the case of severely (physically) disabled people the Government proposed that additional help "which could extend up to 100 per cent. of the community charge" would be available (see *Hansard*, H.L. Vol. 486, col. 1655). Necessarily, these adjustments would be on a national basis and would not take direct account of local levels of community charge.

Para. (b)

Under s.30 of the Social Security Act there is provision for the payment of rating authorities of rate rebate subsidy. That section will have to be amended, for Scotland, to create a community charge rebate subsidy. Responding to an attempt to ensure a 100 per cent. subsidy, Lord Glenarthur declined to promise subsidy at this level but saw no reason to provide a different statutory basis for reimbursement from that which was as yet resolved for rate rebates but under discussion with local authorities (*Hansard*, H.L. Vol. 487, col. 458). It seems probable that the standard rate of "scheme" (*i.e.* reimbursement) subsidy may be 97 per cent. but with lower rates for back-dated payments. "Administration" subsidy will also be payable—at perhaps 80 per cent.

PART V

WATER AND SEWERAGE CHARGES

Water and sewerage charges

25.—(1) With effect from 1st April 1989 the public water rate and the domestic water rate mentioned in section 39 of the 1980 Act shall be abolished.

(2) Parts I to III of Schedule 5 to this Act shall have effect in relation to water and sewerage charges.

(3) The 1980 Act shall have effect subject to the amendments made in Part IV of Schedule 5 to this Act.

DEFINITIONS
  "domestic water rate": see Water (Scotland) Act 1980, s.109(1) (repealed by Sched. 6).
  "the 1980 Act": see s.26(1).
  "public water rate": see Water (Scotland) Act 1980, s.109(1) (repealed by Sched. 6).

COMMENCEMENT
Subs. (1) on September 14, 1987, subss. (2) and (3) on September 14, 1987, but only for the purpose of bringing into force the paragraphs of Sched. 5 indicated in the notes on that Schedule as coming into force on September 14, 1987 and subject to the restrictions of purpose indicated in relation to them in those notes.

Subss. (2) and (3) are to be fully in force on April 1, 1989.

GENERAL NOTE

For notes on the new water and sewerage charges and associated amendments, see Sched. 5.

PART VI

MISCELLANEOUS AND GENERAL

Interpretation

26.—(1) In this Act, unless the context otherwise requires—

"apportionment note" has the meaning assigned to it in paragraph 2 of Schedule 1 to this Act;

"community charge" means a community charge imposed under section 7 of this Act;

"community water charges" shall be construed in accordance with the provisions of paragraph 6 of Schedule 5 to this Act;

"domestic rates" means rates which are leviable on lands and heritages which are domestic subjects;

"domestic subjects" has the meaning assigned to it in section 2(3) of this Act;

"financial year" means the financial year of a local authority;

"housing body" means—
(a) a district council;
(b) the Scottish Special Housing Association;
(c) a development corporation within the meaning of the New Towns (Scotland) Act 1968;

"levying authority" has the meaning assigned to it in paragraph 1 of Schedule 2 to this Act;

"local authority", except in Schedule 5, means a regional, islands or district council;

"net annual value" shall be construed in accordance with the provisions of section 6 of the 1956 Act;

"order" means an order made by statutory instrument;

"part residential subjects" means lands and heritages which are used partly as the sole or main residence of any person, other than
(a) domestic subjects;
(b) such other class or classes of lands and heritages as may be prescribed;

"prescribed" means prescribed by regulations under this Act, and cognate expressions shall be construed accordingly;

"public sewage treatment works" has the meaning assigned to it in section 59(1) of the 1968 Act;

"public sewer" has the meaning assigned to it in section 59(1) of the 1968 Act;

"rateable value" shall be construed in accordance with the provisions of section 6 of the 1956 Act;

"register" means a Community Charges Register established under section 13 of this Act;

"registration area" means the area of a regional or islands council;

"registration officer" means a Community Charges Registration Officer within the meaning of section 12 of this Act;

"sewage" has the meaning assigned to it in section 59(1) of the 1968 Act;

"the Valuation Acts" means the Lands Valuation (Scotland) Act 1854, the Acts amending that Act and any other enactment relating to valuation;

"the 1947 Act" means the Local Government (Scotland) Act 1947;

"the 1956 Act" means the Valuation and Rating (Scotland) Act 1956;

"the 1966 Act" means the Local Government (Scotland) Act 1966;

"the 1968 Act" means the Sewerage (Scotland) Act 1968;

"the 1973 Act" means the Local Government (Scotland) Act 1973;

"the 1975 Act" means the Local Government (Scotland) Act 1975;

"the 1980 Act" means the Water (Scotland) Act 1980; and

"water authority" has the meaning assigned to it in section 3 of the 1980 Act.

(2) In this Act and in any other enactment, whether passed or made before or after the passing of this Act, and unless the context otherwise requires—

(a) the word "rate" shall mean—

   (i) the non-domestic rate,

   (ii) the non-domestic water rate, and

   (iii) the non-domestic sewerage rate;

(b) the expression "non-domestic rate" shall be construed in accordance with the provisions of section 3 of this Act;

(c) the expression "non-domestic water rate" shall be construed in accordance with the provisions of section 40 (non-domestic water rate) of the Water (Scotland) Act 1980 (as substituted by paragraph 29 of Schedule 5 to this Act); and

(d) the expression "non-domestic sewerage rate" shall be construed in accordance with the provisions of paragraph 19 of the said Schedule 5,

and cognate expressions shall be construed accordingly.

COMMENCEMENT

Subs. (1) came wholly into force on September 14, 1987. Subs. (2) came into force on that date but "only for the purpose of the provisions of the Act and any other enactment in relation to rates leviable in respect of the financial year 1989–90 and each subsequent financial year."

GENERAL NOTE

Subs. (1)

Most of the terms listed in the subsection refer directly to another section in the Act for a full definition. These require no comment. Others include:

Financial year. This term is further defined in s.96(5) of the Local Government (Scotland) Act 1973 as amended by s.18 of the Local Government (Scotland) Act 1975. The financial year of all local authorities is now defined as "the period of twelve months ending with 31st March." Before the amendment, the financial year began on May 16.

Housing body. For the deployment of this term in the Act, see s.17 and Sched. 2, para. 5. It is a term which embraces the 53 district councils established under ss.1 and 2 of, and Sched. 1 to, the Local Government (Scotland) Act 1973 but not the three islands councils which, although housing authorities, are also levying authorities under the Act. For a previous use of the term, there including islands councils, see S.I. 1985 No. 246, Art. 2.

Local authority. In Sched. 5, adopting the terminology of the Water (Scotland) Act 1980, a local authority is a regional or islands council only.

Net annual value. See in particular s.6(6)–(8) of the Valuation and Rating (Scotland) Act 1956 in which the net annual value of lands and heritages other than dwelling houses is defined as "the rent at which the lands and heritages might reasonably be expected to let from year to year if no grassam or consideration other than the rent were payable in respect of the lease and if the tenant undertook to pay all rates and to bear the cost of the repairs nd insurance and the other expenses, if any, necessary to maintain the lands and heritages n a state to command that rent".

Note also s.5(10) of this Act which preserves, for the purposes of that section, the meaning ot only of "net annual value" and "rateable value" in s.6 of the 1956 Act but also of "gross nnual value" repealed by Sched. 6.

Order. The standard means in this Act of requiring the promulgation of rules by statutory nstrument is by use of the term "prescribed" (see definition below and s.31) or, directly by 'regulations" (see ss.24 and 31 and Sched. 2, para. 5(6)). S.31 imports the negative esolution procedure in Parliament. "Order made by statutory instrument" does not. The ommencement order under s.35 was not subject to parliamentary supervision.

Part residential subjects. For "lands and heritages" and discussion of the probable use of he power of prescription see the notes on s.2. For "sole or main residence" see notes on .8(1). The system for the apportionment of value of part residential subjects is contained n Sched. 1 but note that subjects may be part residential (thus attracting a community harge to residents) whether or not such an apportionment has been made.

Prescribed. See s.31 and the note on "order" above.

Public sewage treatment works. S.59(1) of the Sewerage (Scotland) Act 1968 defines these as "sewage treatment works which are vested in a local authority."

Public sewer. The same section defines "public sewer" to mean "any sewer which is vested n a local authority".

Rateable value. See the note on "net annual value" above. Notice that a different meaning of "rateable value," that contained in s.7 of the Local Government (Scotland) Act 1975 (as amended by Sched. 1, para. 32 of this Act) is incorporated into s.3(1).

Sewerage. This is defined in s.59(1) of the 1968 Act to include "domestic sewage, surface water and trade effluent."

The Valuation Acts. Note the insertion of the same definition (by making minor amend- nents) into s.43(1) of the Valuation and Rating (Scotland) Act 1956 (by para. 20 of Sched. 1); into s.46(1) of the Local Government (Scotland) Act 1966 (para. 23); s.116 of the Local Government (Scotland) Act 1973 (para. 26); and s.37 of the Local Government Scotland) Act 1975 (para. 33). What is lost in the new formula is any explicit confirmation hat the Act in which the definition appears is itself a "Valuation Act".

Presumably the amendment of the formula is in no way intended to render the Acts eferred to any less "Valuation Acts" and this Act too is presumably a "Valuation Act"? As used in this Act (see ss.2(3), 2(5), 4(1), and 5(7)) the term must be intended to achieve the ncorporation into those sections the whole body of valuation law and practice not evidently n conflict with this Act—even if, as noted in those sections, the result of that incorporation nay not be unambiguous.

Water authority. S.3(1) of the Water (Scotland) Act 1980 defines "water authority for any area" as, normally, "the regional or islands council for that area."

Subs. (2)

This subsection was inserted into the Act in this form in the House of Lords (*Hansard,* H.L. Vol. 486, cols. 464 and 539). It serves two main purposes. In the first place, it provides in paras. (b), (c) and (d)) the source of definitions for "non-domestic rate", "non-domestic water rate", and "non-domestic sewerage rate."

Secondly, it determines that, unless the context demands otherwise, all those three rates hall in this Act, or in any other enactment before or after, be included within the generic erm "rate."

Grant for rate relief given to certain recreational clubs

27. The following paragraph shall be inserted after paragraph 2 of Part I of Schedule 1 to the Local Government (Scotland) Act 1966—

"2A. Notwithstanding the provisions of paragraph 1 above, the Secretary of State may, as respects the year 1988–89, make provision for the apportionment of a prescribed part of the needs element to any local authority which, under paragraph (c) of subsection (5) of section 4 of the Local Government (Financial Provisions etc.) (Scotland) Act 1962, reduces or remits rates leviable for that year in respect of the lands and heritages mentioned in the said paragraph (c) or such class as he may determine of such lands and heritages, and such an apportionment shall be by reference to the amount of the reduction or remission granted by the authority as estimated by

the Secretary of State or so much of that amount as he ma
determine to be appropriate to be taken into account for th
purposes of this paragraph.".

DEFINITIONS

"lands and heritages": see Lands Valuation (Scotland) Act 1854, s.42.
"local authority": see Local Government (Scotland) Act 1966, s.46(1), *i.e.* same meanin
as in s.26(1) of this Act.
"needs element": see Local Government (Scotland) Act 1966, s.2(4) and Sched. 1.
"year": see Local Government (Financial Provisions) (Scotland) Act 1963, s.26(2) a
amended; *i.e.* financial year of a local authority.

GENERAL NOTE

This section has no direct relationship to the general scheme of the Act. It was inserte
as a new clause in the House of Lords (see *Hansard,* H.L. Vol. 486, col. 1198) in order t
respond to concerns about the rating of sports clubs raised in the Commons. In that House
the Government had said that it would be inappropriate to amend other provisions of th
Act to ensure mandatory rating relief for sports clubs but had undertaken to give furthe
consideration to the problem (*Hansard,* H.C. Vol. 111, cols. 962–969).

The principal cause of concern was that although rating authorities are empowered (unde
s.4(5)(c) of the Local Government (Financial Provisions etc.) (Scotland) Act 1962) to reduc
or remit any rate leviable in respect of "any lands and heritages occupied for the purpose
of a club, society or other organisation not established or conducted for profit, and whic
are wholly or mainly used for purposes of recreation" the power was only patchily exercise
It was not, unlike the obligation to grant 50 per cent. relief to charities, mandatory
Furthermore, many authorities were compelled to bear the whole cost themselves (both th
rating authority, if a region, and the district council lost rate income) without any gran
assistance from central government. The only recognition in the rate support grant whic
could be given to the reliefs allowed was in the resources element since any such reliefs wer
built into the calculation of the rate product of authorities (see Local Government (Rat
Product) (Scotland) Regulations 1985, S.I. 1985 No. 246). Thus only those authorities i
receipt of resources element were able to benefit. In order to encourage, but still not t
compel, all authorities to grant rate relief to sports (recreational) clubs, the addition mad
by this section to Pt. I of Sched. 1 to the Local Government (Scotland) Act 1966 enables th
Secretary of State to make special payments out of the *needs element* to authorities usin
their powers under the 1962 Act (and the 1985 Regulations above will require amendment
The only other special provision made hitherto by means of "the apportionment of
prescribed part of the needs element" has been, under para. 2 of the Schedule, in relatio
to "extraordinary expenses". This has been used for oil-related expenditure.

Whilst authorities which remit rates will benefit from additional needs element grant, th
size of rate support grants overall will not be increased. The relief of sports clubs will be
the cost of other local authority services in Scotland.

As stated in the amendment, the arrangement operates with effect from 1988–89. Tha
will, in fact, also be its last year of operation. From 1989–90 and the introduction of revenu
support grants, it is understood that account will be taken of these rating reliefs at the poin
that non-domestic rate income is "netted off" in the process of calculating the grant to b
paid to each authority (see *Hansard,* H.L. Vol. 486, col. 1198 and the notes on Sched.
below). Sched. 1 of the 1966 Act is repealed (from April 1, 1994) by Sched. 6 of this Act
(That repeal will remove a slight unorthodoxy of style in the amendment. As in Sched. 5
para. 47, the singular "authority *which . . . reduces* or *remits*" has infiltrated itself!).

Neither the shorter nor the longer term answer to the problem satisfied all critics. Fo
some, the true answer to the problem of the overrated sports club will come only when thei
values in the roll are reduced. Harmonisation down to the English level would remove mos
of the difficulties at source (see *Hansard,* H.L. Vol. 486, col. 1200).

Prohibition on arrangements for making of certain determinations unde
　　this Act

28. In section 56(6) of the 1973 Act (certain local authority functions t
be discharged only by the local authority themselves) for the word
"determining the rate or" there shall be substituted the words—
　　"(a)　determining a rate;
　　(b)　determining the amount of—

(i) the personal community charge;
(ii) the personal community water charge;
(c) determining the standard community charge multiplier (within the meaning of section 10 of the Abolition of Domestic Rates Etc. (Scotland) Act 1987); or
(d) ".

DEFINITIONS
"the 1973 Act": see s.26(1).
"personal community charge": see ss.26(1), 7(1).
"personal community water charge": see s.26(1) and Sched. 5, para. 6.
"rate": see s.26(2).

GENERAL NOTE
This section was added to the Bill as a new clause at the House of Lords (see *Hansard,* H.L. Vol. 487, col. 77). Had it been contained in the Bill as originally drafted, it would presumably have been included in Pt. III of Sched. 1.

S.56 of the Local Government (Scotland) Act 1973 is the provision which, *inter alia*, gives all local authorities the power to "arrange for the discharge" of their functions by a committee, sub-committee, officer or, indeed, another local authority in Scotland. It is on the strength of this section that most local authority decision-making is routinely delegated to committees and sub-committees and, to a lesser extent, officers.

An exception to the general authority to delegate has been, since the 1973 Act came into effect in 1975, in relation to "determining a rate or borrowing of money". These are functions which, in terms of s.56(6), may be exercised only by the local authority (the council) itself.

This section now extends the functions covered by s.56(6) to include the full range of decisions to be made from 1989. It should be remembered that "rate" is defined to mean the non-domestic rate, the non-domestic water rate and the non-domestic sewerage rate (s.26(2)). "Borrowing money" now becomes the fourth category (d).

Appeals

29.—(1) An appeal to the sheriff under this Act shall be by way of summary application and shall be lodged with the sheriff clerk within 28 days of the determination, refusal, imposition, requirement, designation or, as the case may be, other matter appealed against or within such longer period as the sheriff may allow.

(2) An appeal shall lie to the Court of Session, but only on a question of law, from the decision of the sheriff on an appeal to him under this Act.

GENERAL NOTE
Appeals to the sheriff are provided by the Act as follows:—
(a) S.16(1)(b)—against the determination by the Community Charges Registration Officer of an appeal to him against an entry or amendment of an entry in the register.
(b) S.16(2)(a) (read with s.16(3))—against the refusal by the registration officer of a request to make or to amend an entry in the register.
(c) S.16(2)(b) (read with s.16(3))—against the deemed refusal of a request as in (b).
(d) S.17(9)—against the determination by the registration officer of an appeal against designation as a "responsible person".
(e) S.17(12)—against the imposition by the registration officer on a "responsible person" of a civil penalty (£50 or £200) for failure to provide information or for giving false information.
(f) S.18(5)—against the requirement by the levying authority to pay a sum of money for community charges for a "backdated period".
(g) Sched. 2, para. 3(b)—against the determination of the levying authority (or a housing body under para. 5(2)) of an appeal to it against the amount of community charges stated in a demand notice.
In respect of all these classes of appeal, this section makes three supplementary provisions:
Firstly, it prescribes that the procedure be by way of summary application. (See Sheriff Courts (Scotland) Act 1907, ss.3 and 50).

Secondly, the section prescribes a time-limit of 28 days within which the appeal must be lodged with the sheriff clerk—subject to extension by the sheriff (but see note on subs. (1) below).

Thirdly, there is provision for a further appeal "on a question of law" to the Court of Session. Such appeals are to the Inner House under Chapter 5 of the Rules of Court 196 (S.I. 1965 No. 321). No other appeal from the sheriff is provided for. It must be assumed that an appeal will not normally lie from sheriff to sheriff principal (although the first appeal would be competently heard by either). (For an analogous decision to this effect under the Licensing (Scotland) Act 1976, see *Troc Sales* v. *Kirkcaldy D.L.B.,* 1982 S.L.T.(Sh.Ct. 77).

The section unsurprisingly fails to define what is meant by a "question of law". The phrase occurs frequently in relation to statutory appeals and relies upon the distinction which can supposedly be drawn between "questions of law" which are appealable to the higher court and "questions of fact" which are not. "Questions of law" would be expected to embrace mixed questions of fact and law. As Mr. Ancram pointed out in debate (see 1st Scot.S.C. col. 1342) disputed questions both of fact and of law can be taken in the initial appeal to the sheriff—although the example he appears to cite as a question of fact well illustrates the difficulties in this area. He refers to the question of "whether a person is solely or mainly resident in a specific area." Clearly this issue does involve questions of fact but the interpretation of what, in law, amounts to sole or main residence is itself a question of law

The question of whether the appeals under the Act should go to the sheriff at all in preference to some other new or existing tribunal has already been discussed (see notes on s.16). See also the views of Mr. Ancram: "We considered what were the best appeal mechanisms and came to the conclusion that this established appeal mechanism would work well for the sort of cases likely to be heard, under this legislation. That is the Government's judgment, and unless evidence was brought forward which strongly suggested that this was wrong, I certainly believe that we should stand with the sheriff court appeals, which are to the advantage of those who will require to use them" (1st Scot.S.C., col. 1344).

For discussion of other appellate provisions in the Act see (in addition to the notes on sections creating appeals to the sheriff) the notes on s.2(6) and on Sched. 1, para. 14. Both of these relate primarily to appeals under the Valuation Acts but it is pointed out, under s.2(6), that valuation appeals and community charge appeals may arise from the same facts—and may not necessarily be decided in ways compatible with each other. Notice too the discussion under s.2(6) of the possible use of judicial review proceedings as an alternative to appeal. This possibility may also arise in relation to the decisions of registration officers

Subs. (1)

This subsection was amended at House of Commons Report stage (*Hansard,* H.C. Vol. 111, col. 1105) to incorporate the term "designation" which presumably refers to designation as a responsible person under s.17. That section was, however, itself further amended at House of Lords Report stage to alter the appeal to the sheriff to one against a "determination" rather than a "designation". For debate about the period of 28 days within which an appeal must normally be lodged and suggestions that it may be unsatisfactorily short and then subject only to extension by the sheriff which may not be granted (see 1st Scot.S.C cols. 1342–1344).

A further complication raised by the appeal under s.16(1) and (2) in particular (although it might arise in others) is that of the possible emergence of different decisions from different sheriffs. Under s.16(3) the appeal lies to "the sheriff [presumably "any sheriff"] of any sheriffdom which wholly or partly falls within any of the registration areas".

Subs. (2)

This subsection was also amended at House of Commons Report stage (*Hansard,* H.C Vol. 111, col. 1105) to delete words which declared the decision of the Court of Session on further appeal "to be final". The revised wording leaves open the possibility of appeal to the House of Lords. For "a question of law" see the general note above.

The obligation of the registration officer under s.16(4) presumably extends to the situation following appeal to the higher courts.

Crown application

30.—(1) Parts I and V of this Act apply to Crown land in which there is an interest other than that of the Crown, but this subsection does not render the Crown liable under any of those provisions of this Act.

(2) Persons solely or mainly resident in Crown land who would, but for this subsection, be liable to pay the personal community charge or personal community water charge shall be exempt from that liability if they are within such class or classes of person as may be prescribed.

(3) The premises in respect of which the standard or the collective community charge or the standard or collective community water charge is payable include Crown land, but this subsection does not render the Crown liable to these charges.

(4) In this section "Crown land" means land in which there is any interest belonging to Her Majesty in right of the Crown or to a Government department or to a Minister of the Crown or held on behalf of Her Majesty for the purposes of a Government department.

(5) This section is without prejudice to section 8 of the Crown Private Estates Act 1862.

DEFINITIONS
  "community charge": see ss.26(1) and 7.
  "community water charge": see s.26(1) and Sched. 5, para. 6.
  "prescribed": see ss.26(1) and 31.

GENERAL NOTE
  These provisions dealing with the application of the Act to Crown land achieve five purposes:—
  1. The latter part of subs. (1) maintains the general exemption of the Crown from liability to taxation under the Act. However, under subs. (5) this is to be read subject to s.8 of the Crown Private Estates Act 1862 which provides that the *private estates* of the sovereign (such as Balmoral) are subject to all taxes and rates.
  It should also be noted that the new arrangements for non-domestic rates will not alter the practice under which payments are made by the Crown in respect of Crown property in lieu of rates. (See Armour, *Valuation for Rating 1985*, 5th ed., edited by Clyde and Hope, para. 16–12).
  2. Subs. (1) also extends the taxing provisions of the Act to Crown land "in which there is an interest other than that of the Crown" thus ensuring a liability in those circumstances to non-domestic rates.
  3. Subs. (2) confirms that residence in Crown land will not normally exempt a person, otherwise liable, from liability to pay the personal community charge and personal community water charge.
  4. That subsection, however, also enables a class or classes of person to be exempt if so prescribed. This is the device which will be used to exempt prisoners in custody and long-term patients in N.H.S. hospitals. As Lord Glenarthur said in the House of Lords (*Hansard,* H.L. Vol. 487, col. 80), "The argument here is that those categories are so far removed from the democratic process that the imposition of liability to pay the personal community charge would be inappropriate". In this respect, the exemptions will parallel those which, for properties in rating, will be achieved by prescription under s.2(3)(b) (for the position of these categories of residents within the overall scheme of exemptions envisaged under the Act, see the general note on s.8). On the other hand, liability to community charges will certainly attach to, for example, members of the armed forces and their families. The special position of visiting forces was considered at *Hansard,* H.L. Vol. 487, col. 81.
  5. Subs. (3) confirms a parallel liability to standard and collective community (and water) charges where the premises concerned are on Crown land.

Additional powers exercisable by, and procedure for, regulations

31.—(1) Such provisions as appear to the Secretary of State to be necessary or expedient for the purposes of rendering this Act of full effect may be prescribed.

(2) Regulations under this Act may make—
  (a) such supplemental, consequential or transitional provision as the Secretary of State thinks fit;
  (b) different provision for different cases or classes of case.

(3) Regulations under this Act shall be made by the Secretary of State by statutory instrument subject to annulment in pursuance of a resolution of either House of Parliament.

DEFINITION
"prescribed": see s.26(1) and this section.

GENERAL NOTE
In many areas, this Act produces only a very skeletal pattern of rules. Most of its provisions require to be supplemented by further rules to be "prescribed" by the Secretary of State. S.26(1) defines "prescribed" as "prescribed by regulations under this Act". This section requires such regulations to be by statutory instrument made subject to annulment by resolution of either House.

It will have been noticed that, at many points, during the passage of the Bill through Parliament, the wide powers of prescription attracted criticism. Some of the most trenchant attacks were reserved for this section and, with reference, to the broad language in subs. (1), Lord Ross of Marnock asked, "Why bother to have a Bill at all? Why not just state the general principles and then say, 'Well, anything that we think we need to do for the purposes of introducing these charges may be prescribed'?" (*Hansard,* H.L. Vol. 487, col. 82). He went on to point out that only the negative resolution procedure is involved.

The Government's reply (Lord Glenarthur, *Hansard,* H.L. Vol. 487, col. 84) was that similarly wide powers to ensure that "full effect" be given to an Act were frequently granted. He cited examples in s.215 of the Local Government (Scotland) Act 1973 and s.35 of the Local Government (Scotland) Act 1975.

As to the negative resolution procedure in subs. (3), this extends to all prescription by regulations under the Act. Commencement orders, however, under s.35 are not subject to any parliamentary supervision. The only affirmative resolution procedure in the Act at all is that required, under para. 2(5) of Sched. 4, for revenue support grant orders. (An affirmative resolution is also required for the reports presented to the House of Commons under Sched. 3 to require the reduction of community charges. It has already been pointed out that either House of Parliament would be able to negative the prescription under s.3(2) of maximum non-domestic rates). The power to prescribe amendments to the Social Security Act 1986 under s.24 is subject only to the negative resolution procedure under this section.

Although calculations of the number of prescriptive powers in the Act have produced different results, the total appears to be about 80 (see, *e.g.,* the estimate of 78 at 1st Scot.S.C., col. 1367) but the Government have indicated that they will be exercised in groups. In the House of Lords (*Hansard,* H.L. Vol. 486, col. 371), Lord Glenarthur envisaged the need for about seven main groups of regulations.

More recently a ministerial statement in the House of Commons (*Hansard,* H.C. Vol. 119, cols. 876–877) referred to the need for "about half a dozen main sets of regulations". The most significant would be:—

1. Regulations dealing with domestic subjects. These are the important powers in ss.2(3)(b), 2(4) and 26(1) (part residential subjects).

2. Registration procedures. These are the powers in ss.13–20 relating to the form and content of the register, the canvass and appeals.

3. Definitions of liability of certain groups. The regulations under s.2 will have defined liability to community charges where this is by reference to residence but regulations are required under s.8 (especially concerning students) and s.30 (prisoners and long-stay hospital patients).

4. Regulations governing the time-table for setting community charges and non-domestic rates (principally under ss.3(1) and 9(1)).

5. Regulations governing the collection of community charges (Sched. 2).

Finance

32. There shall be defrayed out of money provided by Parliament—
   (a) sums required for the payment of revenue support grant;
   (b) sums required for the payment of subsidies by virtue of section 24(b) of this Act; and
   (c) any increase attributable to this Act in the sums payable under any other Act out of money so provided.

DEFINITION
"revenue support grants": see Sched. 4.

GENERAL NOTE

This is a standard form of clause to authorise the funding of the Act's provisions. The principal new contributions from central government are identified in (a) as the new revenue support grants to be made from 1989–90 under Sched. 4 and in (b) as the subsidies to local authorities for the community charges rebates under s.24.

In the Explanatory and Financial Memorandum on the Bill as originally introduced into the House of Commons, additional expenditure for local authorities was anticipated for local authorities in the light of their new registration, collection and other duties. It also foresaw an increase in the cost of rebates—perhaps from £15m. per year for the rate rebates expected from April 1, 1988, to £20m. The cost of extra workload in the sheriff courts would be less than £1m. per year. There would be some, unquantifiable, extra cost on legal advice and assistance.

Amendments to Debtors (Scotland) Act 1987

33. The Debtors (Scotland) Act 1987 shall be amended as follows—
(a) in section 1(5) (which relates to time to pay directions), after the word "rates" in paragraph (e) there shall be added—
"(ee) in an action by or on behalf of a—
(i) levying authority for the payment of any community charge or community water charge within the meaning of section 26 of the Abolition of Domestic Rates Etc. (Scotland) Act 1987 (which defines terms used in that Act) or any amount payable under section 18(3) (payment of community charges in respect of backdated period, with surcharge and interest) of that Act; or
(ii) regional or islands council for payment of any amount payable as a civil penalty under section 17(10) or (11) (failure to provide information to a registration officer) of that Act,"
(b) in section 5(4) (which relates to time to pay orders), after the word "authority" in paragraph (e) there shall be added—
"(ee) in relation to a debt including any sum due to—
(i) a levying authority in respect of any community charge or community water charge within the meaning of section 26 of the Abolition of Domestic Rates Etc. (Scotland) Act 1987 (which defines terms used in that Act) or any amount payable under section 18(3) (payment of community charges in respect of backdated period, with surcharge and interest) of that Act; or
(ii) a regional or islands council in respect of any amount payable as a civil penalty under section 17(10) or (11) (failure to provide information to a registration officer) of that Act,"
(c) in section 106 (interpretation)—
(i) after the definition of "employer" there shall be inserted—
" "levying authority" has the meaning assigned to it in paragraph 1 of Schedule 2 to the Abolition of Domestic Rates Etc. (Scotland) Act 1987 and, in relation to community water charges, means the regional or islands council;" and
(ii) in the definition of "summary warrant", after the word "of", where first occurring, there shall be inserted the words "paragraph 7 of Schedule 2 to the Abolition of Domestic Rates Etc. (Scotland) Act 1987 or"; and
(d) in paragraph 35 of Schedule 5, in the definition of "creditor" there shall be inserted at the end—
"(d) for the purposes of—
(i) paragraph 7 of Schedule 2 to the Abolition of Domestic Rates Etc. (Scotland) Act 1987, the levying authority;
(ii) that paragraph as read with section 17(10) or (11) of that Act, the regional or islands council.".

DEFINITIONS
"civil penalty": s.17(10)–(11).
"community charge": ss.7 and 26.
"community water charge": s.26 and Sched. 5, para. 6.
"levying authority": s.26 and Sched. 2, para. 2.

GENERAL NOTE
This section makes a number of amendments to the Debtors (Scotland) Act 1987 which implemented many of the findings of the Report of the Scottish Law Commission on Diligence and Debtor Protection (Scot. Law Com. No. 95, 1985). It was introduced at Committee Stage in the Lords in recognition of the fact that the law of debt in Scotland was about to be restructured in the light of the Scottish Law Commission report and that it should be properly co-ordinated with the new legal framework introduced by the present Act (*Hansard,* H.L. Vol. 486, cols. 1159–1160, *per* the Lord Advocate). This process of co-ordination involves a dual pronged strategy; first, the introduction of a number of amendments to the present Act incorporating some of the changes in methods of recovery of debt precipitated by the Debtors (Scotland) Act 1987 into the procedures available for recovery of community charges under Sched. 2, paras. 7 and 8; secondly, the insertion of the present section which complements and completes this process by amending the Debtors (Scotland) Act 1987 itself in order that relevant aspects of the reformed system of diligences may be applied to community charges, and, in particular, that recovery of community charges is treated in the same manner as recovery of rates under the reformed system.

Para. (a)
This amends s.1(5) of the Debtors (Scotland) Act 1987 so as to provide that it is incompetent for a court, on granting decree for payment of any principal sum of money, to make a time-to-pay direction in an action provided for under this Act, either on behalf of the levying authority for the payment of any amount of community charge together with any interest and surcharge thereupon, or on behalf of the regional or islands council for payment of any amounts payable as a civil penalty under s.17(10) and (11) of this Act. Other situations where it is not competent to make a time-to-pay direction under s.1(5) of the Debtors (Scotland) Act 1987 include: actions by or on behalf of a rating authority for payment of rates; by or on behalf of the Inland Revenue for the recovery of tax; for payment of duty under the Betting and Gaming Duties Act 1981, or of car tax or value added tax; in connection with a maintenance order; where the decree contains an award of a capital sum in divorce or on the granting of a declaration of nullity of marriage; where the sum of money decerned for exceeds £10,000 or such other amount as may be prescribed by the Lord Advocate.

Para. (b)
This amends s.5(4) of the Debtors (Scotland) Act 1987 so as to provide that it is incompetent for a sheriff to make a time-to-pay order in respect of a debt due under a decree or other document in respect of which a charge for payment has been served on a debtor, an arrestment has been executed, or an action of adjudication has been commenced, where the debt due is one of community charge or of civil penalty under the present Act and the creditor is the levying authority or the regional or islands council as the case may be. The class of actions in respect of which a time-to-pay order is incompetent is identical to the class of actions, identified in para. (a) above, in respect of which a time-to-pay direction is incompetent.

Para. (c)
This introduces two amendments to s.106 of the Debtors (Scotland) Act 1987, which is an interpretation section. The first amendment merely defines the term "levying authority" which is incorporated in the amendments in paras. (a) and (b) above, in the manner provided for in the present Act: the second amendment extends the definition of "summary warrant" to include a warrant granted by virtue of para. 7 of Sched. 2 to the present Act, which paragraph deals with the procedure for recovery of community charge as authorised by summary warrant. The effect of this amendment is to ensure that the application to the present Act of the new procedure for the granting of a summary warrant and of the new forms of diligence which are available upon granting of such a decree, as introduced by the Debtors (Scotland) Act 1987, and as is already explicitly provided for in Sched. 2, paras. 7(2) and (3) of the present Act (see the note on Sched. 2, para. 7 below) is also provided for within the terms of the Debtors (Scotland) Act 1987 itself.

Para. (d)

This introduces an amendment to the definition of "creditor" in Sched. 5, para. 35, to the Debtors (Scotland) Act 1987 so as to provide that, for the purposes of that Schedule, which deals with poinding and sales in pursuance of summary warrants, the term shall be extended to include the levying authority concerned with the recovery of community charges under Sched. 2, para. 7, to the present Act and also the islands or regional council concerned with the recovery of civil penalties under s.17(10) and (11) of the present Act. Again, the effect is to put the levying authority or islands or regional council in relation to payments under the present Act on the same footing as a rating authority and indeed any collector of tax for the purposes of recovering money by means of the various forms of diligence.

Repeals

34. The enactments specified in Schedule 6 to this Act are repealed to the extent specified in the third column of that Schedule.

COMMENCEMENT

This section comes into force (a) on September 14, 1987, for the purpose of bringing into force the repeals indicated in the notes on Sched. 6 as coming into force on that date but subject to the restrictions of purpose also indicated; (b) on April 1, 1989, to implement the repeals effective on that date; and (c) on April 1, 1994, when it will be fully in force.

Citation, commencement and extent.

35.—(1) This Act may be cited as the Abolition of Domestic Rates Etc. (Scotland) Act 1987.

(2) This Act shall come into force on such day as the Secretary of State may by order appoint and different days may be so appointed for different provisions or for different purposes.

(3) An order under subsection (2) above may include such transitional provision as appears to the Secretary of State to be necessary or expedient in connection with the provisions thereby brought into force.

(4) This Act applies to Scotland only.

DEFINITION

"order": see s.26(1).

GENERAL NOTE

The section provides for the short title, commencement and extent—Scotland only.

An order, The Abolition of Domestic Rates Etc. (Scotland) Act 1987 Commencement Order 1987 (S.I. 1987 No. 1489) was made on August 18, 1987. It provides for the whole Act to come into force on different dates between September 14, 1987, and April 1, 1994. The appropriate date of commencement is included in the notes on each section and Schedule.

The Act's provisions will be seen to fall broadly into five groups:—

1. Those sections which came into force without qualification on September 14, 1987. These were ss.1–5, 9, 12–17, 21–25(1), 26(1), 27–33, 35 (this section), certain paragraphs in Sched. 1, and all of Scheds. 2, 3, and 4.

2. Those sections which come into force on September 14, 1987, but for restricted purposes only—ss.6–8, 10, 11, 25(2) and (3), 26(2), 34, and certain paragraphs in Scheds. 1, 5 and 6.

The restriction of purpose is principally to ensure that powers in sections fully effective from April 1, 1989 (for the financial year 1989–90) are available beforehand to enable preparations to be made for full implementation—whether of community charges or of the new water and sewerage charges.

3. Three sections—s.18 (Obtaining of information from individual residents), s.19 (Effect of register), and s.20 (Inspection of register)—which will come into force on October 1, 1988.

4. The remainder of the Act (except the provisions in 5 below) which will come into force on April 1, 1989.

5. A limited number of the repeals in Sched. 6 which will come into force on April 1, 1994. Although virtually the whole Act will be in force on April 1, 1989, when the new system of community charges, non-domestic rates, revenue support grants, and water and

sewerage charges will be fully operational, the implementation of some repeals is delayed to allow the final settlement of entitlements to rate support grants.

In Parliament there was a last ditch attempt to make the commencement of the whole Act subject to a referendum (see *Hansard,* H.L. Vol. 486, col. 1202).

SCHEDULES

Sections 2 and 6   SCHEDULE 1

VALUATION AND RATING

PART I

PART RESIDENTIAL SUBJECTS

Apportionment notes

1. Subject to paragraph 2 below, the assessor for each valuation area shall, by such date before 1st April 1989 as may be prescribed, apportion the net annual value and the rateable value of those lands and heritages entered in the valuation roll which are part residential subjects as between the residential and non-residential use made of them.

2. The assessor shall, by such date before 1st April 1989 as may be prescribed, alter the valuation roll by adding to the entry of lands and heritages which are part residential subjects a note (an "apportionment note") showing, separately from their net annual value and their rateable value, the parts of each of those values which relate respectively to the residential and non-residential use of the lands and heritages.

Addition, deletion or amendment of apportionment notes

3. Where, on or after the date prescribed under paragraph 2 above, the assessor alters the valuation roll by entering therein lands and heritages which are part residential subjects, he shall apportion the net annual value and the rateable value of those lands and heritages as between the residential and non-residential use made of them and shall include in the entry an apportionment note.

4. Subject to paragraph 9 below, where, on or after the date prescribed under paragraph 2 above—

(a) lands and heritages included in the valuation roll become or cease to be part residential subjects; or

(b) there is such a change as between the residential and non-residential use of the lands and heritages that the apportionments of the net annual value and the rateable value shown in the valuation roll are incorrect,

the assessor shall apportion or, as the case may be, re-apportion the net annual value and the rateable value of those lands and heritages as between the residential and non-residential use made of them, and shall alter the roll by adding an apportionment note to the entry in respect of those lands and heritages or, as the case may be, by deleting or amending the existing note.

5. Subject to paragraph 9 below, where, under any of the provisions of section 2(1) of the 1975 Act (which provides for the alteration of the valuation roll in certain circumstances), the assessor alters the net annual value and the rateable value of any lands and heritages which are part residential subjects, he shall apportion the new net annual value and the new rateable value as between the residential and non-residential use of the subjects, and shall amend the apportionment note accordingly.

Date of coming into effect of addition, deletion or amendment of apportionment note

6. Where the valuation roll is altered under paragraph 2 above by the addition of an apportionment note to any entry relating to lands and heritages in the valuation roll, the alteration shall take effect from 1st April 1989.

7. Where an apportionment note is included under paragraph 3 above as part of an entry relating to any lands and heritages in the valuation roll, the note shall take effect—

(a) where the entry is made before that date, from 1st April 1989; and

(b) where the entry is made on or after 1st April 1989, from—

(i) the date when the lands and heritages to which the entry relates come into existence or occupancy, or

(ii) the beginning of the financial year in which the entry is made,

whichever is the later.

8. Subject to paragraph 9 below, where the valuation roll is altered by the addition or deletion of, or by an amendment to, an apportionment note under paragraph 4 above, or by an amendment to an apportionment note under paragraph 5 above, the alteration shall take effect from—

(a) the date of the event by reason of which the addition, deletion or amendment is made, or

(b) the beginning of the financial year in which the addition, deletion or amendment is made,

whichever is the later.

9. No alteration to the valuation roll consisting of an amendment to an apportionment note shall be made or take effect until three months, or such other period as may be prescribed, after the date when that apportionment note is made or takes effect, whichever is the later.

Revaluations

10. Where the assessor makes up a valuation roll in respect of a financial year which is a year of revaluation within the meaning of section 37(1) of the 1975 Act (which defines terms used in that Act), he shall apportion the new net annual value and the new rateable value of any lands and heritages which are part residential subjects as between the residential and non-residential use of the subjects, and shall include in the entry relating to those lands and heritages a new apportionment note.

General

11. For the purposes of this Part of this Schedule the extent to which subjects are used residentially shall be determined by reference to the use made of the subjects as the sole or main residence of any person, and criteria may be prescribed by reference to which any apportionment or re-apportionment of net annual values and rateable values under this Part of this Schedule is to be carried out.

12. No rates shall be leviable in respect of such part of their rateable value as relates to the residential use of any lands and heritages which are part residential subjects.

DEFINITIONS

"assessor": see Local Government (Scotland) Act 1973, s.116(2).

"financial year": see s.26(1) and Local Government (Scotland) Act 1973, s.96(5) as amended; *i.e.* the year from April 1.

"lands and heritages": see Lands Valuation (Scotland) Act 1854, s.42.

"net annual value": see s.26(1).

"the 1975 Act": see s.26(1).

"part residential subject": see s.26(1).

"prescribed": see ss.26(1) and 31.

"rateable value": see s.26(1).

"valuation area": see Local Government (Scotland) Act 1973, s.116(1).

"valuation roll": see Local Government (Scotland) Act 1975, s.1.

GENERAL NOTE

Pts. I and II of Sched. 1, to which effect is given by s.2(7), supplement the provisions made in s.2 itself for the extrication of what are there defined as "domestic subjects" from the valuation roll.

The deletion from the roll of domestic subjects which is at the heart of Pt. I of the Act is discussed in the notes on s.2. Another related provision is s.4 (which deals with the removal from the roll of parts of properties whose value has already been apportioned between a part occupied "as a dwelling-house" and a part not so occupied).

As already mentioned in the notes on s.2, yet another concept, that of "part residential subjects", is used to deal with the position, after April 1, 1989, of properties which will be on the valuation roll but in respect of which rates will be levied only in relation to the value of their non-residential use. This leaves those persons who are solely or mainly resident in the premises vulnerable in principle to the personal or collective community charge under ss.8 or 11. The device of part residential subjects seeks to maintain the general dichotomy between liability to rates and liability to community charges at which the Act as a whole is aimed.

Notes on paragraphs in the Schedule are set out below in numerical order. For a more immediate understanding, however, a reordering of the reading of the paragraphs may be advisable.

Thus para. 12 sets out the most general proposition: no rates are leviable on the value of the residential use of "part residential subjects". For the definition of "part residential subjects" we look to s.26(1). This defines them as "lands and heritages which are used partly as the sole or main residence of any person, other than (a) domestic subjects, and (b) such other class or classes of lands and heritages as may be prescribed." "Domestic subjects" can be neither on the valuation roll nor, therefore, rateable by virtue of ss.1 and 2—although it will also be recalled that the scope of "domestic subjects" can be either extended (s.2(3)(b)) or restricted (s.2(4)) by prescription by the Secretary of State. See also the rules under s.2(5) for the extrication of *parts* of lands and heritages prescribed under either s.2(3)(b) or 2(4) but which belong on the other side of the domestic/non-domestic line.

What the concept of part residential subjects does is to enable a further means of extricating from subjects which are rated a part attributable to residential use—a part which cannot be extracted as separate domestic subjects and removed from the roll but a part identified as a proportion of the total *value* of the subjects. The typical example may be the hotel which contains within it accommodation for a manager who uses that accommodation as his sole or main residence (see, *e.g., Hansard,* H.L. Vol. 486, col. 463). The hotel will comprise non-domestic subjects and rated. It will also, however, be regarded as part residential—requiring apportionment of its value under this Schedule and leaving the manager liable to a community charge.

The final limb of the definition (in s.26(1)) of part residential subjects allows the Secretary of State to prescribe exceptions in addition to domestic subjects. As mentioned in the note on s.2, this will probably be done in relation to residential care homes and nursing homes. In order to achieve exemption from community charges for their occupants, these homes will first be *excepted* from the general prescription of "domestic subjects" (s.2(3)(b)) but then prescribed as *not* part residential (s.26(1)).

One curiosity suggested by this process is that if any form of residential home (other than a home for those thought not properly liable to a community charge) is not prescribed as a domestic subject by virtue of s.2(3)(b) and is, therefore, rated, it might be not only "partly" but "wholly" residential. Presumably it would still fall within the definition of "part residential subjects"?

Returning to the Schedule itself, the actual process of apportionment is probably best approached by way of paras. 1 and 2 (apportionment notes) and 11 (criteria for apportionment). These provisions are then supported by paras. 3–5 (addition, deletion, amendment of apportionment notes) and paras. 6–9 (dates of effect). These two groups of paragraphs should be read with paras. 13 and 14 in Pt. II of the Schedule. The general note on Pt. II explains that these are best seen as integrated within Pt. I. Finally, para. 10 relates to the effect of a revaluation.

Paras. 1 and 2

These two paragraphs define the assessor's principal functions under this Part of the Schedule.

Although this is not explicitly stated, he has first to identify those subjects entered in the roll which are part residential. This will be determined in the light of the definition in s.26(1) and will depend upon their use as a "sole or main residence" and upon whether the class of subject has been excluded from the part-residential category by prescription. Depending upon the extent and nature of any such prescriptions this latter criterion may not be expected to be the cause of great difficulty. Ascertaining the actual use of premises for the purpose of this Schedule may be much more difficult.

Secondly, the assessor has to apportion the value of the premises as between their residential and non-residential use. Notice that para. 11 defines "residential use" as the "use made of the subjects as the sole or main residence of any person". Other types of residential use do not qualify for this purpose. Para. 11 goes on to empower the Secretary of State to prescribe the criteria according to which the apportionment of values should proceed. In the absence of such criteria, assessors will have to evolve their own tests and doubtless these will vary. Placing a value on a room or a few rooms (especially if the extent of occupation varies during the year as it may, for instance, in the case of the resident proprietors of a boarding house) is not easily done with precision.

The apportionment of values of all these premises has to be achieved by a date before April 1, 1989, to be prescribed. No doubt, in some cases, the status of premises as part residential subjects or the degree of residential use within them will change between that date and April 1, 1989, or thereafter (see paras. 4 and 9).

Once the apportionment is made, the assessor must, again by a (different?) date to be prescribed, alter the roll by the addition of an "apportionment note" showing the apportioned net annual and rateable values. Notice that, in addition, the assessor must, in terms of para.

13, add a note of the date on which the apportionment must take effect (on that, see para. 6).

To complete this review of the assessor's initial duties, it should be noted that under para. 14 he must give notice to the rating authority and also to what the paragraph describes as "other persons affected" of the addition of the apportionment note. This duty incorporates the terms of s.3 of the Local Government (Scotland) Act 1975 which actually identifies as "other persons affected" each person who is a "proprietor, tenant, or occupier" of the lands and heritages. (This is also the designation built into the appeals under s.2(6) of this Act). S.3(2) of the 1975 Act then goes on to confer a right of appeal upon any such person who is aggrieved by an entry of which he has received notice. The appeal is to the valuation appeal committee and, from there, as described in the note on s.2(6) above.

The main interest of the appellant will no doubt be normally that of reducing the proportion of the value of the premises attributed to non-residential use in order to reduce his liability to rates. In other circumstances, however, it might be in the appellant's (ratepayer's) interest to challenge the designation of the premises as part residential at all. By that means he would, if successful, remove the liability of residents to community charges.

This, in turn, raises the question of who is, or should be, a competent appellant, or, if not appellant, complainant in such proceedings for it might be a "resident" in the premises but not a "proprietor, tenant or occupier" on the roll who wishes to challenge the designation as part residential and thus avoid liability to pay a community charge.

An appeal by such another person under s.3(2) would appear not to be competent. Nor does it seem inevitable that such a person could, as a "person interested" complain under s.22 of the Local Government (Scotland) Act 1966 because such a complaint has to be on the grounds that "particular lands and heritages are not included in the valuation roll for that area and that they ought to be included". It must also be doubtful whether a complaint that an erroneous value has been entered (under s.13 of the Lands Valuation (Scotland) Act 1854) would be the answer. Perhaps, however, a complaint by "any person interested" under s.6 of the Valuation of Lands (Scotland) Amendment Act 1879 that some particular, other than valuation, is inaccurate would be a possible route to the valuation appeal committee.

As also explained in relation to s.2(6) of this Act, it should not be forgotten that the parallel procedures of appeal to the sheriff against liability to a community charge and of application to the Court of Session for judicial review may, in appropriate circumstances, be available.

Paras. 3–5

As already acknowledged, one feature of the apportionment of values of part residential subjects is that circumstances change and this imposes further duties upon the assessor. Three categories of change are addressed by paras. 3–5.

Para. 3 deals with lands and heritages added to the roll after the date to be prescribed for para. 2. If they are part residential, their values must be apportioned and a note added to the entry as above.

Similarly, para. 4 requires a change by way of addition, deletion or amendment of an apportionment note when either (a) premises in the roll become or cease to be part residential subjects or (b) there is such a change in the balance of use that the former apportionment between residential and non-residential use is incorrect. This duty to amend (but not to add or delete) an apportionment note is subject to para. 9 which prohibits such amendment within three months (or other period to be prescribed) of the making (or taking effect if later) of the apportionment note. But see the note on para. 9 below.

Para. 5 (which is again to be read subject to para. 9) addresses the third main class of change—when the value of the premises themselves is altered as a result of a decision of the assessor under s.2(1) of the Local Government (Scotland) Act 1975. This provides for alteration of the roll in a range of circumstances including the correction of an error and also "to give effect to any alteration in the value of any lands and heritages which is due to a material change of circumstances" (discussed in the note on s.5). Such alteration of the values on the roll requires an amendment apportionment role.

In relation to all three paragraphs, see paras. 7–8 (on date of effect), 13 (on the note of date of effect) and 14 (principally in relation to notification and appeals).

Paras. 6–9

These paragraphs determine the date of effect of the addition, deletion or amendment of apportionment notes under earlier paragraphs.

Para. 6 provides that initial apportionments under para. 2 take effect on April 1, 1989.

Para. 7 deals with the new apportionment notes under para. 3. If the entry in the roll is made before April 1, 1989, it is effective from that date. If made on or after that date, then the entry is effective from the later of the date of existence or occupancy of the premises or the beginning of the financial year.

Similar provision is made by para. 8 (subject to para. 9) in relation to changes under para. 4 or 5 save that the "date of the event by reason of which" the change is made is substituted for the date of existence or occupancy of the premises.

The three month restriction imposed upon alterations under paras. 4, 5 and 8 has been referred to above. Presumably the purpose of the restriction was to prevent too great a frequency of modification of the roll and the burdens upon assessors and the uncertainty which would result (see *Hansard*, H.L. Vol. 486, cols. 462–463.) Trivial and short-lived alterations would be prevented. However, what does not appear to be precluded is frequent alteration once the initial apportionment note has been made or has taken effect and three months elapsed. The paragraph does not seem to prevent an amendment within three months of an earlier *amendment* (*cf.* s.15(1)(b)).

Para. 10

This paragraph has a similar effect in relation to changes in years of revaluation as para. 5 does for changes during the currency of a valuation roll. Plainly a new valuation and also a new apportionment is required.

Paras. 11, 12

These paragraphs have been mentioned in both the general note on this Part of the Schedule and the note on paras. 1 and 2.

Notice that one consequence of the introduction to the roll of part residential subjects is that the "rateable value" of subjects in s.7 of the Local Government (Scotland) Act 1975 (which relates to the levying of rates) has been extended (by the addition of a new subsection (1A) by para. 32 of this Schedule) to include the ambiguously styled "apportioned rateable value of part residential subjects". Presumably any ambiguity in that phrase is displaced by the categorical prohibition of the levying of rates on the "residential" portion in para. 12?.

Notice too that the concept of part residential subjects is extended to the new non-domestic water and sewerage rates (see Sched. 5 especially paras. 19 and 29).

PART II
GENERAL
Noting of date on which alterations take effect

13. Where the assessor has altered the entry in the valuation roll relating to any lands and heritages by adding, deleting or amending an apportionment note, he shall also alter the entry by adding thereto a note of the date on which the alteration takes effect.

Notification of addition, deletion or alteration of apportionment notes

14. Section 3 of the 1975 Act (which requires the assessor to notify the rating authority and other persons affected of any alterations in the roll, and provides for a right of appeal against any such alterations) shall apply to any addition, deletion or amendment of apportionment notes made under Part I of this Schedule as it applies to deletions and alterations made under section 1 or 2 of that Act.

DEFINITIONS
See the terms and sources of definitions listed under Sched. 1, Pt. I.

GENERAL NOTE
As indicated in the general note on Pt. I of this Schedule, paras. 13 and 14 which constitute Pt. II are provisions which were contained in Pt. III of the original Bill and were "General" in that they were designed to relate not only to the part residential material in what was then Pt. II but also the original Pt. I of Sched. 1 which dealt with "domestic subjects notes". These were a part of the apparatus included to deal with the transitional period 1989–1992 during which domestic subjects would have remained on the valuation roll. With the abandonment of all the transitional arrangements at the Commons Report stage the original Pt. I of the Schedule fell away.

With it went the references in what is now Pt. II to "domestic subjects notes". The rump of Pt. II is now better viewed as provisions supplemental to Pt. I and their effect has been considered in the notes on that Part.

Para. 13

For the assessor's duties to alter an entry in the valuation roll under this Schedule, see paras. 2, 3, 4 and 5. For the corresponding dates of effect, see paras. 6, 7, 8 and 9.

See para. 14 for the service of notice and appeals.

Para. 14

This is an extremely important supplement to the provisions in Pt. I of the Schedule. The circumstances in which a notice to "persons affected" is required have been referred to in the notes on Pt. I. See, in particular, the notes on paras. 1 and 2 where some further difficulties are discussed.

PART III

AMENDMENT OF ENACTMENTS

The Local Government (Scotland) Act 1974 (c.43)

15. In section 237 of the 1947 Act (which relates to the demand note for rates), in subsection (2)(*b*)—
(a) before the word "annual" insert "net";
(b) for the word "domestic" substitute "non-domestic"; and
(c) for the words "1949" substitute "1980".

16. In section 234B of the 1947 Act (which relates to the relief of rates in respect of non-domestic lands and heritages not in active use), in subsection (1)(b), for the words "sections 24 to 27" substitute "sections 24 and 25".

The Local Government Act 1948 (c.26)

17. In section 145(2) of the Local Government Act 1948 (which defines terms used in the Act for the purposes of its application to Scotland), for the definition of "rate" substitute—
" "rate" means the non-domestic rate and, for the purposes of Part V of this Act, includes the non-domestic water rate and the non-domestic sewerage rate;".

Valuation and Rating (Scotland) Act 1956 (c.60)

18. In section 7(2) of the 1956 Act (which defines terms in relation to agricultural lands and heritages and dwelling houses occupied in connection therewith), for the definition of "pertinent" substitute "in relation to a dwelling house shall be taken to include all land occupied therewith and used for the purposes thereof".

19. In section 22 of the 1956 Act (which relates to the exemption of churches etc. from rates)—
(a) in subsection (2), for the word "gross", in both places where it occurs, substitute "net"; and
(b) in subsection (4)(a), for the words "a domestic water rate" substitute "the non-domestic water rate or the non-domestic sewerage rate".

20. In section 43(1) of the 1956 Act (which defines terms used in the Act), for the definition of "the Valuation Acts" there shall be substituted—
" "the Valuation Acts" means the Lands Valuation (Scotland) Act 1954, the Acts amending that Act and any other enactment relating to valuation;".

The Local Government (Financial Provisions etc.) (Scotland) Act 1962 (c.9)

21. In section 4(10) of the Local Government (Financial Provisions etc.) (Scotland) Act 1962 (which relates to the reduction and remission of rates payable by charitable and other organisations), for paragraph (*b*) substitute—
"(*b*) "rate" means the non-domestic rate.".

The Public Works Loans Act 1965 (c.63)

22. For paragraph (b) of section 2(1) of the Public Works Loans Act 1965 (which relates to new form of local loan and the automatic charge for securing it), there shall be substituted—
"(b) in Scotland—
(i) any local authority within the meaning of the Local Government (Scotland) Act 1973,
(ii) any joint board or joint committee within the meaning of that Act, and

(iii) any other authority having the power to requisition any sum from any such local authority.".

The Local Government (Scotland) Act 1966 (c.51)

23. In section 46(1) of the 1966 Act (which defines terms used in the Act),—
(a) for the definition of "rate" substitute—
   " "rate" means the non-domestic rate," and
(b) in the definition of "Valuation Acts"—
   (i) the word "and" shall be omitted, and
   (ii) at the end there shall be inserted the words "and any other enactment relating to valuation".
24. In paragraph 1(2)(a) of Schedule 3 to the 1966 Act (which relates to the determination of rateable values), for the word "gross" substitute "net".

The National Loans Act 1968 (c.13)

25. In paragraph 1 of Schedule 4 to the National Loans Act 1968 (which relates to local loans), for sub-paragraph (c) there shall be substituted—
"(c) in Scotland—
   (i) any local authority within the meaning of the Local Government (Scotland) Act 1973;
   (ii) any joint board or committee within the meaning of that Act; and
   (iii) any other authority having the power to requisition any sum from such local authority.".

The Local Government (Scotland) Act 1973 (c.65)

26. For subsection (8) of section 116 of the 1973 Act (which relates to valuation areas and authorities and the appointment of assessors, etc.) there shall be substituted—
   "(8) In this section the expression "the Valuation Acts" means the Lands Valuation (Scotland) Act 1854, the Acts amending that Act and any other enactment relating to valuation.".
27. In section 83(4) of the 1973 Act (which relates to the power of local authorities to incur expenditure for certain purposes not otherwise authorised), for the words "that year", in both places where they occur, substitute "the financial year 1988–89".
28. In section 109 of the 1973 Act (which relates to rating authorities)—
(a) in subsection (1)—
   (i) for the words from "such rates" to the first "this Act" substitute "rates,";
   (ii) for the words "regional rate and the district rate" substitute "non-domestic regional and district rates";
   (iii) for the words "general rate" substitute "non-domestic islands rate";
   (iv) after the words "the islands council;" insert—
      "(c) in the case of the non-domestic water rate, the regional council or the islands council which determined it; and
      (d) in the case of the non-domestic sewerage rate, the regional council or the islands council which determined it;"; and
(b) in subsection (2), for the words "district rate" substitute "non-domestic district rate".
29. In section 110 of the 1973 Act (which relates to payments by the regional council to the district council in respect of district rates) for the words "district rate", wherever they appear, substitute "non-domestic district rate".
30. In section 111 of the 1973 Act (which empowers the Secretary of State to make regulations with respect to rates), in subsection (1)—
(a) in paragraphs (a) and (b), for the words "107 to 110" substitute "109 and 110";
(b) in paragraph (b), the words ", or section 5(4) and (5) of the Local Government (Scotland) Act 1966," shall cease to have effect;
(c) in paragraph (d), for the words "the district rate" substitute "the non-domestic district rate"; and
(d) paragraph (f) shall cease to have effect.
31. In section 118(1)(b) of the 1973 Act (which relates to local financial returns) for the words "district rate" substitute "non-domestic district rate".

The Local Government (Scotland) Act 1975 (c.30)

32. After subsection (1) of section 7 of the 1975 Act (which relates to the levying of rates) insert—

"(1A) References in subsection (1) above to "rateable value" include the apportioned rateable value of part residential subjects and, in the case of the non-domestic water rate, the net annual value and the apportioned net annual value of part residential subjects.".

33. In subsection (1) of section 37 of the 1975 Act (which defines terms used in that Act) n the definition of "the Valuation Acts" for the words "any other Act relating to valuation and includes this Act" there shall be substituted "and any other enactment relating to valuation".

34. In paragraph 6(2)(a) of Schedule 3 to the 1975 Act (which relates to borrowing and ending by local authorities), for the words "the regional, general, or district rate, as the case may be," substitute "rates, the community charges and the community water charges".

35. In paragraph 20(2) of the said Schedule 3—

   (a) for the words "or their proper officer of levying rates" substitute "of levying rates, the community charges and the community water charges"; and

   (b) for the words "rating authorities" substitute "other local authorities".

36. In paragraph 31 of the said Schedule 3 (which defines terms used in the Schedule) after the definition of "borrowing account" insert—

   " "community charges" shall be construed in accordance with section 7 (creation and purpose of community charges) of the Abolition of Domestic Rates Etc. (Scotland) Act 1987;

   "community water charges" shall be construed in accordance with paragraph 6 of Schedule 5 to the said Act of 1987;".

The Rating (Caravan Sites) Act 1976 (c.15)

37. In sections 3(3) and 4(1)(e) of the Rating (Caravan Sites) Act 1976 (which relate to the valuation and rating of caravan sites in Scotland), for the word "rate" substitute "non-domestic rate".

The Local Government, Planning and Land Act 1980 (c.65)

38. In paragraph 33(4) of Schedule 32 to the Local Government, Planning and Land Act 1980 (which relates to lands and heritages exempt from rates), for the word "domestic" where it second appears there shall be substituted "the non-domestic".

The Civic Government (Scotland) Act 1982 (c.45)

39. For subsection (9) of section 90 of the Civic Government (Scotland) Act 1982 (which relates to the lighting of common stairs etc.) substitute—

   "(9) A district or islands council who have, under subsection (2), (3) or (7) above, provided or maintained lighting or lit or extinguished lights shall be entitled to recover—

   (a) from the owner of the lands or premises the expense incurred by the council; or

   (b) where there is more than one owner of the lands or premises, that is, where the lands or premises are common property, from each owner such proportion of the expense thereby incurred by the council as the council may determine,

but the council may remit any sum or part of any sum due to them under this subsection.".

GENERAL NOTE
This Part of the Schedule (to which effect is given by s.6) consists of a number of "minor" amendments consequential upon the provisions in Pt. I of the Act. Repeals (on the authority of s.34) are contained in Sched. 6 and amendments to the Water (Scotland) Act 1980 are in Sched. 5, Pt. IV.

Para. 15
Commencement. September 14, 1987, but, "Only for the purposes of and in relation to the determination and levying of the non-domestic rate, the non-domestic water rate and the non-domestic sewerage rate in respect of the financial year 1989–90 and each subsequent financial year." Otherwise, April 1, 1989.

This paragraph makes a number of minor amendments to s.237 of the Local Government (Scotland) Act 1947 (demand note for rates). Subs. (2)(b) has already been amended by s.8 of the Local Government (Financial Provisions) (Scotland) Act 1962. All three new amendments relate to the water rate. Para. (a) ensures that non-domestic water rates are levied on *net* annual value; para. (b) converts old terminology "domestic water rate" to new terminology "non-domestic water rate"; para. (c) updates, somewhat belatedly, the reference to the Water (Scotland) Act 1949 to a reference to the 1980 Act.

Para. 16
Commencement. April 1, 1989.
S.243B of the 1947 Act was inserted by s.7 of the Rating and Valuation (Amendment) (Scotland) Act 1984 and relates to rating relief for "non-domestic" lands and heritages now in active use.
This amendment is directly consequential upon the repeal by Sched. 6 of ss.26 and 27 of the Local Government (Scotland) Act 1966.

Para. 17
Commencement. September 14, 1987 (as for para. 15) and April 1, 1989.
This amendment inserts a new definition of "rate" in the 1948 Act so far as it applies to Scotland and remains in force. In relation to Pt. V only of the 1948 Act the rate is defined to include the water rate. This position, updated to refer to the "non-domestic water rate" and to include the "non-domestic sewerage rate", is maintained.

Para. 18
Commencement. April 1, 1989.
Sched. 6 to this Act repeals, *inter alia* s.6(11) of the 1956 Act, together with much of the rest of that section. S.6(11) is a definition subsection which includes a definition of "pertinent" used in s.6(2) which is also repealed. The definition in s.7(2) of "pertinent" (in relation to agricultural lands) is achieved by incorporating that in the repealed s.6(11). The new definition repeals the old wording (and retains the tautologous double reference to occupation). The point of the section is to keep agricultural lands (but not dwelling-house and their pertinents) off the valuation roll. Presumably such houses are now, in any event, to be off the roll in terms of s.2 of this Act.

Para. 19
Commencement. September 14, 1987 (as for para. 15) and April 1, 1989.
S.22 of the 1956 Act exempts churches (and church related places) from rates but not from (old) "domestic" water rates. On the question of whether *parish* churches may be entered in the roll and rated *at all*, see Armour, *Valuation for Rating* (edited by Clyde and Hope, 5th ed., 1985, paras. 8–15, 8–16).
The amendment in sub-para. (b) retains the position in relation to payment of the new "non-domestic" water rate and extends liability to the "non-domestic" sewerage rate.
The amendment in sub-para. (a) replaces "gross" with "net" as part of the general abandonment of gross values with the end of rating of dwelling houses. The subs. (2) referred to deals with apportionment of values where exempt religious property is part of other property.

Para. 20
Commencement. September 14, 1987.
This amends the 1956 Act to insert the same definition of "the Valuation Acts" as is used in s.26(1) of this Act. *N.B.* the repeals of other parts of s.43(1) by Sched. 6.

Para. 21
Commencement. September 14, 1987 (as for para. 15) and April 1, 1989.
The 1962 Act provides for the reduction and remission of rates payable by charities but "rates" in that Act are defined by s.4(10) *not* to include the (old) domestic water rate. This amendment maintains the position by referring only to the new "non-domestic rate" but not to the "non-domestic water rate".

Para. 22
Commencement. September 14, 1987.
This paragraph (together with para. 25) was added to the Schedule in the House of Lords (*Hansard*, H.L. Vol. 486, col. 468). They were both described as technical amendments. Both have the effect of broadening the scope of (iii) to include the requisition of "any sum" rather than a rate.

Para. 23

Commencement. (1) September 14, 1987 (as for para. 15) and April 1, 1989; (2) September 14, 1987.

These amendments bring relevant definitions in the Local Government (Scotland) Act 1966 into line with those now used in this Act. See s.26(1) and (2). *N.B.* repeal of other definitions in s.46(1) of the 1966 Act by Sched. 6.

Para. 24

Commencement. April 1, 1989.

Sched. 3 to the Local Government (Scotland) Act 1966 is concerned with the rating of unoccupied property. References to "gross annual values" which become meaningless after April 1, 1989, Act comes into effect are replaced by references to "net annual values".

Para. 25

Commencement. September 14, 1987.

See note on para. 22 above.

Para. 26

Commencement. September 14, 1987.

The definition in s.116(8) of the Local Government (Scotland) Act 1973 is brought into line with s.26(1) of this Act.

Para. 27

Commencement. April 1, 1989.

One of the secondary uses of the valuation process (see note on s.5) is part of the definition of the limits of discretionary spending available to all local authorities under s.83 of the Local Government (Scotland) Act 1973. Subject to certain other limitations, local authorities are permitted to incur expenditure, not otherwise authorised by statute, which is in their opinion in the interests of their area, or any part of it, or in the interests of all or some of its inhabitants. The section does not make any extra money available to authorities and imposes an additional constraint. It limits (in subs. (4)) an authority's total annual expenditure under the section to the equivalent of the product of a 2p. rate. That total is clearly something which has varied (upwards) in years of revaluation but would be greatly reduced when domestic subjects are removed from the roll in 1989. Thus this amendment effectively freezes the maximum amount to be spent under the section at the level authorised for 1988–89.

Para. 28

Commencement. September 14, 1987 (as for para. 15) and April 1, 1989.

S.109 of the Local Government (Scotland) Act 1973 defines rating authorities and provides for district councils to intimate to regional councils (rating authorities) their requirements. These are amendments consequential upon the repeal of s.108 of the 1973 Act (see Sched. 6); the introduction of new duties to levy rates under s.3(1) and the redefinition of those rates in s.3(10).

Para. 29

Commencement. April 1, 1989.

This makes similar consequential amendments to s.110 of the Local Government (Scotland) Act 1973.

Para. 30

Commencement. April 1, 1989.

These amendments to s.111 of the Local Government (Scotland) Act 1973 are consequential upon (a) the repeal by Sched. 6 of ss.107–108C, and (b) of s.5 of the Local Government (Scotland) Act 1966; (c) the change of terminology produced by s.3; and (d) the repeal by Sched. 6 of s.108A of the 1973 Act.

Para. 31

Commencement. April 1, 1989.

Similarly consequential upon s.3 of this Act.

Para. 32
Commencement. September 14, 1987 (as for para. 15) and April 1, 1989.
S.7 of the Local Government (Scotland) Act 1975 requires rating authorities to levy rates according to "rateable value". This new subs. (1A) is designed to ensure that "rateable value" includes only the duly apportioned value of part residential subjects (see s.26(1) and Sched. 1, Pts. I and II); and, secondly, in relation to the new non-domestic water rate (see Sched. 5), the net annual value (apportioned for part residential subjects).

Para. 33
Commencement. September 14, 1987.
This brings the definition in the 1975 Act into line with that in s.26(1) of this Act.

Para. 34
Commencement. April 1, 1989.
Para. 6 of Sched. 3 to the 1975 Act is concerned with the limits on short term (up to 12 months) borrowing by local authorities by the issue of bills. The limit is expressed by reference to the amount of estimated gross income from rates. The effect of this amendment is to translate "rates" into "rates, the community charges and the community water charges". By virtue of s.26(2) of this Act, "rates" includes non-domestic water and sewerage rates.

Para. 35
Commencement. April 1, 1989.
Para. 20(2) of Sched. 3 to the 1975 Act is concerned with the recovery of debts by someone who has lent to a local authority. Measures include appointment by the Court of Session of a judicial factor who is given the powers of the authority to levy rates. The amendment ensures that this power is extended to include all rates, community charges and community water charges; and that the power to make requisitions on "rating authorities" is extended to all "other local authorities."

Para. 36
Commencement. April 1, 1989.
Because of the amendments in paras. 34 and 35, a further amendment is necessary to insert definitions of the terms "community charges" and "community water charges" into Sched. 3 to the 1975 Act. The term "rate" or "rates" in any Act is now defined (by s.26(2)) to include all three non-domestic rates.

Para. 37
Commencement. September 14, 1987 (as for para. 15) and April 1, 1989.
Amendment to the Rating (Caravan Sites) Act 1976 consequential upon s.3 of this Act.

Para. 38
Commencement. September 14, 1987 (as for para. 15) and April 1, 1989.
Added at House of Lords Report stage (*Hansard,* H.L. Vol. 486, col. 1436). Sched. 32 to the Local Government, Planning and Land Act 1980 deals with enterprise zones and, in para. 33, with their exemption from rates in Scotland. Para. 33(4) defines rates as excluding (old style) "domestic water rate". In line with the terminology in Sched. 5 to this Act, this is renamed "the non-domestic water rate."

Para. 39
Commencement. April 1, 1989.
S.90(9) of the Civic Government (Scotland) Act 1982 (which deals with a local authority's powers to provide lighting on common stairs) supplies an example of a secondary use of the valuation system (see note on s.5 of this Act). An authority's power to recover expenditure under the Act is achieved by way of an apportionment of the bill by reference to the rateable values of the properties—subject to a power to remit.
With the ending of rateable values of domestic subjects this amendment leaves councils free to determine the basis of apportionment for themselves—and with a continuing power to remit. For discussion of the use of this power to give relief to the blind man for his "stair head gas," see *Hansard,* H.L. Vol. 486, col. 1456.

SCHEDULE 2

LEVY, COLLECTION, PAYMENT AND RECOVERY OF COMMUNITY CHARGES

Levying authorities

1.—(1) The local authority for the purpose of levying the regional, islands or district community charges shall be known as the "levying authority" and shall be—

(a) in the case of the regional community charges and the district community charges, the regional council; and

(b) in the case of the islands community charges, the islands council.

(2) In respect of the financial year 1989–90 and of each subsequent financial year, every district council shall, before such date as may be prescribed, intimate to the regional council within whose region their district falls—

(a) the amount of the—
  (i) personal community charge; and
  (ii) standard community charge multiplier,
  which the district council have determined in respect of that financial year; and

(b) such further information with respect to the district community charges as may reasonably be needed by the regional council for the purpose of issuing demand notices.

(3) In this paragraph "regional community charges" means the community charges imposed by a regional council and "islands community charges" and "district community charges" have the corresponding meanings.

Community charge demand notices

2.—(1) Every levying authority shall, in respect of the financial year 1989–90 and of each subsequent financial year, issue, before such date in relation to each of those years as may be prescribed, to every person liable to pay—

(a) a community charge imposed in respect of that year by the regional or islands council which is that levying authority;

(b) a community charge imposed in respect of that year by a district council whose area falls within that of the regional council which is that levying authority

a notice in respect of that liability (in this Act referred to as a "demand notice").

(2) Where a levying authority are satisfied that a person liable to pay a community charge in respect of a financial year has (for whatever reason) not been issued with a demand notice in respect of that liability they shall, notwithstanding that the date prescribed under sub-paragraph (1) above in relation to that year has passed, issue him with a demand notice.

(3) Where, after the issue of a demand notice, a levying authority are satisfied that there has been, or may be, a change in the amount of any community charge which the person to whom the notice was issued is, or will be, liable to pay under this Act, they may issue to that person a further such notice which shall supersede the previous one.

(4) The form and content of demand notices shall be such as may be prescribed.

Appeals consequent on issue of demand notices

3. A person to whom a demand notice has been issued may appeal—

(a) within such period and in such manner as may be prescribed, to the levying authority which issued the demand notice against the amount stated in it as that which he is liable to pay;

(b) to the sheriff against the determination of the levying authority of an appeal by him under sub-paragraph (a) above.

Payment of community charges

4.—(1) A community charge in respect of any financial year shall, subject to this paragraph, be payable by 12 equal monthly instalments on such day of each month of that year as the levying authority may determine.

(2) Where a person is liable to pay a community charge in respect only of part of a financial year, the amount for which he is liable shall, subject to this paragraph, be calculated by apportionment on a daily basis.

(3) Where a person is liable to pay a community charge in respect of a financial year or of part of a financial year and the demand notice in respect of that liability is issued—

(a) on or after 1st April but before 1st January in that year, the community charge to which the notice relates shall be payable by monthly instalments payable on such day of such months of the year as the levying authority may determine;

(b) on or after 1st January in that year, the community charge to which the notice relates shall be payable in full on such day as the levying authority may determine.

(4) Instalments (except the first) of the personal community charge and standard community charge payable in accordance with sub-paragraph (3)(a) above shall, subject to this paragraph, be equal to the standard monthly amount of the personal community charge or, as the case may be, of the standard community charge; the first instalment shall be equal to the difference between the total amount of the personal community charge or, as the case may be, standard community charge payable and the sum of the other instalments.

(5) In sub-paragraph (4) above—

"standard monthly amount of the personal community charge" means, in relation to the personal community charge determined in respect of any financial year by a local authority, an amount equal to that of each (except the first) of the monthly instalments by which each personal community charge due to the authority in respect of that year is payable in accordance with sub-paragraph (1) above; and

"standard monthly amount of the standard community charge" has the corresponding meaning.

(6) The levying authority may round off the amount of the instalments payable under sub-paragraph (1) above (except the first) to the nearest 5p (or such other sum as may, in substitution, be prescribed) and adjust the amount of the first instalment accordingly.

(7) Where an amount due in respect of a financial year or part thereof or any instalment of such an amount is, after taking account of any rebate under or by virtue of section 24 of this Act from that amount or instalment, less than the minimum amount or, as the case may be, the minimum instalment (these minima being such as may be prescribed), that amount shall not be payable in accordance with sub-paragraphs (1) to (4) above but shall be payable in accordance with whichever of the following ways the levying authority may determine (whether generally or in relation to any case or cases or class or classes of case)—

(a) in full on such day as the levying authority may determine of the month next following that in which the demand notice relating to the amount due is issued;

(b) in such instalments (each of which being equal to or greater than the sum prescribed under this sub-paragraph as the minimum instalment) and on such day of such months as the levying authority may determine.

(8) Where an amount is due in respect of any period before a demand notice relating to that amount or to an amount including it is issued, then the amount due shall be payable in full on the first day of the month next following that in which the notice was issued.

(9) Where—

(a) a community charge is payable by a person in accordance with sub-paragraphs (1) to (8) above;

(b) any three instalments thereof are due but unpaid; and

(c) the levying authority give the person notice in writing of the effect of this sub-paragraph,

then, if these instalments have not been paid within seven days of the sending of that notice, the whole amount of that charge for the financial year in respect of which it was imposed shall, so far as not paid, thereupon become payable by him.

(10) A community charge (or any outstanding balance thereof) shall not be payable in accordance with sub-paragraphs (1) to (9) above if—

(a) the person liable to pay it has agreed in writing with the levying authority that he will pay it otherwise than in accordance with those sub-paragraphs; or

(b) it is payable to a housing body under paragraph 5 below.

Arrangements with housing bodies

5.—(1) Subject to sub-paragraph (3) below, a levying authority may make arrangements with a housing body for the exercise by the housing body on behalf of the levying authority of any of the authority's functions under this Schedule.

(2) Arrangements under sub-paragraph (1) above may, without prejudice to the generality of that sub-paragraph—

(i) provide for the receipt, collection or recovery by the housing body of any amount for which a person is liable under section 18(3) of this Act;

(ii) in relation to the functions to be exercised by the housing body, provide that appeals under paragraph 3(a) above be to, and appeals under paragraph 3(b) above be from, the housing body;

(iii) provide as to the terms upon which, instalments by which and manner in which community charges are to be payable to and collected and recovered by the housing body.

(3) Arrangements under this paragraph for the exercise of functions under paragraph 7(1)(a) below may be made only with a district council.

(4) Every person by whom a community charge is payable to a housing body under arrangements under this paragraph shall pay it to the housing body in accordance with those arrangements.

(5) Arrangements under sub-paragraph (1) above shall be on such terms as may be agreed between the levying authority and the housing body or, failing agreement, as may be determined by the Secretary of State.

(6) Where the Secretary of State is satisfied that a levying authority wish to make arrangements under sub-paragraph (1) above with a housing body but the housing body have not agreed to enter into them, he may, by regulations made after consultation with the levying authority and the housing body, require the housing body to do so.

Accounting for district community charges

6.—(1) A regional council shall be liable to pay to the council of each district in their region, in respect of the district community charges for any financial year, the amount produced in the district by those charges; and shall, in accordance with such arrangements as may be prescribed, make payments to the district council on account of that liability.

(2) For the purposes of sub-paragraph (1) above, the amount produced in a district by the district community charges for a financial year shall, subject to sub-paragraph (3) below, be ascertained after the end of that year in such manner as may be prescribed, and—

(a) if that amount exceeds the aggregate amount of payments on account made under sub-paragraph (1) above, the balance shall be paid by the regional council to the district council; and

(b) if that amount is less than the said aggregate amount, the balance shall be set off against payments on account under sub-paragraph (1) above in respect of the next following financial year.

(3) The cost of, and any losses on, the levying and collection of district community charges levied by a regional council shall, in such manner and to such extent as may be prescribed, be treated as deductions in estimating and ascertaining the amounts produced by each of the district community charges levied by the regional council.

(4) There shall be taken into account, in the calculation of the amount which a regional council are liable, under sub-paragraph (1) above, to pay to a district council, the amount of any community charge which has been collected by the district council under paragraph 5 above and is due but has not been paid to the regional council.

(5) The amount which a regional council are liable to pay under sub-paragraph (1) above to a district council shall, if not paid by such date as may be prescribed, attract interest at such rate as may be prescribed.

(6) In this paragraph, "district community charges" has the same meaning as in paragraph 1 above.

Recovery of arrears of community charges

7.—(1) Subject to sub-paragraphs (4) to (6) below, arrears of community charges may be recovered by the levying authority by diligence—

(a) authorised by summary warrant granted under sub-paragraph (2) below; or

(b) in pursuance of a decree granted in an action of payment.

(2) Subject to sub-paragraph (4) below, the sheriff, on an application by the levying authority accompanied by a certificate by them—

(a) stating that the persons specified in the application have not paid the community charges specified in the application;

(b) stating that the authority have given written notice to each such person requiring him to make payment of the amount due by him within a period of 14 days after the date of the giving of the notice;

(c) stating that the said period of 14 days has expired without payment of the said amounts; and

(d) specifying the amount due and unpaid by each such person,

shall grant a summary warrant in a form provided for by Act of Sederunt authorising the recovery, by any of the diligences mentioned in sub-paragraph (3) below, of the amount of community charges remaining due and unpaid by each such person along with a surcharge of 10 per cent. (or such percentage as may, in substitution, be prescribed) of that amount.

(3) The diligences referred to in sub-paragraph (2) above are—

(a) a poinding and sale in accordance with Schedule 5 to the Debtors (Scotland) Act 1987;

(b) an earnings arrestment;

(c) an arrestment and action of furthcoming or sale.

(4) Sub-paragraph (1)(a) above does not apply to the recovery from a person of arrears of community charge for which that person is liable by virtue only of section 8(7) of this Act.

(5) It shall be incompetent for the sheriff to grant a summary warrant under sub-paragraph (2) above in respect of community charges due by a person if an action has already been raised for the recovery of those charges; and, without prejudice to sub-paragraph (6) below, on the raising of an action for the recovery of community charges, any existing summary warrant in so far as it relates to the recovery of community charges shall cease to have effect.

(6) It shall be incompetent to raise an action for the recovery of community charges if, in pursuance of a summary warrant, any of the diligences mentioned in sub-paragraph (3) above for the recovery of those charges has been executed.

(7) In any proceedings for the recovery of community charges, whether by summary warrant or otherwise, no person shall be entitled to found upon failure of the levying authority or any other authority or body to comply with any provision of this Schedule or requirement under it relating to the date by which something shall be done, not being a provision in this paragraph or a provision regulating the diligence.

(8) No misnomer or inaccurate description of any person or place or mistake or informality in any notice or other document or communication relating to the levy or collection of any community charge or in any proceedings for the payment thereof shall prejudice the recovery thereof.

Expenses of recovery of community charges

8.—(1) Subject to sub-paragraph (2) below and without prejudice to paragraphs 25 to 34 of Schedule 5 to the Debtors (Scotland) Act 1987, the sheriff officer's fees, together with the outlays necessarily incurred by him, in connection with the execution of a summary warrant under paragraph 7 above shall be chargeable against the debtor.

(2) No fees shall be chargeable by the sheriff officer against the debtor for collecting, and accounting to the levying authority for, sums paid to him by the debtor in satisfaction of an amount owing to the levying authority by way of community charges.

Repayment of sums not due

9. A levying authority to whom there has been paid by way of any community charge any sum which (for whatever reason) is not due shall repay that sum or arrange for its repayment.

GENERAL NOTE

This schedule sets out the arrangements for the levy, collection, payment and recovery of community charges. Para. 1 introduces the concept of the levying authority, which is to be either the regional or the islands council, and stipulates that the district council is to provide such information to the regional council about district community charges as is necessary for the execution of the functions of the regional council as levying authority. Para. 2 provides for the issue of demand notices and revised demand notices by the levying authority, while para. 3 deals with the rights of appeal afforded to persons who receive such demand notices. Para. 4 sets out the system for payment of community charges to the levying authority, including the procedure to be followed in the case of arrears and backdated payments. Para. 5 provides for the possibility of the delegation of the duties of the levying authority to housing bodies, including district councils. Para. 6 specifies the accounting arrangements necessary to regulate the distribution of the proceeds of collection between regional councils as levying authorities who are entitled to the proceeds of regional community charges, and district councils, who are entitled to the proceeds of district community charges. Para. 7 sets out the procedures for recovery of arrears of community charges from persons liable, while para. 8 specifies who is to pay the expenses of recovery of community charges. Finally, para. 9 provides a general right to repayment of sums not due under any of the community charges.

As it is largely concerned with the implementation of the principles enunciated elsewhere in the Act, it might appear that this Schedule is of limited intrinsic interest. However, both in a general sense and in several more specific respects, the Schedule is worthy of attention in its own right. At the general level, to the extent that the issue of practicality is subsumed under the heading of technical efficacy, which in turn is one of the central criteria by which the Government itself intends the new proposals to be judged, then the issues treated in this Schedule assume central rather than peripheral significance.

More specifically, a number of points of interest emerge. First, in a formal sense, as was repeatedly underlined by Government spokesmen during debates, this Schedule displays a greater degree of continuity with the rating system which—in the case of domestic subjects—it replaces, than any of the sections in Pt. II of the Act. However, the nature of the measure to be applied and enforced is so radically different that the considerations which might render the enforcement system functional for rating purposes can seldom be guaranteed to be similarly applicable in the context of the new tax. Secondly, para. 4 and, in particular, para. 7, usefully inform and highlight the controversies and debates surrounding the introduction of a universally applicable tax, by suggesting the methods to be used to combat certain difficulties arising from the construction of a substantial class of taxpayers having characteristics which tend to make the collection and payment more burdensome, namely, relative mobility, relative poverty, and lack of experience of similar modes of taxpaying. Thirdly, paras. 5 and 6 attempt to regulate the relationship between regional and district authorities for the purposes of administration and enforcement of the Act, and so provide an important focus for a lively debate which has emerged concerning what may be termed the political sub-text of the new Act, that is, how the manifest principles and pragmatics of the protagonists of various positions in relation to the Act may have consequences, intended or unintended, and may raise possibilities, whether or not previously contemplated, for the wider political strategies of the political actors involved. In particular, what implications will the network of new administrative relations between governmental units necessitated by and provided for under the Act have for the strength and development of numerous ideological positions *vis-à-vis* the legitimate scope and functions of local government which are held by various interested parties (see *e.g. Glasgow Herald*, August 11 and 12, 1987).

It should be noted that, by virtue of para. 11 of Sched. 5, this Schedule applies with adaptations to be prescribed, to community water charges.

Para. 1
This paragraph provides that regional and islands councils are to be levying authorities for the purposes of administration of the community charge, and that, in order to allow the regional council to perform its functions where it is the levying authority, any district council falling within the region must supply it with sufficient information for these purposes.

Sub-para. (1)
This sub-paragraph, which is referred to in the interpretation section, s.26, defines a "levying authority". A regional council is to be the levying authority for the purposes of levying regional and district community charges, while an islands council is to be the levying authority for the purposes of levying its own community charges.

Sub-para. (2)
This sub-paragraph provides that, as of the year 1989–90 and all subsequent financial years, the district council will provide information to the regional council as levying authority as to the amount of the personal community charge and the standard charge multiplier determined by the district council under ss.9(1) and 10(6) of this Act respectively, and also such other information as may reasonably be required by the regional council to enable it to issue demand notices. This information is to be provided before such date as may be prescribed. It is envisaged that this power will be used to prescribe a date early in the calendar year so as to allow sufficient time for the preparation of notices and their prompt issue at the commencement of the financial year.

Sub-para. (3)
This sub-paragraph defines "regional community charges," "islands community charges" and "district community charges" as the community charges imposed by the regional, islands and district councils respectively.

Para. 2
This paragraph provides for the issue of demand notices both prior to and, where necessary, during a financial year, and also provides for the issue of revised demand notices when a change in liability occurs. The provisions included in this paragraph are similar to those provided for in relation to rates by virtue of s.237 of the Local Government (Scotland) Act 1947.

Sub-para. (1)
This requires a levying authority to issue a demand notice, in respect of 1989–90 and of subsequent years, to every person liable to pay a community charge imposed for that year

by the levying authority and, where the levying authority is the regional authority, to every person who is also liable to pay a community charge imposed by a district council whose area falls within that of the regional council. The annual date of issue of the demand note is as is to be prescribed, and it is envisaged that this date will be shortly before the beginning of the financial year to which the notice relates, so as to allow a sufficient period for those liable to pay to make the necessary payment arrangements. As the normal basis of payment of the new charge will be twelve equal monthly payments (para. 4(1)) commencing in the first month of the financial year so eliminating a fallow period in the first and last months of the financial year which is the consequence of the normal method of paying rates by ten monthly instalments (Local Government (Scotland) Act 1975, s.8), it will be imperative that the demand notice is sent out at an earlier date than is necessary under the rating system.

Sub-para. (2)

This sub-paragraph permits a levying authority to issue demand notices after the date prescribed in sub-para. (1). It requires a levying authority, where it is satisfied that a person liable to pay a community charge in respect of a financial year has, for whatever reason, not in fact been issued with a demand notice in respect of that liability, to issue a demand notice to him, even if the date prescribed in sub-para. (1) has passed.

This provision was omitted from the original Bill and was only inserted at Report stage in the Commons (*Hansard,* H.C. Vol. 111, col. 1051, *per* Michael Ancram M.P.). It is envisaged that it will be used to deal with those situations where, on account of the rolling principle (see s.8 above) liability does not commence until after the start of the financial year. Presumably, however, it would also be open to the levying authority to use the facility here provided in circumstances where a person has been liable since the beginning of the financial year, but where, on account of failure to notify either on his part or on the part of the "reasonable person" (see s.18(1) and (2), and s.17(5) above respectively), or of administrative error, such liability has not been previously recorded or acted upon.

Sub-para. (3)

This sub-paragraph permits the levying authority to issue a further demand notice to supersede one which has previously been issued, if it is satisfied that there has been, or will be, a change in the amount which the person concerned is liable to pay. It is envisaged that this power will be exercised where, for example, a person leaves the registration area during the course of the financial year, or where the eligibility of someone for rebate under s.24 changes on account of income fluctuations—or where a collective community charge multiplier is altered (1st Scot.S.C., col. 1140, *per* Michael Ancram M.P.). Unlike that which is provided in sub-para. (2), therefore, the use of the power provided in the present sub-paragraph is limited to circumstances where the levying authority believes there to have been an actual change in the amount of liability of a person.

Sub-para. (4)

This sub-paragraph provides that the form and content of demand notices are to be prescribed. It is envisaged that this power will be used to ensure that demand notices contain the information necessary to explain and illuminate the liabilities to which they relate. There will be included the name and address of the person liable, the point of liability to which the notice relates, a breakdown of the various charges involved including a specification of the information applicable to the case of the collective and standard charges, details of any rebate entitlement, and the time by which and the manner in which payment may be made (1st Scot.S.C., col. 1145, *per* Michael Ancram M.P.).

An amendment moved by the Opposition at Committee stage in the Commons to the effect that it should be obligatory to consult bodies representing local authorities (*i.e.* the Convention of Scottish Local Authorities) prior to the prescription of the form or content of demand notices, was resisted by the Government on the grounds that such consultation would take place in any case. In the light of the breakdown of relations between C.O.S.L.A. and the Government over the new tax—between November 1986 and August 1987, C.O.S.L.A. suspended consultations with the Government over the new tax and remain vigorously opposed to it in principle—a belief in the possibility of constructive voluntary negotiation might appear naive, although by the same token, compulsory negotiations are unlikely to be productive in such a climate either.

Para. 3

This paragraph provides for appeals, first to the levying authority, and then to the sheriff, against the amount mentioned in the demand notice. The provisions of the paragraph are

omparable to those made in relation to rates under s.238 of the Local Government
Scotland) Act 1947.

The period within which and the manner in which an appeal may be made to the levying
authority are to be prescribed. It is envisaged that these terms will be used to prescribe a
reasonable period from the date of receipt of the demand notice for appeals to be lodged,
and for appeals to be made in writing stating the grounds on which they are made.

Presumably, the majority of actions raised under this provision will relate merely to
technical errors (including errors of calculation) in demand notices. This is so on account of
the fact that the other factors having a bearing upon the amount of liability as specified in
the demand notice, consist of the basic conditions of liability—for the three charges as set
out in ss.8, 10 and 11; as these matters are set out in the Community Charges Register by
virtue of s.13, and as the register is, by virtue of s.19, conclusive as to the fact and date of
commencement of liability subject only to the registration appeals system under s.16 which
provides for appropriate amendments of the register to be made, then it is this latter avenue
which must be explored by anyone whose reason for disagreeing with the amount specified
in the demand notice is a more basic disagreement as to liability and the contents of his
register entry. To use the powers available under this paragraph in such circumstances would
be a fruitless endeavour, as the levying authority must treat the register as conclusive by
virtue of s.19 and has no power either to look beyond the register or to alter it in order to
come to a revised judgment on the question of the fact and extent of liability, and so will
have no grounds for altering the demand notice on account only of perceived disparity
between the position of a person's liability as recorded in the register, and his actual liability.
For one possibility of an appeal on a matter of substance, however, see note on s.10(8)
above).

Para. 4

This paragraph sets out the system for payment of the community charge to the levying
authority. In the normal case, the charge is to be payable by 12 equal monthly instalments.
If the liability is only in respect of part of a year, then the monthly instalment system still
applies, except where the demand notice is issued on or after January 1, during the financial
year in question. Five additional exceptions to the equal monthly instalment system apply.
First, if the actual amount of liability is below a certain minimum, then the levying authority
may demand that it is paid either as a lump sum or in a small number of larger instalments.
Secondly, any amount due in a demand notice which includes an element of backdated
liability is to be met in full upon receipt of a notice. Thirdly, where arrears of three months
or more have built up, then they must be met in full and rights to instalment payments are
suspended for the remainder of the year. Fourthly, where the liable person and the levying
authority agree to make a different arrangement for paying, then none of the provisions set
out in the paragraph will apply. Finally, where a housing body is carrying out the functions
of a levying authority, then the procedures set out in this paragraph are inapplicable, and
reference should instead be made to the arrangements provided in para. 5.

Sub-para. (1)

This provides that, subject to the provisions of the rest of the paragraph, the normal
method of payment of a community charge is to be by 12 equal monthly instalments. The
levying authority is to determine the day of the month on which payment is to be made. The
introduction of a system of 12 monthly instalments—rather than the system of 10 instalments
per annum as is the norm under the rating system (Local Government (Scotland) Act 1975,
s.8), was defended on account of the fact that it accords more with general understandings
of the appropriate periodisation of payments, and that the greater mobility of the class of
community charge payees compared with the class of ratepayers means that it is important
to ensure that payment is aligned to liability as it is incurred, so minimising the need for
extensive adjustments upon apportionment (1st Scot.S.C., col. 1147, *per* Michael Ancram
M.P., *Hansard*, H.L. Vol. 486, col. 1153, *per* Lord Glenarthur).

Sub-para. (2)

This provides that, subject to the rest of the paragraph, where liability is for less than a
full year's community charge, the amount due is to be calculated by apportionment of the
annual charge on a daily basis.

Sub-para. (3)

This provides that where a demand notice is issued on or after April 1, but before January
1, in the financial year to which it relates, then the community charge is to be payable by
monthly instalments on such day of such months as the levying authority may determine.

Where, however, the demand notice is issued on or after January 1, the community charge is to be payable in full on such day as the levying authority may determine, although in such cases it is within the discretion of the levying authority by virtue of sub-para. (10) to make alternative arrangements, including arrangements for payment by instalment. This sub paragraph applies in respect of liability either for part of or for a complete financial year and so contemplates situations not only where someone becomes liable during a financial year, but also where the liability of a person, although applicable for the entire year, is only recognised at a point after the commencement of the financial year.

Sub-para. (4)

This sub-paragraph provides that all but one instalments of the personal or standard community charge payable under sub-para. (3)(a) will be equal to the "standard monthly amount" of the personal or standard community charge as defined in sub-para. (4). The exception is with regard to the first instalment, which is to be calculated by reference to the difference between the total sum due and the total of the standard monthly instalments payable.

Sub-para. (5)

This defines the term "standard monthly amount of the personal community charge" introduced in sub-para. (4), to mean the amount of each of the monthly instalments of the personal community charge due in respect of sub-para. (1), which monthly instalments are to be equal with the exception of the first.

Sub-para. (6)

This allows the levying authority to round off the amount of any instalment payable under sub-para. (1) to the nearest 5p. or whatever alternative sum is prescribed. There is to be an exception in respect of the last instalment, which is to be adjusted to take account of the rounding off of the other instalments so as to ensure that the aggregate amount payable is as specified in the demand notice under para. 2.

Sub-para. (7)

This sub-paragraph allows for the prescription of a minimum amount due in respect of a financial year, or part of a year, and a minimum instalment. Specifically, where the amount due after any rebate payable under the provisions of s.24, or an instalment of the amount thereby due, is less than the prescribed minimum, then the method of payment by 12 equal instalments under sub-para. (1) is not to apply, and the levying authority may determine that payment should be made in either of two ways. It may be payable in full, on whatever day is determined by the levying authority, in the month after the month in which the relevant demand notice is issued, or, in such instalments on such days of such months as the levying authority determines, provided that each instalment is equal to or more than the minimum prescribed under this sub-paragraph.

Presumably, by implication, a third option is available under sub-para. (10), namely to arrange for payment in accordance with any other scheme agreed between the levying authority and the liable person. Such a scheme could be used to reinstate the normal procedure under sub-para. (1), and it is submitted that, where a liable person requested this, then it would be the only equitable solution. To explain, the provision contained in this sub-paragraph is justified on the grounds that if very small sums were required to be collected by normal instalment arrangements, the administrative costs would be greater than the amounts received. However, surely this is to put administrative expediency before considerations of individual fairness. If the system is intended to permit some adjustment of liability in accordance with ability to pay, then presumably any instalment due to be paid by any person in receipt of a rebate ought, in proportionate terms, to be judged to impose as onerous a financial burden as any instalment due from any person not in receipt of a rebate. Therefore, to allow for a more onerous method of payment in the case of persons receiving rebates, is to discriminate unfairly against members of this group.

Sub-para. (8)

This provides that, where a demand notice relates entirely or partly to an amount due in respect of a period prior to the date of the demand notice, the amount due is to be paid in full on the first day of the month following the month in which the notice was issued. The extension of the duty to make full payment to include payment in respect of the remaining part of the financial year, and not only the backdated element, might be argued to place an unduly onerous responsibility upon the liable person. This is especially so, when this

rovision is compared with that set out in sub-para. (10) below, which permits a similar
measure to be imposed by the levying authority in a situation where arrears are payable, but
which, in that case, is accompanied by a number of safeguards against arbitrary imposition.
n that the factors which give rise to arrears are more likely to be attributable to the conduct
f a liable person than the factors which give use to the need to make backdated payment
although the latter consequence might also be ultimately attributable to an error on the
part of a liable person in some circumstances, for example, a failure to give notice of a
relevant change in circumstances to the registration officer under s.18(2)), it would seem
anomalous that the quasi-punitive measure is more difficult to invoke in the former case
than the latter.

Presumably, again, levying authorities will take advantage of their powers to make
alternative arrangements, under sub-para. (10) in order to mitigate the harsh impact of this
provision.

Sub-para. (9)

This deals with the situation where a liable person falls into arrears. If three instalments
are due but have not been paid, provided the levying authority has given the person written
notice of the effect of this sub-paragraph, then these instalments must be paid within seven
days of the sending of that notice, otherwise the whole of the charge for the financial year
becomes payable.

The rationale for this measure is that it imposes a "sensible discipline" upon the liable
person, focussing his mind on the need to pay (1st Scot.S.C., col. 1153, *per* Ian Lang M.P.).
Furthermore, it is administratively convenient in that if a levying authority feels compelled
to take legal action to recover the debt under sub-para. (7), then it will not be restricted to
the precise sum outstanding, with the prospect of having to take further legal action in the
case of default of payment of the remainder of the charge due for that year (*Hansard,* H.C.
Vol. 111, col. 1052, *per* Ian Lang M.P.).

Generally, this is intended as a last resort provision. It is envisaged that local authorities
will use their discretion under sub-para. (10) to provide for repayment of the balance by
other means, and, only upon the breakdown of such an arrangement, will they invoke the
quasi-punitive measure here provided. The duty to give prior notice was introduced only at
Report Stage in the Commons after pressure from the Opposition. Again, it is envisaged
that the formal notice procedure will be a last resort to be invoked only after informal
reminders have failed to induce payment of the relevant debt.

Sub-para. (10)

This specifies the circumstances in which a community charge, including any outstanding
balance of a charge for the relevant financial year, is not to be payable in accordance with
the arrangements set out in sub-paras. (1)–(9): first, where the liable person has made other
arrangements for payment in writing with the levying authority and, secondly, where the
charge is payable to a housing body under para. 5 (see below).

As regards the first circumstance, this may be applicable either in the normal case where
alternative arrangements are made at the beginning of the financial year, or in respect of
payments due for part of a financial year. Within this latter category will fall, *inter alia*, all
of the situations described in sub-paras. (3), (8) and (9) above. Accordingly this measure is
initially important in respect of those types of case, in providing a means of avoiding an
otherwise harsh system of peremptory repayment.

The extension of this sub-paragraph to liabilities for amounts due for part of the year was
only achieved by a Government amendment at Report Stage in the Commons (*Hansard,*
H.C. Vol. 111, col. 1053, *per* Ian Lang M.P.).

Para. 5

This paragraph provides for arrangements to be made between the levying authority and
any housing body, defined under s.26(1), for the housing body to exercise any of the
functions of the levying authority under this Schedule. Quite apart from the general
delegation of the functions of levy, collection, receipt and recovery of the charges, such
arrangements shall specifically provide for the receipt, collection and recovery of arrears by
a housing body and that such bodies should be treated as the levying authority for the
purposes of the appeals system provided in para. 3 above in so far as any appeal relates to
matters delegated to such bodies. Furthermore, these arrangements shall stipulate the terms
upon which and the manner in which such bodies shall exercise those delegated functions.
The only type of housing body authorised to invoke the summary warrant procedure is to
be a district council. In general terms, the arrangements will be such as may be agreed
between the levying authority and the housing body in question. If, however, there is a

bilateral failure to agree or a unilateral failure on the part of the housing body to contemplate any such arrangements, then the Secretary of State may intervene to determine the arrangements and compel the district council or other housing body to participate.

The provisions of this paragraph gave rise to extensive debate during the course of the Bill's passage. Two issues, in particular, were the focus of controversy. In the first place, there was the question of the appropriate degree of flexibility in the relationship between the levying authority and housing bodies, in particular, a district council. Secondly, and relatedly, there was the question of the responsibility of the housing body for non-tenants. In the original Bill, the delegation of certain of the functions of the levying authority to housing bodies was mandatory, as was a requirement that such housing bodies should collect community charge payments from non-tenants residing in dwelling houses let by it. After representations by Opposition parties, and by groups such as the Scottish Rating Forum of the Rating and Valuation Association and the Chartered Institute of Public Finance and Accountancy, more flexible arrangements were introduced at Committee stage in the Lords (*Hansard,* H.L. Vol. 486, cols. 1149–1151). There is no longer any express stipulation dealing with the case of non-tenants, and, generally, the assumption of responsibility by housing bodies in this area is to be treated as a matter for agreement between the parties concerned, rather than a duty be imposed upon the housing body; however, the element of compulsion remains in the last analysis, through the powers exercisable by the Secretary of State under sub-paras. (5) and (6), and so the net effect of this change may be slight.

The original justification for the imposition of duties upon housing bodies was based upon traditional practice and the experience gained therefrom, in that normally such bodies were already responsible for collecting rates along with rents from their tenants. The rationale for the extension of this duty to non-tenants residing in houses let by housing bodies contained two elements; the desire for uniformity of treatment between tenants and non-tenants so as to avoid confusion, and the recognition that housing bodies, being responsible for the administration of housing benefit, would already have both expertise relevant to the calculation of charge payments and information relevant to non-tenants (since, under the Social Security and Housing Benefits Act 1982, the presence of non-tenants, whether dependants and non-dependants, is relevant to the calculation of housing benefit due to the tenant). The expertise in the field of calculation of housing benefit would be useful in calculating the amount of charge due as the rebate scheme under s.24 will operate through the medium of housing benefit, while the information available to it would be relevant not only for the housing body's own purposes in carrying out its delegated functions, but also as an aid to the registration officer under s.17 to facilitate the fulfilment of his function of keeping registration details up-to-date under s.12(4).

Over and above these practical benefits, the mandatory allocation of functions in this area was also defended on a broad point of principle: since, in the case of a district council, it was entitled to receive community charge payments, it had a direct interest in, and indirect obligation to take part in, the collection of such payments (1st Scot.S.C., cols. 1158–1166, *per* Michael Ancram M.P.).

Arguments against the mandatory system are similarly available both at the practical level and at the level of principle. At the practical level, it might be contended that the element of continuity of practices relevant to the rating system are overstated. The community charge, not being a property tax, and on account of the accountability principle which insists upon the high visibility of the charge, would have to be specifically identified and separately billed for, even in the case of tenants. In the case of the 350,000–400,000 non-tenants residing in houses let by housing bodies, an entirely new collection machinery would have to be installed in relation to a section of the population whose average income is likely to be relatively low and whose experience of making regular payments to public agencies is likely to be very limited. As such, as yet unknown administrative difficulties would beset housing bodies and friction between them and the levying authorities—in the majority of cases the regional council—would be bound to develop. Moreover, considerable expense would be incurred in setting up the relevant machinery for enforcement.

At the level of principle, it might be argued that, whether or nor the notion of making the beneficiaries of the community charge responsible for its collection embodies a worthwhile ideal, the mechanism used to achieve it in the Act is ill-fitted to the task in hand. First, only one type of housing body, namely a district council, may determine its own community charge, and so the argument is inapplicable to the others. Secondly, if the principle of aligning benefit from payment with responsibility for collection is crucial, then district councils should be responsible for collecting that element of the community charge which relates to the district community charge from all liable persons in their areas, rather than the whole of the community charge, including the element of regional community charge, from some liable persons (*i.e.* their own tenants and other persons resident in premises let by them) within their areas.

It is arguable that the issues raised by this debate are still very relevant, since, although the amendments specified render the responsibilities of housing bodies are less unequivocal, the overall tenor of the paragraph still favours the delegation of a substantial part of the functions of the levying authority to housing bodies.

Sub-para. (1)

Subject to certain limitations pertaining to the methods of recovery of arrears, a levying authority may make arrangements with a housing body for the exercise by the latter of any of the functions of the former under this Schedule. It is envisaged that the degree of responsibility of the housing body might vary considerably:

"At one end of the spectrum the housing body could do the whole thing. It could issue community charge bills and undertake all collections and this collection need not be confined to those living in public housing. At the other end of the spectrum, the levying authority might issue bills and do most of the work, with the housing body simply providing collection points in its local offices." (*Hansard,* H.L. Vol. 486, col. 1150, *per* Baroness Carnegy of Lour).

However, it may be that the power of the Secretary of State to impose an arrangement in the case of disagreement between the relevant bodies might be used to bring about a more uniform structure than that contemplated in the above quote.

Sub-para. (2)

This sub-paragraph, without prejudice to the range of matters which might be covered under sub-para. (1), specifically details three matters which may be provided for under the arrangements. First, the receipt, collection or recovery by the housing body of backdated charge and interest and surcharge thereupon, as specified under s.18(3) of the Act; secondly, that where functions are delegated to a housing body under this Schedule, then appeals under para. 3(a) and (b) of the Schedule should be to and from the housing body respectively; thirdly, the terms upon which, the instalments by which, and the manner in which community charges are to be payable to and collected and recovered by the housing body. This lack of specification of the details of payment contrast strongly with the situation where the levying authority assumes direct responsibility, as described under para. 4.

Sub-para. (3)

The effect of this provision is to extend to the district council, but not other housing bodies, the power to use summary warrant procedure for the recovery of arrears of community charge. A summary warrant is a warrant for the recovery of debt which is obtained by an *ex parte* application to the sheriff rather than as a result of obtaining decree for payment in a court action. As such, from the perspective of the debtor, it is a draconian remedy, which previously has only been available to a limited number of public, revenue-collecting bodies, namely rating authorities, the Inland Revenue, and H.M. Customs and Excise. It was felt appropriate to extend the use of such warrants to district councils as they too are now, by virtue of this Act, "tax raising authorities in their own right" (*Hansard,* H.L. Vol. 486, col. 1151, *per* Baroness Carnegy of Lour).

Sub-para. (4)

This imposes an obligation upon liable persons to make payments of community charge to housing bodies in accordance with arrangements made under this paragraph.

Sub-para. (5)

This provides that arrangements between the housing body and the levying authority which are made under sub-para. (1) shall be on such terms as may be agreed between the levying authority and the housing body. Failing such agreement, the terms are to be determined by the Secretary of State.

Sub-para. (6)

This extends the principle introduced under sub-para. (5) to the situation of unilateral default on the part of the housing body. Where the Secretary of State is satisfied that a levying authority wishes to make arrangements with a housing body under sub-para. (1) above, but the housing body has refused, he may, by means of regulations made after consultation with both parties, require the housing body to acquiesce in such arrangements. Regulations are to be made by statutory instrument (s.31(3)).

Para. 6

This paragraph provides for the accounting arrangements necessary between a regional council, which as levying authority has collected district community charges, and the relevant district council. It specifies the arrangements to be made for making payment to the district council in the course of the financial year and for accounting for district community charges at the end of each financial year. In such accounting, regard is to be had not only to sums paid on account, but also to the costs of and losses on collection, and any payments made directly to the district council under para. 5. If the regional authority does not make payment to the district council timeously during the course of the financial year, then it will be liable to make interest payments.

Sub-para. (1)

This provides that a regional council is to pay to each district council within its area the amount produced by any of the district community charges for the financial year in question which are applicable to them, and will make payments on account of that liability to the district council in question, in accordance with such arrangements as may be prescribed. It is envisaged that this prescriptive power will be used to prescribe arrangements for regular payments to be made to district councils during the financial year in anticipation of the total amount to be collected.

Sub-para. (2)

This provides that for the purposes of sub-para. (1), the amount produced in a district by the district community charges for a financial year is to be ascertained after the end of that year in a manner to be prescribed. If the amount concerned is greater than the sum of payments on account under sub-para. (1), then the regional council is to pay the balance to the district council. If it is less, then the balance is carried forward by the district council to be set off against payments made on account under sub-para. (1) to the district council in respect of the following financial year. It is envisaged that the arrangements to be prescribed will be in line with standard accounting practice.

Sub-para. (3)

This provides that, in estimating and ascertaining the amounts produced by each of the district community charges which it has levied, the regional council is to make reductions to take account of the costs it has incurred in levying and collecting each of those charges, together with any losses which it has sustained. The manner in which and the extent to which this is done may be prescribed. It is envisaged that this power will be used to allow for reasonable expenses and losses to be taken into account in the calculation. Presumably, an additional factor which will be taken into account in calculating the extent to which the expenses of the regional council in collecting the district charge are to be deducted in ascertaining payments to a district, are the corresponding costs borne by the district council in collecting the regional charge under para. 5. Under that paragraph, the specific provision allowing for reimbursement of the expenses of housing bodies was deleted at Committee Stage in the Lords. Therefore, it would appear that, in the case of district councils, the most convenient way of having such expenses defrayed, in the absence of a specific provision, is to have them set off against expenses reciprocally incurred by the regional authority under this sub-paragraph.

Sub-para. (4)

This provides that there is to be taken into account in the calculation of the amount payable by the regional council to a district council under sub-para. (1) the amount of any community charges which have been collected by the district council as a housing body under para. 5, and which are due but have not yet been paid by the regional council.

Sub-para. (5)

This stipulates that interest will be paid on any amount which a regional council is liable to pay to a district council by virtue of sub-para. (1), if it has not been paid by the date to be prescribed. The rate of interest is also a matter which is to be prescribed.

Sub-para. (6)

This defines "district community charge" by reference to para. 1.

Para. 7

This paragraph makes provision for the recovery of arrears of community charge by summary warrant procedure or by the raising of an action in court. The arrangements made this paragraph are broadly similar to those applicable in relation to the recovery of rates under s.247 at the Local Government (Scotland) Act 1947. The Debtors (Scotland) Act 1987, enacted in the light of the Scottish Law Commission's Report on Diligence and Debtor Protection (Scot. Law Com. No. 95, 1985), includes some amendments of the detailed procedures involved in the law relating to the recovery of debts, and in so far as they are relevant these are incorporated into this paragraph and, indeed, into the Act generally (see .33 and sub-para. (8) below).

During the passage of the Bill, a number of bodies, such as the Society of Messengers-at-Arms and Sheriff Officers and the Law Society of Scotland, expressed misgivings as to the efficacy of the new provisions for enforcing payment of community charges. The Scottish Consumer Council was also pessimistic about the rate of default and the effectiveness of the enforcement mechanisms: in one study commissioned by it of a sample of vulnerable groups under the new legislation, it was found that as many as 26 per cent. of the over 25-year-olds believed they would have problems in paying their community charge; as regards the resources available to meet community charge debts, 12·6 per cent. of the total sample stated that they had no possessions worth more than £20, a figure which rose to 70·2 per cent. when the unemployed members of the sample were considered separately. Presumably, then, poinding would be an ineffective form of diligence to use against these groups, so reducing drastically the chances of successful recovery of debt in such cases. (*The Community Charge: A Report to C.O.S.L.A. and S.C.C.*, Dundee University, February 1987). However, one should be cautious of extrapolating from these figures, since, as said, they represent findings from a selective rather than a random sample. In a general sense, however, they do point to difficulties amongst particular sections of the population.

In broad terms, and bearing in mind the above comments, two sets of problems are confronted in the analysis of this paragraph. First, any projection as to the impact of effectiveness of the recovery procedures is inevitably speculative. While it is unsound to derive general conclusions from a limited and unrepresentative sample, it is no more legitimate to draw them from the expense of recovery of arrears of rates, as has been attempted by the Government (1st Scot.S.C., cols. 1180–1181, *per* Michael Ancram M.P.) since the characteristics of the population subject to rates differs markedly from the characteristics of those subject to the community charge, the latter incorporating a much larger section of economically vulnerable persons as it is a broad-based tax unrelated to indices of relative economic stability such as ownership or long term occupation of property. Furthermore, the amendment of the law relating to the enforcement of debt under the Debtors (Scotland) Act 1987 entails that, even if it is permissible to extrapolate from the experience of ratepayers and the apprehensions of vulnerable groups, it must also be borne in mind that the legal structure in relation to which such experiences have been gained and in respect of which such apprehensions have been generated has also been altered in ways which might make past practice and experience an unreliable yardstick.

Secondly, it is very difficult to dissociate criticism of this paragraph from a general critique of the Act. A reading of the parliamentary debates would suggest that, from the perspective of the Opposition parties, considerations of fairness to the individual debtor are seen to vary inversely with considerations of the effectiveness of the legal mechanisms available. Whether or not it is accepted that debt recovery procedures in respect of economically disadvantaged members of the population which are successful tend also to be draconian and oppressive, it must be conceded that such a view inevitably flows from a critique of the distributive principle underpinning the new Act, namely the imposition of a broad-based local tax which is bound to impinge upon those economically disadvantaged groups. To look at the paragraph on its own merits may involve difficult choices between considerations of effectiveness and comprehensiveness on the one hand, and individual life-chances on the other, and any analysis which rejects the contemplation of such a balance must be seen as separate from and irrelevant to an analysis which is prepared to contemplate such weighing-up and to find the appropriate point of balance.

Sub-para. (1)

This provides that the levying authority may recover arrears of community charge, including arrears payable to a housing body under para. 5, by means of diligence which may be authorised either by summary warrant granted under sub-para. (2), or in pursuance of a decree granted in an action of payment raised in the normal way. This provision is subject to sub-paras. (4) to (6) below.

Arrears of community charges may be recovered. In Parliament, some attention was given to the apparently permissive character of this provision. For the Government, it was acknowledged (*Hansard*, H.C. Vol. 111, col. 1067) that there was no express statutory obligation upon levying authorities to take steps to recover arrears of community charges.

This reflected the position in relation to the recovery of rates under s.247 of the Local Government (Scotland) Act 1947. *Roberts* v. *Hopwood* [1925] A.C. 578 was, however, invoked in support of the existence of a fiduciary duty (owed to ratepayers and, presumably, now to community chargees) requiring local authorities to carry out their functions in a businesslike manner.

Whether or not the existence of such a fiduciary duty is to be acknowledged in quite this form (on which see C. M. G. Himsworth "The Fiduciary Duties of Local Authorities in Scotland", 1982 S.L.T. (News) 241 and 249), there must be little doubt that a complete or substantial failure to take steps to recover arrears would attract the attentions of the Controller of Audit under s.102 of the Local Government (Scotland) Act 1973. What will amount to a sufficient response by a levying authority, in the light of what may be very large numbers of small debts persistently unpaid, remains to be seen. It is more likely to be a question of obtaining "value for money" (soon to be made part of the remit of the Controller under the current Local Government Bill) than of strict adherence to the demands of the law.

Sub-para. (2)

This sub-paragraph sets out the procedure which must be followed in order for a summary warrant to be granted. Subject only to sub-para. (4), which deals with situations of joint and several liability, a sheriff may grant a summary warrant if an application is submitted to him by the levying authority, or a district council carrying out the function of a levying authority (para. 5(3)), which states that the persons specified in the application have not paid the community charges specified in the application, that the authority has given written notice to each person specified requiring him to pay the amount due within 14 days of the giving of the notice, that the 14-day period has expired without payment being made, and which specifies the amount due and unpaid by each person. The summary warrant to be granted by the sheriff is to be in a form provided by Act of Sederunt and will authorise the recovery of the amount of community charges outstanding on the part of each person, together with a surcharge of 10 per cent. or whatever other percentage may be prescribed, of the outstanding amount, by means of any of the diligences mentioned in sub-para. (3).

Summary warrant is an uncommon form of proceedings for the recovery of debt only available to rating authorities (Local Government (Scotland) Act 1947, s.247), the Inland Revenue (Taxes Management Act 1970, s.63), and H.M. Customs and Excise (Value Added Tax (General) Regulations 1980 (S.I. 1980 No. 1536), reg. 59; Value Added Tax Act 1983, Sched. 7, para. 6; Car Tax Regulations 1983 (S.I. 1983 No. 1751), reg. 26; Car Tax Act 1983, Sched. 1, para. 3) and now, to the community charge levying authority. The justification of the extension of this procedure to rating authorities, and by analogy to levying authorities under the present Act, lies in the fact that they cannot choose their debtors, and so should be given all assistance necessary to recover the charges deemed to be appropriate for the services which they provide: as they cannot refuse to give credit for services provided, then they should not be penalised if a debtor does not prove to be creditworthy (see Law Reform Committee for Scotland, 14th Report, (Cmnd. 2343 (1964)) para. 30; *Second Memorandum on Diligence, Poindings and Warrant Sales*, Scot. Law Com No. 48, 1980). (See also, para. 5(3) above.)

Sub-para. (3)

This sub-paragraph sets out the three diligences referred to in sub-para. (2) as available in summary warrant proceedings: first, a poinding and sale; secondly, an earnings arrestment; thirdly, an arrestment and action of furthcoming or sale.

The first refers to the means by which the corporeal moveables belonging to the debtor which are in the custody or control of the debtor himself are attached, brought within the control of the court, and thereafter possibly sold, with the proceeds being used to pay off the debt.

The second refers to a new diligence created by ss.75–78 of the Debtors (Scotland) Act 1987. Previously an arrestment of wages or salaries, usually the earnings of a debtor in the hands of a third party (employer) which could be attached by the creditor, referred only to a single payment of wages or salary. As such, in order to clear a debt, there was a frequent need for a creditor to repeat an arrestment, and often to avoid repetition or to minimise the number thereof, the amount required by an arrestment to be deducted from the debtor's pay constituted a large proportion of overall wages. The new earnings arrestment, as originally recommended by the Scottish Law Commission (*Report on Diligence and Debtor Protection*, Scot. Law Com. No. 95, pp.67–70 and 323–414), seeks to avoid the need for repetition of the diligence process and the need to deduct an excessive amount from the one payment by providing a system of continuous diligence, requiring the employer to deduct a tatutory fixed sum (related to net earnings) on each pay day until the debt is cleared. As he Debtors (Scotland) Act was passing through its parliamentary stages concurrently with he present Act, it was not posssible to provide for this new form of diligence to be made available under this Act until a relatively late stage in its gestation, namely Committee Stage n the Lords (*Hansard,* H.L. Vol. 486, cols. 1159–1160, *per* Lord Cameron of Lochbroom).

The third diligence refers to the means by which a creditor may attach money or goods belonging to the debtor which are in the hands of a third party, which property may hereafter be made over to him and made available to him to sell upon the raising of an action of furthcoming or sale.

Sub-para. (4)

This provides that the summary warrant procedure under sub-para. (1)(a) shall not apply where the arrears relate to liability for the community charge of another person under s.8(7). As such, a normal action of payment will have to be raised in such circumstances, which will enable a defender to contest the finding that there exists a relationship of such a type as to give rise to joint or several liability. It is important that such an opportunity is provided with his section since, as information relating to joint and several liability is not included in the register (s.13(2)), there exists no alternative means of contesting such a finding under s.16, which deals only with appeals concerning what appears on the face of the register (see note on s.16 above).

Sub-para. (5)

This specifies that the sheriff is not to grant a summary warrant in an application under sub-para. (2) if a court action has already been raised for recovery of the community charges, and that the raising of such an action will render ineffective any existing summary warrant so far as it relates to the community charges concerned.

The operation of this provision is without prejudice to sub-para. (6). Both of these rules also apply to proceedings for the recovery of rates, having been newly applied under Sched. 5 to the Debtors (Scotland) Act 1987 following a recommendation in the Scottish Law Commission Report (p.418).

Sub-para. (6)

This provides that if a summary warrant has been granted in respect of community charges and there has been reached the stage of execution of any of the diligences mentioned in sub-para. (3), then it is incompetent to raise a court action for recovery of these same charges. Again, this provision already applied in relation to rating authorities, under s.247(2) of the Local Government (Scotland) Act 1947.

Sub-para. (7)

The effect of this sub-paragraph and sub-para. (8), is to ensure that recovery of community charges under this paragraph is not to be prejudiced or inhibited by technical irregularities under this Schedule which are unrelated to the diligence process.

This sub-paragraph prevents any person in any proceedings for recovery of community charges from founding upon failure by the levying authority or any other authority or body to comply with any provision of Sched. 2 or requirement under it relating to the date by which something is to be done. However, a person may found upon failure to comply with any provision in the present paragraph or any other provision regulating the diligences, namely those referred to in sub-para. (3) as applied by Sched. 5 to the Debtors (Scotland) Act 1987.

Sub-para. (8)

This provides that misnomers, inaccuracies, mistakes or informalities in notices or any document or communication relating to the levy or collection of any community charge or in any proceedings for payment, are not to prejudice recovery of the charge.

Para. 8

This paragraph provides for the fees and expenses of summary warrant procedure to be chargeable against the defender. It also prevents the sheriff officer from charging fees to the debtor for collecting payment due by way of community charges.

Sub-para. (1)

This provides that, subject to sub-para. (2), and without prejudice to paras. 25–34 of Sched. 5 to the Debtors (Scotland) Act 1987, the fees of the sheriff officer and the outlays which he has necessarily incurred in connection with the execution of a summary warrant under para. 7 of the Schedule, are to be chargeable against the debtor.

Sub-para. (2)

This provides that the sheriff officer may not charge fees to the debtor for collecting, and accounting to the levying authority for sums paid in satisfaction of an amount due to the levying authority in respect of community charges.

Para. 9

This provides for the repayment of sums not due, by or on behalf of the levying authority, to any person who has made an undue payment.

Section 22   SCHEDULE 3

REDUCTION OF COMMUNITY CHARGES

Parliamentary proceedings for reduction of personal community charges

1.—(1) If the Secretary of State is satisfied that the total estimated expenses mentioned in section 9(2) of this Act of a local authority in respect of any financial year are excessive and unreasonable, he may make and cause to be laid before the Commons House of Parliament a report proposing a reduction in the amount of the personal community charge determined by the authority in respect of that year and stating—
  (a) the amount of the reduction so proposed; and
  (b) his reasons for proposing that reduction.
(2) A report under sub-paragraph (1) above shall set out any representations made by the local authority to which it relates with respect to the matters referred to in the report or a summary of these representations.
(3) In determining, for the purposes of sub-paragraph (1) above, whether, in relation to any financial year, the total estimated expenses of a local authority are excessive and unreasonable, the Secretary of State—
  (a) shall have regard to the financial and other relevant circumstances of the area of the authority;
  (b) may take into account the transfer or any sum between the local authority's general fund and any special fund or account maintained by them under any enactment;
  (c) may have regard—
    (i) to the expenditure or estimated expenses, in that or any preceding year, of other local authorities which the Secretary of State is satisfied are comparable with the local authority concerned;
    (ii) to general economic conditions; and
    (iii) to such other financial, economic, demographic, geographical and like criteria as he considers appropriate; and
  (d) may leave out of account such categories of estimated expenses as he thinks fit.
(4) In determining what amount to state under sub-paragraph (1)(a) above, the Secretary of State may have regard to any balances in the general fund of the local authority.

Procedure prior to Parliamentary proceedings

2. The Secretary of State shall not make and cause to be laid a report under paragraph 1 above without having afforded to the local authority to which the report relates an opportunity of making representations on—
  (a) whether the total estimated expenses of the authority are excessive and unreasonable;
  (b) the amount of the reduction proposed in the personal community charge; and
  (c) his reasons for proposing that reduction,
but need not afford them such an opportunity where he has, in proposing the reduction, taken account of representations made by the authority in relation to a reduction previously proposed by him in that personal community charge.

Effect of approval of report

3.—(1) If a report under paragraph 1 above is approved by the Commons House of Parliament, the local authority to which it relates shall forthwith determine under this sub-paragraph a new personal community charge less, by the amount of the reduction proposed in the report or by such smaller amount as the Secretary of State may agree, than the personal community charge determined by them under section 9(2) of this Act.

(2) Where, for any reason whatsoever, by the twenty-eighth day after the Commons House of Parliament approve a report, the local authority to whom the report relates have not made a determination required by sub-paragraph (1) above, the authority shall be deemed to have determined on that day a personal community charge under sub-paragraph (1) above such that the reduction proposed in the report is effected.

(3) If a local authority determine, or are deemed to have determined, a personal community charge under sub-paragraph (1) above—

(a) the amount of that personal community charge and not the amount determined by them under section 9 of this Act shall be the amount of their personal community charge;

(b) the amounts of their standard and collective community charges shall be recalculated accordingly and these amounts, as so recalculated, and not the amounts calculated respectively under sections 10 and 11 of this Act shall be the respective amounts of their standard and collective community charges; and

(c) their community charges shall be levied (and the rights and liabilities of persons liable to those charges shall be construed) accordingly.

Provisions supplementary to paragraphs 1 to 3

4.—(1) A report under paragraph 1 above may relate to more than one local authority and, if a report so relating is approved by a resolution of the Commons House of Parliament, paragraph 3 above shall apply in relation to each of the authorities to which the report relates.

(2) Any reference in this Act (except in paragraph 3 above and paragraphs 6 and 7 below) and in any other enactment, whether passed before or after the passing of this Act, to such community charge as is determined under section 9 or calculated under section 10 or 11 of this Act shall be construed as respectively including a reference to such community charge as has been determined, or is deemed to have been determined, under sub-paragraph (1) of paragraph 3 above or has been recalculated under sub-paragraph (3) of that paragraph.

(3) Paragraph 6 of Schedule 4 to this Act shall apply for the purposes of the Secretary of State's functions under this Schedule as it applies under that paragraph for the purposes of his functions in relation to revenue support grants.

Redetermination of personal community charge

5.—(1) Where a local authority have, in respect of any financial year, determined a personal community charge under section 9 of this Act but the Secretary of State, under paragraph 1 above, makes and causes to be laid before the Commons House of Parliament, a report as regards them or they have reason to believe that such report may be so laid, they may, at any time before such report is approved by the Commons House of Parliament, reassess the total estimated expenses mentioned in subsection (2) of that section and, subject to that subsection, determine under this paragraph in respect of the financial year such personal community charge, lower than that determined under that subsection, as the Secretary of State may agree.

(2) If a local authority determine a personal community charge under sub-paragraph (1) above—

(a) the amount of that personal community charge and not the amount determined by them under section 9 of this Act shall be the amount of their personal community charge;

(b) the amounts of their standard and collective community charges shall be recalculated accordingly and these amounts, as so recalculated, and not the amounts calculated respectively under sections 10 and 11 of this Act shall be the respective amounts of their standard and collective community charges; and

(c) their community charges shall be levied (and the rights and liabilities of persons liable to those charges shall be construed) accordingly.

(3) Any reference in this Act (except in this paragraph and paragraphs 6 and 7 below) and in any other enactment to such community charge as is determined under section 9 or calculated under section 10 or 11 of this Act shall be construed as including a reference to such community charge as is determined under sub-paragraph (1) above or recalculated under sub-paragraph (2) above.

Supplementary

6. Where a local authority have determined or are deemed to have determined their personal community charge under paragraph 3(1) above or determine their personal

community charge under paragraph 5(1) above, they shall, to such extent and in accordance with such procedure as may be prescribed—

(a) repay sums paid by way of any community charge for which any person was liable while their personal community charge remained as determined by them under section 9 of this Act or for which he would have been liable had it so remained; and

(b) pay the cost of levying and collecting the community charges levied in consequence of the determination or deemed determination of their personal community charge under paragraph 3(1) or 5(1) above.

Prohibition of using loans fund to offset reduced personal community charge

7.—(1) A local authority who, in respect of any financial year—

(a) determine, or are deemed to have determined, or anticipate that they will be required to determine, a personal community charge under paragraph 3(1) of this Schedule; or

(b) determine a personal community charge under paragraph 5(1) of this Schedule,

shall neither wholly nor partially offset the difference between—

(i) the amount produced by their community charges in respect of that year; and

(ii) the amount which would have been so produced had their personal community charge been determined by them under section 9 of this Act,

with sums advanced from their loans fund:

Provided that such offsetting may nevertheless be permitted by the Secretary of State in any case on such terms and conditions as he considers appropriate.

(2) If the Secretary of State is of the opinion that sub-paragraph (1) above, or any term or condition imposed under the proviso thereto, has been contravened, the local authority shall, on such opinion being intimated to them, reimburse their loans fund forthwith or within such time as the Secretary of State may allow.

(3) In this paragraph, "loans fund" means the loans fund established under Schedule 3 to the Local Government (Scotland) Act 1975.

DEFINITIONS

"community charge": see ss.26(1) and 7.

"financial year": see s.26(1) and Local Government (Scotland) Act 1973, s.96(5) as amended; *i.e.* the year from April 1.

"general fund": see Local Government (Scotland) Act 1973, s.93(1).

"loans fund": see para. 7(3) and the Local Government (Scotland) Act 1975, Sched. 3.

"local authority": see s.26(1).

"total estimated expenses": see s.9(2).

GENERAL NOTE

Under the law as it applies until 1989, the amount of income receivable by a local authority for payment into its general fund may be reduced by the Secretary of State with parliamentary approval in a number of ways.

One group of powers available to the Secretary of State relate to the payment of rate support grant. Under powers in ss.5 and 5A of the Local Government (Scotland) Act 1966 (see Sched. 1 to the Rating and Valuation (Amendment) (Scotland) Act 1984), the Secretary of State may take steps to reduce the grant otherwise payable to an authority in circumstances where, *inter alia*, he is satisfied that its expenditure has been, or its estimated expenditure is, excessive and unreasonable. This power supplements a power in s.4 of the 1966 Act to vary amounts payable in rate support grant to local authorities in general.

No equivalent of ss.5 and 5A is to be retained under this Act with effect from 1989. See Sched. 4 "Revenue Support Grants" below.

The other powers of the Secretary of State which operate until 1989 relate to the control of the rate income of local authorities. These take two principal forms. On the one hand, the Government have the power conferred by s.108B of the Local Government (Scotland) Act 1973 (inserted by s.3 of the 1984 Amendment Act above). This allowed the Secretary of State to place a general lid (*i.e.* on all authorities or all in a class) on rate increases in any year. Known as "rate-capping", it is a power which has not been exercised in Scotland and the provisions under which it is conferred are repealed by this Act. The much more elaborate system for the "capping" of non-domestic rates from 1989 is, however, introduced by s.3 of this Act. No power for the general "capping" of community charges is introduced. Under the terms of Pt. II of this Act, authorities are not to be restricted by any general ceiling upon the level of community charges.

What, however, is retained is a successor power to that contained in the 1966 Act (also in s.5) under which the Secretary of State can, until 1989, in addition or as an alternative to ordering the reduction of its rate support grant, order that an individual authority whose total estimated expenses are "excessive and unreasonable" should reduce the level of its rate for the year in question. The introduction of this power by the Local Government and Planning (Scotland) Act 1982 (by amendment of s.5 of the 1966 Act) was the result of the Government's frustration in their failure to induce authorities to reduce their rate levels whilst merely under the threat of grant penalties imposed by the Secretary of State under his other powers in s.5 discussed above. Nor was it ever established that an authority which chose to incur a grant penalty rather than cut its rate was acting in breach of its "fiduciary duty" to its ratepayers. (See Himsworth "Fiduciary duties of local authorities" 1982 S.L.T. (News) 241, 249; *Commission for Local Authority Accounts* v. *Stirling District Council*, 1984 S.L.T. 442.)

Although the Secretary of State's power to reduce grant in the light of proposed expenditure which he considered excessive and unreasonable is dispensed with in this Act, the power to order a reduction in community charge is retained. Plainly there would be little need to retain a similar control in relation to non-domestic rates—given the power of the Secretary of State to prescribe a "base-rate" under s.3(5)(a)(ii) and the strict adherence to the retail prices index thereafter. On the power to reduce community charges, however, the Green Paper (Cmnd. 9714 (1986)) referred to the Government's intention to "retain a last-resort power—analogous to that which they have at present—to reduce impositions on the local domestic taxpayer where an authority is clearly planning expenditure which Parliament judges to be excessive and unreasonable" (para. 8.41).

This view of a need to retain a "last-resort power" was the one carried forward into the Bill and the Act but only after some criticism from Opposition Members that it made a "nonsense of the whole Bill" (Mr. Maxton, 1st Scot.S.C., col. 1196) and was not "consistent with the view that the Bill strengthens local accountability" (Mr. McLennan, 1st Scot.S.C., col. 1203). The accountability argument was one to which the Government were even vulnerable from their own benches (see Mr. Fletcher, *Hansard*, H.C. Vol. 107, col. 223). There is plainly a need to justify a power to restrain local decision-making on expenditure *after* radical change (the universal poll tax) which is, above all, supposed to promote *local* democratic accountability.

In its principal features, the procedure to order the reduction of community charges is very similar to that used in s.5 of the 1966 Act to reduce rates. The Secretary of State must make and lay before the House of Commons a report as in para. 1. That paragraph sets out what the report must contain and, with para. 2, sets out the considerations to be taken into account and the consultation to be made with the affected authority.

If the House of Commons approve the report, the local authority must redetermine its personal community charge at the level required by the report. If it fails to do so, the reduction is deemed to be made (para. 3) and repayment of amounts overpaid is, in either case, required (para. 6). The opportunity is given (by para. 5) to a local authority, prior to Commons approval of a report, to negotiate and agree with the Secretary of State a lower charge.

A local authority may not, except with the Secretary of State's consent, offset a reduction in its community charge by having recourse to its loans fund (para. 7).

Para. 1
Sub-para. (1)
Para. 1 has to be read in close conjunction with para. 2 which sets out the required pre-parliamentary procedure. Notice, in particular, that the authority concerned must be afforded the opportunity to make representations on the three crucial matters set out as para. 2(a), (b) and (c). It is not the level of community charge itself which has to be viewed as "excessive and unreasonable" but the authority's "total estimated expenses". Thus, in the event of the level of community charge being inflated not by an increase in overall expenditure but because of the (improbable) determination of a low domestic rate (s.3) or because of a low level of revenue support grant (Sched. 4), measures under Sched. 3 would be inappropriate.

Notice that a report may relate to more than one authority (para. 4(1) below).

Sub-para. (2)
There was some criticism of the option of submitting a report to the House of Commons containing only a summary version of representations made. The response, however, was that this innovation was to avoid waste. It would not be in the Government's own interest, it was argued, for them to summarise the representations unfairly (see *e.g.*, the Earl of

Dundee at *Hansard,* H.L. Vol. 487, col. 42: "The power to summarise representations is not in any way sinister. It may well never be used." He went on to resist an attempt to require a summary of representations "agreed" by both the Secretary of State and the authority).

Sub-para. (3)

This sub-paragraph sets out what the Secretary of State must and may take into account when determining that total estimated expenses are "excessive and unreasonable" and when deciding upon the amount of the proposed reduction. In sub-para. (3)(c)(i) it is no longer required that the authorities used for comparative purposes be "closely comparable". *Cf.* Local Government (Scotland) Act 1966, s.5(1A).

Sub-para. (4)

This is new and is related to the prohibition in para. 7 on the use of an authority's loans fund to cushion the effect of a reduction in community charge.

Para. 2

This imposes the procedural requirement to afford the opportunity of making representations. The final three lines are intended to avoid the need to invite further representations where, for instance, the Secretary of State decides to amend his report after the first representations have been lodged.

Notice again the power under para. 4 to conjoin more than one report. Presumably, representations must be permitted from each authority.

Para. 3

This paragraph sets out the three possible results of the approval of a report by the Commons.

One is that the authority concerned forthwith determine a new personal community charge reduced by the amount proposed in the report.

The second is that the authority determines a new community charge reduced by a *smaller* amount than proposed if this is agreed by the Secretary of State.

Thirdly, if the authority has not taken action within 28 days, a new community charge is deemed to have been determined—reduced by the amount in the report.

By virtue of sub-para. (3) the new amounts of personal community charge are duly substituted and the standard and collective charges are to be recalculated.

See also para. 6 below.

Para. 4

This serves three separate purposes:

Sub-para. (1)

This has been mentioned. It permits the treatment of more than one authority in one report and one Commons approval—stated, for the first time, to be by resolution!

Sub-para. (2)

This (and para. 5(3) is to similar effect) is designed to ensure that in all legislation (other than that dealing with reduced community charges themselves) the reduced charges are regarded as charges determined by the authority under s.9 (and ss.10 and 11) of the Act.

Sub-para. (3)

This incorporates the Secretary of State's powers to obtain information under Sched. 4, para. 6. See the note on that paragraph. The fact that estimated figures may be deemed to be given by the authority but not deemed to be accurate may be even more troublesome and/or pointless in the case of Sched. 3.

Presumably the power under Sched. 4, para. 6 may be used to make estimates of comparative information from authorities *other than* the one on which the report is made. To deem such information to have been given by the other authority might be severely counterproductive if the Secretary of State purports to rely on it thereafter.

Para. 5

This paragraph provides a procedure analogous to that in para. 3 where the authority decides to act to reduce its level of community charge *before* being compelled to do so by the approval by the Commons of a report. This may occur not only where the report is actually made and laid but also where the authority has "reason to believe that such a report may be so laid". (Para. 7 below refers to an authority "anticipating" action against it.) There is no other provision under which an authority may redetermine its community charge once determined under s.9.

Para. 6

Subject to procedures to be prescribed, local authorities are required under this paragraph to repay sums paid to them as community charges prior to their reduction under paras. 3 and 5; and to pay the (additional) costs of levying and collecting the newly determined charges. Presumably this latter requirement relates primarily to a new *district* community charge levied and collected by a regional council (*cf.* Sched. 2, para. 6(3)).

Para. 7

This paragraph is the successor to s.18 of the Local Government (Miscellaneous Provisions) (Scotland) Act 1981 as amended and is designed to achieve the same purpose. The powers in Sched. 3 reflect a concern both with the total estimated expenses of an authority and the level of its community charge. The two are, of course, intimately related but the result of the use of the powers is a redetermination of the charge alone (although, under para. 5(1), a reassessment of total estimated expenses is also required). This paragraph, in effect, declares unacceptable (except with the consent of the Secretary of State) a decision by the authority to offset the amount lost in community charges (and thus retain the same overall expenditure) by drawing upon its loans fund.

Within the terms of Sched. 3 to the Local Government (Scotland) Act 1975, sums from the loans fund may be transferred for revenue purposes but notice that the Secretary of State may take into account transfers of sums between accounts in deciding whether expenditure levels are "excessive and unreasonable" (see para. 1(3)(b)).

The sanction in respect of an unauthorised transfer is an intimation under para. 7(2) of the opinion of the Secretary of State which is required to be implemented. If it is not so implemented, the authority (and its members and officers) would become vulnerable to an adverse report from the auditor and further sanctions under the Local Government (Scotland) Act 1973, ss. 102–104. It would, in addition, be open to the Secretary of State to start default proceedings under s.211 of the 1973 Act.

Section 23   SCHEDULE 4

REVENUE SUPPORT GRANTS

Determination of aggregate amount

1.—(1) For the purpose of determining the estimated aggregate amount of the revenue support grants payable to local authorities for any financial year, the Secretary of State shall determine (and may, from time to time, redetermine)—

(a) the aggregate amount which he estimates is to be available for the payment out of moneys provided by Parliament of grants (other than housing subsidies) to local authorities in respect of their relevant expenditure for that year; and

(b) the portion of that amount which the Secretary of State estimates will be allocated to grants payable for that year in respect of such services as the Secretary of State may determine;

and the amount remaining, after deducting that portion from the aggregate amount aforesaid, shall be the estimated aggregate amount of the revenue support grants so payable for that year.

(2) In this paragraph—

"housing subsidies" means such grants to local authorities out of moneys provided by Parliament for housing as may be determined by the Secretary of State to be housing subsidies for the purposes of this Schedule;

"relevant expenditure", in relation to a financial year, means the total expenditure of a local authority in respect of that year as estimated by the Secretary of State but, in making that estimate, he may leave out of account such categories of expenditure in respect of that year as he may determine.

Amount of revenue support grant payable to each local authority

2.—(1) The amount of revenue support grant payable to each local authority in respect of a financial year shall be such as is determined in relation to the local authority in an order made by the Secretary of State with the consent of the Treasury.

(2) For the purpose of determining the amount of revenue support grant payable to a local authority in respect of a financial year, the Secretary of State shall—

(a) apportion such part of the estimated aggregate amount of revenue support grants among such local authorities and on such basis as he determines, having regard to what, in his opinion, are their respective needs in that year;

(b) apportion the remainder of that amount among local authorities in accordance with sub-paragraph (3) below.

(3) The remainder referred to in sub-paragraph (2)(b) above shall be divided by an amount equal to the Secretary of State's estimate of the adult population of Scotland (the resultant sum being called the "*per capita* amount"); and there shall be apportioned to—

(a) each islands council a sum equal to the product of his estimate of the adult population of their area and the *per capita* amount;

(b) each regional council a sum equal to the product of his estimate of the adult population of their area and such part as the Secretary of State determines of the *per capita* amount; and

(c) each district council a sum equal to the product of his estimate of the adult population of their area and the remaining part of the *per capita* amount.

(4) The Secretary of State may, by reference to such factors as he determines, alter any amount produced under sub-paragraph (2) or (3) above and may do so in relation to all local authorities or such class or classes of local authority or such local authority as he determines.

(5) An order under sub-paragraph (1) above, together with a report of the considerations which led to it provisions, shall be laid before the Commons House of Parliament but shall have no effect until approved by a resolution of that House.

(6) Subject to paragraph 5 below, anything done under this paragraph may, from time to time, be done again and where, as a result of any redetermination under sub-paragraph (1) above, any amount of revenue support grant paid to a local authority falls to be repaid, the Secretary of State may recover it whenever and however he thinks fit.

3. The Secretary of State's functions under paragraphs 1 and 2 above shall be performed only after consultation with such associations of local authorities as appear to him to be concerned.

Payment of revenue support grant

4. Revenue support grant shall be paid to a local authority in such instalments and at such times as the Secretary of State may, with the consent of the Treasury, determine.

5. The Secretary of State may determine that the amount of revenue support grant which has been paid to a local authority in respect of a financial year shall be final and, where he does so, he shall have no power to redetermine that amount.

Secretary of State's power on local authority's failure to provide information

6. Where under section 199 of the Local Government (Scotland) Act 1973 (which provides for reports and returns being made by local authorities and others) the Secretary of State requires a local authority to give information for the purposes of his functions in relation to revenue support grants payable for the financial year 1989–90 or for any financial year thereafter, but that information is not given timeously, he may make an estimate as regards any element of the required information; and, without prejudice to section 211 of that Act (which makes general provision concerning failure by a local authority to do what is required of them), for the said purposes such estimate shall be deemed information given by the local authority.

DEFINITIONS

"financial year": see 26(1) and s.96(5) as amended of the Local Government (Scotland) Act 1973; *i.e.* the year from April 1.

"local authority": see s.26(1).

"order": see s.26(1).

GENERAL NOTE

The replacement of domestic rates by community charges is not intended to remove the dependence of local authorities upon some measure of central funding. Discussing the system of grants which will operate until 1989, the Green Paper (Cmnd. 9714 (1986)) points out that exchequer grants (including grants paid in respect of rate rebates) accounted, in 1985/86 for 59 per cent. of local authority income in Scotland (para. 8.13). Apart from specific grants (*i.e.* grants tied to the support of particular services, most notably the police) which made up 12 per cent. of that total exchequer grant, exchequer grant was paid in the form of rate support grants.

The essential elements of the new system of revenue support grants introduced by this Schedule are very similar to those which the Local Government (Scotland) Act 1966 as amended established for rate support grants and a summary of the procedure noting similarities and differences may serve as a useful introduction to revenue support grants:—

1. Although the detailed rules for grant distribution will, despite the Government's aim to achieve a simpler system, no doubt be quite complex in practice, the provisions in the Act itself are brief and skeletal. Heavy reliance is placed upon subordinate legislation. In particular, rules for the determination of the "needs" of authorities (para. 2(2)) are not specified at all in the Schedule.

2. Grants are to be determined and distributed by reference to the financial year of local authorities (para. 1), *i.e.* April 1 to March 31.

3. Amounts due to each authority are determined by the Secretary of State with the consent of the Treasury in an order which is required to be laid before and approved by resolution of the House of Commons (paras. 2(1) and 2(5)).

4. The order has to be accompanied by a "report of the considerations which led to its provisions" (para. 2(5)).

5. The Secretary of State's functions leading to the making of an order have to be "performed only after consultation with such associations of local authorities as appear to him to be concerned." This means, in effect, the Convention of Scottish Local Authorities (C.O.S.L.A.). See note on para. 3.

6. The determination of the amounts payable to authorities may be seen as being in two stages. In the first, the Secretary of State determines the aggregate amount (*i.e.* the total amount for all authorities) of revenue support grants to be paid for the year in question. This is done by reference to assumptions which he is empowered to make both about the total level of expenditure by local authorities and about the proportion of that total to be paid out of central grants. It is a process which is very similar to that adopted for rate support grants although the criteria according to which the Secretary of State decides the total level of expenditure, whilst very broad before, are now not specified at all.

7. The second stage is that at which the aggregate grant is divided between the authorities and is more complex. It has, however, on its face at least, lost some of the complexities of the rate support grant system. Under that, the aggregate grant was divided three ways. The first portion was the "domestic element" (in 1985/86, £102.3m) which was simply a subsidy to "domestic" ratepayers (*i.e.* in dwellinghouses) whose rate poundages were required to be reduced by a fixed amount by all regional and islands councils (Local Government (Scotland) Act 1966, s.7). That element of rate support grant has no equivalent in the revenue support grant—with the abolition of domestic rates.

The second element was the "resources" element (in 1985/86, £203.5m) which was supposed to act as an equalisation grant. It was "intended to compensate to some extent for the differences in rating resources between local authorities, primarily due to the uneven spread of commercial and industrial development across the country" (Cmnd. 9714 (1986) para. 8.11). That element has no direct successor in the revenue support grant system. Looking ahead to the stage at which a uniform national non-domestic rate would be levied (see notes on s.3), the Green Paper reasoned that the need for an equalisation or resources element would fall away. "The proceeds of non-domestic rates would . . . be redistributed to all local authorities as a fixed sum per adult . . ." (para. 8.36) removing any inequalities in local revenue from the source which was the biggest cause of unequal resources in the past. The revenue support grant rules do not, therefore, contain any explicit reference to a resources element—but see further notes on para. 2 below.

What is maintained is a grant composed in part of an element calculated by reference to the assumed "needs" of each authority. This is an almost direct successor to the former "needs element" in the rate support grant (in 1985/86, £1424.5m). The rules are not spelled out in the Schedule but, in their statements in both the Green Paper (para. 8.36) and Parliament (see *e.g.* Michael Ancram, M.P., 1st Scot.S.C., col. 1280), the Government have said that they will continue the "client group" system of recent years. It is a system for the division of a fixed revenue pool between all authorities "on the basis of client group assessments of relative expenditure need which are built up service by service. The assessments are designed to identify the factors outwith the control of authorities which affect the need for and the cost of services. The assessments are expressed in terms of primary and, where appropriate, secondary indicators. For instance, the primary indicator for school teaching costs is the number of pupils in the authority, the secondary indicator is the settlement pattern of the authority (to measure sparsity). In other services there are factors to reflect the extra cost of providing services in urban areas or areas of deprivation.

The total of assessments for all services is the basis for needs element distribution. Grant is distributed so that after needs element a similar amount remains to be financed from the rates" (Green Paper, Cmnd. 9714 (1986), para. 8.12). For "rates", from 1989 read "community charges".

In addition to a "needs grant" based on these principles, there will also be payable a "standard grant" on a *per capita* basis. The balance between these two grants elements, the balance between regions and districts in the payment of standard grant, and the formulae for the calculation of the client group assessments (not forgetting the initial assumptions of total expenditure and grant) will, no doubt, be as hotly contested by and between local authorities as their predecessor equivalents.

8. Ancillary provisions include what may be an important "safety net" form of transitional protection (para. 2(4) and the power to make amendment orders (para. 2(6)).

9. One feature which is wholly omitted from the scheme of revenue support grants, but which loomed very large in the rate support grant rules, is any mechanism for the imposition of grant penalties upon individual authorities considered by the Secretary of State to be overspending. It has, however, already been observed that many other controls on the expenditure of individual authorities will be retained and, in particular, the power to order a reduction in the level of an authority's community charges. See the notes on Sched. 3.

Para. 1
This relates to what is described above as the first stage for the determination (formerly, for rate support grants, "fixing") of the aggregate amount of revenue support grants. The process may be otherwise expressed:—

1. Estimation by Secretary of State of total "relevant expenditure" of all authorities. Under s.2(3) of the Local Government (Scotland) Act 1966, he was obliged (before making this and the following determinations) to take into consideration, *inter alia*, latest information on the rate of relevant expenditure, probable fluctuation in the demand for services, the need for developing services, and variations in levels of prices, costs and remuneration. Under this Schedule, the Secretary of State makes his estimates unconstrained by such formally ordained considerations. As before, he may exclude such categories of expenditure as he determines.

2. Estimate of aggregate amount of central grant towards that relevant expenditure (other than "housing subsidies" which are to be defined but will be principally payments of housing support grant under s.191 of the Housing (Scotland) Act 1987).

3. Deduction of specific grants.

4. The result is the aggregate amount of revenue support grants for the financial year in question.

The Secretary of State's function under para. 1 must be carried out only after consultation with C.O.S.L.A. (para. 3). As at present, that process will begin some months before the beginning of the financial year on April 1. The making of the revenue support grant order will follow the determination by authorities of their non-domestic rate but precede their determination of community charges (see, *e.g.* Michael Ancram, M.P., *Hansard*, H.C. Vol. 111, col. 1093 *et seq.*).

Notice the powers of the Secretary of State to require authorities to provide him with information (para. 6).

Para. 2
The essential elements here are:
1. The requirement of procedure by order (sub-para. (1)) laid, with the report of "considerations", before the Commons and requiring an affirmative resolution (sub-para. (5))—the only requirement in the Act of an affirmative resolution.

2. The needs grant (sub-para. (2)(a)). This is to be the larger portion of the total grant and is to be determined by reference to "client groups" as above. How the total grant is apportioned between this "needs" grant and the remainder which becomes the "standard" grant is for determination by the Secretary of State.

3. The standard grant (sub-paras. (2)(b) and (3)). As explained above, this supplements the needs grant but is calculated not by reference to presumed relative needs of local authority services but simply to adult population figures in the different areas. For islands this is the product of their estimated population and the national "*per capita* amount" (total standard grant divided by total estimated population of Scotland). The shares for regions and districts are apportioned by the Secretary of State.

4. The "safety net" (sub-para. (4)). As explained by Mr. Ancram at the Commons Report stage (*Hansard*, H.C. Vol. III, col. 1094), this power further to adjust the results of the calculations under sub-paras. (2) and (3) will be used "to avoid or to moderate any change

in grant entitlement, from one year to the next. Sub-para. (2)(4) provides us with an adequate vehicle to avoid odd or quirky results which otherwise might be expected to arise, particularly for the islands councils. On present estimates we would expect all the islands councils to benefit substantially from the safety netting . . ."

5. The provision for redetermination of revenue support grants and, where appropriate, for the recovery of grant overpaid (sub-para. (2)(b)). Notice that sub-para. (2)(b) is to be read subject to para. 5 according to which the determination of grants can be declared to be final.

As with para. 1, the Secretary of State's functions under paragraph 2 are to follow consultation with C.O.S.L.A. (para. 3). In its potential application to para. 2, para. 3 is expressed rather more widely than one might expect. Will the Secretary of State consult with C.O.S.L.A. before recovering overpaid grant from an individual authority?

As explained in the General Note, there is no separate "resources" element in the grant. This is justified in the Green Paper by forward reference to the time when a uniform non-domestic rate will be levied and redistributed. Until that time, there remains some continuing need for the equalisation of resources and this was, in effect, acknowledged by Mr. Ancram (*Hansard*, H.C. Vol. 111, col. 1094) when he spoke not of a resources element as such but of a process of "netting off" of each authority's non-domestic rate income as a part of assessing the amount of needs grant payable. Thus the size of an authority's grant will be reduced by the amount of its rate income which, in the distribution of a fixed pool, will mean that rich authorities will subsidise the poor. An equalisation capacity has thus been retained and the process will achieve many of the purposes of a pooled, nationally-prescribed rate—with the exception of a uniform poundage. See also the note on s.3.

In adopting this approach, the Government must be taken to assume that the power to determine the respective "needs" of authorities (para. 2(2)(a)) includes a power not only to interpret "needs" for the first time to mean, in part, "lack of rateable resources" but also to determine how the resource base of each authority will be calculated for this purpose. Will the Secretary of State take account of the actual *rate* poundage fixed by an authority to calculate a rate product—thus allowing an authority fixing its rate below the s.3 maximum to draw more heavily upon the grant pool—or, as seems more likely in normal circumstances, will the Secretary of State "net off" the rate product upon the assumption of a maximum poundage? Does a statutory power to determine "needs" include the power to assume a particular level of rate income which the Secretary of State has no statutory power to determine, other than to prescribe its maximum level?

Para. 3

See references to this paragraph under paras. 1 and 2 above. There is, in Scotland, only one "such association of local authorities"—C.O.S.L.A.

Para. 4

This provides for the payment of grant to authorities in instalments.

Para. 5

This paragraph enables the Secretary of State to declare an end to the process of redetermination of grant payable to an authority (see para. 2(2)(b) above) by determining an amount of grant to be "final". Such a determination presumably relieves authorities of the possibility of further recovery of grant under para. 2(2)(b). Although the Secretary of State is declared to have no further power to redetermine the amount of grant, his decision would, where appropriate, remain challengeable in proceedings for judicial review.

Para. 6

This paragraph re-enacts, in relation to revenue support grants, s.19 of the Local Government (Miscellaneous Provisions) (Scotland) Act 1981 (see also s.5(9) of the Local Government (Scotland) Act 1966 as amended) which is repealed by Sched. 6.

In the exercise of his functions under this Schedule the Secretary of State will require financial information from local authorities. There is a standard power to require the provision of information (Local Government (Scotland) Act 1973, s.199) but, since 1981, this has been supplemented with the more specific power which requires the submission of information "timeously". S.211 of the 1973 Act gives the Secretary of State a general power to act against an authority where it defaults in the performance of its duties but, again, this is strengthened by the addition of a power to estimate the information sought and to deem it to be given by the authority. The paragraph does not, however, deem the information to be accurate and it is not inconceivable that the inaccuracy of the estimated information could be relied upon subsequently. Nor does this paragraph go as far as s.81 of the Housing

(Scotland) Act 1987 in placing a personal duty upon an officer of an authority to supply information sought by the Secretary of State.

Section 25   SCHEDULE 5

DEFINITIONS
   "apportionment note": see s.26(1).
   "community charges": see s.7.
   "financial year": see s.26(1) and s. 96(5) of the Local Government (Scotland) Act 1973 as amended; *i.e.* the year from April 1.
   "islands area": see Local Government (Scotland) Act 1973, s. 1.
   "lands and heritages": see Lands Valuation (Scotland) Act 1854, s.42.
   "local authority": see para. 1, The definition in s.26(1) does not apply.
   "1980 Act": see s.26(1).
   "1947 Act": see s.26(1).
   "1975 Act": see s.26(1).
   "1973 Act": see s.26(1).
   "1968 Act": see s.26(1).
   "part residential subjects": see s.26(1) and Sched. 1.
   "prescribe", "prescribed": see ss.26(1) and 31.
   "rateable value": see s.26(1) but also s.7 of the Local Government (Scotland) Act 1975.
   "region": see Local Government (Scotland) Act 1973, s.1.
   "valuation roll": see Local Government (Scotland) Act 1975, s.1.

COMMENCEMENT
   See notes on each Part.

GENERAL NOTE
   When considering the provisions of the Act which deal with the community charges and the non-domestic rate, it is not, for the most part, necessary to look separately at the financing of different local authority services. The revenue raised from the charges and the rate as supplemented by the revenue support grant is paid into the general fund maintained by each authority under s.93 of the Local Government (Scotland) Act 1973 and expenditure for the authority's services is paid out of that fund. There is an important exception in the case of the housing function of district and islands councils which are obliged to maintain separate housing revenue accounts under s.203 of the Housing (Scotland) Act 1987. Payments from an authority's general fund to its housing revenue account are regulated by s.204 of that Act. Those arrangements are not directly affected by the abolition of domestic rates.
   Two services do, however, have to be looked at separately. They are the water and sewerage services and are dealt with in s.25 and in this Schedule.
   Until April 1, 1989, the two services will be subject to different financial regimes (for a summary, see Malcolm Rifkind, M.P., *Hansard*, H.C. Vol. 107, cols. 210–211). Water supply services provided by regional and islands councils are financed, under Pt. IV of the Water (Scotland) Act 1980, from three sources. Much of the supply to commercial premises is paid for by metering (s.49). Otherwise (s.39) water is paid for by all ratepayers as a portion of the rates paid to regional and islands councils (the "public water rate") and by an additional separate rate (the "domestic water rate") levied on all lands and heritages, to which there is a water supply, by reference to the net annual value (or, in the case of commercial premises, normally one-half of the net annual value) of the premises. From April 1, 1989, charging by metering will continue but the two rates will be replaced by three new "community water charges" and a new "non-domestic water rate". Provision for these is made by Pt. I of the Schedule (mainly in relation to the community water charges) and by Pt. IV which, by amendment of the 1980 Act, creates the non-domestic water rate.
   The position of sewerage services is different. Until April 1, 1989 the services provided by regional and islands councils under the Sewerage (Scotland) Act 1968 are paid for from the ordinary rate like other local authority services although some non-domestic consumers may, under s.29 of the Act, pay an additional trade effluent charge. From April 1, 1989, sewerage services are to be financed (under Pt. II of the Schedule) partly from the community charges (the community charges established under Pt. II of the Act) and partly from a new "non-domestic sewerage rate" to be levied on lands and heritages connected to public sewers or public sewage treatment works and which are entered in the valuation roll.

The principal distinction between the scheme for the two services under the Act is that, whilst water has its own community charges, sewerage does not. In the view of Government, "the additional administrative complexity of a community sewerage charge could not be justified at this stage" (Mr. Lang, 1st Scot.S.C., col. 1328). Thus, this element of the burden of financing sewerage services cannot be imposed solely on identifiable consumers of the service whereas consumers alone will be liable to pay community water charges.

This leaves the schemes with a number of common elements. Under both, authorities are required to estimate, by a prescribed date in relation to each financial year, the amount of expenditure to be incurred on the service (paras. 2(a), 14(a)) allowing for contingencies etc. (paras. 3, 15). They must then apportion that estimated total between the sources of income available to them (paras. 2(b), 14(b)) but subject to an obligation not to show "undue preference" nor to "discriminate unduly" in doing so (paras. 4, 17). The apportionment has to be "even-handed between classes of consumer" (Ian Lang, M.P., 1st Scot.S.C., col. 1328). In addition, both schemes require that separate accounts are kept for the services and that "tariffs of charges" for the two services are prepared and made public (Pt. III of the Schedule).

From the Government's point of view, a number of general objectives are achieved under the two schemes (see Ian Lang, M.P. above, cols. 1327–1331). For non-domestic consumers, the new water and sewerage rates and accounts keep expenditure on the two services separate from others which paves the way for a "national business rate" established on a uniform basis with England and Wales where water and sewerage are not financed out of local authority rates. Increased use of metering will, at the same time, reduce the significance of the non-domestic water rate. Domestic consumers will, through the separate water community charges and the published tariffs for water and sewerage, be better informed; the charges will be more discernible; and the authorities more accountable.

The possibility that the restructuring of the financing of the services might be additionally related to future plans for privatisation was not overlooked by the Government's critics (see, *e.g.,* 1st Scot.S.C., col. 1325).

Water and Sewerage Charges

Part I

Charges for Water Services

1. Subject to the provisions of this Part of this Schedule, the expenditure incurred by the council of a region or islands area (in this Schedule referred to as a "local authority") in meeting any requisition under Part IV or VIII of the 1980 Act and in the exercise of any of their functions under any enactment in relation to water supply in their region or area shall, insofar as not otherwise met, be met out of—

   (a) the charges (herinafter in this Schedule referred to as "direct charges") made under section 49 of the 1980 Act (which relates to the payment for water supplies by meter);
   (b) the community water charges mentioned in paragraph 6 below; and
   (c) the non-domestic water rate mentioned in paragraph 12 below.

Estimation and apportionment of expenditure

2. In respect of the financial year 1989–90 and each subsequent financial year, each local authority shall, before such date as may be prescribed in relation to each of those years—

   (a) subject to paragraph 3 below, estimate the amount of the expenditure mentioned in paragraph 1 above which they will incur in respect of that year; and
   (b) subject to paragraph 4 below, determine what proportion of that expenditure is to be met from each of the sources mentioned in sub-paragraphs (a) to (c) of the said paragraph 1.

3. In estimating the expenditure mentioned in paragaph 1 above which they will incur in respect of any financial year a local authority shall take into account—

   (a) such additional sum as is in their opinion required—
       (i) to cover expenses previously incurred,
       (ii) to meet contingencies, and
       (iii) to meet any expenses which may fall to be met before the moneys to be received from the sources mentioned in paragraph 1 above in respect of the next following financial year will become available; and
   (b) any means by which any part of that expenditure may otherwise be met or provided for.

4. A local authority may apportion their estimated expenditure under paragraph 2 above on whatever basis they consider appropriate, but they shall ensure that the apportionment

is not such as to show undue preference to, or discriminate unduly against, any class or classes of person liable to pay—

(a) the direct charges;

(b) the community water charges; or

(c) the non-domestic water rate,

respectively.

Direct charges

5. After a local authority have, under paragraph 2 above, determined what proportion of their estimated expenditure in respect of a particular financial year is to be met out of direct charges, they shall, before such date as may be prescribed in relation to that year, determine such rate or rates of direct charges in respect of that year as will, when calculated in accordance with the provisions of section 49 of the 1980 Act (which relates to the payment for water supplied by meter), produce sufficient moneys to meet the said proportion, and different rates of direct charges may be determined for different circumstances.

Community water charges

6. There shall be imposed, in accordance with the provisions of this Part of this Schedule, three community water charges, to be known respectively as the personal community water charge, the standard community water charge and the collective community water charge.

Liability to pay community water charges

7. Where in respect of any financial year or any part of a financial year the qualifying conditions mentioned in paragraph 8 below are met, any person who is liable to pay any of the community charges mentioned in section 7 of this Act (that is, the personal community charge, the standard community charge or the collective community charge) shall also be liable to pay the corresponding community water charge (that is, the personal community water charge, the standard community water charge or the collective community water charge).

8. The qualifying conditions for the purposes of paragraph 7 above are—

(a) that the water authority provides a supply of water for domestic purposes within the meaning of section 7 of the 1980 Act (which defines that term) to premises—

(i) in which that person has his sole or main residence, or

(ii) in respect of which he is liable to pay the standard community charge or, as the case may be, the collective community charge; and

(b) that the water is not wholly supplied to those premises by meter.

Determination of community water charges

9. Every local authority shall, in respect of the financial year 1989–90 and of each subsequent financial year, determine, before such date as may be prescribed in relation to each of those years, the amount of the personal community water charge to be imposed by them in respect of that year.

10. The amount determined under paragraph 9 above shall be such as will provide (account having been taken of the moneys to be produced by the standard and collective community water charges) sufficient moneys to meet such proportion of the authority's estimated expenditure for that year as they have determined under paragraph 2 above is to be met out of the community water charges.

11. Subject to paragraphs 7 and 8 above, the provisions of Part II of and Schedule 2 to this Act shall have effect, subject to such adaptations, exceptions and modifications as may be prescribed, in relation to the community water charges as they have effect in relation to the corresponding community charges.

Non-domestic water rate

12. The provisions of section 40 of the 1980 Act, as substituted by paragraph 29 of this Schedule, shall have effect in relation to the non-domestic water rate.

COMMENCEMENT

This Part and Pt. II of the Schedule were brought into force on September 14, 1987, but "only for the purposes of and in relation to the community charges, the community water charges, the charges to be made under s.49 of the Water (Scotland) Act 1980, the non-domestic water rate and the non-domestic sewerage rate in respect of the financial year

1989–90 and each subsequent financial year" (S.I. 1987 No. 1489). It comes fully into force on April 1, 1989.

Para. 1

This is a statement which, in dealing with expenditure on water services, broadly corresponds with s.7 of the Act in relation to general expenditure.

As indicated in the paragraph the expenditure of regional and islands councils (local authorities) includes that on their water supply functions in general but also the meeting of requisitions from other water authorities under Pt. IV of the 1980 Act (water supplied outside area of authority) and from water development boards under Pt. VIII of the Act.

Direct charges under s.49 have been referred to above and will continue (see para. 5). Provision for the other two forms of charge are dealt with in para. 6.11 (community water charges) and para. 12 and Pt. IV (non-domestic water rate).

Paras. 2–4

These deal with the estimation by a date to be prescribed (paras. 2(a) and 3) of total expenditure for a financial year and its apportionment (paras. 2(b) and 4) between the three sources of revenue.

As regards the considerations relevant to the estimate of expenditure, these will be seen to correspond closely to the terms of s.9(2) and (3). The other means of meeting expenditure (para. 3(b)) would include balances brought forward from the previous year.

The content of para. 4 is not reflected in the rules on the general expenditure of authorities where there is no explicit requirement (or expectation) of any particular balance between community charges and non-domestic rates. If an apportionment is ever challenged in a application for judicial review, it will be interesting to see how the concepts of "undue preference" and "undue discrimination" are treated.

One consequence of the new system of distributing costs between the three forms of charge is that, almost certainly *some* consumers will pay more after April 1, 1989, than they have been used to. For the particular problems of Orkney, see *Hansard*, H.L. Vol. 487, cols. 74 and 468.

Once the proportion of total expenditure to be met from direct charges under s.49 is fixed, the rate or rates of metered charges are to be determined under this paragraph. Calculations under s.49 have to be by reference to the amount of water consumed but may incorporate a fixed minimum charge. *N.B.* the amendments to s.49 made by paras. 41–42 of this Schedule.

Paras. 6–11

These deal with the new community water charges, liability to pay, and their determination.

The names of the three charges in para. 6 correspond with the names of the three community charges in s.7 and, under para. 7, liability to pay is directly consequent upon liability to pay the personal, standard or collective community charge. The only modification is made by the conditions imposed by para. 8 as to the supply of water. There has to be a supply to the relevant premises of water for "domestic purposes" which, under s.7 of the 1980 Act, include water for "drinking, washing, cooking central heating and sanitary purposes". Under para. 8(b) that supply must not be wholly by meter.

As for determination of the level of community water charges, precisely the same principles applied by s.9(1) and (2) to community charges are incorporated by paras. 9 and 10. For good measure, the entire remaining apparatus of liability to and the levying and collection of community charges in Pt. II and Sched. 2 of the Act is incorporated (subject to adaptation by prescription) by para. 11. In terms of s.56(6) of the Local Government (Scotland) Act 1973 as amended by s.28 of this Act, the determination of the amount of the personal community water charge is to be by the whole council.

Para. 12

The enactment of the new non-domestic water rate referred to in the general note above is achieved by the substitution of a new s.40 of the 1980 Act by para. 29 of the Schedule. Consequential and other amendments are also to be found in Pt. V.

PART II

CHARGES FOR SEWERAGE SERVICES

13. The expenditure incurred by a local authority in carrying out any of their functions under the 1968 Act shall, insofar as not otherwise met, be met out of—

(a) the community charges; and

(b) the non-domestic sewerage rate described in paragraphs 19 to 21 below.

Estimation and apportionment of expenditure

14. In respect of the financial year 1989–90 and each subsequent financial year, each local authority shall, before such date as may be prescribed in relation to each of those years—

(a) subject to paragraph 15 below, estimate the amount of the expenditure mentioned in paragraph 13 above which they will incur in respect of that year; and

(b) subject to paragraphs 16 and 17 below, determine what proportion of that expenditure is to be met out of—

   (i) the community charges, and

   (ii) the said non-domestic sewerage rate,

   respectively.

15. In estimating the expenditure mentioned in paragraph 13 above which they will incur in respect of any financial year, a local authority shall take into account—

(a) such additional sum as is in their opinion required—

   (i) to cover expenses previously incurred,

   (ii) to meet contingencies, and

   (iii) to meet any expenses which may fall to be met before the moneys to be received from the sources mentioned in paragraph 13 above in respect of the next following financial year will become available; and

(b) any means by which any part of that expenditure may otherwise be met or provided for.

16. The proportion of the expenditure mentioned in paragraph 13 above which is to be met out of the community charges shall be such proportion as the local authority consider to be reasonably attributable to the provision by them of the sewerage services mentioned in section 1(1) of the 1986 Act to premises in their area—

(a) which are the sole or main residence of any person; or

(b) in respect of which a person is liable to pay a standard community charge or a collective community charge; and

no part of that proportion shall be met out of any other charge or rate leviable by the local authority.

17. Subject to paragraph 16 above, a local authority may apportion their estimated expenditure mentioned in paragraph 13 above on whatever basis they consider appropriate, but they shall ensure that the apportionment is not such as to show undue preference to, or discriminate unduly against, any class or classes of person liable to pay—

(a) the community charges; or

(b) the said non-domestic sewerage rate,

respectively.

18. Where a local authority have determined in respect of any financial year what proportion of their estimated expenditure under the 1968 Act falls to be met out of the community charges, that amount shall form part of the total estimated expenses in respect of that year which are mentioned in section 9(2) of this Act.

Non-domestic sewerage rate

19. Subject to paragraph 22 below, each local authority shall, in respect of the financial year 1989–90 and each subsequent financial year, determine a non-domestic sewerage rate, which shall be levied in respect of lands and heritages whose drains or private sewers are connected with public sewers or public sewage treatment works and which are—

(a) subjects (other than part residential subjects) in respect of which there is an entry in the valuation roll, according to the rateable value of those subjects; or

(b) part residential subjects, according to that part of their rateable value which is shown in the apportionment note as relating to the non-residential use of those subjects.

20. The person who is liable to pay the non-domestic sewerage rate in respect of any premises shall be the person who is liable to pay the non-domestic rate in respect of those premises.

21. Each local authority shall, in respect of the financial year 1989–90 and of each subsequent financial year, determine, before such date as may be prescribed in relation to each of those years, such amount of the non-domestic sewerage rate as will provide sufficient moneys to meet the proportion of their estimated expenditure under the 1968 Act for that year which they have determined under paragraph 14 above is to be met out of that rate.

22. The provisions of

(a) Part XI of the 1947 Act;

  (b) Part VII of the 1973 Act; and

  (c) sections 7 to 10 of the 1975 Act,

(all of which relate to rating) as amended by the provisions of this Act, shall apply, subject to such adaptations and modifications as may be prescribed, to the levying, collection and recovery of the non-domestic sewerage rate.

COMMENCEMENT

See note on Pt. I above.

GENERAL NOTE

Para. 13

The Sewerage (Scotland) Act 1968 as amended defines the functions of the regional and islands councils. As described in the general note, expenditure is to be met from the community charges (s.7) and the new non-domestic sewerage rate.

Note that in Sched. 6 is the repeal of s.18(3) of the 1968 Act (which provides for expenditure to be met from the regional or general (islands) rate.

Paras. 14–17

With necessary modifications, these paragraphs replicate for sewerage services paras. 2–4 on water services.

Paras. 14(a) and 15 correspond to paras. 2(a) and 3 on estimating total expenditure. Paras. 14(b), 16 and 17 deal with apportionment (*cf.* paras. 2(b) and 4). The principles of apportionment are the same (including no undue preference or discrimination) but, in addition, para. 16 requires the authority to consider how much of the total cost of its sewerage services are reasonably attributable to the provision of services to those (in sub-paras. (a) and (b)) who are liable to pay community charges.

Para. 18

To complete the interrelationship between the cost of sewerage services and community charges, this paragraph ensures that the amount apportioned to be met out of community charges is fed into the "total estimated expenses" in s.9(2).

Paras. 19–22

Whereas the creation of the new non-domestic water rate can be achieved by the substitution of a new s.40 in the 1980 Act (formerly dealing with domestic water rates), the non-domestic sewerage rate has to be created afresh. Heavy reliance is, however, placed upon the machinery (contained particularly in the 1947, 1973 and 1975 Acts) for the (from April 1, 1989) non-domestic rate.

Thus para. 19 ensures that the new non-domestic rate is levied according to their rateable value on lands and heritages in the valuation roll which have a connection with "public sewers" or "public sewerage treatment works" (see s.59(1) of the 1968 Act and the note on s.26(1) of this Act). Although, by para. 22, s.7, of the Local Government (Scotland) Act 1975 which defines "rateable value" for the purpose of the levy of rates is to apply, with modifications, to non-domestic sewerage rates, it is perhaps curious that "rateable value" is not, in this paragraph, defined by reference to the value "as appearing in the roll".

Part residential subjects (see s.26(1) and Sched. 1) have to be rated according to the appropriate (*i.e.* non-residential) apportioned value. *Cf.* the ambiguity now built into s.7 of the 1975 Act by para. 32 of Sched. 1.

Para. 20 incorporates personal liability to pay by reference to the non-domestic rate—although, in this context, the term "premises"(unknown to the non-domestic rate?) may be misplaced (*cf.* the new s.40(3) of the 1980 Act).

Para. 21 performs the same function for the non-domestic sewerage rate is achieved for the different water charges by paras. 5, 10 and 29 (s.40(4) of the 1980 Act).

Para. 22 is messy in that the modifications of the three Acts have to be separately prescribed.

PART III

MISCELLANEOUS PROVISIONS

Accounts

23. Without prejudice to section 96(1) of the 1973 Act (which relates to the keeping of accounts by local authorities), each local authority shall prepare and maintain separate accounts in respect of its functions under the 1968 and 1980 Acts respectively.

24. The provisions of sections 96(2) to (4) (which impose requirements as to the accounts mentioned in section 96(1)) and 105(1) (which empowers the Secretary of State to make regulations as to the said accounts) of the 1973 Act shall apply in relation to the accounts mentioned in paragraph 23 above as they apply to the accounts mentioned in the said section 96(1).

Tariff of charges

25. Each local authority shall, in respect of the financial year 1989–90 and each subsequent financial year, and before such date as may be prescribed in relation to each of those years, prepare a statement, to be known as a tariff of charges, indicating—
    (a) the basis upon which they have apportioned their estimated expenditure under paragraph 2 above as between—
        (i) the direct charges,
        (ii) the community water charges, and
        (iii) the non-domestic water rate;
    (b) the amount determined by them in respect of that year as—
        (i) the rate or rates of the direct charges under paragraph 5 above,
        (ii) the personal community water charge under paragraph 9 above, and
        (iii) the non-domestic water rate under section 40 of the 1980 Act (as substituted by paragraph 29 below);
    (c) the basis upon which they have apportioned their estimated expenditure for that year under paragraph 14 above as between—
        (i) the community charges, and
        (ii) the non-domestic sewerage rate; and
    (d) the amount determined by them for that year as the non-domestic sewerage rate.

26. Each local authority shall make their tariff of charges available for public inspection at all reasonable hours at such places within their area as they may determine, and shall send a copy of the tariff to the Secretary of State.

COMMENCEMENT
    Para. 25 and 26 came into force on September 14, 1987, subject to the same restrictions as Pts. I and II of the Schedule. Paras. 23 and 24 come into force on April 1, 1989.

Paras. 23, 24
    These paragraphs (in force from April 1, 1989) require all regional and islands councils to keep separate accounts for their sewerage and water functions—subject to regulations to be made by the Secretary of State.

Paras. 25 and 26
    The essence of these paragraphs is a duty upon all relevant local authorities to prepare each year a statement (the "tariff of charges") which indicates all the expenditure and apportionments of expenditure under the relevant paragraphs of Pts. I and II of the Schedule and, under paragraph 26, make them available for public inspection and send a copy to the Secretary of State. The word "basis" reflects its use in paras. 4 and 17 but its meaning is not defined.

PART IV

AMENDMENTS TO THE WATER (SCOTLAND) ACT 1980 (c.45)

27. In section 9(6) (which relates to the supply of water for non-domestic purposes), for the word "rates" substitute "non-domestic rates".

28. In section 9A (which relates to the exemption from charges of water for fire fighting), for the words "domestic water rate" substitute "the non-domestic water rate or the community water charges".

29. For section 40 (which provides for liability to the domestic water rate) substitute—

"**Non-domestic water rate**

40.—(1) Subject to the provisions of this Part of this Act, each council of a region or an islands area shall, in respect of the financial year 1989–90 and each subsequent financial year, determine a non-domestic water rate, which shall be levied in respect of those lands and heritages described in subsection (2) below—

(a) where the subjects (other than part residential subjects) in respect of which there is an entry in the valuation roll, according to their net annual value; or

(b) which are part residential subjects, according to that part of their net annual value which is shown in the apportionment note as relating to the non-residential use of those subjects.

(2) The lands and heritages mentioned in subsection (1) above are lands and heritages—

(a) in respect of which the water authority is supplying water, whether for domestic or for non-domestic purposes; and

(b) which are not being—

(i) wholly supplied with water by meter, or

(ii) occupied by a water authority for the purposes of a water undertaking or by a water development board.

(3) The person who is liable to pay the non-domestic water rate in respect of any lands and heritages shall be the person who is liable to pay non-domestic rates in respect of those lands and heritages.

(4) Each council of a region or islands area shall, in respect of the financial year 1989–90 and each subsequent financial year, determine, before such date as may be prescribed in relation to each of those years, such amount of the non-domestic water rate as will provide sufficient moneys to meet the proportion of their estimated expenditure for that year which they have determined under paragraph 2 of Schedule 5 to the Abolition of Domestic Rates Etc. (Scotland) Act 1987 is to be met out of that rate.

(5) The non-domestic water rate shall not be leviable in respect of any premises, being lands and heritages situated within the region or area of a council or a region or islands area, unless a supply of water provided by a water authority is used for any purposes for or in connection with which the premises are used or by or for persons employed or otherwise engaged on or about the premises in connection with such purpose.

(6) Where premises are for the first time provided with a supply of water otherwise than on the first day of a financial year, the person who is liable to pay the non-domestic water rate shall be liable to pay in respect of that year such part only of that rate which would be leviable if a supply had been provided throughout that year as is proportionate to the part of that year which had not elapsed when the supply was provided.

(7) Notwithstanding the foregoing provisions of this section, the non-domestic water rate shall not be leviable in respect of—

(a) the lands and heritages specified in paragraphs 2(1)(c), 3, 4 and 5 (rail, gas, electricity and postal undertakings) of Schedule 1 to the Local Government (Scotland) Act 1975; and

(b) any such lands and heritages specified in paragraph 8 (dock and harbour undertakings) of Schedule 1 to the said Act of 1975 as have their rateable values determined under any order made under sections 6 and 35(3) of that Act."

30. In section 41 (which relates to the levying of domestic water rates on business and commercial premises)—

(a) in subsection (1)—

(i) for "domestic water rate" substitute "non-domestic water rate"; and

(ii) after the words "net annual value" insert "or, in respect of part residential subjects, one half of the part which is shown in the apportionment note as relating to the non-residential use of those subjects".

(b) in subsection (2), at the beginning insert "Subject to subsection (2A) below,"; and

(c) at the end of subsection (2) insert—

"(2A) Where the Secretary of State considers that the amount of the net annual value determined by a water authority under subsection (2) above is too high, he may determine an amount of net annual value in place of that determined by the authority, and subsection (2) shall thereafter have effect accordingly.".

31. For sections 42 and 43 substitute—

"Levy of non-domestic water rate on certain subjects

42. Where the non-domestic water rate is leviable in respect of premises being lands and heritages occupied as waterworks or sewage works, or as a mine or a quarry, or as a public park or recreation ground, it shall be levied according to one quarter of the net annual value or, in respect of part residential subjects, one quarter of the part which is shown in the apportionment note as relating to the non-residential use of those subjects.

Levy of non-domestic water rate on shootings and fishings

43. Where the non-domestic water rate is leviable in respect of premises being lands and heritages occupied as shootings or as fishings it shall be levied according to one eighth of the net annual value thereof.".

32. In section 46(2), for the words "or otherwise", where they first appear, substitute ", community water charge or the non-domestic water rate".

33. In section 47(1) (which relates to the domestic water rate in certain cases), for the words "domestic water rate" substitute "non-domestic water rate".

34. In section 47(2) (which relates to domestic water rate in certain cases)—

(a) for the words "domestic water rate" where they occur for the third time substitute "non-domestic water rate";

(b) after the words "local enactment" where they occur for the fourth time insert "in relation to the domestic water rate"; and

(c) after the words "so specified" where they occur for the second time insert "in relation to the domestic water rate".

35. For the proviso to the said section 47(2) substitute—

"Provided that if in any financial year during the said period the non-domestic water rate levied generally within the region or islands area is lower than the non-domestic water rate falling to be levied for that financial year in accordance with the foregoing provisions of this subsection, the non-domestic water rate to be levied in such area as aforesaid shall not exceed the amount of that rate levied generally within the region or islands area.".

36. In section 47(3), for the words "no domestic water rate shall be payable" substitute "non-domestic water rate shall not be payable".

37. In section 47(7), for the words "domestic water rate" substitute "non-domestic water rate".

38. In section 48(1) (which relates to the levying of, and exemption from, rates), for the words "public water rate and the domestic water rate" substitute "non-domestic water rate".

39. In section 48(2), for the words "domestic water rate" substitute "non-domestic water rate".

40. In section 48(3), after the word "rates" insert "or charges".

41. In section 49 (which relates to payment for water supplied by meter), after subsection (1) insert—

"(1A) Charges payable under this section shall be payable by the occupier of the premises in respect of which they are due.".

42. In section 49(2), for the words "rates levied by the regional or islands council" substitute "non-domestic rates".

43. In section 54(1) (which provides for the register of the meter to be evidence), for the words "prima facie" substitute "sufficient".

44. In section 54(3)(b), for the words "rates levied by the regional or islands council" substitute "non-domestic rates".

45. In section 55(4) (which relates to charges for water supplied by meter), for the words "all ratepayers within the limits of supply of the authority" substitute "the public".

46. In section 58(3) (which relates to the termination of the right to the supply of water on special terms), for the words "the amount of the rate or charge or of the rate and charge" substitute "the amount of any charge under section 49, community water charge or non-domestic water rate".

47. For subsections (1) to (4) of section 61 (which relates to the calculation of the amount to be requisitioned by water authorities) substitute—

"(1) Subject to subsection (2) below, the amount of the requisition made by a requisitioning authority on any contributing authority shall be calculated by—

(a) estimating the cost to the requisitioning authority of supplying the volume of water which is to be supplied to the contributing authority in the financial year; and

(b) deducting therefrom the estimated income which will be received by the requisitioning authority in that financial year by way of charges or other sources (not being community water charges or the non-domestic water rate) from the parts of the contributing authority's area supplied.

(2) In respect of any financial year, the sum of the requisition made on any contributing authority and the estimated income mentioned in subsection (1)(b) above shall bear the same relationship to the expenditure incurred by the requisitioning authority in the exercise of all its water supply functions as the estimated volume of water to be supplied to that contributing authority bears to the total volume of water to be supplied by the requisitioning authority, whether for consumption inside its own area or elsewhere.

(3) For the purposes of this section "requisitioning authority" means a water authority such as is mentioned in section 60(1) above.".

48. In section 61(5) for the words "subsections (2) and (3)" substitute "subsections (1) and 2)".

49. In section 109(1) (which defines terms used in the Act)—

(a) after the definition of "agricultural lands and heritages" insert—
" "apportionment note" has the meaning assigned to it in paragraph 2 of Schedule 1 to the Abolition of Domestic Rates Etc. (Scotland) Act 1987;";

(b) after the definition of "communication pipe" insert—
" "community water charges" shall be construed in accordance with the provisions of paragraph 6 of Schedule 5 to the Abolition of Domestic Rates Etc. (Scotland) Act 1987;"; and

(c) after the definition of "owner" insert—
" "part residential subjects" has the meaning assigned to it in section 26 (interpretation) of the Abolition of Domestic Rates Etc. (Scotland) Act 1987;".

Commencement

Paras. 28, 29, 30(a), 31 to 37, 39 to 41, and 47 to 49 came into force on September 14, 1987, subject to the same restrictions as Pts. I and II of the Schedule. Remaining paragraphs (*i.e.* 27, 30(b) and (c), 38 and 42 to 46) will come into force on April 1, 1989.

Para. 27

See also Sched. 6. Amendment consequential upon change to levy of non-domestic rates only.

Para. 28

S.9A was inserted by s.59 of the Local Government and Planning (Scotland) Act 1982. The "fire fighting" exemption from charge includes both new charges.

Para. 29

This is the most significant single paragraph and, in providing a new s.40 for the 1980 Act establishes the rules for the new non-domestic water rate. The terms of the section have to be read with Pt. I of this Schedule since they are consequential upon the process of estimation and apportionment established in that Part. They also closely resemble the provisions in paras. 19 to 21 concerning the non-domestic sewerage rate. Equally, the section retains, with only minor adaptations, the same limitations upon liability to non-domestic water rates (especially subss. (5), (6) and (7)).

Notice that in subs. (2), there has now to be a reference to the supply of water both for domestic (s.7) and non-domestic (s.9) purposes because there will, from April 1, 1989, be many lands and heritages not classed as "domestic subjects" but to which, in terms of the 1980 Act, water will be supplied for "domestic purposes".

Para. 30

This paragraph contains amendments to s.41 of the 1980 Act. Sub-para. (a) is directly consequential upon the change of non-domestic water rates and the new part residential subjects and para. (b) is consequential upon sub-para. (c). Sub-para. (c) itself permits the Secretary of State to redetermine the threshold amount of the net annual value fixed by the authority to give the occupier the option of water supply by meter.

Para. 31

These are purely technical amendments consequential upon the move to the non-domestic water rate and, in the case of s.42, part residential subjects.

Paras. 32–40
These are all minor consequential amendments to the sections referred to.

Para. 41
This is an amendment designed to remove an ambiguity in s.49 as to who is liable to pay the charges for water supplied by meter.

Para. 42
An amendment consequential upon the change to non-domestic rates.

Para. 43
This small change is designed to substitute the normal phrase in Scots Law "sufficient evidence" for the English equivalent "prima facie evidence" which is currently in s.54. Questions arising are, by subs. (2), determined by the sheriff.

Para. 44
Consequential upon non-domestic rates and their recovery.

Para. 45
This substitutes, for the purposes of access to the register of agreements for the supply of metered water, "the public" for "all ratepayers" which, upon the abolition of rates, becomes a limited category.

Para. 46
Consequential upon the new system of water charges.

Para. 47
This paragraph inserts into s.61 of the 1980 Act an entirely new basis on which a "requisitioning authority" (a water authority which supplies water to another) charges a "contributing authority" (a water authority to which water is supplied).
New subs. (1) requires the amount to be requisitioned to be the difference between the estimated cost of and the estimated income from the water to be supplied in a financial year. Subs. (2) is designed to ensure that the amount of the requisition made is in proportion to the cost of the authority's operations overall. It may be expressed as:

$$\frac{\text{Amount of requisition plus estimated income as in subs. 1(b)}}{\substack{\text{Estimated volume of water supplied to} \\ \text{contributing authority}}} = \frac{\text{Total expenditure on all water supplied}}{\text{Total volume of water supplied}}$$

N.B. Some extraneous singular possessives (the "its") have been allowed into subs. (2).

Para. 48
Consequential upon para. 47.

Para. 49
This gives to the phrases in sub-paras. (a), (b) and (c) the same meanings as they have in this Act. Notice the deletion in Sched. 6 of the definitions of "domestic water rate" and "public water rate".
See too the definitions supplied by s.26(2) of this Act for, *inter alia*, "non-domestic water rate" (by reference to the new s.40 of the 1980 Act substituted by para. 29 of this Schedule).

SCHEDULE 6

REPEALS

Chapter	Short title	Extent of repeal
1926 c.47.	Rating (Scotland) Act 1926.	Section 14(2) and (3).
1947 c.43.	Local Government (Scotland) Act 1947.	In section 379(1), the definitions of "gross annual valuation" and "rate".
1956 c.60. (4 and 5 Eliz. 2)	Valuation and Rating (Scotland) Act 1956.	In section 6(1), the words "the gross annual value,". Section 6(2) to (7). In section 6(8), the words from ", other than" to "this section,". In section 6(9), the words "under subsection (6) or" and ", as the case may be". Section 6(11). In section 7(1), the words "and dwelling houses occupied in connection therewith". Section 7(4) to (8). In section 7A(1), the words "and dwelling houses occupied in connection therewith". Section 7A(4). In section 43(1), the definition of "gross annual valuation" and, in the definition of "rate", the words ", charge and assessment". Schedule 1.
1958 c.64.	Local Government and Miscellaneous Financial Provisions (Scotland) Act 1958.	In section 7(3)(b) and (4), the word "dwelling-houses".
1963 c.12.	Local Government (Financial Provisions) (Scotland) Act 1963.	Sections 7(1) and (2), and 9. In section 10(1) the words "subsection (6) or" and the words ", as the case may be,". In section 15(1A)(b), the words "section 6(2) or, as the case may be," and the words "gross and net annual". Section 26(1). In section 26(2), the definition of "rate".
1966 c.51.	Local Government (Scotland) Act 1966.	Sections 2 to 7. Sections 12 and 14. In section 24(4), in the definition of "relevant lands and heritages", the words "a house,". Section 26. Section 27. In section 46(1), the definitions of "product of a rate of one new penny in the pound" and "standard penny rate product". Schedule 1.
1968 c.47	Sewerage (Scotland) Act 1968.	Section 18(3). In section 59(1), the definitions of "general rate" and "regional rate".
1970 c.4.	Valuation for Rating (Scotland) Act 1970.	In section 1(1), the words ", as ascertained under section 6(6) of the Act of 1956,".

Chapter	Short title	Extent of repeal
1973 c.65.	Local Government (Scotland) Act 1973.	Sections 107 to 108C. In section 111(1), in paragraph (b), the words ", or section 5(4) and (5) of the Local Government (Scotland) Act 1966," and paragraph (f). Sections 119 and 120.
1975 c.30.	Local Government (Scotland) Act 1975.	In section 1, the proviso to subsection (3)(a), subsections (6A) to (6E) and, in subsection (7), the definitions of "specified lands and heritages" and "unspecified lands and heritages". In section 2, in subsection (1)(e), the words "under section 6(7) or 7(7) of the Valuation and Rating (Scotland) Act 1956,", and, in subsection (2)(c), subparagraph (i) and the words "(ii) in any other case". In section 16, the words ", subject to section 18 of the Local Government (Miscellaneous Provisions) (Scotland) Act 1981,". In section 37(1), in the definition of "material change of circumstances", the words "gross or".
1976 c.15.	Rating (Caravan Sites) Act 1976.	Section 3(6), (7) and (10). In paragraph (a) of section 3A(3), the words from "for the purposes" to the end of the paragraph. In section 4(1)(e), the words "(as reduced under section 7(1) of the Local Government (Scotland) Act 1966)".
1976 c.64.	Valuation and Rating (Exempted Classes) (Scotland) Act 1976.	In section 1(4), the words "In this subsection "rate" includes domestic water rates.".
1978 c.40.	Rating (Disabled Persons) Act 1978.	Section 7. In section 8(1), the definition of "rates".
1980 c.45.	Water (Scotland) Act 1980.	In section 9(6), the words "in respect of the premises supplied". Section 39. Section 41(3). In section 41(4), the words "premises occupied wholly as a dwelling house or". Section 44. Section 45. Section 53(3). Section 57. In section 60(1), the words "the aggregate amount by reference to which" and the words "is to be determined". Section 61(6). In section 109(1), the definitions of "domestic water rate" amd "public water rate".
1981 c.23.	Local Government (Miscellaneous Provisions) (Scotland) Act 1981.	Sections 2 to 4. Section 9. Part II. In Schedule 3, paragraphs 1, 11, 25, 27 and 35 and, in paragraph 36, the words "(the schedule mentioned in paragraph 35 above)".
1982 c.43.	Local Government and Planning (Scotland) Act 1982.	Sections 1 to 3. In Schedule 3, paragraphs 5 to 7, 18 to 20 and 43.

Chapter	Short title	Extent of repeal
984 c.31.	Rating and Valuation (Amendment) (Scotland) Act 1984.	Sections 1 to 4. Schedule 1.
984 c.54.	Roads (Scotland) Act 1984.	In section 1(7)(b), the words "either—(i)", the word "or" where it second appears, and sub-paragraph (ii).
987 c.6.	Local Government Finance Act 1987.	Sections 13 and 14.

GENERAL NOTE

The repeals in this Schedule are authorised by s.34 of the Act.

The statutes in the list may be usefully regrouped in accordance with the pattern of implementation of the Act prescribed by the commencement order (S.I. 1987 No. 1489).

The first group were brought into force on September 14, 1987, but "only for the purposes of and in relation to—(a) rates which are, or which but for the Act would be, leviable, and b) other charges which may, or which but for the Act might, be imposed or payable, under any enactment contained in the Act or any other Act in respect of the financial year 1989–90 and each subsequent financial year":

Chapter	Short title	Extent of repeal
1947 c.43.	Local Government (Scotland) Act 1947.	In section 379(1), the definition of "rate".
1956 c.60 (4 and 5 Eliz. 2).	Valuation and Rating (Scotland) Act 1956.	In section 43(1), in the definition of "rate", the words ", charge and assessment".
1963 c.12.	Local Government (Financial Provisions) (Scotland) Act 1963.	In section 26(2), the definition of "rate".
1968 c.47.	Sewerage (Scotland) Act 1968.	Section 18(3).
1973 c.65.	Local Government (Scotland) Act 1973.	Sections 107 and 108.
1976 c.15.	Rating (Caravan Sites) Act 1976.	Section 3(10).
1976 c.64.	Valuation and Rating (Exempted Classes) (Scotland) Act 1976.	In section 1(4), the words "In this subsection "rate" includes domestic water rates.".
1978 c.40.	Rating (Disabled Persons) Act 1978.	In section 8(1), the definition of "rates".
1980 c.45.	Water (Scotland) Act 1980.	Section 39. Section 41(3). In section 41(4), the words "premises occupied wholly as a dwelling house or". Section 44. Section 45. In section 60(1), the words "the aggregate amount by reference to which" and the words "is to be determined". Section 61(6).
1981 c.23.	Local Government (Miscellaneous Provisions) (Scotland) Act 1981.	In Schedule 3, paragraph 25.
1982 c.43.	Local Government and Planning (Scotland) Act 1982.	In Schedule 3, paragraph 18.
1984 c.31.	Rating and Valuation (Amendment) (Scotland) Act 1984.	Section 4.

Chapter	Short title	Extent of repeal
colspan info		

Then, on April 1, 1989, all the above repeals come fully into effect without restriction as to purpose. *In addition*, the following are repealed on that date:

Chapter	Short title	Extent of repeal
1926 c.47.	Rating (Scotland) Act 1926.	Section 14(2) and (3).
1947 c.43.	Local Government (Scotland) Act 1947.	In section 379(1), the definition of "gross annual valuation".
1956 c.60 (4 and 5 Eliz. 2).	Valuation and Rating (Scotland) Act 1956.	In section 6(1), the words "the gross annual value,". Sections 6(2) to (7). In section 6(8), the words from ", other than" to "this section,". In section 6(9), the words "under subsection (6) or" and ", as the case may be". Section 6(11). In section 7(1), the words "and dwelling houses occupied in connection therewith". Section 7(4) to (8). In section 7A(1), the words "and dwelling houses occupied in connection therewith". Section 7A(4). In section 43(1), the definition of "gross annual valuation". Schedule 1.
1958 c.64.	Local Government and Miscellaneous Financial Provisions (Scotland) Act 1958.	In section 7(3)(b) and (4), the word "dwelling-houses".
1963 c.12.	Local Government (Financial Provisions) (Scotland) Act 1963.	In section 10(1) the words "subsection (6) or" and the words ", as the case may be,". In section 15(1A)(b), the words "section 6(2) or, as the case may be," and the words "gross and net annual". Section 26(1).
1966 c.51.	Local Government (Scotland) Act 1966.	Sections 5 and 7. In section 24(4), in the definition of "relevant lands and heritages", the words "a house,". Section 26. Section 27.
1968 c.47.	Sewerage (Scotland) Act 1968.	In section 59(1), the definitions of "general rate" and "regional rate".
1970 c.4.	Valuation for Rating (Scotland) Act 1970.	In section 1(1), the words ", as ascertained under section 6(6) of the Act of 1956,".
1973 c.65.	Local Government (Scotland) Act 1973.	Sections 108A to 108C. In section 111(1), in paragraph (b), the words ", or section 5(4) and (5) of the Local Government (Scotland) Act 1966," and paragraph (f). Section 119.
1975 c.30.	Local Government (Scotland) Act 1975.	In section 1, the proviso to subsection (3)(a), subsections (6A) to (6E) and, in subsection (7), the definitions of "specified lands and heritages" and "unspecified lands and heritages". In section 2, in subsection (1)(e), the words "under section 6(7) or 7(7) of the Valuation and Rating (Scotland) Act 1956,", and, in subsection (2)(c), subparagraph (i) and the words "(ii) in any other case".

Chapter	Short title	Extent of repeal
1976 c.15.	Rating (Caravan Sites) Act 1976.	In section 16, the words ", subject to section 18 of the Local Government (Miscellaneous Provisions) (Scotland) Act 1981,". In section 37(1), in the definition of "material change of circumstances", the words "gross or". Section 3(6) and (7). In paragraph (a) of section 3A(3), the words from "for the purposes" to the end of the paragraph. In section 4(1)(e), the words "(as reduced under section 7(1) of the Local Government (Scotland) Act 1966)".
1978 c.40.	Rating (Disabled Persons) Act 1978.	Section 7.
1980 c.45.	Water (Scotland) Act 1980.	In section 9(6), the words "in respect of the premises supplied". Section 53(3). Section 57. In section 109(1), the definitions of "domestic water rate" and "public water rate".
1981 c.23.	Local Government (Miscellaneous Provisions) (Scotland) Act 1981.	Sections 2 to 4. Section 9. Sections 14 and 15. Section 18 and 19. In Schedule 3, paragraphs 1, 11, 27 and 35 and, in paragraph 36, the words "(the Schedule mentioned in paragraph 35 above)."
1982 c.43.	Local Government and Planning (Scotland) Act 1982.	Sections 1 and 2. In Schedule 3, paragraphs 19, 20 and 43.
1984 c.31.	Rating and Valuation (Amendment) (Scotland) Act 1984.	Section 1. Sections 2 and 3. Schedule 1.
1984 c.54.	Roads (Scotland) Act 1984.	In section 1(7)(b), the words "either—(i)", the word "or" where it second appears, and sub-paragraph (ii).
1987 c.6.	Local Government Finance Act 1987.	Sections 13 and 14.

Finally, on April 1, 1994, the third group of enactments—concerned with the expiring system of rate support grants but requiring to be kept intact until final calculations of entitlement are made—are repealed:

Chapter	Short title	Extent of repeal
1963 c.12.	Local Government (Financial Provisions) (Scotland) Act 1963.	Sections 7(1) and (2), and 9.
1966 c.51.	Local Government (Scotland) Act 1966.	Section 2 to 4. Section 6. Sections 12 and 14. In section 46(1), the definitions of "product of a rate of one new penny in the pound" and "standard penny rate product". Schedule 1.
1973 c.65.	Local Government (Scotland) Act 1973.	Section 120.

Chapter	Short title	Extent of repeal
1981 c.23.	Local Government (Miscellaneous Provisions) (Scotland) Act 1981.	Section 16, 17 and 20.
1982 c.43.	Local Government and Planning (Scotland) Act 1982.	Section 3. In Schedule 3, paragraphs 5 to 7.
1984 c.31.	Rating and Valuation (Amendment) (Scotland) Act 1984.	Section 1(1).

IRISH SAILORS AND SOLDIERS LAND TRUST ACT 1987

(1987 c. 48)

An Act to provide for the distribution of the surplus funds of the Irish Sailors and Soldiers Land Trust; and to make provision for the winding up and dissolution of the Trust.   [15th May 1987]

PARLIAMENTARY DEBATES
   Hansard: H.L. Vol. 486, cols. 1028, 1422; Vol. 487, cols. 11, 423, 815; H.C. Vol. 116, col. 439.

Surplus funds, winding up and dissolution of Irish Sailors and Soldiers Land Trust

1.—(1) It shall be the duty of the Irish Sailors and Soldiers Land Trust—

(a) to pay over in accordance with subsection (2) below any money of the Trust which it at any time considers to be in excess of its requirements for the discharge of its functions; and

(b) when directed to do so by the Secretary of State, to wind up its affairs and to take such steps as are specified in the direction for disposing of its property and rights and discharging or transferring its liabilities.

(2) Any money to be paid over under subsection (1)(a) above shall be divided between the United Kingdom and the Republic of Ireland in the prescribed proportions; and—

(a) two-fifths of the United Kingdom share shall be paid to the Distributory Agency appointed under section 2 below and the remainder to the Secretary of State; and

(b) the Republic of Ireland share shall be paid to the Government of the Republic.

(3) In subsection (2) above "the prescribed proportions" means 68 per cent. as respects the United Kingdom and 32 per cent. as respects the Republic of Ireland or such other proportions as the Secretary of State may direct; and he shall consult the Government of the Republic before giving any direction under this subsection or under subsection (1)(b) above.

(4) If after a direction has been given under subsection (1)(b) above it appears to the Secretary of State that the direction has been fully complied with he may by statutory instrument make an order dissolving the Trust.

(5) Any sums received by the Secretary of State by virtue of this section shall be paid into the Consolidated Fund of the United Kingdom and the Consolidated Fund of Northern Ireland in such proportions as he may with the consent of the Treasury determine.

The Distributory Agency

2.—(1) The Distributory Agency for the purposes of this Act shall be such person or persons as are for the time being appointed under this section by the Secretary of State.

(2) It shall be the duty of the Agency to administer and (so far as not required for the expenses of administration) to apply, or arrange for the application of, the money received by it under this Act for the benefit of persons resident in Northern Ireland or the Republic of Ireland who are former members of Her Majesty's armed forces, their widows or widowers or their children.

(3) The Agency shall comply with such directions relating to the discharge of its functions under this Act as may from time to time be given to it by the Secretary of State.

(4) Without prejudice to the generality of subsection (3) above, directions under that subsection may relate to the investment of money for the time being held by the Agency under this Act but the Secretary of State shall not give directions relating to that matter except with the consent of the Treasury.

(5) In subsection (2) above "children" includes step-children, adopted children and illegitimate children.

Short title, commencement, repeals and extent

3.—(1) This Act may be cited as the Irish Sailors and Soldiers Land Trust Act 1987.

(2) This Act shall come into force on such day as the Secretary of State may appoint by an order made by statutory instrument.

(3) On the coming into force of an order under section 1(4) above the enactments mentioned in the Schedule to this Act shall be repealed to the extent specified in the third column of that Schedule.

(4) This Act extends to Northern Ireland.

Section 3(3)   SCHEDULE

REPEALS

Chapter	Short title	Extent of repeal
9 & 10 Geo.5 c.82.	The Irish Land (Provision for Sailors and Soldiers) Act 1919.	Section 4.
13 Geo.5 Sess. 2 c.2.	The Irish Free State (Consequential Provisions) Act 1922 (Session 2).	Section 3.
13 & 14 Geo.5 c.19 (N.I.)	The Land Trust (Powers) Act (Northern Ireland) 1923.	The whole Act.
15 & 16 Geo.5 c.3 (N.I.)	The Administrative Provisions Act (Northern Ireland) 1925.	Section 2(1).
1950 c.3 (N.I.)	The Exchequer and Financial Provisions Act (Northern Ireland) 1950.	Section 34.
16 Geo.6 & 1 Eliz.2 c.58.	The Irish Sailors and Soldiers Land Trust Act 1952.	The whole Act.
1967 c.67.	The Irish Sailors and Soldiers Land Trust Act 1967.	The whole Act.

TERRITORIAL SEA ACT 1987

(1987 c. 49)

An Act to provide for the extent of the territorial sea adjacent to the
British Islands.   [15th May 1987]

PARLIAMENTARY DEBATES
  Hansard: H.L. Vol. 483, col. 634; Vol. 484, cols. 381, 1212; Vol. 485, cols. 442, 939; H.C.
Vol. 115, col. 697; Vol. 116, col. 442.

Extension of territorial sea

1.—(1) Subject to the provisions of this Act—
  (a) the breadth of the territorial sea adjacent to the United
      Kingdom shall for all purposes be 12 nautical miles; and
  (b) the baselines from which the breadth of that territorial sea is
      to be measured shall for all purposes be those established by
      Her Majesty by Order in Council.
  (2) Her Majesty may, for the purpose of implementing any international
agreement or otherwise, by Order in Council provide that any part of the
territorial sea adjacent to the United Kingdom shall extend to such line
other than that provided for by subsection (1) above as may be specified
in the Order.
  (3) In any legal proceedings a certificate issued by or under the authority
of the Secretary of State stating the location of any baseline established
under subsection (1) above shall be conclusive of what is stated in the
certificate.
  (4) As from the coming into force of this section the Territorial Waters
Order in Council 1964 and the Territorial Waters (Amendment) Order in
Council 1979 shall have effect for all purposes as if they were Orders in
Council made by virtue of subsection (1)(b) above; and subsection (5)
below shall apply to those Orders as it applies to any other instrument.
  (5) Subject to the provisions of this Act, any enactment or instrument
which (whether passed or made before or after the coming into force of
this section) contains a reference (however worded) to the territorial sea
adjacent to, or to any part of, the United Kingdom shall be construed in
accordance with this section and with any provision made, or having effect
as if made, under this section.
  (6) Without prejudice to the operation of subsection (5) above in
relation to a reference to the baselines from which the breadth of the
territorial sea adjacent to the United Kingdom is measured, nothing in
that subsection shall require any reference in any enactment or instrument
to a specified distance to be construed as a reference to a distance equal
to the breadth of that territorial sea.
  (7) In this section "nautical miles" means international nautical miles of
1,852 metres.

Enactments and instruments not affected

2.—(1) Except in so far as Her Majesty may by Order in Council
otherwise provide, nothing in section 1 above shall affect the operation of
any enactment contained in a local Act passed before the date on which
that section comes into force.
  (2) Nothing in section 1 above, or in any Order in Council under that
section or subsection (1) above, shall affect the operation of so much of
any enactment passed or instrument made before the date on which that
section comes into force as for the time being settles the limits within

which any harbour authority or port health authority has jurisdiction o
is able to exercise any power.

(3) Where any area which is not part of the territorial sea adjacent t
the United Kingdom becomes part of that sea by virtue of section 1 abov
or an Order in Council under that section, subsection (2) of section 1 c
the Continental Shelf Act 1964 (vesting and exercise of rights with respec
to coal) shall continue, on and after the date on which section 1 above o
that Order comes into force, to have effect with respect to coal in tha
area as if the area were not part of the territorial sea.

(4) Nothing in section 1 above, or in any Order in Council under tha
section, shall affect—

   (a) any regulations made under section 6 of the Petroleum (Production
      Act 1934 before the date on which that section or Order come
      into force; or

   (b) any licences granted under the said Act of 1934 before that date o
      granted on or after that date in pursuance of regulations mad
      under that section before that date.

(5) In this section—

   "coal" has the same meaning as in the Coal Industry Nationalisatio
      Act 1946;

   "harbour authority" means a harbour authority within the meanin,
      of the Harbours Act 1964 or the Harbours Act (Northeri
      Ireland) 1970; and

   "port health authority" means a port health authority for th
      purposes of the Public Health (Control of Disease) Act 1984.

Amendments and repeals

3.—(1) The enactments mentioned in Schedule 1 to this Act shall hav
effect with the amendments there specified (being minor amendments an
amendments consequential on the provisions of this Act).

(2) Her Majesty may by Order in Council—

   (a) make, in relation to any enactment passed or instrument mad
      before the date on which section 1 above comes into force, an
      amendment corresponding to any of those made by Schedul
      1 to this Act;

   (b) amend subsection (1) of section 36 of the Wildlife and Coun
      tryside Act 1981 (marine nature reserves) so as to include suc
      other parts of the territorial sea adjacent to Great Britain a
      may be specified in the Order in the waters and parts of th
      sea which, by virtue of paragraph 6 of Schedule 1 to this Act
      may be designated under that section;

   (c) amend paragraph 1 of Article 20 of the Nature Conservatio
      and Amenity Lands (Northern Ireland) Order 1985 (marin
      nature reserves) so as to include such other parts of th
      territorial sea adjacent to Northern Ireland as may be specifie
      in the Order in the waters and parts of the sea which, by virtu
      of paragraph 9 of Schedule 1 to this Act, may be designatec
      under that Article.

(3) Her Majesty may by Order in Council make such modifications o
the effect of any Order in Council under section 1(7) of the Continenta
Shelf Act 1964 (designated areas) as appear to Her to be necessary o
expedient in consequence of any provision made by or under this Act.

(4) The enactments mentioned in Schedule 2 to this Act are hereb
repealed to the extent specified in the third column of that Schedule.

Short title, commencement and extent

4.—(1) This Act may be cited as the Territorial Sea Act 1987.

(2) This Act shall come into force on such day as Her Majesty may b

rder in Council appoint, and different days may be so appointed for
ifferent provisions and for different purposes.

(3) This Act extends to Northern Ireland.

(4) Her Majesty may by Order in Council direct that any of the
rovisions of this Act shall extend, with such exceptions, adaptations and
10difications (if any) as may be specified in the Order, to any of the
hannel Islands or to the Isle of Man.

SCHEDULES

ction 3   SCHEDULE 1

MINOR AND CONSEQUENTIAL AMENDMENTS

The Coast Protection Act 1949

1.—(1) In section 18(3) of the Coast Protection Act 1949 (prohibition of excavation etc.
f materials on or under the seashore) for the words "lying to seaward therefrom" there
1all be substituted the words "of the sea-shore lying to seaward of their area but within
1ree nautical miles of the baselines from which the breadth of the territorial sea adjacent
1 Great Britain is measured,".

(2) In section 49(1) of that Act (interpretation) after the definition of "mortgage" there
1all be inserted the following definition—

"'nautical miles' means international nautical miles of 1,852 metres;".

The Mineral Workings (Offshore Installations) Act 1971

2. For the definition of "foreign sector of the continental shelf" in section 1(4) of the
1ineral Workings (Offshore Installations) Act 1971 there shall be substituted the following
efinition—

"'foreign sector of the continental shelf' means an area within which rights are
        exercisable with respect to the sea bed and subsoil and their natural resources
        by a country or territory outside the United Kingdom;".

The Salmon and Freshwater Fisheries Act 1975

3. In section 6(1) of the Salmon and Freshwater Fisheries Act 1975 (offence of placing
nauthorised fixed engine in inland or tidal waters) after the words "inland or tidal waters"
1ere shall be inserted the words "which are within the area of any water authority".

The Customs and Excise Management Act 1979

4.—(1) In section 1(1) of the Customs and Excise Management Act 1979 (interpretation)
fter the definition of "transit shed" there shall be inserted the following definition—

"'United Kingdom waters' means any waters (including inland waters) within the
        seaward limits of the territorial sea of the United Kingdom;".

(2) In section 35(7) of that Act (report inwards of ships and aircraft) for the words "within
2 nautical miles of the coast of the United Kingdom" there shall be substituted the words
1n or over United Kingdom waters".

(3) In that Act the words "in United Kingdom waters" shall be substituted—

(a) in section 64(4) (clearance outwards of ships and aircraft) for the words "within
        the limits of a port or within 3 nautical miles of the coast of the United
        Kingdom";

(b) in section 88 (forfeiture of ship, aircraft or vehicle constructed etc. for concealing
        goods) for the words "within the limits of any port or within 3 or, being a British
        ship, 12 nautical miles of the coast of the United Kingdom";

(c) in section 89(1) and (2) (forfeiture of ship jettisoning cargo etc.) for the words
        "within 3 nautical miles of the coast of the United Kingdom";

(d) in section 142(2) (special provision as to forfeiture of larger ships) for the words
        "within 3 nautical miles of the coast of the United Kingdom".

The Alcoholic Liquor Duties Act 1979

5.—(1) In the Table in section 4(3) of the Alcoholic Liquor Duties Act 1979 (expression defined in the Management Act) after the expression "'tons register'" there shall be inserted the expression "'United Kingdom waters'".

(2) In section 26(4) of that Act (importation and exportation of spirits) for the words " in the case of a British ship, within 12 or, in any other case, within 3 nautical miles of th coast of the United Kingdom" there shall be substituted the words "in United Kingdom waters".

The Wildlife and Countryside Act 1981

6. In section 36 of the Wildlife and Countryside Act 1981 (marine nature reserves)—
   (a) in subsection (1) for the words "in or adjacent to Great Britain up to th seaward limits of territorial waters" there shall be substituted the words "whic are landward of the baselines from which the breadth of the territorial se adjacent to Great Britain is measured or are seaward of those baselines up to distance of three nautical miles"; and
   (b) in subsection (7) after the definition of "local authority" there shall be inserte the following definition—
       "'nautical miles' means international nautical miles of 1,852 metres:".

The Oil and Gas (Enterprise) Act 1982

7—(1) For the definition of "cross-boundary field" in section 22(6) of the Oil and Ga (Enterprise) Act 1982 there shall be substituted the following definition—
       "'cross-boundary field' means a field that extends across the boundary between wate falling within paragraph (a) or (b) of subsection (4) above and a foreign secto of the continental shelf;".

(2) For the definition of "foreign sector of the continental shelf" in section 28(1) of tha Act there shall be substituted the following definition—
       "'foreign sector of the continental shelf' means an area within which rights ar exercisable with respect to the sea bed and subsoil and their natural resource by a country or territory outside the United Kingdom;".

The Public Health (Control of Disease) Act 1984

8. In section 6 of the Public Health (Control of Disease) Act 1984 (under which the Por of London is for the purposes of that Act not to extend outside territorial waters) for th words "are for the time being" there shall be substituted the words "immediately before th coming into force of the Territorial Sea Act 1987 were".

The Nature Conservation and Amenity Lands (Northern Ireland) Order 1985

9. In Article 20 of the Nature Conservation and Amenity Lands (Northern Ireland) Orde 1985 (marine nature reserves)—
   (a) in paragraph (1) for the words "in or adjacent to Northern Ireland up to th seaward limits of territorial waters" there shall be substituted the words "whic are landward of the baselines from which the breadth of the territorial se adjacent to Northern Ireland is measured or are seaward of those baselines u to a distance of three nautical miles"; and
   (b) in paragraph (6) before the definition of "relevant body" there shall be inserte the following definition—
       "'nautical miles' means international nautical miles of 1,852 metres;".

SCHEDULE 2

REPEALS

Chapter	Short Title	Extent of repeal
1 & 42 Vict. c.73.	The Territorial Waters Jurisdiction Act 1878.	In section 7, the definition of "the territorial waters of Her Majesty's dominions", including the words from "and for the purpose of any offence" to "the territorial waters of Her Majesty's dominions".
967 c.41.	The Marine, &c., Broadcasting Offences Act 1967.	Section 9(2).
967 c.72.	The Wireless Telegraphy Act 1967.	Section 9(1).
979 c.2.	The Customs and Excise Management Act 1979.	In section 1(1), the definition of "nautical mile".
979 c.4.	The Alcoholic Duties Act 1979.	In section 4(3), the words "nautical mile".

APPROPRIATION (No. 2) ACT 1987

(1987 c. 50)

An Act to apply a sum out of the Consolidated Fund to the service of the year ending on 31st March 1988, and to appropriate the supplies granted in this Session of Parliament.　　　　　　　　[23rd July 1987]

PARLIAMENTARY DEBATES
Hansard, H.C. Vol. 119, cols. 448, 754; H.L. Vol. 488, cols. 1004, 1486.

GRANT OUT OF THE CONSOLIDATED FUND

Issue out of the Consolidated Fund for the year ending 31st March 1988

1. The Treasury may issue out of the Consolidated Fund of the United Kingdom and apply towards making good the supply granted to Her Majesty for the service of the year ending on 31st March 1988 the sum of £1,064,266,000.

APPROPRIATION OF GRANTS

Appropriation of sums voted for supply services

2. The sum granted by this Act out of the said Consolidated Fund towards making good the supply granted to Her Majesty amounting, as appears by Schedule (A) annexed to this Act, to the sum of £1,064,266,000 is appropriated for the services and purposes in Schedule (B) annexed hereto.

The abstract of schedules and schedules annexed hereto, with the notes (if any) to such schedules, shall be deemed to be part of this Act in the same manner as if they had been contained in the body thereof.

In addition to the said sums granted out of the Consolidated Fund, there may be applied out of any money directed, under section 2 of the Public Accounts and Charges Act 1891, to be applied as appropriations in aid of the grants for the services and purposes specified in Schedule (B) annexed hereto the sums respectively set forth in the last column of the said schedule.

Short title

3. This Act may be cited as the Appropriation (No. 2) Act 1987.

ABSTRACT

OF

SCHEDULES (A) and (B) to which this Act refers

Section 2   SCHEDULE (A)

Grants out of the Consolidated Fund £1,064,266,000

Section 2   SCHEDULE (B).—Appropriation of Grants

	Supply Grants	Appropriations in Aid
	£	£
1987–88 Supplementary, 1987–88 - - - - -	1,064,266,000	22,503,000
Grand Total - - - - -	1,064,266,000	22,503,000

SCHEDULE (A)

Grants out of the Consolidated Fund

	£
For the service of the year ending 31st March 1988— Under this Act	1,064,266,000

Supplementary, 1987–88   SCHEDULE (B)

Supplementary, 1987–88

Schedule of Supplementary Sums granted, and of the sums which may be applied as appropriations in aid in addition thereto, to defray the charges for the Services herein particularly mentioned for the year ended 31st March 1988, viz.:—

	Supply Grants	Appropriations in Aid
	£	£
Vote		
Class I		
1. For expenditure by the Ministry of Defence on personnel costs etc., of the Armed Forces and their Reserves and Cadet Forces etc.; personnel costs etc., of Defence Ministers and of certain civilian staff employed by the Ministry of Defence; on movements; certain stores; supplies and services; plant and machinery; charter of ships; certain research; lands and buildings; sundry grants; payments abroad including contributions and subscriptions to international organisations; and grants in aid - - - - -	2,000,000	—

	Supply Grants	Appropriations in Aid
	£	£

Vote

Class II

5. For expenditure by the Foreign and Commonwealth Office (Overseas Development Administration) on the official United Kingdom Aid Programme including bilateral financial aid, grants in aid and technical co-operation; the cost of in-house Scientific Units; grants and grants in aid to UK institutions, voluntary agencies and individuals, and other expenditure in support of the programme; capital and other subscriptions, other contributions including grants in aid and payments under guarantee, to multilateral development banks and other international and regional bodies; emergency, refugee and other relief assistance; loans to the Commonwealth Development Corporation, and pensions and allowances in respect of overseas service   -   -   -   -   -   - | 1,000 | — |

Class IV

4. For expenditure by the Ministry of Agriculture, Fisheries and Food on commissioned research and development and advice, education and training services, botanical services, assistance to production, marketing and processing, support for the fishing industry, emergency and strategic food services, protective, agency and other services including grants in aid and international subscriptions   -   -   -   -   -   - | 875,000 | 75,000 |

Class V

1. For expenditure by the Department of Trade and Industry on regional development grants, regional selective assistance, selective assistance to individual industries, certain other services including UK contributions to the funding of buffer stock operations of international commodity agreements, a strategic mineral stockpile, the film industry, and support for the aerospace, shipbuilding and steel industries, including loans, grants and the purchase of assets and assistance to redundant steel workers   -   -   -   - | 55,000,000 | — |

2. For expenditure by the Department of Trade and Industry at its research establishments and on the running costs of certain of its headquarters divisions, radiocommunications division and the Patent Office, support for innovation (including industrial research and development, aircraft and aeroengine research and development, and space technology programmes), promotion of standards, export promotion and trade co-operation, miscellaneous support services, grants in aid, international subscriptions, enterprise and job creation, provision of land and buildings, loans, grants and other payments   -   -   - | 9,125,000 | — |

4. For Government investment in British Shipbuilders and grants from the shipbuilding intervention fund to assist public sector yards   -   -   - | 11,000,000 | — |

	Supply Grants	Appropriations in Aid
	£	£
Vote		
CLASS VI		
1. For expenditure by the Department of Energy on assistance to the coal industry including grants to British Coal and payments to redundant workers	114,000,000	—
CLASS VIII		
2. For expenditure by the Department of Transport on assistance to shipping; civil aviation; central administration; certain licensing and testing schemes; research and development; road safety; and certain other transport services including civil defence; and international subscriptions, including grants in aid - - - - - -	1,000,000	—
5. For expenditure by the Department of Transport on transport supplementary grants to Highway Authorities in England, and certain other grants and payments in support of local roads and transport expenditure - - - - - -	1,000	—
6. For residual expenditure by the Department of Transport in connection with the sale of shares in British Airways and for the costs of the second instalment - - - - - - - -	1,000	10,567,000
CLASS X		
2. For expenditure by the Department of the Environment on other environmental services including grants in aid and international subscriptions, on grants in aid to the Development Commission and British Waterways Board, on bridgeworks and on developing Civil Defence water services and grants to New Towns - -	599,000	—
CLASS XI		
3. For expenditure by the Home Office on court services, other services related to crime, probation and aftercare, police, fire, civil defence, control of immigration and nationality, issue of passports etc., other protective services and community services and other miscellaneous services including grants in aid and international subscriptions; and on administrative and operational staff (excluding prisons) and central services - -	1,000	—
5. For expenditure by the Lord Chancellor's Department on the Court Service, the Law Commission, the Office of the Special Commissioners for Income Tax, the Office of the Social Security Commissioners, the VAT tribunals, the immigration appellate authorities, the Public Trustee Office and certain other legal services, including grants in aid to the Council for Licensed Conveyancers and for administration of legal aid - -	1,000	2,736,000
CLASS XII		
3. For expenditure by the Department of Education and Science on universities and certain other institutions, grants for higher and further education, payment of certain licence fees to the Home Office, grants in aid and a subscription to an international organisation - - - - -	43,250,000	59,000

	Supply Grants	Appropriations in Aid
Vote	£	£

CLASS XII—*continued*

5. For a grant in aid of the Agricultural and Food Research Council, and for payment of certain licence fees to the Home Office - - - - 1,500,000 —

6. For a grant in aid of the Medical Research Council including subscriptions to certain international organisations, and for payment of certain licence fees to the Home Office - - - - - 6,300,000 —

7. For a grant in aid of the Natural Environment Research Council, and for payment of certain licence fees to the Home Office - - - - - 800,000 —

8. For a grant in aid of the Science and Engineering Research Council including subscriptions to certain international organisations - - - - 7,500,000 —

9. For a grant in aid of the Economic and Social Research Council - - - - - - 800,000 —

10. For a grant in aid of the British Museum (Natural History) - - - - - - - - 300,000 —

11. For grants in aid of the Royal Society and the Fellowship of Engineering, and the science policy studies programme of the Advisory Board for the Research Councils - - - - - - 300,000 —

CLASS XIV

1. For expenditure by the Department of Health and Social Security on the provision of services under the National Health Service in England, on other health services including grant in aid and on certain other services including research - - 261,060,000 —

3. For expenditure by the Department of Health and Social Security on the national health service in England and on miscellaneous health, personal social and other services (some of which are administered on a United Kingdom basis), including Family Practitioner Committee administration, mental health, medical, scientific and technical services, services for disabled persons, grants to voluntary organisations, etc., grants in aid and subscriptions to international organisations - - - - - - 4,440,000 —

CLASS XV

1. For expenditure by the Department of Health and Social Security on non-contributory retirement pensions, Christmas bonus payments to pensioners, pensions etc., for disablement or death arising out of war or service in the armed forces after 2 September 1939 and on sundry other services, on attendance allowances, invalid care allowance, severe disablement allowance, and mobility allowance - - - - - - - 151,000,000 —

2. For expenditure by the Department of Health and Social Security on supplementary pensions and allowances - - - - - - - 67,000,000 —

4. For expenditure by the Department of Health and Social Security on rent rebate, rent allowance and rate rebate subsidies, to housing, rating and local authorities, and expenditure on subsidies towards the administrative costs incurred by these authorities in operating the housing benefit scheme - 242,000,000 —

	Supply Grants	Appropriations in Aid
	£	£
Vote		
CLASS XV—*continued*		
7. For sums payable out of the Consolidated Fund by way of supplement to the National Insurance Fund - - - - - - - - -	30,000,000	—
CLASS XVI		
2. For expenditure by the Department of Agriculture and Fisheries for Scotland on educational and advisory services, botanical services, assistance to marketing and processing, administration, land management and land settlement, livestock services, assistance to crofters, assistance to the Scottish fishing industry, protective and certain other services including research and development, special services and a grant in aid - -	127,000	—
14. For expenditure by the Scottish Home and Health Department on legal aid administration, certain services relating to crime, prisons, treatment of offenders, civil defence (including grants) and on fire and police services (excluding grants and superannuation), on the provision of services under the national health service, on other health services, on research, services for the disabled and certain other services including a grant in aid - - - - - - - - -	36,000,000	—
17. For expenditure by the Scottish Home and Health Department on the provision of services under the National Health Service in Scotland, on welfare food and certain other services - - -	1,000	—
CLASS XVII		
5. For expenditure by the Welsh Office on tourism, roads and certain associated services including road safety, housing, historic buildings and ancient monuments, other environmental services, civil defence (including grants), education, libraries and museums, health and personal social services, grants in aid, EC agency payments, other grants and certain other services, including research - - - - - - - -	270,000	—
8. For expenditure by the Welsh Office on Hospital and Community Health Services, supporting health services, family practitioner services administration and related services, and services for the disabled - - - - - - -	17,730,000	—
CLASS XIX		
17. To repay to the Contingencies Fund certain miscellaneous advances - - - - - -	283,000	—
CLASS XX		
9. For expenditure by the Land Registry on administrative costs - - - - - - -	1,000	9,066,000
TOTAL SUPPLEMENTARY 1987–88 - £	1,064,266,000	22,503,000

FINANCE (No. 2) ACT 1987*

(1987 c. 51)

ARRANGEMENT OF SECTIONS

PART I

INCOME TAX, CORPORATION TAX AND CAPITAL GAINS TAX

CHAPTER I

PROFIT-RELATED PAY

Preliminary

SECT.
1. Interpretation.
2. Taxation of profit-related pay.

The relief

3. Relief from tax.
4. Exceptions from relief.

Registration

5. Persons who may apply for registration.
6. Excluded employments.
7. Applications for registration.
8. Registration.
9. Change of scheme employer.
10. Cancellation of registration.

Administration

11. Recovery of tax from scheme employer.
12. Annual returns etc.
13. Other information.
14. Information: penalties.
15. Appeals.

Supplementary

16. Partnerships.
17. Independent accountants.

CHAPTER II

PERSONAL PENSION SCHEMES

Preliminary

18. Interpretation.
19. Approval of schemes.

Restrictions on approval: establishment and benefits

20. Establishment of schemes.
21. Scope of benefits.
22. Annuity to member.
23. Lump sum to member.
24. Annuity after death of member.
25. Lump sum on death of member.
26. Return of contributions on death of member.

* Annotations by Christopher Cant, M.A., Barrister; Ian Ferrier, M.A., Barrister; David Goy, LL.M., Barrister and John Shock, M.A., F.C.A., Barrister.

Other restrictions on approval

SECT.
27. Scheme administrator.
28. Transfer payments.
29. Excess contributions.
30. Restriction on contributors.

Tax consequences of approval: member's contributions

31. Deduction from relevant earnings.
32. Limit on deductions.
33. Carry-back of contributions.
34. Carry-forward of relief.
35. Meaning of "relevant earnings".
36. Earnings from pensionable employment.
37. Meaning of "net relevant earnings".

Other tax consequences of approval

38. Employer's contributions.
39. Exemption for scheme investments.
40. Unit trusts.
41. Treatment of annuities.

Miscellaneous

42. Minimum contributions under Social Security Act 1986.
43. Withdrawal of approval.
44. Tax on unauthorised payments etc.
45. Relief by deduction from contributions.
46. Claims for relief.
47. Appeals.
48. Adjustment of relief.
49. Exclusion of double relief.
50. Information about payments.
51. Information: penalties.
52. Remuneration of Ministers and other officers.
53. Contributions under unapproved arrangements.
54. Retirement annuities.
55. Transitional provisions: general.
56. Transitional provisions: approvals.
57. Minor and consequential amendments.

CHAPTER III

GENERAL

Pension and share schemes

58. Occupational pension schemes.
59. Employee share schemes.

Companies

60. Payments of interest etc. between related companies.
61. Apportionment of income etc. of close companies.

Provisions having an overseas element

62. United Kingdom members of partnerships controlled abroad.
63. Limitation of group relief in relation to certain dual resident companies.
64. Limitation of other reliefs in dealings involving dual resident investing companies.
65. Controlled foreign conpanies: acceptable distribution policy.
66. Offshore funds.
67. Double taxation relief: interest on certain overseas loans.
68. Double taxation relief: underlying tax reflecting interest on loans.

Miscellaneous

69. Disclosure of employment information obtained from Inland Revenue.
70. Lloyd's underwriters.
71. Relief for losses on unquoted shares in trading companies.

SECT.
72. Allowances for dwelling-houses let on assured tenancies.
73. Recognised investment exchanges.

CHAPTER IV

CAPITAL GAINS

Companies' chargeable gains

74. General rules.
75. Life assurance business.
76. Gains from oil extraction activities etc.
77. Double taxation relief.

Miscellaneous

78. Collective investment schemes.
79. Building societies: groups of companies.
80. Roll-over relief not available for gains on oil licences.
81. Commodity and financial futures and options.

CHAPTER V

TAXES MANAGEMENT PROVISIONS

Company returns

82. Return of profits.
83. Failure to make return for corporation tax.
84. Assessment of amounts due by way of penalty.

Interest etc.

85. Interest on overdue corporation tax etc.
86. Supplementary provisions as to interest on overdue tax.
87. Interest on tax overpaid.
88. Recovery of overpayment of tax etc.
89. Prescribed rate of interest.

Miscellaneous

90. Corporation tax to be payable without assessment.
91. Close companies: loans to participators.
92. Amendments relating to PAYE.
93. Sub-contractors in the construction industry.
94. Failure to do things within a limited time.
95. Interpretation of Chapter V and consequential and supplementary provisions.

PART II

INHERITANCE TAX ETC.

96. Interests in possession.
97. Acceptance in lieu: capital transfer tax and estate duty.
98. Personal pension schemes.

PART III

MISCELLANEOUS AND SUPPLEMENTARY

 99. Stamp duty: options etc.
100. Stamp duty reserve tax.
101. Oil taxation.
102. Government fees and charges.
103. Consumption in port of goods transhipped for use as stores etc.
104. Short title, interpretation, construction and repeals.

SCHEDULES
Schedule 1—Profit-related pay schemes: conditions for registration.
Schedule 2—Personal pension schemes etc.
Schedule 3—Occupational pension schemes.
Schedule 4—Dual resident investing companies.
Schedule 5—Companies' chargeable gains: transitional provisions.
Schedule 6—Management provisions: supplementary and consequential provisions.
Schedule 7—Inheritance tax: interests in possession.
Schedule 8—Amendments of Schedule 10 to Finance Act 1987.
Schedule 9—Repeals.

An Act to grant certain duties, to alter other duties, and to amend the law relating to the National Debt and the Public Revenue, and to make further provision in connection with Finance.   [23rd July 1987]

PARLIAMENTARY DEBATES
Hansard, H.C. Vol. 118, col. 599; Vol. 119, cols. 356, 976, 1142, 1309; Vol. 120, col. 23; H.L. Vol. 488, cols. 1276, 1486.

PART I

INCOME TAX, CORPORATION TAX AND CAPITAL GAINS TAX

CHAPTER I

PROFIT-RELATED PAY

GENERAL NOTE
Following on an initiative in the 1986 Budget speech, the government issued a Green Paper (Cmnd. 9835) outlining proposals for giving a measure of tax relief to earnings related to the profits of a business. This Chapter implements these proposals with some changes following discussions with interested bodies. Employers will be permitted to set up profit-related pay ("PRP") schemes for an identifiable employment unit. For qualifying schemes, tax relief will be given on half of PRP up to a maximum of 2 per cent. of earnings, subject to a limit of £3,000. Many firms already operate bonus schemes. The PRP system will encourage such schemes by according them a tax incentive and by relating pay to profits could provide a flexibility for management which would reduce the possibility of workers being laid off during a business downturn. For an employee on average earnings the relief could be worth about £6 per week, equivalent to a reduction of 4p in the basic rate of income tax.

Preliminary

Interpretation
1.—(1) In this Chapter—
"employment" means an office or employment whose emoluments fall to be assessed under Schedule E, and related expressions have corresponding meanings;
"employment unit" means an undertaking, or that part of an undertaking, to which a profit-related pay scheme relates;
"pay" (except in the expression "profit-related pay") means emoluments paid under deduction of tax pursuant to section 204 of the Taxes Act (pay as you earn), reduced by any amounts included in them by virtue of Chapter II of Part III of the Finance Act 1976;
"profit period" means an accounting period by reference to which any profit-related pay is calculated;
"profit-related pay" means emoluments from an employment which are paid in accordance with a profit-related pay scheme;

"profit-related pay scheme" means a scheme providing for the payment of emoluments calculated by reference to profits;

"profits" or "losses", in relation to a profit period, means the amount shown in the account prepared for that period in accordance with the relevant profit-related pay scheme as the profit, or as the case may be the loss, on ordinary activities after taxation;

"registered scheme" means a profit-related pay scheme registered under this Chapter;

"scheme employer" means the person on whose application a profit-related pay scheme is or may be registered under this Chapter.

(2) References in this Chapter to the employees to whom a profit-related pay scheme relates are references to the employees who will receive any payments of profit-related pay under the scheme.

GENERAL NOTE

Various basic definitions are provided.

The minimum requirement for constituting an "employment unit" are that accounts meeting Companies Act criteria can be prepared for it. See further Sched. 1, paras. 19 and 20.

Taxation of profit-related pay

2. Any charge to income tax on profit-related pay paid in accordance with a registered scheme shall be made for the year of assessment in which it is paid (rather than the period for which it is paid).

GENERAL NOTE

PRP is to be dealt with through the normal PAYE system and accordingly will be taxed on a cash rather than an accrual basis.

The relief

Relief from tax

3.—(1) One half of any profit-related pay to which this section applies shall be exempt from income tax.

(2) This section applies to any profit-related pay paid to an employee by reference to a profit period and in accordance with a registered scheme, but only so far as it does not exceed the lower of the two limits specified in the following provisions of this section.

(3) The first of the limits referred to in subsection (2) above is one fifth of the aggregate of—

(a) the pay (but not any profit-related pay) paid to the employee in the profit period in respect of his employment in the employment unit concerned (or, if the employee is eligible to receive profit-related pay by reference to part only of the period, so much of his pay, but not any profit-related pay, as is paid in that part), and

(b) the profit-related pay paid to him by reference to that period in respect of that employment.

(4) The second of the limits referred to in subsection (2) above is £3000 (or, if the profit period is less than twelve months or the employee is eligible to receive profit-related pay by reference to part only of the profit period, a proportionately reduced amount).

GENERAL NOTE

This section contains the kernel of the PRP scheme. One half of PRP is exempt from income tax, up to a limit of 20 per cent. of total pay or £3,000 per annum, whichever is less.

Exceptions from relief

4.—(1) Profit-related pay shall not be exempt from income tax by virtue of section 3 above if—

    (a) it is paid to an employee in respect of his employment in an employment unit during a time when he also has another employment, and

    (b) He receives in respect of his other employment during that time profit-related pay which is exempt from income tax by virtue of that section.

(2) Subject to subsection (3) below, profit-related pay in respect of which no secondary Class 1 contributions under Part I of the Social Security Act 1975 or Part I of the Social Security (Northern Ireland) Act 1975 are payable shall not be exempt from income tax by virtue of section 3 above.

(3) Subsection (2) above shall not apply to profit-related pay in respect of which no Class 1 contributions are payable only because the employee's earnings are below the lower earnings limit for such contributions.

GENERAL NOTE

Subs. (1) debars an employee from participating in more than one PRP scheme.

Subss. (2) and (3) prevent earnings not subject to employers' National Insurance contributions, for example because they are paid through a trust, from qualifying for PRP relief, except where they are part of total earnings below the lower earnings limit.

Registration

Persons who may apply for registration

5.—(1) Where the emoluments of all the employees to whom a profit-related pay scheme relates are paid by the same person, an application to register the scheme under this Chapter may be made to the Board by that person.

(2) Where subsection (1) above does not apply to a profit-related pay scheme, no application to register it may be made unless all the persons who pay emoluments to employees to whom the scheme relates are bodies corporate which are members of the same group; and in that case an application may be made by the parent company of the group.

(3) In subsection (2) above "group" means a body corporate and its 51 per cent. subsidiaries, and "parent company" means that body corporate; and in applying for the purposes of this section the definition of "51 per cent. subsidiary" in section 532 of the Taxes Act, any share capital of a registered industrial and provident society (within the meaning of section 340 of the Taxes Act) shall be treated as ordinary share capital.

GENERAL NOTE

Generally, a PRP scheme can only cover employees of a single employer. However, the parent company of a group may apply to register a PRP scheme which covers employees of its subsidiaries.

Excluded employments

6.—(1) No application may be made to register a scheme under this Chapter if any employment to which the scheme relates is—

    (a) employment in an office under the Crown or otherwise in the service of the Crown, or

    (b) employment by an excluded employer.

(2) For the purposes of this section "excluded employer" means—

    (a) a person in an employment within subsection (1) above;

    (b) a body under the control of the Crown, or of one or more persons acting on behalf of the Crown;

(c) a local authority;

(d) a body under the control of one of more local authorities, or of the Crown (or one or more persons acting on behalf of the Crown) and one or more local authorities.

(3) For the purposes of this section a person has control of a body only if one or more of the following conditions is satisfied—

(a) in the case of a body whose affairs are managed by its members, he has the power to appoint more than half of the members;

(b) in the case of a body having a share capital, he holds more than half of its issued share capital;

(c) in the case of a body whose members vote in general meeting, he has the power to exercise more than half of the votes exercisable in general meeting;

(d) the articles of association or other rules regulating the body give him the power to secure that the affairs of the body are conducted in accordance with his wishes.

(4) For the purposes of this section a person shall be taken to possess any rights and powers possessed by—

(a) a person appointed by him to an office by virtue of which the rights or powers are exercisable, or

(b) a body which he controls,

including rights and powers which such an officer or body is taken to possess by virtue of this subsection.

(5) Subsections (3) and (4) above apply with the necessary modifications for the purpose of determining whether persons together have control of a body.

GENERAL NOTE

Employers in the public sector, including central government and local authorities, are excluded from the scope of PRP schemes. This exclusion extends to bodies controlled by central or local government, including trading companies.

Applications for registration

7.—(1) An application for the registration of a profit-related pay scheme under this Chapter—

(a) shall be in such form as the Board may prescribe;

(b) shall contain a declaration by the applicant that the scheme complies with the requirements of Schedule 1 to this Act;

(c) shall contain an undertaking by the applicant that the emoluments paid to any employee to whom the scheme relates and to whom minimum wage legislation applies will satisfy that legislation without taking account of profit-related pay;

(d) shall specify the profit period or periods to which the scheme relates;

(e) shall be supported by such information as the Board may require.

(2) An application for the registration of a profit-related pay scheme under this Chapter shall be accompanied by a report by an independent accountant, in a form prescribed by the Board, to the effect that in his opinion—

(a) the scheme complies with the requirements of Schedule 1 to this Act;

(b) the books and records maintained and proposed to be maintained by the applicant are adequate for the purpose of enabling the documents required by section 12(1) below to be produced.

(3) An application for the registration of a profit-related pay scheme under this Chapter shall be made within the period of six months ending immediately before the beginning of the profit period, or the first of the profit periods, to which the scheme relates.

(4) In subsection (1) above, "minimum wage legislation" means the provisions relating to remuneration in Part II of the Wages Act 1986, the Wages Councils (Northern Ireland) Order 1982, the Agricultural Wage Act 1948, the Agricultural Wages (Scotland) Act 1949 and the Agricultura Wages (Regulation) (Northern Ireland) Order 1977.

GENERAL NOTE

Formal application for registration must be made to a special Revenue PRP Office locate at St. Mungo's Road, Cumbernauld, Glasgow, G67 1YZ. Since it is not the Revenue' intention to become involved in the detailed policing of PRP schemes, a supervisory role i entrusted to independent accountants. See s.17 for the definition of "independen accountant."

The pay of employees participating in a PRP scheme must satisfy the requirements c minimum wage legislation without taking account of the PRP.

Registration

8.—(1) If an application for the registration of a profit-related pa scheme under this Chapter is made more than three months (but not more than six months) before the beginning of the profit period, or the first o the profit periods, to which the scheme relates, then, subject to subsectio (2) below, the Board shall register the scheme before the beginning o that period.

(2) If the Board are not satisfied that an application made as mentione in subsection (1) above complies with the requirements of this Chapter they may within thirty days after the day on which they receive the application—

(a) refuse the application, or

(b) by written notice to the applicant either require him to amend the application or require him to give them such further information a may be specified in the notice, and in either case to do so withi such time, not exceeding thirty days after the day on which the notice is given, as may be so specified.

(3) If a notice under subsection (2) above is complied with and the Board are satisfied that the application complies with the requirements o this Chapter, the Board shall register the scheme before the beginning o the profit period.

(4) If a notice under subsection (2) above is complied with but the Board remain not satisfied that the application complies with the require ments of this Chapter, the Board shall refuse the application.

(5) If a notice under subsection (2) above is not complied with but the Board are before the beginning of the profit period satisfied that the application complies with the requirements of this Chapter, the Board may register the scheme before the beginning of the period; but if they de not do so, the application shall be regarded as having been refused.

(6) If an application for the registration of a profit-related pay scheme under this Chapter is made within the period of three months before the beginning of the profit period, or the first of the profit periods, to which the scheme relates, then—

(a) if before the beginning of the profit period the Board are satisfied that the application complies with the requirements of this Chapter they shall register the scheme before the beginning of the period but

(b) in any other case, the application shall be regarded as having been refused.

(7) After registering a scheme under this Chapter, the Board shall by written notice inform the applicant that they have done so.

(8) The Board shall give written notice to the applicant if they refuse his application under subsection (2) of (4) above.

(9) For the purposes of this section an application does not comply with
he requirements of this Chapter if the scheme to which it relates does not
:omply with the requirements of Schedule 1 to this Act.

GENERAL NOTE
   Normally an application for registration of a PRP scheme should be made between three
and six months before its start. The Revenue then have 30 days to refuse the application or
give a further 30 days' notice to the applicant to amend his application or provide further
nformation. Applications made on less than three months' notice may be approved at the
Revenue's discretion. The requirements for registration are set out in Sched. 1.

Change of scheme employer

9.—(1) Where—
    (a) a scheme employer ceases to fulfil the conditions which section
        5 above requires to be fulfilled by an applicant for registration
        of the scheme, and
    (b) he is succeeded by a person who would be eligible to apply for
        registration of the scheme, and
    (c) there is otherwise no other material change in the employment
        unit or in the circumstances relating to the scheme,
the scheme employer and his successor may make a joint written application to the Board under this section for the amendment of the registration of the scheme.
   (2) If on receiving an application under this section the Board are
satisfied—
    (a) that the conditions in subsection (1)(a), (b) and (c) above are
        fulfilled, and
    (b) that, apart from the change of scheme employer, there would be
        no grounds for cancelling the registration of the scheme,
the Board shall amend the registration of the scheme by substituting the
successor for the previous scheme employer.
   (3) An application under this section shall be made before the end of
the period of one month beginning with the date of the succession.
   (4) Where the Board amend the registration of a scheme under this
section, this Chapter shall (subject to any necessary modifications) have
effect as if the successor had been the scheme employer throughout.
   (5) The Board shall give written notice to the applicants if they refuse
an application under this section.

GENERAL NOTE
   This section caters for the situation arising where an employer changes. On joint
application by both employers to the Revenue within one month of the change, the Revenue
may amend the registration of the scheme by substituting the new employer.

Cancellation of registration

10.—(1) If after a scheme has been registered under this Chapter it
appears to the Board—
    (a) that the scheme has not been or will not be administered in
        accordance with its terms or in accordance with this Chapter in
        relation to a profit period, or
    (b) that the circumstances relating to the scheme have during a profit
        period become such that (if it were not registered) an application
        to register it under this Chapter would be excluded by section 6
        above, or
    (c) in the case of a scheme which employs (as the method of deter-
        mining the distributable pool for a profit period) the method
        described as method B in paragraph 14 of Schedule 1 to this Act,

that losses were incurred in a profit period or in the preceding period of twelve months, or

(d) that the undertaking given in compliance with section 7(1)(c) above has not been complied with in relation to employment at any time during a profit period,

the Board may cancel the registration and, subject to subsection (5) below, the cancellation shall have effect from the beginning of that profit period.

(2) If after a scheme has been registered under this Chapter it appears to the Board—

(a) that at the time of registration the scheme did not comply with the requirements of Schedule 1 to this Act or that the application did not comply with the requirements of this Chapter, or

(b) in the case of a scheme which employs (as the method of determining the distributable pool for a profit period) the method described as method A in paragraph 13 of Schedule 1, that losses were incurred in the base year specified in the scheme,

the Board may cancel the registration with effect from the beginning of the profit period (or first profit period) to which the scheme related.

(3) If after a scheme has been registered under this Chapter the scheme employer fails to comply with the requirements of section 12 below in relation to a profit period, the Board may cancel the registration with effect from the beginning of that profit period.

(4) If the scheme employer, by written notice, requests the Board to cancel the registration of the scheme with effect from the beginning of a profit period specified in the notice, the Board shall comply with the request.

(5) Where—

(a) the scheme employer has given to the Board in accordance with section 13(3) below notice of a change in the employment unit, or in the circumstances relating to the scheme, which is a ground for cancellation of the registration of the scheme by virtue of subsection (1)(a) or (b) above, and

(b) the Board are satisfied that the change is not brought about with a view to the registration of a new scheme, and

(c) in the notice the scheme employer requests the Board to cancel the registration of the scheme with effect from the date of the change,

then, if the notice is given before the end of the period of one month beginning with that date, the Board shall comply with the request.

(6) The Board shall give written notice to the scheme employer of the cancellation of a scheme's registration.

GENERAL NOTE

Registration of a scheme may be cancelled, either on the initiative of the Revenue, or at the instance of the employer, on various grounds. These include:

(i) failure to administer the scheme in accordance with its own or the statutory requirements;

(ii) the employment unit concerned becomes controlled by the public sector, or is running at a loss;

(iii) the employer is not complying with minimum wage legislation;

(iv) the scheme did not in fact comply with the statutory requirements for registration;

(v) the employer fails to make annual returns in accordance with s.12.

Subs. (5) restricts deregistration in cases where the circumstances bringing it about have been contrived with a view to the registration of a new scheme.

Administration

Recovery of tax from scheme employer

11.—(1) This section applies where—

(a) payments of profit-related pay are made to an employee in accordance with a registered scheme, and

(b) in consequence of the relief given by this Chapter in respect of registered schemes, less income tax is deducted from the payments in accordance with section 204 of the Taxes Act (pay as you earn) than would have been deducted if the scheme had not been registered, and

(c) the registration of the scheme is subsequently cancelled with effect from a time before that relevant for the purposes of the relief.

(2) Where this section applies, an amount equal to the shortfall in the deductions made in accordance with section 204 shall be payable by the scheme employer to the Board; and regulations under that section may include provision as to the collection and recovery of any such amount.

GENERAL NOTE

Where registration of a scheme is cancelled with retrospective effect, the employer will be responsible for paying over to the Revenue any under-deduction of PAYE.

Annual returns etc.

12.—(1) After every profit period of a registered scheme, the scheme employer shall, within the period allowed by subsection (2) below, send to the Board—

(a) a return in such form and containing such information as the Board may prescribe, and

(b) a report by an independent accountant in such form and containing such information as the Board may prescribe, and stating that in his opinion the terms of the scheme have been complied with in respect of the profit period.

(2) Subject to subsection (3) below, the period allowed for complying with subsection (1) above is—

(a) seven months from the end of the profit period if the employment unit to which the scheme relates is an undertaking or part of an undertaking of a public company, and

(b) ten months from the end of the profit period in any other case.

(3) If before the end of the period allowed by subsection (2) above the scheme employer gives the Board written notice that an extension of three months has been allowed under section 242(3) of the Companies Act 1985, or under Article 250(3) of the Companies (Northern Ireland) Order 1986, in relation to a financial year of the employer which corresponds with the profit period in question, then the period allowed by subsection (2) above shall be correspondingly extended.

(4) In subsection 2(a) above, "public company" has the meaning given by section 1(3) of the Companies Act 1985 or Article 12(3) of the Companies (Northern Ireland) Order 1986.

GENERAL NOTE

The Revenue will not be involved in the day-to-day operation of PRP schemes. Accordingly, the annual return to be submitted by employers is of crucial importance. It must be submitted within seven months of the end of the period in question in the case of a plc, and 10 months in the case of any other undertaking, subject to the statutory three months' extension under Companies Act 1985, s.242(3) in the case of a company with involvements outside the British Isles. The return must be supported by a report by an independent accountant, as to whom, see s.17.

Other information

13.—(1) The Board may by written notice require any person to give them, within a period of thirty days or such longer period as may be specified in the notice, any information which is so specified and which—

(a) that person has or can reasonably be required to obtain, and

(b) the Board consider they need to have in order to perform their functions under this Chapter.

(2) Without prejudice to the generality of subsection (1)(b) above, the Board may in particular require a person under subsection (1) to give them—

(a) information to enable them to determine whether the registration of a scheme should be cancelled;

(b) information to enable them to determine the liability to tax of any person who is or has been an employee to whom a registered scheme relates or who pays or has paid emoluments to such an employee;

(c) information about the administration of a profit-related pay scheme which is or has been a registered scheme;

(d) information about any change of person paying emoluments to employees to whom a registered scheme relates.

(3) The scheme employer of a registered scheme shall by written notice inform the Board without delay if he becomes aware of anything that is or may be a ground for cancellation of the registration of the scheme.

GENERAL NOTE

A wide power, modelled on that relating to approved share option schemes in F.A. 1984, Sched. 10, para. 14, is given to the Revenue to require information from anyone to enable them to police the operation of PRP schemes. Also an obligation is laid on employers to inform the Revenue of any circumstances giving grounds for cancellation of registration. For such grounds, see s.10.

Information: penalties

14.—(1) At the end of the first column in the Table in section 98 of the Taxes Management Act 1970 (penalties for failure to furnish information etc.) there shall be added—

"Section 13(1) of the Finance (No. 2) Act 1987".

(2) At the end of the second column of that Table there shall be added—

"Section 12(1) of the Finance (No. 2) Act 1987".

GENERAL NOTE

The sanctions for failure to supply information to the Revenue provided by T.M.A. 1970, s.98 are extended to the requirements of ss.12 and 13.

Appeals

15.—(1) An appeal to the Special Commissioners may be made by a scheme employer—

(a) against a refusal by the Board under section 8(2) or (4) above of an application for registration of the scheme;

(b) against a refusal by the Board of an application under section 9 above;

(c) against the cancellation by the Board of the registration of the scheme.

(2) An appeal under this section shall be made by written notice given to the Board within thirty days of the day on which the scheme employer was notified of the refusal or, as the case may be, the cancellation.

An appeal against a refusal by the Revenue to register a scheme, or to amend a registration on a change of employer, or against the cancellation of a registration, may be made to the Special Commissioners by notice within 30 days.

Supplementary

Partnership

16.—For the purposes of this Chapter the members of a partnership which is a scheme employer shall be treated as a single continuing body of persons notwithstanding any change in their identity.

GENERAL NOTE
Partnerships can participate in the PRP system on the same basis as companies and changes in the membership of the partnership are ignored for this purpose.

Independent accountants

17.—(1) For the purposes of this Chapter, "independent accountant", in relation to a profit-related pay scheme, means a person who—

(a) is within section 389(1)(a) or (b) of the Companies Act 1985 or Article 397(1)(a) or (b) of the Companies (Northern Ireland) Order 1986 (qualification for appointment as auditor), and

(b) is not excluded by subsections (2) to (5) below.

(2) A person is not an independent accountant in relation to a profit-related pay scheme if—

(a) he is the employer of employees to whom the scheme relates, or

(b) he is a partner or an employee of, or a partner of an employee of, a person within subsection (3) below, or

(c) he is an employee of a person within paragraph (b) above.

(3) The persons within this subsection are—

(a) any person having employees to whom the scheme relates;

(b) any body corporate which is the subsidiary or holding company of a body corporate within paragraph (a) above or a subsidiary of such a body's holding company.

(4) For the purposes of this section—

(a) an auditor of a company is not to be regarded as an employee of it, and

(b) "holding company" and "subsidiary" are to be construed in accordance with section 736 of the Companies Act 1985 or Article 4 of the Companies (Northern Ireland) Order 1986.

(5) A body corporate cannot be an independent accountant in relation to a scheme.

(6) For the purposes of this Chapter, "independent accountant", in relation to a scheme, includes a Scottish firm all the partners of which are independent accountants in relation to the scheme.

GENERAL NOTE
The "independent accountant" plays a crucial role in the operation of the PRP system, both in certifying the application for registration (s.7(2)) and in supporting the annual return with a report (s.12(1)(b)). He must be qualified to act as an auditor within Companies Act 1985, s.389. Further conditions are specified to prevent conflict of interest. A company's auditor is able to act as the independent accountant for this purpose.

CHAPTER II

PERSONAL PENSION SCHEMES

Preliminary

Interpretation

18. In this Chapter—
"approved"—
    (a) in relation to a scheme, means approved by the Board
        under this Chapter, and
    (b) in relation to arrangements, means made in accordance
        with a scheme which is for the time being, and was when
        the arrangements were made, an approved scheme,
but does not refer to cases in which approval has been
withdrawn;
"authorised insurance company" means either—
    (a) a person authorised under section 3 or 4 of the Insurance
        Companies Act 1982 to carry on long term business and
        acting through a branch or office in the United Kingdom,
        or
    (b) a society registered as a friendly society under the
        Friendly Societies Act 1974 or the Friendly Societies Act
        (Northern Ireland) 1970;
"member", in relation to a personal pension scheme, means an
    individual who makes arrangements in accordance with the
    scheme;
"personal pension arrangements" means arrangements made by an
    individual in accordance with a personal pension scheme;
"personal pension scheme" means a scheme whose sole purpose is
    the provision of annuities or lump sums under arrangements
    made by individuals in accordance with the scheme;
"scheme administrator" means the person referred to in section 27
    below.

GENERAL NOTE

This Chapter contains the provisions relating to the introduction of the new personal
pension schemes. These will enable employees to take out individual personal pension
policies which will not be tied to their particular employment. The provisions operate in a
similar fashion to those already in operation for self-employed individuals.

Approval of schemes

19.—(1) An application to the Board for their approval of a personal
pension scheme shall be in such form, shall contain such information, and
shall be accompanied by such documents (in such form) as the Board may
prescribe.

(2) The Board may at their discretion grant or refuse an application for
approval of a personal pension scheme, but their discretion shall be
subject to the restrictions set out in sections 20 to 30 below.

(3) The Board shall give written notice to the applicant of the grant or
refusal of an application; and in the case of a refusal the notice shall state
the grounds for the refusal.

(4) If an amendment is made to an approved scheme without being
approved by the Board, their approval of the scheme shall cease to have
effect.

    All schemes intended to take the benefits conferred by this Chapter of the Act must be approved by the Board and any unauthorised amendment of such a scheme will cause the approval automatically to cease.
    The conditions to be satisfied by a scheme before approval is given are set out in ss.20 to 30. A draft memorandum of guidance has been prepared by the Occupational Pensions Board to which is attached a draft set of model rules.
    If approval is refused there is a right of appeal contained in s.47.

Restrictions on approval: establishment and benefits

Establishment of schemes

20.—(1) The Board shall not approve a personal pension scheme established by any person other than—
    (a) a person who is authorised under Chapter III of Part I of the Financial Services Act 1986 to carry on investment business, and who carries on business of a kind mentioned in subsection (2) below;
    (b) a building society within the meaning of the Building Societies Act 1986;
    (c) an institution authorised under the Banking Act 1987;
    (d) a recognised bank or licensed institution within the meaning of the Banking Act 1979.
  (2) The kinds of business referred to in subsection (1)(a) above are—
    (a) issuing insurance policies or annuity contracts;
    (b) managing unit trust schemes authorised under section 78(1) of the Financial Services Act 1986.
  (3) Subsection (1) above shall not apply in relation to a scheme approved by the Board by virtue of section 226(5) of the Taxes Act if it is established before 4th January 1988.
  (4) The Treasury may by order amend this section as it has effect for the time being.
  (5) An order under this section shall be made by statutory instrument, which shall be subject to annulment in pursuance of a resolution of the House of Commons.

    In order to qualify for Revenue approval the scheme must be operated by one of the institutions specified in this section. There is excluded any scheme set up pursuant to s.226(5) I.C.T.A. 1970 before January 4, 1988. These are schemes which are for the benefit of individuals "engaged in or connected with a particular occupation" and their dependents provided that it is established by a trust by "a body of persons comprising or representing a substantial proportion of the individuals so engaged in the U.K."
    Any institution within this section can administer the scheme but only an authorised insurance company can provide the annuity to a member (see s.22 below).

Scope of benefits

21.—(1) The Board shall not approve a personal pension scheme which makes provision for any benefit other than—
    (a) the payment of an annuity satisfying the conditions in section 22 below;
    (b) the payment to a member of a lump sum satisfying the conditions in section 23 below;
    (c) the payment after the death of a member of an annuity satisfying the conditions in section 24 below;
    (d) the payment on the death of a member of a lump sum satisfying the conditions in section 25 below;
    (e) the payment on the death of a member of a lump sum satisfying the conditions in section 26 below.

(2) Subsection (1) above shall not prevent the approval of a scheme which makes provision for insurance against a risk relating to the non payment of contributions.

GENERAL NOTE
   The benefits provided under a scheme must be limited to the following if approval is to be obtained, namely:
   (i) annuities payable to the member or after the member's death;
   (ii) lump sum payments to the member or on the member's death;
   (iii) insurance against the risk of the future premiums not being paid—for example, due to ill health.

Annuity to member

22.—(1) The annuity must be payable by an authorised insurance company which may be chosen by the member.
   (2) Subject to subsection (3) below, the annuity must not commence before the member attains the age of 50 or after he attains the age of 75.
   (3) The annuity may commence before the member attains the age of 50 if—
   (a) it is payable on his becoming incapable through infirmity of body or mind of carrying on his own occupation or any occupation of a similar nature for which he is trained or fitted, or
   (b) the Board are satisfied that his occupation is one in which persons customarily retire before that age.
   (4) Subject to subsection (5) below, the annuity must be payable to the member for his life.
   (5) The annuity may continue for a term certain not exceeding ten years, notwithstanding the member's death within that term; and for this purpose an annuity shall be regarded as payable for a term certain notwithstanding that it may terminate, after the death of the member and before the expiry of that term, on the happening of any of the following—
   (a) the marriage of the annuitant;
   (b) his attaining the age of eighteen;
   (c) the later of his attaining that age and ceasing to be in full-time education.
   (6) The annuity must not be capable of assignment or surrender, except that an annuity for a term certain may be assigned by will or by the annuitant's personal representatives in the distribution of his estate so as to give effect to a testamentary disposition, or to the rights of those entitled on an intestacy, or to an appropriation of it to a legacy or to a share or interest in the estate.

GENERAL NOTE
   The annuity payable under the terms of the scheme to a member must be limited so that:
   (i) it is paid by an authorised insurance company which the member has the right to select;
   (ii) it must be payable not earlier than the age of 50 (unless due to ill-health, or the member's occupation is such that persons customarily retire under the age of 50) and must not start after the age of 75; (iii) it must be either an annuity for life or for a term satisfying subs. (5); (iv) the annuity must not be capable of being dealt with by the member save as regards an annuity for a term after the member's death.

Lump sum to member

23.—(1) The lump sum must be payable only if the member so elects on or before the date on which an annuity satisfying the conditions in section 22 above is first payable to him under the arrangements made in accordance with the scheme.
   (2) The lump sum must be payable when that annuity is first payable.

(3) The lump sum must not exceed one quarter of the total value, at the time when the lump sum is paid, of the benefits for the member provided for by the arrangements made by him in accordance with the scheme.

(4) The lump sum must not exceed £150,000 or such other sum as may for the time being be specified in an order made by the Treasury; and an order under this subsection shall be made by statutory instrument, which shall be subject to annulment in pursuance of a resolution of the House of Commons.

(5) The right to payment of the lump sum must not be capable of assignment or surrender.

GENERAL NOTE

As with self-employed individuals' pension plans it is open to a member to elect on or before the date when the annuity becomes payable for up to one quarter of the value of the pension benefits or £150,000 (whichever is the lower) to be paid by way of lump sum.

There are further restrictions contained in ss.25 and 26 covering a payment in the event of the death of a member.

The lump sum payment is not taxable under Schedule E (Sched. 2, para. 3).

Annuity after death of member

24.—(1) The annuity must be payable by an authorised insurance company which may be chosen by the member or by the annuitant.

(2) The annuity must be payable to the surviving spouse of the member, or to a person who was at the member's death a dependant of his.

(3) The aggregate annual amount (or, if that amount varies, the aggregate of the initial annual amounts) of all annuities to which this section applies and which are payable under the same personal pension arrangements shall not exceed—

(a) where before his death the member was in receipt of an annuity under the arrangements, the annual amount (or if it varied, the highest annual amount) of that annuity, or

(b) where paragraph (a) above does not apply, the highest annual amount of the annuity that would have been payable under the arrangements to the member (ignoring any entitlement of his to commute part of it for a lump sum) if it had vested on the day before his death.

(4) Subject to subsections (5) to (9) below, the annuity must be payable for the life of the annuitant.

(5) Where the annuity is payable to the surviving spouse of the member and at the time of the member's death the surviving spouse is under the age of 60, the annuity may be deferred to a time not later than—

(a) the time when the surviving spouse attains that age, or

(b) where the member's annuity is payable to the surviving spouse for a term certain as mentioned in section 22(5) above and the surviving spouse attains the age of 60 before the time when the member's annuity terminates, that time.

(6) The annuity may cease to be payable on the marriage of the annuitant.

(7) Where the annuity is payable to the surviving spouse of the member, it may cease before the death of the surviving spouse if—

(a) the member was survived by one or more dependants under the age of 18 and at the time of the member's death the surviving spouse was under the age of 45, and

(b) at some time before the surviving spouse attains that age no such dependant remains under the age of 18.

(8) Where the annuity is payable to a person who is under the age of 18 when it is first payable, it must cease to be payable either—

   (a) on his attaining that age, or

   (b) on the later of his attaining that age and ceasing to be in full-time education,

unless he was a dependant of the member otherwise than by reason only that he was under the age of 18.

   (9) The annuity may continue for a term certain not exceeding ten years, notwithstanding the original annuitant's death within that term; and for this purpose an annuity shall be regarded as payable for a term certain notwithstanding that it may terminate, after the death of the original annuitant and before the expiry of that term, on the happening of any of the following—

   (a) the marriage of the annuitant to whom it is payable;

   (b) his attaining the age of eighteen;

   (c) the later of his attaining that age and ceasing to be in full-time education.

   (10) The annuity must not be capable of assignment or surrender, except that an annuity for a term certain may be assigned by will or by the annuitant's personal representatives in the distribution of his estate so as to give effect to a testamentary disposition, or to the rights of those entitled on an intestacy, or to an appropriation of it to a legacy or to a share or interest in the estate.

GENERAL NOTE

The scheme may provide for annuities to be payable to the member's surviving spouse or dependants at the date of the member's death.

As with the member the annuity must be payable for life or for a certain term save: (i) it may be determinable on the marriage of the annuitant; (ii) in the case of a surviving spouse aged under 45 at the member's death with one or more dependants under 18 the annuity may determine if before the spouse reaches 45 there ceases to be any dependant under 18; (iii) in the case of dependants under 18 the annuity can cease in the circumstances specified in subs. (8).

If the annuitant is a surviving spouse under 60 then he or she has the right to defer the payment of the annuity until the attainment of that age or, in the case of an annuity for a term certain, the time when the member's annuity terminates.

Lump sum on death of member

   25.—(1) The lump sum must be payable by an authorised insurance company.

   (2) The lump sum must be payable on the death of the member before he attains the age of 75.

GENERAL NOTE

The payment of a lump sum to someone other than the member may be provided for but only if the member dies under 75. It is not restricted to payments to the surviving spouse or dependants.

Return of contributions on death of member

   26.—(1) The lump sum must be payable only if no annuity satisfying the conditions in either section 22 or section 24 above has become payable.

   (2) Subject to subsection (3) below, the lump sum must represent no more than the return of contributions, together with reasonable interest on contributions or bonuses out of profits.

   (3) To the extent that contributions are invested in units under a unit trust scheme, the lump sum may represent the sale or redemption price of the units.

GENERAL NOTE

The lump sum payment to someone other than the member can only be made if no annuity has been payable.

The amount of the payment must not exceed the amount of contributions plus either asonable interest or bonuses out of profits (in the case of schemes linked to units this may the amount realised from their sale or redemption).

Other restrictions on approval

cheme administrator

27. The Board shall not approve a personal pension scheme unless they re satisfied that there is a person resident in the United Kingdom who ill be responsible for the management of the scheme.

ENERAL NOTE

There must be at least one U.K. resident responsible for the administration of a scheme.

ransfer payments

28.—(1) The Board shall not approve a personal pension scheme unless makes such provision for the making, acceptance and application of ransfer payments as satisfies any requirements imposed by or under egulations made by the Board.

(2) Regulations under this section shall be made by statutory instrument, /hich shall be subject to annulment in pursuance of a resolution of the louse of Commons.

GENERAL NOTE

This is to enable an employee upon a change of employment to transfer his or her pension enefits from one scheme to another.

It will be necessary to have regulations to cover transfers from an approved occupational cheme to a new personal pension scheme.

Excess contributions

29.—(1) The Board shall not approve a personal pension scheme unless makes provision, in relation to arrangements made in accordance with he scheme, for ensuring that—

(a) the aggregate amount of the contributions that may be made in a year of assessment by the member and an employer of his under the arrangements, together with the aggregate amounts of such contributions under other approved personal pension arrangements made by the member, does not exceed the permitted maximum for that year, and

(b) any excess is repaid to the member to the extent of his contributions and otherwise to his employer.

(2) In subsection (1) above "the permitted maximum" for a year of ssessment means an amount equal to the aggregate of—

(a) the relevant percentage of the member's net relevant earnings for the year, and

(b) so much of any relief given under section 31 below for that year as is given by virtue of section 34;

nd references in subsection (1) to contributions by the member do not nclude references to contributions treated by virtue of section 42(3) below s paid by him.

(3) In subsection (2) above "the relevant percentage" means 17·5 per cent. or, in a case where section 32(2) below applies, the relevant ercentage there specified.

GENERAL NOTE

It is necessary for a scheme to make provision for monitoring contributions from members vith a view to ensuring that any contributions do no exceed the maximum allowed in any rear of assessment and in so far as they do repaying such excess.

The maximum amount permitted is 17·5 per cent. of a member's net relevant earning (see ss.35 and 37) save for members over 50 (see s.32(2)).

Restriction on contributors

30.—(1) The Board shall not approve a personal pension scheme which permits the acceptance of contributions other than—

(a) contributions by members;

(b) contributions by employers of members;

(c) minimum contributions paid by the Secretary of State under Part I of the Social Security Act 1986 or by the Department of Health and Social Services for Northern Ireland under Part II of the Social Security (Northern Ireland) Order 1986.

(2) The Board shall not approve a personal pension scheme which permits the acceptance of minimum contributions paid as mentioned in subsection (1)(c) above in respect of an individual's service—

(a) as director of a company, if his emoluments as such are within section 35(5) below; or

(b) in an office or employment to which section 36 below applies.

GENERAL NOTE

Contributions to a scheme can only be made by the member, the member's employer and the Department of Health and Social Security (subject to the restrictions in subs. (2)).

Tax consequences of approval: member's contributions

Deduction from relevant earnings

31. A contribution paid by an individual under approved personal pension arrangements made by him shall, subject to the provisions of this Chapter, be deducted from or set off against any relevant earnings of his for the year of assessment in which the payment is made.

GENERAL NOTE

The tax benefit for a member making a contribution to an approved scheme is that it is deducted from the member's relevant earnings in the year of assessment in which the payment is made (subject to the right to carry back (s.33) or forward (s.34)) thereby reducing the member's taxable income.

It is subject to the restrictions contained in s.32 below.

Limit on deductions

32.—(1) The maximum amount that may be deducted or set off in any year of assessment by virtue of section 31 above shall be 17·5 per cent. of the individual's net relevant earnings for that year.

(2) In the case of an individual whose age at the beginning of the year of assessment is within a range specified in the first column of the following table, subsection (1) above shall have effect with the substitution for 17·5 per cent. of the relevant percentage specified in the second column.

51 to 55	20 per cent.
56 to 60	22·5 per cent.
61 or more	27·5 per cent.

(3) Without prejudice to subsection (1) above, the maximum amount that may be deducted or set off in any year of assessment in respect of contributions paid by an individual to secure benefits satisfying the conditions in section 25 above shall be 5 per cent. of the individual's net relevant earnings for that year.

(4) Where personal pension arrangements are made by an employee whose employer makes contributions under the arrangements, the maximum amount that may be deducted or set off in any year of assessment

hall be reduced by the amount of the employer's contributions in the ear.

(5) Any minimum contributions treated by virtue of section 42(3) below s paid by the individual in respect of whom they are paid shall be isregarded for the purposes of this section.

GENERAL NOTE
    This section imposes certain upper limits on the amount of the contributions which can be educted. This upper limit is increased as specified in subs. (2) in respect of members nearer ɔ retirement.
    Any contributions by an employer will be taken into account when determining whether he limit has been used up but not the contracting-out rebate payable by the Department of Iealth and Social Security.
    There is a separate 5 per cent. limit in respect of contributions securing the payment of lump sum in the event of the member's death.

Carry-back of contributions

33.—(1) An individual who pays a contribution under approved personal ɔension arrangements in a year of assessment (whether or not a year for vhich he has relevant earnings) may elect that the contribution, or part ɔf it, shall be treated as paid—

(a) in the year of assessment preceding that year, or
(b) if he had no net relevant earnings in that preceding year of assessment, in the year of assessment before that.

(2) Where for any year of assessment an individual—

(a) has relevant earnings as an underwriting member of Lloyd's or by way of commission calculated by reference to the profits of Lloyd's underwriting business, and
(b) there is an amount of unused relief attributable to those earnings,

the individual may elect that there shall be treated as paid in that year so much of any contributions paid by him under approved personal pension arrangements in the next year of assessment but two as does not exceed the amount of the unused relief.

(3) In subsection (2) above, references to an amount of unused relief attributable to the earnings mentioned in subsection (2)(a) are to an amount which could have been deducted from or set off against those earnings under section 31 above if—

(a) the individual had paid contributions under approved personal pension arrangements in the year of assessment for which he has the earnings, or
(b) any such contributions paid by him in that year had been greater.

(4) An election under this section must be made not later than three months after the end of the year of assessment in which the contributions treated as paid in another year are actually paid.

(5) Where an election is made under this section in respect of a contribution or part of a contribution, the other provisions of this Chapter shall have effect as if the contribution or part had been paid in the year specified in the election and not in the year in which it was actually paid.

GENERAL NOTE
    A member may elect to carry back his contributions to an approved scheme to the preceding year of assessment, or if the member has no net relevant earnings in that year of assessment then to the year of assessment before that.
    This right must be exercised not later than three months after the end of the year of assessment in which the contributions are paid.
    There are special rules in subs. (2) if the member has earnings as a Lloyd's underwriter or receives commissions based on the profits of a Lloyd's underwriting business.

Carry-forward of relief

34.—(1) Where—

    (a) for any year of assessment an individual has relevant earnings from any trade, profession, vocation, office or employment carried on or held by him, and

    (b) there is an amount of unused relief for that year,

relief may be given under section 31 above, up to the amount of the unused relief, in respect of so much of any contributions paid by him under approved personal pension arrangements in any of the next six years of assessment as exceeds the maximum applying for that year under section 32 above.

(2) In this section, references to an amount of unused relief for any year are to an amount which could have been deducted from or set off against the individual's relevant earnings for that year under section 31 above if—

    (a) the individual had paid contributions under approved personal pension arrangements in that year, or

    (b) any such contributions paid by him in that year had been greater.

(3) Relief by virtue of this section shall be given for an earlier year rather than a later year, the unused relief taken into account in giving relief for any year being deducted from that available for giving relief in subsequent years and unused relief derived from an earlier year being exhausted before unused relief derived from a later year.

(4) Where a relevant assessment to tax in respect of a year of assessment becomes final and conclusive more than six years after the end of that year and there is an amount of unused relief for that year which results from the making of the assessment—

    (a) that amount shall not be available for giving relief by virtue of this section for any of the six years following that year; but

    (b) the individual may, within the period of six months beginning with the date on which the assessment becomes final and conclusive, elect that relief shall be given under section 31 above, up to that amount, in respect of so much of any contributions paid by him under approved personal pension arrangements within that period as exceeds the maximum applying under section 32 above for the year of assessment in which they are paid;

and to the extent to which relief in respect of any contributions is given by virtue of this subsection it shall not be given by virtue of subsection (1) above.

(5) In this section "a relevant assessment to tax" means an assessment on the individual's relevant earnings or on the profits or gains of a partnership from which the individual derives relevant earnings.

GENERAL NOTE

If a member does not utilise the full amount of relief available under s.32 in any year of assessment then so much as is not used may be carried forward to be used in respect of contributions made in any of the next six years of assessment in so far as those contributions exceed the maximum relief available in that year of assessment.

Any relief carried forward in this manner should be used as soon as is possible.

Meaning of "relevant earnings"

35.—(1) In this Chapter, "relevant earnings", in relation to an individual, means any income of his which is chargeable to tax for the year of assessment in question and is within subsection (2) below.

(2) Subject to subsections (3) to (5) below, income is within this subsection if it is—

    (a) emoluments chargeable under Schedule E from an office or employment held by the individual;

(b) income from any property which is attached to or forms part of the emoluments of an office or employment held by him;

(c) income which is chargeable under Schedule D and is immediately derived by him from the carrying on or exercise by him of his trade, profession or vocation (either as an individual or as a partner acting personally in a partnership);

(d) income treated as earned income by virtue of section 383 of the Taxes Act (patent rights).

(3) Where section 36 below applies to an office or employment held by the individual, neither emoluments from the office or employment nor income from any property which is attached to it or forms part of its emoluments are within subsection (2) above.

(4) The following are not income within subsection (2) above—

(a) anything in respect of which tax is chargeable under Schedule E and which arises from the acquisition or disposal of shares or an interest in shares or from a right to acquire shares;

(b) anything in respect of which tax is chargeable by virtue of section 187 of the Taxes Act (payments on termination of employment, etc.).

(5) Emoluments of an individual as director of a company are not income within subsection (2) above if—

(a) the income of the company consists wholly or mainly of investment income, and

(b) the individual, either alone or together with any other persons who are or have been at any time directors of the company, controls the company.

(6) For the purposes of subsection (5) above—

"director" includes any person occupying the position of director by whatever name called;

"investment income" shall be construed in accordance with paragraph 11 of Schedule 16 to the Finance Act 1972;

"controls" shall be construed in accordance with section 534 of the Taxes Act.

(7) For the purposes of this Chapter, a married woman's relevant earnings shall not be treated as her husband's relevant earnings, notwithstanding that her income chargeable to tax is treated as his income.

GENERAL NOTE

This section defines an individual's relevant earnings and then s.37 determines what his or her "net relevant earnings" are.

Subs. (2) specifies what income comes within this term—it does not include income derived from land or woodlands.

Subs. (4) excludes from the definition certain types of income. Any profits from shares or rights relating to shares which are chargeable under Schedule E are excluded—this will include income chargeable under s.186 I.C.T.A. 1970 (share options); ss.77 and 79 F.A. 1972 (share incentive schemes); s.67 F.A. 1976 (employee shareholdings); s.55 F.A. 1978 (approved share option schemes). Income from the commercial letting of furnished holiday accommodation is included (see Sched. 2, para. 6).

In addition the fees of a director are excluded if the individual (whether alone or with others) control the company and its income is mainly investment income.

For the purposes of the application of these provisions spouses are treated as separate individuals and the wife's relevant earnings are not treated as her husband's.

Earnings from pensionable employment

36.—(1) This section applies to an office or employment held by an individual if—

(a) service in it is service to which a relevant superannuation scheme relates,

(b) the individual is a participant in the scheme, and

(c) neither subsection (4) nor subsection (5) below applies to h participation in the scheme.

(2) This section applies whether or not the duties of the office c employment are performed wholly or partly in the United Kingdom c the individual is chargeable to tax in respect of it.

(3) In subsection (1) above "a relevant superannuation scheme" mear a scheme or arrangement—

(a) the object or one of the objects of which is the provision, in respec of persons serving in particular offices or employments, of relevar benefits within the meaning of section 26(1) of the Finance Ac 1970, and

(b) which is established by a person other than the individual.

(4) This subsection applies to an individual's participation in a schem if the scheme provides no benefits in relation to him other than—

(a) an annuity payable to his surviving spouse or a dependant of his;

(b) a lump sum payable on his death in service.

(5) This subsection applies to an individual's participation in a schem if any sums paid pursuant to the scheme with a view to the provision c relevant benefits for him are treated as his income for the purposes of th Income Tax Acts.

GENERAL NOTE

Any income from pensionable employment is excluded from the computation of relevar earnings (s.35(3)). This section provides what is pensionable employment for these purposes

A scheme which only provides the benefits specified in subs. (4) will not cause a membe to be treated as in pensionable employment (subs. (4)). Similarly if a member is taxable o contributions to a scheme he or she will not be treated as in pensionable employment (subs (5)).

Meaning of "net relevant earnings"

37.—(1) Subject to subsections (3) to (7) below, in this Chapter "ne relevant earnings", in relation to an individual, means the amount of hi: relevant earnings for the year of assessment in question, less the amoun of any deductions within subsection (2) below which fall to be made fron the relevant earnings in computing for the purposes of income tax hi total income for that year.

(2) Deductions are within this subsection if they are—

(a) deductions which but for section 130(1), (n) or (o) of the Taxe: Act (annuities, royalties, rents etc.) could be made in comput ing the profits or gains of the individual;

(b) deductions made by virtue of section 189, section 192 or sectior 194(3) of the Taxes Act (necessary expenses etc.);

(c) deductions in respect of relief under Schedule 9 or 10 to the Finance Act 1981 (stock relief);

(d) deductions in respect of losses or capital allowances, being losses or capital allowances arising from activities profits o: gains of which would be included in computing relevant earn ings of the individual or the individual's wife or husband.

(3) For the purposes of this section, an individual's relevant earning: shall be taken to be those earnings before giving effect to any capital allowances, other than deductions allowable in computing profits or gains but after taking into account the amounts on which charges fall to be made under the Capital Allowances Act 1968 (including the enactments which under the Taxes Act are to be treated as contained in Part I of the Capital Allowances Act 1968); and in subsections (4) and (5) below references to income (other than references to total income) shall be construed similarly.

(4) In the case of an individual's partnership profits, the amount to be included in arriving at his net relevant earnings shall be his share of the partnership income (estimated in accordance with the Income Tax Acts) after making from it any such deductions in respect of—

(a) payments made by the partnership,

(b) relief given to the partnership under Schedule 9 or 10 to the Finance Act 1981, and

(c) capital allowances falling to be made to the partnership,

as would be made in computing the tax payable in respect of that income.

(5) Where, in a year of assessment for which an amount is deducted or set off under section 31 above against the net relevant earnings of an individual,—

(a) a deduction in respect of such a loss or allowance of the individual as is mentioned in subsection (2)(d) above falls to be made in computing the total income of the individual or the individual's wife or husband, and

(b) the deduction or part of it falls to be so made from income other than relevant earnings,

the amount of the deduction made from that other income shall be treated as reducing the individual's net relevant earnings for subsequent years of assessment in accordance with subsection (6) below.

(6) The deduction shall be made so far as possible from the individual's net relevant earnings for the first of the subsequent years of assessment (whether or not he is entitled to relief under section 31 above for that year), and then, so far as it cannot be so made, from those of the next year, and so on.

(7) An individual's net relevant earnings for any year of assessment shall be computed without regard to any deduction or set-off under section 31 above which falls to be made for that year in respect of the individual or the individual's wife or husband.

GENERAL NOTE

S.35 defined an individual's relevant earnings. There is then deducted from this the items specified in subs. (2) to arrive at the individual's net relevant earnings. It is this figure which is then used to calculate the amount of relief available for the individual (see s.32).

Other tax consequences of approval

Employer's contributions

38. Where contributions are paid by an employer under approved personal pension arrangements made by his employee, those contributions shall not be regarded as emoluments of the employment chargeable to tax under Schedule E.

GENERAL NOTE

Any contributions by an employer to a scheme will not be taxable as emoluments but will reduce the amount of relief available to the employee (s.32(4)).

Exemption for scheme investments

39.—(1) Income derived by a person from investments or deposits held by him for the purposes of an approved personal pension scheme shall be exempt from income tax.

(2) A gain accruing to a person on his disposal of investments held by him for the purposes of an approved personal pension scheme shall not be a chargeable gain for the purposes of capital gains tax.

(3) In section 323(4) of the Taxes Act (which lists the premiums referable to an insurance company's pension business) after paragraph (aa) there shall be inserted—

"(ab) any contract made under approved personal pension arrange
     ments within the meaning of Chapter II of Part I of the financ
     (No. 2) Act 1987";
and nothing in the preceding provisions of this section shall be construe
as affording relief in respect of any sums to be brought into account unde
section 314 of the Taxes Act.

(4) In section 6 of the Finance Act 1975 (investment by pension func
in building societies) at the end of subsection (3) there shall be adde
"and section 39 of the Finance (No. 2) Act 1987".

GENERAL NOTE
   The profits and income arising from the investments subject to the scheme will not t
chargeable to income tax or corporation tax or capital gains tax.
   See also Sched. 2, para. 5 regarding dealings in financial futures and traded options.

Unit trusts

40.—(1) Subsection (2) of section 354 and subsection (3) of sectio
354A of the Taxes Act (which treat unit holders under unit trust scheme
as receiving certain payments) shall not apply to any authorised unit tru:
which is also an approved personal pension scheme.

(2) A gain accruing to a unit holder on his disposal of units in a
authorised unit trust which is also an approved personal pension schem
shall not be a chargeable gain for the purposes of capital gains tax.

GENERAL NOTE
   This provides certain tax advantages if the approved scheme is also an authorised un
trust.

Treatment of annuities

41.—(1) An annuity payable under approved personal pension arrange
ments shall be treated as earned income of the annuitant.

(2) Subsection (1) above applies only in relation to the annuitant t
whom the annuity is made payable by the terms of the arrangements.

(3) In section 230 of the Taxes Act (which gives special treatment t
purchased life annuities) at the end of subsection (7) (exclusions) ther
shall be added—
     ", or
   (e) to any annuity payable under approved personal pension arrange
       ments within the meaning of Chapter II of Part I of the Financ
       (No. 2) Act 1987.".

GENERAL NOTE
   Any annuity paid under an approved scheme shall be taxable as earned income and wi
not be within the special provisions relating to purchased life annuities.

Miscellaneous

Minimum contributions under Social Security Act 1986

42.—(1) Where under Part I of the Social Security Act 1986 th
Secretary of State pays minimum contributions for the purposes o
approved personal pension arrangements, the amount of the employee'
share of those contributions shall, instead of being the amount provide
for in that part, be the grossed-up equivalent of the amount so provide
for.

(2) For the purposes of this section—
     "the employee's share" of minimum contributions is so much of th
        contributions as is attributable to the percentage mentioned i

paragraph (a) of the definition of "rebate percentage" in section 3(3) of the Social Security Act 1986;
"the grossed-up equivalent" of an amount is such sum as, after deduction of income tax at the basic rate in force for the year of assessment for which the contributions are paid, is equal to that amount.

(3) The employee's share of minimum contributions paid for a year of assessment by the Secretary of State for the purposes of approved personal pension arrangements shall be treated for the purposes of income tax—

(a) as income for that year of the individual in respect of whom it is paid, and

(b) as contributions paid in that year by that individual under those arrangements.

(4) The Board may make regulations—

(a) providing for the recovery by the Secretary of State from the Board, in such circumstances as may be prescribed by the regulations, of any increase attributable to this section in the sums paid by the Secretary of State out of the National Insurance Fund;

(b) requiring the Secretary of State to give the Board such information as may be so prescribed about minimum contributions paid by the Secretary of State;

(c) prescribing circumstances in which this section or any provision of it shall not apply;

(d) making such provision as appears to the Board to be necessary or expedient for the purposes of supplementing the provisions of this section.

(5) Any payment received by the Secretary of State by virtue of this section shall be paid into the National Insurance Fund.

(6) Regulations under this section shall be made by statutory instrument, which shall be subject to annulment in pursuance of a resolution of the House of Commons.

(7) In relation to Northern Ireland, this section shall have effect as if—

(a) references to the Secretary of State were references to the Department of Health and Social Services for Northern Ireland;

(b) references to Part I and section 3(3) of the Social Security Act 1986 were references to Part II and Article 5(3) of the Social Security (Northern Ireland) Order 1986; and

(c) references to the National Insurance Fund were references to the Northern Ireland National Insurance Fund.

General Note
Under s.1 of the Social Security Act 1986 a minimum contribution may be paid to an approved scheme of which an employed earner is a member for any period that that person is over 16 and, if a married woman or widow, has not chosen to pay the reduced rate of national insurance contribution.
This will be treated as part of the individual's income and as a contribution made by that individual save that they will be disregarded for the purposes of imposing the limits contained in s.32 (subs. (5) thereof and s.29(2)).

Withdrawal of approval

43.—(1) If in the opinion of the Board the facts concerning an approved personal pension scheme or its administration or arrangements made in accordance with it do not warrant the continuance of their approval of the scheme, they may at any time by written notice given to the scheme administrator withdraw their approval of the scheme.

(2) If in the opinion of the Board the facts concerning any approved personal pension arrangements do not warrant the continuance of their

approval in relation to the arrangements, they may at any time by written notice given to the individual who made them and to the scheme administrator withdraw their approval in relation to the arrangements.

(3) Without prejudice to the generality of subsection (2) above, the Board may withdraw their approval in relation to any personal pension arrangements if they are of the opinion that securing the provision of benefits under the arrangements was not the sole purpose of the individual in making them.

(4) A notice under subsection (1) or subsection (2) above shall state the grounds on which, and the date from which, approval is withdrawn.

(5) The Board may not withdraw their approval from a date earlier than the date when the facts were first such that they did not warrant the continuance of their approval (so, however, that in a case within subsection (3) above their approval may be withdrawn from the day the arrangements in question were made).

GENERAL NOTE

The Board may withdraw its approval in respect of either a scheme or an individual's pension arrangements. However, reasons must be given.

Such withdrawal can be retrospective if it is considered that the securing of the provision of pension benefits was not the sole purpose in making the arrangements. In such a case the withdrawal can be back to the date when the arrangements are made. Otherwise it can be back to the date when the facts first occurred giving cause for approval to be withdrawn. There is a right of appeal against the withdrawal of relief (s.47).

Tax on unauthorised payments etc.

44.—(1) This section applies to any payment within subsection (2) below which is made—

  (a) out of funds which are or have been held for the purposes of a personal pension scheme which is or has at any time been approved, and

  (b) to or for the benefit of an individual who has made personal pension arrangements in accordance with the scheme.

(2) A payment is within this subsection if—

  (a) it is not expressly authorised by the rules of the scheme, or

  (b) it is made at a time when the scheme or the arrangements are not approved and it would not have been expressly authorised by the rules of the scheme or by the arrangements when the scheme or, as the case may be, the arrangements were last so approved.

(3) The individual referred to in subsection (1)(b) above, whether or not he is the recipient of the payment, shall be chargeable to tax under Schedule E on the amount of the payment for the year of assessment in which the payment is made.

(4) This section applies to a transfer of assets or other transfer of money's worth as it applies to a payment, and in relation to such a transfer the reference in subsection (3) above to the amount of the payment shall be read as a reference to the value of the transfer.

GENERAL NOTE

Any unauthorised dealings with assets of an approved scheme to or for the benefit of the individual who made the pension arrangements will be chargeable to income tax under Schedule E. The individual does not have to be the recipient of the asset but he or she must benefit from the transaction.

Relief by deduction from contributions

45.—(1) In such cases and subject to such conditions as the Board may prescribe in regulations, relief under section 31 above shall be given in accordance with subsections (2) and (3) below.

(2) An individual who is entitled to such relief in respect of a contribution may deduct from the contribution when he pays it, and may retain, an amount equal to income tax at the basic rate on the contribution.

(3) The scheme administrator—

    (a) shall accept the amount paid after the deduction in discharge of the individual's liability to the same extent as if the deduction had not been made, and

    (b) may recover an amount equal to the deduction from the Board.

(4) Regulations under this section may make provision for carrying subsections (2) and (3) above into effect and, without prejudice to the generality of that, may—

    (a) provide for the manner in which claims for the recovery of a sum under subsection (3)(b) may be made;

    (b) provide for the giving of such information, in such form, as may be prescribed by or under the regulations;

    (c) provide for the inspection by persons authorised by the Board of books, documents and other records.

(5) Regulations under this section shall be made by statutory instrument, which shall be subject to annulment in pursuance of a resolution of the House of Commons.

GENERAL NOTE

Regulations will be needed to bring this section into operation and when they are passed it is likely that they will cover only employees.

Relief on contributions may be obtained by deducting from the contribution an amount equal to basic rate tax which the scheme administrator will then recover from the Revenue. This will be a similar procedure to that already operating in respect of interest relief on home loans.

Claims for relief

46. Except where section 45 above applies, relief under section 31 above in respect of a contribution shall be given only on a claim made for the purpose.

GENERAL NOTE

Unless and until s.45 is brought into operation it will be necessary to make a claim for relief under s.31 before the benefit of the relief will be available.

Appeals

47.—(1) Where the Board—

    (a) refuse an application by notice under section 19 above, or

    (b) withdraw an approval by notice under section 43 above,

the person to whom the notice is given may appeal to the Special Commissioners against the refusal or, as the case may be, the withdrawal.

(2) An appeal under this section shall be made by written notice stating the grounds for the appeal and given to the Board before the end of the period of thirty days beginning with the day on which the notice of refusal or withdrawal was given to the appellant.

(3) On an appeal under this section against the withdrawal of an approval, the Special Commissioners may, instead of allowing or dismissing the appeal, order that the withdrawal shall have effect from a date other than that determined by the Board.

(4) The bringing of an appeal under this section shall not affect the validity of the decision appealed against pending the determination of the proceedings.

GENERAL NOTE

There is a right of appeal if

    (i) the Board refuses to approve a scheme; and

(ii) the Board withdraws approval.

The Special Commissioners may change the decision of the Board or in the case of a withdrawal of approval substitute a different date when it should take effect.

Adjustment of relief

48. Where relief under section 31 above for any year of assessment is claimed and allowed (whether or not it then falls to be given for that year), and afterwards an assessment, alteration of an assessment, or other adjustment of the claimant's liability to tax is made, there shall also be made such consequential adjustments in the relief allowed or given under section 31 for that or any subsequent year as are appropriate.

GENERAL NOTE

In the event that an individual's tax liability for any year of assessment is altered then consequential amendments will be made in respect of the relief allowed for any contributions to an approved personal pension scheme.

Exclusion of double relief

49.—(1) Where relief under section 31 above is claimed and allowed for any year of assessment in respect of a contribution, relief shall not be given in respect of it under any other provision of the Income Tax Acts for the same or any subsequent year, nor (in the case of a contribution under an annuity contract) in respect of any other premium or consideration for an annuity under the same contract.

(2) References in the Income Tax Acts to relief in respect of life assurance premiums shall not be taken to include relief under section 31 above.

GENERAL NOTE

This prevents any contribution to a personal pension scheme giving rise to a double tax advantage.

Information about payments

50.—(1) An inspector may give notice to a scheme administrator requiring him to provide the inspector with—

    (a) such particulars as the notice may require relating to contributions paid under approved personal pension arrangements made in accordance with the scheme;

    (b) such particulars as the notice may require relating to payments by way of return of contributions;

    (c) copies of such accounts as the notice may require.

(2) A person to whom a notice is given under this section shall comply with the notice within the period of thirty days beginning with the day on which it is given.

Information: penalties

51.—(1) A person who knowingly makes a false statement or false representation on making an application under section 19 above or for the purpose of obtaining for himself or any other person any relief from or repayment of tax under this Chapter shall be liable to a penalty not exceeding £500.

(2) At the end of the first column in the Table in section 98 of the Taxes Management Act 1970 (penalties for failure to furnish information etc.) there shall be added—

    "Regulations under section 45 of the Finance (No. 2) Act 1987
    Section 50 of that Act."

(3) At the end of the second column of that Table there shall be added—
"Regulations under section 45 of the Finance (No.2) Act 1987".

Remuneration of Ministers and other officers

52.—(1) This section applies to any salary—
    (a) payable to the holder of a qualifying office who is also a Member of the House of Commons, and
    (b) payable for a period in respect of which the holder is not a participant in relation to that office in arrangements contained in the Parliamentary pension scheme but is a participant in relation to his membership of the House of Commons in any such arrangements, or for any part of such a period.

(2) So much of any salary to which this section applies as is equal to the difference between a Member's pensionable salary and the salary which (in accordance with any such resolution as is mentioned in subsection (4)(a) below) is payable to him as a Member holding that qualifying office, shall be treated for the purposes of this Chapter as remuneration from the office of Member and not from the qualifying office.

(3) In this section—
    "Member's pensionable salary" means a Member's ordinary salary under any resolution of the House of Commons which, being framed otherwise than as an expression of opinion, is for the time being in force relating to the remuneration of Members or, if the resolution provides for a Member's ordinary salary thereunder to be treated for pension purposes as being at a higher rate, a notional yearly salary at that higher rate;
    "qualifying office" means an office mentioned in paragraph (b), (c) or (d) of subsection (2) of section 2 of the Parliamentary and other Pensions Act 1987;
    "the Parliamentary pension scheme" has the same meaning as in that Act;
and, without prejudice to the power conferred by virtue of paragraph 13 of Schedule 1 to that Act, regulations under section 2 of that Act may make provision specifying the circumstances in which a person is to be regarded for the purposes of this section as being or not being a participant in relation to his membership of the House of Commons, or in relation to any office, in arrangements contained in the Parliamentary pension scheme.

(4) In subsection (3) above "a Member's ordinary salary", in relation to any resolution of the House of Commons, means—
    (a) if the resolution provides for salary to be paid to Members at different rates according to whether or not they are holders of particular offices, or are in receipt of salaries or pensions as the holders or former holders of particular offices, a Member's yearly salary at the higher or highest rate; and
    (b) in any other case, a Member's yearly salary at the rate specified in or determined under the resolution.

GENERAL NOTE
    The salaries of government ministers and other M.P.s who are not members of the Parliamentary pension scheme are not to be treated as income arising from a pensionable employment for the purposes of this legislation.

Contributions under unapproved arrangements

53. Where contributions are paid by an employer under personal pension arrangements made by his employee then, if those arrangements are not approved arrangements and the contributions are not otherwise chargeable to income tax as income of the employee, the contributions shall be regarded for all the purposes of the Income Tax Acts as emoluments of the employment chargeable to tax under Schedule E.

GENERAL NOTE
This ensures that contributions made by an employer to an unapproved pension scheme will be taxable as emoluments under Schedule E.

Retirement annuities

54.—(1) Nothing in Chapter III of Part IX of the Taxes Act shall apply in relation to—

(a) a contract made or trust scheme established on or after 4th January 1988, or

(b) a person by whom contributions are first paid on or after that date under a trust scheme established before that date.

(2) For the year 1987–88 and subsequent years of assessment the Taxes Act shall have effect with the substitution of the following section for section 228—

"Amount of relief for persons over fifty

228. In the case of an individual whose age at the beginning of a year of assessment is within a range specified in the first column of the following table, section 227(1A) above shall have effect for that year with the substitution for 17·5 per cent. of the relevant percentage specified in the second column.

51 to 55	20 per cent.
56 to 60	22·5 per cent.
61 or more	27·5 per cent.".

(3) Subject to subsection (5) below, the terms of a contract made, or the rules of a trust scheme established, on or after 17th March 1987 and before 4th January 1988 and approved by the Board under section 226 of the Taxes Act shall have effect (notwithstanding anything in them to the contrary) as if they did not allow the payment to the individual by whom the contract is made, or an individual paying contributions under the scheme, of a lump sum exceeding £150,000 or such other sum as may for the time being be specified in an order under section 23(4) above.

(4) Subject to subsection (6) below, the rules of a trust scheme established before 17th March 1987 and approved by the Board under section 226 of the Taxes Act shall have effect (notwithstanding anything in them to the contrary) as if they did not allow the payment to any person first paying contributions under the scheme on or after 17th March 1987 of a lump sum such as is mentioned in subsection (3) above.

(5) Subsection (3) above shall not apply—

(a) to a contract if, before the end of January 1988, the persons by and to whom premiums are payable under it jointly give written notice to the Board that subsection (3) is not to apply, or

(b) to a scheme if, before the end of January 1988, the trustees or other persons having the management of the scheme give written notice to the Board that subsection (3) is not to apply;

and where notice is given to the Board under this subsection, the contract or scheme shall, with effect from the date with effect from which it was approved, cease to be approved.

(6) Subsection (4) above shall not apply in the case of any person paying contributions under a scheme if, before the end of January 1988, he and the trustees or other persons having the management of the scheme jointly give written notice to the Board that subsection (4) is not

to apply; and where notice is given to the Board under this subsection, the scheme shall cease to be approved in relation to the contributor with effect from the date on which he first paid a contribution under it or (if later) the date with effect from which it was approved.

GENERAL NOTE

Subs. (1) is to deal with the change over from the rules contained in ss.226 to 229 I.C.T.A. 1970 to these rules. The old rules will not apply to contracts or schemes made or established after January 3, 1988 or to contributions first paid by or on behalf of an individual after that date.

Subs. (2) changes the calculation of the relief available to persons over the age of 50 as presently contained in section 228 I.C.T.A. 1970.

Subs. (3) to (6) introduce the new ceiling on lump sum payments of £150,000 for retirement benefit schemes. With existing contracts and schemes there is an option to continue without such a restriction but in that event the contract or scheme will lose its approval.

Transitional provisions: general

55.—(1) Where approved personal pension arrangements are made by an individual who pays qualifying premiums within the meaning of section 226(1)(b) of the Taxes Act—

(a) the amount that may be deducted or set off by virtue of section 31 above in any year of assessment shall be reduced by the amount of any qualifying premiums which are paid in the year by the individual and in respect of which relief is given for the year under section 227 of the Taxes Act; and

(b) the relief which, by virtue of section 227A of the Taxes Act, may be given under section 227 by reference to the individual's unused relief for any year shall be reduced by the amount of any contributions paid by him in that year under the approved personal pension arrangements.

(2) Where an individual elects under section 33 above that a contribution or part of a contribution shall be treated as paid in the year of assessment 1984–85, 1985–86 or 1986–87, the payment shall be treated as the payment of a qualifying premium for the purposes of Chapter III of Part IX of the Taxes Act; and in such a case references in section 33 to an amount of unused relief shall be construed in accordance with section 227A of that Act.

(3) The references in section 34 above to unused relief for any year are, for years of assessment before 1987–88, references to unused relief within the meaning of section 227A of the Taxes Act.

GENERAL NOTE

This section provides for the situation where an individual is entitled to relief both in respect of a personal pension scheme and a retirement annuity policy.

The rules are

(i) the amount of any premium payable under such a retirement annuity policy qualifying for relief will reduce the maximum allowable amount of any contributions to a personal pension scheme in that year of assessment;

(ii) any unused relief in respect of premiums paid under a retirement annuity policy which has been carried forward will be reduced by any contributions paid under an approved personal pension scheme.

Any contributions to an approved personal pension policy which are carried back to 1986–87, 1985–86 or 1984–85 are to be treated as qualifying premiums under a retirement annuity policy.

Transitional provisions: approvals

56.—(1) The Board may grant or refuse an application for approval of a personal pension scheme under section 19 above at any time on or after

1st August 1987, but they shall not grant an application so as to approve a scheme with effect from a date earlier than 4th January 1988.

(2) The Board may by regulations make provision for applications for approval of personal pension schemes to be granted provisionally in cases where the applications are made before 1st August 1989, notwithstanding that the Board have not satisfied themselves that the schemes comply with the requirements of sections 20 to 30 above; and such regulations may, in particular, provide—

(a) for the contents and form of certificates or other documents which the Board may require the applicant to give them before they grant an application provisionally;

(b) for the making of such amendments of the rules of the scheme after the provisional grant of an application as are necessary to enable the scheme to comply with the requirements of sections 20 to 30 above, and for those amendments to have effect as from the date of approval of the scheme;

(c) for the withdrawal of approval of the scheme as from that date if it does not comply with the requirements of sections 20 to 30 above and such amendments as are mentioned in paragraph (b) above are not made;

and may make such supplementary provision as appears to the Board to be necessary or expedient.

(3) Regulations under this section shall be made by statutory instrument, which shall be subject to annulment in pursuance of a resolution of the House of Commons.

GENERAL NOTE
After August 1, 1987, the Board may grant approvals but they cannot take effect before January 4, 1988. Provisional approvals can have been given before then but amendments may be required subsequently to the schemes.

Minor and consequential amendments

57. Schedule 2 to this Act (which makes minor and consequential amendments to certain enactments relating to retirement annuities etc.) shall have effect.

CHAPTER III

GENERAL

Pension and share schemes

Occupational pension schemes

58. Schedule 3 to this Act (which makes amendments to enactments relating to occupational pension schemes and amends certain existing schemse) shall have effect.

Employee share schemes

59.—(1) In subsection (2A) of section 47 of the Finance Act 1980 (savings-related share option schemes) and in subsection (6A) of section 38 of the Finance Act 1984 (approved share option schemes), both of which subsections are set out in Part III of Schedule 4 to the Finance Act 1987,—

(a) for the words "exchanged for" there shall be substituted "released in consideration of the grant of"; and

(b) for the word "exchange" there shall be substituted "transaction".

(2) In Schedule 10 to the Finance Act 1980, paragraph 10A (which was inserted by paragraph 1(1) of Schedule 4 to the Finance Act 1987) shall be amended as follows—
(a) in sub-paragraph (1), in the words following paragraph (c), for the words "transfer to the acquiring company" there shall be substituted "release";
(b) in sub-paragraph (3)(b) for the word "exchange" there shall be substituted "release of the old rights"; and
(c) in sub-paragraph (3)(c) for the word "exchange", in the first place where it occurs, there shall be substituted "release" and for the word "exchange", in the second place where it occurs, there shall be substituted "grant";
and the amendment of paragraph 11 of the said Schedule 10 made by paragraph 1(2) of Schedule 4 to the Finance Act 1987 shall be deemed not to have been made.

(3) In Schedule 10 to the Finance Act 1984, paragraph 4A (which was inserted by paragraph 2(1) of Schedule 4 to the Finance Act 1987) shall be amended as follows—
(a) in sub-paragraph (1), in the words following paragraph (c), for the words "transfer to the acquiring company" there shall be substituted "release";
(b) in sub-paragraph (3)(b) for the word "exchange" there shall be substituted "release of the old rights"; and
(c) in sub-paragraph (3)(c) for the word "exchange", in the first place where it occurs, there shall be substituted "release" and for the word "exchange", in the second place where it occurs, there shall be substituted "grant";
and the amendment of paragraph 12 of the said Schedule 10 made by paragraph 2(2) of Schedule 4 to the Finance Act 1987 shall be deemed not to have been made.

GENERAL NOTE

S.33 and Sched. 4 F.A. 1987 amended the rules relating to savings related share option schemes (s.47 and Sched. 10 F.A. 1980) and approved share option schemes (F.A 1984, s.38 and Sched. 10). The amendments permit such rights to be exchanged for similar rights over shares in the acquiring company. This section changes the amendment so that it permits the existing rights to be released in return for the grant of new rights in the shares of an acquiring company.

Companies

Payments of interest etc. between related companies

60.—(1) This section applies where—
(a) the relationship between two companies is as mentioned in subsection (2) below;
(b) one of the companies makes to the other a payment which, for the purposes of corporation tax, is a charge on income of the company making it; and
(c) in the hands of the company receiving it, the payment is chargeable to tax under Case III of Schedule D.

(2) The relationship between two companies which is referred to in subsection (1)(a) above is—
(a) that one company controls the other; or
(b) that another person controls both companies; or
(c) that one company is a 51 per cent. subsidiary of the other; or
(d) that both companies are 51 per cent. subsidiaries of another company;
and section 534 of the Taxes Act (meaning of "control") applies for the purposes of this section.

(3) In a case where this section applies, the payment referred to in subsection (1)(b) above shall be treated for the purposes of corporation tax as received by the company to which it is paid on the same day as that on which it is for those purposes treated as paid by the company paying it.

(4) Subject to subsection (5) below, where the payment referred to in subsection (1)(b) above is a "relevant payment" for the purposes of Schedule 20 to the Finance Act 1972 (collection of income tax on company payments which are not distributions), it shall be treated for the purposes of that Schedule as received on the same day as that on which, by virtue of subsection (3) above, it is treated as received for the purposes of corporation tax; and the reference in paragraph 5(1) of that Schedule to the accounting period in which the payment is received shall be construed accordingly.

(5) Subsection (4) above does not apply if the day on which the payment would be treated as received apart from that subsection falls within the same accounting period (of the receiving company) as the day on which it would be treated as received under that subsection.

(6) This section applies to payments made on or after 17th March 1987.

GENERAL NOTE
Interest can be paid by one company and thus qualify for relief as a charge on income at a different date from the date at which it is received and thus brought into charge to corporation tax in the hands of the payee. This point had been utilised in a number of cases in order for deferral of tax to be obtained by one company in a group paying interest to another before the end of the payer's accounting period with the interest being received after the beginning of the payee's accounting period. This section now precludes such a course being followed where the companies concerned are members of the same group. In such cases the payments are to be treated as paid and received on the same day.

It should be noted that the section is not limited to interest but extends to other payments taxable under Case III of Schedule D.

Apportionment of income etc. of close companies

61.—(1) The provisions of this section have effect for the purpose of, and in connection with, converting into obligations certain powers conferred on inspectors by Schedule 16 to the Finance Act 1972 (apportionment of income etc. of close companies).

(2) In the heading to Part I of Schedule 16, the words "Powers of" shall be omitted.

(3) In sub-paragraphs (1) to (4) of paragraph 1 of Schedule 16 (apportionment of excess of company's relevant income over its distributions) for the word "may" there shall be substituted "shall", and, accordingly, in the heading to that paragraph for the words "Power to apportion" there shall be substituted "Apportionment of".

(4) In paragraphs 3(1) and 3A(1) of Schedule 16 (apportionment of amounts deducted in respect of annual payments and of interest) for the word "may" there shall be substituted "shall" and, accordingly, for the heading preceding paragraph 3 there shall be substituted "Apportionment of amounts deducted in respect of annual payments of interest".

(5) In paragraph 17 of Schedule 16 (revision of apportionment) in sub-paragraphs (1) and (2) for the words "may serve on the company" there shall be substituted "shall serve on the company".

(6) In sub-paragraph (1) of paragraph 20 (power of Board to exercise powers of the inspector) and in the heading to that paragraph for the word "powers" there shall be substituted "functions".

(7) This section has effect with respect to accounting periods beginning on or after 17th March 1987.

As a result of the decision in *R.* v. *H.M. Inspector of Taxes, ex p. Lansing Bagnall* [1986] S.T.C. 453 it appeared that the provisions of F.A. 1972, Sched. 16, created no general obligation on the Revenue to apportion income or annual payments, etc., but merely a power to do so which the Revenue was obliged to exercise properly. This section substitutes general obligations to apportion income, etc., in place of mere powers.

Provisions having an overseas element

United Kingdom members of partnerships controlled abroad

62.—(1) At the end of section 153 of the Taxes Act (partnerships controlled abroad) there shall be added the following subsections—
"(4) In any case where—
    (a) a person resident in the United Kingdom (in this subsection and subsection (5) below referred to as "the resident partner") is a member of a partnership which resides or is deemed to reside outside the United Kingdom, and
    (b) by virtue of any arrangements falling within section 497 of this Act (double taxation relief) any of the income or capital gains of the partnership is relieved from tax in the United Kingdom,
the arrangements referred to in paragraph (b) above shall not affect any liability to tax in respect of the resident partner's share of any income or capital gains of the partnership.
(5) If, in a case where subsection (4) above applies, the resident partner's share of the income of the partnership consists of or includes a share in a qualifying distribution, within the meaning of Part V of the Finance Act 1972, made by a company resident in the United Kingdom, then, notwithstanding anything in the arrangements, the resident partner (and not the partnership as a whole) shall be regarded as entitled to that share of the tax credit in respect of the distribution which corresponds to his share of the distribution."
(2) Nothing in subsection (1) above affects—
    (a) the determination of any Commissioners or the judgment of any court made or given before 17th March 1987, or
    (b) the law to be applied in proceedings on appeal to the Court of Appeal or the House of Lords where the judgment of the High Court or the Court of Session which is in issue was given before that date,
but, subject to that, the amendment made by subsection (1) above shall be deemed always to have been made.

This section is designed to reverse the decision in *Padmore* v. *I.R.C.* [1987] S.T.C. 36 in which a U.K. resident partner in a foreign partnership was held to be protected from charge to United Kingdom tax by a double tax treaty. Of particular note is that the section is of retrospective effect, subject to the exceptions referred to in subs. (2).

Limitation of group relief in relation to certain dual resident companies

63.—(1) Notwithstanding anything in the enactments relating to group relief, no loss or other amount shall be available for set off by way of group relief in accordance with section 259 of the Taxes Act if, in the material accounting period of the company which would otherwise be the surrendering company, that company is for the purposes of this section a dual resident investing company.
(2) In this section "the material accounting period" means, according to the kind of group relief which would be appropriate, the accounting period—

    (a) in which the loss is incurred; or

    (b) for which the capital allowances fall to be made; or

    (c) for which the expenses of management are disbursed; or

    (d) for which the amount is paid by way of charges on income;

but subsection (1) above does not have effect unless the material accounting period is an accounting period which begins on or after 1st April 1987.

    (3) In Schedule 4 to this Act,—

        (a) Part I has effect where an accounting period of a company in which it is a dual resident investing company begins before and ends on or after 1st April 1987 and references in subsections (1) and (2) above to the material accounting period shall be construed accordingly; and

        (b) Part II has effect with respect to the time at which certain interest and other payments are to be treated as paid.

    (4) A company is for the purposes of this section a dual resident company in any accounting period in which—

    (a) it is resident in the United Kingdom; and

    (b) it is also within a charge to tax under the laws of a territory outside the United Kingdom,—

        (i) because it derives its status as a company from those laws; or

        (ii) because its place of management is in that territory; or

      (iii) because, under those laws, it is for any other reason regarded as resident in that territory for the purposes of that charge.

    (5) In any accounting period throughout which it is not a trading company, a dual resident company is for the purposes of this section an investing company.

    (6) In any accounting period of a dual resident company in which it is a trading company, the company is nevertheless for the purposes of this section an investing company if—

    (a) in that period it carries on a trade of such a description that its main function or one of its main functions consists of all or any of the following, namely,—

        (i) acquiring and holding, directly or indirectly, shares, securities or investments of any other description, including interests in companies (resident outside, as well as in, the United Kingdom) with which the dual resident company is connected, within the terms of section 533 of the Taxes Act;

        (ii) making payments which, by virtue of any enactment, are charges on income for the purposes of corporation tax;

       (iii) making payments (of interest or other sums) which are similar to those referred to in sub-paragraph (ii) above but which are deductible in computing the profits of the company for the purposes of corporation tax;

       (iv) obtaining funds (by borrowing or in any other manner whatsover) for the purpose of, or otherwise in connection with, any of the activities referred to in sub-paragraphs (i) to (iii) above; or

    (b) it does not fall within paragraph (a) above, but in that accounting period it carries on all or any of the activities referred to in sub-paragraphs (i) to (iv) of that paragraph and does so—

        (i) to an extent which does not appear to be justified by any trade which it does carry on; or

        (ii) for a purpose which does not appear to be appropriate to any such trade; or

    (c) in that period—

        (i) the amount paid by the company by way of charges on income exceeds its profits of the period, determined as mentioned in section 259(7) of the Taxes Act (group relief); and

(ii) those charges include an amount which falls to be treated as a charge on income by virtue of section 42(2) of the Finance Act 1984 (discounts on bills of exchange) or paragraph 3(2) of Schedule 9 to that Act (deep discount securities); and
the paying of those charges by the company is its main activity or one of its main activities.

(7) In this section and Schedule 4 to this Act "the enactments relating ɔ group relief" means sections 258 onwards of Chapter I of Part XI of ɩe Taxes Act; and, except where the context otherwise requires, any xpression to which a meaning is assigned for the purposes of those nactments has the same meaning in this section and that Schedule.

ɪENERAL NOTE

Dual resident companies have been used in the past as a means of obtaining allowances ɔr losses made in two different countries. Typically a company was set up resident in two ɔuntries as part of a multinational group in order to arrange finance for the group. While ɩe company paid interest it regularly had limited taxable sources of income hence losses ɩrose. These losses were then relieved in both of the countries in which the company was ɛsident.

This section precludes group relief for a loss, capital allowances, management expenses or ɩarges on income accruing to a dual resident company. It only applies to investment ɔmpanies not trading companies, but for this purpose certain trading companies are ɛvertheless treated as investment companies (see subs. (6)).

ᴊimitation of other reliefs in dealings involving dual resident investing companies

64.—(1) In Schedule 7 to the Capital Allowances Act 1968 (special ʀules for sales of property between connected persons etc.) at the end of ʊub-paragraph (3) of paragraph 4 (which in certain cases excludes the ʀight to elect to substitute a sale price or other sum for market value for ɩe purposes of Parts I and II of that Act) there shall be added the words 'nor may such an election be made if the buyer is a dual resident investing ɔompany, within the meaning of section 63 of the Finance (No. 2) Act 987".

(2) In section 252 of the Taxes Act (company reconstructions without 'hange of ownership) at the beginning of subsection (2) (which, in relation ɔ capital allowances, provides for continuity as between the successor ɩnd the predecessor) there shall be inserted the words "Subject to ʊubsection (2A) below" and at the end of that subsection there shall be ɪnserted the following subsection—

"(2A) Subsection (2) above does not apply if the successor is a dual resident investing company, within the meaning of section 63 of the Finance (No. 2) Act 1987."

(3) In section 273 of the Taxes Act (disposals of assets within a group ɔf companies to be on a no-gain/no-loss basis) in subsection (2) (exclu-ʊions) at the end of paragraph (c) there shall be inserted the words "or

(d) a disposal to a dual resident investing company, within the meaning
. of section 63 of the Finance (No. 2) Act 1987".

(4) In section 276 of the Taxes Act (replacement of business assets by ɩembers of a group) at the beginning of subsection (1) there shall be ɪnserted the words "Subject to subsection (1A) below" and at the end of ɩat subsection there shall be inserted the following subsection—

"(1A) Subsection (1) above does not apply where so much of the consideration for the disposal of the old assets as is applied in acquiring the new assets or the interest in them is so applied by a member of the group which is a dual resident investing company; and in this subsection—

(a) "the old assets" and "the new assets" have the same meaning as in section 115 of the Capital Gains Tax Act 1979; and

    (b) "dual resident investing company" has the same meaning as in section 63 of the Finance (No. 2) Act 1987."

    (5) In subsection (6) of section 44 of the Finance Act 1971 (disposal value of machinery or plant in relation to capital allowances) in paragraph (b) (if sale is at an undervalue, disposal value is equal to market value except where, among other matters, the buyer's expenditure qualifies for capital allowances) in sub-paragraph (i) after the words "(scientific research allowances)" there shall be inserted "and the buyer is not a dual resident investing company, within the meaning of section 63 of the Finance (No. 2) Act 1987, which is connected with the seller within the terms of section 533 of the Taxes Act".

    (6) In paragraph 13 of Schedule 8 to the Finance Act 1971 (right of connected persons to elect, in relation to capital allowances, for continuity as between the successor and the predecessor) after the words "Taxes Act" there shall be inserted "and the successor is not a dual resident investing company, within the meaning of section 63 of the Finance (No. 2) Act 1987".

    (7) In this section—

    (a) subsections (1) and (5) above apply in relation to sales on or after 1st April 1987;

    (b) subsections (2) and (6) above apply where the successor in question begins to carry on the trade on or after that date;

    (c) subsection (3) above applies in relation to disposals on or after that date; and

    (d) subsection (4) above applies where the new assets (within the meaning of section 115 of the Capital Gains Tax Act 1979) are acquired on or after that date.

GENERAL NOTE

    This section contains further provisions precluding a variety of reliefs from being available to a dual resident company.

Controlled foreign companies: acceptable distribution policy

    65.—(1) In Schedule 17 to the Finance Act 1984 (controlled foreign companies: cases excluded from direction-making powers) Part I (acceptable distribution policy) shall be amended in accordance with this section.

    (2) In sub-paragraph (1) of paragraph 2 (payment of dividend for accounting period of controlled foreign company) after paragraph (b) there shall be inserted the following paragraph—

    "(bb) the dividend is paid at a time when the company is not resident in the United Kingdom (whether or not it is at that time a controlled foreign company); and".

    (3) In sub-paragraph (1) of paragraph 4 (payment of dividend by a third company) after paragraph (b) there shall be inserted the following paragraph—

    "(bb) the subsequent dividend is paid at a time when the company paying it is not resident in the United Kingdom. and".

    (4) This section applies in any case where the dividend concerned is paid on or after 17th March 1987.

GENERAL NOTE

    The charge to tax on controlled foreign companies does not apply if the company pays a certain level of dividend in respect of the profit made in an accounting period. The aim of this is that while the profits of the foreign company may not be subject to tax in the U.K. the dividend will be so that there is no need to raise any additional charge. Such an aim has been thwarted in certain instances by foreign companies being imported into the U.K. prior to a dividend being paid so that the dividend when paid is not in fact subject to U.K. tax by virtue of an election for the group income provisions of s.256 of I.C.T.A. being made. This

ection now amends the law so that the requirements of an acceptable distribution policy
will only be met by the payment of a dividend at a time when a company is not resident in
the U.K.

Offshore funds

66.—(1) In paragraph 1 of Schedule 19 to the Finance Act 1984 (the
distribution test for offshore funds) in sub-paragraph (1)(c) (distribution
for an account period to be made during that period or not more than six
months after its expiry) after the words "six months" there shall be
inserted "or such longer period as the Board may in any particular case
allow".

(2) At the end of Part II of the said Schedule 19 (modifications of
conditions for certification in certain cases) there shall be inserted the
following paragraph—

"Power of Board to disregard certain breaches of conditions

12B. If, in the case of any account period of an offshore fund, it
appears to the Board that there has been a failure to comply with any
of the conditions in paragraphs (a) to (c) of subsection (3) of section
95 of this Act (as modified, where appropriate, by the preceding
provisions of this Part of this Schedule) but the Board are
satisfied—
   (a) that the failure occurred inadvertently, and
   (b) that the failure was remedied without unreasonable delay,
the Board may disregard the failure in determining whether to certify
the fund as a distributing fund in respect of that account period."

(3) This section has effect with respect to periods which—
   (a) for the purposes of Chapter VII of Part II of the Finance Act
       1984 are account periods of offshore funds; and
   (b) end after the passing of this Act.

GENERAL NOTE
This section provides for certain relaxations in the legislative provisions regarding offshore
funds. Such a fund is not subject to the offshore fund legislation if it is a "distributing fund"
and for this purpose Sched. 19, Pt. I, F.A. 1984, sets down various requirements that need
to be satisfied before it can qualify as such. Para. 1 has in the past required distributions of
a specified amount to be made in respect of an accounting period no later than six months
after its expiry. Subs. (1) of this section amends this rule so as to permit payment later if the
Board allows. Subs. (2) gives a general power to the Board to disregard a failure to satisfy
any conditions if the failure occurred inadvertently and was remedied without unreasonable
delay.

Double taxation relief: interest on certain overseas loans

67.—(1) Section 65 of the Finance Act 1982 (restriction of double
taxation relief in relation to interest on certain overseas loans) shall be
amended in accordance with this section.

(2) In subsection (1), in paragraph (a) the words "in a territory" shall
be omitted and at the end of that subsection there shall be added "and for
the purpose only of determining whether the condition in paragraph (b)
above is fulfilled in a case where the lender has in fact incurred no
expenditure related to the earning of the foreign loan interest, it shall be
assumed that he has incurred such expenditure".

(3) After subsection (1) there shall be inserted the following
subsection—

"(1A) In subsection (1) above "interest", in relation to a loan,
includes any introductory or other fee or charge which is payable in
accordance with the terms on which the loan is made or is otherwise

payable in connection with the making of the loan; and any referenc
in this section to foreign loan interest shall be construed accordingly.
(4) In subsection (4) for paragraph (b) there shall be substituted—
"(b) the amount of tax exceeds—
  (i) the amount of credit which, by virtue of Chapter II c
    Part XVIII of the Taxes Act (but disregarding subsectio
    (5) below), is allowed for that foreign tax against incom
    tax or corporation tax, or
  (ii) if it is less, 15 per cent. of the foreign loan interest
    computed without regard to any increase or reductio
    under this section".

(5) For subsection (5) there shall be substituted the followin
subsections—
"(5) Where this section applies, the amount of the credit for foreig
tax referred to in subsection (1)(c) above which, in accordance wit
Chapter II of Part XVIII of the Taxes Act, is to be allowed agains
income tax or corporation tax—
(a) shall be limited by treating the amount of the foreign loa
  interest (as increased or reduced under subsection (2) o
  subsection (4) above) as reduced (or further reduced) for th
  purposes of that Chapter by an amount equal to so much o
  the lender's financial expenditure in relation to the loan con
  cerned as is properly attributable to the period for which th
  interest is paid; and
(b) shall not exceed 15 per cent. of the foreign loan interest
  computed without regard to paragraph (a) above or to an
  increase under subsection (2) or any reduction under subsectio
  (4) above.
(5A) For the purposes of this section the lender's financial expen
diture in relation to a loan is the aggregate of—
(a) the financial expenses (consisting of interest or similar sums
  incurred by the lender in or in connection with the provisio
  of the loan, so far as those expenses consist of payments whic
  either are charges on income for the purposes of corporatio
  tax or are deductible in computing profits of the lender whic
  are brought into charge to income tax or corporation tax; and
(b) where the loan is financed by the issue of securities at ₤
  discount by the lender, so much of the amount of the discoun
  as either constitutes such a charge as is mentioned in paragrap
  (a) above or is deductible as mentioned in that paragraph; and
(c) so much as it is just and reasonable to attribute to the loan o
  any interest or other return forgone by a person connected o
  associated with the lender in connection with the provision o
  funds to the lender, either interest free or in other circum
  stances more favourable to the lender than if the parties wer
  at arm's length; and
(d) any other sum, whether paid by way of refund of tax or interes
  or by way of commission, which—
  (i) is paid by the lender or a person connected or associate
    with him;
  (ii) is paid directly or indirectly to the borrower or a perso
    connected or associated with him;
  (iii) is deductible as mentioned in paragraph (a) above;
  (iv) would not, apart from this paragraph, be taken int
    account in determining the amount of the foreign loa
    interest; and
  (v) it is reasonable to regard as referable to the loan or th
    foreign loan interest (or both).

(5B) In a case where the amount of the lender's financial expenditure in relation to a loan is not readily ascertainable, that amount shall be taken, subject to subsection (5C) below, to be such sum as it is just and reasonable to attribute to the financing of the loan, having regard, in particular, to any market rates of interest by reference to which the rate of interest on the loan is determined.

(5C) The Board may by regulations supplement subsection (5B) above—
  (a) by specifying matters to be taken into account in determining such a just and reasonable attribution as is referred to in that subsection; and
  (b) by making provision with respect to the determination of market rates of interest for the purposes of that subsection;
and any such regulations may make different provision for different cases.

(5D) Regulations under subsection (5C) above shall be made by statutory instrument which shall be subject to annulment in pursuance of a resolution of the House of Commons.

(5E) For the purposes of this section—
  (a) section 533 of the Taxes Act (connected persons) applies; and
  (b) subsection (10) of section 494 of that Act (associated persons) applies as it applies for the purposes of that section."

(6) Where the loan on which the foreign loan interest is payable was made pursuant to an agreement entered into before 1st April 1987, this section does not apply in relation to interest payable before 1st April 1989 but, subject thereto, this section (including the power to make regulations conferred by subsection (5) above) applies in relation to interest payable on or after 1st April 1987.

GENERAL NOTE
  F.A. 1982, s.65, restricts the entitlement to credit foreign tax on interest received from foreign loans to 15 per cent. of the gross interest received. This section further restricts the right of set off by allowing such set off only against the tax payable on the profit of the particular loan in respect of which the credit is obtained. The effect of the new subs. (5) is that the credit is limited to whichever is the lesser of corporation tax on the foreign loan interest less "the lender's financial expenditure in relation to the loan concerned" and 15 per cent. of the foreign loan interest.

Double taxation relief: underlying tax reflecting interest on loans

68.—(1) Section 66 of the Finance Act 1982 (restriction of double taxation relief in respect of underlying tax on certain dividends) shall be amended in accordance with this section.

(2) After subsection (1) there shall be inserted the following subsections—

"(1A) In a case where this section applies, the amount of the credit for that part of the foreign tax which consists of the tax referred to in subsection (1)(c) above shall not exceed an amount determined under subsection (1B) below.

(1B) The amount referred to in subsection (1A) above is a sum equal to corporation tax, at the rate in force at the time the foreign tax referred to in paragraph (c) of subsection (1) above was chargeable, on so much of the interest on the loan as exceeds the amount of the lender's relevant expenditure which is properly attributable to the period for which that interest is paid.

(1C) In subsection (1B) above—
  (a) "interest", subject to subsection (1D) below, has the meaning assigned to it by section 65(1A) above; and
  (b) "the lender's relevant expenditure" means the amount which,

if the company referred to in subsection (1)(d) above were resident in the United Kingdom (and liable to tax accordingly) would be its financial expenditure in relation to the loan, as determined in accordance with subsections (5) to (5E) of section 65 above.

(1D) If, in accordance with subsection (2) or subsection (4) below the amount of the dividend would be treated for the purposes of corporation tax as increased or reduced by any amount, then the amount which, apart from this subsection, would be the amount of the interest referred to in subsection (1B) above shall be taken to be increased or reduced by the same amount as the dividend is so treated as increased or reduced."

(3) Where the loan referred to in paragraph (c) of subsection (1) of section 66 of the Finance Act 1982 was made pursuant to an agreement entered into before 1st April 1987, this section does not apply in relation to tax payable as mentioned in that paragraph by reference to interest payable before 1st April 1989 but, subject thereto, this section applies in relation to tax so payable by reference to interest payable on or after 1st April 1987.

GENERAL NOTE

The aim of F.A. 1982, s.66, is to prevent banks lending through foreign subsidiaries as a means of avoiding F.A. 1982, s.65. In the same way as s.65 has been modified by s.67 of this Act this section makes similar modifications to s.66. It limits the credit for underlying tax to a sum equal to corporation tax on so much of the interest on the loan as exceeds the lender's "relevant expenditure".

Miscellaneous

Disclosure of employment information obtained from Inland Revenue

69.—(1) Section 58 of the Finance Act 1969 (disclosure of information for statistical purposes by Board of Inland Revenue) shall be amended in accordance with this section.

(2) At the end of subsection (4) (cases in which information obtained under the section may be disclosed by officers of the Department of Employment or Manpower Services Commission to other persons) there shall be added "or

(c) to an authorised officer of any body specified in the first column of the following Table for the purposes of functions of that body under any enactment specified in relation to it in the second column of the Table.

TABLE

Body	Enactment
A local education authority in England and Wales.	Section 8 of the Employment and Training Act 1973.
An education authority in Scotland.	Section 126 of the Education (Scotland) Act 1980.
The Northern Ireland Training Authority.	The Industrial Training (Northern Ireland) Order 1984.
A local planning authority within the meaning of the Town and Country Planning Act 1971 and any board which exercises for any area the functions of such an authority.	Part II of the Town and Country Planning Act 1971.

Body	*Enactment*
A planning authority as defined in section 172(3) of the Local Government (Scotland) Act 1973.	Part II of the Town and Country Planning (Scotland) Act 1972.
The Welsh Development Agency.	The Welsh Development Agency Act 1975.
The Scottish Development Agency.	The Scottish Development Agency Act 1975.
The Development Board for Rural Wales.	The Development of Rural Wales Act 1976.
The Highlands and Islands Development Board.	The Highlands and Islands Development (Scotland) Acts 1965 and 1968.
A development corporation within the meaning of the New Towns Act 1981.	Section 4 of the New Towns Act 1981.
A development corporation within the meaning of the New Towns (Scotland) Act 1968.	Section 3 of the New Towns (Scotland) Act 1968.
A new town commission within the meaning of the New Towns Act (Northern Ireland) 1965.	Section 7 of the New Towns Act (Northern Ireland) 1965.''

(3) In subsection (6) for the words "or paragraph (b) of subsection (4)" there shall be substituted "paragraph (b) or paragraph (c) of subsection (4) above".

GENERAL NOTE

F.A. 1969, s.58, permits the Revenue to disclose information for the purposes of statistical surveys carried out by other government departments. This section extends the persons to whom officers of these other government departments can disclose information to include the variety of bodies' specified in the Table.

Lloyd's underwriters

70.—(1) This section applies where, in accordance with the rules or practice of Lloyd's and in consideration of the payment of a premium, one underwriter agrees with another to meet liabilities arising from the latter's business for an underwriting year so that the accounts of the business for that year may be closed.

(2) In computing for the purposes of income tax the profits or gains of his business, the amount of the premium shall be deductible as an expense of the underwriter by whom it is payable only to the extent that it is shown not to exceed a fair and reasonable assessment of the value of the liabilities in respect of which it is payable.

(3) Any part of a premium which, by virtue of subsection (2) above, is not deductible as an expense of the underwriter by whom it is payable shall be disregarded in computing for the purposes of income tax the profits or gains of the business of the underwriter to whom it is payable.

(4) The assessment referred to in subsection (2) above shall be taken to be fair and reasonable only if it is arrived at with a view to producing the result that a profit does not accrue to the underwriter to whom the premium is payable but he does not suffer a loss.

(5) In this section "underwriter" means an underwriting member of Lloyd's, and expressions used in Schedule 10 to the Taxes Act have the same meanings as in that Schedule.

(6) This section has effect in relation to premiums payable in connection with the closing of the accounts of an underwriter's business for an underwriting year ending in the year of assessment 1985–86 or any later year of assessment.

This section restricts the reinsurance to close of Lloyds Syndicates allowable in computing profits.

When the original 1987 Finance Bill was introduced the reinsurance to close that was i future to be allowable was to be limited to an amount equal to provisions for the liabilitie concerned worked out on the basis that the business was continuing. The section was heavil criticised by Lloyds as permitting inadequate relief. The original proposal has now bee scrapped and a limitation on the relief available will only operate if the premium pai exceeds a fair and reasonable assessment of the value of the liabilities in respect of which i is payable. Some sort of general provision will still be able to be made.

Insofar as a limitation is placed by this section on the amount deductible by the paying underwriter, the non-allowed part of the premium is not subject to tax in the hands of the recipient underwriter.

Relief for losses on unquoted shares in trading companies

71. Section 37 of the Finance Act 1980 (relief for losses on unquoted shares in trading companies) shall have effect, and be deemed always to have had effect, with the addition, at the end of the definition of "excluded company" in subsection (12), of the words "or
  (c) which is a building society, within the meaning of the Building Societies Act 1986, or a registered industrial and provident society as defined in section 340 of the Taxes Act".

GENERAL NOTE
F.A. 1980, s.37 provides an income tax relief for losses on unquoted shares in trading companies. This section precludes any such relief being available in respect of shares in building societies or industrial and provident societies.

Allowances for dwelling-houses let on assured tenancies

72.—(1) In section 76 of the Finance Act 1982 (capital allowances for dwelling-houses let on assured tenancies) in subsection (2) (provisions to have effect only where expenditure is incurred before 1st April 1987) for "1987" there shall be substituted "1992".
  (2) In any case where—
    (a) by reason only of the enactment (by the Housing and Planning Act 1986) of section 56B of the Housing Act 1980 (extension of assured tenancies scheme to cases where works have been carried out) an approved body is entitled to an initial allowance in respect of any expenditure under Schedule 12 to the Finance Act 1982 (capital allowances for dwelling-houses let on assured tenancies); and
    (b) effect has not been and, apart from this subsection, no longer can be given to the initial allowance referred to in paragraph (a) above,
then, if a claim is made in that behalf before 1st April 1988, all such adjustments shall be made as may be necessary to give effect to that initial allowance.
  (3) Expressions used in subsection (2) above have the same meaning as in Schedule 12 to the Finance Act 1982.

GENERAL NOTE
F.A. 1982, s.76, provided for allowances in respect of dwelling-houses let on assured tenancies in relation to expenditure before April 1, 1987. That date is now altered to April 1, 1992. This section also provides that, in certain cases, an approved body entitled to initial allowances may claim them before April 1, 1988.

Recognised investment exchanges

73.—(1) The Board may by regulations make provision securing that enactments relating to income tax, corporation tax or capital gains tax and referring to The Stock Exchange have effect, for such purposes and subject to such modifications as may be prescribed by the regulations, in relation to all other recognised investment exchanges (within the meaning of the Financial Services Act 1986), or in relation to such of those exchanges as may be so prescribed.

(2) The power to make regulations under this section shall be exercisable by statutory instrument, which shall be subject to annulment in pursuance of a resolution of the House of Commons.

CHAPTER IV

CAPITAL GAINS

Companies' chargeable gains

General rules

74.—(1) This section has effect with respect to the liability of a company to corporation tax where a chargeable gain accrues to the company on or after 17th March 1987; and in the following provisions of this section—
   (a) "the 1987 date" means 17th March 1987; and
   (b) a "new accounting period" means an accounting period beginning on or after the 1987 date.

(2) With respect to any new accounting period, section 85 of the Finance Act 1972 (set off of advance corporation tax against liability to corporation tax on income) shall have effect as follows—
   (a) in subsections (1) to (3), for the word "income", in each place where it occurs, there shall be substituted "profits"; and
   (b) in subsection (6) for the word "income", in the first place where it occurs, there shall be substituted "profits" and the words from "exclusive" onwards shall be omitted.

(3) Section 93 of the Finance Act 1972 (reduction of corporation tax liability in respect of chargeable gains) shall not apply with respect to any new accounting period.

(4) With respect to any new accounting period, section 95 of the Finance Act 1972 (mitigation of corporation tax liability of small companies) shall have effect as follows—
   (a) in subsections (1) and (2) for the word "income", in each place where it occurs, there shall be substituted "basic profits";
   (b) in subsection (7), after the word "profits", in the first place where it occurs, there shall be inserted "(but not the basic profits)"; and
   (c) in subsection (8), for the word "income", in the first place where it occurs, there shall be substituted "basic profits" and for the words from "is its income", onwards there shall be substituted "shall be taken to be the amount of its profits for that period on which corporation tax falls finally to be borne".

(5) With respect to any new accounting period, in sections 101(2) and 103(4) of the Finance Act 1972 (each of which refer to income as defined in section 85(6) of that Act) for the word "income" there shall be substituted "profits".

(6) In Schedule 5 to this Act—
   (a) Part I has effect with respect to the operation of the provisions of the Finance Act 1972 referred to in subsections (2) to (5)

above in relation to any accounting period of a company which begins before and ends on or after the 1987 date; and
(b) Part II has effect with respect to the operation of the enactments referred to in sections 75 and 76 below in relation to any such period.

GENERAL NOTE

This section contains the changes to the taxation of chargeable gains accruing to companies. They apply to accounting periods which fall wholly after March 17, 1987. In the case of an accounting period straddling that date the transitional provisions contained in Pt. 1 of Sched. 5 apply.

The changes are:
(i) advance corporation tax paid by a company in respect of a distribution may be set off against corporation tax charged on chargeable gains and not just the company's chargeable income. This is achieved by substituting profit for income in F.A. 1972, s.85, and deleting the exclusion of chargeable gains contained in subs. (6) (see subs. (2)). This applies not only to the set off of advance corporation tax paid in the same accounting period but also to any unused advance corporation tax paid in a previous accounting period and carried forward as "surplus advance corporation tax";
(ii) the reduction of corporation tax on chargeable gains achieved by reducing the amount of the gain included in the company's total profits for an accounting period in accordance with F.A. 1972, s.93, will no longer apply. A chargeable gain of a company will accordingly be charged to corporation tax in full, subject to the different rules for small companies;
(iii) the smaller companies rate (applicable if a company's profits are below a specified limit) now applies to chargeable gains and not just the company's income. There will be no reduction in the amount of the gains so charged to tax;
(iv) in the event that an accounting period is treated as split into two due to a change of ownership then the above changes apply to either or both of the deemed accounting periods if they fall wholly after March 17, 1987.

Life assurance business

75.—(1) In Schedule 18 to the Finance Act 1972 (taxation of insurance companies) in paragraph 2(4) (modifications of section 85 of that Act)—
(a) for the word "income", in the first place where it occurs, there shall be substituted "profits"; and
(b) for the words from "an amount" onwards there shall be substituted "deducting therefrom such fraction thereof as is equal to the fraction of the profits of the company in respect of its life assurance business which, under section 309 of the Taxes Act, is excluded from the computation of those profits or would be so excluded if the profits were computed in accordance with the provisions applicable to Case I of Schedule D".

(2) In subsection (2) of section 26 of the Finance Act 1974 (corporation tax on balance of policy holders' share of life assurance gains)—
(a) for the words from the beginning to "that share" there shall be substituted "Corporation tax charged on so much of the policy holders' share of the life assurance gains"; and
(b) for the words from "as if" onwards there shall be substituted "on the basis of a rate of corporation tax of 30 per cent".

(3) In subsection (3) of the said section 26—
(a) in paragraph (a) the words "so much of" and the words from "as remains" to "1972" shall be omitted; and
(b) in paragraph (b) the words "as so reduced" shall be omitted.

(4) Subsections (1) to (3) above have effect with respect to accounting periods beginning on or after 17th March 1987.

This section introduces a number of changes in respect of the taxation of insurance
companies. The changes apply to accounting periods wholly after March 17, 1987, and those
which straddle that date are subject to the transitional provisions contained in Sched. 5.
The changes are:
  (i) the amount of the insurance company's profits chargeable to corporation tax for
      the purposes of F.A. 1972, s.85 (set off of advance corporation tax) is to be
      calculated in a different manner. Instead of reducing the profits by an amount
      equal to the part of the company's unrelieved income specified in I.C.T.A. 1970,
      s.310(6) (being the part referable to that company's life assurance business),
      now there is to be a deduction calculated as set out in subs. (1)(*b*);
  (ii) a fixed rate of 35 per cent. at which corporation tax is charged on the policy
      holder's share of the life assurance gains (see F.A. 1974, s.26(4)).

Gains from oil extraction activities etc.

76.—(1) The provisions of this section have effect with respect to
accounting periods beginning on or after 17th March 1987.

(2) Section 16 of the Oil Taxation Act 1975 (restriction on setting
advance corporation tax against income from oil extraction activities etc.)
shall be amended as follows—
  (a) in subsection (1) the words "on its income" shall be omitted; and
  (b) in subsection (3) for the words "the company's income", in each
      place where they occur, there shall be substituted "the company's
      profits".

(3) In section 79 of the Finance Act 1984 (gains on certain disposals
related to oil fields) subsection (5) shall be amended as follows—
  (a) the words from "(reduced" to "Finance Act 1972)" shall be omitted;
      and
  (b) for the words from "section 15" to "income)" there shall be
      substituted "sections 15 and 16 of the Oil Taxation Act 1975".

(4) Section 44 of the Finance Act 1987 (limited right to carry back
surrendered advance corporation tax) shall be amended as follows—
  (a) in subsection (1), in paragraph (e) for the words from "income",
      in the first place where it occurs, to the end of the paragraph there
      shall be substituted "profits which consist of or include ring fence
      profits";
  (b) in subsection (7) for the word "income" there shall be substituted
      "profits"; and
  (c) at the end there shall be added the following subsection—
        "(9) In this section "ring fence profits" has the meaning given
      by section 79(5) of the Finance Act 1984."

(5) In section 45 of the Finance Act 1987 (surrender of advance
corporation tax where oil extraction company etc. owned by a consortium)
in subsection (4)—
  (a) for the word "income", in the first two places where it occurs, there
      shall be substituted "profits"; and
  (b) for the words from "that income" onwards there shall be substituted
      "those profits as consists of ring fence profits, as defined in section
      79(5) of the Finance act 1984".

This section makes certain changes in oil taxation consequent upon the changes in the
taxation of chargeable gains contained in s.74. The Oil Taxation Act 1975, s.16, which
restricts the set off of ACT against CT liability, in respect of ring fence activities, is amended
to cover capital gains.

Double taxation relief

77.—(1) Section 100 of the Finance Act 1972 (double taxation relief) shall be amended in accordance with this section.

(2) With respect to accounting periods of a company beginning on or after 17th March 1987—

(a) in subsection (6) for the word "income", in the first place where it occurs, there shall be substituted "profits (within the meaning of that section)";

(b) in paragraphs (a) and (b) of subsection (6) for the word "income", in each place where it occurs, there shall be substituted "income or gain";

(c) in subsection (6) in the final words, for the words "income of the company" there shall be substituted "profits of the company" and for the words "relevant income" there shall be substituted "relevant income or gain"; and

(d) in subsection (6A) for the word "income", in each place where it occurs, there shall be substituted "income or gain".

(3) With respect to an accounting period of a company which begins before and ends on or after 17th March 1987, subsection (6) shall have effect as follows—

(a) any reference to the company's income for the accounting period shall be construed as a reference to its income as determined for the purposes of section 85 of the Finance Act 1972, in accordance with paragraph 3 of Schedule 5 to this Act; and

(b) if a relevant gain accrues to the company on or after 17th March 1987, the subsection shall apply in relation to that relevant gain as it applies in relation to relevant income;

and in paragraph (b) above "relevant income" and "relevant gain" have the meaning assigned by subsection (3) of section 100.

(4) Where the accounting period referred to in subsection (3) above began before 3rd June 1986, any reference in that subsection to subsection (6) of section 100 is a reference to that subsection as it had effect before the amendment made by section 49(2) of the Finance Act 1986.

(5) Where the accounting period referred to in subsection (3) above began on or after 3rd June 1986 then (without prejudice to the modifications of subsection (6) of section 100 set out in subsection (3) above), subsection (6A) of section 100 (as set out in section 49(3) of the Finance Act 1986)—

(a) shall apply in relation to the amount of a relevant gain (as defined in subsection (3) of section 100) accruing on or after 17th March as it applies in relation to an amount of income; and

(b) shall have effect as if the reference in paragraph (a) to income for the relevant accounting period were a reference to that income as determined for the purposes of section 85 of the Finance Act 1972, in accordance with paragraph 3 of Schedule 5 to this Act.

General Note

F.A. 1972, s.100, provides for double taxation relief in respect of corporation tax on gains accruing to companies. The amendments contained in this section arise from the changes effected by s.74.

Miscellaneous

Collective investment schemes

78. Where arrangements within section 75 of the Financial Services Act 1986 provide for pooling of the kind mentioned in subsection (3)(a) of that section in relation to different parts of the property concerned, any question whether the arrangements constitute a single collective invest-

ıent scheme shall be determined for the purposes of capital gains tax
ithout regard to any entitlement of the participants to exchange rights in
ne part of the property for rights in another.

GENERAL NOTE

Chapter VIII of the Fianancial Services Act 1986 imposes restrictions on the promotion
f "collective investment schemes." These are defined by s.75(1) to be arrangements in
espect of any type of property enabling persons to participate in the profits or income
rising from the property. Those participants must not have day to day control over the
management of the property. Certain types of arrangement are excluded by subss. (5) and
5).

To come within the definition an arrangement must have either or both of the character-
tics mentioned in subs. (3), namely: (a) there is a pooling of the participants' contributions
nd the profits and income from the property; and (b) the property subject to the
rrangements is managed as a whole by or on behalf of the operator of the scheme.

In the event that the participants pool contributions and profits in relation to separate
arts of the property then the arrangements will not be a single collective investment scheme
nless the participants have the right to exchange rights in one part of the property for rights
n another part (s.75(3)).

In their press release dated April 8, the Revenue have said that the purpose behind this
ection is to make "it explicit that established tax law will continue to apply where an
nvestor in a multi-portfolio unit trust switches from one portfolio to another."

Building societies: groups of companies

79. In section 272 of the Taxes Act (groups of companies: definitions)
ıt the end of subsection (2) (references to a company) there shall be
ıdded "and

    (e) a building society within the meaning of the Building Societies Act
       1986.".

GENERAL NOTE

I.C.T.A. 1970, ss.272–281, impose special rules in respect of transactions between groups
of companies. Building societies may now have subsidiaries and so they have been included
n the definition of company for the purposes of these sections.

Roll-over relief not available for gains on oil licences

80.—(1) A licence under the Petroleum (Production) Act 1934 or the
Petroleum (Production) Act (Northern Ireland) 1964 is not and, subject
to subsection (2) below, shall be assumed never to have been an asset
falling within any of the classes in section 118 of the Capital Gains Tax
Act 1979 (classes of assets for the purposes of roll-over relief under section
115 of that Act).

(2) Nothing in subsection (1) above affects the determination of any
Commissioners or the judgment of any court made or given before 14th
May 1987.

(3) A reference in subsection (1) above to a provision of the Capital
Gains Tax Act 1979 includes a reference to the corresponding enactment
in Part III of the Finance Act 1965 which is re-enacted in that provision.

GENERAL NOTE

Gains on the disposal of oil licences are not capable of being rolled-over under C.G.T.A.
1979, s.115.

Commodity and financial futures and options

81.—(1) In section 72 of the Finance Act 1985 (commodity and financial
futures and traded options) in subsection (1) for the words "traded
options" and "traded option" there shall be substituted respectively
"qualifying options" and "qualifying option".

(2) In subsection (2) of that section, for paragraph (b) (definition o "traded option") there shall be substituted—

"(b) "qualifying option" means a traded option or financial optio as defined in section 137(9) of that Act."

(3) After that subsection there shall be inserted the following subsections—

"(2A) Notwithstanding the provisions of subsection (2)(a) above where, otherwise than in the course of dealing on a recognised future exchange, within the meaning of the principal Act,—

(a) an authorised person or listed institution enters into a commodity or financial futures contract with another person, or

(b) the outstanding obligations under a commodity or financia futures contract to which an authorised person or listed institution is a party are brought to an end by a further contrac between the parties to the futures contract,

then, except in so far as any gain or loss arising to any person from that transaction arises in the course of a trade, that gain or loss shal be regarded for the purposes of subsection (1) above as arising to him in the course of dealing in commodity or financial futures.

(2B) In subsection (2A) above—

"authorised person" has the same meaning as in the Financial Services Act 1986, and

"listed institution" has the same meaning as in section 43 of that Act."

(4) In subsection (4) of section 137 of the Capital Gains Tax Act 1979 (options and forfeited deposits) for paragraph (aa) there shall be substituted the following paragraph—

"(aa) a traded option or financial option, or".

(5) For subsection (9) of section 137 of the Capital Gains Tax Act 1979 (definitions) there shall be substituted the following subsections—

"(9) In subsection (4) above and sections 138 and 139 below—

(a) "quoted option" means an option which, at the time of the abandonment or other disposal, is quoted on a recognised stock exchange;

(b) "traded option" means an option which, at the time of the abandonment or other disposal, is quoted on a recognised stock exchange or a recognised futures exchange; and

(c) "financial option" means an option which is not a traded option, as defined in paragraph (b) above, but which, subject to subsection (10) below,—

(i) relates to currency, shares, securities or an interest rate and is granted (otherwise than as agent) by a member of a recognised stock exchange, by an authorised person within the meaning of the Financial Services Act 1986 or by a listed institution within the meaning of section 43 of that Act; or

(ii) relates to shares or securities which are dealt in on a recognised stock exchange and is granted by a member of such an exchange, acting as agent; or

(iii) relates to currency, shares, securities or an interest rate and is granted to such an authorised person or institution as is referred to in sub-paragraph (i) above and concurrently and in association with an option falling within that sub-paragraph which is granted by that authorised person or institution to the grantor of the first-mentioned option; or

(iv) relates to shares or securities which are dealt in on a recognised stock exchange and is granted to a member of

such an exchange, including such a member acting as
agent;
and in this subsection "recognised stock exchange" has the meaning
given by section 535 of the Taxes Act.

(10) If the Treasury by order so provide, an option of a description
specified in the order shall be taken to be within the definition of
"financial option" in subsection (9)(c) above; and the power to make
an order under this subsection shall be exercisable by statutory
instrument which shall be subject to annulment in pursuance of a
resolution of the House of Commons."

(6) In subsection (1) of section 138 of the Capital Gains Tax Act 1979
(application of rules as to wasting assets) for paragraph (aa) there shall be
substituted the following paragraph—

"(aa) to a traded option or financial option, or".

(7) In subsection (4) of section 138 of the Capital Gains Tax Act 1979
(definitions for the purpose of that section) for paragraph (a) there shall
be substituted the following paragraph—

"(a) "financial option", "quoted option" and "traded option" have
the meaning given by section 137(9) above, and".

(8) This section shall come into force on such day as the Treasury may
by order made by statutory instrument appoint.

GENERAL NOTE

This section will only come into force when a statutory instrument appoints a commencement date.

It causes the scope of F.A. 1985, s.72, to be extended to financial options which are
defined by the new subs. (9) of s.137 of the Capital Gains Tax Act 1979 (see subs. (5)). This
extension covers: (i) commodity and financial futures to which one party is an authorised
person as defined by the Financial Services Act 1986 or a listed institution within s.43 of that
Act; (ii) options relating to quoted shares and securities arranged through a Stock Exchange
member; (iii) financial options involving an authorised person or a listed institution.

Any gains or losses arising from such transactions will be chargeable to tax under the
capital gains tax legislation unless arising in the course of a trade.

Such contracts will not be treated as wasting assets for the purposes of capital gains tax
(see subs. (6)).

The expiry of such a contract will now also be a disposal (see F.A. 1985, s.72(4)).

CHAPTER V

TAXES MANAGEMENT PROVISIONS

GENERAL NOTE

The greater part of this Chapter (ss.82–90), together with Sched. 6, is concerned with
laying the legislative groundwork for the introduction of the so-called "Pay and File" system
for corporation tax. Many companies have not prepared their accounts by the time tax
becomes payable. The Revenue then have to raise estimated assessments, which are
frequently appealed, occasioning further delays and administrative costs. Under the "Pay
and File" system, companies will be required to pay their tax on the due date on an
estimated basis if necessary and to file their accounts within a limited period thereafter.
Both requirements are backed up by a penalty system. To allow companies and the Revenue
ample time to prepare, "Pay and File" will not be introduced before March 31, 1992.

Company returns

Return of profits

82.—(1) With respect to any notice served after the appointed day,
section 11 of the Management Act (return of profits) shall be amended in
accordance with this section.

(2) In subsection (1) for the words from "within the time limited by the notice" to the end there shall be substituted "not later than the final day determined under subsection (4) below a return of the profits and losses of the company containing such information and accompanied by such accounts, statements and reports as, subject to subsection (6) below, may be required in pursuance of the notice."

(3) For subsection (2) there shall be substituted the following subsection—

"(2) A notice under this section may require a return of profits and losses arising in any period specified in the notice (in this subsection referred to as "the specified period") but, if the specified period does not coincide with an accounting period of the company and the company is within the charge to corporation tax in the whole or some part of the specified period, then—

(a) if an accounting period of the company ends in or at the end of the specified period, the notice shall be taken to require a return for that accounting period or, if there is more than one, for each of them;

(b) if no accounting period of the company ends in or at the end of the specified period but there is a part of the specified period which does not fall within an accounting period of the company, the notice shall be taken to require a return for that part of the specified period; and

(c) if the specified period begins in or at the beginning of an accounting period of the company and ends before the end of that period, the notice shall be of no effect and, accordingly, the company shall not be required to make any return pursuant to it."

(4) For subsections (4) to (6) there shall be substituted the following subsections—

"(4) Subject to subsection (5) below, the final day for the delivery of any return required by a notice under this section shall be whichever is the later of—

(a) the first anniversary of the last day of the period to which the return relates;

(b) the first anniversary of the last day of that period of account of the company in which falls the last day of the accounting period (if any) to which the return relates; and

(c) the end of the period of three months beginning on the day following that on which the notice was served.

(5) In paragraph (b) of subsection (4) above "period of account" has the same meaning as in the principal Act, but for the purposes of that paragraph the last day of a period of account which is longer than eighteen months shall be treated as the day on which expires the period of eighteen months beginning on the first day of the period of account.

(6) In relation to a company which—

(a) is resident in the United Kingdom throughout the period to which the return relates (in this subsection referred to as "the return period"); and

(b) is required under the Companies Act 1985 to prepare accounts for a period consisting of or including the return period,

the reference to accounts in subsection (1) above is a reference only to such accounts, containing such particulars and having annexed to them such documents, as are required under that Act to be so prepared.

(7) The statements which may be required in pursuance of a notice under this section include statements showing the amount of tax (if any) chargeable.

(8) Different information, accounts, statements and reports may be required in pursuance of a notice under this section in relation to different descriptions of company or different descriptions of profits and losses; and, in particular, information may be so required with respect to tax recoverable by virtue of section 286 of the principal Act (loans to participators) as if it were corporation tax, to advance corporation tax and to corporation tax already paid.

(9) In the application of this section to a company registered in Northern Ireland, references to the Companies Act 1985 shall be construed as references to the Companies (Northern Ireland) Order 1986."

GENERAL NOTE
This section lays the foundation for the "File" part of the "Pay and File" system by setting deadline for the submission of accounts to the Revenue by companies. This will normally e 12 months after the end of the company's financial year. Generally, the accounts to be ubmitted will be those prepared in accordance with the Companies Act 1985.

Failure to make return for corporation tax

83. With respect to failures to deliver returns required by notices served under section 11 of the Management Act after the appointed day, for section 94 of that Act (failure to make return for corporation tax) there shall be substituted the following section—

"Failure to make return for corporation tax

94.—(1) If a company has been required by a notice served under section 11 of this Act (or under that section as extended by section 12 of this Act) to deliver a return for any period (in this section referred to as "the return period") and the company fails to make proper delivery of the return, then, subject to subsections (3) and (5) below, the company shall be liable to a penalty which,—

(a) if the return is delivered before the expiry of the period of three months beginning on the day following the final day for the delivery of the return, shall be £100; and

(b) in any other case, shall be £200.

(2) In relation to a return required by such a notice as is referred to in subsection (1) above,—

(a) any reference in this section (however expressed) to the delivery of the return is a reference to its delivery together with the accompanying accounts, statements and reports referred to in section 11(1) of this Act; and

(b) any reference in this section to making proper delivery of the return is a reference to the delivery of the return on or before the day which (in accordance with section 11(4) of this Act) is the final day for the delivery of the return.

(3) In a case where—

(a) a company is required to deliver a return for a return period, and

(b) the return period is a period for which, under the Companies Act 1985, the company is required to deliver accounts to the Registrar of Companies,

the company shall not be liable to a penalty under subsection (1) above by reason of a failure to make proper delivery of the return if the return is delivered on or before the day which is the last day for the delivery to the Registrar of the accounts referred to in paragraph (b) above.

(4) In the application of this section to a company registered in Northern Ireland, the reference in subsection (3) above to the Companies Act 1985 shall be construed as a reference to the Companies (Northern Ireland) Order 1986 and references to the Registrar of Companies shall be construed accordingly.

(5) In any case where—

(a) a company is within the charge to corporation tax for three consecutive accounting periods, each of which is a return period, and

(b) at no time between the beginning of the first of those periods and the end of the last is the company outside the charge to corporation tax, and

(c) the company fails to make proper delivery of the return for the third of those periods, and

(d) the company was liable to a penalty under this section in respect of each of the first two of those periods,

subsection (1) above shall have effect in relation to the failure referred to in paragraph (c) above as if for "£100" there were substituted "£500" and for "£200" there were substituted "£1,000".

(6) If a company which has been required as mentioned in subsection (1) above to deliver a return fails to deliver the return before the expiry of the period of eighteen months beginning on the day following the last day of the return period, then (without prejudice to any penalty under the preceding provisions of this section) the company shall be liable to a penalty which,—

(a) if the return is delivered before the expiry of the period of two years beginning on the day following that last day, shall be 10 per cent. of the tax unpaid at the end of the eighteen months referred to above; and

(b) in any other case, shall be 20 per cent. of the tax unpaid at the end of those eighteen months.

(7) In subsection (6) above "the tax unpaid" at any time means the amount by which the corporation tax chargeable on the profits of the company for the return period which then remains unpaid exceeds any income tax borne by deduction from payments included in those profits.

(8) In determining for the purposes of subsection (7) above how much of the corporation tax chargeable on the profits of a company for the return period remains unpaid at any time, no account shall be taken of the discharge of any liability for that tax which, pursuant to a claim under subsection (3) of section 85 of the Finance Act 1972, is attributable to an amount of surplus advance corporation tax, as defined in that subsection, unless it is a surplus for an accounting period ending not later than two years after the end of the return period."

GENERAL NOTE

The relatively ineffective system of maximum penalties under T.M.A. 1970, s.94 is replaced by a much more stringent regime of fixed penalties. If a return is made within three months after the due date, the penalty is £100, increasing to £200, thereafter. In the third year of such default, these penalties increase to £500 and £1000 respectively.

Further, if the return is delivered between 18 months and two years late, there is an additional penalty amounting to 10 per cent. of any tax unpaid as at the end of the 18 months, increasing to 20 per cent. of that tax after two years.

Although the penalties are fixed, the Revenue have a general power to mitigate under T.M.A. 1970, s.102, and will do so where there is a reasonable excuse (see T.M.A., s.118(2), as amended by s.94, *infra*).

Their ruling on this point can be appealed to commissioners (see ministerial statement in *ınsard*, Vol. 119, col. 1325).

ssessment of amounts due by way of penalty

84.—(1) Where it appears to the inspector or the Board that any person liable to a penalty under any provision of section 94 of the Management ct, the amount appearing to be due may be assessed by the inspector or ıe Board as if it were tax; and, subject to the provisions of this section, ıe provisions of the Management Act and section 247 of the Taxes Act ·lating to the assessment and collection of tax shall have effect :cordingly.

(2) An amount assessed under this section by way of penalty shall be ıe at the end of the period of thirty days beginning with the date of the sue of the notice of assessment.

(3) In any case where—

(a) an assessment under this section relates to a penalty the amount of which falls to be determined under subsections (6) to (8) of section 94 of the Management Act, and

(b) after the assessment has been made, it appears to the inspector or the Board that the amount which was taken into account in the making of the assessment as the tax unpaid (as defined in subsection (7) of that section) was incorrect,

l such adjustments shall be made, whether by way of amending the ssessment, making a further assessment, repayment or otherwise as may e necessary to take account of the correct amount.

(4) At the end of section 70 of the Management Act (evidential :rtificates) there shall be inserted the following subsection—

   "(5) Where an amount has been assessed by way of penalty under section 94 of this Act and either no appeal has been brought against that assessment or the amount assessed has been confirmed or varied on appeal,—

   (a) a certificate of an inspector or other officer of the Board that an amount is due by way of penalty under that section, and

   (b) a certificate of a collector that payment of that amount has not been made to him or, to the best of his knowledge and belief, to any other collector, or to a person acting on his behalf or on behalf of another collector,

   shall be sufficient evidence that the amount mentioned in the certificates is unpaid and is due to the Crown; and any document purporting to be such a certificate as is mentioned in this subsection shall be deemed to be such a certificate unless the contrary is proved."

(5) Where there is a failure to make proper delivery of a return, within ıe meaning of section 94 of the Management Act, as assessment of an mount due by way of penalty under any provision of that section may be ıade at any time within six years beginning on the day on which the ıilure began or, in the case of a penalty under subsection (6) of that :ction, at any later time within three years beginning at the time of the ıal determination of the amount which is the unpaid tax for the purposes f that subsection.

(6) On an appeal against an assessment of an amount by way of penalty nder section 94 of the Management Act, subsections (6) to (8) of section 0 of that Act shall not apply but the Commissioners—

(a) may confirm the amount of the assessment or, if it appears to them that the amount assessed is greater or smaller than the penalty provided for under the said section 94, may reduce it or increase it to such an amount as is appropriate having regard to the provisions of that section; and

(b) if it appears to them that no penalty has been incurred, may set t
assessment aside.

(7) Nothing in sections 34 to 40 (time limits) of the Management A
applies to an assessment made by virtue of this section and nothing
section 55 of that Act (recovery of tax not postponed) applies to an appe
against such an assessment.

(8) Section 100 of the Management Act (procedure for recovery
penalties) shall not apply to a penalty under section 94 of that Act.

(9) This section has effect with respect to penalties incurred after t
appointed day.

GENERAL NOTE

Penalties under s.83 may levied by way of assessment and subject to the appeal procedur
are payable within 30 days. The onus is on the Revenue to prove that a penalty is applicab
Although the commissioners have no power to mitigate the amount of penalties establish
by the statute, they can review the Revenue's exercise or non-exercise of their discreti
under T.M.A. 1970, s.102. See ministerial statement referred to in commentary to s.
supra.

Interest etc.

Interest on overdue corporation tax etc.

85. With respect to accounting periods ending after the appointed da
after section 87 of the Management Act there shall be inserted t
following section—

"Interest on overdue corporation tax etc.

87A.—(1) Corporation tax shall carry interest at the prescribed ra
from the date when the tax becomes due and payable (in accordan
with section 243(4) of the principal Act) until payment.

(2) Subsection (1) above applies even if the date when the ta
becomes due and payable (as mentioned in that subsection) is
non-business day within the meaning of section 92 of the Bills
Exchange Act 1882.

(3) In relation to corporation tax assessed by virtue of secti
266(2), section 267(3C), section 277(1) or section 278(5) of the Tax
Act or section 87(4) of the Capital Gains Tax Act 1979 (which enab
unpaid corporation tax assessed on a company to be assessed on oth
persons in certain circumstances), the reference in subsection (
above to the date when the tax becomes due and payable is
reference to the date when it became due and payable by t
company.

(4) In any case where—

(a) there is in any accounting period of a company (in th
subsection referred to as "the later period") an amount
surplus advance corporation tax, as defined in subsection (
of section 85 of the Finance Act 1972, and

(b) pursuant to a claim under the said subsection (3), the whole
any part of that amount is treated for the purposes of the sa
section 85 as discharging liability for an amount of corporatic
tax for an earlier accounting period (in this subsection referre
to as "the earlier period"), and

(c) disregarding the effect of the said subsection (3), an amount
corporation tax for the earlier period would carry interest
accordance with this section,

then, in determining the amount of interest payable under this sectic
on corporation tax unpaid for the earlier period, no account shall b
taken of any reduction in the amount of that tax which results fro

the said subsection (3) except so far as concerns interest for any time
after the date on which any corporation tax for the later period
became due and payable (as mentioned in subsection (1) above).

(5) A sum assessed on a company by such an assessment as is
referred to in subsection (2) of section 102 of the Finance Act 1972
(recovery of payment of tax credit or interest on such a payment)
shall carry interest at the prescribed rate from the date when the
payment of tax credit or interest was made until the sum assessed is
paid."

GENERAL NOTE
    The general rule in the fiscal system has been that interest runs from the date when
assessments become due and payable. Under the "Pay and File" system interest runs from
the date when the corporation tax is due and payable.
    Subs. (3) applies the provisions to cases where another person becomes liable to pay
corporation tax on chargeable gains in circumstances involving tax avoidance.
    Subs. (4). Surplus advance corporation tax ("A.C.T.") in a later accounting period may
not be set against unpaid mainstream corporation tax in earlier periods for the purpose of
determining the amount of interest payable. A.C.T. is deducted by companies from
dividends at the standard rate applicable to income tax.
    Subs. (5). Interest on an assessment to recover an excessive set-off of A.C.T. or tax credit
will run from the date of the set-off or credit rather than from the assessment becoming due.

Supplementary provisions as to interest on overdue tax

86.—(1) At the end of section 69 of the Management Act (recovery of
interest on tax) there shall be added the words "or, if it is interest on tax
which is not in fact assessed, as if it were tax charged and due and payable
under an assessment".

(2) In section 86 of the Management Act (interest on overdue tax),
subsection (2)(d) and paragraph 5 of the Table (which relate to assessed
corporation tax) shall be omitted.

(3) References to section 86 of the Management Act in—
    (a) sections 70(2) and 92 of that Act (evidence, and remission of
        interest in certain cases), and
    (b) paragraph 4 of Schedule 15 to the Finance Act 1973 (territorial
        extension of tax),
shall include a reference to section 87A of the Management Act.

(4) In section 88 of the Management Act (interest on tax recovered to
make good loss due to taxpayer's fault)—
    (a) in subsection (2) (exclusion of certain non-assessed tax) after the
        words "in relation to" there shall be inserted "corporation tax or";
        and
    (b) in subsection (5), paragraph (e) (which relates to corporation tax)
        shall be omitted.

(5) In section 91 of the Management Act (effect on interest of reliefs)
after subsection (1) there shall be inserted the following subsections—
    "(1A) Where interest is payable under section 87A of this Act in
respect of an amount of corporation tax for an accounting period,
and relief from tax is given by a discharge of any of that corporation
tax—
    (a) such adjustment shall be made of the amount of interest
        payable under that section in respect of corporation tax for
        that accounting period, and
    (b) such repayment shall be made of any amounts of interest
        previously paid under that section in respect of that corporation
        tax,
as are necessary to secure that the total sum (if any) paid or payable
under that section in respect of corporation tax for that accounting

period is the same as it would have been if the tax discharged had never been charged.

(1B) Subsection (1A) above has effect subject to section 87A(4) of this Act."

(6) At the beginning of subsection (2) of that section there shall be inserted the words "Subject to subsection (2A) below" and at the end of that subsection there shall be added the following subsection—

"(2A) In any case where—

(a) relief from corporation tax is given to any person by repayment and

(b) that tax was paid for an accounting period ending after the day which is the appointed day for the purposes of section 90 of the Finance (No. 2) Act 1987,

that person shall be entitled to require that the amount repaid shall be treated for the purposes of this section, so far as it will go, as if it were a discharge of the corporation tax charged on him for that period."

(7) This section has effect with respect to accounting periods ending after the appointed day.

GENERAL NOTE

This section makes a series of amendments to the T.M.A. 1970 to reflect the fact that interest on overdue mainsteam corporation tax will run automatically after the due date of payment rather than requiring the raising of an assessment.

Interest on tax overpaid

87.—(1) In any case where—

(a) a repayment falls to be made of corporation tax paid by a company for an accounting period which ends after the appointed day, or

(b) a repayment of income tax falls to be made in respect of a payment received by a company in such an accounting period or

(c) a payment falls to be made to a company of the whole or part of the tax credit comprised in any franked investment income received by the company in such an accounting period,

then, from the material date until that repayment or payment is made the repayment or payment shall carry interest at the rate which, under section 89 of the Management Act, is for the time being the prescribed rate for the purposes of this section.

(2) In relation to corporation tax paid by a company for an accounting period, the material date for the purposes of this section is the date on which the corporation tax was paid or, if it is later, the date on which corporation tax for that accounting period became (or, as the case may be, would have become) due and payable in accordance with section 243(4) of the Taxes Act.

(3) In relation to a repayment of income tax falling within subsection (1)(b) above or a payment of the whole or part of a tax credit falling within subsection (1)(c) above, the material date is the date on which corporation tax became (or, as the case may be, would have become) due and payable for the accounting period in which the payment referred to in subsection (1)(b) above or, as the case may be, the franked investment income referred to in subsection (1)(c) above was received by the company.

(4) For the purposes of this section a repayment of tax made on a claim under subsection (5) of section 286 of the Taxes Act (loans to participators etc.) shall be treated as if it were a repayment of corporation tax for the accounting period in which the repayment of, or of the part in question

of, the loan or advance mentioned in that subsection was made but, in relation to such a repayment of tax, the material date for the purposes of this section is—

(a) the date on which the loan or advance (or part thereof) is repaid; or

(b) if it is later, the date on which the tax which is to be repaid was in fact paid.

(5) Interest paid under this section shall be paid without any deduction of income tax and shall not be brought into account in computing any profits or income.

(6) Where a repayment of corporation tax is a repayment of tax paid by a company on different dates, the repayment shall as far as possible be treated for the purposes of this section as a repayment of tax paid on a later rather than an earlier date among those dates.

(7) In any case where—

(a) there is in any accounting period of a company (in this subsection referred to as "the later period") an amount of surplus advance corporation tax, as defined in subsection (3) of section 85 of the Finance Act 1972, and

(b) pursuant to a claim under the said subsection (3), the whole or any part of that amount is treated for the purposes of the said section 85 as discharging liability for an amount of corporation tax for an earlier accounting period (in this subsection referred to as "the earlier period"), and

(c) a repayment falls to be made of corporation tax paid for the earlier period,

then, in determining the amount of interest (if any) payable under this section on the repayment of corporation tax for the earlier period, no account shall be taken of any increase in the amount of the repayment resulting from the said subsection (3) except so far as concerns interest for any time after the date on which any corporation tax for the later period became due and payable (as mentioned in subsection (2) above).

(8) In consequence of the preceding provisions of this section, no repayment supplement, within the meaning of section 48 of the Finance (No. 2) Act 1975, shall be paid in respect of any repayment of tax or payment of tax credit where the relevant accounting period, within the meaning of that section, ends after the appointed day.

GENERAL NOTE

Interest will be payable to companies when corporation tax is repaid after an overpayment under the "Pay and File" system. The interest will run from the due date at the rate prescribed under T.M.A. 1970, s.89. This is rather more generous than the existing regime for repayment supplements under F. (No. 2) A. 1975, s.48, which it replaces. It is designed as a commercial restitution in the circumstances where a company accidentally overpays tax against what is eventually assessed.

Recovery of overpayment of tax etc.

88.—(1) In section 30 of the Management Act (recovery of overpayment of tax etc.) after subsection (2) there shall be inserted the following subsection—

"(2A) In any case where—

(a) interest has been paid under section 87 of the Finance (No.2) Act 1987 on a repayment of tax, and

(b) the whole or any part of that repayment has been paid to any person but ought not to have been paid to him, and

(c) interest ought not to have been paid on that repayment, either at all or to any extent, then the amount of the repayment assessed under subsection (1) above may include an amount equal to the interest that ought not to have been paid."

(2) After subsection (3) of that section there shall be inserted the following subsection—

"(3A) If, in a case not falling within subsection (2A) above,—

(a) interest has been paid under section 87 of the Finance (No. 2) Act 1987 on a repayment of tax, and

(b) that interest ought not to have been paid, either at all or to any extent,

then an amount equal to the interest that ought not to have been paid may be assessed and recovered as if it were unpaid corporation tax."

(3) At the end of subsection (4) of that section there shall be added the words "and an assessment to recover—

(a) an amount of corporation tax repaid to a company in respect of an accounting period, or

(b) an amount of income tax repaid to a company in respect of a payment received by the company in any accounting period, or

(c) interest on any such repayment of tax,

shall be treated as an assessment to corporation tax for the accounting period referred to in paragraph (a) or (b) above, as the case may be, and the sum assessed shall carry interest at the prescribed rate for the purposes of section 87A of this Act from the date when the payment being recovered was made until payment."

(4) After subsection (4) of that section there shall be inserted the following subsection—

"(4A) Where an assessment is made under this section to recover—

(a) corporation tax repaid to a company in respect of an accounting period, or

(b) income tax repaid to a company in respect of payments received by the company in an accounting period,

and more than one repayment of that tax has been made in respect of that period, any sum recovered in respect of income tax or corporation tax repaid shall as far as possible be treated as relating to a repayment of that tax made later rather than to a repayment made earlier."

(5) In section 102 of the Finance Act 1972 (rectification of excessive set-off etc. of advance corporation tax or tax credit) after subsection (1) there shall be inserted the following subsections—

"(1A) In any case where—

(a) interest has been paid under section 87 of the Finance (No. 2) Act 1987 on a payment of tax credit, and

(b) interest ought not to have been paid on that payment, either at all or to any extent,

an assessment under this section may be made for recovering any interest that ought not to have been paid.

(1B) Where—

(a) an assessment is made under this section to recover tax credit paid to a company in respect of franked investment income received by the company in an accounting period, and

(b) more than one payment of tax credit has been made in respect of that period,

any sum recovered shall as far as possible be treated as relating to a payment of tax credit made later rather than to a payment made earlier."

(6) In subsection (2) of that section after the words "tax credit" there shall be inserted "or interest on such a payment".

(7) Subsections (1) to (4) above have effect with respect to the recovery of

    (a) repayments of corporation tax paid for accounting periods ending after the appointed day,

    (b) repayments of income tax on payments received by a company in any such accounting period, and

    (c) interest on such repayments;

and subsections (5) and (6) above have effect with respect to recovery of interest on payments of tax credit (within the meaning of Part V of the Finance Act 1972) claimed in respect of accounting periods ending after the appointed day.

GENERAL NOTE

Provision is made for the recovery by way of assessment of corporation tax repaid under the "Pay and File" system which should not have been repaid and of the interest paid on such repayments.

Prescribed rate of interest

89.—(1) In section 89 of the Management Act (prescribed rate of interest) for subsection (1) there shall be substituted the following subsection—

"(1) For the purposes of any provision of this Part of this Act and of section 87 of the Finance (No. 2) Act 1987 "the prescribed rate" means such rate as may for the time being be prescribed for the purposes of the provision in question by order made by the Treasury."

(2) In subsection (2) of that section—

    (a) for the words "The Treasury may, by order in a" there shall be substituted "The power to make an order under this section shall be exercisable by"; and

    (b) for the words from "from time to time" to "either" there shall be substituted "and any such order may be framed either so as to prescribe a single rate".

(3) In subsection (3) of that section for the words from the beginning to "(2) above" there shall be substituted "Any rate of interest prescribed by order under this section".

GENERAL NOTE

This section provides for the prescribed rate of interest under T.M.A. 1970, s.89, to apply to repayments under s.87, *supra*, and effects some tidying-up amendments to s.89. At present interest is payable after six months if a company underpays, and after 12 months if it overpays, but the rate of interest is the same. Consideration will be given to introducing a differential under the new system, to discourage deliberate overpayments of tax.

Miscellaneous

Corporation tax to be payable without assessment

90.—(1) With respect to accounting periods ending after the appointed day, corporation tax shall be payable without the making of an assessment and, with respect to such periods—

    (a) in subsection (3) of section 243 of the Taxes Act (which provides for assessments by reference to accounting periods) for the words from "assessments" to "a company" there shall be substituted "corporation tax shall be computed and chargeable (and any assessments shall accordingly be made)"; and

    (b) in subsection (4) of that section (which specifies the date when corporation tax assessed for an accounting period is to be paid) the word "assessed" and the words from "or if it is later" onwards shall be omitted and for the words "paid within" there shall be substituted "due and payable on the day following the expiry of".

(2) With respect to loans or advances made (or treated as made) in an accounting period ending after the appointed day, in subsection (1) of section 286 of the Taxes Act (loans to participators etc.) for the words "assessed on and recoverable" there shall be substituted "due".

(3) With respect to loans or advances made (or treated as made) as mentioned in subsection (2) above, for subsection (4) of the said section 286 there shall be substituted—

"(4) Tax due by virtue of this section shall be due and payable within fourteen days after the end of the accounting period in which the loan or advance was made".

(4) Notwithstanding that, by virtue of the preceding provisions of this section, any corporation tax (or any amount due as if it were corporation tax) is due without the making of an assessment, no proceedings for collecting that tax (or other amount) shall be instituted—

(a) unless it has been assessed; and

(b) until the expiry of the period of thirty days beginning on the date on which the notice of assessment is issued;

and the reference in this subsection to proceedings for collecting tax or any other amount includes a reference to proceedings by way of distraint or poinding for that tax or other amount.

(5) If, with respect to any accounting period,—

(a) a company has paid an amount of corporation tax without the making of an assessment; and

(b) at any time before an assessment to corporation tax for the period becomes final, the company has grounds for believing that, by reason of a change in the circumstances of the case since the tax was paid, the amount paid exceeds the company's probable liability for corporation tax,

the company may, by notice in writing given to the inspector on or after the date which, under section 87 above, is the material date in relation to that tax, make a claim for the repayment to the company of the amount of that excess; and a notice under this subsection shall state the amount which the company considers should be repaid and the grounds referred to in paragraph (b) above.

(6) If, apart from this subsection, a claim would fall to be made under subsection (5) above at a time when the company concerned has appealed against such an assessment as is referred to in paragraph (b) of that subsection but that appeal has not been finally determined, that subsection shall have effect as if, for the words from "make a claim" to "excess" there were substituted "apply to the Commissioners to whom the appeal stands referred for a determination of the amount which should be repaid to the company pending a determination of the company's liability for the accounting period in question"; and such an application shall be determined in the same way as the appeal.

(7) Where, on an appeal against an assessment to corporation tax, a company makes an application under subsection (3) or subsection (4) of section 55 of the Management Act (postponement of tax charged but not paid etc.) that application may be combined with an application under subsections (5) and (6) above (relating to tax which was paid prior to the assessment).

GENERAL NOTE

Although placed under the heading "miscellaneous", this section in fact contains the heart of the "Pay" limb of the "Pay and File" system by amending I.C.T.A. 1970, s.243(4) to make corporation tax payable by effluxion of time rather than by the raising of an assessment.

Subss. (2) and (3) apply the same regime to the corporation tax on loans to participators made by close companies.

Subs. (4) requires the raising of an assessment before proceedings are commenced for the collection of unpaid corporation tax.

Subss. (5)–(7) provide a system whereby a company can file a claim for tax overpaid either to the inspector or to the Commissioners, if the matter has gone to appeal, and such a claim can be combined with an application for postponement of payment.

Close companies: loans to participators

91.—(1) In section 109 of the Management Act (close companies: loans to participators) subsection (2) shall be omitted.

(2) In subsection (3) of that section for "88" there shall be substituted "87A" and for the words from "charged" onwards there shall be substituted "under the said section 286 became due and payable shall be that determined in accordance with subsection (4) of that section".

(3) After subsection (3) of that section there shall be inserted the following subsection—

"(3A) If there is such a repayment of the whole or any part of a loan or advance as is referred to in subsection (5) of section 286 of the principal Act, interest under section 87A of this Act on so much of the tax under the said section 286 as is referable to the amount repaid shall not be payable in respect of any period after the date on which the repayment was made."

(4) This section has effect with respect to loans or advances made (or treated as made) in any accounting period ending after the appointed day.

<small>GENERAL NOTE</small>

This section makes further amendments to the T.M.A. 1970 consequential on the bringing of loans to participators by close companies under I.C.T.A. 1970, s.286, within the "Pay and File" regime for corporation tax.

Amendments relating to PAYE

92.—(1) Section 204 of the Taxes Act (pay as you earn) shall be amended in accordance with this section.

(2) In subsection (2) (regulations) after paragraph (c) there shall be inserted the following paragraph—

"(cc) for requiring the payment of interest on sums due to the Board—

(i) which are not paid by the due date, and

(ii) of which the amount is determined by the inspector (before or after the due date) in accordance with the regulations,

and for determining the date (being not less than 14 days after the end of the year of assessment in respect of which the sums are due) from which such interest is to be calculated".

(3) After subsection (3) there shall be inserted the following subsection—

"(3A) Any reference in the preceding provisions of this section to a payment of, or on account of, any income assessable under Schedule E includes a reference to anything which, in accordance with regulations under subsection (2) above, is to be treated as a payment of, or on account of, any such income."

<small>GENERAL NOTE</small>

Two changes are made to the PAYE system.

<small>*Subs. (2)*</small>

Interest will be chargeable on PAYE underdeducted on the same general footing as on corporation tax unpaid in the "Pay and File" system.

Subs. (3)

It will be made clear that "payment" for PAYE purposes includes sums credited to an employee's account or remuneration voted to him. It has in any case been held that a bonus credited to a director's account in the company's books is a payment to him (*Garforth* v. *Newsmith Stainless* (1978) 52 T.C. 522).

It is proposed to make April 20, 1988, the effective date for these changes.

Sub-contractors in the construction industry

93.—(1) Section 70 of the Finance (No. 2) Act 1975 (certificates securing exemption from the deduction scheme applicable to sub-contractors in the construction industry) shall be amended as follows.

(2) After subsection (4) there shall be inserted the following subsection—

"(4A) Where it appears to the Board that there has been a change in the control of a company holding or applying for a certificate, the Board may make any such direction as is referred to in subsection (4) above."

(3) In subsection (5) (cancellation of certificates) at the end of paragraph (c) there shall be inserted "or

(d) in the case of a certificate issued to a company, there has been a change in the control of the company and information with respect to that change has not been furnished in accordance with regulations under subsection (7) below".

(4) In subsection (6) (appeals against refusal of certificate)—

(a) after the words "certificate under this section" there shall be inserted "or the cancellation of such a certificate"; and

(b) after the word "refusal", in the second place where it occurs, there shall be inserted "or as the case may be, cancellation".

(5) In subsection (7) after paragraph (c) there shall be inserted the following paragraph—

"(cc) requiring the furnishing of information with respect to changes in the control of a company holding or applying for such a certificate";

and after paragraph (f) there shall be inserted the following paragraph—

"(ff) with respect to the production, copying and removal of, and the making of extracts from, any records kept by virtue of any such requirement as is referred to in paragraph (f) above and with respect to rights of access to or copies of any such records which are removed; and".

(6) At the end of the section there shall be added the following subsection—

"(13) In this section "control" has the same meaning as in section 534 of the Taxes Act."

GENERAL NOTE

Various minor changes are made to the regime for sub-contractors in the construction industry, known as "the lump."

Subss. (2), (3), (5) and (6) enable the Revenue to require information regarding changes in control of a company holding a sub-contractor's certificate and to take protective measures in consequence of such a change or in default of information.

Subs. (4) introduces a right of appeal to the General or Special Commissioners against the cancellation of a certificate as well as against a refusal to grant one.

Failure to do things within a limited time

94. In section 118(2) of the Management Act (cases where persons are deemed not to have failed to do things which are required to be done within a limited time), after the word "deemed", in the second place where it occurs, there shall be inserted "not to have failed to do it unless the excuse ceased and, after the excuse ceased, he shall be deemed".

GENERAL NOTE

T.M.A. 1970, s.118(2), is amended to make it clear that a person cannot be deemed to have failed to do something within a limited time so long as a reasonable excuse for not doing it subsists.

Interpretation of Chapter V and consequential and supplementary provisions

95.—(1) In this Chapter "the Management Act" means the Taxes Management Act 1970.

(2) Subject to subsection (3) below, any reference in this Chapter to the appointed day is a reference to such day as the Treasury may by order made by statutory instrument appoint, and different days may be so appointed for different provisions of this Chapter.

(3) No day may be appointed by virtue of subsection (2) above which falls earlier than 31st March 1992.

(4) The provisions of Schedule 6 to this Act shall have effect, being provisions consequential on and supplementary to the provisions of this Chapter.

GENERAL NOTE

The "Pay and File" system is not to be introduced prior to March 31, 1992, and may be phased in by stages thereafter.

PART II

INHERITANCE TAX ETC.

Interests in possession

96.—(1) With respect to transfers of value made, and other events occurring, on or after 17th March 1987, the Inheritance Tax Act 1984 shall be amended in accordance with this section.

(2) In section 3A (potentially exempt transfers)—
 (a) in subsection (2)(a) the words "otherwise than as settled property" shall be omitted;
 (b) in subsection (2)(b) the words from "otherwise" onwards shall be omitted; and
 (c) in subsection (6) after the words "this Act" there shall be inserted "other than section 52".

(3) At the end of section 3A there shall be added the following subsection—
 "(7) In the application of this section to an event on the happening of which tax is chargeable under section 52 below, the reference in subsection (1)(a) above to the individual by whom the transfer of value is made is a reference to the person who, by virtue of section 3(4) above, is treated as the transferor."

(4) In section 49 (treatment of interests in possession) subsection (3) (which was added by paragraph 14 of Schedule 19 to the Finance Act 1986) shall be omitted.

(5) In section 55 (reversionary interest acquired by beneficiary) in subsection (2) the words "and such a disposition is not a potentially exempt transfer" (being words added by paragraph 15 of the said Schedule 19) shall be omitted.

(6) Schedule 7 to this Act shall have effect for the purpose of making further amendments of the Inheritance Tax Act 1984 relating to interests in possession in settled property.

GENERAL NOTE

The relief given by F.A. 1986 to *inter vivos* gifts of property, denominated as "potentially exempt transfers" ("PETs"), is now extended to gifts of settled property where the donee has an interest in possession. Under the 1986 Act the PET had to be either an outright gift to another individual or a gift into an accumulation and maintenance trust or a trust for the disabled under I.H.T.A. 1984, ss.71 or 89. Elaborate anti-avoidance provisions are contained in Sched. 7. See further the commentary to that Schedule.

Acceptance in lieu: capital transfer tax and estate duty

97.—(1) If, under paragraph 17 of Schedule 4 to the Finance Act 1975, the Commissioners of Inland Revenue agree to accept property in satisfaction of an amount of capital transfer tax on terms that the value to be attributed to the property for the purposes of that acceptance is determined as at a date earlier than that on which the property is actually accepted, the terms may provide that the amount of capital transfer tax which is satisfied by the acceptance of that property shall not carry interest under paragraph 19 of that Schedule from that date.

(2) If, under any of the enactments set out in paragraphs (a) to (c) of subsection (3) of section 8 of the National Heritage Act 1980, the Commissioners of Inland Revenue agree to accept property in satisfaction of an amount of estate duty on terms that the value to be attributed to the property for the purposes of that acceptance is determined as at a date earlier than that on which the property is actually accepted, the terms may provide that the amount of estate duty which is satisfied by the acceptance of that property shall not carry interest under section 18 of the Finance Act 1896 from that date.

(3) Subsections (1) and (2) above apply in any case where the acceptance of the property in question occurs on or after 17th March 1987 and paragraph 19 of Schedule 4 to the Finance Act 1975 or, as the case may be, section 18 of the Finance Act 1896 shall have effect subject to any such terms as are referred to in subsection (1) or subsection (2) above.

(4) In this section "estate duty" and "property" have the meaning assigned by section 272 of the Inheritance Tax Act 1984.

GENERAL NOTE

F.A. 1987, s.60, provided that where heritage property was offered in lieu of I.H.T., the value of the property could be determined as at the date of offer, and interest would cease to run from that date. Previously, this option did not exist; interest continued to run until the offer was accepted by the authorities and the property was valued as at the date of acceptance. The option is now extended to heritage property subsisting from the estate duty and capital transfer tax regimes. An Inland Revenue press release of April 8, 1987, described how they intended to operate the new system.

Personal pension schemes

98.—(1) The Inheritance Tax Act 1984 shall be amended as follows.

(2) At the end of section 12(2) (dispositions by employers that are not transfers of value) there shall be added—

"or
  (c) it is a contribution under approved personal pension arrangements within the meaning of Chapter II of Part I of the Finance (No. 2) Act 1987 entered into by an employee of the person making the disposition".

(3) In section 12(3), for the words "both paragraph (a) and (b)" there shall be substituted the words "more than one paragraph", and for the word "either" there shall be substituted the words "any one".

(4) In section 151 (treatment of pension rights etc.) after subsection (1) there shall be inserted—

"(1A) This section also applies to approved personal pension arrangements within the meaning of Chapter II of Part I of the Finance (No. 2) Act 1987; and references in the following provisions of this section to a scheme shall be construed accordingly."

(5) In section 152 (cash options) for the words from "under a contract" to "annuities)" there shall be substituted the words—

"(a) under approved personal pension arrangements within the meaning of Chapter II of Part I of the Finance (No. 2) Act 1987, or

(b) under a contract or trust scheme approved by the Board under section 226 or 226A of the Taxes Act or (before the commencement of that Act) under section 22 of the Finance Act 1956,".

GENERAL NOTE

Personal pension schemes under Pt. I, Chapter II, of this Act are accorded the same favourable treatment for I.H.T. purposes as occupational pension schemes under F.A. 1970, Pt. II, Chapter II, retirement annuities under I.C.T.A. 1970, ss.226 and 226A, and other similar arrangements.

PART III

MISCELLANEOUS AND SUPPLEMENTARY

Stamp duty: options etc.

99.—(1) In section 50 of the Finance Act 1987 (stamp duty exemption for options to acquire, and other interests in, exempt securities), in subsection (1), after the word "acquire" there shall be inserted the words "or to dispose of".

(2) In subsection (3) of that section, after the words "the Finance Act (Northern Ireland) 1967" (in both places) there shall be inserted the words "or section 79(2) of the Finance Act 1986".

GENERAL NOTE

Two amendments are made to F.A. 1987, s.50, which extended the stamp duty exemption for gilt edged securities and most categories of loan stock to options to acquire such stock.

Subs. (1) extends the exemption to options to dispose of such securities, *i.e.* the exemption will cover "put" as well as "call" options.

Subs. (2). The exemption under F.A. 1987, s.50, covered bearer instruments relating to stock expressed in the currency of a territory outside the scheduled territories, exempted from stamp duty by F.A. 1987, s.30. It is now extended to cover all bearer instruments relating to loan capital, exempted from stamp duty by F.A. 1986, s.79(2). The earlier exemption is in any case obsolete, since the definition of "scheduled territories" has disappeared from the statute book by virtue of the repeal of Exchange Control Act 1947 by F.A. 1987, s.68 and Sched. 16, Part XI.

Stamp duty reserve tax

100.—(1) The Finance Act 1986 shall have effect in relation to agreements to transfer securities made on or after 8th May 1987 with the insertion of the following section after section 89—

"Section 87: exceptions for public issues

89A.—(1) Section 87 above shall not apply as regards an agreement to transfer securities other than units under a unit trust scheme to B or B's nominee if—

(a) the agreement is part of an arrangement, entered into by B in the ordinary course of B's business as an issuing house, under which B (as principal) is to offer the securities for sale to the public,

(b) the agreement is conditional upon the admission of the securities to the Official List of The Stock Exchange,

(c) the consideration under the agreement for each security is the same as the price at which B is to offer the security for sale, and

(d) B sells the securities in accordance with the arrangement referred to in paragraph (a) above.

(2) Section 87 above shall not apply as regards an agreement if the securities to which the agreement relates are newly subscribed securities other than units under a unit trust scheme and—

(a) the agreement is made in pursuance of an offer to the public made by A (as principal) under an arrangement entered into in the ordinary course of A's business as an issuing house,

(b) a right of allotment in respect of, or to subscribe for, the securities has been acquired by A under an agreement which is part of the arrangement,

(c) both those agreements are conditional upon the admission of the securities to the Official List of The Stock Exchange, and

(d) the consideration for each security is the same under both agreements;

and for the purposes of this subsection, "newly subscribed securities" are securities which, in pursuance of the arrangement referred to in paragraph (a) above, are issued wholly for new consideration.

(3) Section 87 above shall not apply as regards an agreement if the securities to which the agreement relates are registered securities other than units under a unit trust scheme and—

(a) the agreement is made in pursuance of an offer to the public made by A,

(b) the agreement is conditional upon the admission of the securities to the Official List of The Stock Exchange, and

(c) under the agreement A issues to B or his nominee a renounceable letter of acceptance, or similar instrument, in respect of the securities.

(4) The Treasury may by regulations amend paragraph (b) of subsection (1) above, paragraph (c) of subsection (2) above, and paragraph (b) of subsection (3) above (as they have effect for the time being); and the power to make regulations under this section shall be exercisable by statutory instrument subject to annulment in pursuance of a resolution of the House of Commons."

(2) Section 91 of the Finance Act 1986 (liability to tax) shall have effect, and shall be deemed always to have had effect, with the omission of subsection (2).

GENERAL NOTE

Stamp duty reserve tax ("S.D.R.T.") was introduced by F.A. 1986, ss.86–99, to protect the revenue by imposing a charge on agreements to transfer securities in cases where no transfer document liable for stamp duty was subsequently produced. Two amendments are now made to these provisions.

Subs. (1) inserts a new s.89A which excepts from S.D.R.T. agreements to transfer securities entered into in the course of an offer for sale to the public. S.89A(1), (2) and (3) apply the exception respectively to existing securities and newly subscribed securities offered through an issuing house and securities issued directly under renounceable letters of acceptance. Where an issuing house is involved, the consideration under each agreement must be the same. The exception applies only to securities on the Stock Exchange Official List, but the Treasury is given power to modify this condition by statutory instrument. The effective date of the change is May 8, 1987, when an amending clause was put down to the spring Finance Bill.

Subs. (2). F.A. 1986, s.91(2) provided that where a transferee was acting as a nominee, is principal was liable for S.D.R.T. This restriction of liability is removed retrospectively. Regulations for the management of S.D.R.T. in pursuance of F.A. 1986, s.98 were made by .I. 1986, No. 1711.

Oil taxation

101.—(1) Schedule 10 to the Finance Act 1987 (nomination scheme for disposals and appropriations of oil) shall have effect subject to the amendments in Schedule 8 to this Act.

(2) In section 62 of the Finance Act 1987 (market value of oil to be determined on a monthly basis) subsection (6) (meaning of relevant sale of oil in relation to the additional return required by subsection (4) of that section) shall have effect subject to the following modifications—

(a) after the words "sale of oil", in the second place where they occur, there shall be inserted the words "at arm's length"; and

(b) in paragraph (b) after the words "sub-paragraph (3A) thereof" there shall be inserted "or otherwise".

(3) Section 63 of the Finance Act 1987 (blends of oil from two or more fields) shall have effect with the omission from subsection (1) of the words from "and in" onwards and with the addition, at the end of that subsection, of the following subsection—

"(1A) In this section—

(a) "oil field" includes an area which is a foreign field for the purposes of section 12 of the Oil Taxation Act 1983;

(b) "oil" includes any substance which would be oil if the enactments mentioned in section 1(1) of the principal Act extended to such an area as is referred to in paragraph (a) above;

(c) "blended oil" means oil which has been mixed as mentioned in subsection (1) above; and

(d) "the originating fields", in relation to any blended oil, means the oil fields from which the blended oil is derived."

(4) In paragraph 5 of Schedule 2 to the Oil Taxation Act 1975 (returns by the responsible person for an oil field) after sub-paragraph (2A) there shall be inserted the following sub-paragraph—

"(2B) If in any chargeable period oil won from the oil field is mixed as mentioned in section 63 of the Finance Act 1987 so as to give rise to blended oil, within the meaning of that section, then, as respects that chargeable period, for paragraph (a) of sub-paragraph (2) above there shall be substituted the following paragraph—

'(a) state the total of the shares of the participators in the oil field of the oil won from the field during the period less so much of the oil won from the field as is not saved'."

(5) Subsections (2) to (4) above have effect with respect to chargeable periods ending after 1st January 1987 and, subject to subsection (6) below, Schedule 8 to this Act has effect with respect to calendar months in chargeable periods beginning with March 1987.

(6) Paragraph 5 of Schedule 8 to this Act has effect with respect to chargeable periods ending after such date as the Treasury may by order made by statutory instrument appoint; but no order shall be made under this subsection unless a draft of it has been laid before and approved by a resolution of the House of Commons.

GENERAL NOTE

The spring Finance Bill (later enacted as F.A. 1987) contained provisions designed to tighten up the rules relating to valuation and pricing of oil for the purposes of petroleum revenue tax ("P.R.T."). The calling of the June 11 general election foreshortened discussion of these provisions, contained in F.A. 1987, ss.61–63 and Sched. 10. This section and Sched. 8 make mainly technical amendments which might have been otherwise dealt with on the committee stage of the earlier Bill.

Subs. (1). See the note to Sched. 8.

Subss. (2) to (4) make clarifying amendments to the relevant legislation.

Subs. (5). As with the provisions in F.A. 1987, the amendments have effect from January 1, 1987 in relation to valuation and from March 1987 in relation to pricing.

Subs. (6). Sched. 8, para. 5 introduces provisions designed to prevent manipulation of the new pricing rules. These provisions may only be brought into effect by Treasury order subject to affirmative resolution by the House of Commons.

Government fees and charges

102.—(1) This section applies where a Minister of the Crown or any other person has power under any enactment (whenever passed) to require the payment of, or to determine by subordinate legislation the amount of, any fee or charge (however described) which is payable to the Minister or to any other person who is required to pay the fee or charge into the Consolidated Fund (whether the obligation is so expressed or is expressed as a requirement to make the payment into the Exchequer).

(2) In the following provisions of this section, a power falling within subsection (1) above is referred to as a "power to fix a fee" and, in relation to such a power,—

    (a) "fee" includes charge;

    (b) "the appropriate authority" means, if the power is exercisable by a Minister of the Crown or any Commissioners, that Minister or those Commissioners and, in any other case, such Minister of the Crown as the Treasury may determine; and

    (c) "the recipient" means the Minister or other person to whom the fee is payable.

(3) In relation to any power to fix a fee, the appropriate authority or any Minister of the Crown with the consent of the appropriate authority may, by order made by statutory instrument, specify functions, whether of the recipient or any other person and whether arising under any enactment, by virtue of any Community obligation or otherwise, the costs of which, in addition to any other matters already required to be taken into account, are to be taken into account in determining the amount of the fee.

(4) In relation to any functions the costs of which fall to be taken into account on the exercise of any power to fix a fee (whether by virtue of subsection (3) above or otherwise), the appropriate authority or any Minister of the Crown with the consent of the appropriate authority may, by order made by statutory instrument, specify matters which, in addition to any matters already required to be taken into account, are to be taken into account in determining those costs, and, without prejudice to the generality of the power conferred by this subsection, those matters may include deficits incurred before as well as after the exercise of that power, a requirement to secure a return on an amount of capital and depreciation of assets.

(5) No order shall be made under subsection (3) or subsection (4) above unless a draft of the order has been laid before, and approved by a resolution of, the House of Commons.

(6) An order under subsection (3) or subsection (4) above has effect in relation to any exercise of the power to fix the fee concerned after the making of the order; but no earlier exercise of that power shall be regarded as having been invalid if, had the order been made before that exercise of the power, the exercise would have been validated by the order.

(7) In this section—

    (a) "Minister of the Crown" has the same meaning as in the Ministers of the Crown Act 1975;

(b) "Commissioners" means the Commissioners of Customs and Excise or the Commissioners of Inland Revenue;

(c) "enactment" does not include Northern Ireland legislation, as defined in section 24(5) of the Interpretation Act 1978; and

(d) subject to paragraph (c) above "subordinate legislation" has the same meaning as in the Interpretation Act 1978.

(8) An Order in Council under paragraph 1(1)(b) of Schedule 1 to the Northern Ireland Act 1974 (legislation for Northern Ireland in the interim period) which states that it is made only for purposes corresponding to those of this section—

(a) shall not be subject to sub-paragraphs (4) and (5) of paragraph 1 of that Schedule (affirmative resolution of both Houses of Parliament); but

(b) shall be subject to annulment in pursuance of a resolution of either House.

ENERAL NOTE

This section does not relate to taxation as such. It authorises government departments when fixing fees or charges under any statute to take into account functions other than those already provided for, pre-existing deficits, a requirement to secure a return on capital and depreciation of assets. The power is exercisable in pursuance of a statutory instrument subject to the affirmative procedure, except in relation to legislative functions under direct rule in Northern Ireland, where the order is subject to negative resolution in either House.

Consumption in port of goods transhipped for use as stores etc.

103.—(1) Subject to subsection (2) below and to any directions given by the Commissioners under section 61 of the Customs and Excise Management Act 1979, goods transhipped for use as stores on a ship which is of not less than 40 tons register and which is to make a voyage to a country outside the United Kingdom may be used while the ship is in port without payment of duty.

(2) Subsection (1) above does not apply to—

(a) dutiable alcoholic liquor other than beer and cider; or

(b) tobacco products;

and the reference in subsection (1) above to a country outside the United Kingdom does not include a reference to the Isle of Man.

(3) In section 1(1) of the Customs and Excise Management Act 1979, at the end of the definition of "transit or transhipment" there shall be added "or transhipment of those goods for use as stores".

(4) In subsection (1) of section 61 of that Act, after paragraph (a) there shall be added—

"(aa) as to the descriptions of vessel on which goods carried as stores may be used in port without payment of duty in accordance with section 103(1) of the Finance (No. 2) Act 1987;

(ab) as to the quantity of any goods which may be carried as stores for use in port as mentioned in paragraph (aa) above and as to the time within which such goods or any specified quantities of them may be so used; and";

and in paragraph (b) of that subsection after the words "paragraph (a)" there shall be inserted "or paragraph (aa)".

(5) In subsection (5) of the said section 61 after the words "United Kingdom", in the first place where they occur, there shall be inserted "or for use in port without payment of duty".

(6) Subsections (1) and (2) above shall be construed as one with the Customs and Excise Management Act 1979.

(7) Notwithstanding the generality of section 24 of the Value Added Tax Act 1983 (application of customs and excise enactments in relation to

value added tax), subsections (1) and (2) above are excluded from th enactments to which that section applies.

GENERAL NOTE
Fish processing ships, known as Klondykers, from foreign countries, have been enter British waters for extended periods in connection with purchases from local fishermen. T charging of customs duty on supplies to such factory ships has threatened to drive the away from British ports. To protect this loss of trade supplies of stores, other than wir spirits or tobacco, to these ships are relieved from duty.

Short title, interpretation, construction and repeals

104.—(1) This Act may be cited as the Finance (No. 2) Act 1987.

(2) In this Act "the Taxes Act" means the Income and Corporatic Taxes Act 1970.

(3) Part I of this Act, so far as it relates to income tax, shall I construed as one with the Income Tax Acts, so far as it relates corporation tax, shall be construed as one with the Corporation Tax Ac and, so far as it relates to capital gains tax, shall be construed as one wi the Capital Gains Tax Act 1979.

(4) The enactments specified in Schedule 9 to this Act (which inclue enactments which are spent or otherwise unnecessary) are hereby repeale to the extent specified in the third column of that Schedule, but subje to any provision at the end of any Part of that Schedule.

SCHEDULES

Section 7 etc.   SCHEDULE 1

PROFIT-RELATED PAY SCHEMES:

CONDITIONS FOR REGISTRATION

Form

1. The terms of the scheme must be set out in writing.

Employer and employment unit

2. The scheme must identify the scheme employer.

3. If the scheme employer does not pay the emoluments of all the employees to whom t scheme relates, the scheme must identify each of the persons who pays the emoluments any of those employees.

4.—(1) The scheme must identify the undertaking to which the scheme relates, and th undertaking must be one which is carried on with a view to profit.

(2) The references in sub-paragraph (1) above to an undertaking include references part of an undertaking; and the provisions of a scheme identifying part of an undertaki must do so in such a way as to distinguish it, otherwise than by name only, from other pa of the undertaking.

Employees

5. The scheme must contain provisions by reference to which the employees to whom t scheme relates may be identified.

6. The scheme must contain provisions ensuring that no payments are made under it reference to a profit period if the employees to whom the scheme relates constitute less th 80 per cent. of all the employees in the employment unit at the beginning of that pro period; but for this purpose any person who is at that time within paragraph 7 or 8 belo shall not be counted.

7.—(1) The scheme must contain provisions ensuring that no payments are made und it to any person who is employed in the employment unit by a company and who has, or an associate of a person who has, a material interest in the company.

(2) For the purposes of this paragraph a person shall be treated as having a material interest in a company

(a) if he, either on his own or with any one or more of his associates, or if any associate of his with or without such other associates, is the beneficial owner of, or able (directly or through the medium of other companies or by any other indirect means) to control, more than 25 per cent. of the ordinary share capital of the company, or

(b) if, in the case of a close company, on an amount equal to the whole distributable income of the company falling to be apportioned under Chapter III of Part XI of the Taxes Act for the purpose of computing total income, more than 25 per cent. of that amount could be apportioned to him together with his associates (if any), or to any associate of his, or to any such associates taken together.

(3) In this paragraph "associate" has the same meaning as in section 303(3) of the Taxes Act and "control" has the meaning given by section 534 of that Act; and the definition of 'control" in section 534 applies (with the necessary modifications) in relation to a company which is an unincorporated association as it applies in relation to one that is not.

8.—(1) The persons within this paragraph are any of the following employees who are excluded by the scheme from receiving any payment of profit-related pay—

(a) those who are not required, under the terms of their employment, to work in the employment unit for twenty hours or more a week;

(b) those who have not been employed by a relevant employer for a minimum period (of not more than three years) specified in the scheme;

and for this purpose "relevant employer" means the scheme employer or any person who pays the emoluments of any of the employees to whom the scheme relates.

Profit periods

9. The scheme must identify the accounting period or periods by reference to which any profit-related pay is to be calculated.

10.—(1) Subject to sub-paragraphs (2) and (3) below, any such accounting period must be a period of twelve months.

(2) If the scheme is a replacement scheme, the first of two profit periods may be a period of less than twelve months, but the scheme may not provide for more than two profit periods.

(3) The scheme may make provision for a profit period to be abbreviated where registration of the scheme is cancelled with effect from a day after the beginning of the period; and a scheme making such provision may exclude the operation of all or any of the provisions of paragraph 13(4) and (5) or (as the case may be) paragraph 14(3)(b), (4) and (5) below in relation to the determination of the distributable pool for an abbreviated period.

(4) For the purposes of this paragraph, a scheme is a replacement scheme if—

(a) it succeeds another scheme (or two or more other schemes) registration of which was cancelled under section 10(1)(a) of this Act on the ground of a change in the employment unit or in the circumstances relating to the scheme, and

(b) that change occurred not more than three months before the beginning of the first (or only) profit period of the new scheme, and the Board are satisfied that it was not brought about with a view to the registration of the new scheme or in circumstances satisfying the conditions in section 9(1)(a), (b) and (c) of this Act, and

(c) not less than one half of the employees to whom the new scheme relates were employees to whom the previous scheme (or any of the previous schemes) related at the time of that change.

Distributable pool

11. The scheme must contain provisions by reference to which the aggregate sum that may be paid to employees in respect of a profit period ("the distributable pool") may be determined.

12. Except where the scheme is a replacement scheme (within the meaning of paragraph 10 above), the provisions for the determination of the distributable pool must employ either the method specified in paragraph 13 below ("method A") or the method specified in paragraph 14 below ("method B").

13.—(1) Method A is that the distributable pool is equal to a fixed percentage of the profits of the employment unit in the profit period.

(2) That percentage must be such that, on the assumption as to profits mentioned i
sub-paragraph (3) below, it will produce a distributable pool equal to not less than 5 pe
cent. of the standard pay of the employment unit.

(3) The assumption referred to in sub-paragraph (2) above is that the profits in the profi
period are the same as those in a base year specified in the scheme; and that base year mus
be a period of twelve months ending at a time within the period of two years immediatel
preceding the profit period, or the first of the profit periods, to which the scheme relates.

(4) Notwithstanding sub-paragraph (1) above, a scheme employing method A may includ
provision for disregarding profits in the profit period so far as they exceed 160 per cent. (o
such greater percentage as may be specified in the scheme) of—

    (a) if the profit period is the first or only period to which the scheme relates, the profit
        for the base year referred to in sub-paragraph (3) above;

    (b) in any other case, the profits for the previous profit period.

(5) Notwithstanding sub-paragraph (1) above, a scheme employing method A may includ
provision to the effect that there shall be no distributable pool if the profits in the profi
period are less than an amount specified in, or ascertainable by reference to, the scheme
but that amount must be less than the amount which would produce a distributable pool o
5 per cent. of the standard pay of the employment unit.

(6) The references in this paragraph to the standard pay of the employment unit ar
references to the amount which the scheme employer, at the time when he applies fo
registration of the scheme, reasonably estimates will be the annual equivalent of the pay, a
the beginning of the profit period or first profit period, of the employees to whom th
scheme will then relate; and for this purpose an estimate shall (in the absence of evidenc
to the contrary) be taken to be a reasonable one if it is based on the most recent informatio
available to the employer as to the monthly or annual pay of the relevant employees.

14.—(1) Method B is that the distributable pool is—

    (a) if the profit period is the first or only profit period to which the scheme relates, a
        percentage of a notional pool of an amount specified in the scheme;

    (b) in any other case, a percentage of the distributable pool for the previous profit period

(2) The amount of the notional pool referred to in sub-paragraph (1) above must not b
less than 5 per cent. of the standard pay of the employment unit.

(3) The percentage referred to in sub-paragraph (1) above must be either—

    (a) that arrived at by expressing the profits in the profit period as a percentage of th
        profits in the preceding period of twelve months, or

    (b) the percentage mentioned in paragraph (a) above reduced (if it is more than 100) o
        increased (if it is less than 100) by a specified fraction of the difference between it an
        100;

and the reference in paragraph (b) above to a specified fraction is a reference to a fractio
of not more than one half specified in the scheme.

(4) Notwithstanding sub-paragraph (1) above, a scheme employing method B may includ
provision for disregarding profits in the profit period so far as they exceed 160 per cent. (o
such greater percentage as may be specified in the scheme) of the profits in the precedin
period of twelve months.

(5) Notwithstanding sub-paragraph (1) above, a scheme employing method B may includ
provision to the effect that there shall be no distributable pool if the profits in the profi
period are less than an amount specified in, or ascertainable by reference to, the scheme
but that amount must be less than the amount which would produce a distributable pool o
5 per cent. of the standard pay of the employment unit.

(6) Where by virtue of a provision of the kind described in sub-paragraph (5) above there
is no distributable pool for a profit period, any comparison required in accordance with
sub-paragraph (1)(b) to be made with the distributable pool for that period shall be made
with what would have been the pool but for sub-paragraph (5).

(7) In this paragraph "standard pay of the employment unit" has the same meaning as i
has in paragraph 13 above.

15. If the scheme is a replacement scheme (within the meaning of paragraph 10 above)
it must provide for the distributable pool for a profit period to be equal to a specifiec
percentage of the profits for the period.

Payments from distributable pool, etc.

16. The scheme must provide for the whole of the distributable pool to be paid tc
employees in the employment unit.

17. The scheme must make provision as to when payments will be made to employees.

18.—(1) The provisions of the scheme must be such that employees participate in the
scheme on similar terms.

(2) For the purposes of sub-paragraph (1) above, the fact that the payments to employees vary according to the levels of their remuneration, the length of their service or similar factors shall not be regarded as meaning that they do not participate on similar terms.

Ascertainment of profits

19.—(1) The scheme must provide for the preparation of a profit and loss account in respect of—

(a) each profit period of the employment unit, and

(b) any other period the profits for which must be ascertained for the purposes of this Chapter.

(2) The profit and loss account must give a true and fair view of the profit or loss of the employment unit for the period to which it relates.

(3) Subject to sub-paragraph (2) above, the requirements of Schedule 4 to the Companies Act 1985 shall apply (with any necessary modifications) to a profit and loss account prepared for the purposes of the scheme as they apply to a profit and loss account of a company for a financial year.

(4) Notwithstanding the preceding provisions of this paragraph, a profit and loss account prepared for the purposes of the scheme must not make any deduction, in arriving at the profits or losses of the employment unit, for the remuneration of any person excluded from the scheme by virtue of paragraph 7 above.

(5) Notwithstanding the preceding provisions of this paragraph, if the scheme so provides in relation to any of the items listed in sub-paragraph (6) below, a profit and loss account prepared for the purposes of the scheme may, in arriving at the profits or losses of the employment unit,—

(a) leave the item out of account notwithstanding that Schedule 4 to the Companies Act 1985 requires it to be taken into account, or

(b) take the item into account notwithstanding that Schedule 4 to the Companies Act 1985 requires it to be left out of account.

(6) The items referred to in sub-paragraph (5) above are—

(a) interest receivable and similar income;

(b) interest payable and similar charges;

(c) goodwill;

(d) tax on profit or loss on ordinary activities (but not any penalty under the Taxes Acts);

(e) research and development costs;

(f) profit-related pay payable under the scheme;

(g) extraordinary income;

(h) extraordinary charges;

(i) extraordinary profit or loss;

(j) tax on extraordinary profit or loss.

(7) References in this paragraph to Schedule 4 to the Companies Act 1985 shall be construed, in relation to Northern Ireland, as references to Schedule 4 to the Companies (Northern Ireland) Order 1986.

20.—(1) The scheme must provide that, in preparing a profit and loss account for the purposes of this Schedule, no changes may be made from the accounting policies used in preparing accounts for any earlier period relevant for those purposes, or in the methods of applying those policies, if the effect of the changes (either singly or taken together) would be that the amount of profits (or losses) differed by more than 5 per cent. from what would be that amount if no changes were made.

(2) Sub-paragraph (1) above has effect subject to paragraph 19(2) above.

GENERAL NOTE

This Schedule contains the basic "nuts and bolts" of PRP schemes. Once a scheme is approved, it will generally operate on a self-regulatory basis, subject to annual reports to the Revenue. Accordingly the registration conditions are of paramount importance. Many of the conditions are virtually self-evident, *e.g.* the rule under para. 1 that the terms must be set out in writing. The more important specific requirements are noted below.

Para. 6. At least 80 per cent. of the employees in the unit connected must be eligible for payments under the PRP scheme, subject to the exclusions under paras. 7 and 8.

Para. 7. No employee of a company is eligible to participate in a PRP scheme if he and his associates have more than a 25 per cent. interest.

Para. 8. Employees who work for less than 20 hours a week or have been with the employer for less than three years may be excluded from the scheme.

Para. 10. Except in the case of replacement or terminated schemes, PRP schemes must operate with reference to a 12 month accounting period. A replacement scheme may be registered where changes of circumstance make it impracticable to operate the original scheme, provided at least half the employees in the original scheme are included in the replacement scheme. See further para. 15.

Para. 11 sets out the subject matter of the P.R.P. scheme as "the distributable pool" of profits.

Para. 12 introduces two methods of calculating the distributable pool.

Para. 13 sets out Method A. Under this the distributable pool is a percentage of the profits, set so that if the profits are the same as in a base year within the two preceding years, the pool will not be less than 5 per cent. of the pay of the employees concerned at the beginning of the period. The scheme may include cut-off points if the profits for any period rise by more than 60 per cent. or fall below the 5 per cent. threshold.

Para. 14 sets out Method B. Under this the distributable pool is arrived at by applying to a fixed sum, which must meet the 5 per cent. test mentioned above, a percentage arrived at by expressing the profit for the period as a percentage of the profit in the previous period, or by applying a fraction of not more than one half to the difference between that percentage and 100. The same upper and lower cut-off points are available as for Method A.

Para. 15. For a replacement scheme (see para. 10), the distributable pool must be a specified percentage of the profits.

Paras. 16 and 17 provide that the distributable pool must all be paid out to employees at specified times. The Revenue envisage that payments may be made in a lump sum when the profits for the period have been ascertained or by instalments during the period based on estimated results or management accounts, with adjustments as necessary.

Para. 18. As with employee share schemes, the participation of employees in the distributable pool may vary with their pay levels, length of service or similar factors.

Para. 19. Accounts used for the purposes of PRP schemes must comply with the requirements of Companies Act 1985, Sched. 4, but a number of items, including interest, tax, R&D costs and extraordinary income or charges, may be left out of the computation. The logical standard for a unit would appear to be net trading income before interest, tax and extraordinary items.

Para. 20. Accounting policies may not be changed if the change would produce more than a 5 per cent. variation in profits.

Section 57   SCHEDULE 2

Personal Pension Schemes Etc.

1. In section 226(13) of the Taxes Act, after "means" there shall be inserted "(a)", and at the end there shall be added—
> "and
> (b) annuities or lump sums under approved personal pension arrangements within the meaning of Chapter II of Part I of the Finance (No. 2) Act 1987".

2.—(1) In section 332(2) of the Taxes Act (exceptions to registered friendly societies' exemption from income tax and corporation tax), after paragraph (a) and before the word "and" which follows it there shall be inserted—
> "(aa) shall not apply to profits arising from pension business,".

(2) In section 337 of the Taxes Act (interpretation of Chapter III of Part XII of that Act etc.)—
> (a) in subsection (2), after the words "the Friendly Societies Act 1974" there shall be inserted the words ", any pension business",
> (b) paragraph (b) of subsection (2) shall be omitted, and
> (c) in subsection (3), after the definition of "tax exempt life or endowment business" there shall be inserted—
>> "'pension business' shall be construed in accordance with section 323 above,".

3. In section 14(1) of the Finance Act 1973 (lump sum benefits on retirement not chargeable under Schedule E), at the end there shall be added "; or
> (c) it is paid under approved personal pension arrangements (within the meaning of Chapter II of Part I of the Finance (No. 2) Act 1987)".

4.—(1) In section 26 of the Finance Act 1978 (open market option for retirement annuities) in subsection (1), for the words from "may require" to the end there shall be substituted—
> "(a) may agree with the person with whom it is made that a sum representing the value

of the individual's accrued rights under it should be applied as the premium or other consideration either under another annuity contract made between them and approved by the Board under section 226 of the Taxes Act, or under personal pension arrangements made between them and approved by the Board under Chapter II of Part I of the Finance (No. 2) Act 1987, or

(b) may require the person with whom it is made to pay such a sum to such other person as the individual may specify, to be applied by that other person as the premium or other consideration either under an annuity contract made between the individual and him and approved by the Board under section 226 of the Taxes Act, or under personal pension arrangements made between the individual and him and approved by the Board under Chapter II of Part I of the Finance (No. 2) Act 1987.".

(2) This paragraph shall be deemed to have come into force on 6th April 1987.

5. In section 45(2) of the Finance Act 1984, after paragraph (c) there shall be added—
"(d) subsections (1) and (2) of section 39 of the Finance (No. 2) Act 1987".

6. In paragraph 1 of Schedule 11 to the Finance Act 1984 (treatment of lettings as a trade for the purposes of certain provisions), at the end of sub-paragraph (2) there shall be added—
"(k) subsection (2)(c) of section 35 of the Finance (No. 2) Act 1987 (personal pension schemes).".

GENERAL NOTE

This contains a number of miscellaneous amendments consequent upon the introduction of the new relief for approved personal pension arrangements. In particular:

(i) the general exemption in favour of friendly societies will not cover profits from pension business (para. 2);

(ii) the lump sum paid to a member on retirement is not chargeable to income tax under Schedule E (para. 3);

(iii) the funds of such schemes invested in financial futures and trade options will be covered by the exemption contained in F.A. 1984, s.45 (para. 5);

(iv) income from the commercial letting of furnished holiday accommodation is included in a member's relevant earnings (para. 6).

Section 58   SCHEDULE 3

OCCUPATIONAL PENSION SCHEMES

PART I

AMENDMENTS OF FINANCE ACT 1970 ETC.

The Finance Act 1970

1.—(1) In subsection (2A) of section 19 of the Finance Act 1970 (mandatory approval of schemes) in paragraph (d), after the words "final remuneration" there shall be inserted the words "(disregarding any excess of that remuneration over the permitted maximum)"; and after that subsection there shall be inserted—
"(2B) In subsection (2A) above "the permitted maximum" means £100,000 or such other sum as may for the time being be specified in an order made by the Treasury; and an order under this subsection shall be made by statutory instrument, which shall be subject to annulment in pursuance of a resolution of the House of Commons."

(2) This paragraph shall be deemed to have come into force on 17th March 1987.

2.—(1) In subsection (3) of section 19 (withdrawal of approval) after the words "such date" there shall be inserted the words "(which shall not be earlier than the date when those facts first ceased to warrant the continuance of their approval)".

(2) This paragraph shall be deemed to have come into force on 17th March 1987, but shall not authorise the withdrawal of an approval from a day before that day.

3.—(1) Section 20 (discretionary approval) shall be amended as follows.

(2) At the end of subsection (1) there shall be added the words "; but this subsection has effect subject to subsection (4) below.".

(3) For paragraph (g) of subsection (2), there shall be substituted—
"(g) which provides in certain contingencies for securing relevant benefits (but no other benefits) by means of an annuity contract approved by the Board and made with an insurance company of the employee's choice,".

(4) After paragraph (g) of subsection (2) there shall be added—
"or

    (h) to which the employer is not a contributor and which provides benefits additional to those provided by a scheme to which he is a contributor.".

(5) At the end of the section there shall be added—

"(4) The Board shall not approve a scheme by virtue of this section if to do so would be inconsistent with regulations made for the purposes of this section.

(5) Regulations made for the purposes of this section may restrict the Board's discretion to approve a scheme by reference to the benefits provided by the scheme, the investments held for the purposes of the scheme, the manner in which the scheme is administered, or any other circumstances whatever.

(6) The power to make regulations for the purposes of this section shall be exercisable by the Board by statutory instrument, which shall be subject to annulment in pursuance of a resolution of the House of Commons.".

4.—(1) In subsection (4) of section 21 (tax relief for ordinary annual contributions) the words "ordinary annual" shall be omitted; and after that subsection there shall be inserted—

"(4A) The amount allowed to be deducted by virtue of subsection (4) above in respect of contributions paid by an employee in a year of assessment (whether under a single scheme or under two or more schemes) shall not exceed 15 per cent., or such higher percentage as the Board may in a particular case prescribe, of his remuneration for that year.".

(2) This paragraph shall have effect in relation to contributions paid on or after 6th April 1987.

5. After subsection (7) of section 21 there shall be inserted—

"(7A) Subsection (2) of section 354 and subsection (3) of section 354A of the Taxes Act (which treat unit holders under unit trust schemes as receiving certain payments) shall not apply to any authorised unit trust which is also an exempt approved scheme if the employer is not a contributor to the exempt approved scheme and that scheme provides benefits additional to those provided by another exempt approved scheme to which he is a contributor.

(7B) A gain accruing to a unit holder on his disposal of units in an authorised unit trust to which subsection (7A) above applies shall not be a chargeable gain for the purposes of capital gains tax."

6.—(1) In subsection (2) of section 22 (tax relief for ordinary annual contributions) the words "ordinary annual" shall be omitted, and for the words "chargeable period" there shall be substituted the words "year of assessment"; and after that subsection there shall be inserted—

"(2A) The amount allowed to be deducted by virtue of subsection (2) above in respect of contributions paid by a person in a year of assessment (whether under a single scheme or under two or more schemes) shall not exceed 15 per cent., or such higher percentage as the Board may in a particular case prescribe, of his remuneration for that year.".

(2) This paragraph shall have effect in relation to contributions paid on or after 6th April 1987.

7.—(1) Section 26(1) shall be amended as follows.

(2) After the definition of "pension" there shall be inserted—

" 'the permitted maximum' has the meaning given by section 19(2B) above;".

(3) After the definition of "relevant benefits" there shall be inserted—

"'remuneration' does not include—

    (a) anything in respect of which tax is chargeable under Schedule E and which arises from the acquisition or disposal of shares or an interest in shares or from a right to acquire shares, or

    (b) anything in respect of which tax is chargeable by virtue of section 187 of the Taxes Act (payments on termination of employment, etc.);".

8. In section 26(2), after the words "the employer" there shall be inserted the words "or the employee", and at the end there shall be added the words "; and any reference to pensions or contributions paid, or payments made, under a scheme includes a reference to pensions or contributions paid, or payments made, under such a contract entered into for the purposes of the scheme".

9.—(1) In Schedule 5 to the Finance Act 1970, in paragraph 3(1)(i), after the words "final remuneration" there shall be inserted the words "(disregarding any excess of that remuneration over the permitted maximum)".

(2) This paragraph applies to any payments made on or after 17th March 1987 except payments made under schemes approved or established before that date to employees who became members before that date.

10. In paragraph 3 of that Schedule, at the end there shall be added—

"(7) Where the pension has been secured by means of an annuity contract with an insurance company and the sum receivable is payable under that contract by the insurance company, the references to the administrator of the scheme in sub-paragraph (2) above and paragraph 2(2) and (4) above as applied by sub-paragraph (2) are to be read as references to the insurance company.

(8) In sub-paragraph (7) above "insurance company" means—

(a) a person authorised under section 3 or 4 of the Insurance Companies Act 1982 to carry on long term business and acting through a branch or agency in the United Kingdom, or

(b) a society registered as a friendly society under the Friendly Societies Act 1974 or the Friendly Societies Act (Northern Ireland) 1970."

11. In paragraph 6 (which shall become paragraph 6(1)) of that Schedule, for the word "supported" there shall be substituted the word "accompanied"; and at the end there shall be added—

"(2) The form in which an application for approval is to be made, or in which any information is to be given, in pursuance of this paragraph may be prescribed by the Board.".

12. After paragraph 6 of that Schedule there shall be inserted—

"Relief by deduction from contributions

6A.—(1) Relief under section 21(4) of this Act shall be given in accordance with sub-paragraphs (2) and (3) below in such cases and subject to such conditions as the Board may prescribe by regulations under paragraph 10 below in respect of schemes—

(a) to which employees, but not their employers, are contributors, and

(b) which provide benefits additional to benefits provided by schemes to which their employers are contributors.

(2) An employee who is entitled to relief under section 21(4) in respect of a contribution may deduct from the contribution when he pays it, and may retain, an amount equal to income tax at the basic rate on the contribution.

(3) The administrator of the scheme—

(a) shall accept the amount paid after the deduction in discharge of the employee's liability to the same extent as if the deduction had not been made, and

(b) may recover an amount equal to the deduction from the Board.

(4) Regulations under paragraph 10 below may, without prejudice to the generality of that paragraph,—

(a) provide for the manner in which claims for the recovery of a sum under sub-paragraph (3)(b) above may be made;

(b) provide for the giving of such information, in such form, as may be prescribed by or under the regulations;

(c) provide for the inspection by persons authorised by the Board of books, documents and other records."

13. In paragraph 7 (which shall become paragraph 7(1)) of that Schedule, at the end there shall be added—

"(2) Where benefits provided for an employee under an approved scheme or a statutory scheme have been secured by means of an annuity contract with an insurance company (within the meaning given by paragraph 3 above), the insurance company shall, within thirty days from the date of a notice from the inspector requiring it to do so, prepare and deliver to the inspector a return containing particulars of—

(a) any payments under the contract by way of commutation of, or in lieu of, a pension, or any other lump sum payments under the contract, and

(b) any payments made under the contract to the employer.".

14. In paragraph 8(2)(a) of that Schedule, after the words "such scheme" there shall be inserted the words "to which he contributes".

15. In paragraph 9 of that Schedule, after sub-paragraph (1) there shall be inserted—

"(1A) Sub-paragraph (1) above does not apply if the employer is not a contributor to the scheme.".

The Taxes Act

16. In section 323(4) of the Taxes Act (insurance companies: interpretation of "pension business"), after paragraph (ab) there shall be inserted—

"(ac) any annuity contract entered into for the purposes of—

(i) a scheme which is approved or is being considered for approval under Chapter II of Part II of the Finance Act 1970,

(ii) a statutory scheme as defined in section 26 of that Act, or

(iii) a fund to which section 36 of the Finance Act 1980 applies,

being a contract which is approved by the Board and made with the persons having the management of the scheme or fund (or those persons and a member of or contributor to the scheme or fund) and by means of which relevant benefits as defined in section 26 of the Finance Act 1970 (but no other benefits) are secured,

(ad) any annuity contract approved by the Board which is entered into in substitution for a contract within paragraph (ac) above,".

The Taxes Management Act 1970

17. In both columns in the Table in section 98 of the Taxes Management Act 1970, after the reference to provisions of Schedule 5 to the Finance Act 1970 there shall be inserted—
"Regulations under paragraph 10 of that Part of that Schedule".

PART II

SCHEMES APPROVED BEFORE THE PASSING OF THIS ACT

Preliminary

18.—(1) This Part of this Schedule shall be deemed to have come into force on 17th March 1987 and, subject to sub-paragraphs (2) and (3) below, applies in relation to any retirement benefits scheme approved by the Board before the passing of this Act.

(2) The Board may by regulations provide that this Part of this Schedule, or any provision of it, shall not apply in relation to a scheme or to an employee—

(a) in circumstances prescribed in the regulations;

(b) in any case where in the opinion of the Board the facts are such that it would be appropriate for this Part of this Schedule, or the provision in question, not to apply;

and regulations under this sub-paragraph shall be made by statutory instrument, which shall be subject to annulment in pursuance of a resolution of the House of Commons.

(3) This Part of this Schedule shall not apply to a retirement benefits scheme if, before the end of 1987, the administrator of the scheme gives written notice to the Board that it is not to apply.

(4) Where a notice is given to the Board under sub-paragraph (3) above, the scheme shall, with effect from 17th March 1987 or (if later) the date with effect from which it was approved, cease to be approved.

Accelerated accrual

19.—(1) This paragraph applies where an employee becomes a member of the scheme on or after 17th March 1987.

(2) Notwithstanding anything to the contrary in the rules of the scheme, they shall have effect as if they did not allow the provision for the employee of a pension exceeding one-thirtieth of his relevant annual remuneration for each year of service up to a maximum of 20.

20.—(1) This paragraph applies where an employee becomes a member of the scheme on or after 17th March 1987 and the scheme allows him to commute his pension or part of it for a lump sum or sums.

(2) If the employee's full pension (that is, the pension before any commutation) is equal to or less than a basic rate commutable pension, the rules of the scheme shall have effect (notwithstanding anything in them to the contrary) as if they did not allow him to obtain by way of commutation a lump sum or sums exceeding in all a basic rate lump sum.

(3) If the employee's full pension is greater than a basic rate commutable pension but less than a maximum rate commutable pension, the rules of the scheme shall have effect (notwithstanding anything in them to the contrary) as if they did not allow him to obtain by way of commutation a lump sum or sums exceeding in all the aggregate of—

(a) a basic rate lump sum, and

(b) an amount equal to the relevant percentage of the difference between a basic rate lump sum and a maximum rate lump sum.

(4) In this paragraph, as it applies in relation to an employee—

    (a) a "basic rate commutable pension" means a pension of one-sixtieth of his relevant annual remuneration for each year of service up to a maximum of 40;

    (b) a "maximum rate commutable pension" means a pension of one-thirtieth of his relevant annual remuneration for each year of service up to a maximum of 20;

    (c) a "basic rate lump sum" means a lump sum of three-eightieths of his relevant annual remuneration for each year of service up to a maximum of 40;

    (d) a "maximum rate lump sum" means a lump sum of such amount as may be determined by or under regulations made by the Board for the purposes of this paragraph and paragraph 21 below;

    (e) "the relevant percentage" means the difference between a basic rate commutable pension and the employee's full pension expressed as a percentage of the difference between a basic rate commutable pension and a maximum rate commutable pension.

(5) Regulations under this paragraph shall be made by statutory instrument.

21.—(1) This paragraph applies where an employee becomes a member of the scheme on or after 17th March 1987 and the scheme provides a lump sum or sums for him otherwise than by commutation of his pension or part of it.

(2) If the employee's pension is equal to or less than a basic rate non-commutable pension, the rules of the scheme shall have effect (notwithstanding anything in them to the contrary) as if they did not allow the payment to him, otherwise than by way of commutation, of a lump sum or sums exceeding in all a basic rate lump sum.

(3) If the employee's pension is greater than a basic rate non-commutable pension but less than a maximum rate non-commutable pension the rules of the scheme shall have effect (notwithstanding anything in them to the contrary) as if they did not allow the payment to him, otherwise than by way of commutation, of a lump sum or sums exceeding in all the aggregate of—

    (a) a basic rate lump sum, and

    (b) an amount equal to the relevant percentage of the difference between a basic rate lump sum and a maximum rate lump sum.

(4) In this paragraph, as it applies in relation to an employee—

    (a) a "basic rate non-commutable pension" means a pension of one-eightieth of his relevant annual remuneration for each year of service up to a maximum of 40;

    (b) a "maximum rate non-commutable pension" means a pension of one-fortieth of his relevant annual remuneration for each year of service up to a maximum of 20;

    (c) "basic rate lump sum" and "maximum rate lump sum" have the same meanings as in paragraph 20 above; and

    (d) "the relevant percentage" means the difference between a basic rate non-commutable pension and the employee's actual pension expressed as a percentage of the difference between a basic rate non-commutable pension and a maximum rate non-commutable pension.

Final remuneration

22.—(1) This paragraph applies where an employee who is a member of the scheme retires on or after 17th March 1987.

(2) The rules of the scheme shall have effect as if they provided that in determining the employee's relevant annual remuneration for the purpose of calculating benefits, no account should be taken of anything excluded from the definition of "remuneration" in section 26(1) of the Finance Act 1970.

(3) In the case of an employee—

    (a) whose employer is a company and who at any time in the last ten years of his service is a controlling director of the company, or

    (b) whose relevant annual remuneration for the purpose of calculating benefits, so far as the remuneration is ascertained by reference to years beginning on or after 6th April 1987, would (apart from this Schedule) exceed the permitted maximum,

the rules of the scheme shall have effect as if they provided that his relevant annual remuneration must not exceed his highest average annual remuneration for any period of three or more years ending within the period of ten years which ends with the date on which his service ends.

(4) In the case of an employee within paragraph (b) of sub-paragraph (3) above who retires before 6th April 1991, the rules of the scheme shall have effect as if they provide that his relevant annual remuneration must not exceed the higher of—

(a) the average annual remuneration referred to in that sub-paragraph, and

(b) his remuneration (within the meaning given in section 26(1) of the Finance Act 1970 assessable to income tax under Schedule E for the year of assessment 1986–87.

(5) For the purposes of this paragraph a person is a controlling director of a company if—

(a) he is a director as defined in section 26 of the Finance Act 1970, and

(b) he is within paragraph (c) of section 303(5) of the Taxes Act,

in relation to the company.

Lump sums

23.—(1) This paragraph applies where an employee becomes a member of the scheme on or after 17th March 1987.

(2) If the rules of the scheme allow the employee to obtain (by commutation of his pension or otherwise) a lump sum or sums calculated by reference to his relevant annual remuneration, they shall have effect as if they included a rule that in calculating a lump sum an excess of that remuneration over the permitted maximum should be disregarded.

Additional voluntary contributions

24.—(1) This paragraph applies where—

(a) the rules of the scheme make provision for the payment by employees of voluntary contributions, and

(b) on or after 8th April 1987 an employee enters into arrangements to pay such contributions.

(2) Notwithstanding anything in the rules of the scheme, they shall have effect as if they did not allow the payment to the employee of a lump sum in commutation of a pension if or to the extent that the pension is secured by the voluntary contributions.

25.—(1) This paragraph applies where an employee who is a member of the scheme ("the main scheme") is also a member of an approved scheme ("the voluntary scheme") which provides additional benefits to supplement those provided by the main scheme and to which no contributions are made by any employer of his.

(2) Any rules of the main scheme imposing a limit on the amount of a benefit provided for the employee shall have effect (notwithstanding anything in them to the contrary) as if they provided for the limit to be reduced by the amount of any like benefit provided for the employee by the voluntary scheme.

Supplementary

26.—(1) In this Part of this Schedule "relevant annual remuneration" means final remuneration or, if the scheme provides for benefits to be calculated by reference to some other annual remuneration, that other annual remuneration.

(2) Expressions used in this Part of this Schedule and in Chapter II of Part II of the Finance Act 1970 have the same meanings in this Part as they have in that Chapter.

GENERAL NOTE

This Schedule is designed to tighten up some of the rules relating to occupational pension schemes.

1. No tax free lump sums will be able to exceed £150,000 as regards people joining schemes after Budget Day. Subject to this the normal rule of $1\frac{1}{2}$ times "final remuneration" continues.

2. Para. 2 makes clear that any withdrawal of approval can take effect from the date when the facts warranted such withdrawal.

3. Para. 3 confers a power for regulations to be made which will set out conditions which will need to be satisfied if the discretion to approve schemes not satisfying all the requirements for mandatory approval is to be exercisable.

4. Para. 4 enacts the Revenue practice imposing a limit on the amount of contributions by an employer which is a deduction when calculating the employer's profits.

5. The definition of "final remuneration" is allowed so as to exclude share options and other matters referred to in para. 7. This is to prevent manipulation of the last years income before retirement with a view to increasing benefits. As regards employees earning over £100,000 and persons who in the last 10 years of service have been controlling directors,

final remuneration is only to be based as the highest average annual remuneration within the last 10 years of service. In the past a more flexible rule of taking remuneration to be that received in any single year in the last five years before retirement was allowed for all save persons who were controlling directors at retirement. The new rule prevents directors leaving to be such prior to retirement and obtaining the benefit of the more relaxed rule. In addition by not allowing very highly paid employees to benefit from the more relaxed rule it is thought that manipulation of final year remuneration with a view to increasing reliefs will generally be reduced.

6. An important feature of the Schedule is the introduction in para. 12 of free standing pension schemes as receptacles for "additional voluntary contribution" by employees. The new arrangement only applies where a scheme is additional to one to which an employer is already a contributor. In the past such an arrangement has only been possible where the employer has himself set up the scheme. The normal limits on total benefits and contributions continue.

7. Pt. II of the Schedule relates to approved retirement benefits schemes established before July 23, 1987. The administrator may give notice to the Board that the changes contained in this part of the Schedule are not apply to the scheme in which case it will lose its approval. There is a power for the Board to provide that a change contained in this part of the Schedule will not apply to the scheme but first regulations must be made.

The changes are:

(i) any employee joining a scheme after March 16, 1987, must not receive a pension scheme which in amount exceeds the limits in para. 19(2);

(ii) such an employee will not be able to obtain by commutation a lump sum payment exceeding the limitations contained in para. 20(2) and (3);

(iii) similar rules are introduced in respect of lump sums payable otherwise than by reason of commutation (para. 21);

(iv) restrictions are imposed when calculating the final remuneration of an employee retiring after March 16, 1987, and the lump sum a member may obtain if he or she became a member after March 16, 1987;

(v) an employee entering an arrangement after April 7, 1987, to pay additional voluntary contributions shall not be entitled to a lump sum payment secured by those contributions.

Section 63   SCHEDULE 4

DUAL RESIDENT INVESTING COMPANIES

PART I

DIVISION OF ACCOUNTING PERIODS COVERING 1ST APRIL 1987

1.—(1) This Part of this Schedule has effect in the circumstances set out in subsection (3)(a) of the principal section.

(2) In this Part of this Schedule—

(a) "the principal section" means section 63 of this Act;

(b) "the straddling period" means the accounting period of the dual resident investing company which begins before and ends on or after 1st April 1987; and

(c) "dual resident investing company" has the same meaning as in the principal section.

(3) It shall be assumed for the purposes of subsections (1) and (2) of the principal section, the enactments relating to group relief and Part II of this Schedule,—

(a) that an accounting period of the company ends on 31st March 1987; and

(b) that a new accounting period begins on 1st April 1987, the new accounting period to end with the end of the straddling period.

(4) In this Part of this Schedule "the component accounting periods" means the two accounting periods referred to in sub-paragraph (3) above.

2. Subject to paragraph 5 below, for the purposes referred to in paragraph 1(3) above, the losses and other amounts of the straddling period of a dual resident investing company, excluding any such excess of charges on income as is referred to in section 259(6) of the Taxes Act, shall be apportioned to the component accounting periods on a time basis according to their lengths.

3. If, in the straddling period of a dual resident investing company, the company has paid any amount by way of charges on income, then, for the purposes referred to in paragraph

1(3) above, the excess of that amount referred to in section 259(6) of the Taxes Act shall be apportioned to the component accounting periods—

(a) according to the dates on which, subject to paragraph 6 below, the interest or other payments giving rise to those charges were paid (or were treated as paid for the purposes of section 248 of that Act); and

(b) in proportion to the amounts of interest or other payments paid (or treated as paid on those dates.

PART II

EARLY PAYMENTS OF INTEREST ETC AND CHARGES ON INCOME

Interpretation

4. In this Part of this Schedule—

(a) "the principal section" means section 63 of this Act;

(b) a "1986 accounting period" means an accounting period which begins or ends (or begins and ends) in the financial year 1986,

(c) a "post-1986 accounting period" means an accounting period which begins on or after 1st April 1987, and

(d) "dual resident investing company" has the same meaning as in the principal section.

Early payment of interest etc

5.—(1) If the conditions in sub-paragraph (2) or sub-paragraph (3) below are fulfilled and if the Board so direct, this paragraph applies in relation to a 1986 accounting period of a dual resident investing company.

(2) The conditions in this sub-paragraph are applicable only if the company is carrying on a trade in the 1986 accounting period, and those conditions are—

(a) that in that accounting period the company has incurred a loss, computed as for the purposes of section 177(2) of the Taxes Act, in carrying on that trade; and

(b) that in that period the company has made a payment falling within subsection (6)(a)(iii) of the principal section; and

(c) that the payment referred to in paragraph (b) above either did not fall due in that period or would not have fallen due in that period but for the making, on or after 5th December 1986, of arrangements varying the due date for payment.

(3) The conditions in this sub-paragraph are applicable only if the company is an investment company in the 1986 accounting period, and those conditions are—

(a) that for that accounting period the company has (apart from this paragraph) such an excess as is referred to in section 259(3) of the Taxes Act (excess of management expenses over profits); and

(b) that one or more of the sums which for that accounting period may be deducted as expenses of management under section 304(1) of the Taxes Act either did not fall due in that period or would not have fallen due in that period but for the making, on or after 5th December 1986, of arrangements varying the due date for payment.

(4) The Board shall not give a direction under this paragraph with respect to a 1986 accounting period of a dual resident investing company unless it appears to the Board that the sole or main benefit that might be expected to accrue from the early payment or, as the case may be, from the arrangements was that (apart from this paragraph) the company would, for that period, have an amount or, as the case may be, a larger amount available for surrender by way of group relief.

(5) If this paragraph applies in relation to a 1986 accounting period of a dual resident investing company which is carrying on a trade then, for the purposes of the enactments relating to group relief and, where appropriate, any apportionment under paragraph 2 above,—

(a) the loss (if any) of the company for that period shall be computed (as mentioned in section 259(1) of the Taxes Act) as if any payment falling within sub-paragraph (2)(b) above had not been made in that period; and

(b) the loss (if any) of the company for its first post-1986 accounting period shall be computed as if any such payment were made in that period.

(6) If this paragraph applies in relation to a 1986 accounting period of a dual resident investing company which is an investment company, then, for the purposes referred to in sub-paragraph (5) above,—

(a) the amount which may be deducted as expenses of management for that period, as mentioned in section 259(3) of the Taxes Act, shall be computed as if any sum falling within sub-paragraph (3)(b) above had not been disbursed; and

(b) the amount which may be so deducted as expenses of management for the first of the company's post-1986 accounting periods shall be computed as if any such sum were disbursed in that period.

Early payment of charges on income

6.—(1) If, in the case of a dual resident investing company, either of the following conditions is fulfilled,—

(a) that any interest or other payment which is, or is treated as, a charge on income falls due in a post-1986 accounting period but is paid (or treated for the purposes of section 248 of the Taxes Act as paid) in a 1986 accounting period, or

(b) that, on or after 5th December 1986, arrangements have been made such that any such interest or other payment which, but for the arrangements, would have fallen due in a post-1986 accounting period, fell due in a 1986 accounting period,

the interest or other payment shall, if the Board so direct, be treated for the purposes of the enactments relating to group relief and, where appropriate, paragraph 3 above as paid in the post-1986 accounting period referred to in paragraph (a) or, as the case may be, paragraph (b) above.

(2) The Board shall not give a direction under this paragraph unless it appears to them that the sole or main benefit that might be expected to accrue from the early payment or, as the case may be, from the arrangements was that (apart from the direction) the interest or other payment would be attributed or apportioned to a 1986 accounting period rather than a post-1986 accounting period, so that, for the 1986 accounting period, the dual resident investing company would have an amount or, as the case may be, a larger amount available for surrender by way of group relief.

Appeals

7. Notice of the giving of a direction under paragraph 5 or paragraph 6 above shall be given to the dual resident investing company concerned; and any company to which such a notice is given may, by giving notice of appeal in writing to the Board within sixty days of the date of the notice given to the company, appeal to the Special Commissioners against the direction on either or both of the following grounds,—

(a) that the conditions applicable to the company under sub-paragraph (2) or sub-paragraph (3) of paragraph 5 above are not fulfilled or, as the case may be, that neither of the conditions in paragraph 6(1) above is fulfilled;

(b) that the sole or main benefit that might be expected to accrue from the early payment or, as the case may be, the arrangements was not that stated in paragraph 5(4) or, as the case may be, paragraph 6(2) above.

General

8. The preceding provisions of this Schedule have effect in priority to section 262 of the Taxes Act (companies joining or leaving group or consortium) and, accordingly, each of the component accounting periods resulting from the operation of Part I of this Schedule shall be regarded as true accounting periods for the purposes of that section.

GENERAL NOTE

This Schedule, introduced by s.63(3), deals with two matters in relation to the anti-avoidance provisions regarding the obtaining of loss relief for interest payments in two countries (usually the U.S.A. and the U.K.) by investing companies with dual residence for fiscal purposes. Part I deals with accounting periods which straddle April 1, 1987, the effective date of the new provisions. Part II is designed to prevent forestalling of the provisions by early payment of interest or charges on income.

Part I. It is assumed for the purposes of the legislation that the accounting period straddling April 1, 1987, is divided in two as at that date, and the losses in question are apportioned to the two periods on a time basis.

Part II. The Revenue consultative document on Dual Resident Companies, which incorporated draft clauses, was published on December 5, 1986. To prevent forestalling of the anti-avoidance provisions, the Revenue are given power to direct that advance payments of interest or charges on income, or payments in pursuance of a re-arrangement made after December 5, prior to April 1, shall be treated as if they were made after that date. The power applies only in cases where the sole or main motive for the advance payment or the re-arrangement is the obtaining of group loss relief. An appeal against a Revenue direction to the Special Commissioners is available.

Sections 74 to 76   SCHEDULE 5

<h3 align="center">COMPANIES' CHARGEABLE GAINS:</h3>

<h3 align="center">TRANSITIONAL PROVISIONS</h3>

<h3 align="center">PART I</h3>

<h3 align="center">GENERAL RULES</h3>

Interpretation

1. In this Part of this Schedule—
  - (a) a "straddling period" means an accounting period of a company which begins before and ends on or after the 1987 date;
  - (b) "the principal section" means section 74 of this Act;
  - (c) "the 1987 date" means 17th March 1987;
  - (d) references to "section 85", "section 93" and "section 95" are references to those sections of the Finance Act 1972.

Chargeable gains comprised in profits

2.—(1) It shall be assumed for the purposes of this paragraph that the straddling period of the company consists of two separate accounting periods—
  - (a) the first beginning at the beginning of the straddling period and ending immediately before the 1987 date; and
  - (b) the second beginning on the 1987 date and ending at the end of the straddling period.

(2) In this Part of this Schedule those two notional accounting periods are referred to as "component periods".

(3) A separate computation shall be made under section 265 of the Taxes Act (computation of company's chargeable gains) for each of the component periods and, by virtue of subsection (3) of the principal section, only the amount (if any) computed for the first component period shall be reduced under section 93.

(4) If, in accordance with sub-paragraph (3) above,—
  - (a) a positive amount is computed for the first component period, and
  - (b) the amount computed for the second component period is nil,

any excess for the second component period of allowable losses over chargeable gains shall be treated for the purposes of this paragraph as an allowable loss of the first component period and the amount originally computed for that period shall be recalculated accordingly.

(5) The amount which is to be included in respect of chargeable gains in the company's total profits for the straddling period—
  - (a) shall be the sum of the amounts computed as mentioned above for the two component periods; and
  - (b) shall not itself be subject to any reduction under section 93.

(6) The preceding provisions of this paragraph have effect in place of any provision of section 93 under which the amount to be included in respect of chargeable gains in the company's total profits for the straddling period would fall to be apportioned between different parts of that period.

Advance corporation tax and liability of small companies

3.—(1) This paragraph has effect to determine for the purposes of section 85 the income of the company charged to corporation tax for the straddling period and, accordingly (by virtue of subsection (8) of section 95), the income of the company for that period for the purposes of section 95.

(2) For the straddling period, subsection (6) of section 85 (meaning of the income of the company charged to tax for any period) shall have effect as if—
  - (a) the reference to the part of the profits attributable to chargeable gains were a

reference only to the part of the profits attributable to chargeable gains of the first component period; and

(b) the reference to the amount brought into the company's profits for that period for the purposes of corporation tax in respect of chargeable gains were a reference to the amount computed for the first component period under paragraph 2(3) above.

(3) As it applies to the straddling period, the reference in subsection (8) of section 95 to subsection (6) of section 85 shall be construed as a reference to that subsection as it has effect by virtue of sub-paragraph (2) above.

Other references to the income of a company charged to corporation tax

4. For the straddling period, any reference in any enactment, other than sections 85 and 5, to subsection (6) of section 85 shall be construed as a reference to that subsection as it has effect by virtue of paragraph 3(2) above.

Part II

Special Cases

Interpretation

5. In this Part of this Schedule "straddling period" has the meaning assigned to it by paragraph 1(a) above and sub-paragraphs (1) and (2) of paragraph 2 above apply for the purposes of this Part.

Life assurance companies

6.—(1) Subject to the following provisions of this paragraph, where an accounting period of an insurance company carrying on life assurance business is a straddling period, section 26 of the Finance Act 1974 (life assurance gains etc.) shall apply separately in relation to each of the component periods and—

(a) for the first component period, section 26 shall have effect without regard to subsections (2) and (3) of section 75 of this Act; and

(b) for the second component period, section 26 shall have effect as amended by those subsections.

(2) For the purposes of the separate application of section 26 in accordance with sub-paragraph (1) above, the relevant reliefs (within the meaning of that section) of the straddling period shall be apportioned to the two component periods on a time basis according to their lengths.

(3) If, on a computation under section 26 in accordance with sub-paragraphs (1) and (2) above,—

(a) the policy holders' share of the life assurance gains for one of the component periods exceeds the relevant reliefs apportioned to that period, and

(b) the relevant reliefs apportioned to the other component period exceed the policy holders' share of the life assurance gains of that period,

the excess for the component period referred to in paragraph (a) above shall be treated for the purposes of this paragraph as reduced or, as the case may be, extinguished by deducting from that excess so much of the excess referred to in paragraph (b) above as does not exceed it.

(4) Section 26 of the Finance Act 1974 shall not apply to the straddling period taken as a whole.

7.—(1) For a straddling period of an insurance company carrying on life assurance business, sub-paragraph (4) of paragraph 2 of Schedule 18 to the Finance Act 1972 shall have effect as if the amount of the reduction provided for by that sub-paragraph were increased by the policy holders' share of the life assurance gains of the second component period (determined under section 26 of the Finance Act 1974, as applied to that period by paragraph 6 above).

(2) Sub-paragraph (1) above is without prejudice to the operation of paragraph 4 above in relation to the said sub-paragraph (4).

Companies carrying on oil extraction activities etc.

8.—(1) Subject to the following provisions of this paragraph, a separate computation shall be made under subsections (3) and (7) of section 79 of the Finance Act 1984 (gains on certain disposals related to oil fields) for each of the component periods.

(2) If, by virtue of paragraph (a) of subsection (7) of section 79 of the Finance Act 1984, a loss which accrues on a material disposal to a connected person is excluded from those which are taken into account in the computation under subsection (3) of that section for the second component period, then—

    (a) for the purposes of the application of section 62 of the Capital Gains Tax Act 1979 as modified by paragraph (b) of the said subsection (7), in relation to that loss, the first component period shall be treated as if it were subsequent to the second (so as to permit the loss to be set against an appropriate chargeable gain of the first component period); and

    (b) paragraph (c) of subsection (7) of the said section 79 shall apply accordingly in relation to the gains which are taken into account in the computation under subsection (3) of that section for the first component period.

(3) If, on the initial computation in accordance with sub-paragraphs (1) and (2) above there would be an aggregate gain for one of the component periods and an aggregate loss for the other, then, for the purposes of this paragraph, that aggregate loss shall be set against that aggregate gain so as to produce—

    (a) for one of the component periods neither an aggregate gain nor an aggregate loss; and

    (b) for the other component period either an aggregate gain or an aggregate loss (according as the original aggregate gain was greater or smaller than the original aggregate loss);

or, if the original aggregate gain was equal to the original aggregate loss, neither an aggregate gain nor an aggregate loss for either component period.

(4) Section 93 of the Finance Act 1972 (corporation tax liability in respect of chargeable gains) shall not apply to either component period.

(5) The amounts computed for the two component periods in accordance with sub-paragraphs (1) to (4) above shall themselves be aggregated to give an aggregate gain or aggregate loss for the straddling period as a whole and that aggregate gain or loss shall not itself be subject to any reduction under section 93 of the Finance Act 1972 except in accordance with sub-paragraph (7) below.

(6) Subsections (4) and (5) of section 79 of the Finance Act 1984 shall apply in relation to the aggregate gain or aggregate loss of the straddling period as a whole (as determined under sub-paragraph (5) above) as if it were the aggregate gain or loss referred to in (and derived from) subsection (3) of that section.

(7) If there is an aggregate gain of the straddling period as a whole, only so much (if any) of that gain as does not exceed the aggregate gain of the first component period shall be reduced under section 93 of the Finance Act 1972, and the reference in subsection (5) of section 79 of the Finance Act 1984 to reduction in accordance with the said section 93 shall be construed accordingly.

(8) As respects the straddling period, for the purposes of—

    (a) section 16 of the Oil Taxation Act 1975 (restriction on setting advance corporation tax against income from oil extraction activities),

    (b) section 44 of the Finance Act 1987 (limited right to carry back surrendered advance corporation tax), and

    (c) section 45(4) of the Finance Act 1987 (surrender of advance corporation tax where oil extraction company etc. owned by a consortium),

any reference to income arising from oil extraction activities or from oil rights shall be taken to include a reference to the aggregate gain (if any) of the second component period, as determined under sub-paragraphs (1) to (4) above.

GENERAL NOTE

This Schedule contains the transitional provisions to deal with the capital gains tax changes effected by ss. 74 to 76. It applies to a company's accounting period which straddles March 17, 1987. This accounting period is to be split into two separate periods—the first ending immediately before March 17, 1987, and the second beginning on that date. There is then to be a separate computation of the company's chargeable gains under I.C.T.A. 1970, s.265 (subject to paragraph 2(4)) for each period.

There will be no reduction of the company's chargeable gains pursuant to F.A. 1972, s.93 but advance corporation tax may be set off against chargeable gains accruing in the second but not in the first period. Similarly the small company rate will apply to the chargeable gains of the company in that second period but not the first.

There are special rules to deal with the straddling period of a life insurance company and the changes contained in s.75 (paragraphs 6 and 7) and similarly with a company making gains from oil extraction activites and the changes contained in s.76 (paragraph 8).

SCHEDULE 6

Management Provisions: Supplementary and Consequential Provisions

Companies' capital gains

1.—(1) With respect to chargeable gains accruing in accounting periods ending after the appointed day, section 266 of the Taxes Act (corporation tax attributable to chargeable gains: recovery from shareholder) shall be amended as follows.

(2) In subsection (2) for the words "the date when it becomes payable by the company" there shall be substituted "the date determined under subsection (2A) below".

(3) After subsection (2) there shall be inserted the following subsection—

"(2A) The date referred to in subsection (2) above is whichever is the later of—
(a) the date when the tax becomes due and payable by the company; and
(b) the date when the assessment was made on the company."

(4) In subsection (3) for the words from "a sum" onwards there shall be substituted "from the company a sum equal to that amount together with any interest paid by him under section 87A of the Taxes Management Act 1970 on that amount".

2. With respect to chargeable gains accruing in accounting periods ending after the appointed day, in subsection (3C) of section 267 of the Taxes Act (company reconstruction or amalgamation: transfer of assets)—
(a) for the words "when it is payable" there shall be substituted "when it is due and payable or, if later, the date when the assessment is made on the company";
(b) for the words "the time when the tax became payable" there shall be substituted "the later of those dates"; and
(c) for the words from "a sum" onwards there shall be substituted "from the chargeable company a sum equal to that amount together with any interest paid by him under section 87A of the Taxes Management Act 1970 on that amount".

3.—(1) With respect to chargeable gains accruing in accounting periods ending after the appointed day, section 277 of the Taxes Act (tax on company recoverable from other members of group) shall be amended as follows.

(2) In subsection (1) for the words "the date when it becomes payable by the company" there shall be substituted "the date determined under subsection (1A) below" and for the words "the time when the tax became payable" there shall be substituted "the date determined under subsection (1A) below".

(3) After subsection (1) there shall be inserted the following subsection—

"(1A) The date referred to in subsection (1) above is whichever is the later of—
(a) the date when the tax becomes due and payable by the company; and
(b) the date when the assessment is made on the company."

(4) After subsection (2) there shall inserted the following subsection—

"(2A) Any reference in subsection (2) above to an amount of tax includes a reference to any interest paid under section 87A of the Taxes Management Act 1970 on that amount."

4.—(1) Section 278 of the Taxes Act (company ceasing to be a member of a group) shall be amended as follows.

(2) In subsection (3) at the beginning of the words following paragraph (b) there shall be inserted "then, subject to subsection (3A) below", and after that subsection there shall be inserted the following subsection—

"(3A) Any chargeable gain or allowable loss which, apart from this subsection, would accrue to the chargeable company on the sale referred to in subsection (3) above shall be treated as accruing to the chargeable company as follows—
(a) for the purposes for which the assumptions in section 262(2) of this Act apply, it shall be assumed to accrue in the notional or actual accounting period which ends when the company ceases to be a member of the group; and
(b) subject to paragraph (a) above, it shall be treated as accruing immediately before the company ceases to be a member of the group."

(3) In subsection (5)—
(a) the words "of the", in the first place where they occur, shall be omitted;
(b) for the words "the date when it becomes payable" there shall be substituted "the date determined under subsection (5A) below";
(c) for the words "the time when the tax became payable" there shall be substituted "the said date"; and
(d) for the words "a sum" onwards there shall be substituted "from the chargeable

company a sum equal to that amount together with any interest paid by the company concerned under section 87A of the Taxes Management Act 1970 on that amount".

(4) After subsection (5) there shall be inserted the following subsection—

"(5A) The date referred to in subsection (5) above is whichever is the later of—

(a) the date when the tax becomes due and payable by the company; and

(b) the date when the assessment was made on the chargeable company."

(5) In subsection (6) the words from the beginning to "group, and" shall be omitted.

(6) This paragraph has effect where the accounting period in which the chargeable company ceases to be a member of the group ends after the appointed day.

5.—(1) With respect to chargeable gains accruing in chargeable periods ending after the appointed day, section 87 of the Capital Gains Tax Act 1979 (restriction on application of sections 85 and 86 of that Act) shall be amended as follows.

(2) In subsection (4)—

(a) for the words "the date when it it payable" there shall be substituted "the date determined under subsection (4A) below";

(b) for the words "the time when the tax became payable" there shall be substituted "that date"; and

(c) for the words from "a sum" onwards there shall be substituted "from the chargeable person a sum equal to that amount together with any interest paid by him under section 87A of the Taxes Management Act 1970 on that amount".

(3) After subsection (4) there shall be inserted the following subsection—

"(4A) The date referred to in subsection (4) above is whichever is the later of—

(a) the date when the tax becomes due and payable by the chargeable person; and

(b) the date when the assessment was made on the chargeable person."

Relief for unremittable income

6.—(1) Section 418 of the Taxes Act (relief for unremittable income) shall be amended as follows.

(2) At the beginning of subsection (2) there shall be inserted the words "Subject to subsection (2A) below".

(3) After subsection (2) there shall be inserted the following subsections—

"(2A) Where the tax chargeable is corporation tax, subsection (2) above shall have effect as if—

(a) for the word "assessed", in the second place where it occurs, there were substituted "assessable";

(b) for the words from "on the Board ceasing" to "take account" there were substituted "on the said conditions ceasing to be satisfied as respects any part of the income, it shall be treated as income arising on the date when those conditions cease to satisfied with respect to it and account shall be taken"; and

(c) for the words from "the date" onwards there were substituted "that date".

(2B) Where a company becomes chargeable to corporation tax in respect of income from any source by virtue of subsections (2) and (2A) above after it has ceased to possess that source of income, the income shall be chargeable under Case VI of Schedule D."

(4) In subsection (5) for the words "subsection (2)" there shall be substituted "subsections (2) and (2A)".

(5) This paragraph has effect where the accounting period in which the conditions in subsection (2) of section 418 cease to be satisfied in relation to any income ends after the appointed day.

Charges on non-residents

7. With respect to tax in respect of accounting periods ending after the appointed day and interest on such tax, at the end of section 85 of the Management Act (application to corporation tax of provisions of Part VIII of that Act) there shall be added the following subsection—

"(2) Subsection (2) of section 83 above shall apply—

(a) to corporation tax to which a person is chargeable in respect of a non-resident company and which has become due and payable without the making of an assessment; and

(b) to interest to which he is chargeable on such tax under section 87A below, as it applies (by virtue of subsection (1) above) to corporation tax which has been assessed on him in respect of such a company."

Lloyd's underwriting agents

8.—(1) The Treasury may by regulations made by statutory instrument modify any of the provisions specified in sub-paragraph (2) below in their application to companies permitted by the Council of Lloyd's to act as underwriting agents at Lloyd's.

(2) The provisions referred to in subsection (1) above are—
  (a) section 11 of the Management Act (return of profits);
  (b) section 87A of that Act (interest on overdue corporation tax); and
  (c) section 243(4) of the Taxes Act (date for payment of corporation tax).

(3) A statutory instrument made under this paragraph shall be subject to annulment in pursuance of a resolution of the House of Commons.

(4) This paragraph has effect with respect to accounting periods ending after the appointed day.

GENERAL NOTE

This Schedule is designed to make provision for certain special cases where the normal Pay and File rules on interest for late payment would produce an inequitable result.

Paras. 1 to 5 deal with the situation which may arise under I.C.T.A. ss.266, 267, 277 and 278 and C.G.T.A. s.87 where, usually in the context of a tax avoidance scheme, corporation tax on chargeable gains is assessed on a company which was not primarily liable to pay the tax in question. Since the company on which the assessment is raised will not have been directly responsible for any delay, interest in such a case will run from the date of the assessment.

Para. 6. In relation to the relief for unremittable overseas income, the date on which the income will be treated as arising for Pay and File purposes is the date on which it becomes remittable. If the source has ceased in the meantime, the income will be chargeable under Case VI of Schedule D.

Para. 7 extends to a resident agent charged in the name of a non-resident company a right to recoup himself in respect of tax payable under Pay and File and interest.

Para. 8 Lloyd's poses special problems because accounts are finalised well in arrears. The Treasury is empowered to make regulations to cater for companies acting as underwriting agents.

Section 96   SCHEDULE 7

INHERITANCE TAX: INTERESTS IN POSSESSION

1. After section 54 of the Inheritance Tax Act 1984 (in this Schedule referred to as "the 1984 Act") there shall be inserted the following sections—

"Special rate of charge where settled property affected by potentially exempt transfer
  54A.—(1) If the circumstances fall within subsection (2) below, this section applies to any chargeable transfer made—
    (a) under section 52 above, on the coming to an end of an interest in possession in settled property during the life of the person beneficially entitled to it, or
    (b) on the death of a person beneficially entitled to an interest in possession in settled property;
and in the following provisions of this section the interest in possession mentioned in paragraph (a) or paragraph (b) above is referred to as "the relevant interest".
  (2) The circumstances referred to in subsection (1) above are—
    (a) that the whole or part of the value transferred by the transfer is attributable to property in which the relevant interest subsisted and which became settled property in which there subsisted an interest in possession (whether the relevant interest or any previous interest) on the making by the settlor of a potentially exempt transfer at any time on or after 17th March 1987 and within the period of seven years ending with the date of the chargeable transfer; and
    (b) that the settlor is alive at the time when the relevant interest comes to an end; and
    (c) that, on the coming to an end of the relevant interest, any of the property in which that interest subsisted becomes settled property in which no qualifying

51–93

interest in possession (as defined in section 59 below) subsists, other than property to which section 71 below applies; and

(d) that, within six months of the coming to an end of the relevant interest, any of the property in which that interest subsisted has neither—

    (i) become settled property in which a qualifying interest in possession subsists or to which section 71 below applies, nor

    (ii) become property to which an individual is beneficially entitled.

(3) In the following provisions of this section "the special rate property", in relation to a chargeable transfer to which this section applies, means the property in which the relevant interest subsisted or, in a case where—

(a) any part of that property does not fall within subsection (2)(a) above, or

(b) any part of that property does not become settled property of the kind mentioned in subsection (2)(c) above,

so much of that property as appears to the Board or, on appeal, to the Special Commissioners to be just and reasonable.

(4) Where this section applies to a chargeable transfer (in this section referred to as "the relevant transfer"), the tax chargeable on the value transferred by the transfer shall be whichever is the greater of the tax that would have been chargeable apart from this section and the tax determined in accordance with subsection (5) below.

(5) The tax determined in accordance with this subsection is the aggregate of—

(a) the tax that would be chargeable on a chargeable transfer of the description specified in subsection (6) below, and

(b) so much (if any) of the tax that would, apart from this section, have been chargeable on the value transferred by the relevant transfer as is attributable to the value of property other than the special rate property.

(6) The chargeable transfer postulated in subsection (5)(a) above is one—

(a) the value transferred by which is equal to the value transferred by the relevant transfer or, where only part of that value is attributable to the special rate property, that part of that value;

(b) which is made at the time of the relevant transfer by a transferor who has in the preceding seven years made chargeable transfers having an aggregate value equal to the aggregate of the values transferred by any chargeable transfers made by the settlor in the period of seven years ending with the date of the potentially exempt transfer; and

(c) for which the applicable rate or rates are one-half of the rate or rates referred to in section 7(1) above.

(7) This section has effect subject to section 54B below.

Provisions supplementary to section 54A

54B.—(1) The death of the settlor, at any time after a chargeable transfer to which section 54A above applies, shall not increase the tax chargeable on the value transferred by the transfer unless, at the time of the transfer, the tax determined in accordance with subsection (5) of that section is greater than the tax that would be chargeable apart from that section.

(2) The death of the person who was beneficially entitled to the relevant interest, at any time after a chargeable transfer to which section 54A above applies, shall not increase the tax chargeable on the value transferred by the transfer unless, at the time of the transfer, the tax that would be chargeable apart from that section is greater than the tax determined in accordance with subsection (5) of that section.

(3) Where the tax chargeable on the value transferred by a chargeable transfer to which section 54A above applies falls to be determined in accordance with subsection (5) of that section, the amount referred to in paragraph (a) of that subsection shall be treated for the purposes of this Act as tax attributable to the value of the property in which the relevant interest subsisted.

(4) Subsection (5) below shall apply if—

(a) during the period of seven years preceding the date on which a chargeable transfer to which section 54A above applies ("the current transfer") is made, there has been another chargeable transfer to which that section applied, and

(b) the person who is for the purposes of the current transfer the settlor mentioned in subsection (2)(a) of that section is the settlor for the purposes of the other transfer (whether or not the settlements are the same);

and in subsections (5) and (6) below the other transfer is referred to as the "previous transfer".

(5) Where this subsection applies, the appropriate amount in relation to the previous transfer (or, it there has been more than one previous transfer, the aggregate of the appropriate amounts in relation to each) shall, for the purposes of calculating the tax chargeable on the current transfer, be taken to be the value transferred by a chargeable transfer made by the settlor immediately before the potentially exempt transfer was made.

(6) In subsection (5) above "the appropriate amount", in relation to a previous transfer, means so much of the value transferred by the previous transfer as was attributable to the value of property which was the special rate property in relation to that transfer.

(7) In this section—

"the relevant interest" has the meaning given by subsection (1) of section 54A above; and

"the special rate property" has the meaning given by subsection (3) of that section.".

2. In section 56 of the 1984 Act (exclusion of certain exemptions) in subsection (5) after the word "disposition" there shall be inserted "for such consideration".

3.—(1) Section 201 of the 1984 Act (liability for tax relating to settled property) shall be amended as follows.

(2) In subsection (2) after the word "death" there shall be inserted "but is not a potentially exempt transfer".

(3) After subsection (3) there shall be inserted the following subsection—

"(3A) Subsection (1)(d) above shall not apply in relation to the tax chargeable on the value transferred by a potentially exempt transfer which proves to be a chargeable transfer in a case where the settlement was made before 17th March 1987 if the trustees were resident in the United Kingdom when the settlement was made, but have not been resident there at any time between 16th March 1987 and the death of the transferor."

4.—(1) Section 216 of the 1984 Act (delivery of accounts) shall be amended as follows.

(2) In subsection (1) after paragraph (bc) there shall be inserted the following paragraph—

"(bd) is liable under section 201(1)(b), (c) or (d) above for tax on the value transferred by a potentially exempt transfer which is made under section 52 above and which proves to be a chargeable transfer, or would be so liable if tax were chargeable on that value, or"

(3) In subsection (6)(aa) of that section after the words "subsection (1)(bb)" there shall be inserted "or (bd)".

5. In section 265 of the 1984 Act (chargeable transfers affecting more than one property) after the words "subject to" there shall be inserted "section 54B(3) above and to".

GENERAL NOTE

The purpose of this Schedule is to prevent the avoidance of I.H.T. by the creation of short-lived interests in possession which might be used as a conduit to transfer property into discretionary trusts. Through the use of "men of straw" substantial sums could be transferred into such trusts without a charge to I.H.T.

S.54A attacks these devices by providing that on the termination of such an interest during the life of the settlor the tax charged shall be such as if the settlor had made the transfer into the discretionary trust directly. Trustees are given a six months grace period during which the settlement may be discretionary.

S.54B caters for the situation where either the settlor or the short-term beneficiary involved in such a scheme dies.

Section 101   SCHEDULE 8

AMENDMENTS OF SCHEDULE 10 TO FINANCE ACT 1987

1. At the end of paragraph 1 (interpretation) there shall be added the following sub-paragraph—

"(3) Where an amount of oil is required to be delivered to the Secretary of State pursuant to a notice served by him, any oil which is inadvertently delivered to him in excess of the amount required shall be treated for the purposes of sub-paragraph (2) above as delivered pursuant to the notice.".

2.—(1) In paragraph 5 (content of nomination) in sub-paragraph (1)(b)—

(a) for the words "except in the case of a proposed appropriation" there shall be substituted "in the case of a proposed sale"; and

(b) for the word "delivered" there shall be substituted "sold".

(2) At the end of sub-paragraph (3) of paragraph 5 (penalty for fraudulent or negligent furnishing of information etc. in connection with a nomination) there shall be added the words "and the nomination shall not be effective".

3.—(1) In paragraph 8 (revision of nominations) after sub-paragraph (2) there shall be inserted the following sub-paragraphs—

"(2A) If a participator who has made a nomination of a proposed supply, proposed appropriation or a proposed transaction falling within paragraph 2(1)(d) above fails, in whole or in part, to supply, to appropriate or otherwise to complete the proposed transaction by the delivery or appropriation of oil forming part of his equity production for the proposed delivery month, then, in accordance with regulations made by the Board, he may amend or withdraw the nomination as mentioned in sub-paragraph (2B) below.

(2B) The circumstances in which, in a case falling within sub-paragraph (2A) above, a participator may amend or withdraw a nomination are,—

(a) in the case of a nomination of a proposed supply or proposed appropriation, if the participator is of the opinion that the failure referred to in that sub-paragraph was caused by circumstances over which neither he nor any person connected or associated with him had control; or

(b) in the case of a nomination of a proposed transaction falling within paragraph 2(1)(d) above, in such circumstances as may be prescribed by regulations made by the Board; or

(c) in any case where the nomination is of a proposed supply or proposed appropriation and the participator is either the field operator or the operator of a relevant system, if the participator is of the opinion that the failure referred to in sub-paragraph (2A) above was caused by action necessarily taken by him in the interests of safety or the prevention of pollution or in accordance with good oil field practice.

(2C) In relation to such a nomination as is referred to in sub-paragraph (2B)(c) above,—

(a) a participator is the field operator if, in relation to the field specified in the nomination, he is the person having the function of organising or supervising operations for searching or boring for or getting oil in pursuance of a licence; and

(b) the expression "relevant system" is applicable only where the oil to which the nomination relates is blended oil and is a reference to any system by which blended oil (in relation to which the field specified in the nomination is one of the originating fields) is transported, treated or stored prior to its disposal or relevant appropriation; and

(c) a participator in an oil field is an operator of a relevant system, as defined above, if he is the person charged, or principally charged, with the operation of the system;

and expressions used in paragraph (b) above have the same meaning as in section 63 of this Act."

(2) In sub-paragraph (3) of paragraph 8—

(a) for the words "sub-paragraph (2)", in the first place where they occur, there shall be substituted "the preceding provisions of this paragraph";

(b) in paragraph (a) after the word "above" there shall be inserted "or, where sub-paragraph (2B) above applies, that the failure was caused as mentioned in paragraph (a) or paragraph (c) of that sub-paragraph or that the circumstances prescribed for the purposes of paragraph (b) of that sub-paragraph exist"; and

(c) in paragraph (b), for the words "if sub-paragraph (2)(a)" there shall be substituted "except where sub-paragraph (2)(b) or sub-paragraph (2B)(a)".

(3) In sub-paragraph (4) of paragraph 8 after the words "sub-paragraph (2)(b)" there shall be inserted "and sub-paragraph (2B)".

(4) In sub-paragraph (5) of paragraph 8 for the words "preceding provisions of this Schedule" there shall be substituted "provisions of this Schedule (other than this paragraph)".

4. In paragraph 9 (effective volume for nominated transactions) for sub-paragraph (4) there shall be substituted the following sub-paragraphs—

"(4) In relation to a proposed supply or proposed appropriation where the nominal volume is expressed as mentioned in paragraph 7(5) above and oil is in fact supplied

or, as the case may be, relevantly appropriated as proposed in the nomination, the effective volume is whichever is the greater of—
   (a) the minimum nominal volume; and
   (b) so much of the total volume of oil supplied or relevantly appropriated as does not exceed the maximum nominal volume.
   (5) In relation to a proposed supply or proposed appropriation which does not fall within sub-paragraph (4) above, the effective volume is the nominal volume."
   5.—(1) In paragraph 11 (which defines the aggregate nominated proceeds for a month) at the beginning of paragraph (b) of sub-paragraph (1) (market value of excess of equity production over proceeds of nominated transactions) there shall be inserted the words "subject to sub-paragraph (1A) below" and at the end of that sub-paragraph there shall be inserted the following sub-paragraph—
   "(1A) If for any month—
   (a) a participator has made a nomination of a proposed sale, and
   (b) he has an excess falling within sub-paragraph (3) below,
   then for that month the reference in sub-paragraph (1)(b) above to the market value of the excess shall be construed as a reference to the market value multiplied by the designated fraction for that month."
   (2) At the beginning of sub-paragraph (2) of paragraph 11 there shall be inserted "Subject to sub-paragraph (2A) below" and at the end of that sub-paragraph there shall be inserted the following sub-paragraph—
   "(2A) In the case of a nominated transaction consisting of a proposed supply or proposed appropriation, the proceeds of the transaction shall not have the meaning assigned by sub-paragraph (2) above unless the participator satisfies the Board—
   (a) that the whole of the effective volume of oil has been or is to be used for refining as mentioned in paragraph 2(1)(b) above or, as the case may be, has been or is to be relevantly appropriated; or
   (b) that, in so far as any of the effective volume of oil has not been or is not to be so used or appropriated, that is occasioned by circumstances over which neither the participator nor any company associated with him, as mentioned in paragraph 2(1) above, has (or had at any material time) control;
   and if the Board are not so satisfied with respect to any such nominated transaction, the proceeds of that transaction means the market value (determined in accordance with Schedule 3 to the principal Act) of the effective volume of oil, multiplied by the designated fraction for the month in question."
   (3) At the end of paragraph 11 there shall be inserted the following sub-paragraphs—
   "(5) For any month the designated fraction is such fraction as may be specified for the purposes of that month by order made by the Treasury.
   (6) An order under sub-paragraph (5) above—
   (a) shall not specify a fraction smaller than unity or greater than 3/2;
   (b) may be made to have effect for any month in the chargeable period in which falls the date on which the order is made (whether that month begins before, on or after that date);
   (c) if it has effect for a month earlier than the date on which it is made, may contain such transitional provisions as the Treasury consider appropriate; and
   (d) shall be made by statutory instrument which shall be subject to annulment in pursuance of a resolution of the House of Commons."
   6. In paragraph 12 (nominations of blended oil by a participator in two or more fields)—
   (a) for the words from the beginning to "this Act" there shall be substituted "(1) If a person is a participator in two or more oil fields which, in relation to any blended oil, are or are included among the originating fields, then, in accordance with regulations made by the Board, he may make a nomination, having effect with respect to all the originating fields in which he is a participator, of a proposed sale, supply or appropriation of the blended oil"; and
   (b) at the end there shall be added—
      "(2) In sub-paragraph (1) above "blended oil" and "the originating fields" have the same meaning as in section 63 of this Act."

GENERAL NOTE
For the background to this Schedule, see the note to s.101, *supra*. Amendments of substantial importance to F.A. 1987, Sched. 10, are as follows.
Para. 1 makes allowance for inadvertent over-delivery of oil to the Secretary of State.

Para. 2 makes it clear that the nomination system applies to sales rather than deliveries and that fraud or negligence negates the nomination as well as incurring a substantial penalty.

Para. 3 allows for the amendment or withdrawal of nominations in cases where the failure to deliver is due to circumstances beyond a participator's control or where it has resulted from action taken in the interests of safety or the prevention of pollution or good oil field practice.

Para. 5 permits the Treasury to introduce an overriding system for determining aggregate nominated proceeds for any month where the Revenue is not satisfied that deliveries to associated companies are for the purpose of refining. Under s.101(6) this anti-avoidance provision can only be activated by the affirmative resolution procedure.

Section 104

SCHEDULE 9

REPEALS

PART I

INCOME TAX AND CORPORATION TAX: GENERAL

Chapter	Short title	Extent of repeal
1970 c. 10.	The Income and Corporation Taxes Act 1970.	In section 337(2), paragraph (b).
1970 c. 24.	The Finance Act 1970.	In section 21(4), the words "ordinary annual". In section 22(2), the words "ordinary annual".
1982 c. 39.	The Finance Act 1982.	In section 65(1)(a), the words "in a territory".
1987 c. 16.	The Finance Act 1987.	In Schedule 4, paragraphs 1(2) and 2(2).

1. The repeals in section 21 and 22 of the Finance Act 1970 have effect in relation to contributions made on or after 6th April 1987.

2. The repeal in section 65 of the Finance Act 1982 has effect in accordance with section 67(6) of this Act.

PART II

CAPITAL GAINS

Chapter	Short title	Extent of repeal
1972 c. 41.	The Finance Act 1972.	In section 85(6) the words from "exclusive" onwards. Section 93.
1974 c. 30.	The Finance Act 1974.	In section 26(3), in paragraph (a), the words "so much of" and the words from "as remains" to "1972" and, in paragraph (b), the words "as so reduced".
1975 c. 22.	The Oil Taxation Act 1975.	In section 16(1), the words "on its income".
1980 c. 48.	The Finance Act 1980.	Section 84(2) to (4).
1984 c. 43.	The Finance Act 1984.	Section 18(6). Section 65. In section 79(5), the words from "(reduced" to "Finance Act 1972)".
1985 c. 54.	The Finance Act 1985.	Section 72(5).

1. The repeals of section 84(2) to (4) of the Finance Act 1980, section 65 of the Finance Act 1984 and section 72(5) of the Finance Act 1985 come into force on the day appointed under section 81(8) of this Act.

2. The remaining repeals have effect with respect to accounting periods beginning on or after 17th March 1987.

PART III

INHERITANCE TAX

Chapter	Short title	Extent of repeal
1984 c. 51.	The Inheritance Tax Act 1984.	In section 3A, in subsection (2), in paragraph (a) the words "otherwise than as settled property" and in paragraph (b) the words from "otherwise" onwards. Section 49(3). In section 55(2), the words "and such a disposition is not a potentially exempt transfer".
1986 c.41.	The Finance Act 1986.	In Schedule 19, paragraphs 14 and 15.

These repeals have effect in relation to transfers of value made, and other events occuring, on or after 17th March 1987.

PART IV

STAMP DUTY RESERVE TAX

Chapter	Short title	Extent of repeal
1986 c. 41.	The Finance Act 1986.	Section 91(2).

This repeal has effect in accordance with section 100(2) of this Act.

PART V

OIL TAXATION

Chapter	Short title	Extent of repeal
1987 c. 16.	The Finance Act 1987.	In section 63(1), the words from "and in" onwards.

This repeal has effect for chargeable periods ending after 1st January 1987.

BRITISH SHIPBUILDERS (BORROWING POWERS) ACT 1987

(1987 c. 52)

An Act to raise the limits imposed by section 11(7) of the Aircraft and
Shipbuilding Industries Act 1977 in relation to the finances of British
Shipbuilders and its wholly owned subsidiaries.   [23rd July 1987]

PARLIAMENTARY DEBATES
Hansard, H.C. Vol. 118, col. 155; Vol. 119, cols. 545, 1338; H.L. Vol. 488, col. 1271.

Limit on borrowing etc. of British Shipbuilders

1.—(1) Section 11(7) of the Aircraft and Shipbuilding Industries Act
1977 (which imposes an overall limit, increased from £1300 million to
£1400 million by the British Shipbuilders Borrowing Powers (Increase of
Limit) Order 1986, on certain sums borrowed by British Shipbuilders and
its wholly owned subsidiaries and on its public dividend capital) shall be
amended as follows—

(a) for "£1300 million" there shall be substituted "£1550 million";

(b) for "£100 million" (the maximum by which that limit may be
  increased or further increased by order) there shall be substituted
  "£150 million"; and

(c) for "£1400 million" (the maximum to which that limit may be
  increased by order) there shall be substituted "£1800 million".

(2) The British Shipbuilders (Borrowing Powers) Act 1986 is hereby
repealed and the British Shipbuilders Borrowing Powers (Increase of
Limit) Order 1986 is hereby revoked.

Short title and extent

2.—(1) This Act may be cited as the British Shipbuilders (Borrowing
Powers) Act 1987.

(2) This Act extends to Northern Ireland.

CHANNEL TUNNEL ACT 1987

(1987 c. 53)

ARRANGEMENT OF SECTIONS

PART I

PRELIMINARY

SECT.
1. Construction and operation of a tunnel rail link between the United Kingdom and France.
2. No government funds or guarantees for the tunnel system.
3. Provision for further definition of the tunnel system and for applying this Act to a new Concession.
4. Notice with respect to operation, expiry or termination of the Concession.

PART II

WORKS AND LAND FOR THE TUNNEL SYSTEM AND CONNECTED ROAD AND RAIL WORKS

5. Construction of the scheduled works.
6. Supplementary provisions as to the scheduled works and other authorised works.
7. Vesting of seaward section of tunnel system in Secretary of State, subject to Concession lease.
8. Acquisition of land for the scheduled works and other authorised works.
9. Planning permission, etc.

PART III

STATUS, OPERATION AND REGULATION OF THE TUNNEL SYSTEM

Status of tunnel system

10. Incorporation of part of the tunnel system into the United Kingdom and general application of law.

Application and enforcement of law

11. Regulation of the tunnel system: application and enforcement of law, etc.
12. Controls on board trains engaged on international services.
13. Provisions supplementary to sections 11 and 12.
14. Arrangements for the policing of the tunnel system.

Application of English law to Concession agreements and leases to be subject to international arrangements

15. Contract law and arbitration law.
16. Landlord and tenant law.

Intergovernmental supervision of construction and operation

17. Supervision by Intergovernmental Commission and Safety Authority.
18. Intergovernmental Commission and Safety Authority: supplementary.

Regulation of operation of the system

19. Operation by the Concessionaires.
20. Byelaws of the Concessionaires.
21. Confirmation of byelaws by Secretary of State.
22. Application of Railways Board's byelaws to their services in the tunnel system.
23. Control of traffic within the tunnel system.
24. Approval of trains.

Termination of construction or operation

SECT.
25. Maintenance of the tunnel system on termination of construction by Concessionaires.
26. Operation of the tunnel system on a temporary basis where practicable on terminatio of the Concession.
27. Limitations on exercise of Secretary of State's powers under sections 25 and 26.
28. Provisions supplementary to sections 25 to 27.
29. Scheme for land on abandonment of construction or operation.

Miscellaneous

30. Rating.
31. Building regulations.
32. Exclusion of exercise of rights under telecommunications code in relation to tunne system land under the sea.
33. Competition, etc.
34. Supplementary provisions with respect to orders under Part III.

PART IV

CONSTRUCTION AND IMPROVEMENT OF ROADS NEAR FOLKESTONE

35. The A20 improvement works.
36. Acquisition of land for the A20 improvement works.

PART V

MISCELLANEOUS AND GENERAL

37. Supplementary provisions with respect to acquisition of land.
38. Time within such powers of compulsory acquisition may be exercised.
39. Extension of Railways Board's powers in connection with through services.
40. Railways Board's plan for international through services.
41. Railway services: consultative committees and closures.
42. No government grants to Railways Board in respect of international railway services.
43. Application of railway regulation enactments.
44. Modification of enactments relating to coast protection, safety of navigation and th powers of harbour authorities.
45. Protection of interests.
46. Determination of questions referred to arbitration under this Act.
47. Offences by bodies corporate.
48. Financial provisions.
49. Interpretation.
50. Short title and extent.
  SCHEDULES:
    Schedule 1—The scheduled works.
      Part I—The Concessionaires' scheduled works.
      Part II—The County Council's scheduled works.
      Part III—The Railways Board's scheduled works.
      Part IV—Supplementary.
    Schedule 2—Supplementary provisions as to the scheduled works and other author ised works.
      Part I—Application of enactments.
      Part II—Regulation of scheduled works and subsidiary provisions.
      Part III—Highways, roads, etc.
    Schedule 3—Planning permission.
    Schedule 4—The A20 improvement works.
      Part I—The authorised works.
      Part II—Interference with highways.
      Part III—Miscellaneous.
    Schedule 5—Supplementary provisions as to acquisition of land.
      Part I—Purposes for which certain land may be acquired or used under section 8.
      Part II—Purposes for which certain land may be acquired or used under section 36.
      Part III—Supplementary.
    Schedule 6—Application of railway regulation enactments.

Schedule 7—Protective provisions.
    Part I—Highways and traffic.
    Part II—Protection of the Railways Board.
    Part III—Protection of navigation.
    Part IV—Protection of Dover Harbour Board.
    Part V—Protection of sewers.
    Part VI—Protection of certain statutory undertakers.
   Part VII—Protection of land drainage.
  Part VIII—Further protection of Southern Water Authority.
  Part IX—Further protection of the Folkestone and District Water Company.
    Part X—Protection of telecommunications operators.

An Act to provide for the construction and operation of a railway tunnel system under the English Channel, together with associated works; to provide for connected improvements in the road network near Ashford, in Kent, and in the rail network in South Eastern England; to incorporate part of the railway tunnel system into the United Kingdom and to provide for the application and enforcement of law in relation to, and otherwise for the regulation of, that system and matters connected with it; to provide for the construction of certain highways and associated works in the vicinity of Folkestone; and for connected purposes.   [23rd July 1987]

PARLIAMENTARY DEBATE
  Hansard, H.C. Vol. 95, col. 1035; Vol. 98, col. 1101; Vol. 103, col. 877; Vol. 109, col. 363; Vol. 116, col. 378; Vol. 119, col. 470; Vol. 120, col. 217; H.L. Vol. 484, cols. 205, 897; Vol. 487 col. 711; Vol. 488, cols. 350, 463, 834, 1160, 1529.
  The Bill was considered in Standing Committee A from December 2, 1986 to January 22, 1987.

Part I

Preliminary

Construction and operation of a tunnel rail link between the United Kingdom and France

1.—(1) The primary purpose of this Act is to provide for the construction and operation of a tunnel rail link (together with associated works, facilities and installations) under the English Channel between the United Kingdom and France, in accordance with—

(a) the Treaty between the United Kingdom of Great Britain and Northern Ireland and the French Republic concerning the Construction and Operation by Private Concessionaires of a Channel Fixed Link, signed at Canterbury on 12th February 1986, together with its supplementary protocols and arrangements; and

(b) the Concession between Her Majesty's Government in the United Kingdom and the Government of the French Republic on the one hand and private Concessionaires on the other hand which, in accordance with Article 1 of that Treaty, regulates, together with that Treaty, the construction and operation of the Channel fixed link referred to in that Article.

(2) In connection with the primary purpose mentioned in subsection (1) above, Part II of this Act also makes provision for enabling—

(a) the road network in the vicinity of Ashford, in Kent; and

(b) the rail network in South Eastern England;

to be improved with a view to accommodating traffic using the tunnel rail link when it comes into operation.

(3) Subject to section 3 of this Act, the expressions defined below in this section have the meanings there given for the purposes of this Act.

(4) "The Treaty" means the Treaty mentioned in paragraph (a) of subsection (1) above, including its supplementary protocols and arrangements, and "the Concession" means the Concession mentioned in paragraph (b) of that subsection.

(5) "Concession agreement" means any agreement or arrangement which for the time being constitutes, or is included among the agreements or arrangements which together for the time being constitute, the Concession.

(6) "Concession lease" means any lease granted by the Secretary of State to the Concessionaires in pursuance of the Concession, and references to a Concession lease include any provisions of a Concession agreement providing for the grant of a lease of any land by the Secretary of State to the Concessionaires.

(7) "The tunnel system" means the tunnel rail link, together with its associated works, facilities and installations, to be constructed in pursuance of the Treaty, and incorporating—

(a) tunnels under the English Channel between Cheriton, Folkestone in Kent and Fréthun in the Pas de Calais, comprising two main tunnels capable of carrying both road traffic on shuttle trains and rail traffic, and an associated service tunnel;

(b) two terminal areas, for controlling access to and egress from the tunnels, located at the portals of the tunnels in the vicinity of Cheriton, Folkestone and Fréthun respectively;

(c) a service and maintenance area at the Old Dover Colliery site;

(d) an inland clearance depot at Ashford, in Kent, for the accommodation, in connection with the application to them of customs and other controls, of freight vehicles which have been or are to be conveyed through the tunnels on shuttle services;

(e) necessary links with the road and rail networks of each country; and

(f) the fixed and movable equipment needed for the operation of the tunnels and the associated works, facilities and installations mentioned in paragraphs (b) to (e) above or for the operation of shuttle services using the tunnels.

(8) "The Concessionaires" means the person or persons who, under the Concession, have for the time being the function of constructing and operating or (as the case may be) of operating the tunnel system.

(9) "Shuttle train" means a train designed for the purpose of carrying road traffic between Cheriton, Folkestone and Fréthun by way of the tunnels and "shuttle service" means a service operated by means of a shuttle train.

(10) Where the Concessionaires for the time being are two or more persons, any provision of this Act conferring or imposing upon them any right, power, liability or duty shall have effect (except where the context otherwise requires) so as to confer or impose it upon them jointly; but anything done by or in relation to any one of them which purports to be done by or in relation to both or all of them shall have effect for the purposes of this Act as if done by or in relation to them jointly.

No government funds or guarantees for the tunnel system

2.—(1) Subject to subsection (2) below, no Minister of the Crown or Government department shall provide funds to the Concessionaires, or guarantees of a financial or commercial nature relating to the performance of any obligations of the Concessionaires, in respect of the construction or operation of the tunnel system or any part of it.

(2) Subject to subsection (3) below, subsection (1) above shall not preclude the provision of funds to the Concessionaires, or the provision of guarantees relating to the performance of any of their obligations, if they are provided under any enactment conferring a power or imposing a duty on any such Minister or department to provide such funds or guarantees—

(a) to or for the benefit of persons of any class or description which includes the Concessionaires; or

(b) in respect of expenditure of any class or description which includes expenditure on the construction or operation of the tunnel system or any part of it.

(3) Subsection (1) above shall preclude the making by the Secretary of State under section 56(1) of the Transport Act 1968 (grants towards capital expenditure on public passenger transport facilities) of grants towards expenditure incurred or to be incurred by the Concessionaires for the purpose of the provision, improvement or development of the tunnel system or any part of it.

(4) Where anything in contravention of subsection (1) above is done or proposed by or on behalf of a Minister of the Crown or Government department, any person who has suffered, or may suffer, loss in consequence of it may bring an action against the Minister or department concerned.

(5) In such an action the court may—

(a) grant a declaration that the thing done or proposed is or would be in contravention of that subsection; or

(b) subject to subsection (6) below, make an award of damages.

(6) The court may only make an award of damages if the person bringing the action has suffered loss in consequence of something done and if, at the time when it was done, the Minister or Government department concerned knew—

(a) that it was in contravention of subsection (1) above; and

(b) that it would cause loss of the description suffered either to the person bringing the action or to persons of a class to which he belongs.

(7) The Crown Proceedings Act 1947 shall have effect as if anything done in contravention of subsection (1) above were a tort committed by the Minister, or by the Minister in charge of the department, by whom or on whose behalf the thing was done.

(8) Where in any proceedings a question arises as to the construction of subsection (1) above, the court shall have regard in determining the question to any construction of the corresponding provision in Article 1(1) of the Treaty for the time being adopted by the arbitral tribunal which appears to the court to be relevant.

(9) The reference in subsection (8) above to the corresponding provision in Article 1(1) of the Treaty is a reference to the provision of Article 1(1) which requires the Channel fixed link referred to in that Article to be financed without recourse to government funds or to government guarantees of a financial or commercial nature.

(10) In this Act "the arbitral tribunal" means the arbitral tribunal constituted under the Treaty.

Provision for further definition of the tunnel system and for applying this Act to a new Concession

3.—(1) The Secretary of State may, from time to time, by order define (by reference to its boundaries or situation, the area it occupies or any other characteristics of any kind whatsoever) any element of the tunnel system.

(2) The reference in subsection (1) above to an element of the tunnel system is a reference to any area, facility or work, and any description of equipment, incorporated in the tunnel system by virtue of section 1(7) of this Act.

(3) Where on or following the expiry or termination of the original Concession, as defined by section 1(4) above, there is agreement on a new Concession, references in this Act (other than section 1(1)(b) and (4)) to the Concession shall be read, in relation to any matter occurring after the new Concession comes into operation, as references to the new Concession.

(4) Subsection (3) above shall apply in relation to the expiry or termination of any such new Concession as it applies in relation to the expiry or termination of the original Concession.

(5) In this Act—

(a) references to agreement on a new Concession are references to the conclusion of any agreements or arrangements between Her Majesty's Government in the United Kingdom and the Government of the French Republic on the one hand and any other persons on the other hand for the operation (and, where it has not yet been completed, the construction) by those persons of the tunnel system; and

(b) references to a new Concession are references to any such agreements or arrangements.

(6) The power to make an order under this section shall be exercisable by statutory instrument which shall be subject to annulment in pursuance of a resolution of either House of Parliament.

Notice with respect to operation, expiry or termination of the Concession

4.—(1) The Secretary of State shall as soon as practicable after the coming into operation or (as the case may be) the expiry or termination of the Concession publish notice of that fact and of the date on which it came into operation or (as the case may be) expired or terminated; and any such notice shall specify in such manner as the Secretary of State thinks fit any Concession agreements.

(2) A notice required by this section shall be published—

(a) in the London Gazette; and

(b) in such newspapers circulating in the City of Canterbury, the borough of Ashford and the districts of Dover, Shepway and Thanet, in the county of Kent, as the Secretary of State thinks fit.

(3) For the purposes of this Act, the Concession shall be taken to have come into operation or (as the case may be) to have expired or terminated on the relevant date specified in any notice published under this section in relation to the Concession.

Part II

Works and Land for the Tunnel System and Connected Road and Rail Works

Construction of the scheduled works

5.—(1) The Concessionaires may, subject to and in accordance with the provisions of this Act, construct and maintain in the borough of Ashford and in the districts of Dover and Shepway in the county of Kent and under the English Channel the works specified in Part I of Schedule 1 to this Act.

(2) The Kent County Council may, subject to and in accordance with the provisions of this Act, construct and maintain in the borough of Ashford the works specified in Part II of that Schedule.

(3) The British Railways Board (referred to below in this Act as the Railways Board) may, subject to and in accordance with the provisions of this Act, construct and (in so far as they do not have power to do so apart from this Act) maintain and operate the works specified in Part III of that Schedule.

(4) The works specified in Parts I, II and III of that Schedule are referred to below in this Act, where no distinction is drawn between them, as the scheduled works, and otherwise as the Concessionaires' scheduled works, the County Council's scheduled works or the Railways Board's scheduled works, as the case may require.

(5) Subject to Part IV of that Schedule (which gives the limits of deviation for the works and also permits deviation from the levels shown on the deposited sections), the scheduled works shall be constructed in the lines or situations shown on the deposited plans and in accordance with the levels shown on the deposited sections.

Supplementary provisions as to the scheduled works and other authorised works

6.—(1) Part I of Schedule 2 to this Act shall have effect—
- (a) for applying Part II of the Public Utilities Street Works Act 1950 to works for the construction or maintenance of certain of the Concessionaires' scheduled works; and
- (b) for incorporating with this Act the Railways Clauses Consolidation Act 1845 and Part I of the Railways Clauses Act 1863, subject to modifications there specified.

(2) Part II of that Schedule shall have effect—
- (a) for regulating the manner in which the scheduled works and any installations connected with the scheduled works are to be constructed and maintained;
- (b) for authorising or regulating the carrying out of subsidiary works; and
- (c) for conferring or imposing, in connection with the construction or maintenance of those works and installations, certain supplementary powers and certain incidental duties.

(3) Part III of that Schedule shall have effect—
- (a) for making in connection with the scheduled works and other works authorised by this Act provision in relation to highways and roads; and
- (b) for making provision as to compensation for, and mitigation of, adverse effects of such works.

(4) Any activities carried on by the Concessionaires for or in connection with the construction or maintenance of their scheduled works or any other works of theirs authorised by this Act shall be treated (if they would not be so treated apart from this subsection) as the carrying on by the Concessionaires of the railway undertaking they are authorised by virtue of section 19 of this Act to carry on.

Vesting of seaward section of tunnel system in Secretary of State, subject to Concession lease

7.—(1) The land comprising the seaward section of the tunnel system shall, as it becomes occupied by or on behalf of the Concessionaires working from England, vest in the Secretary of State, together with so much of the surrounding subsoil as is necessary for the security of the part of the system so occupied.

(2) Where the land agreed to be granted under a Concession lease consists of or includes the land and subsoil mentioned in subsection (1) above, the interest in that land and subsoil shall vest in the Concessionaires under the lease as that land becomes so occupied, as if granted by the Secretary of State immediately on the vesting in him of that land and subsoil by virtue of subsection (1) above.

(3) The Secretary of State shall, at such time or times as may be agreed by him and the Crown Estate Commissioners, pay to those Commissioners, in respect of the vesting in him by virtue of subsection (1) above of any land of the Crown Estate, such an amount as those Commissioners would have obtained for it on a sale in accordance with section 3(1) of the Crown Estate Act 1961 (duty as to consideration).

(4) In subsection (3) above "land of the Crown Estate" means land which, immediately before the vesting of that land in the Secretary of State by virtue of subsection (1) above, was vested in Her Majesty in right of the Crown.

(5) References in this section to the seaward section of the tunnel system are references to that system, so far as lying under the foreshore and the bed of the sea as far as the frontier.

Acquisition of land for the scheduled works and other authorised works

8.—(1) The Secretary of State is authorised by this section to acquire compulsorily—

(a) so much of the land shown on the deposited plans within the limits of deviation for the Concessionaires' scheduled works as may be required for the construction and maintenance of those works and other works in connection with those works, or otherwise for any purposes of the construction or operation by the Concessionaires of the tunnel system; and

(b) so much of the land so shown within the limits of land to be acquired as may be so required;

being in neither case land which falls to be vested in the Secretary of State by virtue of section 7 of this Act.

(2) The Secretary of State is authorised by this section to acquire by agreement any land which he is not otherwise authorised to acquire and which is required for the construction and maintenance of the Concessionaires' scheduled works and other works in connection with those works, or otherwise for any purposes of the construction or operation by the Concessionaires of the tunnel system.

(3) The Kent County Council are authorised by this section to acquire compulsorily—

(a) so much of the land shown on the deposited plans within the limits of deviation for their scheduled works as may be required for the construction of those works and other works in connection with those works; and

(b) so much of the land so shown within the limits of land to be acquired as may be so required.

(4) The Railways Board are authorised by this section to acquire compulsorily—

(a) so much of the land shown on the deposited plans within the limits of deviation for their scheduled works as may be required for the construction and maintenance of those works and other works in connection with those works, or otherwise for the purposes of their undertaking; and

(b) so much of the land so shown within the limits of the land to be acquired as may be so required.

(5) The preceding provisions of this section are subject to section 37 of this Act.

Planning permission, etc.

9.—(1) Planning permission shall be deemed to have been granted under Part III of the Act of 1971 for the carrying out by the Concessionaires of such development as may be necessary or expedient for—

(a) the construction of their scheduled works within the limits of deviation for those works; and

(b) the construction of the works, the provision of the facilities and the carrying out of the operations mentioned in section A of Part I of Schedule 5 to this Act within the limits of the land to be acquired for those purposes;

except to the extent that it consists of or includes the erection, construction, alteration or extension of any hotel or any building which is not required for or in connection with the movement through the tunnel system of passengers or of vehicles or other goods (including their handling, control or accommodation).

(2) For the purposes of the Town and Country Planning General Development Order 1977 or any order replacing that order—

(a) any development for which planning permission is deemed by subsection (1) above to have been granted shall be treated as not being development of a class for which planning permission is granted by the order; and

(b) any land which is the subject of a Concession lease shall be treated as operational land of the Concessionaires unless it is land required—

(i) for the purposes of or in connection with the inland clearance depot to be constructed at Ashford, in Kent; or

(ii) for purposes which do not include the Concessionaires' operation of the tunnel system.

(3) Planning permission shall be deemed to have been granted under Part III of the Act of 1971 for the carrying out by the Kent County Council of such development as may be necessary or expedient for the construction of their scheduled works within the limits of deviation for those works.

(4) The provisions of the Town and Country Planning General Development Order 1977 regarding development permitted by the order, or the equivalent provisions of any order replacing that order, shall apply in relation to the Railways Board's works as if this Act were a local or private Act.

(5) Schedule 3 to this Act shall have effect in relation to planning permission deemed by subsection (1) or (3) above to have been granted or granted by virtue of subsection (4) above and, in particular, the requirements there set out with respect to any development to which such permission relates shall be conditions to which the permission is subject.

(6) Nothing in section 41 of the Act of 1971 (limit on duration of planning permissions) shall apply to the planning permission deemed by subsection (1) or (3) above to have been granted under Part III of that Act.

(7) Section 28(5) and 29(3) of the Wildlife and Countryside Act 1981 (prohibitions of operations likely to be injurious to the flora, fauna or features of areas of special scientific interest) shall not apply in relation to any operation which is connected with the carrying out of any works authorised to be carried out by this Act and which is carried out within the limits of land to be acquired for any of those works.

(8) In this section and in Schedule 3 to this Act—

"the Act of 1971" means the Town and Country Planning Act 1971;
"building" includes any bridge, aqueduct, pier, mast or dam or
fence, wall or other means of enclosure; and
"the Railways Board's works" means their scheduled works and any
other works or operations which they are authorised to carry
out by this Act.

PART III

STATUS, OPERATION AND REGULATION OF THE TUNNEL SYSTEM

Status of the tunnel system

Incorporation of part of the tunnel into the United Kingdom and general application of law

10.—(1) The land comprising the tunnel system as far as the frontier,
so far as not forming part of the United Kingdom before the passing of
this Act, shall, as it becomes occupied by or on behalf of the Concessionaires working from England, together with so much of the surrounding
subsoil as is necessary for the security of the part of the system so
occupied, be incorporated into England and form part of the district of
Dover in the county of Kent, and the law of England shall apply
accordingly.

(2) Subsections (3) and (4) below apply if any part of the tunnel system
constructed by or on behalf of the Concessionaires working from England
("the English section") extends beyond the frontier before it effectively
joins the part of the tunnel system constructed by or on behalf of the
Concessionaires working from France ("the French section") and subsections (5) to (7) below apply if the converse case occurs.

Any land comprising any such part of the English or (as the case may
be) of the French section is referred to in those subsections as a cross-
frontier extension of that section.

(3) Until the English section effectively joins the French section, any
cross-frontier extension of the English section shall be treated as being in
England and, except for rating purposes, as forming part of the county of
Kent and the law of England shall apply there.

(4) When the English section effectively joins the French section, the
law of England shall continue to apply in relation to things done or
omitted while the cross-frontier extension was treated by virtue of subsection (3) above as being in England and any proceedings may be brought
or continued, any punishment may be imposed and carried out and any
remedy may be granted and enforced in respect of such things accordingly.

(5) Subject to subsection (6) below, until the English section effectively
joins the French section, no part of the law of England that would
otherwise apply in relation to things done or omitted in, over or under
the bed of the sea above any cross-frontier extension of the French section
shall apply in relation to anything done or omitted in that extension or in
so much of the surrounding subsoil as is necessary for the security of that
extension.

(6) Subsection (5) above shall not exclude the application of any
enactment or rule of law that applies irrespective of the country or
territory in which any acts or omissions with which it is concerned take
place.

(7) On the date on which the English section effectively joins the French
section, section 7 of this Act and subsection (1) above shall apply to the
cross-frontier extension of the French section as if it had become occupied
on that date by or on behalf of the Concessionaires working from England.

(8) For the purposes of this section, the date on which the English section effectively joins the French section shall be taken to be such date as the Secretary of State may by order certify as being that date.

Application and enforcement of law

Regulation of the tunnel system: application and enforcement of law, etc.

11.—(1) The appropriate Minister may by order make such provision as appears to him to be necessary or expedient—

(a) for the purpose of implementing the international arrangements, or enabling those arrangements to be implemented;

(b) for the transfer to, and the vesting by virtue of the order in, any person or persons specified in the order (referred to below in this section as the transferee), on such terms (if any) as may be provided by the order—

    (i) on any substitution of Concessionaires under the Concession or on the expiry or termination of the Concession, of the interest of the former Concessionaires in all movable property and intellectual property rights necessary for the construction or operation of the tunnel system;

    (ii) on any such substitution, of all rights and liabilities of the former Concessionaires under the Concession or any Concession lease; and

    (iii) on any substitution which takes place in such circumstances as may be specified in the order, of liabilities of the former Concessionaires (other than liabilities within subparagraph (ii) above) of such description as may be so specified;

and for securing effective possession or control by the transferee of any movable property or rights in which any interest transferred by the order subsists;

(c) in relation to the construction, operation or use of the tunnel system or any part of the tunnel system, so far as relates to activities carried on, persons employed or engaged in work, things done or omitted or other matters arising anywhere within the system (whether in England or in France), including in particular (without prejudice to the generality of the preceding provision) provision with respect to controls in relation to persons or goods within the system;

(d) for the purpose of applying any provisions of the law of England (with or without modifications), or excluding or modifying any of those provisions, in relation to things done or omitted or other matters arising anywhere within the tunnel system (whether in England or France);

(e) with respect to controls in relation to persons or goods—

    (i) on trains engaged on international services; or

    (ii) at authorised terminal control points for such services;

outside the tunnel system (whether in the United Kingdom or elsewhere);

(f) in relation to persons employed or engaged on work outside the tunnel system (whether in the United Kingdom or elsewhere)—

    (i) on any train engaged on an international service, in or for the purposes of or in connection with the operation of that service; or

    (ii) in or for the purposes of or in connection with the exercise, on any such train or at any authorised terminal control point for such services, of any controls in relation to persons or goods such as are mentioned in paragraph (e) above;

(g) for the purpose of dealing with any matters arising out of or connected with any provision within the powers conferred by any of paragraphs (a) to (f) above (whether or not those matters arise within the tunnel system, on any such train or at any such control point); or

(h) otherwise in relation to, or for regulating any matters arising out of or connected with, the tunnel system.

(2) Subject to subsection (5) below—

(a) the provision authorised by any of paragraphs (a) to (c) and (e) to (h) of subsection (1) above includes provision applying any provisions of the law of England (with or without modifications) or excluding or modifying the application of any of those provisions; and

(b) for the purposes of paragraph (a) above and paragraph (d) of that subsection—

(i) "modification" includes, in relation to an enactment, any amendment of it; and

(ii) provision excluding or modifying the application of any provision of the law of England includes, in relation to an enactment, provision amending or repealing it (in either case with or without savings).

(3) Without prejudice to the generality of subsection (1) above, the kind of provision that may be made by an order under this section includes the following—

(a) provision creating new criminal offences punishable as may be provided by the order or imposing penalties otherwise than in respect of criminal offences;

(b) provision imposing, or providing for the imposition of, fees or charges;

(c) provision conferring power on any Minister of the Crown or Government department to make orders, rules, regulations or other subordinate instruments of a legislative character;

(d) provision for, or authorising any such order, rule, regulation or other subordinate instrument to provide for, the delegation of any functions conferred or imposed by or in pursuance of any order under this section or by any enactment;

(e) provision, subject to subsection (4) below, for or in connection with the enforcement or execution outside the United Kingdom of any provision of the law of England or within the United Kingdom of any provision of the law of any other country, including in particular—

(i) provision conferring powers on any officer belonging to the United Kingdom to arrest and detain outside the United Kingdom persons suspected of having committed offences under the law of England and bring them to lawful custody in England;

(ii) provision conferring powers on any such officer to arrest and detain within the United Kingdom persons suspected of having committed offences under the law of any other country and surrender them to the custody of officers belonging to that country without the authority of any order of a court in any part of the United Kingdom; and

(iii) provision for or in connection with the exercise in the United Kingdom by officers belonging to any other country of powers corresponding to those mentioned in sub-paragraph (i) above; and

(f) provision conferring jurisdiction on courts or tribunals in any part of the United Kingdom or limiting the jurisdiction otherwise exercisable by any such courts or tribunals.

(4) An order under this section may not make provision for or in connection with the exercise of powers by officers belonging to one country in any other country except—

    (a) within the tunnel system;

    (b) on trains engaged on international services; or

    (c) at authorised terminal control points for such services.

(5) So far as relates to enactments contained in this Act, only the following may be amended or repealed by an order under this section, that is to say, sections 12, 14 to 18, 20 to 22, 31 and 43 and Schedule 6.

(6) An order made by virtue of subsection (1)(b) above may provide for any interest or right transferred by the order—

    (a) to vest in the transferee free of any security to which it is subject immediately before the order comes into force, other than one created in accordance with the Concession; or

    (b) to be treated on vesting in the transferee as subject to a security of such a description, held by such person or persons, as may be provided by or specified in the order.

(7) An order so made may provide for applying any provisions of the order relating to the interest of the former Concessionaires in any movable property or intellectual property rights necessary for the construction or operation of the tunnel system, subject to any modifications specified in the order, in relation to—

    (a) any interest in any such property or rights of a liquidator of any company which is, or is included among, the former Concessionaires; or

    (b) any interest of any such liquidator of any description specified in the order

(8) No liquidator of, or other person exercising functions under insolvency law in relation to, any company which is, or is included among, the Concessionaires shall sell or otherwise dispose of any interest of the company in any such property or rights without the consent of the Secretary of State; and any sale or other disposal in contravention of this subsection shall be void.

(9) Where in any proceedings a question arises as to what constitutes for the purposes of this section an interest in movable property or intellectual property rights necessary for the construction or operation of the tunnel system, the court shall have regard in determining the question to any construction of the corresponding references in the Concession for the time being adopted by the arbitral tribunal.

(10) For the purposes of subsection (9) above, the corresponding references in the Concession are the references to the interest of the Concessionaires in all movable property and intellectual property rights necessary for the construction or operation of the Fixed Link.

(11) For the purposes of this section—

    (a) a substitution of Concessionaires under the Concession occurs at any time when any person or persons become the Concessionaires in substitution for any person or persons who were the Concessionaires immediately before that time;

    (b) "the former Concessionaires" means, in relation to any such substitution or in relation to the expiry or termination of the Concession, the person or persons who cease to be the Concessionaires on that substitution or on that expiry or termination;

    (c) "liabilities" includes duties and obligations;

    (d) "company" means a British company or a French company;

    (e) "British company" means a company formed and registered under the Companies Act 1985;

(f) "French company" means a body corporate incorporated under the law of France;

(g) "liquidator" means, in relation to a company, a person appointed as liquidator or provisional liquidator of the company under any provision of the Insolvency Act 1986 or exercising in relation to the company functions under the law France corresponding to those of a person so appointed, and the reference in subsection (8) above to any person other than a liquidator exercising functions under insolvency law in relation to a company is a reference to—

    (i) any person appointed as the administrator of the company under any provision of that Act;

    (ii) an administrative receiver of the company within the meaning of Chapter I of Part III of that Act;

    (iii) any person acting as supervisor of any voluntary arrangement (within the meaning of section 7 of that Act) relating to the company's affairs; or

    (iv) any person exercising in relation to the company functions under the law of France corresponding to those exercisable by any person of a description within any of sub-paragraphs (i) to (iii) above; and

(h) "security" means any mortgage, charge, lien or other security.

Controls on board trains engaged on international services

12.—(1) It shall be duty of the appropriate Minister to secure that, where this subsection applies, controls exercisable in relation to—

(a) passengers carried on a train engaged on an international service on a journey beginning or intended to end at a place in Great Britain other than London or Cheriton, Folkestone or any place between those places; or

(b) things contained in the baggage of such passengers;

shall be exercised on the train.

(2) Subject to subsection (3) below, subsection (1) above applies where—

(a) the person operating the service has made a request to the appropriate Minister that the controls in question should be exercised on trains engaged on the service in question;

(b) the appropriate Minister has approved as satisfactory arrangements made by that person for the provision of facilities to enable the controls in question to be exercised on such trains;

(c) facilities enabling the exercise of the controls in question are provided on the train in question in accordance with such approved arrangements; and

(d) the controls are exercised by customs officers or immigration officers.

(3) Subsection (1) above does not apply.

(a) in the case of passengers carried on a particular train or part of a particular train, or things contained in the baggage of such passengers, if in the opinion of a customs officer or immigration officer exercising the controls it is not reasonably practicable effectively to exercise the controls in question on the train or part of a train; and

(b) in the case of any particular passenger or things contained in the baggage of any particular passenger, if in the opinion of any such officer it is not reasonably practicable effectively to exercise the controls in question in relation to the passenger or his baggage on the train.

(4) An order under section 11 of this Act may include provision imposing, or providing for the imposition of, fees or charges on persons operating international services in respect of the exercise of controls in relation to passengers or things such as are mentioned in subsection (1) above on trains engaged on the services.

(5) In this section—

"customs officer" means an officer or other person acting under the authority of the Commissioners of Customs and Excise; and

"immigration officer" means an immigration officer appointed for the purposes of the Immigration Act 1971.

Provisions supplementary to sections 11 and 12

13.—(1) Subject to subsection (2) below, in sections 11 and 12 of this Act "the appropriate Minister" means, in relation to any matter, the Minister in charge of any Government department concerned with that matter or, where more than one such department is concerned with that matter, the Ministers in charge of those departments, acting jointly.

(2) Where the Commissioners of Customs and Excise or the Forestry Commissioners are concerned with any matter (whether alone or together with any other Government department) subsection (1) above shall apply as if the references to the Minister or Ministers in charge of any Government department or departments concerned with that matter were or included references to those Commissioners.

(3) The validity of any order purporting to be made under section 11 of this Act shall not be affected by any question whether or not the order fell by virtue of subsection (1) above to be made by the Minister or department (or any of the Ministers or departments) purporting to make it.

(4) In sections 11 and 12 of this Act "controls" means prohibitions, restrictions or requirements of any description, and any reference to the exercise of controls is a reference to the exercise or performance of any functions conferred or imposed by any enactment, or otherwise under any lawful authority, for or in connection with the enforcement of prohibitions, restrictions or requirements of any description.

(5) For the purposes of those sections a train is engaged on an international service at any time when the whole or any part of the train is being used in the operation of such a service and a place is an authorised terminal control point for international services if it is designated as such in accordance with the international arrangements.

(6) In those sections and this section—

"the international arrangements" includes any agreements or arrangements between Her Majesty's Government in the United Kingdom and the Government of any country on the Continent of Europe other than France which for the time being apply for regulating any matters arising out of or connected with the operation of international services; and

"international service" means any service (including a shuttle service) for the carriage of passengers or goods by way of the tunnel system.

Arrangements for the policing of the tunnel system

14.—(1) The policing of the tunnel system shall be undertaken by constables under the direction and control of the Chief Constable of the police force for the county of Kent.

(2) The Railways Board may, on the application of the Chief Constable of the police force for the county of Kent, provide constables or other assistance for the policing of the tunnel system.

(3) Any constable so provided shall, when he is engaged in the policing of the tunnel system, be under the direction and control of the Chief Constable of the police force for the county of Kent and have the same powers as a constable who is a member of that force.

(4) The Concessionaires shall—

    (a) make to the police committee for the county of Kent such payments in respect of the policing of the tunnel system; and

    (b) provide for use in connection with the policing of the system such accommodation and facilities;

as the Concessionaires and that committee may agree or as may, in default of agreement, be determined by the Secretary of State.

(5) The police committee for the county of Kent shall make to the Railways Board such payments in respect of any assistance provided under subsection (2) above as the committee and the Board may agree or as may, in default of agreement, be determined by the Secretary of State.

Application of English law to Concession agreements and leases to be subject to international arrangements

Contract law and arbitration law

15.—(1) Subject to subsection (3)(a) below, English law shall not apply for the determination of any question with respect to the formation, discharge, validity or effect of any Concession agreement except to the extent and in the circumstances (if any) provided by or determined under any provision of the international arrangements.

(2) For the purposes of all legal proceedings—

    (a) any Concession agreement specified in any notice published under section 4 of this Act with respect to the coming into operation of the Concession shall be taken to be valid and effective at any time on or after the date specifed in that notice; and

    (b) any Concession agreement other than one so specified shall be taken to be valid and effective at any time on or after the date on which it expressed to take effect;

until any date specified in a notice so published as being the date on which the Concession expired or terminated.

(3) Where any Concession agreement provides for the determination of a dispute by the arbitral tribunal—

    (a) the provisions of Part I of the Arbitration Act 1950 and the Arbitration Act 1979 specified in subsection (4) below shall apply in relation to that agreement, or to the enforcement of an award on that agreement, subject to the modifications specified in that subsection and except so far as excluded by, and subject to any modifications contained in, the agreement or any provision of the international arrangements; but

    (b) without prejudice to subsection (1) above, no other provision of Part I of the Act of 1950 or the Act of 1979 shall apply in relation to that agreement, or to the enforcement of an award on that agreement, except so far as applied by, and subject to any modifications contained in, that agreement or any provision of the international arrangements.

(4) The provisions are—

    (a) section 4(1) of the Act of 1950 (staying court proceedings on matters subject to arbitration) with the substitution of the words "shall make an order staying the proceedings" for the words from "if satisfied" to the end;

    (b) section 26 of that Act (enforcement of arbitration award by court); and

(c) section 2 of the Act of 1979 (determination by court of preliminary point of law arising on arbitration) with—

(i) the omission of the words "Subject to subsection (2) and section 3 below," in subsection (1) and of subsection (2); and

(ii) the substitution of the words "with the consent of the arbitral tribunal" for paragraphs (a) and (b) of subsection (1);

and any other provisions of Part I of the Act of 1950 or the Act of 1979 so far as affecting the operation of the provisions mentioned in any of paragraphs (a) to (c) of this subsection.

(5) Subject to subsection (3)(a) above and except to the extent and in the circumstances (if any) provided by or determined under the agreement in question or any provision of the international arrangements, no court in any part of the United Kingdom shall have jurisdiction (whether by virtue of any enactment or at common law)—

(a) to determine any matter over which the arbitral tribunal assumes jurisdiction;

(b) to set aside or remit an award made on any Concession agreement on the ground of errors of fact or law on the face of the award, excess of jurisdiction, procedural irregularities or on any other ground whatsoever; or

(c) to determine whether anything purporting to be such an award is a valid award;

and in all legal proceedings anything purporting to be such an award shall be taken to be a valid award and shall not be questioned on any ground whatsoever.

Landlord and tenant law

16.—(1) The purpose of this section is to secure that the application of English law to any Concession lease does not have effect so as to prejudice the operation of the international arrangements, so far as relates to the provision for use by the Concessionaires of the land required in England for the construction and operation of the tunnel system by the grant to the Concessionaires of a Concession lease on terms determined in pursuance of those arrangements.

(2) No enactment or rule of law regulating the rights and obligations of landlords and tenants shall apply in relation to the rights and obligations of the parties to a Concession lease—

(a) so as to exclude or in any respect modify any of the rights and obligations of those parties under the terms of the lease, whether with respect to the termination of the tenancy or any other matter;

(b) so as to confer or impose on either party any right or obligation arising out of or connected with anything done or omitted on or in relation to land which is the subject of the lease, in addition to any such right or obligation provided for by the terms of the lease; or

(c) so as to restrict the enforcement (whether by action for damages or otherwise) by either party to the lease of any obligation of the other party under the lease.

Intergovernmental supervision of construction and operation

Supervision by Intergovernmental Commission and Safety Authority

17.—(1) Any person authorised by a supervisory body to exercise the powers under this section for the purpose of the performance by that body of any of their functions under the Treaty (referred to below in this section as an authorised person) shall have the powers conferred by

subsection (3) below, subject to any conditions or limitations in th
instrument by which he is so authorised.

(2) An authorised person shall, if so required when exercising or seekin
to exercise any of the powers conferred by subsection (3) below, produc
his instrument of authority or a duly authenticated copy of it.

(3) The powers of an authorised person under this subsection are th
following—

(a) at any reasonable time (or, in a situation which in his opinion is c
  may be dangerous, at any time) to enter the tunnel system or an
  premises, place or vehicle in the tunnel system for the purpose c
  carrying out any inspection, examination or investigation wit
  respect to any matter concerning the construction or operation c
  that system;

(b) to take in connection with any such inspection, examination c
  investigation samples of any articles or substances found in an
  premises, place or vehicle in the tunnel system and of the atmo:
  phere in or in the vicinity of any such premises, place or vehicle;

(c) in the case of any article or substance which is so found and whic
  appears to him to have caused or be likely to cause danger t
  health or safety, to cause it to be dismantled or subjected to an
  process or test (but not so as to damage or destroy it unless this
  in the circumstances necessary for the performance of any functio
  under the Treaty of the supervisory body by whom he
  authorised);

(d) in the case of any such article or substance, to take possession c
  it and detain it for so long as is necessary for all or any of th
  following purposes—

  (i) to examine it and to do anything which he has the powe
  to do under paragraph (c) above;

  (ii) to ensure that it is not tampered with before his examina
  tion of it is completed;

  (iii) to ensure that it is available for use as evidence in an
  legal proceedings;

(e) to require any person whom he has reasonable cause to believe t
  be able to give any information relevant to any inspection, exam
  nation or investigation with respect to any matter concerning th
  construction or operation of the tunnel system to answer suc
  questions as the authorised person thinks fit to ask;

(f) to require the production of, inspect and take copies of any entr
  in, any books or documents which it is necessary for him to see fo
  the purposes of any such inspection, examination or investigatior
  and

(g) to require any person to afford him such facilities and assistanc
  with respect to any matters or things within that person's contrc
  or in relation to which that person has responsibilities as ar
  necessary to enable the authorised person to exercise any of th
  powers conferred on him by this section.

(4) Without prejudice to subsection (3)(g) above, it shall be the duty c
the Concessionaires or, where the Concessionaires for the time being ar
two or more persons, of each of them, and of their servants and agents
to afford to an authorised person such facilities and assistance as ar
necessary to enable him to exercise any of those powers.

(5) For the purpose of the performance of any of their functions unde
the Treaty, a supervisory body may give directions to any person wit
respect to any matter concerning the construction or operation of th
tunnel system.

(6) Directions given by a supervisory body under subsection (5) abov
shall be given in writing.

(7) It is an offence for any person, without reasonable excuse—

    (a) to refuse or fail to comply with a requirement made by an authorised person under this section;

    (b) to refuse or fail to afford to an authorised person any facilities or assistance that person is required to afford to the authorised person under subsection (4) above; or

    (c) to refuse or fail to comply with a direction given by a supervisory body under subsection (5) above.

(8) It is an offence for any person intentionally to obstruct an authorised person in the exercise of his powers under this section.

(9) A person who commits an offence under this section shall be liable on summary conviction to a fine not exceeding the statutory maximum or, on conviction on indictment, to imprisonment for a term not exceeding two years or a fine or both.

(10) Proceedings for an offence under this section shall not be brought in England and Wales except by or with the consent of the Director of Public Prosecutions or in Northern Ireland except by or with the consent of the Director of Public Prosecutions for Northern Ireland.

(11) References in this section to a supervisory body are references to the Intergovernmental Commission or the Safety Authority; but in relation to the powers of the Safety Authority and a person authorised by that authority references in this section to matters concerning the construction or operation of the tunnel system shall be read as limited to such matters so far as they affect health or safety.

Intergovernmental Commission and Safety Authority: supplementary

    18.—(1) For the purposes of all legal proceedings—

    (a) any instrument of authority, direction or certificate purporting to be issued by the Intergovernmental Commission or by the Safety Authority; and

    (b) any other thing purporting to be done by or on behalf of that Commission or Authority;

shall be taken as having been so issued or done without proof that the instrument, direction, certificate or other thing was validly issued or done in accordance with the Treaty or any procedure adopted by that Commission or Authority in pursuance of the Treaty.

(2) For the purposes of all legal proceedings, anything purporting to be done on behalf of that Commission or Authority by a person authorised to do it by that Commission or Authority shall be taken as having been so done without proof of the authorisation of the person by whom it purports to be done.

(3) Evidence of any direction or certificate issued by the Intergovernmental Commission or by the Safety Authority may be given in any legal proceedings by production of a copy—

    (a) which purports to be a copy of a direction or certificate so issued; and

    (b) on which is endorsed a statement purporting to be signed by a person authorised to do so by that Commission or Authority that it is a copy of a direction or certificate so issued and that the copy is a true copy of that direction or certificate.

(4) Any such statement, and any other document purporting to be signed by a person authorised to do so by that Commission or Authority, shall be taken for the purposes of all legal proceedings as having been signed by the person purporting to sign it without proof of that person's handwriting.

(5) Any legal proceedings may be brought by and against that Commission or Authority under the name by which it was established by the Treaty.

Regulation of operation of the system

Operation by the Concessionaires

19.—(1) Subject to the provisions of this Act, the Concessionaires are authorised by this section to manage, operate, maintain and develop the tunnel system.

(2) The Concessionaires shall not be regarded as common carriers.

(3) The Concessionaires shall make provision for the conveyance by means of shuttle trains of pedal bicycles and of motorcycles of which the cylinder capacity of the engine is less than 50 cubic centimetres.

(4) The Concessionaires shall not convey any passengers by means of shuttle trains at any time when there is not in force a certificate issued by the Intergovernmental Commission stating—

(a) that the Commission are satisfied with a code of practice relating to the conveyance by means of shuttle trains of persons who are disabled which has for the time being been adopted by the Concessionaires; and

(b) that the code of practice has been published in a manner approved by the Commission.

(5) Such a code of practice must contain—

(a) a statement of any description of such persons not intended to be conveyed by means of shuttle trains, with reasons;

(b) details of provision for ensuring the safety of such persons in the tunnel system, in particular the safety in the event of an emergency of such persons being conveyed by means of shuttle trains; and

(c) information relating to such other matters affecting the conveyance by means of shuttle trains of persons who are disabled as the Commission may specify.

(6) Contravention of the restriction imposed by subsection (4) above may be restrained by an order of the High Court made on an application by the Intergovernmental Commission.

Byelaws of the Concessionaires

20.—(1) The Concessionaires may make byelaws regulating the operation and use of the tunnel system (including the use of shuttle trains), the maintenance of order in the system and the conduct of all persons while using or otherwise in the system and, in particular, byelaws—

(a) with respect to interference with or obstruction of the operation of the tunnel system;

(b) with respect to the prevention of nuisances and of damage to property;

(c) prohibiting or restricting access to any premises, place or vehicle in the tunnel system;

(d) prohibiting the smoking of tobacco in any such premises, place or vehicle;

(e) prohibiting the admission of any description of vehicle specified in the byelaws to, or requiring the removal of any such description of vehicle from, the tunnel system or any premises, place or other vehicle in it;

(f) regulating the use or conveyance of vehicles and prohibiting or regulating the conveyance of goods other than vehicles, in particular dangerous goods;

(g) for requiring any person, if required by a constable or a person authorised for the purpose by the Concessionaires, to state his name and address and the purpose of his being in the tunnel system;

(h) for requiring any person, if required by a constable or a person so authorised, to leave the tunnel system or any premises, place or vehicle in it and to remove any goods which he has with him; and

(i) for securing the safe custody and redelivery of any property which, while not in proper custody, is found within the tunnel system, and in particular—

(i) for requiring charges to be paid in respect of any such property before it is redelivered; and

(ii) for authorising the disposal of any such property if it is not redelivered before the end of such period as may be specified in the byelaws.

(2) Byelaws under this section may provide—

(a) for the punishment on summary conviction of contraventions of any of the byelaws with a fine not exceeding a maximum fixed by the byelaws; and

(b) for any defence specified in the byelaws to be available in proceedings for a contravention of any byelaw, either generally or in circumstances so specified.

(3) Different provision may be made by virtue of subsection (2)(a) or (b) above in relation to different byelaws; but the greatest maximum fine that may be fixed for contravention of any byelaw shall not exceed level 4 on the standard scale.

(4) A constable or a person authorised for the purpose by the Concessionaires may remove from the tunnel system or any premises, place or vehicle in it any person whom he reasonably suspects to be contravening or to have contravened any byelaw made under this section and any goods which he has with him.

(5) A person so authorised may take steps to remove or obviate any danger being caused or likely to be caused by the contravention of any byelaw made under this section.

(6) Byelaws under this section shall not come into operation until they have been confirmed by the Secretary of State under section 21 of this Act.

(7) When any byelaws under this section have been so confirmed—

(a) a copy of the byelaws shall be printed and deposited at such place or places as may be specified in a direction given to the Concessionaires by the Secretary of State and shall at all reasonable hours be open to public inspection free of charge; and

(b) a copy of the byelaws, or any part of them, shall be supplied to any person on request on payment of such reasonable fee as the Concessionaires may determine.

(8) The production of a printed copy of a byelaw purporting to be made by the Concessionaires on which is endorsed a certificate purporting to be signed by a person authorised to do so by the Concessionaires stating—

(a) that the byelaw is made by the Concessionaires;

(b) that the copy is a true copy of the byelaw;

(c) that on a specified date the byelaw was confirmed by the Secretary of State; and

(d) the date, if any, fixed by the Secretary of State for the coming into operation of the byelaw;

shall be evidence of the facts stated in the certificate, without proof of the handwriting or authorisation of the person by whom it purports to be signed.

Confirmation of byelaws by Secretary of State

21.—(1) At least one month before making an application for confirmation of any byelaws under section 20 of this Act the Concessionaires shall publish notice of their intention to apply for confirmation and of the place at which and the time during which a copy of the byelaws will be open for public inspection—

(a) in such newspapers circulating in the City of Canterbury, the borough of Ashford and the districts of Dover, Shepway and Thanet, in the county of Kent; and

(b) in such other manner;

as may be approved by the Secretary of State.

(2) Any person affected by any of the byelaws shall be entitled to make representations on the byelaws to the Secretary of State within a period of not less than one month which must be specified in the notice published under subsection (1) above.

(3) For at least one month before the making of any such application a copy of the byelaws in question shall be deposited at such place or places as may be specified in a direction given to the Concessionaires by the Secretary of State and shall at all reasonable hours be open to public inspection free of charge.

(4) A copy of those byelaws, or any part of them, shall be supplied to any person on request on payment of such reasonable fee as the Concessionaires may determine.

(5) Subject to the following provisions of this section, the Secretary of State may confirm with or without modification, or refuse to confirm, any byelaws submitted to him for confirmation, and may fix the date on which a byelaw confirmed by him is to come into operation; and if no such date is so fixed the byelaw shall come into operation at the expiration of one month beginning with the date of its confirmation.

(6) The Secretary of State shall not confirm any byelaw submitted to him for confirmation unless he has consulted the Kent County Council and the council of any district in which it appears to him that the byelaw would have effect.

(7) Where the Secretary of State proposes to make a modification of any byelaws submitted to him for confirmation which appears to him to be substantial—

(a) he shall inform the Concessionaires and require them to take any steps he considers necessary for informing persons likely to be concerned with the modification; and

(b) he shall not confirm the byelaws until such period has elapsed as he thinks reasonable for consideration of, and comment upon, the proposed modification by the Concessionaires and by other persons who have been informed of it.

Application of Railways Board's byelaws to their services in the tunnel system

22. Byelaws made by the Railways Board under section 67 of the Transport Act 1962 (general power to make byelaws for their railways and premises) shall apply in relation to persons and goods being conveyed by the Railways Board on any railway of the Concessionaires as they apply in relation to persons and goods being conveyed on any railway of the Board.

Control of traffic within the tunnel system

23.—(1) Subject to the following provisions of this section, the enactments relating to road traffic shall apply in relation to any tunnel system road to which the public does not have access as they apply in relation to a road to which the public does have access.

(2) Those enactments shall apply in relation to any tunnel system road subject to such exceptions and modifications as the Secretary of State may by order specify.

(3) An order under subsection (2) above may, in particular, confer on the Concessionaires functions exercisable under those enactments by a highway authority or a local authority.

(4) The Secretary of State may by order provide that those enactments shall not apply in relation to any tunnel system road specified in the order and may require the Concessionaires to indicate any such road in a manner so specified.

(5) Those enactments shall not, in the case of any tunnel system road, apply in relation to it until such date as the Secretary of State may by order specify.

(6) Before making an order under this section, the Secretary of State shall consult the Concessionaires.

(7) In this section, "tunnel system road" means any length of road comprised in the tunnel system.

Approval of trains

24. Any train used for conveying passengers or goods through the tunnel system (including any shuttle train) shall be of such a description and conform to such specifications as may for the time being be approved by the Secretary of State.

Termination of construction or operation

Maintenance of the tunnel system on termination of construction by Concessionaires

25.—(1) Subject to section 27 of this Act, on termination of the Concession at any time before the construction of the Concessionaires' scheduled works is completed, the Secretary of State is authorised by this section to take such steps as appear to him to be appropriate for maintaining the tunnel system, so far as already constructed, in a safe and satisfactory condition.

(2) During any period when this section has effect—

    (a) the Secretary of State is responsible, subject to subsection (1) above, for the exercise of any relevant functions of the Concessionaires under this Act in relation to the tunnel system; and

    (b) references in provisions of this Act relating to those functions to the Concessionaires shall be read as references to the Secretary of State.

Operation of the tunnel system on a temporary basis where practicable on termination of the Concession

26.—(1) Subject to section 27 of this Act and the following provisions of this section, if on the expiry or termination of the Concession the construction of the Concessionaires' scheduled works has been completed or has reached a stage so near completion that it is practicable to operate the tunnel system or any part of it, the Secretary of State is authorised by this section—

    (a) in collaboration with any Minister or department of the Government of the French Republic; and

    (b) in accordance with any arrangements made, in pursuance of Article 17 of the Treaty, between that Government and Her Majesty's

Government in the United Kingdom with respect to the continued operation of the tunnel system by those Governments;

to manage, operate and maintain the tunnel system or (as the case may be) such part of it as it is practicable to operate.

(2) The Secretary of State may not by virtue of this section continue to participate in the management, operation or maintenance of the tunnel system after the end of the period of three months beginning with the date of the expiry or termination of the Concession.

(3) During any period when this section has effect—

   (a) the Secretary of State is responsible for the exercise of any relevant functions of the Concessionaires under this Act in relation to the tunnel system or (as the case may be) in relation to any part of it to which the arrangements mentioned in subsection (1)(b) above apply; and

   (b) references in provisions of this Act relating to those functions to the Concessionaires shall be read as references to the Secretary of State.

Limitations on exercise of Secretary of State's powers under sections 25 and 26

27.—(1) Section 25 or (as the case may be) section 26 of this Act only has effect—

   (a) if on the termination or (as the case may be) on the expiry or termination of the Concession the Secretary of State is satisfied that there is a reasonable prospect of agreement on a new Concession in the near future; and

   (b) until either there is such agreement and the new Concession comes into operation or (as the case may be) he ceases to be so satisfied.

(2) Where either of those sections ceases to have effect on the coming into operation of a new Concession, this section is without prejudice to the subsequent operation of either of those sections on the expiry or termination of the new Concession.

Provisions supplementary to sections 25 to 27

28.—(1) The Secretary of State may by order make such modifications of the provisions of this Act, as they apply during any period when section 25 or 26 of this Act has effect, as appear to him to be necessary or expedient for the purposes or in consequence of the exercise by him of any relevant functions of the Concessionaires under this Act.

(2) References in sections 25 and 26 and in subsection (1) above to relevant functions of the Concessionaires under this Act are references—

   (a) in relation to the exercise by the Secretary of State of his powers under section 25(1); to functions of the Concessionaires under Part II or V of this Act; and

   (b) in relation to the exercise by the Secretary of State of his powers under section 26(1), to functions of the Concessionaires under this Part of this Act or under Part V of this Act.

(3) Below in this section—

   (a) references to an authority responsible for the tunnel system are references to the Secretary of State, in relation to any period during which section 25 or 26 of this Act has effect, and otherwise to the Concessionaires;

   (b) "a transfer of responsibility" means the expiry or termination of the Concession or the coming into operation of a new Concession (as the case may be); and

   (c) "relevant functions" means, in relation to any such transfer, functions conferred by or under this Act for the exercise of which by virtue of that transfer one such authority ceases to be, and another such authority becomes, responsible.

(4) On any transfer of responsibility—

(a) all subsisting rights and duties conferred or imposed by any provision of this Act relating to any relevant functions on the person who ceases on that transfer to be the authority responsible for the tunnel system shall become rights and duties of the person who on that transfer becomes the authority so responsible; and

(b) anything done by any person before that transfer in the exercise of any of those functions which is in force, valid or subsisting immediately before the transfer shall continue in force and have effect as if done by the person who on that transfer becomes the authority responsible for the tunnel system.

(5) In particular, but without prejudice to the generality of paragraph (b) of subsection (4) above, any byelaws or other instrument made by one authority responsible for the tunnel system in exercise of any of the relevant functions may by virtue of that paragraph be varied or revoked by another authority so responsible, notwithstanding that the procedure applicable in relation to the making, variation or revocation of those byelaws or that instrument may, by virtue of any order made under this section with respect to the exercise of those functions by the Secretary of State, vary from one such authority to another.

Scheme for land on abandonment of construction or operation

29.—(1) Where on or at any time after the expiry or termination of the Concession it appears to the Secretary of State that the construction or operation of the tunnel system will not be resumed in the near future, the Secretary of State shall notify the district planning authority of that fact and, after consultation with them, shall make in relation to any land on which work has been done under this Act a scheme for putting it into such a condition as the scheme may provide and shall put into such a condition in accordance with the scheme.

(2) A scheme under this section may be revoked or varied by a subsequent scheme made under this section by the Secretary of State after consultation with the district planning authority.

Miscellaneous

Rating

30. In Schedule 3 to the Local Government Act 1974 (hereditaments in relation to which a method for fixing or determining rateable value may be specified by the Secretary of State under section 19 of that Act), there shall be inserted at the end—

"10.—(1) Any hereditament consisting of channel tunnel premises occupied by the Concessionaires or by any subsidiary of theirs.

(2) For the purposes of this paragraph—

(a) "channel tunnel premises" means premises comprised in the tunnel system within the meaning of the Channel Tunnel Act 1987;

(b) "Concessionaires" has the same meaning as in that Act; and

(c) "subsidiary", in relation to the Concessionaires—

(i) means a body corporate which is a subsidiary of theirs or, where the Concessionaires are for the time being two or more persons, of any of them, within the meaning of the Companies Act 1985; and

(ii) where the Concessionaires are for the time being two or more persons, includes a body corporate which would be a subsidiary of theirs within the meaning of that Act if the Concessionaires were a single body corporate."

Building regulations

31.—(1) Nothing in Part I of the Building Act 1984 (building regulations), and nothing in any building regulations, shall apply in relation to any building comprised in the tunnel system unless the building is, within the meaning of that Act, a house or a hotel.

(2) Section 4 of that Act (exemption from building regulations of certain buildings, other than houses, which belong to statutory undertakers) shall not apply in relation to any building comprised in the tunnel system.

Exclusion of exercise of rights under telecommunications code in relation to tunnel system land under the sea

32. Notwithstanding anything in section 10 of the Telecommunications Act 1984 (the telecommunications code) or in any licence granted by the Secretary of State under section 7 of that Act (licensing of telecommunication systems), no rights shall be exercisable by any person by virtue of the telecommunications code in relation to any land comprised in the tunnel system and lying in or under the bed of the sea.

Competition, etc.

33.—(1) The Act of 1976 shall not apply to any Concession agreement and shall be deemed never to have applied to any such agreement.

(2) Where the Concessionaires are for the time being two or more persons, the Secretary of State may, after consultation with the Director General of Fair Trading, by order provide that—

(a) the Concessionaires and any body corporate which is a member of the same group as any of them shall be deemed to be members of one and the same group of interconnected bodies corporate for the purposes of section 6(1)(b) (monopoly situation in relation to the supply of goods by or to members of one and the same group of interconnected bodies corporate) and 7(1)(b) (corresponding provision in relation to the supply of services) of the Act of 1973;

(b) the Concessionaires and any body corporate which is a member of the same group as any of them shall be deemed to be interconnected bodies corporate for the purposes of the Act of 1976 in relation to any specified channel tunnel agreement, any such specified class of channel tunnel agreements or all such agreements; and

(c) the Concessionaires and any body corporate which is a member of the same group as any of them shall be deemed to be persons who are to be treated as associated for the purposes of section 2 of the Act of 1980 (anti-competitive practices).

(3) In the case of any channel tunnel agreement—

(a) the Secretary of State shall consult the Director General of Fair Trading before approving the agreement under section 29 of the Act of 1976 (exemption from registration under that Act of agreements which are of importance to the national economy and approved by the Secretary of State for the purposes of that section); and

(b) that section shall apply as if for the condition set out in subsection (2)(b) there were substituted a condition that the object or main object of the agreement is the facilitation of the construction or operation of the tunnel system.

(4) In the case of any channel tunnel agreement made before, or within the period of six months beginning with, the date of passing of this Act, the Secretary of State may, before the expiration of that period, approve the agreement under section 29 by order made after it has been concluded; and, if he does so, the Act of 1976 shall be deemed not to have applied to the agreement at any time before that order comes into force.

(5) In connection with the approval of any channel tunnel agreement for the purposes of section 29, the Secretary of State may, after consultation with the Director General of Fair Trading, by order provide that—

(a) in relation to any specified description of goods or services supplied in connection with the construction or operation of the tunnel system, such of the parties to that agreement as he may specify and any body corporate which is a member of the same group as any of them shall be deemed to be members of one and the same group of interconnected bodies corporate for the purposes of sections 6(1)(b) and 7(1)(b) of the Act of 1973;

(b) in relation to any specified class of agreement which is made in pursuance or furtherance of that agreement, such of the parties to that agreement as he may specify and any body corporate which is a member of the same group as any of them shall be deemed to be interconnected bodies corporate for the purposes of the Act of 1976; and

(c) in relation to any course of conduct engaged in in connection with the construction or operation of the tunnel system, such of the parties to that agreement as he may specify and any body corporate which is a member of the same group as any of them shall be deemed to be persons who are to be treated as associated for the purposes of section 2 of the Act of 1980.

(6) An order under subsection (2) or (5) above may impose, on any person to whom any provision made under that subsection relates, such requirements as the Secretary of State considers it expedient to impose in connection with that provision.

(7) Section 93(3) and (4) of the Act of 1973 (which enables the Secretary of State to apply to the court for an order to enforce certain directions given by him under that Act and make provision with respect to the expenses of such an application) shall apply in relation to requirements imposed by an order under subsection (2) or (5) above as it applies in relation to directions given under section 90(7) of that Act.

(8) Where, before the expiration of the period mentioned in subsection (4) above, the Secretary of State makes such provision as is mentioned in subsection (5)(b) above in connection with the approval of any agreement for the purposes of section 29, the Act of 1976 shall be deemed not to have applied, at any time before the order making the provision comes into force, to any agreement made in pursuance or furtherance of that agreement if, by virtue of that provision, the agreement so made is one to which that Act does not apply on the coming into force of that order.

(9) Where an order under subsection (2) or (5) above is revoked, section 24 of the Act of 1976 (time for registering particulars of agreements subject to registration) shall apply in relation to any agreement which becomes subject to registration under that Act by virtue of the revocation of that order as it applies in relation to any agreement which becomes subject to registration under that Act by virtue of the expiry or revocation of an order under section 29 of that Act.

(10) In section 137(3) of the Act of 1973 (which defines "the supply of services" for the purposes of that Act and, by virtue of section 33(2) of the Act of 1980, for the purposes also of sections 2 to 24 of the latter Act) there shall be added after paragraph (d)—

"and

(e) includes the making of arrangements permitting use of the tunnel system (within the meaning of the Channel Tunnel Act 1987) by a person operating services for the carriage of passengers or goods by rail."

(11) In paragraph 5 of Schedule 5 to the Act of 1973 (which lists the carriage of goods or passengers by rail as among the services in respect of which a reference to the Consumer Protection Advisory Committee or the Monopolies and Mergers Commission is excluded or subject to special restrictions) there shall be added at the end "otherwise than on shuttle services (within the meaning of the Channel Tunnel Act 1987)."

(12) In this section—

"the Act of 1973" means the Fair Trading Act 1973;

"the Act of 1976" means the Restrictive Trade Practices Act 1976;

"the Act of 1980" means the Competition Act 1980;

"channel tunnel agreement" means any agreement connected with the construction or operation of the tunnel system;

"group" means a body corporate and all other bodies corporate which are its subsidiaries within the meaning of the Companies Act 1985; and

"specify" and "specified" mean specify and specified in an order.

Supplementary provisions with respect to orders under Part III

34.—(1) Any power to make an order conferred on the Secretary of State or the appropriate Minister by any provision of this Part of this Act shall be exercisable by statutory instrument.

(2) Subject to subsection (3) below, any statutory instrument containing an order made under any such provision shall be subject to annulment in pursuance of a resolution of either House of Parliament.

(3) Subsection (2) above—

(a) shall not apply to a statutory instrument containing an order under section 10(8), 23(5) or 33 of this Act; and

(b) shall not apply to a statutory instrument containing an order made under section 11 of this Act if a draft of the instrument containing the order has been approved by resolution of each House of Parliament before the order is made.

(4) Any order made by the Secretary of State or the appropriate Minister under this Part of this Act may make different provision for different cases or classes of case to which the order applies.

(5) It is hereby declared that, notwithstanding that orders under section 11 of this Act may affect individuals or bodies corporate outside the United Kingdom, any provision made by any such order that does affect such individuals or bodies corporate applies whether or not those individuals are British subjects or those bodies corporate are incorporated in any part of the United Kingdom.

PART IV

CONSTRUCTION AND IMPROVEMENT OF ROADS NEAR FOLKESTONE

The A20 improvement works

35.—(1) The Secretary of State may, subject to and in accordance with the provisions of this Act, construct the works specified in Part I of Schedule 4 to this Act (referred to below in this Act as the A20 improvement works).

(2) Part II of that Schedule shall have effect for conferring on the Secretary of State powers in relation to—

(a) the stopping up of highways and the extinguishment of rights of way over them; and

(b) temporary interference with highways;

for the purpose of or in connection with the construction of any of the A20 improvement works.

(3) Part III of that Schedule shall have effect—

    (a) for treating highways constructed by the Secretary of State in pursuance of that Schedule as highways of the descriptions there specified;

    (b) for transferring such of those highways as do not become trunk roads to the Kent County Council;

    (c) for treating the construction of highways and other things done in pursuance of that Schedule as authorised under the provisions of the Highways Act 1980 there specified;

    (d) for treating certain provisions of that Schedule as provisions of instruments made under that Act of the descriptions there specified; and

    (e) for enabling traffic on any highway constructed in pursuance of that Schedule to be subject to regulation under the Road Traffic Regulation Act 1984 as soon as it is open for public use.

(4) Subject to paragraph 2 of that Schedule (which gives the limits of deviation for the works and also permits deviation from the levels shown on the deposited sections), the A20 improvement works shall be constructed in the lines or situations shown on the deposited plans and in accordance with the levels shown on the deposited sections.

Acquisition of land for the A20 improvement works

36. Subject to section 37 of this Act, the Secretary of State is authorised by this section to acquire compulsorily—

    (a) so much of the land shown on the deposited plans within the limits of deviation for the A20 improvement works as may be required for the construction of those works and other works in connection with those works; and

    (b) so much of the land so shown within the limits of land to be acquired as may be so required.

Part V

Miscellaneous and General

Supplementary provisions with respect to acquisition of land

37.—(1) The purposes for which land may be acquired under section 8 of this Act include, in the case of any land specified in columns 1 and 2 of section A or B of Part I of Schedule 5 to this Act, the purpose specified in relation to that land in column 3 of section A or B as one for which that land may be acquired or used.

(2) The purposes for which land may be acquired under section 36 of this Act include, in the case of any land specified in columns 1 and 2 of Part II of that Schedule, the purpose specified in relation to that land in column 3 of that Schedule as one for which that land may be acquired or used.

(3) Part III of that Schedule shall have effect for supplementing sections 8 and 36 of this Act and for regulating or (in certain circumstances) restricting the exercise of the powers conferred by those sections.

(4) Subject to Part III of that Schedule and to subsection (5) below, Part I of the Compulsory Purchase Act 1965 (except sections 4 and 27 and paragraph 3(3) of Schedule 3), in so far as it is applicable for the purposes of this Act and is not inconsistent with the provisions of this Act, shall apply to the acquisition of land under section 8 or 36 of this Act, as it applies to a compulsory purchase to which Part II of the Acquisition of Land Act 1981, or Schedule 1 to that Act, applies and as if this Act were a compulsory purchase order under the latter Act.

(5) Section 11(1) of the Compulsory Purchase Act 1965 (power to enter on and take possession of land the subject of a notice to treat after giving not less than fourteen days' notice) shall have effect—

> (a) in its application by virtue of subsection (4) above to any of the land specified in the table in paragraph 2(3) of Part III of Schedule 5 to this Act, as if for the words "fourteen days" there were substituted the words "one month"; and
>
> (b) in its application by virtue of that subsection to any other land, as if for the words "fourteen days" there were substituted the words "three months".

(6) The Lands Clauses Consolidation Act 1845 shall not apply to the acquisition of land under section 8 or 36 of this Act.

Time within which powers of compulsory acquisition may be exercised

38.—(1) Subject to subsection (3) below, a notice to treat under the Compulsory Purchase Act 1965 (as applied by section 37 of this Act and whether or not as extended by Part III of Schedule 5 to this Act) for the purpose of acquiring any land under section 8 or 36 of this Act shall not be served after 31st December 1992 or such later date as may for the time being be authorised by an order made by the Secretary of State.

(2) An order under subsection (1) above shall be subject to special Parliamentary procedure.

(3) Where the Secretary of State has issued a certificate under the following provisions of this section, a notice to treat under the Act of 1965 (as so applied and whether or not as so extended) for the purpose of acquiring under section 8(1) of this Act the land specified in the certificate may be served at any time before the date specified in the certificate.

(4) The Concessionaires may in relation to any land which they require for purposes of safety in connection with any railway or siding comprised in the tunnel system apply to the Secretary of State for an extension of the time allowed under subsection (1) above for serving a notice to treat for the purpose of acquiring the land under section 8(1) of this Act.

(5) Before making such an application, the Concessionaires shall serve on every owner, lessee and occupier (except tenants for a month or less than a month) of the land in relation to which they propose to seek the extension a notice in a form approved by the Secretary of State—

> (a) stating that they propose to make an application under subsection (4) above in relation to the land;
>
> (b) stating what the effect will be if their application is granted; and
>
> (c) specifying the time, which shall not be less than fourteen days from service of the notice, within which and the manner in which representations about the application can be made.

(6) Where the Secretary of State is satisfied—

> (a) that the Concessionaires have complied with the requirements of subsection (5) above; and
>
> (b) that all or some part of the land to which the application relates is required for purposes of safety in connection with any railway or siding comprised in the tunnel system;

he may, after taking into consideration any representations about the application duly made by the recipient of a notice under that subsection, issue a certificate specifying which of the land to which the application relates is in his opinion required for those purposes.

(7) The Secretary of State shall specify in any certificate which he issues under this section such date as he thinks fit as the date before which any notice to treat for the purpose of acquiring the land specified in the certificate must be served.

Extension of Railways Board's powers in connection with through services

39.—(1) In section 3(3) of the Transport Act 1962 (powers of the Railways Board) there shall be substituted for paragraph (a) (power to carry goods and passengers within Great Britain)—

"(a) to carry goods and passengers by rail within, to or from Great Britain,

(aa) to carry goods and passengers by rail between places outside Great Britain in so far as they consider it expedient to do so in connection with the exercise of their powers under paragraph (a) above,";

and there shall be added at the end—

"(g) to do anything which appears to the Board to be expedient for the purposes of or in connection with the provision by the Board of railway services outside Great Britain."

(2) It is within the power of the Railways Board to enter into a contract with any person operating railway services through the tunnel system for the passage of any train of any such person over or along any railway of the Board; and this section gives any person with whom the Board have entered into such a contract authority to use any railway of the Board in accordance with that contract in so far as such authority is not given by any other enactment.

(3) The assumption by the Railways Board, under any contract with the Concessionaires under which the Board are permitted to use the tunnel system, of any obligations with respect to the exercise of any of their powers, shall not be regarded (if it would be so regarded apart from this provision) as incompatible with the proper exercise of those or any other of their powers.

Railways Board's plan for international through services

40.—(1) It shall be the duty of the Railways Board to prepare a plan stating measures which the Board propose to take, and any proposals as to measures which the Board consider ought to be taken by any person in the United Kingdom or France, with the aim of securing—

(a) the provision or improvement of international through services serving various parts of the United Kingdom; and

(b) an increase in the proportion of the passengers and goods carried between places in the United Kingdom and places outside the United Kingdom that is carried by international through services.

(2) The measures referred to in subsection (1) above are—

(a) measures relating to the operation of international through services;

(b) measures relating to the carrying out of works or other development connected with international through services (including collection and distribution centres for goods and inland clearance depots); and

(c) measures relating to the provision or improvement of facilities or other services connected with international through services.

(3) The Railways Board—

    (a) shall prepare the plan under this section not later than 31st December 1989;

    (b) shall keep the plan under review and from time to time revise it; and

    (c) shall cause the plan and any revisions of it to be published in such manner as they think fit.

(4) In preparing the plan and any revisions of it the Railways Board shall have regard to the financial resources likely to be available to them and to any restrictions likely to be imposed on them with respect to the application of such resources.

(5) The duties imposed by this section shall not apply at any time when the original Concession, as defined by section 1(4) of this Act, has expired or terminated and no new Concession is in operation.

(6) In this section "international through services" means services for the carriage of passengers or goods by rail by way of the tunnel system, other than shuttle services.

Railway services: consultative committees and closures

41.—(1) The duty—

    (a) of the Central Transport Consultative Committee for Great Britain and each of the Area Transport Users Consultative Committees under section 56(4) of the Transport Act 1962; and

    (b) of the London Regional Passengers' Committee under section 40(4) of the London Regional Transport Act 1984;

to consider and, where it appears to them to be desirable, make recommendations with respect to any matter affecting the services and facilities there mentioned shall apply in relation to services and facilities within this subsection as it applies in relation to services and facilities provided by the Railways Board or any subsidiary of theirs.

(2) The services and facilities within subsection (1) above are—

    (a) international railway passenger services which are provided otherwise than by the Concessionaires or the Railways Board or any subsidiary of theirs; and

    (b) facilities so provided which are intended for use primarily in connection with such services.

(3) In relation to any services or facilities to which by virtue of subsection (1) above the duty under section 56(4) or 40(4) applies—

    (a) section 56(4) shall have effect as if references in it to a Board or to the Board concerned were references to the person providing those services and facilities; and

    (b) section 40(5) to (7) and (9) and section 41(3) and (5) to (7) of the Act of 1984 shall have effect as if references in any of those provisions to the Railways Board or to the Railways Board or any subsidiary of theirs were references to that person.

(4) The reference to services and facilities in section 56(4) shall not include railway services and facilities provided by the Railways Board or any subsidiary of theirs so far as they are provided outside Great Britain.

(5) The references to railway passenger services in section 56(7) of the Act of 1962 (procedure in case of proposal to discontinue all railway passenger services from a station or on a line) shall not include international railway passenger services.

(6) In this section "international railway passenger services" means services provided in Great Britain for the carriage of passengers by rail between any place in Great Britain and any place outside Great Britain by way of the tunnel system.

No government grants to Railways Board in respect of international railway services

42.—(1) No obligation with respect to international railway services shall be imposed on the Railways Board under section 3 of the Railways Act 1974 (imposition of obligations in connection with certain Community regulations giving rise to payments by way of compensation).

(2) In ascertaining any relevant deficit of the Railways Board's railway undertaking for the purposes of section 1 of the Transport (Financial Provisions) Act 1977 (power of Secretary of State to make grants in respect of such a deficit) there shall be disregarded so much of the revenue and expenditure properly attributable to revenue account as is referable to the provision of international railway services.

(3) No grants shall be made by the Secretary of State under section 56(1) of the Transport Act 1968 (grants towards capital expenditure on public passenger transport facilities) towards expenditure incurred or to be incurred by the Railways Board for the purpose of the provision, improvement or development of international railway services.

(4) In this section "international railway services" means services for the carriage of passengers or goods by way of the tunnel system.

Application of railway regulation enactments

43. Schedule 6 to this Act shall have effect for making miscellaneous provisions about the application of railway regulation enactments in relation to the tunnel system, the Concessionaires and certain other persons operating services by way of the tunnel system.

Modification of enactments relating to coast protection, safety of navigation and the powers of harbour authorities

44.—(1) Section 16(1) of the Coast Protection Act 1949 (consent of coast protection authority required for carrying out coast protection work) shall not apply to the carrying out of any work by the Concessionaires for the construction or protection of any part of the tunnel system, but section 17(2) to (9) of that Act (restrictions imposed on the carrying out of work excluded from section 16(1) by section 17(1) of that Act) shall apply to any such work of the Concessionaires as it applies to work so excluded by section 17(1)(d) of that Act (work carried out by certain bodies for the protection of a railway).

(2) Section 18 of that Act (prohibition of excavation or removal of materials from the seashore) shall not apply to any excavation or removal by the Concessionaires in the course of constructing, maintaining or altering the tunnel system of any materials on, under or forming part of any portion of the seashore within the limits of deviation for their scheduled works.

(3) Section 34(1) of that Act (restriction of works detrimental to navigation) shall not apply in relation to anything done in the course of carrying out any work which the Concessionaires are authorised by this Act to carry out.

(4) Nothing in that Act or any order under that Act shall authorise or require any person to carry out any work within 150 metres of the centre line of the tunnel system, so far as lying under the foreshore or the bed of the sea, without the consent of the Concessionaires.

(5) Subject to subsection (6) below, any power conferred on the Dover Harbour Board by any enactment to raise or destroy wrecks, dredge or deepen the foreshore or the bed of the sea or carry out any blasting operations shall not without the consent of the Concessionaires be exercised—

   (a) in the case of any operation involving the use of explosives having an explosive force greater than that of 100 pounds of trinitrotoluene (TNT), within 1,000 metres;

   (b) in the case of any other operation involving the use of any explosives, within 500 metres; and

   (c) in any other case, within 150 metres;

of the centre line of the tunnel system, so far as lying under the foreshore or the bed of the sea.

(6) Subsection (5) above shall not apply in relation to the exercise by the Dover Harbour Board in, or within 200 metres of any entrance to, Dover Harbour of any power to carry out blasting operations if the Board—

   (a) have given to the Concessionaires such notice of their intention to carry out the operations as is reasonably practicable; and

   (b) have consulted the Concessionaires with a view to agreeing the time at which and the manner in which the operations are carried out.

(7) The Concessionaires shall not unreasonably withhold their consent in any case where it is required under subsection (4) or (5) above.

(8) Any difference arising between the Concessionaires and any person seeking their consent under subsection (4) or (5) above shall be determined by arbitration.

Protection of interests

45. Schedule 7 to this Act shall have effect for protecting the interests of the bodies and persons specified in that Schedule (being bodies and persons who may be affected by other provisions of this Act).

Determination of questions referred to arbitration under this Act

46. Where under this Act any difference (other than a difference which falls to be determined by the Lands Tribunal) is to be determined by arbitration, then, subject to any other provision of this Act, the difference shall be referred to, and settled by, a single arbitrator to be agreed between the parties or, in default of agreement, to be appointed on the application of either party, after notice in writing to the other, by the President of the Institution of Civil Engineers.

Offences by bodies corporate

47.—(1) Where a body corporate is guilty of an offence under this Act or of an offence created by an order made under section 11 of this Act and the offence is proved to have been committed with the consent or connivance of or to be attributable to any neglect on the part of a director, manager, secretary or other similar officer of the body corporate or person who was purporting to act in any such capacity, he as well as the body corporate shall be guilty of that offence and liable to be proceeded against and punished accordingly.

(2) Where the affairs of a body corporate are managed by its members, this section shall apply in relation to the acts and defaults of a member in connection with his functions of management as if he were a director of the body corporate.

Financial provisions

48.—(1) Any expenditure incurred by the Secretary of State—

   (a) in making payments for land vested in or acquired by him under this Act;

   (b) for the purpose of or in connection with the discharge by the

Intergovernmental Commission or the Safety Authority of their
functions under the Treaty;

(c) by virtue of section 25 or 26 of this Act;

(d) in making payments for the purpose of restoring any land in
pursuance of this Act;

(e) in making any payments of compensation that fall under any
provision of this Act to be made by him; and

(f) in meeting any obligations or exercising any rights to which he
is or from time to time becomes subject or entitled in pursuance
of the Treaty or the Concession, being obligations or rights
arising in connection with the tunnel system;

shall be met out of money provided by Parliament.

(2) Any increase attributable to this Act—

(a) in the sums payable out of money so provided under any other
enactment; and

(b) in the administrative expenses of any government department;

shall be met out of money so provided.

(3) Any sums received by the Secretary of State—

(a) in reimbursement of any expenditure mentioned in subsection
(1)(a), (d) or (e) above;

(b) in consideration of the disposal by him of any land acquired
under this Act or otherwise in connection with the construction
of the tunnel system;

(c) by way of receipts arising from the operation of the tunnel
system or any part of it under section 26 of this Act; or

(d) in pursuance of the Treaty or the Concession;

shall be paid by him into the Consolidated Fund.

Interpretation

49.—(1) In this Act, except where the context otherwise requires—

"A20 improvement works" has the meaning given by section 35;

"the appropriate authority" means—

(a) in relation to the acquisition of land required for the
Concessionaires' scheduled works and other works in connec-
tion with those works, or for any purpose of Part IV of this
Act, the Secretary of State;

(b) in relation to any other matter concerning the Concessionaires' scheduled works or such other works, the
Concessionaires;

(c) in relation to the County Council's scheduled works and
other works in connection with those works, that Council; and

(d) in relation to the Railways Board's scheduled works and
other works in connection with those works, the Railways
Board;

"the arbitral tribunal" has the meaning given by section 2(10);

"bridleway" has the same meaning as in the Highways Act 1980;

"the Concession", "Concession agreement", "Concession lease" and
"the Concessionaires" have the meanings given by the relevant
provisions of section 1 (read with section 3(3));

"deposited plans" and "deposited sections" mean respectively the
plans and sections shown on Sheets Nos. 1 to 15 and 21 to 34
of the plans and sections deposited in connection with the
Channel Tunnel Bill in the Office of the Clerk of the Parliaments and the Private Bill Office of the House of Commons in
April 1986 and the plans and sections so deposited in July
1986;

"Dover Harbour" has the same meaning "harbour" has in the Dover Harbour Consolidation Act 1954;

"enactment" includes an enactment contained in this Act or in any Act passed on or after the date on which this Act is passed, and any subordinate legislation within the meaning of the Interpretation Act 1978;

"footpath" has the same meaning as in the Highways Act 1980;

"frontier" means the frontier between the United Kingdom and France fixed by the Treaty;

"functions" includes powers, duties and obligations;

"goods" includes vehicles (notwithstanding that they may be being used for the carriage of other goods or of persons), animals, plants and any other creature, substance or thing capable of being transported;

"the Intergovernmental Commission" means the Intergovernmental Commission established by the Treaty;

"the international arrangements" means—
    (a) the Treaty and the Concession; and
    (b) any other agreements or arrangements between Her Majesty's Government in the United Kingdom and the Government of the French Republic which for the time being apply for regulating any matters arising out of or connected with the tunnel system;

"land" includes buildings and other structures, land covered with water, and any estate, interest, easement, servitude or right in or over land;

"limits of deviation" means the limits of deviation shown on the deposited plans and "limits of land to be acquired" means the limits of land to be acquired so shown;

"modification" includes addition, omission and alteration, and related expressions shall be construed accordingly;

"nature conservation" means the conservation of flora, fauna or geological or physiographical features;

"the Railways Board" has the meaning given by section 5(3);

"the Safety Authority" means the Safety Authority established by the Treaty;

"shuttle service" and "shuttle train" have the meanings given by section 1(9);

"substance" means any natural or artificial substance, whether in solid or liquid form or in the form of a gas or vapour;

"train" includes any locomotive and railway rolling stock of any description;

"the Treaty" has the meaning given by section 1(4);

"the tunnel system" has the meaning given by section 1(7); and

"vehicle" includes a railway vehicle.

(2) References in this Act to—
    (a) the scheduled works;
    (b) the Concessionaires' scheduled works;
    (c) the County Council's scheduled works; and
    (d) the Railways Board's scheduled works;
shall be read in accordance with section 5(4) of this Act.

(3) References in this Act to the expiry of the Concession are references to the expiry of the maximum period for which, in accordance with its terms, the Concession would remain in force in default of earlier termination under any of its provisions providing for premature termination of that maximum period.

(4) References in this Act to the termination of the Concession are references to the termination of the Concession before the end of that maximum period.

(5) References in this Act to agreement on a new Concession, and to a new Concession, shall be read in accordance with section 3(5) of this Act.

(6) In this Act—

    (a) references to the M20 are references to the special road so designated; and

    (b) references to specified distances or lengths shall be construed as if the words "or thereabouts" were inserted after each such distance or length, distances between points on a road or railway being measured along the centre line of the road or railway.

(7) Unless the context otherwise requires, a reference in this Act to a work identified by a number shall be read as a reference to the scheduled work or (as the case may be) the A20 improvement work of that number.

(8) In this Act—

    (a) any reference specifying any land or point shown on the deposited plans shall be taken as a reference to the land or point identified on those plans by the numbers or letters or the numbers and letters so specified;

    (b) unless the context otherwise requires, any reference to any land specifying a range of consecutive numbers shall include a reference to any land identified on the deposited plans by a number within the range of numbers so specified whether or not a letter is added to that number for the purpose of identification; and

    (c) any reference to any land specifying a single number with the addition of a range of alphabetically consecutive letters shall include a reference to any land identified on the deposited plans by that number with the addition of any letter within the range of letters so specified.

(9) Any reference in this Act to Part I or II of the Land Compensation Act 1973 or any provision of either Part shall include a reference to that Part or provision as modified by section 84(1) of that Act.

Short title and extent

50.—(1) This Act may be cited as the Channel Tunnel Act 1987.

(2) This Act extends to Northern Ireland.

SCHEDULES

Section 5

SCHEDULE 1

THE SCHEDULED WORKS

PART I

THE CONCESSIONAIRES' SCHEDULED WORKS

In the district of Dover (town of Dover and parishes of Capel-le-Ferne and Hougham Without) and the district of Shepway (town of Folkestone and parishes of Hawkinge, Newington and Saltwood), in the county of Kent—

    Work No. 1—A railway (3225 metres in length), including a viaduct, commencing by a junction with Work No. 30 at a point 565 metres east of the northern end of the existing bridge carrying the B2065 over the railway between Ashford and Folkestone West, passing by means of the viaduct over the M20 at a point 155 metres north-west of the bridge carrying the bridleway from the A20 at Stone Farm, Newington, to Dibgate Camp and then over the A20 (Work No. 9A), continuing in an easterly direction and terminating at a point 85 metres west of a point on the road known as Castle Hill 170 metres north of its junction with the Castle Hill Roundabout:

Work No. 2—A railway (5862 metres in length), commencing by a junction with Work No. 1 at its termination, diverging in a south-westerly direction from that work, then turning in a north-westerly direction to pass under that work in tunnel, then turning in a northerly and then in an easterly direction and terminating by a junction with Work No. 1 at its said termination:

Work No. 3—A railway (1146 metres in length), commencing by a junction with Work No. 1 at its termination, passing under Castle Hill and terminating at a point 240 metres west of a point on Canterbury Road 620 metres from its junction with Churchill Avenue:

Work No. 4—A railway (8400 metres in length), commencing by a junction with Work No. 3 at its termination, passing in a north-easterly direction under Sugarloaf Hill, then in an easterly and then in a south-easterly direction and terminating below a point on the line of the level of mean high water springs below Shakespeare Cliff 580 metres east of the western portal of the Shakespeare Tunnel of the Railways Board:

Partly in the district of Dover (town of Dover and parish of Hougham Without), in the county of Kent—

Work No. 5—A railway (19250 metres in length), commencing by a junction with Work No. 4 at its termination and extending under the English Channel to terminate by a junction with a railway constructed from France:

Work No. 6—An adit, commencing at a point on the Old Dover Colliery site 360 metres south-west of the western portal of the said Shakespeare Tunnel, passing in a north-east by easterly direction and terminating by a junction with Work No. 5 at the commencement of that work:

Work No. 7—A sea wall between Abbot's Cliff and the Old Dover Colliery site, commencing at a point on the line of the level of mean high water springs 255 metres south-west by west of the eastern portal of the Abbotscliff Tunnel of the Railways Board, extending seaward in a south-easterly direction to a line near the level of mean low water springs, then turning in an east by north-easterly direction to a point seaward of the Old Dover Colliery site and then turning in a north-easterly direction and terminating at a point on the line of the level of mean high water springs 130 metres south of the western portal of the said Shakespeare Tunnel:

In the district of Shepway (town of Folkestone and parishes of Hythe, Newington and Saltwood), in the county of Kent—

Work No. 9A—A diversion of the A20, including a roundabout at its junction with the B2065 (Work No. 10A) commencing at a point 40 metres west of the access from the A20 to Truck's Hall, passing in a north-easterly and then easterly direction to the said junction with the B2065 at a point 45 metres north of Beachborough Crossroads, thence passing in a south-east by easterly direction to join the line of the existing A20 near its junction with Frogholt Lane, thence in a south-easterly direction, south of the existing A20, and terminating by a junction with that road at a point 530 metres west of its termination at the Cheriton Roundabout:

Work No. 9B—A slip road commencing by a junction with Work No. 9A at a point 340 metres south-east of the junction of the existing A20 with Frogholt Lane and terminating by a junction with the existing A20 at a point 30 metres west of the junction of that road with Newington Road:

Work No. 9C—An access road commencing by a junction with the existing A20 at a point 850 metres west of its said termination, passing in a north-easterly and then easterly direction and terminating at the bridge forming part of Work No. 9D:

Work No. 9D—An access road, including a bridge over the railway (Work No. 2), commencing by a junction with Work No. 9C at its termination and terminating at a point 60 metres north of the building known as Longport:

Work No. 9E—An access road comprising a slip road, including a crossing over the A20 as diverted (Work No. 9A), commencing by a junction with the northern carriageway of the M20 at a point 170 metres east of the bridge carrying over that road the bridleway from Saltwood to the A20 at Stone Farm, Saltwood, passing in a north-east by easterly, easterly and then south-easterly direction, crossing Work No. 9A at a point 720 metres west of its termination, thence passing in an easterly and then northerly direction and terminating at a point 70 metres east of the building known as Shelton:

Work No. 9F—An access road comprising a slip road, including a crossing over the M20 and the A20 as diverted (Work No. 9A), commencing by a junction with the southern carriageway of the M20 at a point 150 metres east of the said bridge carrying over that road the bridleway from Saltwood to the A20, passing in a north-east by easterly, south-easterly and then easterly direction, crossing the M20 and Work No. 9A at a point 660 metres west of the termination of that work, then passing in a north-east by easterly direction and terminating at a point 160 metres north of the said building known as Longport:

Work No. 9G—A slip road commencing by a junction with the A20 as diverted (Work No. 9A) at the roundabout at its junction with the B2065, passing in a westerly, southerly and then easterly direction and terminating by a junction with the slip road (Work No. 9E) at a point 105 metres east of the existing bridge carrying the B2065 over the M20:

Work No. 10A—A diversion of the B2065, including a bridge over Works Nos. 9E to 9G and the M20, commencing at a point 220 metres north of Beachborough Crossroads, passing in a southerly direction to the roundabout (part of Work No. 9A), thence in a southerly direction over the slip road (Work No. 9G), the access road (Work No. 9E), the M20 and the access road (Work No. 9F) and terminating at the commencement of Work No. 11:

Work No. 11—A diversion of the B2065, including a viaduct over Works Nos. 30 and 30A and the railway between Ashford and Folkestone West (including Work No. 30B), commencing at a point 25 metres south of the southern end of the bridge carrying that road over the M20 and terminating at a point 140 metres south of the southern end of the existing bridge carrying that road over the said railway:

Work No. 14—An access road commencing at a point 10 metres west of a point on the access road (Waterworks Lane) leading to the Cherry Garden Reservoir of the Folkestone and District Water Company 220 metres north of the M20, passing in a south-easterly direction and terminating by a junction with the new road (Work No. 34H):

Work No. 15—An access road commencing by a junction with Churchill Avenue on its north side at a point 230 metres east of the entrance from that road to Cannon House and terminating at a point on the surface of the ground at the termination of Work No. 3:

Work No. 16—A drainage lagoon in the enclosures numbered 0794, 1684, 1085, 0584, 1174, 1136, 0571, 0272, 0576, 0083, 0002, 8200, 8585 and 0095 on the 1/2500 Ordnance Map of Kent, sheets TR1736 and TR1737 (editions of 1971) and TR 1836 (edition of 1958) to be formed by an embankment across Seabrook Stream immediately to the east of the footbridge carrying the bridleway from the A20 at Stone Farm to Dibgate Camp across that stream:

In the borough of Ashford (town of Ashford and parishes of Kingsnorth and Sevington), in the county of Kent—

Work No. 17—A road comprising dual carriageways, including a bridge over the Ashford to Folkestone West railway, commencing at a roundabout at a point 350 metres south by south-west from the southernmost corner of the moat at Old Boys Hall, passing in an easterly, then north-easterly, direction to cross over that railway at a point 450 metres north-west of the bridge carrying Highfield Lane over that railway, then passing in a northerly direction and terminating by a junction with the slip roads by which the road from Sevington joins Junction No. 10 on the M20, the existing road from that junction to the entrance to Ashford Park at a point 330 metres north-east of the said railway forming part of the northern carriageway of the said dual carriageway road:

Work No. 17A—A road commencing by a junction with the roundabout at the commencement of Work No. 17 and terminating, within the entrance to an intended inland clearance depot, at a point 85 metres south-east of that point of commencement.

PART II

THE COUNTY COUNCIL'S SCHEDULED WORKS

In the borough of Ashford (town of Ashford and parishes of Kingsnorth and Sevington), in the county of Kent—

Work No. 18—A road comprising dual carriageways, including a bridge over th river Great Stour, two bridges over the river East Stour and duplication of th bridge carrying Beaver Road over the Tonbridge to Ashford railway, commenc ing at the existing roundabout in Beaver Road at a point 65 metres north of th northern end of that bridge, passing over that railway to a roundabout south o that bridge, then turning south-east to pass over the rivers Great Stour and Eas Stour to a roundabout at a point 80 metres north-west of the bridge carrying th Ashford to Rye railway over New Town Road, then turning south-south-wes along a line to the east of the river East Stour, then crossing that river an continuing on the same line and terminating at a roundabout 550 metres o the junction of Kingsnorth Road with Ashford Road:

Work No. 18A—A road commencing by a junction with Work No. 18 at th roundabout south of the bridge over the Tonbridge to Ashford railway an terminating in Beaver Road at the northern end of the bridge carrying that roa over the river Great Stour:

Work No. 18B—A road commencing by a junction with Work No. 18 at th roundabout north-west of the railway bridge over New Town Road and termi nating by a junction with that road 35 metres north-east of that commencement

Work No. 18C—A road commencing by a junction with Work No. 18 at a roundabou at a point 280 metres south-east of the junction of Riversdale Road and Whitfiel Road and terminating at a point 40 metres east of that commencement, formin the access to an intended road vehicle park on land owned by the Railway Board:

Work No. 18D—A road, including a bridge over the river East Stour, commencing by a junction with Work No. 18 at the roundabout at the commencement o Work No. 18C, passing west across the river East Stour and terminating by junction with Beaver Road at a point 70 metres east of the junction of that road with Park Place:

Work No. 18E—A road commencing by a junction with Work No. 18 at the roundabout at the termination of that work and terminating by a junction with Ashford Road (A2070) at a point 770 metres south-east of that roundabout:

Work No. 19—A road commencing by a junction with Work No. 18 at the roundabout at the termination of that work, passing in a north-westerly direction and terminating at a roundabout forming a junction with Wotton Road at a point 300 metres from Kingsnorth Road:

Work No. 20—A road comprising dual carriageways, including bridges over the Ashford to Rye railway and the river East Stour, commencing by a junction with Work No. 18 at the roundabout at the termination of that work, passing in an easterly direction across the Ashford to Rye railway at a point 420 metres south of the bridge carrying that railway over the river East Stour, and across that river and terminating by a junction with Work No. 17 at the roundabout at the commencement of that work.

PART III

THE RAILWAYS BOARD'S SCHEDULED WORKS

In the London borough of Lambeth—

Work No. 21—A railway (705 metres in length), at Waterloo station on the west side of the railway between that station and Clapham Junction, commencing at a point on platforms 19 and 20 serving two of the Windsor lines of the said railway 61 metres south of the buffer stops of those two lines and terminating by a junction with the said Windsor lines at a point 15 metres north of the bridge carrying the said railway over Carlisle Lane at its junction with Hercules Road, including bridges over Westminster Bridge Road, Upper Marsh, Carlisle Lane, Centaur Street and Virgil Street and viaducts over lands between or adjoining those roads:

Work No. 21A—An access road at Waterloo station, commencing at a point on the arched structure carrying the said station 115 metres south-west of the buffer stop of the Windsor line served by platform 21 and terminating by a junction with Leake Street at a point 26 metres south-east of the junction of that street with York Road:

Work No. 21B—An access road at Waterloo station, commencing at a point in the existing access road serving the said station 28 metres east of its junction with Westminster Bridge Road and terminating at the point in Addington Street where that street branches to join Westminster Bridge Road:

In the London borough of Wandsworth—

Work No. 23—A railway (984 metres in length) at Stewart's Lane, Battersea, commencing by a junction with the Windsor lines of the railway between Waterloo and Clapham Junction at a point 480 metres north-east of the bridge carrying that railway over Thessaly Road and terminating by a junction with the railway between Victoria and Ashford at a point 225 metres south-east of the bridge carrying that railway over the said railway between Waterloo and Clapham Junction, including bridges over the access road to Covent Garden Market, Thessaly Road and Stewart's Road and viaducts over lands between or adjoining those roads and the said railway between Waterloo and Clapham Junction:

Work No. 23A—A railway (1012 metres in length) at Stewart's Lane, Battersea, on the north-west side of the railway between Waterloo and Clapham Junction, commencing by a junction with the Windsor lines of that railway at a point 480 metres north-east of the bridge carrying that railway over Thessaly Road and terminating by a junction with those lines at a point 1 metre north-east of the viaduct carrying the South London line between London Bridge and Victoria over that railway, including a viaduct and bridges over the said access road and Thessaly Road:

Work No. 23B—A railway (328 metres in length) at Stewarts' Lane, Battersea, on the south-east side of the railway between Waterloo and Clapham Junction, commencing by a junction with the Weymouth lines of that railway at a point 1 metre south-west of the bridge carrying that railway over Thessaly Road and terminating by a junction with those lines at a point 1 metre north-east of the viaduct carrying the railway between Victoria and Ashford over that railway, including bridges over Stewart's Road and the railway between Victoria and Stewart's Lane Junction:

Work No. 24—A railway (489 metres in length) at Clapham Junction (being a reinstatement of a former railway), commencing by a junction with the Windsor lines of the railway between Waterloo and Clapham Junction at a point 5 metres south-west of the bridge carrying those lines over Culvert Road and terminating by a junction with the West London Extension railway, between Longhedge Junction and Kensington Olympia, at a point 3 metres south-east of the bridge carrying that railway over Latchmere Road:

In the London boroughs of Ealing and Hammersmith and Fulham and the Royal borough of Kensington and Chelsea—

Work No. 25A—A railway (1716 metres in length) at Old Oak Common, commencing in the London borough of Ealing at a point 205 metres south-west of the bridge carrying the railway between Reading and Paddington over the Central Line railway between North Acton and East Acton and terminating in the London borough of Hammersmith and Fulham by a junction with the West London railway, between Mitre Bridge Junction and Kensington Olympia, at a point 3 metres north-west of the bridge carrying that railway over Scrubs Lane, including bridges over the said Central Line and Old Oak Common Lane:

Work No. 25B—A railway (2300 metres in length) at Old Oak Common, commencing in the London borough of Ealing by a junction with Work No. 25A at a point 260 metres east of Old Oak Common Lane, passing through the London borough of Hammersmith and Fulham and terminating in the Royal borough of Kensington and Chelsea at a point 100 metres north-east of the junction of Barlby Gardens with Barlby Road:

Work No. 25C—A railway (290 metres in length) at Old Oak Common, commencing by a junction with the railway between Reading and Paddington at a point 138 metres west of the bridge carrying the said West London railway over that railway and terminating by a junction with the Victoria branch railway at a point 85 metres south-east of the eastern portal of Mitre Tunnel on that railway, including the removal of that tunnel and the substitution of bridges to carry Scrubs Lane and the said West London railway over the said Victoria branch railway:

In the district of Tandridge (parishes of Bletchingley and Nutfield), in the county of Surrey—

Work No. 26—A railway (1120 metres in length) at Nutfield on the north side of the railway between Redhill and Ashford, commencing by a junction with that railway at a point 63 metres east of the bridge carrying that railway over Coopers Hill Road and terminating by a junction with that railway at a point 20 metres west of the bridge carrying Outwood Lane over that railway:

Work No. 26A—A cut (115 metres in length) at Nutfield forming a diversion of Nutfield Brook, commencing at a point 22 metres north of the southern head-wall of the culvert conducting that stream under the railway between Redhill and Ashford and terminating at a point 98 metres north-east of that point of commencement:

In the borough of Maidstone (parish of Lenham), in the county of Kent—

Work No. 28A—A railway (543 metres in length) on the north side of the railway between London and Ashford, commencing by a junction with that railway at a point 560 metres north-west of the bridge carrying Ham Lane over that railway and terminating by a junction with that railway at a point 18 metres north-west of that bridge:

Work No. 28B—A railway (543 metres in length) on the south side of the railway between London and Ashford, commencing by a junction with that railway at a point 170 metres north-west of the bridge carrying Lenham Road over that railway and terminating by a junction with that railway at a point 365 metres south-east of that bridge:

In the borough of Ashford (town of Ashford), in the county of Kent—

Works Nos. 29A and 29B—Widenings on the north sides of the bridges carrying the railways between Ashford and Canterbury, Folkestone West and Rye over the rivers Great Stour and East Stour:

In the district of Shepway (parishes of Newington and Saltwood), in the county of Kent—

Work No. 30—A railway (700 metres in length) at Dolland's Moor, commencing by a junction with the railway between Ashford and Folkestone West at a point 135 metres west of the existing bridge carrying the B2065 over that railway and terminating by a junction with Work No. 1 at its commencement:

Work No. 30A—A railway (1270 metres in length) at Dolland's Moor, commencing by a junction with the railway between Ashford and Folkestone West at a point 375 metres east of the eastern portal of Saltwood Tunnel and terminating by a junction with Work No. 30 at a point 125 metres from the termination of that work:

Work No. 30B—A railway (558 metres in length), being a deviation of the railway between Ashford and Folkestone West, commencing by a junction with that railway at the said point 135 metres west of the existing bridge carrying the B2065 over that railway and terminating by a junction with that railway at a point 415 metres east of that bridge.

PART IV

SUPPLEMENTARY

Interpretation

1. In this Schedule—

"A20" means the road from Ashford to Folkestone so classified; and
"B2065" means the road from Hythe to Bishopsbourne so classified.

Limits of deviation

In their construction–

(a) each scheduled work may deviate from the line or situation shown for that work on the deposited plans to the extent of the limits of deviation so shown:

(b) Work No. 5 may deviate from the level shown for that work on the deposited sections to the extent of 10 metres upwards and to any extent downwards; and

(c) each of the scheduled works other than Work No. 5 may deviate from the level so shown for the work in question to the extent of 3 metres upwards and to any extent downwards.

SCHEDULE 2

SUPPLEMENTARY PROVISIONS AS TO THE SCHEDULED WORKS AND OTHER
AUTHORISED WORKS

PART I

APPLICATION OF ENACTMENTS

Application of Part II of the Public Utilities Street Works Act 1950

1.—(1) Part II of the Public Utilities Street Works Act 1950 (public utilities' street works code where apparatus is affected by road, bridge or transport works) shall apply to any works for the construction or maintenance of Works Nos. 9A, 10A, 11 and 17 as if the Concessionaires were a highway authority.

(2) This paragraph does not prejudice the application, in accordance with that Act, of Part II of that Act to works required for the purposes of any transport undertaking within the meaning of that Act.

Application of Railways Clauses Acts

2.—(1) Subject to the following provisions of this paragraph, the Railways Clauses Consolidation Act 1845 and Part I of the Railways Clauses Act 1863, insofar as they are applicable for the purposes of this Act and are not inconsistent with its provisions, are hereby incorporated into this Act.

(2) The following provisions of the Railways Clauses Consolidation Act 1845 are excepted from incorporation by virtue of sub-paragraph (1) above—
sections 1, 5, 7 to 9, 11, 12, 15, 17, 19, 20, 22, 23, 162 and 163;
but of the provisions of that Act which are so incorporated the following shall not apply to the Concessionaires—
sections 13, 14, 47, 48, 59 to 62, 75, 77 to 85, 94, 95 and 112 to 124.

(3) The following provisions of Part I of the Railways Clauses Act 1863 are excepted from incorporation by virtue of sub-paragraph (1) above—
sections 13 to 19;
but of the provisions of that Part of that Act which are so incorporated sections 4 to 7 shall not apply to the Concessionaires.

(4) For the purposes of the provisions of the said Clauses Acts so incorporated and applicable to the Concessionaires—
(a) references to the company are references to the Concessionaires;
(b) "the railway" means Works Nos. 1 to 5 and other works and things constructed, provided or used for or in connection with those works and, for the purposes of sections 16 and 30 to 44 of the said Act of 1845, includes Work No. 6;
(c) section 6 of the said Act of 1845 shall have effect as if the words "and to take lands for that purpose" and the words "for the value of the lands so taken or used and" were omitted;
(d) section 46 of the said Act of 1845 shall have effect as if the proviso were omitted; and
(e) section 68 of the said Act of 1845 shall have effect as if the word "gates" where first occurring, the words "or leading to or from" and the words from "together with all necessary gates" to "all necessary stiles" were omitted.

(5) For the purposes of the provisions of the said Clauses Acts so incorporated and applicable to the Railways Board—
(a) references to the company are references to the Railways Board;
(b) "the railway" means the Railways Board's scheduled works other than Works Nos. 21A, 21B and 26A and, for the purposes of sections 16 and 30 to 44 of the said Act of 1845, includes those last-mentioned works.

(6) For the purposes of the provisions of the said Clauses Acts so incorporated and applicable to the Concessionaires and the Railways Board—
(a) section 87 of the said Act of 1845 shall have effect as if for the words from "company, being" to "other railway" there were substituted the word "body" and for the words "other company", where secondly occurring, there were substituted the words "other body"; and
(b) section 88 of the said Act of 1845 shall have effect as if for the word "companies", in both places where it occurs, there were substituted the word "bodies" and for the word "company" there were substituted the word "body".

(7) Sections 18 and 21 of the said Act of 1845 as incorporated by subparagraph (1) above shall not apply in any case where the relations between either the Concessionaires or the

Railways Board and any other persons are regulated by Part II of the Public Utilities Street Works Act 1950 or by Part VI of Schedule 7 to this Act.

PART II

REGULATION OF SCHEDULED WORKS AND SUBSIDIARY PROVISIONS

SECTION A

PROVISIONS APPLICABLE TO CONCESSIONAIRES

Use of electrical energy

3.—(1) The following provisions of this paragraph shall apply in respect of the use of electrical energy for the purposes of Works Nos. 3, 4 and 5 (in this section referred to as "the authorised railway").

(2) All reasonable precautions shall be taken in constructing, placing and maintaining electric lines and circuits, and in working the authorised railway, to prevent—
  (a) injurious affection (by the discharge of electrical currents into the ground, fusion or electrolytic action) of any gas or water pipes, electric lines or other metallic pipes, structures or substances; or
  (b) interference with, or with the working of, any wire, line or apparatus used for the purpose of transmitting electrical energy or of telecommunications.

(3) The Secretary of State may make regulations under this paragraph for regulating the use of electrical energy for the operation of the authorised railway, including regulations—
  (a) for preventing injurious affection (by the discharge of electrical currents into the ground, fusion or electrolytic action) of gas or water pipes, electric lines or other metallic pipes, structures or substances; and
  (b) for minimising, so far as is reasonably practicable, interference with, and with the working of, electric wires, lines and other apparatus whether such apparatus does, or does not, use the earth as a return.

(4) All reasonable precautions against interference with, or with the working of, any wire, line or apparatus shall be deemed to have been taken if and so long as use is made of either such insulated returns, or of such uninsulated metallic returns of low resistance and of such other means of preventing injurious interference with, and with the working of, electric wires, lines and apparatus, as may be prescribed by the said regulations; and in prescribing such means the Secretary of State shall have regard to the expense involved in relation to the protection afforded.

(5) The provisions of this paragraph shall not give any right of action in respect of injurious interference with, or the working of any electric wire, line or apparatus, or the currents therein, unless in the construction, erection, maintaining and working of such wire, line or apparatus all reasonable and proper precautions, including the use of an insulated return, have been taken to minimise injurious interference therewith, and with the currents therein, by or from other electric currents.

(6) If any difference arises between the Concessionaires and any other person with respect to anything in the foregoing provisions of this paragraph, the difference shall, unless the parties otherwise agree, be determined by the Secretary of State or, at his option, by an arbitrator to be appointed by him, and the costs of such determination shall be in the discretion of the Secretary of State or of the arbitrator, as the case may be.

(7) The power to make regulations conferred on the Secretary of State by this paragraph shall be exercisable by statutory instrument.

(8) In this paragraph reference to an insulated return includes a reference to a return by means of a combined neutral and earth cable which is covered by a sheath suitable for protection against corrosion and is approved for use below ground by the Secretary of State for the purpose of any regulations relating to the supply of electricity.

Concessionaires' subsidiary works

4.—(1) The Concessionaires may, for the purposes of or in connection with their scheduled works, do any of the following things within the limits of deviation for those works, that is to say—
  (a) make, provide and maintain all such approaches, bridges, subways, interchanges, roundabouts, lifts, stairs, escalators, ramps, passages, means of access, shafts, stagings, buildings, apparatus, plant and machinery as may be necessary or convenient;
  (b) make junctions and communications (including the provision of steps or ramps for the use of persons on foot) with any existing highway or access way intersected or

interfered with by, or contiguous to, any of those works, and widen or alter the line or level of any existing highway or access way for the purpose of connecting it with any of those works or another highway, or of crossing under or over the existing highway or access way;

(c) construct, provide and maintain all such embankments, aprons, abutments, retaining walls, wing walls, culverts and other works as may be necessary or convenient;

(d) carry out any works, and do any things necessary, for the protection of any adjoining land;

(e) alter or remove any structure erected upon any highway or adjoining land and plant trees, shrubs or other vegetation; and

(f) raise, sink or otherwise alter the position of any of the steps, areas, cellars, boundary-walls, railings, fences, windows, sewers, drains, watercourses, pipes, spouts or wires of, or connected with, any building, and remove any other obstruction.

(2) The Concessionaires shall pay compensation for any damage done in exercise of the powers conferred by this paragraph.

(3) Any question of disputed compensation payable under the provisions of this paragraph shall be determined under and in accordance with Part I of the Land Compensation Act 1961.

Use of lagoon for drainage

5.—(1) Subject to the requirements of sub-paragraph (2) below, the Concessionaires may—

(a) raise, lower or regulate the water, or the level or flow of water, in the Seabrook Stream in such manner as may be necessary or expedient for the construction, maintenance or operation of the drainage lagoon (Work No. 16); and

(b) discharge water from the lagoon into the stream at a point immediately below the embankment by which that work is formed.

(2) In the construction of that embankment, and thereafter in the maintenance and operation of that work, the Concessionaires shall take such steps as may be necessary to ensure compliance with the requirement that the rate at which water is discharged from that work into the stream is never more than such maximum rate nor less than such minimum rate as may be agreed between the Concessionaires and the Southern Water Authority or, in default of agreement or on notice being given by the Secretary of State to the Concessionaires and the water authority, shall be determined by him; and in the exercise of any of the powers of sub-paragraph (1) above the Concessionaires shall comply with such conditions as may be so agreed or determined.

(3) Before agreeing rates of discharge or conditions under sub-paragraph (2) above the water authority shall consult the Nature Conservancy Council, the Shepway District Council and the Kent County Council.

(4) For the purposes of the Water Resources Act 1963 the provisions of this Act authorising the construction, maintenance and operation of the drainage lagoon shall be treated as if contained in a licence to construct impounding works granted to the Concessionaires subject to the requirement, and to any conditions relating to the exercise of the powers of sub-paragraph (1)(a) above, agreed or determined under sub-paragraph (2) above.

(5) For the purposes of Part II of the Control of Pollution Act 1974 the discharge of water under sub-paragraph (1)(b) above shall be treated as if made with the consent of the water authority given in pursuance of that Act subject to such conditions relating to the discharge as may be agreed or determined under sub-paragraph (2) above.

(6) In any proceedings for failure to comply with any such requirement or condition as is mentioned in sub-paragraph (4) above, it shall be a defence to prove that the failure was wholly or mainly attributable to exceptional shortage of rain, frost, accident or other unavoidable cause.

Safety of lagoon

6. For the purposes of the Reservoirs Act 1975 (which makes special provision about the construction, use, alteration and inspection of large reservoirs), the drainage lagoon (Work No. 16) shall be treated as a large raised reservoir within the meaning of that Act.

SECTION B

PROVISIONS APPLICABLE TO COUNTY COUNCIL

County Council's subsidiary works

7.—(1) The County Council may, for the purposes of or in connection with their scheduled works, do any of the following things within the limits of deviation for those works, that is to say—

  (a) make, provide and maintain all such approaches, bridges, subways, roundabouts, ramps, passages and means of access as may be necessary or convenient;

  (b) make junctions and communications (including the provision of steps or ramps for the use of persons on foot) with any existing highway or access way intersected or interfered with by, or contiguous to, any of those works, and widen or alter the line or level of any existing highway or access way for the purpose of connecting it with any of those works or another highway, or of crossing under or over the existing highway or access way;

  (c) construct, provide and maintain all such embankments, aprons, abutments, retaining walls, wing walls, culverts and other works as may be necessary or convenient;

  (d) carry out any works, and do any things necessary, for the protection of any adjoining land;

  (e) alter or remove any structure erected upon any highway or adjoining land and plant trees, shrubs or other vegetation; and

  (f) raise, sink or otherwise alter the position of any of the steps, areas, cellars, boundary-walls, railings, fences, windows, sewers, drains, watercourses, pipes, spouts or wires of, or connected with, any building, and remove any other obstruction.

(2) The County Council shall pay compensation for any damage done in exercise of the powers conferred by this paragraph.

(3) Any question of disputed compensation payable under the provisions of this paragraph shall be determined under and in accordance with Part I of the Land Compensation Act 1961.

SECTION C

PROVISIONS APPLICABLE TO RAILWAYS BOARD

Passenger station at Ashford

8.—(1) Without prejudice to section 16 of the Railways Clauses Consolidation Act 1845, as applicable to them, the Railways Board may, on land in the borough of Ashford (town of Ashford) in which they have sufficient right or interest—

  (a) make, maintain and operate a new passenger station adjacent to their existing station at Ashford on any part of the lands in that town numbered 21 on the deposited plans;

  (b) construct and maintain facilities in connection with the said new passenger station, including a terminal building with frontier control facilities, footbridges linking that station with their said existing station and other works and conveniences, including road vehicle parks, on the lands in that town numbered 3, 16, 18, 20 and 21 on the deposited plans and means of access for vehicles provided in accordance with sub-paragraph (2) below;

  (c) lay out a new road vehicle park on any part of the lands in that town numbered 25, 27 and 28 to 31 on the deposited plans with means of access for vehicles either to the new road (Work No. 18C) or to such other road as may be agreed between the Railways Board and the Kent County Council or in default of agreement determined by the Secretary of State.

(2) The means of access for vehicles to the facilities mentioned in sub-paragraph (1)(b) above shall be provided at such points as may be agreed between the Railways Board and the County Council or in default of agreement determined by the Secretary of State.

Passenger station at Waterloo

9.—(1) In connection with the construction of Works Nos. 21, 21A and 21B, the Railways Board may, within the limits of deviation for those works in the London borough of Lambeth—

  (a) enlarge, improve, and provide frontier control facilities at their existing Waterloo station with all necessary works and conveniences connected therewith;

  (b) make junctions with and alter the line or level of any street or way adjoining, or affected by the construction of, those works;

(c) provide means of access for vehicles to Carlisle Lane at the points marked C and D on the deposited plans and to Upper Marsh at the points so marked E and F; and

(d) appropriate, hold and use, for the purposes of Work No. 21 and the works at the station under paragraph (a) above, any lands within the said limits, including any works on those lands previously authorised by any enactment.

(2) In connection with the construction of Work No. 21, the Railways Board may in the London borough of Lambeth—

(a) reduce to a width not less than 1·83 metres so much of the footpath known as Leake Court as lies between the points marked G and H on the deposited plans;

(b) reduce to a width not less than 15 metres so much of Carlisle Lane as lies within the limits of deviation for that work between the points marked I and J on the deposited plans; and

(c) remove the parapets on the western sides of the existing bridges over Westminster Bridge Road and Upper Marsh.

Railways at Stewart's Lane, Wandsworth

10.—(1) In connection with the construction of Works Nos. 23, 23A and 23B, the Railways Board may in the London borough of Wandsworth—

(a) construct the bridge over Thessaly Road (part of Work No. 23A) so as to provide a headroom not less than 4·40 metres over the surface of the street under the bridge;

(b) alter the level of Stewart's Road under the bridge over that road (part of Work No. 23B) so as to provide a headroom not less than 4·57 metres over the surface of the street;

(c) provide means of access for vehicles to Ascalon Street at the points marked A and B on the deposited plans, to Stewart's Road at the point so marked C and to Ponton Street at the point so marked D; and

(d) appropriate, hold and use, for the purposes of Works Nos. 23A and 23B, any lands within the limits of deviation for those works and any works on those lands previously authorised by any enactment.

(2) In connection with the construction of Works Nos. 23, 23A and 23B or other works of the Railways Board in the vicinity thereof, the Railways Board may in the London borough of Wandsworth provide, for the purposes of such construction and of the maintenance and operation of those works, means of access for vehicles to Corunna Terrace at the point marked J on the deposited plans.

Works Nos. 25A and 25B: nature consultations

11. The Railways Board shall not begin to construct Work No. 25A or Work No. 25B until they have consulted—

(a) the councils of the London borough of Ealing, the London borough of Hammersmith and Fulham and the Royal borough of Kensington and Chelsea; and

(b) the London Wildlife Trust;

as to the likely effect of the construction of the works on nature conservation.

Further works and powers

12. The Railways Board may make and maintain the following further works (in so far as they are shown on the deposited plans and sections, in the lines or situations, and according to the levels, so shown) and may exercise the following powers—

(1) In connection with the construction of Work No. 24, they may in the London borough of Wandsworth—

(a) provide means of access for vehicles to Sheepcote Lane at the points marked A and B on the deposited plans; and

(b) appropriate, hold and use, for the purposes of that work, any lands within the limits of deviation for that work, including any works on those lands previously authorised by any enactment.

(2) In connection with the construction of Works Nos. 25A, 25B and 25C, they may, within the limits of deviation for those works, in the London boroughs of Ealing and Hammersmith and Fulham and the Royal borough of Kensington and Chelsea—

(a) make, maintain and operate a maintenance depot; and

(b) provide means of access for vehicles to Scrubs Lane and Mitre Way at the points marked B and C respectively on the deposited plans.

(3) In connection with the construction of Works Nos. 25A, 25B and 25C and of other works of the Railways Board in the vicinity thereof, they may in those boroughs provide

means of access for vehicles to Old Oak Common Lane and Barlby Road at the points marked A and D respectively on the deposited plans.

(4) On the completion of Work No. 26A they may, in the parish of Bletchingley in the district of Tandridge, in the county of Surrey, fill in so much of Nutfield Brook between the points marked B and C on the deposited plans as will be rendered unnecessary by that work.

(5) In connection with the construction of Works Nos. 30, 30A and 30B, they may in the parishes of Newington and Saltwood, in the district of Shepway, in the county of Kent—

- (a) provide facilities for making emergency repairs to rolling stock on any part of the lands numbered, in the parish of Newington, 4 to 7, 12, 25, 26, 33 and 36 and, in the parish of Saltwood, 7 and 8 on the deposited plans; and

- (b) provide means of access for vehicles for construction purposes to the road from Hythe to Bishopsbourne (B2065) at the point marked K on the deposited plans.

Temporary possession of land

13.—(1) Subject to the provisions of this paragraph the Railways Board may, in connection with the construction of their scheduled works specified in column (1) of the following table or any works in connection with those works, enter upon and take possession of the lands in the areas specified in columns (2) and (3) of that table for such purposes as are specified in column (4) of that table and may, for any such purpose, remove any structures on those lands and provide means of access to those lands.

THE TABLE

(1) Works Nos.	(2) Area	(3) Number of land shown on deposited plans	(4) Purpose for which temporary possession may be taken
23, 23A and 23B	London borough of Wandsworth	26	The provision of vehicular access for construction.
		48	The provision of a working site and vehicular access for construction.
25A, 25B and 25C	London borough of Hammersmith and Fulham	4 and 8	The provision of a working site and vehicular access for construction.
26 and 26A	District of Tandridge (parish of Nutfield)	1, 2 4 to 7 and 7A	The provision of a working site and vehicular access for construction to Coopers Hill Road at the point marked A on the deposited plans.
	District of Tandridge (parish of Bletchingley)	1, 2 and 5 to 7	The provision of a working site and vehicular access for construction to Outwood Lane at the point marked B on the deposited plans.
28A and 28B	Borough of Maidstone (parish of Lenham)	2 and 4	The provision of a working site and vehicular access for construction to Ham Lane at the point marked A on the deposited plans.
		10 and 11	The provision of a working site and vehicular access for construction to Lenham Road at the point marked B on the deposited plans.

(2) Not less than 28 days before entering upon and taking temporary possession of any land under this paragraph the Railways Board shall give notice to the owners and occupiers of the land.

(3) The Railways Board shall not, without the agreement of the owners and occupiers, remain in possession of any part of any land under this paragraph after a period of one year from the completion of the work or (as the case may be) all the works specified in relation to that land in column (1) of the table in sub-paragraph (1) above.

(4) Except in the case of the land in the London borough of Wandsworth numbered 26 on the deposited plans, all private rights of way over any land of which the Railways Board take temporary possession under this paragraph shall be suspended and unenforceable for so long as the Railways Board remain in lawful possession of the land.

(5) Before giving up possession of any land of which they have taken temporary possession under this paragraph, the Railways Board shall remove all temporary works and restore the land to the reasonable satisfaction of the owners and occupiers of the land.

(6) The Railways Board shall not be empowered to purchase compulsorily, or be required to purchase, any part of any land of which they have taken temporary possession under this paragraph.

(7) The Railways Board shall pay compensation to—

    (a) the owner or occupier of any land of which they take temporary possession under this paragraph for any damage resulting from the exercise of the powers of this paragraph in relation to that land; and

    (b) any person who suffers damage by reason of the suspension of any right under this paragraph.

(8) Nothing in this paragraph shall affect liability to compensate under section 6 or 43 of the Railways Clauses Consolidation Act 1845, as incorporated with this Act, or section 10(2) of the Compulsory Purchase Act 1965, as applied by section 37 of this Act, or under any other enactment, except so far as compensation is payable under sub-paragraph (7) above.

(9) Any dispute as to a person's entitlement to compensation under this paragraph, or as to the amount of the compensation, shall be determined under and in accordance with Part of the Land Compensation Act 1961.

SECTION D

PROVISIONS APPLICABLE TO CONCESSIONAIRES, COUNTY COUNCIL AND RAILWAYS BOARD

Use of sewers, etc. for removing water

14.—(1) The appropriate authority may use for the discharge of any water pumped or found during the construction of the scheduled works or any works in connection with those works any available stream or watercourse or any public sewer, and for that purpose may lay down, take up and alter conduits, pipes and other works and may make any convenient connections with any such stream, watercourse or public sewer within the limits of deviation or their scheduled works.

(2) The appropriate authority shall not under the powers of this paragraph discharge any water into any sewer vested in or under the control of a water authority, internal drainage board or local authority except with the consent of that authority or board (which shall not be unreasonably withheld) and subject to such terms and conditions as that authority or board may reasonably impose; and the appropriate authority shall not make an opening into any such sewer except in accordance with plans reasonably approved by, and under the superintendence (if given) of, that authority or board.

(3) The discharge of water under the powers conferred by this paragraph into any stream shall not prejudice the application of Part II of the Control of Pollution Act 1974 but section 1 of that Act shall have effect in relation to discharges under the powers of this paragraph into any relevant waters within the meaning of that section as if no matter so discharged were trade or sewage effluent or other matter mentioned in subsection (2)(e) of that section.

(4) In the exercise of their powers under this paragraph the appropriate authority shall not damage or interfere with—

    (a) the bed of any watercourse forming part of the main river of a water authority or the banks thereof within the meaning of section 116 of the Land Drainage Act 1976; or

    (b) a metropolitan watercourse within the meaning of paragraph 1 of Schedule 5 to that Act.

(5) The appropriate authority shall take all such steps as may be reasonably required to secure that any water discharged under the powers of this paragraph shall be as free as may be reasonably practicable from any gravel, chalk, soil or other solid substance or matter in suspension.

(6) Any difference arising between the appropriate authority and a water authority,

internal drainage board or local authority under this paragraph shall be determined **
arbitration.

Underpinning of buildings

15.—(1) If in the construction of any of the scheduled works or any works in connectic
with any such work ("the work in question") it becomes necessary to do so, the appropria
authority may, and if required by the owner or lessee shall, underpin or otherwise strengthe
any building within 35 metres of the work in question in accordance with the provisions
this paragraph.

(2) Except in case of emergency, the appropriate authority shall give to the owner, less
or occupier of a building, or the owner or lessee of a building shall give to the appropria
authority, at least 28 days' notice in writing of the intention or (as the case may b
requirement, to underpin or otherwise strengthen that building under this paragraph, and
within 21 days of the giving of such notice the owner, lessee or occupier or (as the case m:
be) the appropriate authority give a counter-notice in writing disputing the necessity of tl
underpinning or strengthening, the question of necessity shall be settled by arbitration.

(3) The appropriate authority may, at any time after the underpinning or strengthening
any building under the foregoing provisions of this paragraph is completed and before tl
expiration of a period of five years from the bringing into use of the work in question, ent
upon and survey the building and, after complying with the foregoing provisions of th
paragraph, carry out such further underpinning or strengthening of the building as they m:
deem necessary or expedient or, if the owner, lessee or occupier of the building disputes tl
necessity or expediency, as may be settled by arbitration.

(4) Where any question of necessity or expediency is referred to arbitration under tl
foregoing provisions of this paragraph and the arbitrator, after inspecting the buildin;
decides that the underpinning or strengthening is necessary or (as the case may be) that tl
further underpinning or strengthening is necessary or expedient, the arbitrator may, and
so required by the owner, lessee or occupier shall, prescribe the manner in which tl
underpinning or strengthening is to be carried out and the appropriate authority sha
underpin or strengthen the building accordingly.

(5) For the purpose of determining how to exercise their powers and duties under th
paragraph the appropriate authority may at any reasonable time enter and survey an
building within 35 metres of any of their scheduled works.

(6) The appropriate authority shall pay compensation to the owner, lessee and occupie
of every building underpinned or strengthened in pursuance of the powers conferred by th
paragraph for any damage which they may suffer by reason of the exercise of those power:

(7) Nothing in this paragraph shall affect liability to compensate under section 6 of th
Railways Clauses Consolidation Act 1845, as incorporated with this Act, or section 10(2) c
the Compulsory Purchase Act 1965, as applied by section 37 of this Act, or under any othe
enactment, except so far as compensation is payable under sub-paragraph (6) above.

(8) Any dispute as to a person's entitlement to compensation under this paragraph, or a
to the amount of the compensation, shall be determined under and in accordance with Pa:
I of the Land Compensation Act 1961.

(9) Section 30 of the Compulsory Purchase Act 1965 shall apply to the service of notice
under this paragraph with any necessary modifications.

(10) In this paragraph "building" includes any structure and, in the case of a work unde
the surface of the ground, reference to a building within 35 metres of that work include
reference to any building within 35 metres of the point on the surface below which the wor
is situated.

PART III

HIGHWAYS, ROADS, ETC.

Stopping up of highways by Concessionaires, County Council and Railways Board

16.—(1) Subject to the provisions of this paragraph, the Concessionaires may, i
connection with the construction of their scheduled works, stop up each of the highways o
parts thereof specified, by reference to the letters and numbers shown on the deposite
plans, in columns (1) and (2) of Section A in Part I or II of the following table and any othe
bridleways or footpaths within the limits of land to be acquired.

(2) Subject to the provisions of this paragraph, the County Council may, in connectio
with the construction of their scheduled works, stop up each of the highways or parts thereo
specified as aforesaid in columns (1) and (2) of Section B in Part I or II of the followin;
table and any other bridleways or footpaths within the limits of land to be acquired.

(3) Subject to the provisions of this paragraph, the Railways Board may stop up each of
e highways or parts thereof specified as aforesaid in columns (1) and (2) of Section C in
art I or II of the following table and any other bridleways or footpaths within the limits of
nd to be acquired.

(4) The stopping up under this paragraph of the existing highways or parts thereof
ecified in columns (1) and (2) of Part II of the following table is subject to the requirements
paragraph 18 below—

(a) with respect to the new highway to be substituted therefor, specified as aforesaid or
by reference to scheduled works, in column (3) of that Part of the table in relation to
each such existing highway or part thereof; or

(b) where that new highway is not a scheduled work, with respect either to that new
highway or to such other new highway as may be approved by the County Council as
the highway to be substituted for any such existing highway or part thereof;

nd references in paragraph 18, in relation to any such existing highway or part thereof, to
a alternative approved highway are references to any other new highway approved as
entioned in paragraph (b) above as the highway to be substituted for it.

THE TABLE

PART I

HIGHWAYS TO BE STOPPED UP

SECTION A

In connection with the Concessionaires' scheduled works

(1) Area	(2) Highway or part to be stopped up
District of Shepway, parish of Newington	Footpath from A4 to A5 Footpath and access from C5 to C6 Footpath from C3 to C4
town of Folkestone	Access road (Waterworks Lane) from N3 to N5 Footpath and track from P3 to P4
Borough of Ashford, parish of Sevington	Road (Church Road) from S5 to S6 Road used as public path from T1 to T2 Footpath from T2 to U1 Footpath from W1 to W2 Footpath from V1 to V2 Footpath from Z3 to Y2

SECTION B

In connection with the County Council's scheduled works

(1) Area	(2) Highway or part to be stopped up
Borough of Ashford, town of Ashford	Road (New Town Road) from KA1 to KA2 Footpath from KB1 to KB2 Road (Rugby Gardens) from KB3 to KB4 Track from KB5 to KB6 Track from KB7 to KB8
town of Ashford and parish of Kingsnorth parish of Sevington	Footpath from KD1 to KD6 Footpath from KE2 to KE3 Footpath from KE1 to U1

Section C

In connection with the Railways Board's scheduled works

(1) Area	(2) Highway or part to be stopped up
London borough of Lambeth	Road (Addington Street) from A to B

Part II

Highways to be stopped up and new highways substituted therefor

Section A

In connection with the Concessionaires' scheduled works

(1) Area	(2) Highway or part to be stopped up	(3) New highway to be substituted therefor
Disrict of Shepway, parish of Newington	Footpath from A2 to A3	New footpath from A1 to A?
	Road (A20) from CA1 to CA3	Works Nos. 9A and 9B
	Road (B2065) from CC3 to CC1	Work No. 10A
	Road (B2065) from CC1 to CC2	Work No. 11
	Road (A20) from CE1 to CE2	Works Nos. 9A and 9B
	Footpath and access road from F6 to F2	New footpath from F6 to CE1
	Bridleway from F5 to F7	New bridleway from CE1 to F4 to F5
parishes of Hythe and Newington	Bridleway from G1 to G2	New bridleway on embankment from G1 to G2
town of Folkestone and parish of Newington	Footpath from H1 to H2	
	Footpaths from J1 to J2	
	Track from J1 to J3	
	Road (Danton Lane) from J4 to J5	New footpath from H3 to L1
	Bridleway from J4 to L2	
	Footpath from K1 to K2	
	Bridleway from L1 to L2	
town of Folkestone	Footpath from M1 to M2	
	Footpath from N1 to N2	New footpath from N3 to N4
	Footpath from P1 to P2	New footpath from P1 to P2
Borough of Ashford, parish of Sevington	Footpath from S1 to S2	New footpath from S1 to S3 to S4 to S2
	Footpath from U1 to Z2	New footpath from X1 to X2
	Footpath from Z1 to Z4	New footpath from Y1 to Y2

SECTION B

In connection with the County Council's scheduled works

(1) Area	(2) *Highway or part to be stopped up*	(3) *New highway to be substituted therefor*
Borough of Ashford, parish of Kingsnorth	Footpath from KC1 to KC2	New footpath from KC2 to KC3

town of Ashford and par-
  ishes of Kingsnorth and
  Sevington
	Bridleway from KD2 to KD7	New bridleway from KD2 to KD4 to KD5 to KD7 to U1 to T1

SECTION C

In connection with the Railways Board's scheduled works

(1) Area	(2) *Highway or part to be stopped up*	(3) *New highway to be substituted therefor*
Borough of Maidstone, parish of Lenham	Footpath from C to D	New footpath from E to D
Borough of Ashford, town of Ashford	Footpath and track from B to C	New footpath from B to D

(5) No part of any highway shall be stopped up under this paragraph until the appropriate authority are in possession of all lands abutting on both sides of that part of the highway except so far as the owners, lessees and occupiers of those lands may otherwise agree.

(6) On the stopping up of any highway or part thereof under this paragraph, all rights of way over or along the highway or part so stopped up shall be extinguished.

(7) After the extinguishment of all rights of way over or along any highway or any part thereof under the foregoing provisions of this paragraph the land forming the site of the highway or part so stopped up may be appropriated without payment thereof and may be used by the appropriate authority for the purposes of Part II or III of this Act.

(8) Any person who suffers loss by the extinguishment of any private right under this paragraph shall be entitled to compensation to be determined, in case of dispute, under and in accordance with Part I of the Land Compensation Act 1961.

(9) Compensation in respect of the extinguishment of any private right payable under sub-paragraph (8) above shall be paid by that one of the Concessionaires, the County Council and the Railways Board by whose action the private right is extinguished.

17.—(1) The Concessionaires may, with the written consent of the Secretary of State, stop up in connection with the construction of any of the works authorised by this Act any part of the M20 within the limits of land to be acquired other than any part of its carriageways.

(2) On the stopping up of any part of the M20 under sub-paragraph (1) above, all rights of way over or along that part shall be extinguished.

Construction and completion of new or substituted highways

18.—(1) None of the following parts of highways to which sub-paragraph (4) of paragraph 16 above applies, namely—

(a) the parts of the A20 road from Ashford to Folkestone for which parts of Work No. 9A and Work No. 9B are to be substituted; and

(b) the parts of the B2065 road from Hythe to Bishopsbourne for which Works Nos. 10A and 11 are to be substituted;

shall be stopped up under that paragraph until the County Council have certified the date on which the new highway concerned has been completed and is open for public use or, on application made to the Secretary of State by the Concessionaires after refusal by the County Council so to certify, he has so certified.

(2) If within 28 days after an application has been made to the County Council for them

to certify a date under sub-paragraph (1) above they have neither done so nor refused to do so, they shall be deemed for the purposes of that sub-paragraph to have refused to do so.

(3) The part of the A20 road from Ashford to Folkestone for which Work No. 9A is to be substituted shall not be stopped up under paragraph 16 above until, in addition, the County Council have certified that—

(a) the new bridleway between CE1 and F5; or

(b) an alternative approved highway;

has been completed in accordance with their reasonable requirements and is open for public use or, in the case of a difference between the Concessionaires and the County Council as to whether a certificate has been unreasonably withheld or as to the reasonableness of their requirements, until the difference has been determined by the Secretary of State, on application made to him by the Concessionaires after not less than 28 days' notice to the County Council, and he has certified that the new bridleway or alternative approved highway has been completed in accordance with his determination and is open for public use.

(4) No part of any highway specified in Section A of Part II of the table in paragraph 16 above, other than one mentioned in sub-paragraph (1) above, and no part of the highways specified in Section C of Part II of that table shall be stopped up under that paragraph until the County Council have certified that—

(a) the new highway to be substituted therefor; or

(b) an alternative approved highway;

has been completed in accordance with their reasonable requirements and is open for public use or, in the case of a difference between the Concessionaires or the Railways Board and the County Council as to whether a certificate has been unreasonably withheld or as to the reasonableness of their requirements, until the difference has been determined by the Secretary of State, on application made to him by the Concessionaires or the Railways Board after not less than 7 days' notice to the County Council, and he has certified that the new highway or alternative approved highway has been completed in accordance with his determination and is open for public use.

(5) No part of any highway specified in Section B of Part II of the table in paragraph 16 above shall be stopped up under that paragraph until the County Council are satisfied that—

(a) the new highway to be substituted therefor; or

(b) an alternative approved highway;

has been completed and is open for public use.

19.—(1) Before commencing the construction of any of Works Nos. 9A, 9B, 10A, 11 or 17 the Concessionaires shall submit to the County Council for their approval plans, sections and specifications (below in this paragraph referred to as "plans") of the work and, unless the Concessionaires and the County Council otherwise agree, it shall not be constructed except in accordance with the plans submitted to the County Council and approved by them or, on application made to the Secretary of State by the Concessionaires after disapproval of the plans by the County Council, approved by him.

(2) If within 28 days after the plans have been submitted the County Council have not approved or disapproved them, they shall be deemed to have approved the plans as submitted.

20.—(1) If it appears to the County Council that the construction of Work No. 17 will not be completed on or before the date on which their scheduled works will be completed and open for public use, they may by notice require the Concessionaires to complete the construction of that work by such reasonable date as they may specify in the notice.

(2) Any difference about the reasonableness of any date specified in a notice under sub-paragraph (1) above shall be determined by the Secretary of State.

(3) The Secretary of State shall certify the date on which the construction of Work No. 17 has been completed.

Repair of highways and agreements with highway authorities

21.—(1) Notwithstanding anything in section 46 of the Railways Clauses Consolidation Act 1845, as incorporated with this Act, the appropriate authority shall not be liable to maintain the surface of any highway under or over which the scheduled works shall be constructed or the immediate approaches thereto.

(2) Except as provided in sub-paragraph (3) below, any new highway constructed by the Concessionaires or the Railways Board under this Act in substitution for an existing highway or part thereof shall, unless otherwise agreed between the Concessionaires or the Railways Board and the County Council, be maintained by and at the expense of the Concessionaires or the Railways Board for a period of twelve months from the date certified as the date on which it has been completed and is open for public use and, at the end of that period, shall be maintained by and at the expense of the County Council.

(3) The new bridleway between the points G1 and G2 shown on the deposited plans to be substituted for the part of the existing bridleway in the district of Shepway (parishes of Hythe and Newington) between those points shall, when completed, be maintained by and at the expense of the Concessionaires.

(4) Sections 116 and 117 of the Transport Act 1968 (responsibility for the maintenance of highway bridges over railways) shall apply to the Concessionaires as if they were one of the boards mentioned in those sections.

(5) Where under this Act the appropriate authority are authorised to stop up or interfere with an existing highway or part thereof, they may enter into agreements with the persons having the charge, management or control of the highway concerning the construction, or a contribution towards the expense of the construction, of any new highway to be provided in substitution therefor or of any alteration of the existing highway and any other related matters.

(6) The appropriate authority may, by agreement with any such persons, delegate to them the power of constructing any such new highway or any such alteration of an existing highway, including any bridge over any railway, and, where the appropriate authority are responsible for maintaining the new or altered highway (or bridge), the power to maintain it.

Temporary interference with highways

22.—(1) The appropriate authority may, for the purpose of constructing or maintaining works which they are authorised to construct under this Act, temporarily stop up, break up or interfere with, or alter or divert, the whole or any part of any highway within the limits of land to be acquired or used and may carry out and do all necessary works and things for, or in connection with, the stopping up, opening, breaking up, interference, alteration or diversion and for keeping the highway open for traffic.

(2) The appropriate authority shall provide reasonable access for all persons, with or without vehicles, going to or returning from premises abutting on any highway affected by the exercise of the powers conferred by this paragraph.

Power to use subsoil of highways

23. Subject to the provisions of this Act the appropriate authority may enter upon, take and use for the purposes of this Act so much of the subsoil and under-surface of any highway within the limits of deviation for their scheduled works as shall be required for the purpose of the construction or maintenance of those works, without being required to acquire that subsoil and under-surface or any interest therein.

Status of certain highways constructed by the Concessionaires

24.—(1) The Secretary of State shall certify points on Works Nos. 9E and 9F to which each of those works from their commencement shall be special roads.

(2) On the date certified by the Secretary of State as the date on which the roads forming the parts of those works from their commencement to those points have been completed and are open for public use, those roads shall become trunk roads and special roads for the exclusive use of traffic of Classes I and II of the classes of traffic specified in Schedule 4 to the Highways Act 1980 as if they had been provided by the Secretary of State in pursuance of a scheme made by him under section 16 of that Act—

(a) prescribing the route of those roads as the route for the special roads to be provided under the scheme;

(b) prescribing both those classes of traffic; and

(c) specifying that date as the date on which those special roads were to become trunk roads.

(3) The provisions of sub-paragraph (2) above shall be treated for the purposes of that Act as provisions of a scheme under that section.

(4) On the date certified in relation to any new highway under paragraph 18(1) above the road which is the highway shall be transferred to the Kent County Council.

(5) Where the construction of any part of the road forming Work No. 17 has been completed the Secretary of State may, if the part concerned was not a highway at the passing of this Act, certify a date on which it is to be transferred to that Council.

(6) In the case of any new road constructed by the Concessionaires in pursuance of this Schedule, other than one to which sub-paragraph (2), (4) or (5) above applies, the Secretary of State may certify a date on which that road is to be transferred to that Council.

(7) On the date certified in relation to any road or part of a road under sub-paragraph (5) or (6) above, that road or part of a road shall be transferred to that Council.

(8) Subject to paragraph 27(4)(b) below, following a transfer under sub-paragraph (4) or (7) above the road or part of a road transferred shall be treated as if it had been constructed by that Council in exercise of their powers under section 24(2) of the Highways Act 1980.

(9) The Secretary of State may classify any road proposed to be constructed which may be transferred to that Council under this paragraph in any manner in which, and for any purposes for which, he could under section 12(3) of that Act classify a proposed highway for which that Council are the highway authority.

(10) On the date of its transfer to that Council any road classified under sub-paragraph (9) above shall become a highway classified in the manner and for the purposes in question as if so classified under section 12(3) of that Act.

Status of the County Council's works

25. The construction by the Kent County Council of a highway in pursuance of this Act shall be treated as the construction of a highway in pursuance of section 24(2) of the Highways Act 1980.

Regulation of traffic on new roads

26.—(1) Subject to sub-paragraph (2) below, any power under the Road Traffic Regulation Act 1984 to make an order or to give a direction with respect to any road shall be exercisable in relation to any road forming or forming part of any of the Concessionaires' or the County Council's scheduled works before that road is open for public use, in any case where it appears to the Secretary of State to be expedient that the order or (as the case may be) the direction should have effect immediately on the road's becoming open for public use.

(2) The procedure otherwise applicable under that Act in relation to the making of any such order or the giving of any such direction shall apply in any such case with such modifications as the Secretary of State may determine; and he shall publish notice of those modifications in such manner as appears to him to be appropriate for bringing them to the notice of persons likely to be affected by the provisions of any such order or (as the case may be) by any such direction.

Compensation for, and mitigation of, adverse effects of certain authorised works

27.—(1) Subject to the following provisions of this paragraph, the Secretary of State is the responsible authority for the purposes of Parts I and II of the Land Compensation Act 1973 (compensation for, and mitigation of, injurious effects of public works) as respects the Concessionaires' scheduled works and any other works of the Concessionaires authorised by this Act (including the construction or alteration of any highway).

(2) Where a claim under Part I of that Act relates to depreciation caused by use of the road forming Work No. 17—

  (a) if and so far as it relates to depreciation that would not have been caused but for the opening to public traffic of Kent County Council's scheduled works, that Council shall be the responsible authority in relation to it; and

  (b) if and so far as the Secretary of State is the responsible authority in relation to it, no account shall be taken in assessing compensation of any use or expected intensification of use of that road due to that opening.

(3) If and so far as the Kent County Council are the responsible authority in relation to a claim under that Part of that Act by virtue of sub-paragraph (2)(a) above, that Part of that Act shall have effect in relation to the claim as if—

  (a) the relevant date were the date on which all of their scheduled works were first open to public traffic;

  (b) the increase in value to be taken into account under section 6 were any increase that would not have been caused but for the opening to public traffic of those works; and

  (c) subsection (1) of section 8 did not preclude the payment of compensation unless the previous claim was in respect of depreciation that would not have been caused but for that opening and subsection (2) of that section did not preclude the payment of compensation.

(4) Subject to the following provisions of this paragraph, the Noise Insulation Regulations 1975 shall have effect as if—

  (a) the Secretary of State were the appropriate highway authority in relation to all of the Concessionaires' scheduled works and other works of the Concessionaires authorised by this Act which are highways, except the road forming Work No. 17;

  (b) Work No. 17 were, as from the commencement of its construction, the construction of a highway by the Kent County Council; and

(c) the relevant noise level, in relation to the road forming that work, did not include any level of noise caused or expected to be caused by traffic using or expected to use it before the date on which all of Kent County Council's scheduled works are first open to public traffic.

(5) Notwithstanding anything in sub-paragraph (1) or (4) above, the Secretary of State—

(a) is not liable to satisfy any claim under Part I of the Land Compensation Act 1973 in connection with the use of any highway for which he is not the highway authority; and

(b) does not have any obligation or power under the Noise Insulation Regulations 1975 in connection with the use or alteration of any such highway;

if and so far as the claim, obligation or power arises in connection with the alteration of the highway otherwise than in pursuance of this Act.

(6) Subject to the following provisions of this paragraph, in the case of any of the Concessionaires' scheduled works and any other works of the Concessionaires authorised by this Act which involve the construction or alteration of a highway, the Secretary of State shall have the powers and duties of a highway authority under—

(a) section 28 of that Act (power to pay expenses of persons moving temporarily during construction works); and

(b) sections 246, 253 and 282 of the Highways Act 1980 (which relate respectively to acquisition of land, agreements with respect to use of land and execution of works for the purpose of mitigating adverse effects of highways);

as if he were constructing or altering, or proposing to construct or alter, the highway, and references in those sections to a highway authority shall be construed accordingly.

(7) The Secretary of State may with the consent of the Kent County Council by order made by statutory instrument transfer to that Council, on such terms as may be provided in the order—

(a) any land acquired by him under section 246 of the Highways Act 1980; and

(b) any rights and liabilities acquired by or accrued to him under that section, section 253 or 282 of the Highways Act 1980 or the Noise Insulation Regulations 1975;

by virtue of this paragraph.

(8) For the purposes of section 26 of the Land Compensation Act 1973 (power of responsible authority to acquire land by agreement for the purpose of mitigating any adverse effects of public works) the Concessionaires' and the Railways Board's scheduled works and any other works of the Concessionaires or (as the case may be) of the Railways Board authorised by this Act shall be treated as public works notwithstanding that they form part of a statutory undertaking as defined by section 290(1) of the Town and Country Planning Act 1971.

Section 9   SCHEDULE 3

PLANNING PERMISSION

Preliminary

1. In this Schedule—

"authorised development" means development to which the planning permission deemed by section 9(1) of this Act to have been granted under Part III of the Act of 1971 relates;

"spoil" means spoil from tunnelling works; and

"surplus spoil" means spoil which is not used for the purposes of any of the works authorised by this Act.

Scheme of operation for authorised development

2. Any authorised development shall be carried out in accordance with a scheme of operation consisting of the arrangements with respect to the matters mentioned in the left-hand column of the following table which the appropriate planning authority have, at the request of the Concessionaires, for the time being approved as the arrangements which are to be adopted in carrying out the development to which the scheme relates.

The only grounds on which the authority may refuse to approve arrangements with respect to any matter so mentioned (including arrangements modifying or replacing any arrangements previously approved) are—

(a) that the arrangements relate to development which, for the purposes of regulating the matter in question, ought to and can reasonably be considered in conjunction with other authorised development which is to be carried out in the authority's area; and

(b) the ground specified in relation to that matter in the right-hand column of the table.

THE TABLE

Matters	Grounds
The sites, other than sea bed sites, from which any minerals and aggregates required for carrying out the development are to be obtained.	That the arrangements ought to be modified— (a) to control the depletion of mineral resources in the authority's area; (b) to prevent or reduce prejudicial effects on the free flow of traffic in their area; or (c) to preserve the amenity of their area or in the interests of nature conservation; and are reasonably capable of being so modified.
The means and routes by which any minerals, aggregates, bulk materials other than minerals or aggregates and tunnel lining segments so required are to be transported to construction and storage sites within the limits of land to be acquired.	That the arrangements ought to be modified— (a) to prevent or reduce prejudicial effects on the free flow of traffic in their area; or (b) to preserve the amenity of their area or in the interests of nature conservation; and are reasonably capable of being so modified.
The handling during removal, storage and re-use of any topsoil removed in the course of carrying out the development.	That the arrangements ought to be modified to ensure that the topsoil remains in good condition and are reasonably capable of being so modified.
The sites, within the limits of land to be acquired, at which any minerals and aggregates required for carrying out the development are to be stored until used. The sites, within those limits, at which any topsoil removed in the course of carrying out the development is to be stored until re-used. The hours during which, and the days on which, work is to be carried out within those limits for the purpose of carrying out the development. The suppression of noise and dust caused by any operations carried on within those limits for the purpose of carrying out the development. The measures to be taken within those limits to prevent mud being carried on to any highway as a result of carrying out the development. The use within those limits of artificial lighting for the purpose of carrying out the development. The sites, within those limits, which are to be used for camps for the accommodation of persons engaged in carrying out the development.	That the arrangements ought to be modified to preserve the amenity of the neighbourhood or in the interests of nature conservation or of the preservation of a site of archaeological or historic interest and are reasonably capable of being so modified. (*Note*: This ground applies in relation to the matters mentioned in all succeeding entries in the left-hand column of this table.)

In this paragraph "the appropriate planning authority" means, in relation to the first two matters mentioned in the left-hand column of the table, the county planning authority, and otherwise the district planning authority.

Detailed plans and specifications for certain authorised development

3. To the extent that any authorised development consists of any operation or work mentioned in the left-hand column of the following table it shall be carried out in accordance with detailed plans and specifications approved, at the request of the Concessionaires, by the appropriate planning authority.

The only ground on which the authority may refuse, or impose conditions on the grant of, any approval of plans or specifications of any operation or work so mentioned is that specified in relation to that operation or work in the right-hand column of the table.

THE TABLE

Operation or work	Grounds
The erection, construction, alteration or extension of any building, road vehicle park or noise screening. Terracing or other earthworks.	That— (a) the design or external appearance of the building, road vehicle park, noise screening, terracing or other earthworks ought to be modified to preserve the amenity of the neighbourhood and is reasonably capable of being so modified; or (b) the development ought to and could reasonably be carried out elsewhere within the limits of land on which the works of which it forms part may be carried out under this Act.
The erection, construction or installation of lighting equipment	That— (a) the design of the equipment, with respect to the emission of light, ought to be modified to preserve the amenity of the neighbourhood and is reasonably capable of being so modified; or (b) the development ought to and could reasonably be carried out elsewhere within the limits of land on which the works of which it forms part may be carried out under this Act.
The formation, laying out or alteration of any means of access to any highway used, or proposed highway proposed to be used, by vehicular traffic.	That the development would be prejudicial to road safety or the free flow of traffic and is reasonably capable of modification so as to avoid such prejudice.
The construction of Work No. 7, referred to below in this Schedule as the sea wall.	That its elevation, situation or external appearance ought to be modified to preserve the amenity of the neighbourhood or the marine environment or in the interests of nature conservation and is reasonably capable of being so modified having regard to all the circumstances (including any relevant requirements for the protection of navigation).

Note:

1. The operations and works specified in the entries in the left-hand column of the table preceding the last such entry do not include anything to which that last entry applies or the deposit of spoil on the landward side of the sea wall.

2. The grounds in paragraph (b) of the first and second entries in the right-hand column of the table do not apply in the case of any development which forms part of a scheduled work or of railway sidings constructed in connection with such a work.

In this paragraph—

    (a) "the appropriate planning authority" means, in relation to the construction of the sea wall, the county planning authority, and otherwise the district planning authority; and

(b) the reference to relevant requirements for the protection of navigation is a reference to—

(i) the requirements of paragraph 2 of Part III and paragraphs 4 and 5 of Part IV of Schedule 7 to this Act with respect to the approval of such part of the sea wall as is on the surface of lands below the level of mean high water springs; and

(ii) any conditions or restrictions imposed in relation to any such part of the sea wall under any of those provisions.

Spoil

4.—(1) No surplus spoil shall be deposited except on the landward side of the sea wall.

(2) No more than the maximum permitted amount of spoil shall be deposited there (whether or not as surplus spoil.)

(3) The maximum permitted amount of spoil is the amount deriving from the excavation of 3.75 million cubic metres of unexcavated material.

(4) The functions of a local planning authority of issuing enforcement notices under section 87 of the Act of 1971 or serving stop notices under section 90 of that Act shall be exercisable by the county planning authority so far as they relate to a breach of planning control consisting of failure to comply with the requirement imposed by sub-paragraph (2) above.

(5) The county planning authority may by notice in writing require the Concessionaires to give in writing twenty-one days after the date on which the notice is served, or such longer time as may be specified in the notice or as the authority may allow, such information as may be so specified as to—

(a) the amount of spoil has been deposited on the landward side of the sea wall; and

(b) the rate at which spoil is to be deposited there in the future;

and any information as to an amount of spoil shall be given by reference to the volume of the material from which it derives in its unexcavated state.

(6) Subsections (2) and (3) (offences) of section 284 of the Act of 1971 shall have effect in relation to notices under sub-paragraph (5) above as they have effect in relation to notices under subsection (1) of that section.

5.—(1) The methods to be employed in, and the timing of, the deposit of spoil on the landward side of the sea wall shall be in accordance with arrangements approved, at the request of the Concessionaires, by the county planning authority.

(2) The height of the spoil deposited on the landward side of the sea wall shall not exceed the maximum specified in those arrangements.

(3) Finishing treatment shall be applied to the surface of the spoil deposited there in accordance with those arrangements.

(4) The county planning authority shall not refuse, or impose conditions on the grant of, any approval required for the purposes of this paragraph unless they are satisfied that it is expedient to do so on the ground that the arrangements ought to be modified to preserve the amenity of the neighbourhood or the marine environment or in the interests of nature conservation and are reasonably capable of being so modified.

6. Once the tunnel system has been brought into operation, the Concessionaires shall, in accordance with a scheme agreed with the county planning authority or, in default of agreement or on notice being given by the Secretary of State to the authority and the Concessionaires, settled by him, put so much of the area on the landward side of the sea wall as consists of land reclaimed by the deposit of spoil and is not required for or in connection with the operation of the tunnel system into such a condition as the scheme may provide.

Protection of site at Holywell Coombe

7.—(1) No part of Work No. 3 shall be constructed in any part of the protected site.

(2) Nothing shall be done in any part of the protected site in connection with the construction of that work except necessary drainage work and landscaping of the site.

(3) No part of that work shall be constructed, and nothing shall be done in connection with the construction of that work, anywhere else unless—

(a) the southern boundary of the protected site is fenced; or

(b) that boundary has been fenced but the fencing has been temporarily removed because it was necessary to remove it in order to carry out necessary drainage work or landscaping of the site.

(4) In this paragraph "the protected site" means the area of land at Holywell Coombe in the district of Shepway (town of Folkestone) bounded on the southern side by a straight line

between National Grid reference points 622058E 138078N and 622138E 138095N, on the western and eastern sides by straight lines passing due north from each of those points to the limit of deviation of Work No. 3 and on the northern side by that limit.

Arrangements and schemes for certain authorised development

8.—(1) Where the bringing into use of any building, facility or work comprised in any authorised development will result in the emission of significant levels of noise, the building, facility or work shall not be brought into use unless measures for the suppression of that noise have been taken in accordance with arrangements approved, at the request of the Concessionaires, by the district planning authority.

(2) The district planning authority shall not refuse any approval required for the purposes of sub-paragraph (1) above unless they are satisfied that it is expedient to do so on the ground that the arrangements ought to be modified to preserve the amentiy of the neighbourhood and are reasonably capable of being so modified.

9.—(1) The land associated with any building, facility or work comprised in any authorised development shall be landscaped in accordance with a scheme approved, at the request of the Concessionaires, by the district planning authority.

(2) No building, facility or work so comprised shall be brought into use unless—
    (a) a scheme for the landscaping of the land associated with it has been so approved; and
    (b) any landscaping operations required by the scheme to have been completed before the building, facility or work is brought into use have been completed in accordance with the scheme.

(3) The district planning authority shall not refuse any approval required for the purposes of this paragraph unless they are satisfied that it is expedient to do so on the ground that the scheme ought to be modified to enhance the amenity of the neighbourhood or in the interests of nature conservation or of the preservation of a site of archaeological or historic interest and is reasonably capable of being so modified.

Consultation regarding County Council development

10. None of the development to which the planning permission deemed by section 9(3) of this Act to have been granted under Part III of the Act of 1971 relates shall be begun until the County Council have consulted the district planning authority with regard to the design of the development and the landscaping and noise screening to be undertaken in connection with the development.

Certificates for construction or use of certain authorised development

11.—(1) Subject to sub-paragraph (2) below, the construction of the terminal area at Cheriton, Folkestone shall cease at the end of the period of six months beginning with the day it began unless the Secretary of State has, before the end of that period, certified either—
    (a) that, in his opinion, adequate facilities for and in connection with public viewing of the construction have been provided; or
    (b) that, in his opinion, the Concessionaires have taken all reasonable steps to provide such facilities;
and it shall not be begun again unless the Secretary of State has certified as mentioned either in paragraph (a) above or in paragraph (b) above.

(2) If it is intended to provide facilities for or in connection with public viewing of the construction of the terminal area within that area, sub-paragraph (1) above shall not apply in relation to the construction of the terminal area so far as it consists of work in connection with the provision of the facilities.

12. The inland clearance depot to be constructed at Ashford, in Kent, shall not be brought into use until the Secretary of State has—
    (a) certified either—
        (i) that, in his opinion, adequate refreshment and sleeping facilities for the use of drivers of vehicles using the depot have been provided within the limits of land to be acquired for the purposes of or in connection with the depot; or
        (ii) that, in his opinion, the Concessionaires have taken all reasonable steps to provide such facilities; and
    (b) certified, under paragraph 20(3) of Schedule 2 to this Act, completion of the construction of Work No. 17.

13. The tunnel system shall not be brought into use until the Secretary of State has certified either—

(a) that, in his opinion, adequate facilites for and in connection with public viewing of the operation of the terminal area at Cheriton, Folkestone have been provided; or

(b) that, in his opinion, the Concessionaires have taken all reasonable steps to provide such facilities.

14.—(1) The Secretary of State shall consult the county and district planning authorities before giving any certificate for the purposes of paragraph 11, 12(a) or 13 above.

(2) Where the Secretary of State gives any such certificate as is mentioned in sub-paragraph (1) above he shall give a copy of the certificate to each of the authorities whom he was required by that sub-paragraph to consult before giving it.

(3) No failure on the part of the Secretary of State to comply with his obligations under sub-paragraph (1) or (2) above shall affect the validity of any certificate given by him for the purposes of paragraph 11, 12(a) or 13 above.

Working sites: discontinuance of operations and putting into condition

15.—(1) Where any authorised development consists of or includes the carrying out on any working site within the limits of land to be acquired of operations ancillary to the construction of the tunnel system—

(a) those operations shall be discontinued before the end of the relevant period; and

(b) the Concessionaires shall, in accordance with a scheme agreed with the district planning authority or, in default of agreement or on notice being given by the Secretary of State to the authority and the Concessionaires, settled by him, put the site, except any part which is required for use for or in connection with the operation of the tunnel system or for any of the Railways Board's works, into such a condition as the scheme may provide.

(2) The relevant period is the period of ten years beginning with the date of the passing of this Act or such longer period as the Secretary of State may specify, after consultation with the district planning authority, at any time before the end of the period of ten years or of any period previously specified by him.

16. Where any development to which any planning permission granted by virtue of section 9(4) of this Act relates consists of or includes the carrying out on any working site within the limits of land to be acquired of operations ancillary to any of the Railways Board's works—

(a) those operations shall be discontinued before the end of the period of ten years beginning with the date of passing of this Act; and

(b) the Railways Board shall, in accordance with a scheme agreed, in the case of a working site in a London borough, with the borough planning authority and, in the case of a working site anywhere else, by the district planning authority or, in default of agreement or on notice being given by the Secretary of State to the authority and the Railways Board, settled by him, put the site, except any part which is required for any of the Railways Board's works, into such a condition as the scheme may provide.

Nature, the countryside and archaeological and historic sites

17.—(1) Where a request is made—

(a) for an approval under paragraphs 2, 3, 5 or 9 above;

(b) for an approval of detailed plans and specifications which is required for the exercise of any planning permission granted by virtue of section 9(4) of this Act;

the planning authority shall, within five days of receiving it, commence any appropriate consultation with respect to it.

(2) The authority shall not take any decision in relation to the request until either they have received any representations which the body or bodies consulted wish to make or the period of 21 days from the commencement of consultation has ended.

(3) Before a planning authority agree a scheme under paragraph 6, 15 or 16 above they shall undertake any appropriate consultation with respect to it.

(4) In this paragraph "appropriate consultation" means—

(a) where the authority consider that nature conservation may be affected, consultation with the Nature Conservancy Council;

(b) where they consider that the conservation of the natural beauty and amenity of the countryside (including nature conservation) may be affected, consultation with the Countryside Commission;

(c) where they consider that a site of archaeological or historic interest may be affected, consultation with the Historic Buildings and Monuments Commission for England.

Approvals: supplementary

18. A planning authority shall not be required to entertain any request for an approval required for the purposes of any provision of this Schedule unless the Concessionaires have deposited with them both—

(a) a plan showing the Concessionaires' current proposals regarding the layout of the authorised development; and

(b) a schedule setting out the Concessionaires' current proposals regarding the timetable for carrying it out.

19.—(1) The Secretary of State may give directions to a planning authority requiring any request by the Concessionaires for an approval required for the purposes of any provision of this Schedule to be referred to him instead of being dealt with by them.

(2) A direction under this paragraph may relate either to a particular request or to requests of a class specified in the direction.

(3) A request in respect of which such a direction has effect shall be referred to the Secretary of State accordingly.

(4) The Secretary of State may refuse or impose conditions on an approval only on the grounds open to the authority required to refer the request for it.

(5) The determination by the Secretary of State of the request shall be final.

20. The Secretary of State may give directions to a planning authority restricting the grant, either indefinitely or during such period as may be specified in the directions, of a particular approval required for the purposes of any provision of this Schedule or of approvals so required of a class specified in the directions.

21.—(1) Where the Concessionaires are aggrieved by the decision of a planning authority on any request for an approval required for the purposes of any provision of this Schedule, they may by notice under this sub-paragraph appeal to the Secretary of State whose decision on the appeal shall be final.

(2) Any notice under sub-paragraph (1) above shall be in writing and be served, within 28 days of notification of the decision to which it relates, on the Secretary of State and the authority whose decision is appealed against.

(3) On an appeal under this paragraph, the Secretary of State may allow or dismiss the appeal or vary the decision of the authority whose decision is appealed against but may make a determination involving the refusal of, or imposition of conditions on, an approval only on the grounds open to that authority.

(4) Where the authority to whom a request for approval is made fail to notify the Concessionaires of their decision on that request within—

(a) the period of two months beginning with the date on which that request was made; or

(b) such extended period as may from time to time be agreed upon in writing between the authority and the Concessionaires;

the provisions of this paragraph shall apply in relation to the request as if the authority had refused it and as if they had notified the Concessionaires of their decision on the last day of the two month period or, where an extended period has been agreed, on the last day of that extended period.

(5) No appeal under section 36 of the Act of 1971 may be made against any decision in relation to which a right of appeal arises under this paragraph.

Section 35   SCHEDULE 4

The A20 Improvement Works

Part I

The Authorised Works

Description of works

1. The works which the Secretary of State is authorised by section 35 of this Act to construct are the following—

In the district of Dover (town of Dover and parishes of Capel-le-Ferne and Hougham Without) and the district of Shepway (town of Folkestone and parish of Hawkinge), in the county of Kent—

Work No. 31—A road forming the northern carriageway of a dual carriageway road, including a viaduct, commencing by a junction with the northern carriageway of the M20 at a point 90 metres west of the underpass whereby the footpath from Elvington Road to Biggins Wood Road passes under the M20, passing east and turning north-east over land known as Holywell Coombe by means of the viaduct, then in tunnel under Round Hill and Crete Road West (Pilgrims Way) and terminating on the west side of Canterbury Road (A260) at a point 55 metres north-west of the junction of that road with Alkham Valley Road (B2060):

Work No. 32—A road forming the southern carriageway of the said dual carriageway road, including a viaduct, commencing by a junction with the southern carriageway of the M20 at the said point 90 metres west of the said underpass, passing east and turning north-east over the said land known as Holywell Coombe by means of the viaduct, then in tunnel under Round Hill and Crete Road West (Pilgrims Way) and terminating at a point 45 metres north-west of the junction of Canterbury Road with Alkham Valley Road:

Work No. 33—A road comprising dual carriageways, commencing by junctions with Works Nos. 31 and 32 at their termination, passing north-east under Canterbury Road at a point 50 metres north of its junction with Alkham Valley Road, then along a line to the north of Alkham Valley Road, then crossing over that road by a bridge at a point 125 metres north-west of the entrance to Havenfield Lodge, then passing east, crossing under Cauldham Lane, Capel Street and Satmar Lane, then turning south-east and terminating at a roundabout forming a junction with the A20 (Works Nos. 44A and 44B) at a point 480 metres south-west of the entrance from that road to Court Wood:

Work No. 34—A grade separated junction comprising—

Work No. 34A—A slip road commencing by a junction with Work No. 31 at a point 220 metres from its commencement and terminating at the entry to a northern junction roundabout (part of Work No. 34C) at a point 80 metres north of the northern end of the bridge carrying the M20 over Waterworks Lane;

Work No. 34B—A slip road commencing at the exit from the said northern junction roundabout and terminating by a junction with Work No. 31 at a point 280 metres east of the existing junction of Castle Hill with the Castle Hill Roundabout.

Work No. 34C—A road, including junction roundabouts at its commencement and termination and a bridge over Works Nos. 31 and 32, commencing at the said northern junction roundabout at the termination of Work No. 34A and terminating at a southern junction roundabout at a point 85 metres south of the said existing junction of Castle Hill with the Castle Hill Roundabout;

Work No. 34D—A realignment and alteration of the southern carriageway of the M20 to form a slip road, commencing at a point in the said carriageway 270 metres west of the southern end of the said bridge carrying the M20 over Waterworks Lane and terminating at the exit from the said southern junction roundabout;

Work No. 34E—A slip road commencing at the entry to the said southern junction roundabout and terminating by a junction with Work No. 32 at a point 400 metres east of the said existing junction of Castle Hill with the Castle Hill Roundabout;

Work No. 34F—A road in substitution for part of Churchill Avenue commencing by a junction with the said southern junction roundabout and terminating by a junction with the southern carriageway of Churchill Avenue at a point 440 metres east of that roundabout;

Work No. 34G—A realignment of Cherry Garden Avenue, commencing at the said southern junction roundabout and terminating at the junction of that road with Papworth Close;

Work No. 34H—A road in substitution for part of Castle Hill at its junction with the Castle Hill Roundabout, commencing by a junction with that road at a point 260 metres north of that roundabout, passing south-west and west and terminating at the northern junction roundabout at the termination of Work No. 34A:

Work No. 35—A diversion and extension of Park Farm Road, commencing by a junction with Work No. 34F at a point 150 metres west of the termination of that work and terminating at a point in Park Farm Road 75 metres from its commencement:

Work No. 36—A widening on the north side of Crete Road West (Pilgrims Way) between its junction with Gibraltar Lane and its junction with Canterbury Road at a point 235 metres south of the junction of that road with Alkham Valley Road:

Work No. 37—A realignment of Canterbury Road and regrading of its junction with Alkham Valley Road, including a bridge over Works Nos. 33, 38A and 38C, commencing at a point in Canterbury Road 420 metres north of that road junction as existing and terminating at a point 250 metres south of that road junction:

Work No. 38—Junctions of Works Nos. 31, 32 and 33 with Canterbury Road and Alkham Valley Road comprising—

Work No. 38A—A slip road commencing by a junction with Work No. 31 at a point 190 metres south-west of the termination of that work, passing under Canterbury Road and turning north and west to terminate at a roundabout forming a junction with that road at a point 240 metres north of its junction with Alkham Valley Road;

Work No. 38B—A slip road commencing at the said roundabout forming a junction with Canterbury Road at the termination of Work No. 38A and terminating by a junction with the northern carriageway of Work No. 33 at a point 385 metres south-west of the existing junction of Church Hill with Alkham Valley Road;

Work No. 38C—A slip road commencing by a junction with Work No. 32 at a point 80 metres south-west of the termination of that work, passing under Canterbury Road and terminating at a roundabout forming a junction with Alkham Valley Road at a point 340 metres from its junction with Canterbury Road;

Work No. 38D—A slip road commencing at the said roundabout forming a junction with Alkham Valley Road at the termination of Work No. 38C and terminating by a junction with the southern carriageway of Work No. 33 at a point 220 metres south-west of the said existing junction of Church Hill with Alkham Valley Road:

Work No. 39—A road, including a bridge over Works Nos. 33 and 38D, in substitution for part of Church Hill at its junction with Alkham Valley Road, commencing by a junction with Alkham Valley Road at a point 100 metres north-east of the existing entrance to Coombe Farm, passing north, then turning north-east and terminating at a point in Church Hill 100 metres from the existing junction of that road with Alkham Valley Road:

Work No. 40—A road in substitution for part of Crete Road East at its junction with Alkham Valley Road, commencing by a junction with Alkham Valley Road at a point 30 metres east of the existing entrance to Havenfield Lodge and terminating at a point in Crete Road East 15 metres south-west of the entrance to Havenfield Hall:

Work No. 41—A diversion of Cauldham Lane, including a bridge over Work No. 33, commencing at a point in that road 125 metres south of its junction with the road to Lower Stenden Farm and terminating at a point in Cauldham Lane at its junction with Hurst Lane:

Work No. 42—A realignment and regrading of Capel Street, including a bridge over Work No. 33, commencing at a point in that road 150 metres south-west of its junction with Satmar Lane and terminating at a point in Capel Street 180 metres north of its junction with Hurst Lane:

Work No. 43—A diversion of Satmar Lane, including a bridge over Work No. 33, commencing at a point in that road 560 metres south-west of its junction with Crook's Court Lane and terminating at a point in Satmar Lane 300 metres north-east of Ivy Farm:

Work No. 44—A junction of Work No. 33 with the A20 at Court Wood comprising—

Work No. 44A—A diversion of the A20 as existing, commencing at a point in that road 310 metres east of the existing entrance to Abbots Land Farm and terminating at the said roundabout at the termination of Work No. 33;

Work No. 44B—A diversion of the A20 as existing, commencing at the said roundabout at the termination of Work No. 33 and terminating at a point in the A20 95 metres west of the entrance to Court Wood.

Limits of deviation

2. In their construction—

(a) each of the works described in paragraph 1 above may deviate from the line o situation shown for that work on the deposited plans to the extent of the limi of deviation so shown;

(b) so much of each of Works Nos. 31 and 32 as lies between its commencemer and the point at which it passes into tunnel under Round Hill may deviate fror the level shown for that part of that work on the deposited sections to the exter of 1.5 metres upwards and to any extent downwards; and

(c) each of the works described in paragraph 1 above, other than the parts of Work Nos. 31 and 32 specified in sub-paragraph (b) above, may deviate from the leve shown for that work or, in the case of Work Nos. 31 and 32, that part of tha work on the deposited sections to the extent of 3 metres upwards and to an extent downwards.

Interpretation of Part I

3. In paragraph 1 above, "A20" means the trunk road from Folkestone to Dover s classified.

PART II

INTERFERENCE WITH HIGHWAYS

Stopping up of highways

4.—(1) Subject to the provisions of this paragraph, the Secretary of State may, i connection with the construction of the A20 improvement works, stop up each of th highways or parts thereof specified, by reference to the letters and numbers shown on th deposited plans, in columns (1) and (2) of the following table and any other bridleways o footpaths within the limits of deviation for the works authorised by Part IV of this Act, an thereupon all rights of way over or along the highway or part thereof so stopped up shall b extinguished.

(2) The existing highways or part thereof specified in columns (1) and (2) of Part II of th following table shall not be stopped up under this paragraph until the new highway to b substituted therefor specified as aforesaid, or by reference to works authorised by Part IV of this Act, in column (3) of that Part of the table in relation to each such existing highway or part thereof has been completed in accordance with sub-paragraph (4) below.

THE TABLE

PART I

Highway to be stopped up

(1) Area	(2) Length of highway to be stopped up
District of Shepway, town of Folkestone	Footpath and access track from DB1 to DB: Road (Castle Hill) from DC1 to DC2 Road (part of Churchill Avenue (A20)) from DD1 to DD2 Road (Park Farm Road) from DE1 to DE2 Road (Crete Road West) from DF1 to DF2 Footpath from DG1 to DG2
District of Shepway, parish of Hawkinge	Footpath from DH1 to DH2 Footpath and access track from DI1 to DI2
District of Dover, parish of Capel-le-Ferne	Footpath from DL1 to DL4 Footpath from DN1 to DN2 Footpath from DP1 to DP2 Footpath from DP3 to DP4 Road (Satmar Lane) from DR1 to DR2 Footpath from DS1 to DS2

PART II

Highways to be stopped up and new highways substituted therefor

(1) Area	(2) Highway or part to be stopped up	(3) New highway to be substituted therefor
District of Shepway, town of Folkestone	Footpath and access track from DA1 to DA2	New footpath from DA1 to N3
District of Shepway, parish of Hawkinge	Road (Church Hill) from DJ1 to DJ2	Work No. 39
	Road (Crete Road East) from DK1 to DK2	Work No. 40
District of Dover, parish of Capel-le-Ferne	Footpath from DL2 to DL3 Road (Cauldham Lane) from DM1 to DM2 Footpath from DO1 to DO4 and DO2 to DO5	New footpath from DL2 to DL5 Work No. 41 New footpath from DO1 to DO3
District of Dover, parishes of Capel-le-Ferne and Hougham Without	Byway from DT1 to DT2, footpath from DW1 to DW2 and footpath from DX1 to DX2	New bridleway from DT1 to DT3 to DW1 to DX2
	Road (Satmar Lane) from DU1 to DU2	Work No. 43 New footpath from DV2 southward along the line of the existing road to the new bridleway between DT3 and DW1
District of Dover, parish of Hougham Without	Road (A20) from DY1 to DY2	Works Nos. 44A and 44B New footpath from DY1 to DY2 (part of Works Nos. 44A and 44B)

(3) No part of any highway shall be stopped up under this paragraph until the Secretary of State is in possession of all lands abutting on both sides of that part of the highway except so far as the owners, lessees and occupiers of those lands may otherwise agree.

(4) No part of any highway specified in Part II of the above table in this paragraph shall be stopped up under this paragraph until the Secretary of State is satisfied that the new highway to be substituted therefor has been completed and is open for public use.

(5) Any person who suffers loss by the extinguishment of any private right under this paragraph shall be entitled to compensation to be determined, in case of dispute, under and in accordance with Part I of the Land Compensation Act 1961.

Temporary interference with highways

5.—(1) The Secretary of State may, for the purpose of constructing or maintaining the A20 improvement works, temporarily stop up, open, break up or interfere with, or alter or divert, the whole or any part of any highway within the limits of deviation for the works authorised by Part IV of this Act or the limits of land to be acquired, and may carry out and do all necessary works and things for, or in connection with, the stopping up, opening, breaking up, interference, alteration or diversion and for keeping the highway open for traffic.

(2) The Secretary of State shall provide reasonable access for all persons, with or without vehicles, going to or returning from premises abutting on any highway affected by the exercise of the powers conferred by this paragraph.

PART III

MISCELLANEOUS

Status of new highways

6.—(1) On the date on which this Act is passed the roads mentioned in sub-paragraph (2) below shall become trunk roads and special roads for the exclusive use of traffic of Classes I and II of the classes of traffic specified in Schedule 4 to the Highways Act 1980 as if the provision by him of special roads along the route of those roads had been authorised by a scheme made by the Secretary of State under section 16 of that Act—

(a) prescribing that route as the route for the special roads;

(b) prescribing both those classes of traffic; and

(c) specifying that date as the date on which those special roads were to become trunk roads.

(2) The roads to which sub-paragraph (1) above applies are—

(a) so much of the roads forming Works Nos. 31 and 32 as lie, in the case of Work No. 31, between its commencement and a point on the road 690 metres from that commencement and, in the case of Work No. 32, between its commencement and a point on the road 875 metres from that commencement; and

(b) the slip roads forming or forming part of Works Nos. 34A and 34D.

(3) On the date on which this Act is passed the roads mentioned in sub-paragraph (4) below shall become trunk roads as if they had become so by virtue of an order under section 10(2) of the Highways Act 1980 specifying that date as the date on which they were to become trunk roads.

(4) Those roads are—

(a) such parts of the roads forming Works Nos. 31 and 32 as do not on that date become trunk roads and special roads by virtue of sub-paragraph (1) above;

(b) the roads forming Works Nos. 33, 34F, 44A and 44B; and

(c) the slip roads forming or forming part of Works Nos. 34B and 34E and the trunk road parts of Works Nos. 38A, 38B, 38C and 38D.

(5) The roads forming—

(a) in the case of each of Works Nos. 38A and 38C, the part from its commencement to a point certified the Secretary of State for the purposes of sub-paragraph (4)(c) above; and

(b) in the case of each of Works Nos. 38B and 38D, the part from a point so certified to its termination;

shall be the trunk road parts of those works for those purposes.

7.—(1) On the date certified by the Secretary of State as the date on which any highway constructed in pursuance of this Schedule, other than one to which paragraph 6 above applies, is open for public use, that highway shall be transferred to the Kent County Council and, following that transfer, shall be treated for the purposes of the Highways Act 1980 as if it had been so transferred by virtue of an order made under the provision of that Act which applies in relation to its construction by virtue of paragraph 8 below.

(2) The Secretary of State may classify any highway proposed to be constructed in pursuance of this Schedule, other than one to which paragraph 6 above applies, in any manner in which, and for any purposes for which, he could classify that highway under section 12(3) of that Act.

(3) On the date of its transfer under sub-paragraph (1) above to the Kent County Council any highway classified under sub-paragraph (2) above shall become a highway classified in the manner and for the purposes in question as if so classified under section 12(3) of that Act.

Regulation of construction of works

8. The construction by the Secretary of State of a highway in pursuance of this Act shall be treated as the construction of a highway in pursuance of—

(a) a scheme under section 16 of the Highways Act 1980, in the case of the roads mentioned in paragraph 6(2) above;

(b) section 24(1) of that Act, in the case of the roads mentioned in paragraph 6(4) above;

(c) an order under section 18 of that Act made in relation to the roads which become trunk roads and special roads by virtue of paragraph 6(1) above, in the case of the road forming Work No. 34C; and

(d) an order under section 14 of that Act made in relation to the roads which become trunk roads by virtue of paragraph 6(3) above, in any other case.

Status of ancillary operations and works

9.—(1) The carrying out of any of the A20 improvement works which is not the construction of a highway and the stopping up of any highway in pursuance of Part II of this Schedule shall be treated as having been authorised by an order under section 14 of the Highways Act 1980 made in relation to the roads which become trunk roads by virtue of paragraph 6(3) above.

(2) Subject to sections 21 and 22 of that Act as they apply by virtue of sub-paragraph (1) above, the stopping up of any highway in pursuance of Part II of this Schedule shall not affect any rights—

(a) of statutory undertakers in respect of any apparatus of theirs which immediately before the date on which this Act is passed is under, in, on, over, along or across that highway; or

(b) of any sewerage authority in respect of any sewers or sewage disposal works of theirs which immediately before that date are under, in, on, over, along or across that highway.

Application of Highways Act powers to provisions of this Schedule

10.—(1) Any provision of Part I or II of this Schedule relating to any operation or work which by virtue of any of the preceding provisions of this Part of this Schedule is to be treated as authorised by an order under section 14 or 18 of the Highways Act 1980 shall be treated for the purposes of that Act as provisions of such an order.

(2) The provisions of paragraph 6(1) above shall be treated for those purposes as provisions of a scheme under section 16 of that Act.

Regulation of traffic on new roads

11.—(1) Subject to sub-paragraph (2) below, any power under the Road Traffic Regulation Act 1984 to make an order or to give a direction with respect to any road shall be exercisable in relation to any road forming or forming part of any of the A20 improvement works before that road is open for public use, in any case where it appears to the Secretary of State to be expedient that the order or (as the case may be) the direction should have effect immediately on the road's becoming open for public use.

(2) The procedure otherwise applicable under that Act in relation to the making of any such order or the giving of any such direction shall apply in any such case with such modifications as the Secretary of State may determine; and he shall publish notice of those modifications in such manner as appears to him to be appropriate for bringing them to the notice of persons likely to be affected by the provisions of any such order or (as the case may be) by any such direction.

Section 37

SCHEDULE 5

SUPPLEMENTARY PROVISIONS AS TO ACQUISITION OF LAND

PART I

PURPOSES FOR WHICH CERTAIN LAND MAY BE
ACQUIRED OR USED UNDER SECTION 8

SECTION A

PURPOSES OF THE CONCESSIONAIRES

(1) *Area*	(2) *Number of land shown on deposited plans*	(3) *Purpose for which land may be acquired or used*
Borough of Ashford— parish of Sevington	1 to 8	The construction of an inland clearance depot, the provision of road vehicle parks and landscaping and a working site and access for construction purposes.

(1) *Area*	(2) *Number of land shown on deposited plans*	(3) *Purpose for which land may be acquired or used*
District of Shepway— parish of Newington	4, 5, 7, 25 26, 35 and 36 30 to 35 and 37	The provision of a working site and access for construction purposes. The provision of drainage, a working site and access for construction and maintenance purposes.

District of Shepway—
   town of Folkestone
   parish of Newington
	3 to 37,
	48 to 52,
	60 to 65
	and 82
		The construction of a terminal area (including loading platforms, bridges, railway sidings and premises) at Cheriton, Folkestone and the provision of working sites and access for construction purposes.

District of Shepway— town of Folkestone	30 to 44 51 and 55 51 and 54	The provision of drainage and access for construction and maintenance purposes. The provision of a working site and access for construction purposes. The provision of facilities north of Churchill Avenue for operation and maintenance purposes, the provision of a working site and access for construction purposes.
District of Dover— town of Dover	7, 8 and 9 9 to 18 22 to 31 35 and 36 33 and 34 33 to 36	The provision of a working site and access for construction purposes. The provision of working and camp sites and access for construction purposes. The provision of a working site and access for construction purposes and the construction and maintenance of a shaft and facilities for operation and maintenance purposes. The construction of railway sidings at the Old Dover Colliery site, the provision of a working site and the provision of facilities for operation and maintenance purposes. The operation and maintenance of the existing road access tunnel between the Old Folkestone Road and the Old Dover Colliery site and the existing adit from the Old Dover Colliery site. The provision of working sites and access for construction and maintenance purposes.

SECTION B

PURPOSES OF THE RAILWAY BOARD

(1) *Area*	(2) *Number of land shown on deposited plans*	(3) *Purpose for which land may be acquired or used*
London borough of Hammersmith and Fulham	2	The construction of a retaining wall and provision of access for vehicles for the purposes of maintenance.
London borough of Wandsworth	9 to 13 and 16 to 18	The provision of a working site for construction of Works Nos. 23, 23A and 23B, and means of access for vehicles for the purposes of maintenance, to Stewart's Road at the point marked E on the deposited plans, Corunna Terrace at the point so marked F, and Linford Street at the points so marked G and H.
District of Shepway— parish of Newington	25, 26 and 35	The construction of railway sidings at Dolland's Moor.

PART II

PURPOSES FOR WHICH CERTAIN LAND MAY BE ACQUIRED OR
USED UNDER SECTION 36

(1) *Area*	(2) *Number of land shown on deposited plans*	(3) *Purpose for which land may be acquired or used*
District of Dover— parish of Capel-le-Ferne	107	The landscaping of the works and land formation.
parish of Hougham Without	2	The landscaping of the works and land formation.

PART III

SUPPLEMENTARY

Provision enabling owners and lessees to require purchase of their interests

1.—(1) If the Secretary of State makes an order under section 38(1) of this Act extending the time within which a notice to treat may be served in respect of any land the following provisions of this paragraph shall have effect as from the coming into operation of that order.

(2) If any owner or lessee of any of that land gives notice in writing to the appropriate authority that he desires his interest in any part of the land specified in the notice to be acquired by the appropriate authority, the appropriate authority shall, within the period of three months after the receipt of such notice—

(a) enter into an agreement with him for the acquisition of his interest in the land or such part thereof as may be specified in the agreement; or

(b) serve on him a notice to treat for the compulsory acquisition of his interest in the land specified in his notice, or in such part thereof as may be required by the appropriate authority; or

(c) serve on him notice in writing of their intention not to proceed with the purchase of his interest in the land specified in his notice.

(3) Where notice is given under sub-paragraph (2) above by an owner or lessee in respect of his interest in land specified in the notice, then—

    (a) if the appropriate authority—

        (i) fails to comply with the requirements of that sub-paragraph; or

        (ii) withdraws a notice to treat served in compliance with paragraph (b) of that sub-paragraph; or

        (iii) serves on him notice in compliance with paragraph (c) of that sub-paragraph; the power of the appropriate authority to serve a notice to treat in respect of that person's interest in the land so specified shall cease; or

    (b) if the owner's or lessee's interest in part only of that land is acquired in pursuance of an agreement under paragraph (a) of that sub-paragraph, or a notice to treat served by virtue of paragraph (b) of that sub-paragraph, the power of the appropriate authority to serve a notice to treat in respect of that person's interest in the remainder of that land shall cease.

(4) In this paragraph "lessee" means a person who holds an interest under a lease for a period of which not less than 21 years is unexpired at the date of the giving of any notice by that person under sub-paragraph (2) above.

(5) This paragraph shall not apply to any subsoil or under-surface of land required only for the construction of a work at a level more than 9 metres below the surface of the land or, in the case of a work below a watercourse or other area of water, the surface of the adjoining ground which is at all times above water level.

Acquisition of subsoil or rights in land

2.—(1) The appropriate authority may, under section 8 or 36 of this Act—

    (a) acquire only so much as may be required for the purposes mentioned in those sections of the subsoil and under-surface of; or

    (b) create and acquire such easements or rights as may be required for those purposes in;

any land to which that section relates, not being land specified in the table in sub-paragraph (3) below, without being required to acquire any greater interest.

(2) The provisions of Part I of the Compulsory Purchase Act 1965, as applied by section 37 of this Act, and the enactments relating to compensation for the compulsory purchase of land, shall with the necessary modifications (including the adaptations of that Part of that Act specified in paragraph 8 below) have effect in relation to the creation and acquisition of such easements or rights as if it were the purchase of land within the meaning of that Part of that Act, and any notice to treat in respect of any such easement or right shall describe its nature.

(3) Notwithstanding the provisions of section 8 of this Act, the Secretary of State shall not acquire compulsorily under that section any interest in any part of any land specified in the following table, except the subsoil or under-surface or easements or rights in the subsoil and under-surface as provided by sub-paragraph (1) above—

THE TABLE

(1) Area	(2) Number of land shown on deposited plans
District of Shepway—	
town of Folkestone	59 to 88
parish of Hawkinge	1 to 17
District of Dover—	
parish of Capel-le-Ferne	1 to 98
parish of Hougham Without	1 and 3 to 51
town of Dover	1 to 6, 19, 20, 21 and 32

(4) For the purposes of sub-paragraph (3) above the subsoil and under-surface of any land specified in the table in that sub-paragraph shall not include any subsoil or under-surface which is within 9 metres of the level of the surface of the ground or, in the case of a building on the land, the level of the surface of the ground adjoining the building or, in the case of a watercourse or other area of water, the level of the surface of the adjoining ground which is at all times above water level.

Acquisition of part only of certain properties

3.—(1) Where a copy of this paragraph is endorsed on, or annexed to, a notice to treat served under Part I of the Compulsory Purchase Act 1965, as applied by section 37 of this Act, the following provisions of this paragraph shall apply to the land subject to the notice instead of section 8(1) of that Act.

(2) Where the land subject to the notice is part only of a house, building or factory, or part only of land consisting of a house together with any park or garden belonging thereto, then, if the person on whom the notice is served, within the period of two months beginning with the day on which the notice is served on him, serves on the appropriate authority a counter-notice objecting to the sale of the part and stating that he is willing and able to sell the whole (in this paragraph below referred to as "the land subject to the counter-notice"), the question whether he shall be required to sell the part shall, unless the appropriate authority agrees to take the land subject to the counter-notice, be referred to the Lands Tribunal.

(3) If the said person does not serve such a counter-notice as aforesaid within the period of two months beginning with the day on which the notice to treat is served on him, or if on such a reference to the Lands Tribunal the tribunal determines that the part subject to the notice to treat can be taken without material detriment to the remainder of the land subject to the counter-notice or, in the case of part of any land consisting of a house together with a park or garden belonging thereto, without material detriment to the remainder of the land subject to the counter-notice and without seriously affecting the amenity and convenience of the house, the said person shall be required to sell the part.

(4) If, on such a reference to the Lands Tribunal, the tribunal determines that part only of the land subject to the notice to treat can be taken without material detriment to the remainder of the land subject to the counter-notice, or, as the case may be, without material detriment to the remainder of the land subject to the counter-notice and without seriously affecting the amenity and convenience of the house, the notice to treat shall be deemed to be a notice to treat for that part.

(5) If, on such a reference to the Lands Tribunal, the tribunal determines that the land subject to the notice to treat cannot be taken without material detriment to the remainder of the land subject to the counter-notice but that the material detriment is confined to a part of the land subject to the counter-notice, the notice to treat shall be deemed to be a notice to treat for the land to which the material detriment is confined in addition to the land already subject to the notice, whether or not the additional land is land which the appropriate authority is authorised to acquire compulsorily under section 8 or 36 of this Act.

(6) If the appropriate authority agrees to take the land subject to the counter-notice, or if the Lands Tribunal determines that—

(a) none of the land subject to the notice to treat can be taken without material detriment to the remainder of the land subject to the counter-notice or (as the case may be) without material detriment to the remainder of the land subject to the counter-notice and without seriously affecting the amenity and convenience of the house; and

(b) the material detriment is not confined to a part of the land subject to the counter-notice;

the notice to treat shall be deemed to be a notice to treat for the land subject to the counter-notice, whether or not the whole of that land is land which the appropriate authority is authorised to acquire compulsorily under section 8 or 36 of this Act.

(7) In any case where, by virtue of a determination by the Lands Tribunal under sub-paragraph (4), (5) or (6) above, a notice to treat is deemed to be a notice to treat for part of the land specified in the notice or for more land than is specified in the notice, the appropriate authority may, within six weeks after the tribunal makes its determination, withdraw the notice to treat and, if this is done, shall pay to the person on whom the notice to treat was served compensation for any loss or expense occasioned to him by the giving and withdrawal of the notice, to be determined in default of agreement by the tribunal.

(8) For the purposes of sub-paragraph (7) above, the determination shall not be deemed to be made so long as—

(a) the time for requiring the tribunal to state a case with respect to the determination has not expired;

(b) any proceedings on points raised by a case so stated have not been concluded; or

(c) any proceedings on appeal from any decision on points raised by a case so stated have not been concluded.

(9) Where a person is required under this paragraph to sell part only of a house, building or factory, or of land consisting of a house together with any park or garden belonging thereto, compensation shall be payable to him for any loss sustained by him due to the severance of that part in addition to the value of his interest therein.

Minerals

4.—(1) Subject to sub-paragraph (2) below, Parts II and III of Schedule 2 to the Acquisition of Land Act 1981 (exception of minerals from compulsory purchase and regulation of the working of mines or minerals underlying an authorised undertaking) shall have effect in relation to lands within the limits of land to be acquired as if those lands were comprised in a compulsory purchase order providing for the incorporation with that order of those Parts of that Schedule.

(2) In the application of that Schedule to lands which the Secretary of State is authorised to acquire under section 36 of this Act, the prescribed distance in relation to any seam of minerals lying under land adjoining works forming part of the A20 improvement works shall be such a lateral distance from those works on every side as is equal at every point along those works to one half of the depth of the seam below the natural surface of the ground at that point or forty yards, whichever is the greater.

Extinguishment of private rights of way

5.—(1) All private rights of way over any land which may be acquired compulsorily under this Act shall be extinguished on the acquisition of the land, whether compulsorily or by agreement, or on the entry on the land in pursuance of section 11(1) of the Compulsory Purchase Act 1965, as applied by section 37 of this Act, whichever is sooner.

(2) Any person who suffers loss by the extinguishment of any right under this paragraph shall be entitled to compensation.

Provisions as to compensation

6.—(1) In determining a question with respect to compensation claimed in consequence of the compulsory acquisition of land under this Act, the Lands Tribunal shall not take into account—

(a) any interest in land; or

(b) any enhancement of the value of any interest in land by reason of any building erected, works executed or improvement or alteration made, whether on the land acquired or on any other land with which the claimant is (or was at the time of the erection, execution or making of the building, works, improvement or alteration) directly or indirectly concerned;

if the tribunal are satisfied that the creation of the interest, or (as the case may be) the erection of the building, the execution of the works or the making of the improvement or alteration was not reasonably necessary and was undertaken with a view to obtaining compensation or increased compensation.

(2) Any dispute as to a person's entitlement to compensation under any provision of this paragraph, or as to the amount of the compensation, shall be determined under and in accordance with Part I of the Land Compensation Act 1961.

Correction of deposited plans

7.—(1) If the deposited plans or the book of reference to those plans are inaccurate in their description of any land, or in their statement or description of the ownership or occupation of any land, the appropriate authority, after giving not less than ten days' notice to the owner, lessee and occupier of the land in question, may apply to two justices having jurisdiction in the place where the land is situated for the correction thereof.

(2) If on any such application it appears to the justices that the misstatement or wrong description arose from mistake or inadvertence, the justices shall certify accordingly and shall in their certificate state in what respect any matter is misstated or wrongly described.

(3) The certificate shall be deposited in the office of the Clerk of the Parliaments and a copy thereof in the Private Bill Office of the House of Commons and with the proper officer

of each County Council or London Borough Council in whose area is situated the land to which the certificate relates, and thereupon the deposited plans or the book of reference thereto (as the case may be) shall be deemed to be corrected according to the certificate, and it shall be lawful for the appropriate authority, in accordance with the certificate, to proceed under this Act as if the deposited plans or the book of reference had always been in the corrected form.

(4) A person with whom a copy of the certificate is deposited under this paragraph shall keep it with the documents to which it relates.

Adaptation of Part I of the Compulsory Purchase Act 1965

8. In relation to the compulsory creation and acquisition of an easement or right in land (in any enactment amended by this paragraph referred to as "a right over land") by virtue of paragraph 2 above, Part I of the Compulsory Purchase Act 1965 applies with the following modifications—

(a) For section 7 (which relates to compensation) there shall be substituted the following—

"7.—(1) In assessing the compensation to be paid by the acquiring authority under this Act regard shall be had not only to the extent (if any) to which the value of the land over which the right is purchased is depreciated by the purchase but also to the damage, if any, to be sustained by the owner of the land by reason of injurious affection of other land of the owner by the exercise of the right.

(2) The modifications subject to which subsection (1) of section 44 of the Land Compensation Act 1973 is to have effect, as applied by subsection (2) of that section to compensation for injurious affection under this section, are that for the words 'land is acquired or taken' there shall be substituted 'a right over land is purchased' and for the words 'acquired or taken from him' there shall be substituted 'over which the right is exercisable'.";

(b) For section 8(1) (which relates to cases in which a vendor cannot be required to sell part only of a building or garden) there shall be substituted the following—

"8.—(1) Where in consequence of the service on a person under section 5 of this Act of a notice to treat in respect of a right over land consisting of a house, building or factory or of a park or garden belonging to a house (hereafter in this subsection referred to as 'the relevant land')—

(a) a question of disputed compensation in respect of the purchase of the right would apart from this section fall to be determined by the Lands Tribunal (hereafter in this section referred to as 'the Tribunal'); and

(b) before the Tribunal has determined that question the person satisfies the Tribunal that he has an interest which he is able and willing to sell in the whole of the relevant land; and—

(i) where that land consists of a house, building or factory, that it cannot be made subject to the right without material detriment to it; or

(ii) where that land consists of such a park or garden, that it cannot be made subject to the right without seriously affecting the amenity or convenience of the house to which it belongs;

the compulsory purchase order shall, in relation to that person, cease to authorise the purchase of the right and be deemed to authorise the purchase of that person's interest in the whole of the relevant land including, where the land consists of such a park or garden, the house to which it belongs, and the notice shall be deemed to have been served in respect of that interest on such a date as the Tribunal directs.

(1A) Any question as to the extent of the land in which the compulsory purchase order is deemed to authorise the purchase of an interest by virtue of subsection (1) above shall be determined by the Tribunal.

(1B) Where in consequence of a determination of the Tribunal that it is satisfied as mentioned in subsection (1) above the compulsory purchase order is deemed by virtue of that subsection to authorise the purchase of an interest in land, the acquiring authority may, at any time within the period of six weeks beginning with the date of the determination, withdraw the notice to treat in consequence of which the determination was made; but nothing in this subsection prejudices any other power of the acquiring authority to withdraw the notice.

(1C) The modifications subject to which subsection (1) of section 58 of the Land Compensation Act 1973 is to have effect, as applied by subsection (2) of that section to the duty of the Tribunal in determining whether it is satisfied as mentioned in subsection (1) above, are that at the beginning of paragraphs (a) and (b) there shall be inserted the words 'a right over', for the word 'severance' there shall be substituted 'right on the whole of the house, building or factory or of the house and the park or garden' and for the words 'part proposed' and 'part is' there shall be substituted respectively 'rights proposed' and 'right is'.";

(c) The following provisions stating the effect of a deed poll executed in various circumstances where there is no conveyance by persons with interests in the land, namely—

    section 9(4) (failure of owners to convey);

    paragraph 10(3) of Schedule 1 (owners under incapacity);

    paragraph 2(3) of Schedule 2 (absent and untraced owners); and

    paragraphs 2(3) and 7(2) of Schedule 4 (common land);

shall be so modified as to secure that, as against persons with interests in the land which are expressed to be overridden by the deed, the right which is to be purchased compulsorily is vested absolutely in the acquiring authority;

(d) Section 11 (powers of entry) shall be so modified as to secure that, as from the date on which the acquiring authority have served notice to treat in respect of any right, they have power, exercisable in the like circumstances and subject to the like conditions, to enter for the purpose of exercising that right (which shall be deemed for this purpose to have been created on the date of service of the notice); and sections 12 (penalty for unauthorised entry) and 13 (entry on sheriff's warrant in the event of obstruction) shall be modified correspondingly;

(e) Section 20 (compensation for short term tenants) shall apply with the modifications necessary to secure that persons with such interests as are mentioned in that section are compensated in a manner corresponding to that in which they would be compensated on a compulsory acquisition of the interests but taking into account only the extent (if any) of such interference with such interests as is actually caused, or likely to be caused, by the exercise of the right in question;

(f) Section 22 (protection of acquiring authority's possession of land where by inadvertence an interest in the land has not been purchased) shall be so modified as to enable the acquiring authority, in circumstances corresponding to those referred to in that section, to continue to be entitled to exercise the right in question, subject to compliance with that section as represents compensation; and

(g) Paragraph 2(1) of Schedule 1 (power of owners to sell to the acquiring authority) shall be modified to empower all persons who are seised or possessed of or entitled to any of the land over which a right is required by the acquiring authority to grant that right to the authority and to enter all necessary agreements for the purpose.

Section 43   SCHEDULE 6

APPLICATION OF RAILWAY REGULATION ENACTMENTS

Tunnel system railway to be a "railway" under the Regulation of Railways Act 1871

1. In section 2 of the Regulation of Railways Act 1871 (interpretation of terms), in the definition of "railway" there shall be inserted after the word "Parliament", where it first occurs, the words "the Channel Tunnel Act 1987".

Disapplication of enactments in the case of the Concessionaires and through service operators

2. Sections 4 (duty of railway company to make returns of overtime worked by certain employees) and 6 (passenger tickets issued by railway company in the United Kingdom to be printed with the fare) of the Regulation of Railways Act 1889 and the Railway Companies (Accounts and Returns) Act 1911 shall not apply to the Concessionaires or to any through service operator.

Extension of enactments in relation to through service operators

3. In the following enactments, the expressions "company" and "railway company" shall be treated as including (in so far as they do not already do so) any through service operator—

    section 16 of the Railway Regulation Act 1840 (obstruction of officers of railway company);

    sections 22 (provision and improper use of means of communication) and 25 (arbitration of compensation for railway accidents) of the Regulation of Railways Act 1868;

sections 3 and 4 (inspection of railways) and 6 and 7 (returns of and inquiries into railway accidents) of the Regulation of Railways Act 1871;

sections 1(1)(c) (power of Secretary of State to make orders in relation to the provision and use of brakes on passenger trains) and 5 (penalty for avoiding payment of fare) of the Regulation of Railways Act 1889; and

section 43 of the Road and Rail Traffic Act 1933 (which modifies section 6 of the Act of 1871).

Modification of enactments applying to Concessionaires and through service operators

4.—(1) In their application to—

(a) the Concessionaires or any through service operator;

(b) any railway of the Concessionaires or any station or other works or premises connected therewith; or

(c) any train of the Concessionaires or any through service operator;

the enactments specified in column (1) of the following table (which create the offences broadly described in column (2) of the table) shall each have effect as if the maximum fine which may be imposed on summary conviction of any offence specified in the enactment were, instead of that specified in column (3) of the table, a fine not exceeding the level specified in column (4) of the table.

THE TABLE

(1) Enactment	(2) Description of offence	(3) *Maximum fine otherwise applicable (level on standard scale)*	(4) *Maximum fine (level on standard scale)*
Section 16 of the Railway Regulation Act 1840.	Obstruction of officers of railway company or trespass upon railway.	Level 1	Level 3
Section 17 of the Railway Regulation Act 1842.	Misconduct of persons employed on railways.	Level 1	Level 3
Section 22 of the Regulation of Railways Act 1868.	Provision and improper use of means of communication.	Level 1	Level 2
The Regulation of Railways Act 1889— section 5(1).	Failure to produce ticket, to pay fare or to give name and address.	Level 1	Level 2
section 5(3).	Travel with intent to avoid payment of fare.	Level 2	Level 3

(2) In such application—

(a) section 16 of the Act of 1840 shall have effect as if the court had, as an alternative to imposing a fine, the power to award imprisonment for a period not exceeding one month; and

(b) section 17 of the Act of 1842 shall have effect as if, instead of the power to award imprisonment for a period not exceeding two months, the court had power to award imprisonment for a period not exceeding three months; and

(c) section 5(2) of the Act of 1889 (power to arrest passenger who fails to produce ticket and refuses to give his name and address) shall have effect as if after the word "refuses" there were inserted the words "or fails".

Extension of sections 55 and 56 of the British Transport Commission Act 1949 in relation to the tunnel system railway

5. Sections 55 (penalty for trespass on railways, etc.) and 56 (penalty for stone throwing, etc., on railways) of the British Transport Commission Act 1949 shall apply in relation to any railway, siding, tunnel, railway embankment, cutting or similar work comprised in the tunnel system as they apply in relation to any railway, siding, tunnel, railway embankment, cutting or similar work belonging to the Railways Board.

Interpretation

6. In this Schedule "through service operator" means a person, other than the Concessionaires or the Railways Board, operating services for the carriage of passengers or goods by rail by way of the tunnel system.

Section 45   SCHEDULE 7

PROTECTIVE PROVISIONS

PART I

HIGHWAYS AND TRAFFIC

1.—(1) The following provisions of this Part of this Schedule shall, unless otherwise agreed in writing between the appropriate authority and the highway authority concerned, have effect for the protection of the highway authorities referred to in this Part.

(2) In this Part of this Schedule—

"appropriate authority" does not include the Secretary of State or the County Council;

"highway" means a highway maintainable by the highway authority;

"highway authority" means—

(a) in the case of a trunk road, the Secretary of State;
and

(b) in the case of other highways, the local highway authority.

2. Wherever in this Part of this Schedule provision is made with respect to the approval or consent of the highway authority, that approval or consent shall be in writing and subject to such reasonable terms and conditions as the highway authority may require, but shall not be unreasonably withheld.

3. Before carrying out any work for the construction or maintenance of any part of the works authorised by this Act which will involve interference with a highway, or the traffic in any highway, or before temporarily stopping up any highway, the appropriate authority shall consult the highway authority—

(a) as to the time when the work shall be commenced, and as to the extent of the surface of the highway which it may be reasonably necessary for the appropriate authority to occupy, or the nature of the interference which may be caused to traffic in the carrying out of the work, or as to the time during which, and the extent to which, the highway shall be stopped up (as the case may be); and

(b) as to the conditions under which the work shall be carried out or the highway shall be stopped up (as the case may be);

so as to reduce so far as possible inconvenience to the public and to ensure the safety of the public.

4.—(1) Any such work involving interference with a highway shall not be carried out, the surface of the highway shall not be occupied, the highway shall not be stopped up by the appropriate authority and the interference with traffic shall not be caused except at such time, to such extent and in accordance with such conditions as may be submitted to and approved by the highway authority.

(2) If, within 28 days after the submission to them of proposals for compliance with this paragraph, the highway authority have not approved them or disapproved them, they shall be deemed to have approved the proposals as submitted.

5. The highway authority may require that the works authorised by this Act, so far as they involve any serious interference with the movement of traffic in any highway, shall be carried on, so far as reasonably practicable, continuously day and night and the appropriate authority shall take all such steps as may be reasonably necessary to reduce so far as possible the period of such interference.

6. It shall not be lawful for the appropriate authority in exercise of their powers under this Act to place any hoardings on any part of any highway except for such period and in such manner as shall be reasonably necessary.

7.—(1) The appropriate authority shall not, without the consent of the highway authority, make a junction between any road and a highway or an intended highway except in accordance with plans, sections and specifications submitted to and approved by the highway authority and if, within 28 days after such plans, sections and specifications have been submitted, the highway authority have not approved or disapproved them, they shall be deemed to have approved the plans, sections and specifications as submitted.

(2) For the purposes of this paragraph the plans, sections and specifications of a junction with a highway or intended highway shall include plans, sections and specifications of all

orks within the highway or (as the case may be) intended highway which are required for ιe purposes of or in connection with the junction.

8. The appropriate authority shall not, without the consent of the highway authority, onstruct any part of the works authorised by this Act under and within 8 metres of the urface of any highway except in accordance with plans and sections submitted to, and pproved by, the highway authority and if within 28 days after such plans and sections have een submitted the highway authority have not approved or disapproved them, they shall be eemed to have approved the plans and sections as submitted.

9. In the construction of any part of the said works under a highway no part thereof shall, xcept with the consent of the highway authority, be so constructed as to interfere with the rovision of proper means of drainage of the surface of the highway or be nearer than two ιetres to the surface of the highway.

10.—(1) The provisions of this paragraph have effect in relation to, and to the construction f, any new bridge, or any extension or alteration of an existing bridge, carrying any part of he works authorised by this Act over a highway or carrying a highway over any part of hose works, and any such new bridge, or (as the case may be) any bridge so extended or ltered, is in this paragraph referred to as "the bridge".

(2) Before commencing the construction of, or the carrying out of any work in connection ʋith, the bridge which involves interference with a highway, the appropriate authority shall ubmit to the highway authority for their approval plans, sections, drawings and particulars below in this paragraph referred to as "plans") relating thereto, and the bridge shall not be onstructed and the works shall not be carried out except in accordance with the plans ubmitted to, and approved by, the highway authority.

(3) If within 28 days after the plans have been submitted the highway authority have not pproved or disapproved them, they shall be deemed to have approved the plans as ubmitted.

(4) Any part of the construction of the bridge or any part of any work as aforesaid which nvolves interference with a highway shall be carried out under the supervision (if given) and o the reasonable satisfaction of the highway authority.

(5) In constructing the bridge, or in carrying out any work in connection therewith which nvolves interference with any highway, the appropriate authority shall, in such manner and ιt such time as the highway authority may reasonably require, make good all damage caused o the highway by reason or in consequence of the construction of the bridge or the carrying ut of the work.

(6) If the bridge carries any part of the works authorised by this Act over any ιighway—

(a) it shall be constructed in such manner as to prevent so far as may be reasonably practicable the dripping of water from the bridge; and

(b) the highway authority may, at the cost of the appropriate authority, provide and place such lamps and apparatus as may from time to time be reasonably necessary for efficiently lighting any highway under or in the vicinity of the bridge.

11. The appropriate authority shall secure that so much of the works authorised by this Act as is constructed under any highway shall be so designed, constructed and maintained ιs to carry the appropriate loading recommended for highway bridges by the Secretary of ·tate at the time of construction of the works, and the appropriate authority shall indemnify he highway authority against, and make good to the highway authority, the expenses which he highway authority may reasonably incur in the maintenance or repair of any highway, ɔr any tunnels, sewers, drains or apparatus therein, by reason of non-compliance with the ɔrovisions of this paragraph.

12. It shall be lawful for an officer of the highway authority duly appointed for the ɔurpose, at all reasonable times, on giving to the appropriate authority such notice as may n the circumstances be reasonable, to enter upon and inspect any part of the works ιuthorised by this Act which is in or over any highway, or which may affect any highway or ιny property of the highway authority, during the carrying out of the work, and the ιppropriate authority shall give to such engineer or surveyor or officer all reasonable ʰacilities for such inspection and, if he shall be of opinion that the construction of the work s attended with danger to any highway or to any property of the highway authority on or ιnder any highway, the appropriate authority shall adopt such measures and precautions as ιnay be reasonably necessary for the purpose of preventing any damage or injury thereto.

13. The appropriate authority shall not alter, disturb or in any way interfere with any ɔroperty of the highway authority on or under any highway, or the access thereto, without the consent of the highway authority, and any alteration, diversion, replacement or reconstruction of any such property which may be necessary shall be made by the highway ιuthority or the appropriate authority as the highway authority think fit, and the expense

reasonably incurred by the highway authority in so doing shall be repaid to the highway authority by the appropriate authority.

14. The appropriate authority shall not remove any soil or material from any highway except so much as must be excavated in the carrying out of the works authorised by this Act.

15. If the highway authority, after giving to the appropriate authority not less than 2 days' notice (or, in the case of emergency, such notice as is reasonably practicable) of their intention to do so, incur any additional expense in the signposting of traffic diversions or the taking of other measures in relation thereto, or in the repair of any highway by reason of the diversion thereto of traffic from a road of a higher standard, in consequence of the construction of the works authorised by this Act, the appropriate authority shall repay to the highway authority the amount of any such expense reasonably so incurred.

16.—(1) The appropriate authority shall not, except with the consent of the highway authority, deposit any soil or materials, or stand any vehicle or plant, on or over any highway so as to obstruct or render less safe the use of the highway by any person, or except with the like consent, deposit any soil or materials on any highway outside a hoarding and, unless the consent of the highway authority is given within 28 days after request therefor, it shall be deemed to have been refused.

(2) The expense reasonably incurred by the highway authority in removing any soil or materials deposited on any highway in contravention of this paragraph shall be repaid to the highway authority by the appropriate authority.

17. The appropriate authority shall, if reasonably so required by the highway authority provide and maintain to the reasonable satisfaction of the highway authority, during such time as the appropriate authority may occupy any part of a highway for the purpose of the construction of any part of the works authorised by this Act, temporary bridges and temporary ramps for vehicular or pedestrian traffic over any part of the works or in such other position as may be necessary to prevent undue interference with the flow of traffic in the highway.

18.—(1) Where any part of any highway shall have been broken up or disturbed by the appropriate authority and not permanently stopped up or diverted they shall make good the subsoil, foundations and surface of that part of the highway to the reasonable satisfaction of the highway authority, and shall maintain the same to the reasonable satisfaction of the highway authority for such time as may be reasonably required for the permanent reinstatement of the highway.

(2) The reinstatement of that part of the highway shall in the first instance be of a temporary nature only and the permanent reinstatement thereof shall be carried out by the highway authority so soon as reasonably practicable after the completion of the temporary reinstatement, and the expense reasonably incurred by the highway authority in so doing shall be repaid to the highway authority by the appropriate authority.

19. The appropriate authority shall make compensation to the highway authority for any subsidence of, or damage to, any highway or any property of the highway authority on or under any highway which may be caused by, or in consequence of, any act or default of the appropriate authority, their contractors, servants or agents, whether such damage or subsidence shall happen during the construction of the works authorised by this Act or at any time thereafter.

20. The fact that any act or things may have been done in accordance with plans approved by the highway authority or under their supervision shall not (if it was not attributable to the act, neglect or default of the highway authority or of any person in their employ or their contractors or agents) exonerate the appropriate authority from any liability, or affect any claim for damages, under this Part of this Schedule or otherwise.

21.—(1) Except as provided in sub-paragraph (2) below, any difference arising between the appropriate authority and the highway authority under this Part of this Schedule shall be determined by the Secretary of State or, at his option, by arbitration.

(2) Where the Secretary of State is the highway authority concerned any such difference shall be determined by arbitration.

PART II

PROTECTION OF THE RAILWAYS BOARD

1.—(1) The following provisions of this Part of this Schedule shall, unless otherwise agreed in writing between the appropriate authority and the Railways Board, have effect for the protection of that board.

(2) In this Part of this Schedule—

"appropriate authority" does not include the Railways Board;

"railway property" means any railway of the Railways Board, and any works connected therewith for the maintenance or operation of which the Railways Board are responsible, and includes any land held or used by the Railways Board for the purposes of any such railway or works;

"the specified works" means so much of any of the works authorised by this Act (other than the A20 improvement works) as may be situated upon, across, under or over, or within 15 metres of, railway property or may in any way affect railway property;

"construction" includes reconstruction and for the purposes of paragraphs 8, 11 and 12 below includes maintenance and repair of the specified works;

"plans" includes sections, drawings, particulars and schedules of construction.

2. The appropriate authority shall not under the powers conferred by section 8 of this Act acquire compulsorily any railway property but may create and acquire such easements and rights as may reasonably be required for the purposes specified in that section in any such property delineated on the deposited plans.

3.—(1) The appropriate authority shall, before commencing the construction of the specified works, supply to the Railways Board such proper and sufficient plans thereof as may reasonably be required and shall not commence the specified works until plans thereof have been approved in writing by the engineer of the Railways Board or settled by arbitration.

(2) If within 28 days after such plans have been supplied to the Railways Board their engineer shall not have notified his disapproval thereof and the grounds of his disapproval, he shall be deemed to have approved the plans as submitted.

4. If within 28 days after such plans have been supplied to the Railways Board the Railways Board give notice to the appropriate authority that the Railways Board desire themselves to construct any part of the specified works forming part of Work No. 1 which, in the opinion of the engineer of the Railways Board, will or may affect the stability of railway property then, if the appropriate authority desire such part of the specified works to be constructed, the Railways Board shall construct it with all reasonable dispatch on behalf of, and to the reasonable satisfaction of, the appropriate authority in accordance with the plans approved or deemed to be approved or settled as aforesaid and under the supervision (if given) of the appropriate authority.

5. Upon signifying his approval or disapproval of the plans the engineer of the Railways Board may specify any protective works, whether temporary or permanent, which in his opinion should be carried out before the construction of the specified works to ensure the safety and stability of railway property; and such protective works as may be reasonably necessary for those purposes shall be constructed by the Railways Board with all reasonable dispatch, and the appropriate authority shall not commence the construction of the specified works until the Railways Board shall have notifed the appropriate authority that the protective works have been completed.

6. The appropriate authority shall give to the engineer of the Railways Board not less than 28 days' notice of their intention to commence the construction of any of the specified works and, except in emergency (when they shall give such notice as may be reasonably practicable), of their intention to carry out any works for the repair or maintenance of the specified works in so far as such works of repair or maintenance affect or interfere with railway property.

7.—(1) The construction of the specified works shall, when commenced, be carried out with all reasonable dispatch in accordance with the plans approved or deemed to be approved or settled as aforesaid and under the supervision (if given), and to the reasonable satisfaction, of the engineer of the Railways Board, and in such manner as to cause as little damage to railway property as may be and as little interference as may be with the conduct of traffic on the railways of the Railways Board.

(2) If any damage to railway property or any such interference shall be caused by the carrying out of the specified works, the appropriate authority shall, notwithstanding any such approval as aforesaid, make good such damage and pay to the Railways Board reasonable expenses to which they may be put and compensation for any loss which they may sustain by reason of any such damage or interference.

(3) Nothing in this paragraph shall impose any liability on the appropriate authority with respect to any damage, costs, expenses or loss attributable to the act, neglect or default of the Railways Board or their servants, contractors or agents.

8. The appropriate authority shall at all times afford reasonable facilities to the engineer of the Railways Board for access to the specified works during their construction and shall supply to him all such information as he may reasonably require with regard to the specified works or the method of construction thereof.

9. The Railways Board shall at all times afford reasonable facilities to the appropriate authority and their agents for access to any works carried out by the Railways Board under this Part of this Schedule during their construction, and shall supply to the appropriate authority such information as they may reasonably require with regard to such works or the method of construction thereof.

10.—(1) If any alteration or addition, whether permanent or temporary, to railway property shall be reasonably necessary during the construction of the specified works, or during a period of twelve months after their completion in consequence of their construction such alterations and additions may be carried out by the Railways Board.

(2) If the Railways Board give to the appropriate authority reasonable notice of their intention to carry out such alterations or additions, the appropriate authority shall pay to the Railways Board the reasonable cost thereof including, in respect of permanent alteration and additions, a capitalised sum representing any increase in the costs which may be expected to be reasonably incurred by the Railways Board in maintaining, working and when necessary, renewing any such alterations or additions.

(3) If the cost of maintaining, working or renewing railway property is reduced in consequence of any such alterations or additions, a capitalised sum representing such saving shall be set off against any sum payable by the appropriate authority to the Railways Board under this Part of this Schedule.

11. The appropriate authority shall repay to the Railways Board costs reasonably incurred by the Railways Board—

(a) in constructing any part of the specified works on behalf of the appropriate authority as provided by paragraph 4 above or in constructing any protective works under paragraph 5 above including, in respect of any permanent protective works, capitalised sum representing the costs which may be expected to be reasonably incurred by the Railways Board in maintaining and renewing such works;

(b) in respect of the employment of any inspectors, signalmen, watchmen and other persons whom it shall be reasonably necessary to appoint for inspecting, watching and lighting railway property and signalling railway traffic and for preventing, so far as may be reasonably practicable, interference, obstruction, danger or accident arising from the construction of the specified works;

(c) in respect of any special traffic working upon any existing railways of the Railways Board resulting from any speed restrictions, or any substitution or diversion of services, which may, in the opinion of the Railways Board, be required by reason of in consequence of the construction of the specified works;

(d) in respect of any additional temporary lighting of railway property in the vicinity of the specified works, being lighting made reasonably necessary by reason or in consequence of the construction of the specified works;

(e) in respect of the supervision by the engineer of the Railways Board of the construction of the specified works.

12.—(1) Subject to sub-paragraph (2) below, the appropriate authority shall be responsible for, and make good to the Railways Board, costs, charges, damages and expenses not otherwise provided for in this Part of this Schedule which may be occasioned to, or reasonably incurred by, the Railways Board—

(a) by reason of the construction of the specified works; or

(b) by reason of any act or omission of the appropriate authority, or of any person in their employ, or of their contractors or others whilst engaged upon the construction of the specified works;

and the appropriate authority shall indemnify the Railways Board from and against claims and demands arising out of, or in connection with, the construction of the specified works or any such act or omission.

(2) The fact that any act or thing may have been done in accordance with plans approved by the engineer of the Railways Board, or in accordance with any requirement made by him, or under his supervision, shall not (if it was not attributable to the act, neglect or default of the Railways Board, or of any person in their employ, or of their contractors or agents) excuse the appropriate authority from any liability under this Part of this Schedule.

(3) The Railways Board shall give to the appropriate authority reasonable notice of any claim or demand as aforesaid and no settlement or compromise thereof shall be made without the prior consent of the appropriate authority.

13. Any difference arising between the appropriate authority and the Railways Board under this Part of this Schedule shall be determined by arbitration.

PART III

PROTECTION OF NAVIGATION

1.—(1) The following provisions of this Part of this Schedule shall have effect in relation tidal works for the protection of navigation.

(2) In this Part of this Schedule—

"tidal work" means so much of the works authorised by this Act as is on the surface of lands below the level of mean high water springs;

"the Trinity House" has the meaning given in section 742 of the Merchant Shipping Act 1894.

2.—(1) A tidal work shall not be constructed, extended, enlarged, altered, renewed, placed or reconstructed except in accordance with plans and sections approved by the cretary of State and subject to any conditions and restrictions imposed by the Secretary State before the work is begun.

(2) The Secretary of State's primary concern in exercising his powers under sub-paragraph) above shall be to prevent danger to navigation; but he shall have regard, in exercising ose powers in relation to such part of the sea wall as is a tidal work, to—

(a) any factors that have been or may be taken into account by the county planning authority in deciding under paragraph 3 of Schedule 3 to this Act whether to approve plans and specifications of the sea wall;

(b) any decision of that authority with respect to the approval of any such plans and specifications; and

(c) any conditions imposed on the grant of any such approval;

ith a view to securing that his exercise of those powers is consistent so far as practicable ith any decision that has been or may be made by that authority under that paragraph.

(3) In case of contravention of this paragraph or of any condition or restriction imposed nder this paragraph—

(a) the Secretary of State may by notice in writing require the Concessionaires, at their own expense, to remove the tidal work or any part thereof and restore the site thereof to its former condition; and if, on the expiration of 30 days from the date when the notice is served upon the Concessionaires, they have failed to comply with the requirements of the notice the Secretary of State may execute the works specified in the notice; or

(b) if it appears to the Secretary of State urgently necessary to do so, he may himself remove the tidal work or part of it and restore the site to its former condition;

nd any expenditure incurred by the Secretary of State in so doing shall be recoverable from ie Concessionaires.

3. The Secretary of State may at any time if he deems it expedient order a survey and xamination of a tidal work, or of the site upon which it is proposed to construct the work, nd any expenditure incurred by the Secretary of State in any such survey and examination hall be recoverable from the Concessionaires.

4.—(1) The Concessionaires shall, at or near a tidal work, during the whole time of the onstruction, extension, enlargement, alteration, renewal, replacement or reconstruction hereof, exhibit every night from sunset to sunrise such lights, if any, and take such other teps for the prevention of danger to navigation as the Secretary of State shall from time to ime direct.

(2) If the Concessionaires fail to comply in any respect with a direction given under this aragraph they shall be liable on summary conviction to a fine not exceeding the statutory naximum and on conviction on indictment to a fine.

5.—(1) After the completion of a tidal work the Concessionaires shall, at the outer xtremity thereof, exhibit every night from sunset to sunrise such lights, if any, and take uch other steps for the prevention of danger to navigation as the Trinity House shall from ime to time direct.

(2) If the Concessionaires fail to comply in any respect with a direction given under this aragraph they shall be liable on summary conviction to a fine not exceeding the statutory naximum and on conviction on indictment to a fine.

6.—(1) Where a tidal work is abandoned, or suffered to fall into decay, the Secretary of tate may by notice in writing require the Concessionaires at their own expense either to epair and restore the work, or any part thereof, or to remove the work and restore the site hereof to its former condition, to such an extent and within such limits as the Secretary of tate may think proper.

(2) Where part of a work is situated on or over land above the level of mean high water prings and that part is in such condition as to interfere, or to cause reasonable apprehension hat it may interfere, with the right of navigation or other public rights over the foreshore,

the Secretary of State may include that part of the work, or any portion thereof, in an notice under this paragraph.

(3) If on the expiration of 30 days from the date on which a notice under this paragraph is served upon the Concessionaires they have failed to comply with the requirements of th notice, the Secretary of State may execute the works specified in the notice and an expenditure incurred by him in so doing shall be recoverable from the Concessionaires.

7.—(1) In case of injury to or destruction or decay of a tidal work, or any part thereof the Concessionaires shall forthwith notify the Trinity House and shall lay down such buoys exhibit such lights and take such other steps for preventing danger to navigation as th Trinity House shall from time to time direct.

(2) If the Concessionaires fail to notify the Trinity House as required by this paragraph o to comply in any respect with a direction given under this paragraph, they shall be liable o summary conviction to a fine not exceeding the statutory maximum and on conviction o indictment to a fine.

8.—(1) In proceedings for an offence under paragraph 4, 5 or 7 above it shall be a defenc for the Concessionaires to prove that they took all reasonable precautions and exercised al due diligence to avoid the commission of the offence.

(2) If in any case the defence provided by sub-paragraph (1) above involves the allegatio that the commission of the offence was due to the act or default of another person, th Concessionaires shall not, without leave of the court, be entitled to rely on that defenc unless, within a period of seven days before the hearing, they have served on the prosecuto a notice in writing giving such information identifying or assisting in the identification of tha other person as was then in their possession.

PART IV

PROTECTION OF DOVER HARBOUR BOARD

1. The following provisions of this Part of this Schedule shall, unless otherwise agreed ir writing between the Concessionaires and the Dover Harbour Board (in this Part referred to as "the Harbour Board"), have effect for the protection of the Harbour Board.

2. In this Part of this Schedule—

    "plans" includes sections, drawings and specifications;

    "the Harbour Board's shore" means that part of the shore above mean low water springs which is vested in the Harbour Board.

    "the protected beach" means that part of the Harbour Board's shore which lies within 100 metres westward of the Admiralty Pier;

    "the specified works" means Work No. 7 and any other works authorised by this Act which are on the surface of lands below the level of mean high water springs and within one international nautical mile from the seaward limits of Dover Harbour.

3. The Concessionaires shall consult the Harbour Board as to the methods and timetable for the construction of any of the specified works or the carrying out of operations relating thereto so as to avoid so far as practicable any interference with navigation in Dover Harbour or in the approaches thereto and any damage to the Harbour Board's shore or to any works forming part of the Harbour Board's undertaking.

4.—(1) Before commencing to construct any of the specified works the Concessionaires shall submit to the Harbour Board for their reasonable approval proper and sufficient plans of that work and such work shall not be constructed otherwise than in accordance with such plans as may be reasonably approved in writing by the principal engineer of the Harbour Board and subject to such conditions as he may reasonably require so as to avoid so far as practicable any interference with navigation in Dover Harbour or in the approaches thereto and any damage to the works forming part of the Harbour Board's undertaking, or in accordance with such plans and subject to such conditions as may be determined under paragraph 10 below.

(2) In the event of the principal engineer of the Harbour Board failing to express his disapproval of any plans within one month after such plans have been delivered to the Harbour Board in pursuance of this paragraph, he shall be deemed to have approved the plans as submitted.

5.—(1) If there shall be any inconsistency between the plans of any tidal work approved under paragraph 4 above and the plans approved by the Secretary of State under paragraph 2 of Part III of this Schedule, or between any conditions required under paragraph 4 above and any conditions or restrictions imposed by the Secretary of State under the said paragraph 2, the inconsistency shall be referred to the Secretary of State by the Concessionaires after not less than 14 days' notice to the Harbour Board, and the work shall be constructed in accordance with the plans, and subject to the conditions and restrictions, then determined by the Secretary of State.

(2) A determination by the Secretary of State under sub-paragraph (1) above shall be made in accordance with the said paragraph 2 and shall have effect as if it were an approval of plans and sections, subject to conditions and restrictions (if any) imposed, under that paragraph.

6. The Concessionaires shall compensate the Harbour Board for any damage to any work forming part of the Harbour Board's undertaking or to Dover Harbour or its approaches caused by or arising in consequence of the construction or maintenance of any of the specified works or of the failure or want of repair thereof or in consequence of any act or omission of the Concessionaires, their contractors, agents, workmen or servants whilst engaged upon a specified work and shall indemnify the Harbour Board from all claims, demands or expenses which may be made on or against them or which they may have to pay by reason or in consequence of any such damage:

Provided that the Harbour Board shall give to the Concessionaires reasonable notice of any such claim or demand as aforesaid and no settlement or compromise thereof shall be made without the agreement of the Concessionaires.

7. If at any time any damage or diminution shall occur to the protected beach and such damage or diminution shall be caused wholly or substantially by the construction of the specified works, the Concessionaires shall make good or cause to be made good such damage or diminution to the reasonable satisfaction of the principal engineer of the Harbour Board.

8. The fact that any act or thing may have been done in accordance with plans approved by the principal engineer of the Harbour Board, or in accordance with a requirement made by him, or under his supervision, shall not (if it was not attributable to the act, neglect or default of the Harbour Board, or of any person in their employ, or of their contractors or agents) excuse the Concessionaires from any liability under this Part of this Schedule.

9. Except in connection with the arrangements for the deposit of spoil approved under paragraph 5 of Schedule 3 to this Act and without prejudice to any other obligations and liabilities of the Concessionaires under this Part of this Schedule, the Concessionaires shall not deposit spoil anywhere below the level of mean high water springs within one international nautical mile of the seaward limits of Dover Harbour.

10. Any difference arising between the Concessionaires and the Harbour Board under this Part of this Schedule shall be determined by the Secretary of State or, at his option, by an arbitrator to be appointed by him, and the costs of final determination shall be in the discretion of the Secretary of State or of the arbitrator, as the case may be.

PART V

PROTECTION OF SEWERS

1.—(1) The following provisions of this Part of this Schedule shall, unless otherwise agreed in writing between the appropriate authority and the sewerage authority concerned, have effect for the protection of the sewerage authorities.

(2) In this Part of this Schedule—

"appropriate authority" does not include the Secretary of State in respect of the A20 improvement works;

"sewer" includes any main used for the conveyance of sewage sludge or sewage effluent and any pipe, subway or storm overflow or other apparatus vested in, or maintained by, the sewerage authority for the purposes of sewerage or sewage disposal, but does not include any such apparatus in respect of which the relations between the appropriate authority and the sewerage authority are regulated by the provisions of Part II of the Public Utilities Street Works Act 1950;

"the sewerage authority" means the Southern Water Authority and the Thames Water Authority, or either of them, in their capacity as authorities responsible for sewerage and sewage disposal, and includes a local authority as a relevant authority for the purposes of section 15 of the Water Act 1973;

"specified work" means so much of any of the works authorised by this Act (other than the A20 improvement works) as may be situated over, or within 15 metres measured in any direction of, or impose any load directly upon, any sewer.

2.—(1) Before commencing the construction or renewal of any specified work the appropriate authority shall submit to the sewerage authority plans thereof as described in paragraph 3 below (in this Part of this Schedule referred to as "the said plans") and shall not commence that work until the sewerage authority have signified their approval of the said plans.

(2) The sewerage authority's approval shall not be unreasonably withheld and, if within 56 days after the submission of the said plans the sewerage authority have not approved or disapproved them, they shall be deemed to have approved them.

3.—(1) The plans to be submitted to the sewerage authority shall be detailed plans drawings, sections and specifications describing the position and manner in which, and the level at which, any specified work is proposed to be carried out and the position of all sewers of the sewerage authority within the limits of deviation for that work, and shall comprise detailed drawings of every alteration which the appropriate authority propose to make in any such sewers.

(2) For the purpose of the preparation of the said plans the sewerage authority shall, on application by the appropriate authority, permit them to have access to plans in the possession of the sewerage authority and to any of their sewers.

4. The appropriate authority shall give to the sewerage authority not less than 28 days notice of their intention to commence the construction or renewal of a specified work and, except in case of emergency (when they shall give such notice as may be reasonably practicable), of their intention to carry out works of repair or maintenance of a specified work.

5. In carrying out any specified work the appropriate authority shall comply with all reasonable requirements of the sewerage authority of which due notice is given to the appropriate authority and shall provide new, altered or substituted sewers, or works for the protection of any sewers of the sewerage authority, in such manner as the sewerage authority shall reasonably require for the protection of, and for preventing injury or impediment to, any such sewer by reason of the specified work.

6. All works for the provision of new, altered or substituted sewers or protective works in pursuance of paragraph 5 above shall, where so required by the sewerage authority, be carried out by or under the supervision (if given) of an officer of the sewerage authority duly appointed for the purpose, and all reasonable costs, charges and expenses to which the sewerage authority may be put by reason of such works, whether in the course of the carrying out of the works, or in the preparation or examination of plans or designs or in such supervision as aforesaid, or otherwise, shall be paid to the sewerage authority by the appropriate authority.

7. Nothing in paragraphs 5 and 6 above shall require the appropriate authority to provide new or substituted works of better type, of greater dimensions or of greater capacity than those of the works in place of which they are provided except in so far as the placing of works of such type, dimensions or capacity has been specified as necessary in a specification of works settled under paragraph 2 above.

8. When works for the provision of any such new, altered or substituted sewers or protective works have been completed in accordance with paragraph 5 above they shall be maintainable by the sewerage authority.

9. The sewerage authority may require such modifications to be made in the said plans as may be reasonably necessary to secure their sewerage system against interference or risk of damage and to provide convenient means of access to their sewers.

10.—(1) Subject to sub-paragraphs (2) and (3) below, if by reason or in consequence of the construction or failure of any of the works authorised by this Act, or any subsidence resulting from any of those works, any damage to any sewer (other than a sewer intended for removal for the purposes of those works) of the sewerage authority shall be caused, the appropriate authority shall pay the cost reasonably incurred by the sewerage authority in making good such damage and shall—

    (a) make reasonable compensation to the sewerage authority for loss sustained by them; and

    (b) indemnify the sewerage authority against claims, demands, proceedings, costs, damages and expenses which may be made or taken against, or recovered from or incurred by, the sewerage authority;

by reason or in consequence of any such damage.

(2) Nothing in sub-paragraph (1) above shall impose any liability on the appropriate authority with respect to any damage to the extent that it is attributable to the act, neglect or default of the sewerage authority, their officers, servants, contractors or agents.

(3) The sewerage authority shall give to the appropriate authority reasonable notice of any claim or demand as aforesaid and no settlement or compromise shall be made without the prior consent of the appropriate authority.

11. If, in the carrying out of any specified work, or any work for the provision of new, altered or substituted sewers or protective works in pursuance of paragraph 5 above, the appropriate authority damage or, without the consent of the sewerage authority, alter or in any way interfere with any of their existing sewers the appropriate authority shall—

(a) pay to the sewerage authority any additional expense to which they may be put in the maintenance, management or renewal of any new, altered or substituted sewer which may be necessary in consequence of the construction of the specified work; and

(b) subject to paragraph 13 below, give to the sewerage authority uninterrupted access to any such new, altered or substituted sewer and such facilities as may be reasonably required for the inspection, maintenance, alteration and repair thereof.

12. An officer of the sewerage authority duly appointed for the purpose may, subject to paragraph 13 below, enter upon and inspect any specified work or any other works constructed under this Part of this Schedule.

13. Access to any sewer under paragraph 11(b) above or entry upon any specified work under paragraph 12 above shall be subject to supervision and control by the appropriate authority but shall be afforded by the appropriate authority as soon as possible and at any reasonable time at which it is required.

14. The approval by the sewerage authority of any plans, drawings, sections or specifications or the supervision by them of any work under this Part of this Schedule shall not exonerate the appropriate authority from any liability or affect any claim for damages by the sewerage authority.

15. As soon as reasonably practicable after the completion of the carrying out of a specified work, the appropriate authority shall deliver to the sewerage authority a plan and section showing the position and level of that work as constructed and all new, altered or substituted works provided in pursuance of paragraph 5 above.

16. Any difference arising between the appropriate authority and the sewerage authority under this Part of this Schedule shall be determined by arbitration.

PART VI

PROTECTION OF CERTAIN STATUTORY UNDERTAKERS

1.—(1) The following provisions of this Part of this Schedule shall, unless otherwise agreed in writing between the appropriate authority and the undertakers concerned, have effect for the protection of the undertakers.

(2) In this Part of this Schedule—

"appropriate authority" does not include the Secretary of State in respect of the A20 improvement works;

"the undertakers" means any person authorised to carry on an undertaking for the supply of electricity, gas or water within any area within which land is to be acquired or works are to be constructed under this Act and—

(a) in relation to water undertakers, includes a water authority in their capacity as an authority to carry on an undertaking for the supply of water within their area; and

(b) in relation to any apparatus, means the undertakers to whom the apparatus belongs or by whom the apparatus is maintained;

"apparatus" means—

(a) in the case of electricity undertakers, electric lines and works (as respectively defined in the Electric Lighting Act 1882) belonging to, or maintained by, those undertakers; or

(b) in the case of gas or water undertakers, mains, pipes or other apparatus belonging to, or maintained by, those undertakers for the purposes of gas or water supply;

(not being in any case apparatus in respect of which the relations between the appropriate authority and the undertakers are regulated by the provisions of Part II of the Public Utilities Street Works Act 1950), and includes any structure for the lodging therein of apparatus;

"alternative apparatus" means alternative apparatus adequate to enable the undertakers to fulfil their statutory functions in a manner not less efficient than previously;

"in" in a context referring to apparatus includes under, over, across, along or upon.

2. Notwithstanding anything in this Act or shown on the deposited plans, the appropriate authority shall not acquire any apparatus under section 8 of this Act otherwise than by agreement.

3. If the appropriate authority in the exercise of the powers conferred by this Act acquire any interest in or temporarily occupy any lands in which any apparatus is placed, that apparatus shall not be removed under this Part of this Schedule, and any right of the undertakers to maintain, repair, renew or inspect that apparatus in those lands shall not be

extinguished, until any necessary alternative apparatus has been constructed and is in operation to the reasonable satisfaction of the undertakers.

4. If—

(a) the appropriate authority, for the purpose of carrying out any work authorised by this Act in, on or under any land, require the removal of any apparatus placed in that land, and give to the undertakers not less than 56 days' written notice of that requirement, together with a plan and section of the proposed work, and of the proposed position of the alternative apparatus to be provided or constructed; or

(b) in consequence of the exercise of any of the powers conferred by this Act, the undertakers reasonably require to remove any apparatus;

the appropriate authority shall afford to the undertakers the necessary facilities and rights for the construction of any necessary alternative apparatus in other land held by the appropriate authority, or in which the appropriate authority have sufficient rights or interests, and thereafter for the maintenance, repair, renewal and inspection of such apparatus:

Provided that, if the alternative apparatus or any part thereof is to be constructed elsewhere than in other land held by the appropriate authority and the appropriate authority are unable to afford such facilities and rights as aforesaid, the undertakers shall, on receipt of a written notice to that effect from the appropriate authority, forthwith use their best endeavours to obtain the necessary facilities and rights.

5. Any alternative apparatus to be constructed in land held by the appropriate authority in pursuance of paragraph 4 above shall be constructed in such manner, and in such line or situation, as may be agreed between the undertakers and the appropriate authority or, in default of agreement, determined by arbitration.

6. The undertakers shall, after the manner of construction and the line and situation of any necessary alternative apparatus have been agreed or determined as aforesaid, and after the grant to the undertakers of any such facilities and rights as are referred to in paragraph 4 above, proceed with all reasonable dispatch to construct and bring into operation the alternative apparatus and thereafter to remove any apparatus required by the appropriate authority to be removed under the provisions of this Part of this Schedule and, in default, the appropriate authority may remove the apparatus.

7.—(1) Notwithstanding anything in paragraphs 5 and 6 above, if the appropriate authority give notice in writing to the undertakers that they desire themselves to carry out any part of so much of the work necessary in connection with the construction of the alternative apparatus, or the removal of the apparatus required to be removed, as will be situate in any lands held by the appropriate authority, such work, instead of being carried out by the undertakers, shall be carried out by the appropriate authority with all reasonable dispatch under the superintendence (if given) and to the reasonable satisfaction of the undertakers.

(2) Nothing in this paragraph shall authorise the appropriate authority to carry out the placing, erection, installation, bedding, packing, removal, connection or disconnection of any apparatus or to carry out any filling around the apparatus extending (where the apparatus is laid in a trench) within 300 millimetres above the apparatus.

8.—(1) Where, in accordance with the provisions of this Part of this Schedule, the appropriate authority afford to the undertakers facilities and rights for the construction, maintenance, repair, renewal and inspection on land held by the appropriate authority of alternative apparatus, those facilities and rights shall be granted upon such terms and conditions as may be agreed between the appropriate authority and the undertakers or, in default of agreement, determined by arbitration.

(2) In determining such terms and conditions as aforesaid in respect of alternative apparatus to be constructed across or along any works authorised by this Act the arbitrator shall—

(a) give effect to all reasonable requirements of the appropriate authority for ensuring the safety and efficient operation of those works and for securing any subsequent alterations or adaptations of the alternative apparatus which may be required to prevent interference with any proposed works of the appropriate authority or the use of the same; and

(b) so far as it may be reasonable and practicable to do so in the circumstances of the case, give effect to the terms and conditions (if any) applicable to the apparatus for which the alternative apparatus is to be substituted.

(3) If the facilities and rights to be afforded by the appropriate authority in respect of any alternative apparatus, and the terms and conditions subject to which those facilities and rights are to be granted are, in the opinion of the arbitrator, more or less favourable on the whole to the undertakers than the facilities, rights, terms and conditions applying to the apparatus to be removed, the arbitrator shall make such provision for the payment of

compensation to or by the appropriate authority by or to the undertakers in respect thereof as shall appear to him to be reasonable having regard to all the circumstances of the case.

9.—(1) Not less than 56 days before commencing to carry out any work authorised by this Act which is near to, or will or may affect, any apparatus the removal of which has not been required by the appropriate authority under paragraph 4 above, the appropriate authority shall submit to the undertakers a plan, section and description of the work to be carried out.

(2) The work shall be carried out in accordance with the plan, section and description submitted as aforesaid and in accordance with such reasonable requirements as may be made by the undertakers for the alteration or otherwise for the protection of the apparatus, or for securing access thereto, and the undertakers shall be entitled by their officer to watch and inspect the carrying out of the work.

(3) If the undertakers, within 28 days after the submission to them of any such plan, section and description, shall, in consequence of the work proposed by the appropriate authority, reasonably require the removal of any apparatus and give written notice to the appropriate authority of that requirement, the foregoing provisions of this Part of this Schedule shall have effect as if the removal of such apparatus had been required by the appropriate authority under paragraph 4 above.

(4) Nothing in sub-paragraphs (1) to (3) above shall preclude the appropriate authority from submitting at any time, or from time to time, but in no case less than 28 days before commencing to carry out the work, a new plan, section and description thereof instead of the plan, section and description previously submitted, and thereupon the provisions of those sub-paragraphs shall apply to, and in respect of, that new plan, section and description.

(5) The appropriate authority shall not be required to comply with sub-paragraphs (1) to (3) above in a case of emergency but in such a case they shall give notice to the undertakers so soon as reasonably practicable and a plan, section and description of the works so soon as reasonably practicable thereafter, and shall otherwise comply with those sub-paragraphs so far as reasonably practicable in the circumstances.

10. If in consequence of the exercise of the powers of this Act the access to any apparatus is materially obstructed the appropriate authority shall, so far as reasonably practicable, provide alternative means of access to such apparatus.

11. Where, in consequence of this Act, any part of any highway in which any apparatus is situate ceases to be part of a highway, the undertakers may exercise the same rights of access to such apparatus as they enjoyed immediately before the passing of this Act, but nothing in this paragraph shall prejudice or affect any right of the appropriate authority or of the undertakers to require removal of that apparatus under this Part of this Schedule or the power of the appropriate authority to carry out works in accordance with paragraph 9 above.

12.—(1) Subject to sub-paragraph (2) below, the appropriate authority shall repay to the undertakers the reasonable expenses incurred by the undertakers in, or in connection with—

(a) the removal and relaying or replacing, alteration or protection of any apparatus or the provision and construction of any new apparatus under any of the provisions of this Part of this Schedule;

(b) the cutting off of any apparatus from any other apparatus; and

(c) any other work or thing rendered reasonably necessary in consequence of the exercise by the appropriate authority of any of the powers of this Act.

(2) Section 23(3) and (4) of the Public Utilities Street Works Act 1950 (limitations on undertakers' right to payments) shall, so far as applicable, apply to any payment to be made by the appropriate authority under sub-paragraph (1) above as if the works or operations mentioned in that sub-paragraph were such undertakers' works as are referred to in the said subsection (3), and as if in that subsection for the words "specified as so necessary in a specification of the works settled under Part I of the Fourth Schedule to this Act or agreed so to be by the promoting authority" there were substituted the words "agreed or determined by arbitration under Part VI of Schedule 7 of the Channel Tunnel Act 1987".

13.—(1) Subject to sub-paragraphs (2) and (3) below, if by reason or in consequence of the construction of any of the works authorised by this Act, or any subsidence resulting from any of those works, any damage to any apparatus (other than apparatus the repair of which is not reasonably necessary in view of its intended removal for the purposes of those works) or property of the undertakers, or any interruption in the supply of electricity, gas or water (as the case may be) by the undertakers or, in the case of the Central Electricity Generating Board, by or to that board, shall be caused, the appropriate authority shall bear and pay the cost reasonably incurred by the undertakers in making good such damage or restoring the supply and shall—

(a) make reasonable compensation to the undertakers for loss sustained by them; and

(b) indemnify the undertakers against claims, demands, proceedings, costs, damages and expenses which may be made or taken against, or recovered from, or incurred by, the undertakers;

by reason or in consequence of any such damage or interruption.

(2) Nothing in sub-paragraph (1) above shall impose any liability on the appropriate authority with respect to any damage or interruption to the extent that such damage or interruption is attributable to the act, neglect or default of the undertakers, their officers, servants, contractors or agents.

(3) The undertakers shall give to the appropriate authority reasonable notice of any claim or demand as aforesaid and no settlement or compromise thereof shall be made without the prior consent of the appropriate authority.

14. The appropriate authority shall, so far as is reasonably practicable, so exercise their powers under paragraph 15 of Schedule 2 above as not to obstruct or render less convenient the access to any apparatus.

15. Notwithstanding the temporary stopping up or diversion of any highway under paragraph 22 of Schedule 2 above, the undertakers shall be at liberty at all times to execute and do all such works and things in, upon or under any such highway as may be reasonably necessary to enable them to inspect, repair, maintain, renew, remove or use any apparatus which at the time of the stopping up or diversion was in that highway.

16. Nothing in this Part of this Schedule shall prejudice or affect the provisions of any enactment or agreement regulating the relations between the appropriate authority and the undertakers in respect of any apparatus in land held by the appropriate authority at the commencement of this Act.

17.—(1) Any difference arising between the appropriate authority and the undertakers under this Part of this Schedule shall be determined by arbitration.

(2) In determining any such difference the arbitrator may, if he thinks fit, require the appropriate authority to carry out any temporary or other works so as to avoid, so far as may be reasonably possible, interference with the use of any apparatus.

PART VII

PROTECTION OF LAND DRAINAGE

1.—(1) The following provisions of this Part of this Schedule shall, unless otherwise agreed in writing between the appropriate authority and the drainage authority concerned, have effect for the further protection of the drainage authority.

(2) In this Part of this Schedule—

"appropriate authority" does not include the Secretary of State in respect of the A20 improvement works;

"drainage authority" means the Southern Water Authority or, within the area of the River Stour (Kent) Internal Drainage Board, that board except in relation to a drainage work forming part of a main river as defined in the Land Drainage Act 1976;

"drainage work" means any watercourse as defined in that Act and any structure or appliance under the control of the drainage authority constructed or used for defence against water (including sea water);

"plans" includes sections, drawings and specifications;

"specified work" means so much of any work authorised by this Act as will affect any drainage work in the drainage authority's area or the flow of water in, to or from any such drainage work.

2.—(1) Not less than 56 days before beginning to construct any specified work, the appropriate authority shall submit to the drainage authority plans of the work and the work shall not be constructed except in accordance with plans approved by the drainage authority or settled by arbitration and in accordance with any reasonable requirements made by the drainage authority for the protection of any drainage work and for the prevention of flooding.

(2) The requirements which the drainage authority may make under sub-paragraph (1) above include conditions requiring the construction of such protective works by, and at the expense of, the appropriate authority during the construction of the specified work as are reasonably necessary to safeguard a drainage work against damage or to secure that the efficiency of a drainage work for land drainage purposes is not impaired.

(3) If within a period of 28 days after the submission of any plans under sub-paragraph (1) above the drainage authority do not inform the appropriate authority in writing that they disapprove of those plans, stating the grounds of their disapproval, they shall be treated for the purposes of this paragraph as having approved them.

3. Any specified work, and all protective works required by the drainage authority under paragraph 2 above, shall be constructed to the reasonable satisfaction of the drainage authority and the drainage authority shall be entitled by their officer to watch and inspect the construction of such works.

4. If by reason of the construction of any specified work the efficiency of any drainage work for land drainage purposes is impaired or that work is otherwise damaged, such damage shall be made good by the appropriate authority to the reasonable satisfaction of the drainage authority and, if the appropriate authority fail to do so, the drainage authority may make good the same and recover from the appropriate authority the expense reasonably incurred by them in so doing.

5.—(1) The appropriate authority shall indemnify the drainage authority from all claims, demands, proceedings, costs, damages and expenses which may be made or taken against, or recovered from or incurred by, the drainage authority by reason or in consequence of—

(a) any damage to any drainage work so as to impair its efficiency for the purposes of land drainage; or

(b) any raising of the water table in lands adjoining the works authorised by this Act or any sewers, drains or watercourses; or

(c) any flooding or increased flooding of any such lands;

which may be caused by or result from the construction of any work authorised by this Act or any act or omission of the appropriate authority, their contractors, agents, workmen or servants whilst engaged upon the work.

(2) The drainage authority shall give to the appropriate authority reasonable notice of any such claim or demand and no settlement or compromise thereof shall be made without the agreement of the appropriate authority.

6. The fact that any work or thing has been executed or done in accordance with a plan approved or deemed to be approved by the drainage authority or to their satisfaction or in accordance with any directions or award of an arbitrator shall not relieve the appropriate authority from any liability under the provisions of this Part of this Schedule.

7. Any difference arising between the appropriate authority and the drainage authority under this Part of this Schedule shall be determined by arbitration.

PART VIII

FURTHER PROTECTION OF SOUTHERN WATER AUTHORITY

1. The following provisions of this Part of this Schedule shall, unless otherwise agreed in writing between the Concessionaires and the Southern Water Authority (in this Part referred to as "the Authority"), have effect for the further protection of the Authority.

2. If within six months from the passing of this Act the Authority notify the Concessionaires that they have decided to proceed with the construction of a public sewer and other works for the improvement of drainage sufficient to provide for the disposal of surface water from the terminal area at Cheriton, Folkestone and that it is their intention to complete the works within the period of three years thereafter, the Concessionaires shall not, so long as the Authority proceed with the construction of those works in accordance with that intention, construct the drainage lagoon (Work No. 16) and, on the completion of those works, the powers of this Act for the construction of the lagoon shall cease to have effect.

3. Any right of the Concessionaires under section 34 of the Public Health Act 1936 to drain surface water from the terminal area to any public sewer other than the public sewer mentioned in paragraph 2 above shall not be exercisable except with the written consent of the drainage authority.

4.—(1) Not less than 56 days before beginning to construct the drainage lagoon or other drainage works for the terminal area the Concessionaires shall submit to the Authority a description of the terminal area together with plans and full particulars of the drainage lagoon or such other drainage works or, as the case may be, both the lagoon and such other drainage works as they may propose for or in connection with the discharge of surface water.

(2) The said works shall not be constructed except in accordance with a specification and plans approved by the Authority or settled by arbitration and in accordance with any reasonable requirements made by the Authority for the protection from pollution of any watercourse or underground strata.

(3) The requirements which the Authority may make under sub-paragraph (2) above include the construction of such works by and at the expense of the Concessionaires as are reasonably necessary for the interception, treatment and disposal of any poisonous, noxious or polluting matter contained in the run-off from the terminal area.

(4) If within a period of 28 days after the submission of the specification and any plans under sub-paragraph (1) above the Authority do not inform the Concessionaires in writing that they disapprove of those plans, stating the grounds of their disapproval, they shall be treated for the purposes of this paragraph as having approved them.

5. The drainage lagoon and other works constructed by the Concessionaires for or in connection with the discharge of surface water from the terminal area shall be constructed, maintained and operated by the Concessionaires to the reasonable satisfaction of the Authority and the Authority shall be entitled by their officer to watch and inspect the same.

6. Not less than six months before commencing the construction of Works Nos. 3 and 4 and any underground ancillary works associated with those works, the Concessionaires shall, subject to any necessary consents, construct such number of observation boreholes in such positions and equipped with such monitoring equipment as the Authority may reasonably require for the purpose of monitoring the effect of any of those works on groundwater.

7. Except as otherwise agreed in writing by the Authority, the Concessionaires shall not construct buildings on, or raise the level of the surface of the ground within, so much of the site of the inland clearance depot as is within the area designated by the Authority as the 100 year flood plain of the river East Stour without providing equivalent compensatory flood storage capacity elsewhere.

8. Except as provided in paragraph 3 above, nothing in this Part of this Schedule shall prejudice or affect the provisions of any other enactment in their application to the Concessionaires and the Authority.

9. Any difference arising between the Concessionaires and the Authority under this Part of this Schedule shall be determined by arbitration.

Part IX

Further Protection of the Folkestone and District Water Company

1. The following provisions of this Part of this Schedule shall, unless otherwise agreed in writing between the Concessionaires and the Folkestone and District Water Company (in this Part referred to as "the Company"), have effect for the further protection of the Company.

2. Part VI of this Schedule shall have effect as if references therein to apparatus of the Company included the existing drain and telecommunication line serving the Company's house at Cherry Garden.

3. No part of the access road known as Waterworks Lane in the district of Shepway (town of Folkestone) shall be stopped up under paragraph 16 of Schedule 2 to this Act until Work No. 14 has been completed and is open for use by the Company.

4.—(1) Where the Concessionaires propose to construct, as part or for the purpose of Work No. 3 or 4, any underground work within a radius of three kilometres of any of the Company's existing sources of supply, they shall take steps—

    (a) to prevent or restrict the flow of water into that work from the stratum through which the work is to be constructed; and

    (b) to prevent pollution of water in that stratum from the work;

and, not less than three months before beginning to construct that work, shall submit to the Company a description of the work and of the steps which they propose to take for the purposes mentioned in paragraphs (a) and (b) above.

(2) Any underground work mentioned in sub-paragraph (1) above shall not be constructed except in accordance with the descriptions submitted to, and either approved by the Company or settled by arbitration, and in accordance with any reasonable requirements made by the Company for the protection of the water which they are authorised to abstract from the source of supply in question or which as been so abstracted by them.

(3) If within the period of two months from the submission of any description of an underground work under sub-paragraph (1) above the Company do not inform the Concessionaires in writing that they disapprove of the underground work stating the grounds of their disapproval they shall be treated for the purposes of this paragraph as having approved of it.

(4) If it appears to the Company that—

    (a) by reason of the construction by the Concessionaires of an underground work (whether a work such as is mentioned in sub-paragraph (1) above or not) there has been or will be a material reduction in the yield of any of the Company's existing sources of supply; or

    (b) by reason of anything done or omitted by the Concessionaires, their servants or agents in relation to an underground work, either in the course of constructing it or otherwise, the water in the stratum through which the work is being or has been constructed has or will become polluted;

the Company may by notice in writing require the Concessionaires—

    (i) to take such measures as are specified in the notice for the purpose of preventing or mitigating the reduction in the yield of their sources or for preventing or abating the pollution (as the case may be); or

    (ii) if no measures are capable of being required for this purpose, to cease the construction of the underground work for such time as is specified in the notice.

(5) On the receipt of notice under sub-paragraph (4)(a) above the Concessionaires shall forthwith cease such construction for such period as may be agreed in writing between the Company and the Concessionaires or in default of agreement for such period as may be determined by arbitration.

(6) On the receipt of notice under sub-paragraph (4)(b) above the Concessionaires shall take the measures therein specified subject only to such modifications (if any) as may be agreed in writing between the Company and the Concessionaires.

(7) Paragraph 13 of Part VI of this Schedule shall apply to any pollution of or reduction in the yield of water from any of the Company's existing sources of supply which is within a radius of three kilometres from any undergound work mentioned in sub-paragraph (1) above as it applies in relation to any damage to property of the Company, and any approval given in relation to that work under this paragraph shall not exonerate the Concessionaires from any liability to the Company under the said paragraph 13 as applied by this sub-paragraph.

5. The Company shall be entitled by their officers or agents to watch and inspect the carrying out of any work authorised by this Act which is within the limits within which the Company are for the time being authorised to supply water.

6. Any difference arising between the Concessionaires and the Company under this Part of this Schedule shall, except as otherwise provided in this Part of this Schedule, be determined by arbitration.

PART X

PROTECTION OF TELECOMMUNICATIONS OPERATORS

1.—(1) The following provisions of this Part of this Schedule shall, unless otherwise agreed in writing between the appropriate authority and a telecommunications operator, have effect for the protection of that operator.

(2) In this Part of this Schedule "telecommunications operator" means the operator of a telecommunications code system and "telecommunication apparatus", "telecommunications code system" and "telecommunication system" have the meanings as in Schedule 4 to the Telecommunications Act 1984.

2.—(1) Subject to sub-paragraph (2) below, any electrical works or equipment constructed, erected, laid, maintained, worked or used under this Act shall be so constructed, erected or laid and so maintained, worked and used, and Works Nos. 3, 4 and 5 ("the railway") shall be so worked, that any electricity conveyed by, or used in, or in connection with, any such works or equipment, and the working of the railway, does not cause avoidable interference (whether by induction or otherwise) with any telecommunication apparatus kept installed for the purposes of a telecommunications code system or the service provided by such a system.

(2) Sub-paragraph (1) above does not apply to any telecommunication apparatus kept or installed for the purposes of a telecommunication system and installed in any part of the railway.

3.—(1) Where in pursuance of paragraph 16 of Schedule 2 to this Act the appropriate authority stop up and discontinue the whole or any part of any highway the following provisions of this paragraph shall have effect in relation to so much of any telecommunication apparatus as is in the land which by reason of the stopping up ceases to be a highway or part thereof (in this paragraph referred to as "the affected apparatus").

(2) The rights of the telecommunications operator of the system for the purposes of which the apparatus is used to remove the affected apparatus shall be exercisable notwithstanding the stopping up, but those rights shall not be exercisable as respects the whole or any part of the affected apparatus after the expiration of a period of 28 days from the date of the service of the notice referred to in sub-paragraph (6) below unless, before the expiration of that period, the operator has given notice to the appropriate authority of its intention to remove the affected apparatus, or that part of it, as the case may be.

(3) The operator of the system for the purposes of which the apparatus is used may, by notice in that behalf to the appropriate authority, abandon the affected apparatus, or any part of it, and shall be deemed, as respects the affected apparatus, or any part of it, to have abandoned it at the expiration of the said period of 28 days unless, before the expiration of that period, the operator has removed it or served notice of intention to remove it.

(4) The operator of the system for the purposes of which the apparatus is used shall be entitled to recover from the appropriate authority the expense of providing, in substitution for the affected apparatus and any apparatus connected with it which is rendered useless in consequence of the removal or abandonment of the affected apparatus, telecommunication apparatus in such other place as the operator may reasonably require.

(5) Where under sub-paragraph (3) above the operator of the system for the purposes of which the apparatus is used has abandoned the whole or any part of the affected apparatus, it shall vest in the appropriate authority and shall be deemed with its abandonment to cease to be kept installed for the purposes of a telecommunications code system.

(6) So soon as is practicable after the whole or any part of a highway has been stopped up under paragraph 16 of Schedule 2 to this Act the appropriate authority shall serve notice of the stopping up on any telecommunications operator which has notified the appropriate authority of its interest in the highway.

4. The powers conferred by paragraph 15 of Schedule 2 to this Act shall, so far as reasonably practicable, be so exercised as not to obstruct or render less convenient the access to any telecommunication apparatus kept installed for the purposes of a telecommunications code system.

5. The exercise of the powers conferred by paragraph 22 of Schedule 2 to this Act in relation to a highway shall not affect the rights of the operator of any telecommunications code system, for the purposes of which the apparatus is used, to maintain, inspect, repair, renew or remove telecommunication apparatus in the highway or to open or break up that highway for any of those purposes.

6.—(1) Subject to sub-paragraphs (2) and (3) below, if, by reason or in consequence of the construction of any of the works authorised by this Act or any subsidence resulting from any of those works, any damage to any telecommunication apparatus kept installed for the purposes of a telecommunications code system (other than apparatus the repair of which is not reasonably necessary in view of its intended removal), or any interruption in the service provided by that telecommunications system, shall be caused, the appropriate authority shall bear and pay the cost reasonably incurred by the telecommunications operator of that system in making good such damage or restoring that service and shall—

(a) make reasonable compensation to the operator for loss sustained by it; and

(b) indemnify the operator against claims, demands, proceedings, costs, damages and expenses which may be made, or taken against, or recovered from, or incurred by, the operator;

by reason or in consequence of any such damage or interruption.

(2) Nothing in sub-paragraph (1) above shall impose any liability on the appropriate authority with respect to any damage or interruption affecting any telecommunications code system to the extent that such damage or interruption is attributable to the act, neglect or default of the operator of that system, its officers, servants, contractors or agents.

(3) The operator shall give to the appropriate authority reasonable notice of any claim or demand as aforesaid and no settlement or compromise thereof shall be made without the prior consent of the appropriate authority.

7. Any difference arising between the appropriate authority and any telecommunications operator under this Part of this Schedule shall be determined by arbitration.

CONSOLIDATED FUND (No. 2) ACT 1987

(1987 c. 54)

An Act to apply a sum out of the Consolidated Fund to the service of the year ending on 31st March 1988.   [17th November 1987]

Issue out of the Consolidated Fund for the year ending 31st March 1988

1. The Treasury may issue out of the Consolidated Fund of the United Kingdom and apply towards making good the supply granted to Her Majesty for the service of the year ending on 31st March 1988 the sum of £1,000.

Short title

2. This Act may be cited as the Consolidated Fund (No. 2) Act 1987.

CONSOLIDATED FUND (No. 3) ACT 1987

(1987 c. 55)

An Act to apply certain sums out of the Consolidated Fund to the service
of the years ending on 31st March 1988 and 1989.

[10th December 1987]

Issue out of the Consolidated Fund for the year ending 31st March 1988

1. The Treasury may issue out of the Consolidated Fund of the United
Kingdom and apply towards making good the supply granted to Her
Majesty for the service of the year ending on 31st March 1988 the sum of
£1,196,459,000.

Issue out of the Consolidated Fund for the year ending 31st March 1989

2. The Treasury may issue out of the Consolidated Fund of the United
Kingdom and apply towards making good the supply granted to Her
Majesty for the service of the year ending on 31st March 1989 the sum of
£47,440,004,000.

Short title

3. This Act may be cited as the Consolidated Fund (No. 3) Act 1987.

SCOTTISH DEVELOPMENT AGENCY ACT 1987

(1987 c. 56)

An Act to make provision with respect to the limit on sums borrowed by, or paid by the Secretary of State to, the Scottish Development Agency and its subsidiaries, on sums paid by the Treasury in pursuance of guarantee of loans to the Agency and on loans guaranteed by the Agency or its subsidiaries   [17th December 1987]

Increase of financial limit

1. In section 13(3) of the Scottish Development Agency Act 1975 (which sets out the limit on the aggregate of certain amounts outstanding as regards the Scottish Development Agency), for the words "£700 million" (which were substituted by section 2(1) of the Industry Act 1981) there shall be substituted the words "£1,200 million".

Short title and extent

2.—(1) This Act may be cited as the Scottish Development Agency Act 1987.

(2) This Act extends to Scotland only.

URBAN DEVELOPMENT CORPORATIONS
(FINANCIAL LIMITS) ACT 1987

(1987 c. 57)

An Act to remove the limit on the amount of grants that may be made to urban development corporations and to provide a new limit applicable only to the amounts for the time being outstanding in respect of sums borrowed by them and sums issued by the Treasury in fulfilment of guarantees of their debts.   [17th December 1987]

Alteration of financial limits of urban development corporations

1.—(1) For paragraph 8 of Schedule 31 to the Local Government, Planning and Land Act 1980 (financial limits of urban development corporations) there shall be substituted—

"**8.**—(1) The aggregate amount of the sums mentioned in subparagraph (2) below shall not exceed £30 million or such greater sum not exceeding £100 million as the Secretary of State may by order made by statutory instrument specify.

(2) The sums are—

(a) sums borrowed by all corporations under paragraph 4 above minus repayments made in respect of those sums; and

(b) sums issued by the Treasury in fulfilment of guarantees under paragraph 5 above of debts of all corporations.

(3) No order under sub-paragraph (1) above shall have effect until approved by a resolution of the House of Commons."

(2) Section 12 of the New Towns and Urban Development Corporations Act 1985 is hereby repealed and the Urban Development Corporations (Financial Limits) Order 1983 and the Urban Development Corporations (Financial Limits) Order 1987 are hereby revoked.

Short title, commencement and extent

2.—(1) This Act may be cited as the Urban Development Corporations (Financial Limits) Act 1987.

(2) This Act shall come into force at the end of the period of two months beginning with the day on which it is passed.

(3) This Act does not extend to Northern Ireland.

CURRENT LAW
STATUTE CITATOR 1987

This is the third part of the Current Law Statute Citator 1987 and is up to date to December 31, 1987.

It comprises in a single table:
  (i) Statutes passed between January 1 and December 31, 1987;
  (ii) Statutes affected during this period by Statutory Instrument;
  (iii) Statutes judicially considered during this period;
  (iv) Statutes repealed and amended during this period.

(S.) Amendments relating to Scotland only.

ACTS OF THE PARLIAMENT OF SCOTLAND

CAP.
6. Leases Act 1449.
Bells Exrs. v. *Inland Revenue*, 1987 S.L.T. 625.
45. Diligence Act 1503.
repealed: 1987, c.18, sch. 8.
13. Registration Act 1579.
repealed: 1987, c.18, sch. 8.
45. Hornings Act 1579.
repealed: 1987, c.18, sch. 8.
26. Convention of Burghs Act 1581.
repealed: 1987, c.18, sch. 8.
15. Execution of Decrees Act 1584.
repealed: 1987, c.18, sch. 8.
30. Officers of Arms Act 1587.
repealed: 1987, c.18, sch. 8.
29. Lyon King of Arms Act 1592.
ss. (3)(5), repealed in pt.: 1987, c.18, sch. 8.
34. Hornings Act 1593.
repealed: 1987, c.18, sch. 8.
22. Hornings Act 1600.
repealed: 1987, c.18, sch. 8.

CAP.
13. Convention of Burghs Act 1607.
repealed: 1987, c.18, sch. 8.
20. Hornings Act 1621.
repealed: 1987, c.18, sch. 8.
218. Poinding Act 1661.
repealed: 1987, c.18, sch. 8.
5. Poinding Act 1669.
repealed: 1987, c.18, sch. 8.
95. Lyon King of Arms Act 1669.
repealed in pt.: 1987, c.18, sch. 8.
47. Lyon King of Arms Act 1672.
repealed in pt.: 1987, c.18, sch. 8.
5. Subscription of Deeds Act 1681.
repealed in pt.: 1987, c.18, sch. 8.
86. Bills of Exchange Act 1681.
repealed in pt.: 1987, c.18, sch. 8.
21. Winter Herding Act 1686.
repealed: 1987, c.9, sch.
6. Criminal Procedure Act 1701.
see *Dunbar, Petr.* 1986 S.C.C.R. 602.

ACTS OF THE PARLIAMENTS OF ENGLAND, GREAT BRITAIN, AND THE UNITED KINGDOM

CAP.

35 Edw. 3 (1361)

1. Justices of the Peace Act 1361.
see *R.* v. *Randall* [1987] Crim.L.R. 254, C.A. and D.C.; *Hughes* v. *Holley* [1987] Crim.L.R. 253, D.C.

29 Car. 2 (1677)

3. Statute of Frauds 1677.
s. 4, see *Decouvreur* v. *Jordan, The Times*, May 25, 1987, C.A.; *Perrylease* v. *Imecar A.G.* [1987] 2 All E.R. 373, Scott J.

8 Anne (1709)

16. Circuit Courts (Scotland) Act 1709.
repealed: 1987, c.41, sch. 2.

CAP.

20 Geo. 2 (1746)

43. Heritable Jurisdictions (Scotland) Act 1746.
s. 28, repealed: 1987, c.18, sch. 8.
ss. 32–34, 36, 37, 40, repealed: 1987, c.41, sch. 2.
50. Tenures Abolition Act 1746.
ss. 12, 13, repealed (S.): 1987, c.18, sch. 8.

5 Geo. 3 (1765)

49. Bank Notes (Scotland) Act 1765.
s. 4, amended: 1987, c.18, sch. 6.
s. 6, repealed in pt.: *ibid.*, sch. 8.

12 Geo. 3 (1772)

72. Bill of Exchange (Scotland) Act 1772.
ss. 42, 43, repealed in pt.: 1987, c.18, sch. 8.

(1)

CAP.

14 Geo. 3 (1774)

48. Life Assurance Act 1774.
s. 2, see *Arif* v. *Excess Insurance Group* (O.H.), 1987 S.L.T. 473.

9 Geo. 4 (1828)

29. Circuit Courts (Scotland) Act 1828.
ss. 15, 24, repealed: 1987, c.41, sch. 2.

1 & 2 Will. 4 (1831)

37. Truck Act 1831.
s. 3, see *Topping* v. *Warne Surgical Products* [1986] 9 N.I.J.B. 14, Hutton J.
43. Turnpike Roads (Scotland) Act 1831.
see *Moncrieff* v. *Tayside Regional Council* (O.H.), 1987 S.L.T. 374.

2 & 3 Will. 4 (1832)

68. Game (Scotland) Act 1832.
s. 1, see *Ferguson* v. *Macphail*, 1987 S.C.C.R. 52.
71. Prescription Act 1832.
s. 4, see *Goldsmith* v. *Burrow Construction Co., The Times*, July 31, 1987, C.A.

3 & 4 Will. 4 (1833)

85. Government of India Act 1833.
s. 112, order 87/1268.

6 & 7 Will. 4 (1836)

76. Stamp Duties on Newspapers Act 1836.
s. 19, see *Ricci* v. *Chow, The Times*, June 19, 1987, C.A.

1 & 2 Vict. (1837–38)

114. Debtors (Scotland) Act 1838.
ss. 2–15, repealed: 1987, c.18, sch. 8.
s. 22, amended: *ibid.*, sch. 6.
ss. 23–31, 32 (in pt.), 35, schs. repealed: *ibid.*, sch. 8.
s. 26, see *Roboserve* v. *Akerman*, 1987 S.L.T.(Sh.Ct.) 137.

8 & 9 Vict. (1845)

19. Lands Clauses Consolidation (Scotland) Act 1845.
s. 116, amended: 1987, c.26, sch. 7.
109. Gaming Act 1845.
ss. 10–14, sch. 3, repealed: 1987, c.19, sch.

9 & 10 Vict. (1846)

67. Citations (Scotland) Act 1846.
s. 1, repealed in pt.: 1987, c.18, sch. 8.

10 & 11 Vict. (1847)

27. Harbours, Docks and Piers Clauses Act 1847.
s. 57, amended (S.): 1987, c.18, sch. 6.
s. 71, order 87/37.
s. 74, see *B. P. Petroleum Development* v. *Esso Petroleum Co.* (O.H.), 1987 S.L.T. 345.

CAP.

10 & 11 Vict. (1847)—cont.

89. Town Police Clauses Act 1847.
s. 37, see *Tudor* v. *Ellesmere Port an Neston B.C., The Times*, May 8, 198' D.C.

11 & 12 Vict. (1848)

79. Justiciary (Scotland) Act 1848.
s. 5, repealed: 1987, c.41, sch. 2.

17 & 18 Vict. (1854)

91. Lands Valuation (Scotland) Act 1854.
s. 42, see *Pauls Malt* v. *Grampian Assessc* [1987] R.A. 16, Lands Valuation Appea Ct.

19 & 20 Vict. (1856)

56. Exchequer Court (Scotland) Act 1856.
ss. 28 (in pt.), 29–34, 36, 42, repealed 1987, c.18, s.74, sch. 8.
schs. G–K, repealed: *ibid.*, sch. 8.
60. Mercantile Law Amendment (Scotland) Ac 1856.
s. 8, see *Scottish Metropolitan Property* v *Christie*, 1987 S.L.T.(Sh.Ct.) 18.
91. Debts Securities (Scotland) Act 1856.
s. 6 repealed in pt.: 1987, c.18, sch. 8.

24 & 25 Vict. (1861)

86. Conjugal Rights (Scotland) Amendmen Act 1861.
s. 9, see *Hogg* v. *Dick* (O.H.), 1987 S.L.T 716.
100. Offences against the Person Act 1861.
s. 16, see *R.* v. *Williams (Clarence)* (1987 84 Cr.App.R. 299, C.A.
s. 24, see *R.* v. *Hill* [1986] Crim.L.R. 815 (1986) 83 Cr.App.R. 386, H.L.; *R.* v *Nalty*, June 16, 1987, C.A.
ss. 42, 46, 47, see *R.* v. *Blyth Valley Justices, ex p. Dobson, The Times*, Nov ember 7, 1987, D.C.

30 & 31 Vict. (1867)

17. Lyon King of Arms Act 1867.
s. 2, amended (S.): 1987, c.18, sch. 6.

31 & 32 Vict. (1868)

100. Court of Session Act 1868.
s. 14, amended (S.): 1987, c.18, sch. 6.
101. Titles to Land Consolidation (Scotland) Act 1868.
s. 138, amended: 1987, c.18, sch. 6.

32 & 33 Vict. (1869)

115. Metropolitan Public Carriage Act 1869.
s. 8, order 87/999.

33 & 34 Vict. (1870)

35. Apportionment Act 1870.
s. 2, see *Parry* v. *Robinson-Wyllie* (1987) 283 E.G. 559; (1987) 54 P. & C.R. 187, Browne-Wilkinson V.-C.

CAP.

33 & 34 Vict. (1870)—cont.

52. Extradition Act 1870.
s. 2, orders 87/451, 453–456, 2041, 2046.
s. 8, see *R.* v. *Governor of Ashford Remand Centre, ex p. Postlethwaite, The Times,* April 14, 1987, D.C.
s. 9, see *R.* v. *Governor of Pentonville Prison, ex p. Syal, The Times,* May 18, 1987, D.C.
s. 10, see *Government of Belgium* v. *Postlethwaite* [1987] 3 W.L.R. 365, H.L.
ss. 10, 15, see *Lee* v. *Governor of Pentonville Prison and the Government of the U.S.A.* [1987] Crim.L.R. 635, D.C.
s. 14, see *R.* v. *Governor of Ashford Remand Centre, ex p. Postlethwaite, The Times,* July 14, 1987, H.L.
s. 15, see *R.* v. *Governor of Ashford Remand Centre, ex p. Postlethwaite, The Times,* July 14, 1987, H.L.
ss. 17, 21, orders 87/451, 453–456, 2041, 2046.

63. Wages Arrestment Limitation (Scotland) Act 1870.
repealed: 1987, c.18, sch. 8.

34 & 35 Vict. (1871)

78. Regulation of Railways Act 1871.
s. 2, amended: 1987, c.53, sch. 6.

35 & 36 Vict. (1872)

94. Licensing Act 1872.
s. 75, repealed: 1987, c.19, sch.

37 & 38 Vict. (1874)

62. Infants Relief Act 1874.
repealed: 1987, c.13, ss.1, 4.

81. Great Seal (Offices) Act 1874.
s. 9, order 87/1464.

38 & 39 Vict. (1875)

17. Explosives Act 1875.
ss. 15, 18, 21, 26, amended: regs. 87/52.
s. 31, amended: 1987, c.43, sch. 4.
ss. 34, 36, repealed in pt.: order 87/37.
s. 80, amended: 1987, c.43, sch. 4.
s. 97, order 87/37.
s. 115, repealed: *ibid.*

39 & 40 Vict. (1876)

36. Customs Consolidation Act 1876.
s. 42, see *Conegate* v. *H.M. Customs and Excise* [1987] 2 W.L.R. 39, Kennedy J.

40 & 41 Vict. (1877)

40. Writs Execution (Scotland) Act 1877.
s. 3, substituted: 1987, c.18, s.87.

41 & 42 Vict. (1878)

73. Territorial Waters Jurisdiction Act 1878.
s. 7, repealed in pt.: 1987, c.49, sch. 2.

CAP.

42 & 43 Vict. (1879)

11. Bankers' Books Evidence Act 1879.
ss. 7, 9, see *Williams* v. *Williams; Tucker* v. *Williams* [1987] 3 W.L.R. 790, C.A.
s. 9, amended: 1987, c.22, sch. 6.

43 & 44 Vict. (1880)

20. Inland Revenue Act 1880.
s. 47, repealed: 1987, c.19, sch.

34. Debtors (Scotland) Act 1880.
s. 4, amended: 1987, c.18, sch. 6; repealed in pt.: *ibid.*, sch. 8.

45 & 46 Vict. (1882)

42. Civil Imprisonment (Scotland) Act 1882.
s. 5, repealed: 1987, c.18, sch. 8.

56. Electric Lighting Act 1882.
see *R.* v. *Midlands Electricity Board, ex p. Busby; Same* v. *Same, ex p. Williamson, The Times,* October 28, 1987, Schiemann J.
s. 17, see *Mayclose* v. *Central Electricity Generating Board* (1987) 283 E.G. 192, C.A.

61. Bills of Exchange Act 1882.
ss. 26, 83, see *Claydon* v. *Bradley* [1987] 1 All E.R. 522, C.A.

46 & 47 Vict. (1883)

22. Sea Fisheries Act 1883.
s. 20, amended (S.): 1987, c.18, sch. 6.

57. Patents, Designs and Trade Marks Act 1883.
s. 29, see *Williamson* v. *Moldline* [1986] R.P.C. 556, C.A.

49 & 50 Vict. (1886)

29. Crofters Holdings (Scotland) Act 1886.
s. 29, rules 87/643.
sch., amended: 1987, c.26, sch. 23.

50 & 51 Vict. (1887)

54. British Settlement Act 1887.
order 87/1268.

71. Coroners Act 1887.
s. 3, see *R.* v. *Greater Manchester North District Coroner, ex p. Worth, The Times,* August 1, 1987, C.A.
ss. 4, 6, see *R.* v. *West London Coroners' Court, ex p. Gray; Same* v. *Same, ex p. Duncan* [1987] 2 W.L.R. 1020, D.C.
s. 6, see *Att.-Gen,* v. *Harte (J.D.)* (1987) 151 J.P.N. 750, Taylor J: *R.* v. *H.M. Coroner for South Glamorgan, ex p. B.P. Chemicals* (1987) 151 J.P.N. 808, D.C.

52 & 53 Vict. (1889)

45. Factors Act 1889.
ss. 2, 9, see *National Employers Mutual General Insurance Association* v. *Jones* [1987] 3 All E.R. 385, C.A.

53 & 54 Vict. (1890)

39. Partnership Act 1890.
s. 5, see *United Bank of Kuwait* v. *Hammoud* (1987) 137 N.L.J. 921, Stuart-Smith J.

55 & 56 Vict. (1892)

4. Betting and Loans (Infants) Act 1892.
repealed: 1987, c.13, ss.1, 4.

17. Sheriff Courts (Scotland) Extracts Act 1892.
s. 7, amended: 1987, c.18, s.87; repealed in pt.: *ibid.*, sch. 8.

43. Military Lands Act 1892.
Pt. II (ss. 14–18), see *D.P.P.* v. *Bugg* [1987] Crim.L.R. 625, D.C.
ss. 14, 17, see *Francis* v. *Cardle*, 1987 S.C.C.R. 1.

57 & 58 Vict. (1894)

30. Finance Act 1894.
s. 8, amended: order 87/892.

60. Merchant Shipping Act 1894.
s. 373, order 87/1284.
s. 669, order 87/171.
s. 693, amended (S.): 1987 c.18, sch. 6.
s. 735, orders 87/932, 933, 1267, 1827.
s. 738, orders 87/1263, 1284.

58 & 59 Vict. (1895)

14. Courts of Law Fees (Scotland) Act 1895.
s. 2, orders 87/38, 39, 771, 772.

59 & 60 Vict. (1896)

44. Truck Act 1896.
ss. 1, 2, 4, see *Bristow* v. *City Petroleum* [1987] 1 W.L.R. 529, H.L.

48. Light Railways Act 1896.
s. 3, orders 87/1443, 1984.
ss. 7, orders 87/75, 950, 1088, 1443, 1984.
s. 8, order, 87/1443.
s. 9, orders 87/75, 950, 1088, 1443, 1984.
s. 10, orders 87/950, 1088, 1443.
s. 11, orders, 87/950, 1088.
s. 12, orders 87/75, 950, 1088, 1984.
s. 24, orders 87/75, 950.

60 & 61 Vict. (1897)

38. Public Health (Scotland) Act 1897.
s. 157, see *Renfrew District Council* v. *McGourlick* (O.H.), 1987 S.L.T. 538.

61 & 62 Vict. (1898)

36. Criminal Evidence Act 1898.
s. 1, see *R.* v. *Phillips, The Times*, January 31, 1987, C.A.

40. Circuit Clerks (Scotland) Act 1898.
repealed: 1987, c.41, sch. 2.

44. Merchant Shipping (Mercantile Marine Fund) Act 1898.
s. 5, regs. 87/244, 746.

62 & 63 Vict. (1899)

19. Electric Lighting (Clauses) Act 1899.
see *R.* v. *Midlands Electricity Board, ex p Busby; Same* v. *Same, ex p. Williamson The Times*, October, 28, 1987, Schiemann J.
s. 57, regs. 87/901.

63 & 64 Vict. (1900)

14. Colonial Solicitors Act 1900.
s. 2, order 86/1986 (S.).

6 Edw. 7 (1906)

14. Alkali, etc. Works Regulation Act 1906.
s. 27, amended and repealed in pt.: regs. 87/180.

32. Dogs Act 1906.
s. 1, repealed in pt.: 1987, c.9, sch.

41. Marine Insurance Act 1906.
s. 41, see *Euro Diam* v. *Bathurst* [1987] 2 All E.R. 113, Staughton J.
s. 83, see *C. T. Bowring Reinsurance* v. *Baxter, Financial Times*, March 25, 1987, Hirst J.

55. Public Trustee Act 1906.
s. 9, order 87/403.
s. 14, rules 87/1891.

7 Edw. 7 (1907)

51. Sheriff Courts (Scotland) Act 1907.
s. 3, see *Squire Light & Sound* v. *Vidicom Systems* (Sh.Ct.), 1987 S.C.L.R. 538.
s. 27, see *Trolland* v. *Trolland*, 1987 S.L.T.(Sh.Ct.) 42.
s. 38A, added: 1987, c.26, sch. 23.
s. 40, Acts of Sederunt 87/865, 1078.
sch. 1, see *Anderson Brown & Co.* v. *Morris* 1987 S.L.T. (Sh.Ct.) 96; *Burmy* v. *White*, 1987 S.L.T.(Sh.Ct.) 120; *Strang* v. *Ross, Harper & Murphy* (Sh.Ct.), 1987 S.C.L.R. 10; *Kristiansen* v. *Kristiansen* (Sh.Ct.), 1987 S.C.L.R. 462; *C.J.M. Manufacturing* v. *Gordon* (Sh.Ct.), 1987 S.C.L.R. 534; *Kinnerslay* v. *Husband* (Sh.Ct.), 1987 S.C.L.R. 544.

55. London Cab and Stage Carriage Act 1907.
s. 1, order 87/999.

8 Edw. 7 (1908)

53. Law of Distress Amendment Act 1908.
ss. 1, 3, 6, see *Offshore Ventilation, Re* (1987) 3 BCC 486, Harman J.

9 Edw. 7 (1909)

30. Cinematograph Act 1909.
s. 1, see *British Amusement Catering Trades Association* v. *Westminster City Council* [1987] 1 W.L.R. 977, C.A.

34. Electric Lighting Act 1909.
see *R.* v. *Midlands Electricity Board, ex p. Busby; Same* v. *Same, ex p. Williamson, The Times*, October 28, 1987, Schiemann J.

AP.

10 Edw. 7 & 1 Geo. 5 (1910)

8. Finance (1909–10) Act 1910.
ss. 77–79, repealed (prosp.): 1987, c.16, s.49, sch. 16.

1 & 2 Geo. 5 (1911)

27. Protection of Animals Act 1911.
s. 1, amended: 1987, c.35, s.1.

28. Official Secrets Act 1911.
s. 2, see *R.* v. *Galvin* [1987] 3 W.L.R. 93, C.A.

46. Copyright Act 1911.
see *Butterworth & Co.* v. *Ng Sui Nam, The Financial Times*, May 1, 1987, High Court of the Republic of Singapore.
s. 15, order 87/698; regs. 87/918.

57. Maritime Conventions Act 1911.
s. 8, see *Gaz Fountain, The,* [1987] F.T.L.R. 423, Sheen J.

2 & 3 Geo. 5 (1912–13)

14. Protection of Animals (Scotland) Act 1912.
s. 1, see *Tudhope* v. *Ross*, 1986 S.C.C.R. 467.

17. Protection of Animals Act (1911) Amendment Act 1912.
repealed: 1987, c.35, s.2.

19. Light Railways Act 1912.
order 87/1443.

30. Trade Union Act 1913.
s. 3, see *Paul* v. *National Association of Local Government Officers, The Times*, June 4, 1987, Browne-Wilkinson V.-C.

3 & 4 Geo. 5 (1913)

17. Fabrics (Misdescription) Act 1913.
repealed: 1987, c.43, s.48, sch. 5.

20. Bankruptcy (Scotland) Act 1913.
s. 97, see *Dickson* v. *United Dominions Trust* (O.H.) February 7, 1986.

4 & 5 Geo. 5 (1914)

31. Housing Act 1914.
repealed (S.): 1987, c.26, sch. 24.

59. Bankruptcy Act 1914.
see *Eyre* v. *Hall* (1986) 18 H.L.R. 509, C.A.
s. 25, see *Tucker (A Bankrupt), ex p. Tucker, Re* [1987] 2 All E.R. 23, Scott J.
ss. 55, 56, see *Weddell* v. *Pearce (J. A.) and Major* [1987] 3 W.L.R. 592, Scott J.

61. Special Constables Act 1914.
s. 1, S.R. 1987 No. 380.

5 & 6 Geo. 5 (1914–15)

18. Injuries in War Compensation Act 1914 (Session 2).
s. 1, scheme 87/529.

90. Indictments Act 1915.
s. 5, see *R.* v. *Phillips, The Times*, January 31, 1987, C.A.

CAP.

9 & 10 Geo. 5 (1919)

82. Irish Land (Provision for Sailors and Soldiers) Act 1919.
s. 4, repealed: 1987, c.48, sch.

10 & 11 Geo. 5 (1920)

33. Maintenance Orders (Facilities for Enforcement) Act 1920.
s. 6, amended: 1987, c.42, sch. 2.

11 & 12 Geo. 5 (1921)

55. Railways Act 1921.
Pt. V (ss.68–74), orders 87/1088, 1443.

58. Trusts (Scotland) Act 1921.
s. 2, see *Fraser, Petr.(O.H.),* 1987 S.C.L.R. 577.

13 Geo. 5, Sess. 2 (1922)

2. Irish Free State (Consequential Provisions) Act 1922.
s. 3, repealed: 1987, c.48, sch.

13 & 14 Geo. 5 (1923)

8. Industrial Assurance Act 1923.
s. 43, regs. 87/377.

11. Special Constables Act 1923.
s. 3, amended and repealed in pt.: 1987, c.4, s.7.

15. Alderney (Transfer of Property etc.) Act 1923.
s. 1, order 87/1273.

17. Explosives Act 1923.
s. 4, repealed: order 87/37.

15 & 16 Geo. 5 (1924–25)

19. Trustee Act 1925.
s. 33, amended: 1987, c.42, sch. 2.

20. Law of Property Act 1925.
s. 3, repealed in pt.: 1987, c.15, s.8, sch.
s. 7, repealed in pt.: *ibid.*, sch.
s. 14, see *City of London Building Society* v. *Flegg* [1987] 2 W.L.R. 1266, H.L.
s. 30, see *Mott, Re, ex p. Trustee of the Property of the Bankrupt* v. *Mott and McQuitty*, March 30, 1987, Hoffmann J.
s. 62, see *Kumar* v. *Dunning* (1987) 283 E.G. 59, C.A.; *M.R.A. Engineering* v. *Trimster Co., The Times*, October 22, 1987, C.A.
s. 84, see *Stockport Metropolitan Borough Council* v. *Alwiyah Developments* (1983) 52 P. & C.R. 278, C.A.
s. 142, see *City and Metropolitan Properties* v. *Greycroft* [1987] 1 W.L.R. 1085, Mr. John Mowbray Q.C.
s. 146, see *Hill* v. *Griffin* (1987) 282 E.G. 85, C.A.
s. 189, see *Coastplace* v. *Hartley* [1987] 2 W.L.R. 1289, French J.; *Kumar* v. *Dunning* (1987) 283 E.G. 59, C.A.
s. 198, see *Rignall Developments* v. *Halil* [1987] 3 W.L.R. 394, Millett J.

STATUTE CITATOR 1987

15 & 16 Geo. 5 (1924–25)—cont.

21. Land Registration Act 1925.
ss. 49, 64, amended: 1987, c.31, sch. 4.
s. 70, see *Winkworth* v. *Baron (Edward) Development Co.* [1986] 1 W.L.R. 1512, H.L.; *City of London Building Society* v. *Flegg* [1987] 2 W.L.R. 1266, H.L.; *Regent Indemnity Co.* v. *Fishley and Fishley,* July 21, 1987; Mr. Recorder Walton; Birmingham County Ct.
s. 110, see *Naz* v. *Raja, The Times,* April 11, 1987, C.A.
s. 112, amended: 1987, c.31, s.51.
s. 112C, added: *ibid.*, s.51.
s. 120, order 87/939.
ss. 132, 133, order 87/360.

23. Administration of Estates Act 1925.
ss. 50, 52, amended: 1987, c.42, sch. 2.

49. Supreme Court of Judicature (Consolidation) Act 1925.
s. 50, see *Williamson* v. *Moldline* [1986] R.P.C. 556, C.A.

86. Criminal Justice Act 1925.
s. 13, see *R.* v. *O'Laughlin and McLaughlin* [1987] Crim.L.R. 632, Central Criminal Ct.

16 & 17 Geo. 5 (1926)

16. Execution of Diligence (Scotland) Act 1926.
ss. 1, 2, amended: 1987, c.18, sch. 6.

47. Rating (Scotland) Act 1926.
s. 14, repealed in pt.: 1987, c.47, sch. 6.

59. Coroners (Amendment) Act 1926.
s. 19, see *Att.-Gen.* v. *Harte (J.D.)* (1987) 151 J.P.N. 750, Taylor J.; *R.* v. *H.M. Coroner for South Glamorgan, ex p. B.P. Chemicals* (1987) 151 J.P.N. 808, D.C.
s. 21, see *R.* v. *Greater Manchester North District Coroner, ex p. Worth, The Times,* August 1, 1987, C.A.

17 & 18 Geo. 5 (1927)

39. Medical and Dentists Acts Amendment Act 1927.
repealed: order 87/2047.

18 & 19 Geo. 5 (1928)

21. Dogs (Amendment) Act 1928.
s. 1, repealed in pt.: 1987, c.9, sch.

32. Petroleum (Consolidation) Act 1928.
s. 4, amended: regs. 87/52.
ss. 7, 8, order 87/37.
sch. 1, repealed: regs. 87/52.

43. Agricultural Credits Act 1928.
s. 5, amended: 1987, c.22, sch. 6.

44. Rating and Valuation (Apportionment) Act 1928.
s. 3, see *Assessor for Strathclyde Region* v. *B.S.R.*, 1987 S.L.T. 250.

19 & 20 Geo. 5 (1929)

13. Agricultural Credits (Scotland) Act 1929.
s. 9, amended: 1987 c.22, sch. 6.

19 & 20 Geo. 5 (1929)—cont.

34. Infant Life (Preservation) Act 1929.
see *C.* v. *S.* [1987] 1 All E.R. 1230, C.A.

22 & 23 Geo. 5 (1931–32)

12. Destructive Imported Animals Act 1932.
s. 10, order 87/2196.

23 & 24 Geo. 5 (1932–33)

12. Children and Young Persons Act 1933.
s. 1, see *R.* v. *Beard, The Times,* May 22, 1987, C.A.
s, 53, see *R.* v. *Mckenna* (1985) 7 Cr.App.R.(S) 348, C.A.; *R.* v. *Fairhurst* [1986] 1 W.L.R. 1374, C.A.; *R.* v. *Padwick and New* (1985) 7 Cr.App.R.(S) 452, C.A.; *R.* v. *Ealand and Standing* (1986) 83 Cr.App.R. 241, C.A.

13. Foreign Judgments (Reciprocal Enforcement) Act 1933.
see *Interpool* v. *Galani* [1987] 2 All E.R. 981, C.A.
ss. 1, 3, order 87/468.
s. 8, see *Maples (Formerly Melamud)* v. *Maples; Maples (Formerly Melamud)* v. *Melamud* [1987] 3 W.L.R. 487, Latey J.

36. Administration of Justice (Miscellaneous Provisions) Act 1933.
s. 2, see *R.* v. *Liverpool Crown Court, ex p. Bray* [1987] Crim.L.R. 51, D.C.
s. 2, amended: 1987, c.38, sch. 2.

41. Administration of Justice (Scotland) Act 1933.
s. 4, Act of Sederunt 87/40.
s. 16, Acts of Sederunt 87/871, 1079, 1206.

24 & 25 Geo. 5 (1933–34)

36. Petroleum (Production) Act 1934.
ss. 1, 11, repealed in pt.: 1987, c.12, sch. 3.
s. 3, see *B.P. Petroleum Development* v. *Ryder, The Times,* June 27, 1987, Peter Gibson J.

26 Geo. 5 & 1 Edw. 8 (1935–36)

27. Petroleum (Transfer of Licences) Act 1936.
s. 1, amended: regs. 87/52.

49. Public Health Act 1936.
s. 17, see *R.* v. *Secretary of State for Wales and A.B. Hutton (Secretary to the Maes Gerddi Residents Association)* [1987] J.P.L. 711, Macpherson J.
s. 72, see *Mattison* v. *Beverley Borough Council, The Times,* February 16, 1987, C.A.; *Dear* v. *Newham London Borough Council* (1987) 19 H.L.R. 391, Wright Q.C.
ss. 92, 99, see *Birmingham District Council* v. *McMahon* (1987) 19 H.L.R. 452, D.C.
s. 222, see *Bradford Metropolitan City Council* v. *Brown* (1987) 19 H.L.R. 16, C.A.

AP.

'6 Geo. 5 & 1 Edw. 8 (1935–36)—cont.

49. Public Health Act 1936—*cont.*
s. 301, see *Cook* v. *Southend Borough Council, The Times,* April 14, 1987, Simon Brown J.

1 Edw. 8 & 1 Geo. 6 (1936–37)

5. Trunk Roads Act 1936.
see *Moncrieff* v. *Tayside Regional Council* (O.H.), 1987 S.L.T. 374.

6. Public Order Act 1936.
s. 5, see *G.* v. *Chief Superintendent of Police, Stroud, Gloucestershire* [1987] Crim.L.R. 269, D.C.

37. Children and Young Persons (Scotland) Act 1937.
s. 58A, repealed: 1987, c.41, s.59, sch. 2.

67. Factories Act 1937.
s. 47, see *Bryce* v. *Swan Hunter Group, The Times,* February 19, 1987, Phillips J.

1 & 2 Geo. 6 (1937–38)

22. Trade Marks Act 1938.
ss. 4, 8, see *Mars G.B.* v. *Cadbury* [1987] R.P.C. 387, Whitford J.
ss. 9, 10, see *Unilever's (Striped Toothpaste No. 2) Trade Marks* [1987] R.P.C. 13, Hoffmann J.; *Exxate Trade Mark* [1987] R.P.C. 597, Whitford J.; *Photo-Scan Trade Mark* [1987] R.P.C. 213, Board of Trade.
s. 11, see *Photo-Scan Trade Mark* [1987] R.P.C. 213, Board of Trade; *Lancer Trade Mark* [1987] R.P.C. 303, C.A.; *Reckitt and Colman Products* v. *Borden Inc. (No. 3)* [1987] F.S.R. 505, Walton J.
s. 12, see *Lancer Trade Mark* [1987] R.P.C. 303, C.A.
s. 13, see *Mars G.B.* v. *Cadbury* [1987] R.P.C. 387, Whitford J.
s. 26, see *Warrington Inc.'s Application, Re, The Times,* February 9, 1987, C.A.; *Concord Trade Mark* [1987] F.S.R. 209, Falconer J.; *Kodiak Trade Mark* [1987] R.P.C. 269, C.A.
ss. 28, 29, see *Dristan Trade Mark* [1986] R.P.C. 161, Supreme Court of India.
s. 39A, order 87/170.
ss. 40, 41, rules 87/751, 964.
s. 68, see *Unilever's (Striped Toothpaste No. 2) Trade Marks* [1987] R.P.C. 13, Hoffmann J.

73. Nursing Homes Registration (Scotland) Act 1938.
s. 1, repealed: 1987, c.40, s.6.
s. 1A, added: *ibid.*
s. 2A, added: *ibid.,* s.5.

2 & 3 Geo. 6 (1938–39)

21. Limitation Act 1939.
see *Arnold* v. *Central Electricity Generating Board, The Times,* October 23, 1987, H.L.

CAP.

2 & 3 Geo. 6 (1938–39)—cont.

21. Limitation Act 1939—*cont.*
ss. 4, 10, 16, see *B.P. Properties* v. *Buckler, The Times,* August 13, 1987, C.A.

69. Import, Export and Customs Powers (Defence) Act 1939.
s. 1, orders 87/215, 271, 1350, 2070.

75. Compensation (Defence) Act 1939.
s. 7, see *McDermott* v. *Department of Agriculture for Northern Ireland and H.M. Treasury* (R/11/1986).

82. Personal Injuries (Emergency Provisions) Act 1939.
ss. 1, 2, scheme 87/191.

83. Pensions (Navy, Army, Air Force and Mercantile Marine) Act 1939.
s. 4, amended: 1987, c.21, sch. 2.
s. 7, scheme 87/585.

3 & 4 Geo. 6 (1939–40)

42. Law Reform (Miscellaneous Provisions) (Scotland) Act 1940.
s. 3, see *Comex Houlder Diving* v. *Colne Fishing Co.,* House of Lords, 1987 S.L.T. 433.

7 & 8 Geo. 6 (1943–44)

31. Education Act 1944.
s. 24, see *McGoldrick* v. *Brent London Borough Council* [1987] I.R.L.R. 67, C.A.
ss. 36, 37, see *Enfield London Borough Council* v. *F.* (1987) 85 L.G.R. 526, D.C.
ss. 39, 55, see *R.* v. *Devon County Council, ex p. C., The Independent,* April 29, 1987, Mann J.
s. 80, regs. 87/1285.
s. 100, regs. 87/1126, 1138, 1182, 1314.
sch. 1, see *R.* v. *Kirklees Metropolitan Borough Council, ex p. Molloy, The Independent,* July 28, 1987, C.A.; *R.* v. *Croydon London Borough Council, ex p. Leney* (1987) 85 L.G.R. 466, D.C.

8 & 9 Geo. 6 (1944–45)

28. Law Reform (Contributory Negligence) Act 1945.
s. 1, see *Banque Keyser Ullman S.A.* v. *Skandia (U.K.) Insurance Co.* [1987] 2 W.L.R. 1300, Steyn J.; *Fitzgerald* v. *Lane* [1987] 2 All E.R. 455, C.A.

42. Water Act 1945.
s. 23, orders 87/234, 1434.
s. 32, order 87/234.
ss. 33, 50, orders 87/234, 1434.
s. 59, order 87/1434.

9 & 10 Geo. 6 (1945–46)

7. British Settlement Act 1945.
order 87/1268.

30. Trunk Roads Act 1946.
see *Moncrieff* v. *Tayside Regional Council* (O.H.), 1987 S.L.T. 374.

CAP.

9 & 10 Geo. 6 (1945–46)—cont.

36. Statutory Instruments Act 1946.

s. 1, see *R.* v. *Secretary of State for Social Services, ex p. Camden London Borough Council, The Times,* March 6, 1987, C.A.

59. Coal Industry Nationalisation Act 1946.

ss. 1–4, 27–31, 36–38, amended: 1987, c.3, sch. 1.

s. 46, see *National Coal Board* v. *National Union of Mineworkers* [1986] I.C.R. 736, Scott J.; *R.* v. *National Coal Board, ex p. The Union of Democratic Mineworkers, The Independent,* April 2, 1987, D.C.

ss. 46–54, 64, sch. 2A, amended: 1987, c.3, sch. 1.

64. Finance Act 1946.

s. 54, repealed in pt.: 1987, c.16, sch. 16.

s. 57, amended: *ibid.,* s.48.

73. Hill Farming Act 1946.

s. 20, order 87/1208.

10 & 11 Geo. 6 (1946–47)

14. Exchange Control Act 1947.

repealed: 1987, c.16, s.68, sch. 16.

39. Statistics of Trade Act 1947.

s. 5, order 87/669.

sch., amended: *ibid.*

41. Fire Services Act 1947.

s. 26, order 87/1302.

42. Acquisition of Land (Authorisation Procedure) (Scotland) Act 1947.

sch. 1, see *Martin* v. *Bearsden and Milngavie District Council* (O.H.), 1987 S.L.T. 300.

43. Local Government (Scotland) Act 1947.

ss. 237, 243B, amended: 1987, c.47, sch. 1.

ss. 247, 247A, substituted: 1987, c.18, sch. 4.

s. 248, repealed: *ibid.,* s.74, sch. 8.

s. 249, repealed: *ibid.,* sch. 8.

s. 250, amended: *ibid.,* sch. 4; repealed in pt.: *ibid.,* sch. 8.

ss. 251, 252, repealed: *ibid.*

s. 379, repealed: 1987, c.47, sch. 6.

44. Crown Proceedings Act 1947.

s. 2, see *Jones* v. *Department of the Environment, The Times,* November 27, 1987, C.A.

s. 10, see *Pearce* v. *Secretary of State for Defence, The Times,* August 5, 1987, C.A.

s. 10, repealed: 1987, c.25, s.1.

s. 46, repealed in pt. (S.): 1987, c.18, sch. 8.

54. Electricity Act 1947.

see *R.* v. *Midlands Electricity Board, ex p. Busby; Same* v. *Same, ex p. Williamson, The Times,* October 28, 1987, Schiemann J.

CAP.

11 & 12 Geo. 6 (1947–48)

10. Emergency Laws (Miscellaneous Provisions) Act 1947.

sch. 2, amended and repealed in pt.: 1987 c.4, s.7.

26. Local Government Act 1948.

s. 145, amended (S.): 1987, c.47, sch. 1.

29. National Assistance Act 1948.

s. 22, regs. 87/364(S.), 370.

s. 42, amended: 1987, c.42, sch. 2 repealed in pt.: *ibid.,* sch. 4.

s. 43, amended: *ibid.,* sch. 2.

s. 44, repealed: *ibid.,* schs. 2, 4.

s. 56, amended: *ibid.,* sch. 2.

36. House of Commons Members' Fund Act 1948.

s. 3, resolution 87/511.

38. Companies Act 1948.

ss. 223, 224, see *Furmston, Petr.,* 1987 S.L.T.(Sh.Ct.) 10.

s. 227, see *Tramway Building and Construction Co., Re* (1987) 3 BCC 443, Scott J.

s. 268, see *Rhodes (John T.), Re* [1986] P.C.C. 366, Hoffmann J.

s. 327, see *Commercial Aluminium Windows* v. *Cumbernauld Development Corporation,* 1987 S.L.T. (Sh.Ct.) 91.

s. 353, see *A.G.A. Estate Agencies, Re* [1986] P.C.C. 358, Harman J.

41. Law Reform (Personal Injuries) Act 1948.

s. 2, see *Jackman* v. *Corbett* [1987] 2 All E.R. 699, C.A.

43. Children Act 1948.

s. 2, see *R.* v. *Corby Juvenile Court, ex p. M* [1987] 1 W.L.R. 55, Waite J.

44. Merchant Shipping Act 1948.

s. 5, regs. 87/63.

63. Agricultural Holdings Act 1948.

s. 2, see *Watts* v. *Yeend* [1987] 1 W.L.R. 323, C.A.

sch. 6, see *Burton* v. *Timmis* (1987) 281 E.G. 795, C.A.

12, 13 & 14 Geo. 6 (1948–49)

5. Civil Defence Act 1948.

ss. 3, 8, regs. 87/622, 677(S.).

10. Administration of Justice (Scotland) Act 1948.

s. 2, Act of Sederunt 87/40.

25. Tenancy of Shops (Scotland) Act 1949.

s. 1, see *McMahon* v. *Associated Rentals,* 1987 S.L.T (Sh.Ct.) 94.

27. Juries Act 1949.

s. 25, amended (S.): 1987, c.41, sch. 1.

42. Lands Tribunal Act 1949.

s. 3, see *Imperial College of Science and Technology* v. *Ebdon (V.O.) and Westminster City Council* [1986] R.A. 233, C.A.

s. 3, rules 87/1139 (S.).

43. Merchant Shipping (Safety Convention) Act 1949.

s. 33, regs. 87/63, 548, 854.

12, 13 & 14 Geo. 6 (1948–49)—cont.

53. Coal Industry Act 1949.
s. 1, amended: 1987, c.3, sch. 1.

54. Wireless Telegraphy Act 1949.
s. 1, regs. 87/775, 776.
ss. 1, 14, see *Rudd* v. *Secretary of State for Trade and Industry* [1987] 1 W.L.R. 786, H.L.

62. Patents and Designs Act 1949.
s. 33, see *Fairfax (Dental) Equipment* v. *Filhol (S.J.)* [1986] R.P.C. 499, C.A.

74. Coast Protection Act 1949.
ss. 18, 49, amended: 1987, c.49, sch. 1.

75. Agricultural Holdings (Scotland) Act 1949.
s. 7, see *MacKenzie* v. *Bocardo S.A.*, 1986 S.L.C.R. 53; *McGill* v. *Bury Management*, 1986 S.L.C.R. 32; *Buccleuch Estates and Kennedy*, 1986 S.L.C.R. 1.
s. 20, see *Macrae* v. *MacDonald*, 1986 S.L.C.R. 69.
ss. 25, 26, see *Edmondton* v. *Smith*, 1986 S.L.C.R. 97.
s. 49, see *MacEwen and Law*, 1986 S.L.C.R. 109.
s. 52, see *Renwick* v. *Roger*, 1986 S.L.C.R. 126.

76. Marriage Act 1949.
ss. 3, 16, amended: 1987, c.42, sch. 2.
s. 27, order 87/50.
s. 28, amended: 1987, c.42, sch. 2.
ss. 32, 41, 51, order 87/50.
s. 78, amended: 1987, c.42, sch. 2.
sch. 2, amended: *ibid.*, s.9, sch. 2.

87. Patents Act 1949.
ss. 1, 5, see *Ishihara Sangyo Kaisha* v. *Dow Chemical Co.* [1987] F.S.R. 137, C.A.
s. 29, see *Waddington's Patent* [1986] R.P.C. 158, Patent Office.
ss. 35, 36, see *Glaverbel's Patent* [1987] F.S.R. 153, C.A.
ss. 35, 41, see *Allen & Hanbury (Salbutamol) Patent* [1987] R.P.C. 327, C.A.
s. 41, see *Syntex Corporation's Patent* [1986] R.P.C. 585, Whitford J.
ss. 69, 101, see *Ishihara Sangyo Kaisha* v. *Dow Chemical Co.* [1987] F.S.R. 137, C.A.

88. Registered Designs Act 1949.
see *Sommer Allibert (U.K.)* v. *Flair Plastics, The Times*, June 6, 1987, C.A.
s. 1, see *Gardex* v. *Sorata* [1986] R.P.C. 623, Falconer J.
ss. 1, 4, see *Interlego A.G.* v. *Folley (Alex) (Vic) Pty.* [1987] F.S.R. 283, Whitford J.
ss. 36, 39, rules 87/287.

101. Justices of the Peace Act 1949.
s. 41, repealed in pt.: 1987, c.19, sch.

14 Geo. 6 (1950)

12. Foreign Compensation Act 1950.
s. 3, order 87/663.
s. 4, instrument 87/143.
s. 7, orders 87/164, 1028.
s. 8, instrument 87/143.

14 Geo. 6 (1950)—cont.

27. Arbitration Act 1950.
s. 4, see *Cunningham-Reid* v. *Buchanan-Jardine, The Times*, June 27, 1987, C.A.; *Chatbrown* v. *Alfred McAlpine Construction (Southern)* (1987) 35 Build.L.R. 44, C.A.
s. 19A, see *Food Corp. of India* v. *Marastro Cia Naviera S.A.; Trade Fortitude, The* [1986] 3 All E.R. 500, C.A.
s. 24, see *Cunningham-Reid* v. *Buchanan-Jardine, The Times*, June 27, 1987, C.A.
s. 27, see *Mariana Islands Steamship Corp.* v. *Marimpex Mineraloel-Handelsgesellschaft mbH & Co. K.G.; Medusa, The* [1986] 2 Lloyd's Rep. 328, C.A.; *Irish Agricultural Wholesale Society* v. *Partenreederei: M.S. Eurotrader; Eurotrader, The* [1987] 1 Lloyd's Rep. 418, C.A.

28. Shops Act 1950.
see *Wychavon District Council* v. *Midland Enterprises (Special Events), The Times*, February 28, 1987, Millett J.
ss. 47, 59, see *B. & Q. (Retail)* v. *Dudley Metropolitan Borough Council, The Times*, July 15, 1987, D.C.

34. Housing (Scotland) Act 1950.
repealed: 1987, c.26, sch. 24.

37. Maintenance Orders Act 1950.
s. 3, repealed: 1987, c.42, sch. 4.
s. 16, amended: *ibid.*, sch. 2; repealed in pt.: *ibid.*, schs. 2, 4.
s. 18, amended: *ibid.*, sch. 2.

14 & 15 Geo. 6 (1950–51)

26. Salmon and Freshwater Fisheries (Protection) (Scotland) Act 1951.
ss. 1–3, 13, see *MacDougall* v. *Livingstone*, 1986 S.C.C.R. 527.
s. 19, see *Bain* v. *Wilson*, 1987 S.C.C.R. 270.

65. Reserve and Auxiliary Forces (Protection of Civil Interests) Act 1951.
s. 2, amended: 1987, c.42, sch. 2.

15 & 16 Geo. 6 & 1 Eliz. 2 (1951–52)

12. Judicial Offices (Salaries etc.) Act 1952.
s. 2, amended (S.): 1987, c.41, sch. 1.

23. Miners' Welfare Act 1952.
ss. 13, 14, 16, amended: 1987, c.3, sch. 1.

52. Prison Act 1952.
s. 4, see *R.* v. *Secretary of State for the Home Department, ex p. Dew, The Independent*, February 19, 1987, McNeill J.
ss. 25, 47, rules 87/1256.

58. Irish Sailors and Soldiers Land Trust Act 1952.
repealed: 1987, c.48, sch.

61. Prisons (Scotland) Act 1952.
s. 12, see *McAllister* v. *H.M. Advocate*, 1986 S.C.C.R. 688.

67. Visiting Forces Act 1952.
s. 8, order 87/928.

1 & 2 Eliz. 2 (1952–53)

14. Prevention of Crime Act 1953.

s. 1, see *Southwell* v. *Chadwick, The Times*, January 8, 1987, D.C.; *Campbell* v. *H.M. Advocate*, 1986 S.C.C.R. 516; *Ralston* v. *Lockhart*, 1986 S.C.C.R. 400; *Smith* v. *Wilson*, 1987 S.C.C.R. 191; *Houghton* v. *Chief Constable of Greater Manchester* (1987) 84 Cr.App.R. 320, C.A.; *Glendinning* v. *Guild*, 1987 S.C.C.R. 304.

20. Births and Deaths Registration Act 1953.

s. 9, amended: 1987, c.42, sch. 2.

s. 10, substituted: *ibid.*, s.24.

s. 10A, substituted: *ibid.*, s.25.

s. 14, amended and repealed in pt.: *ibid.*, sch. 2.

s. 14A, added: *ibid.*, s.26.

ss. 23, 29, see *Att.-Gen.* v. *Harte (J. D.)* (1987) 151 J.P.N. 750, Taylor J.

s. 34, amended: 1987, c.42, sch. 2.

25. Local Government Superannuation Act 1953.

s. 15, see *Hertfordshire County Council* v. *Retirement Lease Housing Association, The Independent*, February 19, 1987, Hoffmann J.

36. Post Office Act 1953.

s. 16, repealed in pt.: 1987, c.16, sch. 16.

2 & 3 Eliz. 2 (1953–54)

17. Royal Irish Constabulary (Widow's Pensions) Act 1954.

s. 1, regs. 87/1461.

32. Atomic Energy Authority Act 1954.

sch. 3, amended: 1987, c.4, s.7.

36. Law Reform (Limitation of Actions) Act 1954.

ss. 1, 7, see *Arnold* v. *Central Electricity Generating Board* [1987] 2 W.L.R. 245, C.A.

50. Housing (Repairs and Rents) (Scotland) Act 1954.

repealed: 1987, c.26, sch. 24.

56. Landlord and Tenant Act 1954.

s. 11, see *Dinefwr Borough Council* v. *Jones, The Times*, June 27, 1987, C.A.

s. 23, see *Nozari-Zadeh* v. *Pearl Assurance* (1987) 283 E.G. 457, C.A.

s. 24, see *Hill* v. *Griffin* (1987) 282 E.G. 85, C.A.

s. 24A, see *Follett (Charles)* v. *Cabtell Investments* (1987) 283 E.G. 195, C.A.

s. 29, see *Nurit Bar* v. *Pathwood Investments* (1987) 282 E.G. 1538; (1987) 54 P. & C.R. 178, C.A.

s. 30, see *J. W. Thornton* v. *Blacks Leisure Group* (1987) 53 P. & C.R. 223, C.A.; *Capocci* v. *Goble* (1987) 284 E.G. 230, C.A.

s. 31A, see *Cerex Jewels* v. *Peachey Property Corp.* (1986) 52 P. & C.R. 127, C.A.

s. 34, see *Oriani* v. *Dorita Properties* (1987) 282 E.G. 1001, C.A.

2 & 3 Eliz. 2 (1953–54)—cont.

56. Landlord and Tenant Act 1954—*cont.*

s. 37, see *Breeze* v. *Elden & Hyde*, December 3, 1986; Mr. Deputy Registrar Sheriff; *Norwich County Ct.; Department of the Environment* v. *Royal Insurance* (1987) 282 E.G. 208; (1987) 54 P. & C.R. 26, Falconer J.

s. 69, amended: 1987, c.3, sch. 1.

61. Pharmacy Act 1954.

ss. 2, 4, amended: order 87/2202.

s. 4A, added: *ibid.*

ss. 5, 8, amended: *ibid.*

sch. 1A, added: *ibid.*

70. Mines and Quarries Act 1954.

s. 82, see *Ewing* v. *National Coal Board* (O.H.), 1987 S.L.T. 414.

3 & 4 Eliz. 2 (1954–55)

18. Army Act 1955.

continued in force: order 87/1262.

s. 150, repealed in pt.: 1987, c.42, sch. 4.

sch. 5A, regs. 87/1999.

19. Air Force Act 1955.

continued in force: order 87/1262.

s. 103, rules 87/2000.

s. 150, repealed in pt.: 1986, c.42, sch. 4.

s. 209, rules 87/2000.

sch. 5A, regs. 87/1999.

21. Crofters (Scotland) Act 1955.

sch. 2, see *Macaskill* v. *Basil Baird & Sons*, 1987 S.L.T.(Land Ct.) 34; *Crofters Sharing in Keil Common Grazings* v. *MacColl*, 1986 S.L.C.R. 142.

sch. 5, amended: 1987, c.26, sch. 23.

4 & 5 Eliz. 2 (1955–56)

16. Food and Drugs Act 1955.

ss. 91, 108, see *Arun District Council* v. *Argyle Stores* (1987) 85 L.G.R. 59, D.C.

30. Food and Drugs (Scotland) Act 1956.

ss. 4, 7, regs. 87/26.

s. 13, regs. 87/800, 1957.

s. 26, regs. 87/26, 800.

s. 56, regs. 87/26, 800, 1957.

46. Administration of Justice Act 1956.

s. 47, see *William Batey (Exports)* v. *Kent*, 1987 S.L.T. 557.

52. Clean Air Act 1956.

s. 11, orders 87/383 (S.), 1394.

ss. 12, 31, amended (S.): 1987, c.26, sch. 23.

s. 33, order 87/1394.

s. 34, regs. 87/625, 2159.

sch. 3, amended (S.): 1987, c.26, sch. 23.

60. Valuation and Rating (Scotland) Act 1956.

s. 6, repealed in pt.: 1987, c.47, sch. 6.

s. 7, amended: *ibid.*, sch. 1; repealed in pt.: *ibid.*, sch. 6.

s. 7A, repealed in pt.: *ibid.*

s. 13, orders 87/432, 794.

s. 22, amended: 1987, c.47, sch. 1.

s. 42, order 87/794.

s. 43, amended: 1987, c.47, sch. 1; repealed in pt.: *ibid.*, sch. 6.

sch. 1, repealed: *ibid.*

4 & 5 Eliz. 2 (1955–56)—cont.

69. Sexual Offences Act 1956.
s. 13, see *R.* v. *Spight* [1986] Crim.L.R. 817; *Chief Constable of Hampshire* v. *Mace* (1987) 84 Cr.App.R. 40, D.C.

s. 14, see *R.* v. *Court* [1986] 3 W.L.R. 1029, C.A.

s. 30, see *R.* v. *Stewart* [1986] Crim.L.R. 805; (1986) 83 Cr.App.R. 327, C.A.

s. 33, see *Stevens and Stevens* v. *Christy* [1987] Crim.L.R. 503, D.C.

s. 45, see *R.* v. *Hall (John Hamilton), The Times,* July 15, 1987, C.A.

74. Copyright Act 1956.
s. 1, see *Def-Lepp Music* v. *Stuart-Brown* [1986] R.P.C. 273, Browne-Wilkinson V.-C.

s. 2, see *Williamson Music* v *Pearson Partnership* [1987] F.S.R. 97, Judge Paul Baker Q.C.

s. 3, see *Howard Clark* v. *David Allan & Co.* (O.H.), February 6, 1986.

s. 4, see *Plix Products* v. *Winstone (Frank M.) (Merchants)* [1986] F.S.R. 608, N.Z.C.A.; *Gardex* v. *Sorata* [1986] R.P.C. 623, Falconer J.

s. 5, see *Def-Lepp Music* v. *Stuart-Brown* [1986] R.P.C. 273, Browne-Wilkinson V.-C.

s. 6, see *Associated Newspapers Group* v. *News Group Newspapers* [1986] R.P.C. 515, Walton J.

s. 9, see *Howard Clark* v. *David Allan & Co.* (O.H.), February 6, 1986; *Rubycliff* v. *Plastic Engineers* [1986] R.P.C. 573, Browne-Wilkinson V.-C.

s. 10, see *Interlego A.G.* v. *Folley (Alex) (Vic) Pty.* [1987] F.S.R. 283, Whitford J.

s. 12, see *Def-Lepp Music* v. *Stuart-Brown* [1986] R.P.C. 273, Browne-Wilkinson V.-C.; *CBS/Sony Hong Kong* v. *Television Broadcasts* [1987] F.S.R. 262, Supreme Ct. Hong Kong.

s. 13, see *Musa* v. *Le Maitre* [1987] F.S.R. 212, D.C.; *CBS/Sony Hong Kong* v. *Television Broadcasts* [1987] F.S.R. 262, Supreme Ct. Hong Kong.

s. 16, see *Def-Lepp Music* v. *Stuart-Brown* [1986] R.P.C. 273, V.-C.

s. 17, see *Paterson Zochonis & Co.* v. *Merfarken Packaging* [1986] 3 All E.R. 522, C.A.

s. 18, see *Rubycliff* v. *Plastic Engineers* [1986] R.P.C. 573, Browne-Wilkinson V.-C.; *Musa* v. *Le Maitre* [1987] F.S.R. 212, D.C.

s. 19, see *Western Front* v. *Vestron Inc.* [1987] F.S.R. 66, Gibson J.

s. 21, see *C.B.S. Songs* v. *Amstrad Consumer Electronics* [1987] 1 F.T.L.R. 488, C.A.; *Musa* v. *Le Maitre* [1987] F.S.R. 212, D.C.

s. 31, orders 87/940, 1030, 1826, 1833, 2060.

s. 32, orders 87/940, 1030, 2060.

4 & 5 Eliz. 2 (1955–56)—cont.

74. Copyright Act 1956—cont.
s. 36, see *Western Front* v. *Vestron Inc.* [1987] F.S.R. 66, Gibson J.

s. 47, orders 87/940, 1030, 1826, 2060.

s. 49, see *Musa* v. *Le Maitre* [1987] F.S.R. 212, D.C.; *Williamson Music* v. *Pearson Partnership* [1987] F.S.R. 97, Judge Paul Baker Q.C.

5 & 6 Eliz. 2 (1957)

11. Homicide Act 1957.
s. 3, see *R.* v. *Doughty* (1986) 83 Cr.App.R. 319, C.A.

31. Occupier's Liability Act 1957.
s. 2, see *Ferguson* v. *Welsh* [1987] 3 All E.R. 777, H.L.

48. Electricity Act 1957.
see *R.* v. *Midlands Electricity Board, ex p. Busby; Same* v. *Same, ex p. Williamson, The Times,* October 28, 1987, Schiemann J.

s. 30, order 87/730.

53. Naval Discipline Act 1957.
continued in force: order 87/1262.

s. 101, repealed in pt.: 1987, c.42, sch. 4. sch. 4A, regs. 87/1999.

55. Affiliation Proceedings Act 1957.
repealed: 1987, c.42, s.17, sch. 4.

s. 4, see *McV* v. *B., The Times,* November 28, 1987, Wood J.

56. Housing Act 1957.
s. 9, see *R.* v. *Lambeth London Borough Council, ex p. Claythorpe Properties* (1987) 19 H.L.R. 426, C.A.

Pt. V (ss.91–134), see *Hemsted* v. *Lees and Norwich City Council* (1986) 18 H.L.R. 424, McCowan J.

s. 111, see *Wandsworth London Borough Council* v. *Winder (No. 2)* (1987) 137 New L.J. 124, Mervyn Davies J.

59. Coal-Mining (Subsidence) Act 1957.
s. 1, amended: 1987, c.3, sch. 1; 1987, c.26, sch. 23 (S.).

ss. 1, 13, see *Knibb* v. *National Coal Board* [1986] 3 W.L.R. 895, C.A.

ss. 2–13, 15, 17, amended: 1987, c.3, sch. 1.

schs. 1, 2, amended: *ibid.,* 1987, c.26, sch. 23 (S.).

6 & 7 Eliz. 2 (1957–58)

30. Land Powers (Defence) Act 1958.
s. 25, see *McDermott* v. *Department of Agriculture for Northern Ireland and H.M. Treasury* (R/11/1986).

32. Opticians Act 1958.
s. 7, order 87/1887.

s. 21, see *S.A. Magnivision NV* v. *General Optical Council, The Times,* February 19, 1987, D.C.

39. Maintenance Orders Act 1958.
s. 3, amended: 1987, c.42, sch. 2.

s. 21, repealed in pt.: *ibid.,* sch. 4.

CAP.

6 & 7 Eliz. 2 (1957–58)—cont.

40. Matrimonial Proceedings (Children) Act 1958.
s. 12, see *Hunt* v. *Hunt* (O.H.), 1987 S.L.T. 672.

42. Housing (Financial Provisions) Act 1958.
s. 43, see *Harris* v. *Wyre Forest District Council* (1987) 1 E.G.L.R. 231, Schiemann J.

44. Dramatic and Musical Performers' Protection Act 1958.
s. 2, see *Rickless* v. *United Artists Corp.* [1987] 1 All E.R. 679, C.A.

47. Agricultural Marketing Act 1958.
s. 2, sch. 1, order 87/282, 740 (S.).

51. Public Records Act 1958.
s. 2, regs. 87/444.
sch. 1, amended: 1987, c.3, sch. 1; repealed in pt.: *ibid.*, sch. 3.

53. Variation of Trusts Act 1958.
see *Practice Direction (Ch.D.) (Procedure: Applications under the Variation of Trusts Act 1958) (No. 3 of 1987)*, December 8, 1987.

60. Chequers Estate Act 1958.
s. 2, amended: order 87/2039.

62. Merchant Shipping (Liability of Shipowners and Others) Act 1958.
s. 3, see *McDermid* v. *Nash Dredging and Reclamation Co.* [1987] 3 W.L.R. 212, H.L.

64. Local Government and Miscellaneous Financial Provisions (Scotland) Act 1958.
s. 7, repealed in pt.: 1987, c.47, sch. 6.

69. Opencast Coal Act 1958.
ss. 3, 14A, amended: 1987, c.3, sch. 1.
ss. 4, 15A, regs. 87/1915.
s. 35, order 87/700.
s. 49, order 87/700; regs. 87/1915.
s. 51, amended: 1987, c.3, sch. 1; repealed in pt.: *ibid.*, sch. 3.

7 & 8 Eliz. 2 (1958–59)

5. Adoption Act 1958.
ss. 4, 5, see *A.* v. *B.*, 1987 S.L.T.(Sh.Ct.) 121.
s. 50, see *Adoption Application (Payment for Adoption)*, *Re* [1987] 3 W.L.R. 31, Latey J.

24. Building (Scotland) Act 1959.
s. 2, regs. 87/1232.
s. 3, regs. 87/1231.
ss. 20, 29, regs. 87/1232.
sch. 4, regs. 87/1231.
sch. 6, amended: 1987, c.26, sch. 23.

33. House Purchase and Housing Act 1959.
repealed (S.): 1987, c.26, sch. 24.

49. Chevening Estate Act 1959.
s. 2, amended: 1987, c.20, s.4.

53. Town and Country Planning Act 1959.
s. 26, see *R.* v. *Plymouth City Council, ex p. Freeman, The Independent,* April 22, 1987, C.A.

73. Legitimacy Act 1959.
repealed: 1987, c.42, sch. 4.

CAP.

8 & 9 Eliz. 2 (1959–60)

16. Road Traffic Act 1960.
s. 146, see *Steff* v. *Beck* [1987] R.T.R. 61, D.C.

21. Wages Arrestment Limitation (Amendment) (Scotland) Act 1960.
repealed: 1987, c.18, sch. 8.

52. Cyprus Act 1960.
sch., repealed in pt.: 1987, c.16, sch. 16.

58. Charities Act 1960.
s. 28, see *Bradshaw* v. *University College of Wales, Aberystwyth* [1987] 3 All E.R. 200, Hoffmann J.
sch. 2, order 87/1823.

65. Administration of Justice Act 1960.
s. 12, see *S. (Minors) (Wardship: Police Investigation), Re* [1987] 3 W.L.R. 847, Booth J.

9 & 10 Eliz. 2 (1960–61)

33. Land Compensation Act 1961.
s. 32, regs. 87/405, 889.

34. Factories Act 1961.
s. 4, see *Hornett* v. *Associated Octel*, November 6, 1986, Russell J., Manchester Crown Ct.
s. 14, see *T.B.A. Industrial Products* v. *Lainé* [1987] I.C.R. 75, D.C.; *Price* v. *Steinberg*, January 27, 1987, H.H. Judge Hywel Robert, Pontypridd County Ct.; *Clews* v. *B. A. Chemicals* (O.H.), July 21, 1987.
s. 28, see *Allen* v. *Avon Rubber Co.* [1986] I.C.R. 695, C.A.; *McCart* v. *Queen of Scots Knitwear*, 1987 S.L.T.(Sh.Ct.) 57.
s. 29, see *Allen* v. *Avon Rubber Co.* [1986] I.C.R. 695, C.A.; *Harkins* v. *McCluskey* (O.H.), 1987 S.L.T. 289; *Kirkpatrick* v. *Scott Lithgow* (O.H.), 1987 S.L.T. 654.
s. 63, see *Hornett* v. *Associated Octel*, November 6, 1986, Russell J., Manchester Crown Ct.
s. 72, see *Power* v. *Greater Glasgow Health Board* (O.H.), 1987 S.L.T. 567.
s. 155, see *R.* v. *A.I. Industrial Products* [1987] I.C.R. 418, C.A.

35. Police Pensions Act 1961.
s. 1, regs. 87/1698(S.)

40. Consumer Protection Act 1961.
s. 3, see *Riley* v. *Webb* [1987] Crim.L.R. 477, D.C.

62. Trustee Investments Act 1961.
see *Fraser, Petr.* (O.H.), 1987 S.C.L.R. 577.

65. Housing Act 1961.
ss. 15, 19, see *R.* v. *Hackney London Borough Council, ex p. Thrasyvoulou* (1986) 84 L.G.R. 823, C.A.; *R.* v. *Hackney London Borough Council, ex p. Evenbray, The Times,* September 15, 1987, Kennedy J.
s. 17, see *Berg* v. *Trafford Borough Council, The Times,* July 14, 1987, C.A.
s. 32, see *Murray* v. *Birmingham City Council* (1987) 283 E.G. 962, C.A.

CAP.

10 & 11 Eliz. 2 (1961–62)

9. Local Government (Financial Provisions etc.) (Scotland) Act 1962.
s. 4, amended: 1987, c.47, sch. 1.

12. Education Act 1962.
s. 1, regs. 87/1261.
s. 3, regs. 87/96, 499, 1365, 1393.
s. 4, regs. 87/96, 499, 1261, 1365, 1393.
s. 9, order 87/275.
sch. 1, regs. 87/1261.

19. West Indies Act 1962.
s. 5, orders 87/934, 1271, 1829.

28. Housing (Scotland) Act 1962.
repealed: 1987, c.26, sch. 24.

35. Shops (Airports) Act 1962.
s. 1, order 87/837 (S.), 1983.

36. Local Authorities (Historic Buildings) Act 1962.
s. 2, see *Canterbury City Council* v. *Quine* (1987) 284 E.G. 507, C.A.

46. Transport Act 1962.
s. 3, amended: 1987, c.53, s.39.
s. 56, see *R.* v. *British Railways Board, ex p. Bradford Metropolitan City Council, The Times,* December 8, 1987, C.A.
s. 67, see *Grieve* v. *Hillary,* 1987 S.C.C.R. 317.

58. Pipe-lines Act 1962.
s. 26A, added: 1987, c.12, s.26.
s. 30, amended (S.): 1987, c.26, sch. 23.
s. 47, repealed in pt.: 1987, c.12, sch. 3.
ss. 58, 59, amended: *ibid.,* s.26.
sch. 1, amended: *ibid.,* s.25; repealed in pt.: *ibid.,* s.25, sch. 3.

11 Eliz. 2 (1962)

4. Foreign Compensation Act 1962.
s. 3, order 87/164.

6. Coal Industry Act 1962.
s. 2, amended: 1987, c.3, sch. 1.

1963

2. Betting, Gaming and Lotteries Act 1963.
s. 56, repealed in pt.: 1987, c.19, sch.
sch. 1, orders 87/93 (S.), 95; amended: order 87/95.

12. Local Government (Financial Provisions) (Scotland) Act 1963.
ss. 7, 10, 15, 26, repealed in pt.: 1987, c.47, sch. 6.

25. Finance Act 1963.
s. 71, repealed in pt.: 1987, c.16, sch. 16.

31. Weights and Measures Act 1963.
s. 11, see *Evans* v. *Clifton Inns* (1987) 85 L.G.R. 119, D.C.
sch. 6, see *Gaunt* v. *Nelson* [1987] R.T.R. 1, D.C.

33. London Government Act 1963.
s. 23, see *R.* v. *Secretary of State for the Environment, ex p. Newham London Borough Council* (1987) 19 H.L.R. 298, C.A.
ss. 80, 90, order 87/939.
sch. 12, amended: 1987, c.27, s.42, sch. 3; repealed in pt.: *ibid.,* schs. 3, 4.

CAP.

1963—cont.

36. Deer Act 1963.
s. 10, amended: 1987, c.28, s.1.

38. Water Resources Act 1963.
ss. 12, 82, order 87/1360.

41. Offices, Shops and Railway Premsies Act 1963.
s. 14, see *Wray* v. *Greater London Council,* January 16, 1986, Mr. M. Ogden Q.C. (sitting as a deputy High Court judge).

47. Limitation Act 1963.
s. 1, see *Arnold* v. *Central Electricity Generating Board* [1987] 2 W.L.R. 245, C.A.

51. Land Compensation (Scotland) Act 1963.
s. 12, see *McLean* v. *City of Glasgow District Council,* 1987 S.L.T.(Lands Tr.) 2; *Mclaren's Discretionary Tr.* v. *Secretary of State for Scotland,* 1987 S.L.T.(Lands. Tr.) 25.
s. 15, amended: 1987, c.26, sch. 23.
s. 40, regs. 87/397, 890, 1842.
sch. 2, substituted: 1987, c.26, sch. 23.

1964

5. International Headquarters and Defence Organisations Act 1964.
s. 1, order 87/927.

14. Plant Varieties and Seeds Act 1964.
s. 16, regs. 87/188, 498(S.), 547, 649, 1091–1093, 1097, 1098, 1148.
s. 17, regs. 87/1091–1093, 1097.
ss. 24, 26, regs. 87/1098.
s. 36, regs. 87/547, 1091–1093, 1097, 1098.

24. Trade Union (Amalgamations, etc.) Act 1964.
s. 7, regs. 87/258.

26. Licensing Act 1964.
s. 3, see *London Borough of Haringey* v. *Sandhu, The Times,* May 6, 1987, D.C.
s. 5, see *Patel* v. *Wright, The Times,* November 19, 1987, D.C.
s. 56, amended: 1987, c.3, sch. 1.
s. 68, amended: 1987, c.2, s.1.
s. 74, see *Workman George Grosvenor* v. *Blaenau Ffestiniog Magistrates' Court, The Times,* January 28, 1987, Taylor J.
s. 87, order 87/1982.
s. 94, amended: 1987, c.2, s.1.
s. 182, repealed in pt.: 1987, c.19, sch.
s. 201, see *Grieve* v. *Hillary,* 1987 S.C.C.R. 317.

29. Continental Shelf Act 1964.
s. 1, order 87/1265.
s. 1, amended: 1987, c.3, sch. 1; repealed in pt.: 1987, c.12, sch. 3.
s. 3, see *Johnston* v. *Heerema Offshore Contractors* (O.H.), 1987 S.L.T. 407; *Fraser* v. *John N. Ward & Son* (O.H.), 1987 S.L.T. 513.

40. Harbours Act 1964.
s. 14, orders 87/420, 1016, 1514, 1790.
s. 15A, order 87/222.

CAP.
1964—cont.

41. Succession (Scotland) Act 1964.
s. 37, see *MacMillan, Petr.*, 1987 S.L.T.(Sh.Ct.) 50.

48. Police Act 1964.
s. 4, see *R. v. Secretary of State for the Home Department, ex p. Northumbria Police Authority* [1987] 2 W.L.R. 998, Q.B.D.
s. 14, see *R. v. Secretary of State for the Home Department, ex p. Devon and Cornwall Police Authority, The Times,* March 16, 1987, D.C.
s. 15, see *Harris v. Sheffield United Football Club* [1987] 3 W.L.R. 305, C.A.
s. 33, see *R. v. Chief Constable of South Wales, ex p. Thornhill* [1987] I.R.L.R. 313, C.A.
s. 33, regs. 87/851, 1753.
s. 34, regs. 87/159, 343.
s. 35, regs. 87/157, 158, 342, 1754.
s. 41, see *R. v. Secretary of State for the Home Department, ex p. Northumbria Police Authority, The Times,* November 19, 1987, C.A.
s. 44, regs. 87/1062.
s. 48, see *Hill v. Chief Constable of West Yorkshire* [1987] 1 All E.R. 1173, C.A.
s. 51, see *G. v. Chief Superintendent of Police, Stroud, Gloucestershire* [1987] Crim.L.R. 269, D.C.; *Nicholas v. Parsonage* [1987] R.T.R. 199, D.C.

56. Housing Act 1964.
s. 101, repealed (S.): 1987, c.26, sch. 24.

75. Public Libraries and Museums Act 1964.
ss. 7, 10, see *R. v. Ealing London Borough, ex p. Times Newspapers; R. v. Hammersmith and Fulham London Borough Council, ex p. Same; R. v. Camden London Borough Council, ex p. Same* (1987) 85 L.G.R. 316, D.C.

81. Diplomatic Privileges Act 1964.
sch. 1, see *Fayed v. Tajir* [1987] 2 All E.R. 396, C.A.
sch. 1, amended: 1987, c.46, sch. 2.

1965

2. Administration of Justice Act 1965.
sch. 1, repealed in pt.: 1987, c.16, sch. 16.

3. Remuneration of Teachers Act 1965.
repealed in pt.: 1987, c.1, s.1, sch. 2.
ss. 2, 7, orders 87/137, 236, 398.

12. Industrial and Provident Societies Act 1965.
ss. 70, 71, regs. 87/393, 394.

14. Cereals Marketing Act 1965.
s. 13, order 87/1194.
s. 16, order 87/671.
s. 23, orders 87/671, 1194.

24. Severn Bridge Tolls Act 1965.
ss. 1, 3, 4, sch. 2, see *R. v. Secretary of State for Transport, ex p. Gwent County Council* [1987] 1 All E.R. 161, C.A.

CAP.
1965—cont.

25. Finance Act 1965.
s. 19, see *Craven v. White; I.R.C. v. Bowater Property Developments; Baylis v. Gregory; Baylis v. Gregory and Weare* [1987] 1 F.T.L.R. 551, C.A.
s. 22, see *Kirby (Inspector of Taxes) v. Thorn E.M.I.* [1987] S.T.C. 621, C.A.; *Welbeck Securities v. Powlson (Inspector of Taxes)* [1987] S.T.C. 468, C.A.
s. 56, see *Elliss (Inspector of Taxes) v. B.P. Oil Northern Ireland Refinery; Ellis (Inspector of Taxes) v. B.P. Tyne Tanker Co.* [1987] 1 F.T.L.R. 253; [1987] S.T.C. 52, C.A.
sch. 7, see *Welbeck Securities v. Powlson (Inspector of Taxes)* [1987] S.T.C. 468, C.A.; *Westcott (Inspector of Taxes) v. Woolcombers* [1987] S.T.C. 600, C.A.; *Dunstan (Inspector of Taxes) v. Young, Austen & Young, The Times,* October 21, 1987, Warner J.
sch. 13, see *Westcott (Inspector of Taxes) v. Woolcombers* [1987] S.T.C. 600, C.A.

32. Administration of Estates (Small Payments) Act 1965.
s. 6, repealed in pt.: 1987, c.45, sch. 4.

45. Backing of Warrants (Republic of Ireland) Act 1965.
s. 1, see *Malinowski, Re* [1987] Crim.L.R. 324, D.C.
s. 7, see *Hawkins (Francis), Re, The Times,* February 11, 1987, D.C.

51. National Insurance Act 1965.
s. 36, amended: orders 87/45, 1978.
s. 110, regs. 87/1850 (S.).

56. Compulsory Purchase Act 1965.
s. 11, sch. 6, see *Chilton v. Telford Development Corp.* (1987) 281 E.G. 1443, C.A.

57. Nuclear Installations Act 1965.
s. 21, amended: regs. 87/2171.
s. 28, order 87/668.
sch. 1, amended and repealed in pt.: 1987, c.4, s.7.

59. New Towns Act 1965.
sch. 6, see *Chilton v. Telford Development Corp.* [1987] 1 W.L.R. 872, C.A.

63. Public Works Loans Act 1965.
s. 2, amended (S.): 1987, c.47, sch. 1.

66. Hire Purchase Act 1965.
ss. 33, 34, see *Chartered Trust v. Pitcher, The Independent,* February 13, 1987, C.A.

74. Superannuation Act 1965.
s. 38, rules 87/376.

82. Coal Industry Act 1965.
ss. 1, 2, 4, amended: 1987, c.3, sch. 1.

1966

4. Mines (Working Facilities and Support) Act 1966.
s. 1, amended: 1987, c.3, sch. 1.
ss. 1, 3, 5, 8, see *B.P. Petroleum Development v. Ryder, The Times,* June 27, 1987, Peter Gibson J.

CAP.
1966—cont.

4. Mines (Working Facilities and Support) Act 1966—*cont.*
s. 2, amended: 1987, c.12, s.27; repealed in pt.: *ibid.*, s.27, sch. 3.
ss. 4, 9, amended: 1987, c.3, sch. 1.

19. Law Reform (Miscellaneous Provisions) (Scotland) Act 1966.
ss. 2, 3, repealed: 1987, c.18, sch. 8.
s. 8, see *McGuire* v. *McGuire* (Sh.Ct.), 1987 S.C.L.R. 378.

27. Building Control Act 1966.
sch., amended: 1987, c.3, sch. 1.

34. Industrial Development Act 1966.
sch. 2, amended: 1987, c.3, sch. 1.

35. Family Provision Act 1966.
s. 1, order 87/799.

36. Veterinary Surgeons Act 1966.
sch. 1A, amended: order 87/447.

47. National Coal Board (Additional Powers) Act 1966.
s. 1, amended: 1987, c.3, sch. 1.

49. Housing (Scotland) Act 1966.
repealed: 1987, c.26, sch. 24.

51. Local Government (Scotland) Act 1966.
ss. 2–7, 12, 14, repealed: 1987, c.47, sch. 6.
ss. 3, 4, order 87/1329.
s. 15, see *Assessor for Central Region* v. *Fleming's Trs.*, 1987 S.L.T. 793.
ss. 24 (in pt.), 26, 27, repealed: 1987, c.47, sch. 6.
s. 45, order 87/1329.
s. 46, amended: 1987, c.26, sch. 23; c.47, s.27.
sch. 1, order 87/1329.
sch. 1, amended: 1987, c.47, s.27; repealed in pt.: *ibid.*, sch. 6.
sch. 3, amended: 1987, c.26, sch. 23; c.47, sch. 1.

1967

7. Misrepresentation Act 1967.
s. 2, see *Highlands Insurance Co.* v. *Continental Insurance Co.* [1987] 1 Lloyd's Rep. 109, Steyn J.; *Corner* v. *Mundy*, January 7, 1987, Judge Hewitt, Middlesbrough County Ct.

8. Plant Health Act 1967.
s. 1, orders 87/428, 880 (S.).
ss. 2, 3, orders 87/19, 340, 428, 880 (S.), 1679.
s. 4A, order 87/340.

9. General Rate Act 1967.
see *Rendall* v. *Duke of Westminster* (1987) 19 H.L.R. 345, C.A.
s. 2, see *R.* v. *Hackney London Borough Council, ex p. Fleming* (1986) 26 R.V.R. 182, Woolf J.; *Lloyd* v. *McMahon* (1986) 26 R.V.R. 188, C.A.
s. 3, see *R.* v. *Hackney London Borough Council, ex p. Fleming* (1986) 26 R.V.R. 182, Woolf J.
s. 6, see *Trendworthy Two* v. *Islington London Borough Council* (1987) 282 E.G. 1125, C.A.

CAP.
1967—cont.

9. General Rate Act 1967—*cont.*
s. 7, see *Polo Pictures* v. *Trafford Metropolitan Borough Council* (1987) 27 R.V.R. 74, Manchester Crown Court.
s. 9, see *R.* v. *Tower Hamlets London Borough Council, ex p. Chetnik Developments* [1987] 1 W.L.R. 593, C.A.
s. 11, see *Lloyd* v. *McMahon* (1986) 26 R.V.R. 188, C.A.
s. 17, see *Trendworthy Two* v. *Islington London Borough Council* (1987) 282 E.G. 1125, C.A.
s. 19, see *Imperial College of Science and Technology* v. *Ebdon (V.O) and Westminster City Council* [1986] R.A. 233, C.A.
ss. 19, 20, see *Addis* v. *Clement (Valuation Officer)* (1987) 85 L.G.R. 489; (1987) 281 E.G. 683, C.A.
s. 19A, order 87/604.
s. 26, see *Hemens (V.O.)* v. *Whitsbury Farm and Stud* [1987] 1 All E.R. 430, C.A.
s. 37, see *Rendall* v. *Duke of Westminster* (1987) 281 E.G. 1197, C.A.
s. 53, see *Polo Pictures* v. *Trafford Metropolitan Borough Council* (1987) 27 R.V.R. 74, Manchester Crown Court.
ss. 67, 70, see *R.* v. *Valuation Officer, ex p. High Park Investments* (1987) 27 R.V.R. 84, Nolan J.
s. 68, order 87/921.
s. 79, see *Rendall* v. *Duke of Westminster* (1987) 281 E.G. 1197, C.A.
sch. 1, see *Debenhams* v. *Westminster City Council* [1986] 3 W.L.R. 1063, H.L.; *London Merchant Securities* v. *Islington London Borough Council* [1987] 3 W.L.R. 173, H.L.; *Trendworthy Two* v. *Islington London Borough Council* (1987) 282 E.G. 1125, C.A.

10. Forestry Act 1967.
ss. 10, 17B, 24, 25, 32, regs. 87/632.

13. Parliamentary Commissioner Act 1967.
order 87/661.
s. 1, amended: 1987, c.39, s.2.
s. 3, amended: *ibid.*, s.3.
s. 3A, added: *ibid.*, s.6.
s. 4, substituted: *ibid.*, s.1.
s. 5, order 87/661.
s. 11, amended: 1987, c.39, s.4.
s. 11A, added: *ibid.*
ss. 13, 14, amended: *ibid.*, s.1.
sch. 2, substituted: 1987, c.39, s.1, sch. 1; amended and repealed in pt.: order 87/2039.
sch. 3, amended: order 87/661; 1987, c.39, s.1; repealed in pt.: order 87/661.

20. Housing (Financial Provisions, Etc.) (Scotland) Act 1967.
repealed: 1987, c.26, sch. 24.

22. Agriculture Act 1967.
s. 13A, order 87/1303.

27. Merchant Shipping (Load Lines) Act 1967.
s. 26, regs. 87/63.

CAP.
1967—cont.

28. Superannuation (Miscellaneous Provisions) Act 1967.
s. 13, regs. 87/157, 158, 1699(S.), 1700(S.).

41. Marine, etc., Broadcasting Offences Act 1967.
s. 9, repealed in pt.: 1987, c.49, sch. 2.

43. Legal Aid (Scotland) Act 1967.
s. 1, see *McLachlan, Petr.*, 1987 S.C.C.R. 195.
s. 2, see *Jeffrey* v. *Jeffrey*, 1987 S.L.T. 488.
ss. 13, 14, 20, see *Walker* v. *Walker* (O.H.), 1987 S.L.T. 129.
ss. 14A, 15, regs. 87/894, 1355, 1357.

45. Uniform Laws on International Sales Act 1967.
s. 1, order 87/2061.

52. Tokyo Convention Act 1967.
s. 8, order 87/456.

54. Finance Act 1967.
s. 30, amended: 1987, c.16, s.51; repealed in pt.: *ibid.*, s.51, sch. 16.
s. 40, orders 87/513, 898, 1492, 1988.

58. Criminal Law Act 1967.
s. 4, see *Holtham* v. *Commissioner of Police for the Metropolis, The Independent*, November 26, 1987, C.A.
s. 6, see *R.* v. *Saunders* [1987] 3 W.L.R. 355, H.L.; *R.* v. *Whiting* (1987) 85 Cr.App.R. 78; [1987] Crim.L.R. 473, C.A.

60. Sexual Offences Act 1967.
ss. 1, 4, see *R.* v. *Spight* [1986] Crim.L.R. 817, C.A.

64. Anchors and Chain Cables Act 1967.
s. 1, regs. 87/854.

66. Welsh Language Act 1967.
s. 2, orders 87/561, 562.

67. Irish Sailors and Soldiers Land Trust Act 1967.
repealed: 1987, c.48, sch.

68. Fugitive Offenders Act 1967.
ss. 9, 11, see *R.* v. *Governor of Pentonville Prison, ex p. Oscar, The Times*, May 29, 1987, D.C.
s. 17, orders 87/451–455.
s. 20, order 87/452.

72. Wireless Telegraphy Act 1967.
s. 7, order 87/774.
s. 9, repealed in pt.: 1987, c.49, sch. 2.

77. Police (Scotland) Act 1967.
s. 26, regs. 87/423, 1698, 1914.
s. 27, regs. 87/424, 1699, 1700, 1878.
ss. 36, 48, order 87/1537.

80. Criminal Justice Act 1967.
s. 11, amended: 1987, c.38, sch. 2.
s. 60, see *R.* v. *Mckinnon (William Harold)* [1987] 1 W.L.R. 234, C.A.
s. 61, see *R.* v. *Secretary of State for the Home Department, ex p. Handscomb, The Times*, March 4, 1987, D.C.
s. 62, see *R.* v. *Mckinnon (William Harold)* [1987] 1 W.L.R. 234, C.A.
s. 67, see *R.* v. *Towers, The Times,* July 24, 1987, C.A.
sch. 3, repealed in pt.: 1987, c.43, sch. 5.

CAP.
1967—cont.

83. Sea Fisheries (Shellfish) Act 1967.
s. 1, regs. 87/217, 218.

84. Sea Fish (Conservation) Act 1967.
s. 4, orders 87/1564, 1565.
s. 5, orders 87/718, 1227, 1900.
s. 6, order 87/1566.
ss. 15, 20, orders 87/1564–1566, 1900.

87. Abortion Act 1967.
s. 1, see *C.* v. *S.* [1987] 1 All E.R. 1230, C.A.
s. 4, see *R.* v. *Salford Health Authority, ex p. Janaway, The Times*, February 13, 1987, Nolan J.

88. Leasehold Reform Act 1967.
see *Dixon* v. *Allgood* (1987) 19 H.L.R. 124, C.A.; *Rendall* v. *Duke of Westminster* (1987) 19 H.L.R. 345, C.A.
s. 1, see *McFarquhar* v. *Phillimore; Marks* v. *Phillimore* (1986) 18 H.L.R. 397, C.A.; *Rendell* v. *Duke of Westminster* (1987) 281 E.G. 1197, C.A.; *Gratton-Storey* v. *Lewis* (1987) 137 N.L.J. 789; (1987) 283 E.G. 1562, C.A.
s. 2, see *Sharpe* v. *Duke Street Securities N.V.* (1987) 283 E.G. 1558, C.A.
s. 4, see *Griffiths* v. *Birmingham City District Council*, January 26, 1987, H.H. Judge Clive Taylor, Q.C., Stafford County Ct.; *MacDonald* v. *Trustees of Henry Smith's Charity, The Times*, July 30, 1987, C.A.; *Dixon* v. *Allgood, The Times*, November 27, 1987, H.L.
ss. 4, 6, 37, see *McFarquhar* v. *Phillimore; Marks* v. *Phillimore* (1986) 18 H.L.R. 397, C.A.
s. 8, see *Gratton-Storey* v. *Lewis* (1987) 137 N.L.J. 789; (1987) 283 E.G. 1562, C.A.
s. 39, see *Investment & Freehold English Estates* v. *Casement* (1987) 283 E.G. 748, H.H. Judge Paul Baker, Q.C.
sch. 4A, regs. 87/1940.

91. Coal Industry Act 1967.
s. 4, amended: 1987, c.3, sch. 1.
s. 7, repealed in pt.: *ibid.*, sch. 3.

1968

3. Capital Allowances Act 1968.
s. 34, amended: 1987, c.16, sch. 15.
s. 84, order 87/362.
s. 91, see *Gaspet (formerly Saga Petroleum (U.K.))* v. *Elliss (Inspector of Taxes)* [1987] 1 W.L.R. 769, C.A.
s. 95, order 87/362.
sch. 7, amended: 1987, c.51, s.64.

7. London Cab Act 1968.
s. 1, order 87/999.

13. National Loans Act 1968.
sch. 4, amended (S.): 1987, c.26, sch. 23; c.47, sch. 1.

14. Public Expenditure and Receipts Act 1968.
s. 5, sch. 3, orders 87/50, 353.

CAP.

1968—cont.

16. New Towns (Scotland) Act 1968.
s. 6, repealed in pt.: 1987, c.26, schs. 23, 24.
s. 38B, added: *ibid.*, sch. 23.

18. Consular Relations Act 1968.
sch. 1, amended: 1987, c.46, sch. 2.

19. Criminal Appeal Act 1968.
s. 2, see *R.* v. *Stewart* (1986) 83 Cr.App.R. 327, C.A.; *R.* v. *Garwood* [1987] 1 W.L.R. 319, C.A.; *R.* v. *Gorman* [1987] 1 W.L.R. 545, C.A.; *McVey, The Times*, October 24, 1987, C.A.
ss. 33, 36, 38, amended: 1987, c.38, sch. 2.

27. Firearms Act 1968.
s. 1, see *R.* v. *Thorpe* [1987] 1 W.L.R. 383, C.A.
s. 5, see *Flack* v. *Baldry, The Times,* November 7, 1987, D.C.
s. 16, see *Urquhart* v. *H.M. Advocate*, 1987 S.C.C.R. 31.
s. 17, see *R.* v. *McGrath* [1987] Crim.L.R. 143, C.A.
s. 20, see *Ferguson* v. *Macphail*, 1987 S.C.C.R. 52.
s. 57, see *R.* v. *Thorpe* [1987] 1 W.L.R. 383, C.A.
sch. 6, see *R.* v. *McGrath* [1987] Crim.L.R. 143, C.A.

29. Trade Descriptions Act 1968.
s. 1, see *Wolkind and Northcott* v. *Pura Foods, The Times,* January 30, 1987, D.C.; *Hirschler* v. *Birch* [1987] R.T.R. 13, D.C.; *Denard* v. *Abbas* (1987) 151 J.P.N. 348, D.C.; *Blunden* v. *Gravelle* (1987) 151 J.P.N. 348, D.C.; *R.* v. *Southwood, The Times,* July 1, 1987, C.A.; *Newham London Borough Council* v. *Singh, The Times,* December 10, 1987, D.C.
ss. 1, 2, see *R.* v. *Coventry City Justices, ex p. Farrand* (1987) 151 J.P.N. 702, D.C.
s. 2, amended: 1987, c.43, sch. 4.
s. 11, repealed: *ibid.*, sch. 5.
s. 14, see *Best Travel Co.* v. *Patterson* (1987) 151 J.P.N. 348, D.C.
ss. 20, 23, see *Hirschler* v. *Birch* [1987] R.T.R. 13, D.C.
s. 24, see *Hirschler* v. *Birch* [1987] R.T.R. 13, D.C.; *Denard* v. *Abbas* [1987] Crim.L.R. 424, D.C.; *R.* v. *Southwood, The Times,* July 1, 1987, C.A.
s. 28, amended: 1987, c.43, sch. 4.

31. Housing (Financial Provisions) (Scotland) Act 1968.
repealed, except ss.20, 67, 71: 1987, c.26, sch. 24.

34. Agriculture (Miscellaneous Provisions) Act 1968.
s. 2, regs. 87/114, 2020, 2021.

39. Gas and Electricity Act 1968.
s. 2, repealed in pt.: 1987, c.16, sch. 16.
sch. 12, see *Burman (Inspector of Taxes)* v. *Westminster Press* [1987] S.T.C. 669, Knox J.

CAP.

1968—cont.

47. Sewerage (Scotland) Act 1968.
ss. 18, 59, repealed in pt.: 1987, c.47, sch. 6.

49. Social Work (Scotland) Act 1968.
s. 32, see *S.* v. *Kennedy*, 1987 S.L.T. 667; *B.* v. *Kennedy,* Second Division, June 5, 1987.
ss. 32, 42, see *Merrin* v. *S.*, 1987 S.L.T. 193.
ss. 34, 35, rules 86/2291.
s. 42, See *B.* v. *Kennedy*, 1987 S.L.T. 765.
s. 61, amended: 1987, c.40, s.1.
s. 61A, added: *ibid.*, s.2.
s. 62, amended: *ibid.*, s.3.
s. 63A, added: *ibid.*, s.4.
s. 63B, added: *ibid.*, s.5.
s. 64A, added: *ibid.*, s.6.
s. 65, amended: *ibid.*, s.7.
s. 80, repealed in pt.: 1987, c.18, sch. 8.
s. 94, amended: 1987, c.40, s.6.
sch. 2, repealed in pt.: 1987, c.41, sch. 2.

52. Caravan Sites Act 1968.
s. 10, see *Stubbings* v. *Beaconsfield JJ.* (1987) 284 E.G. 223, C.A.
s. 12, orders 87/73, 556, 1639–1641, 1709.

59. Hovercraft Act 1968.
ss. 1, 3, order 87/1835.

60. Theft Act 1968.
s. 1, see *R.* v. *Shelton* (1968) 83 Cr.App.R. 379, C.A.
s. 5, see *Lewis* v. *Lethbridge* [1987] Crim.L.R. 59, D.C.
s. 6, see *R.* v. *Coffey* [1987] Crim.L.R. 498, C.A.
s. 9, see *R.* v. *Whiting* [1987] Crim.L.R. 473; (1987) 85 Cr.App.R. 78, C.A.
s. 15, see *R.* v. *Silverman, The Times*, April 3, 1987, C.A.
s. 16, see *R.* v. *Bevan* [1987] Crim.L.R. 129; (1987) 84 Cr.App.R. 143, C.A.; *R.* v. *King (David); R.* v. *Stockwell* [1987] 2 W.L.R. 746, C.A.
s. 20, see *R.* v. *Nanayakkara; R.* v. *Khor; R.* v. *Tan* [1987] 1 W.L.R. 265, C.A.
s. 21, see *R.* v. *Garwood* [1987] 1 W.L.R. 319, C.A.; *R.* v. *Bevans (Ronald), The Times*, December 1, 1987, C.A.
s. 22, see *R.* v. *Roberts (William)* (1987) 84 Cr.App.R. 117, C.A.; *R.* v. *Shelton* (1986) 83 Cr.App.R. 379, C.A.
s. 25, see *Minor* v. *Crown Prosecution Service, The Times,* August 28, 1987, D.C.
s. 27, see *R.* v. *Wood (William Douglas)* [1987] 1 W.L.R. 779, C.A.; *R.* v. *Fowler, The Independent*, July 21, 1987, C.A.

62. Clean Air Act 1968.
s. 8, amended (S.): 1987, c.26, sch. 23.

63. Domestic and Appellate Proceedings (Restriction of Publicity) Act 1968.
s. 2, amended: 1987, c.42, sch. 2; repealed in pt.: *ibid.*, sch. 4.

(17)

1968—cont.

64. Civil Evidence Act 1968.

s. 11, see *Union Carbide Corp.* v. *Naturin* [1987] F.S.R. 538, C.A.

s. 12, amended: 1987, c.42, s.29.

65. Gaming Act 1968.

s. 14, regs. 87/609, 631 (S.).

s. 18, amended and repealed in pt.: 1987, c.11, s.1.

s. 20, order 87/608, 630 (S.).

s. 20, amended: order 87/608.

Pt. III (ss.26–39), s.30, see *Chief Constable, Tayside* v. *Dundee Snooker Centre*, 1987 S.L.T. (Sh.Ct.) 65.

s. 32, see *Mecca Leisure* v. *City of Glasgow District Licensing Board* (O.H.), 1987 S.L.T. 483.

s. 51, orders 87/242, 255 (S.), 608, 631 (S.); regs. 87/609.

s. 52, amended: 1987, c.3, sch. 1.

sch. 2, see *Patmor* v. *City of Edinburgh District Licensing Board* (O.H.), 1987 S.L.T. 492.

schs. 7, 8, see *Chief Constable, Tayside* v. *Dundee Snooker Centre*, 1987 S.L.T. (Sh.Ct.) 65.

67. Medicines Act 1968.

s. 1, order 87/1980.

s. 15, order 87/2217.

s. 20, see *R.* v. *Secretary of State for Social Services, ex p. Wellcome Foundation, The Independent*, February 18, 1987, Webster J.

s. 51, order 87/910.

s. 57, orders 87/1123, 1980.

s. 58, orders 87/674, 1250.

s. 70, amended: order 87/2202.

s. 71, amended and repealed in pt.: *ibid.*

s. 87, regs. 87/877.

s. 129, orders 87/674, 910, 1123, 1250, 1980; regs. 87/877.

69. Justices of the Peace Act 1968.

s. 1, see *R.* v. *Inner London Crown Court, ex p. Benjamin, The Times*, January 5, 1987, D.C.

73. Transport Act 1968.

s. 9A, see *R.* v. *Merseyside Passenger Transport Authority, ex p. Crosville Motor Services, The Times*, April 4, 1987, D.C.

s. 60, regs. 87/841.

s. 69, amended: *ibid.*

ss. 85, 89, 91, regs. 87/841.

s. 96, regs. 87/28, 98.

s. 97, see *Gaunt* v. *Nelson* [1987] R.T.R. 1, D.C.

ss. 97, 98, see *Weir* v. *Tudhope*, 1987 S.C.C.R. 307.

ss. 98, 101, regs. 87/1421.

s. 121, order 87/1443.

ss. 127, 130, sch. 14, see *Lowe* v. *Lester* [1987] R.T.R. 30, D.C.

77. Sea Fisheries Act 1968.

s. 12, amended (S.): 1987, c.18, sch. 6.

1969

27. Vehicles and Driving Licences Act 1969.

s. 16, see *Lowe* v. *Lester* [1987] R.T.R. 30, D.C.

32. Finance Act 1969.

s. 58, amended: 1987, c.51, s.69.

33. Housing Act 1969.

s. 80, see *Investment & Freehold English Estates* v. *Casement* (1987) 283 E.G. 748, H.H. Judge Paul Baker, Q.C.

34. Housing (Scotland) Act 1969.

repealed: 1987, c.26, sch.24.

37. Employer's Liability (Defective Equipment) Act 1969.

s. 1, see *Coltman* v. *Bibby Tankers, Derbyshire, The* [1987] 1 All E.R. 932, C.A.; *Ralston* v. *Greater Glasgow Health Board* (O.H.), 1987 S.L.T. 386.

46. Family Law Reform Act 1969.

s. 6, amended: 1987, c.42, sch. 2; repealed in pt.: *ibid.*.

ss. 14, 15, repealed: *ibid.*, sch. 4.

s. 17, repealed: *ibid.*, s.20, sch. 4.

s. 20, amended: *ibid.*, s.23, sch. 2.

ss. 21–24, amended: *ibid.*, sch. 2.

s. 22, regs. 87/1199.

s. 25, amended: 1987, c.42, s.23.

s. 27, repealed: *ibid.*, sch. 4.

48. Post Office Act 1969.

s. 93, repealed in pt.: 1987, c.39, sch. 2.

sch. 4, amended (S.): 1987, c.26, sch. 23.

54. Children and Young Persons Act 1969.

s. 1, see *D (A Minor) Re* [1986] 3 W.L.R. 1080, H.L.; *B. (A Minor) (Wardship: Sterilisation), Re* [1987] 2 W.L.R. 1213, H.L.; *R.* v. *Bedfordshire County Council, ex p. C.; R.* v. *Hertfordshire County Council, ex p. B.* (1987) 85 L.G.R. 218, Ewbank J.

ss. 1, 2, see *R.* v. *Croydon Juvenile Court, ex p. N.* (1987) J.P.N. 151, Garland J.

s. 2, see *R.* v. *Birmingham City Juvenile Court, ex p. Birmingham City Council, The Times*, September 3, 1987, C.A.

s. 22, see *Northamptonshire County Council* v. *H., The Times*, November 7, 1987, Sheldon J.

s. 28, see *R.* v. *Bristol Justice, ex p. Broome* [1987] 1 W.L.R. 352, Booth J.

s. 32A, see *R.* v. *Croydon Juvenile Court, ex p. N.* (1987) J.P.N. 151, Garland J.

s. 70, amended: 1987, c.42, s.8, sch. 2.

1970

4. Valuation for Rating (Scotland) Act 1970.

s. 1, repealed in pt.: 1987, c.47, sch. 6.

9. Taxes Management Act 1970.

s. 11, amended: 1987, c.51, s.82.

s. 30, amended: *ibid.*, s.89.

s. 36, see *Pleasants* v. *Atkinson (Inspector of Taxes), The Times*, November 13, 1987, Hoffmann J.

s. 42, see *Decision No. R(SB) 25/86*.

s. 56A, order 87/1422.

ss. 63, 63A, substituted (S.): 1987, c.18, sch. 4.

1970—cont.

9. Taxes Management Act 1970—*cont.*
- s. 69, amended: 1987, c.51, s.86.
- s. 70, amended: *ibid.*, s.84.
- s. 85, amended: *ibid.*, sch. 6.
- s. 86, repealed in pt.: 1987, c.16, sch. 16; c.51, s.86.
- s. 87A, added: *ibid.*, s.85.
- s. 88, amended: *ibid.*, s.86; repealed in pt.: *ibid.*
- s. 89, orders 87/513, 898, 1492, 1988.
- s. 89, amended: 1987, c.51, s.89.
- s. 91, amended: *ibid.*, s.86.
- s. 94, substituted: *ibid.*, s.83.
- s. 95, see *Brodt* v. *Wells General Comrs. and I.R.C.* [1987] S.T.C. 207, Scott J.
- s. 98, amended: 1987, c.16, s.35; c.51, ss.14, 51, sch. 5.
- s. 100, see *Brodt* v. *Wells General Comrs. and I.R.C.* [1987] S.T.C. 207, Scott J.
- s. 109, amended: 1987, c.51, s.91; repealed in pt.: *ibid.*
- s. 114, see *Baylis (Inspector of Taxes)* v. *Gregory, The Times,* April 2, 1987, C.A.
- s. 118, amended: 1987, c.51, s.94.

10. Income and Corporation Taxes Act 1970.
- s. 8, amended: order 87/434; 1987, c.16, ss.26, 27.
- s. 14, amended: 1987, c.16, s.26, sch. 15.
- s. 18, amended: *ibid.*, s.28, sch. 15.
- s. 20, amended: *ibid.*, sch. 15; repealed in pt.: *ibid.*, schs. 15, 16.
- s. 21, amended: *ibid.*, sch. 15.
- s. 34, repealed in pt.: *ibid.*, sch. 16.
- ss. 52, 53, see *I.R.C.* v. *Crawley* [1987] S.T.C. 147, Vinelott J.
- s. 54, see *Hafton Properties* v. *McHugh (Inspector of Taxes)* [1987] S.T.C. 16, Gibson J.
- s. 73, amended: 1987, c.16, sch. 15.
- s. 103, amended: *ibid.*
- s. 105, repealed in pt.: *ibid.*, sch. 16.
- s. 108, see *Marson* v. *Morton* [1986] 1 W.L.R. 1343, Browne-Wilkinson V.-C.
- ss. 108, 114, see *Dawson* v. *I.R.C.* [1987] 1 W.L.R. 716, Vinelott J.
- s. 117, amended: 1987, c.16, sch. 15.
- s. 122, repealed in pt.: *ibid.*, sch. 16.
- s. 130, see *Mackinlay (Inspector of Taxes)* v. *Arthur Young McClelland Moores & Co.* [1986] 1 W.L.R. 1468, Vinelott J.; *Bott (E.)* v. *Price (Inspector of Taxes)* [1987] S.T.C. 100; Hoffmann J.; *Beauchamp (Inspector of Taxes)* v. *Woolworth (F. W.)* [1987] S.T.C. 279, Hoffmann J.; *R.T.Z. Oil and Gas* v. *Elliss (Inspector of Taxes* [1987] 1 W.L.R. 1442, Vinelott J.
- s. 130, amended: 1987, c.16, sch. 15.
- s. 133, amended and repealed in pt.: *ibid.*
- s. 153, amended: 1987, c.51, s.62.
- s. 168, amended: 1987, c.16, sch. 15.
- s. 175, repealed in pt.: *ibid.*, sch. 16.
- s. 181, see *Bray (Inspector of Taxes)* v. *Best, Financial Times,* November 6, 1987, C.A.

1970—cont.

9. Taxes Management Act 1970—*cont.*
- ss. 181, 183, see *Hamblett* v. *Godfrey (Inspector of Taxes)* [1987] 1 W.L.R. 357, C.A.
- s. 189, see *Bhadra* v. *Ellam (Inspector of Taxes), The Times,* November 30, 1987, Knox J.
- s. 194, amended: 1987, c.16, sch. 15.
- s. 204, amended: 1987, c.51, s.92.
- s. 211, amended: 1987, c.45, sch. 3.
- s. 212, repealed in pt.: 1987, c.16, sch. 16.
- s. 213, amended: *ibid.*, sch. 15.
- s. 214, amended: *ibid.*, repealed in pt.: *ibid.*, sch. 16.
- ss. 216, 217, amended: *ibid.*, sch. 15.
- s. 219, amended: *ibid.*, s.29.
- s. 226, amended: 1987, c.51, sch. 2; repealed in pt.: 1987, c.16, sch. 16.
- s. 227, repealed in pt.: *ibid.*
- s. 228, substituted: 1987, c.51, s.54.
- s. 229, amended: 1987, c.45, sch. 3; repealed in pt.: 1987, c.16, sch. 16.
- s. 230, amended: 1987, c.51, s.41.
- s. 243, amended: *ibid.*, s.90; repealed in pt.: *ibid.*, sch. 16.
- s. 244, repealed: *ibid.*, s.36, sch. 16.
- s. 248, repealed in pt.: *ibid.*, sch. 16.
- s. 252, amended: 1987, c.51, s.64.
- ss. 266, 267, amended: *ibid.*, sch. 6.
- s. 272, amended: *ibid.*, s.79.
- ss. 273, 276, amended: *ibid.*, s.64.
- s. 277, amended: *ibid.*, sch. 6.
- s. 278, amended and repealed in pt.: *ibid.*
- s. 286, amended: *ibid.*, s.90.
- s. 303, amended: 1987, c.16, s.37; repealed in pt.: *ibid.*, s.37, sch. 16.
- ss. 312, repealed in pt.: *ibid.*, sch. 16.
- s. 323, amended: 1987, c.51, s.39, sch. 3.
- s. 325, repealed: 1987, c.16, sch. 16.
- s. 332, amended: *ibid.*, s.30; c.51, sch. 2.
- s. 337, amended: *ibid.*; repealed in pt.: *ibid.*, schs. 2, 9.
- s. 338, amended: 1987, c.16, s.31.
- s. 340, amended: *ibid.*, s.41.
- s. 343, see *R.* v. *I.R.C., ex p. Woolwich Equitable Building Society* [1987] S.T.C. 654, Nolan J.
- s. 343, regs. 87/844.
- s. 344, repealed (prosp.): 1987, c.16, s.36.
- ss. 345, 352, repealed in pt.: *ibid.*, sch. 16.
- s. 353, see *Essex County Council* v. *Ellam (Inspector of Taxes), The Times,* November 6, 1987, Hoffmann J.
- s. 354, substituted: 1987, c.16, s.38.
- s. 354A, added: *ibid.*, s.39.
- s. 358, substituted: *ibid.*, s.40.
- ss. 362 (in pt.), 375 (in pt.), 388 (in pt.), 403, 404, repealed: *ibid.*, sch. 16.
- s. 418, amended: 1987, c.51, sch. 6.
- ss. 420 (in pt.), 422–424, repealed: 1987, c.16, sch. 16.
- ss. 433, 434, 438, amended: *ibid.*, sch. 15.
- ss. 460, 461, see *Bird* v. *I.R.C.; Breams Nominees* v. *Same* [1987] 1 F.T.L.R. 361, C.A.

CAP.

1970—cont.

9. Taxes Management Act 1970—cont.
ss. 460 (in pt.), 467 (in pt.), 468, repealed: 1987, c.16, sch. 16.
s. 478, see *I.R.C.* v. *Brackett* [1987] 1 FTLR 8, Hoffmann J.
s. 482, see *R.* v. *H.M. Treasury, ex p. Daily Mail and General Trust* [1987] 1 FTLR, Macpherson J.
s. 488, see *Sugarwhite* v. *Budd (Inspector of Taxes)* [1987] S.T.C. 491, Vinelott J.
s. 495, repealed in pt.: 1987, c.16, sch. 16.
s. 497, see *Padmore* v. *I.R.C.* [1987] S.T.C. 36, Gibson J.
s. 497, orders 87/169, 466, 467, 2054–2058.
s. 497, amended: 1987, c.16, s.70.
ss. 497, 501, 505, see *Collard* v. *Mining and Industrial Holdings, Financial Times*, December 1, 1987, C.A.
s. 503, repealed in pt.: 1987, s.16, sch. 15.
s. 514, repealed: *ibid.*, sch. 16.
s. 516, amended: *ibid.*, sch. 15.
s. 517, regs. 87/2071.
s. 519, repealed in pt.: 1987, c.16, sch. 16.
s. 526, see *Marson* v. *Morton* [1986] 1 W.L.R. 1343, Browne-Wilkinson V.-C.
s. 526, amended: 1987, c.16, s.40, sch. 15.
s. 528, see *I.R.C.* v. *Crawley* [1987] S.T.C. 147, Vinelott J.
s. 530, amended: 1987, c.16, sch. 3.
s. 533, repealed in pt.: *ibid.*, sch. 16.
sch. 10, amended: *ibid.*, sch. 15; repealed in pt.: *ibid.*, sch. 16.
sch. 12, amended: *ibid.*, sch. 15.
sch. 15, repealed in pt.: *ibid.*, sch. 16.

24. Finance Act 1970.
s. 19, amended: 1987, c.51, sch. 3.
s. 20, amended: 1987, c.16, sch. 15; c.51, sch. 3.
ss. 21, 22, amended: *ibid.*; repealed in pt.: *ibid.*, schs. 3, 9.
s. 26, amended: *ibid.*, sch. 3.
s. 30, order 87/892.
sch. 5, regs. 87/1749.
sch. 5, amended: 1987, c.51, sch. 3.
sch. 7, repealed in pt.: 1987, c.16, sch. 16.

27. Fishing Vessels (Safety Provisions) Act 1970.
s. 6, regs. 87/63, 548, 854.

31. Administration of Justice Act 1970.
s. 32, see *O'Sullivan* v. *Herdmans* [1987] 1 W.L.R. 1047, H.L.
s. 36, see *Citibank Trust* v. *Ayivor* [1987] 1 W.L.R. 1157, Mervyn Davies J.
sch. 8, amended: 1987, c.42, sch. 2; repealed in pt.: *ibid.*, schs. 2, 4.

35. Conveyancing and Feudal Reform (Scotland) Act 1970.
ss. 24, 29, see *Mountstar Metal Corporation* v. *Cameron*, 1987 S.L.T.(Sh.Ct.) 106; *Bradford and Bingley Building Society* v. *Roddy*, 1987 S.L.T.(Sh.Ct.) 109.
sch. 3, see *Bradford and Bingley Building Society* v. *Roddy*, 1987 S.L.T.(Sh.Ct.) 109.

CAP.

1970—cont.

36. Merchant Shipping Act 1970.
s. 11, repealed in pt. (S.): 1987, c.18, sch. 8.
s. 43, regs. 87/884.
ss. 70, 71, regs. 87/408.
s. 84, regs. 87/63, 548, 854.
s. 92, regs. 87/884.
s. 99, regs. 87/408.

40. Agriculture Act 1970.
s. 28, order 87/1948, 1949.
s. 29, order 87/1949.

41. Equal Pay Act 1970.
s. 1, see *Rainey* v. *Greater Glasgow Health Board* [1986] 3 W.L.R. 1017; 1987 S.L.T. 146, H.L.; *Hayward* v. *Cammell Laird Shipbuilders (No. 2)* [1986] I.C.R. 862, E.A.T.; *Leverton* v. *Clwyd County Council* [1987] 1 W.L.R. 65, E.A.T.; *Forex Neptune (Overseas)* v. *Miller* [1987] I.C.R. 170, E.A.T.; *Thomas* v. *National Coal Board; Barker* v. *National Coal Board, The Times*, May 20, 1987, E.A.T.; *Hayward* v. *Cammell Laird Shipbuilders* [1987] 2 All E.R. 344, C.A.; *Bromley* v. *Quick (H. & V.), The Times*, August 24, 1987, E.A.T.; *McGregor* v. *General Municipal Boilermakers and Allied Trades Union* [1987] I.C.R. 505, E.A.T.; *Lawson* v. *Britfish* [1987] I.C.R. 726, E.A.T.; *Pickstone* v. *Freemans* [1987] 3 W.L.R. 811, C.A.; *R.* v. *Secretary of State for Social Services, ex p. Clark, The Times*, November 13, 1987, D.C.
s. 2, see *Dennehy* v. *Sealink U.K.* [1987] I.R.L.R. 120, E.A.T.
s. 2A, see *R.* v. *Secretary of State for Social Services, ex p. Clark, The Times*, November 13, 1987, D.C.
s. 8, sch. 1, see *Lawson* v. *Britfish* [1987] I.C.R. 726, E.A.T.

42. Local Authority Social Services Act 1970.
sch. 1, amended (S.): 1987, c.26, sch. 23.

44. Chronically Sick and Disabled Persons Act 1970.
s. 3, amended (S.): 1987, c.26, sch. 23; repealed in pt. (S.): *ibid.*, sch. 24.

55. Family Income Supplements Act 1970.
ss. 2, 3, regs. 87/32.
s. 6, regs. 87/281.
s. 10, regs. 87/32.

1971

3. Guardianship of Minors Act 1971.
text as amended: 1987, c.42, s.32, sch. 1.
amended: *ibid.*, sch. 2.
s. 1, see *W.* v. *P., The Times*, October 26, 1987, Ewbank J.
s. 5, amended: 1987, c.42, sch. 2.
s. 9, see *M. and H. (Minors) (Local Authority: Parental Rights), Re* [1987] 3 W.L.R. 759, C.A.
s. 9, substituted: 1987, c.42, s.10.
ss. 10, 11, substituted: *ibid.*, s.11.

1971—cont.

3. Guardianship of Minors Act 1971—cont.
s. 11A, amended: *ibid.*, sch. 2.
s. 11B, added: *ibid.*, s.12.
s. 11C, added: *ibid.*, s.13.
s. 11D, added: *ibid.*, s.14.
ss. 12, 12A, amended: *ibid.*, sch. 2.
s. 12B, amended: *ibid.*; repealed in pt.:
    ibid., schs. 2, 4.
s. 12C, amended: *ibid.*, sch. 2.
s. 12D, added: *ibid.*
ss. 13, 13A, amended: *ibid.*
s. 13B, added: *ibid.*
s. 14, repealed: *ibid.*, schs. 2, 4.
s. 14A, amended: *ibid.*, sch. 2.
s. 15A, amended: *ibid.*; repealed in pt.:
    ibid., schs. 2, 4.
ss. 16, 20, amended: *ibid.*, sch. 2.

10. Vehicles (Excise) Act 1971.
s. 8, see *Guyll* v. *Bright* [1987] R.T.R.
    104, D.C.; *Algar* v. *Shaw* [1987] R.T.R.
    229, D.C.
s. 9, repealed in pt.: 1987, c.16, schs. 1,
    16.
s. 16, amended: *ibid.*, s.2, sch. 1; repealed
    in pt.: *ibid.*, schs. 1, 16.
s. 18A, amended: *ibid.*, sch. 1; repealed in
    pt.: *ibid.*, schs. 1, 16.
s. 23, amended: 1987, c.16, sch. 1.
s. 28, see *Algar* v. *Shaw* [1987] R.T.R.
    229, D.C.
s. 37, sch. 3, amended: 1987, c.16, sch. 1.
sch. 4, amended: *ibid.*, s.2, sch. 1.
sch. 7, amended: *ibid.*, sch. 1; repealed in
    pt.: *ibid.*, schs. 1, 16.

13. Mr. Speaker King's Retirement Act 1971.
s. 1, amended: 1987, c.45, s.4.

16. Coal Industry Act 1971.
ss. 4, 6–10, amended: 1987, c.3, sch. 1.

19. Carriage of Goods by Sea Act 1971.
sch. see *China Ocean Shipping Co.
    (Owners of Xingcheng)* v. *Andros
    (Owners of the Andros)* [1987] 1 W.L.R.
    1213, P.C.

22. Animals Act 1971.
ss. 4, 5, see *Matthews* v. *Wicks, The Times,*
    May 25, 1987, C.A.

23. Courts Act 1971.
s. 10, see *Sampson, Re* [1987] 1 W.L.R.
    194, H.L.

27. Powers of Attorney Act 1971.
s. 7, see *Clause* v. *Pir* [1987] 2 All E.R.
    752, Francis Ferrie Q.C.

28. Rent (Scotland) Act 1971.
s. 2, see *Gavin* v. *Lindsay*, 1987
    S.L.T.(Sh.Ct.) 12.

29. National Savings Bank Act 1971.
s. 4, order 87/329, 330.

32. Attachment of Earnings Act 1971.
s. 22, amended: order 87/2039.
sch. 1, amended: 1987, c.42, sch. 2;
    repealed in pt.: *ibid.*, schs. 2, 4.

34. Water Resources Act 1971.
s. 1, orders 87/107, 1354.

1971—cont.

38. Misuse of Drugs Act 1971.
s. 4, see *R.* v. *Maginnis* [1987] 2 W.L.R.
    765, H.L.; *Trotter* v. *H.M. Advocate,*
    1987 S.C.C.R. 131.
s. 5, see *R.* v. *Hunt (Richard)* [1986] 3
    W.L.R. 1115, H.L.; *Campbell* v. *H.M.
    Advocate*, 1986 S.C.C.R. 403; *R.* v.
    Maginnis [1987] 2 W.L.R. 765, H.L.;
    Young v. *H.M. Advocate,* 1986
    S.C.C.R. 583; *R.* v. *Walker* [1987]
    Crim.L.R. 565, C.A.; *Grundison* v.
    Brown, 1987 S.C.C.R. 186.
s. 7, S.Rs. 1987 Nos. 66, 68.
s. 10, regs. 87/67; S.R. 1987 No. 68.
s. 20, see *R.* v. *Panayi; R.* v. *Karte, The
    Times,* July 24, 1987, C.A.
s. 27, see *R.* v. *Llewellyn (Kevin Anthony)*
    (1985) 7 Cr.App.R.(S.) 225, C.A.; *R.* v.
    Cox [1987] Crim.L.R. 141, C.A.; *R.* v.
    Boothe [1987] Crim.L.R. 347, C.A.; *R.*
    v. *Churcher* (1986) 8 Cr.App.R.(S.) 94,
    C.A.; *R.* v. *Askew* [1987] Crim.L.R.
    584, C.A.
s. 30, regs. 87/298.
s. 31, regs. 87/67, 298; S.R. 1987 No. 68.
s. 37, regs. 87/298.
s. 38, regs. 87/67; S.R. 1987 No. 68.
sch. 2, see *R.* v. *Walker* [1987] Crim.L.R.
    565, C.A.

39. Rating Act 1971.
s. 2, see *Hemens (V.O.)* v. *Whitsbury
    Farm and Stud* [1987] 1 All E.R. 430,
    C.A.
s. 5, see *Lothian Regional Assessor* v.
    Hood (1987) 27 R.V.R. 132, Lands Val-
    uation Appeal Ct.

40. Fire Precautions Act 1971.
s. 1, amended: 1987, c.27, s.1.
s. 2, repealed in pt.: *ibid.*, s.13, sch. 4.
s. 5, amended: *ibid.*, ss.1, 4, 8; repealed
    in pt.: *ibid.*, s.15, sch. 4.
ss. 5A, 5B, added: *ibid.*, s.1.
s. 6, repealed in pt.: *ibid.*, sch. 4.
s. 7, see *R.* v. *Mabbott, The Times,* August
    4, 1987, C.A.
s. 7, amended: 1987, c.27, ss.8, 14.
s. 8A, added: *ibid.*, s.2.
s. 8B, added: *ibid.*, s.3.
s. 9A, substituted: *ibid.*, s.5.
ss. 9B, 9C, added: *ibid.*, s.6.
ss. 9D, 9E, 9F, added: *ibid.*, s.7.
s. 10, substituted: *ibid.*, s.9.
ss. 10A, 10B, amended: *ibid.*
s. 12, amended: *ibid.*, s.13; repealed in
    pt.: *ibid.*, s.13, sch. 4.
ss. 14, 17, amended: *ibid.*, s.7.
s. 18, amended: *ibid.*, s.10.
s. 19, amended: *ibid.*, s.2.
s. 21, amended: *ibid.*, s.11.
s. 27A, added: *ibid.*, s.12.
s. 28A, added: *ibid.*, s.16.
s. 34, amended: *ibid.*
s. 35, amended: *ibid.*, s.17.
s. 40, amended: *ibid.*, s.18.

1971—cont.

40. Fire Precautions Act 1971—cont.
s. 43, amended: *ibid.*, ss.4, 9; repealed in pt.: *ibid.*, ss.12, 16, sch. 4.
sch., renumbered sch. 1: *ibid.*, s.16, sch. 1.
sch. 2, added: *ibid.*.

48. Criminal Damage Act 1971.
s. 1, see *Chief Constable of Avon and Somerset Constabulary* v. *Shimmen* (1987) 84 Cr.App.R. 7, D.C.; *R.* v. *Steer* [1987] 3 W.L.R. 205, H.L.

55. Law Reform (Jurisdiction in Delict) (Scotland) Act 1971.
see *Kirkcaldy District Council* v. *Household Manufacturing* (O.H.), 1987 S.L.T. 617.

56. Pensions (Increase) Act 1971.
s. 5, see *Hertfordshire County Council* v. *Retirement Lease Housing Association, The Independent*, February 19, 1987, Hoffman J.
sch. 2, amended: 1987, c.45, sch. 3.

58. Sheriff Courts (Scotland) Act 1971.
s. 35, see *Monklands District Council* v. *Johnstone* (Sh.Ct.), 1987 S.C.L.R. 480.
s. 36, repealed in pt.: 1987, c.18, sch. 8.
s. 37, see *Monklands District Council* v. *Baird* (Sh.Ct.), 1987 S.C.L.R. 88.
s. 38, see *Webster Engineering Services* v. *Gibson*, 1987 S.L.T.(Sh.Ct.) 101.

59. Merchant Shipping (Oil Pollution) Act 1971.
s. 18, order 87/1263.

60. Prevention of Oil Pollution Act 1971.
s. 20, amended (S.): 1987, c.18, sch. 6.

61. Mineral Workings (Offshore Installations) Act 1971.
s. 1, amended: 1987, c.49, sch. 1.
s. 6, regs. 87/129.

62. Tribunals and Inquiries Act 1971.
s. 8, sch. 1, amended: 1987, c.22, sch. 6.
s. 11, rules 87/1522 (S.).

68. Finance Act 1971.
s. 32, amended: order 87/434; 1987, c.16, s.20.
s. 36, see *I.R.C.* v. *Crawley* [1987] S.T.C. 147, Vinelott J.
ss. 41, 44, see *Thomas (Inspector of Taxes)* v. *Reynolds* [1987] S.T.C. 135, Walton J.
s. 44, amended: 1987, c.51, s.64.
sch. 4, amended: 1987, c.16, ss.26, 27.
sch. 8, amended: 1987, c.51, s.64.

69. Medicines Act 1971.
s. 1, regs. 87/1439.

72. Industrial Relations Act 1971.
s. 167, see *Express & Star* v. *Bunday, The Times*, July 28, 1987, C.A.

76. Housing Act 1971.
repealed (S.): 1986, c.26, sch. 24.

77. Immigration Act 1971.
see *R.* v. *Secretary of State for the Home Department, ex p. H., The Times*, August 5, 1987, D.C.; *R.* v. *Immigration Appeal Tribunal, ex p. Jones (Ross), The Times*, December 9, 1987, C.A.

1971—cont.

77. Immigration Act 1971—cont.
s. 1, see *R.* v. *Immigration Appeal Tribunal, ex p. Haque; Same* v. *Same, ex p. Ruhul; Same* v. *Same, ex p. Rahman, The Independent*, August, 6, 1987, C.A.; *R.* v. *Secretary of State for the Home Department, ex p. Ullah and other Applications* [1987] 1 All E.R. 1025, Taylor J.; *R.* v. *Secretary of State for the Home Department, ex p. Huseyin (Zalihe), The Times*, October 31, 1987, C.A.
s. 3, see *Owusu-Sekyere's Application, Re, The Times*, April 22, 1987, C.A.; *R.* v. *Immigration Appeal Tribunal, ex p. Sheikh, The Times*, April 29, 1987, D.C.; *R.* v. *Immigration Appeal Tribunal, ex p. Patel, The Independent*, August 21, 1987, C.A.
s. 4, see *Baljinder Singh* v. *Hammond* [1987] 1 W.L.R. 283, D.C.; *R.* v. *Secretary of State for the Home Office, ex p. Betancourt, The Times*, October 5, 1987, Kennedy J.
ss. 4, 13, see *Bugdaycay* v. *Secretary of State for the Home Department; Nelidow Santis* v. *Same; Norman* v. *The Same; Musisi, Re* [1987] 2 W.L.R. 606, H.L.
s. 11, see *R.* v. *Secretary of State for the Home Department, ex p. Coonhye, The Independent*, May 14, 1987, D.C.
s. 19, see *R.* v. *Immigration Appeal Tribunal, ex p. Hassanin, Kandemir and Farooq* [1986] 1 W.L.R. 1448, C.A.
s. 24, see *Manickavasagar* v. *Comr. of Metropolitan Police* [1987] Crim.L.R. 50, D.C.; *Gursan*, April 3, 1987, H.H. Judge Phillips, Knutsford Crown Ct.
s. 26, see *Baljinder Singh* v. *Hammond* [1987] 1 W.L.R. 283, D.C.
s. 33, order 87/177.
sch. 2, see *R.* v. *Secretary of State for the Home Department, ex p. Kaur, The Independent*, February 27, 1987, D.C.; *Baljinder Singh* v. *Hammond* [1987] 1 W.L.R. 283, D.C.; *Kaur* v. *Secretary of State for the Home Department* (O.H.), 1987 S.C.L.R. 550; *R.* v. *Secretary of State for the Home Department, ex p. Malik, The Independent*, October 6, 1987, Kennedy J.

78. Town and Country Planning Act 1971.
see *Surrey Heath Borough Council* v. *Secretary of State for the Environment* (1987) 53 P. & C.R. 428, Kennedy J.
s. 1, see *R.* v. *Basildon District Council, ex p. Martin Grant Homes* (1987) 53 P. & C.R. 397, McCowan J.
s. 10, see *Groveside Homes* v. *Elmbridge Borough Council* (1987) 284 E.G. 940, D.C.
s. 12A, regs. 87/1760.
s. 14, see *R.* v. *Secretary of State for the Environment, ex p. Southwark London Borough Council* (1987) 54 P. & C.R. 226, D.C.

1971—cont.

78. Town and Country Planning Act 1971—
cont.

s. 22, see *R.* v. *Runnymede Borough Council, ex p. Sarvan Singh Seehra* (1987) 151 J.P. 80, Schiemann J.; *Somak Travel* v. *Secretary of State for the Environment, The Times,* June 2, 1987, Stuart-Smith J.; *R.* v. *Basildon District Council, ex p. Martin Grant Homes* (1987) 53 P. & C.R. 397, McCowan J.

s. 22, order 87/764.

s. 24, orders 87/265, 702, 738, 1343–1345.

s. 24E, order 87/1849.

s. 29, see *R.* v. *Basildon District Council, ex p. Martin Grant Homes* (1987) 53 P. & C.R. 397, McCowan J.

s. 36, order 87/702.

s. 52, see *Martin's Application, Re* (No. LP/40/1985) (1987) 53 P. & C.R. 146, Lands Tribunal.

s. 54, see *Debenhams* v. *Westminster City Council* [1986] 3 W.L.R. 1063, H.L.; *Leominster District Council* v. *British Historic Buildings and S.P.S. Shipping* [1987] J.P.L. 350, Hoffmann J.

ss. 54, 56B, regs. 87/349.

s. 55, see *R.* v. *Wells Street Magistrates, ex p. Westminster City Council* (1987) 53 P. & C.R. 421, D.C.

s. 63, regs. 87/804.

s. 87, see *R.* v. *Runnymede Borough Council, ex p. Sarvan Singh Seehra* (1987) 151 J.P. 80, Schiemann J.

s. 88, see *Masefield* v. *Taylor, The Times,* December 16, 1986, D.C.; *R.* v. *Runnymede Borough Council, ex p. Sarvan Singh Seehra* (1987) 151 J.P. 80; (1987) 53 P. & C.R. 281, Schiemann J.; *R.* v. *Secretary of State and Bromley London Borough Council, ex p. Jackson* [1987] J.P.L. 790, Macpherson J.

s. 89, see *R.* v. *Jefford* [1986] J.P.L. 912, Judge Rubin; *Coventry Scaffolding Co. (London)* v. *Parker (John Brian)* [1987] J.P.L. 127, D.C.; *R.* v. *Keeys, The Times,* July 17, 1987, C.A.; *R.* v. *Fyfield Equipment* [1987] Crim.L.R. 507, Snaresbrook Crown Ct.

s. 90, see *R.* v. *Runnymede Borough Council, ex p. Sarvan Singh Seehra* (1987) 151 J.P. 80, Schiemann J.; *Runnymede Borough Council* v. *Smith* (1987) 53 P. & C.R. 132, Millett J.

s. 91, regs. 87/349.

s. 93, see *R.* v. *Fyfield Equipment* [1987] Crim.L.R. 507, Snaresbrook Crown Ct.

s. 94, see *Bristol City Council* v. *Secretary of State for the Environment, The Times,* March 19, 1987, D.C.

ss. 96, 97, see *Leominster District Council* v. *British Historic Buildings and S.P.S. Shipping* [1987] J.P.L. 350, Hoffmann J.

s. 99, regs. 87/349.

1971—cont.

78. Town and Country Planning Act 1971—
cont.

s. 102, see *Groveside Homes* v. *Elmbridge Borough Council, The Times,* September 5, 1987, D.C.

s. 109, regs. 87/804.

s. 112, see *R.* v. *Secretary of State for the Environment, ex p. Leicester City Council* [1987] J.P.L. 787, McCullough J.

ss. 171–173, regs. 87/349.

s. 174, see *Bell* v. *Canterbury City Council* (Ref. No. 166/1985) (1986) 52 P. & C.R. 428, Lands Tribunal.

s. 190, regs. 87/349.

ss. 192, 205, see *R.* v. *Secretary of State for the Environment, ex p. Bournemouth Borough Council* (1987) 281 E.G. 539, Mann J.

ss. 192, 216, amended: 1987, c.3, sch. 1.

s. 243, see *R.* v. *Keeys, The Times,* June 17, 1987, C.A.

s. 246, see *London Parachuting and Rectory Farm (Pampisford)* v. *Secretary of State for the Environment and South Cambridgeshire District Council* (1986) 52 P. & C.R. 376, C.A.; *Newbury District Council* v. *Secretary of State for the Environment, The Times,* July 2, 1987, Kennedy J.

s. 264, amended: 1987, c.3, sch. 1.

s. 270, see *R.* v. *Lambeth London Borough Council, ex p. Sharp* [1987] J.P.L. 440, C.A.

s. 271, regs. 87/349.

s. 273, regs. 87/1936.

s. 273, amended: 1987, c.3, sch. 1.

s. 277A, regs. 87/349.

s. 282B, regs. 87/701.

s. 283, see *R.* v. *Secretary of State and Bromley London Borough Council, ex p. Jackson* [1987] J.P.L. 790, Macpherson J.

s. 287, regs. 87/349, 804, 1750, 1760; orders 87/702, 764.

s. 290, see *R.* v. *Plymouth City Council, ex p. Freeman, The Independent,* April 22, 1987.

s. 290, regs. 87/349, 1750, 1760.

sch. 7, see *R.* v. *Secretary of State for the Environment, ex p. Great Grimsby Borough Council* [1986] J.P.L. 910, Russell J.

sch. 8A, regs. 87/1750.

sch. 11, regs. 87/349.

80. Banking and Financial Dealings Act 1971.

s. 2, amended: 1987, c.16, s.69.

1972

11. Superannuation Act 1972.

ss. 7, 8, 12, regs. 87/1850 (S.).

ss. 12, 15, regs. 87/157, 158, 1698(S.)–1700 (S.).

18. Maintenance Orders (Reciprocal Enforcement) Act 1972.

s. 3, repealed in pt.: 1987, c.42, sch. 4.

1972—cont.

18. Maintenance Orders (Reciprocal Enforcement) Act 1972—cont.

s. 8, amended: *ibid.*, sch. 2.

s. 27, amended: *ibid.*; repealed in pt.: *ibid.*, schs. 2, 4.

ss. 28, 28A, amended: *ibid.*, sch. 2.

s. 30, amended: *ibid.*; repealed in pt.: *ibid.*, schs. 2, 4.

s. 33, amended: *ibid.*, sch. 2.

ss. 40, 45, order 87/1282.

s. 41, amended: 1987, c.42, sch. 2; repealed in pt.: *ibid.*, schs. 2, 4.

20. Road Traffic Act 1972.

see *Gumbley* v. *Cunningham; Gould* v. *Castle, The Independent*, July 29, 1987, D.C.

s. 2, see *R.* v. *Denton* [1987] R.T.R. 129, C.A.

s. 3, see *Farquhar* v. *MacKinnon*, 1986 S.C.C.R. 524.

s. 5, see *Pearson* v. *Comr. of Police of the Metropolis, The Times*, June 29, 1987, D.C.; *D.P.P.* v. *Webb, The Times*, October 19, 1987, D.C.

s. 6, see *Gunn* v. *Brown*, 1987 S.L.T. 94; *O'Brien* v. *Ferguson*, 1987 S.L.T. 96; *MacLeod* v. *Fraser*, 1987 S.L.T. 142; *Wright* v. *Tudhope*, 1986 S.C.C.R. 431; *Jones* v. *Thomas (John Barrie)* [1987] Crim.L.R. 133; [1987] R.T.R. 111, D.C.; *Newton* v. *Woods* [1987] R.T.R. 41, D.C.; *McKoen* v. *Ellis* [1987] R.T.R. 26, D.C.; *Sivyer* v. *Parker* [1987] R.T.R. 169, D.C.; *Wakeley* v. *Hyams* [1987] R.T.R. 49, D.C.; *Haghigat-Khou* v. *Chambers* [1987] Crim.L.R. 340, D.C.; *Pearson* v. *Comr. of Police of the Metropolis, The Times*, June 29, 1987, D.C.; *Rawlins* v. *Brown* [1987] R.T.R. 238, D.C.; *R.* v. *Brentford Magistrates' Court, ex p. Clarke* [1987] R.T.R. 205, D.C.; *R.* v. *Tower Bridge Metropolitan Stipendiary Magistrate, ex p. D.P.P., The Times*, May 15, 1987, D.C.; *Smith* v. *Mellors and Soar* (1987) 84 Cr.App.R. 279, D.C.; *Stephenson* v. *Clift, The Times*, July 28, 1987, D.C.; *Badkin* v. *Chief Constable of South Yorkshire, The Times*, August 29, 1987, D.C.; *Donnelly* v. *Hamilton*, 1987 S.C.C.R. 313.

s. 7, see *Gallagher* v. *MacKinnon*, 1986 S.C.C.R. 704; *Gull* v. *Scarborough* (Note) [1987] R.T.R. 261, D.C.

s. 8, see *Beveridge* v. *Allan*, 1986 S.C.C.R. 542; *Sutch* v. *Crown Prosecution Service*, January 30, 1987, H.H. Judge Compton, Wood Green Crown Ct.; *McLeod* v. *Murray*, 1986 S.C.C.R. 369; *Hynd* v. *Guild*, 1986 S.C.C.R. 406; *Goldie* v. *Tudhope*, 1986 S.C.C.R. 414; *Douglas* v. *Stevenson*, 1986 S.C.C.R. 519; *Tudhope* v. *O'Kane*, 1986 S.C.C.R. 538; *Newton* v. *Woods* [1987] R.T.R. 41, D.C.; *Chief Constable of Avon and*

1972—cont.

20. Road Traffic Act 1972—cont.

Somerset Constabulary v. *Singh, The Times*, April 11, 1987, D.C.; *R.* v. *Ashford and Tenterden Magistrates' Court, ex p. Wood, The Times*, May 8, 1987, D.C.; *McGrath* v. *Field* [1985] Crim.L.R. 275, D.C.; *Gallagher* v. *MacKinnon*, 1986 S.C.C.R. 704; *Dye* v. *Manns* [1987] R.T.R. 90, D.C.; *Kemp* v. *Chief Constable of Kent* [1987] R.T.R. 66, D.C.; *Sivyer* v. *Parker* [1987] R.T.R. 169, D.C.; *Wakeley* v. *Hyams* [1987] R.T.R. 49, D.C.; *Chief Constable of Avon and Somerset* v. *O'Brien* [1987] R.T.R. 182, D.C.; *Cotgrove* v. *Cooney* [1987] R.T.R. 124, D.C.; *Haghigat-Khou* v. *Chambers* [1987] Crim.L.R. 340, D.C.; *Cole* v. *Boon, The Times*, June 19, 1987, D.C.; *Sharp* v. *Spencer* [1987] Crim.L.R. 420, D.C.; *D.P.P.* v. *Billington, Chappell, Rumble and East, The Independent*, July 22, 1987, D.C.; *Pearson* v. *Comr. of Police of the Metropolis, The Times*, June 29, 1987, D.C.; *Grix* v. *Chief Constable of Kent* [1987] R.T.R. 193, D.C.; *Gull* v. *Scarborough* (Note) [1987] R.T.R. 261, D.C.; *Oxford* v. *Baxendale* [1987] R.T.R. 247, D.C.; *Rawlins* v. *Brown* [1987] R.T.R. 238, D.C.; *R.* v. *Brentford Magistrates' Court, ex p. Clarke* [1987] R.T.R. 205, D.C.; *Hartland* v. *Alden* [1987] R.T.R. 253, D.C.; *Badkin* v. *Chief Constable of South Yorkshire, The Times*, August 29, 1987, D.C.; *D.P.P.* v. *Webb, The Times*, October 19, 1987, D.C.; *Davis* v. *D.P.P., The Times*, October 23, 1987, D.C.; *Aitchison* v. *Johnstone*, 1987 S.C.C.R. 225; *Fraser* v. *McLeod*, 1987 S.C.C.R. 294; *Reynolds* v. *Tudhope*, 1987 S.C.C.R. 340; *Nugent* v. *Ridley* [1987] Crim.L.R. 640, D.C.

s. 9, see *D.P.P.* v. *Fountain, The Times*, October 10, 1987, D.C.

s. 10, see *Gunn* v. *Brown*, 1987 S.L.T. 94; *O'Brien* v. *Ferguson*, 1987 S.L.T. 96; *MacLeod* v. *Fraser*, 1987 S.L.T. 142; *Newton* v. *Woods* [1987] R.T.R. 41, D.C.; *Wakeley* v. *Hyams* [1987] R.T.R. 49, D.C.; *Tobi* v. *Nicholas, The Independent*, July 3, 1987, D.C.; *R.* v. *Brentford Magistrates' Court, ex p. Clarke* [1987] R.T.R. 205, D.C.; *Badkin* v. *Chief Constable of South Yorkshire, The Times*, August 29, 1987, D.C.; *Dear* v. *D.P.P., The Times*, November 27, 1987, D.C.

s. 12, see *Newton* v. *Woods* [1987] R.T.R. 41, D.C.; *Oxford* v. *Baxendale* [1987] R.T.R. 247, D.C.; *R.* v. *Brentford Magistrates' Court, ex p. Clarke* [1987] R.T.R. 205, D.C.

s. 15, regs. 87/346 (S.).

s. 18, see *Nicholas* v. *Parsonage* [1987] R.T.R. 199, D.C.

1972—cont.

20. Road Traffic Act 1972—cont.
s. 25, see *Selby* v. *Chief Constable of Avon and Somerset, The Times*, February 18, 1987, D.C.; *Singh* v. *McLeod*, 1986 S.C.C.R. 656.
s. 33A, see *Webb* v. *Crane, The Times*, October 14, 1987, D.C.
s. 33AA, regs. 87/675.
s. 40, see *Valentine* v. *MacBrayne Haulage*, 1986 S.C.C.R. 692; *Carmichael* v. *Hannaway*, 1987 S.C.C.R. 236.
s. 40, regs. 87/675, 1133, 1315.
s. 41, regs. 87/1315.
s. 42, order 87/1327.
s. 43, regs. 87/1144.
ss. 45, 46, see *Weir* v. *Tudhope*, 1987 S.C.C.R. 307.
s. 47, see *British Leyland* v. *E.C. Commission (Merson Intervening) (No. 226/84)* [1987] R.T.R. 136, European Ct.
s. 47, regs. 87/1508, 1509.
s. 50, regs. 87/315, 1508, 1509, 1556.
ss. 57, 58, regs. 87/1149.
s. 84, regs. 87/1378.
s. 85, regs. 87/560, 1378.
ss. 86–89, regs. 87/1378.
s. 93, see *Sutch* v. *Crown Prosecution Service*, January 30, 1987; H.H. Judge Compton; Wood Green Crown Ct.; *Tudhope* v. *O'Kane*, 1986 S.C.C.R. 538; *Grix* v. *Chief Constable of Kent* [1987] R.T.R. 193, D.C.
s. 94, see *Taylor* v. *Comr. of Police of the Metropolis* [1987] R.T.R. 118, D.C.
s. 96, regs. 87/1378.
s. 99, see *McKenzie* v. *Lockhart*, 1986 S.C.C.R. 663.
s. 101, see *Sutch* v. *Crown Prosecution Service*, January 30, 1987; H.H. Judge Compton; Wood Green Crown Ct.; *Chief Constable of West Mercia Police* v. *Williams* [1987] R.T.R. 188, D.C.; *Barnett* v. *Fieldhouse* [1987] R.T.R. 266, D.C.
s. 101, amended (S.): 1987, c.41, sch. 1.
s. 107, regs. 87/560, 1378.
s. 108, regs. 87/1378.
ss. 143, 144, see *Jones* v. *Chief Constable of Bedfordshire* [1987] Crim.L.R. 502, D.C.
ss. 145, 149, amended: regs. 87/2171.
ss. 154, 155, amended: order 87/353.
s. 158, amended: regs. 87/2171.
s. 168, see *Clarke* v. *Allan*, 1987 S.C.C.R. 333.
s. 172, regs. 87/1326.
s. 190, see *Chief Constable of Avon and Somerset* v. *Fleming* [1987] 1 All E.R. 318, D.C.
s. 199, regs. 87/1149.
sch. 4, see *Sutch* v. *Crown Prosecution Service*, January 30, 1987; H.H. Judge Compton; Wood Green Crown Ct.; *Tudhope* v. *O'Kane*, 1986 S.C.C.R. 538.

1972—cont.

20. Road Traffic Act 1972—cont.
sch. 4, repealed in pt. (S.): 1987, c.41, sch. 2.
34. Trade Descriptions Act 1972.
repealed: 1987, c.43, s.48, sch. 5.
41. Finance Act 1972.
s. 7, see *Pattni (Purshotam M.) & Sons* v. *Customs and Excise Comrs.* [1987] S.T.C. 1, Russell J.
s. 76, repealed: 1987, c.16, sch. 16.
ss. 84, 85, 100, see *Collard* v. *Mining and Industrial Holdings, Financial Times*, December 1, 1987, C.A.
s. 85, amended: 1987, c.51, s.74; repealed in pt.: *ibid.*, s.74, sch. 9.
s. 93, repealed: *ibid.*
s. 95, amended: *ibid.*, s.74.
s. 100, amended: *ibid.*, s.77.
s. 101, amended: *ibid.*, s.74.
s. 102, amended: *ibid.*, s.88.
s. 103, amended: *ibid.*, s.74.
sch. 3, see *Customs and Excise Commissioners* v. *Teknequip* [1987] S.T.C. 664, Otton J.
sch. 16, amended: 1987, c.16, sch. 15; c.51, s.61; repealed in pt.: 1987, c.16, sch. 16; c.51, s.61.
sch. 18, amended: 1987, c.51, s.75.
46. Housing (Financial Provisions) (Scotland) Act 1972.
repealed, except ss.69, 78, 81, sch. 9 (in pt.): 1987, c.26, sch. 24.
s. 23A, order 87/11.
47. Housing Finance Act 1972.
s. 12, sch. 1, see *Hemsted* v. *Lees and Norwich City Council* (1986) 18 H.L.R. 424, McCowan J.
48. Parliamentary and other Pensions Act 1972.
Pt. I (ss.1–25), repealed: 1987, c.45, sch. 4.
s. 27, amended: *ibid.*, sch. 3.
ss. 30, 31 (in pt.), 33, 34, 35 (in pt.), 36 (in pt.), schs. 1–4, repealed: *ibid.*, sch. 4.
49. Affiliation Proceedings (Amendment) Act 1972.
repealed: 1987, c.42, sch. 4.
52. Town and Country Planning (Scotland) Act 1972.
ss. 52, 54D, regs. 87/1529.
s. 88, see *Midlothian District Council* v. *Stevenson* [1986] J.P.L. 913, Court of Session.
s. 98, see *White* v. *Hamilton*, 1987 S.C.C.R. 12.
ss. 160–162, regs. 87/1529.
s. 173, see *Strathclyde Regional Council* v. *Secretary of State for Scotland*, 1987 S.L.T. 724.
s. 179, regs. 87/1529.
s. 181, amended: 1987, c.3, sch. 1.
s. 186, amended: 1987, c.26, sch. 23.

1972—cont.

52. Town and Country Planning (Scotland) Act 1972—cont.

ss. 205, 251, amended: 1987, c.3, sch. 1.

s. 257, regs. 87/1529.

s. 259, regs. 87/1937.

s. 259, amended: 1987, c.3, sch. 1.

s. 262A, regs. 87/1529.

s. 267, amended: 1987, c.18, sch. 6.

ss. 273, 275, regs. 87/1529, 1531, 1532.

sch. 6A, regs. 87/1532.

sch. 7, regs. 87/1531.

sch. 10, regs. 87/1529.

59. Administration of Justice (Scotland) Act 1972.

s. 1, Act of Sederunt 87/1206.

s. 3, see *O'Neill* v. *Scottish Joint Negotiating Committee for Teaching Staff* (O.H.), 1987 S.L.T. 648.

61. Land Charges Act 1972.

s. 5, see *Perez-Adamson* v. *Perez-Rivas* [1987] 2 W.L.R. 500, C.A.

63. Industry Act 1972.

s. 7, see *Ryan (Inspector of Taxes)* v. *Crabtree Denims* [1987] S.T.C. 402, Hoffmann J.

s. 10, amended: regs. 87/1807.

65. National Debt Act 1972.

s. 3, regs. 87/1635.

67. Companies (Floating Charges and Receivers) (Scotland) Act 1972.

s. 15, see *Shanks* v. *Central Regional Council* (O.H.), 1987 S.L.T. 410.

68. European Communities Act 1972.

ss. 1, 2, see *British Leyland* v. *E.C. Commission (Merson Intervening) (No. 226/84)* [1987] R.T.R. 136, European Ct.

s. 2, see *R.* v. *H.M. Treasury, ex p. Daily Mail and General Trust* [1987] 1 F.T.L.R. 394, Macpherson J.

s. 2, regs. 87/27, 97, 116, 149, 410, 425 (S.), 442, 524, 735, 763, 800 (S.), 805, 881 (S.), 909, 949, 1497, 1521, 1523, 1755, 1771, 1783, 1807, 1824, 1843, 1902, 1991, 2118, 2130, 2171, 2202; orders 87/447, 448, 926, 973; S.Rs. 1987 Nos. 78, 85, 92, 114, 154–156, 217, 218, 225, 306, 317, 328, 351, 352, 383, 407.

s. 5, orders 87/1053, 1125, 1218, 1804.

sch. 1, see *British Leyland* v. *E.C. Commission (Merson Intervening) (No. 226/84)* [1987] R.T.R. 136, European Ct.

sch. 2, orders 87/1053, 1125, 1804.

70. Local Government Act 1972.

see *Bradford Metropolitan City Council* v. *Brown* (1987) 19 H.L.R. 16, C.A.

s. 13, see *Taylor* v. *Masefield* (1987) 85 L.G.R. 108, C.A.

s. 51, orders 87/221, 305, 338, 339, 1576, 1598, 1737.

s. 67, orders 87/124, 221, 305, 338, 339, 1576, 1598, 1737.

1972—cont.

70. Local Government Act 1972—cont.

s. 123, see *R.* v. *Doncaster Metropolitan Borough Council, ex p. Braim* (1987) 85 L.G.R. 233, McCullough J.; *Manchester City Council* v. *Secretary of State for the Environment* (1987) 27 R.V.R. 75; (1987) 54 P. & C.R. 212, C.A.

s. 151, see *R.* v. *Hackney London Borough Council, ex p. Fleming* (1986) 26 R.V.R. 182, Woolf J.

ss. 173, 177, 177A, regs. 87/1483.

s. 247, order 87/162.

s. 262, order 87/1533.

sch. 10, order 87/124.

sch. 12, rules 87/1, 262.

sch. 29, repealed in pt.: 1987, c.43, sch. 5.

1973

4. Atomic Energy Authority (Weapons Group) Act 1973.

see *Pearce* v. *Secretary of State for Defence, The Times,* August 5, 1987, C.A.

5. Housing (Amendment) Act 1973.

repealed (S.): 1987, c.26, sch. 24.

8. Coal Industry Act 1973.

ss. 2, 10, amended: 1987, c.3, sch. 1.

14. Costs in Criminal Cases Act 1973.

s. 2, see *R.* v. *Nottingham JJ., ex p. Fohmann* (1987) 84 Cr.App.R. 316, D.C.

ss. 3, 4, see *Sampson, Re, The Independent,* February 12, 1987, H.L.

s. 12, see *Patel* v. *Blakey, The Times,* February 26, 1987, D.C.

15. Administration of Justice Act 1973.

s. 8, see *Citibank Trust* v. *Ayivor* [1987] 1 W.L.R. 1157, Mervyn Davies J.

s. 10, sch. 3, regs. 87/101, 160.

16. Education Act 1973.

s. 3, regs. 87/1261.

s. 2, repealed in pt.: 1987, c.15, sch.

18. Matrimonial Causes Act 1973.

s. 23, see *Board (Orse Checkland)* v. *Checkland (Board Intervening), The Times,* January 10, 1987, C.A.; *R.* v. *Rushmoor Borough Council, ex p. Barrett* [1986] 3 W.L.R. 998, Reeve J.; *Dinch* v. *Dinch* [1987] 1 W.L.R. 252, H.L.; *Sherdley* v. *Sherdley* [1987] 2 W.L.R. 1071, H.L.

s. 24, see *R.* v. *Rushmoor Borough Council, ex p. Barrett* [1986] 3 W.L.R. 998; Reeve J.; *Dinch* v. *Dinch* [1987] 1 W.L.R. 252, H.L.

s. 24A, see *R.* v. *Rushmoor Borough Council, ex p. Barrett* [1986] 3 W.L.R. 998, Reeve J.; *Burton* v. *Burton* (1986) 2 F.L.R. 419, Butler-Sloss J.

ss. 25, 25A, see *Suter* v. *Suter and Jones* [1987] 3 W.L.R. 9, C.A.

s. 27, amended: 1987, c.42, sch. 2.

22. Law Reform (Diligence) (Scotland) Act 1973.

repealed: 1987, c.18, sch. 8.

1973—cont.

29. Guardianship Act 1973.
amended: 1987, c.42, sch. 2.
s. 1, amended: *ibid*, ss.2, 5.
s. 2, amended: *ibid.*, s.3, sch. 2; repealed in pt.: *ibid.*, schs. 2, 4.
s. 3, amended: *ibid.*, s.6.
s. 4, amended: *ibid.*, s.6, sch. 2; repealed in pt.: *ibid.*, schs. 2, 4.
s. 5, amended: *ibid.*, s.6, sch. 2.
s. 5A, amended: *ibid.*, sch. 2.
s. 8A, added: *ibid.*

32. National Health Service Reorganisation Act 1973.
ss. 19, 54, 56, order 87/1428.

36. Northern Ireland Constitution Act 1973.
s. 38, orders 87/168, 1628.

37. Water Act 1973.
s. 29, order 87/2022.
ss. 29–31, see *Severn Trent Water Authority* v. *Cardshops* (1987) 27 R.V.R. 133, C.A.

38. Social Security Act 1973.
s. 64, amended: regs. 87/1116.
s. 65, orders 87/373, 374.
ss. 66, 67, regs. 87/1114.
sch. 16, amended: regs. 87/1116.

41. Fair Trading Act 1973.
see *R.* v. *Monopolies and Mergers Commission, ex p. Brown (Matthew)* [1987] 1 All E.R. 463, Macpherson J.
s. 130, amended: 1987, c.43, sch. 4.
s. 133, see *R.* v. *Monopolies and Mergers Commission, ex p. Elders IXL* [1987] 1 All E.R. 451, Mann J.

43. Hallmarking Act 1973.
ss. 2, 21, 22, order 87/1892.

45. Domicile and Matrimonial Proceedings Act 1973.
s. 16, see *Maples (Formerly Melamud)* v. *Maples; Maples (Formerly Melamud)* v. *Melamud* [1987] 3 W.L.R. 487, Latey J.
sch. 1, see *K.* v. *K.* (1986) 2 F.L.R. 411, Hollis J.; *De Dampierre* v. *De Dampierre* [1987] 2 W.L.R. 1006, H.L.

50. Employment and Training Act 1973.
sch. 3, repealed in pt.: 1987, c.39, sch. 2.

51. Finance Act 1973.
s. 14, amended: 1987, c.51, sch. 2.
s. 17, see *Stevenson (Inspector of Taxes)* v. *Wishart* [1987] 2 All E.R. 428, C.A.
s. 23, see *Ward-Stemp* v. *Griffin (Inspector of Taxes), The Times,* December 1, 1987, Walton J.
ss. 31 (in pt.), 44, repealed: 1987, c.16, sch. 16.
s. 56, regs. 87/315, 802, 803, 869, 1556, 2012; order 87/1131; S.Rs. 1987 Nos. 217, 383, 390.
s. 90, sch. 8, order 87/1131.
sch. 12, amended: 1987, c.16, sch. 15.

52. Prescription and Limitation (Scotland) Act 1973.
s. 6, see *Kirkcaldy District Council* v. *Household Manufacturing* (O.H.), 1987 S.L.T. 617; *Lieberman* v. *G. W. Tait and Sons* (O.H.), 1987 S.L.T. 585.

1973—cont.

52. Prescription and Limitation (Scotland) Act 1973—*cont.*
ss. 6, 9, see *Shanks* v. *Central Regional Council* (O.H.), 1987 S.L.T. 410.
s. 7, amended: 1987, c.43, sch. 1.
s. 9, amended and repealed in pt.: 1987, c.36, s. 1.
s. 10, see *Lieberman* v. *G. W. Tait and Sons* (O.H.), 1987 S.L.T. 585.
s. 16A, added: 1987, c.43, sch. 1.
s. 17, see *Grimason* v. *National Coal Board,* 1987 S.L.T. 714.
s. 18, see *Hamill* v. *Newalls Insulation Co.* (O.H.), 1987 S.L.T. 478.
s. 19A, see *Anderson* v. *City of Glasgow District Council,* 1987 S.L.T. 279; *Forbes* v. *House of Clydesdale* (O.H.), 1987 S.C.L.R. 136.
ss. 22A–22D, added: 1987, c.43, sch. 1.
s. 23, repealed: *ibid.*, schs. 1, 5.
sch. 1, amended: *ibid.*, sch. 1.

56. Land Compensation (Scotland) Act 1973.
s. 27, amended and repealed in pt.: 1987, c.26, sch. 23.
ss. 29, 34, 36, 38, 39, 53, 69, 80, amended: *ibid.*

62. Powers of Criminal Courts Act 1973.
s. 1, see *R.* v. *West London Stipendiary Magistrate, ex p. Watts, The Times,* May 30, 1987, D.C.
s. 2, see *R.* v. *Barnett* (1986) 86 Cr.App.R. 365, C.A.
s. 16, see *Jones* v. *Kelsey* [1987] Crim.L.R. 392, D.C.
s. 19, see *Lewisham London Borough* v. *W. & P.,* May 15, 1987, Pearlman J.
s. 43, see *R.* v. *Boothe* [1987] Crim.L.R. 347, C.A.; *R.* v. *Neville* [1987] Crim.L.R. 585, C.A.
s. 54, sch. 3, orders 87/356, 1855.

65. Local Government (Scotland) Act 1973.
s. 17, orders 87/112, 334, 1943.
s. 45, regs. 87/1381.
s. 49, regs. 87/308.
ss. 49A, 50, regs. 87/1381.
s. 56, amended: 1987, c.47, s.28.
s. 83, amended: *ibid.*, sch. 1.
s. 94, order 87/943.
ss. 107–108C, repealed: 1987, c.47, sch. 6.
ss. 109, 110, amended: *ibid.*, sch. 1.
s. 111, amended: *ibid.*; repealed in pt.: *ibid.*, schs. 1, 6.
ss. 116, 118, amended: *ibid.*, sch. 1.
ss. 119, 120, repealed: *ibid.*, sch. 6.
s. 130, amended: 1987, c.26, sch. 23.
s. 131, repealed in pt.: *ibid.*, schs. 23, 24.
s. 235, regs. 87/1381.
s. 236, amended: 1987, c.47, sch. 23.
schs. 9, 12, repealed in pt.: *ibid.*, schs. 23, 24.
sch. 27, repealed in pt.: 1987, c.43, sch. 5.

1974

4. Legal Aid Act 1974.
s. 1, regs. 87/627; amended: *ibid.*

1974—cont.

4. Legal Aid Act 1974—*cont.*
s. 4, regs. 87/396; amended: *ibid.*
ss. 6, 9, regs. 87/628; amended: *ibid.*
s. 9, see *Simpson* v. *The Law Society* [1987] 2 W.L.R. 1390, H.L.
s. 10, see *Harris* v. *Harris*, February 11, 1987, H.H. Judge Whitley, Portsmouth Crown Ct.
s. 13, see *Adams & Adams* v. *Riley (M.G.), The Times*, October 12, 1987, Hutchison J.
s. 20, regs. 87/388, 396, 443, 627, 628, 2098.
s. 28, amended: 1987, c. 38, sch. 2.
ss. 28, 31, see *R.* v. *Huntingdon Magistrates' Court, ex p. Yapp* (1987) 84 Cr.App.R. 90, D.C.
s. 37, see *R.* v. *Boswell; R.* v. *Halliwell* [1987] 1 W.L.R. 705, Leggatt J.
s. 39, regs. 87/369, 422.
sch. 1, repealed in pt.: 1987, c.42, sch. 4.
sch. 2, regs. 87/2098; amended: *ibid.*

7. Local Government Act 1974.
s. 21, see *Appeal of Maudsley (V.O.), Re* (Ref. LVC/184/1982) (1986) 26 R.V.R. 181.
s. 34, see *R.* v. *Local Commissioner for Administration for the South, the West, the West Midlands, Leicestershire, Lincolnshire and Cambridgeshire, ex p. Eastleigh Borough Council, The Times*, July 14, 1987, Nolan J.
sch. 3, amended: 1987, c.3, sch. 1; c.53, s.30.

14. National Insurance Act 1974.
s. 6, regs. 87/214.

23. Juries Act 1974.
s. 18, see *R.* v. *Bliss* (1987) 84 Cr.App.R. 1, C.A.

24. Prices Act 1974.
s. 4, order 87/8.

28. Northern Ireland Act 1974.
Commencement orders: S.Rs. 1987 Nos. 6, 20, 308.
s. 1, order 87/1207.
sch. 1, S.Rs. 1987 Nos. 6, 20, 21, 121, 137, 161, 184, 185, 200, 271, 308.

30. Finance Act 1974.
s. 26, amended: 1987, c.51, s.71; repealed in pt.: *ibid.*, s.71, sch. 9.
s. 27, amended: 1987, c.16, sch. 15.

37. Health and Safety at Work etc. Act 1974.
s. 3, see *R.* v. *Mara* [1987] 1 W.L.R. 87, C.A.; *Sterling-Winthrop Group* v. *Allan*, 1987 S.C.C.R. 25.
s. 6, amended: 1987, c.43, sch. 3.
s. 11, regs. 87/605.
s. 15, regs. 87/180; orders 87/37, 52.
s. 22, amended: 1987, c.43, sch. 3.
ss. 25A, 27A, added: *ibid.*
ss. 28, 33, amended: *ibid.*
ss. 33, 36, see *West Cumberland By Products* v. *D.P.P., The Times*, November 12, 1987, D.C.

1974—cont.

37. Health and Safety at Work etc. Ac 1974—*cont.*
s. 43, regs. 87/605; orders, 87/37, 52.
s. 50, regs. 87/180.
s. 53, amended: 1987, c.43, sch. 3 repealed in pt.: *ibid.*, sch. 5.
s. 78, repealed in pt.: 1987, c.27, sch. 4.
s. 80, order 87/37.
s. 82, regs. 87/180, 605; orders 87/37, 52.
sch. 3, order 87/37.
sch. 9, repealed in pt.: 1987, c.39, sch. 2.

38. Land Tenure Reform (Scotland) Act 1974.
s. 8, amended: 1987, c.26, sch. 23.

39. Consumer Credit Act 1974.
s. 16, order 87/1578.
s. 16, amended: 1987, c.22, s.88; c.26, sch 23(S.).
s. 93A, added (S.): 1987, c.18, sch. 6.
s. 113, amended: 1987, c.13, s.4.
s. 129, amended (S.): 1987, c.18, sch. 6.
s. 173, amended: 1987, c.22, s.87.
s. 174, amended: 1987, c.43, sch. 4.
s. 182, order 87/1578.
s. 187, amended: 1987, c.22, s.89.
s. 189, amended: *ibid.*, s.88.

40. Control of Pollution Act 1974.
ss. 3, 17, regs. 87/402.
s. 25, amended: 1987, c.3, sch. 1.
s. 30, regs. 87/402.
s. 32, order 87/1782.
Pt. 3 (ss.57–74), s.60, see *Lloyds Bank* v *Guardian Assurance and Trollope & Colls* (1987) 35 Build.L.R. 34, C.A.
s. 58, see *R.* v. *Birmingham Justices, ex p Guppy, The Times*, October 8, 1987 D.C.
s. 71, order 87/1730.
s. 100, regs. 87/783.
s. 104, regs. 87/783; orders 87/1730, 1732.

43. Merchant Shipping Act 1974.
s. 5, order 87/220.
s. 16, regs. 87/306, 311.
s. 17, sch. 5, regs. 87/63, 306, 311, 548 854, 1603.
s. 20, order 87/1263.

44. Housing Act 1974.
repealed, except ss. 11, 18 (in pt.) 129–131, sch. 3 (in pt.), (S.): 1987, c.26 sch. 24.
s. 71A, see *R.* v. *Lambeth London Borough, ex p. Clayhope Properties* (1987) 283 E.G. 739, C.A.
ss. 75, 82, see *R.* v. *Westminster City Council, ex p. Hazan, The Independent,* December 10, 1987, C.A.
sch. 8, see *R.* v. *Westminster Valuation Officer, ex p. Rendall* (1986) 26 R.V.R. 220, C.A.
sch. 13, repealed in pt. (S.): 1987, c.26, sch.24.

45. Housing (Scotland) Act 1974.
repealed: 1987, c.26, sch. 24.

46. Friendly Societies Act 1974.
s. 64, amended: 1987, c.16, s.30.
s. 104, regs. 87/392.

CAP.

1974—cont.

47. Solicitors Act 1974.
see *Solicitor, A, Re, The Times*, July 7, 1987, C.A.
ss. 20, 22, 25, 27, 39, 87, see *Reiss Engineering* v. *Harris* [1987] R.P.C. 171, Patents Ct.
s. 70, see *Harrison* v. *Tew, The Independent*, July 7, 1987, C.A.
s. 71, see *Ingrams* v. *Sykes, The Independent*, November 12, 1987, C.A.
s. 87, amended: 1987, c.22, sch. 6; repealed in pt.: *ibid.*, schs. 6, 7.

48. Railways Act 1974.
see *R.* v. *Secretary of State for Transport, ex p. Sherrif and Sons Ltd., The Times*, December 18, 1986, Taylor J.

49. Insurance Companies Act 1974.
ss. 3, 83, see *Phoenix General Insurance Co. of Greece S.A.* v. *Halvanon Insurance Co.; Same* v. *Administratia Asigurarilor de Stat* [1987] 2 W.L.R. 512, C.A.

50. Road Traffic Act 1974.
sch. 3, repealed in pt.(S.): 1974, c.41, sch. 2.

52. Trade Union and Labour Relations Act 1974.
s. 2, see *Goring* v. *British Actors Equity Association* [1987] I.R.L.R. 122, Browne-Wilkinson V.-C.
ss. 2, 28, see *British Association of Advisers and Lecturers in Physical Education* v. *National Union of Teachers* [1986] I.R.L.R. 497, C.A.
s. 8, regs. 87/258.
ss. 13, 15, see *News Group Newspapers* v. *Society of Graphical and Allied Trades '82 (No. 2)* [1987] I.C.R. 181, Stuart-Smith J.
s. 30, see *Falconer* v. *A.S.L.E.F. and N.U.R.* [1986] I.R.L.R. 331, Sheffield County Ct.

53. Rehabilitation of Offenders Act 1974.
ss. 4, 7, see *Francey* v. *Cunninghame District Council* (Sh.Ct.), 1987 S.C.L.R. 6.
s. 7, repealed in pt.: 1987, c.22, sch. 7.

1975

3. Arbitration Act 1975.
s. 1, see *World Star, The* [1986] 2 Lloyd's Rep. 274, Sheen J.; *Zambia Steel & Building Supplies* v. *Clark (James) Eaton* [1986] 2 Lloyd's Rep. 225, C.A.; *Etri Fans Co.* v. *NMB (U.K.)* [1987] 2 All E.R. 763, C.A.
s. 7, order 87/1029.

7. Finance Act 1975.
s. 6, amended: 1987, c.51, s.39.
s. 12, amended: 1987, c.16, sch. 15.
s. 20, see *MacPherson* v. *I.R.C.* [1987] S.T.C. 73, C.A.
ss. 22, 23, see *Miller* v. *I.R.C.* [1987] S.T.C. 108, Ct. of Session; *sub nom. Roberton's Trs.* v. *I.R.C.*, 1987 S.L.T. 534.

CAP.

1975—cont.

7. Finance Act 1975—cont.
sch. 5, see *Macpherson* v. *I.R.C.* [1987] S.T.C. 73, C.A.; *Robertson's Trs.* v. *Inland Revenue Comrs.*, 1987 S.L.T. 534.

8. Offshore Petroleum Development (Scotland) Act 1975.
s. 6, repealed in pt.: 1987, c.21, schs. 2, 3.
s. 18, amended: *ibid.*, sch. 2.

14. Social Security Act 1975.
s. 1, order 87/48; amended: *ibid.*
s. 2, order 87/935.
s. 3, regs. 87/413, 606, 1590.
s. 4, regs. 87/413; amended: order 87/46.
ss. 7–9, amended: *ibid.*
s. 13, regs. 87/316, 411, 413, 687, 914.
s. 14, see *Decision No. R(S) 6/86.*
s. 17, see *Decisions Nos. R(S) 6/86; R(U) 3/86.*
s. 17, regs. 87/317, 327, 688, 878.
s. 19, see *Decisions Nos. R(U) 5/86; R(U) 1/87.*
s. 22, regs. 87/416.
s. 25, amended: 1987, c.42, sch. 2.
s. 29, regs. 87/1854.
s. 35, see *Decision No. R(A) 3/86; Moran* v. *Secretary of State for Social Services, The Times*, March 14, 1987, C.A.
s. 35, regs. 87/1426.
s. 37A, see *Decision No. R(M) 3/86; Decision No. R(M) 4/86.*
s. 39, regs. 87/1854.
s. 41, amended: order 87/45.
s. 49, regs. 87/355.
s. 58, regs. 87/327.
s. 59A, regs. 87/415.
ss. 76, 77, regs. 87/335.
s. 79, regs. 87/878.
ss. 81, 82, regs. 87/1683.
s. 84, regs. 87/355.
s. 85, regs. 87/31, 1683.
s. 101, regs. 87/214.
s. 104, regs. 87/1424, 1973.
ss. 106, 112, regs. 87/214.
s. 113, regs. 87/335.
s. 114, regs. 87/214, 1967, 1970.
s. 115, regs. 87/214, 409, 1970.
s. 116, regs. 87/1967.
s. 117, see *Jones* v. *Department of Employment, The Times*, November 27, 1987, C.A.
s. 119, regs. 87/1970.
ss. 120, 121, 123A, order 87/46.
s. 131, regs. 87/327, 417.
s. 134, order 87/48, amended: *ibid.*
s. 143, orders 87/935, 1830, 1831.
s. 146, see *R.* v. *Highbury Corner Stipendiary Magistrate, ex p. D.H.S.S., The Times*, February 4, 1987, D.C.
s. 165A, regs. 87/878, 1968.
s. 166, regs. 87/36, 317, 355, 358, 606, 659, 687, 878, 1325, 1440, 1854, 1917, 1968, 1970, 1973; order 87/1910.
s. 167, order 87/48.

CAP.

1975—cont.

14. Social Security Act 1975—cont.

s. 168, regs. 87/106, 411, 413, 657, 687, 914, 1099–1107, 1110–1114, 1590, 1854.

sch. 1, regs. 87/413.

sch. 4, amended: order 87/45.

sch. 13, regs. 87/409, 1970.

sch. 20, regs. 87/31, 106, 214, 316, 327, 335, 355, 409, 411, 413, 415–417, 606, 657, 688, 878, 914, 1100, 1102, 1106, 1110–1112, 1424, 1590, 1683, 1854.

15. Social Security (Northern Ireland) Act 1975.

s. 1, S.R. 1987 No. 25.

ss. 3, S.Rs. 1987 No. 143, 201, 348.

s. 4, S.R. 1987 No. 143.

s. 13, S.Rs. 1987 Nos. 115, 138, 143, 220.

s. 17, S.Rs. 1987 Nos. 90, 128, 221.

s. 22, S.R. 1987 No. 170.

s. 29, S.R. 1978 No. 404.

s. 35, S.Rs. 1987 Nos. 322, 413.

s. 39, S.R. 1987 No. 404.

s. 49, S.R. 1987 No. 129.

s. 58, S.R. 1987 No. 128.

s. 59A, S.R. 1987 No. 142.

ss. 76, 77, S.R. 1987 No. 116.

ss. 81, 82, S.R. 1987 No. 391.

s. 84, S.R. 1987 No. 129.

s. 85, S.Rs. 1987 Nos. 12, 391, 413.

s. 97, S.R. 1987 No. 61.

ss. 98, 100, S.R. 1987 No. 82.

s. 101, S.Rs. 1987 Nos. 82, 112.

s. 104, S.R. 1987 No. 325.

s. 105, S.R. 1987 No. 82.

s. 106, S.Rs. 1987 Nos. 82, 112.

ss. 108–110, S.R. 1987 No. 82.

s. 112A, S.Rs. 1987 Nos. 81, 112.

s. 113, S.Rs. 1987 Nos. 82, 116.

s. 114, S.Rs. 1987 Nos. 82, 100, 112.

s. 115, S.Rs. 1987 Nos. 82, 112, 117.

s. 119, S.R. 1987 No. 82.

s. 120, S.R. 1987 No. 26.

s. 126, S.Rs. 1987 Nos. 128, 151.

s. 128, S.R. 1987 No. 25.

s. 134, S.Rs. 1987 Nos. 231, 399, 402.

s. 155, S.R. 1987 No. 61.

sch. 1, S.R. 1987 No. 143.

sch. 10, S.R. 1987 No. 61.

sch. 12, S.R. 1987 No. 82.

sch. 13, S.Rs. 1987 Nos. 112, 117.

sch. 17, S.Rs. 1987 Nos. 112, 129, 404.

16. Industrial Injuries and Diseases (Old Cases) Act 1975.

s. 2, schemes 87/419, 429, amended: orders 87/45, 1978.

s. 4, schemes 87/419, 429.

s. 5, scheme 87/400.

s. 7, amended: orders 87/45, 1978.

17. Industrial Injuries and Diseases (Northern Ireland Old Cases) Act 1975.

ss. 2, 4, S.Rs. 1987 Nos. 118, 152.

18. Social Security (Consequential Provisions) Act 1975.

s. 2, order 87/935.

sch. 3, S.R. 1987 No. 413.

CAP.

1975—cont.

21. Criminal Procedure (Scotland) Act 1975.

s. 2, amended: 1987, c.41, s.58.

s. 5, amended: *ibid.*, sch. 1; repealed in pt.: *ibid.*, schs. 1, 2.

s. 86, amended: *ibid.*, sch. 1.

ss. 87, 88, repealed: *ibid.*, sch. 2.

s. 101, see *H.M. Advocate* v. *Sinclair*, 1987 S.L.T. 161; *H.M. Advocate* v. *Shevlin*, 1987 S.L.T. 314; *Sandford* v. *H.M. Advocate*, 1987 S.L.T. 399; *Mallison* v. *H.M. Advocate*, 1987 S.C.C.R. 320.

s. 104, amended: 1987, c.41, s.58.

s. 112, substituted: *ibid.*, s. 57.

s. 113, amended: *ibid.*, sch. 1; repealed in pt.: *ibid.*, sch. 2.

s. 114, substituted: *ibid.*, s.57.

ss. 115–119, repealed: *ibid.*, sch. 2.

s. 123, see *Keane* v. *H.M. Advocate*, 1987 S.L.T. 220.

s. 129, amended: 1987, c.41, sch. 1.

s. 139A, added: *ibid.*, s.63.

s. 141, see *Fleming* v. *H.M. Advocate*, 1986 S.C.C.R. 577.

ss. 141, 149, amended: 1987, c.41, sch. 1.

s. 143, see *B.* v. *Kennedy* 1987 S.L.T. 765.

s. 160, see *Deeney* v. *H.M. Advocate*, 1986 S.C.C.R. 393.

s. 170, see *Merrin* v. *S.*, 1987 S.L.T. 193.

s. 183, amended: 1987, c.41, s.65, sch. 1.

s. 186, amended: *ibid.*, s.65.

s. 193B, repealed: *ibid.*, sch. 2.

s. 212, amended and repealed in pt.: *ibid.*, sch. 1.

s. 215, amended: *ibid.*

s. 216, amended: *ibid.*, s.64.

s. 218, see *Campbell* v. *H.M. Advocate*, 1986 S.C.C.R. 403.

s. 221, amended: 1987, c.41, s.58.

s. 228, see *McDonald* v. *H.M. Advocate*, 1987 S.C.C.R. 153; *Salusbury-Hughes* v. *H.M. Advocate*, 1987 S.C.C.R. 38.

s. 231, amended: 1987, c.41, s.45.

ss. 245, 246, amended: *ibid.*, sch. 1.

s. 263, repealed in pt.: *ibid.*, sch. 2.

s. 264, amended: *ibid.*, s.68.

s. 268, amended: *ibid.*, sch. 1.

s. 280A, see *H.M. Advocate* v. *Sinclair*, 1987 S.L.T. 161.

s. 282, Act of Adjournal 87/1328.

s. 289B, amended: 1987, c.41, sch. 1; repealed in pt.: *ibid.*, sch. 2.

s. 289D, repealed in pt.: *ibid.*, sch. 2.

s. 289G, amended: *ibid.*, s.66.

ss. 289GA, 289GB, added: *ibid.*

s. 300, amended: *ibid.*, s.62; repealed in pt.: *ibid.*, sch. 2.

ss. 314, 315, see *Keily* v. *Tudhope*, 1987 S.L.T. 99.

ss. 328, 329, amended: 1987, c.41, s.62.

s. 331, see *Keily* v. *Tudhope*, 1987 S.L.T. 99; *Ross Inns* v. *Smith*, 1987 S.L.T. 121.

s. 335, see *MacArthur* v. *MacNeill*, 1987 S.L.T. 299; *Tudhope* v. *Fulton*, 1986 S.C.C.R. 567; *Belcher* v. *MacKinnon*,

1975—cont.

21. Criminal Procedure (Scotland) Act 1975—
cont.
1987 S.L.T. 298; *Brown* v. *McLeod,*
1986 S.C.C.R. 615; *Duffy* v. *Ingram,*
1987 S.C.C.R. 286.
s. 337, amended: 1987, c.41, s.62.
s. 342A, added: *ibid.,* s.63.
s. 346, amended: *ibid.,* sch. 1.
s. 357, see *Carmichael* v. *Monaghan,* 1987
S.L.T. 338.
s. 369, see *Merrin* v. *S.,* 1987 S.L.T. 193.
s. 384, amended: 1987, c.41, s.65, sch. 1.
s. 387, amended: *ibid.,* s.65.
s. 407, amended: *ibid.,* s.67.
s. 411, amended: 1987, c.18, sch. 6.
s. 413, substituted: 1987, c.41, s.59.
s. 426, amended: *ibid.,* sch. 1.
s. 428, amended: *ibid.,* s.64.
s. 431, see *Morrison* v. *Scott,* 1987
S.C.C.R. 376.
s. 442, see *Courtney* v. *Mackinnon,* 1986
S.C.C.R. 545; *Marshall* v. *Macdougall,*
1987 S.L.T. 123; *Moore* v. *Tudhope,*
1987 S.C.C.R. 371.
s. 443A, added: 1987, c.41, s.68.
s. 444, see *Singh, Petr.,* 1987 S.L.T. 63.
s. 447, see *Gordon* v. *Allan,* 1987 S.L.T.
400.
s. 452, see *Marshall* v. *Macdougall,* 1987
S.L.T. 123.
ss. 452A, 452B, see *Courtney* v. *Mackinnon,* 1986 S.C.C.R. 545.
s. 453C, see *Briggs* v. *Guild,* 1987
S.C.C.R. 141.
s. 463, amended: 1987, c.41, s.59.
sch. 1, see *B.* v. *Kennedy,* 1987 S.L.T.
765.
schs. 7C, 7D, repealed in pt.: 1987, c.26,
sch. 24.

22. Oil Taxation Act 1975.
s. 2, amended: 1987, c.16, s.62, sch. 13;
repealed in pt.: *ibid.,* s.62, sch. 16.
s. 3, see *I.R.C.* v. *Mobil North Sea* [1987]
1 W.L.R. 389, C.A.
s. 3, amended: 1987, c.16, sch. 13.
s. 5A, repealed in pt.: *ibid.,* s.62, sch. 16.
s. 5B, added: *ibid.,* s.64, sch. 13.
s. 9, amended: *ibid.*
s. 14, repealed in pt.: *ibid.,* s.62, sch. 16.
s. 16, amended: *ibid.,* s.46; c.51, s.76;
repealed in pt.: *ibid.,* s.76, sch. 9.
sch. 2, amended: 1987, c.16, s.62, schs.
10, 13; c.51, s.101; repealed in pt.: 1987,
c.16, s.62, sch. 16.
sch. 3, amended: *ibid.,* s.62, sch. 11:
repealed in pt.: *ibid.,* schs. 11, 16.
sch. 7, amended: *ibid.,* s.67, sch. 13.

**24. House of Commons Disqualification Act
1975.**
s. 5, order 87/449.
sch. 1, amended: 1987, c.1, sch. 1; c.3,
sch. 1; order 87/449; repealed in pt.:
1987, c.3, sch. 3; c.21, sch. 3.

1975—cont.

**25. Northern Ireland Assembly Disqualifica-
tion Act 1975.**
sch. 1, amended: 1987, c.3, sch. 1;
repealed in pt.: *ibid.,* sch. 3; c.21, sch.
3.

26. Ministers of the Crown Act 1975.
s. 1, orders 87/465, 2039.

27. Ministerial and other Salaries Act 1975.
s. 1, orders 87/941, 2039; amended: order
87/941.

**28. Housing Rents and Subsidies (Scotland) Act
1975.**
repealed, except sch. 3 (in pt.): 1987, c.26,
sch. 24.

30. Local Government (Scotland) Act 1975.
ss. 1, 2, repealed in pt.: 1987, c.47, sch. 2.
s. 2, see *Assessor for Strathclyde Region* v.
B.S.R., 1987 S.L.T. 250; *Assessor for
Central Region* v. *Fleming's Trs.,* 1987
S.L.T. 793.
ss. 2, 3, 37, see *W. R. Whitwell* v. *Assessor
for Strathclyde Region,* Lands Valuation
Appeal Court, October 24, 1985.
ss. 3, 37, see *Dalgleish* v. *Assessor for
Strathclyde Region,* Land Valuation
Appeal Court, October 24, 1985.
s. 7, amended: 1987, c.47, sch. 1.
s. 16, repealed in pt.: *ibid.,* sch. 6.
s. 37, amended: *ibid.,* sch. 1; repealed in
pt.: *ibid.,* sch. 6.
sch. 1, amended: 1987, c.3, sch. 1.
sch. 3, amended: 1987, c.47, sch. 1;
repealed in pt.: 1987, c.26, schs. 23, 24.

**34. Evidence (Proceedings in Other Jurisdic-
tions) Act 1975.**
s. 10, orders 87/662, 1266.

45. Finance (No. 2) Act 1975.
s. 38, see *Bhadra* v. *Ellam (Inspector of
Taxes), The Times,* November 30, 1987,
Knox J.
s. 41, repealed: 1987, c.16, sch. 16.
s. 42, amended: *ibid.,* sch. 15.
s. 44, repealed in pt.: *ibid.,* sch. 16.
ss. 47, 48, orders 87/513, 898, 1492, 1988.
ss. 47, 48, repealed in pt.: 1987, c.16, sch.
16.
s. 69, amended: *ibid.,* s.23.
s. 70, amended: 1987, c.51, s.93.
sch. 12, amended: 1987, c.16, sch. 15.

49. Mobile Homes Act 1975.
see *Stroud* v. *Weir Associates* (1987) 19
H.L.R. 151, C.A.

51. Salmon and Freshwater Fisheries Act 1975.
s. 6, amended: 1987, c.49, sch. 1.
s. 28, orders 87/99, 612, 745, 1054.

52. Safety of Sports Grounds Act 1975.
s. 1, order 87/1689.
s. 1, amended: 1987, c.27, s.20, sch. 2.
s. 2, amended: *ibid.,* ss. 19, 21, sch. 2.
ss. 3, 4, amended: *ibid.,* sch. 2.
s. 5, amended: *ibid.,* s.22; repealed in pt.:
ibid., s.22, sch. 4.
s. 6, regs. 87/1941.
s. 6, amended: 1987, c.27, s.22.
s. 7, amended and repealed in pt.: *ibid.*

CAP.

1975—cont.

52. Safety of Sports Grounds Act 1975—cont.
ss. 8, 9, amended: *ibid.*, sch. 2.
s. 10, substituted: *ibid.*, s.23.
s. 10A, regs. 87/1941.
s. 10A, added: 1987, c.27, s.24.
s. 10B, added: *ibid.*, s.25.
s. 12, amended: *ibid.*, ss.23, 25, sch. 2; repealed in pt.: *ibid.*, schs. 2, 4.
s. 15, repealed: *ibid.*, s.15, sch. 4.
s. 15A, added: *ibid.*, s.15.
s. 17, amended: *ibid.*, s.23, sch. 2; repealed in pt.: *ibid.*, schs. 2, 4.
s. 18, amended: *ibid.*, s.15.

54. Limitation Act 1975.
s. 1, see *Arnold* v. *Central Electricity Generating Board* [1987] 2 W.L.R. 245, C.A.

55. Statutory Corporations (Financial Provisions) Act 1975.
sch. 2, amended: 1987, c.3, sch. 1.

56. Coal Industry Act 1975.
s. 1, sch. 1, amended: 1987, c.3, sch. 1.

60. Social Security Pensions Act 1975.
s. 6, regs. 87/316.
s. 6, amended: orders 87/45, 1978.
s. 12, regs. 87/1854.
s. 21, order 87/861.
s. 27, amended: order 87/656.
s. 28, order 87/656.
s. 29, regs. 87/1113.
s. 30, regs. 87/1101; amended: order 87/1978.
s. 31, regs. 87/1104, 1114.
s. 32, regs. 87/1101, 1114.
s. 35, regs. 87/411; amended: order 87/1978.
s. 36, regs. 87/1100.
s. 38, regs. 87/1099, 1114.
s. 39, regs. 87/1114.
s. 41, amended: order 87/1978.
ss. 41B, 41C, regs. 87/1114.
s. 43, regs. 87/1106, 1114.
ss. 44, 44A, regs. 87/657.
s. 44ZA, regs. 87/657, 1103.
s. 45, regs. 87/657, 1114.
s. 49, amended: regs. 87/1116.
s. 51, regs. 87/1114.
s. 52, regs. 87/1104, 1111, 1114.
s. 52A. order 87/1981.
s. 52C, regs. 87/1106.
s. 56A, regs. 87/1105, 1110.
s. 56P, regs. 87/1102.
s. 59, order 87/130.
s. 62, regs. 87/1099.
s. 66, regs. 87/1114.
sch. 1, regs, 87/1854.
sch. 1, amended: orders 87/45, 1978.
sch. 1A, regs. 87/1107, 1112.
sch. 2, regs. 87/657, 1104, 1111.
sch. 2, amended: regs. 87/1116.
sch. 3, amended: order 87/656.
sch. 4, amended: order 87/1978.

61. Child Benefit Act 1975.
ss. 2, 4, regs. 87/357.
s. 6, regs. 87/1968.

CAP.

1975—cont.

61. Child Benefit Act 1975—cont.
s. 15, order 87/1831.
ss. 22, 24, sch. 1, regs. 87/357.

63. Inheritance (Provision for Family and Dependants) Act 1975.
see *Rajabally* v. *Rajabally, The Times*, March 18, 1987, C.A.
s. 4, see *Johnson (Paul Anthony) Decd., Re*, May 8, 1987, Latey J.

65. Sex Discrimination Act 1975.
s. 1, see *Rainey* v. *Greater Glasgow Health Board*, 1987 S.L.T. 146; *Cornelius* v. *University College of Swansea, The Times*, February 14, 1987, C.A.; *R.* v. *Secretary of State for Education, ex p. Schaffter* [1987] I.R.L.R. 53, Schiemann J.; *Francis* v. *Tower Hamlets Borough Council* (1987) L.S.Gaz. 2530, E.A.T.; *Turner* v. *Labour Party and the Labour Party Superannuation Society* [1987] I.R.L.R. 101, E.A.T.; *Cornelius* v. *University College of Swansea* [1987] I.R.L.R. 141, C.A.
ss. 4, 5, see *Cornelius* v. *University College of Swansea* [1987] I.R.L.R. 141, C.A.
s. 6, see *Parsons* v. *East Surrey Health Authority* [1986] I.C.R. 837, E.A.T.; *Duke* v. *Reliance Systems* [1987] 2 W.L.R. 1225, C.A.; *Foster* v. *British Gas* [1987] I.C.R. 52, Industrial Tribunal; *Francis* v. *Tower Hamlets Borough Council* (1987) L.S.Gaz. 2530, E.A.T.; *Turner* v. *Labour Party and the Labour Party Superannuation Society* [1987] I.R.L.R. 101, E.A.T.; *Cornelius* v. *University College of Swansea* [1987] I.R.L.R. 141, C.A.; *Snowball* v. *Gardner Merchant* [1987] I.C.R. 719, E.A.T.
s. 10, order 87/930.
s. 51, see *R.* v. *Secretary of State for Education, ex p. Schaffter* [1987] I.R.L.R. 53, Schiemann J.
ss. 65, 66, see *Turner* v. *Labour Party and the Labour Party Superannuation Society* [1987] I.R.L.R. 101, E.A.T.
s. 81, order 87/930.
sch. 1, see *Rainey* v. *Greater Glasgow Health Board*, 1987 S.L.T. 146.

69. Scottish Development Agency Act 1975.
s. 13, amended: 1987, c.56, s.1.

70. Welsh Development Agency Act 1975.
s. 27, amended: 1987, c.3, sch. 1.

71. Employment Protection Act 1975.
s. 8, regs. 87/258.
s. 99, see *Association of University Teachers* v. *University of Newcastle-upon-Tyne* [1987] I.C.R. 317, E.A.T.
ss. 99, 101, see *Transport & General Workers Union* v. *Ledbury Preserves (1828)* [1986] I.C.R. 855, E.A.T.
sch. 16, repealed in pt.: 1987, c.1, sch. 2.

72. Children Act 1975.
Commencement order: 87/1242.
s. 3, see *S. (A Minor) (Adoption), Re, The Times*, August 26, 1987, C.A.

1975—cont.

72. Children Act 1975—cont.

s. 12, see *J. (A Minor) (Adoption Application), Re* (1987) 151 J.P.N. 62, Sheldon J.; *A. (A Minor) (Adoption: Parental Consent), Re* (1987) 131 S.J. 194, C.A.; *A. (A Minor) (Adoption: Parental Consent), Re* [1987] 1 W.L.R. 153, C.A.; *M. (A Minor) (Custodianship: Jurisdiction), Re* [1987] 1 W.L.R. 162, C.A.; *R. (A Minor) (Adoption or Custodianship), Re* (1987) 151 J.P.N. 175, Sheldon J.

s. 33, see *J. (A Minor) (Adoption Application), Re* (1987) 151 J.P.N. 62, Sheldon J.

s. 33, amended: 1987, c.42, sch. 2.

s. 34, amended: *ibid.*, sch. 2; repealed in pt.: *ibid.*, schs. 2, 4.

s. 35, amended: *ibid.*, sch. 2.

s. 36, repealed in pt.: *ibid.*, schs. 2, 4.

s. 37, see *J. (A Minor) (Adoption Application), Re* (1987) 151 J.P.N. 82, Sheldon J.; *A. (A Minor) (Adoption: Parental Consent), Re* [1987] 1 W.L.R. 153, C.A.; *M. (A Minor) (Custodianship: Jurisdiction), Re* [1987] 1 W.L.R. 162, C.A.; *R. (A Minor) (Adoption or Custodianship), Re* (1987) 151 J.P.N. 175, Sheldon J.; *S. (A Minor) (Adoption or Custodianship), Re* [1987] 2 W.L.R. 977, C.A.

ss. 37, 43, amended: 1987, c.42, sch. 2.

s. 45, repealed: *ibid.*, schs. 2, 4.

ss. 85, 93, repealed in pt.: *ibid.*, sch. 4.

s. 108, order 87/1242.

sch. 3, repealed in pt.: 1987, c.42, sch. 4; c.45, sch. 4.

74. Petroleum and Submarine Pipe-lines Act 1975.

ss. 34–39, repealed: 1987, c.12, s.28, sch. 3.

schs. 2, 3, amended and repealed in pt.: *ibid.*, sch. 1.

76. Local Land Charges Act 1975.

s. 14, rules, 87/389.

1976

1. National Coal Board (Finance) Act 1976.

s. 2, amended: 1987, c.3, sch. 1; repealed in pt.: *ibid.*, sch. 3.

s. 4, amended: *ibid.*, sch. 1.

8. Prevention of Terrorism (Temporary Provisions) Act 1976.

see *R. v. Secretary of State for the Home Office, ex p. Stitt, The Times*, February 3, 1987, D.C.

13. Damages (Scotland) Act 1976.

s. 1, sch. 1, see *Forbes v. House of Clydesdale* (O.H.), 1987 S.C.L.R. 136.

15. Rating (Caravan Sites) Act 1976.

s. 3, amended (S.): 1987, c.47, sch. 1; repealed in pt. (S.): *ibid.*, sch. 6.

s. 3A, repealed in pt. (S.): *ibid.*

s. 4, amended (S.): *ibid.*, sch. 1; repealed in pt. (S.): *ibid.*, sch. 6.

1976—cont.

21. Crofting Reform (Scotland) Act 1976.

see *Macaskill v. Basil Baird & Sons*, 1987 S.L.T.(Land Ct.) 34.

s. 9, see *Vestey v. Blunt*, 1986 S.L.C.R. 150.

s. 17, amended: 1987, c.18, sch. 6.

24. Development Land Tax Act 1976.

s. 28, see *Worthing Rugby Football Club Trustees v. I.R.C.* [1987] 1 W.L.R. 1057, C.A.

sch. 3, see *Taddale Properties v. I.R.C.* [1987] S.T.C. 411, Scott J.

26. Explosives (Age of Purchase etc.) Act 1976.

s. 1, repealed in pt.: 1987, c.43, sch. 5.

28. Congenital Disabilities (Civil Liability) Act 1976.

s. 4, order 87/668.

31. Legitimacy Act 1976.

s. 1, amended: 1987, c.42, s.28.

32. Lotteries and Amusements Act 1976.

s. 8, repealed in pt.: 1987, c.6, sch. 5.

ss. 18, 24, order 87/243.

sch. 3, see *Hunt v. City of Glasgow District Council* (Sh.Ct.), 1987 S.C.L.R. 244.

35. Police Pensions Act 1976.

s. 1, regs. 87/156, 256, 257, 341, 1462, 1907.

s. 2, regs. 87/256, 257.

s. 3, regs. 87/156, 256, 257, 341, 1462, 1907.

s. 4, regs. 87/156, 256, 257, 341.

s. 5, regs. 87/256, 257, 1462.

s. 6, regs. 87/156, 256, 257, 341.

ss. 7, 8, regs. 87/256, 257.

36. Adoption Act 1976.

Commencement order: 87/1242.

ss. 18, 72, amended: 1987, c.42, s.7, sch. 2.

s. 74, order 87/1242.

sch. 3, repealed in pt.: 1987, c.42, sch. 4.

39. Divorce (Scotland) Act 1976.

s. 1, see *Stewart v. Stewart*, 1987 S.L.T. (Sh.Ct.) 48.

s. 5, see *Stewart v. Stewart* (O.H.), 1987 S.L.T. 246; *Wilson v. Wilson*, 1987 S.L.T. 721; *Caven v. Caven* (O.H.), 1987 S.L.T. 761.

s. 6, see *Leslie v. Leslie* (O.H.), 1987 S.L.T. 232.

40. Finance Act 1976.

s. 33, repealed in pt.: 1987, c.16, sch. 16.

s. 36, amended: *ibid.*, s.26.

s. 38, amended: *ibid.*, sch. 15.

s. 64, order 87/1897.

s. 66, orders 87/512, 886, 1493, 1989.

sch. 4, amended: 1987, c.16, sch. 15.

sch. 5, see *General Motors Acceptance Corp. (U.K.) v. I.R.C.* [1987] S.T.C. 22, C.A.; *Ashworth (Inspector of Taxes) v. Mainland Car Deliveries* [1987] S.T.C. 481, Knox J.

sch. 7, amended: order 87/1897.

48. Parliamentary and other Pensions and Salaries Act 1976.

schs. 1–4, repealed: 1987, c.45, sch. 4.

1976—cont.

50. Domestic Violence and Matrimonial Proceedings Act 1976.
see *Wiseman* v. *Simpson, The Independent,* October 6, 1987, C.A.

52. Armed Forces Act 1976.
sch. 3, order 87/2001.

57. Local Government (Miscellaneous Provisions) Act 1976.
ss. 15, 26, amended: 1987, c.3, sch. 1.

58. International Carriage of Perishable Foodstuffs 1976.
ss. 3, 4, regs. 87/1066.

63. Bail Act 1976.
s. 3, amended: 1987, c.38, sch. 2.
ss. 3, 6, see *R.* v. *Reader* (1987) 84 Cr.App.R. 294, C.A.
s. 8, see *R.* v. *Warwick Crown Court, ex p. Smalley* (1987) 84 Cr.App.R. 51, D.C.

64. Valuation and Rating (Exempted Classes) (Scotland) Act 1976.
s. 1, repealed in pt.: 1987, c.47, sch. 6.

66. Licensing (Scotland) Act 1976.
s. 5, see *Main* v. *City of Glasgow District Licensing Board* (O.H.), 1987 S.L.T. 305.
s. 6, see *Hart* v. *City of Edinburgh District Licensing Board,* 1987 S.L.T. (Sh.Ct.) 54; *Clive* v. *Nithsdale District Licensing Board,* 1987 S.L.T.(Sh.Ct.) 113.
s. 8, order 87/1738.
s. 10, see *Ballantyne* v. *City of Glasgow District Licensing Board* (O.H.), 1987 S.L.T. 745.
ss. 10, 13, see *Tait* v. *City of Glasgow District Licensing Board* (O.H.), 1987 S.L.T. 340; *M. Milne* v. *City of Glasgow District Licensing Board,* 1987 S.L.T.(Sh.Ct.) 145.
s. 17, see *Hart* v. *City of Edinburgh District Licensing Board,* 1987 S.L.T.(Sh.Ct.) 54; *Clive* v. *Nithsdale District Licensing Board,* 1987 S.L.T.(Sh.Ct.) 113.
s. 25, see *Archyield* v. *City of Glasgow Licensing Board* (O.H.), 1987 S.L.T. 547.
s. 35, see *Tennent Caledonian Breweries* v. *City of Aberdeen District Licensing Board,* 1987 S.L.T. (Sh.Ct.) 2.
s. 63, order 87/838.
s. 64, see *Archyield* v. *City of Glasgow Licensing Board* (O.H.), 1987 S.L.T. 547.
s. 135, order 87/1738.

67. Sexual Offences (Scotland) Act 1976.
s. 2D, repealed in pt.: 1987, c.41, sch. 2.
s. 5, see *B.* v. *Kennedy,* 1987 S.L.T. 765.

70. Land Drainage Act 1976.
s. 11, orders 87/555, 815.
s. 13, orders, 87/1928, 1929.
s. 49, order 87/318.
s. 109, orders 87/555, 815, 1928, 1929.
s. 112, amended: 1987, c.3, sch. 1.

1976—cont.

71. Supplementary Benefits Act 1976.
s. 1, regs. 87/659, 1325.
ss. 1, 3, see *Scottish Old People's Welfare Council, Petrs.* (O.H.), 1987 S.L.T. 179.
s. 2, see *Secretary of State for Social Services* v. *Elkington, The Independent,* March 18, 1987, C.A.; *Decision No. R(SB) 22/86.*
s. 2, regs. 87/17, 49, 659, 660, 1325.
s. 3, regs. 87/36, 481, 2010.
s. 4, regs. 87/481.
ss. 5, 6, regs. 87/358.
s. 14, regs. 87/36, 2010.
s. 18, see *Secretary of State for Social Services* v. *McMillan,* 1987 S.L.T. (Sh.Ct.) 52; *Secretary of State for Social Services* v. *Ritchie,* 1987 S.L.T.(Sh.Ct.) 98.
s. 33, regs. 87/1325.
ss. 33, 34, see *R.* v. *Secretary of State for Social Services, ex p. Camden London Borough Council, The Times,* March 6, 1987, C.A.
s. 34, regs. 87/17, 36, 49, 358, 481, 659, 660, 1325, 2010.
sch. 1, see *R.* v. *Secretary of State for Social Services, ex p. Camden London Borough Council, The Times,* March 6, 1987, C.A.
sch. 1, regs. 87/17, 49, 659, 660, 1325.

74. Race Relations Act 1976.
s. 1, see *Tower Hamlets London Borough Council* v. *Qayyum* [1987] I.C.R. 729, E.A.T.; *Irving & Irving* v. *The Post Office* [1987] I.R.L.R. 289, C.A.
ss. 1, 3, see *Gwynedd County Council* v. *Jones* [1986] I.C.R. 833, E.A.T.; *Tejani* v. *Superintendent Registrar for the District of Peterborough* [1986] I.R.L.R. 502, C.A.
ss. 2, 3, 11, 78, see *Aziz* v. *Trinity Street Taxis* [1986] I.R.L.R. 435, E.A.T.
s. 3, see *Tower Hamlets London Borough Council* v. *Qayyum, The Times,* May 2, 1987, E.A.T.
ss. 8, 74, order 87/929.

75. Development of Rural Wales Act 1976.
s. 34, sch. 3, amended: 1987, c.3, sch. 1.

77. Weights and Measures Act 1976.
s. 8, sch. 4, see *Gaunt* v. *Nelson* [1987] R.T.R. 1, D.C.

80. Rent (Agriculture) Act 1976.
s. 15, sch. 6, repealed: order 87/264.
ss. 27–29, see *R.* v. *Agricultural Dwelling-House Advisory Committee for Bedfordshire, Cambridgeshire and Northamptonshire, ex p. Brough* (1987) 282 E.G. 1542; (1987) 19 H.L.R. 367, Hodgson J.

82. Sexual Offences (Amendment) Act 1976.
ss. 1, 2, see *R.* v. *Barton* (1987) 85 Cr.App.R. 5; [1987] Crim.L.R. 399, C.A.
s. 2, see *R.* v. *Cox (David)* (1987) 84 Cr.App.R. 132, C.A.

CAP.

1976—cont.

82. Sexual Offences (Amendment) Act 1976—cont.
s. 4, see *R.* v. *Gilligan* [1987] Crim.L.R. 501, Nottingham Crown Ct., Boreham J.

1977

3. Aircraft and Shipbuilding Industries Act 1977.
s. 11, amended: 1987, c.52, s.1.

5. Social Security (Miscellaneous Provisions) Act 1977.
s. 12, order 87/165.

7. Nuclear Industry (Finance) Act 1977.
s. 2, order 87/875; amended: *ibid.*

8. Job Release Act 1977.
s. 1, order 87/1339; continued in force: *ibid.*

12. Agricultural Holdings (Notices to Quit) Act 1977.
s. 2, see *Burton* v. *Timmis* (1987) 281 E.G. 795, C.A.

15. Marriage (Scotland) Act 1977.
ss. 13, 23A, see *Saleh* v. *Saleh* (O.H.), 1987 S.L.T. 633.

32. Torts (Interference with Goods) Act 1977.
s. 1, amended: 1987, c.43, sch. 4.
s. 3, see *Rubycliff* v. *Plastic Engineers* [1986] R.P.C. 573, Browne-Wilkinson V.-C.
s. 5, see *Macaulay* v. *Screenkarn* [1987] F.S.R. 257, Falconer J.
s. 8, see *De Franco* v. *Commissioner of Police of the Metropolis, The Times,* May 8, 1987, C.A.

36. Finance Act 1977.
s. 58, repealed: 1987, c.16, sch. 16.

37. Patents Act 1977.
ss. 1–3, see *Ward's Applications* [1986] R.P.C. 50, Patent Office.
ss. 2, 7, see *James Industries' Patent* [1987] R.P.C. 235, Patent Office.
ss. 7, 13, see *Nippon Piston Ring Co.'s Applications* [1987] R.P.C. 120, Patents Ct.
s. 13, see *Sonic Tape's Patent* [1987] R.P.C. 251, Patent Office.
s. 14, see *Chinoin's Application* [1986] R.P.C. 39, Falconer J.; *Intera Corp.'s Application* [1986] R.P.C. 45a, C.A.; *Peabody International's Application* [1986] R.P.C. 521, Patent Appeal; *Raychem's Applications* [1986] R.P.C. 547, Falconer J.
s. 15, see *Raychem's Applications* [1986] R.P.C. 547, Falconer J.; *Van der Lely's Application* [1987] R.P.C. 61, Patents Ct.
s. 16, see *Intera Corp.'s Application* [1986] R.P.C. 45a, C.A.: *Peabody International's Application* [1986] R.P.C. 521, Patent Appeal.
s. 17, see *Application Des Gaz's Application* [1987] R.P.C. 297, Falconer J.
s. 19, see *Intera Corp.'s Application* [1986] R.P.C. 45a, C.A.

CAP.

1977—cont.

37. Patents Act 1977—cont.
ss. 25, 28, see *Deforeit's Patent* [1986] R.P.C. 142, Patent Office.
s. 27, see *Waddington's Patent* [1986] R.P.C. 158, Patent Office; *Philips Electronic and Associated Industries Patent* [1987] R.P.C. 244, Patent Office.
s. 37, see *James Industries' Patent* [1987] R.P.C. 235, Patent Office.
s. 38, see *Borg-Warner Corp.'s Patent* [1986] R.P.C. 137, Patent Office.
s. 46, see *Allen & Hanbury* v. *Generics (U.K.) and Gist Brocades, Brocades (Great Britain); Beecham Group; Comptroller General of Patents* [1986] R.P.C. 203, H.L.; *Ciba-Geigy A.G.'s Patent* [1986] R.P.C. 403, Patents Ct.; *Syntex Corporation's Patent* [1986] R.P.C. 585, Whitford J.; *Diamond Shamrock Technologies S.A.'s Patent* [1987] R.P.C. 91, Patents Ct.; *Roussel-Uclaf (Clemence & Le Martret's) Patent* [1987] R.P.C. 109, Patents Ct.; *Allen & Hanburys (Salbutamol) Patent* [1987] R.P.C. 327, C.A.
s. 48, see *Enviro Spray System Inc.'s Patents* [1986] R.P.C. 147, Patent Office; *Allen & Hanbury* v. *Generics (U.K.) and Gist Brocades, Brocades (Great Britain); Beecham Group; Comptroller General of Patents* [1986] R.P.C. 203, H.L.; *Ciba-Geigy A.G.'s Patent* [1986] R.P.C. 403, Patents Ct.; *Syntex Corporation's Patent* [1986] R.P.C. 585, Whitford J.; *Allen & Hanburys (Salbutamol) Patent* [1987] R.P.C. 327, C.A.
s. 50, see *Enviro Spray System Inc.'s Patents* [1986] R.P.C. 147, Patent Office; *Allen & Hanbury* v. *Generics (U.K.) and Gist Brocades, Brocades (Great Britain); Beecham Group; Comptroller General of Patents* [1986] R.P.C. 203, H.L.; *Ciba-Geigy A.G.'s Patent* [1986] R.P.C. 403, Patents Ct.; *Syntex Corporation's Patent* [1986] R.P.C. 585, Whitford J.
ss. 50, 55, see *Allen & Hanburys (Salbutamol) Patent* [1987] R.P.C. 327, C.A.
s. 72, see *James Industries' Patent* [1987] R.P.C. 235, Patent Office.
s. 76, see *Waddington's Patent* [1986] R.P.C. 158, Patent Office; *Chinoin's Application* [1986] R.P.C. 39, Falconer J.; *Ward's Applications* [1986] R.P.C. 50, Patent Office; *Raychem's Applications* [1986] R.P.C. 547, Falconer J.; *Van der Lely's Application* [1987] R.P.C. 61, Patents Ct.; *Philips Electronic and Associated Industries Patent* [1987] R.P.C. 244, Patent Office.
s. 77, see *Deforeit's Patent* [1986] R.P.C. 142, Patent Office; *Amersham International* v. *Corning* [1987] R.P.C. 53, Patents Ct.
ss. 77, 78, rules 87/288.

1977—cont.

37. Patents Act 1977—*cont.*

s. 89, see *Masuda's Application* [1987] R.P.C. 37, Patents Ct.

s. 93, amended (S.): 1987, c.18, sch. 6.

ss. 97, 99, see *Allen & Hanburys (Salbutamol) Patent* [1987] R.P.C. 327, C.A.

s. 101, see *Intera Corp.'s Application* [1986] R.P.C. 45a, C.A.

ss. 102–104, see *Reiss Engineering* v. *Harris* [1987] R.P.C. 171, Patents Ct.

s. 104, see *Rockwell International* v. *Serck Industries* [1987] R.P.C. 89, Falconer J.; *Sonic Tape's Patent* [1987] R.P.C. 251, Patent Office.

s. 107, amended (S.): 1987, c.18, sch. 6.

s. 108, see *Allen & Hanburys (Salbutamol) Patent* [1987] R.P.C. 327, C.A.

s. 117, see *Masuda's Application* [1987] R.P.C. 37, Patents Ct.

s. 118, see *Diamond Shamrock Technologies S.A.'s Patent* [1987] R.P.C. 91, Patents Ct.

s. 120, rules 87/288.

s. 123, see *Waddington's Patent* [1986] R.P.C. 158, Patent Office; *Intera Corp.'s Application* [1986] R.P.C. 45a, C.A.

s. 123, rules 87/288, 753.

ss. 125, 130, see *Philips Electronic and Associated Industries Patent* [1987] R.P.C. 244, Patent Office.

s. 130, see *Intera Corp.'s Application* [1986] R.P.C. 45a, C.A.; *Van der Lely's Application* [1987] R.P.C. 61, Patents Ct.

sch. 1, see *Ciba-Geigy A.G.'s Patent* [1986] R.P.C. 403, Patents Ct.; *Masi A.G.* v. *Coloroll* [1986] R.P.C. 483, Patents Ct.; *Allen & Hanburys (Salbutamol) Patent* [1987] R.P.C. 327, C.A.

sch. 2, see *Allen & Hanbury* v. *Generics (U.K.) and Gist Brocades, Brocades (Great Britain); Beecham Group; Comptroller General of Patents* [1986] R.P.C. 203, H.L.

sch. 4, see *Allen & Hanbury* v. *Generics (U.K.) and Gist Brocades, Brocades (Great Britain); Beecham Group; Comptroller General of Patents* [1986] R.P.C. 203, H.L.

sch. 4, rules 87/610, 753.

39. Coal Industry Act 1977.

s. 6, repealed: 1987, c.3, sch. 3.

s. 7, order 87/1258.

ss. 7, 9–11, 14, amended: 1987, c.3, sch. 1.

schs. 2, 4 (in pt.), repealed: *ibid.*, sch. 3.

42. Rent Act 1977.

s. 2, see *Duke and Duke* v. *Porter* (1987) 19 H.L.R. 1, C.A.; *Hall* v. *King* (1987) 19 H.L.R. 440, C.A.; *Sefton Holdings* v. *Cairns, The Times,* November 3, 1987, C.A.

s. 5A, regs. 87/1940.

1977—cont.

42. Rent Act 1977—*cont.*

s. 7, see *Otter* v. *Norman, The Times,* August 3, 1987, C.A.

s. 13, see *Crown Estate Commissioners* v. *Connor and the London Rent Assessment Panel* (1987) 19 H.L.R. 35, McCowan J.

s. 25, see *MacFarquhar* v. *Phillimore; Marks* v. *Phillimore* (1986) 18 H.L.R. 397, C.A.; *Griffiths* v. *Birmingham City District Council,* January 26, 1987; H.H. Judge Clive Taylor, Q.C., Stafford County Ct.; *Dixon* v. *Allgood, The Times,* November 27, 1987, H.L.

s. 44, amended: order 87/264.

s. 45, amended and repealed in pt.: *ibid.*

s. 49, regs. 87/266.

ss. 51 (in pt.), 55, repealed: order 87/264.

ss. 60, 61, regs. 87/266.

Pt. IV (ss. 62–75), see *Crown Estate Commissioners* v. *Connor and the London Rent Assessment Panel* (1987) 19 H.L.R. 35, McCowan J.

s. 71, repealed in pt.: order 87/264.

s. 98, see *Minchburn* v. *Fernandez* (1987) 19 H.L.R. 29, C.A.; *Roberts* v. *Macilwraith-Christie* (1987) 1 E.G.L.R. 244, C.A.; *Appleton* v. *Aspin, The Times,* December 1, 1987, C.A.

s. 106A, see *Bryant* v. *Best* (1987) 283 E.G. 843, C.A.

sch. 1, see *Swanbrae* v. *Elliott* (1987) 281 E.G. 917; (1987) 19 H.L.R. 87, C.A.; *Portman Registrars & Nominees* v. *Mohammed Latif,* April 23, 1987, H.H. Judge Hill-Smith, Willesden County Ct.; *Sefton Holdings* v. *Cairns, The Times,* November 3, 1987, C.A.; *Chios Investment Property Co.* v. *Lopez, The Times,* November 3, 1987, C.A.

sch. 8, repealed in pt.: order 87/264.

sch. 15, see *Bissessar* v. *Ghosn* (1986) 18 H.L.R. 486, C.A.; *Fowler* v. *Minchin* (1987) 19 H.L.R. 224, C.A.; *Reid and Reid* v. *Andreou,* February 14, 1986, H.H. Judge Tibber; Edmonton County Ct.; *Bostock* v. *de la Pagerie, sub nom. Bostock* v. *Tacher de la Pagerie* (1987) 19 H.L.R. 358, C.A.; *Hodges* v. *Blee* (1987) E.G. 1215, C.A.; *Coombs* v. *Parry* (1987) 19 H.L.R. 384, C.A.; *Roberts* v. *Macilwraith-Christie* (1987) 1 E.G.L.R. 224, C.A.

sch. 20, amended and repealed in pt.: order 87/264.

43. Protection from Eviction Act 1977.

s. 1, see *R.* v. *Ahmad (Zafar)* (1986) 52 P. & C.R. 346, C.A.

45. Criminal Law Act 1977.

s. 5, repealed in pt.: 1987, c.38, s.12.

s. 9, amended: 1987, c.46, s.7.

sch. 6, repealed in pt.: 1987, c.35, s.2.

46. Insurance Brokers (Registration) Act 1977.

ss. 27, 28, order 87/1496.

CAP.
1977—cont.

48. Housing (Homeless Persons) Act 1977.
repealed (S.): 1987, c.26, sch. 24.
ss. 1, 2, 17, see *Stewart* v. *Monklands District Council* (O.H.), 1987 S.L.T. 630.
ss. 4, 17, see *Mazzacherini* v. *Argyll and Bute District Council* (O.H.), 1987 S.C.L.R. 475.

49. National Health Service Act 1977.
s. 11, orders 87/6, 151, 192, 808.
s. 13, regs. 87/245.
s. 16, regs. 87/401.
s. 18, regs. 87/245.
s. 29, regs. 87/5, 407, 1425.
s. 35, regs. 87/445, 736, 1512, 1965.
s. 36, regs. 87/445, 1512, 1965.
s. 37, regs. 87/445.
ss. 41, 42, regs. 87/5, 401, 1425.
s. 42, amended: order 87/2202.
ss. 77, 83, regs. 87/368.
s. 106, amended: 1987, c.39, s.2.
s. 108A, added: *ibid.*, s.6.
s. 109, order 87/1272.
s. 117, amended: 1987, c.39, s.7.
s. 118, amended: *ibid.*, s.4.
s. 119, amended: *ibid.*, s.5.
s. 121, regs. 87/371.
s. 126, regs. 87/736, 1512.
sch. 5, regs. 87/7, 152, 401, 1425.
sch. 13, amended: 1987, c.39, s.4.

50. Unfair Contract Terms Act 1977.
s. 2, see *Thompson* v. *Lohan (T.) (Plant Hire), The Times*, February 12, 1987, C.A.; *Smith* v. *Eric S. Bush (A Firm), The Times*, March 18, 1987, C.A.; *Phillips Products* v. *Hyland (Note)* [1987] 1 W.L.R. 659, C.A.
s. 11, see *Smith* v. *Eric S. Bush (A Firm), The Times*, March 18, 1987, C.A.; *Phillips Products* v. *Hyland (Note)* [1987] 1 W.L.R. 659, C.A.
ss. 20, 24, see *Continental Tyre & Rubber Co.* v. *Trunk Trailer Co.*, 1987 S.L.T. 58.

1978

2. Commonwealth Development Corporation Act 1978.
s. 3, order 87/1253.

5. Northern Ireland (Emergency Provisions) Act 1978.
continued in force, except s.12, sch. 1; order 87/30.
repealed (prosp.): 1987, c.30, s.13.
s. 2, substituted: *ibid.*, s.1.
s. 3A, added: *ibid.*, s.2.
s. 5A, added: *ibid.*, s.3.
s. 6, substituted: *ibid.*, s.4.
s. 8, substituted: *ibid.*, s.5.
s. 11, substituted: *ibid.*, s.6.
ss. 13, 14, amended: *ibid.*, sch. 1.
s. 15, amended: *ibid.*, s.7, sch. 1.

CAP.
1978—cont.

5. Northern Ireland (Emergency Provisons) Act 1978—cont.
s. 18, amended: *ibid.*, sch.1.
s. 19A, added: *ibid.*, s.8.
s. 21, amended: *ibid.*, s.9.
s. 22, amended: *ibid.*, s.10; repealed in pt.: *ibid.*, s.10, sch. 2.
s. 25, substituted: *ibid.*, s.11.
s. 26, amended: *ibid.*
ss. 28, 28A, substituted: *ibid.*, s.12.
s. 31, repealed in pt.: *ibid.*, schs. 1, 2.
s. 32, amended: *ibid.*, sch. 1.
s. 33, order 87/30.
s. 33, amended: 1987, c.30, s.13, sch. 1.
sch. 4, amended: *ibid.*, ss.11, 17, sch. 1.

6. Employment Subsidies Act 1978.
s. 1, continued in force: order 87/1124.
s. 3, order 87/1124; S.R. 1987 No. 215.

10. European Assembly Elections Act 1978.
sch. 1, order 87/20.

14. Housing (Financial Provisions) (Scotland) Act 1978.
repealed, except sch. 2 (in pt.): 1987, c.26, sch. 24.
ss. 1, 2, orders 87/331, 332.

17. Internationally Protected Persons Act 1978.
ss. 3, 4, order 87/454.

22. Domestic Proceedings and Magistrates' Courts Act 1978.
s. 3, see *Day* v. *Day,* November 26, 1986, Wood J.
s. 20, repealed in pt.: 1987, c.42, sch. 4.
s. 20A, added: *ibid.*, sch. 2.
s. 32, amended: *ibid.*
ss. 36 (in pt.), 38 (in pt.), 41, 45 (in pt.), repealed: *ibid.*, sch. 4.
s. 88, sch. 1, amended: *ibid.*, sch. 2.
sch. 2, repealed in pt.: *ibid.*, sch. 4.

23. Judicature (Northern Ireland) Act 1978.
s. 55, S.R. 1987 No. 304.
s. 62, order 87/1283.
s. 116, S.Rs. 1987 Nos. 270, 412.
sch. 5, amended: 1987, c.30, sch. 1; repealed in pt.: 1987, c.16, sch. 16; c.30, sch. 2.

26. Suppression of Terrorism Act 1978.
s. 7, order 87/2045.
s. 8, order 87/2137.

27. Home Purchase Assistance and Housing Corporation Guarantee Act 1978.
repealed (S.): 1987, c.26, sch. 4.
ss. 1, 2, order 87/268(S.).
sch., amended: 1987, c.22, sch. 6.

28. Adoption (Scotland) Act 1978.
s. 11, see *A.* v. *Children's Hearing for the Tayside Region,* 1987 S.L.T.(Sh.Ct.) 126.
s. 16, see *A.* v. *B.*, 1987 S.L.T.(Sh.Ct.) 121; *A. and B.* v. *C.*, 1987 S.C.L.R. 514.
s. 39, see *A.B.* v. *M.* (O.H.), 1987 S.C.L.R. 389.
s. 65, see *A.* v. *Children's Hearing for the Tayside Region,* 1987 S.L.T.(Sh.Ct.) 126.

CAP.

1978—cont.

29. National Health Service (Scotland) Act 1978.
s. 19, regs. 87/386, 1382.
s. 25, regs. 87/1634.
s. 27, regs. 87/385, 1382.
s. 27, amended: order 87/2202.
ss. 69, 75, regs. 87/367.
s. 90, amended: 1987, c.39, s.2.
s. 92A, added: *ibid.*, s.6.
s. 94, amended: *ibid.*, s.8.
s. 95A, added: *ibid.*, s.4.
s. 96, amended: *ibid.*, s.5.
s. 98, regs. 87/387.
s. 100, amended: 1987, c.26, sch. 23.
s. 108, regs. 87/367, 386, 387, 1382.

30. Interpretation Act 1978.
s. 6, see *Lewis* v. *Surrey County Council, The Times,* October 17, 1987, H.L.
s. 7, see *Secretary of State for Employment* v. *Milk & General Haulage (Nottingham)* (1987) 84 L.S.Gaz. 2118, E.A.T.; *T. & D. Transport (Portsmouth)* v. *Limburn* [1987] I.C.R. 696, E.A.T.
s. 17, see *R.* v. *Corby Juvenile Court, ex p. M* [1987] 1 W.L.R. 55, Waite J.
sch. 1, amended: 1987, c.16, sch. 15; c.42, sch. 2.
sch. 2, amended: 1987, c.42, sch. 2; repealed in pt.: *ibid.*, schs. 2, 4.

31. Theft Act 1978.
s. 3, see *Troughton* v. *Metropolitan Police* [1987] Crim.L.R. 138, D.C.

33. State Immunity Act 1978.
s. 3, see *Rayner (J. H.) (Mincing Lane)* v. *Department of Trade and Industry, The Independent,* June 26, 1987, Staughton J.
s. 13, see *Forth Tugs* v. *Wilmington Trust Co.,* 1987 S.L.T. 153.

37. Protection of Children Act 1978.
s. 1, see *R.* v. *Owen, The Times,* October 10, 1987, C.A.

38. Consumer Safety Act 1978.
repealed: 1987, c.43, sch. 5.
see *Sarwan Singh Deu* v. *Dudley Metropolitan Borough Council,* July 10, 1987; Sedgley Crown Ct.
s. 1, regs. 87/286, 603, 1337.
s. 12, order 87/1681.
sch. 2, regs. 87/286, 603.

40. Rating (Disabled Persons) Act 1978.
s. 2, see *Nottinghamshire County Council* v. *Nottinghamshire City Council* (1987) 27 R.V.R. 82, Nottingham County Ct.
ss. 7, 8 (in pt.), repealed (S.): 1987, c.47, sch. 6.

42. Finance Act 1978.
s. 12, see *T. H. Knitwear (Wholesale), Re* [1987] 1 W.L.R. 371, Browne-Wilkinson V.-C.
s. 26, amended: 1987, c.51, sch. 2.
ss. 30, 59, amended: 1987, c.16, sch. 15.
sch. 9, repealed in pt.: *ibid.*, sch. 16.

CAP.

1978—cont.

44. Employment Protection (Consolidation) Act 1978.
see *Caledonian Mining Co.* v. *Bassett* [1987] I.C.R. 425, E.A.T.
s. 8, see *Chapman* v. *CPS Computer Group, The Times,* June 30, 1987, C.A.
s. 18, order 87/1757.
s. 23, see *National Coal Board* v. *Ridgway, sub nom. Ridgway and Fairbrother* v. *National Coal Board* [1987] I.C.R. 641, C.A.
s. 33, see *Secretary of State for Employment* v. *Ford (A.) and Sons (Sacks)* [1986] I.C.R. 882, E.A.T.
ss. 45–48, see *Dowuona* v. *John Lewis* [1987] I.R.L.R. 310, C.A.
s. 49, see *Lanton Leisure* v. *White and Gibson* [1987] I.R.L.R. 119, E.A.T.
s. 53, see *Smith* v. *City of Glasgow District Council* (H.L.), 1987 S.L.T. 605; *Ladbroke Entertainments* v. *Clark* [1987] I.C.R. 585, E.A.T.
ss. 54, 55, see *Karim* v. *Sunblest Bakeries, The Daily Telegraph,* November 2, 1987, C.A.
s. 55, see *Bridgen* v. *Lancashire County Council* [1987] I.R.L.R. 58, C.A.; *Cardinal Vaughan Memorial School Governors* v. *Alie* [1987] I.C.R. 406, E.A.T.; *Batchelor* v. *British Railways Board* [1987] I.R.L.R. 136, C.A.; *Lanton Leisure* v. *White and Gibson* [1987] I.R.L.R. 119, E.A.T.
ss. 55, 56, see *Dowuona* v. *John Lewis* [1987] I.R.L.R. 310, C.A.
s. 57, see *Polkey* v. *Dauton (A. E.) Services* [1987] 1 All E.R. 948, C.A; *Smiths Industries Aerospace and Defence Systems* v. *Brookes* [1986] I.R.L.R. 434, E.A.T.; *Moyes* v. *Hylton Castle Working Men's Social Club and Institute* [1986] I.R.L.R. 482, E.A.T.; *Pritchett* v. *McIntyre (J.)* [1978] I.C.R. 359, C.A.; *Polkey* v. *Edmund Walker (Holdings)* [1987] I.R.L.R. 13, C.A.; *Labour Party* v. *Oakley, The Daily Telegraph,* October 30, 1987, C.A.; *Smith* v. *City of Glasgow District Council* [1987] I.R.L.R. 326, H.L.; *Brown* v. *Stockton-on-Tees Borough Council* [1987] I.R.L.R. 230, C.A.
s. 58, see *Crossville Motor Services* v. *Ashfield* [1986] I.R.L.R. 475, E.A.T.; *National Coal Board* v. *McGinty* (1987) 84 L.S.Gaz. 2455, E.A.T.; *Ridgway and Fairbrother* v. *National Coal Board* [1987] I.R.L.R. 80, C.A.
ss. 59, 61, see *Brown* v. *Stockton-on-Tees Borough Council* [1987] I.R.L.R. 230, C.A.
s. 62, see *Campey & Sons* v. *Bellwood* [1987] I.C.R. 311, E.A.T.; *Munir* v. *Jang Publications* (1987) 84 L.S.Gaz. 2450, E.A.T.; *Express & Star* v. *Bunday, The Times,* July 28, 1987, C.A.

CAP.

1978—cont.

44. Employment Protection (Consolidation) Act 1978—*cont.*

s. 64, see *Lanton Leisure* v. *White and Gibson* [1987] I.R.L.R. 119, E.A.T.; *Mauldon* v. *British Telecommunications* [1987] I.C.R. 450, E.A.T.

s. 64A, see *Harford* v. *Swiftrim* [1987] I.C.R. 439, E.A.T.

s. 67, see *Batchelor* v. *British Railways Board* [1987] I.R.L.R. 136, C.A.

s. 69, see *Boots Co.* v. *Lees-Collier* [1986] I.C.R. 728, E.A.T.

s. 74, see *Crossville Motor Services* v. *Ashfield* [1986] I.R.L.R. 475, E.A.T.; *Moyes* v. *Hylton Castle Working Men's Social Club and Institute* [1986] I.R.L.R. 482, E.A.T.; *Polkey* v. *Edmund Walker (Holdings)* [1987] I.R.L.R. 13, C.A.; *Babcock F.A.T.A.* v. *Addison* [1987] 1 F.T.L.R. 505, C.A.

s. 77, see *National Coal Board* v. *McGinty* (1987) 84 L.S.Gaz. 2455, E.A.T.; *Ridgway and Fairbrother* v. *National Coal Board* [1987] I.R.L.R. 80, C.A.

s. 79, see *National Coal Board* v. *McGinty* (1987) 84 L.S.Gaz. 2455, E.A.T.

ss. 81, 91, see *Willcox* v. *Hastings* [1987] I.R.L.R. 298, C.A.

s. 84, see *Elliot* v. *Stump (Richard)*, (1987) 84 L.S.Gaz. 1142, E.A.T.

ss. 104, 104A, see *Secretary of State for Employment* v. *Milk & General Haulage (Nottingham)* (1987) 84 L.S.Gaz. 2118, E.A.T.

s. 136, see *Smith* v. *City of Glasgow District Council* (H.L.), 1987 S.L.T. 605.

s. 140, see *Karim* v. *Sunblest Bakeries, The Daily Telegraph*, November 2, 1987, C.A.

s. 146, see *Lewis* v. *Surrey County Council, The Times*, October 17, 1987, H.L.

s. 153, see *Secretary of State for Employment* v. *Ford (A.) & Son (Sacks)* [1986] I.C.R. 882, E.A.T.; *Batchelor* v. *British Railways Board* [1987] I.R.L.R. 136, C.A.; *Harford* v. *Swiftrim* (1987 I.C.R. 439, E.A.T.; *National Coal Board* v. *Ridgway, sub nom. Ridgway and Fairbrother* v. *National Coal Board* [1987] I.C.R. 641, C.A.

sch. 2, see *Dowuona* v. *John Lewis Partnership* [1987] I.R.L.R. 310, C.A.

sch. 13, see *Secretary of State for Employment* v. *Ford (A.) & Son (Sacks)* [1986] I.C.R. 882, E.A.T.; *Girls' Public Day School Trust* v. *Khanna* [1987] I.C.R. 339, E.A.T.; *Express & Star* v. *Bunday, The Times*, July 28, 1987, C.A.; *Secretary of State for Employment* v. *Cohen* [1987] I.C.R. 570, E.A.T.; *Byrne* v. *Birmingham City District Council* [1987] I.C.R. 519, C.A.; *Lewis* v. *Surrey County Council* [1987] 3 W.L.R. 927, H.L.

CAP.

1978—cont.

47. Civil Liability (Contribution) Act 1978.

s. 1, see *Benarty, The, The Times*, June 23, 1987, Hobhouse J.; *Kapetin Georgis, The; sub nom. Virgo Steamship Co. S.A.* v. *Skaarup Shipping Corp., The Financial Times*, October 21, 1987, Hirst J.

48. Homes Insulation Act 1978.

repealed (S.): 1987, c.26, sch. 24.

49. Community Service by Offenders (Scotland) Act 1978.

ss. 3–5, see *H.M. Advocate* v. *Hood*, 1987 S.C.C.R. 63.

s. 7, repealed in pt.: 1987, c.41, sch. 2.

50. Inner Urban Areas Act 1978.

ss. 1, 15, order 87/115.

56. Parliamentary Pensions Act 1978.

repealed: 1987, c.45, sch. 4.

1979

2. Customs and Excise Management Act 1979.

s. 1, regs. 87/2114.

s. 1, amended: 1987, c.49, sch. 1; c.51, s.103; repealed in pt.: 1987, c.49, sch. 2.

ss. 20, 25, amended: 1987, c.16, s.6.

s. 22, order 87/1982.

ss. 27, 28, amended: 1987, c.16, sch. 7.

s. 35, amended: 1987, c.49, sch. 1.

s. 48, regs. 87/1781.

ss. 58A, 58D, amended: 1987, c.16, s.8.

s. 61, amended: 1987, c.51, s.103.

s. 64, amended: 1987, c.49, sch. 1.

s. 75A, added: 1987, c.16, s.9.

s. 77, repealed in pt.: *ibid.*, s.10, sch. 16.

s. 77A, added: *ibid.*, s.10.

s. 78, see *Comrs. of Customs and Excise* v. *Claus, The Times*, July 6, 1987, D.C.

s. 86, see *R.* v. *Jones (Keith Desmond)* [1987] 1 W.L.R. 692, C.A.

ss. 88, 89, amended: 1987, c.49, sch. 1.

s. 102, amended: 1987, c.16, sch. 1.

s. 117, amended (S.): 1987, c.18, sch. 6.

s. 142, amended: 1987, c.49, sch. 1.

s. 151, see *R.* v. *Clacton Justices, ex p. Commissioners of Customs and Excise, The Times*, October 5, 1987, D.C.

s. 167, see *R.* v. *Cross* [1987] Crim.L.R. 43, C.A.

s. 170, see *R.* v. *Collins* [1987] Crim.L.R. 256, C.A.; *R.* v. *Ellis, Street and Smith* [1987] Crim.L.R. 44; (1987) 84 Cr.App.R. 235, C.A.

sch. 4, repealed in pt.: 1987, c.16, sch. 16.

3. Customs and Excise Duties (General Reliefs) Act 1979.

s. 1, order 87/1785.

s. 4, orders 87/134, 1122, 1785.

4. Alcoholic Liquor Duties Act 1979.

ss. 2, 3, regs. 87/314.

s. 4, amended: 1987, c.49, sch. 1; repealed in pt.: *ibid.*, sch. 2.

s. 26, amended: *ibid.*, sch. 1.

s. 36, regs. 87/314.

s. 77, regs. 87/2009.

CAP.

1979—cont.

5. Hydrocarbon Oil Duties Act 1979.
s. 13A, added: 1987, c.16, s.1.
ss. 24, 27, amended: *ibid.*

10. Public Lending Right Act 1979.
s. 3, order 87/1908.

11. Electricity (Scotland) Act 1979.
s. 27, repealed in pt.: 1987, c.16, sch. 16.

14. Capital Gains Tax Act 1979.
s. 5, order 87/436.
s. 5, amended: *ibid.*
s. 87, amended: 1987, c.51, sch. 6.
s. 92, amended: 1987, c.16, s.40.
ss. 101, 102, see *Markey (Inspector of Taxes)* v. *Sanders* [1987] 1 W.L.R. 864, Walton J.; *Williams (Inspector of Taxes)* v. *Merrylees, The Times,* June 30, 1987, Vinelott J.
s. 115, see *Todd (Inspector of Taxes)* v. *Mudd* [1987] S.T.C. 141, Vinelott J.
ss. 137, 138, amended: 1987, c.51, s.81.
s. 150, repealed in pt.: 1987, c.16, sch. 16.
sch. 2, order 87/259.

33. Land Registration (Scotland) Act 1979.
ss. 20, 21, see *Ferguson* v. *Gibbs,* 1987 S.L.T. (Lands Tr.) 32.
sch. 2, repealed in pt.: 1987, c.26, sch. 24.

34. Credit Unions Act 1979.
s. 8, amended: 1987, c.22, sch. 6.
s. 31, amended: *ibid.*; repealed in pt.: *ibid.*, schs. 6, 7.
sch. 3, repealed: *ibid.*, sch. 7.

36. Nurses, Midwives and Health Visitors Act 1979.
s. 13, see *Slater* v. *United Kingdom Central Council for Nursing Midwifery and Health Visitors, The Independent,* June 9, 1987, D.C.
s. 22, orders 87/446, 944.

37. Banking Act 1979.
repealed, except ss. 38, 47, 51, 52, sch. 6; 1987, c.22, sch. 7.
s. 1, see *S.C.F. Finance Co.* v. *Masri* [1986] 2 Lloyd's Rep. 366, C.A.; *S.C.F. Finance Co.* v. *Masri (No. 2)* [1987] 2 W.L.R. 58, C.A.
s. 2, regs. 87/65.
s. 34, regs. 87/64.

38. Estate Agents Act 1979.
s. 10, amended: 1987, c.43, sch. 4.

39. Merchant Shipping Act 1979.
Commencement orders: 87/635, 719.
s. 14, order 87/855.
s. 16, orders 87/635, 670, 855.
s. 20, orders 87/470, 664.
s. 21, regs. 87/63, 548, 549, 854, 884, 1298, 1591, 1961.
s. 22, regs. 87/549, 1591, 1886, 1961.
s. 39, repealed in pt. (S.): 1987, c.18, sch. 8.
s. 50, repealed in pt.: 1987, c.21, sch. 3.
s. 52, orders 87/635, 719.
sch. 1, repealed: 1987, c.21, sch. 3.
sch. 3, orders 87/703, 855, 931.
sch. 3, amended and repealed in pt.: order 87/670.

CAP.

1979—cont.

42. Arbitration Act 1979.
s. 1, see *Universal Petroleum Co.* v. *Handels and Transport Gesellschaft m.b.H., Financial Times* [1987] 1 F.T.L.R. 429, C.A.; *Warrington and Runcorn Development Corp.* v. *Greggs* (1987) 281 E.G. 1075, Warner J.; *Triumph Securities* v. *Reid Furniture Co.* (1987) 283 E.G. 1071, Harman J.

43. Crown Agents Act 1979.
s. 8, amended: 1987, c.22, sch. 6; repealed in pt.: 1987, c.16, sch. 16.

46. Ancient Monuments and Archaeological Areas Act 1979.
s. 61, amended: 1987, c.3, sch. 1.

48. Pensioners' Payments and Social Security Act 1979.
s. 4, order 87/1305.

50. European Assembly (Pay and Pensions) Act 1979.
s. 8, amended: 1987, c.45, sch. 3.

53. Charging Orders Act 1979.
s. 1, see *Mercantile Credit Co.* v. *Ellis, The Independent,* March 17, 1987, C.A.

54. Sale of Goods Act 1979.
s. 2, see *National Employers Mutual General Insurance Association* v. *Jones* [1987] 3 All E.R. 385, C.A.
s. 11, see *Bernstein* v. *Pamson Motors (Golders Green)* [1987] 2 All E.R. 220, Rougier J.
s. 14, see *M/S Aswan Engineering Establishment Co.* v. *Lupdine* [1987] 1 W.L.R. 1, C.A.; *Rogers* v. *Parish (Scarborough)* [1987] 2 W.L.R. 353, C.A.; *N.V. Devos Gebroeder* v. *Sunderland Sportswear* (O.H.), 1987 S.L.T. 331; *Bernstein* v. *Pamson Motors (Golders Green)* [1987] 2 All E.R. 220, Rougier J.; *Shine* v. *General Guarantee Corporation, The Times,* August 18, 1987, C.A.; *Wormell* v. *R.H.M. Agriculture (East)* [1987] 1 W.L.R. 1091, C.A.; *Lutton* v. *Saville Tractors (Belfast)* [1986] 12 N.I.J.B. 1, Carswell J.
s. 21, see *Shaw* v. *Commissioner of Police for the Metropolis* [1987] 1 W.L.R. 1332, C.A.
s. 25, see *National Employers Mutual General Insurance Association* v. *Jones* [1987] 3 All E.R. 385, C.A.
s. 32, see *D. L. Electrical Supplies (Mitcham)* v. *G. L. Group,* 1987 S.L.T. (Sh.Ct.) 36.
s. 35, see *Bernstein* v. *Pamson Motors (Golders Green)* [1987] 2 All E.R. 220, Rougier J.
s. 40, repealed (S.): 1987, c.18, sch. 8.
s. 61, see *National Employers Mutual General Insurance Association* v. *Jones* [1987] 3 All E.R. 385, C.A.

55. Justices of the Peace Act 1979.
s. 18, rules 87/1137.

CAP.

1979—cont.

55. Justices of the Peace Act 1979—*cont.*
s. 23, orders 87/184, 519, 1201, 1688, 1739, 1786, 1796, 1797, 1912, 1913, 1925, 1962.
s. 33, repealed in pt.: 1987, c.21, sch. 3.

1980

1. Petroleum Revenue Tax Act 1980.
sch., amended: 1987, c.16, sch. 13.
4. Bail etc. (Scotland) Act 1980.
s. 3, see *Baird* v. *Lockhart*, 1986 S.C.C.R. 514; *Allan* v. *Lockhart*, 1986 S.C.C.R. 395; *H.M. Advocate* v. *Kerr*, 1987 S.C.C.R. 283; *Montgomery* v. *H.M. Advocate*, 1987 S.C.C.R. 264.
5. Child Care Act 1980.
s. 2, see *R.* v. *Tower Hamlets London Borough Council, ex p. Monaf, Ali and Miah, The Times*, August 6, 1987, D.C.
s. 3, see *M. and H. (Minors), (Local Authority: Parental Rights) Re* [1987] 3 W.L.R. 759, C.A.
s. 8, amended: 1987, c.42, s.8.
s. 10, see *R.* v. *Befordshire County Council, ex p. C.; R.* v. *Hertfordshire County Council, ex p. B.* (1987) 85 L.G.R. 218, Ewbank J.
ss. 12A, 12C, see *R.* v. *Corby Juvenile Court, ex p. M* [1987] 1 W.L.R. 55, Waite J.
s. 13, amended: 1987, c.42, s.8.
s. 21A, see *M* v. *Lambeth Borough Council (No. 3)* (1986) 2 F.L.R. 136, C.A.
s. 24, amended: 1987, c.42, s.8.
s. 46, see *R.* v. *Essex County Council, ex p. Washington* (1987) 85 L.G.R. 210, McCowan J.
s. 47, amended: 1987, c.42, sch. 2.
ss. 49, 50, repealed: *ibid.*, schs. 2, 4.
ss. 52, 54, 55, repealed in pt.: *ibid.*, sch. 2.
s. 64, amended: *ibid.*, s.8.
s. 86, amended: *ibid.*, sch. 2.
s. 87, amended: *ibid.*; repealed in pt.: *ibid.*, schs. 2, 4.
sch. 2, repealed in pt.: *ibid.*, sch. 4.
12. Bees Act 1980.
s. 1, order 87/867.
20. Education Act 1980.
s. 17, regs. 87/1312
s. 18, regs. 87/1313
s. 27, regs. 87/879.
s. 35, regs. 87/879, 1312, 1313.
21. Competition Act 1980.
s. 19, amended: 1987, c.43, sch. 4.
22. Companies Act 1980.
s. 48, see *Joint Receivers and Managers of Niltan Carson* v. *Hawthorne* (1987) 3 B.C.C. 454, Hodgson J.
23. Consular Fees Act 1980.
s. 1, order 87/1264.
30. Social Security Act 1980.
s. 14, regs. 87/214; S.R. 1987 No. 112.
s. 15, regs. 87/214.

CAP.

1980—cont.

33. Industry Act 1980.
s. 5, order 87/520.
s. 5, amended: *ibid.*
43. Magistrates' Courts Act 1980.
see *R.* v. *Avon Magistrates' Court Committee, ex p. Bath Law Society, The Independent*, July 16, 1987, D.C.
s. 6, see *R.* v. *Newcastle-under-Lyme JJ., ex p. Hemmings* [1987] Crim.L.R. 416, D.C.
s. 10, see *R.* v. *Ali, The Times*, July 6, 1987, D.C.; *Arthur* v. *Stringer* (1987) 84 Cr.App.R. 361, C.A.
s. 12, see *R.* v. *Epping and Ongar J.J., ex p. Breach; R.* v. *Same, ex p. Shippam (C.)* [1986] Crim.L.R. 810; [1987] R.T.R. 233, D.C.
s. 22, see *R.* v. *Braden, The Times*, October 14, 1987, C.A.
s. 24, see *R.* v. *Hammersmith Juvenile Court, ex p. O. (A Minor), The Times*, April 7, 1987, D.C.; *R.* v. *Crown Court at Doncaster, ex p. South Yorkshire Prosecution Service, sub nom. R.* v. *Doncaster Crown Court, ex p. Crown Prosecution Service* (1987) 85 Cr.App.R. 1; [1987] Crim.L.R. 395, D.C.
s. 44, see *Smith* v. *Mellors and Soar* (1987) 84 Cr.App.R. 279, D.C.
s. 58, amended: 1987, c.42, sch. 2.
s. 59, repealed in pt.: *ibid.*, sch. 4.
s. 64, amended: *ibid.*, sch. 2.
s. 65, amended: *ibid.*; repealed in pt.: *ibid.*, schs. 2, 4.
s. 80, amended: *ibid.*, sch. 2.
s. 82, see *R.* v. *Norwich JJ., ex p. Tigger (formerly Lilly), The Times*, June 26, 1987, D.C.
s. 92, repealed in pt.: 1987, c.42, sch. 4.
ss. 93–95, amended: *ibid.*, sch. 2.
s. 97, see *R.* v. *Peterborough Magistrates' Court, ex p. Willis, The Times*, June 23, 1987, D.C.
s. 100, amended: 1987, c.42, sch. 2.
s. 101, see *Guyll* v. *Bright* [1987] R.T.R. 104, D.C.
ss. 102, 104, see *R.* v. *Governor of Ashford Remand Centre, ex p. Postlethwaite, The Times*, July 14, 1987, H.L.
s. 114, see *R.* v. *Newcastle upon Tyne JJ., ex p. Skinner* [1987] 1 All E.R. 349, D.C.
s. 121, see *R.* v. *Malvern JJ., ex p. Evans; R.* v. *Evesham JJ., ex p. McDonagh, The Times*, August 1, 1987, D.C.
s. 125, see *Jones* v. *Kelsey* [1987] Crim.L.R. 392, D.C.
s. 142, see *Jane* v. *Broome, The Times*, November 2, 1987, D.C.
s. 150, amended: 1987, c.42, sch. 2; repealed in pt.: *ibid.*, schs. 2, 4.
sch. 2, see *R.* v. *Braden, The Times*, October 14, 1987, C.A.

1980—cont.

43. Magistrates' Courts Act 1980—*cont.*
sch. 6, repealed in pt.: 1987, c.19, sch.; c.21, sch. 3.
sch. 7, repealed in pt.: 1987, c.22, sch. 7; c.43, sch. 7.

44. Education (Scotland) Act 1980.
s. 2, regs. 87/290.
ss. 21, 22, 22C, 22D, see *Scottish Hierarchy of the Roman Catholic Church* v. *Highland Regional Council,* 1987 S.L.T. 169, 708, House of Lords, July 16, 1987.
s. 48A, order 87/1140.
s. 49, regs. 87/1366.
s. 54, see *Shaw* v. *Strathclyde Regional Council* (O.H.), 1987 S.C.L.R. 439.
s. 73, regs. 87/208, 291, 309, 644, 864, 1146, 1801.
s. 74, regs. 87/291, 309, 644, 864, 1146, 1801.
s. 75, regs. 87/291, 644.
ss. 75A, 75B, regs. 87/1147.
s. 77, regs. 87/309.
s. 135, amended: 1987, c.40, s.2.
sch. 1, amended: 1987, c.18, sch. 6.

45. Water (Scotland) Act 1980.
s. 9, amended: 1987, c.47, sch. 5; repealed in pt.: *ibid.,* sch. 6.
s. 9A, amended: *ibid.,* sch. 5.
s. 17, orders 87/1032, 1390–1392, 1763, 1879.
s. 29, orders 87/1390–1392, 1763, 1879.
s. 39, repealed: 1987, c.47, sch. 6.
s. 40, substituted: *ibid.,* sch. 5.
s. 41, amended: *ibid.*; repealed in pt.: *ibid.,* sch. 6.
ss. 42, 43, substituted: *ibid.,* sch. 5.
ss. 44, 45, repealed: *ibid.,* sch. 6.
ss. 46–49, amended: *ibid.,* sch. 5.
s. 53, repealed in pt.: *ibid.,* sch. 6.
ss. 54, 55, amended: *ibid.,* sch. 5.
s. 57, repealed: *ibid.,* sch. 6.
s. 58, amended: *ibid.,* sch. 5.
s. 60, repealed in pt.: *ibid.,* sch. 6.
s. 61, amended: *ibid.,* sch. 5; repealed in pt.: *ibid.,* sch. 6.
s. 107, orders 87/1032, 1879.
s. 109, amended: 1987, c.47, sch. 5; repealed in pt.: *ibid.,* sch. 6.

46. Solicitors (Scotland) Act 1980.
s. 35, amended: 1987, c.22, sch. 6; repealed in pt.: *ibid.,* schs. 6, 7.
s. 53, order 87/333.

47. Criminal Appeal (Northern Ireland) Act 1980.
s. 29, see *R.* v. *Ellis* [1986] 10 N.I.J.B. 117, C.A.

48. Finance Act 1980.
s. 24, order 87/434.
s. 24, amended: 1987, c.16, ss.24, 26.
s. 35, amended: 1987, c.21, sch. 2.
s. 36, repealed in pt.: 1987, c.16, sch. 16.
s. 37, amended: 1987, c.51, s.71.
s. 46, repealed in pt.: 1987, c.16, sch. 16.
s. 47, amended: 1987, c.51, s.59.

1980—cont.

48. Finance Act 1980—*cont.*
s. 53, amended: 1987, c.16, sch. 15.
s. 60, repealed in pt.: *ibid.,* sch. 16.
s. 84, repealed in pt.: 1987, c.51, sch. 9.
s. 97, amended: 1987, c.16, s.54.
sch. 10, amended: *ibid.,* s.33, schs. 4, 15; c.51, s.59; repealed in pt.: 1987, c.16, sch. 16.
sch. 17, amended: *ibid.,* sch. 13.

50. Coal Industry Act 1980.
s. 2, amended: 1987, c.3, sch. 1.
ss. 6, 10 (in pt.), repealed: *ibid.,* sch. 3.

51. Housing Act 1980.
repealed (S.): 1987, c.26, sch. 24.
s. 28, see *R.* v. *Plymouth City Council, ex p. Freeman, The Independent,* April 22, 1987, C.A.
ss. 40, 41, see *Palmer* v. *Sandwell Metropolitan Borough, The Times,* October 12, 1987, C.A.
s. 52, see *Paterson* v. *Aggio* (1987) 284 E.G. 508, C.A.
s. 52, order 87/265.
s. 52, repealed in pt.: *ibid.*
s. 56, orders 87/737, 822, 1164, 1525.
s. 56B, order 87/122.
s. 60, order 87/264.
s. 147, see *Berg* v. *Trafford Borough Council, The Times,* July 14, 1987, C.A.
s. 151, order 87/264.
sch. 3, see *South Holland District Council* v. *Keyte* (1985) 19 H.L.R. 97, C.A.
sch. 8, see *Crown Estate Commissioners* v. *Connor and the London Rent Assessment Panel* (1986) 19 H.L.R. 35, McCowan J.
sch. 24, see *Berg* v. *Trafford Borough Council, The Times,* July 14, 1987, C.A.

52. Tenants' Rights, Etc. (Scotland) Act 1980.
Pts. I–III (ss.1–32), V (ss.66–81), except s.74, VI (ss.82–86), except s.86, schs. A1, 1–4, repealed: 1987, c.26, sch. 24.
s. 2, see *Hannan* v. *Falkirk District Council,* 1987 S.L.T. (Lands Tr.) 18.
s. 4, see *Popescu* v. *Banff and Buchan District Council,* 1987 S.L.T. (Lands Tr.) 20; *Morrison* v. *Stirling District Council,* 1987 S.L.T. (Lands Tr.) 22.
s. 7. see *Hannan* v. *Falkirk District Council,* 1987 S.L.T. (Lands Tr.) 18.
ss. 12, 14, see *Monklands District Council* v. *Johnstone* (Sh.Ct.), 1987 S.C.L.R. 480.
s. 14, see *City of Edinburgh District Council* v. *Davis,* 1987 S.L.T. (Sh.Ct.) 33.
s. 31. order 87/1388.
s. 82, see *Hannan* v. *Falkirk District Council,* 1987 S.L.T. (Lands Tr.) 18.
sch. 1, see *Barron* v. *Borders Regional Council,* 1987 S.L.T. (Lands Tr.) 36.

55. Law Reform (Miscellaneous Provisions) (Scotland) Act 1980.
s. 6, see *MacMillan, Petr.,* 1987 S.L.T. (Sh.Ct.) 50.
s. 22, see *Saleh* v. *Saleh* (O.H.), 1987 S.L.T. 633.

CAP.

1980—cont.

58. Limitation Act 1980.

see *Arnold* v. *Central Electricity Generating Board, The Times,* October 23, 1987, H.L.

s. 11, see *Wilkinson* v. *Ancliff (B.L.T.)* [1986] 1 W.L.R. 1352, C.A.

s. 11A, added: 1987, c.43, sch. 1.

s. 12, amended: *ibid.*

s. 14, see *Rule* v. *Atlas Stone Co.,* December 11, 1984, Simon Brown J.; *Wilkinson* v. *Ancliff (B.L.T.)* [1986] 1 W.L.R. 1352, C.A.; *Young* v. *G.L.C. and Massey,* December 19, 1986, Owen J.

s. 14, amended: 1987, c.43, sch. 1.

s. 15, see *BP Properties* v. *Buckler, The Times,* August 13, 1987, C.A.

s. 21, see *Att.-Gen.* v. *Cocke, The Times,* November 9, 1987, Harman J.

ss. 28, 32, amended: 1987, c.43, sch. 1.

s. 33, see *Rule* v. *Atlas Stone Co.,* December 11, 1984, Simon Brown J.; *Young* v. *G.L.C. and Massey,* December 19, 1986, Owen J.

s. 33, amended: 1987, c.43, sch. 1.

s. 35, see *Kenya Railways* v. *Antares Pte., The Times,* February 12, 1987, C.A.; *Fannon* v. *Backhouse, The Times,* August 22, 1987, C.A.

60. Civil Aviation Act 1980.

s. 7, order 87/747.

61. Tenants' Rights, Etc. (Scotland) Amendment Act 1980.

repealed: 1987, c.26, sch. 24.

62. Criminal Justice (Scotland) Act 1980.

s. 2, see *Wilson* v. *Robertson,* 1986 S.C.C.R. 700.

s. 2, amended: 1987, c.41, sch. 1.

s. 14, see *Sandford* v. *H.M. Advocate,* 1986 S.C.C.R. 573.

s. 32, amended: 1987, c.41, s.61.

s. 41, amended: *ibid.,* sch. 1.

s. 74, see *Barrett* v. *Allan,* 1986 S.C.C.R. 479.

sch. 1, amended: 1987, c.41, sch. 1.

sch. 2, see *Salusbury-Hughes* v. *H.M. Advocate,* 1987 S.C.C.R. 38; *McDonald* v. *H.M. Advocate,* 1987 S.C.C.R. 153; *Briggs* v. *Guild,* 1987 S.C.C.R. 141.

sch. 3, see *Courtney* v. *Mackinnon,* 1986 S.C.C.R. 545.

63. Overseas Development and Co-operation Act 1980.

s. 2, sch. 1, amended: 1987, c.3, sch. 1.

s. 4, order 87/1252.

65. Local Government, Planning and Land Act 1980.

see *R.* v. *Secretary of State for the Environment, ex p. Birmingham City Council, The Independent,* February 25, 1987, D.C.

ss. 7, 9, regs. 87/181.

s. 54, amended: 1987, c.6, sch. 4; repealed in pt.: *ibid.,* schs. 4, 5.

s. 56, amended: *ibid.,* sch. 4; repealed in pt.: *ibid.,* sch. 5.

CAP.

1980—cont.

65. Local Government, Planning and Land Act 1980—cont.

s. 58, amended: *ibid.,* sch. 4.

s. 59, see *R.* v. *Secretary of State for the Environment, ex p. Greenwich London Borough Council, The Times,* February 27, 1987, Taylor J.

ss. 59–62, 65, see *R.* v. *Hackney London Borough Council, ex p. Fleming* (1986) 26 R.V.R. 182, Woolf J.

s. 62, repealed: 1987, c.5, s.1.

s. 65, substituted: *ibid.,* sch. 4.

s. 68, repealed in pt.: *ibid.,* sch. 5.

s. 71, see *R.* v. *Greater London Council, ex p. London Residuary Body* (1987) 19 H.L.R. 175, Macpherson J.

Pt. VIII (ss.71–85), see *R.* v. *Secretary of State for the Environment, ex p. Newham London Borough Council* (1987) 19 H.L.R. 298, C.A.

s. 72, regs. 87/351.

s. 75, see *R.* v. *Secretary of State for the Environment, ex p. Newham London Borough Council, The Times,* March 28, 1987, C.A.

s. 75, regs. 87/351.

s. 78, amended and repealed in pt.: 1987, c.44, sch.

ss. 79, 80, amended: *ibid.*

s. 80A, regs. 87/1583.

ss. 80A, 80B, added: 1987, c.44, s.1, sch.

s. 82, amended: *ibid.,* sch.

s. 84, regs. 87/351, 1583.

ss. 84, 85, amended: 1987, c.44, sch.

s. 87, regs. 87/101.

s. 98, see *Manchester City Council* v. *Secretary of State for the Environment* (1987) 27 R.V.R. 75; (1987) 54 P. & C.R. 212, C.A.

ss. 108, 120, amended: 1987, c.3, sch. 1.

ss. 134, 135, orders 87/179, 646, 922–924.

s. 141, see *Mersey Docks and Harbour Co.* v. *Merseyside Development Corporation* (Ref./12/1983) (1987) 27 R.V.R. 97.

s. 148, orders 87/738, 1343–1435.

s. 149, orders 87/739, 1340–1342.

ss. 152, 153, 156, amended (S.): 1987, c.26, sch. 23.

s. 170, amended: 1987, c.3, sch. 1.

s. 179, see *Addis* v. *Clement (Valuation Officer)* (1987) 85 L.G.R. 489, C.A.

sch. 10, regs. 87/347, 359.

sch. 10, amended and repealed in pt.: 1987, c.44, s.2.

sch. 12, see *R.* v. *Greater London Council, ex p. London Residuary Body* (1987) 19 H.L.R. 175, Macpherson J.

sch. 12, regs. 87/351.

sch. 16, amended: 1987, c.3, sch. 1.

sch. 26, orders 87/179, 646, 922–924.

sch. 27, see *Mersey Docks and Harbour Co.* v. *Merseyside Development Corporation* (Ref./12/1983) (1987) 27 R.V.R. 97.

sch. 31, order 87/1238.

1980—cont.

65. Local Government, Planning and Land Act 1980—cont.
sch. 31, amended: 1987, c.51, s.1.
sch. 32, see *Addis* v. *Clement (Valuation Officer)* (1987) 85 L.G.R. 489, C.A.
sch. 32, amended (S.): 1987, c.47, sch. 1.

66. Highways Act 1980.
s. 16, scheme 87/1429.
s. 106, instruments 87/251, 1954.
s. 131, see *Greenwich London Borough Council* v. *Millcroft Construction* (1987) 85 L.G.R. 66, D.C.
s. 137, see *Hertfordshire County Council* v. *Bolden, The Times,* December 9, 1986, D.C.; *Pugh* v. *Pidgen; Same* v. *Powley, The Times,* April 2, 1987, D.C.; *Hirst and Agu* v. *Chief Constable of West Yorkshire* [1987] Crim.L.R. 330, D.C.
s. 290, amended: 1987, c.3, sch. 1.
s. 325, instrument 87/1954.

67. Anguilla Act 1980.
s. 1, order 87/450.

1981

7. House of Commons Members' Fund and Parliamentary Pensions Act 1981.
s. 1, amended: 1987, c.45, sch. 3.
s. 2, resolution 87/511.
ss. 4, 5 (in pt.), repealed: 1987, c.45, sch. 4.

14. Public Passenger Vehicles Act 1981.
ss. 9, 51, 60, 61, regs. 87/1150.

20. Judicial Pensions Act 1981.
s. 21, order 87/209.
s. 23, regs. 87/375.

22. Animal Health Act 1981.
s. 1, orders 87/74, 135(S.), 232, 233, 790, 836, 905, 1447, 1601.
s. 6, order 87/135(S.)
s. 7, orders 87/74, 233, 790, 836, 1447.
s. 8, orders 87/135(S.), 232, 233, 790, 836, 1601.
s. 11, orders 87/211, 248, 1808.
s. 14, order 87/836.
ss. 15, 17, orders 87/790, 836.
s. 23, orders 87/74, 790, 836, 1447.
s. 25, orders 87/233, 836.
ss. 28, 35, order 87/790.
s. 50, order 87/709.
s. 72, orders 87/790, 905.
s. 84, order 87/361.
s. 86, orders 87/135(S.), 1601.
s. 87, orders 87/135(S.), 790.
s. 88, orders 87/790, 905.

23. Local Government (Miscellaneous Provisions) (Scotland) Act 1981.
ss. 2–4, 9, Pt. II (ss.14–20), repealed: 1987, c.47, sch. 6.
ss. 21–23, 34, 35, sch. 2 (in pt.), repealed: 1987, c.26, sch. 24.
sch. 3, repealed in pt.: *ibid.*; c.47, sch. 6.

1981—cont.

29. Fisheries Act 1981.
ss. 15, 18, schemes 87/1135, 1136.
s. 30, orders 87/213, 292, 1536.
s. 31, scheme 87/1134.

31. Insurance Companies Act 1981.
sch. 4, repealed in pt.: 1987, c.22, sch. 7.

35. Finance Act 1981.
s. 27, repealed: 1987, c.16, sch. 16.
ss. 28, 29, amended: *ibid.*, sch. 3.
ss. 48, 58, amended: *ibid.*, sch. 15.
s. 111, see *Mobil North Sea* v. *I.R.C.* [1987] 1 W.L.R. 1065, H.L.
s. 111, repealed in pt.: 1987, c.16, schs. 13, 16.
s. 136 (in pt.), sch. 18, repealed: *ibid.*, sch. 16.

36. Town and Country Planning (Minerals) Act 1981.
s. 33, repealed: 1987, c.12, sch. 3.

38. British Telecommunications Act 1981.
s. 67, amended: 1987, c.22, sch. 6.

45. Forgery and Counterfeiting Act 1981.
s. 1, see *R.* v. *Utting* [1987] 1 W.L.R. 1375, C.A.; *R.* v. *Gold; R.* v. *Schifreen* [1987] 3 W.L.R. 803, C.A.
s. 3, see *Chief Constable of West Mercia Police* v. *Williams* [1987] R.T.R. 188, D.C.; *R.* v. *Garcia, The Times,* November 3, 1987, C.A.
s. 8, see *R.* v. *Gold; R.* v. *Schifreen* [1987] 3 W.L.R. 803, C.A.
s. 9, see *R.* v. *Lack* (1987) 84 Cr.App.R. 342, C.A.; *R.* v. *Moore, The Times,* November 9, 1987, H.L.
s. 10, see *R.* v. *Garcia, The Times,* November 3, 1987, C.A.
s. 15, see *McLeod* v. *Allan,* 1986 S.C.C.R. 666.

47. Criminal Attempts Act 1981.
s. 1, see *Chief Constable of Hampshire* v. *Mace* (1987) 84 Cr.App.R. 40, D.C.; *R.* v. *Gullefer* [1987] Crim.L.R. 195, C.A.; *R.* v. *Millard and Vernon* [1987] Crim.L.R. 393, C.A., *R.* v. *Boyle (G.) and Boyle (J.)* (1987) 84 Cr.App.R. 270, C.A.

49. Contempt of Court Act 1981.
s. 4, see *Keane* v. *H.M. Advocate,* 1986 S.C.C.R. 491.
s. 10, see *Maxwell* v. *Pressdram* [1987] 1 W.L.R. 298, C.A.; *Enquiry under the Company Securities (Insider Dealing) Act 1985, An, Re, The Times,* May 7, 1987, C.A.
s. 11, see *R.* v. *Malvern JJ., ex p. Evans; R.* v. *Evesham JJ., ex p. McDonagh, The Times,* August 1, 1987, D.C.
s. 14, see *Lewisham London Borough* v. *W. & P.,* May 15, 1987, Pearlman J.; *R.* v. *Reader* (1987) 84 Cr.App.R. 294, C.A.
s. 15, amended (S.): 1987, c.41, sch. 1.

54. Supreme Court Act 1981.
see *Rover International* v. *Cannon Films Sales, The Times,* March 30, 1987, Harman J.

1981—cont.

54. Supreme Court Act 1981—*cont.*

ss. 2, 4, order 87/2059; amended: *ibid.*

s. 16, see *R.* v. *Secretary of State for the Home Department, ex p. Dew, The Independent,* February 19, 1987, McNeill J.

s. 18, see *Crosby* v. *Crosby* (1986) 16 Fam. Law 328, C.A.; *Allette* v. *Allette* (1986) 2 F.L.R. 427, C.A.; *R.* v. *Central Criminal Court, ex p. Carr, The Independent,* May 19, 1987, C.A.; *Warren* v. *Kilroe (T.) & Sons, The Times,* July 3, 1987, C.A.; *Carr* v. *Atkins* [1987] 3 W.L.R. 529, C.A.; *Infabrics* v. *Jaytex* [1987] F.S.R. 529, C.A.

ss. 20, 21, see *River Rima, The* [1987] 3 All E.R. 1, C.A.

s. 31, see *R.* v. *Secretary of State for the Home Department, ex p. Dew* [1987] 2 All E.R. 1049, McNeill J.; *R.* v. *H.M. Coroner for North Northumberland, ex p. Armstrong* (1987) 151 J.P. 773, D.C.

s. 33, see *Huddleston* v. *Control Risks Information Services* [1987] 1 W.L.R. 701, Hoffmann J.

s. 35A, see *Mewis* v. *Woolf,* September 12, 1986, Sir Hugh Park sitting as a Deputy High Court Judge at Exeter.

s. 37, see *Company, A (No. 00596 of 1986), Re* [1987] BCLC 133, Harman J.; *I. (A Minor) (Surrogacy), Re* (1987) 151 J.P.N. 334, Sir John Arnold P.; *Company, A (No. 003318 of 1987), Re* [1987] 3 BCC 564, Harman J.

s. 40, amended: 1987, c.22, sch. 6.

s. 48, see *Arthur* v. *Stringer* (1987) 84 Cr.App.R. 361, C.A.

s. 49, see *Att.-Gen.* v. *Arthur Anderson & Co., The Times,* October 13, 1987, Steyn J.

s. 51, see *Davies (Joseph Owen)* v. *Eli Lilley & Co., The Times,* June 6, 1987, C.A.

s. 69, see *Viscount De L'Isle* v. *Times Newspapers, The Times,* April 16, 1987; *The Independent,* April 28, 1987, C.A.

s. 72, see *Crest Homes* v. *Marks* [1987] 3 W.L.R. 293, H.L.

s. 75, see *Practice Direction, (C.A.) (Crown Court Business: Classification)* [1987] 1 W.L.R. 1671.

ss. 76, 77, 81, amended: 1987, c.38, sch. 2.

s. 84, rules 87/716, 1423, 1977.

s. 86, rules 87/716, 1977.

s. 87, rules 87/1977.

s. 138, see *Bankers Trust Co.* v. *Galadari; Chase Manhattan Bank N.A. (Intervener)* [1986] 3 W.L.R. 1099, C.A.

s. 150, order 87/1263.

sch. 1, repealed in pt.: 1987, c.42, sch. 4.

sch. 5, repealed in pt.: 1987, c.16, sch. 16.

56. Transport Act 1981.

see *Jones* v. *Thomas (John Barrie)* [1987] Crim.L.R. 133, D.C.

1981—cont.

56. Transport Act 1981—*cont.*

s. 19, see *Owen* v. *Jones, The Times,* January 28, 1987, D.C.; *Railton* v. *Houston,* 1986 S.C.C.R. 428; *Miller* v. *Ingram,* 1986 S.C.C.R. 437; *Robinson* v. *Aitchison,* 1986 S.C.C.R. 511; *McFadyen* v. *Tudhope,* 1986 S.C.C.R. 712; *Briggs* v. *Guild,* 1987 S.C.C.R. 141.

s. 25, see *Sutch* v. *Crown Prosecution Service,* January 30, 1987, H.H. Judge Compton, Wood Green Crown Ct.; *Newton* v. *Woods* [1987] R.T.R. 41, D.C.; *McKeon* v. *Ellis* [1987] R.T.R. 26, D.C.

s. 30, see *Barnett* v. *Fieldhouse* [1987] R.T.R. 266, D.C.

sch. 8, see *Sutch* v. *Crown Prosecution Service,* January 30, 1987, H.H. Judge Compton, Wood Green Crown Ct.; *Douglas* v. *Stevenson,* 1986 S.C.C.R. 519; *Tudhope* v. *Fulton,* 1986 S.C.C.R. 567; *Newton* v. *Woods* [1987] R.T.R. 41, D.C.; *McKeon* v. *Ellis* [1987] R.T.R. 26, D.C.; *Gallagher* v. *Mackinnon,* 1986 S.C.C.R. 704; *Fraser* v. *McLeod,* 1987 S.C.C.R. 294.

sch. 9, see *Barnett* v. *Fieldhouse* [1987] R.T.R. 266, D.C.

59. Matrimonial Homes (Family Protection) (Scotland) Act 1981.

s. 3, see *Welsh* v. *Welsh,* 1987 S.L.T. (Sh.Ct.) 30.

s. 4, see *Mather* v. *Mather* (O.H.), 1987 S.L.T. 565.

s. 7, see *O'Neill* v. *O'Neill,* 1987 S.L.T. (Sh.Ct.) 26; *Fyfe* v. *Fyfe,* 1987 S.L.T. (Sh.Ct.) 38.

s. 13, amended: 1987, c.26, sch. 23.

s. 18, see *Clarke* v. *Hatten* (Sh.Ct.), 1987 S.C.L.R. 527.

s. 19, see *Hall* v. *Hall,* 1987 S.L.T. (Sh.Ct.) 15.

60. Education Act 1981.

ss. 1, 2, 4, 5, 7, 9, see *R.* v. *Secretary of State for Education and Science, ex p. L.* [1987] 85 L.G.R. 333, D.C.

s. 7, see *R.* v. *Hereford and Worcester County Council, ex p. Lashford, The Times,* May 13, 1987, C.A.

61. British Nationality Act 1981.

s. 2, order 87/611.

63. Betting and Gaming Duties Act 1981.

s. 1, amended: 1987, c.16, s.3; repealed in pt.: *ibid.*, s.3, sch. 16.

s. 3, repealed: *ibid.*, sch. 16.

s. 12, regs. 87/312, 1963.

s. 21, amended; 1987, c.16, s.5; repealed in pt.: *ibid.*, sch. 16.

s. 23, amended: *ibid.*, s.4.

s. 26, amended: *ibid.*, s.5.

s. 29, amended (S.): 1987, c.18, sch. 6.

sch. 1, regs. 87/312, 1963.

sch. 1, amended: 1987, c.16, s.3.

sch. 4, amended: *ibid.*, s.5; repealed in pt.: *ibid.*, sch. 16.

1981—cont.

64. New Towns Act 1981.
s. 2, order 87/104.

67. Acquisition of Land Act 1981.
ss. 7, 10–12, 15, 22, 29, regs. 87/1915.
ss. 17, 29, amended: 1987, c.3, sch. 1.

68. Broadcasting Act 1981.
s. 2, order 87/673.
s. 2, amended: *ibid.*
s. 19, amended: 1987, c.10, s.1.
s. 66, order 87/2205.

69. Wildlife and Countryside Act 1981.
s. 1, see *Kirkland* v. *Robinson* [1987]
Crim.L.R. 643, D.C.
s. 3, order 87/1163.
s. 5, see *Robinson* v. *Hughes* [1987]
Crim.L.R. 644, D.C.
s. 36, amended: 1987, c.49, sch. 1;
repealed in pt.: 1987, c.21, sch. 3.

72. Housing (Amendment) (Scotland) Act 1981.
repealed: 1987, c.26, sch. 24.

1982

9. Agricultural Training Board Act 1982.
s. 4, amended: 1987, c.29, s.1.
s. 5A, added: *ibid.*
ss. 7, 8, amended: *ibid.*

15. Coal Industry Act 1982.
s. 3, amended and repealed in pt.: 1987,
c.3, sch. 1.

16. Civil Aviation Act 1982.
ss. 4, 64, 66, see *Air Ecosse* v. *Civil Aviation Authority*, Second Division, July 3,
1987.
s. 7, regs. 87/379.
ss. 73, 74, regs. 87/269.
s. 88, orders 87/1377, 2229.
s. 108, order 87/456.

22. Gaming (Amendment) Act 1982.
s. 2, sch. 2, repealed: 1987, c.19, sch.

23. Oil and Gas (Enterprise) Act 1982.
Commencement order: 87/2272.
s. 21, orders 87/4, 53–59, 61, 62, 66–72,
199, 200–206, 591–595, 812–814,
974–989, 1094, 1095, 1399–1416,
1418–1420.
s. 21, repealed: 1987, c.12, s.24, sch. 3.
s. 22, amended: *ibid.*, s.24; c.49, sch. 1.
s. 27, amended: 1987, c.12, s.24; c.21, sch.
2; repealed in pt.: 1987, c.12, s.24,
sch. 3.
s. 28, amended: 1987, c.49, sch. 1.
s. 38, order 87/2272.
sch. 3, repealed in pt.: 1987, c.12, sch. 3.

24. Social Security and Housing Benefits Act 1982.
s. 1, regs. 87/372.
s. 3, regs. 87/868.
s. 7, regs. 87/33.
s. 7, amended: *ibid.*; orders 87/45, 1978.
s. 9, regs. 87/92, 413.
s. 26, regs. 87/92, 372, 868.
s. 28, see *R.* v. *Kensington and Chelsea London Borough Council, ex p. Woolrich, The Times,* September 1, 1987,
Kennedy J.

1982—cont.

34. Social Security and Housing Benefits Act 1982—cont.
s. 28, regs. 87/1440.
s. 32, see *R.* v. *Secretary of State for Social Services, ex p. Waltham Forest London Borough Council; Same* v. *Same, ex p. Worcester City Council, The Independent,* July 9, 1987, D.C.
s. 32, order 87/1805.
s. 34, amended: 1987, c.6, sch. 4.
s. 45, regs. 87/92.
s. 47, regs. 87/92, 372, 413, 868.
sch. 1, regs. 87/868.
sch. 4, repealed in pt.: 1987, c.42, sch. 4.

25. Iron and Steel Act 1982.
s. 30, amended: 1987, c.3, sch. 1.

27. Civil Jurisdiction and Judgments Act 1982.
see *Silver Athens (No. 1), The* [1986] 2
Lloyd's Rep. 580, Sheen J.
s. 2, see *Porzelack K.G.* v. *Porzelack (U.K.)* [1987] 1 W.L.R. 420, Browne-Wilkinson V.-C.
s. 5, amended: 1987, c.42, sch. 2; repealed
in pt.: *ibid.*, sch. 2.
s. 9, order 87/468.
s. 18, amended (S.): 1987, c.41, s.45.
s. 26, see *Silver Athens (No. 2), The* [1986] 2 Lloyd's Rep. 583; *Jalamatsya, The* [1987] 2 Lloyd's Rep. 164, Sheen J.
s. 27, see *World Star, The* [1986] 2 Lloyd's
Rep. 274, Sheen J.

27. Civil Jurisdiction and Judgments Act 1982.
ss. 41–46, sch. 1; see *St. Michael Financial Services* v. *Michie* (Sh.Ct.), 1987
S.C.L.R. 376.
sch. 8, amended (S): 1987, c.47, s.16.

28. Taking of Hostages Act 1982.
ss. 3, 5, order 87/455.

29. Supply of Goods and Services Act 1982.
s. 13, see *Metaalhandel Ja Magnus BV* v. *Ardfields Transport, Financial Times,*
July 21, 1987, Gatehouse J.

30. Local Government (Miscellaneous Provisions) Act 1982.
s. 2, see *R.* v. *Peterborough City Council, ex p. Quietlynn* (1987) 85 L.G.R. 249, C.A.; *Plymouth City Council* v. *Quietlynn; Portsmouth City Council* v. *Quietlynn; Quietlynn* v. *Oldham Borough Council* [1987] 3 W.L.R. 189, D.C.
s. 10, amended: 1987, c.27, s.47.
sch. 1, see *R.* v. *Tyneside Justices, ex p. North Tyneside Borough Council, The Times,* November 7, 1987, Schiemann J.
sch. 1, amended: 1987, c.27, ss.43, 46.
sch. 3, see *R.* v. *Peterborough City Council, ex p. Quietlynn* (1987) 85 L.G.R. 249, C.A.; *Plymouth City Council* v. *Quietlynn; Portsmouth City Council* v. *Quietlynn; Quietlynn* v. *Oldham Borough Council* [1987] 3 W.L.R. 189, D.C.; *Sheptonhurst* v. *City of Wakefield Metropolitan District Council, The Times,* November 18, 1987, C.A.

1982—cont.

32. Local Government Finance Act 1982.
s. 3, amended: 1987, c.6, sch. 4.
ss. 5, 8, see *R.* v. *Hackney London Borough Council, ex p. Fleming* (1986) 26 R.V.R. 182, Woolf J.
s. 8, amended: 1987, c.6, sch. 4.
s. 9, repealed in pt.; *ibid.*, sch. 5.
s. 20, see *Lloyd* v. *McMahon* [1987] 2 W.L.R. 821, H.L.
sch. 2, repealed in pt.: 1987, c.6, sch. 5.

33. Cinematograph (Amendment) Act 1982.
see *British Amusement Catering Trades Association* v. *Westminster City Council, The Times,* March 27, 1987, C.A.

34. Forfeiture Act 1982.
s. 2, see *Cross, Petr.* (O.H.), 1987 S.L.T. 384.
s. 4, regs. 87/214.

36. Aviation Security Act 1982.
s. 9, orders 87/451, 2041.
s. 39, orders 87/451, 456, 2041.

39. Finance Act 1982.
s. 29, regs. 87/404.
s. 32, repealed: 1987, c.16, sch. 16.
s. 65, amended: 1987, c.51, s.67; repealed in pt.: *ibid.*, sch. 9.
s. 66, amended: *ibid.*, s.68.
s. 76, amended: *ibid.*, s.72.
s. 142, sch. 6, repealed in pt.: 1987, c.16, sch. 16.
sch. 7, orders 87/1224, 2127.
sch. 7, amended: 1987, c.22, sch. 16.

41. Stock Transfer Act 1982.
s. 1, regs. 87/1294.
s. 3, regs. 87/1293.
s. 6, sch. 2, repealed in pt.: 1987, c.16, sch. 16.

42. Derelict Land Act 1982.
s. 1, order 87/1653.

43. Local Government and Planning (Scotland) Act 1982.
ss. 1–3, repealed: 1987, c.47, sch. 6.
s. 24, amended: 1987, c.26, sch. 23.
ss. 51–55, repealed: *ibid.*, sch. 24.
sch. 3, repealed in pt.: *ibid.*, c.47, sch. 6.

44. Legal Aid Act 1982.
s. 1, regs. 87/388, 433.
s. 7, regs. 87/422.
ss. 7, 8, see *Sampson, Re* [1987] 1 W.L.R. 194, H.L.
s. 9, see *R.* v. *Huntingdon Magistrates' Court, ex p. Yapp* (1987) 84 Cr.App.R. 90, D.C.

45. Civic Government (Scotland) Act 1982.
s. 7, see *Gregan* v. *Tudhope,* 1987 S.C.C.R. 57; *Joseph Dunn (Bottlers)* v. *MacDougall,* 1987 S.C.C.R. 290; *McInnes* v. *Tudhope,* 1987 S.C.C.R. 368.
s. 9, amended: 1987, c.27, s.44.
ss. 10, 13, see *McDowall* v. *Cunninghame District Council,* 1987 S.L.T. 662.
s. 39, see *Joseph Dunn (Bottlers)* v. *MacDougall,* 1987 S.C.C.R. 290; *McInnes* v. *Tudhope,* 1987 S.C.C.R. 368.

1982—cont.

45. Civic Government (Scotland) Act 1982—cont.
ss. 39, 41, see *Thomson* v. *Kirkcaldy District Council* (O.H.), 1987 S.L.T. 372.
s. 41, amended: 1987, c.27, s.44.
s. 41A, added: *ibid.*
s. 58, see *Allan* v. *Bree,* 1987 S.C.C.R. 228.
ss. 67–69, see *Fleming* v. *Chief Constable of Strathclyde* (Sh.Ct.), 1987 S.C.L.R. 303.
s. 87, see *University Court of the University of Edinburgh* v. *City of Edinburgh District Council,* 1987 S.L.T.(Sh.Ct.) 103.
s. 87, amended: 1987, c.26, sch. 23.
s. 90, amended: 1987, c.47, sch. 1.
s. 98, amended: 1987, c.27, s.48.
ss. 99, 103, see *Purves* v. *City of Edinburgh District Council,* 1987 S.L.T. 366.
s. 108, amended: 1987, c.26, sch. 23.
s. 123, amended: 1987, c.3, sch. 1.
s. 129, repealed in pt.: 1987, c.9, sch.
sch. 1, see *McDowall* v. *Cunninghame District Council,* 1987 S.L.T. 662; *Holmes* v. *Hamilton District Council* (Sh.Ct), 1987 S.C.L.R. 407.
sch. 3, repealed in pt.: 1987, c.26, sch. 24.

46. Employment Act 1982.
s. 16, amended: 1987, c.43, sch. 4.

47. Duchy of Cornwall Management Act 1982.
s. 6, amended: 1987, c.22, sch. 6.

48. Criminal Justice Act 1982.
s. 1, see *R.* v. *Passmore* (1985) 7 Cr.App.R.(S.) 377, C.A.; *R.* v. *Munday* (1985) 7 Cr.App.R.(S.) 216, C.A.; *R.* v. *Roberts* [1987] Crim.L.R. 581, C.A.
s. 7, see *R.* v. *Fairhurst* [1986] 1 W.L.R. 1374, C.A.; *R.* v. *Ealand and Standing* (1986) 83 Cr.App.R. 241, C.A.

50. Insurance Companies Act 1982.
ss. 2, 15, regs. 87/2130; amended: *ibid.*
ss. 5, 17, 32, 33, regs. 87/2130.
s. 49, amended: regs. 87/2118.
s. 94A, regs. 87/350.
s. 97, regs. 87/350, 2130.
sch. 2, amended: regs. 87/2130.
sch. 5, repealed in pt.: 1987, c.22, sch. 7.

53. Administration of Justice Act 1982.
s. 8, see *Forsyth's Curator Bonis* v. *Govan Shipbuilders* (O.H.), 1987 S.C.L.R. 604.
s. 12, see *Potter* v. *McCulloch* (O.H.), 1987 S.L.T. 308; *White* v. *Inveresk Paper Co.* (O.H.), 1987 S.L.T. 586; *White* v. *Inveresk Paper Co. (No. 2)* (O.H.), February 5, 1987.
s. 38, rules 87/821.
s. 62, see *Duke* v. *Plessey* (O.H.), 1987 S.L.T. 638.

1983

2. Representation of the People Act 1983.
s. 29, regs. 87/899, 900.
s. 36, rules 87/1, 260, 261.
ss. 76A, 197, order 87/903.
ss. 78, 197, amended: *ibid.*

1983—cont.

8. British Fishing Boats Act 1983.
s. 5, amended (S.): 1987, c.18, sch. 6.

13. Merchant Shipping Act 1983.
s. 5, sch., regs. 87/63.

19. Matrimonial Homes Act 1983.
s. 1, see *Hall* v. *King* (1987) 283 E.G. 1400; (1987) 19 H.L.R. 440, C.A.

20. Mental Health Act 1983.
s. 70, see *R.* v. *Mental Health Review Tribunal, ex p. Secretary of State for the Home Department, The Times,* March 25, 1987, Farquharson J.
s. 72, 145, see *R.* v. *Mersey Mental Health Review Tribunal, ex p. D., The Times,* April 13, 1987, D.C.
s. 73, see *Campbell* v. *Secretary of State for the Home Department, sub nom. R.* v. *Oxford Regional Mental Health Review Tribunal, ex p. Secretary of State for the Home Department* [1987] 3 W.L.R. 522, H.L.
s. 96, see *B. (Court of Protection: Notice of Proceedings), Re* [1987] 1 W.L.R. 552, Millett J.
sch. 4, repealed in pt.: 1987, c.45, sch. 4.

21. Pilotage Act 1983.
repealed: 1987, c.21, sch. 3.
s. 3, order 87/295.
s. 9, orders 87/843 (S.), 1484, 1576 (S.).

25. Energy Act 1983.
s. 33, order 87/668.

28. Finance Act 1983.
s. 7, repealed in pt.: 1987, c.16, sch. 16.
s. 28, amended: *ibid.*, s.34.
sch. 5, amended: *ibid.*, ss.42, 43, sch. 15.
sch. 8, repealed in pt.: *ibid.*, sch. 16.

34. Mobile Homes Act 1983.
ss. 1, 5, sch. 1, see *West Lothian District Council* v. *Morrison,* 1987 S.L.T. 361.

35. Litter Act 1983.
s. 1, see *Camden London Borough Council* v. *Shinder, The Times,* July 4, 1987, C.A.

40. Education (Fees and Awards) Act 1983.
ss. 1, 2, regs. 87/1364, 1383 (S.).

44. National Audit Act 1983.
sch. 4, amended: 1987, c.3, sch. 1; repealed in pt.: *ibid.*, sch. 3.

47. National Heritage Act 1983.
s. 31, order 87/1945.

53. Car Tax Act 1983.
s. 2, see *R.* v. *Customs and Excise Comrs., ex p. Nissan (U.K.), The Times,* November 23, 1987, C.A.
sch. 1, amended (S.): 1987, c.18, sch. 4.

54. Medical Act 1983.
s. 1, order 87/457.
s. 32, order of council 87/102.
s. 36, see *Finegan* v. *General Medical Council* [1987] 1 W.L.R. 121, P.C.
sch. 1, orders 87/457, 1120.

1983—cont.

55. Value Added Tax Act 1983.
s. 2, see *Nasim (Trading as Yasmine Restaurant)* v. *Customs and Excise Comrs.* [1987] S.T.C. 387, Simon Brown J.
s. 2, amended: 1987, c.16, s.13.
ss. 3, 6, order 87/1806.
s. 6, amended: 1987, c.16, s.12.
s. 7, amended: *ibid.*, s.19, sch. 2.
s. 14, see *Flockton (Ian) Developments* v. *Customs and Excise Comrs.* [1987] S.T.C. 394, Stuart-Smith J.; *R.* v. *Customs and Excise Comrs., ex p. Strangewood* [1987] S.T.C. 502, Otton J.
s. 14, orders 87/510, 781, 1072, 1427, 1916.
s. 14, amended: 1987, c.16, s.11.
s. 15, order 87/510.
s. 15, amended: 1987, c.16, s.12.
s. 16, regs. 87/150, 1916; orders 87/437, 518, 781, 1072, 1806.
s. 17, orders 87/517, 860, 1259.
s. 19, orders 87/154, 155, 1916.
s. 22, see *Euro-Academy* v. *Comrs. of Customs and Excise* [1987] 2 C.M.L.R. 29, VAT Tribunal.
s. 23. regs. 87/2015.
s. 23, amended: 1987, c.16, sch. 2.
s. 29A, added: *ibid.*, s.15.
s. 33, amended: *ibid.*, sch. 2.
s. 34, order 87/806.
s. 35, amended: 1987, c.16, s.12.
s. 37A, order 87/1806.
s. 37A, added: 1987, c.16, s.16.
s. 40, amended: *ibid.*, sch. 2.
s. 45, amended: *ibid.*, s.16.
s. 48, orders 87/437, 517, 518, 781, 1072, 1259, 1806.
s. 48, amended: 1987, c.16, s.13.
sch. 1, see *Customs and Excise Commissioners* v. *Shingleton, The Times,* December 8, 1987, Brown J.
sch. 1, order 87/438; regs. 87/1916.
sch. 1, amended: order 87/438; 1987, c.16, ss.13, 14; repealed in pt.: *ibid.*, s.14, sch. 16.
sch. 4, amended: *ibid.*, s.17.
sch. 5, see *Pimblett (John) and Sons* v. *Comrs. of Customs and Excise* [1987] S.T.C. 202, Taylor J.; *Customs and Excise Comrs.* v. *Great Shelford Free Church (Baptist)* [1987] S.T.C. 249, Kennedy J.; *Customs and Excise Commissioners* v. *Quaker Oats* [1987] S.T.C. 638, Kennedy J.; *Customs and Excise Commissioners* v. *Willmott (John) Housing* [1987] S.T.C. 692, Webster J.
sch. 5, amended: orders 87/437, 518, 718, 1072, 1806; repealed in pt.: 1987, c.16, s.13, sch. 16; orders 87/437, 518.
sch. 6, see *Customs and Excise Commissioners* v. *Zinn, The Daily Telegraph,* November 30, 1987, Nolan J.
sch. 6, amended: 1987, c.16, s.18; orders 87/517, 860, 1259; repealed in pt.: order 87/860.

CAP.

1983—cont.

55. Value Added Tax Act 1983—cont.
sch. 7, see *Schlumberger Inland Services Inc.* v. *Customs and Excise Comrs.* [1987] S.T.C. 228, Taylor J.; *Grunwick Processing Laboratories* v. *Customs and Excise Comrs.* [1987] S.T.C. 357, C.A.
sch. 7, regs. 87/1427, 1712, 1916.
sch. 7, amended: 1987, c.16, s.11; c.18, sch. 4(S.).

56. Oil Taxation Act 1983.
ss. 9, 12, order 87/545.

60. Coal Industry Act 1983.
s. 3, repealed: 1987, c.3, sch. 3.

1984

8. Prevention of Terrorism (Temporary Provisions) Act 1984.
continued in force: order 87/273.
see *R.* v. *Secretary of State for the Home Office, ex p. Stitt, The Times*, February 3, 1987, D.C.
s. 12, see *Hanna* v. *Chief Constable of the Royal Ulster Constabulary* [1986] 13 N.I.J.B. 71, Carswell J.
ss. 13, 14, orders 87/119, 1209.
s. 17, order 87/273.
sch. 3, see *H.M. Advocate* v. *Copeland,* 1987 S.C.C.R. 232.
sch. 3, orders 87/119, 1209.

10. Town and Country Planning Act 1984.
ss. 1, 6, regs. 87/1529(S.).

11. Education (Grants and Awards) Act 1984.
ss. 1, 3, regs. 87/1960.

12. Telecommunications Act 1984.
s. 7, order 87/3, 827.
ss. 28, amended: 1987, c.43, sch. 4.
s. 85, order 87/774.
s. 85, amended: 1987, c.43, sch. 4.
s. 101, amended: *ibid.*; repealed in pt.: *ibid.*, sch. 5.
sch. 1, repealed in pt.: 1987, c.39, sch. 1.
sch. 4, repealed in pt.(S.): 1987, c.26, sch. 24.

18. Tenants' Rights, etc. (Scotland) Amendment Act 1984.
repealed: 1987, c.26, sch. 24.

22. Public Health (Control of Disease) Act 1984.
s. 6, amended: 1987, c.49, sch. 1.
ss. 10, 11, 15, see *Lyons* v. *East Sussex County Council, The Times*, July 27, 1987, Farquharson J.

24. Dentists Act 1984.
s. 3, repealed in pt.: order 87/2047.
s. 4, amended and repealed in pt.: *ibid.*
s. 27, see *Doughty* v. *General Medical Council* [1987] 3 W.L.R. 769, P.C.
s. 49, order 87/2047.
sch. 1, amended: *ibid.*
schs. 3, 5, repealed in pt.: *ibid.*

26. Inshore Fishing (Scotland) Act 1984.
s. 8, amended: 1987, c.18, sch. 6.

CAP.

1984—cont.

27. Road Traffic Regulation Act 1984.
s. 5, see *Rodgers* v. *Taylor* [1987] R.T.R. 86, D.C.
s. 6, order 87/897.
s. 17, see *Mawson* v. *Oxford* [1987] Crim.L.R. 131, D.C.
ss. 25, 64, regs. 87/16.
s. 65, regs. 87/16; directions 87/1706.
s. 131, order 87/363.
sch. 9, order 87/897.
sch. 12, see *McInnes* v. *Allan,* 1987 S.C.L.R. 99.

28. County Courts Act 1984.
s. 40, see *Weston* v. *Briar*, May 15, 1987, Hoffmann J.
s. 42, see *Habib Bank A.G. Zurich* v. *Mindi Investments, The Times*, October 9, 1987, C.A.
s. 50, see *H.H. Property Co.* v. *Rahim,* (1987) 282 E.G. 455, C.A.
s. 75, rules 87/1119, 1397.
s. 86, see *Mercantile Credit Co.* v. *Ellis, The Independent*, March 17, 1987, C.A.
s. 147, amended: 1987, c.22, sch. 6.

30. Food Act 1984.
s. 2, see *McDonald's Hamburgers* v. *Windle* [1987] Crim.L.R. 200, D.C.
ss. 4, 7, regs. 87/1986, 1987.
s. 8, see *Barton* v. *Unigate Dairies* [1987] Crim.L.R. 121, D.C.; *Gateway Foodmarkets* v. *Simmonds, The Times*, March 26, 1987, D.C.
ss. 33, 38, regs. 87/212.
s. 68, order 87/310.
s. 73, regs. 87/133.
s. 102, see *Gateway Foodmarkets* v. *Simmonds, The Times*, March 26, 1987, D.C.
s. 118, regs. 87/212, 1986, 1987.
s. 119, regs. 87/1986.
sch. 10, repealed in pt.: 1987, c.43, sch. 5.

31. Rating and Valuation (Amendment) (Scotland) Act 1984.
ss. 1–4, repealed: 1987, c.47, sch. 6.
s. 8, repealed: 1986, c.26, sch. 24.
s. 12, see *Imperial Chemical Industries* v. *Central Region Valuation Appeal Committee* (O.H.), August 5, 1986.
s. 20, see *Dalgleish* v. *Assessor for Strathclyde Region*, Lands Valuation Appeal Court, October 24, 1985; *W. R. Whitwell* v. *Assessor for Strathclyde Region*, Lands Valuation Appeal Court, October 24, 1985.
sch. 1, repealed: 1987, c.47, sch. 6.

32. London Regional Transport Act 1984.
s. 13, order 87/125.

33. Rates Act 1984.
ss. 1–3, 6, 8, see *R.* v. *Hackney London Borough Council, ex p. Fleming* (1986) 26 R.V.R. 182, Woolf J.
s. 2, orders 87/785, 786, 1251.
s. 2, amended: order 87/1251.
ss. 7, 19, amended: 1987, c.6, sch. 4.

35. Data Protection Act 1984.
s. 6, regs. 87/1304.

(49)

CAP.

1984—cont.

35. Data Protection Act 1984—cont.
s. 8, regs. 87/272, 1304.
s. 21, regs. 87/1507.
s. 29, orders 87/1903, 1904.
s. 30, order 87/1905.
s. 34, order 87/1906.
s. 40, order 87/272, 1304, 1906.
s. 41, regs. 87/272, 1304, 1507.

36. Mental Health (Scotland) Act 1984.
ss. 18, 24, 26, see *B.* v. *F.* (2nd Div.), 1987 S.C.L.R. 395.
s. 29, see *Ferns* v. *Management Committee and Managers, Ravenscraig Hospital,* 1987 S.L.T. (Sh.Ct.) 76; *T.* v. *Secretary of State for Scotland* (Sh.Ct.), 1987 S.C.L.R. 65.
ss. 33, 34, see *A.B. and C.B.* v. *E.* (Sh.Ct.), 1987 S.C.L.R. 419.

37. Child Abduction Act 1984.
see *R.* v. *Mousir* [1987] Crim.L.R. 561, C.A.

39. Video Recordings Act 1984.
Commencement orders: 87/123, 160, 1142, 1249(S.), 2155.
s. 23, orders 87/123, 160, 1142, 1249(S.), 2155.

40. Animal Health and Welfare Act 1984.
s. 10, regs. 87/390, 904.
s. 11, regs. 87/390.

42. Matrimonial and Family Proceedings Act 1984.
s. 12, see *Chebaro* v. *Chebaro* [1987] 1 All E.R. 999, C.A.
s. 39, see *N. and L. (Minors) (Adoption Proceedings: Venue), Re* [1987] 1 W.L.R. 829, C.A.

43. Finance Act 1984.
s. 16, repealed (S.): 1987, c.18, sch. 8.
s. 18, repealed in pt.: 1987, c.51, sch. 9.
s. 38, amended: *ibid.*, s.59.
s. 45, amended: *ibid.*, sch. 2.
s. 65, repealed: *ibid.*, sch. 9.
s. 79, amended: *ibid.*, s.76; repealed in pt.: *ibid.*, s.76, sch. 9.
ss. 92, 94, repealed in pt.: 1987, c.16, sch. 16.
s. 96, amended: *ibid.*, sch. 15.
s. 113, amended: *ibid.*, sch. 13; repealed in pt.: *ibid.*, schs. 13, 16.
sch. 3, repealed in pt.: *ibid.*, sch. 16.
sch. 8, amended: *ibid.*, sch. 15; c.22, sch. 6.
sch. 9, amended: *ibid.*, sch. 15.
sch. 10, amended: *ibid.*, s.33, sch. 4; c.51, s.59; repealed in pt.: 1987, c.16, sch. 10.
sch. 11, amended: 1987, c.51, sch. 2.
sch. 17, amended: *ibid.*, s.65.
sch. 19, amended: *ibid.*, s.66.

46. Cable and Broadcasting Act 1984.
Commencement order: 87/672.
s. 59, order 87/672.
sch. 5, repealed in pt.: 1987, c.22, sch. 7.

CAP.

1984—cont.

47. Repatriation of Prisoners Act 1984.
ss. 1, 3, 10, see *R.* v. *Secretary of State for the Home Department, ex p. Read (Gary John), The Times,* November 2, 1987, D.C.
s. 9, order 87/1828.

49. Trade Union Act 1984.
s. 10, see *Monsanto* v. *Transport and General Workers' Union* [1987] 1 All E.R. 358, C.A.; *Longley* v. *National Union of Journalists* [1987] I.R.L.R. 109, C.A.
ss. 10, 11, see *Falconer* v. *A.S.L.E.F. and N.U.R.* [1986] I.R.L.R. 331, Sheffield County Ct.

50. Housing Defects Act 1984.
repealed (S.): 1987, c.26, sch. 24.
ss. 2, 27, see *McSweeney* v. *Dumbarton District Council,* 1987 S.L.T.(Sh.Ct.) 129.
sch. 4, amended: 1987, c.3, sch. 1.

51. Inheritance Tax Act 1984.
s. 3A, amended: 1987, c.51, s.96; repealed in pt.: *ibid.*, s.96, sch. 9.
s. 8, order 87/435.
s. 10, amended: 1987, c.16, sch. 8.
s. 12, amended: 1987, c.51, s.98.
s. 49, repealed in pt.: *ibid.*, s.96, sch. 9.
ss. 54A, 54B, added: *ibid.*, sch. 7.
s. 55, repealed in pt.: *ibid.*, s.96, sch. 9.
s. 56, amended: *ibid.*, sch. 7.
s. 57A, added: 1987, c.16, sch. 9.
ss. 98, 100, 104, 105, 107, amended: *ibid.*, sch. 8.
s. 109A, added: *ibid.*
ss. 113A, 124A, 136, 140, amended: *ibid.*
ss. 151, 152, amended: 1987, c.51, s.98.
s. 157, amended: 1987, c.22, sch. 6.
s. 158, amended: 1987, c.16, s.70.
ss. 168, 178, amended: *ibid.*, sch. 8; repealed in pt.: *ibid.*, schs. 8, 16.
s. 180, amended: *ibid.*, sch. 8.
ss. 201, 216, amended: 1987, c.51, sch. 7.
ss. 227, 228, amended: 1987, c.16, sch. 8.
s. 233, order 87/887.
s. 256, regs. 87/1127, 1128 (S.), 1129 (N.I.).
s. 265, amended: 1987, c.51, sch. 7.
s. 272, amended: 1987, c.16, sch. 8.
sch. 1, amended: order 87/435; 1987, c.16, s.57.
sch. 4, amended: 1987, c.16, sch. 9.

52. Parliamentary Pensions etc. Act 1984.
ss. 1–11, 15 (in pt.), 16, sch., repealed: 1987, c.45, sch. 4.

54. Roads (Scotland) Act 1984.
s. 1, repealed in pt.: 1987, c.47, sch. 6.
s. 87, see *Lord Advocate* v. *Strathclyde Regional Council* (O.H.), 1987 S.C.L.R. 171.
s. 140, amended: 1987, c.3, sch. 1.

55. Building Act 1984.
ss. 1, 3, 8, regs. 87/798, 1445.
ss. 16, 17, 35, regs. 87/798.

(50)

1984—cont.

55. Building Act 1984—cont.

s. 36, see *Rickards* v. *Kerrier District Council, The Times*, April 7, 1987, Schiemann J.

s. 47, regs. 87/798.

s. 48, amended: 1987, c.27, s.7; regs. 87/798.

ss. 49–54, 56, regs. 87/798.

sch. 1, regs. 87/798, 1445.

schs. 3, 4, regs. 87/798.

58. Rent (Scotland) Act 1984.

s. 5, amended: 1987, c.26, sch. 23; repealed in pt.: *ibid.*, sch. 24.

s. 6, amended: *ibid.*, sch. 23.

s. 37, see *North* v. *Allan Properties (Edinburgh)*, 1987 S.L.T. (Sh.Ct.) 141.

ss. 59, 63, amended: 1987, c.26, sch. 23; repealed in pt.: *ibid.*, sch. 24.

ss. 63, 66, 101, 106, amended: *ibid.*, sch. 23.

s. 110, substituted: 1987, c.18, sch. 6.

sch. 2, amended: 1987, c.26, sch. 23.

59. Ordnance Factories and Military Services Act 1984.

s. 11, sch. 3, repealed: 1987, c.4, s.7.

60. Police and Criminal Evidence Act 1984.

s. 9, see *R.* v. *Central Criminal Court, ex p. Carr, The Independent*, May 19, 1987, C.A.; *R.* v. *Bristol Crown Court, ex p. Bristol Press and Picture Agency* [1987] Crim.L.R. 329, D.C.; *Carr* v. *Atkins* [1987] 3 W.L.R. 529, C.A.; *R.* v. *Leicester Crown Court, ex p. D.P.P.* [1987] 1 W.L.R. 1371, D.C.

s. 10, see *R.* v. *Crown Court, ex p. Baines and White* (1987) 137 New L.J. 945, D.C.

s. 17, see *Kynaston* v. *D.P.P.; Heron (Joseph)* v. *D.P.P.; Heron (Tracey)* v. *D.P.P., The Times*, November 4, 1987, D.C.

s. 18, see *R.* v. *Badham* [1987] Crim.L.R. 202, Wood Green Crown Court.

ss. 25, 28, see *Nicholas* v. *Parsonage* [1987] R.T.R. 199, D.C.

s. 32, see *R.* v. *Badham* [1987] Crim.L.R. 202, Wood Green Crown Ct.

s. 43, see *R.* v. *Slough Justices, ex p. Stirling* [1987] Crim.L.R. 576, D.C.

s. 56, see *R.* v. *McIvor* [1987] Crim.L.R. 409, Sheffield Crown Ct.

s. 58, see *D.P.P.* v. *Billington, Chappell, Rumble and East, The Independent*, July 22, 1987, D.C.; *Walters, Re* [1987] Crim.L.R. 577, D.C.; *R.* v. *Smith (Eric)* [1987] Crim.L.R. 579, Stafford Crown Ct.

s. 66, see *Walters, Re* [1987] Crm.L.R. 577, D.C.

s. 68, see *R.* v. *O'Laughlin and McLaughlin* [1987] Crim.L.R. 632, Central Criminal Ct.

s. 69, see *Sophocleous* v. *Ringer* [1987] Crim.L.R. 422, D.C.

s. 74, see *R.* v. *Robertson; R.* v. *Golder* [1987] 3 W.L.R. 327, C.A.

1984—cont.

60. Police and Criminal Evidence Act 1984— cont.

ss. 74, 75, see *R.* v. *O'Connor* [1987] Crim.L.R. 260, C.A.

s. 76, see *R.* v. *Oxford City JJ., ex p. Berry* [1987] 1 All E.R. 244, Q.B.D.; *R.* v. *Fulling* [1987] 2 W.L.R. 923, C.A.; *R.* v. *Millard* [1987] Crim.L.R. 196, Central Criminal Ct.; *R.* v. *McIvor* [1987] Crim.L.R. 409, Sheffield Crown Ct.; *R.* v. *Liverpool Juvenile Court, ex p. R.* [1987] 2 All E.R. 668, D.C.; *R.* v. *Mason (Carl)* [1987] 3 All E.R. 481, C.A.

s. 78, see *R.* v. *H.* [1987] Crim.L.R. 47, Winchester Crown Court, Gatehouse J.; *R.* v. *O'Connor* [1987] Crim.L.R. 260, C.A.; *R.* v. *Deacon* [1987] Crim.L.R. 404, Guildford Crown Ct.; *R.* v. *Beveridge* [1987] Crim.L.R. 401, C.A.; *Vel* v. *Owen, sub nom. Vel (Kevin)* v. *Chief Constable of North Wales* [1987] Crim.L.R. 496, D.C.; *R.* v. *Robertson; R.* v. *Golder* [1987] 3 W.L.R. 327, C.A.; *R.* v. *Smith (Eric)* [1987] Crim.L.R. 579, Stafford Crown Ct.; *R.* v. *Mason (Carl)* [1987] 3 All E.R. 481, C.A.; *R.* v. *O'Laughlin and McLaughlin* [1987] Crim.L.R. 632, Central Criminal Ct.; *Matto (Jit Singh)* v. *D.P.P.* [1987] Crim.L.R. 641, D.C.

s. 81, rules 87/716.

s. 84, see *Vel (Kevin)* v. *Chief Constable of North Wales, The Times*, February 14, 1987, D.C.

s. 114, order 87/439.

s. 116, see *R.* v. *McIvor* [1987] Crim.L.R. 409, Sheffield Crown Ct.; *R.* v. *Smith (Eric)* [1987] Crim.L.R. 579, Stafford Crown Ct.

sch. 1, see *R.* v. *Central Criminal Court, ex p. Carr, The Independent*, May 19, 1987, C.A.; *R.* v. *Bristol Crown Court, ex p. Bristol Press and Picture Agency* [1987] Crim.L.R. 329, D.C.; *R.* v. *Crown Court, ex p. Baines and White* (1987) 137 New L.J. 945, D.C.; *Carr* v. *Atkins* [1987] 3 W.L.R. 529, C.A.; *R.* v. *Leicester Crown Court, ex p. D.P.P.* [1987] 1 W.L.R. 1371, D.C.

sch. 5, see *R.* v. *Smith (Eric)* [1987] Crim.L.R. 579, Stafford Crown Ct.

62. Friendly Societies Act 1984.

s. 4, order 87/1276.

1985

1. Consolidated Fund Act 1985.

repealed: 1987, c.17, sch. (C).

4. Milk (Cessation of Production) Act 1985.

s. 1, schemes 87/882(S.), 908.

s. 5, scheme 87/882(S.).

5. New Towns and Urban Development Corporations Act 1985.

s. 12, repealed: 1987, c.57, s.1.

1985—cont.

6. Companies Act 1985.

ss. 2, 18, 45, see *Scandinavian Bank Group, Re* [1987] 2 W.L.R. 752, Harman J.

s. 6, regs. 87/752.

s. 36, see *Rover International* v. *Cannon Film Sales* (1987) 3 BCC 369, Harman J.

ss. 54, 88, regs. 87/752.

s. 121, see *Scandinavian Bank Group, Re* [1987] 2 W.L.R. 752, Harman J.

ss. 122, 123, 128, 129, regs. 87/752.

s. 135, see *Willaire Systems, Re* [1987] BCLC 67, C.A.

s. 136, see *House of Fraser* v. *A.C.G.E. Investments*, [1987] 2 W.L.R. 1083, H.L.(Sc.)

s. 137, see *Willaire Systems, Re* [1987] BCLC 67, C.A.

ss. 151, 153, see *Brady* v. *Brady* (1987) 3 BCC 535, C.A.

ss. 157, 169, 176, 190, regs. 87/752.

s. 209, amended: 1987, c.22, sch. 6.

ss. 212, 216, see *Geers Gross, Re* (1987) 3 BCC 528, C.A.

ss. 224, 225, regs. 87/752.

s. 232, amended: 1987, c.22, sch. 6.

s. 233, amended: *ibid.*, s.90.

ss. 234, 247, 257, amended: *ibid.*, sch. 6.

s. 300, see *Eurostem Maritime, Re*, 1987 PCC 190, Mervyn Davies J.; *Dawson Print Group, Re* (1987) 3 BCC 322, Hoffmann J.; *Stanford Services, Re* (1987) 3 BCC 326, Vinelott J.

s. 317, see *Guinness* v. *Saunders, The Independent*, April 16, 1987, Browne-Wilkinson V.-C.; *Guinness* v. *Saunders (No. 2)* (1987) 3 BCC 520, Browne-Wilkinson V.-C.

ss. 318, 325, regs. 87/752.

s. 331, repealed in pt.: 1987, c.22, sch. 7.

ss. 338, 339, 343, 344, amended: *ibid.*, sch. 6.

s. 353, regs. 87/752.

s. 359, see *Willaire Systems, Re* [1987] BCLC 67, C.A.

ss. 362, 386, regs. 87/752.

ss. 395, 396, see *Specialist Plant Services* v. *Braithwaite* [1987] BCLC 1, C.A.

ss. 400, 403, 416, 419, regs. 87/752.

s. 427A, added: regs. 87/1991.

ss. 428, 429, regs. 87/752.

s. 440, amended: 1987, c.41, s.55.

s. 449, orders 87/859, 1141.

s. 449, amended: 1987, c.22, sch. 6.

ss. 454, 456, see *Geers Gross, Re* (1987) 3 BCC 528, C.A.

s. 459, see *Company, A, (No. 00477 of 1986), Re*, 1986 PCC 372, Hoffmann J.; *Company, A, (No. 004377 of 1986), Re* [1987] 1 W.L.R. 102, Hoffmann J.; *Company, A, (No. 005136 of 1986), Re* [1987] BCLC 82, Hoffmann J.; *Postgate & Denby (Agencies), Re* [1987] BCLC 8, Hoffmann J.; *Kenyon Swansea, Re*,

1985—cont.

6. Companies Act 1985—*cont.*

The Times, April 29, 1987, Vinelott J.; *Company, A, (No. 007281 of 1981), Re*, *The Times*, April 13, 1987, Vinelott J.; *Company, A (No. 001761 of 1986), Re* [1987] BCLC 141, Harman J.; *XYZ, Re*, 1987 PCC 92, Hoffmann J.; *Mossmain, Re*, 1987 PCC 104, Hoffmann J.; *Company, A (No. 00596 of 1986), Re* [1987] BCLC 133, Harman J.; *Company, A (No. 004175 of 1986), Re* [1987] 1 W.L.R. 585, Scott J.; *Malaga Investments, Petrs.* (V.C.), April 16, 1987; *Company No. 007281 of 1986, Re* (1987) 3 BCC 375, Vinelott J.

s. 461, see *Company, A (No. 004175 of 1986), Re* [1987] 1 W.L.R. 585, Scott J.

ss. 469, 471, 473, see *Callaghan (Myles J.) (In Receivership)* v. *City of Glasgow District Council* (1987) 3 BCC 337, Ct. of Session.

s. 522, see *Company, A (No. 007523 of 1986), Re* [1987] BCLC 200, Mervyn Davies J.; *French's (Wine Bar), Re* [1987] B.C.L.C. 499, Vinelott J.

s. 561, see *Company, A (No. 003318 of 1987), Re* [1987] 3 BCC 564, Harman J.

ss. 618, 619, see *A.E. Realisations (1985), Re* [1987] BCLC 486, Vinelott J.

s. 665, see *International Tin Council, Re* [1987] 1 All E.R. 890, Millet J.

s. 711, amended: regs. 87/1991.

s. 726, see *Stewart* v. *Steen*, 1987 S.L.T. (Sh.Ct.) 60; *Aquila Design (GRB) Products* v. *Cornhill Insurance* (1987) 3 BCC 364.

s. 735, see *Rover International* v. *Cannon Film Sales* (1987) 3 BCC 369, Harman J.

s. 738, see *Scandinavian Bank Group, Re* [1987] 2 W.L.R. 752, Harman J.

s. 741, see *Eurostem Maritime, Re*, 1987 PCC 190, Mervyn Davies J.

s. 744, amended: 1987, c.22, sch. 6; repealed in pt.: *ibid.*, sch. 7.

sch. 6, amended: *ibid.*, sch. 6; repealed in pt.: *ibid.*, sch. 7.

schs. 13, 14, regs. 87/752.

sch. 15A, added: regs. 87/1991.

9. Companies Consolidation (Consequential Provisions) Act 1985.

s. 4, regs. 87/752.

s. 20, sch. 2 (in pt.), repealed: 1987, c.22, sch. 7.

11. Consolidated Fund (No. 2) Act 1985.

repealed: 1987, c.17, sch. (C).

23. Prosecution of Offences Act 1985.

s. 1, see *R.* v. *Liverpool Crown Court, ex p. Bray* [1987] Crim.L.R. 51, D.C.

s. 3, amended: 1987, c.38, sch. 2.

s. 14, regs. 87/902, 1636, 1851.

s. 16, see *R.* v. *Jain, The Times*, December 10, 1987, C.A.

ss. 16, 18, amended: 1987, c.38, sch. 2.

ss. 22, 29, regs. 87/299.

1985—cont.

27. Coal Industry Act 1985.
s. 2, repealed: 1987, c.3, sch. 3.
29. Enduring Powers of Attorney Act 1985.
ss. 1, 4, 6, see *K., Re; F., Re, The Independent*, November 3, 1987, Hoffmann J.
s. 2, regs. 87/1612.
s. 7, amended: order 87/1628.
33. Rating (Revaluation Rebates) (Scotland) Act 1985.
s. 1, order 87/345.
37. Family Law (Scotland) Act 1985.
s. 1, see *Nixon* v. *Nixon* (O.H.), 1987 S.L.T. 602; *Inglis* v. *Inglis* (Sh.Ct.), 1987 S.C.L.R. 608.
s. 4, see *Inglis* v. *Inglis* (Sh.Ct.), 1987 S.C.L.R. 608.
s. 5, see *Nixon* v. *Nixon* (O.H.), 1987 S.L.T. 602.
s. 6, see *Neill* v. *Neill*, 1987 S.L.T.(Sh.Ct.) 143.
ss. 8, 9, see *Thirde* v. *Thirde* (Sh.Ct.), 1987 S.C.L.R. 335; *Wilson* v. *Wilson*, 1987 S.L.T. 721.
ss. 11, 13, see *Thirde* v. *Thirde* (Sh.Ct.), 1987 S.C.L.R. 335.
s. 28, see *Smith* v. *Smith* (O.H.), 1987 S.L.T. 199; *Grindlay* v. *Grindlay* (O.H.), 1987 S.L.T. 264; *Collins* v. *Collins* (O.H.), 1987 S.L.T. 224; *Wilson* v. *Wilson*, 1987 S.L.T. 721; *Caven* v. *Caven* (O.H.), 1987 S.L.T. 761; *Gow* v. *Gow* (O.H.), 1987 S.L.T. 798.
47. Further Education Act 1985.
Commencement order: 87/1335 (S.).
s. 7, order 87/1335 (S.).
48. Food and Environment Protection Act 1985.
s. 1, orders, 87/153, 182, 249, 263, 885, 906, 1165 (S.), 1181, 1436, 1450, 1515, 1555, 1567, 1568, 1638, 1682, 1687, 1696, 1697, 1802, 1837, 1888(S.), 1893, 1894; S.Rs. 1987 Nos. 367, 395.
s. 16, S.Rs. 1987 Nos. 341, 342, 414.
s. 24, orders 87/153, 182, 249, 263, 270, 885, 906, 1165 (S.), 1181, 1436, 1450, 1515, 1555, 1567, 1568, 1638, 1682, 1687, 1696, 1697, 1802, 1837, 1888(S.), 1893; S.Rs. 1987 No. 367, 395, 414.
s. 26, orders 87/665–667.
sch. 5, S.R. 1987 No. 342.
50. Representation of the People Act 1985.
Commencement order: 87/207.
s. 29, order 87/207.
51. Local Government Act 1985.
s. 49, order 87/118.
s. 56, see *R.* v. *Secretary of State for the Environment, ex p. Camden London Borough Council, The Times*, July 14, 1987, D.C.
s. 67, orders 87/15, 117, 651, 1077, 1288, 1446, 1451, 1463, 1579.
s. 69, repealed in pt.: 1987, c.6, sch. 5.
s. 77, order 87/118.
s. 100, order 87/117.

1985—cont.

51. Local Government Act 1985—*cont.*
s. 101, orders 87/118, 1463.
sch. 13, see *R.* v. *Secretary of State for the Environment, ex p. Camden London Borough Council, The Times*, July 14, 1987, D.C.
sch. 13, amended: 1987, c.31, sch. 4; repealed in pt.: *ibid.*, schs. 4, 5; c.39, sch. 2.
sch. 15, amended: 1987, c.6, sch. 4.
54. Finance Act 1985.
s. 15, see *Neal* v. *Customs and Excise Commissioners, The Times*, November 11, 1987, Simon Brown J.; *Customs and Excise Commissioners* v. *Shingleton, The Times*, December 8, 1987, Brown J.
s. 41, amended: 1987, c.16, s.30.
s. 72, amended: 1987, c.51, s.81; repealed in pt.: *ibid.*, sch. 9.
s. 87, regs. 87/516.
schs. 5, 11, repealed in pt.: 1987, c.16, sch. 16.
sch. 20, amended: *ibid.*, s.47.
sch. 23, repealed in pt.: *ibid.*, sch. 16.
55. Appropriation Act 1985.
repealed: 1987, c.17, sch. (C).
57. Sporting Events (Control of Alcohol etc.) Act 1985.
s. 9, order 87/1520.
58. Trustee Savings Banks Act 1985.
s. 6, repealed: 1987, c.22, sch. 7.
sch. 1, amended: *ibid.*, sch. 6; repealed in pt.: *ibid.*, schs. 6, 7.
sch. 3, repealed: *ibid.*, sch. 7.
60. Child Abduction and Custody Act 1985.
s. 1, see *Viola* v. *Viola* (O.H.), 1987 S.C.L.R. 529.
s. 2, see *Kilgour* v. *Kilgour* (O.H.), 1987 S.L.T. 568.
s. 2, orders 87/163, 1825.
sch. 1, see *Kilgour* v. *Kilgour* (O.H.), 1987 S.L.T. 568; *A.* v. *A.; A (A Minor), Re, The Times*, June 13, 1987, C.A.; *Viola* v. *Viola* (O.H.), 1987 S.C.L.R. 529; *B. (Minors), Re, The Times*, October 29, 1987, Waterhouse J.
sch. 3, amended: 1987, c.42, sch. 2.
61. Administration of Justice Act 1985.
Commencement order: 87/787.
s. 48, see *Practice Direction (Ch.D.) (No. 1 of 1987)*, January 28, 1987.
s. 69, order 87/787.
sch. 4, rules 87/788, 789.
65. Insolvency Act 1985.
sch. 8, repealed in pt.: 1987, c.16, sch. 16.
66. Bankruptcy (Scotland) Act 1985.
ss. 5, 7, amended: 1987, c.41, s.45.
s. 37, amended: 1987, c.18, sch. 6.
s. 73, amended: 1987, c.22, sch. 6.
sch. 7, amended: 1987, c.18, sch, 6; repealed in pt.: 1987, c.16, sch. 16.
67. Transport Act 1985.
Commencement order: 87/1228.
s. 10, orders 87/784, 839, 1535.

1985—cont.

67. Transport Act 1985—*cont.*

s. 16, see *Tudor* v. *Ellesmere Port and Neston B.C.*, *The Times*, May 8, 1987, D.C.; *R.* v. *Reading Borough Council, ex p. Egan; Same* v. *Same, ex p. Sullman, The Times*, June 12, 1987, Nolan J.; *R.* v. *Great Yarmouth Borough Council, ex p. Sawyer, The Times*, June 18, 1987, C.A.

s. 47, order 87/1613.

s. 129, order 87/337.

s. 140, order 87/1228.

68. Housing Act 1985.

see *R.* v. *Tower Hamlets London Borough Council, ex p. Monaf, Ali and Miah, The Times*, August 6, 1987, D.C.

Pt. II (ss. 8–57), see *R.* v. *Hammersmith and Fulham London Borough, ex p. Beddowes* (1986) 18 H.L.R. 458, C.A.; *R.* v. *Plymouth City Council and Cornwall County Council, ex p. Freeman* (1987) 19 H.L.R. 328, C.A.

s. 17, see *R.* v. *Secretary of State for the Environment, ex p. Kensington and Chelsea Royal Borough Council, The Times*, January 30, 1987, Taylor J.

ss. 21, 24, see *Wandsworth London Borough Council* v. *Winder (No. 2)* (1987) 19 H.L.R. 204, Mervyn Davies J.

s. 22, see *R.* v. *Canterbury City Council, ex p. Gillespie* (1987) 19 H.L.R. 7, Simon Brown J.

s. 32, see *R.* v. *Hammersmith and Fulham London Borough, ex p. Beddowes* (1986) 18 H.L.R. 458, C.A.

s. 45, amended: 1987, c.31, sch. 4; repealed in pt.: *ibid.*, schs. 4, 5.

ss. 49, 50 (in pt.), repealed: *ibid.*

Pt. III (ss. 58–78), see *R.* v. *Lambeth London Borough, ex p. Ly* (1987) 19 H.L.R. 51, Simon Brown J.; *R.* v. *Wandsworth Borough Council, ex p., Banbury* (1987) 19 H.L.R. 76, Russell J.; *South Holland District Council* v. *Keyte* (1987) 19 H.L.R. 97, C.A.; *R.* v. *Hillingdon London Borough, ex p. Thomas* (1987) 19 H.L.R. 197, Taylor J.; *R.* v. *Christchurch Borough Council, ex p. Conway* (1987) 19 H.L.R. 238, Taylor J.

s. 59, see *R.* v. *Reigate and Banstead Borough Council, ex p. Di Domenico, The Independent*, October 21, 1987, Mann J.; *R.* v. *Lambeth London Borough Council, ex p. Carroll, The Guardian*, October 8, 1987, Webster J.

s. 60, see *R.* v. *East Hertfordshire District Council, ex p. Bannon* (1986) 18 H.L.R. 515, Webster J.; *R.* v. *London Borough of Wandsworth, ex p. Henderson and Hayes* (1986) 18 H.L.R. 525, McNeill J.; *R.* v. *London Borough of Croydon, ex p. Toth* (1986) 18 H.L.R. 493, Simon Brown J.; *R.* v. *Christchurch Borough*

1985—cont.

67. Transport Act 1985—*cont.*

Council, ex p. Conway (1987) 19 H.L.R. 238, Taylor J.

s. 65, see *R.* v. *Croydon London Borough, ex p. Wait* (1986) 18 H.L.R. 434, McCowan J.; *R.* v. *London Borough of Wandsworth, ex p. Lindsay* (1986) 18 H.L.R. 502, Simon Brown J.

s. 69, see *R.* v. *Camden London Borough, ex p. Wait* (1986) 18 H.L.R. 434, McCowan J.

s. 76, amended (S.): 1987, c.26, sch. 23.

ss. 79, 81–84, see *R.* v. *London Borough of Croydon, ex p. Toth* (1986) 18 H.L.R. 493, Simon Brown J.

s. 82, see *Thompson* v. *Elmbridge Borough Council* (1987) 84 L.S.Gaz. 2456, C.A.

s. 83, regs. 87/755.

s. 84, see *Second W.R.V.S. Housing Society* v. *Blair* (1986) 19 H.L.R. 104, C.A.; *Wandsworth London Borough Council* v. *Fadayomi* [1987] 3 All E.R. 474, C.A.; *Wansbeck District Council* v. *Marley, The Times*, November 30, 1987, C.A.

s. 85, see *Governors of the Peabody Donation Fund* v. *Hay* (1986) 19 H.L.R. 145, C.A.

s. 105, see *R.* v. *Hammersmith and Fulham London Borough, ex p. Beddowes* (1986) 18 H.L.R. 458, C.A.

s. 106, see *R.* v. *Canterbury City Council, ex p. Gillespie* (1987) 19 H.L.R. 7, Simon Brown J.

s. 156, orders 87/1203, 1810.

s. 160, see *R.* v. *Rushmoor Borough Council, ex p. Barrett* [1986] 3 W.L.R. 998, Reeve J.

s. 171, order 87/1732.

s. 187, repealed in pt. (S.): 1987, c.26, schs. 23, 24.

Pt. VI (ss. 189–208), see *R.* v. *London Borough of Lambeth, ex p. Clayhope Properties* (1986) 18 H.L.R. 541, Hodgson J.

s. 190, see *R.* v. *London Borough of Lambeth, ex p. Clayhope Properties* (1986) 18 H.L.R. 541, Hodgson J.

ss. 268, 270, 276, 304, see *Beaney* v. *Branchett* (1987) 283 E.G. 1063, C.A.

Pt. XI (ss. 345–400), see *Mayor and Burgesses of Wandsworth London Borough* v. *Orakpo* (1987) 19 H.L.R. 57, C.A.; *R.* v. *Secretary of State for the Environment, ex p. Royal Borough of Kensington and Chelsea* (1987) 19 H.L.R. 161, Taylor J.

s. 369, see *Wandsworth London Borough Council* v. *Sparling, The Times*, November 21, 1987, D.C.

Pt. XIII (ss. 417–434), see *Hemsted* v. *Lees and Norwich City Council* (1986) 18 H.L.R. 424, McCowan J.

1985—cont.

67. Transport Act 1985—*cont.*
s. 444, orders 87/1204, 1811.
s. 445, order 87/268.
s. 447, orders 87/1202, 1809.
s. 458, amended (S.): 1987, c.26, sch. 23.
ss. 503, 504, see *R.* v. *Camden London Borough Council, ex p. Christey* (1987) 19 H.L.R. 420, Macpherson J.
ss. 509, 517, order 87/1379.
s. 573, amended: 1987, c.3, sch. 1.
s. 622, amended: 1987, c.22, sch. 6.
sch. 2, see *R.* v. *London Borough of Croydon, ex p. Toth* (1986) 18 H.L.R. 493, Simon Brown J.; *Second W.R.V.S. Housing Society* v. *Blair* (1986) 19 H.L.R. 104, C.A.; *Wandsworth London Borough Council* v. *Fadayomi* [1987] 3 All E.R. 474, C.A.; *Wansbeck District Council* v. *Marley, The Times*, November 30, 1987, C.A.
sch. 4, amended (S.): 1987, c.26, sch. 23.
sch. 14, see *Hemsted* v. *Lees and Norwich City Council* (1986) 18 H.L.R. 424, McCowan J.

69. Housing Associations Act 1985.
ss. 8, 10, 39, 44, 45, 52, 59, 69A, 88, amended (S.): 1987, c.26, sch. 23.
s. 86, order 87/1389 (S.).
s. 106, amended: 1987, c.22, sch. 6.
s. 107, amended: 1987, c.31, sch. 4.

70. Landlord and Tenant Act 1985.
see *Boldmark* v. *Cohen and Cohen* (1985) 19 H.L.R. 135, C.A.
s. 3, amended: 1987, c.31, s.50.
s. 4, amended: *ibid.*, s.45.
s. 11, see *McClean* v. *Liverpool City Council* (1987) 283 E.G. 1395, C.A.; *Dinefwr Borough Council* v. *Jones* (1987) 19 H.L.R. 445, C.A.
ss. 18, 19, amended: 1987, c.31, sch. 2.
s. 19, see *Delahay* v. *Maltlodge*, March 9, 1987; P. St. J. Langan Q.C., West London County Court.
s. 20, substituted: 1987, c.31, sch. 2
ss. 20B, 20C, added: *ibid.*
ss. 21, 22, 24, 27, 28, amended: *ibid.*
s. 29, see *R.* v. *London Rent Assessment Panel, ex p. Trustees of Henry Smith's Charity Kensington Estate, The Independent*, October 30, 1987, Schiemann J.
s. 29, amended: 1987, c.31, sch. 2.
s. 30, amended: *ibid.*; repealed in pt.: *ibid.*, schs. 2, 5.
s. 30A, added: *ibid.*, s.43, sch.3.
s. 30B, added: *ibid.*, s.44.

71. Housing (Consequential Provisions) Act 1985.
sch. 2, repealed in pt. (S.): 1987, c.26. sch. 24.

72. Weights and Measures Act 1985.
ss. 4, 5, regs. 87/51.
s. 15, regs. 87/1538.
s. 22, order 87/216.
s. 23, regs. 87/1538.

1985—cont.

72. Weights and Measures Act 1985—*cont.*
s. 24, order 87/216.
ss. 48, 66, 86, regs. 87/1538.
s. 86, regs. 87/51, 1538; order 87/216.
s. 94, regs. 87/51, 1538.
sch. 5, amended: 1987, c.3, sch. 1.

73. Law Reform (Miscellaneous Provisions) (Scotland) Act 1985.
s. 39, repealed: 1987, c.41, sch. 2.

74. Consolidated Fund (No. 3) Act 1985.
repealed: 1987, c.17, sch. (C).

1986

1. Education (Amendment) Act 1986.
s. 2, repealed: 1987, c.1, sch. 2.

5. Agricultural Holdings Act 1986.
sch. 3, regs. 87/711.
sch. 3, amended: 1987, c.3, sch. 1.
sch. 4, order 87/710.
sch. 6, order 87/1465.

9. Law Reform (Parent and Child) (Scotland) Act 1986.
ss. 2–4, see *Montgomery* v. *Lockwood* (Sh.Ct.) 1987 S.C.L.R. 525.
ss. 3, 8, see *A.B.* v. *M. (O.M.)*, 1987 S.C.L.R. 389.

10. Local Government Act 1986.
Commencement order: 87/2003.
s. 5, order 87/2004.
s. 12, order 87/2003.

14. Animals (Scientific Procedures) Act 1986.
ss. 12, 29, S.R. 1987 No. 2.

19. British Shipbuilders (Borrowing Powers) Act 1986.
repealed: 1987, c.52, s.1.

21. Armed Forces Act 1986.
Commencement order: 87/1998.
s. 1, order 87/1262.
s. 17, order 87/1998.

29. Consumer Safety (Amendment) Act 1986.
repealed: 1987, c.43, sch. 5.

31. Airports Act 1986.
s. 32, order 87/874.
s. 63, orders 87/380, 1132, 2246.
s. 74, amended: 1987, c.43, sch. 4; repealed in pt.: *ibid.*, sch. 5.
s. 79, order 87/874.
sch. 2, amended (S.): 1987, c.26, sch. 23.

32. Drug Trafficking Offences Act 1986.
ss. 2, 8, amended (S.): 1987, c.41, s.45.
ss. 8, 9, see *Defendant, A, Re, The Independent*, April 2, 1987, Webster J.
ss. 13, 15, repealed in pt.(S.): 1987, c.41, sch. 2.
s. 16, amended (S.): *ibid.*, s.45; repealed in pt.(S.): *ibid.*, sch. 2.
s. 17, repealed in pt.(S.): *ibid.*
s. 19, amended (S.): *ibid.*, s.45.
ss. 20–23, repealed (S.): *ibid.*, sch. 2.
s. 24A, amended (S.): *ibid.*, s.31.
ss. 27–29, repealed in pt.(S.): *ibid.*, sch. 2.
ss. 33, 40, amended (S.): *ibid.*, s.45; repealed in pt.(S.): *ibid.*, sch. 2.

CAP.

1986—cont.

33. Disabled Persons (Services, Consultation and Representation) Act 1986.
Commencement orders: 87/564, 729, 911 (S.).
s. 18, orders 87/564, 729, 911 (S.).

35. Protection of Military Remains Act 1986.
s. 10, order 87/1281.

41. Finance Act 1986.
s. 27, amended: 1987, c.16, s.32.
s. 66, order 87/512.
s. 70, amended: 1987, c.16, s.52.
s. 82, amended: *ibid.*, s.53.
ss. 87–89, amended: *ibid.*, sch. 7.
s. 89A, added: 1987, c.51, s.100.
s. 90, amended: 1987, c.16, sch. 7.
s. 91, repealed in pt.: 1987, c.51, s.100, sch. 9.
s. 92, orders 87/514, 883, 888, 1494, 1990.
s. 92, amended: 1987, c.16, sch. 7.
s. 104, regs. 87/1130.
sch. 7, amended: 1987, c.22, sch. 6.
sch. 9, amended: 1987, c.16, sch. 15.
sch. 11, regs. 87/530.
sch. 12, regs. 87/352, 412.
sch. 19, repealed in pt.: 1987, c.51, sch. 9.
sch. 20, amended: 1987, c.16, s.58, sch. 8; repealed in pt.: *ibid.*, sch. 16.

44. Gas Act 1986.
s. 42, amended: 1987, c.43, sch. 4; repealed in pt.: *ibid.*, sch. 5.
s. 54, order 87/866.
sch. 1, repealed in pt.: 1987, c.39, sch. 2.

45. Insolvency Act 1986.
s. 8, see *Charnley Davies Business Services, Re* (1987) 3 BCC 408, Harman J.
s. 8, amended: 1987, c.22, sch. 6.
Pt. II (ss. 8–27), see *Company A, (No. 00175 of 1987), Re* [1987] BCLC 467, Vinelott J.
s. 11, see *Air Ecosse* v. *Civil Aviation Authority* (1987) 3 BCC 492, Ct. of Session.
ss. 23, 27, see *Charnley Davies Business Services, Re* (1987) 3 BCC 408, Harman J.
s. 108, see *Keypack Homecare, Re* [1987] B.C.L.C. 409, Millett J.
s. 109, regs. 87/752.
s. 127, see *Company, A (No. 007523 of 1986), Re* [1987] BCLC 200, Mervyn Davies J.; *French's (Wine Bar), Re* [1987] B.C.L.C. 499, Vinelott J.
s. 140, see *Charnley Davies Business Services, Re* (1987) 3 BCC 408, Harman J.
ss. 178, 179, see *A. E. Realisations (1985), Re* [1987] BCLC 486, Vinelott J.
s. 221, see *Company, A (No. 00359 of 1987), Re* [1987] 3 W.L.R. 339, Gibson J.
s. 236, see *Company, A (No. 003318 of 1987), Re* [1987] 3 BCC 564, Harman J.
s. 253, see *Peake, Re,* July 16, 1987, Mr. Registrar Ashworth, Blackburn County Ct.
s. 281, amended: 1987, c.43, sch. 4.

CAP.

1986—cont.

45. Insolvency Act 1986—cont.
s. 411, rules 87/1919, 1921(S.).
s. 412, rules 87/1919.
s. 422, amended: 1987, c.22, sch. 6.
ss. 439, 441, order 87/1398.
sch. 1, see *Charnley Davies Business Services, Re* (1987) 3 BCC 408, Harman J.
sch. 14, repealed in pt.: 1987, c.16, sch. 16.

46. Company Directors Disqualification Act 1986.
s. 8, amended: 1987, c.41, s.55.

47. Legal Aid (Scotland) Act 1986.
Commencement order: 87/289.
s. 9, regs. 87/642.
s. 11, regs. 87/704.
s. 12, regs. 87/382, 883.
ss. 14A, 15, regs. 87/825, 826.
ss. 17, 19, 20, regs. 87/381.
s. 31, regs. 87/307.
s. 33, regs. 87/365, 366, 382, 823, 824, 883, 895, 1356, 1358.
s. 36, regs. 87/307, 381, 382, 384, 431, 704, 705.
s. 37, regs. 87/883.
s. 38, Acts of Sederunt 87/427, 492; Act of Adjournal 87/430.
s. 42, regs. 87/381, 382.
s. 45, regs. 87/894.
s. 46, order 87/289.
sch. 2, amended: 1987, c.18, s.98.
sch. 4, regs. 87/894.

48. Wages Act 1986.
see *Staffordshire County Council* v. *Secretary of State for Employment, The Times,* August 19, 1987, E.A.T.
s. 13, order 87/801.
s. 19, regs. 87/863, 1852.
s. 25, regs. 87/862, 863, 1852.
s. 27, sch. 6, see *Secretary of State for Employment* v. *Milk & General Haulage (Nottingham)* (1987) 84 L.S.Gaz. 2118, E.A.T.
sch. 2, regs. 87/862.
sch. 3, regs. 87/863, 1852.

49. Agriculture Act 1986.
s. 18, orders 87/653(S.), 654(S.).
sch. 1, order 87/626.
sch. 2, order 87/870 (S.).

50. Social Security Act 1986.
Commencement orders: 87/354, 543, 1096, 1853.
s. 1, regs. 87/1109, 1933.
s. 2, regs. 87/1101, 1109, 1118, 1933.
s. 3, regs. 87/1109, 1115, 1933.
s. 4, regs. 87/1113.
s. 5, regs. 87/657, 658, 1111.
s. 7, regs. 87/1115.
s. 9, regs. 87/1100.
s. 12, regs. 87/1108, 1933.
s. 14, regs. 87/1115, 1117.
s. 15, regs. 87/1108.
s. 16, regs. 87/657, 658.
s. 17, regs. 87/1116.
s. 17, repealed in pt.: 1987, c.45, sch. 4.
s. 20, regs. 87/1967, 1971, 1973.

CAP.
1986—cont.

50. Social Security Act 1986—*cont.*
s. 21, regs. 87/1968, 1971, 1973.
s. 22, regs. 87/1967, 1971, 1973.
s. 23, regs. 87/1967.
s. 24, amended: 1987, c.42, sch. 2; repealed in pt.: *ibid.*, sch. 4.
s. 25, repealed: *ibid.*, schs. 2, 4.
s. 25A, added (S.): 1987, c.18, s.68.
s. 26, amended: 1987, c.42, sch. 2.
s. 27, regs. 87/491.
ss. 28, 29, regs. 87/1971.
s. 30, order 87/1910.
s. 30, amended: 1987, c.6, sch. 4.
s. 32, regs. 87/481.
s. 32, amended: 1987, c.7, s.1.
s. 49, regs. 87/235.
s. 51, regs. 87/372, 491, 1967, 1968, 1971, 1973.
s. 52, regs. 87/1970.
s. 53, regs. 87/491.
s. 54, regs. 87/1102.
s. 60, regs. 87/250.
s. 63, orders 87/45, 1978.
s. 64, regs. 87/327.
s. 67, regs. 87/33.
s. 74. regs. 87/413.
s. 80, regs. 87/418.
s. 83, regs. 87/250, 491; order 87/45.
s. 84, regs. 87/235, 250, 372, 406, 411, 413, 415, 416, 418, 481, 491, 914, 1100–1102, 1108, 1109, 1111, 1113, 1115–1118, 1692, 1933, 1967–1970, 1972, 1974.
s. 88, orders 87/354, 543, 1096, 1853.
s. 89, regs. 87/33, 372, 406, 411, 415, 416, 481, 491, 914, 1109, 1692, 1854, 1969, 1970, 1972, 1974.
sch. 1, regs. 87/1117.
sch. 4, regs. 87/235, 413.
sch. 10, repealed in pt.: 1987, c.6, sch. 5; c.16, sch. 16.

51. British Council and Commonwealth Institute Superannuation Act 1986.
Commencement order: 87/588.
s. 3, order 87/588.

52. Dockyard Services Act 1986.
ss. 1, 2, see *Institution of Professional Civil Servants* v. *Secretary of State for Defence, The Times*, April 30, 1987, Millett J.
s. 3, repealed in pt.: 1987, c.4, s.7.

53. Building Societies Act 1986.
order 87/1872.
s. 2, regs. 87/391.
s. 7, orders 87/378, 1670, 2131.
s. 7, amended: order 87/378, 1670; repealed in pt.: order 87/378.
s. 12, order 87/1671.
s. 14, order 87/1498.
ss. 15, 16, amended: order 87/1975.
s. 17, order 87/1942.
s. 18, order 87/1871.
s. 18, amended: 1987, c.22, sch. 6.
s. 19, order 87/1975.
s. 21, regs. 87/1499
s. 25, amended: 1987, c.22, sch. 6; repealed in pt.: *ibid.*, schs. 6, 7.

CAP.
1986—cont.

53. Building Societies Act 1986—*cont.*
s. 27, order 87/1349.
s. 27, amended: 1987, c.22, sch. 6; order 87/1349.
s. 34, orders 87/172, 1670, 1848, 1976, 2019.
s. 48, regs. 87/891.
s. 53, order 87/1500.
s. 53, amended: 1987, c.22, sch. 6.
s. 54, repealed in pt.: *ibid.*, sch. 7.
s. 96, order 87/2005.
ss. 98, 102, 107, amended: 1987, c.22, sch. 6.
s. 116, regs. 87/391.
s. 121, orders 87/395, 426.
sch. 1, repealed in pt.: 1987, c.39, sch. 2.
sch. 8, order 87/1848.
sch. 8, amended: orders 87/172, 1670, 1976, 2019; 1987, c.22, sch. 6; repealed in pt.: *ibid.*, schs. 6, 7.
sch. 10, order 87/723.
sch. 18, repealed in pt.: 1987, c.22, sch. 24(S.).

54. Rate Support Grants Act 1986.
ss. 1–3, sch. 1, see *R.* v. *Secretary of State for the Environment, ex p. Greenwich London Borough Council* (1987) 27 R.V.R. 48, Taylor J.
sch. 1, repealed in pt.: 1987, c.5, s.1; c.6, sch. 5.

55. Family Law Act 1986.
ss. 1, 3, amended: 1987, c.42, sch. 2.
s. 56, substituted: *ibid.*, s.22.
s. 60, amended: *ibid.*, sch. 2.

56. Parliamentary Constituencies Act 1986.
s. 4, orders 87/462, 469, 937.

57. Public Trustee and Administration of Funds Act 1986.
sch., repealed in pt.: 1987, c.39, sch. 2.

59. Sex Discrimination Act 1986.
s. 2, see *Duke* v. *Reliance Systems, The Times*, February 23, 1987, C.A.

60. Financial Services Act 1986.
Commencement orders: 87/623, 907, 1997, 2157, 2158.
ss. 75, 105, amended: 1987, c.22, sch. 6.
s. 114, order 87/942.
s. 118, orders 87/942, 2035.
s. 172, regs. 87/752.
s. 178, see *Enquiry under the Company Securities (Insider Dealing) Act 1985, An, Re, The Times*, May 7, 1987, C.A.
s. 178, order 87/942.
s. 180, orders 87/859, 1141.
s. 180, amended: 1987, c.22, sch. 6.
s. 185, amended: *ibid.*; repealed in pt.: *ibid.*, sch. 6.
s. 186, amended: *ibid.*, sch. 6; repealed in pt.: *ibid.*, schs. 6, 7.
s. 190, order 87/1905.
s. 193, repealed: 1987, c.22, sch. 7.
ss. 199, 201, 206, order 87/942.
s. 211, orders 87/623, 907, 1997, 2158.
sch. 5, amended: 1987, c.22, sch. 6.
sch. 11, order 87/925; S.R. 1987 No. 228.

CAP.

1986—cont.

60. Financial Services Act 1986—*cont.*
sch. 13, repealed in pt.: 1987, c.22, sch. 7.
sch. 15, orders 87/925, 2157.
61. Education (No. 2) Act 1986.
Commencement orders: 87/344, 1159.
ss. 8, 16, 36, regs. 87/1359.
s. 47, regs. 87/1183.
s. 50, regs. 87/96.
s. 54, regs. 87/34.
s. 61, regs. 87/1160.
s. 62, regs. 87/1160, 1359.
s. 63, regs. 87/96, 1160, 1359.
s. 66, order 87/344, 1159.
sch. 2, regs. 87/1359.
63. Housing and Planning Act 1986.
Commencement orders: 87/304, 348, 754,
1554, 1607(S.), 1759, 1939.
s. 3, repealed: 1987, c.26, sch. 24.
s. 57, orders, 87/1554, 1607(S.), 1759,
1939.
sch. 5, repealed in pt.: 1987, c.26, sch. 24.
64. Public Order Act 1986.
Commencement orders: 87/198, 852.
ss. 34, 36, order 87/853.
s. 41, orders. 87/198, 852.
65. Housing (Scotland) Act 1986.
ss. 1–12, 18–21, schs. 1, 2 (in pt.),
repealed: 1987, c.26, sch. 24.
**66. National Health Service (Amendment) Act
1986.**
Commencement order: 87/399.
s. 1, regs. 87/2(S.), 18.
s. 8, order 87/399.
2. Ecclesiastical Fees Measure 1986.
s. 4, orders 87/1296, 1297.

1987

1. Teachers' Pay and Conditions Act 1987.
Royal Assent, March 2, 1987.
s. 3, orders 87/650, 1433.
2. Licensing (Restaurant Meals) Act 1987.
Royal Assent, March 2, 1987.
3. Coal Industry Act 1987.
Royal Assent, March 5, 1987.
s. 3, order 87/770.
4. Ministry of Defence Police Act 1987.
Royal Assent, March 5, 1987.
5. Rate Support Grants Act 1987.
Royal Assent, March 12, 1987.
6. Local Government Finance Act 1987.
Royal Assent, March 12, 1987.
ss. 13, 14, repealed (S.): 1987, c.47, sch. 6.
**7. Social Fund (Maternity and Funeral
Expenses) Act 1987.**
Royal Assent, March 17, 1987.
8. Consolidated Fund Act 1987.
Royal Assent, March 25, 1987.
9. Animals (Scotland) Act 1987.
Royal Assent, April 9, 1987.
10. Broadcasting Act 1987.
Royal Assent, April 9, 1987.

CAP.

1987—cont.

11. Gaming (Amendment) Act 1987.
Royal Assent, April 9, 1987.
Commencement order: 87/1200.
s. 2, order 87/1200.
12. Petroleum Act 1987.
Royal Assent, April 9, 1987.
Commencement orders: 87/820, 1330.
s. 23, regs. 87/1331, 1332.
s. 31, orders 87/820, 1330.
13. Minors' Contracts Act 1987.
Royal Assent, April 9, 1987.
14. Recognition of Trusts Act 1987.
Royal Assent, April 9, 1987.
Commencement order: 87/1177.
s. 3, order 87/1177.
15. Reverter of Sites Act 1987.
Royal Assent, April 9, 1987.
Commencement order: 87/1260.
s. 9, order 87/1260.
16. Finance Act 1987.
Royal Assent, May 15, 1987.
s. 16, regs. 87/1338.
ss. 44, 45, amended: 1987, c.51, s.76.
s. 50, amended: *ibid.*, s.99.
s. 62, amended: *ibid.*, s.101.
s. 63, amended: *ibid.*; repealed in pt.:
ibid., s.101, sch. 9.
sch. 4, repealed in pt.: *ibid.*, sch. 9.
sch. 10, regs. 87/1338.
sch. 10, amendment: 1987, c.51, sch. 8.
17. Appropriation Act 1987.
Royal Assent, May 15, 1987.
18. Debtors (Scotland) Act 1987.
Royal Assent, May 15, 1987.
Commencement order: 87/1838.
ss. 1, 5, 106, amended: 1987, c.47, s.33.
s. 109, order 87/1838.
sch. 5, amended: 1987, c.47, s.33.
**19. Billiards (Abolition of Restrictions) Act
1987.**
Royal Assent, May 15, 1987.
20. Chevening Estate Act 1987.
Royal Assent, May 15, 1987.
Commencement order: 87/1254.
s. 5, order 87/1254.
21. Pilotage Act 1987.
Royal Assent, May 15, 1987.
Commencement orders: 87/1306, 2138.
s. 9, order 87/1143.
s. 33, orders 87/1306, 2138.
22. Banking Act 1987.
Royal Assent, May 15, 1987.
Commencement orders: 87/1189, 1664.
s. 30, regs. 87/1336(S.)
s. 84, order 87/1292.
s. 110, orders 87/1189, 1664.
23. Register of Sasines (Scotland) Act 1987.
Royal Assent, May 15, 1987.
24. Immigration (Carriers' Liability) Act 1987.
Royal Assent, May 15, 1987.
**25. Crown Proceedings (Armed Forces) Act
1987.**
Royal Assent, May 15, 1987.
26. Housing (Scotland) Act 1987.
Royal Assent, May 15, 1987.

1987—cont.

27. **Fire Safety and Safety of Places of Sport Act 1987.**
Royal Assent, May 15, 1987.
Commencement order: 87/1762.
s. 50, order 87/1762.
28. **Deer Act 1987.**
Royal Assent, May 15, 1987.
29. **Agricultural Training Board Act 1987.**
Royal Assent, May 15, 1987.
30. **Northern Ireland (Emergency Provisions) Act 1987.**
Royal Assent, May 15, 1987.
Commencement order: 87/1241.
repealed in pt. (prosp.): 1987, c.30, s.26.
s. 26, order 87/1241.
31. **Landlord and Tenant Act 1987.**
Royal Assent, May 15, 1987.
32. **Crossbows Act 1987.**
Royal Assent, May 15, 1987.
33. **AIDS (Control) Act 1987.**
Royal Assent, May 15, 1987.
34. **Motor Cycle Noise Act 1987.**
Royal Assent, May 15, 1987.
sch., amended: 1987, c.43, sch. 4.
35. **Protection of Animals (Penalties) Act 1987.**
Royal Assent, May 15, 1987.
36. **Prescription (Scotland) Act 1987.**
Royal Assent, May 15, 1987.
37. **Access to Personal Files Act 1987.**
Royal Assent, May 15, 1987.
38. **Criminal Justice Act 1987.**
Royal Assent, May 15, 1987.
Commencement order: 87/1061.
s. 16, order 87/1061.
39. **Parliamentary and Health Service Commissioners Act 1987.**
Royal Assent, May 15, 1987.
40. **Registered Establishments (Scotland) Act 1987.**
Royal Assent, May 15, 1987.
41. **Criminal Justice (Scotland) Act 1987.**
Royal Assent, May 15, 1987.
Commencement orders: 87/1468, 1594.
s. 72, orders 87/1468, 1594.
42. **Family Law Reform Act 1987.**
Royal Assent, May 15, 1987.
43. **Consumer Protection Act 1987.**
Royal Assent, May 15, 1987.
Commencement orders: 87/1680, 1681.
s. 11, regs. 87/1911, 1920, 1979.
s. 12, order 87/1681.
s. 50, order 87/1680.

1987—cont.

44. **Local Government Act 1987.**
Royal Assent, May 15, 1987.
45. **Parliamentary and other Pensions Act 1987.**
Royal Assent, May 15, 1987.
Commencement order: 87/1311.
s. 7, order 87/1311.
46. **Diplomatic and Consular Premises Act 1987.**
Royal Assent, May 15, 1987.
Commencement orders: 87/1022, 2248.
s. 9, orders 87/1022, 2248.
47. **Abolition of Domestic Rates Etc. (Scotland) Act 1987.**
Royal Assent, May 15, 1987.
Commencement order: 87/1489.
s. 35, order 87/1489.
48. **Irish Sailors and Soldiers Land Trust Act 1987.**
Royal Assent, May 15, 1987.
Commencement order: 87/1909.
s. 3, order 87/1909.
49. **Territorial Sea Act 1987.**
Royal Assent, May 15, 1987.
Commencement order: 87/1270.
s. 1, order 87/1269.
s. 4, order 87/1270.
50. **Appropriation (No. 2) Act 1987.**
Royal Assent, July 23, 1987.
51. **Finance (No. 2) Act 1987.**
Royal Assent, July 23, 1987.
s. 56, regs. 87/1765.
sch. 3, regs. 87/1513.
52. **British Shipbuilders (Borrowing Powers) Act 1987.**
Royal Assent, July 23, 1987.
53. **Channel Tunnel Act 1987.**
Royal Assent, July 23, 1987.
s. 33, order 87/2068.
54. **Consolidated Fund (No. 2) Act 1987.**
Royal Assent, November 17, 1987.
55. **Consolidated Fund (No. 3) Act 1987.**
Royal Assent, December 10, 1987.
56. **Scottish Development Agency Act 1987.**
Royal Assent, December 17, 1987.
57. **Urban Development Corporations (Financial Limits) Act 1987.**
Royal Assent, December 17, 1987.

INDEX

This is the third part of the Current Law Statute Index 1987 and is up to date to December 31, 1987. References, e.g. 31/44 are to the Statutes of 1987, Chapter 31, section 44

Abolition of Domestic Rates Etc. (Scotland) Act 1987 (c.47)
Access to Personal Files Act 1987 (c.37)
ADMINISTRATIVE LAW,
Health Service Commissioner,
complaints: references to, **39**/7, 8
functions, **39**/4–6
Parliamentary Commissioner,
functions, **39**/3
incapacity, removal for, **39**/2
jurisdiction, **39**/1
Agricultural Training Board Act 1987 (c.29)
AGRICULTURE,
Training Board, **29**/1, 2
AIDS (Control) Act 1987 (c.33)
ANIMALS,
deer, **28**/1, 2
protection: penalties, **35**/1, 2
Scotland, **9**/1–9, sch.
Animals (Scotland) Act 1987 (c.9)
Appropriation Act 1987 (c.17)
Appropriation (No. 2) Act 1987 (c.50)
ARMED FORCES,
Crown proceedings, **25**/1–5

BANKING,
Act,
injunctions under, **22**/93
interpretation, **22**/5–7, 74, 105, 106
Northern Ireland, application, **22**/109
offences, **22**/96
summary proceedings, **22**/97
unincorporated associations, by, **22**/98
orders and regulations, **22**/102
Board of Banking Supervision, **22**/2, sch. 1
Consumer Credit Act 1974, application, **22**/88, 89
deposit, meaning, **22**/5, 7
Deposit Protection Board, **22**/50, sch. 4
borrowing powers, **22**/64
information, power to obtain, **22**/65
Deposit Protection Fund, **22**/51
contributions to, **22**/52–57
payments out of, **22**/58–62
repayments in respect of contributions, **22**/63
Deposit Protection Scheme, **22**/50–66
deposit-taking business,
accounts and auditors, **22**/45–47
authorisation, **22**/8–18
appeals, **22**/27–31
minimum criteria, **22**/sch. 3
Bank of England: functions and duties, **22**/1
controllers, objections to, **22**/21–26
directions, **22**/19–20, 23, 33
appeals, **22**/27–31

BANKING—*cont.*
deposit-taking business—*cont.*
information, **22**/8, 36–38
power to obtain, **22**/39, 40
investigations, **22**/41–44
meaning, **22**/6, 7
regulation, **22**/1 *et seq.*
deposits,
exempted persons and transactions, **22**/4, sch. 2
invitations to make, **22**/32–35
restriction on acceptance, **22**/3
unauthorised acceptance, **22**/48, 49
descriptions: restrictions on use, **22**/69, 73
electronic transfer of funds, **22**/89
evidence in proceedings, **22**/101
financial dealings: regulation, **16**/69
information,
false and misleading, **22**/94
restriction on disclosure, **22**/82–87
municipal banks, **22**/103
names: restriction on use, **22**/67, 68, 70–73
overseas institutions, **22**/76, 78
overseas institution,
information, etc., duty to provide, **22**/79
meaning, **22**/74
representative office, with, **22**/74–81
reciprocal facilities, powers for enforcing, **22**/91
Rehabilitation of Offenders Act 1974: restriction, **22**/95
Scottish savings banks, **22**/104
service of notices, **22**/100
Bank, on, **22**/99
transactions, disclosure of, **22**/90
winding up on Bank petition, **22**/92
Banking Act 1987 (c.22)
BANKRUPTCY,
drug trafficking proceeds, realisable [S], **41**/34
Billiards (Abolition of Restrictions) Act 1987 (c.19)
British Shipbuilders (Borrowing Powers) Act 1987 (c.52)
Broadcasting Act 1987 (c.10)
BUILDING SOCIETIES,
corporation tax: payment dates, **16**/36, sch. 6
groups of companies, **51**/79

CAPITAL GAINS TAX,
collective investment schemes, **51**/78
commodity futures, **51**/81
employee share schemes, **16**/33, sch. 4, **51**/59
financial futures, **51**/81
oil licences, gains on: no roll-over relief, **51**/80
options, **51**/81

CAPITAL GAINS TAX—*cont.*
personal pension scheme, **51**/39
recovery [S], **18**/74, sch. 4
retirement relief, **16**/47
CAPITAL TRANSFER TAX,
acceptance in lieu, **51**/97
CAR TAX,
recovery [S], **18**/74, sch. 4
CARRIERS,
immigration: liability, **24**/1, 2
Channel Tunnel Act 1987 (c.53)
CHARITIES,
payroll deduction scheme, **16**/32
religious education: trusts, **15**/5
trusts for sale, **15**/1
    Charity Commissioners' schemes, **15**/2–4
    right of reverter replaced by, **15**/1
Chevening Estate Act 1987 (c.20)
Coal Industry Act 1987 (c.3)
COMMUNITY CHARGES,
Scotland. *See* SCOTLAND.
COMPANY LAW,
close company: associate, meaning, **16**/37
corporation tax. *See* CORPORATION TAX.
employee share schemes, **16**/33, sch. 4, **51**/59
groups of companies: building societies, **51**/79
stamp duty. *See* STAMP DUTY.
trading companies: losses on unquoted shares,
    51/71
unit trusts, **16**/38–40
    stamp duty, **16**/48
winding up: drug trafficking proceeds realis-
    able [S], **41**/35
Consolidated Fund Act 1987 (c.8)
Consolidated Fund (No. 2) Act 1987 (c.54)
Consolidated Fund (No. 3) Act 1987 (c.55)
CONSUMER CREDIT,
Banking Act 1987 and, **22**/88, 89
CONSUMER PROTECTION,
consumer safety, **43**/10–19
    act or default of another, **43**/40
    defence of due diligence, **43**/39
    enforcement, **43**/27–35
    forfeiture, **43**/16, 17
    information, power to obtain, **43**/18
    interpretation, **43**/19
    notices to warn, **43**/13, sch. 2
    prohibition notices, **43**/13, sch. 2
    regulations, **43**/11
        civil proceedings, **43**/41
        offences, **43**/12
    suspension notices, **43**/14, 15
defective products, liability for, **43**/2–4
    Crown, application, **43**/9
    damage giving rise to, **43**/5
    enactments: application, **43**/6
    exclusions: prohibition, **43**/7
    limitation of actions, **43**/6, sch. 1
Health and Safety at Work etc. Act 1974:
    amendments, **43**/36, sch. 3
information, disclosure of, **43**/37, 38
interpretation, **43**/19, 45, 46
misleading price indications, **43**/20
    accommodation, etc.: provision, **43**/23
    act or default of another, **43**/40
    code of practice, **43**/25

CONSUMER PROTECTION—*cont.*
misleading price indications—*cont.*
    defence of due diligence, **43**/39
    defences, **43**/24
    enforcement, **43**/27–35
    regulations, **43**/26
    services and facilities: provision, **43**/22
Northern Ireland, **43**/49
privileges, savings for certain, **43**/47
product liability, **43**/1–9
reports by Secretary of State, **43**/42
service of documents etc., **43**/44
Consumer Protection Act 1987 (c.43)
CONTRACT,
minor, **13**/1–5
CORPORATION TAX,
Acts: pre-consolidation amendments, **16**/71,
    sch. 15
advance,
    oil extraction activities, **51**/76, sch. 5
    oil industry, **16**/44–46
    set-off, corporation tax, against, **51**/74, sch.
        5
charge, **16**/21
chargeable gains, **51**/74, sch. 5
close companies,
    apportionment of income, **51**/61
    loans to participators, **51**/91
double taxation relief, **51**/77
    foreign loan interest, **51**/67
    underlying tax reflecting interest on loans,
        51/68
dual resident companies,
    dealings: reliefs, **51**/64
    group relief, **51**/63, sch. 4
employees seconded to educational bodies,
    16/34
group relief: dual resident companies, **51**/63,
    sch. 4
interest,
    overdue tax, on, **51**/85, 86
    overpaid tax, on, **51**/87
    prescribed rate of, **51**/89
investment companies, **16**/41
life assurance business, **51**/75, sch. 5
management, **51**/82 *et seq.*, sch. 6
payable without assessment, **51**/90
payment dates, **16**/36, sch. 6
recovery [S], **18**/74, sch. 4
recovery of overpayment, **51**/88
registered friendly societies, **16**/30
related companies: interest payments, **51**/60
return of profits, **51**/82
    failure to make, **51**/83, 84
small companies, **16**/22
trade unions, **16**/31
unit trusts, **16**/38–40
COUNTY COURT,
landlord and tenant: jurisdiction, **31**/52
CRIMINAL EVIDENCE AND PROCEDURE,
Crown Court, transfer of fraud cases to,
    38/4–6
fraud,
    conspiracy to defraud, **38**/12
    Crown Court, transfer of cases to, **38**/4–6
    director's investigation powers, **38**/2

CRIMINAL EVIDENCE AND PROCEDURE—*cont.*
  fraud—*cont.*
    information: disclosure, **38**/3
    preparatory hearing, **38**/7–10
    reporting restrictions, **38**/11
    Scotland: investigation, **41**/51–55
    Serious Fraud Office, **38**/1, sch. 1
    Scotland, **41**/60, 61
Criminal Justice Act 1987 (c.38)
Criminal Justice (Scotland) Act 1987 (c.41)
CRIMINAL LAW,
  Scotland. *See* SCOTLAND.
Crossbows Act 1987 (c.32)
CROWN,
  Abolition of Domestic Rates Etc. (Scotland) Act 1987, application, **47**/30
  Animals (Scotland) Act 1987, application, **9**/6
  Consumer Protection Act 1987, application, **43**/9
  Debtors (Scotland) Act 1987, application, **18**/105
  Fire Safety etc. Act 1987, application, **27**/18, 40
  Housing (Scotland) Act 1987, application, **26**/105, 301, 335
  Landlord and Tenant Act 1987, application, **31**/56
  proceedings: armed forces, **25**/1–5
  product liability, **43**/9
  sports grounds, safety at: provisions, **27**/40
  stamp duty, **16**/55
  trusts, recognition of, **14**/3
Crown Proceedings (Armed Forces) Act 1987 (c.25)
CUSTOMS AND EXCISE,
  approved wharves, access to, **16**/6
  Commissioners: information, disclosure of, **43**/37
  consumer protection: enforcement, **43**/30, 37
  detention by customs officers,
    drug trafficking [S], **41**/48
    goods: consumer protection, **43**/31
  export,
    local control, **16**/8
    records relating to, **16**/9
  gaming machine licence duty, **16**/4, 5
  general betting duty, **16**/3
  importation: records, **16**/9
  information powers, **16**/10
  transhipped stores, consumption in port, **51**/103
  transit sheds, access to, **16**/6
  unleaded petrol: rebate, **16**/1
  vehicles excise duty, **16**/2, sch. 1
  vehicles: search and access, **16**/7

Debtors (Scotland) Act 1987 (c.18)
Deer Act 1987 (c.28)
DEFINITIONS,
  accessible personal information, **37**/2, schs. 1, 2
  adjudication for debt [S], **18**/15
  AIDS, **33**/4
  animal [S], **9**/7
  associate (body corporate), **22**/105

DEFINITIONS—*cont.*
  associate (close company), **16**/37
  British Coal Corporation, **2**/1
  chief executive (institution), **22**/105
  close relative, **21**/5
  community charges [S], **47**/7
  competent harbour authority, **21**/1
  confiscation order [S], **41**/1
  conjoined arrestment order [S], **18**/46
  consular post, **46**/5
  consular premises, **46**/5
  consumer goods, **43**/10
  controller (institution), **22**/105
  co-operative housing association [S], **26**/300
  Crown property, **4**/2
  current maintenance arrestment [S], **18**/46
  debt [S], **18**/15
  decree or other document [S], **18**/15, 73
  defect (product liability), **43**/3
  defective dwelling [S], **26**/257
  deposit (banking), **22**/5, 7
  deposit-taking business, **22**/6, 7
  diplomatic premises, **46**/5
  director (institution), **22**/105
  dockyard property, **4**/2
  domestic subjects [S], **47**/1
  drug trafficking [S], **41**/1
  dwelling [S], **26**/302
  earnings arrestment [S], **18**/46
  flat, **31**/60
  food (consumer safety), **43**/19
  foreign currency, **16**/69
  goods (consumer protection), **43**/45
  HIV, **33**/4
  harbour, **21**/1
  harbour authority, **21**/1, 31
  homeless [S], **26**/24
  homeless intentionally [S], **26**/26
  house [S], **26**/302, 338
  housing co-operative [S], **26**/22
  improvement (house) [S], **26**/236
  insolvency, **22**/59
  institution, **22**/106
  international defence property, **4**/2
  keeper (animal) [S], **9**/5
  landlord, **31**/2, 59, 60
  lease, **31**/59
  legitimated person, **42**/22
  livestock [S], **9**/4
  local authority, **22**/106, [S] **26**/338
  long lease, **31**/59
  maintenance agreement, **42**/15
  maintenance order [S], **18**/106
  manager (institution), **22**/105
  member of family [S], **26**/83
  misleading (price indication), **43**/21
  officer of court [S], **18**/106
  offshore installation, **12**/16
  ordnance company, **4**/2
  ordnance property, **4**/2
  overcrowding [S], **26**/135–137
  overseas institution (banking), **22**/74
  owner (house) [S], **26**/338
  personal information, **37**/2
  personal pension scheme, **51**/19
  pilot, **21**/31

DEFINITIONS—*cont.*
poinding schedule [S], **18**/20
priority need (for accommodation) [S], **26**/25
profit-related pay, **51**/1
public sector authority [S], **26**/300
rate [S], **47**/26
recovery vehicle, **16**/sch. 1
representative office (banking), **22**/74
resident landlord, **31**/58
restraint order (drug trafficking proceeds) [S], **41**/9
safe (goods), **43**/19
school teacher, **1**/7
secure tenancy [S], **26**/44
service charge, **31**/42
sheriff [S], **18**/15, 73
species (animals) [S], **9**/1
sport, **27**/42, 43
stand (sports ground), **27**/26
submarine pipe-line, **12**/16
suitable alternative accommodation [S], **26**/151, sch. 3
summary warrant [S], **18**/106
supply (goods), **43**/46
Taxes Act, **51**/104
teacher in further education, **1**/7
tenancy, **31**/59, 60
tenant, **31**/59
terrorism provisions (Northern Ireland), **30**/16
threatened with homelessness [S], **26**/24
threatened with homelessness intentionally [S], **26**/26
time to pay direction [S], **18**/1
time to pay order [S], **18**/5
tolerable standard (housing) [S], **26**/86
trust, **14**/sch.
unit trust scheme, **16**/39, 40, 48
warrant of sale [S], **18**/30
warrant sales, **18**/30
work required to reinstate a defective dwelling [S], **26**/303
Diplomatic and Consular Premises Act 1987 (c.46)
DIVORCE AND CONSISTORIAL CAUSES,
maintenance. *See* SCOTLAND.

EDUCATION,
block grant, adjustments, **44**/2, 3
religious: trusts, **15**/5
teachers' pay and conditions,
existing arrangements: termination, **1**/1
further education, in, **1**/4
Interim Advisory Committee, **1**/2, sch. 1
Secretary of State: powers, **1**/3
EMPLOYMENT,
employee share schemes, etc., **16**/33, sch. 4, **51**/59
employees,
seconded to educational bodies: tax, **16**/34
tax relief for training costs, **16**/35, sch. 5
profit-related pay, **51**/1–17
ENTERTAINMENTS,
indoor sports licences, **27**/42–44, sch. 3
licences,
fees for variation, **27**/46
Royal Albert Hall, **27**/45

ENTERTAINMENTS—*cont.*
luminous tube signs, **27**/47, 48
sports grounds: safety. *See* SPORTS GROUNDS.
ENTRY, POWERS OF,
Consumer Protection Act 1987, under, **43**/29
drug trafficking, investigation, **41**/39
fraud, investigation, **38**/2
Scotland, **41**/51
Housing (Scotland) Act 1987, under, **26**/317
sports grounds, safety of stands at, **27**/34
ESTATE DUTY,
acceptance in lieu, **51**/97
EVIDENCE,
criminal. *See* CRIMINAL EVIDENCE AND PROCEDURE.
paternity in civil proceedings, of, **42**/29
EXPENSES,
Scotland. *See* SCOTLAND.

FAMILY LAW,
adoption: rights, **42**/7
affiliation proceedings, abolition, **42**/17
artificial insemination, **42**/27
birth outside marriage: general principle, **42**/1, 30
child in care: rights, **42**/8
custody orders, **42**/10, 11
dispositions of property, **42**/19
trustees and personal representatives, by, **42**/20
financial relief orders, **42**/12–14
grant of probate etc., entitlement to, **42**/21
guardians, appointment, **42**/6
intestate succession, **42**/18
maintenance agreements: alteration, **42**/15, 16
marriage, consent to, **42**/9
1971 Act, amendments, **42**/32, sch. 1
parentage,
declaration of, **42**/22
re-registration of birth, **42**/26
scientific tests: provisions, **42**/23
parental rights and duties, **42**/2–17
agreements as to exercise, **42**/3
construction of enactments, **42**/2
parents not married, **42**/4–9
paternity: evidence in civil proceedings, **42**/29
property right, **42**/18
registration of births, **42**/24–26
relationships, determination of, **42**/22, 23
void marriages, children of, **42**/28
Family Law Reform Act 1987 (c.42)
Finance Act 1987 (c.16)
Finance (No. 2) Act 1987 (c.51)
FIRE SAFETY,
Act,
civil and other liability, **27**/12
Crown, application to, **27**/18
extension of power to apply, **27**/17
fire certificate,
breaches of requirements: defence, **27**/14
requirement: exemption, **27**/1, 2
fire certification work: charges, **27**/3
fire fighting: means, **27**/5
automatic, **27**/15
codes of practice, **27**/6

FIRE SAFETY—*cont.*
  improvement notices, **27**/7
  luminous tube signs, **27**/47, 48
  means of escape, **27**/4, 5
    codes of practice, **27**/6
  premises,
    factory, office etc.: provision, **27**/16, sch. 1
    information obtained in, disclosure, **27**/11
    inspection, **27**/10, 11
    interim duties, **27**/8
    public religious worship, **27**/3
    serious risk: prohibition notices, **27**/9
Fire Safety and Safety of Places of Sport Act 1987 (c.27)
FRAUD. *See also* CRIMINAL EVIDENCE AND PROCEDURE.
  Scotland: investigation, **41**/51–55
FRIENDLY SOCIETIES,
  registered: tax exemptions, **16**/30

Gaming (Amendment) Act 1987 (c.11)
GAMING AND WAGERING,
  billiards: abolition of licensing, **19**/1, 2, sch.
  gaming hours, **11**/1, 2

HEALTH AND SAFETY AT WORK,
  1974 Act, amendments, **43**/36, sch. 3
HOUSING,
  associations, registered: management, **31**/45
  assured tenancies: capital allowances, **51**/61
  flats. *See* LANDLORD AND TENANT.
  Scotland. *See* SCOTLAND.
  service charges, **31**/41, sch. 2
Housing (Scotland) Act 1987 (c.26)
HUMAN RIGHTS,
  access to personal files, **37**/1–5, schs. 1, 2

Immigration (Carriers' Liability) Act 1987 (c.24)
INCOME TAX,
  Acts: pre-consolidation amendments, **16**/71, sch. 15
  capital allowances: assured tenancies, **51**/72
  charge, **16**/20
  charities: payroll deduction scheme, **16**/32
  construction industry: sub-contractors, **16**/23, **51**/93
  controlled foreign company: distribution policy, **51**/65
  double taxation relief: foreign loan interest, **51**/67
  employees: training costs, relief, **16**/35, sch. 5
  interest relief, **16**/25
  occupational pension schemes, **51**/58, sch. 3
  offshore funds, **51**/66
  partnership controlled abroad, **51**/62
  PAYE: amendments, **51**/92
  personal pension schemes, **51**/18 *et seq.*
    amendments, **51**/57, sch. 2
    appeals, **51**/47
    approval, **51**/19, 56
      member's contributions, **51**/31–34
      restrictions on, **51**/20–30

INCOME TAX—*cont.*
  personal pension schemes—*cont.*
    approval—*cont.*
      tax consequences, **51**/31–41
      withdrawal, **51**/43
    benefits, **51**/21–26
    contributions under Social Security Act 1986, **51**/42
    earnings from pensionable employment, **51**/36
    establishment, **51**/20
    information about payments, **51**/50, 51
    interpretation, **51**/18
    Ministers, etc.: remuneration, **51**/52
    net relevant earnings, meaning, **51**/35
    relevant earnings, meaning, **51**/35
    relief, **51**/45, 46, 48, 49
    retirement annuities, **51**/54, sch. 2
    transitional provisions, **51**/55, 56
    unapproved arrangements: contributions, **51**/53
    unauthorised payments etc.: tax on, **51**/44
  personal reliefs,
    age relief, **16**/26
    blind persons, **16**/28
    income support, etc., **16**/29, sch. 3
    invalid care allowance, **16**/27
    PAYE: operative date, **16**/24
    unemployment benefit, **16**/27
  profit-related pay,
    annual returns, etc., **51**/12
    appeals, **51**/15
    independent accountant, **51**/7, 17
    information, **51**/12–14
    interpretation, **51**/1
    partnership, **51**/16
    recovery of tax, **51**/11
    registration of scheme, **51**/5–10, sch. 1
    relief, **51**/3, 4
    taxation, **51**/2
  recovery [S], **18**/74, sch. 4
  registered friendly societies, **16**/30
  trade unions, **16**/31
INHERITANCE TAX,
  acceptance in lieu, **16**/60
  gifts with reservation, **16**/58, sch. 8
  historic buildings: maintenance funds, **16**/59, sch. 9
  interests in possession, **51**/96, sch. 7
  personal pension schemes, **51**/98
  rates, **16**/57
INSURANCE,
  landlord and tenant, **31**/43, sch. 3
  life assurance business: corporation tax, **51**/75, sch. 5
INTERNATIONAL LAW,
  diplomatic and consular premises, **46**/1–9, schs. 1, 2
  territorial sea, extension, **49**/1, 2
  trusts, recognition: Convention, **14**/1–3, sch.
Irish Sailors and Soldiers Land Trust Act 1987 (c.48)

LANDLORD AND TENANT,
  Act,
    county courts, jurisdiction, **31**/52

LANDLORD AND TENANT—*cont.*
Act—*cont.*
Crown land, application, **31**/56
interpretation, **31**/20, 58–60
Isles of Scilly, application, **31**/55
notices, **31**/54
regulations and orders, **31**/53
assured tenancies: capital allowances, **51**/61
flats, tenants' rights of first refusal, **31**/1–4
enforcement of obligations, **31**/19
enforcement of rights,
new landlords, against, **31**/11–15, sch. 1
subsequent purchasers, against, **31**/16
interpretation, **31**/20
notices conferring, **31**/5–10
prospective purchasers: notices, **31**/18
termination, **31**/17
information to tenants, **31**/46–51, **37**/1
insurance, **31**/43, sch. 3
landlord's interest, compulsory acquisition by
tenants, **31**/25–34, sch. 1
management of leasehold property, **31**/41–45
managers, appointment by court, **31**/21–24
managing agents, **31**/44
registered housing associations, management,
31/45
Scotland. *See* SCOTLAND.
service charges, **31**/41, sch. 2
variation of leases, **31**/35–40
Landlord and Tenant Act 1987 (c.31)
LICENSING,
billiards: abolition, **19**/1, 2, sch.
indoor sports premises, **27**/42–44, sch. 3
petroleum: production, **12**/17–20, schs. 1, 2
restaurant meals, **2**/1–3
Licensing (Restaurant Meals) Act 1987 (c.2)
LOCAL GOVERNMENT,
block grant: education, **44**/2, 3
capital expenditure: payments, **44**/1, sch.
community charges, rates replaced by. *See*
SCOTLAND.
rating and valuation, **5**/1–3, **6**/1–16, schs. 1–5
Local Government Act 1987 (c.44)
Local Government Finance Act 1987 (c.6)
LONDON,
licensing, indoor sports premises, **27**/42

MINING LAW,
British Coal Corporation, **3**/1
grants to, **3**/2–4
coal industry,
social welfare bodies, **3**/6, 8
superannuation schemes, etc., **3**/7, 8
trusts, **3**/5
Ministry of Defence Police Act 1987 (c.4)
MINORS,
contracts, **13**/1–5
Minors' Contracts Act 1987 (c.13)
Motor Cycle Noise Act 1987 (c.34)

NATIONAL HEALTH,
AIDS: control, **33**/1–4, sch.
Health Service Commissioner,
complaints: references to, **39**/7, 8
functions, **39**/4–6

NORTHERN IRELAND,
AIDS: control, **33**/2, 4
Banking Act 1987, application, **22**/109
broadcasting, **10**/2
Consumer Protection Act 1987, application,
43/49
crossbows: offences, **32**/7, 8
Crown proceedings: armed forces, **25**/1–5
diplomatic and consular premises, **46**/4, 9,
sch. 1
drug trafficking proceeds: orders, enforcement [S], **41**/29
emergency provisions,
commencement, continuation, etc., **30**/26
detainees in police custody: rights, **30**/14–16
1978 Act, amendments, **30**/1–13
security services, provision: regulation,
30/17–24
fraud, investigation and trials, **38**/13, 17
immigration: carriers' liability, **24**/2
Irish Sailors and Soldiers Land Trust Act
1987, application, **48**/3
Ministry of Defence police, **4**/8
petroleum, **12**/32
Pilotage Act 1987, application, **21**/33
social fund: maternity and funeral expenses,
7/2
trusts, recognition of, **14**/2
**Northern Ireland (Emergency Provisions) Act
1987 (c.30)**

PARLIAMENT,
Parliamentary Contributory Pension Fund,
continuance, **45**/1
exchequer contributions to, **45**/3
regulations, power to make, **45**/2, sch. 1
pensions, provision for members, etc., **45**/1–7,
schs. 1–4
**Parliamentary and Health Service Commission-
ers Act 1987 (c.39)**
**Parliamentary and other Pensions Act 1987
(c.45)**
PARTNERSHIP,
controlled abroad: United Kingdom members, **51**/62
profit-related pay scheme, **51**/16
PENSIONS AND SUPERANNUATION,
occupational pension schemes, **51**/58, sch. 3
Parliamentary pensions, **45**/1–7, schs. 1–4
personal pension schemes, **51**/18 *et seq.*, 98
PETROLEUM,
advance corporation tax: oil industry,
16/44–46
offshore installations: abandonment, **12**/1–16
oil extraction activities etc., chargeable gains,
51/76, sch. 5
oil licences, gains on: no roll-over relief, **51**/80
oil taxation, **16**/61–67, schs. 10–14, **51**/101,
sch. 8
pipe-lines, **12**/25–27
production: licences, **12**/17–20, schs. 1, 2
refineries, **12**/28
safety zones, **12**/21–24
Petroleum Act 1987 (c.12)
Pilotage Act 1987 (c.21)

POLICE,
Defence Police Federation, **4**/3
Ministry of Defence, **4**/1
disaffection, causing, **4**/6
disciplinary proceedings, **4**/3, 4
impersonation, etc., **4**/5
jurisdiction, **4**/2
Prescription (Scotland) Act 1987 (c.36)
Protection of Animals (Penalties) Act 1987 (c.35)

Rate Support Grant Act 1987 (c.5)
RATING AND VALUATION,
block grant entitlement, **5**/1–3
community charges. *See* SCOTLAND.
rate support grants, **5**/1–3, **6**/1–5, 9, 10, schs.
1, 3
Scotland: replacement, **47**/23
rates, **6**/6–8, sch. 2
community charges, replaced by. *See*
SCOTLAND.
domestic: abolition [S], **47**/1, 2, sch. 1
non-domestic [S], **47**/3
rateable values, etc., references to [S], **47**/5
recovery [S], **18**/74, sch. 4
valuation: part premises dwelling house [S],
47/4
Scotland, **6**/13, 14, **47**/1 *et seq.*
water and sewerage charges [S], **47**/25, sch. 5
water rates: abolition [S], **47**/25
Recognition of Trusts Act 1987 (c.14)
Register of Sasines (Scotland) Act 1987 (c.23)
**Registered Establishments (Scotland) Act 1987
(c.40)**
REVENUE AND FINANCE,
capital gains tax. *See* CAPITAL GAINS TAX.
capital transfer tax: acceptance in lieu, **51**/97
car tax: recovery [S], **18**/74, sch. 4
community charges. *See* SCOTLAND.
corporation tax. *See* CORPORATION TAX.
customs and excise. *See* CUSTOMS AND EXCISE.
double taxation relief, **16**/70, **51**/67, 68, 77
estate duty: acceptance in lieu, **51**/97
exchange control, **16**/68
financial dealings: regulation, **16**/69
Government fees and charges, **51**/102
income tax. *See* INCOME TAX.
inheritance tax. *See* INHERITANCE TAX.
Inland Revenue: employment information,
disclosure, **51**/69
oil taxation, **16**/61–67, schs. 10–14, **51**/101,
sch. 8
personal pension schemes, **51**/18 *et seq.*, 98
profit-related pay, **51**/1–17
recognised investment exchanges, **51**/73
rate support grants, **5**/1–3, **6**/1–5, 9, 10, schs.
1, 3
rates, **6**/6–8, sch. 2
Scotland. *See* SCOTLAND.
Scottish Development Agency, **56**/1, 2
stamp duty. *See* STAMP DUTY.
taxes management provisions, **51**/82–95, sch.
6
failure to do things within a limited time,
51/94
urban development corporations, **57**/1, 2
value added tax. *See* VALUE ADDED TAX.

Reverter of Sites Act 1987 (c.15)
ROAD TRAFFIC,
Channel Tunnel, provisions for, **53**/1 *et seq.*
motor cycles: noise, **34**/1, 2, sch.

SCOTLAND,
accessible personal information, **37**/2, sch. 2
aiding and abetting, **41**/64
animals, **9**/1–9, sch.
Crown, application of Act to, **9**/6
injury or damage: strict liability, **9**/1, 2
keeper, meaning, **9**/5
killing, etc., defence, **9**/4
straying: detention, **9**/3
children: detention, **41**/59
community charges,
appeals, **47**/16
collection, **47**/21, sch. 2
collective, **47**/7, 11
creation and purpose, **47**/7
interpretation, **47**/26
levy, **47**/21, sch. 2
payment, **47**/21, sch. 2
personal, **47**/7–9
rebates, **47**/24
recovery, **47**/21, sch. 2
reduction, **47**/22, sch. 3
register, **47**/13–16
registration: duties, **47**/17–20
registration officer, **47**/12
standard, **47**/7, 10
conjoined arrestment orders, **18**/60–66, sch. 3
current maintenance arrestment and, **18**/62
diligences: equalisation, **18**/67
earnings arrestment and, **18**/62
consumer protection: limitation of actions,
43/6, sch. 1
consumer safety: forfeiture, **43**/17
current maintenance arrestment, **18**/51–56
conjoined arrestment orders and, **18**/62
diligences: equalisation, **18**/67
earnings arrestment and, **18**/58, 60–66
failure to comply with, **18**/57
meaning, **18**/46
priority among arrestments, **18**/59
debtors,
Act,
Crown, application to, **18**/105
interpretation, **18**/15, 45, 73, 106, **47**/33
proceedings, assistance, **18**/96–101
regulations, **18**/104
appeals, **18**/103
current maintenance arrestment, **18**/46,
51–67
diligence against earnings, **18**/46–73
earnings arrestment, **18**/46–50, 57–67
expenses: recovery from, **18**/93
payment, extension of time for, **18**/1–15,
47/33
poinding. *See* poinding, *infra.*
warrant sales. *See* warrant sales, *infra.*
debts, extension of time to pay, **18**/1–15, **47**/33
decree, directions on, **18**/1–4, 12–15, **47**/33
orders following charge or diligence
18/5–15, **47**/33

Scotland—*cont.*
  detention,
    children, of, **41**/59
    customs officers, by, **41**/48
    drug smuggling offences, **41**/50
    right to have someone informed of, **41**/49
  diligence,
    ascription of sums recovered, **18**/94
    drug trafficking proceeds: administration,
      effect, **41**/19
    earnings, against, **18**/46 *et seq.*
    expenses, **18**/93
    interim order: effect, **18**/8
    proceedings: procedure, **18**/102
    termination on payment, etc., **18**/95
    time to pay direction: effect, **18**/2
    time to pay order: effect, **18**/9
    warrants for, **18**/87, 88
  diplomatic and consular premises, **46**/4, sch.
    1
  disqualification: suspension, **41**/68
  drug trafficking proceeds,
    administrators, **41**/13–22
      exercise of powers, **41**/23
    amendments, **41**/45
    confiscation orders, **41**/1–7
      reciprocal enforcement, **41**/27, 28, 31
      variation, **41**/25
    Court of Session: exercise of powers, **41**/23,
      24
    England and Wales: orders, enforcement,
      41/31
    external orders: enforcement, **41**/30
    information: disclosure by government
      departments, **41**/41
    interdict, **41**/11, 12
    interpretation, **41**/47, 69
    investigations, **41**/38–40, 42
    Northern Ireland orders: enforcement,
      41/29
    notices and service, **41**/46
    offences, **41**/42–44
    proceedings unjustified: compensation,
      41/26
    realisable property: sequestration, etc.,
      41/33–37
    restraint orders, **41**/8–11
  earnings,
    arrested, diversion to Secretary of State,
      18/68
    diligence against, **18**/46 *et seq.*
  earnings arrestment, **18**/47–50, sch. 2
    charges for payment, **18**/90
    conjoined arrestment orders and, **18**/62
    current maintenance arrestment and, **18**/58,
      60–66
    diligences: equalisation, **18**/67
    failure to comply with, **18**/57
    meaning, **18**/46
    priority among arrestments, **18**/59
  evidence, **41**/60, 61
  expenses,
    court proceedings, **18**/92
    debtors, recovery from, **18**/93
  fire safety: luminous tube signs, **27**/48
  fixed penalty: conditional offer, **41**/56

Scotland—*cont.*
  forfeiture: suspension, **41**/68
  fraud, serious, etc.: investigation, **41**/51–55
  High Court sittings, **41**/57
  housing,
    accommodation: provision, **26**/1–8
    acquisition of land, **26**/9–12, sch. 1
    Act,
      byelaws, **26**/313–316
      Crown, application, **26**/105, 301, 335
      entry, powers of, **26**/317
      interpretation, **26**/43, 82, 83, 133, 190,
        302, 303, 311, 338
      offences, **26**/318–321, 325
      Secretary of State: powers, **26**/329–333
      service of orders, notices, **26**/325, 326
    action areas, **26**/89–93, 97, 98, sch. 7
      grants, **26**/250
      improvement, loans for, **26**/217
      landlords and tenants, in, **26**/99–104
    agricultural tenants, etc.: grants, **26**/256
    agricultural workers, accommodation: bye-
      laws, **26**/314
    allocation, **26**/19–21
    assistance, **26**/229–235
      defective housing: owners, **26**/257 *et seq.*
      first time buyers, for, **26**/222–228
      reinstatement grant, **26**/269–274
      repurchase of defective, **26**/275–286,
        sch. 20
    byelaws, **26**/313–316
    closing orders, **26**/114, 116–122, 127–133,
      307
    compensation,
      compulsory purchase of land, **26**/10, 95,
        278, 279, schs. 1, 8
      local authorities: payments to other,
        26/312
      multiple occupation: control order,
        26/183
      repayment, **26**/307
      tolerable standard, houses not meeting,
        26/308–311
      well-maintained houses, **26**/304–307
    co-operative housing association, **26**/45, 300
    defective: owners, assistance, **26**/257 *et seq.*,
      sch. 21
    demolition orders, **26**/115–119, 121,
      123–133, 307
    disposal of land, **26**/13–16
    fire escapes, **26**/162–165
      grants, **26**/249
    first-time buyers: assistance, **26**/222–228
    grants,
      agricultural tenants, etc., **26**/256
      amenities: improvement, **26**/251
      Exchequer contributions, **26**/254, 255
      fire escapes, **26**/249
      housing action areas, **26**/250
      improvement, **26**/88, 236–247
      local authorities, by, **26**/236 *et seq.*, schs.
        18, 19
      local authorities, to, **26**/191–193, 198,
        199, sch. 12

SCOTLAND—*cont.*
  housing—*cont.*
    grants—*cont.*
      reinstatement, **26**/269–274
      repairs, **26**/248
      Scottish Special Housing Association, **26**/194–196, 198, 199
      thermal insulation, **26**/252, 253
      voluntary organisations, to, **26**/197
    heir of entail: power to sell land, **26**/334
    homeless persons, **26**/24–43
    improvement,
      amenities: grants, **26**/251
      execution of works by local authorities, **26**/106
      grants, **26**/88, 236–247, schs. 18, 19
      loans: housing action areas, **26**/217
      secure tenancies, **26**/57–59, sch. 5
      sub-standard houses, **26**/88
    listed buildings,
      closing orders, **26**/119
      housing action areas, **26**/93, sch. 7
    loans, **26**/88, 214–221, sch. 17
      improvement: housing action areas, **26**/217
      interest rates, **26**/219–221
      repairs, **26**/218
    local authorities,
      accommodation: provision, **26**/1–8
        contracts: fair wages clause, **26**/337
      accounts, **26**/203–209, schs. 15, 16
      charging orders, **26**/109, 131, sch. 9
      duties and powers, **26**/1 *et seq.*
      expenses, recovery of, **26**/109, 131, 164, 336, sch. 9
      grants by, **26**/236 *et seq.*, schs. 18, 19
      grants to, **26**/191–193, 198, 199, sch. 12
      homelessness, **26**/24–43
      loans, **26**/214–221, sch. 17
      management and allocation, **26**/17–21
      overcrowding: powers, **26**/142, 143, 146–150, 166–170
      repairs: powers, **26**/108, 109
      secure tenants, **26**/44 *et seq.*, sch. 2
        right to buy, **26**/44 *et seq.*
      sub-standard houses, **26**/85–93, 95–98, sch. 8
    management, **26**/17, 18
    multiple occupation, **26**/152 *et seq.*
      byelaws, **26**/313
      control orders, **26**/178–190, sch. 11
      fire escapes: grants, **26**/246
      management code, **26**/156–160, 172
      overcrowding, **26**/135
      multiple occupation, where, **26**/166–170
    provision of, **26**/1 *et seq.*
    reinstatement grants, **26**/269–274
    rents: public sector housing, **26**/210, 212, 213
    repairs, **26**/108–113, sch. 10
      grants, **26**/248
      loans, **26**/218
      secure tenancies, **26**/57–60, sch. 5
    Scottish Special Housing Association,
      grants to, **26**/194–196, 198, 199
      powers, **26**/23

SCOTLAND—*cont.*
  housing—*cont.*
    seasonal workers, accommodation: bye-laws, **26**/315
    service charges, **26**/211
    sheriff: powers, **26**/322–324
    slum clearance,
      revenue account, **26**/207, sch. 16
      subsidy, **26**/200
    subsidy,
      payment, **26**/201, schs. 13, 14
      power to vary, etc., **26**/202
      slum clearance, **26**/200
    sub-standard houses, **26**/85 *et seq.*
      Crown interest: exclusion, **26**/105
      housing action areas, **26**/89–93, 97–104 sch. 7
      improvement order, **26**/88
      local authority: powers, **26**/95–98, sch. 8
      sale: conditions, **26**/107
      Secretary of State: powers, **26**/94
      tolerable standard, **26**/85–87
    thermal insulation grants, **26**/252, 253
  housing co-operatives, **26**/22
  imprisonment, non-payment of fine, etc., for **41**/67
  landlord and tenant,
    housing action areas, in, **26**/99–104
    landlord's identity, **26**/327, 328
    possession, grounds for, **26**/47, 48, sch. 3
    public sector tenants, rights, **26**/44 *et seq.*
    right to buy, **26**/44 *et seq.*
      discount: recoverability, **26**/72, 73
      exceptions, **26**/61, 69, 70
      landlord: duties, **26**/74–76
      Lands Tribunal: reference to, **26**/71
      loans for purchase, **26**/216
      notices, **26**/84
      price, **26**/62
      procedure, **26**/63–68
      Secretary of State: powers, **26**/77–81, sch. 6
    secure tenancies, **26**/44 *et seq.*
      assignment, **26**/55, 56, sch. 4
      co-operative housing associations, **26**/45
      death: succession on, **26**/52
      exchanges: contributions towards costs, **26**/80
      repairs and improvements, **26**/57–60, sch. 5
      right to buy, **26**/44 *et seq.*
      subletting, **26**/55, 56, sch. 4
      tenancies not secure, **26**/sch. 2
      transfers: contributions towards costs, **26**/80
      variation of terms, **26**/54
      written lease, right to, **26**/53
    security of tenure, **26**/44 *et seq.*
  letters of horning, etc.: abolition, **18**/89
  licensing, indoor sports premises, **27**/44
  maintenance, order,
    enforcement. *See* current maintenance arrestment, *supra.*
    meaning, **18**/106
  messengers-at-arms, **18**/75–86
  nursing homes, registration, **40**/5, 6

SCOTLAND—*cont.*
offences, summary conviction: penalties, **41**/66
officers of court, **18**/75–86
ordaining to appear, **41**/62
poinded articles, removal, etc., **18**/28, 29, sch. 5
poinding, **18**/16–27
  charges for payment, **18**/90
  common ownership, articles in, **18**/41, sch. 5
  conjoining of further, **18**/43
  expenses, **18**/44, sch. 1
  procedure, **18**/20, 21, sch. 5
  release from, **18**/40, 41, sch. 5
  summary warrant, in pursuance of, **18**/74, sch. 5
  third party, articles belonging to, **18**/40, sch. 5
precepts, enforcement, **18**/91
prescription, **36**/1, 2
probation order: compensation requirements, **41**/65
rate support grants, replacement, **47**/23
rates,
  community charges, replaced by. *See* community charges, *supra.*
  domestic: abolition, **47**/1, 2, sch. 1
    Crown land, **47**/30
  non-domestic, **47**/3
  rateable values, etc., references to, **47**/5
  recovery, **18**/74, sch. 4
  recreational clubs, relief: grant, **47**/27
  valuation: part premises dwelling house, **47**/4
rating and valuation, **6**/13, 14
Register of Sasines, **23**/1–3
registered establishments: 1968 Act provision, **40**/1–6
revenue support grants, **47**/23, sch. 4
savings banks, **22**/104
Scottish Development Agency, **56**/1, 2
sewerage charges, **47**/25, sch. 5
sheriff: sentencing power, **41**/58
sheriff officers, **18**/75–86
taxes, recovery, **18**/74, sch. 4
warrant sales, **18**/30
  common ownership, articles in, **18**/41, sch. 5
  expenses, **18**/44, schs. 1, 5
  proceedings: postponement, **18**/42, sch. 5
  summary warrant, in pursuance of, **18**/74, sch. 5
warrants,
  diligence, for, **18**/87, 88
  enforcement, **18**/91
water charges, **47**/25, sch. 5
water rates: abolition, **47**/25
  Crown land, **47**/30
witness in court during trial, **41**/63
Scottish Development Agency Act 1987 (c.56)
SEA AND SEASHORE,
  territorial sea, extension, **49**/1, 2
SHERIFF COURT PRACTICE. *See* SCOTLAND.

SHIPPING AND MARINE INSURANCE,
  British Shipbuilders, limit on borrowing etc. of, **52**/1, 2
  pilotage,
    accounts, **21**/14
    charges, **21**/10
    compulsory, **21**/7–9, 15, 16
    deep sea, **21**/23
    existing organisation: winding-up, **21**/24–29
    harbour authorities: functions, **21**/1–14
      agents and joint arrangements, **21**/11–13
    interpretation, **21**/31
    reorganisation: funding, **21**/29
    services, provision, **21**/2
  pilotage authorities,
    abolition, **21**/24
    transfer of staff, **21**/25
  Pilotage Commission, abolition, **21**/26, 27
  pilots,
    compensation scheme, **21**/28
    liability: limitation, **21**/22
    misconduct, **21**/21
    rights, **21**/17–20
Social Fund (Maternity and Funeral Expenses) Act 1987 (c.7)
SOCIAL SECURITY,
  funeral expenses, **7**/1, 2
  maternity expenses, **7**/1, 2
SPORTS GROUNDS,
  safety, **27**/19–25
    certificates, **27**/21, 22
    designation: spectator capacity, **27**/20
    enforcement: inspections and obstruction, **27**/25
    1975 Act, application, **27**/19, sch. 2
    serious risk: prohibition notices, **27**/23, 24
  safety of stands at, **27**/26–41
    alterations and extensions, **27**/32
    appeals, **27**/30
    civil and other liability, **27**/37
    Crown, application to, **27**/40
    enforcement, **27**/34
    entry and inspection, powers of, **27**/34
    interpretation, **27**/41
    offences, **27**/36
    provisions: power to modify, **27**/39
    regulations, **27**/31
    safety certificates, **27**/26–29
    service of documents, **27**/38
    statutory requirements: exclusion of other, **27**/33
STAMP DUTY,
  bearer instruments: stock in foreign currencies, **16**/51
  clearance services, **16**/52
  contract notes, **16**/49
  Crown exemption, **16**/55
  exempt stock: warrants to purchase, **16**/50
  market makers: borrowing of stock, **16**/53
  options to acquire etc. exempt securities, **51**/99
  reserve tax, **16**/56, sch. 7, **51**/100
  shared ownership transactions, **16**/54
  unit trusts, **16**/48

Teachers' Pay and Conditions Act 1987 (c.1)
TELECOMMUNICATIONS,
  Independent Broadcasting Authority: programme contracts, **10**/1, 2
Territorial Sea Act 1987 (c.49)
TRADE UNIONS,
  tax relief, **16**/31
TRANSPORT,
  Channel Tunnel, provisions for, **53**/1 *et seq.*
TRUSTS,
  charitable: reverter of sites and, **15**/1–9, sch.

Urban Development Corporations (Financial Limits) Act 1987 (c.57)

VALUE ADDED TAX,
  accounting for, and payment, **16**/11
  amendments, **16**/19, sch. 2
  appeals, **16**/sch. 2

VALUE ADDED TAX—*cont.*
  credit for input tax, **16**/12
  customs enactments: application, **51**/103
  going concerns: transfers, **16**/sch. 2
  recovery [S], **18**/74, sch. 4
  registration, **16**/14
  repayment, **16**/sch. 2
  securities: issue, **16**/18
  supplies,
    abroad, etc., **16**/13, sch. 2
    groups, to, **16**/15
    valuation, **16**/17
  tour operators, **16**/16

WATER AND WATERWORKS,
  charges [S], **47**/25, sch. 5
WEIGHTS AND MEASURES,
  authority, consumer protection: enforcement, **43**/27